UPDATE EDITION

INTRODUCTION TO
Comparative Government

FIFTH EDITION

Michael Curtis, General Editor
Rutgers University

Jean Blondel
European University Institute

Bernard E. Brown
City University of New York

Joseph Fewsmith
Boston University

Roger E. Kanet
University of Miami

Donald Kommers
University of Notre Dame

A. James McAdams
University of Notre Dame

Theodore McNelly
University of Maryland

Martin C. Needler
University of the Pacific

John S. Reshetar, Jr.
University of Washington

Stephen Wright
Northern Arizona University

PEARSON
Longman

New York San Francisco Boston
London Toronto Sydney Tokyo Singapore Madrid
Mexico City Munich Paris Cape Town Hong Kong Montreal

Executive Editor: Eric Stano
Senior Marketing Manager: Elizabeth Fogarty
Production Manager: Stacey Kulig
Text Design: Electronic Publishing Services Inc., NYC
Project Coordination and Electronic Page Makeup: Pre-Press Company, Inc.
Cover Design Manager: Wendy Ann Fredericks
Cover Designer: John Callahan
Cover Photo: ©PhotoDisc
Photo Researcher: Photosearch, Inc.
Senior Manufacturing Buyer: Alfred C. Dorsey
Printer and Binder: Hamilton Printing Company
Cover Printer: Phoenix Color Corp.

Library of Congress Cataloging-in-Publication Data

Introduction to comparative government / Michael Curtis, general editor; Jean Blondel
... [et al.].—5th ed.
    p. cm.
  Includes bibliographical references and index.
  ISBN 0-321-10478-1 (pbk.)
  1. Comparative government. I. Curtis, Michael, 1923–II. Blondel, Jean, 1929–

  JF51 .I58 2003
  320.3—dc21

2002072996

Please visit our Web site at http://www.ablongman.com.

ISBN 0-321-36481-3

1 2 3 4 5 6 7 8 9 10—HT—05 04 03 02

For
Ann and Kenny

Brief Contents

Detailed Contents

Part 1   INDUSTRIAL DEMOCRACIES

Part 2   COMMUNIST AND POST-COMMUNIST SYSTEMS

CHAPTER **7**   **THE GOVERNMENT OF THE RUSSIAN FEDERATION**

Roger E. Kanet and John S. Reshetar Jr. **357**

Part 3   DEVELOPING COUNTRIES

Preface

OUR APPROACH

This book introduces students to the subject of comparative government and politics through both an analytical and institutional approach. The authors believe it is desirable, even essential, to use this double approach to provide a valid and meaningful understanding of the subject. A wise bird uses both wings to fly. Our approach allows unusual flexibility for purposes of instruction, since students can benefit from exposure to alternative ways of comparing political systems.

The book therefore is not based on any narrow or rigid theoretical approach. It does not force the material into categories that do not provide understanding or that make learning difficult for beginning students. This book allows each instructor and student to choose the comparative approach that he or she thinks is most helpful for understanding the whole or parts of political systems.

To help that understanding, the authors have written with clarity and have throughout tried to avoid unnecessary jargon, unfamiliar terminology, and unduly complex classifications. What is important about this book is that the authors have used a more *descriptive, accessible style* than other texts available at the present time so that all can learn about the realities and performances of the countries we cover.

Each chapter is divided into three discrete sections. The first is the history and socioeconomic development of the country and the bases on which the regimes rest, the norms and rules of each society. The second section is devoted to political processes and institutions, a subject that so many other texts have neglected or relegated to minor significance. The third section looks at various aspects of public policies, including economic, social, and foreign affairs. By this method, we can obtain comparisons among the chapters as well as within them, a method that again provides instructors and students with flexibility.

OUR COUNTRIES

This updated edition provides introductions to countries familiar in the previous edition, but it also adds an analysis for the first time of Middle East systems. We examine the politics of some important industrialized democratic countries (Great Britain, France, Germany, and Japan), two communist and post-communist countries (Russia and China), and three developing countries in different continents (India, Mexico, and Nigeria). We also focus on the dramatic changes taking place in Western Europe with the recent transformation of the European Community into the European Union, and with the discussion of the role and status of the North Atlantic Treaty Organization. We believe that the new chapter on governments and politics in the Middle East is now crucial for students. The Middle East has become a prominent part of political discussion after the dramatic attacks on New York and Washington, D.C., on September 11, 2001, and the U.S. actions in Afghanistan and Iraq.

The chapters exemplify the politics, policies, and problems of democratic and industrialized states, past and present communist systems, and developing countries. Why have these countries been chosen? The reason is partly that they are or have been of great historical or contemporary significance, and partly because of the wealth of political experience and diverse behavior patterns they represent. The study of these countries is interesting in itself, but it is also instructive for those wanting to understand the world in which we live, especially at this time of unusual flux in a number of the major political systems, and in international politics generally with new threats to security.

OUR FEATURES

This edition introduces a number of new features, helpful for understanding factual material and theoretical approaches.

Country Profile

The chapters begin with a profile of the country or region, constructed in a consistent way across the chapters, thus providing uniformity for the whole book. We recognize that the statistics in these profiles, taken from official sources, may not always correspond exactly to those provided by international organizations that may appear elsewhere within a chapter, but the small differences do not detract from their essential validity.

Thinking Critically

The authors have provided a number of questions for instructors to use and students to ponder at the end of each of the three sections of a chapter. Students will therefore be encouraged to think about the reading, apply and review what they have learned, and be prepared for the next section.

Web Sites

Each chapter provides a list of relevant Web sites that students can use for up-to-date, detailed information on the individual system or parts of it. These sites can serve as the starting point for student research or as a first step to additional exploration of the countries examined in the book.

"A Closer Look" and "Review" Boxes

This edition introduces two new features, "A Closer Look" and "Review" boxes, both of which provide succinct information on a particular aspect of each system.

Visuals

All tables and statistics have been brought up-to-date, including electoral results up to the point of publication. The photos in each chapter illustrate significant people and institutions. The maps have been drawn for easy comprehension.

SUPPLEMENTS

Instructor's Manual/Test Bank

Written by Dwayne Woods of Purdue University, the Instructor's Manual/Test Bank includes chapter summaries, key terms, multiple-choice questions, true/false questions, and essay questions.

Longman Comparative Politics Web Site, *www.ablongman.com/ comparativepolitics*

On this Web site students can take interactive geography quizzes, find out how much they know about the 24 countries featured on the site, and learn how to use the narrative and statistical data in the country profiles.

ACKNOWLEDGMENTS

Both individually and collectively, the 11 authors of the book owe intellectual debts to many colleagues who have given valuable advice, and also to our students at different institutions. We also want to thank the various readers of drafts of the manuscript, whose comments and suggestions improved the end result. The reviewers to whom we are indebted are as follows:

Donald Barry, Lehigh University

Richard E. Chard, State University of New York at Stony Brook

Mark Cichock, University of Texas at Arlington

Edward DeClair, Gettysburg College

Mark W. Delancy, University of South Carolina

Manoutchehr Eskandari-Qajar, Santa Barbara City College

Michael W. Foley, Catholic University of America

Sumit Ganguly, Hunter College

William Garner, Southern Illinois University

Bertil L. Hanson, Oklahoma State University

Stephen P. Hoffman, Taylor University

Alana Jadel, North Carolina State University

Michael Levy, Southeast Missouri University

Frank Meyers, State University of New York at Stony Brook

Sofia Perez, Boston University

Richard Piper, University of Tampa

Jonas Pontusson, Cornell University

George Romoser, University of New Hampshire

Nirvikar Singh, Delhi School of Economics

Dale Story, University of Texas at Arlington

James White, University of North Carolina

Paul Wallace, University of Missouri–Columbia

Ife Williams, Savannah State College

Dwayne Woods, Purdue University

Michael Curtis

Introduction

Michael Curtis

On September 11, 2001, attacks on the World Trade Center in New York City, a symbol of American wealth, and on the Pentagon, a symbol of American strength, killed thousands of civilians. This was the worst single episode of terrorism on U.S. territory. The United States responded by declaring a war on terrorism and taking military and economic action, starting in Afghanistan against those who had unleashed the attacks in support of their version of Islam—which for them meant overcoming the forces of modernity, materialism, and secularism and spreading their idea of the true faith, the core of their identity and behavior. For the student of comparative politics, the September 11 attacks are a salutary reminder that knowledge and assessment of foreign countries, their political systems, behavior patterns, religious and political beliefs, are essential in our twenty-first century. George Washington, in his Farewell Address in 1796, warned that "it is our true policy to steer clear of permanent alliances with any portion of the foreign world." Yet the September 11 events are only the most vivid incidents illustrating that in a world in which globalization is so important and in which the nature of war has dramatically changed, isolation is not viable and international cooperation is imperative, as is knowledge of other countries, for students as well as for those concerned with national security issues.

It is not easy in our complex world to become familiar with all of the dramatic events that occur, or even all of the major ones. In the last few years we have witnessed ethnic wars in the Balkans, militant insurgencies in the Philippines and other countries, revolt in Chechnya against Russian control, internal hostilities in Kashmir that have involved India and Pakistan, turmoil in the Middle East, and international terrorism. Nevertheless, students as well as practitioners of politics must try to understand the various political systems of the world, the beliefs, values, and cultures of foreign countries, and the relationship between different social and economic factors such as the degree of poverty, population increase, treatment of women, growth of large cities, and extent of corruption, and attitudes of rage, hatred, envy, religious extremism, resentment of Western mores and practices, and the political and military action resulting from such factors and attitudes.

WHY STUDY COMPARATIVE POLITICS AND GOVERNMENT?

Why should we study the political systems, behavior, and values of other countries? Why should we try to make comparisons between countries? A simple answer is that an essential part of being educated today is knowing something about the politics of foreign countries. For many there is also a fascination and intellectual excitement in the study of foreign systems and in the discovery of political ways of life different from our own.

Study of foreign political systems, or comparative politics, is useful for additional reasons. We can understand better our own system if we can appreciate its similarities to and differences from other systems. We can see, for example, and try to understand why the United States Supreme Court can declare legislation unconstitutional while the highest court in Britain cannot. We can observe that the central authorities in the former Soviet Union up to 1991 controlled the republics making up that country to a greater degree than the U.S. federal government controls the states. In both cases we are led to general conclusions about the nature of power in the United States as well as in the other countries. Knowledge of the politics of foreign countries allows us both as citizens and as students to discuss and evaluate more intelligently U.S. policy and attitudes to those countries.

Study of different systems lets us compare the ways in which governments and political participants face similar problems and respond to them and to the needs and demands of their citizens. All societies deal with crucial matters such as health, control over the economy, management of production, or changes caused by new technology and by modernization. Students will be interested in the distinctive ways in which different societies deal with problems of this kind. We can learn both positive and negative lessons from

experiences such as the National Health Service in Britain, government proposals for economic planning in France, workers' participation in industrial management in Germany, the relationship between religion and politics in the Middle East, the cooperation of the state and the industrial sector in the development of technology in Japan, the problems of modernization in Communist countries or countries influenced by Communism, the efforts of a changing, diverse society such as India to maintain a democratic form of government, or the attempts of African countries such as Nigeria to create stable political systems.

An effective comparison of systems must accurately describe and satisfactorily explain the similarities and differences of the systems being compared. The first step in this process is to understand how individual systems, or parts of those systems, function, and how individuals behave, react to, and are involved in politics. From the specific information and understanding of the political institutions and the political processes of different countries, we may then pose questions of a more general nature. We can ask questions as to the extent and ways in which systems are democratic, their level of political development, their degree of stability or effectiveness in making decisions, or the manner in which political ideologies and other factors influence their policy.

To answer questions of this kind we need to decide on some criteria for analysis of the similarities and differences between countries and political behavior in them. Such criteria, in turn, may often influence policy.

What criteria should be used to provide generalizations? Since Aristotle (384–322 B.C.E.) began the study of comparative politics, countless students have analyzed the nature and quality of political regimes. They have looked at the way the functions of government are performed and the relationship between rulers and ruled. Students have also examined the kinds of rules that exist and actions that are taken. They ask if the ruling groups are acting in their own interest or the interest of the whole community. They observe how much force and how much persuasion are being exercised.

REVIEW

1.1 APPROACHES TO THE STUDY OF COMPARATIVE GOVERNMENT

- *Systems theory:* political activity seen as an interrelated system in which *inputs* stemming from demands and supports from individuals and groups lead to *outputs* or policies, and a continuing feedback process.
- *Communication theory:* political activity responding to interrelated messages, and to changing factors.
- *Structural functionalism:* political systems understood as requiring similar functions performed by political structures of different kinds.
- *Behavioralism:* use of rigorous methods in concept formation and quantitative resting.
- *Rational choice:* individuals and groups seen as maximizing rational utility in politics.
- *Institutional analysis:* detailed or "thick" description and comparison of political institutions.
- *Statistical analysis:* comparing political variables across countries, in different settings, and at different times.
- *Political development:* the ongoing process of modernization viewed in different ways.
- *Dependency theory:* developing countries, especially in Latin America, explained by dependence on actions of advanced industrial countries.
- *Political culture:* attitudes of citizens to politics and political personalities.
- *Political cleavages:* divisions resulting from differences in class, religion, ethnicity, territory, nationality, tribe.
- *Globalization:* impact of international factors, information, and communications developments on political action.

The modern method of political science has sought to formulate general statements applicable to the large numbers of particular cases. It argues that a necessary scientific approach means a search for generalizations, regularities of behavior, and—even more ambitiously—laws of the social and political process. The search for generalizations is necessary and, indeed, essential if comparative analysis is to be valuable, but it is not easy because of the multiplicity and diversity of human activities and because of the play of chance factors that affect the political process. The house of comparative government and politics has many mansions and can be analyzed in different ways.

In recent years two major additions have been made in the study of comparative politics. The area of interest was once largely limited to those few countries in Western Europe and the English-speaking world with highly developed institutions and a familiar history. These coun-

tries were the principal powers of the world; now there are 192 nation-states. Students are, therefore, also interested in the politics of the newer nation-states, in which an increasing part of the world's population lives, and try to include these states within the scope of the generalizations about comparative politics. About 5 billion of the world's 6 billion population live in these states. Moreover, students are not content merely with descriptions of political institutions and constitutional arrangements; more attention is now paid to nongovernmental and social organizations and to the political behavior of individuals and groups.

TOWARD A THEORY OF COMPARATIVE GOVERNMENT

What do we want to know about politics, and what is the best way to obtain information about crucial questions such as who governs, how do people govern, what objectives do they have, and what is the relationship between the government and the people? Answers to these questions must take account of the ever changing nature of politics throughout the world, unpredicted events, and new factors that affect political behavior. To list all these factors would be beyond the scope of this book, but it is well to indicate some of the more recent important factors. Prominent among these are the process of globalization, the revolution in communications technology, and the downfall of the Soviet Union. The ongoing and rapidly increasing process of globalization, the international integration of markets in goods, capital, and services, has meant similar experi- ence or knowledge of behavior patterns, food, music, dress, television programs, and movies. It may also mean immediate diffusion of informa- tion of political activities throughout the world. (see Table 1.1). Communications technology has directly affected politics in many ways: cassettes helped bring about the revolution in Iran in 1979, and email helped topple the president of the Philippines in 2001.

At the end of the 1980s, 16 states were ruled by Communist parties or some version of a con- cept of Marxism-Leninism, and a number of other states were influenced by that concept. Commu- nist states ruled over a third of the world's popu- lation. The 1989 revolutions in Eastern and Central Europe and the unexpected downfall and

TABLE 1.1

GLOBAL INSTITUTIONS

Institution		Membership	Nations' Share of World GDP (%)	Nations' Share of World Population (%)
P-5	UN Security Council	Five permanent members (China, France, Russian Federation, United Kingdom, United States) plus 10 others elected for two-year term	40.9	30.6
G-8	Major industrial democracies	Canada, France, Germany, Italy, Japan, United Kingdom, United States, Russia	64.0	11.8
G-7		Major industrial lands without Russia		
G-10	Major economic powers	Belgium, Canada, France, Germany, Italy, Japan, Netherlands, Sweden, Switzerland, United Kingdom, United States	67.8	12.5
G-22	Major economic powers and emerging markets	Argentina, Australia, Brazil, Canada, China, France, Germany, Hong Kong, India, Indonesia, Italy, Japan, Republic of Korea, Malaysia, Mexico, Poland, Russian Federation, Singapore, South Africa, Thailand, United Kingdom, United States	81.7	64.8
G-24	Major developing countries	Algeria, Argentina, Brazil, Colombia, Democratic Republic of the Congo, Côte d'Ivoire, Egypt, Ethiopia, Gabon, Ghana, Guatemala, India, Iran, Lebanon, Mexico, Nigeria, Pakistan, Peru, Philippines, Sri Lanka, Syria, Trinidad and Tobago, Venezuela, Yugoslavia	8.93	34.6
	Developing and transition countries	133 countries	16.9	76.0

REVIEW
1.2

GLOBALIZATION—WHAT'S REALLY NEW?

Some argue that globalization is not new, and that the world was more integrated a century ago. Trade and investment as a proportion of GDP were comparable, and with borders open, many people were migrating abroad. What's new this time?

NEW MARKETS

- Growing global markets in services—banking, insurance, transport.
- New financial markets—deregulated, globally linked, working around the clock, with action at a distance in real time, with new instruments such as derivatives.
- Deregulation of antitrust laws and proliferation of mergers and acquisitions.
- Global consumer markets with global brands.

NEW ACTORS

- Multinational corporations integrating their production and marketing, dominating world production.
- The World Trade Organization—the first multilateral organization with authority to enforce national governments' compliance with rules.
- An international criminal court system in the making.
- A booming international network of NGOs.
- Regional blocs proliferating and gaining importance—European Union, Association of South-East Asian Nations, Mercosur, North American Free Trade Association, Southern African Development Community, among many others.
- More policy coordination groups—G-8, G-10, G-22, G-77, OECD.

NEW RULES AND NORMS

- Market economic policies spreading around the world, with greater privatization and liberalization than in earlier decades.
- Widespread adoption of democracy as the choice of political regime.
- Human rights conventions and instruments building up in both coverage and number of signatories—and growing awareness among people around the world.
- Consensus goals and action agenda for development.
- Conventions and agreements on the global environment—biodiversity, ozone layer, disposal of hazardous wastes, desertification, climate change.
- Multilateral agreements in trade, taking on such new agendas as environmental and social conditions.
- New multilateral agreements—for services, intellectual property, communications—more binding on national governments than any previous agreements.
- The Multilateral Agreement on Investment under debate.

(continues)

dissolution of the Soviet Union in 1991 led to the creation of new regimes in 12 states in Europe formerly under Soviet influence, and 15 states formed from the Soviet Union (see Table 1.2). The events of 1989–1991 also led to a discrediting of and decline in support for communist politics, the Leninist view of a single party as the vanguard of the population, and a state-controlled economy.

Other factors influencing recent political action may be briefly mentioned. The aging Western populations and the decline in birth-rates in the developed countries and the correspondingly higher birthrates in Africa, the Middle East, and Asia; the greater longevity in almost all countries; the changing lifestyle of women and their increasing role in public affairs and in the economy; the attempts to introduce democratic institutions in previously authoritar-

ian systems in Latin America, Asia, and Russia; the creation of a united Germany with its capital in Berlin; the increasing immigration into the Western European countries; the prominent role of television in political campaigns and reliance on polling in the choice of leaders; the continuing high level of spending on social security; the end of apartheid in South Africa and the election in 1994 as its president of Nelson Mandela, leader of the African National Congress; the Taliban regime in Afghanistan, its imposition of Islamic law, its oppression of women, and its overthrow by a U.S.-supported coalition in 2001; the greater concern for civil rights in many countries; the more moderate policies of the political left regarding public ownership of enterprises, intervention in the economy, taxes, and public spending; the rise of a fundamentalist form of

A CLOSER LOOK

1.1

GEOGRAPHY AND DEVELOPMENT

The geography of a country may not determine its level of economic development but clearly they are related. In tropical countries, factors such as poor soil, unreliable climate, and vulnerability to infectious diseases help explain the lack of development. In the substantial and growing gap between rich and poor countries, the richest 20 percent of the world's population now has over 70 times the income of the poorest 20 percent. The latter group live in tropical regions or have problems in access to world markets. The people of tropical countries have less income, a lower rate of economic growth, poorer health, and a shorter life expectancy than do the people of temperate countries.

TABLE 1.2

FIVE EX-SOVIET ASIAN REPUBLICS, 2002

	Population (millions)	% Muslim	GDP per Capita (dollars)
Uzbekistan	25.7	88	1,670
Kazakhstan	15.5	47	5,870
Tajikistan	6.2	85	980
Kyrgyzstan	3.3	75	1,620
Turkmenistan	4.8	89	4,300

Islam; the use of terrorism. This book takes these considerations into account.

Our Analytical Approach

Each chapter deals with four essential aspects of a particular country or region in the following order:

1. *Factors that have helped shape political behavior:* historical background, geography, economic and social conditions, ethnic and caste groups, religious beliefs and ideologies.

2. *The political process:* the ways in which leaders are chosen, the role of political parties and interest groups, the manner in which individual citizens participate in politics.

3. *The major political institutions:* the way they exercise power, the interrelationship between them, and the restraints on them.

4. *Public policy:* certain basic functions performed by political institutions in all systems, such as maintaining internal order and external security, resolving the competitive demands of individuals and groups, raising expenditure to pay for services provided by government, regulating the behavior of citizens in differing ways.

The author of each of the country studies provides basic information about these four aspects without the use of jargon or unhelpful methodologies so that the political system and its policies can be comprehensible.

With information and analysis of this kind, we can formulate generalizations that are the heart of comparative politics. Our studies of Western and non-Western countries can be used for that purpose in a variety of ways:

1. The countries can be compared on the basis of the various political, social, and economic problems they have encountered, and they can be compared according to their different paths to political development and modernity.

2. The three most important West European countries can be compared with the

REVIEW 1.3

A CHOICE OF SUBJECTS TO STUDY

- Single county or political system.
- A number of countries on basis of geographical area, culture, ethnicity, nationalism, religion.
- Major political institutions (executive, legislative, judicial) or processes.
- Typologies of political systems or units in those systems.
- Patterns of political activities.
- Global political and socioeconomic variables, analyzed statistically.
- Middle-range theories, examining and comparing limited ranges of data and different forms of behavior.
- Ideological bases of political regimes.
- Public policies.

EUROPEAN COUNTRIES FORMERLY UNDER SOVIET INFLUENCE

Albania	Macedonia (formerly part of Yugoslavia)
Bosnia-Herzegovina	Poland
Bulgaria	Romania
Croatia	Serbia and Montenegro
Czech Republic	Slovakia
Hungary	Slovenia

non-Western countries. Questions can be raised about general differences in the nature and style of politics in Western and non-Western nations.

3. The two foremost past and present Communist countries—the Soviet Union–Russia and China—can be compared with the non-Communist countries and also with each other as differences and rivalries emerged between them.

4. The states created after World War II can be compared with the older states. India and Nigeria, two of the most important of the less developed countries, can illustrate the problems facing the newer nation-states in creating stable and effective political systems.

5. The liberal democratic countries can be compared with the nondemocratic countries. Thus, questions can be posed about why some countries are more likely to be democratic than others and what factors are likely to foster democratic systems.

6. The states illustrate different kinds of party systems—one, two, or multiparty—and the relations between those systems and governmental institutions and policy.

7. The Middle East states illustrate the interaction between religion and politics, and the problems of modernization.

What Theory to Use

Comparison is inevitable in life, and people differ in their assessments of individuals, ideas, and policies. Not surprisingly, analysts differ on the subject of comparative government, how it should be studied, and what themes to examine. Should we fight a civil war over this? The most ambitious would enter battle carrying a banner calling for grand, general theories and models to frame characteristics common to all political systems. The most well known of these attempts at grand theory was the structural-functionalism approach, which defines systems in terms of functions that are performed by different structures in political systems.

Doubts about the usefulness of such grandiose theories led to a more modest approach, usually referred to as "middle-range theory," seeking generalizations based on cross-national studies and empirical data of specific organizations and institutions and behavior patterns. Since no useful generalization can be drawn from information from a single country, institution, or group, cross-national comparisons are needed to provide sufficient data on which such generalizations and explanations can be based.

What should be the subject matter of those generalizations? At one point, comparative analysis was largely limited to constitutional structures, political institutions, and their interaction and to the precise description of institutions, processes, and policies in particular countries. Themes now are much broader, if ever changing. Analysis must acknowledge the multifaceted nature of comparative government, the multicausal factors that are relevant, and the overlapping of the study with other intellectual disciplines, especially sociology, economics, and psychology. If the central concerns of comparative government are with decision making and the absence of decision making, with rights and duties, with the rules and conventions to deal with conflicts of many kinds (over resources, rewards, power, and distribution) and resolve them in various ways (some violent, some persuasive, some by influence), many factors are relevant. Comparative government cannot neglect the social, economic, cultural, ethnic, national, and religious factors that affect and can help explain political behavior. No one factor, whether it be economics or culture, is sufficient unto itself for full explanation.

In this book, we have tried to take account of these factors, combining the precise, up-to-date description of political systems and a theoretical framework in which those systems can be compared and understood. We recognize that the focus of attention changes: if the economy is important, so are themes of globalization, feminism, identity, ethnicity, and religion. We believe that students and instructors will find it most useful to begin with the classification of the various systems.

CLASSIFICATION OF SYSTEMS

Every political system is at once unique and different from all others and is in flux. Britain presents an interesting mixture of traditional and modern forms of organization and behavior. France, though an old state, has had its political continuity disrupted by frequent changes of system and internal divisions. The former Soviet Union was the first Communist system to be established; its ruling party controlled not only its own system but also the policies of Communist parties in other countries for many years, until the collapse of its system in 1990–1991. In China, the most populous Communist state, the vast majority of the people are peasants, not proletarians as Marxist theory suggests. Germany and Japan are prosperous democracies that were rapidly successful after the devastation and collapse of their systems from defeat in World War II; Japan now has the second highest gross domestic product (GDP) per capita of any industrialized country.

India is the most populous state emerging from colonial rule after the war that has remained essentially democratic in character. India is a democracy that, while still a developing country, has one of the six largest economies in the world.

Nigeria, with a fifth of black Africans, has alternated between civilian rule and dominant military rule. Mexico experienced a historic peaceful political change in 2000 with the election as president for the first time of someone outside the previously dominant party. The Middle East countries face difficulties in resolving problems of regional peace and security and, more recently, in coping with religious extremists.

Since political systems do not fit neatly in rigid categories, all classification is at best partial and temporary. Nevertheless, classification serves to illuminate some politically meaningful similarities and dissimilarities. Of the many ways to classify political systems, a few are discussed here.

The Number and Kinds of Rulers

Aristotle is usually regarded as the father of comparative political analysis. His classification (see Table 1.3) was based on the number of people who participated in governing (one, few, or many); on the ethical quality of their rule, depending on whether it was in the general interest or in their self-interest (A or B); and on their socioeconomic status (C). Those regimes that served only the interests of the ruling group were perversions of the true constitutional forms.

Aristotle clearly preferred the aristocratic form (2A) because the mean and moderate were most desirable. Other classical theorists in ancient Rome thought that simple and moderate forms of government would degenerate and that stability depended on the existence of a "mixed state" with all the social classes either participating or being represented to some degree.

The Aristotelian theory has been useful in indicating the number and nature of the governing group. Modern democracies, including the United States, would be in category 3A. But in all systems a relatively small number of people either rule or dominate the political process. This group is sometimes termed the political elite. The

TABLE 1.3

THE ARISTOTELIAN DIVISION OF GOVERNMENTS

Number of Rulers	A Rule in the General Interest	B Self-Interest Rule	C Social Group
1. One	Monarchy	Tyranny	King
2. Few	Aristocracy	Oligarchy	The wealthy
3. Many	Polity or democracy	Ochlocracy	The poor

elite may remain closed to outsiders as in aristo-cratic systems or as in communist, one-party, or military-dominated systems. In such a case the system is likely to be monolithic in that only a single or a limited political point of view is allowed. In other systems the elite is open to the emergence of individuals from a diversity of backgrounds and with different views. The elite then consists not of members of one group but of a number of groups and individuals competing for political power. Systems of this kind, which allow for choice among competing elite groups, are known as pluralistic (see Figure 1.1).

Political Culture

Anthropologists have used the concept of culture to provide a total picture of the life, actions, and beliefs of a community. For comparative politics

the concept of political culture has been used to clarify those community-held beliefs, feelings, and values that influence political behavior. In each community there are sets of attitudes toward the political system. They depend on knowledge of the way in which the system operates, its personnel, and its policies. They also depend on the ability of people to participate in the political process and on the degree to which the system is accepted as legitimate (the right of the government to exercise power).

In all countries the political values, norms, and behavior patterns, or political culture, are transmitted to present and future citizens. This political socialization is produced by a variety of agencies such as the family, school system, religious bodies, mass media, popular literature and art, fable, heroes, and popular mythology. In developed systems, such as the United States, the

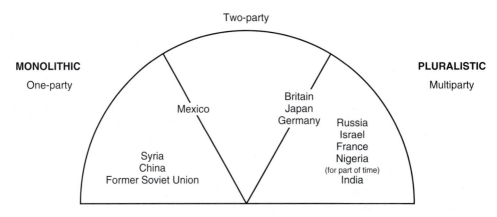

Figure 1.1 MONOLITHIC, PLURALISTIC, AND PARTY SYSTEMS IN OUR COUNTRIES

THE CLASH OF CIVILIZATIONS

In an influential book *The Clash of Civilizations and the Making of World Order* (1996), Samuel Huntington suggested that cultures based on civilizations would be a source of future conflict in the world. He divided the countries of the world into seven or eight major civilizations: Western, Confucian, Japanese, Islamic, Hindu, Slavic-Orthodox, Latin American, and perhaps African. The main divisions in the world and the dominating source of conflict will be cultural, between nations and groups of different civilizations. Huntington defines a civilization as the highest cultural grouping of people and the broadest level of cultural identity people have. This identity results from objective factors (language, history, religion, customs, etc.) and from subjective self-identification of people. Over the centuries, Huntington argues, differences among civilizations have generated the most prolonged and the most violent conflicts.

family has been thought of as the dominant factor in the process of socialization, though this view has been qualified. Socialization can take place either unconsciously, such as by membership in a caste in India, or more deliberately, as in the communes in China or the kibbutzim in Israel. The impact of all these agencies of socialization varies according to changes in population, and according to social relations, technological innovation, and political events.

Political Development

Attempts to classify systems according to stages of political development have been stimulated by the creation, since 1945, of a large number of states, now the majority in the world, all trying to establish viable political systems and modernize their economies and societies. One influential early theory of political leadership types was formulated by Max Weber, who classified societies as follows:

Traditional: based on conformity of the people, rule on the basis of tradition or divine law by a monarch or aristocracy whose power is made legitimate by status or heredity. Examples of this type are Saudi Arabia and Thailand.

Charismatic: political leadership based on personal magnetism and devotion, and often exercised by a military leader or religious prophet. Examples

here might be Egypt under Nasser, Cuba under Castro, and Indonesia under Sukarno.

Bureaucratic: a constitutional regime in which the legal rules are established and officials adhere to those rules and exercise authority according to known procedures. Most Western political systems are of this kind.

Economic and social modernization is relatively easy to define, but it is more difficult to define political development. Many recent studies compare two "ideal types" of societies—traditional and modern—to help explain economic, social, and political differences.

Some of the comparisons made are the following:

1. In traditional societies the vast majority of the population is engaged in agriculture, which accounts for a large part of the gross national product (GDP) of the country. In modern societies, such as that of the United States, only a small percentage of the population works in agriculture, which accounts for a small part of the GDP; in the United States it is now under 3 percent. Instead, the population works in industry and, to an even larger degree, in providing services, which in some countries now account for the majority of the workforce.

2. In traditional societies the chief social relationships are the family, the tribe, or the clan, from which the dominant values derive. In modern societies there is a more complex and diverse set of relationships. Individuals belong to a variety of different groups, such as trade unions, business associations, religious faiths, and political and social organizations. The chief values come from a wide variety of sources. Science and technology are significant factors, though religious and traditional values may still remain to some extent.

3. In traditional countries the population is less literate, on average much poorer, shorter-lived, and more rural than in modernized countries.

4. Politics in traditional countries have been less differentiated than in modern systems, where political functions are carried out by different categories of people and where political rule is justified by rational principles rather than by concepts like divine right or heredity.

The distinction between traditional and modern does not imply any judgment of inferiority or superiority regarding individuals or societies. Many traditional societies have produced significant cultures, elaborate political structures, and efficient administrative systems.

Factors such as greater industrialization, application of technology and science, economic growth leading to increases in gross national product and per capita income, more education for a larger part of the population, independence of women, increasing urbanization, improved transportation, and Western influence have disrupted traditional societies and changed the economic, social, and political structure in those countries (see Table 1.4).

Countries have taken different paths to modernity. In some cases the path has been Western-style democracy, in others fascism or communism, and in many of the newer countries different forms of nationalism and social change.

No exact correlation exists between economic and social change and political development. Earlier studies that tried to explain political development simply by trends in a society toward

TABLE 1.4

TEN COUNTRIES: POPULATION AND ECONOMY, 2004

Country	Land Area (thousand km)	Population (millions)	Urban % of Total	GDP per Capita ($ thousand)	Public Spending (% of GDP)		
					Education	Health	Defense
Britain	244	59	89	26.1	4.6	6.3	2.4
China	9,561	1,294	37.7	4.5	N/A	2.0	2.5
France	547	59.8	76.1	26.9	5.7	7.3	2.5
Germany	356	82.4	87.9	27.1	4.6	8.1	1.5
India	3,288	1,049	28.1	2.6	4.1	0.9	2.3
Japan	378	127.2	65.3	26.9	3.6	6.2	1.0
Mexico	1,958	102	75.2	8.9	5.1	2.7	0.5
Nigeria	924	102.9	45.9	0.8	N/A	0.8	N/A
Russia	17,075	144.1	73.3	8.2	3.1	3.7	4.0
United States	9,373	291	79.8	35.7	5.6	6.2	3.4

Source: Human Development Report, 2004.

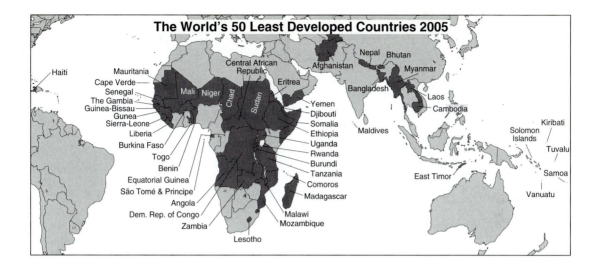

urbanization, industrialization, greater communication, and more education have now proved inadequate explanations of a complex process.

One important recent development is the economic growth of East Asia, particularly in the now-prosperous states of Indonesia, Japan, Hong Kong and Taiwan, Malaysia, Singapore, South Korea, and Thailand. These countries have not had one economic model, but rather a mix of policies with varying state intervention. Moreover, most of these states are more authoritarian than democratic, with a combination of some democratic political framework with a one-party system and with strong controls over freedom of expression and public behavior.

All states have differing mixtures of traditional and modern elements and are at different stages of political development. There is no single way in which the process of political development occurs or any one group that is crucial in that process. Change was fostered in Japan by the aristocratic oligarchy, in Western Europe by commercial traders and capitalists, in Latin America by strong leaders, in revolutionary countries by leaders of a political party or movement, in some countries such as Morocco by traditional authorities, in some African countries by bureaucratic-military elites, and in other new

countries such as Nigeria by a variety of groups and institutions.

In all countries the process of political development leads to certain changes, of which some important ones are usually the following:

1. A complex governmental structure in which different institutions and people perform different functions, such as legislative, executive, judicial, and military actions.

2. Attempts to integrate the whole community to achieve a coherent and stable system.

3. A claim to legitimacy of the leadership group based on a secular and rational view of the right to govern.

4. A widening of political participation in some way to the whole population, which helps choose the leadership group.

5. The ability of government to manage tensions within the system and to implement policies.

The UN Development Program compares systems using an index of human development rather than relying simply on statistics of productivity or income. The three key indicators would be life expectancy and a healthy life; degree of literacy and knowledge; and purchasing power of individuals or GDP per capita. The index compares the quality and welfare of societies by taking account of factors such as education, nutrition, social welfare, degree of inequality, cultural norms; social problems such as drugs, divorce, and homelessness; and extent of political participation and freedom (See A Closer Look 1.5).

Development is affected by many factors. These would include the different rates of economic growth, population increase (now about 2 percent in developing countries and 0.5 percent in industrial countries), degree of political stability, extent of ethnic or internal strife, the democratic or authoritarian nature of the political system, and the effect of world trade on a country.

In the developing countries as a whole, average life expectancy has increased by 16 years and adult literacy by 40 percent since 1960. Many of these countries have made striking gains in health and education and have increased average income. Yet other developing countries have done poorly, and about one-quarter have actually suffered a fall in living standards. Poverty, especially in Africa, remains a serious problem for more than 1 billion people, nearly one-fifth of the world's population, many of whom lack primary health care and are illiterate. In the world as a whole, and in developing countries in particular, women still lag behind men in power, wealth, and opportunity, though there have been important changes in the lives of women over the last 20 years.

Is there any correlation between human development and human freedom and civil liberties in societies? There does not appear to be an exact causal relation between the two, but it is clear that countries that rank high on the freedom index, based on compliance with international treaties and conventions of human

A CLOSER LOOK 1.4

AFRICA, 2005

- Poorest continent in the world: in sub-Saharan Africa, 49 percent are very poor.
- High birthrate and population increase.
- South Africa's GDP is 4 times the combined GDPs of the 10 other countries in southern Africa.
- Ethnic divisions in many countries.
- About 2,000 language groups, of which 50 are important. 85% of people speak 15 core languages.
- Countries are in 11 different economic organizations with overlapping membership.
- In the 1990s, over 10 countries declined in terms of human development; many had a decline in income per capita and in life expectancy, partly due to a considerable increase in HIV/AIDS.
- More multiparty elections in the 1990s; peaceful transfer of power in 13 countries where leaders lost an election.
- According to Freedom House survey, 6 countries in "free" category, 16 "party free," and 25 "not free."
- Francophone countries, former colonies of France and Belgium where French is the official language, account for about half the area of sub-Saharan Africa and 17 countries in West and Central Africa.
- Islam is the dominant religion in West Africa.
- Why has democracy been difficult to achieve? Legacy of colonial rule, failures of individual African leaders, corruption, weak institutions that cannot guarantee democratic changes of power, lack of independent bureaucracy and judiciary.

A CLOSER LOOK
1.5

THE HUMAN DEVELOPMENT INDEX, 2004

The index produced by the United Nations Development Program covers 177 countries. The countries we examine are ranked as follows: Japan (9), France (16), Britain (12), Germany (19), Israel (22), Bahrain (40), Mexico (53), Russia (57), Libya (58), Saudi Arabia (77), China (94), Jordan (90), Iran (101), Syria (106), India (127), Nigeria (151). Norway is 1 and the United States is 8.

In terms of high, medium, and low levels of human development, the countries we examine can be characterized as follows:

High: Britain, France, Germany, Japan, United States, Israel, Bahrain, UAR, Qatar, Kuwait
Medium: China, India, Mexico, Russia, Libya, Lebanon, Saudi Arabia, Jordan, Iran, Syria, Sudan
Low: Nigeria, Yemen

rights, tend to rank high in human development. Comparison also shows that between 1985 and 2002 a number of countries became more democratic and enjoyed greater political freedom.

Men and Women

The lives of men and women differ in terms of their access to resources, health care, education, and professional opportunities. Great disparities still remain between the sexes in spite of recent progress toward equality.

Education   Increasing numbers of women have been educated at the secondary level and beyond. Progress has been most rapid in Latin America, with a female literacy rate over 75 percent, and least in sub-Saharan Africa. In some areas women outnumber men in post-secondary schools.

Fertility   Higher education, family planning, and the increase in the number of women who work have led to lower fertility for women in most parts of the world. During the 25 years between 1970 and 1995, average global fertility declined from 6 to 4 births per woman.

REVIEW
1.4

WORLD POPULATION PROFILE, 2004

- World population 6.4 billion, expected to be 7.5 billion in 2020: developed countries have about 20 percent of population, and developing regions account for an increasing proportion of world population.

- Adolescents constitute a large proportion of the population in most developing regions and number more than previously in history. Under 30, the population numbers 3.4 billion.

- Population of the world is aging, especially in the West, as fewer children are born.

- Life expectancy has increased for women and men except in southern Africa.

- Population of people over 60 has increased, with many more older women than men.

- Urban population has increased to 47 percent of total population.

- Migration to world's richest countries is increasing.

Work   Women are still less active economically than are men. While in Africa and Asia 77–84 percent of men are economically active, only 29 percent of women in North Africa are active, and only 33–62 percent in Asia.

Women rarely account for more than 1–2 percent of senior executive positions, but their numbers have increased in the general category of administration and management. In the health and teaching professions, women are well represented, though usually at the lower levels of the status and wage hierarchy. Women are increasingly visible in the media as reporters and anchors but less well represented as program managers and senior editors. They are also less visible as Nobel Prize winners. Since 1901, when Nobel prizes began to be awarded, women have received only 34 of the total 634, and 12 of those shared the prize with a man.

Power   Women have rarely reached the highest levels of influence in the public and private sector. In the 1990s, only 10 of the 191 countries in the world had women as heads of government. About 8 percent of cabinet ministers were women and a larger number of women have been appointed to subministerial positions. In the legislatures of the world, progress for women has been mixed and varies widely among regions (see Table 1.6). The average proportion of women in national legislatures in 2001 was 14 percent (Table 1.7). It was highest in Sweden, where over half the cabinet ministers were women. In Western Europe as a whole, about 21 percent of legislators were women; in the European Parliament it was 30 percent. But in only 16 countries is women's representation in national assemblies over 25 members. The number of women in legislatures declined in Eastern Europe after 1987 and in Asia, but increased in Africa and Latin America.

Since 1974, when Argentina became the first state to have a woman president, 16 other states have chosen a women president or head of state. In 45 countries women have not held any ministerial position, and in another 13 they have not had junior positions. In only 16 countries have

they held over 20 percent of ministerial positions. Women have been most prominent in social ministries (health, education, housing, and welfare) and in the law and justice departments.

Women are underrepresented in the higher levels of political parties and senior legislative positions. About two-thirds of 871 parties in 80 countries have no woman in the governing bodies. Some countries, to remedy this, have recently introduced a more equitable quota for women in governing bodies.

Women have become influential in nongovernmental organizations (NGOs) at the grassroots, national, and international levels. Social issues previously largely ignored, such as violence against women and rights of choice, have entered the mainstream of public policy discussion.

TABLE 1.5

FREEDOM IN OUR COUNTRIES, 2005

| Comparative Measures, 1 is top | | | | Rank in World |
Country	Political Rights	Civil Rights	Rank	Economic Freedom
Britain	1	1	F	7
China	7	6	NF	112
France	1	1	F	44
Germany	1	1	F	18
India	2	3	F	118
Japan	1	3	F	39
Mexico	2	2	F	63
Nigeria	4	4	PF	141
Russia	6	5	NF	124
United States	1	1	F	12

F = Free, PF = Partly Free, NF = Not Free

In the world in 2005, 89 countries (with 44 percent of world's population) are free, 54 (19 percent of world's population) are partly free, and 49 (37 percent of world's population) are not free.

Source: Freedom House and Heritage Foundation.

TABLE 1.6

WOMEN IN THE LEGISLATURES OF SELECTED COUNTRIES, 2005

Country	Legislative Seats Held by Women (%) Upper House	Lower House	Year Given the Vote
Britain	18	18	1918, 1928
China	—	20	1949
France	17	12	1944
Germany	18	32	1918
India	11	8	1950
Japan	13	7	1945
Mexico	15	22	1947
Nigeria	2	6	1958
Russian Federation	3	9	1918
United States	14	15	1920
Israel	18	(one chamber)	1948

TABLE 1.7

WOMEN IN LEGISLATURES WORLDWIDE, 2005

World Average

Both Houses Combined	
Total legislators	42,704
Gender breakdown known for	41,139
Men	34,703
Women	6,436
Percentage of women	15.6%
Single House or Lower House	
Total legislators	36,222
Gender breakdown known for	35,032
Men	29,507
Women	5,525
Percentage of women	15.8%
Upper House or Senate	
Total legislators	6,382
Gender breakdown known for	6,107
Men	5,196
Women	911
Percentage of women	14.9%

Regional Averages

	Single House or Lower House (%)	Upper House or Senate (%)	Both Houses Combined (%)
Europe	18.7	17.1	18.4
Asia	15.2	13.5	15.0
Americas	18.5	18.3	18.4
Sub-Saharan Africa	14.5	11.7	14.2
Pacific	10.9	24.8	12.8
Arab States	6.8	7.8	7.0

Source: Inter-Parliamentary Union.

The Economic System

For some analysts, the chief characteristic of political systems is the nature of the economic system. Many socialists hold this view, but it is particularly important for Marxists, who stress the nature of the production process and the social or class relationships that are bound up with particular historical phases of that process. The Marxist philosophy sees history as propelled by the struggles between classes, the essential conflict always being between those who own the means of production and those who do not. The state is seen as the reflection of the interests of the dominant economic class and the support of the interests of that class. In contemporary capitalist systems, such as that of the United States, all organs of power would be seen mainly as organs of the capitalist class; opposing them would be socialist or communist systems.

There is an obvious connection among social relationships, the economic system, and political institutions. But there is no automatic correlation between an economic basis such as private ownership of property and political institutions or actions. Marxist theory has not taken account of the complexity and hetero-

REVIEW
1.5

WOMEN IN SOCIETY AND POLITICS, 2005

- Minority in world, 49.3 percent of population; a majority in developed areas; women live longer than men.
- Literacy rates increased, but illiteracy among women still high in much of Africa and parts of Asia; in rural areas much higher illiteracy than in urban areas; women outnumber men in higher education in many developed regions; nearly two-thirds of illiterates in the world are women.
- Marrying later, fewer children; in developed regions 1.9 births per woman, in Africa 6.
- Marriage less frequent and less stable; more divorce.
- Households smaller in size.
- More single-parent families; in developed countries women are the single parent in 75 percent of families.
- Increase in percent of workforce; now 40 percent in developed regions.
- Work in different occupations than men, usually lower pay and status; in developing countries many work as unpaid family laborers in agriculture and household.
- Earn less per hour than men, and earn less in general; often work part-time; still a considerable gender gap in income and activity.
- Major responsibility for household work and care of children.
- Often work more hours than men; working time fluctuates widely because of domestic obligations and work outside the home; women are unemployed more often than men.
- Work in occupations that are losing status, while men dominate new occupations of higher status.
- Underrepresented in production jobs in large cities; work mainly in professional, clerical, and especially service occupations, teaching, health.
- Constitute 70 percent of world's poor.
- Lack access to economic and political opportunities, including senior managerial jobs.
- Very underrepresented in all political positions and offices.
- Fewer women than men are employers.
- Minority among administrative and managerial workers, less than 30 percent in most regions of the world.

geneity of modern societies and regimes in three main ways. First, nothing in Marxism effectively explains the considerable diversity of political forms that capitalist countries have taken or the mixture of public and private enterprise in those countries. Second, even at their zenith, Communist regimes were not a monolithic group. The acute disagreements and intermittent hostility between the Soviet and Chinese regimes reflected both ideological and tactical differences about communism as well as tension

between two great rival powers. For almost 20 years, China referred to the Soviet Union as hegemonic, interested in worldwide expansion. Similarly, the dispute between China and Vietnam, based on different geopolitical interests and historical enmity, led to hostilities in 1979. Third, conflict in politics has resulted from many factors other than class differences. The most important of these, which have often been more meaningful for a political system than class, are as follows:

A CLOSER LOOK
1.6

WOMEN HEADS OF STATE AND GOVERNMENT UP TO 2005

PRESIDENTS

Argentina (1974–76), Bolivia (1979–80), Finland (2000), Germany (1990), Guyana (1997–1999), Haiti (1991), Iceland (1980–), Indonesia (2001–), Ireland (1990–), Latvia (1999), Liberia (1996), Malta (1982), Nicaragua (1990–), Panama (1999), Philippines (1986–92) and (2001–), Sri Lanka (1994), Switzerland (1999), Yugoslavia (1982–86)

PRIME MINISTERS

Bangladesh (1991–), Britain (1979–90), Bulgaria (1994), Burundi (1993), Canada (1993), Central African Republic (1974–76), Dominica (1980–), France (1991–92), Guyana (1997), Haiti (1995–1996), (5) India (1966–1977, 1980–1984), Israel (1969–74), Lithuania (1990–1991), New Zealand (1997–1999), Norway (1981, 1986–89, 1990–1996), Pakistan (1988–90, 1993–1996), Poland (1992–93), Portugal (1981–85), Rwanda (1993–94), Senegal (2001–), Sri Lanka (1960–1965, 1970–1977, 1994, 2000), Turkey (1993–1996), Yugoslavia (1982–1986)

Source: Division for the Advancement of Women of the United Nations Secretariat.

---

1. *Religion:* Catholics and Protestants in Northern Ireland; Muslims and Hindus in Asia; Muslims and Christians or Jews. Most of the conflicts around the world in recent years have resulted from religious discord.

2. *Race:* Blacks and whites in South Africa; blacks and Asians in Uganda.

3. *Language:* English- and French-speaking populations in Canada; Flemish- and French-speaking populations in Belgium.

4. *Tribe:* Yorubas, Ibos, and Hausa-Fulanis in Nigeria.

5. *Caste:* The four major castes and thousands of subcastes in India.

6. *Nation:* Basques and Catalans in Spain; Serbs and Croats in former Yugoslavia; Kurds in Turkey and Iraq.

7. *Ethnic group:* Balkan peoples; groups in Afghanistan.

8. *Population change:* 700 million people in Africa and the number may rise to 2 billion by 2050. In Europe the population is expected to decline, but the makeup will change because of increasing number of immigrants;

in Luxembourg about a third of the population is now foreign-born.

Economics, Democracy, and History

Francis Fukuyama in *The End of History* argued that a move had occurred over the centuries toward modernity, characterized by liberal democracy and capitalism, the mode of production and economic activity oriented to private profit. Capitalism has continued to experience sustained growth, a prominent middle class, and a high per capita GNP, due to factors including innovation, risk taking, entrepreneurship, and competition. By contrast, systems based on Marxist economics, communism, and state control of the economy have failed. Fukuyama's argument is that no great challenges to Western-style liberal capitalism are likely to arise and that, from an ideological point of view, history has ended, and no alternative is likely with the discrediting of communism, socialism, and fascism. Democracy and free markets will continue to expand over time as the dominant organizational principles for much of the world.

It is perilous to make predictions, especially about the future. Yet it is certainly true that the democratic countries in North America and Europe are the most economically free countries and the richest, apart from oil-rich Middle East emirates. At the top is Luxembourg with a GDP per capita of nearly $35,000, and the United States with $28,000. Countries with the most economic freedom also have higher rates of long-term economic growth. They also exhibit greater tolerance and civility than economically and politically repressed countries that are devoid of a rule of law. However, on balance, the world is growing freer economically in terms of liberal trade policy, lower taxes and regulations, sound monetary policy, and property rights.

Nevertheless, the relationship between economics and politics is complicated. Democracies used to be rare in the less developed countries, but they are increasing, especially after the fall of the Soviet Union in 1989. A number of countries in Central and South America, Southeast Asia, Africa, and the former Soviet bloc have established democratic systems, with differing degrees of success. In some, the institutions, ethics, and practices of modernity did not develop.

Some non-Western societies have been resistant to modernity or may prefer the economic and technical part of modernity but not democratic politics or Western cultural values (China and Singapore), or have difficulty embracing both democracy and modernity (Russia). The most recent challenge to modernity has come from Islamic fundamentalism, stressing the return of religion to centrality and making faith the chief determinant of identity and behavior. The process of globalization, inherently identified with American values, has been criticized as embodying cultural homogeneity, materialism, secularism, and sexual permissiveness.

The question of democracy and liberal capitalism is also affected by features of the contemporary world, two of which may be dealt with here. One is the sustained, unprecedented economic growth of the late twentieth century, and the uneven nature of that growth across the world. The consequence is the relative power and the changing relationships of countries. In some countries the extraordinary disparity between wealth and poverty affects the trend toward democracy. Much of the growth in market economies has resulted from competition, innovation, and research and development, which have generated new products and processes.

A second feature is the changing nature of the world's economy. Much of the industrial production in the world is moving from the developed countries—the United States, Western Europe, and Japan—to countries in Latin America, Southeast Asia, and East Asia, where labor is cheaper. The most conspicuous example is textiles. For mass-production processes, large Western-owned companies may have more employees in poor than in rich countries; about a quarter of IBM's employees are non-Americans. In the rich OECD countries, economic activity has changed from manufacturing to services. More than two-thirds of the output in the OECD countries and up to four-fifths of employment in them is now in the service sector. Political behavior correspondingly changes, as shown in political party membership and policies and in participation of voters.

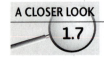

A CLOSER LOOK 1.7

THE SUM TOTALS: GDP AND GNP

Gross Domestic Product (GDP) is the value of all final goods and services produced in a country in one year. It is usually measured by adding up all of an economy's incomes, wages, interests, profits, and rents.

Gross National Product (GNP) is GDP plus income that residents have received from abroad, minus income claimed by nonresidents. GNP may therefore be higher or lower than GDP.

Constitutional Democracies

All countries have written constitutions or, in a few cases such as Britain and Israel, basic laws which set up the major political institutions, the structure of the political system, the basic principles on which the system rests, and often a declaration of rights. Constitutions are recognized as legally supreme over other law, and they are more difficult to change or amend than ordinary law. However, *constitution* does not mean or imply *constitutional,* since constitutions are framed for dictatorial, totalitarian, and authoritarian systems as well as for democratic ones. Constitutional systems imply government by law, limits on governmental power, opportunities to challenge that power, individual rights, and freedom of speech and association without coercion.

Many contemporary systems describe themselves as democratic. Self-description, however, is not always accurate. The "people's democracies" of Central and Eastern Europe or Yemen after World War II could more accurately be classified as forms of dictatorship.

Constitutional democracies have certain characteristics. There are free elections with competing candidates and a political opposition that is free to criticize the government. The press and other media are free, and censorship is rare. People are able to write and speak as they like and to practice any religion they choose. Personal and civil rights are usually respected. A wide variety of unofficial associations exists, and no single group or element in society is dominant. The military does not intervene in politics and is under the control of the political leaders. Political change takes place by a peaceful process. The rule of law ensures impartial justice for all.

In all constitutional democracies, officials who make and enforce law are themselves subject to the law. All government actions must be performed in a legal manner and can be controlled by appropriate authorities. These authorities may include the ordinary courts and the system of common law as in the United States and Britain, an elaborate code of law as in the German *Rechtsstaat,* or special administrative courts such as the *Conseil d'Etat* in France.

Constitutional democracies exist, with few exceptions, in the older and more developed political systems and in some countries influenced by them. Of the 6.4 billion people in the world, about 50 percent live under constitutional democracies, 40 percent in one-party or one-person regimes, and 8 percent in military regimes (see Table 1.5).

Authoritarian Systems

Authoritarian systems or dictatorships may exist because a country has no tradition or standard of constitutional behavior, because there is no general consensus about the desirability of freedom, or because a limited and closed elite dominates the political process. Dictatorship may result from the instability or ineffectiveness of a democratic government, from the desire to put a particular ideology into effect, or from the reaction to economic changes and instability or to defeat in war.

In authoritarian regimes political activity is controlled, all the media are subject to censorship, liberty is restricted, there is no legally recognized opposition, public criticism is rare, and parliamentary institutions are absent or meaningless. Power is exercised by small groups such as military leaders, party officials, bureaucrats, or religious figures. But economic activities can usually be pursued with some independence, a certain degree of cultural freedom is allowed, and voluntary internal and external travel is possible. A large number of modern regimes embody similar characteristics. In many Latin American countries in the past, political parties have been barred or suspended, the press has been censored, and opponents have been imprisoned arbitrarily.

Some authoritarian regimes are personal or party dictatorships supported by a considerable part of the population and interested in general social or economic reform. Such regimes may be based on a particular doctrine or may be more pragmatic and less doctrinaire, such as the Latin American populist systems that have been both nationalist and socially reformist. The regime led by General Juan Peron and his wife Eva Duarte, known as Evita, in Argentina from 1946 to 1955 combined nationalism and a populist appeal by a charismatic leader. The Peron movement was run by the Justicialista Party, which mobilized *los descamisados* (the "shirtless" working masses) and the labor unions. Peron combined policies said to be those of social justice with his admiration of Italian Fascism. Peron created a coalition of organized labor, industrialists, and military officers, strongly nationalist, which led to state intervention in industrialization, income redistribution, and nationalization of public utilities, railroads, and foreign trade. Peronism also meant an authoritarian system that restricted political opposition and censored the press.

Of a different kind are the bureaucratic-authoritarian or authoritarian-corporativist regimes which appeared in Latin America in the 1960s. They were dominated by technocrats, bureaucrats, and military personnel and were not based on labor's political support. Often the economies of the countries ruled by these regimes were dependent on foreign capital.

Other authoritarian regimes are military dictatorships. Throughout history the military has interested itself in politics, in exercising power, or in influencing political decisions. In past Asian or Middle Eastern regimes, there was little distinction between civil and military authority; the monarch was absolute ruler and controlled the army. The military has often intervened on behalf of politicians, usually those of a conservative disposition. Sometimes civilian political leaders themselves urge the intervention of the military or depend on the approval of the military, as in Turkey in 1908, 1960, 1971, 1980, and 1997. In some Latin American constitutions the military is given the task of guaranteeing the constitutional powers. Thirteen of the 19 Latin American countries were under some form of military rule in 1983. By 1991 there were none. Similarly, in every country in Central Africa, civilian governments are now in power, and the role of the military has been reduced.

Sometimes the military leadership, regarding itself as the most honest, most efficient, and most advanced organization in a nation, may turn out the politicians or civilian rulers it believes to be corrupt, misguided, or inefficient. It may do so where political instability results from irreconcilable political divisions or contin-

ual political crises, or when the nation has been humiliated by defeat in war, or when governments have lacked sufficient legitimacy to establish an efficient administration. Yet the decline in the number of military regimes in the world has been significant, though resort to such regimes still occurs, as in Pakistan in 1999.

Totalitarian Systems

The existence of some similar important features in the Communist regime of the Soviet Union under Stalin, the Fascist regime of Italy, and the Nazi regime of Germany led some analysts to suggest a new concept of totalitarianism. This concept implies the existence of a new twentieth-century type of system based on a dominant leader supported by a mass party acting on an aggressive ideology that explains and influences political actions.

According to this concept, a totalitarian system differs from an authoritarian regime in that it attempts to control behavior totally and subordinates all organizations and individuals to the ruling group. Whereas authoritarian regimes allow individuals and groups some independence of action, the central feature of totalitarian systems is that the state attempts to control the whole of society, minds as well as bodies, and to this end mobilizes the population, youth as well as adults.

The totalitarian system concentrates power in the hands of an individual or group. It eliminates all opposition parties, controls communication and the mass media, exercises control over the economy and over highly centralized planning, uses religion for its own purpose even though it is fundamentally irreligious, and makes deliberate use of terror as a controlling factor through the secret police, concentration or labor camps, and the completely amoral use of force. A single official ideology and a single party lead to the elimination of dissension, even within the one ruling party, and the refusal to allow any standard of morality other than that of the party or the leader.

The three regimes regarded as prime examples of the totalitarian model—Nazi Germany,

Fascist Italy, and the Soviet Union under Stalin, if not after his death—did not embody all characteristics of the model to the same degree. Moreover, there was in reality less coherence and unity in decision making in these systems than is suggested in the model. Nevertheless, despite the differences in ideology, purpose, and kind of support they obtained, these three regimes were similar in their ruthlessness and extreme dictatorial behavior, and they may be regarded as models of a particular kind of political system, which can be distinguished from authoritarian systems. Moreover, while authoritarian regimes have sometimes evolved into democracies as in the recent cases of Greece, Spain, and Portugal, no totalitarian system had done so until 1989.

After the collapse of the Soviet Union and its Eastern European associate countries and the dissolution of their communist system, and with the recent moves in China to a more market economy, no major power can be considered totalitarian today. In the current world, North Korea and perhaps Cuba might be categorized in this way.

Communist and Non-Communist Systems

A classification of system into communist and non-communist has been of great political significance in the making of U.S. foreign policy in the post–World War II period, as well as for theoretical analysis. Communism today is purportedly based on the principles of Marxism-Leninism. From Karl Marx (1818–1883) is derived the belief, or ideology, that capitalism will be overthrown by a revolution of the proletariat, or working class, and be replaced by a classless communist system after a transitional stage of socialism. In this system the guiding principle would be "from each according to his ability, to each according to his needs."

It was Lenin (1870–1924) who called for the creation of a highly centralized and disciplined revolutionary party to lead the proletariat. His principle of democratic centralism means in practice that all members of the party must adhere to central party policy. The Russian party, which

successfully carried out the revolution in 1917, became the model for all communist parties in both Communist and non-communist systems.

In the Soviet Union the Communist Party exercised control not only over the state and over all social organizations and all forms of communication. Under Stalin (1879–1953) this control was more complete than it was after his death.

For many years the Soviet Union controlled the policies of foreign Communist parties and the activities of regimes created in Eastern Europe after World War II. In the latter systems a Communist party based on Marxist-Leninist principles was the ruling group. All factories were nationalized and agriculture was largely under collective control. Communism was therefore regarded as a monolithic bloc with its center in Moscow.

Starting in the 1960s, the Communist movement began to fragment. The Communist parties in non-Communist systems such as Italy, Spain, and sometimes even France showed a degree of independence and were occasionally critical of the Soviet Union. Some of these parties—sometimes called Eurocommunist—declared that they believed in the democratic process and would allow free elections and abide by electoral decisions if they came to power.

In 1948, Yugoslavia, under its Communist leader, Tito, refused to accept orders from the Soviet Union and was expelled from the international Communist movement. The most significant division in the Communist movement, however, was between the Soviet Union and China. In spite of their common claimed inheritance of Marxism-Leninism, the two countries were divided by ideological issues and rivalry for leadership of the international Communist movement, as well as by a dispute over their common border.

The last few years have seen dramatic changes in the former Soviet Union and in China, and the collapse of the Communist systems in Eastern Europe. These systems toppled when it became clear that the Soviet Union would no longer use force to maintain the monopoly of power and privileged position of their Communist rulers. The East European states have, at different speeds, introduced elements of a market economy, and some have moved to a more democratic regime.

The political and economic changes during the 1980s in the Soviet Union stemmed from the policies of *glasnost* (openness) and *perestroika* (restructuring) of the Soviet leader, Mikhail Gorbachev. But the policies were accompanied by violence, internal turmoil, civil war in some parts of the country, and an attempt to overthrow the leader in a coup in August 1991. Gorbachev, who had tried to preserve the Union, resigned in December 1991.

The stagnation of the Soviet economy, marked by scarcity of goods and inefficient modes of production and distribution, led to a call for a move from the centralized command economy under state control to a more market-oriented economy, in which controls would be reduced and individual farming and private business would be encouraged. Total control of resources was regarded as incompatible with the process of modernization and with a modern economy that requires the free flow of information and decentralized decision making.

During the *glasnost* period, one-party rule by the Communist Party and democratic centralism gave way to looser political control, competition between different political groups and ideas, relaxation of censorship, open discussion and criticism of official policy, abandonment of Marxism-Leninism as the official creed, some contested elections, and the opening of borders to allow people to travel and emigrate. The Soviet Union also disintegrated as a political structure with the rise of nationalism in many of the republics, marked by ethnic group assertion and religious enthusiasm. The republics have become independent states and the Soviet Union was replaced in December 1991 by the Commonwealth of Independent States, a grouping of most of the former republics in a loose alliance, 12 in 2005.

The former Communist systems are in different phases of transition to some other form of political system. Russia, under Boris Yeltsin in the 1990s, decentralized economic decision making for most of the economy and encouraged private ownership. Its new constitution, drafted in 1993, provides for a Russian Federation with democratic characteristics.

China today is difficult to categorize in any simple way. For 30 years under Mao Zedong, its totalitarian system controlled the economy, the life and movements of its citizens, the allocation of jobs, and decisions on production in agriculture and industry. The Communist Party, never more than 5 percent of the population, is a disciplined, loyal, and secretive force that monopolizes political power, state activities, and the media. Since the late 1970s economic reforms have sparked rapid growth, increase in GDP, lessening of central control, strengthening of the influence of cities and provinces, and a considerable increase in the numbers of people employed in the private sector, which now accounts for a large part of industrial and other production in the country. Yet this liberalizing of the economy and growth of a competitive free market with free prices, stock markets, and private businesses is still accompanied by the authoritarian control of a single party, the Communist Party, with centralized decision making. If central economic planning no longer exists, central political control still does, with some qualifications such as a freer process, multicandidate elections for the party's Central Committee, and elections for local people's congresses with competing candidates.

Third World or Developing Countries

The classification of systems as communist or non-communist neglects the large number of nations, now the majority in the world, that are neither communist states nor Western democracies. Since the Bandung Conference of 1955, when 29 African and Asian nations met to discuss their common interests, a group now known as third world or developing countries—most of which achieved political independence since 1945—emerged, with some exceptions, as nonaligned in conflicts between the other two groups.

Containing a majority of the world's population, these countries vary considerably in wealth,

USEFUL CLASSIFICATIONS IN COMPARATIVE POLITICS

- Number and kind of rulers
- Political culture
- Political development
- Economic systems
- Constitutional democracies

- Authoritarian systems
- Totalitarian systems
- Communist and non-Communist systems
- Third world or developing countries

---

ranging from oil-rich Saudi Arabia to impoverished Bangladesh, and in level of political development and importance. But all of them reject any form of colonialism, advocate political and economic independence, and stress the need for nation building.

THE POLITICAL PROCESS

For comparative analysis it is useful to study the ways in which the electoral process works in different countries and the parties and groups that play a part in that process. Even nondemocratic countries hold elections, which supposedly demonstrate the solidarity of the people with the existing political leadership and are intended to promote consensus. But to be meaningful, elections must present voters with alternative candidates, parties, or issues from which to choose, and they must be fairly and honestly organized. Elections must also allow peaceful change of government, meaning that all will accept the electoral decision and that, at the same time, the minority will be permitted to oppose the policies of the successful majority.

Political development has meant that an increasing proportion of the population obtains the vote and that there is greater political equality. Gradually, disqualifications for representation based on religion, property, education, and sex are removed. Ownership of property and educational degrees are no longer necessary to vote, and in all but a few countries women are no longer excluded from suffrage. The minimum age limit of 21, once generally accepted, has been lowered in many countries.

People generally take part in political activities through membership in a party or interest group, as well as by voting. In a number of systems, opportunities are provided for direct political participation of the people in deciding some issues. The chief forms of such participation are referendums or plebiscites, approval of constitutions, initiatives presenting petitions or bills, and recall of elected officials. In addition to these devices, governments and politicians may take account of the views of citizens expressed in public opinion polls and change their policies or attitudes accordingly. Nevertheless, in all systems the extent of direct participation by any considerable part of the people is limited.

Functional Representation

Earlier assemblies consisted of representatives from the legally defined and hierarchical groups of "estates" into which society was divided. Gradually, in most countries, assemblies began to represent citizens as individuals rather than as members of groups and occupations.

The case for some form of functional representation is still argued by part of the Left, especially guild Socialists; by some pluralists who think representation should take account of occupational activity; and by those advocating a corporate system. Corporatism, which has been prominent in Latin systems, is a system of interest representation in which certain occupational categories participate in official bodies and decisions emerge from the interaction between government and those interest associations. In Austria, all employees belong to associations of commerce, labor, and agriculture. In corporatism, groups are generally organized nationally, and they work and negotiate with the state on policy issues.

The supporters of functional representation believe that geographically oriented parliaments and parties are not sufficiently representative of the economic interests of the community. In spite of the practical difficulty in selecting the functional groups to be represented and in deciding on the relative weight of the different occupations, a number of countries, including France and Germany, have set up various kinds of economic and social councils to represent interest groups. In most countries such councils have been limited to giving advice and possess no real power. Moreover, interest groups have found that they are better able to influence political decisions through direct contacts with governments or parliaments or through membership in official advisory committees than through economic and social councils.

Not surprisingly, functional representation existed in some Communist systems. In the for-

mer Soviet Union the system of soviets, or councils, supposedly representative of the workers, was not very meaningful in reality. In the former Yugoslavia, however, the workers' councils in industry and the agricultural cooperatives were of some significance for a time. Yet, even there, the "workers' democracy," which was supposed to be responsive to the demands of workers in factories, was in fact controlled by the Communist Party.

Territorial Representation

There are many different methods of territorial representation, whether in single-member or multimember constituencies.

Single-Member Constituencies   These are relatively small geographic areas, often approximately equal in population, which elect one representative. The usual method, as in the United States, is that the candidate with the highest number of votes wins—the plurality system, or first past the post. This has the virtue of simplicity, tends to limit the number of parties that win seats, and generally fosters a two-party system. One party may gain an absolute majority of seats. Logically, this electoral method can lead to the formation of strong single-party governments and make coalitions unnecessary. But the system can be mathematically inequitable. A candidate may win with a minority of the total votes cast, as shown in Table 1.8.

A CLOSER LOOK 1.8

REFERENDUMS

Referendums are now widely used in democratic and nondemocratic countries. Most countries of Western Europe provide for them in their constitutions. Citizens in Italy and New Zealand forced changes in voting methods on the government. Australians voted in 1999 to maintain the British monarchy. Switzerland has voted more frequently than any other country, rejecting among other proposals membership in the UN and links with the European Union. President de Gaulle of France used them to establish the legitimacy of the Fifth Republic. Denmark rejected the Maastricht Treaty. Scotland and Wales voted for devolution. Governments in a number of countries have submitted moral or lifestyle issues such as abortion, divorce, or consumption of alcohol to referendums in order to avoid making decisions on controversial matters. Referendums may be advisory, testing public opinion, or mandatory, part of the lawmaking process. Petitions by voters, initiatives, can put a referendum on the ballot.

TABLE 1.8

SINGLE-MEMBER CONSTITUENCY ELECTION RESULTS: MANHATTAN, EAST SIDE

Stano	25,463
Harper	23,185
Collins	14,694
Michel	8,247
Costello is the winner with 35.5 percent of the votes.	

Other methods include a second-ballot system, as in France when no candidate has won an overall majority at the first ballot, and the alternative-vote system, which allows for electors to rank the various candidates and for their preferences to be transferred from the lowest candidates until one candidate obtains a majority.

Multimember Constituencies In some areas a number of representatives are chosen by each voter. When this system is followed in its most extreme form, the whole country might be one constituency, as in Weimar Germany (1919–1933) and in Israel. The least extreme examples are constituencies that elect between two and five members, as in France during the Fourth Republic.

The most common electoral system in multimember areas is proportional representation (PR). Seats in the legislature are allocated to parties in proportion to their share of the electoral vote. A more accurate representation of electoral opinion is thus produced. But PR also produces or perpetuates a multiparty system, thereby usually making government coalitions of different parties necessary because it is extremely rare for one party to obtain an overall majority. Government is thus often less likely to be stable or effective than in the plurality system, though the Scandinavian countries are an exception in this regard. Italy, for example, has had over 60 governments in 55 years. Every country using PR has at least four parties of some importance in its legislature. PR also allows small extremist parties to obtain representation.

What is the most desirable electoral system for a nation? The answer is that electoral systems are methods, not ends in themselves. Their value must be related to the political system as a whole. A single-member plurality system, such as the U.S. system, tends to reduce the number of parties. In Britain it has, with some qualification, allowed a strong government to emerge with a coherent policy. The PR method tends to lead to a multiparty system that accurately reflects electoral divisions, but it also tends to preserve those divisions and to make strong government less probable.

INTEREST GROUPS

Students of comparative politics examine the different kinds of interest groups and the various ways that such groups formulate demands, express political views, and make claims on government.

Pressure on governments has always taken a variety of forms, ranging from riots, acts of violence, and rebellions to social movements, political parties, and peaceful presentation of petitions. What is distinctive in modern times is the powerful, sustained role of groups in getting or preventing action and in influencing decisions and policy. Interest groups are now necessary for the running of the modern state.

Interest groups are very diverse in character. Many have a formal structure and organization, but some are informal. Some are temporary bodies organized for one specific purpose and often disband when that is achieved. Others are permanent organizations concerned with a continuing problem or issue. Some are concerned primarily with the interests of one part of society, while others are concerned with a common interest or a general problem relevant to the whole society or even to the international community. Some, such as ecological, civil rights, or women's groups, can be regarded as social movements.

The impact of groups depends on a number of factors:

1. The demands of the group and the way those demands are seen by the politicians and officials handling the issue.

2. The functions performed or planned by the state and the degree to which groups are consulted about those functions or can supply information about them.

3. The size, reputation, and cohesiveness of the group and the amount of money and energy it is prepared to expend on the issue.

4. The degree of concern of the members of the group about some particular problem.

This is not a complete list of the relevant factors, but it is helpful to analyze some of these factors when comparing interest groups.

Some pressure groups have access to the political actors; some influence policy in a private manner; some bargain with the executive or legislature before legislation is framed. Some, as in Germany, have a semiofficial status; they must be consulted by the executive, and sometimes are given seats on official supervisory boards. Some, as in France, affect the political process directly by mass demonstrations, strikes, or disrupting public services. Some, as in Japan, are able to obstruct or block potential legislation in a variety of areas, such as farming and education.

POLITICAL PARTIES

An interest group is concerned with influencing decisions on a limited number of issues; a political party, in addition to this function, is also concerned with running candidates, contesting elections, and holding office. But it is sometimes easier to distinguish between them in theory than in practice. In Weimar Germany, the German Farmers' Party was essentially an interest group. In the United States, an antiabortion group became the Right-to-Life Party. In Britain, a close relationship exists between the Labour Party and the trade unions, which provide over five-sixths of the membership and about 80 percent of the financing of the party.

How then can we define a party? A starting point is to see it as a group of people who hold certain political beliefs in common or who are prepared to support official candidates of the party. They formulate policies and recruit the political elite. Members of a party work together to win elections in order to gain and maintain political power. Parties struggle for power as well as to achieve certain policies and goals.

Parties have been compared in different ways. One method is to see them as either traditional, representative, or mobilizing. Traditional parties reflect the social and economic control of a hereditary or oligarchic elite and last until that control is ended. Representative parties, such as those in the United States, put forward the views of followers of the parties at a particular time. Mobilizing parties, such as the parties of the third world and most Communist parties until the late 1980s, aim at converting the population to a particular point of view.

A CLOSER LOOK 1.9

CAN YOU TELL YOUR LEFT FROM YOUR RIGHT?

The frequently used terms Left and Right stem from the differences among political groups in the French Revolution. The more radical or extreme sat to the left of the presiding officer and the less radical to his right in the parliamentary assembly. The Left is more likely to favor political, economic, and social change, to support government intervention to get change, and to propose a more egalitarian society and economic redistribution. The Right is more likely to limit government intervention, to regard private property as the basis of political and economic liberty, and to believe in a market economy where individuals and firms respond to consumer demands for goods and services. However, these theoretical distinctions do not altogether relate to current political reality and practice. Left and center-left parties in democratic systems, constrained by budgetary concerns, have not renounced the market economy or a consensus on macro-economic policies.

The reason for the creation of parties and their main base varies widely as Table 1.9 shows. The types of party systems are shown in Table 1.10.

POLITICAL INSTITUTIONS

All political systems carry out certain basic functions. Although these functions have been defined in different ways, it is still most useful for beginning students of comparative politics to think of them in the traditional language of legislative, executive, and judicial functions or powers. The legislative function involves discussion of public affairs and enactment of general rules and laws. The executive function involves the application of those general rules to specific cases and the formulation of policy based on those rules. The judicial function involves resolution of disputes between individuals or between individuals and the state.

Constitutions usually determine what institutions are to carry out these functions as well as the extent and limit of their powers. The interrelationship between functions and institutions

TABLE 1.9

THE MAIN BASES OF SELECTED POLITICAL PARTIES

Main Basis	Party
Ideology	Communist, Nazi
Economic Interest	U.S. Republican Party, Lok Dal (Indian Farmers)
Religion	Muslim Brotherhood (Egypt), BJP (India)
Nationalism	Scottish National Party, Parti Quebecois
Ethnic	People's Progressive Party (Guyana), Tamil Federal Party (Sri Lanka)
Caste	Parts of the Indian Congress Party, Janata Dal
Specific Issue	Green Party (Germany)
Faction	Japanese Liberal Democratic Party, Italian Christian Democratic Party
Mobilization	TANU (Tanzania)
Clientele	Blancos and Colorados (Uruguay)

TABLE 1.10

MODELS OF PARTY SYSTEMS

Type	Characteristics
Two party	Two major parties get most of the seats in the elected chamber and usually most of the votes in the country. Examples—Britain, the United States.
Two party qualified	Two major parties, but two or more other parties get a significant part of the vote. Examples—Germany, Canada, Belgium, Ireland.
Multiparty with dominant party	Over party gets about 40 percent of the vote, and a number of others share the rest. Examples—Scandinavian countries, India, Italy.
Multiparty with no dominant party	A number of parties share the vote with none usually getting over 25 percent. Examples—France Third and Fourth Republics, Finland, Switzerland.
One party or none	Only one party allowed in reality. Examples—former Soviet Union and communist countries, Nazi Germany, some sub-Saharan African countries, Syria.

depends on (1) whether the system is unitary or federal (see Figure 1.2), and (2) whether there is a separation or nonseparation of functions, or powers (which is the word usually used).

A unitary system is one in which a set of central institutions exercises authority, as in Great Britain, China, or France. Local and regional authorities obtain their powers from the central authority, which can amend those powers if it desires.

A federal system is one in which powers are divided between a central government and state or provincial governments. Both levels of government have certain powers of their own derived from the constitution or interpretations of it. The states do not get their powers from the central government; power is shared between the central and state institutions. Federalism is thus more complex than a unitary system.

For comparison, the distinction between federal and unitary systems is useful, but modern trends in government have sometimes blurred the distinction. In many federal systems, such as that of the United States, the central institutions have grown stronger, while in some unitary states, such as Britain and France, some decentralization and devolution of power has occurred to countries, regions, and local authorities.

The concept of separation of powers originated in the seventeenth and eighteenth centuries as a method of controlling excessive use of power by one group or institution. It involves the establishment of three separate institutions—a legislature, an executive, and a judiciary—each almost exclusively responsible for the exercise of its separate function. It may also entail separation of personnel by forbidding any person to be a member of more than one branch of government at the same time. The United States is a model of this concept of separation of powers.

In systems that do not embody a separation of powers, such as the British, the members of one institution, the executive, are also members of the legislature. The executive usually controls a majority of the legislature and, because of party discipline, can control the legislative process as well as decision making in general. This concentration of power has often led to strong government.

Again, it is important to remember that these are types of systems rather than exact reality. In all modern systems each institution exercises some functions associated with the other two institutions. Some degree of cooperation between the three institutions is necessary to perform the work of government. A separation of powers need not necessarily result in weak or stalemated government, which may result from a variety of other factors, such as political parties, a strong legislature, an active high court that declares legislation invalid, or the mores of political behavior.

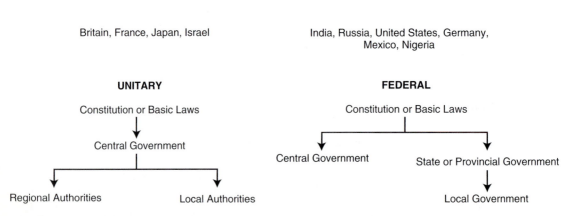

FIGURE 1.2 UNITARY AND FEDERAL SYSTEMS: DIVISION OF POWER

A CLOSER LOOK

1.10

FEDERALISM IN GERMANY

Germany has 16 Länder (states). Each Land has its own constitution, government, and legislature. The Länder can make law on matters not granted by the Basic Law of 1949 to the federal government, now in Berlin. Those matters extend to police, education, agriculture, tax collection, culture, electoral system, local judiciary, regional development, school system, and graduation examinations. The Länder send representatives, appointed by their governments, to the Federal Bundesrat. The heads of government in the Länder meet regularly to coordinate matters and can enter into some agreements with foreign countries.

THE POLITICAL EXECUTIVE

The executive branch of government is the major organ of modern political leadership. Its prominence reflects the increase in the activities of the state in domestic affairs and its special role in foreign policy.

The kind of executive branch found in a system is shaped by many factors. A useful beginning method of comparison is to examine the relationship between the executive and legislature. In nondemocratic systems, the executive is likely to have almost complete control over the legislature. In democratic systems, a more varied relationship exists. Five familiar types are the following:

1. *Parliamentary-cabinet government:* The classical model of this type is the British system, but Germany, Japan, and India also illustrate it in different ways. Political leadership is provided by the cabinet ministers, a small group of leaders of the party or parties headed by a prime minister who control a majority in the legislature, of which they

are also members (see Table 1.11). The link between the executive and the legislature is crucial. The cabinet is collectively responsible to the legislature for political decisions, government policies, and legislative programs. Individual ministers are responsible for the conduct of their administrative departments and for their political actions.

2. *Presidential system:* The United States is the model for the presidential system, which has been imitated by many other countries. A single head of the executive, the popularly elected president, is both the political leader and the head of state, hence the major policy-maker (see Table 1.12). The president appoints all the chief members of the government and executive agencies. The members of the cabinet are all subordinate and responsible to the president. Collective responsibility to the legislature does not exist. The present Fifth Republic of France is an interesting mixture of the presidential and cabinet systems.

3. *Assembly government:* In this type of system the legislature dominates the executive, which has little disciplined control over legisla-

A CLOSER LOOK

1.11

CENTRAL GOVERNMENT GROWS WEAKER

Decentralization	Central government functions are carried out by local and regional authorities.
Devolution	Central government cedes power to regions to make decisions and legislation on certain issues, as in France, Italy, and Spain, or as in Britain to Scotland and Wales.

TABLE 1.11

PRESIDENTIAL AND PARLIAMENTARY-CABINET GOVERNMENTS

Presidential	Parliamentary-Cabinet
• President is directly elected and chooses the cabinet, which he leads.	• Government stems from the party or parties controlling a majority in the legislative. The cabinet is a collegial executive.
• Both the president and the legislature have fixed terms of office: neither can dismiss the other.	• The executive can be forced to resign by a parliamentary vote of no confidence.
• Individuals cannot be members of both the executive and the legislature.	• Members of the executive are usually drawn from the legislature, in which they remain members.

tive and financial matters. The legislature is in many ways the real decision-making body in the system. The regimes most characteristic of this type were the French Third (1875–1940) and Fourth (1946–1958) Republics, with weak political executives, constant government instability—102 governments in the Third and 24 in the Fourth Republic—and few disciplined parties. The legislature saw itself, rather than the executive, as the true representative of the sovereignty

of the people. The postwar Italian system has had similar features.

4. *Consociation government:* This system entails proportional sharing of government and other public positions on the basis of ethnic, racial, or religious groups at elite levels. The usual arrangements are a government coalition including the important groups and a sharing of decisions by them on general issues. Each group usually has autonomy on issues of particular con-

TABLE 1.12

HEADS OF STATE IN SELECTED COUNTRIES

	Position	Method of Selection	Tenure
Britain	Monarch	Heredity	Life
China	President	Elected by National People's Congress	5 years
Egypt	President	Nominated by People's Assembly and validated by national referendum	6 years
France	President	Elected by people	5 years (formerly 7 years)
Germany	President	Elected by lower house and states	5 years
India	President	Elected by federal and state assemblies	5 years
Israel	President	Elected by legislature	5 years
Japan	Monarch	Heredity	Life
Jordan	Monarch	Heredity	Life
Mexico	President	Elected by people	6 years, nonrenewable
Nigeria	President	Elected by people (since 1999 after military rule)	4 years
Russia	President	Elected by people	5 years, limit of 2 terms
United States	President	Elected by electoral college	4 years, limit of 2 terms

cern to its members. These arrangements have been made in a number of countries: Netherlands (1917–1967), Austria (1945–1966), Lebanon (1943–1975), Canada and India at different times.

5. *Council government:* Systems of collective leadership are rare. The oldest example is the Federal Council of Switzerland (see Table 1.13). This political executive of seven, elected by the legislature, shares ministerial duties and administers the country. Communist systems have also experimented with this type. In the Soviet Union, after Stalin, collective leadership existed for short periods before an individual leader consolidated his political position.

LEGISLATURES AND PARLIAMENTARY ASSEMBLIES

Almost all political systems have legislative bodies or parliamentary assemblies of some kind, with members either elected or appointed. Their significance varies over time in an individual system as well as comparatively between one system and another. Assemblies play different roles and

TABLE 1.13

SWITZERLAND'S COUNCIL GOVERNMENT: A COALITION OF FOUR PARTIES, 2005

Executive Branch

The Federal Council, the executive authority, is composed of 7 members, 2 each from the SD, FD, and CD parties, and 1 from the SPP.

Legislative Branch
Distribution of Seats in Both Chambers (2005)

Party	National Council	Council of States
Social Democrats	52	9
Free Democrats	36	14
Christian Democrats	28	15
Swiss People's Party	55	8
Others	27	—

exercise functions of different kinds (see Tables 1.14 and 1.15).

Countries have either a single assembly (unicameral) or two (bicameral). A strong bicameral system would be one where the upper chamber has the same or similar powers as the lower chamber, as in the United States and Australia. A second chamber may provide for representation of different interests, for members who are more independent of the government than members of the lower chamber, and for expressing reservations about and delaying government proposals.

Assemblies have declined in power and prestige in most countries in recent years, the United States being the major exception. This decline has occurred for a number of reasons. Government functions and expenditures have greatly increased since World War II. The complexity of both internal and international affairs often prevents members of the legislature from fully understanding issues or having sufficient information about them because of the inadequate research facilities and staff available to them.

The executive can claim to be as representative of the people as is the legislature. The bureaucracy, or permanent administration, at the disposal of the executive has grown substantially in number and significance. The leaders of organized parties have dominated politics, and the mass media, especially television, have tended to concentrate on the personalities of the leaders. In the newer nations, the executive is usually viewed as the instrument through which modernization can most rapidly occur.

Parliaments are therefore no longer the dominant bodies in political life. Rarely do they control the legislative program, act as a watchdog over government spending and the financial process, or control ministerial behavior in any continuous real way. Democratic governments are created and normally fall as a result of electoral decisions, and only rarely as the result of parliamentary debate. The power of party organizations in generating political leadership and creating disciplined political forces has reduced the possibility of independent behavior on the part of parliamentarians once a party decision on an issue has been made.

TABLE 1.14

MAIN FUNCTIONS OF PARLIAMENTS OR ASSEMBLIES

Activity	Some Examples
Select head of state	Italy, Soviet Union
Approve head of government	Germany, Israel
Approve individual ministers of government	United States
Hold ministers accountable by motions of no confidence or censure	Britain, Italy
Impeach the executive	United States
Support the executive	Former Soviet Union
Pass legislation	Most systems
Debate	India, Switzerland, Israel
Question ministers	Canada, Netherlands
Hold committees of inquiry into government action	United States
Provide criticism as loyal opposition	Britain
Maintain financial control	United States
Act as ombudsman or parliamentary commissioner	Sweden, New Zealand
Help constituents	United States
Modify government proposals	Germany

THE JUDICIAL BRANCH

The system of courts of law, with its apex in a high or supreme court, constitutes the third branch of government. In nondemocratic systems, the judiciary is likely to be subordinate to and controlled by the executive authorities, whether in authoritarian, communist, or military regimes. In the emerging democracies in Latin America, the judiciary has been trying to establish a true rule of law.

In constitutional democracies, judges have tended to decide cases on the basis of judicial restraint, applying the law strictly with less heed to policy or their own views. More recently, they have engaged to a greater degree than in previous years in judicial activism, interpreting the law to influence public policy. This latter role has

TABLE 1.15

HOW THE UPPER CHAMBER IS CHOSEN

Hereditary and Life Term	House of Lords in Britain until 1999
Direct election	United States, Japan, Australia, Switzerland; often in federal states
Indirect election	France, by electoral college composed of National Assembly deputies, departmental councilors, and city councils
Election by lower chamber	Norway, Iceland
Group election	Ireland, representatives of economic and social interests
Appointed by state governments	Germany
Appointed by prime minister	Canada

expanded for two reasons: the increase in government regulation and the challenge to it by individuals, interest groups, and civic organizations; and the increased number of international agreements and treaties that provide opportunity for judges to make decisions.

Decisions by the courts on constitutional issues and executive actions take two essential forms: *judicial review,* deciding the constitutionality of laws and regulations; and *administrative review,* deciding the legality and appropriate nature of actions by the executive and other public sector bodies. Judicial review, a power asserted first in the U.S. case of *Marbury v. Madison* (1803), allows courts to evaluate laws and possibly strike them down as unconstitutional, as contrary to the fundamental constitution, thus giving an authoritative, binding interpretation of a law. Judges balance the requirement for governmental power in a particular case and time with the need to protect civil liberties and individual rights of citizens.

The courts also resolve conflicts between the different branches of central government and between the different levels of government in the system. This function can be done either in the highest or supreme court in the regular court system, as in the United State or Britain, or by a special constitutional court, as in Germany, France, Austria, Spain, or Greece. The German Federal Constitutional Court has been particularly important in this respect: between 1951 and 1990 it judged 198 federal laws to be contrary to the Basic Law (or constitution), including the banning of the Communist and Neo-Nazi parties. Constitutional courts can nullify legislation as unconstitutional, either before it goes into effect as in France, or after it has been passed, the usual case.

Administrative review has increased in significance with the expansion of government activity and power in many areas of life, including social security, immigration, tax and planning issues, and the challenge to that increased activity by citizens and private organizations. Judges decide if officials have the right to take the challenged action, and they decide on possible remedies. Some countries deal with these challenges primarily in the ordinary courts. France, with its *Conseil d'Etat*, and Germany and Italy have special administrative tribunals to deal with these matters.

International courts have increased in importance (see A Closer Look 1.12).

PUBLIC POLICY

Comparison of what different countries do—their public policy—is as significant as comparison of the political culture, processes, ideas, or institutions already discussed. Public policy is inevitably related to those other aspects of political systems and can only be explained in the context of the rest of the system. Only then can one attempt to answer such questions as why the United States does not have a national health insurance system while Germany has had one since 1883, or why it has traditionally been easier to get support for public housing in

A CLOSER LOOK 1.12

INTERNATIONAL COURTS

The Court of Justice of the European Union (EU), in Luxembourg, decides on laws and regulations by reference to the treaties on which the EU is founded.

The European Court of Human Rights, in Strasbourg, is the final court of appeal on human rights for most of the European countries.

The International Court of Justice, in The Hague since 1946, is the chief judicial organ of the United Nations.

The International Criminal Court, in The Hague since 2002, is intended to deal with war crimes and crimes against humanity.

Western Europe than in the United States, or why the United States has been so far ahead of other countries in the development of a public education system extending to the whole population.

Multiple Affairs of State

It is true of all countries that the state is no longer limited, as in earlier times, largely to maintaining internal order and external defense, providing a minimum of basic services, and raising taxation to pay for these activities. Government has expanded for a wide variety of reasons: economic recession, war, social justice, help for the underprivileged, protection of minority rights, demands for the redistribution of income or wealth, and the ideas of social reformers.

States are now concerned with a mix of policies concerning social welfare, economic management, and protection of the environment. A substantial part of government budgets is spent on defense, either directly on the armed forces and weaponry or indirectly on research and the development of technology. But spending on social services is now the largest item in many budgets and continues to grow as people live longer and more is spent on pensions and hospitals.

In all states—liberal, socialist, conservative, or communist—there is some economic planning, though to considerably different degrees. Attempts are made to stimulate economic growth, to increase employment, to check inflation, to get a favorable balance of trade with foreign countries, and to regulate industry and other economic activities from mining coal to making cigarettes. Governments have recently become increasingly aware of ecological and esthetic issues and of the need to improve the quality of life in their countries.

In some countries a backlash has occurred against the rising cost of programs that have necessitated both an increase of taxation to pay for them and a larger bureaucracy. Government spending accounts for a considerable part of the GDP of modern states—in Sweden it reached 68

percent of GDP—though countries differ in the size of welfare and health services, taxation policies, industrial policies, and public ownership. The main areas of growth include pensions, health care, unemployment benefits, and family support. Wealthier countries tend to spend a larger part of their national income on medical care than poorer ones. In the wealthy OECD countries, health care for medical goods and services presently amounts to about 8 percent of GDP. The United States spends about 14 percent of GDP.

Why Do Public Policies Differ?

Political scientists differ in the importance given to political and other variables in explaining the diversity of public policies. The following paragraphs look at some of the relevant factors without ranking them in order of importance.

Political Structure and Institutions   The likelihood and kind of actions taken by the state will be affected by the system of government, separation or nonseparation of powers, national or locally based parties, democratic or nondemocratic politics, the nature of the elite political groups, and the qualities and interests of the civil service.

The Political Process   Relevant here is whether political decisions are based on ideology or are more pragmatic and the result of bargaining, as in the United States. Public policies will also depend on the strength of interest groups and the nature of the party system.

The Prevailing Ideas in the Community
Public policy will differ depending on whether the dominant ideas are those of liberalism, democratic socialism, communism, conservatism, nationalism, religious fundamentalism, fascism, or anticolonialism. Conservatives, for example, want the state to play a limited role. Policy ideas are partly a response to current social problems and to the external concerns of the country and its international role.

A CLOSER LOOK 1.13

THE WELFARE STATE

Many states provide increasing degrees and varieties of welfare for citizens. Welfare systems embrace social security, social assistance, and welfare services. Benefits are provided by the state for sickness, unemployment, disability, pensions, death, housing, and family allowances. Systems of health care and comprehensive education are established. Assistance is provided for the aged, for single parents, and for low-cost public housing. Services include social work, legal counsel, rehabilitation, and training for employment. The extent and cost of welfare systems depend on a number of factors: the demographic character of society, the relative proportion of older and younger people, rapidly increasing health care provisions, the changing labor market, changing gender relationships, and patterns of household and living arrangements. Because of the cost of welfare systems today, most countries have sought to introduce a more efficient allocation of resources, better management, and an increase in the qualification needed to obtain benefits.

The Basic Elements of the Social System

Factors such as the geography of a country, demographic and racial composition of the population, economic and occupational distribution, and the degree of literacy will affect policy. Some studies argue, for example, that factors like economic development, the age structure of the population, and the age of the social security system explain most of the differences in the social security expenditures in different countries.

CONCLUSION

We have now reviewed why individual political systems should be studied and why comparisons are useful. We have looked at the various bases on which comparison may proceed, at some major differences among systems, and at some major categories in which different systems may be analyzed. The reader is now invited to begin the challenging and exciting task of understanding a number of the major countries in the world and to compare their political systems in a meaningful way.

Thinking Critically

1. What do you think should be compared when you study comparative politics and government? What difficulties would you encounter in this study?
2. How has the emergence of new countries since the end of World War II affected the character of the study of comparative government?
3. What do you consider the major divisions in Western and non-Western societies? What are the major points of connection?
4. If you were founding a new political system, what electoral system would you choose?
5. What factors account for the rise and decline of military regimes?
6. What problems do non-Western systems face in the process of development and modernization?
7. What do you think is the most desirable relationship between the executive and legislative branches of government?
8. What is the effect of globalization on comparative politics?

KEY TERMS

administrative review *(35)*
assembly government *(32)*
authoritarian *(21)*
bureaucracy *(11)*
cabinet government *(31)*
communist *(23)*
constitutional democracy *(21)*
developing countries *(25)*
federal system *(30)*
functional representation *(26)*
globalization *(4)*
gross domestic product (GDP) *(20)*
gross national product (GNP) *(20)*
interest groups *(27)*
judicial review *(35)*
liberal *(8)*
Marxism *(18)*
multimember constituency *(27)*
parliamentary government *(31)*
party system *(28)*
political culture *(10)*
presidential system *(32)*
proportional representation (PR) *(27)*
separation of powers *(30)*
single-member constituency *(27)*
socialist *(18)*
third world countries *(25)*
totalitarian *(22)*
unitary system *(30)*

FURTHER READINGS

Adams, Francis. *Deepening Democracy* (Westport: Praeger, 2003).

Brooker, Paul. *Non-democratic Regimes: Theory, Government and Politics* (New York: St. Martin's, 2000).

Budge, Ian, et al. *Parties, Policies and Democracy* (Boulder: Westview, 1994).

Castles, Francis G. *The Future of the Welfare State: Crisis Myths and Crisis Realities* (Oxford: Oxford University Press, 2004).

Crick, Bernard. *Democracy, a Very Short Introduction* (Oxford: Oxford University Press, 2002).

Dalton, Russell J., and Martin J. Wattenberg. *Parties without Partisans: Political Change in Advanced Industrial Democracies* (New York: Oxford University Press, 2000).

Diamond, Larry, ed. *Democracy in Developing Countries* (Boulder: Rienner, 1999).

Dogan, Mattei, and Ali Kazancigil, eds. *Comparing Nations: Concepts, Strategies, Substance* (Cambridge: Blackwell, 1994).

Duke, Lois L., ed, *Women in Politics: Outsiders or Insiders?* (Englewood Cliffs: Prentice-Hall, 1993).

Esping-Andersen, Gosta. *Welfare States in Transition: National Adaptations in Global Economies* (Thousand Oaks: Sage, 1996).

Esser, Frank, and Barbara Pfetsch, eds. *Comparing Political Communication: Theories, Cases, and Challenges.* (Cambridge: Cambridge University Press, 2004).

Farrell, David M. *Electoral Systems: A Comparative Introduction* (New York: Palgrave, 2001).

Fetzer, Joel S., and J. Christopher Soper. *Muslims and the State in Britain, France, and Germany* (Cambridge: Cambridge University Press, 2004).

Finer, S. E., et al. *Comparing Constitutions* (New York: Oxford University Press, 1995).

Forster, Anthony, et al., eds. *Soldiers and Societies in Postcommunist Europe* (London: Palgrave Macmillan, 2003).

Gunther, Richard, and Anthony Mughan, eds. *Democracy and the Media: A Comparative Perspective* (New York: Cambridge University Press, 2000).

Heywood, Andrew. *Political Ideologies: An Introduction,* 2nd ed. (Basingstoke: Macmillan, 1998).

Huntington, Samuel P. *The Third Wave: Democratization in the Late Twentieth Century* (Norman: University of Oklahoma Press, 1993).

Ignazi, Piero. *Extreme Right Parties in Western Europe* (Oxford: Oxford University Press, 2003).

Lewis, Bernard. *What Went Wrong? Western Impact and Middle Eastern Response* (New York: Oxford University Press, 2002).

Lijphart, Arend, et al. *Electoral Systems and Party Systems: A Study of 27 Democracies, 1945–90* (New York: Oxford University Press, 1994).

Lipset, Seymour M., and Jason M. Laikin. *The Democratic Century* (Norman: University of Oklahoma, 2004).

Madeley, John T. S., ed. *Religion and Politics* (Aldershot: Ashgate, 2003).

Mair, Peter, et al., eds. *Political Parties and Electoral Change* (Thousand Oaks: Sage, 2004).

Mendelsohn, Matthew, and Andrew Parkin, eds. *Referendum Democracy* (New York: Palgrave, 2001).

Norris, Pippa, ed. *Critical Citizens: Global Support for Democratic Government* (New York: Oxford University Press, 1999).

Norton, Philip, ed. *Legislatures and Legislators* (Brookfield: Ashgate, 1998).

Norton, Philip, ed. *Parliaments in Contemporary Western Europe* (Portland: Cass, 1999).

Page, Edward C., and Vincent Wright, eds. *Bureaucratic Elites in Western European States: A Comparative Analysis of Top Officials* (New York: Oxford University Press, 1999).

Peeler, John A. *Building Democracy in Latin America* (Boulder: Rienner, 1998).

Pharr, Susan J., and Robert Putnam, eds. *Disaffected Democracies: What's Troubling the Trilateral Countries?* (Princeton: Princeton University Press, 2001).

Pierson, Christopher. *Hard Choices: Social Democracy in the 21st Century* (Malden: Blackwell, 2001).

Richardson, Jeremy J., ed. *Pressure Groups* (New York: Oxford University Press, 1993).

Siedentop, Larry. *Democracy in Europe* (London: Allen Lane, 2000).

Sykes, Robert, et al., eds. *Globalization and European Welfare States* (New York: Palgrave, 2001).

Wilson, Graham. *Interest Groups* (Cambridge: Blackwell, 1990).

North
Atlantic
Ocean

Voe Shetland Islands

Orkney
Islands

100 km

0   100 Miles

Hebrides

SCOTLAND

Aberdeen

Dundee

Grangemouth

Edinburgh

Glasgow

North Sea

Newcastle
upon Tyne

NORTHERN

Londonderry

Belfast

IRELAND

Middlesbrough

Isle
of Man

Hull

Irish Sea

Liverpool

Manchester

IRELAND

Birmingham

ENGLAND

WALES

London

Cardiff

Dover

Bristol

Southampton
Portsmouth

Channel
Tunnel

English Channel

FRANCE

Guernsey

Jersey

CHAPTER

2

THE GOVERNMENT OF
Great Britain

Michael Curtis

INTRODUCTION

Background: Great Britain, the dominant industrial and maritime power of the 19th century, played a leading role in developing parliamentary democracy and in advancing literature and science. At its zenith, the British Empire stretched over one-fourth of the earth's surface. The first half of the 20th century saw the UK's strength seriously depleted in two World Wars. The second half witnessed the dismantling of the Empire and the UK rebuilding itself into a modern and prosperous European nation. As one of five permanent members of the UN Security Council, a founding member of NATO, and of the Commonwealth, the UK pursues a global approach to foreign policy; it currently is weighing the degree of its integration with continental Europe. A member of the EU, it chose to remain outside of the European Monetary Union for the time being. Constitutional reform is also a significant issue in the UK. Regional assemblies with varying degrees of power opened in Scotland, Wales, and Northern Ireland in 1999.

GEOGRAPHY

Location: Western Europe, islands including the northern one-sixth of the island of Ireland between the North Atlantic Ocean and the North Sea, northwest of France

Area: 244,820 sq km

Area—comparative: slightly smaller than Oregon

Land boundaries: 360 km

   border countries: Ireland 360 km

Climate: temperate; moderated by prevailing southwest winds over the North Atlantic Current; more than one-half of the days are overcast

Terrain: mostly rugged hills and low mountains; level to rolling plains in east and southeast

41

Elevation extremes: *lowest point:* Fenland –4 m
highest point: Ben Nevis 1,343 m

Geography note: lies near vital North Atlantic sea lanes; only 35 km from France and now linked by tunnel under the English Channel; because of heavily indented coastline, no location is more than 125 km from tidal waters

PEOPLE, 2005

Population: 60,270,000

Age structure: *0–14 years:* 18.89% (male 5.5 million; female 5.3 million)
15–64 years: 66.3% (male 20.1 million; female 19.7 million)
65 years and over: 15.7% (male 4.0 million; female 5.4 million)

Population growth rate: 0.29%

Birthrate: 10.88 births/1,000 population

Sex ratio: 0.98 male/female

Life expectancy at birth: 78.27 years
male: 75.84 years
female: 80.83 years

Nationality: *noun:* Briton, Britons, British (collective plural)
adjective: British

Ethnic groups: English 81.5%, Scottish 9.6%, Irish 2.4%, Welsh 1.9%, Ulster 1.8%, West Indian, Indian, Pakistani, and other 2.8%

Religions: Anglican 27 million, Roman Catholic 9 million, Muslim 1.5 million, Presbyterian 800,000, Methodist 760,000, Sikh 500,000, Hindu 500,000, Jewish 300,000

Languages: English, Welsh (about 26% of the population of Wales), Scottish form of Gaelic (about 60,000 in Scotland)

Literacy: *definition:* age 15 and over has completed five or more years of schooling
total population: 99%

GOVERNMENT

Country name: *conventional long form:* United Kingdom of Great Britain and Northern Ireland

conventional short form: United Kingdom, Great Britain
abbreviation: UK, GB

Government type: constitutional monarchy

Capital: London

Dependent areas: Anguilla, Bermuda, British Indian Ocean Territory, British Virgin Islands, Cayman Islands, Falkland Islands, Gibraltar, Guernsey, Jersey, Isle of Man, Montserrat, Pitcairn Islands, Saint Helena, South Georgia and the South Sandwich Islands, Turks and Caicos Islands

Independence: England has existed as a unified entity since the 10th century; the union between England and Wales was enacted under the Statute of Rhuddlan in 1284; in the Act of Union of 1707, England and Scotland agreed to permanent union as Great Britain; the legislative union of Great Britain and Ireland was implemented in 1801, with the adoption of the name the United Kingdom of Great Britain and Ireland; the Anglo-Irish treaty of 1921 formalized a partition of Ireland; six northern Irish counties remained part of the United Kingdom as Northern Ireland and the current name of the country, the United Kingdom of Great Britain and Northern Ireland, was adopted in 1927

Constitution: unwritten; partly statutes, partly common law and practice

Legal system: common law tradition with early Roman and modern continental influences; no judicial review of Acts of Parliament; accepts compulsory International Court of Justice jurisdiction, with reservations; British courts and legislation are increasingly subject to review by European Union courts

Suffrage: 18 years of age; universal

Executive branch: *chief of state:* Queen Elizabeth II (since 6 February 1952); Heir Apparent Prince Charles (son of the queen, born 14 November 1948)

head of government: Prime Minister Anthony (Tony) Blair (since 2 May 1997) *cabinet:* Cabinet of Ministers appointed by the prime minister

elections: none; the monarch is hereditary; the prime minister is the leader of the majority party in the House of Commons (assuming there is no majority party, a prime minister would have a majority coalition or at least a coalition that was not rejected by the majority)

Legislative branch: bicameral Parliament comprised of House of Lords (consists of approximately 500 life peers, 92 hereditary peers and 26 clergy) and House of Commons (659 seats; members are elected by popular vote to serve five-year terms unless the House is dissolved earlier)

Judicial branch: House of Lords (highest court of appeal; several Lords of Appeal in Ordinary are appointed by the monarch for life); Supreme Courts of England, Wales, and Northern Ireland (comprising the Courts of Appeal, the High Courts of Justice, and the Crown Courts); Scotland's Court of Session and Court of the Justiciary

ECONOMY

Overview: The UK, a leading trading power and financial center, deploys an essentially capitalistic economy, one of the quartet of trillion dollar economies of Western Europe. Over the past two decades the government has greatly reduced public ownership and contained the growth of social welfare programs. Agriculture is intensive, highly mechanized, and efficient by European standards, producing about 60% of food needs with only 1% of the labor force. The UK has large coal, natural gas, and oil reserves; primary energy production accounts for 10% of GDP, one of the highest shares of any industrial nation. Services, particularly banking, insurance, and business services, account by far for the largest proportion of GDP while industry continues to decline in importance. The economy has grown steadily, at just above or below 3%, for the last several years.

GDP: purchasing power parity—$1.66 trillion

GDP—real growth rate: 2.2%

GDP—per capita: purchasing power parity—$27,700

GDP—composition by sector: *agriculture:* 0.9%
industry: 26.5%
services: 72.6%

Population below poverty line: 17%

Labor force: 29.6 million

Labor force—by occupation: agriculture 1%, industry 25%, services 74%

Unemployment rate: 5.1%

Currency: British pound (GBP)

A. POLITICAL DEVELOPMENT

HISTORICAL BACKGROUND

Why study the British political system? There are a number of answers to this understandable question. Britain has the oldest operating political system in the world; some of its governmental institutions have been in continuous existence for nearly a thousand years. Symbolically this is illustrated by the memorials to many notable figures in public and cultural life in Westminster Abbey, the building of which was begun in the eleventh century. No one needs to be reminded of the intellectual and literary influence of Britain's writers, such as Chaucer, Shakespeare, Milton, Austen, Dickens, Shaw, Woolf, and Auden, and its philosophers, such as Hobbes, Locke, Hume, Mill, Bentham, and Russell. Its political influence, both directly and indirectly, has been equally important.

Through its former control of about one-quarter of the world's population on every continent, Britain has directly influenced many countries, including the United States. From Britain, the United States has absorbed a similar idea of the rule of law and a concern for personal freedoms. There are similar political institutions, such as a single-member-constituency electoral system for the lower house, a two-chamber legislature, a two-major-party system, a cabinet, and a civil service based on merit. Oscar Wilde once said that Britain and the United States were two countries separated by a common language. Certainly there are great differences in the way that political power is exercised and institutions function in the two countries. Nevertheless, it was appropriate that the British memorial to President John F. Kennedy be placed at Runnymede, where King John was tamed by the feudal barons into signing the Magna Carta in 1215.

Today the British Empire, on which the sun never set, no longer exists. But most of the countries once ruled by Britain belong to the 54-member Commonwealth with its population of over 1.7 billion. Though not a political power in itself, the Commonwealth is a unique multiracial association.

Indirectly, Britain has influenced other countries by its political ideals and values and by some of its political practices, such as a meaningful parliament which could control the excesses of executive power, an officially recognized loyal opposition, political moderation and tolerance, and a process of change by gradual and peaceful means.

The British system is also instructive for those interested in modernization and political development. Britain was the world's first industrialized country, a process which began at the end of the eighteenth century. For Karl Marx, Britain was the model of the capitalist system in the middle of the nineteenth century. The proportion of the working population employed in factories and manufacturing rose while that in agriculture declined. With the repeal of the Corn Laws in 1846, allowing the entry of cheap food, and the adoption of free-trade principles, Britain lived by exporting its manufactured goods and by importing food and raw materials. As a result, the country has been very concerned with problems of foreign trade and international exchange. London became the financial center of the world in banking, insurance, and shipping: the British

A CLOSER LOOK
2.1

MAGNA CARTA

No freeman shall be taken, imprisoned … or in any other way destroyed … except by the lawful judgment of his peers, or by the law of the land. To no one will we sell, to none will we deny or delay, right or justice.

currency, the pound sterling, became the medium for much of the world's trade.

A century ago Britain was the workshop of the world, producing two-thirds of the world's coal, half of its iron, over half of its steel, half of its cotton goods, and almost all of its machine tools. Britain's exports of capital goods—machines and technology—led to industrialization in other major countries, which soon became competitors and began to supplant Britain technologically and industrially. Yet with the industrial exports had also gone other exports such as ideas, institutions, and ways of life. Britain was the foremost example of the process of modernization and industrialization without a revolution from either above or below.

But Britain has also paid a heavy price for having the first mature industrial system and for being dependent on international trade. Its cap-

ital equipment became outmoded, and its relative economic position in the world weakened as other countries advanced industrially. Its dependence on imports of food and raw materials made it vulnerable to outside forces.

In the modern age, Britain has become a postindustrial society with a mixed economy and a significant social welfare system, in which private enterprise coexists with a public sector and public expenditure now amounts to about 40 percent of the gross national product. In the 1980s Britain was acutely troubled by problems such as inflation, less-than-full employment, and comparatively slow economic growth, which have plagued other advanced nations to differing degrees. Yet productivity grew by over 3 percent a year between 1980 and 2001. The British economy is still the sixth largest in the world, and Britain is still the fifth largest trading nation.

No. 10 Downing Street, the residence and office of the prime minister, is located in a small street off Whitehall about half a mile from Parliament. The only other houses in the street are occupied by the chancellor of the Exchequer and by the office of the government chief whip.

Political demonstration in Trafalgar Square in London.

EVOLUTION OF THE POLITICAL SYSTEM

The British political system illustrates the gradual evolution from internal chaos and divisions, which resulted in the Wars of the Roses between rival contenders for the throne in the fifteenth century and the Civil War between the king and parliament and the peaceful "Glorious Revolu-tion" in the seventeenth century, to a stable unitary system with a long process of development of political structures, institutions, and behavior (see Figure 2.1). The country changed from a mainly rural, isolated, religious nation to a democratic, largely urban, industrial society, essentially secular in practice, and the center of an empire.

Britain exemplifies political change from a strong monarchy with an important aristocratic

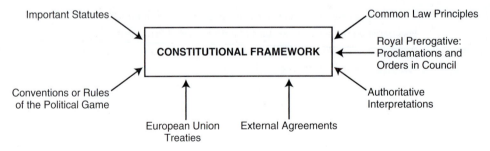

Figure 2.1 THE CONSTITUTIONAL FRAMEWORK OF BRITISH GOVERNMENT

class to a political democracy. A constitutional monarch reigns over a country in which the parliamentary cabinet system and political parties are the dominant political organizations representing the different political expressions of the power of the people. With the gradual expansion of rights and privileges and the removal of civil and religious disabilities, all can legally participate in politics without discrimination (see Table 2.1).

All political systems retain certain traditional practices and institutions that seem to run counter to the logic of political development. In Britain these would include anomalies such as the presence until 1999 of over 700 hereditary peers in the House of Lords; the rebuilding of the destroyed House of Commons after World War II so that it physically resembles the old chamber and can seat only half of its members; and the uses until recently of eighteenth-century wigs by the Speaker of the House of Commons and by the judges and barristers in the High Courts of Law. Indeed, it is ironic that the leading political figure, the prime minister, was long paid for holding an office, First Lord of the Treasury, which no longer has a function, but was not paid for being prime minister, the functions of which are nowhere legally or precisely defined.

In recent years the British system has changed. Innovations such as the referendum on the European Community in 1975, the devolution of power to Scotland and Wales in 1998, and the restoration of direct rule in Northern Ireland in 1972 and then the creation of a Northern Ireland Assembly in 1998, the direct election of a mayor of London and the establishment of a Greater London Authority, and setting up of Regional Development Agencies have been just some of the responses. New parties of the political center such as the Social Democrats and later the Liberal Democrats came on the scene. The nationalist parties in Wales and particularly in Scotland obtained greater support from the electorates in the two countries, though the support has fluctuated. The Greens, a group and party reflecting the growing concern about environmental issues, emerged in the 1980s. The UK Independence Party was formed in 1993 to oppose British membership of the EU.

TABLE 2.1

REMOVAL OF POLITICAL AND CIVIL DISABILITIES

1656	Jews allowed back into the country
1689	Toleration Act—members of all religious orders except Catholics and Unitarians permitted freedom of worship
1774	Residency qualifications for members of Parliament declared unnecessary
1778	Some restrictions against Roman Catholic worship removed
1779	Dissenters relieved from subscribing to some of the 39 Articles
1807	Slave trade abolished
1828	Dissenters allowed to become members of Parliament
1829	Catholics permitted to become members of both houses of Parliament
1858	Jews permitted to become members of both houses of Parliament
	Property qualification for members of Parliament ended
1871	University religious tests abolished
1872	Secret ballot instituted
1888	Atheists allowed to become members of Parliament
1918	Women over 30 obtain the vote
1928	Women over 21 obtain the vote
2004	Same-sex couples can obtain legal recognition of their relationship by a civil partnership

BRITAIN AS A MODEL IN POLITICS

For the student of politics, Britain has long been useful as an example in the comparison of different systems. Britain with its constitutional and civilian government, essentially two-party system, and representative democracy has been instructive for this purpose. The British system has sometimes been called the "Westminster model" after the area of London in which Parliament is located.

Britain has adhered for three centuries to the subordination of the military to political power, and the military has been loyal to governments of all political complexions. Not since Oliver Cromwell's government (1653–1658) has Britain had a military dictator or been seriously threatened by fear of a military coup. Britain had also been an example of an essentially two-party system as distinct from regimes with one dominant party, a number of parties, or none at all. In Britain, as in the United States, only two parties have, in effect, been strong enough to share the bulk of the electoral vote and exert political control while alternating in the exercise of executive power. However, a third party is still an important presence.

Britain is a constitutional democracy as well as a constitutional monarchy. All citizens, individually and through organizations, can participate and attempt to influence political decisions. For the most part this is done indirectly through the electoral system, by which the representatives of the people are sent to the House of Commons, the powerful chamber of Parliament, the supreme legal power in the country. The representative system based on the majority principle, by which a plurality is sufficient to win, is also based on the permitted existence of political minorities, which have the right to try to become the majority in their turn, and on basic freedoms of speech, meeting, and the press which allow political commentary of all kinds.

Britain is one of few countries which do not have a single formal document regarded as a constitution to define the political system and state the rights and duties of citizens. Unlike most other systems, all changes of a constitutional nature take place without any special legal provision for them; nor is there a supreme or constitutional court to decide on the constitutionality of legislation passed by Parliament. But Britain is the classical example of a system that is "constitutional" in the sense of adherence to rules and to accepted ways of political behavior as contrasted with countries that are nonconstitutional, or arbitrary, in their political practices.

The British constitutional framework results from the following different components (see Figure 2.1).

1. A number of legislative statutes and documents of outstanding importance have provided the foundations of a considerable number of political institutions. These include the Magna Carta, 1215; the Petition of Right, 1628; the Bill of Rights, 1689; the Habeas Corpus Act, 1679; the Act of Settlement, 1701; the Acts of Union with Scotland in 1707 and with Ireland in 1801; the Franchise Acts of 1832, 1867, 1884, 1918, 1928, 1948, 1958, 1963, and 1969; the Parliament Acts, 1911 and 1949; the Crown Proceedings Act, 1947; the Ministers of the Crown Act, 1937; the Nationalization Acts between 1947 and 1950; the European Communities Act, 1972; the British Nationality Act, 1981; the European Communities (Amendment) Act, 1986; the House of Lords Act, 1999. They differ from other statutes, not in a technical sense, but only in their political importance.

2. Certain principles have been established by common law, which comprises the decisions of judges and the courts in individual cases. Personal liberties of speech, press, and assembly are to a considerable degree the result of judicial decisions over the last two centuries.

The most important principle is the rule of law, which implies the certainty of legal rules rather than arbitrary judgments in determining the rights of individuals and in examining the behavior of authorities. There is no punishment unless a breach of the law has been established in a court of law. False imprisonment is prevented by a writ of habeas corpus, by which an individual obtains an explanation of the reason for detainment. The rule of law also implies that everyone is subject to the law, including officials. No one can plead the orders of a superior official in defense of illegal actions or can claim the right to be tried in a special court under a different code for official actions.

The demand for a more formal bill of rights has grown, largely as a result of two of Britain's external agreements. Britain ratified the European Convention of Human Rights in 1951 and has thus been subject to grievances taken before the European Commission on Human Rights. Furthermore, British membership in the European Union, the laws of which may take precedence over British law, has allowed judges to decide on conflicts between the two sets of law.

Though the British judiciary since the 1970s occasionally ruled against the interpretation by ministers of the extent of their powers, it still cannot rule on the validity of statutes passed by Parliament. Britain does not have a court like the United States Supreme Court that can declare legislation unconstitutional. However, the British courts in recent years have reviewed some actions of government ministers and administrative officials to see if they have exceeded the powers allowed them by parliamentary statute and encroached on rights of individuals. The courts have sometimes declared such actions *ultra vires* (beyond legal power) and even exercised some judicial review.

3. Certain books written by constitutional experts are regarded as so authoritative that some of their views on constitutional issues are commonly accepted. They include such works as Walter Bagehot's *The English Constitution,* A. V. Dicey's *Introduction to the Study of the Law of the Constitution,* and Erskine May's *Parliamentary Practice.*

4. Numerous political rules and practices, known collectively as conventions, are observed by all participating in the system. Though they have never been passed in any formal or legal manner, they are usually observed as completely as any laws. Occasionally, however, there may be differences about the exact meaning of a convention. Among the most important of these conventions are the following:

a. The real heads of the government are the prime minister and the cabinet.

b. The government is formed from the party that can control a majority in the House of Commons.

c. Cabinet ministers will normally be chosen from the two houses of Parliament, and the prime minister will come from the House of Commons.

d. The cabinet will operate on the basis of collective responsibility to ensure political unity.

e. The government will resign or ask for a dissolution of Parliament if defeated in the House of Commons on a motion of no confidence.

f. The monarch will ultimately accept the wishes of his or her government.

g. Only the government can propose votes on grants of money in the House of Commons.

h. Those affected by a proposed action will normally be consulted by the government before a final decision is made.

Without these conventions, regular and orderly government in its present form could not function. They create harmony between the executive and legislative branches of the government through various understandings about the workings of the parliamentary cabinet system. The conventions ensure that government is ultimately responsible to the will of the people because an election decides which party is to form the government and thus who is to be prime minister. In a society such as the British, in which traditional institutions have survived changing political circumstances, as the monarchy has done in a political democracy, conventions allow institutions to adjust to political reality.

Conventions are observed not because it is illegal to disregard them, but because they enable the political system to work in accordance with the agreed fundamental principles on which consensus exists.

THE IMPORTANCE OF CONSENSUS AND ITS LIMITS

Britain until very recently has been a model of political stability and consensus on the nature of the regime and on the method of change. British politics has depended on all participants abiding by "the rules of the political game" or understandings. These rules include the pragmatic working and adaptation by gradual change of political institutions and organizations; tolerance of different political positions; the belief that government should govern and have adequate powers; agreement on procedural matters, the validity of political dissent and of trade union organization, through which the working class has a stake in the system; the view that the people should be consulted about political action, through their representatives and groups to which they belong; and moderation in political behavior.

The essence of the British political system is a stable democracy which provides for the exercise of strong power by the government, but which also allows substantial personal freedoms and rights. There has been an alternation of political power between the parties in a system characterized by a limited constitutional monarchy, a bicameral parliament, the supremacy of parliament, the linking of the executive and the legislature through the members of the government sitting in parliament, the responsibility of the government to parliament and indirectly to the people, and on an independent nuclear deterrent.

There has also been acceptance of the welfare state, the need for full employment and adequate incomes, free collective bargaining, a mixed economy with both private and state enterprises, and a foreign policy based on membership in the Western alliance.

POLITICAL STABILITY

The last revolution was in 1688 when the struggle between the king and the parliament led to the overthrow of the monarch. The principle was established that Parliament, not the king, had supreme power. The monarch could not suspend laws, levy taxes without parliamentary consent or maintain a standing army in peace-time. How is this remarkable political stability to be explained? There are various explanations of why the British people accepted the political institutions and those classes which controlled

them. Some of them are analyzed in the following paragraphs.

Political Culture

The acceptance by the population of political authority, on the one hand, and the existence of individual rights, on the other, has resulted in political moderation. The balance among the British people between limited political activity and general acquiescence in what government does has led to an attachment to the political system and to agreement on the rules of political behavior. Britain has been regarded as the model of a democratic political culture in which there is regular competition for the control of government (the existence of which is dependent on the electoral will of the people). Training in this civic culture takes place in many social institutions—for example, the family, peer group, school, and workplace—as well as in the political system itself.

Deference of the People

Since Bagehot introduced the idea in the nineteenth century, some have stressed the deference until quite recently of the population, including a significant part of the working class, to the social elite or members of the upper social classes, the well-born or the wealthy, who because of their social position are regarded as the natural or uniquely qualified political leaders by a people that accepts traditional values and authority. In practice, the Conservative Party came to be regarded by many as the embodiment of the natural ruling class or as particularly gifted to govern. But whatever the significance of the deference of people in the past, the fact that the Conservative Party, though it governed from 1979 to 1997, did not win 6 of the 11 elections since 1964 has suggested that deference is less important today and not the sole explanation of the political stability.

Pattern of Authority

Some analysts suggest that there is a correlation between the pattern of authority in government and administration, and that in parties, interest groups, and nonofficial organizations and institutions. In Britain the pattern is strong leadership, which is efficient and can make itself obeyed but which is limited by substantive and procedural restraints. There is minimal direct participation by the vast majority of the population. Voters choose between alternatives presented by party leaders. The parties themselves are not only disciplined but also dominated by the leadership.

Traditional values uphold leadership and authority in politics and society. They permeate the elite institutions such as the monarchy, the established Church, the "public" schools, Oxford and Cambridge, the military and administrative hierarchy, and the senior civil service. The Conservative Party has controlled the government for the majority of years since 1895.

Relative Deprivation

One hypothesis suggests that the feeling of people that they are deprived economically or socially—and their consequent political behavior—depends on which other people or group they compare themselves with rather than on real social conditions. The British working class has usually not taken the nonmanual privileged classes as a comparative reference group. Therefore, the working class's feeling of deprivation has not been as strong as objective inequalities might have led them to believe. This, in turn, has produced a less disruptive and less revolutionary political attitude than in other major countries.

Effect of Geography

Perhaps the most important single factor explaining British stability and the continuity of social and political life is that Britain is an island. Since 1066 the existing political institutions have not been disrupted by military invasion. This happy fact permitted the creation of stable borders, a luxury not enjoyed by other European countries that were forced into wars to create or maintain national unity. Moreover, this island power developed both a navy (until 1939 the

largest in the world) for its protection, as well as a shipping fleet that became the basis for its commercial expansion, capital accumulation, and the conquest of an empire, which at its height consisted of over 15 million square miles of territory on every continent of the world.

THE UNIFIED SYSTEM

The process of unification of the country took more than five centuries. The United Kingdom is now composed of four national units on two main islands and surrounding small islands. England constitutes 52 percent, Wales 9 percent, Scotland 33 percent, and Northern Ireland 6 percent of the total area. Northern Ireland, or Ulster, constitutes 16 percent of the area of the second island, the rest of which is occupied by the Republic of Ireland (see Table 2.2).

The British population is a heterogeneous multiracial society of Celts, Romans, Scots, Picts, Angles, Jutes, Danes, Norsemen, Normans, East Europeans, West Indians, Asians, and other groups. But the prospect of much greater immigration from the Caribbean and Asian Commonwealth countries such as India, Pakistan, and Bangladesh led to limitations on that immigration by statutes in 1962, 1968, and 1971, which were passed after a certain amount of opposition, and by political policies.

Though English is the standard language (the form spoken in the southeast is the most prestigious norm), other languages are also spoken. About 20 percent of the Welsh population

TABLE 2.2

THE UNITED KINGDOM, 2005

	Area (square miles)	Population (millions)
England	50.3	49.8
Scotland	30.4	5.0
Wales	8.0	2.9
Northern Ireland	5.4	1.7
Total	94.1	59.5

speaks Welsh, a form of British Celtic which is of equal validity with English in the administration of justice and the conduct of government business in Wales. Some 2 percent of the population of Scotland, mainly in the Highlands and western coastal regions, speak Gaelic, and about 2 percent in Northern Ireland speak the Irish form of Gaelic. The newer Asian communities speak a variety of languages.

A NEW PLURALISTIC SYSTEM?

Although Britain is a pluralistic society in ethnic origin, language, religion, and race, the differences have rarely caused political problems affecting the unity and centralization of the system. But in recent years the issues of race, ethnicity, and religion and the emergence of nationalist sentiment have upset the stability of the political order.

After World War II the presence of the new nonwhite communities, with their different languages, religions, lifestyles, and tendency to remain in certain inner-city areas, has caused friction and riots and led to statutes such as the 1976 Race Relations Act, which makes discrimination unlawful on grounds of color, race, or ethnic and national origins in employment, housing, education, and provision of goods and services (see Table 2.3). Some extreme members of the Islamic community called for the recognition by the state of Islamic laws on marriage, divorce, and inheritance.

The areas of Scotland, Wales, and Northern Ireland until the late 1990s were ruled by departments of the central government in London. The centralized, unitary political system has been troubled in the last decades by the rise of nationalist sentiment in Scotland and Wales, and the constitutional framework has been disturbed by political problems in Northern Ireland.

In Northern Ireland the minority Catholic population, numbering about 670,000, has long objected to discrimination against it in political rights, employment, and housing by the Protestant majority of about 1 million. The Catholic civil rights campaign in 1969 resulted in greater tension between the two separate communities and an increasing level of violence, which led the British government to send army units to maintain order. Though some concessions were made on civil rights, no agreement could be reached on the larger Catholic political demands. As a result of the continuing violence and the terrorist activity by the Irish Republican Army (IRA), the powers of the Northern Irish government and Parliament were suspended, and direct rule by the British government began in March 1972. Britain in 1978 shifted the responsibility for security back to the local police and a part-time civilian corps, almost exclusively Protestant.

An assembly elected in Northern Ireland in 1982 charged with making proposals for devolu-

A CLOSER LOOK
2.2

THE GOOD FRIDAY AGREEMENT

Multiparty negotiations in 1998, aided by former U.S. senator George Mitchell, led to the Good Friday Agreement in Belfast. Under the agreement, the fate of Northern Ireland was to be decided by vote. The Catholic minority would be part of the new power-sharing executive. A council would link Northern Ireland and the Republic of Ireland; another council would link Ireland and Great Britain. In addition, weapons of paramilitary organizations were to be "decommissioned." A Northern Ireland Assembly would be elected, to include 108 members in 18 six-member constituencies. After the Good Friday Agreement was approved by the people through referendum, the Northern Ireland Assembly was elected, with legislative and executive authority for Northern Ireland in those matters devolved by Great Britain. The Assembly is led by a First Minister and Deputy First Minister, chosen by the members.

TABLE 2.3

IMMIGRATION AND CIVIL RIGHTS IN BRITAIN

Immigration and Nationality

From the early seventeenth century, Britons were British subjects by birth within the realm of the monarch; this was extended to British colonies. By the 1940s, over 800 million people were British subjects and had rights in the United Kingdom.

1948	British Nationality Act: 2 classes of citizenship: (1) UK and colonies—full rights of citizens; (2) independent Commonwealth citizens could enter Britain. Citizens of the Republic of Ireland given special status to enter. Over half a million nonwhite British subjects immigrated to Britain in the 1950s and 1960s.
1962	Commonwealth Immigration Act: restricted entry for overseas British subjects. By 1971, over 1.5 million had immigrated.
1971	Immigration Act: entry for those with at least one British grandparent, or who were naturalized, or who had lived in Britain for five years.
1981	Nationality Act: British citizenship limited to those already legally in Britain, or who had one British parent and were registered abroad, or long-standing family connections with UK (patriality).
1990	Citizenship granted to 50,000 Hong Kong "heads of household"; about 135,000 Hong Kong nationals acquire citizenship.
1996	Distinction between "economic" and "political" refugees. Asylum seekers denied social benefits.
1998	Citizens of all dependent territories receive UK citizenship.
2002	Nationality, Immigration, and Asylum Act created new rules on immigration.

Civil Rights

1965	Racial discrimination in housing and jobs outlawed.
1968	Racial discrimination in provision of goods and services outlawed.
1970	Women to get same pay as men for similar work.
1975	Discrimination on grounds of sex forbidden; Equal Opportunities Commission set up.
1976	Criminal offense to incite racial hatred; Race Relations Board to assist conciliation among races; Commission for Racial Equality set up to investigate complaints of racial discrimination.
1976	Discrimination unlawful on grounds of color, race, nationality, or ethnic or national origin.
1986	Amended 1975 Act prohibiting sexual discrimination in housing, training, provision of goods and services, and employment.
1996	Women given right of paid maternity leave.
1998	New offenses of racial harassment and racially motivated violence created. Race Relations Forum established to advise on issues affecting ethnic minority communities.
2001	Anti-terrorism Act gave ministers power to detain foreigners who posed a risk to national security and were linked with an international terrorist group.

tion failed and was dissolved. By a 1985 agreement with Britain, the Republic of Ireland was given a consultative role about the future of Ulster. Attempts in 1991 to foster talks among Britain, the main constitutional parties in Northern Ireland, and the Irish government on home rule for Ulster failed. In December 1993 the British and Irish prime ministers agreed on the Downing Street Declaration for general principles for peace talks on Northern Ireland. These include agreement of the people in both the north and the south (Ireland). Since then the leaders of

THE IRISH PROBLEM

1690	Battle of the Boyne—Catholic King James II beaten by Protestant King William III of Orange. Siege of Derry.
1795	Battle of the Diamond—the two religions clash over land ownership in Armagh. Orange Society formed.
1886	Gladstone introduces Home Rule bill, which fails.
1893	Second Home Rule bill leads to violence.
1912	Protestants sign Ulster Covenant to resist home rule.
1916	Easter rebellion in Dublin against Britain.
1920	Ireland becomes independent, but six northern counties form Northern Ireland or Ulster.
1937	Ireland becomes Eire.
1968	Riots in Londonderry over Catholic civil rights.
1969	Police ban most marches. British troops in streets of Northern Ireland.
1972	Britain suspends Northern Ireland Parliament and assumes direct rule.
1985	Anglo-Irish agreement on search for a peaceful solution.
1993	British and Irish prime ministers agree on the Downing Street Declaration for general principles for peace talks on Northern Ireland, which include agreement of the people in both the north and the south (Ireland).
1995–97	Peace talks break down and then resume with cease-fire.
1997	Parades Commission to deal with contentious parades.
1998	Multiparty negotiations lead to Good Friday Agreement. Assembly to be elected. General de Chastelain appointed to supervise decommissioning of paramilitary arms.
1999	Police Service of Northern Ireland to replace Royal Ulster Constabulary, to get a balance between Protestants and Catholics.
2000	Power-sharing executive in Northern Ireland forms coalition, then suspends, then resumes.
2001	IRA declares it will decommission its weapons; process begins to place them permanently and verifiably beyond use.
2002	Four years of power sharing government between Protestant and Catholic communities in Northern Ireland ended, and direct rule from London imposed.
2003	British and Irish prime ministers try to revive the peace process.

the different parties in Ulster have met with the British government to discuss the peace process. The Good Friday Agreement reached in Belfast in 1998 led to the establishment of the Northern Ireland Assembly and elections to it.

In Scotland after the Act of Union of 1707, the continuation of separate educational, legal, and religious institutions and a local government system provided the country with a distinctive historical and cultural identity. But not until recently has there been a revival of the political nationalism that was strong in the eighteenth century. Economically, industrial production and commerce in Scotland has been tied to the rest of the British economy, with which it trades two-thirds of its imports and exports.

Politically, Scotland sends 72 members to the House of Commons, which is 11 percent of the total members even though Scotland represents only 9.5 percent of Britain's electorate. The British system responded to Scottish concerns by the establishment in London of the position of Secretary of State for Scotland, a cabinet minister who had responsibility for the formulation and execution of a wide range of policies.

The argument that Scotland's problems, especially those of ailing heavy industry and shipbuilding, were due to neglect or exploitation by London, the increased emphasis on national pride, and the discovery of large oil reserves in the North Sea off the Scottish coast stimulated the Scottish National Party (SNP) to become the proponent of self-government in the 1960s.

In the sixteenth century, Wales was united with England and became part of the English system of administration. Nationalist expression had been more literary and cultural than political. But for some years demands were made for administrative arrangements similar to those of Scotland. In 1964 a Welsh Office was set up in Cardiff, the Welsh capital, and a Secretary of State for Wales with a seat in the British cabinet was appointed. In Parliament, to which Wales sends 40 MPs, there was a Welsh Grand Committee to discuss Welsh affairs in general, as well as all legislation pertaining to Wales.

In 1969 a Royal Commission on the Constitution—the Kilbrandon Commission—was appointed to examine the problem of Scotland and Wales. Reporting in 1973, the commission rejected both the division of the United Kingdom into independent states (separatism) and the creation of states sharing sovereignty with Parliament (federalism). It recommended the devolution of political and administrative powers from London for both countries. The British Parliament in 1978 passed two statutes that would establish elected assemblies with responsibility for a wide range of internal affairs in Scotland and Wales.

Both statutes were submitted to referendums in March 1979 with the stipulation that they would only take effect if at least 40 percent of the electorate, as well as a simple majority, approved. The voters in Wales rejected the statute by nearly 4 to 1. Scottish voters approved their statute by 51.6 percent of the voters but only 32.5 percent of the total electorate. Both statutes were therefore repealed in June 1979.

Twenty years later, in 1998, in major constitutional changes, devolution was introduced for both Scotland and Wales with the creation of a Scottish Parliament, the first since 1707, and a Welsh Assembly, the first since 1495, with local executives to follow with responsibilities formerly performed by government departments in London. The Scottish Parliament in Edinburgh, with 129 members, has lawmaking and some tax powers, while the Welsh Assembly in Cardiff, with 60 members, has powers only of secondary legislation and is wholly dependent for its budget on an annual grant from London.

A CLOSER LOOK 2.3

THE WEST LOTHIAN QUESTION

Devolution now exists for Scotland and Wales, but what about England? Raised by a Scottish Labour MP during the devolution debates in the 1970s, the West Lothian question concerned the anomaly of Scottish MPs being able to vote on legislation relating purely to England and Wales when English and Welsh MPs could not vote on purely Scottish issues. Scotland and Wales still send members, in disproportionate numbers, to the House of Commons and therefore deal with issues pertinent to England, but English MPs cannot deal with Scottish or Welsh issues. The question now is whether an English Parliament should be established for the 80 percent of British citizens who live in England.

The government has acknowledged the problem in a number of ways. Among these attempts were the introduction of Regional Development Agencies for England, appointed by ministers, supposedly to coordinate regional economic development; some unelected Regional Chambers; a standing committee on regional affairs in the House of Commons; select committees in the House of MPs from English constituencies; and a joint ministerial committee on devolution. Little visible result was evident by 2005 on this complicated constitutional issue.

TABLE 2.4

THE SCOTTISH PARLIAMENT AND THE WELSH ASSEMBLY, 2003 ELECTIONS

Election to Scottish Parliament: 129 members

Party	First Vote (%)	Second Vote (%)	Seats		
			Constituency	PR	Total
Labour	34.6	29.3	46	4	50
SNP	23.8	20.9	9	18	27
Conservative	16.6	15.5	3	15	18
Liberal Democrat	15.4	11.8	13	4	17
Greens	—	6.9	—	7	7
Others	2.7	11.4	2	8	10
Turnout: 49.4 percent			73	56	129

Election to Welsh Assembly: 60 members

Party	First Vote (%)	Second Vote (%)	Seats		
			Constituency	PR	Total
Labour	39.5	36.6	30	0	30
Plaid Cymru	21.2	19.7	5	7	12
Conservative	20.4	19.2	1	10	11
Liberal Democrat	14.1	12.6	3	3	6
Others	4.8	11.9	1	0	1
Turnout: 38.2 percent			40	20	60

Source: Inter-Parliamentary Union.

Elections took place in both countries in 1999 by a form of proportional representation; each elector cast two votes, (1) in the familiar constituency method of victory by plurality (first past the post), and (2) by regional party lists and proportional share of seats (see Table 2.4).

POLITICAL PROBLEMS

Britain confronts a number of complex political problems. The relationship of the four countries within the United Kingdom is changing. The impact of membership in the European Union on British sovereignty and on the rights and duties of citizens is uncertain. The growing numbers of nonwhite immigrants have led to greater racial tension. There are now six parliamentary constituencies in which nonwhites are a majority, and ten others in which they are prominent.

The British system has been troubled by difficult economic, social, and constitutional issues.

The weakness of the currency was shown when Britain withdrew from the Exchange Rate Mechanism of the European Union in 1992. The downturns in the economic cycle helped increase ethnic tensions which led to urban riots, mostly of blacks, in 1981 and 1985. The monarchy has come under sharp criticism with questioning of the finances and cost of the Queen and her household and concern about the drama of the failure of the marriage of the heir to the throne, Prince Charles, and Princess Diana. The question arises of whether a divorced Charles could become King, and therefore head of the Church of England.

Among the various problems facing Britain today some are high on the political agenda. One is a certain dissatisfaction with some aspects of the political system and of the unwritten constitution. Proposals have been made for modernization of procedures of the House of Commons, change of the electoral system, further reform or abolition of the House of Lords, regional auton-

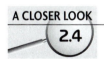

REVIEW

2.2

A SUMMARY OF RECENT CONSTITUTIONAL CHANGE

1998	Devolution to Scotland and Wales, and new Assembly in Northern Ireland.
1999	Regional Development Agencies, and 8 Regional Chambers, voluntary bodies, to scrutinize the RDAs, which are nondepartmental public bodies accountable through ministers to Parliament.
1999	Direct election of mayor of London, with considerable authority but limited financial powers. Creation of a Greater London Authority.
1999	Reform of House of Lords—interim arrangement with elimination of hereditary peers except 92.
1998	Human Rights Act incorporates the 1950 European Convention on Human Rights into British law; British courts will enforce the provisions of the Convention.
1998	Accepted Social Chapter of Maastricht Treaty of European Union; Britain bound to European Union rules on working life, equal treatment of the sexes, and protection of workers.
1998	European Parliament Elections Act adopts proportional representation system and party lists for voting in European Parliament elections.
2001	Anti-terrorism, Crime and Security Act.
2005	Freedom of Information Act came into force.

omy for England, and peace in Northern Ireland. Above all, some call for a bill of rights, on U.S. lines, to provide better protection for basic British freedoms.

A second problem is the increased attempt to decentralize government after the reduction of powers of local authorities, and the more central intervention in decisions about universities, police authorities, and health service regions in postwar policies.

A third issue is the strong difference of opinion in political parties and in the country about the development and powers of the European Union and the extent to which its laws and regulations may limit the sovereignty of Britain.

A continuing economic and political problem is the disparity between an ailing industrial northern England and the more prosperous service economy in southern England. The gap is growing in income, average disposable household income, number of unemployed, and migration patterns. The population of London has grown considerably in the 1990s, while that in the northeast has declined.

A CLOSER LOOK

2.4

BRITISH SOVEREIGNTY

Traditional British sovereignty, the final legal and political authority to make decisions, is affected in a number of ways. International economic globalization, especially freedom of capital movements, has influenced and placed limits on domestic monetary policies and meant more difficulty in controlling exchange and interest rates. Britain is not independent from the continent of Europe politically, nor from the world economically.

Politically, the UK is bound by the European Union treaties and decisions, and by the European Convention on Human Rights (ECHR) and the European Court of Human Rights, which has found the UK guilty in some cases of violation of rights. The 1998 Human Rights Act requires that all British legislation be implemented in a way compatible with the ECHR. British courts have also accepted the ruling of the EU's Court of Justice of the primacy of EU law over national law; a UK statute will not be given effect by the courts if it is incompatible with EU law. In 2004 the Law Lords ruled that the government's detention of foreigners without trial on grounds of national security was incompatible with the 1998 Act.

THE NATURE OF BRITISH SOCIETY

Political systems inevitably reflect economic, social, and cultural forces in the country, though there is no inevitable or automatic link among them. The British system has reflected, among other forces, a prosperous industrialized economy; sharp differences between social classes; the aristocratic values such as obedience, fair play, and sportsmanship that lasted into the present era; the ideal of the gentleman; a working-class subculture; and religious differences.

Certain significant characteristics of and changes in contemporary British society will be discussed in the following sections.

A Postindustrial Society

Britain is now a postindustrial society in which there has been a shift from the production of goods to a service economy, with a very prominent professional and technical class and with a sophisticated technology. Services now account for 74 percent of the workforce of the country, industry for 25 percent, and agriculture for 1 percent. There has been a dramatic increase in the service sector in the last two decades. Services now account for about 72 percent of the gross domestic product, manufacturing for about 26 percent, construction for 6 percent, and agriculture, fishing, and mining for about 1.7 percent.

The public sector grew at a faster rate than the private sector until the late 1970s, after which private employment increased relative to public jobs. Of the 29 million in the current workforce, 23.9 million (82.4 percent) are employed in the private sector, and 5.1 million in the public sector. About 3.5 million of the latter work for the government. The number of self-employed rose from 1.9 million in 1979 to 3.4 million in 2000.

About 7.1 million belong to the 221 trade unions; of these, 7 million in 70 unions are affiliated with the Trades Union Congress (TUC). Union membership has declined 40 percent since 1979, especially among manual workers and par-ticularly in southeast England. This decline can be attributed to the replacement of old industries, a base for strong unionization, by high-technology firms; the increase of the self-employed to 3.4 million; and the privatization which reduced the numbers working in the public sector, a union stronghold. By 2002, only 30 percent of British workers were unionists. The largest union is Unison, public employees, with 1.3 million members. The highest density of union members are those working in public authorities, and the lowest in agriculture and in services.

Women, over 46 percent of the labor force, are now almost as equally unionized as men. With their consciousness raised by the women's liberation movement, women have been more eager to obtain a job than remain in the home. Women in Britain now tend to marry younger, have children later, bear fewer children, and stay in a job at least until their first child is born. Increasingly they return to full- or part-time work after having children. The higher divorce rate has reinforced the trend for women to work.

Women have been protected by law in a number of ways. The 1970 Equal Pay Act states that women are entitled to the same pay as men when performing similar work. The 1975 Sex Discrimination Act makes sexual discrimination unlawful in employment, education, occupational training, and provisions of housing, goods, facilities, and services. With regard to both statutes, the Equal Opportunities Commission exists to promote equal opportunities for women. Through legislation in 1996 and 2000, women have the right of paid time off before and after pregnancy. Yet women are still underrepresented in senior managerial positions and overrepresented in lower paid, part-time work.

There has been a steady rise in the general standard of living and in the consumption of goods, especially of housing, cars, better-quality food and drink, and recreation, and more credit borrowing. At the beginning of the twentieth century only 1 in 10 families owned their own home; in 1952 the proportion was less than 1 in 3; by 2005, 68 percent of the 21 million homes in Britain were owner-occupied. In spite of occupational changes, Britain is still a highly urban as well as densely populated country. About 60 percent of the population lives in cities of over 50,000 people, though only 28 percent of the population of Wales does so. Only one-fifth of the total population lives in rural communities. In recent years there has been an increase in the population of the suburbs and a decline in those in the inner-city areas.

A Class Society

Britain has remained a divided, though changing, society in which people of different occupations, income levels, and education have different lifestyles, modes of dress, speech patterns and accents, favorite games, social habits, ways of leisure, and mortality rates due to different standards of health. It has been dominated by an elite, albeit an open elite into which the successful could enter, that has occupied the key positions in the financial world, the professions, government administration, and the Conservative Party. The principles of the elite have been moderation, fair play, loyalty, and its ideal of the gentleman and the cultivated amateur.

A class theory of politics would argue that class is the major factor influencing voting behavior and that the political parties are representative of the different social classes. In Britain this would mean that the working class would vote for the Labour Party, and the middle and upper classes for the Conservative Party. But this broad generalization is only partly true. About one-third of the working class does not vote Labour, while one-fifth of the middle class does. Nor are the leaders and members of the parties recruited from one class. The programs of the parties do not reflect the interest of one class, as all of them have tried to broaden their appeal.

Britain is still a country with great inequality in the distribution of wealth. About 25 percent of total personal wealth is owned by 1 percent of the adult population and about half by 10 percent. In 1914 the bottom 90 percent of the population owned 8 percent of all personal wealth; by 1974 they owned 37 percent. The top tenth got 30 percent of pretax income in 1987, compared with the 22 percent obtained by the bottom 50 percent.

Britain remains a society in which class differences, due to these inequalities in wealth and income, are strongly felt, and where barriers to social and economic mobility still exist. Yet dramatic changes in the last few years have reduced the old class consciousness, with the shrinkage of the manual working class and with the striking increase in shareholders to 11 million in 1991, compared with 3 million in 1979. This has resulted from three factors: the sale of public enterprises (privatization), employee share schemes, and personal equity plans making it more attractive for small savers to invest.

A Pluralistic Religious Society

Britain is a pluralistic society in its religious diversity after centuries of discrimination (see Table 2.5). There is now no religious disqualification for public office. (The only exception is the monarch, who must be a member of the established Church of England.) About 40 percent of the population regards itself as secular, unattached to any religion.

Protestant   Though few people go to any church on a regular basis, Protestantism is still the dominant religion, with the Anglican Church nominally accounting for 40 percent of the English and 45 percent of the Welsh population. The free or nonconformist churches account for 20 percent of the population in England and 45 percent in Wales.

The Church of England is the established church (the concept of "establishment" derives from this fact) and the monarch is its Supreme Head. The chief dignitaries of the Church—the two archbishops of Canterbury and York, the 43 bishops, and the deans—are formally appointed by the monarch, who accepts the recommendation of the prime minister, who is advised by ecclesiastical representatives. Politically, 26 of the higher clergy sit as members of the House of Lords, but no clergy of the Church of England can sit in the House of Commons. The Church is a large landowner and has considerable possessions in industrial shares and property; however, though many of the senior figures in the Church have

TABLE 2.5
RELIGION IN BRITAIN, 2005

Group	Number	Percentage of Population
Christian	41 million	71.8
Muslim	1.6 million	2.8
Hindu	558,000	1.0
Sikh	336,000	0.6
Jewish	267,000	0.5
Buddhist	150,000	0.3
Others	160,000	0.3

Source: U.K. Government, Stationery Office.

come from elite backgrounds, the Church does not speak with a monolithic voice in political, social, and economic affairs. The former Archbishop of Canterbury, George Carey, came from a working-class background. The monarch is also head of the Presbyterian Church of Scotland, which has been the established Church since 1707.

The free or nonconformist Protestant churches, strong in the west of England and in Wales, have historically been critical of or opposed to the establishment. In general, there has been a correlation between areas of religious nonconformity and those of political dissent, associated first with the Liberal Party and later with the Labour Party. The largest of the free churches are the Methodist Church and the Baptist Church.

Catholicism   There are some 9 million adherents to Roman Catholicism. The religion is strongest in Northern Ireland, where it accounts for about 40 percent of the population, and in northwest England. Though some old aristocratic families are Catholic, as are some prominent converts and members of the upper class, most Catholics are members of the lower middle class and the majority stem from Irish immigrants. Catholicism has not been the politically divisive issue that it has been in

many other political systems, but the Labour Party has sometimes nominated Catholic candidates in heavily Catholic constituencies.

Other Religions   The Jewish community dates from 1656, after being expelled from Britain in 1290. In the twentieth century it was increased by immigration from Eastern Europe after pogroms and anti-Semitic outbreaks and from Germany during the Nazi regime in the 1930s. It now consists of about 300,000 people. As a result of the recent immigration of Asians, there is now a considerable number of non-Christian adherents, primarily Muslims, Buddhists, Hindus, and Sikhs. Most live in large urban areas.

Since World War I, religion has not been a divisive political issue, except in Northern Ireland. In general, the correspondence between a particular religion and a particular party has remained—the Anglican Church with Conservatives, the Catholics with Labour and the nonconformists with the Liberals and Labour—but the ties are much less strong, especially among Anglicans, than in previous generations. In the late 1980s, a small Islamic fundamentalist movement emerged, demanding separate status and insisting on Islamic law.

A Multicultural Society

The population of Britain is not ethnically homogeneous but contains ethnic, religious, and cultural diversities, bringing changes in social structure, geographical mobility, and educational patterns (see Table 2.6). Minority groups can be defined in two ways: Afro-Caribbean (from West Indies and Africa) now about 1 million, and Asian (from India, Pakistan, Bangladesh, Sri Lanka) now about 2 million. The first group tends to be less segregated than the Asian. In East London, public notices are printed in Bengali as well as English. Riots occurred in summer 2001 in northern industrial cities with pockets of poverty and unemployment, where some Asian groups live in self-segregated communities with Islamic schools that receive state funding, halal butchers, and mosques. In Birmingham, where Asian Muslims constitute 12 percent of the total 1 million population, the party based on Pakistani immigrants has won a number of seats in the local council. The three major political parties ran 57 nonwhite candidates in the 2001 election, of whom 12 were elected.

TABLE 2.6

ETHNIC GROUPS IN THE UNITED KINGDOM, 2005

Group	%
White	93.2
Nonwhite	6.7
Caribbean	0.9
African	0.7
Other black	0.5
Indian	1.7
Pakistani	1.2
Bangladeshi	0.5
Chinese	0.2
Others	1.1

Source: U.K. Government, Stationery Office.

Nonwhites are younger on average than whites and are more concentrated in the fertile age groups. They are located in the more populous areas of England. About three-fifths of people from black ethnic groups live in London. Indians and Pakistanis are in the midlands and northern England. About 2 million Muslims live in the United Kingdom. There are over 600 mosques and numerous Muslim community centers.

A Welfare State

The British welfare system developed to deal with problems of poverty and unemployment; to provide for the aged, the sick, and the infirm; and to maintain minimum living standards. The main elements of the current welfare system are the national health service, personal social services, and social security, which now account for about 40 percent of total public expenditure.

The national health service provides almost free treatment for all who want to use it and allows free choice of medical practitioners and hospitals. Personal social services include services for the elderly, the physically disabled and mentally ill, home care, social clubs, and day care for children under age 5. Social security exists to provide a basic standard of living for people in need through nonemployment benefits, retirement pensions, sickness benefit and invalidity pensions, child benefits, benefits to widows, and death grants.

A Mixed Economy

Britain was the first capitalist country in the world when, in the eighteenth and nineteenth centuries, the ownership and control of industry was in private hands. Today it is more appropriate to regard the economy as a mixture of private enterprise and various public controls.

Most manufacturing enterprises are privately owned except for the steel, aeroengine, and (since 1977) most of the aircraft and ship-building industries. Few, since 1945, argued a laissez-faire position and a minimal role for public control over the economy. Although only the left wing of the Labour Party believes in the state ownership of the means of production, distribution, and exchange, most people in the different political parties accepted a substantial role for the state, the largest employer in the country. Since 1979 public policy under the Thatcher and Major governments emphasized the reduction of the state sector, the sale of public enterprises to private ownership, and a freer market economy. This has been continued by the Blair government since 1997.

THE SOCIALIZATION PROCESS

Education and Class

Class distinctions have long been a prominent feature of British society. Though classes have been defined in different ways—the easiest way is to talk of the upper class, the upper middle, the lower middle, and the lower class—they differ in accent and language used, dress, style of life, nature of schooling, and occupations.

The educational system has reflected and helped to perpetuate the class structure. In 1944 the system was reorganized and students were streamed into separate modern secondary, technical, and grammar schools. Most students ended their education between 14 and 16 years of age to become manual workers. The occupational pattern and the working-class status of these youngsters who had left school was in most cases set for life. Those who left school at age 18 entered white-collar or minor managerial jobs and became part of the lower middle, sometimes middle, class. Only those who had further education beyond 18 years of age were likely to enter the professions or become managers and executives, the middle-class occupations.

In the 1970s comprehensive schools, which like high schools in the United States provide a wide range of education and educate students of different backgrounds and abilities together,

replaced many of the selective secondary and grammar schools to help end the class stratification of educational streaming based on passing of examinations at an early age. During the 1980s, Conservative governments removed many of these comprehensive schools from local government control to enable them to become more selective again. Whether schools are comprehensive, as in the United States, and local government controlled, or selective and self-governing, varies on whether the Labour or Conservative Party, respectively, is in power.

Outside the state system are parochial schools, independent grammar schools stressing academic achievement (many have impressive reputations), and the 260 "public" schools, which are expensive and socially significant. The most prominent of the public schools—such as Eton. Harrow, Winchester, and Rugby—are prestigious institutions, consciously training young people for leadership positions in politics and society by discipline, building of character, and inculcation of traditional values. They have been a unique means of recruiting members of elite groups, constituting an "old boy" network in prominent positions. Though they represent only 4 percent of the British student population, graduates of the public schools, like those of the older universities, have occupied a highly disproportionate number of positions in the cabinet, the House of Commons, the senior civil service, the upper ranks of the armed forces, the High Courts, and the Church of England, as well as in major banking and financial institutions. Perhaps more surprisingly, public school graduates also accounted for 42 percent of the Labour Cabinet in 1966–1970 and 18 percent of Labour MPs in 1978. About 75 percent of Conservative MPs in the House of Commons elected in 1987 attended a public school. Between 1900 and 1985 old Etonians alone accounted for almost one-fourth of government ministers and top ambassadors. It is interesting in light of this that none of the last five prime ministers before Blair, including three conservatives, attended a public school.

Traditionally, higher education has been dominated by Oxford and Cambridge, which have provided the political and social elite. Eight of the last ten prime ministers attended Oxford, as did three-quarters of the present senior judges, two-thirds of the top civil servants, and many of the prominent media personalities.

In the last two decades, there has been a considerable expansion of higher education for both social and educational reasons. The full-time student body has increased to over 844,000, about 20 percent of the 18-year-old population. There are now 47 universities attended by about 270,000 students. Another 250,000 take courses on a wide range of topics at the 35 former poly-technics in England and Wales or attend other colleges providing further education in Britain. The most prestigious of the universities remain Oxford, with its 39 individual colleges, and Cambridge, with 29. Graduates of "Oxbridge" still constitute a high proportion of the elite groups in the country, including the Cabinet and the House of Commons. Nevertheless, the Conservative government in 1991 called for abolishing the distinction between universities and polytechnics, which have increased in importance in recent years, thus removing barriers between academic and vocational education.

Class barriers still exist, linked to educational achievement, in spite of more social mobility and emphasis on meritocracy and equal opportunity. Labour and Conservative prime ministers alike have been critical of the class system. Labour leaders have regarded it as responsible for lack of innovation. Margaret Thatcher attacked the upper-class amateurs in her Conservative Party and in the BBC and Foreign Office; John Major spoke of the need for a classless society.

A CHANGING BRITAIN

Britain has long been a free and—despite unnec-essary secrecy in government—open society. It has also generally been a peaceful society in which the police went unarmed. A sign of increased social problems has been the consid-erable rise in crime. The increasing violence and the terrorist acts, perpetrated mostly by the IRA in British cities, have meant that some of the police now carry weapons, though the majority still go unarmed.

Britain is still a significant industrial and economic power. It is the fifth largest trading nation, exporting nearly 9 percent of total exports of manufactured goods by the industrial countries of the world. These exports constitute about one-half of all British exports. Britain still accounts for nearly one-third of all international banking business. About 10 percent of "invisible" trade in the world (banking, insurance, shipping, tourism, and income from overseas investment) is handled by Britain.

As Britain became industrialized, it also became a larger importer of foods and raw mate-rials; today its imports also include a growing proportion of semimanufactured and manufac-tured goods. For almost 200 years the value of British imports of goods was usually larger than the value of exports. The deficit on this balance of "visible" trade was overcome in the total bal-ance of payments by a surplus on invisible trade, the receipts from which are about one-third of total receipts. But as the deficit in visible trade has increased, partly due to the rise in raw mate-rials prices, the dramatic rise in oil prices, the large contribution to the budget of the European Union, the lower exchange rate of sterling, for-eign competition, and the loss of many Com-monwealth markets to other industrialized countries, the earnings on invisible trade were often not enough to overcome the deficit.

Britain has suffered the disadvantages, as well as having gotten the rewards, of being the first mature industrial nation in the world and of now having old capital equipment. Its older industries—coal, textiles, and shipbuilding—have contracted, and productivity per worker remained low compared with that of other advanced nations. It suffered from having exported capital abroad rather than using it internally and for being dependent on the inter-national economy, which has made Britain vul-nerable to external factors. The persistent balance of payments problem discouraged sus-tained investment and limited the rate of growth.

The postwar British performance in production, trade, and growth disappointed its political leaders. In the 1950s Britain was one of the ten richest countries in the world. From the mid-1960s to the mid-1970s, the economy grew by only 2.7 percent per year. By 1976 Britain ranked twenty-fourth in per capita gross national product, which was about half that of the United States.

There have been differing explanations for the low level of productivity per worker and the relatively slow economic growth. Some criticize the overmanning of jobs and the restrictive practices and obstructions of the powerful trade unions, which they see as more interested in job security than in increases in production, as well as the immobility of the labor force. Other critics stress inadequate management that is slow to introduce innovations, insufficient research and development, low levels of replacement of capital goods, reluctance to adapt production to new needs, and poor sales drive. The ethos of the social system and the ideal of the cultivated amateur and gentleman have been blamed for the failure to attract well-educated people as industrial managers and for the view of industrial activity as distasteful. Britain's desire to remain an important world power has meant large expenditure on overseas bases, large military forces, and considerable expenditure on nuclear research and development and on expensive delivery vehicles in the attempt to become a nuclear power.

Government policies have been criticized for many reasons: the disincentive of high tax rates, the lack of effective economic planning, the slowness in retraining unemployed workers, the concentration on prestigious and wasteful items such as supersonic aircraft rather than on more profitable industries likely to grow, and the inability to control inflation. Though there is validity in all of these criticisms, much of the British economic problem has been caused by external factors: the inevitable growth of other countries, many of which are industrializing rapidly and some of which are technologically mature; the rising cost of imports of food and raw materials; the loss of protected markets for exports to the former colonies; the sacrifices made by Britain in the two world wars, which seriously depleted British capital and led to the sale of overseas investments; and large external debts.

All British governments tried to solve the economic problem by increasing productivity, growth, and exports; by reducing the rate of inflation; and by maintaining confidence in the British pound. In the decade after 1979 the Thatcher government tried to encourage growth by cutting taxes, controlling the money supply for a time, approving only those wage settlements connected with increases in productivity, and stressing the value of competition. The economy has grown faster, inflation fell, and strikes declined, while trade unionism was weakened. But the share of manufacturing in the economy has declined, and deficits have occurred in some years.

In addition to economic problems and the issue of sovereignty, a new troubling issue is that of international terrorism. This has led to the Terrorism Act 2000, which allows the Home Secretary to ban organizations engaged in violence, in Britain or abroad, to advance a political religious or ideological cause, or to create a serious risk to public health or safety. This was followed by the Anti-terrorist Act of 2001.

Thinking Critically

1. Can Britain still be considered a unitary state? Do you think that devolution of Scotland and Wales has been helpful from a political and administrative point of view?
2. Do you think that Britain ought to have a written constitution?
3. Is it still valid to talk of British parliamentary sovereignty?
4. From a comparative point of view, would you regard Britain as a class society?
5. Is Britain a country of equal opportunity and affirmative action?

6. Do you believe that Britain should limit immigration?
7. Have economic changes and the increasing concentration of ownership and control of the media in Britain been harmful to free speech and political democracy?

KEY TERMS

Anglican church *(59)*
Bill of Rights *(48)*
class *(59)*
consensus *(49–50)*
constitutional democracy *(48)*
conventions *(48–49)*
deference *(50)*
devolution *(55)*
Magna Carta *(44)*
majority principle *(48)*
mixed economy *(61–62)*
Northern Ireland (Ulster) *(52)*
Oxbridge *(63)*
pluralistic society *(52)*
postindustrial society *(45, 58)*
privatization *(62)*
public school *(62)*
referendum *(55)*
Reform Acts *(48)*
representative system *(47)*
rule of law *(48)*
sovereignty *(57)*
United Kingdom *(51)*
welfare state *(61)*

FURTHER READINGS

Bagehot, Walter. *The English Constitution* (Ithaca, NY: Cornell University Press, 1966).

Blackburn, Robert, and Raymond Plant, eds. *Constitutional Reform: The Labour Government's Constitutional Reform Agenda* (New York: Longman, 1999).

Crick, Bernard, ed. *National Identities* (Oxford: Blackwell, 1991).

Dunleavy, Patrick, et al. eds. *Developments in British Politics 7* (London: Palgrave Macmillan, 2004).

Ewing, Keith, and C. A. Gearty. *Freedom under Thatcher: Civil Liberties in Modern Britain* (New York: Oxford University Press, 1990).

Foley, Michael. *The Politics of the British Constitution* (New York: Manchester University Press, 1999).

Gamble, Allen. *The Free Economy and the Strong State: The Politics of Thatcherism* (London: Macmillan, 1988).

Jones, Nicholas. *Sultans of Spin: The Media and the New Labour Government* (London: Orion, 2000).

Jowell, Jeffery, and Dawn Oliver. *The Changing Constitution,* 4th ed. (London: Oxford University Press, 2000).

Kavanagh, Dennis. *British Politics: Continuities and Change,* 4th ed. (London: Oxford University Press, 2000).

Kearney, Hugh. *The British Isles: A History of Four Nations* (New York: Cambridge University Press, 1989).

Mitchell, James. *Governing Scotland: The Invention of Administrative Devolution* (New York: Palgrave Macmillan, 2004).

O'Neill, Michael, ed. *Devolution and British Politics* (London: Longman, 2004).

Winder, Robert. *Bloody Foreigners: The Story of Immigration to Britain* (London: Little Brown, 2004).

B. POLITICAL PROCESSES AND INSTITUTIONS

VOTING

The electoral system for the House of Commons is a simple one, comprising single-member constituencies, plurality decision or top-of-the-poll winner, and the principle of one person, one vote. Since the first Reform Act of 1832, which began the process of standardizing the qualifications for voting, the suffrage has gradually been extended to the whole citizenry over the age of 18. During the same period, factors such as the necessary ownership of property, double or triple voting based on ownership of a business or possession of an MA degree, residential qualification, feminine gender, and deliberately unequally sized constituencies have been eliminated (see Table 2.7).

Registration of voters is the responsibility of the local authorities, not of the individual, and an annual register of those eligible to vote in each constituency is issued every February. Since 1948, a postal vote has been possible for those who are incapable of voting in person, have moved from the constituency, or will be away on business. Middle-class voters are more likely to register for a postal vote than working-class voters, and the Conservative organization is better able to mobilize postal voters than other parties.

There are now 646 constituencies with boundaries that are a compromise between population and geographical size. In 1944, four boundary commissions—one each for England, Wales, Scotland, and Northern Ireland—were set up to ensure an equitable relationship between

TABLE 2.7

EXTENSION OF THE FRANCHISE

Year	Main Group Enfranchised	Other Features
1832	Industrial middle class	Redistribution of seats from small boroughs to the counties and towns
		Registration of voters necessary
		Increased suffrage by 217,000
1867	Urban workers	Increased suffrage by 1 million
1872		Secret ballot
1883		Bribery and corrupt electoral practices become criminal offenses
1884	Agricultural workers	Increased suffrage by 2 million
1885		Equal-sized constituencies
1918	Women over age 30	Increased suffrage by 12.5 million
		Redistribution of seats
		Limit to two votes (places of residence and business or university)
1928	Women over age 21	Increased suffrage by 7 million
		Universal suffrage over age 21
1948		One person, one vote
		Abolition of university vote and seats
		Abolition of business vote
		Redistribution of seats
1969	Persons over age 18	Increased suffrage by 3 million

representation and population and to recommend, every five to seven years, alteration of constituency boundaries as population shifts. Wales and Scotland are deliberately overrepresented as a concession to nationalist sentiment. An Electoral Commission, an independent body, now oversees controls on donations to and campaign spending by political parties and others, and reviews electoral law and practice.

Election by plurality has helped to sustain the system of two major parties. The Conservative and Labour parties have shared the bulk of the electoral vote and seats in the House of Commons. These two parties alternated in political power for almost the same number of years between 1945 and 1979—the Conservatives remained in power from 1979 to 1997—while until 1983 the third party, the Liberal, had not obtained more than 14 seats (see Figure 2.2).

The plurality system has produced serious inequities and distortions of the will of the people at both the level of the individual single-member constituency and the national level. At the individual constituency level, seats may be won by a minority vote where there are more than two parties and the successful candidate polls fewer votes than those of all the other candidates. In February 1974 there were 408 seats (64.3 percent of the total) won by less than a majority. Between 1945 and 1979, 30 percent of all seats were won by a minority vote. At the national level the opinion of the people may be distorted and political parties may not be truly represented in proportion to the votes they receive in the country, as is shown in Table 2.8.

There is no exact correlation between the votes obtained by a party in the country as a whole and the number of seats it wins in the House of Commons. Indeed, it may even happen, as in 1951 and February 1974, that the party with the smaller percentage of votes in the country may win more seats than the party with a larger percentage of votes. Labour in 2001 won 62 percent of seats with only 40 percent of the vote.

A second problem is that a relatively small change in electoral opinion may produce a much larger proportional change in the distribution of seats between the parties. This disproportionate result is produced by changes in voting in the "marginal seats," those that are normally won by small numbers of votes.

The main inequity in the system is that the Liberals, in spite of considerable support all over the country, have not won more than a few seats in the postwar period until 1997. Unlike a regional party such as the Scottish National Party (SNP) or the Plaid Cymru, whose votes are concentrated in a small number of constituencies, the Liberal and, in 1983 and 1987, the Social Democratic vote was spread throughout the country. The Liberal Democrats only got 62 seats in 2005 with 22 percent of the vote. Minority parties are underrepresented in the House of Commons.

The present system is unfortunate for the Liberal Democrats and other minor parties in two other respects. The first is that candidates lose their deposit—the registration fee paid in order to run for election—if they get less than 5 percent of the constituency vote; in 1992, 897 candidates lost deposits of £500 each. The second is that Liberal Democrat electoral support is very fluid. Persons who might vote Liberal are reluctant to do so if they believe the candidate is likely to lose and the party as a whole will do badly. They might prefer to influence the outcome of the election by voting for a candidate of one of the two major parties. Not surprisingly, the Liberal Party and the former Social Democratic Party (SDP) advocated a change in the electoral system. But the two major parties are still unwilling to approve a change because they benefit from the present system. This method has helped perpetuate the two-party system in the postwar period by normally producing a majority of seats for one of the two major parties, which is then able to form a government. Not since 1935 has one party obtained 50 percent of the total poll, but parties have had comfortable majorities in 12 of the 16 postwar elections. A different electoral system would result in a fairer distribution of seats in relation to the votes cast for the parties; but it would also lead to an increase in the number of parties represented in the House of Commons, make it difficult to obtain a majority, and therefore change the formation and functioning of government.

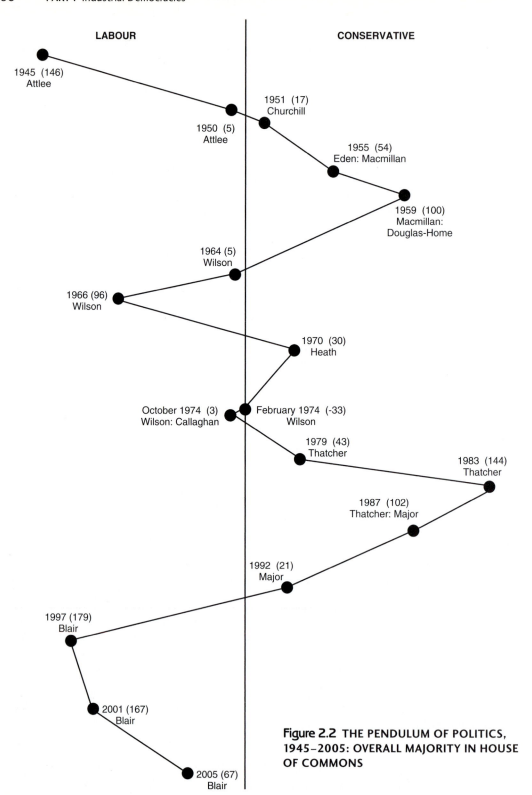

LABOUR

CONSERVATIVE

1945 (146)
Attlee

1951 (17)
Churchill

1950 (5)
Attlee

1955 (54)
Eden: Macmillan

1959 (100)
Macmillan:
Douglas-Home

1964 (5)
Wilson

1966 (96)
Wilson

1970 (30)
Heath

October 1974 (3)
Wilson: Callaghan

February 1974 (-33)
Wilson

1979 (43)
Thatcher

1983 (144)
Thatcher

1987 (102)
Thatcher: Major

1992 (21)
Major

1997 (179)
Blair

2001 (167)
Blair

2005 (67)
Blair

Figure 2.2 THE PENDULUM OF POLITICS,
**1945–2005: OVERALL MAJORITY IN HOUSE
OF COMMONS**

TABLE 2.8

GENERAL ELECTIONS, 1974–2005

Year	% of Votes Cast				Number of Seats Won				Total number of seats	Turnout % of electorate
	Con.	Lab.	Lib.Dem.	Others	Con.	Lab.	Lib.Dem.	Others		
1974 (Feb)	38.2	37.2	19.3	5.7	297	301	14	23	635	78.7
1974 (Oct)	35.8	39.3	18.3	6.7	277	319	13	26	635	72.8
1979	43.9	36.9	13.8	5.4	339	269	11	16	635	72.0
1983	42.4	27.6	25.4[a]	4.6	397	209	23	21	650	72.7
1987	42.3	30.8	22.6[a]	4.3	376	229	22	23	650	75.3
1992	41.8	34.4	17.8[b]	5.8	336	271	20	24	651	77.7
1997	31.4	44.4	17.2	7.0	165	418[c]	46	29	659	71.3
2001	31.7	40.7	18.3	9.3	166	412[c]	52	28	659	59.4
2005	32.4	35.3	22.0	10.3	198	356	62	30	646	61.3

[a]Combined vote of the Liberal and Social Democratic parties (Alliance) [b]Liberal Democratic Party; [c]Excludes the speaker

IS THE ELECTORAL SYSTEM WORKING?

The present electoral system has been defended essentially on the grounds that it provides one of the two major parties with a comfortable majority in the House of Commons. The winning party can then form a strong government which is able to formulate a coherent policy that will be approved by Parliament. This has generally been true in the postwar period when the Conservative and Labour Parties have obtained the bulk of the electoral vote and one of them has obtained a majority of seats. The peak was reached in 1951, when their combined vote was 96.8 percent of the poll and 79.9 percent of the total electorate.

But from 1951 there was a steady drop in their electoral support, as well as a decline in the proportion of those voting in general. The decline in strength of the two major parties resulted in February 1974 in a minority government, with Labour getting 33 seats less than an absolute majority, and in October 1974 in an overall majority of only 3 seats. The two major parties got only 67.7 percent of the poll in 2005 (see Table 2.9).

TABLE 2.9

PERCENT SHARE OF THE VOTE BY THE TWO MAJOR PARTIES, SELECTED ELECTIONS

Election	% Total Electorate	% Actual Vote	Seats Won		% Seats Won by 2 Parties	Total Seats
			Con.	Lab.		
1945	64.6	88.1	213	393	94.1	640
1951	79.9	96.8	321	295	98.6	625
1966	68.1	89.8	253	363	97.8	630
1974 (Oct.)	54.6	75.0	277	319	94.0	635
1983	50.9	70.0	397	209	93.2	650
1992	58.8	76.3	336	271	93.2	651
1997	53.1	75.8	165	419	88.5	659
2001	43.0	72.4	166	412	87.5	659
2005	35.6	67.7	198	356	80.4	646

The decline in recent electoral support for the two major parties is attributable to two main factors: the rise in nationalist sentiment and in Liberal-Social Democratic support, and the decrease in the strength of partisanship for the Conservative and Labour Parties.

The cumulative rise in Scottish nationalist strength has been rapid in recent elections. The SNP slogan "It's Scotland's oil" appealed to those who believe that Scotland should control the North Sea oil revenues. By 1974 the SNP had become a broad-based party drawing support from all social classes, geographical regions, and age groups, and from former voters, especially younger people, from other parties. In 2001 it got the second highest proportion of votes in Scotland (see Table 2.10).

In October 1974 the Welsh Plaid Cymru won three seats, with 10.8 percent of the Welsh vote, and came in second in six constituencies, but its strength was largely confined to the rural, Welsh-speaking part of the country. Influenced by literary figures, the party has been more concerned about the extinction of the Welsh culture and language than about broader political issues. The Welsh protest vote against the major parties—unlike the Scottish, which has increasingly gone to the nationalist party—has often gone to the Liberals and more recently to Labour (see Table 2.10).

The Ulster Unionists, once automatically associated with the Conservative Party, are now more independent. Elections in Northern Ireland had little reference to the rest of the United Kingdom and were primarily concerned with political affairs in Ulster since 1974.

Many electors have a partisan self-image or psychological commitment to one of the two major parties, but there has been a drop in support for them. The Conservative vote fell in 1997, and in 2001 to 31 percent, the lowest in its history. Labour lost considerable support in the 1980s. In 1979 the party got the votes of less than half of the working-class voters. But after 1983 it recovered a considerable part of the working-class vote. Both parties have experienced a decline in membership, a weakening of party allegiance, and expressions of dissatisfaction with their leadership.

Nevertheless, despite the decline in the major party vote of the electorate as a consequence of the rise of minor parties and the decline in partisanship, there has not been a similar decrease in the number of seats gained by the major parties. The working of the present electoral system still allowed Conservatives and Labour to obtain 80 percent of the seats while getting only 67 percent of the electoral vote in 2001.

ELECTIONS

When are general elections held? The whole House of Commons is elected for a period of five years, but only two Parliaments since 1945 have lasted the full allotted time. Most elections are called by the prime minister at a time thought best for the ruling party to win. Campaigns last less than a month, and in recent years, especially because of television coverage, they have concentrated on the major party leaders.

TABLE 2.10

VOTING IN SCOTLAND AND WALES FOR HOUSE OF COMMONS, 2005

Scotland: turnout 60.6%			Wales: turnout 62.4%		
Party	% Vote	Seats	Party	% Vote	Seats
SNP	17.7	6	Plaid Cymru	12.6	3
Labour	39.5	41	Labour	42.7	29
Conservative	15.8	1	Conservative	21.4	3
Liberal Democrat	22.6	11	Liberal Democrat	18.4	4
Others	4.4	0	Others	4.9	0

Source: The Constitutional Unit: Constitutional Update.

A CLOSER LOOK

2.5

THE JUNE 2001 GENERAL ELECTION

Britain in June 2001 had a strong economy, low inflation, low interest rates, an independent Bank of England, a mostly unified Labour Party, a divided Conservative Party, and a new leader of the Liberal Democrats (since 1999). The Labour government had not lost any by-election between 1997 and 2001. The electoral system favored Labour, and the British press was mainly supporting Labour at the election. The Labour campaign was the most effective. Conservative organization was weak at the local level; many constituencies were without a full-time Tory agent. The Liberal Democrats seemed to be left of Labour, calling for more spending on public services and speedy entry into the euro single currency. Labour focused on health, education, transport, law and order, and information technology. The Conservatives called for tax cuts, limits on state intervention, no euro during the next parliamentary term, and no participation in a military structure independent of NATO. Conservative leader William Hague had low rating as "most capable leader." The parties concentrated on marginal seats.

The 3,318 candidates included 375 women and 63 persons of ethnic minorities (blacks and Asians). Almost all constituencies in Great Britain were contested by the three major parties. The Scottish National Party (SNP) contested all 73 seats in Scotland, and the Welsh nationalists, Plaid Cymru, all 40 seats in Wales. The UK Independence Party, an anti–European Union party, put up 420 candidates, the Greens 149, and the far-right British National Party 50, mostly in northern England where racial tensions were high in some cities.

The June 2001 election saw a dramatic drop in turnout; it was 59.4 percent, the lowest since 1918. More people abstained than voted for the winning party. About 60 percent of young people abstained. Many people took a Labour victory for granted. The result was a Labour landslide in terms of seats. Labour was reelected with 40.7 percent of the vote and 412 seats. In 1997, Labour had the biggest overall majority in the House of Commons in recent years. Yet in 2001, with almost the same majority, it got fewer votes (10.7 million) than any government since 1924. In the 1997 and 2001 elections, Labour got less than 50 percent of the vote. Labour won a considerable part of the middle-class vote, marginal seats, and owner-occupiers. The Conservative Party suffered its second consecutive defeat, getting 31.7 percent of the vote and 166 seats in 2001. In 1997 the party had received 31.4 percent of the vote and 165 seats, its worst performance since 1832. Its vote fell from 1992 to 2001 by 40 percent, to 8.3 million. The Conservatives lost the upwardly mobile, skilled working-class male in the southeast, to whom the Tories appealed in the 1980s. They won no seat in Scotland in 1997, and only one in 2001. The Conservatives won no seat in Wales in either election, though they were the second party in terms of votes (21 percent). They won no seat in any large city or town outside London. In some areas the party's candidates came in third. It lost many of its stronghold seats in southeast England, the old conservative working-class, and marginal seats. It suffered in both elections by tactical voting by Labour and Liberal Democrats in some individual constituencies to defeat the Tories though there was no formal pact to do so. William Hague resigned immediately after the 2001 election, the first Conservative leader in 80 years to have resigned without having been prime minister.

The Liberal Democrats made considerable gains in seats in 2001, with 18.3 percent of the vote and 52 seats; in 1997, they had received 17.2 percent and 46 seats. The 2001 result was the best for any third party since 1923. The Liberal Democratic Party now has representation in all regions of the country. It offered the main challenge to Labour in working-class areas, and to Conservatives in rural areas. It got more votes than the Conservatives in Scotland and was second in a number of northern constituencies. The UK Independence Party, the Greens, and the BNP got about 2 percent of the vote and no seats. The SNP got 1.8 percent and 5 seats, and Plaid Cymru 0.7 percent and 4 seats. Parties in Northern Ireland got 2.8 percent and 18 seats.

Women were elected to 118 seats in 2001, down from 120 in 1997. Ethnic minorities, who held 9 seats in 1997, were elected to 12 seats in 2001, all from Labour. The June 2001 election saw considerable class dealignment. Labour got substantial support from the salaried middle class and public sector professionals.

By-elections in an individual constituency are held on the death or resignation of a member of Parliament (MP). The number of by-elections during the life of a Parliament thus depends on the duration of the Parliament and the age of MPs.

There are two interesting features of by-elections. The first is that the vote is always considerably lower than in the same constituency at general elections. The second is that the voters usually register a more antigovernment view than they did at the previous general election, thus decreasing the strength of the government party in the House of Commons. However, Labour between 1997 and 2003 did not lose a single by-election, but it did lose two, in 2003 and 2004.

There are no primaries or nominating conventions in British politics. Primaries are virtually impossible in the British context because of the unpredictable timing of elections. Almost all candidates are sponsored by a political party. It has been rare for a nonparty candidate to run or for a candidate not associated with a major party to win.

Any person over age 21 can stand as a candidate, with certain exceptions: those who are disqualified from voting; clergymen of the churches of England, Scotland, and Ireland, and of the Roman Catholic Church; and people holding certain offices, including judges, civil servants, members of the armed forces, police officers, and various public officials, except members of the government. Candidates need not reside in their constituencies.

One requirement is that each candidate must deposit £500 with the registrar, which is returned if the candidate gets over 5 percent of the total vote in a constituency.

Who Are the Candidates?

An implicit problem in representative democracies is that the candidates and the representatives elected are not a model of their constituents. The British system bears out this generalization. The percentage of male candidates is far greater than the percentage of men in the general population, and candidates are wealthier and better educated than the average constituent (see Table 2.11).

Among Conservative candidates it is noticeable that 57 percent attended a public school, 35 percent went to Oxbridge (Oxford or Cambridge), and 33 percent to some other university. What is perhaps more surprising in a party that gets most of its support from the working class is that 14 percent of the Labour candidates went to public school, 13 percent went to Oxbridge, and 45 percent to some other university.

In 2001 the two dominant occupations among the candidates were business and the professions. Most Conservative professionals were lawyers, while most Labour professionals were teachers at some educational level. The Liberals also had a high proportion of teachers. The Conservatives have become a less aristocratic group and Labour more professional.

A CLOSER LOOK

2.6

SOME RECORD POSTWAR ELECTIONS

- Labour's largest share of the vote: 48.8 percent in 1951.
- Labour's lowest share of the vote: 27.6 percent in 1983.
- Conservatives' lowest share of the vote: 31.4 percent in 1997.
- Largest overall majority: 179 by Labour in 1997; 144 by Conservatives in 1983.
- Best third-party performance: 25.4 percent by the Alliance (Liberals and Social Democrats) in 1983, though only 23 seats.
- Highest voter turnout: 84 percent in 1950.
- Lowest voter turnout: 59.4 percent in 2001.
- Labour lost its first by-election since 1997 in 2003, and a second in 2004.

TABLE 2.11

EDUCATION AND OCCUPATIONS OF CANDIDATES, 2001

	Labour		Conservative		Liberal Democrat	
	Total	Elected	Total	Elected	Total	Elected
Education						
State secondary	461	342	360	60	507	34
Public school	103	68	280	106	132	18
Oxford or Cambridge	88	65	145	79	75	14
All universities	420	275	422	138	356	36
Main Occupations						
Barrister	25	13	46	28	9	2
Solicitor	28	10	47	13	23	4
Accountant	5	2	25	3	31	1
Civil service	51	30	15	2	26	3
Military	2	1	20	11	8	—
University and college teachers	66	49	7	1	34	3
School teachers	81	49	25	6	75	9
Business: directors and executives	29	15	172	49	78	13
Insurance	10	2	52	6	33	—
White collar workers	108	73	31	2	91	1
Politician	60	44	47	18	43	4
Publishers and journalists	51	32	32	14	24	4
Farmer	1	—	17	5	5	1
Skilled Worker	50	37	4	—	17	1
Miner	11	11	1	1	2	—
Total	640	412	640	166	639	52

Source: David Butler and Dennis Kavanagh, *The British General Election of 2001* (New York: Palgrave, 2002).

In all parties there have been a limited number of women candidates, though the number has been increasing. The highest number was the 640, or 19 percent of the total, who ran in 2001 (see Table 2.12).

The Nature of Voting

Though recent changes in voting behavior must be borne in mind, and despite the fluid political situation, certain general statements

TABLE 2.12

WOMEN CANDIDATES AND MPs, 2001

Party	Candidates	MPs
Conservative	95	14
Labour	150	95
Liberal Democrat	139	5
Others	260	4
	644	118

Source: Inter-Parliamentary Union.

about voting in the post–World War II period can be made.

A High but Declining Poll   Voting is not compulsory, but the vote in general elections in the postwar period has tended to be over 72 percent of the electorate, though smaller at by-elections. Turnout reached a peak of 83.9 percent in 1950, but there has been a steady, though irregular, decline. In October 1974, it dropped to 72.8 percent, increased 77 percent in 1992, and dropped to 59.4 percent in 2001.

The abstention rate is higher among younger people, new residents of a constituency, the unmarried or divorced, blacks, the unemployed, and private rather than council tenants. These groups are less involved in political parties, less interested in politics, and less exposed to political information in general. Demographic factors have reinforced an overall decline in political interest and the belief, perhaps temporary, that the outcome of elections is not important. The decline in the poll may also be explained by the greater mobility of the population and the reduction of voting in safe seats in the inner cities.

Class   There has been a strong correlation between class and party voting. Until the late 1990s the Conservatives normally got 90 percent of the upper-middle-class vote and between two-thirds and three-quarters of the middle-class vote. Labour gets some two-thirds of the working-class vote, while the Liberal Democrats draw from all social classes.

Yet the link between class and party voting has never been complete. About one-third of the electorate does not vote according to this premise. The most serious qualification of class-party voting has always been the working-class Conservative vote, which has amounted to about one-third of the total working-class vote. There are a number of possible explanations for this contradiction of class voting. Those among the working class who see themselves as middle class and adopt middle-class values and ways of life are more likely to vote Conservative than those who think of themselves as working class. Members of the working class who have had more than the minimum secondary and further education are more likely to vote Conservative than those who have not. Workers in agricultural areas who have close contacts with their employers, who do not belong to unions, who are religious, who belong to local organizations and are integrated into the local community are more likely to vote Conservative than the average worker.

Another explanation has been the deference of the working class. It used to be argued that this group preferred a socially superior political leadership, which it believed to be a natural ruling group. But it is more likely that this group believes that the Conservative Party is more efficient than its rivals and that its wielding of power will ensure greater material benefits.

Whatever the explanation, the Conservatives have done particularly well in the working class among older people, women until 1979, those who own their own homes, and those who own shares. The increase in home ownership—66 percent of voters now own homes—has meant greater Conservative support. About 44 percent in 1987 and 40 percent in 1992 of the home-owning working class voted Conservative; 32 percent voted Labour in 1987 and 41 percent in 1992. By contrast, about 57 percent of working-class tenants in public housing voted Labour in the same election. In the same way, a majority of first-time shareholders voted Conservative and only 17 percent voted Labour, in 1987. However, in the 1997 and 2001 elections, Labour obtained considerable support from the middle class.

The evidence is mixed at present, but there appears to be less subjective class identification, a weakening of class alignment, especially by young voters, and less acceptance of the basic principles of a party by its supporters. In 1992, 1997, and 2001, the Conservatives did less well than in previous elections with voters of the "new" working class, those who live in the south of England, are homeowners, work in the private sector, and are non-unionists.

Party Identification   The best guide to voting choice for most of the electorate has been identification with a party and psychological commitment to it. This allegiance has been the basis for response to party programs, for evaluation of the competence of party leaders, and for voting and political behavior in general. Among Labour and Conservative voters in 1974, 9 out of 10 thought of themselves as Labour or Conservative. In contrast, only half of the Liberal voters felt a similar identification with the party.

Why do people identify with a party? The strongest single influence has been the party preference of parents, especially if both parents voted the same way. Identification also results from other factors, including the supposed link between the party and a class, and the image of what policies and principles the party represents. For the Conservatives, the image has included capable leadership, skill in foreign policy, patriotism, and maintenance of the free enterprise system. For Labour it has been the pursuit of a more egalitarian society and concern for the underprivileged. Part of the dilemma of the Liberals is that their image is rather diffuse, devoid of specific policy content of general appeal.

In the early 1980s the Labour Party moved to the left and alienated some traditional supporters. In the 1990s it moved to more centrist positions, renounced extreme policies that lost votes, gave up unilateral disarmament, accepted the market economy, and agreed not to revoke privatization of enterprises.

In the recent past the party identification factor has given considerable stability and pre-dictability to the voting pattern for the major parties. But in the 1970s and 1980s strength of party identification appears to have declined and the ties of voters to a particular party to have grown weaker. Voters are less prone to vote for the party of their parents. Changes in the social structure, a general criticism of the performance of governments of both parties, and the presence of new issues that cut across party lines have contributed to this decline in party identification, the rise of the Social Democrats, and perhaps also to a certain cynicism about parties. In particular, part of the decline since 1970 in the Labour and Conservative vote and in turnout has been attributed to two factors: (1) less party identification in the young and newly enfranchised part of the electorate, and (2) a decline in the number of those who define themselves as "very strong identifiers" with a party.

Gender   Women constitute 52 percent of the electorate. Until recently, men have been more politically active than women, with a particularly low political interest among working-class women. Women tended to vote Conservative to a greater degree than did men until 1979. In 1983, for the first time, the Conservatives got less support from women than from men. In recent elections, Labour received a majority of the votes of women.

Race   Nonwhite immigrants have overwhelmingly voted Labour, partly because the vast majority are

A CLOSER LOOK
2.7

PARTY IDENTIFICATION AND CLASS

Social class has been the main form of identity, and British voters have identified in general with the party they think represents the interests of their social class. In elections between 1945 and 1970, nearly two-thirds of all voters voted for their class-party. Since 1974, the percentage has declined, though class remains the single most important factor. On one hand the increase in public sector professions, whose members are more concerned with service than with wealth, meant more middle-class support for Labour. On the other hand, social factors (home ownership, mobility from north to south and from inner cities to suburbs, decline in trade union membership) meant working-class support for non-Labour parties. Moreover, the working class has declined from 41 percent of all voters in 1979 to 30 percent in 2002. The new social cleavages have weakened, though not ended, class voting.

members of the working class. But the presence of a significant number of immigrants in a constituency and the nonwhite immigration issue have another effect on voting. In the 1970 election the Conservatives were believed to have gained about six seats as a result of their being perceived—largely owing to the speeches made by the then-prominent Conservative Enoch Powell—as the more restrictive major party on allowing immigration.

In the 1990s, all mainstream parties increased their number of ethnic minority candidates. In 2001, 12 were elected to the House of Commons.

Religion   In contemporary times, religion has not been a politically divisive issue, except in Northern Ireland and among parts of the Islamic community. But there is a link between class and membership in a particular religion, and thus a link between religion and voting behavior. In general, members of the Anglican Church vote more Conservative than do individuals of other religious denominations; members of the nonconformist churches are likely to support the Labour or Liberal Parties; and Catholics, largely working class, vote strongly Labour.

Age   Younger people tend to vote Labour in greater proportions than their elders, especially those between 50 and 64. But the youngest people also have the lowest rates of turnout. On the whole it is true that the Conservatives are supported more by older than younger voters. This has been explained by the argument that it is the conservation of those political tendencies that were established when young that increases with age, not conservatism itself. Voting habits will therefore be influenced by those tendencies that were dominant when people first entered the electorate. Older people became adults when Labour was still a minor party and therefore have less allegiance to it than younger people.

Regional Variations   For generations, certain areas have been strongholds of particular parties. Labour does well in south Wales, central Scotland, the industrial north of England, and in the inner cities. The Conservatives have been strong in southern and eastern England,

and in the suburbs and country areas, which have grown in population and economic prosperity. In 1987 Labour won only 3 of the 176 seats in southern England, excluding London, but did better in 1997 and 2001. The Liberal Democrats do best in the west of England, Wales, and the Scottish islands. Labour has a plurality in Wales and Scotland. The Conservatives usually have a plurality in England and, until recently, in Northern Ireland. From the 1970s, politics in Ulster have been very fluid because of complex internal problems.

Occupation   Those employed in nationalized industries and public service organizations are more likely to vote Labour than those working in commercial organizations and the self-employed. People in both the working and middle class who have experienced unemployment are more likely than the average to vote Labour. Trade unionists vote Labour to a greater degree than do nonunionists. The strongest working-class support for Labour comes from predominantly working-class constituencies in large towns, industrial areas, and mining villages; union members; workers in large factories and offices with over 250 employees; those with working-class parents; those living in council apartments; and those who have been unemployed for a period of time. However, the number of manual workers and of those working in large factories, and the number of council tenants all have been declining.

Party and Leader   Voting may depend on the images people have of the parties and their leaders and on perceptions of party positions on issues. The assumption that people are more likely to vote for a party than a leader may no longer be true in view of the prominence of the leaders on television and the time given to their speeches and personalities.

POLITICAL PARTIES

British parties have been largely unregulated by law until very recently. The Registration of Political Parties Act 1998 forbade misleading descriptions of candidates who run under labels easily confused with those of other parties. It also provided for noncompulsory registration of parties. The Political Parties, Elections, and Referendums Act 2000 made registration compulsory and set up an independent Electoral Commission with wide executive and investigative powers over party funding, as well as administration of elections and referendums. Each political party must publish annual accounts and information on donations, gifts, subscriptions, and affiliation fees. Donations must not be anonymous nor come from a foreign source.

The British system has often been regarded as the classic example of a two-party system in which the Conservative and Labour Parties—national, large, cohesive, disciplined, ideological but generally moderate—have alternated as the government and the opposition. The Liberals did not win more than 20 seats until 1997. A considerable number of minor parties have existed and run candidates in national and local elections. But none, except the nationalists in recent years, has had much success. Extremist parties have fared poorly. On the left, the Communist Party, founded in 1920, has never gained more than two parliamentary seats and since 1950 has been unrepresented. On the right, the party opposing nonwhite immigration has not been able to win a parliamentary seat. The Green Party emerged in 1985 out of an ecological group. In 1987 it received less than 1 percent of the vote, but in the 1989 election for the European Parliament it obtained 15 percent. In the 2001 election, its candidates got between 1 and 2 percent of the vote.

A possible change to a multiparty system appeared with the formation of the Social Democratic Party (SDP) in 1981 by some prominent Labour politicians who were disturbed by militant leftism in their party and by organizational changes allowing more influence to extraparliamentary forces, extremists in some of the constituency parties, and the trade unions.

The SDP and the Liberals agreed to form an Alliance to support each other electorally. This did well at some by-elections and in local elections. But the Alliance was less successful nationally, though it won 23 seats and came second in 311 constituencies and got 25 percent of the poll

in 1983, and it won 22 seats and came second in 260 constituencies and got 22 percent in 1987.

As a result of this disappointment, a majority in SDP agreed to merge with the Liberals and form a new party, the Social and Liberal Democrats (SLD), who were generally called Liberal Democrats in 1988. In the 1992 election the Liberal Democrats got 17.8 percent of the vote and 20 seats, which in 2001 increased to 18.3 percent and 52 seats. The new UK Independence Party has not yet won a seat, but did win 12 in the 2004 European Parliament.

PARTY ORGANIZATIONS

Local and Regional

All the major parties have the parliamentary constituency as the basic unit of party organization. The Conservative and Liberal constituency associations are composed of individual members who subscribe to the party and who manage the local organizations, elect their own officers, select parliamentary and local government candidates, raise funds, engage in educational work, and conduct the electoral campaign in their area. However, the constituency Labour parties are composed not only of individual members but also of affiliated organizations, such as trade unions, cooperative societies and branches of the Cooperative Party, branches of Socialist societies and some professional organizations, and trade councils.

Total membership of all parties has declined in the last two decades. The Conservative Party has declined from about 3 million in the late 1950s to about 300,000 members, the Liberals now have about 60,000 members, and the Labour Party has about 311,000 individual and 4 million affiliated members. A number of factors may explain this decline away from party membership: other political outlets such as social movements and pressure groups, the lessening of partisan alignment, the erosion of working-class communities, the increase in middle-class working women who are no longer Conservative volunteers, and the reliance on television and not personal activity for electoral campaigns.

National Organization

Each party has a national organization that works through different committees, holds an annual conference in the autumn, has a central headquarters to control the working of the party machinery and prepare publications, and has geographical regional groups and policy committees.

The National Union of Conservative and Unionist Associations is a federation of constituency associations. It is responsible for the organization and growth of these associations and acts as a link between the leader of the party and the associations. The Union is nominally governed by the Central Council, which meets once a year and which, in the postwar period, has chosen the officers of the Union. But because the Central Council is too large a body for effective action, the group that acts on its behalf and meets more frequently is the Executive Committee; this committee is composed of the party leader, chief officials, and representatives of the regional organizations. The Party Board is the ultimate decision-making body, responsible for operational matters.

The Conservatives hold an annual conference. Until recently the conference was usually a platform for the main party leaders rather than a challenge to them. However, the conferences over the last decade have become less placid and more divisive. Since 1998 a Conservative Policy Forum oversees the policy discussions at constituency level. It is characteristic of the Conservative conference that it is usually more right-wing than the leadership.

The Conservative Central Office, the party headquarters, is concerned with the efficient organization of the party. It provides general guidance and technical assistance, helps the formulation of policy by supplying background material through its research department, and offers advice on electioneering. It is headed by a chairperson, appointed by the party leader, and officers who are responsible for the different departments concerned with specific functions.

The Central Office cannot coerce the constituency associations, which operate through local volunteer workers and obtain and spend their own funds. The local associations also, in the main, control the process of selection of parliamentary candidates, though the Central Office supplies a list of available candidates on request and may influence the final choice.

The Labour Party has the most complex organizational structure. It began as, and has remained, a federal body composed of four main groups (see Figure 2.3):

1. The more than 600 constituency associations, which now have about 214,000 members. They are responsible for their own organization and selection of parliamentary candidates. The number of activists is relatively small, and they are usually more left-wing than either the party leaders or their MPs. Most party members spend little or no time at party meetings or activities.

2. The 23 affiliated trade unions, which account for 4 million, or 95 percent, of the members. Not all unions are affiliated with the party—74 unions are now attached to the Trades Union Congress—and not all members of a union that is affiliated want to be members of the party. About one-third of the membership of the affiliated unions have "contracted out," or refused to have part of their union dues go to a political levy for the party. About three-quarters of the Labour Party's funds come from the unions.

Since all organizations are represented at the annual conference in proportion to their membership, the four largest unions constituted a majority if they all voted the same way. But the union vote has been reduced to a third of the whole conference.

A number of unions sponsor parliamentary candidates, most of whose election expenses they pay. Because their constituencies are usually safe seats, those candidates are much more likely to win than nonsponsored candidates. In 1992, of the 634 Labour candidates, the unions sponsored 173. Of these, 143 won, of whom 22 were women.

3. The cooperative organizations linked to the Labour Party. One cooperative society, the Royal Arsenal, has been affiliated since 1927 and another since 1979. There is a separate Cooperative Party, founded in 1917, but it is now in real-

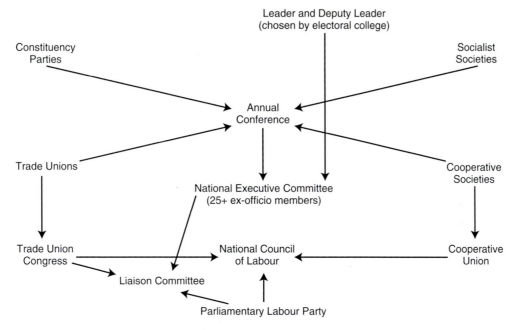

Figure 2.3 ORGANIZATION OF THE LABOUR PARTY

ity an adjunct of the Labour Party. Since 1922 all Cooperative Party parliamentary candidates have been endorsed by the Labour Party and have run as Labour and Cooperative.

4. A number of Socialist societies, small in size and composed largely of professionals or intellectuals. The most well-known of these bodies is the Fabian Society, which was founded in 1884. The total membership of these societies and of the cooperative groups is about 54,000.

The nominal policy-making body in the Labour Party is the annual party conference, which debates resolutions, changes the constitution of the party, and elects the major administrative organ, the National Executive Committee (NEC). The conference is attended by representatives from the four different elements making up the party and by the chief officials of the party, MPs, and parliamentary candidates.

The NEC consists of the leader of the party, the deputy leader, the treasurer, and 28 other members who are elected at the conference. Of

these people, 12 are chosen by the trade union delegates, 7 by those from the constituency parties, 4 by representatives of the cooperative and Socialist societies, and 5 women by the whole conference. At least 11 members must be women.

The NEC is the administrative authority of the party and is the body responsible between annual conferences for deciding policy matters and enforcing the rules of the party. It controls the central organization, supervises the work of the party outside Parliament, decides disputes between members or associations, and manages the party funds. Together with the Parliamentary Labour Party (PLP), the NEC draws up the election manifesto based on conference proposals, but there is sometimes friction between them.

The NEC also plays a role in the selection of parliamentary candidates. Like the Conservative Central Office, it maintains a list of acceptable candidates that the local constituencies can request, but the final choice is made by the local parties.

The NEC can expel a member or disaffiliate an organization for activity contrary to party decisions. In recent years Labour has enforced its rules stringently. Since 1998 the NEC has vetted the voting and absentee record of Labour MPs to see if they are suitable to be reselected as parliamentary candidates. The party expelled two Labour members of the European Parliament who had repeatedly criticized the leadership of Prime Minister Blair and suspended two others for breaking party or parliamentary rules.

THE PARTIES IN PARLIAMENT

The major Conservative organ in Parliament is the 1922 Committee, which is composed of the nongovernmental Conservative MPs and expresses their opinions to the leadership of the party. When the party is in power, its leaders, now members of the government, do not attend the committee's weekly meetings. After the discussion of policy issues or political problems, the chairperson of the committee expresses its views to the leadership.

From 1881, after the death of Disraeli, until 1963 the Conservative leader "emerged" after a series of informal "soundings" of the views of different sections of the party. Of the 11 leaders in this period, 5 were of aristocratic descent and the others came from business or professional politics. The method adopted in 1963 was that the Conservative leader would be elected by the MPs in the House of Commons and then presented for confirmation to a meeting composed of the Conservative MPs and peers, prospective candidates, and members of the Executive Committee of the National Union.

In 1998 new rules were adopted. Each Conservative MP can vote for a candidate to be leader. One or more ballots take place until only two candidates remain. The party members in the country then choose between the two in a postal ballot. The two candidates are allowed campaign managers and can spend up to £100,000. A new leader, Michael Howard, former cabinet minister, was elected in November 2003, the first practicing Jew to head a major British party.

The Parliamentary Labour Party (PLP) consists of Labour members in the House of Commons and those in the House of Lords. It is led, when the party is in opposition, by the Parliamentary Committee, or "shadow cabinet," which consists of the leader and deputy leader, 15 others elected by Labour MPs, and 1 elected representative of Labour peers. The leader and deputy leader of the PLP are the same people who have been elected as the leaders of the party by the electoral college. In this electoral college, the trade unions, the constituency parties, and the PLP each have one-third of the votes.

In recent years most of the members of the shadow cabinet have become cabinet ministers if the party gains power. This custom was reinforced by a party rule, which states that 16 members of the shadow cabinet will be given cabinet positions if the party wins the next election. When the party is in power, a liaison committee links the government and other Labour MPs, who thus have the opportunity to influence the policies of the government. Groups of Labour MPs based on territory and subject matter have also been formed for that purpose.

PARTY LEADERSHIP

In all the parties the parliamentary leader has until recently been regarded as leader of the whole party. Unlike the formal process of democratic decision making in the SLD and Labour Parties, the Conservative Party leader is responsible for deciding party policy and for the choice of the shadow cabinet, or consultative committee, when the party is in opposition. The leader controls the party headquarters and appoints the chief officials, who are responsible to him or her.

The Labour Party has been more loyal to its leaders than have the Conservatives. In the twentieth century the Conservatives have had 13 leaders, 7 of whom were overthrown by a party revolt, while an eighth was almost overthrown twice, and another two resigned after electoral defeats. During the same period Labour had eight leaders, one of whom (MacDonald) left his party, and another (Lansbury) resigned because of disagreements with party policy. All the others died in office or resigned voluntarily. The current leader, Tony Blair, who reflects a moderate liberal position, was elected in July 1994.

Until 1976 the Liberal leader was also elected by the MPs of the party. In that year the Liberals established a new procedure by which the leader was chosen by an electoral college composed of about 20,000 delegates from the constituencies. The new SLD party elects its leader by ballot of all members, using the alternative vote method. The present leader, Charles Kennedy, was elected in this way in the fourth round of balloting in August 1999.

POWER WITHIN THE PARTIES

A complex relationship exists among the different sections of the parties, in which no one element has complete power over the others, and in which each section has some, if unequal, influence on decision making in the party. Differences over policy and personnel exist between the central party organizations and the constituency associations, especially the activists in them; between the organizations in the country and the parliamentary party; and between the leadership of the party, especially when it is in power, and the MPs of the party (see Table 2.13).

Important as the party organizations are, the real power in the formulation of policy has remained with the parliamentary elements of the parties. The Liberal and Conservative parliamentary parties, from which come the prime minister and governmental leaders, existed before the mass organizations in the country were created. The dominance of the Conservative parliamentarians over the rest of the party is understandable in view of the fact that between 1886 and 2002 the Conservatives were in power for 79 years and the party leaders were also prime ministers and cabinet ministers.

Although the Labour Party is different from the others in having begun as a mass organization, by the 1920s the Parliamentary Labour Party had become the strongest element and the body that chose the political leaders. This has been partly due to the strong support of the parliamentary leaders by the trade union leaders, who for the most part held similar political opinions.

Activists of the party, at both the national and local level, have rarely been able to challenge the parliamentary leadership successfully. The political reality is that the national electoral decision and the parliamentary representatives, not the party as a whole, determine who is to be prime minister. The party organizations have been able to influence and sometimes limit the

---

TABLE 2.13

POWER IN THE POLITICAL PARTIES, 2005

	Conservatives	Labour	Liberals
Leader	Michael Howard, leader until 2005, makes policy, controls party HQ, chooses shadow cabinet, chooses cabinet, approves election manifesto	Tony Blair, chooses cabinet	Charles Kennedy, shares policy making, controls party HQ, approves election manifesto
Parliamentary party	Chooses two candidates for leader	Shares in election of leader, chooses shadow cabinet	Shares policy making, approves manifesto
Party conference	—	Makes policy	Makes policy
Party HQ executive	—	Makes policy, approves manifesto, controls party organization	Makes policy, controls party organization
Constituency associations	The constituency associations in all the parties choose or help choose parliamentary candidates		
Individual members	Elect leader		Elect leader

activity for the parliamentary leadership, but they rarely formulate policy.

Skillful manipulation by political and union officials controlled the agenda and the debates of the annual conference, and tended to exalt the parliamentary part of the Labour Party over the mass movement. In recent years the Labour conference has asserted itself and changed the organization of the party. In 1979, when the left wing of the party controlled a majority, resolutions were approved for all Labour MPs to be automatically subject to a reselection process by their constituency parties in order to remain as candidates for the next election and for the NEC to take, after appropriate consultation, the final decision on the contents of the general election manifesto.

A decision at the 2000 conference was that any resolution passed by a two-thirds majority at conferences would be embodied in the party platform from which the electoral manifesto is composed. The Labour Party in 2000 also created a network of policy forums at regional and constituency levels and a National Policy Forum to oversee them, on lines similar to those adopted by the Conservatives two years earlier.

The constituency parties on a number of occasions have attempted, sometimes successfully, not to renominate MPs who differ politically from the activists controlling the local organization. Selection of candidates is now in the hands of the local organizations. Though the central offices keep a list of nationally approved candidates and can veto an undesirable local choice, they cannot force the local organization to accept a candidate, and only very rarely have they exercised a veto even when it involved an individual who had rebelled against party policy or leadership.

The internal struggle for power within the parties continues. This has recently been shown in a number of ways. All the parties have made the choice of the party leader open to wider participation: the Conservatives by choice of two candidates by MPs and then election by party members; the Liberals by bringing the whole membership of the party into the process; and Labour by establishing an electoral college in which the trade unions and other affiliated organizations, the PLP, and the constituency parties would each have one-third of the vote.

INTEREST GROUPS

Interest groups have long existed in British politics and now play a significant role. They are usually differentiated from parties in that they do not hold or seek political office, though some groups sponsor parliamentary candidates. Interest group leaders now participate in consultative or even administrative functions and serve on government committees and advisory boards. In certain matters, they may even have a veto on government decisions.

There are numerous interest groups concerned with all aspects of life. For analytical purposes, a frequently used distinction is between sectional interest and promotional groups. *Sectional interest groups* defend and promote the interests of their members, whether individuals or enterprises. They include organizations concerned with the economic interests of labor, business, and agriculture, with social affairs such as automobile organizations, or with living arrangements such as tenants' groups. *Promotional groups* are concerned with a particular general cause, principle, or policy issue. They advocate a specific conception of the public interest. Examples of such groups are the Howard League for Penal Reform, the National Society for the Prevention of Cruelty to Children, and the Royal Society for the Prevention of Accidents.

Recent years have seen the rise of a number of protest movements, of which the most vocal has been the Campaign for Nuclear Disarmament, and groups concerned with welfare and environmental issues, such as Greenpeace with nearly half a million supporters, and Friends of the Earth, which has a quarter million members.

The most significant interest groups affecting the working of the political system are the business organizations and the trade unions.

Business

There are hundreds of business organizations concerned with a number of functions: providing common services, exchanging information, regulating trade practices, negotiating with trade unions on wages and conditions of work, and representing the business position to the government.

Most employers' groups are organized on an industry rather than product basis. Some are local or deal with a part of or the whole of an industry. There are about 150 national employers' organizations, most of which belong to the Confederation of British Industry (CBI), formed in 1965 of a number of industrial groups. The CBI is the central body representing national business and industry. It acts as an advisory and consultative body for its members and presents their views publicly. Its representatives sit on many official bodies and advisory groups. The CBI has been called the voice of British business, but this is only partly true because of the widely varied interests of industrial and commercial organizations.

The CBI has had little consistent direct influence over government policy as a whole, though it has had an impact on some industrial and business issues. On the other hand, the important financial institutions—usually referred to as the City—have been politically important.

This importance results from two factors. First, the City is still the world's most significant financial and credit center, including the Bank of England and the central offices of many British banks, the largest number of foreign banks, the stock exchange, the largest gold market and international insurance markets, and international insurance and commodity markets. Second, many public issues have been connected with regulation of money, credit, price levels, and currency relationships and balance of payments, all of which need the expertise of the City. The leading persons in the City are usually closely connected with the Conservative Party in the same way that union leaders are with the Labour Party.

Trade Unions

Trade unions began with the Industrial Revolution, but not until the mid-nineteenth century did unions of skilled and semiskilled workers become well organized in their demands for higher wages and better working conditions. In the latter part of the century, unions of unskilled workers that pursued a more active industrial policy were formed. The attacks on the unions by court decisions led to the establishment of a political lobby, the Trades Union Congress (TUC), and later to the Labour Party.

The TUC is a loose confederation which does not direct individual unions and has little power over them, but acts on behalf of the whole union movement to achieve objectives that would be difficult for separate unions to obtain. Since World War II, the TUC has sat on countless governmental committees, advisory bodies on economic issues, agricultural marketing boards, and consumer councils, and has given its views on questions of general economic and social policy. The leaders of the TUC have become members of numerous QUANGOs (Quasi Autonomous Nongovernmental Organizations).

The unions have been linked with the Labour Party since their decision to establish a pressure group in Parliament. The unions still provide the bulk of party membership and financing. Of the 74 unions in the TUC in 2005, 23 are affiliated with the party. About 60 percent of the members of these affiliated unions have paid the political levy which automatically makes them party members, though many do not realize they are doing so. They represent about 4 million members, or over 95 percent of the total party. The large manual and industrial unions form the basis of Labour's main union strength. They supply not only most of the annual funds of the party but also the extra money needed for campaigns. The unions constitute one-third of the electoral college which chooses the leader and deputy leader of the party. The unions also sponsor parliamentary candidates.

But the alliance between the unions and the party has been an uneasy one. There was considerable cooperation between 1945 and 1951, when there was a voluntary restraint on wage demands, largely because of the close personal relations between the government and union leaders. Under the Labour government of 1964–1970, the unions generally supported the government, including its income policy, until 1969, when an attempt was made to introduce legislative controls over unions. Similarly, in the Labour government of 1974–1979, the unions abided by the social contract and restraint in wage increases, until 1978–1979, when they defied the government's income policy that sought to limit wage increases to 5 percent per year.

The significant influence of the unions on policy—especially in 1974, when a series of strikes led the Conservative government to call an election which resulted in its defeat—brought calls for limits on their power; the Conservatives after their return to power in 1979 imposed such limits. The most important of these are ending the legal case for the closed shop; allowing employers the right not to recognize unions; union contributions to political parties have to be approved by secret vote of members; forbidding political strikes; forbidding mass picketing; strikes must be approved and union leaders must be elected by secret ballot. Working days lost through strikes have been substantially reduced. So has the membership of unions, which dropped from 13.3 million in 1979 to 7 million in 2005. The power of unions in relation to government and to employers has greatly declined.

THE EXECUTIVE

About 150 years ago, Bagehot in *The English Government* distinguished between the dignified and efficient parts of the political system. Some institutions, such as the monarchy, were important for symbolic reasons, while others exercised real power.

The British executive can still be viewed in the same fashion. The head of the state is the monarch, who reigns but has virtually no political power and only limited influence. The real political power is centered in the prime minister and the cabinet, with the civil service assisting and influencing the exercise and administration of that power. The British system has been based on the existence or possibility of strong, effective government. Over the last three centuries, the executive power of the king was first restrained by Parliament and then transferred to ministers.

THE MONARCHY

The present monarch, Queen Elizabeth II, can trace her descent back to at least the ninth century. The powers formerly exercised by the monarch are now in the hands of various individuals and institutions. By a series of arrangements beginning in 1760, the monarchy turned over to the government the hereditary revenues derived from the Crown Lands and other sources and has received in return an annual grant (Civil List) to cover the salaries and expenses of the royal household.

Queen Elizabeth II greets her people during the 50th anniversary of her reign, celebrations June 2002.

REVIEW

2.3

LONG LIVE THE QUEEN: A EUROPEAN TIME LINE

In June 2005, Britain's Queen Elizabeth II celebrated 53 years on the throne. During that time she witnessed, among other things:

- Ten British prime ministers.
- The end of the Soviet Union, leading to 8 new republics and 7 dictatorships.
- Two republics in France.
- The end of East Germany as a separate state.
- Over 50 governments in Italy, where these were also four political assassinations and the criminal indictment of two former prime ministers.
- Yugoslavia fragmented into 6 republics.
- Czechoslovakia partitioned into 2 states.
- Spain transformed from an authoritarian dictatorship to a parliamentary democracy, constitutional monarchy, and market economy.
- Portugal changed from an authoritarian regime to a republic.
- Greece transformed from a monarchy and 7 years of dictatorship to a republic.
- Three constitutional changes in Belgium.

The functions of government are now exercised by political ministers who are collectively and individually responsible to Parliament, but the monarch still participates in a formal way in some executive and legislative activities. The monarchy survived in Britain because the sovereign became a constitutional monarch, neither exercising the wide powers of the crown nor being responsible for their exercise. According to constitutional procedure, the sovereign always ultimately accepts the will of the government, although the monarch may make known his or her opinion and can attempt to influence the decision made.

The most important single political power of the sovereign is the choice of a prime minister. When there is a clearly recognized leader of a party that is able to control a majority in the House of Commons, the choice of the individual is obvious and immediate. But where one or both of these conditions are not present, a real choice may exist for the sovereign.

Referring to the monarchy, it used to be said that "we must not let daylight in upon magic," but in this television age, the royal family has been more exposed to the public eye. The monarch today still has a symbolic and ceremonial role to play in the system, but the monarchy has been divested of its former political power, though legally it still has the power to dissolve Parliament.

THE GOVERNMENT

The real power is exercised by the government, composed of the political ministers and junior ministers, of whom the most politically important are the prime minister and the cabinet (see Figure 2.4).

The government consists of about 100 members, all nominated by the prime minister and appointed by the monarch. It essentially consists of holders of administrative posts of a political character and the whips of the government party. It never meets as a whole to discuss policy or to take action. There is no fixed number of departments. These are established to deal with issues

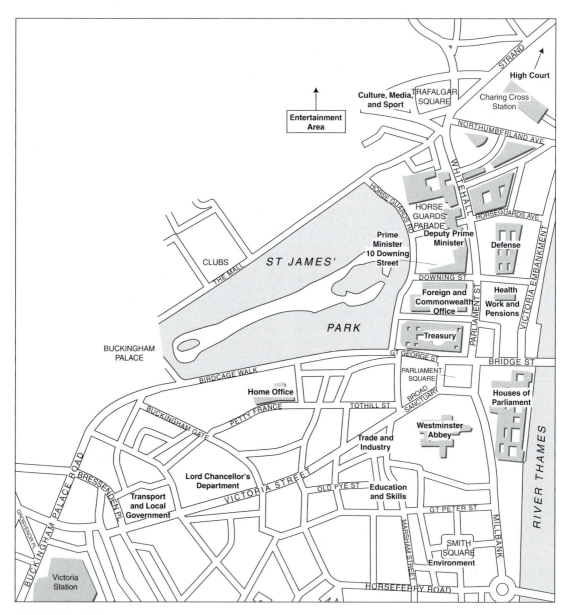

Figure 2.4 LONDON: THE POLITICAL ELITE, 2005

or to meet changing conditions or political and social crises. In the postwar period the number of major departments has been reduced and almost all of them are now in the present cabinet, usually 20 to 25. Five of the 22 persons in the cabinet in 2005 are women, as are 17 of the 67 ministers of state and junior ministers.

Ministers are individually responsible to Parliament for the work of their departments. They introduce legislative proposals, press the concerns of their department, and argue its case and requests for money in cabinet and interdepartmental committees. They discuss departmental issues with interest groups and others affected by or interested in those issues and speak in defense of the department in Parliament. It is their task to see that decisions and policies are correctly implemented by the civil servants in the department.

THE CABINET

The most significant members of the government constitute the cabinet, those ministers who are chosen by the prime minister to attend cabinet meetings and are made privy councillors. The cabinet has replaced the privy council as the chief source of executive power since the eighteenth century, but the latter still exists as an executive organ, largely giving formal effect to policy decisions made by the cabinet and making orders-in-council. A significant heritage from the past is the Judicial Committee of the Privy Council, which is the final court of appeal on certain legal issues arising in the colonies and in those independent countries of the Commonwealth that have decided to retain the arrangement.

The cabinet, which is not a legal body, is based on political understandings or conventions. Its members are normally the leading figures of the party controlling a majority in the House of Commons. The cabinet is the chief single body concerned with the initiation, control, and implementation of political policy and the most important decision-making body. It initiates most legislation and controls the legislative process. It is responsible for the coordination of governmental activity; all ministers must implement cabinet decisions insofar as their departments are affected.

For politicians, the cabinet is the top of the political ladder, except for the position of prime minister. It constitutes the core of the British political elite. A number of conventions underlie the existence and operation of cabinet government:

1. The cabinet is ultimately dependent on the support of the House of Commons that has

come into existence as a result of the general election. A government that is defeated on a major issue or on a vote of censure or no confidence is expected to resign or to ask for a dissolution of Parliament. A government whose party has been clearly defeated at a general election will resign immediately.

2. Unlike the American cabinet, the members of which are drawn from a wide variety of sources and backgrounds, the British cabinet is drawn, with rare exceptions, from members of the two Houses of Parliament. This fusion of executive and legislative functions in the hands of the same people is a striking denial of the concept of the separation of powers. This convention also means that the members of the cabinet are selected from a relatively small pool of available people. Moreover, in recent years most of the members of both Labour and Conservative cabinets have come from the shadow cabinets of the two parties.

3. Except in wartime or in a serious political or economic crisis, the entire cabinet will be members of the same political party if that party can control a majority in the Commons. In this way, political coherence and unity can be obtained. Britain is the only country in Western Europe that has not had a coalition government in the postwar period.

4. The monarch is excluded from the discussions of the cabinet, though he or she is kept informed of its conclusions by the prime minister, who is the acknowledged head of the cabinet. The advice offered by the cabinet, even on personal issues (as in 1936 on the marital plans of King Edward VIII, who was eventually obliged to abdicate), must be accepted by the monarch or a constitutional crisis will result.

5. All members take the oath of privy councillors and are bound to secrecy by this and the Official Secrets Act. There is now a 30-year limitation on the publication of cabinet documents, and secrecy is generally preserved.

6. The members of the cabinet are collectively responsible for all decisions and actions, as well as individually responsible for the performance of the particular department or unit each may head. There is free and frank discussion of issues in the cabinet.

REVIEW 2.4

SOME KEY TERMS IN BRITISH POLITICS

Backbencher—members of the House of Commons (MPs) who are not members of the government or leaders of the opposition; they sit on the back benches of the chamber.

Cabinet—the most senior ministers in the government, usually about 20.

Constituency—the geographical area represented by an MP; there are now 659 constituencies.

Dissolution—the ending of the life of the House of Commons by royal proclamation on the advice of the prime minister (PM).

Government—the ministers, usually about 100, who form the political executive; most are in the House of Commons (HoC).

Great Britain—the countries of England, Scotland, and Wales.

Hansard—the daily official report of the proceedings in Parliament.

Law Lords (Lords of Appeal in Ordinary)—senior judges appointed to the House of Lords to hear appeals in civil and criminal cases.

Money bill—legislation on spending and taxation introduced in HoC; it becomes law within one month.

Opposition—second party in HoC with an officially paid leader and a "shadow cabinet."

Prime minister (PM)—head of the government and the cabinet.

Public bill—proposed legislation on public policy, which affects everyone.

Question time—one hour four times a week when ministers answer questions in HoC.

Shadow cabinet—the group of opposition party leaders in Parliament.

Speaker—presiding officer of the HoC.

10 Downing Street—home of the PM.

United Kingdom—the countries of Great Britain and Northern Ireland.

Usual channels—consultations between whips of different parties on parliamentary business.

Whips—MPs who provide information to and from their party members and leaders and who discipline their party in HoC.

Whitehall—term used for civil service and administration.

Members may and do disagree about the desirability of a policy, but they must support and implement policy decisions once they have been made. The British system is based on the premise that a government that is publicly divided on a given subject cannot govern.

The principle of collective responsibility means that all ministers must support and defend government policy and not speak or act against it. The principle applies now not only to cabinet ministers but also to all members of the government. If ministers continue to oppose or cannot accept a decision made on an important issue, the principle suggests that they should resign. In recent years cabinets have sometimes remained divided but without resignations. In addition, the development of the system of cabinet committees and the dominant role of the prime minister has meant that cabinet members tend to feel less personally committed to every decision.

Collective responsibility also implies that an attack on a minister in regard to important policy, as distinct from criticism of the administration of that minister's department, will be taken as an attack on the whole government unless it disclaims responsibility. If the latter is the case, strong criticism of a minister may lead to resignation, but not to a vote on the government as a whole.

This concept of collective responsibility and decision making is to be distinguished from the principle of ministerial responsibility, which means that individual ministers are responsible for all the work and actions of the government departments that they head. Though it is most improbable that ministers will be familiar with all the work of the department, they must respond to parliamentary criticism of or inquiry about it.

Theoretically, if parliamentary criticism of a department or of a minister's performance or neglect of duties or competence is sufficiently great, the minister is obliged to resign. Resignation has also resulted from ministerial indiscretion, either inadvertent or more blatant, as in sexual escapades such as that by the Home Secretary in 2004, improper behavior, or the use of indiscreet language. But there are many more examples of ministers not resigning in spite of considerable parliamentary criticism of their activity.

Cabinet Membership

The number and members of the cabinet depend on the prime minister, whose appointments result partly from the administrative needs and governmental functions to be performed and partly from political necessity to accommodate the ambitions of colleagues, to have different ideological sections of the party and territorial parts of the country represented, and to include some individuals loyal to himself or herself. The cabinet, which realistically contains the political

rivals and possible successors of the prime minister, is thus the result of administrative, political, and personal factors.

Except during the two world wars, when the size of the cabinet was reduced to 8 or 9, and in 2001 with a War Cabinet, it has numbered between 18 and 23 ministers. Usually, the important departments will be included in the cabinet, though no one becomes a member simply because of his or her office. The minister of a department has been included in one cabinet but excluded from the next, depending on the priority given it by the different cabinets or the political weight of the minister.

Although members of the cabinet are drawn from both Houses, certain ministers, especially those with financial responsibilities, will almost always be chosen from the Commons. Only occasionally will someone outside Parliament be appointed. Ministers are not experts and rarely have executive experience, as they have spent much of their lives in politics.

In reality, the choice of the prime minister is constrained by the existence of the shadow cabinet led by the PM when his party was in opposition. Though there is no compulsion, prime ministers in recent years have appointed most of the members of the shadow cabinet to the cabinet itself. This is now mandatory in the Labour Party.

Procedure in the Cabinet

Cabinet meetings are called by the prime minister, usually once a week. Members ask the cabinet

A CLOSER LOOK

2.8

THE CABINET, 2005

In recent years, the cabinet as a body appears to have become less significant for a wide range of political affairs. It now largely deals with foreign issues, some immediate important questions of the day, any item brought up by the PM, and issues that have not been resolved by cabinet committees or interministerial meetings. The normal process today is for a ministerial proposal to go to the relevant cabinet committee, which virtually decides if it should become policy; that decision is usually accepted as a cabinet decision. Ministers are reluctant to take some matters to the cabinet, and almost always try to get agreement from the Treasury.

secretariat to put items on the agenda and receive copies of it before each meeting. They are thus able to study the issues and to attend meetings with an informed opinion on them. Ministers who are not cabinet members are normally invited to attend when a subject affecting their department is on the agenda.

It has usually been assumed that the cabinet does not vote on issues, but that discussion takes place until a collective decision is reached when the prime minister sums up "the sense of the meeting." But some cabinet ministers have stated that voting did sometimes take place on substantive as well as procedural matters.

There are other qualifications of the principle of collective decision making by the cabinet. First, members do not always participate in discussion, especially as the range of subjects has increased. This is largely the result of the heavy burden of duties imposed on cabinet members, which includes the reading of official papers, attending and speaking in Parliament, supervising the work of their departments and giving directions to officials, attending official functions, maintaining contact with their parliamentary constituencies, and undertaking a round of speeches throughout the country, as well as attending cabinet meetings. Ministers tend to fight in cabinet for their departmental policies and budgets.

Second, not all issues are fully discussed by the cabinet as a whole. Various devices are used to reduce the burden on it. Decisions made by individual ministers have sometimes been accepted by the whole body. Agreement on issues has been reached by interdepartmental ministerial meetings or in private meetings between ministers, including the prime minister. Above all, cabinet committees, consisting of a small number of cabinet members, and occasionally nonmembers, have been established to relieve the burden on the cabinet as a whole and to speed up decision making now that there has been a great increase in governmental activity. Sometimes the real decisions are made by a small committee rather than by the cabinet as a whole. In crisis or wartime, a small cabinet of five or six members is usually set up to make major decisions.

THE PRIME MINISTER

The prime minister is the acknowledged head of the executive. Unlike the U.S. presidency, the office of the prime minister is largely based on conventions. Despite the office now being over 285 years old, there are still few statutes referring to it or to the functions to be performed. The prime minister was once regarded as *primus inter pares* (first among equals) in the cabinet, but this is an inadequate description for an individual who is preeminent in it and is the dominant political personality.

Legally the prime minister is chosen by the monarch, who selects the person capable of forming a government. The choice is obvious if one political party possesses or controls an absolute majority of seats in the House of Commons and if that party has an acknowledged leader. This was the case in 1979 with the appointment of Margaret Thatcher, the first woman to become prime minister, and Tony Blair in 1997.

But there are occasions when the monarch has a real choice between individuals. If the prime minister dies or resigns, the choice of a successor is not always obvious. The monarch had to choose between rival candidates in 1957 and 1963. If no party has an absolute majority in the Commons, as in February 1974, the monarch might have a choice between the leaders of the different parties. In those situations the monarch will not act without directly or indirectly consulting a number of political leaders.

A convention of the twentieth century has limited the monarch's choice to members of the House of Commons. Since 1923, all prime ministers have been members of the lower chamber. When Lord Home was appointed in 1963, he immediately disclaimed his title, left the House of Lords, and won a seat in the Commons. This convention illustrates the predominance of the Commons over the Lords. Governments can be defeated and forced to resign by vote of the Commons but not by the Lords.

Prime ministers differ in personality, energy, political interests, and administrative abilities, but all are seasoned politicians with experience in Parliament. In the twentieth century as a whole, as in the postwar period, the prime minister's average tenure as an MP has been 28 years. Most of them have held a number of other cabinet positions. The average tenure in this century has been three different posts and eight years in the cabinet. Thatcher had only one previous post and four years in cabinet, and Major had only one year in a senior cabinet post before becoming prime minister. Blair had not served in a previous cabinet.

In the twentieth century there have been 20 prime ministers. They have differed in social background: five came from the aristocracy, eight from the middle class, six from the lower middle class, and one from the working class. All the aristocrats and six of the eight middle-class prime ministers went to a public school, five of them went to Eton and two to Harrow. Thirteen attended university at Oxford or Cambridge. It is distinctive that the last five before Blair came from the lower middle class, attended state (non-public) schools, and can be regarded as examples of the principle of meritocracy. John Major, like James Callaghan, Labour PM (1976–1979), is unusual in never having gone to a university.

Functions

The prime minister chooses and can dismiss members of the government. But, unlike the U.S. president, the prime minister's range of choice is restricted; rarely does he or she choose someone from outside Parliament and even more rarely from outside the government party. Many choices will be obvious because the leading members of the successful party, especially many of those who have been in the shadow cabinet, will be appointed; the most important of them may even be consulted by the prime minister in choosing the others. The prime minister must keep the confidence of senior colleagues. He or she can dismiss or demand the resignation of ministers, but may not always be able to get rid of those who have some independent political strength in the party or country.

The prime minister decides the size and composition of the cabinet. He or she forms a cabinet that is satisfactory from both a political and an administrative point of view. Thus, prime ministers will usually include not only people who reflect different elements or political opinions in

A CLOSER LOOK

2.9

TONY BLAIR: LABOUR LEADER AND PRIME MINISTER

- Born in Edinburgh, Scotland, in 1953. Educated at Scottish private school and at Oxford University.
- Lawyer specializing in employment and industrial law; married to fellow lawyer.
- Became Labour MP in 1983 for constituency in northern England, formerly a coal-mining area.
- Member of NEC of Labour Party in 1989; member of shadow cabinet.
- Elected leader of Labour Party in 1994, its youngest leader.
- Self-proclaimed modernizer and moderate, left of center.
- Spoke of "New Labour"—called for reduced influence of trade unions in party policies, removing "common ownership of the means of production, distribution, and exchange" from the party's constitution, closer ties with EU, and devolution.
- Became Prime Minister in 1997 after Labour electoral victory.
- Advocated "the Third Way," a mixture of public and private enterprise, less governmental interference with the economic market balanced with social justice.
- Continued as Prime Minister after Labour's 2001 victory; focus on "tough choices."
- Strongly supports U.S. war on terrorism and the war in Iraq.
- Called in 2004 for dismantling of 1945 welfare state and replacing it with an "opportunity society."

the party but also some on whose loyalty they can rely or whose counsel they value.

The prime minister also establishes and appoints the members of cabinet committees. He or she sets up task forces, working parties, and ad hoc meetings as may seem necessary to deal with issues.

The prime minister calls cabinet meetings, takes the chair, determines the items of business, and controls the agenda, as well as also chairing some cabinet committees. In the task of summing up the sense of the meeting, the prime minister is allowed to interpret to some extent the decision reached. He or she is also the ultimate decider and spokesperson of cabinet policy, controlling the flow of information about the government.

The prime minister reports the conclusions of the cabinet and is the chief channel of political communication to the monarch. By convention, no minister can see the monarch without first informing the prime minister. Many of the prerogatives of the Crown, such as declarations of war and peace and dissolution of Parliament, are, in fact, exercised by the prime minister.

The prime minister acts as an arbiter and tries to resolve disputes between departments. The degree of interest the prime minister today has in any particular department varies, but traditionally he or she is always in close touch with the Foreign Office.

The prime minister dispenses considerable patronage and has a power of appointment that includes not only the members of the government but also the senior members of the civil service, the chief members of the judiciary, military leaders, and the archbishops of the Church of England. Twice yearly an official Honors List bestows some title or honor on individuals chosen by the prime minister for some contribution to public life.

The prime minister controls the major appointments in the civil service, especially those of the permanent secretary to the Treasury and the secretary of the cabinet, who is the prime minister's chief adviser on problems concerning the machinery of government.

The prime minister is also the leader of his or her party within Parliament and in the country. In Parliament he or she answers questions in the House of Commons and speaks on important occasions and in debates. Blair spends less time in the House than did his predecessors and answers questions only once a week.

The prime minister's task is to keep the party as united as possible, and his or her political survival depends on it. When the prime minister loses control of the party, as did Chamberlain in 1940, Eden in 1956–1957, and Thatcher in 1990, he or she is obliged to resign. But normally the prime minister can expect loyalty from his or her party, and he or she is aided in the maintenance of discipline by the whips, who since 1964 are paid and are regarded as part of the government team. Thatcher served as prime minister for 11 years, the longest consecutive term in the twentieth century. In 1995, 1997, and again in 2001, a deputy prime minister was appointed and given special duties in the cabinet. In 2002 he was given additional departmental responsibility. The title, however, does not imply a right to succeed the prime minister.

Is the Prime Minister a Quasi President?

There is universal agreement that the prime minister is the most important political figure in Britain. This has led some to regard the office as similar in the extent and degree of its power to that of the U.S. president. Some argue that the country is governed by the prime minister, who leads, coordinates, and maintains a series of ministers who are advised and supported by the civil service. In this view, prime ministerial government has replaced cabinet government as a result of the increased role of political parties, the influence of the cabinet secretariat, which is close to the prime minister, the control of the prime minister over patronage and major civil service appointments in the departments, and the influence of the mass media and television in particular, which normally focus attention on the leader. In addition, the prime minister has more time for thinking about general policy issues or current problems than do the ministers at the head of particular departments who are responsible for a heavy administrative load.

Certainly it is true that the prime minister has sometimes taken the initiative in foreign affairs and in emergencies and has been personally responsible for political decisions, of which in recent years the Falklands war in 1982 to resist the seizure by Argentina of the Falkland Islands administered by Britain and Blair's support of the war on terrorism and in Iraq were the most striking. In addition, until recently, the cabinet did not discuss the annual budget and was only informed about it a day before the budget was introduced in the House of Commons.

Although the powers of the prime minister are strong, they are qualified in certain respects. The prime minister can retain power only as long as he or she retains control over the party,

REVIEW 2.5

THE CENTER OF BRITISH GOVERNMENT

The center of British government in 2005 comprises the Prime Minister's Office, the Cabinet and its committees, and the Cabinet Office, as well as the Treasury, the Law Officers, and the parliamentary business managers.

THE PRIME MINISTER'S OFFICE

Located in 10 Downing Street, the Prime Minister's Office is run by a chief of staff, appointed as a temporary civil servant. It includes a number of units: the Private Office, the Political Office, the Press Office, the Strategic Communications Unit, and the Policy Unit, and also a small number of special advisers to help with specific areas of policy.

The Private Office manages the flow of business to and from Prime Minister Blair, arranging his timetable and the documents he needs to see, and briefing him before public meetings and the House of Commons. The Political Office handles Blair's relations with the Labour Party in Parliament and in the country; its members are political appointees, not civil servants. The Press Office deals with the government's relations with the media; its head, Alastair Campbell, appointed as a temporary civil servant, was a powerful and controversial figure between 1997 and 2001. The Strategic Communications Unit provides a unified presentation of government policy to reflect the government's overall program. The Policy Unit, staffed by special advisers, is concerned with the main policy issues of the government, proposing and evaluating initiatives taken by the departments.

THE CABINET OFFICE

Created in 1916, the Cabinet Office headed by the PM is run by the Cabinet Secretary, who since 1983 has been the head of the Home Civil Service. The Cabinet Office is at the center of British government, responsible for coordinating government business and for reviewing expenditures on and managing government security and intelligence operations. It assists the PM and ministers on selection of senior civil servants. Its two main functions are to assist the Cabinet and its committees and to manage the civil service and the machinery of government. It ensures the efficient dispatch of business in those bodies, records decisions, and distributes them to relevant ministers and officials.

Connected with the Cabinet Office are innovations by Tony Blair aimed at dealing with issues that cut across a number of departmental lines. The most important of these are the Social Exclusion Unit and the Performance and Innovation Unit.

THE TREASURY

In 2005 the Treasury is headed by Gordon Brown, a political rival of Prime Minister Blair. The Treasury is the guardian of the public purse, coordinating and supervising the spending of public departments and offices. It has considerable influence over the direction of government policy.

and over both the cabinet and Parliament. Unlike the U.S. president, he or she does not have a fixed term of office.

The range of the prime minister's choice of cabinet is very limited compared with that of the U.S. president; moreover, he or she is always aware of potential successors in the cabinet.

The prime minister still relies more than the U.S. president on collective decision making, but the relationship between the prime minister and the cabinet changes with the personality of the individuals and issues involved. Thatcher often appeared to act in an authoritarian way. By contrast, Major was a more tactful and less abrasive person. Blair has been forceful and commanding, and has tended to put less stress on decisions made at the full collective cabinet level. He has been criticized for "presidentialism."

One can conclude that the relationship between the prime minister and the cabinet is molded by the personality and preferences of the prime minister and by the political conditions and problems of the country. Other PMs besides Blair, such as Churchill and Thatcher, have also been accused of being presidential or being elected dictators exercising strong power and leadership, and ignoring both cabinet government and the House of Commons.

THE CIVIL SERVICE

The British civil service has long been admired for its competence, political impartiality, and dedication, and only in recent years have mounting criticisms led to structural changes in its organization. In the nineteenth century, the civil service was based on patronage and was sometimes corrupt and inefficient. The modern civil service is based on the 1854 Northcote-Trevelyan report, most of whose recommendations were implemented. The civil service became a single organization instead of a series of separate departmental staffs. Entry into the service was based on open competition, not on patronage. The successful candidate entered the service, rather than a particular department, and could be transferred from one department to another.

All examinations were conducted by the Civil Service Commission, not the individual departments, and corresponded to both the level and academic content of those taken in the educational system at the same age of applicants. The exams were always general rather than specific.

The civil service is organized into departments according to subject matter. Almost all departments have their headquarters in London in or near Whitehall, and some have branch offices throughout the country. The civil service, based on the distinction between intellectual and routine work, was divided into three servicewide classes: administrative, executive, and clerical. Outside these classifications were the professional, scientific, and technical officials, as well as the manual and manipulative workers, mostly in the postal and telegraph systems.

Criticism of various aspects of civil service organization and behavior mounted in the 1960s, based largely on the elitist nature of the senior civil service, their limited experience, their lack of initiative, the lack of scientists in top administrative positions, narrowness of outlook, and poor methods of training. As a result, the Fulton Committee on the civil service was established. Reporting in 1968, the committee was critical of the civil service's stress on the gifted amateur and generalist who was expected to be able to deal with any subject matter. It was also critical of the division of the civil service into general classes, the inferior status of scientists, the relative lack of specialized experts, and the frequent movement of senior civil servants between departments.

Only some of the changes recommended were introduced. A Civil Service Department was established, taking over the management of the service from the Treasury Department. A Civil Service College was set up to give courses in management techniques to new entrants. The three-class organization was ended, and part of the service was restructured along classless, unified lines. In the 523,000 civil service in 2005, the largest unit is the administrative group, composed of the former three classes. An important change was a new grade, administrative trainee, made to strengthen middle management. The Civil Service Department was abolished by Margaret Thatcher in 1981, but

REVIEW
2.6
QUANGOS (QUASI AUTONOMOUS NONGOVERNMENTAL ORGANIZATIONS) OR NONDEPARTMENTAL PUBLIC BODIES

- About 6,700 QUANGOS in 2005, spending one-third of public expenditure.
- Responsible for administration (e.g., Audit Commission, Medical Research Council, Forest Commission) or advice (e.g., Parole Board, Consumers Panel, Political Honors Scouting Committee).
- Mostly appointed by ministers; many business people appointed.
- Decentralize administration and bring in non–civil servants.
- Not directly accountable to those who use public services.

the prime minister remains in charge of the machinery of government. In 1988, Thatcher proposed a plan for semiautonomous agencies to manage services now administered by departments. By 2005, over 100 such agencies had been set up, employing about three quarters of civil servants. The general idea behind these agencies is to introduce a more entrepreneurial and competitive spirit into administration. Besides the executive agencies a large number of QUANGOs have been set up, run by non–civil servants appointed by a minister.

A constant cause of criticism of the senior civil service—the 3,000 top positions in the home and foreign service—has been that its members come largely from the middle and upper class, with less than 5 percent coming from the working class, and that a high proportion of those in the elite group, the former administrative class, was educated at the public schools and at Oxford and Cambridge. About three-quarters of top officials come from Oxbridge and about half from the public schools. The proportions are even higher for entrants into the senior foreign civil service, of which about 10 percent were educated at Eton. Yet, in 2005, a quarter of top jobs will be held by women, and a quarter will come from ethnic minorities.

The Role of the Civil Service

The senior civil servants advise ministers on formulating policy and decision making. Their role

is based on impartiality and anonymity, though the latter has been eroded in recent years. All governments, irrespective of political persuasion, have been served loyally by the nonpolitical permanent civil servants.

The work of the civil service is anonymous because of the principle of ministerial responsibility; the minister alone is responsible to Parliament for the operation of his or her department, even though in practice the minister may not always be aware of what has been done. Civil servants are free to give unbiased and frank advice to ministers without having to defend their views.

The obverse of anonymity has been the secrecy behind the making of decisions, both in form and content. The shielding of the civil service from the glare of partisan politics has also meant that it is restricted in its political activities. No member of the senior administrative group, above the clerical staff, can participate in national political activity; a member can take part in local politics only with departmental permission.

The determination of policy is the responsibility of ministers; the task of the civil service is to carry out that policy with energy and goodwill. The minister is a politician, not an expert on the issues of his or her department, and he or she must decide policy not only on its own merits, but in light of the government program as a whole and of what is politically rather than administratively possible at a certain point.

A CLOSER LOOK 2.10

CIVIL SERVANTS AND POLICY ADVICE

During the 1990s, and especially during the Blair government since 1997, two new factors have been apparent. One factor is that, ministers, who have tended to appear less frequently before Parliament and who have nonofficial advisers and spin doctors, have seemed less dependent on civil servants, who have become more a vehicle for managerial responsibilities than for policy advice. The other factor is a certain tension between two different views of a proper public service ethos. One view, the traditional one, is that civil servants are concerned with protecting the public good, ensuring good government, which might entail checks on ministers. The second view is that the primary function of civil servants is to serve ministers, whose will and political interests are paramount. The traditional view seems less certain today than in the past.

But the reality of ministerial–civil service relations is often different from the theory. Departmental policy may often result from past administrative experience and the cumulative decisions made by the civil servants while dealing with individual cases. Moreover, civil servants do not merely implement policy; they also play a role in policy making, advising on options for new policies. The long experience and great knowledge of the senior administrators may often lead them to take the initiative in suggesting new policies. Ministers are not experts in the affairs of their departments and have time to pay attention to only a relatively small number of those affairs.

Ministers may often accept the advice or acquiesce in the views of their civil servants. The role of the civil service has grown with the vast increase in government business, owing to the expanded activity of government in internal affairs; the time pressures on ministers; the influence of the cabinet secretariat; the growth of interdepartmental committees, which tend to settle problems at an early stage; and the creation of high-level civil service committees to parallel and give advice to cabinet committees.

But influential as the civil service may be, ministers are not its puppets, nor are civil servants "statesmen in disguise." Senior civil servants are mostly concerned with the administration of existing policies rather than policy planning, with immediate needs rather than long-term policy.

The interaction between ministers and senior civil servants is complex, but the political ministers are still the dominant element in the policy-making process.

THE LEGISLATURE

Parliament—or strictly speaking the Queen-in-Parliament, since the monarch must assent to all legislation—is the supreme legislative body. It has the authority to pass, change, or repeal any law without being subject to restraint or veto by the courts of law or any other body; on the contrary, Parliament can reverse the decisions of the courts. No issues are outside the control of Parliament. It can pass retrospective legislation that legalizes past illegalities and punishes actions that were lawful when performed. By the 1911 Parliament Act, the term of Parliament is fixed at five years, though it can be dissolved at any time. But Parliament is able to prolong its own life as it did during both world wars. One Parliament cannot bind its successors.

In fact, Parliament uses self-restraint in the exercise of this legal supremacy. It is conscious of the common law tradition and of political conventions that foster moderation. The effective power of Parliament is limited in real ways. Parliament rarely passes legislation which is contrary to the views of the population or deprives individuals of rights. The principle of the mandate suggests that the electorate has given general approval of changes proposed by the electoral manifesto of the successful party. Though this does not mean that the electorate has approved of all proposals in the manifesto, it implies that a major change will only rarely be introduced in Parliament if it was not included in the party manifesto, except in a time of emergency or crisis.

Parliamentary action is also affected and influenced by the major interest groups in the country, which by convention are always consulted on legislation related to them. In the 1960s and 1970s some regarded the trade unions as having a virtual veto power on proposals concerning industrial relations and incomes policy. Perhaps most important of all, Parliament is dominated by the government, which, as the majority party, generally controls the time, procedure, and actions of Parliament and is responsible for the initiation of all financial and most legislative proposals.

In the 1970s a new factor, British membership in the European Community (EC), now the European Union (EU), affected parliamentary supremacy. Britain is now pledged to adhere to EU decisions, which signifies qualification of Parliament's legal supremacy. The European Court of Justice ruled in 1990 that British courts could suspend a statute that was incompatible with law of the European Community. The Court ruled in 1991 that parts of a British law breached the law of the EC and therefore had to be changed. Parliamentary supremacy has also been limited by the 1950 European Convention on Human Rights, by which Britain accepted the obligation to recognize certain fundamental rights.

Composition of Parliament

The two chambers of Parliament now at Westminister have existed for seven centuries. Though for some time the House of Commons has been the more significant political body, the House of Lords had an unlimited veto power over legislation until 1911. In that year the Parliament Act limited the veto of the Lords to two years over bills passed by the Commons in three successive sessions and abolished the veto over financial bills. In 1949 this delaying power of the Lords was reduced to one year.

House of Lords

Until 1999, the House of Lords consisted of about 1,330 members. Its heterogeneous composition reflected the nature of its origin with the greater noblemen and higher clergy. The main categories were the following:

1. Some 760 hereditary peers (since 1958 including women) who inherit or have been appointed to the peerage and who pass on the titles to their heirs; since the Peerage Act of 1963 they can disclaim their titles for their lifetime.

2. About 550 life peers, men and women, created under the Life Peerage Act of 1958; their title expires at their death.

3. Twelve Lords of Appeal in Ordinary (Law Lords), who are appointed to act as judges when the House of Lords acts as a court of law; they must have been barristers for at least 15 years and have held high judicial office for at least 2 years.

4. Twenty-six senior dignitaries of the Church of England; they are the archbishops of Canterbury and York, the Bishops of London, Durham, and Winchester, and 21 other bishops in their order of seniority as bishops.

5. In 2005, 126 members are women.

The House of Lords Act 1999 ended the right of all but 92 of hereditary peers to sit in the upper chamber. Further changes are to come. In future, members may be chosen through an electoral system and through appointment.

Although the House of Lords still has the function of considering and approving all legislation, its powers have been significantly limited by the Parliament Acts of 1911 and 1949. The Lords can propose amendments to bills and can delay them by voting against them, but they have no power of absolute veto. Since 1949, a bill passed by the Commons in two successive sessions does not need the consent of the House of Lords. This procedure was used five times between 1911 and 2002, and in 2004 to pass a bill banning foxhunting.

The House of Lords has no power over finances. It can still reject, however, delegated legislation, which requires the approval of both Houses. By convention, it will not vote against the principles of a government bill if the bill was featured in the governing party's electoral manifesto.

The Lords are unpaid; however, since 1957, attending members receive a daily allowance for expenses and lodging. Because of the experience in public affairs and the intellectual caliber of many of the new life peers—as well as the presence of past and present cabinet ministers, other public servants, and former MPs—debate on important topics in the House of Lords may often be on a high level.

The subordination of the Lords to the Commons and to the executive has been accepted in general, but proposed legislation has sometimes been delayed. In 2004, the Lords rejected a bill calling for the abolition of the position of Lord Chancellor.

It is this power of delay and the Conservative majority in the House of Lords that have been the main reasons for criticism. In a democratic system like the British, it seems paradoxical for a nonelected body to delay the legislation passed by the elected lower chamber and to claim it is acting in the best interests of the country. Because of the automatic Conservative plurality in the House of Lords, a Labour government had more to fear in this regard than a Conservative one.

The House of Lords still performs a useful role as an organ of review in the revision of legislation, the initiation of noncontroversial legislation, the discussion of important topics, and the examination of delegated legislation—which all save the time of the Commons. It performs an important judicial function as the final Court of Appeal and Court of Criminal Appeal. By convention, only the Law Lords and the lord chancellor attend these sittings of the House as a court.

House of Commons

There are now 646 members (MPs) of the House of Commons elected from the territorial constituencies of the country. The number and distribution of the seats can be altered according to population changes after recommendations by the four boundary commissions. Currently, 529 represent English, 40 Welsh, 59 Scottish, and 18 Northern Ireland constituencies. Members are elected at a general election or at a by-election on the death or resignation of an MP.

There are no property, religious, sex, or education disqualifications. Any person over 21 can be elected, except members of the House of Lords, aliens, clergy of the established churches and the Catholic Church, felons, and holders of most official positions other than members of the government. Since 1963, an MP who has succeeded to the peerage can disclaim his title and remain in the Commons.

A CLOSER LOOK

2.11

THE HOUSE OF LORDS: INTERIM REFORM

A major constitutional change was made by the House of Lords Act 1999, which removed the automatic right of hereditary peers to sit in the upper house of Parliament, ending 700 years of tradition. By a compromise agreement, the House of Lords will retain 92 hereditary peers until the second stage of its reform. Two of these are ceremonial persons, 15 were elected by the whole house, and 75 were chosen by hereditary peers voting in political party groups. Proposals by a Royal Commission for the second stage of reform were introduced in January 2000; the essential one was that a new chamber would be chosen, part appointed and part elected, to represent the countries and regions of the nation. No immediate action was taken. In terms of declared political affiliation in 2005, the House of Lords has 736 members, consisting of 216 Labours, 211 Conservatives, 74 Liberal Democrats, 218 others, 26 bishops, and 28 current and former Law Lords.

MPs are paid less and have inadequate facilities compared with U.S. congressional members. In 2005 they receive a salary of £57,485, secretarial assistance, travel and stationery costs, and a London supplementary allowance. There is no shortage of candidates for the Commons. People are attracted to it for nonmaterial rewards, including public service, personal prestige, and the opportunity to exert influence on public affairs. However in recent years, as a result of certain improper or questionable behavior, MPs have to register their financial interests and, since 1996, cannot accept payment for lobbying.

The glory of Parliament may have dimmed somewhat in recent years, but the Commons still plays a significant role in the political system (see Table 2.14). Parliament not only possesses legislative supremacy and authorizes all expenditure and taxation; the Commons is politically important because its party composition is the basis for the formation of governments. It enables the leaders of one political party to rule and those of the opposition party to be considered as a possible alternative government. It is the major political arena in which there is continuous interaction among the parties. Ministers explain and defend their policies in it against the attacks of the opposition.

If it is not the real determinant of policy or decisions, Parliament wields influence over the executive which makes concessions to it. For its members, Parliament is a forum for the raising of complaints and grievances on behalf of their constituents, for arguing political views of their own, and for subjecting the executive to criticism. It is also the main path to political distinction and to membership in the government.

TABLE 2.14

THE POWERS AND LIMITS OF THE HOUSE OF COMMONS

Powers

Provides road to political success and to becoming a minister

Main forum for discussion of grievances of constituents

Approves legislation and policy thus giving them greater legitimacy; debates legislation and motions

Allows representation and expression of different views of citizens on policy

Asks questions of ministers

Greater independence of MPs in voting; governments defeated in some standing committees

Departmental select committees in House of Commons investigate administration and recommend policy

Some committees discuss issues of European Union

Limits

Power of executive

Increasing impact of interest groups outside of Parliament

Increasing burden of work

Little impact on decisions of European Union

Who Becomes an MP?

MPs have become increasingly professional in their background and lifestyle and, therefore, less characteristic of their constituents. This is especially true in the Parliamentary Labour Party, where the proportion of manual workers has fallen and that of professionals has increased

A CLOSER LOOK

2.12

DID I HEAR A WORD?

MPs may not utter certain words or phrases about each other in the House of Commons. The forbidden locutions include: *blackguard, cad, criminal, liar, coward, hypocrite, murderer, Pharisee, rat, traitor, guttersnipe, dog, stool-pigeon, swine, ruffian, snail, jackass, jerk, impertinent pup.*

since 1945. The average age of the PLP has fallen; recruiting younger MPs generally means less opportunity for working-class candidates, who tend to emerge later in life.

The Conservative MPs illustrate the postwar shift away from landowners, farmers, and people with an aristocratic background to businesspeople and industrial technocrats. A considerable number have been local councillors. Conservative MPs have rarely had working-class backgrounds.

The number of women MPs in the postwar period was small: about 5 percent until 1987 and 8 percent in 1992. In 1997, a record number of 120 women were elected. Women have always been underrepresented in the Commons, which has been a male-dominated "club." One, Betty Boothroyd, was Speaker, 1992–2000.

There has been a trend for MPs to remain longer in Parliament and thus to be regarded as professional politicians. The House of Commons has always been attractive to people in the professions, who in many cases combine their careers as lawyers, journalists, or businesspeople with afternoon and evening attendance in the House.

MPs and Political Parties

All MPs are members of political parties, and the arrangements in the Commons reflect the fact that its working is interrelated with the party system and the operation of government.

The only exception to the partisan nature of MPs is the Speaker (with three deputies), who is the chief officer of the House of Commons. Unlike the U.S. counterpart, the British Speaker is an impartial, nonpartisan figure who gives up party associations. The general rule is that the Speaker, who is elected at the beginning of a Parliament, will be reelected in subsequent Parliaments irrespective of which party controls a majority. For the first time a woman was elected in 1992.

The chamber in which MPs meet is small and rectangular. It is a political arena in which the opposing parties physically face each other, as shown in Figure 2.5. The Speaker sits at one end of the chamber. The benches to his or her right are used by the government party, while the official opposition party and other parties not

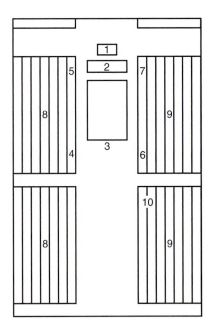

1. Speaker
2. Clerks
3. Mace
4. Prime minister
5. Cabinet
6. Leader of opposition
7. Shadow cabinet
8. Government party MPs (backbenchers)
9. Main opposition party MPs (backbenchers)
10. MPs of other opposition parties

Figure 2.5 HOUSE OF COMMONS

supporting the government sit on his or her left. The members of the government and the shadow cabinet sit on the front benches, with their supporters behind them on the back benches. The physical separation reflects the political differences between the two sides.

The smallness of the chamber, which seats only 350 MPs, together with the fact that MPs speak from their places rather than from a rostrum, has led to a more intimate style of speech than is often the case in other countries. By tradition, MPs do not read speeches or speak boisterously. They refer to colleagues in a dignified and polite way.

With rare exceptions the MPs are organized in parliamentary parties. The Parliamentary Labour Party (PLP) is composed of Labour members of both Houses. The major organ of the Conservative Party in Parliament is the 1922 Committee, composed of all Conservative backbenchers.

The Opposition

The official opposition, the largest nongovernment party in Parliament, is a vital part of the British system. Its leaders are seen inside and outside Parliament, as an alternative government. Its function is both to subject government to criticism and to seek to replace it, as well as to participate in the working of the system.

The opposition acts as a responsible group in criticism of the government. It proposes alternative policies and tries to change government policies, get concessions on government bills, and defeat the government. By convention, governments resign or request dissolution of Parliament if defeated on a major question, though since 1867 only five governments have resigned for this reason. In 1979 the opposition successfully moved a vote of no confidence for the first time since 1892. In Parliament, the opposition is continually addressing itself to the electorate as a whole with its eyes on the next election.

The opposition also cooperates with the government party in formulating the business of the Commons. It chooses the subjects for debate on a number of occasions, currently on the 16

Prime Minister Tony Blair, 2005.

days available to it. It is given time at the committee stage of bills to move amendments and time in the House of Commons itself for both opposition leaders and backbenchers to question ministers. The government even provides the time for the opposition to move motions of censure against it.

Since 1937 there has been an official, paid leader of the opposition who is consulted by the prime minister on political arrangements; by convention, the shadow cabinet receives information from cabinet ministers relevant to the conduct of affairs. There is consultation between the two sides on some questions concerning foreign affairs and defense.

The opposition is represented on standing and select committees, now about 40, in proportion to its membership in the Commons. An accepted rule is that the chairpersons of some committees are members of the opposition.

How Important Is the MP?

Important though MPs are, their prominence has declined for several reasons: the extension of the suffrage, the organization of constituency associations and the rise of disciplined political parties; the increase in the function and activity of government and the growth in power of the bureaucracy; and the nature of modern general elections, which are to a large degree about which party leader will become prime minister.

MPs are aware that the electorate is the ultimate political sovereign and that their reelection depends on their activity in Parliament. Attendance is not compulsory, and no financial loss is attached to nonattendance, but it is rare for MPs to neglect their parliamentary duties. MPs also frequently visit their constituencies, particularly on weekends, and hold "surgeries," at which they meet their constituents. They ask questions in the Commons and speak in debates on matters affecting their areas.

The crucial fact about MPs is that, with rare exceptions, they are members of parties that they are expected to support loyally and without which they could not have been elected. In the Commons, MPs are still subject to the persuasion, if not the discipline, of the whips and rarely engage in a conflict with the parliamentary leadership. Party cohesion exists partly because of agreement by party MPs on policy issues, partly because of ambition for promotion, especially among those of the government party, and partly because of the probable political isolation experienced by those consistently opposing party policy. The ultimate threat by a prime minister, faced by revolt within his party, is to dissolve Parliament, but this is a theoretical rather than a real menace. Nevertheless, some revolts against the leaders, when the party is in power and in opposition, have occurred.

This recent greater assertiveness and independence of MPs can be attributed to a number of factors. MPs found that they were seldom denied readoption as candidates or ministerial promotion because of their rebellious actions. Defeats of the government—65 times between 1972 and 1979, and 26 times a session during the Blair government in 2000—did not mean

resignation or the dissolution of Parliament, which will occur only on a motion of no confidence. The major parties have been internally divided on significant recent issues such as the European Union, devolution, and income policy. MPs have believed, correctly in a number of cases, that fear of defeat may make a government change its mind.

For some time the dominant body in the operation of the Commons has been the government, which controls the timetable, the allocation of time, and the procedure of the Commons and is responsible for the initiation of most legislation. During the years from 1939 to 1948, backbenchers had no legislative initiative; they currently have 12 days to introduce bills as well as 10 days to move motions.

The great increase in the amount of legislation, and in its scope, variety, and technical nature, has meant both that few MPs are knowledgeable about much of the legislation and the wide range of problems with which the Commons deals and that little time is available for the discussion of government legislation. Most amendments of that legislation are minor, and they are made or agreed to by the government. Of those amendments proposed by ministers, almost all are accepted by the Commons; of those proposed by backbenchers, few are successful.

In addition, many rules are now made by ministers in the form of delegated legislation. There are several reasons for this large development of ministerial power: the technical nature of the rules, the speed with which they can be made, the flexibility available to change them, and the opportunity of discretionary choice. Although some opportunity to discuss delegated legislation is available to MPs, there is little parliamentary scrutiny of it.

An Assenting Assembly

MPs participate in the work of the Commons in a variety of ways: through question time, participation in debates on legislation and on policy, membership on standing and select committees, and proposal of motions and initiation of some legislation.

In the parliamentary golden age of the mid-nineteenth century, the Commons regularly defeated governments without being dissolved. Since that period, few governments have been defeated and obliged to resign or have Parliament dissolved as a result of the actions of the House of Commons.

A number of criticisms can be made of the failings of contemporary parliaments. Parliamentary control over administration and finance is ineffective. Most MPs feel inadequately informed about administration. The real initiative in the legislative process and policy making is in the hands of the executive. Procedure in the Commons is still poorly organized and archaic. The majority political party is the real strength underlying the operation of the political system. Nevertheless, recent experience has shown that MPs can exercise some control over governments. The assertiveness and dissent among MPs led to a surprising number of government defeats in the 1970s and 1980s.

JUDGES AND POLITICS

Unlike the United States, Britain does not have a system of judicial review, and courts cannot declare legislation void. As the legal sovereign, Parliament, not the courts, decides on the nature and extent of legislative power. The function of British judges is to apply the law to the particular cases before their courts rather than to decide on the desirability or correctness of the law itself. Some judges interpret the law in a way that upholds individual liberty or in accordance with social and personal justice. But most judges interpret statutes narrowly, holding that it is Parliament, not judicial interpretation, that should change a law that is unjust.

British judges have long had the reputation of being impartial and neutral. The judges' impartiality results partly from the common law tradition and judgment based on precedent and partly from the method of their appointment. Judges are not political appointees; few of them have been MPs, and even fewer have been partisans of a political party, as they come from the ranks of barristers with long and successful careers. In the legal profession, there are now about 5,500 barristers, of whom 750 are women, and over 40,000 solicitors.

Judges are independent of the other branches of government and their salaries are not open to discussion by Parliament. Since 1701, judges have been appointed on "good behavior," meaning until retirement, which since 1959 has been at age 75. They can only be dismissed by resolutions of both Houses, an event that has not yet occurred. They are scrupulous about a fair hearing in court and impartial application of the law.

The qualities of impartiality and neutrality are always present in cases concerning disputes between private individuals. But there are also other cases in which decisions of judges may affect a wider group of people, or in which they can exercise some discretion. These cases have recently included subjects such as immigration, industrial relations, race relations, police powers, and human rights. It is on questions of this kind that the generally conservative view of judges may be felt.

Judges form one of the prominent elite groups of the country. Over 75 percent of senior judges were educated at public schools and at Oxford and Cambridge; over 80 percent come from upper-class or upper-middle-class backgrounds. A conservative position is to be expected from individuals who not only come from these social

TABLE 2.15

BRITISH JUDGES

Position	Men	Women
Lords of Appeal in Ordinary (Law Lords)	12	—
Lords Justice of Appeal	31	1
High Court Judges	88	6
Circuit Judges	486	30
Recorders	853	53
Assistant Recorders	297	52
District Judges	273	29
Deputy District Judges	632	84

Source: The Times, April 10, 1995.

backgrounds but also have had a successful career and adhere to the tradition of the common law and precedent.

Judges have been reluctant to limit the scope of ministerial powers and have habitually upheld the exercise of the discretionary power of ministers (who can take action under a statute if they think it necessary). Judges have approved executive action, provided it was not out of bounds or exercised unfairly, unreasonably, or in bad faith.

But in the last three decades, some judges have tried to control ministerial administrative action and assert judicial discretion in cases on the scope of executive prerogative in war or on ministerial privilege, or if they decided that ministers had exceeded their legal powers and had encroached on individual rights.

Britain does not have a strong system of administrative or constitutional law to control the actions of the political executive or administration. Yet in recent years the judiciary has been more active in scrutinizing and challenging executive actions, largely by reference to "fundamental rights" which need to be safeguarded as well as to the will of Parliament, the traditional basis for judgement. This kind of judicial review, though still rare, results from the increase of powers claimed by an active government and from the impact of European Union laws and charters which judges interpret.

The Human Rights Act 1998 not only provides for individuals to challenge executive actions but also allows the courts wide interpretive powers regarding those actions. Since 1998 the courts have decided on a number of occasions that ministers acted beyond their powers, and decided on issues stemming from British statutes in a way that they thought compatible with the European Convention on Human Rights. In addition to this convention, a series of international agreements such as the UN Convention on Refugees and the UN's Dublin Convention give judges the power to block deportation and repatriation of individuals suspected by the government to be linked to terrorist organizations.

Thinking Critically

1. Is it still true to speak of the British system as cabinet government?
2. Do you think the present electoral system in Britain should be changed?
3. Do you believe that the role of Parliament has been reduced in recent years?
4. Should the House of Lords be abolished?
5. What are the major differences between the British political parties?
6. Do you agree with those who say that civil servants are the real rulers in Britain?

KEY TERMS

backbencher *(101)*
by-election *(72)*
the City *(83)*
civil service *(94–96)*
common law *(96)*
Confederation of British Industry (CBI) *(83)*
Conservative Party *(78)*
constituency *(66)*
Crown *(84–85)*
legislation *(102)*
House of Commons *(98–99)*
House of Lords *(97–98)*
Labour Party *(78–80)*
marginal seat *(67)*
National Executive Committee (NEC) *(79)*
opposition *(101)*
party identification *(74–75)*
Plaid Cymru *(70)*
prime minister *(90–94)*
QUANGO *(95)*
Scottish National Party (SNP) *(70)*
Social and Liberal Democrats (SLD or Liberal Democrats) *(67, 77)*
Trades Union Congress (TUC) *(78, 83)*
Treasury *(93)*
Westminster *(97)*
whip *(102)*
Whitehall *(94)*

*F*URTHER READINGS

Blackburn, Robert. *The Electoral System in Britain* (London: Macmillan, 1995).

Butler, David, and Martin Westlake. *British Politics and European Elections 1999* (New York: St. Martin's 2000).

Butler, David, and Dennis Kavanagh. *The British General Election of 1997* (New York: St. Martin's, 1997).

Conley, Frank. *General Elections Today,* 2nd ed. (New York: Manchester University Press, 1992).

Crewe, Ivor, et al. *The British Electorate 1963–87* (New York: Cambridge University Press, 1991).

Jones, Bill, and Dennis Kavanagh. *British Politics Today,* 7th ed. (Manchester: Manchester University Press, 2003).

Loughlin James, et. al. *The Ulster Question Since 1945,* 2nd ed. (Basingstoke: Houndmills, 2004).

Norris, Pippa. *Electoral Change since 1945* (Oxford: Blackwell, 1997).

Richardson, Jeremy, ed. *Pressure Groups* (New York: Oxford University Press, 1993).

Wright, Anthony. *British Politics* (Oxford: Oxford University Press, 2003).

The Executive and Judiciary

Barber, James P. *The Prime Minister since 1945* (Cambridge: Blackwell, 1991).

Bogdanor, Vernon, ed., *The British Constitution in the 20th Century* (Oxford: Oxford University Press, 2003).

Foley, Michael. *The British Presidency: Tony Blair and the Politics of Public Leadership* (Manchester: Manchester University Press, 2000).

Griffith, J.A.G. *The Politics of the Judiciary,* 5th ed. (London: Fontana, 1997).

Hennessy, Peter. *The Prime Minister: The Office and Its Holders since 1945* (London: Penguin, 2000).

James, Simon. *British Cabinet Government,* 2nd ed. (New York: Routledge, 1999).

Laver, Michael, and Kenneth Shepsie, eds. *Cabinet Ministers and Parliamentary Government* (New York: Cambridge University Press, 1994).

Pilkington, Colin. *The Civil Service in Britain Today* (Manchester: Manchester University Press, 1999).

Seldon, Anthony, et al. *Blair* (London: Free Press, 2004).

Shell, Donald, and Richard Hodder-Williams. *Churchill to Major: The British Prime Ministership since 1945* (Armonk: Sharpe, 1995).

The Legislature

Bluth, Christopher, et al. *The Future of European Security* (Brookfield: Dartmouth, 1995).

Griffith, J.A.G., and Michael Ryle. *Parliament: Functions, Practice and Procedure* (London: Sweet and Maxwell, 1989).

Jogerst, Michael. *Reform in the House of Commons* (Lexington: University of Kentucky, 1993).

Norris, Pippa, and Joni Lovenduski. *Political Recruitment: Gender, Race and Class in the British Parliament* (New York: Cambridge University Press, 1995).

Norton, Philip. *Does Parliament Matter?* (New York: Harvester Wheatsheaf, 1993).

Norton, Philip, and David Wood. *Back from Westminster: British MPs and Their Constituents* (Lexington: University Press of Kentucky, 1993).

Rush, Michael, ed. *Parliament and Pressure Politics* (New York: Oxford University Press, 1990).

Shell, Donald. *The House of Lords,* 2nd ed. (New York: Harvester Wheatsheaf, 1992).

Silk, Paul, and Rhodri Walters. *How Parliament Works,* 4th ed. (New York: Longman, 1998).

Weir, Stuart, and David Beetham. *Political Power and Democratic Control in Britain* (London: Routledge, 1999).

C. PUBLIC POLICY

THE MIXED ECONOMY

Like other Western countries, Britain has a mixed economy. Part of it is owned and administered by public authorities; this public sector employs 5.1 million workers, including central and local government and public corporations. However, most of the economy is under private ownership and control. The private sector has increased since 1979 as the Conservative government cut the public sector and denationalized or "privatized" many enterprises.

Both Labour and Conservative governments intervened in economic affairs in the postwar period in differing degrees. This intervention stemmed partly from the desire to implement social principles such as the public ownership of resources, the welfare of citizens, and the reduction of unemployment, but also from the effort to solve economic problems by increasing production and trade. Governments therefore not only nationalized industries, but also promoted industrial development, supplied money and credits to both public and private enterprises, increased the level of investment, helped firms in trouble, proposed "targets" and planning agreements for industry and the restructuring of industry, and attempted to restrain wage increases.

The public sector today comprises three parts: central government, local government, and public–private partnerships, which have largely replaced the former nationalized industries and aim to deliver public services through private sector management.

Central government is responsible for all spending on social security benefits, health, defense, trade, industry, overseas payments and foreign aid, and central administration (see Table 2.16 and Figure 2.6). It also partly finances housing, education, transport, and law and order programs. The largest spending programs are on social security, health, the environment, education, transport, and defense. Most of the expenditure is paid for by taxation and social security

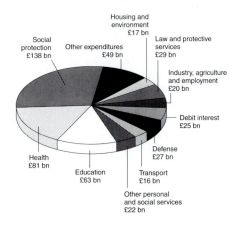

- Other expenditure includes spending on general public services, recreation, culture and religion, international cooperation and development, public service pensions, and other matters.
- Social protection includes tax credit payments.

Figure 2.6 BUDGET, 2004–2005

contributions, which in the late 1990s amounted to about 35–37 percent of GNP.

Local government now accounts for about one-quarter of total public spending. The largest item is education, followed by housing, transport, law and order, and social services. This expenditure is paid for by property taxes and by grants from the central government.

The nationalized industries in 1979 accounted for 10 percent of gross domestic product (GDP), employed almost 2 million (8 percent of the workforce), and took 14 percent of fixed investment. The industries dominated areas such as coal, electricity, gas, broadcasting, public transport, communications, and iron and steel. Because they were producers of basic goods and services, as well as large consumers of raw materials, they significantly affected investment, employment, prices, and cost of living in the whole economy. By 1988, denationalization had reduced them to 6 percent of GDP, 750,000 workers, and 9 percent of investment.

TABLE 2.16

BUDGET (general government transactions, £ million)		(2004 £1 = $1.8)	
Revenue	**2001**	**2002**	**2003**
Tax revenue	364,769	368,113	388,081
Taxes on income and wealth	147,665	142,463	145,725
Household income tax	108,915	109,047	113,142
Petroleum revenue tax	1,526	946	1,146
Other taxes on income	37,224	32,470	31,437
Taxes on production and imports	132,195	138,513	145,883
Value-added tax	63,974	68,778	75,124
Other taxes on products	50,177	50,971	51,662
Tobacco duties	7,638	7,947	8,079
Excise on hydrocarbon oils	22,046	22,070	22,476
Non-domestic rates	16,273	16,878	17, 157
Council Tax	15,068	16,448	18,423
National Insurance Contributions	62,887	63,520	70,629
Gross operating surplus	10,163	10,335	10,722
Interest and dividends from private sector and abroad	4,849	3,836	3,772
Interest and dividends (net) from public sector	5,663	5,732	5,792
Rent	1,862	1,879	1,525
Other current transfers	398	320	273
Total	**387,704**	**390,215**	**410,165**
Expenditure	**2001**	**2002**	**2003**
General public services	21,363	24,579	27,845
Defence	26,465	27,451	30,642
Public order and safety	19,064	21,333	23,193
Education	46,326	52,812	55,802
Health	60,718	67,005	75,588
Social protection	156,475	163,584	176,826
Housing and community amenities	6,131	7,025	8,288
Recreational, cultural, and religious affairs	4,749	5,449	5,808
Economic affairs	27,981	28,799	34,958
Environmental protection	4,832	5,449	5,856
Interest and dividends aid to private sector and abroad	23,492	21,211	22,403
Total	**397,596**	**424,697**	**467,209**

Source: United Kingdom National Accounts.

THE DECLINE OF NATIONALIZED INDUSTRIES

The motives to nationalize industries were varied. They included public control over significant parts of the economic system; efficient organization and development of the economy; influencing the level of investment to achieve full employment; better industrial relations; preventing possible abuse of a monopoly situation; continuation of enterprises, even if unprofitable, to provide a social service or minimize unemployment; or assistance to failing firms. Added to these economic and social reasons was the ideology of the Labour Party, whose constitution (Clause IV) called for "public ownership of the means of production, distribution, and exchange."

A major change took place with the privatization policy of the Thatcher government that consisted of selling off the assets and shares of nationalized industries to private owners. This policy also allowed some services previously administered by public authorities to be performed by private firms. Prime Minister Thatcher argued that privatization brought certain benefits: the industries would be more efficient and profitable in a more competitive market, away from interference of officials; their objectives would not be overridden by irrelevant political, social, and economic factors, thereby increasing business confidence; the government would raise large amounts by sales; Britain would become a property-owning democracy (now 11 million shareholders). By 1991 about 60 percent of state industry had been privatized. The government claimed that output, profits, investment, and industrial relations in those enterprises had all improved.

The Conservative government also sought to promote competition by ending the monopoly of a number of enterprises, such as long distance buses and express delivery services, and of certain professional activity, such as some legal work.

ECONOMIC PLANNING

All postwar British governments accepted the need for planning, which resulted from increased government activity and expenditure. They saw the need for creating nationalized industries and increasing productivity, economic growth, and exports. Governmental intervention took a variety of forms: financial aid and incentives to stimulate industrial investment; taxation changes and loans to strengthen development areas and transfer workers from services to manufacturing; physical controls to induce firms to move to less developed areas; subsidies to aid failing enterprises and controls on wages, prices, and foreign exchange. Bodies such as the National Economic Development Council (NEDC) and the National Enterprise Board were set up to assist the economy and to foster greater efficiency.

These governments sought, mainly through the annual budget, to maintain a high level of economic activity, and strove for full employment, economic growth, and a rising standard of living. They stressed expansion of demand rather than anti-inflationary measures, and relatively little attention was paid to restraint of money supply.

The Thatcher government broke with this approach. It sought, at first, to reduce inflation by restricting the money supply, hoping to increase output and employment. It tried to revitalize the private sector by lowering taxes and interest rates that would result from cuts in public expenditure and borrowing. It emphasized free market forces by reducing the public sector, taming the trade unions, ending controls on prices and wages, and trying to curb the spending of local authorities.

The government from 1979 on was particularly interested in limiting or controlling the power of the trade unions. Unions must now hold secret ballots for the election of union leaders, before a strike is called, and on their political funds. Limits have been set on picketing, secondary strike action, and closed shops. Union funds are now liable for damages in civil actions. Union membership declined substantially during the 1980s.

In the late 1980s, a policy at first called New Steps was introduced to separate executive functions of officials from policy making. The civil service would be reduced to a small core responsible for policy making, while many activities would be transferred to agencies which would deliver services and which would have a good deal of operational and budgetary autonomy, thus replacing civil service departments. By 2005 about 150 such agencies have been set up, employing three-quarters of all civil servants. Regulatory agencies have been set up to get public utility companies to provide good service for consumers and to protect the environment.

REVIEW
2.7

THATCHER AND BLAIR ECONOMICS AND SOCIAL POLICY

THATCHER

- Privatized national industries and utilities.
- Monetarism; minimal government intervention in economic affairs except for control of money supply.
- Chief concern to control inflation, which was linked to supply of money circulating in the economy.
- Curbed power of trade unions, cut taxes, introduced poll tax.

BLAIR

- Continued policy of keeping inflation low.
- Financed expenditure with taxation, usually low indirect tax.
- Accepted that free market, not the state, should be the main provider of goods and services. Brought private sector into public services, and used private firms to provide treatment in national health service.

In 2005 the private sector is employing three-quarters of civilian workers, of whom 19 percent belong to trade unions; by contrast, about 60 percent of public sector employees are union members. Public spending as a proportion of GDP between 1997 and 2000 fell from 41.2 to 37.7 percent but rose in the next year, reaching 42.6% in 2004. Both Major and Blair have wanted to extend private sector management in some major public services, especially in medical care and transport and education; outside contractors provide a range of services.

THE WELFARE STATE

The term *welfare state* implies the provision by the state of benefits and services, elements of social and economic security, including health care, subsidies for housing, sick and unemployment benefits, pensions, disability help, and family allowances. Britain has long concerned itself with the poor. Before 1914, national insurance, old-age pensions, and unemployment insurance were adopted. But it was not until after World War II that the plans for a welfare state and for social improvement were implemented.

The Labour government of 1945–1950 introduced the basic elements of a welfare system. Three elements of this system have been particularly important: social security, the national health service, and personal social services. The last is the responsibility of local authorities and voluntary organizations, though central government is responsible for setting national policies; the first two are the direct responsibility of central government.

Personal services help the elderly, the disabled, children, and young people. Older people represent the fastest growing part of the population, with consequent greater demands for services including advice by social workers, domestic help, provision of meals in homes, day centers, and recreational facilities.

Social Security

The social security system is a complex one with over 30 different benefits. It is the largest single area of government spending. The major postwar reform in this area has been the extension of national insurance to cover unemployment, sickness, maternity, retirement, industrial injuries, and death. A National Insurance Fund was established,

ECONOMIC AND SOCIAL POLICIES OF THE BLAIR GOVERNMENT, 1997–2005

ECONOMIC

- Bank of England given independent control of interest rates; Monetary Policy Committee of Bank of England officials and other economists to decide on those rates.
- Rise in tax burden (37.7 percent of GDP in 2000) though cut in basic rate of income tax.
- Abolished dividend tax credit for pension schemes.
- Abolished mortgage interest tax relief and married couple's allowance; increased child benefits.
- Less government intervention in industrial disputes and wage bargaining; less close collaboration with trade unions.
- Limited stress on redistribution of income.
- Labour Party gives up Clause IV; stress on public–private partnerships: privatization of some state-owned assets, including National Air Traffic Services, Horserace Totalisator Board, Royal Mint.
- Considerable growth in public sector jobs.

SOCIAL

- Increased number of university students, now 35 percent of age group.
- Maintained Conservative policies of national school tests and inspections.
- Abolished system of maintenance grants by which students qualified for help with living expenses.
- Recourse to private sector by National Health Service and some state schools.
- Benefits for employed parents, and maternity leave increased to three months; protection for workers if dismissed.
- New official categories of social class; now seven classes reflecting a person's position in the labor market and the nature of the employment contract.
- Minimum income guarantee for pensioners; free TV licenses for those over 75.
- Welfare spending increased since 1997 by over £40 billion in 2004.

---

to which insured persons and their employers contribute and from which they are paid when necessary. The contributions cover about 90 percent of the benefits paid, with the state paying the rest. The system is universal, applying to everyone, but individuals can have their own private insurance in addition to the national system.

Unemployment benefit is payable for one year in each case of unemployment. Sickness benefits of various kinds cover loss of earnings during absence from work. Maternity pay, normally for 18 weeks, is now usually paid by employers. A variety of different grants, depending on the individuals and relationships, are paid on death. The most significant of these grants go to widows who receive allowances for the first 26 weeks of widowhood, as well as other possible allowances.

Since 1946 pensions have been paid to men at age 65 and women at age 60; individuals may defer retirement for five years and qualify for a higher pension, however. Since 1959, the basic pension has been supplemented by an additional amount in return for larger contributions, an earning-related scheme. Pensions are also paid to disabled veterans. An injured worker receives benefits for a period depending on the disablement.

Family allowances have been given since 1945 to mothers who receive a sum for all children who are below the minimum school-leaving age or in full-time education (now up to the age of 19). In 1977, child benefits replaced family allowances and the income tax allowances, which have been phased out. Children also receive other benefits: medical examinations, free milk (which since 1971 has been limited to those under 7 years of age), and school meals. Benefits introduced in 1988 included income support for families whose income is under a certain level, a family credit for low-income working families with children, and aid for rent and local rates.

The cost of these services has been high. Social security accounts for about 9 percent and retirement pensions alone for 6 percent of GNP. If health and education are included, the social services account for over 23 percent of GNP and 47 percent of total public expenditure. But in spite of the cost, for political reasons Conservative governments did not reduce the services and benefits. Indeed, expenditure increased under Thatcher and Major, partly because of the larger numbers of elderly and unemployed people and single-parent families.

The National Health Service

Introduced in 1946, the National Health Service (NHS) was one of the towering achievements of the Labour government. It was a centrally planned, government-funded institution, providing a full range of medical services available to all residents, regardless of income. It is financed through general taxation, national insurance contributions, and charges for prescribed drugs.

When the NHS was established, the state acquired all hospitals except teaching hospitals. Doctors could no longer sell their practices or set up practice in an area that already had too many doctors. But concessions included the right of doctors to private practice, maintenance of private paying beds in hospitals, the right of the patients to choose their doctor, and local rather than central administration of hospitals. Medical and dental services were free to all who used the service. Doctors in the service receive a basic salary plus a certain fee for each patient. Hospitals have been run by regional boards and committees. Over 90 percent of doctors decided to enter the service.

Residents in Britain can choose to join the system, as over 90 percent have done. They have free choice of an NHS doctor, dentist, optician, and pharmacist and have access to specialists and hospital treatment through their doctor. About 11 percent of the population in 2005 is covered by various forms of private health insurance. Spending on publicly funded patients treated privately currently accounts for about 5 percent of total expenditure on the NHS.

The creation of the NHS and the provision of free medicine resulted initially in higher costs than had been anticipated. Charges, covering only a small part of the cost, were therefore imposed for drug prescriptions, dental treatment, dentures, and spectacles. But over 80 percent of the cost is financed from the regular tax. The most costly item has been the hospitals, which now account for about three-fifths of the total cost; the teaching hospitals are particularly expensive. The NHS, employing 1.4 million people, including 30,000 doctors, accounts in 2005 for 10 percent of public expenditure and 8 percent of GDP, and about $110 billion a year.

Considerable variation exists in the performance of NHS trusts, hospitals, and doctors' surgeries throughout the country. There are now fewer doctors per 1,000 patients than in most Western European countries, and about half the comparable number in the United States. The NHS has faced some difficulties in recent years because of the demands on it. Problems have arisen over pay for medical personnel, industrial disputes, low morale, waiting lists in hospitals and for operations, a shortage of specialists, demands caused by the increasing proportion of older people, and the high cost of medical care and high-technology equipment. The cost of the NHS, which treats 30 million patients a year, rose 50 percent in real terms between 1979 and 1990.

The government has therefore recently tried to shift emphasis from the treatment of illness to the promotion of health and the prevention of disease, and to decentralize the system by allowing some hospitals to administer their own budgets and to become self-governing trusts with their own boards of directors. In 2000 the government agreed that health authorities could arrange for citizens to travel to continental Europe for operations, largely paid for by the NHS.

FOREIGN AFFAIRS

At the end of World War II, Britain was still one of the three major powers; its empire and Commonwealth contained one-quarter of the world's population. It remained the major European economic and military power until the mid-1950s. By 1952 Britain had manufactured atomic bombs, and in 1957 it exploded a thermonuclear bomb. It was the dominant power in the Middle East and the second most important power in the Far East, and had a "special relationship" with the United States.

But in the postwar period, Britain has become an important but middle-sized power. It declined economically, in both production and trade, as other nations developed industrially. British economic growth was lower than that of other major Western European countries. Britain increased its imports not only of raw materials but also of manufactured chemical and semi-manufactured products. Britain never fully recaptured its export markets, over half of which had been lost as a result of World War II. Although Britain has been technologically inventive—for example, television, radar, the jet engine, and the swing-line plane—it has been deficient in exploiting inventions.

The British Empire has been almost completely transformed into independent nations, most of them now members of the Commonwealth. Unable to produce missiles to launch its bombs, Britain became dependent on the United States, which supplied it with the Polaris missile. Britain could not sustain the burden of supporting other countries, such as Greece and Turkey, or of protecting Palestine, from which it withdrew in 1948. It began withdrawing its forces from other areas: the Suez Canal zone in 1956, Jordan in 1957, Iraq in 1958, the Persian Gulf in 1969, Singapore in 1971, and Hong Kong in 1997.

Britain's relative economic decline, as well as the demand for independence of its former colonies, affected its foreign policy. Both major parties agreed that Britain should be a nuclear power and for a time sought to maintain its bases east of Suez. Both Labour and Conservatives intervened to help keep the peace, to safeguard oil, tin, and rubber supply lines, and to protect other countries, such as Malaysia from 1948 on, Kenya between 1952 and 1960, and Kenya and Tanganyika in 1964, as well as the Middle East. About 10 percent of the central government's expenditure was for defense; in 2005 it was 5.5 percent.

Britain had to adjust its foreign policy to three developments: the decline in its special relationship with the United States, the end of the empire and the increase in the Commonwealth, and the creation of the European Community (now the European Union).

From Special Relationship to Ally

The close British-American relationship during World War II was transformed by postwar events, the first of which was the quick termination of the U.S. lend-lease program in 1945; this forced Britain to borrow heavily in the immediate postwar period. The strategic strength and economic might of the United States and its emergence as the dominant world power meant that Britain was an ally, not an equal partner. The relationship is now one of consultation and exchange of information, intelligence, and opinions on issues of common interest. Britain has been a staunch U.S. ally in recent conflicts: the Gulf War of 1991, the war in the Balkans and Kosovo, sanctions against Iraq, and the fight against terrorism following extremist attacks on the United States in 2001.

Britain is one of the few countries in the world with a military nuclear capacity, and it intends to maintain that capacity. The core of its defense effort is now based on its membership in the North Atlantic Treaty Organization (NATO). Britain is committed to the deterrent strategy of NATO and to consultations of the Nuclear Planning Group within it. It contributes forces to all three elements of NATO's strategy: strategic nuclear, theater nuclear, and conventional armaments.

Britain has a Trident submarine force, but has reduced its reliance on nuclear weapons. The Royal Navy, the strongest European navy in NATO, contributes its wide variety of ships—the third largest number of surface combat ships in the world—including aircraft carriers, antisubmarine helicopters, nuclear-powered attack submarines, frigates, and guided missile destroyers to the alliance. In addition to its NATO assignments in the Atlantic and the North Sea, the navy sends task forces into the Indian Ocean, party to help safeguard oil supplies.

Britain has 55,000 regular army troops assigned to NATO's force. It has two divisions in Germany and one in Britain. It is supported by a tactical unit of the Royal Air Force (RAF). The RAF as a whole has some 500 combat aircraft at its disposal, including units in Britain that provide part of NATO's mobile force, a contribution to NATO's Intermediate and Rapid Reaction Forces.

Out of the NATO area, Britain still stations troops or plays a role in a number of areas such as Cyprus, Gibraltar, the Falklands, and in the major oceans. Britain played a significant role in the Gulf War of 1991. With the end of the Warsaw Pact in 1991, Britain made substantial cuts in all its armed forces. In 2002 there were 110,000 in the army, 54,000 in the RAF, and 42,000 in the navy. For Britain, NATO, rather than an EU force, should be Europe's major security unit.

From Empire to Commonwealth

Before World War II the British Commonwealth, as it was then called, consisted of Britain and six dominions, which (except for South Africa) were largely populated by individuals of British extraction, economically modernized and politically developed, with democratic systems and values (again except for South Africa) similar to the British. Preferential trading arrangements, adopted in Ottawa in 1932, were extended to all the dominions.

The rest of Britain's possessions throughout the world were colonies ruled by Britain. They began demanding independence soon after the end of the war, beginning in Asia and then throughout Africa and the rest of the world. Most nations on gaining independence have chosen to be members of the Commonwealth, which in 2005 numbers 53 countries with a population of 1.7 billion. Britain, however, is still responsible for 16 dependent territories around the world.

The Commonwealth, now consisting of diverse races, religions, and cultures, is a voluntary association with members all being equal in status. Some are republics which acknowledge the monarch as head of the Commonwealth, some 16 are constitutional monarchies owing allegiance to the monarch, and four have their own monarchs. Some are political democracies in the British sense, but others have one-party systems or are under military control. Some are based on private ownership, while others regard themselves as socialists. A few are wealthy, but most are poor countries with a low per capita income.

The Commonwealth accounts for 23 percent of world trade and about 20 percent of global investment. It is a loose association of independent nations, all once ruled by Britain, which have in no way chosen each other but are linked by accident. British law no longer extends to the Commonwealth. It does not reach collective decisions or take united political action. It is neither a trade bloc—although some economic privileges do exist—nor a military alliance, though its weapons, uniforms, and military training are similar to Britain's and there are combined exercises and joint research organizations. In the Commonwealth the Queen is the symbol of free association, but this is not a position of executive power. It has no center of sovereignty, no central law-making body or parliament, and no organ to speak for it; in 1965, a secretariat was established, but it does not make decisions that are binding on Commonwealth members. However, a Commonwealth Ministerial Action Group was set up in 1995 which addresses violations of democratic principles in the countries.

The Commonwealth does not have a written constitution but it does have a number of statements outlining its objectives. The most important of these are the Declaration of Commonwealth Principles agreed in Singapore in 1971 and the Harare Declaration in 1991, which committed the Commonwealth to promote democracy, human

The Commonwealth Member Countries
(with date of membership and populations)

1 Antigua and Barbuda (1981) 67,000	11 Cyprus (1961) 760,000	22 Lesotho (1966) 2,105,000
2 Australia (1901) 18,967,000	12 Dominica (1978) 73,000	23 Malawi (1964) 10,788,000
3 The Bahamas (1973) 298,000	13 Fiji Islands (1970) 801,000	24 Malaysia (1957) 22,710,000
4 Bangladesh (1973) 127,669,000	14 The Gambia (1965) 1,251,000	25 Maldives (1982) 269,000
5 Barbados (1966) 267,000	15 Ghana (1957) 18,785,000	26 Malta (1964) 379,000
6 Belize (1981) 247,000	16 Grenada (1974) 97,000	27 Mauritius (1968) 1,174,000
7 Botswana (1966) 1,588,000	17 Guyana (1966) 856,000	28 Mozambique (1995) 17,299,000
8 Brunei Darussalam (1984) 322,000	18 India (1947) 997,515,000	29 Namibia (1990) 1,701,000
9 Cameroon (1995) 14,691,000	19 Jamaica (1962) 2,598,000	30 Nauru (1968) 11,000
10 Canada (1867) 30,491,000	20 Kenya (1963) 29,410,000	31 New Zealand (1907) 3,811,000
	21 Kiribati (1979) 88,000	32 Nigeria (1960) 123,897,000

THE COMMONWEALTH

Source: Commonwealth Secretariat Publications.

rights, gender equality, economic and social development, eradication of poverty, and opposition to racial discrimination.

Tangible and intangible bonds have linked the Commonwealth. The latter result from the use of English by the professional classes, similar educational experiences, and common backgrounds in some cases. More tangible have been the regular meetings of heads of governments, political leaders, and profes-

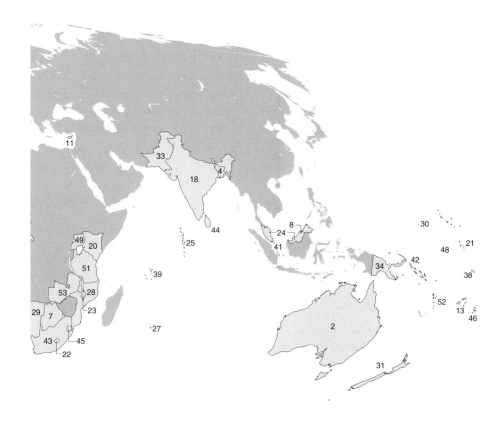

33 Pakistan (1947) 134,790,000
34 Papua New Guinea (1975) 4,705,000
35 St. Kitts and Nevis (1983) 41,000
36 St. Lucia (1979) 154,000
37 St. Vincent and the Grenadines (1979) 114,000
38 Samoa (1970) 169,000
39 Seychelles (1976) 80,000
40 Sierra Leone (1961) 4,949,000
41 Singapore (1965) 3,952,000
42 Solomon Islands (1978) 429,000
43 South Africa (1931) 42,106,000

44 Sri Lanka (1948) 18,985,000
45 Swaziland (1968) 1,019,000
46 Tonga (1970) 100,000
47 Trinidad and Tobago (1962) 1,293,000
48 Tuvalu (1978) 11,000
49 Uganda (1963) 21,479,000
50 United Kingdom 59,501,000
51 United Republic of Tanzania (1961) 32,923,000
52 Vanuatu (1980) 193,000
53 Zambia (1964) 9,881,000

sional people; collaborative functions in areas such as health, especially the fight against HIV/AIDS, education, law, technical cooperation, teacher training, youth groups, sports, arts festivals, and agriculture; and representation of the members by High Commissioners in London. Some preferential trade arrangements still exist. Most of Britain's bilateral and much of its multilateral foreign aid has gone to the Commonwealth.

SPLITTING THE ROCK

Britain still has 15 overseas territories; one of them, Gibraltar, has been British since 1713. A few square miles of rock with a population of 30,000, Gibraltar voted in 1967 to remain British. The British proposal in 2003 to discuss with Spain the possibility of sharing sovereignty over it in return for the lifting of Spanish restrictions on border crossing, air traffic, and telecommunications, was rejected by Spain.

But Britain's ties with the Commonwealth have weakened. The very diversity of its members means that no common ethnic or cultural bonds exist. Controls have been imposed on non-white immigration into Britain. Britain can no longer offer military protection to the members. Few of them retain the Judicial Committee of the Privy Council in London as the final court of appeal from their own courts.

The Commonwealth is a useful bridge among races, areas of the world, and richer and poorer nations. But it has declined in economic value and political importance for Britain. This is especially true in the changing pattern of trade as Britain has turned to Europe, and the Commonwealth countries have begun manufacturing their own products. British exports to the Commonwealth decreased from 37.3 percent of the total in 1958 to 8.5 percent in 1987. In the same period, exports to the European Community increased from 13.9 to 42 percent, and imports from it rose from 9 to 52 percent. British trade has shifted from the Commonwealth to other industrial countries, especially those of Western Europe.

Britain and the European Union

In the immediate postwar period, Britain was not interested in joining in the proposals for greater European unity. Its status as one of the "Big Three" powers, its worldwide role, its Commonwealth, its special relationship with the United States, its higher standard of living and trade pattern, and its insular political tradition and fear of European entanglement—all led Britain to refuse to participate in the Economic Coal and Steel Community in 1951, the proposed European Defense Community in the 1950s, and in the formation of the European Economic Community (EEC) and European Atomic Energy Community (Euratom) in 1957.

Britain preferred to maintain a much looser free-trade area and organized the European Free Trade Association in 1959 as an alternative. But the speedy success of the EEC, popularly known as the Common Market, the rapid recovery of Western Europe after the war—at first assisted by U.S. economic aid—the realization of the importance of a large single market, and weakening relations with the United States and the Commonwealth led Britain to apply for membership in the European Community (EC), which is now the European Union (EU). After being vetoed twice by France, in 1963 and 1967, Britain was accepted and joined the Community in January 1973.

When the Labour Party, split on the issue of the EC, formed the government in 1974, it decided to renegotiate the terms of Britain's membership and then put the issue to a vote by the people. A number of changes were made, including the system of financing the EC budget, the reduction in the cost of the common agricultural program, and better access for certain Commonwealth produce. As a result, the government, though still divided, recommended that Britain remain in the EC. The referendum, the first in British history, was approved by 67 percent of the vote in 1975.

British Eurostar train at Victoria Station in London.

Britain accepted the EC's agricultural policy, which means higher prices for food and the gradual reduction of Commonwealth trade preferences. In return, it hoped that the larger market and progressive removal of European tariff barriers would induce a faster rate of economic growth, a restructuring of the British economy, and greater economies of scale in production.

Membership in the EC did not immediately revive British industry, but trade with it increased. Trade with the EU now accounts for over half of Britain's imports and exports.

Britain was also concerned about the size of its net contribution to the EC budget, as it contributed considerably more than it received in return. The EC raised revenue from customs duties, farm levies, and value-added taxation (VAT), which was costly to Britain, which imports most of its food; most EC expenditure was to

farmers, thus benefiting countries with a larger farming population than Britain's. As a result of vigorous protest by Prime Minister Thatcher, Britain's contribution was reduced in the 1980s.

Britain is now subject to the laws of the European Union; it accepts and gives the force of law to the rules, principles, and procedures of the EU. It is bound by all EU treaties. The Court of Justice of the European Union has ultimate authority to rule on interpretation of the law. In the institutions of the EU, now composed of 25 states. Britain has 1 of the members of the European Commission, the executive of the EU, and 78 of the 732 members of the enlarged European Parliament, elected in 2004.

For Britain some new political problems exist. The historic concept of the supremacy of Parliament is now qualified by the right of EU institutions to make rules applying to Britain without parliamentary consent and by the ability of the EU Court of Justice to rule on whether British law is compatible with European Union law. Though there has not been any serious constitutional clash between Britain and the EU institutions, problems remain now that there is a level of government above that of Britain and now that Britain is for the first time bound to some extent by the written constitution of the European Union. Britain welcomed the EU objective of a free internal market by 1992, and approved of a greater European role in world affairs, but it has been reluctant to become a member of the European Monetary System or to accept the idea of a European bank, let alone a United States of Europe.

It did, however, join the exchange rate mechanism of the European Monetary System in October 1990, though it remained opposed to rapid moves to an economic and monetary union, and to a single European currency (the euro). It also still insists that any such union must be based on free markets and price stability. Equally, the Conservative governments under Thatcher and Major rejected the idea of a federal Europe, and have been concerned about any reduction of British sovereignty. The Conservatives agreed that some common European policies, such as a single market and a negotiating position on world trade, are necessary and that Europe should have a more coordinated foreign policy and a stronger voice in world affairs; they did not accept the view that all European cooperation must take place through the institutions of the European Union. However, the Blair government in 1997 accepted, after the previous Conservative government had refused to do so, the Social Chapter of the Maastricht Treaty, and minimum wage regulations.

Britain has been troubled by the diminution of its sovereignty, as in late 1991 when the Community threatened to take legal action to stop British Rail construction projects for environmental reasons. Parliamentary sovereignty is even more challenged by the European integration process and the move to common European employment, budgetary, taxation, and defense policies, and by the 1999 Amsterdam Treaty.

CONCLUSION

Whether examined from an international, social, economic, or political point of view, the British system has changed in the postwar world. Internationally, Britain cannot be seen as a superpower, though it is still a significant world power with a capacity for independent action as was displayed in the 1982 Falklands war. It has drawn closer to Western Europe and its membership in the European Union now accounts for over half of British trade. Britain maintains a variety of important foreign ties, especially with the United States, with which it shares common political and democratic values as well as military and intelligence-gathering connections.

It is a leading member of NATO and the European Union, a permanent member of the Security Council of the United Nations, and one of the Group of Seven Economic Summit countries. British troops are deployed or stationed in over 40 countries.

Britain is the world's sixth largest economy, though its share of world trade has fallen from 11.5 percent in the early postwar years to 5.5 percent in 2002. It is the world's second biggest foreign investor and the biggest foreign investor in the United States. Promoting trade is as important as diplomatic activity; about a quarter of GDP comes from the overseas market. Over 85 percent of that trade is with OECD countries.

Socially, Britain is a country with a mixture of peoples of different races and background, a less rigid class system, and, for most individuals, a more affluent lifestyle. Economically, Britain has experienced mixed success. Long-term economic growth has averaged about 2.25 percent a year in recent years. Fastest growth has been in the services sector, especially in transport, storage, and communications. Inflation has been kept to a low level. Trade unions, with a declining membership, have in general been less militant. Under both Conservative and Labour governments, the proportion of total GDP spent by government did not diminish significantly.

Britain in the mid-1990s witnessed an increasing centralization of public administration as the Conservative government under John Major reduced the autonomy of local councils, universities, police authorities, health regions, armed forces, and nationalized industry boards. The Blair government reversed this trend by the policy of devolution, thus qualifying the unitary nature of Britain and decreasing centralized authority.

The Thatcher government stressed individual responsibility, encouraged economic initiative, sold off many nationalized industries, and dismantled state controls over the economy. To a considerable degree the Blair government has accepted this and the new consensus on the free market, maximizing individual choice, more concern for costs, no return to nationalization of enterprises, and limits on powers of government in normal times. This has merged with the previous consensus of full employment, a welfare state, and free collective bargaining.

Difficult issues, such as the Irish question, environmental problems, the role of Britain externally (particularly in the EU, which is a very divisive issue), class and ethnic differences, the question of equal opportunity for women, and protective laws for ethnic minorities, remain to be adequately resolved. It is clear that there will be no shortage of difficult problems on the British political agenda.

The need for constitutional and political changes including reform of the House of Lords has been raised. Britain is the only country in Western Europe which does not have a bill of rights providing constitutional protection for individual and group rights. It set up a considerable number of independent government agencies and QUANGOs whose political responsibility is unclear. This has led some to argue that Britain should have a formal bill of rights, a fairer electoral system, and more parliamentary scrutiny of the executive. This has yet to be done.

On the other hand, Britain remains a stable democracy in no danger of military defeat, revolution, or political collapse. In a country where tradition and conventions have played such a large role, peaceful political and constitutional change is taking place.

Thinking Critically

1. Why was Britain reluctant to join the European Community? Why is Britain still unwilling to adopt the euro?
2. How would you explain Britain's changing policies on nationalization and privatization?
3. Does Britain have, and did it ever have, a special relationship with the United States?
4. Has the welfare state changed during the postwar period? Is it working satisfactorily?
5. Is British government expenditure excessive?
6. Should the Commonwealth be ended?

KEY TERMS

Commonwealth *(114–115)*
devolution *(119)*
economic planning *(108)*
European Community (EC) *(116)*
European Monetary System *(118)*
European Union (EU) *(117)*
family allowances *(111)*
mixed economy *(106)*
National Health Service (NHS) *(111)*
nationalized industries *(106)*
North Atlantic Treaty Organization (NATO) *(112)*
privatization *(108)*
public–private partnerships *(108)*
social security *(110)*
special relationship *(112)*
welfare state *(109)*

ABBREVIATIONS

BBC	British Broadcasting Corporation
CAP	Common Agricultural Policy
CBI	Confederation of British Industry
EC	European Community
ECHR	European Convention on Human Rights
EMS	European Monetary System
EMU	European Monetary Union
EP	European Parliament
EU	European Union

GB	Great Britain
GDP	Gross Domestic Product
GNP	Gross National Product
HoC	House of Commons
HoL	House of Lords
Lib Dem	Liberal Democrat
MP	Member of Parliament
NATO	North Atlantic Treaty Organization
NHS	National Health Service
PM	Prime Minister
PR	Proportional Representation
SNP	Scottish National Party
TUC	Trades Union Congress
UK	United Kingdom

FURTHER READINGS

Atkinson, A. B. *Incomes and the Welfare State* (Cambridge: Cambridge University Press, 1996).

Bagilhole, Barbara. *Equal Opportunities and Social Policy* (New York: Longman, 1997).

Bartlett, Christopher J. *British Foreign Policy in the Twentieth Century* (Basingstoke: Macmillan, 1989).

Booth, Alan. *The British Economy in the Twentieth Century* (Basingstoke: Palgrave, 2001).

Curwen, Peter, ed. *Understanding the United Kingdom Economy* (London: Macmillan, 1997).

Deakin, Nicholas, and Richard Parry. *The Treasury and Social Policy* (New York: St. Martin's, 2000).

Ellison, Nick, and Christopher Pierson, eds. *Developments in British Social Policy* (New York: Palgrave Macmillan, 2003).

Gamble, Andrew. *Between Europe and America: The Future of British Politics* (New York: Palgrave Macmillan, 2003).

Geddes, Andrew. *The European Union and British Politics* (New York: Palgrave Macmillan, 2004).

Giddens, Anthony. *The Third Way and Its Critics* (Cambridge: Polity Press, 2000).

Grant, Wyn. *Pressure Groups, Politics and Democracy in Britain* (New York: Allan, 1989).

Grant, Wyn. *Business and Politics in Britain,* 2nd ed. (London: Macmillan, 1993).

Grant, Wyn. *The Politics of Economic Policy* (New York: Harvester Wheatsheaf, 1993).

Hills, John, ed. *The State of Welfare: The Welfare State in Britain Since 1974* (New York: Oxford University Press, 1990).

Kavanagh, Dennis. *The Reordering of British Politics: Politics after Thatcher* (New York: Oxford University Press, 1997).

Kellas, James. *The Politics of Nationalism and Ethnicity* (Basingstoke: Macmillan, 1991).

Kellas, James. *The Scottish Political System,* 4th ed. (New York: Cambridge University Press, 1989).

Lister, Ruth. *Citizenship: Feminist Perspectives*, 2nd ed. (London: Macmillan, 2003).

Louis, Wm. Roger, and Hedley Bull, eds. *The Special Relationship: Anglo-American Relations Since 1945* (New York: Oxford University Press, 1986).

Ludlam, Steve, and Martin J. Smith, eds. *Governing as New Labour: Policy and Politics Under Blair* (New York: Palgrave Macmillan, 2004).

Pierson, Christopher. *Beyond the Welfare State? The New Political Economy of Welfare* (Cambridge: Polity Press, 1991).

Robins, Lynton, and Bill Jones, eds. *Half a Century of British Politics* (Manchester: Manchester University Press, 1997).

Sanders, David. *Losing an Empire, Finding a Role: British Foreign Policy since 1945* (Basingstoke: Macmillan, 1990).

Savage, Stephen P., and R. Atkinson, eds. *Public Policy under Blair* (New York: Palgrave, 2001).

Smith, Michael, et al., eds. *British Foreign Policy: Tradition, Change and Transformation* (Boston: Allen and Unwin, 1988).

Timmins, Nicholas. *The Five Giants: A Biography of the Welfare State* (New York: Harper Collins, 1995).

WEB SITES

www.ukpol.co.uk
information on many subjects
www.pm.gov.uk
information on prime minister
www.parliament.uk
information on Parliament
www.cabinet-office.gov.uk
information on the cabinet
www.parliament.uk/commons
information on House of Commons

www.publications.parliament.uk/pa/ld/ldhome.htm
information on House of Lords and its committees

www.civil-service.gov.uk
information on the civil service

www.hm-treasury.gov.uk
information on Treasury

www.fco.gov.uk
information on Foreign and Commonwealth Office

www.thecommonwealth.org
information on the Commonwealth

www.tuc.org.uk
information on Trades Union Congress

www.humanrights.gov.uk
information on Britain and Human Rights treaties

www.scotland.gov.uk
information on Executive of the Scottish Parliament

www.scottish.parliament.uk
information on Scottish Parliament

www.alba.org.uk
information on Scottish politics

www.wales.gov.uk/assembly.dbs
information on Welsh Assembly

www.nio.gov.uk
information on Northern Ireland Office

www.ni-executive.gov.uk
information on Executive in Northern Ireland

www.niassembly.gov.uk
information on Northern Ireland Assembly

THE GOVERNMENT OF
France

Jean Blondel

INTRODUCTION

Background: Although ultimately a victor in World Wars I and II, France suffered extensive losses in its empire, wealth, manpower, and rank as a dominant nation-state. Nevertheless, France today is one of the most modern countries in the world and is a leader among European nations. Since 1958, it has constructed a presidential democracy resistant to the instabilities experienced in earlier parliamentary democracies. In recent years, its reconciliation and cooperation with Germany have proved central to the economic integration of Europe, including the advent of the euro in January 1999. Presently, France is at the forefront of European states seeking to exploit the momentum of monetary union to advance the creation of a more unified and capable European defense and security apparatus.

GEOGRAPHY

Location: Western Europe, bordering the Bay of Biscay and English Channel between Belgium and Spain, southeast of the UK; bordering the Mediterranean Sea between Italy and Spain

Area: 547,030 sq km

Area—comparative: slightly less than twice the size of Colorado

Land boundaries: 2,889 km

> *border countries:* Andorra 56.6 km, Belgium 620 km, Germany 451 km, Italy 488 km, Luxembourg 73 km, Monaco 4.4 km, Spain 623 km, Switzerland 573 km

Climate: generally cool winters and mild summers, but mild winters and hot summers along the Mediterranean; occasional strong, cold, dry, north-to-northwesterly wind known as mistral

Terrain: mostly flat plains or gently rolling hills in north and west; remainder is mountainous, especially Pyrenees in south, Alps in east

Elevation extremes: *lowest point:* Rhone River delta −2 m

highest point: Mont Blanc 4,807 m

Geography note: largest West European nation

PEOPLE

Population: 60,424,000

Age structure: *0–14 years:* 18.5% (male 5.7 million; female 5.4 million)

15–64 years: 65.19% (male 19.6 million; female 19.6 million)

65 years and over: 16.4% (male 4.0 million; female 5.8 million)

Population growth rate: 0.39%

Birthrate: 12.3 births/1,000 population

Sex ratio: 1.05 male/female

Life expectancy at birth: 79.44 years

male: 75.8 years

female: 83.2 years

Nationality: *noun:* Frenchman (men), French-woman (women)

adjective: French

Ethnic groups: Celtic and Latin with Teutonic, Slavic, North African, Indochinese, Basque minorities

Religions: Roman Catholic 83%, Muslim 10%, Protestant 2%, Jewish 1%, unaffiliated 4%

Languages: French, rapidly declining regional dialects and languages (Provençal, Breton, Alsatian, Corsican, Catalan, Basque, Flemish)

Literacy: *definition:* age 15 and over can read and write

total population: 99%

GOVERNMENT

Country name: *conventional long form:* French Republic

conventional short form: France

Government type: republic

Capital: Paris

Administrative divisions: 22 regions: Alsace, Aquitaine, Auvergne, Basse-Normandie, Bour-gogne, Bretagne, Centre, Champagne-Ardenne, Corse, Franche-Comté, Haute-Normandie, Ile-de-France, Languedoc-Roussillon, Limousin, Lorraine, Midi-Pyrénées, Nord-Pas-de-Calais, Pays de la Loire, Picardie, Poitou-Charentes, Provence-Alpes-Côte d'Azur, Rhône-Alpes

Dependent areas: Bassas da India, Clipperton Island, Europa Island, French Polynesia, French Southern and Antarctic Lands, Glorioso Islands, Juan de Nova Island, New Caledonia, Tromelin Island, Wallis and Futuna

note: the US does not recognize claims to Antarctica

Independence: 486 (unified by Clovis)

National holiday: Bastille Day, 14 July (1789)

Constitution: 28 September 1958, amended concerning election of president in 1962, amended to comply with provisions of EC Maastricht Treaty in 1992, amended to tighten immigration laws 1993

Legal system: civil law system with indigenous concepts; review of administrative but not leg-islative acts

Suffrage: 18 years of age; universal

Executive branch: *chief of state:* President Jacques Chirac (since 17 May 1995)

head of government: Prime Minister Dominique (since May 2002)

cabinet: Council of Ministers appointed by the president on the suggestion of the prime minister

elections: president elected by popular vote for a five-year term; at election June 2002 prime minister nominated by the National Assembly majority and appointed by the president

Legislative branch: bicameral parliament con-sists of the Senate or Senat (321 seats to be increased to 346; members are indirectly elected by an electoral college to serve six-year terms; elected by thirds every three years) and the National Assembly (577 seats; members are elected by popular vote under a single-member majoritarian system to serve five-year terms)

Judicial branch: Supreme Court of Appeals (judges are appointed by the president from nominations of the High Council of the Judiciary); Constitutional Council (three members appointed by the president, three appointed by the president of the National Assembly, and three appointed by the president of the Senate); Council of State

ECONOMY

Overview: France is in the midst of transition, from an economy that featured extensive government ownership and intervention to one that relies more on market mechanisms. The government remains dominant in some sectors, particularly power, public transport, and defense industries, but it has been relaxing its control since the mid-1980s. The Socialist-led government has sold off part of its holdings in France Telecom, Air France, Thales, Thomson Multimedia, and the European Aerospace and Defense Company (EADS). The telecommunications sector is gradually being opened to competition. France's leaders remain committed to a capitalism in which they maintain social equity by means of laws, tax policies, and social spending that reduce income disparity and the impact of free markets on public health and welfare. The government has done little to cut generous unemployment and retirement benefits which impose a heavy tax burden and discourage hiring. It has also shied from measures that would dramatically increase the use of stock options and retirement investment plans; such measures would boost the stock market and fast-growing IT firms as well as ease the burden on the pension system, but would disproportionately benefit the rich. In addition to the tax burden, the reduction of the work week to 35-hours has drawn criticism for lowering the competitiveness of French companies.

GDP: purchasing power parity $1.661 trillion

GDP—real growth rate: 0.5%

GDP—per capita: purchasing power parity $27,600

GDP—composition by sector: *agriculture:* 2.7%
   industry: 24.4%
   services: 72.9%

Labor force: 27 million

Labor force by occupation: services 71%, industry 25%, agriculture 4%

Unemployment rate: 9.7%

Currency: euro (EUR)

   note: on 1 January 1999, the EU introduced the euro as a common currency to be used by financial institutions; the euro has replaced the franc for all transactions in 2002

A. POLITICAL DEVELOPMENT

HISTORY AND SOCIETY: TRADITIONS AND CONTRADICTIONS IN FRENCH POLITICS

The Instability of French Politics through the 1960s

France refuses, almost doggedly, to fit the framework of the rest of Western Europe and of the Atlantic world. The Fifth Republic, set up by Charles de Gaulle in 1958, has been a stable regime, but as recently as 1958 the country seemed on the verge of political catastrophe, with generals in Algiers threatening a military invasion. The previous regime, the Fourth Republic, had ended after 12 years marked by great political instability. During the 150 years before that, France had had about 20 constitutions, of which only one—that of the Third Republic, inaugurated in 1870—lasted more than 20 years. The First Republic was installed at the end of the eighteenth century and lasted 7 years (1792–1799); the Second was established in 1848 and lasted 3 years to 1851; the Fourth Republic was set up after World War II and lasted 12 years (1946–1958).

Indeed, both the Third and Fourth Republics were characterized by instability greater even than that of contemporary Italy. During that period, governments rarely lasted more than half a year and almost never had any real authority. It may be that France has at last acquired real political stability in the Fifth Republic, but at a price. France's political system is somewhat different from those of other Western countries and poses as yet unresolved problems about the respective position of president and government.

Social and Economic Development

Explanations for France's political instability are not easy to find. Economic performance does not provide the answer. France is one of the richest countries in the world. Its per capita GDP of $21,900 in 2000 is the same as that of Denmark (also $21,900), somewhat lower than that of Germany ($22,800), and appreciably lower than that of the Netherlands ($23,200) and Britain ($23,800), though the differences are much smaller if one takes into account the purchasing power parity of the various currencies. If, as political scientists believe, on the basis of considerable evidence, wealth and political stability are closely associated, France should be as stable as the other Western European countries.

The distribution of wealth and the class structure do not provide clues either. Incomes and wealth are somewhat more unevenly distributed in France than in northern Europe, but the large majority of the population has sizeable incomes, and a very substantial proportion are small property owners. Indeed, France has traditionally been a nation of small businesspeople—shopkeepers, artisans, and above all farmers. While in Latin America and the countries of southern Europe political unrest can be attributed to conflict over land reform, in France the land is owned by large numbers of smallholders, making agricultural workers and sharecroppers a tiny minority.

The sources of French contemporary difficulties are therefore not the direct consequence of social and economic characteristics common to Latin or other countries that experience instability. Political unrest is more deeply embedded in the culture of the country, in its history, and in many of its structures, especially the administrative structures. Conflicts appear to arise in large part from a number of contradictions which the French do not seem able to surmount. The result has been that, for a long period at least, the legitimacy of the regime has been relatively low; only recently has the political system been fully accepted by almost all the French citizens.

The Clash between Liberalism and Authoritarianism

Since the eighteenth century, perhaps the most obvious contradiction has been between traditional authoritarianism and liberal democracy. It has left its scars. The Revolution of 1789 stressed the values of republicanism, liberalism, and egalitarianism, but these values had to be imposed on a substantial segment of the French population which did not readily accept them and at times combatted them by force. France was the first continental country to adopt constitutionalism and liberalism; it was also the first country to experience modern authoritarian rule, under the two Napoleons at the beginning and in the middle of the nineteenth century. It escaped with difficulty twentieth-century totalitarianism in peacetime, but did succumb to it, with the so-called Vichy regime, under the impact of the German occupation between 1940 and 1944. Liberal democracy became fully legitimate in the last decades of the twentieth century only.

Nationalism and Internationalism

France sees itself as having an international mission, but this results in another contradiction, between nationalism and internationalism. France's international mission has tended to be to propagate its national values. Thus the Revolution of 1789 was the only time when the contradiction was resolved, since the imperialism of the French was then associated with the desire to spread an idealistic gospel. The armies of the Republic invaded Europe to defeat the "tyrants" and liberate the "people." This same idea existed a hundred years later, as France made "assimilation" its colonial policy. By contrast, British colonial policy was based on the principle of noninterference with local traditions. Opposition to French colonial rule was often held to be wholly misguided as

SYMBOLS OF THE FRENCH REPUBLIC

The Tricolour Flag

Article 2 of the Fifth Republic's Constitution states the national emblem is the blue, red and white flag. This three-coloured flag, visible on public buildings, during commemorations and sports events, results from a long evolution.

The Marseillaise

Product of the Revolution, the French national anthem survived two Empires, the Restoration and the Occupation before finally being officialized by the Republic in 1946.

Bastille Day : 14 July The National Holiday

Bastille Day today means, for all in France, the solemn military parade up the Champs Elysées in the presence of the head of State.

Marianne and the motto of the Republic

Marianne is the embodiment of the French Republic. Marianne represents the permanent values that found her citizens' attachment to the Republic: "Liberty, Equality, Fraternity".

Liberté · Égalité · Fraternité

RÉPUBLIQUE FRANÇAISE

The Gallic rooster

The Latin word Gallus means both "rooster" and "inhabitant of Gaul". Gradually the figure of the rooster became the most widely shared representation of the French people.

it did not recognize the blessings of France's "civilizing mission."

France's view of the outside world reveals a third contradiction: a belief in the greatness of the country that does not correspond to reality. When political power was based on the strength of armies and on cultural prestige, France did rather well. It was the most populous of European countries and it had spread its language and civilization all over Europe; European aristocrats worshipped French culture, while French armies periodically fought and imposed their will. But the Industrial Revolution gradually changed the basis of power, and suddenly a small country like England could control the world by its exports of manufactured goods. France was caught unprepared. Although it had a rich tradition of public works (on roads and urban planning), it entirely lacked one of industrial enterprise. To this day, objects of French national pride are more likely to be grand projects of dubious commercial value, such as the Concorde, rather than successful ventures in light engineering or consumer goods. Hence a bitter resentment and jealousy has extended to this day to the "Anglo-Saxon" countries.

Cultural pride helps to explain the peculiar relationship France had with the former Soviet Union. In the late 1940s, the French Communist Party had over 25 percent of the votes; only very slowly did it fall to under 10 percent four decades later. The French Communist Party was also probably the most Stalinist of Western Communist parties, following quite faithfully the policy dictated by the Soviet Union in the pre-Gorbachev era. Communist Russia exercised some attraction in part because France always wanted to be independent of the United States and wanted the Western nations that form part of the Atlantic alliance to be more independent. In reality, France's geographical position as well as its culture and history make it a part of the West. Thus, it can scarcely be independent. In spite of this, its leaders periodically by various means endeavor to affirm, typically rather symbolically, France's independence.

Centralization and Decentralization

The Role of the Bureaucracy The final fundamental contradiction in French government is the role of the bureaucracy. Historically it has been a major instrument of change and a major hindrance to decentralization and development. Authorities had viewed the centralization of the French state as a necessity dictated by the fact that civil servants and technocrats had been the originators of industrial strength who

---

A CLOSER LOOK

3.1

FRENCH CULTURE AND THE FRENCH LANGUAGE

In some ways, France remains outside the major social and cultural changes that took place in the second half of the twentieth century. The determined resistance to Americanization accounts in large part for the awkwardness with which French governments, but also the French people, react to world developments. Many of the country's elites believe that French culture must be defended against all kinds of encroachments, particularly against the invasion of Anglicisms into the French language. The enduring belief that the French language is a flagship that helps to propagate French culture has prompted French governments to continually extol the "francophonie" (the supposed cultural realm defined by French-speaking peoples throughout the world). In the mid-1990s a law was passed to attempt to protect the language. Such a policy helps to keep some weakening ties from dissolving completely, particularly in Africa, but it isolates France from the rest of the world. Foreign language skills are not seen as essential, and French citizens are often officially told that they must use the French language while abroad.

often saw themselves as agents in the midst of a population that was passive and often markedly antagonistic to their innovations. Further justifications were added. Government centralization meant a uniform structure. Who would want education to be less developed in some parts of the country than in others? Moreover, if the civil service did not intervene, so the argument went, localism would prevail and there would be much patronage and graft. A centralized bureaucracy was thus morally justified. Nevertheless, some decentralization has occurred with the movement away from central control to move decision making by local groups such as municipalities, *départements*, and regions. This decentralization has been recognized in the constitution as "free administration of local collectivities."

These contradictions remain, although they are less acute than in the past. The cultural prestige of France has dwindled and many know it. Many also know that industrial strength is the key to prosperity and world influence, as the growth of West Germany and Japan has shown. Yet, while there is awareness of these realities in some circles, old views about French greatness still linger on, as the utterances of many leaders, even at the beginning of the twenty-first century, clearly demonstrate.

THE HISTORICAL PERSPECTIVE OF FRENCH POLITICS

France's political history has been highly complex. To unravel this jumble, one must begin with the great rent in French history—the Revolution of 1789. With great drama, with a missionary and military zeal that threatened *anciens régimes* in much of the rest of Europe, the French routed the monarchy, the aristocracy, and the privileged Roman Catholic Church in the name of liberty, equality, and the republican form of government. Yet the old order, though defeated, was not destroyed. Its defenders were able to revive the monarchy in the nineteenth century and delay for decades any final regulation of the Church's powers. Meanwhile, the antirepublican tradition resisted through time; after

attempting to undermine all the republics from the First (1792) to the Fifth (1958), its supporters took until the last decades of the twentieth century to reconcile themselves to the processes of popular sovereignty.

The Revolution of 1789

The defenders of the Revolution and Republic were not long in becoming divided over whether they should give priority to equality or liberty. In the early revolutionary period, great effort was made to destroy the political privileges of the titled and aristocratic classes. The Declaration of the Rights of Man and the Citizen, adopted tumultuously in the Revolutionary Assembly of 1789, detailed the expectations of French citizens to be given basic freedoms and to be granted justice on the basis of the law. The Declaration represented the momentary ascendancy of libertarians over egalitarians.

However, strong undercurrents in the Revolution were bent on leveling all economic and social distinctions. The dictatorship of the progressive party of the time, known as the Jacobins (1793–1794), was a move toward the use of the state as an instrument of vigorous social change. The efforts of the Jacobins failed, and Napoleon installed a much more conservative (and stabilizing) regime after taking power in 1799. However, the Jacobins added to the matrix of French political development a powerful political strain.

Traditionalists and Liberals in the Nineteenth Century

For most of the nineteenth century the libertarians had only a shaky hold on France, and the antirevolutionaries came back in 1814–1815. As the returning monarch, Louis XVIII agreed to a considerable dose of liberalism, which did not sit well with his brother and successor, Charles X. Charles's reactionary attempts ended in revolution in 1830, when the French put Louis Philippe d'Orléans on the throne. The new Orleanist monarchy started as a parliamentary regime but ended once more in revolution, after having made too many efforts to manipulate parliament instead of concentrating on the new political aspirations of the French. The Revolution of 1848 (which swept over continental Europe as well) put an end to the liberal monarchy, and to the monarchy altogether.

The Napoleonic Tradition

The most curious intermixture of political strands flowing from the French Revolution was the imperial tradition, into which Napoleon Bonaparte (1799–1814) stumbled, which his nephew Louis Napoleon perfected in the Second Empire (1852–1870), and which some contemporary commentators felt was reincarnated in the Fifth Republic of General de Gaulle (see Table 3.1). Claiming that they were embodying the general will of the nation as expressed in the plebiscites that chose them, the Bonapartes could thus pretend that they were descendants of the revolutionary assemblies.

The imperial tradition, despite some trappings borrowed from the Revolution, was both politically antiliberal and socially conservative. It was aimed essentially at maintaining the rights of the newly enfranchised bourgeoisie. Napoleon I's primary achievement was to develop the bureaucracy inherited from the monarchy. Through him, France was given a well-functioning civil service, codes of law, and a theory of the administrative process that were envied by many countries for several generations. Much of the Napoleonic bureaucracy is still in existence. Political battles have been fought largely over governments and their policies, not over the administrative instruments of government.

The Second Empire went further than the First by placing great emphasis on industrial and commercial development, often with substantial state help. This was the time when some of the great banks were set up, for instance. It was under the Second Empire that France began moving decisively away from being a predominantly agricultural economy.

TABLE 3.1

CHRONOLOGY OF POLITICAL DEVELOPMENT IN FRANCE

To 1789	*Ancien régime* (dates of reign): Louis XIV, 1643–1715. Louis XV, 1715–1774. Louis XVI, 1774–1792.
1789–1792	Constitutional Monarchy. Constituent Assembly. Constitution of 1791. First legislative Assembly.
1792–1799	First Republic. Convention Constitution of 1793 (not applied). Directory Constitution of 1795.
1799–1804	Consulate. Napoleon, first consul. Constitutions of 1799 and 1802.
1804–1814 and 1815	First Empire. Napoleon I, emperor. Constitutions of 1804, 1814 (not applied), and 1815.
1814–1815 and 1815–1830	Restoration. Louis XVIII, 1814–1824. Charter of 1814. Charles X, 1824–1830.
1830–1848	Orleans monarchy. Louis-Philippe I, 1830–1848. Charter of 1830.
1848–1851	Second Republic. Napoleon Bonaparte (nephew of Napoleon I), president. Constitution of 1848.
1852–1870	Second Empire. Napoleon III, emperor. Constitutions of 1852 and 1870.
1870–1940	Third Republic. Constitution of 1875.
1940–1944	Vichy regime. Pétain "head of state."
1945–1958	Fourth Republic. Constitution of 1946.
From 1958	Fifth Republic. Constitution of 1958. Presidents: Charles de Gaulle, 1958–1969; Georges Pompidou, 1969–1974; Valéry Giscard d'Estaing, 1974–1981; François Mitterrand, 1981–1988, reelected, 1988–1995; Jacques Chirac, 1995–2002, reelected 2002.

Republicanism and Its Elements

Nineteenth-century French republicanism originally comprised only a few simple elements: the expression of the public will through a sovereign and directly elected assembly, a society free from the institutionalized influence of the Church, and distrust of executive authority as a threat to freedom, against which the people had an obligation to rise when and if tyranny appeared imminent. Several times the people did take to the barricades. From when the monarchy was returned in 1815 to the Commune of 1870, the people, particularly the people of Paris, took periodically to the streets. On at least two occasions, in 1830 and 1848, civic violence led to the collapse of a regime. A rising of this kind occurred in 1944 when the German occupation forces were leaving Paris; students rose also in the university district of Paris, the Latin Quarter, in 1968.

The egalitarian strand of French republicanism never succeeded for long. The 1793–1794 Reign of Terror eventually led to Napoleon; the 1848 revolution led to the Second Empire. When this regime fell after being defeated by Prussia in 1870, the Paris Commune seized power in the capital, but it was smashed, ending in one of the bloodiest episodes of repression in French history.

Moderate republicanism became truly established after the Paris Commune. A national assembly composed mainly of monarchists drafted constitutional laws, hoping that a monarchical restoration could take place. The republic triumphed by default, and almost by accident, in 1875. The constitution then grudgingly adopted lasted until 1940. It was destroyed by German arms after a series of attacks coming from both Right and Left and by the weakness and internal divisions of its supporters.

The Second World War and Its Consequences: The Vichy Regime, the Resistance, and the Fourth Republic

Modern French history spans the Third, Fourth (1946–1958), and Fifth Republics (since 1958); it was interrupted between 1940 and 1944 by the "corporate state" of Pétain, whose authority derived from the German victory over France and not, despite the appearances of a legal transfer, from the will of the French people. In many ways, the Vichy regime (so called because the seat of government was transferred to Vichy, in central France, while northern France was occupied) symbolized what was antirepublican in French life.

Meanwhile, a Resistance movement against German occupation began organizing. It contained elements from all shades of French republicanism, from conservative nationalists to Communists. Although General de Gaulle had created a government in exile long before, first in London and later in Algiers, at the time of liberation in 1944 the Resistance remained the main political force in the country. The new constitution, adopted in 1946, established the Fourth Republic on the basis of traditional republican principles, but with left-wing overtones inherited from the Resistance. The Left was not strong enough to retain power, however, and the Fourth Republic resembled the Third. It was characterised by a powerful popular assembly, a weak executive, and an administrative apparatus floating in an ambiguous limbo below the government.

The Fall of the Fourth Republic

Being weak and transient, the governments of the Fourth Republic were unable to solve the major political problem of the time: decolonization. Defeat in Indochina in 1954 severely undermined the political system. A strong prime minister, Mendès-France, produced a settlement that effectively disengaged France from its Indochinese colonies, but he remained in power for only six months afterwards. By then, the war had begun in the French possession of Algeria between supporters of the status quo (mostly comprising the million French settlers in Algeria) and those who demanded Algerian independence. Successive governments proved too weak to make any move in the direction of reform. Despite the presence of a million French conscripts on the other side of the Mediterranean, France lost the war. By May 1958, pushed by civilian extremists, commanders in Algiers ceased to recognize the authority of the Paris government and even landed a small military force in Corsica. Rumors of an impending army coup spread throughout France; these created a climate of tension, plots, and counterplots. De Gaulle was recalled to office by a large majority of the Assembly on June 1, 1958, some hoping he could keep Algeria French, others thinking that he alone had the power to solve the problem. The Fifth Republic was born.

THE BACKGROUND OF THE SOCIAL ORDER

In the 1950s and 1960s, France leapt forward both socially and economically. Many consider the tragedy of modern France to be the inability to keep pace with socioeconomic change. At the same time aspects of the traditional background of French society remain visible in many parts of the country. Four characteristics of this traditional social order have special prominence. First, the French population—long static at 40 million and now about 60 million—has peasant origins. Second, France is geographically and even linguistically divided. Third, the class system and particularly the division between bourgeois and worker (*ouvrier*) has long affected lifestyles. Fourth, France is traditionally Roman

Catholic, but it also was fiercely anticlerical in the nineteenth and early twentieth centuries. It was on such a social landscape that the kings first and Napoleon later built a centralized administrative machine and that the Republic imposed a centralized political culture.

Peasant Origins

France was long a peasant nation—indeed perhaps the only peasant nation with a substantial proportion of its population who worked as smallholders instead of farm laborers. By the outbreak of World War II, as many as one-third of the population worked on plots inherited from their parents and to which they were strongly attached (see Table 3.2). Though owners of the land, these farmers had a difficult life. Plots were small and often fragmented because the civil code of Napoleon required that estates be divided equally among all the children. This led to low productivity even in rich areas and to low incomes—a state of affairs that fostered pessimism among large numbers of farmers. This also led to a low birthrate—lower, before 1945, than in all other developed nations.

Migrations from village to city were characteristic of Western Europe, yet in France they had less influence on the new city-dweller than

TABLE 3.2

OCCUPATIONS OF THE FRENCH POPULATION

	Percentage of the Active Population			
	1954	1962	1975	1990
Farmers and farm laborers	26.5	24.0	9.4	4.5
Owners of businesses	12.0	10.0	7.8	7.9
Higher management and professions	3.0	4.0	6.7	11.7
Middle management	6.0	7.5	12.7	20.0
White-collar workers	16.0	17.0	22.3	26.5
Manual workers	33.5	35.0	37.6	29.4
Other (army, police, etc.)	3.0	2.5	3.5	—
	100.0	100.0	100.0	100.0
Total (millions)	19.3	20.1	21.7	22.3

Source: Europa World Yearbook, various years (origin ILO Yearbooks of Social Statistics.)

in other countries. Peasant origins remained very important, and residents of cities often took on attitudes more characteristic of rural than of urban communities. Preconceptions, fears, worries, and a rather negative and anarchistic individualism came to dominate much of the middle and lower-middle levels of French society—shopkeepers, artisans, mechanics, and workers in commerce and even in industry, as well as the many civil servants.

The peasant complex, as this orientation might be called, has been a strong element in that much discussed French characteristic: individualism. It has manifested itself in the negative way in which the French have traditionally reacted to voluntary groupings. They did not believe in them and supported them with great hesitation, thus demonstrating, in a self-fulfilling prophecy, that most groupings conferred few benefits. The respect for negative criticism, the fear of appearing naive, and the suspicion of all men and institutions had considerable drawbacks for the French economy. This individualism rendered experimentation an object of ridicule and it became the very cause of the outside imposition of rules that the peasant community could not and would not establish.

Since World War II the characteristics of the farming community have altered markedly. The flight from the land took such proportions in the late 1950s and the 1960s that the weight of the peasantry in society diminished notably: from 1954 to 1975 the farming population was more than halved, from 5.2 million to under 2 million; there was a further decline to less than 1 million by 2005. Farmers who remained on the land acquired larger plots and mechanization, and the commercialization of farm products gave farmers a different outlook on their role in society. With less than one person in 20 engaged in agriculture and with farms becoming businesses, modern France no longer has a large body of citizens who alone can tilt the scales in elections and generally flavor the political culture. But attitudes die hard and memories are long. The past political order on the land still plays a substantial part in the political life of the present, as can periodically be seen in the way the government defends French farming in the European Union and other international settings.

Regional Sectionalism and the Influence of Paris

The second characteristic of the traditional French social structure is its sectionalism. This was maintained partly by the size of the peasantry, but general historical and geographical characteristics are also at play. Mountains and plateaus separate the country into natural regions and isolate certain areas from the main communication axes. Brittany in the west, the Southwest (sometimes known as Aquitaine), the Alpine area, and Provence (of which the southeastern tip on the Mediterranean has a very hilly interior and is known to tourists as the Côte d'Azur) all constitute sharply differentiated regions. These regions are somewhat isolated from the more accessible northern and northeastern parts of the country, whose wide plains give them an easier agriculture, more industry, and more natural lines of communication. History has in large part been molded by these geographical constraints, and local particularism has been widespread.

French sectionalism manifests itself in many ways. As everywhere, there are differences in accent, in turn often the product of the survival of local dialects, some of which, as in the south, have a Latin origin and are related to Italian (Provençal) or Spanish (Catalan), while others (Alsatian and Flemish) have Germanic roots and yet others (Breton and Basque) have little or nothing in common with the main European languages. But different forms of living are often also the consequences of different climates, which vary sharply as one moves from humid but temperate Brittany to the cold Massif Central or Alsace and to the pleasant, almost Californian Mediterranean coast. Architectural styles make towns and villages in Alsace, Provence, or the Paris area so distinct that they seem to belong to different countries. But these variations are the symbols of other, more profound variations in modes of living; the outdoor life in the clement south and southeast contrasts with the indoor life of the tougher north and east.

These differences naturally led the French to be attached to their *petite patrie*—to their traditional districts—while strangers who come to an area find real human relationships slow to develop. Important consequences follow; for instance, for a long time, political candidates had little chance of being elected if they ran for office in areas where they had no local roots.

The peculiar position of Paris has to be considered in this context. The political, social, economic, and cultural preeminence of the capital is beyond doubt, but it is resented. Paris is much larger than any other French city or metropolitan area. Eight million people live in the Paris area (the city proper has a population of only about 2 million). The next three largest metropolitan areas—Marseilles, Lyons, and Lille—barely reach a million, while the fifth largest town, Toulouse, has about half a million. Provincial capitals are therefore not in a position to challenge the metropolis. Those who have "arrived" have to be in Paris; those who are not in Paris often feel they have not "arrived," although there are exceptions. The weight of Paris, however, is felt even by those who do not wish to move to the capital.

Factors such as the car and television are minimizing sectionalism and bringing Paris nearer to the provinces. The wider economic context of the European Union decreases the preeminence of Paris, but the capital remains a pole of attraction, as well as a drain on the better resources of the provinces, to a much greater extent than in other European countries.

Social Class

Class consciousness, the third main influence on French society, is a function of the cleavages that have torn the fabric of modern society and an outgrowth of the Industrial Revolution, which acquired full momentum in France only at the end of the nineteenth century. Social distinctions run sharp and deep, particularly in the large cities, although these have decreased since the 1950s. The size of the Communist vote was clearly a consequence of the bitterness that these conflicts caused.

Social mobility does occur, of course, indeed at about the same rate as in other developed societies. Moreover, this development is not new. Through education in particular, large numbers of sons and daughters of peasants, of lower-middle-class employees, and of manual workers have entered the middle class. Some educational channels have long made social promotion possible, in particular through prestigious graduate schools, such as the Ecole Polytechnique and the Ecole Normale Supérieure, as well as numerous other schools or examinations leading to the middle ranks of the civil service or the armed forces. Thrifty working-class young people often set up small businesses that they hope slowly to expand.

In France, social class is based to a large extent on occupation, education, and income. Though there is in France a tradition of respect for the crafts (the skills of artisans are often extolled), the esteem for industrial manual work is low. Class tension has decreased somewhat, however, partly as a result of the "embourgeoisement" of many workers who have adopted a middle-class lifestyle, from cars to holidays abroad.

Class tension may also have decreased because large-scale immigration enabled the French to avoid working in the building trades and sections of the automobile and other engineering industries, where they have been replaced by workers from Poland, Italy, Spain, and, since the 1950s, Portugal and, even more, North Africa. This situation may have helped the French avoid less pleasant forms of work, but it is at the root of the major ethnic tensions that have characterized contemporary France. Tension between the native French and North Africans has erupted in violence in many vast suburban high-rise estates where immigrants often are in the majority. While government policy is officially against all forms of discrimination, repressive measures, including forced repatriation, have occasionally been taken against immigrants. Terrorist incidents have from time to time provided authorities with grounds for surveillance and repression of the immigrant population. These measures have been taken in part to compete with and hopefully stop (so far unsuccessfully) the development of a strong extreme-right movement, the National Front, which emerged in the 1980s.

There has also been an increase in the proportion of women in higher-status positions, particularly in the civil service and the professions and more recently in business, but still less so in politics, especially at the parliamentary level. Improvement has taken place despite the fact that there has been markedly less pressure from women's organizations than in Anglo-American countries. Nonetheless, France has not, any more than most industrial countries, ceased to be mainly male dominated.

CHURCH AND STATE

France is nominally a Catholic nation. One million Protestants (Calvinists in the south, Lutherans in Alsace) and fewer than half a million Jews are the only other sizeable indigenous religious groups. While these groups are static or in decline, Muslims have gained appreciably in the course of the last decades. Numbering more than 6 million, they are drawn from among immigrants, mainly from North Africa. The many Muslims born in France may feel religiously but also culturally least at ease in an environment that is often hostile and at best uncomprehending. A number of highly symbolic difficulties have occurred in schools with respect to the right of girls to wear the veil or not to participate fully in physical education classes. However, despite tensions that are often close to the surface, French and non-French Muslims have become somewhat uneasily integrated in the life of the nation.

While France is in theory overwhelmingly a Catholic nation, it also is profoundly anticlerical, in parts wholly dechristianized, and still somewhat affected by the great political battles that led to the separation of church and state in 1905. For the majority of French people, Roman Catholic practice relates only to social rites such as baptisms, marriages, and funerals. Weekly attendance at mass and general observance of religious prescriptions is limited to a rather small minority that is not uniformly spread throughout the nation. Brittany and Alsace are Catholic areas; the western part of the Massif Central and the southeast are antireligious or at best areligious. The historical origins of these variations are complex and are often due less to the priests than to the behavior of the local gentry before or during the Revolution of 1789.

As in most predominantly Roman Catholic countries of Western Europe, church and social order are associated in France. Since the Catholic Church was close to the Right in the nineteenth century, the Left, both moderate and extremist, has always attacked it. The attempt to restore the monarchy in the 1870s was viewed partly as an effort of the Church. Anticlericalism therefore spread among supporters of the Republic. The climax was reached in the 1890s with the Dreyfus case, in which a Jewish military officer was unjustly accused and convicted of treason. In spite of numerous signs that a judicial error had been committed, the case was reopened only after a long and bitter struggle between his defenders and his accusers (the Church, the military, and the conservatives). In 1905, partly in response to the Dreyfus Affair, Parliament passed a law separating church and state. Priests, Protestant ministers, and Jewish rabbis lost their status as civil servants, and various religious orders were disbanded or had to leave the country (among them the Jesuits, who were tolerated again after 1918 and not formally allowed in the country before World War II).

Many Roman Catholics became embittered against the Republic, but others began to realize that a change of attitude had to take place. The pronouncements of Pope Leo XIII helped in this respect, though his successor, Pius X, returned to more traditional ways and condemned a progressive Catholic movement, *Le Sillon,* created in 1894. Development of a strong Christian Democratic party therefore was difficult and was to occur only in the 1940s, too late to enable the party to have a permanent social base, as the country was by then rather dechristianized. On the other hand, progressive Catholics played a large part in the development of some trade unions and other organizations.

The climate has changed since the 1950s, although some antipathy against the Catholic Church still exists. However, the status of Catholics and of the Church has increased and there are no longer the big battles of the early part of the century. Major skirmishes have centered on church schools, to which state subsidies were granted in the 1950s. After the 1981 Socialist victory, when the government attempted to establish greater control over the schools, vast demonstrations occurred—so large that the proposals had to be abandoned. There is still sensitivity with respect to the Catholic Church, but the issue has ceased to be truly central.

THE ADMINISTRATIVE AND CULTURAL CENTRALIZATION OF MODERN FRANCE

Divisions run deep in France. Not all are due to the Revolution, as we have seen; many date back to an earlier period. They cut across each other and lead to a fragmentation of the basic social attitudes, which accounts for much of the ideological and political sectionalism of the country.

The very number and complexity of the social divisions account for state centralization, both administrative and cultural. It is often thought that, had not the French kings and later the Empire set up a strong administrative system, the country would not have survived. It is also often thought that, had not the Republic introduced a uniform political culture cutting across geographical and social barriers, the Republic would not have survived. Administrative centralization was thus practiced by all regimes in order to defend themselves; not surprisingly, the strength of the impressive network of state agencies existing throughout the country has proved difficult to reduce.

The Republic did introduce a new political culture, mostly since the 1880s. This was spread by means of a centralized educational system, which was to be liberal, lay, and egalitarian. It

was not totalitarian, as it aimed at developing critical faculties, but it was uniform. It was largely based on the frame of mind of the writers of the eighteenth-century French Enlightenment, particularly Voltaire, who for about half a century had waged a war against the power of the Church and the state, which were viewed as opposed to rational thinking in order to reduce criticisms of the social order.

This critical ideology clearly undermined the authority on which all states, even republican ones, have to be based; only the centralized administration was therefore able to maintain the state. This, of course, made France more difficult to govern, although one can understand why republican politicians thought it necessary to spread their somewhat negative ideology. By emphasizing the right to criticize, they created problems for their successors. The political system has been bedeviled by the very success of the republicans of the 1880s and 1890s, who bequeathed their political culture to millions of their fellow citizens. But had the republicans not been so successful, France might not have been a republic for long.

Such is the background with which modern French governments have had to contend; not surprisingly, the various traditions reduced the ability of ministers and governments to maneuver. The centralizing tendencies are of course the most visible—and the most overwhelmingly strong—of these traditions. But the weight of tradition can be seen also in the very large part played by the public sector, in its various facets, on the French economy, at least up to the last decade of the twentieth century and even to an extent since then. Centralization brought about a spirit of enlightened despotism and *dirigisme,* the strong role of the state in administering the economy, which has prevailed in the political, administrative, and economic life of the country. France underwent major changes in the second half of the twentieth century, but the impact of the past lies close to the surface. It would be as foolish for observers to forget these traditions as it would be fatal for politicians to disregard them.

Thinking Critically

1. Would you agree with those who say, "All roads in France lead to Paris"?
2. How would you define "anticlericalism" in France?
3. What was the impact of Napoleon on French history and politics?
4. Would you regard France as an example of political instability?
5. What are the major social and political divisions in France?

KEY TERMS

administative centralization *(136)*
church and state *(135)*
class consciousness *(134)*
The Declaration of the Rights of Man and the Citizen *(129)*
The Dreyfus Affair *(135)*
Jacobins *(129)*
Napoleon Bonaparte *(130)*
regional sectionalism *(133)*
republicanism *(131)*
Revolution of 1848 *(130)*
Revolution of 1789/Revolutionary Assembly *(129)*

FURTHER READINGS

Bodley, J. E. *France* (London: Macmillan, 1898).

Brogan, D. W. *The Development of Modern France* (London: Hamish Hamilton, 1940).

Curtis, Michael. *Verdict on Vichy* (New York: Arcade, 2003).

Frears, J. R. *France in the Giscard Presidency* (London: Allen and Unwin, 1981).

de Gaulle, C. *Memoirs* (New York: Simon and Schuster, 1968–1972).

Hall, P. A., J. Hayward, and H. Machin, *Developments in French Politics* 2 (London: Macmillan, 2001).

Hanley, David. *Party, Society and Government: Republican Democracy in France* (New York: Berghahn, 2002).

Hewlitt, Nick. *Democracy in Modern France* (London: Continuum, 2003).

Hoffmann, S., G. Ross, and S. Malzacher, eds. *The Mitterrand Experiment,* (Oxford: Polity Press, 1987).

Howarth, David, and Georgios Varonskakis. *Contemporary France: An Introduction to French Politics and Society* (London: Arnold, 2003).

Milner, Susan, and Nick Parsons, eds., *Reinventing France: State and Society in the 21st Century* (New York: Palgrave Macmillan, 2003).

Safran, William. *The French Polity,* 6th ed. (New York: Longman, 2003).

Todd, E. *The Making of Modern France* (Oxford: Blackwell, 1991).

Williams, P. M. *Crisis and Compromise* (New York: McKay, 1964).

Williams, P. M., and M. Harrison. *Politics and Society in de Gaulle's Republic* (New York: Doubleday, 1973).

Wylie, L. *Village in the Vaucluse* (Cambridge: Harvard University Press, 1964).

B. POLITICAL PROCESSES AND INSTITUTIONS

The advent of the Fifth Republic in 1958 marked the emergence of truly modern politics in France, although as we already noted, elements of the past are still prominent. The constitution was changed, transforming the roles of president, government, and parliament. At the same time, the strength and characteristics of groups and of parties were markedly affected, although these remain weaker and less well-organized than elsewhere in Western Europe.

INTEREST GROUPS

Interest groups have long been frowned upon in France. To this day, they have remained rather weak, at least by comparison with other Western countries. In the 1830s, Tocqueville went to America and saw the part that associations played in bringing about democracy. Nearly 200 years later, France has still not become a truly associational society, and this has important consequences for the democratic character of the society.

The Revolution of 1789 fought the corporate state of the *ancien régime,* in which each trade was organized in closed craft networks that were entered only after long periods of apprenticeship, but which provided their members with monopoly privileges. In the name of liberty the Revolution abolished these guilds and forbade individuals to coalesce to limit production or regulate the entry of others into a profession (with several important exceptions). Trade unions came to be tolerated 75 years after the Revolution, but they had to wait another 25 years to be fully recognized.

Political parties were undermined by the conception that politicians should have direct contacts with electors and remain free from the bureaucratic influence of headquarters and leaders. In the 1950s a major change of attitude occurred, paradoxically as de Gaulle continued to attack groups and parties, but he needed a party to maintain his hold on the country.

While more pluralistic than at any time since 1789, present-day France still has fewer associations than other Western countries. The target of group attacks is often the state, and the typical approach is still to ask the state to meet the demands or to force (for instance, by law) private employers to make concessions. The idea of partnership between economic actors is only slowly gaining ground, and not in a regular manner.

Trade Unions

Workers' Unions The French trade union movement is very divided, largely for political reasons. Its membership is small, proportionately the smallest in Western Europe, indeed smaller than in the United States, though participation is high in works councils mandated by law in firms of a certain size. The relatively late development of the union movement and political divisions account for these weaknesses.

The early history was difficult. Full recognition was achieved only in 1884. Very quickly, trade unions came to be controlled by militants who believed in direct action. By the turn of the twentieth century, they displaced the more reformist or even Marxist elements from the leadership. These "syndicalists" were against employers and against all politicians. The *Confédération Générale du Travail* (CGT), created in 1895 as a federation of all major trade unions, did not look for piecemeal victories through parliament. Rather, it sought one major push through the general strike. The union was never powerful enough to launch any such action and, when war broke out in 1914, even trade unionists rushed to defend the "bourgeois" state.

After World War I, the majority of labor leaders adopted a more reformist stance, but the emergence of Communism brought about a split and introduced party politics into the trade union movement. The CGT followed more closely the Socialist Party, while the more militant elements set up a Communist-led trade union, which was disbanded in 1936 in a "popular front" alliance.

This move enabled Communists to acquire influence gradually in the newly reunited body and to dominate it in 1945. In 1947, when the CGT was openly used for political reasons in a wave of strikes launched by the Communists, the Socialists broke away and set up a new union, the CGT-*Force Ouvrière* (the name of the newspaper of those who held these views).

Meanwhile, a Catholic union, the *Confédération Française des Travailleurs Chrétiens* (CFTC), created in 1918, quickly acquired substantial support among white-collar employees and in strongly Christian parts of the country (Alsace in particular); it then slowly gathered followers in the whole of the country. Having grown to be the second largest trade union, it changed its name in 1964 to widen its appeal and became the *Confédération Française Démocratique du Travail* (CFDT), although a small segment continued under the old name.

There are thus three main trade union organizations catering to manual and white-collar workers. Yet the membership is small, perhaps 2 to 2.5 million for all three organizations. Under 10 percent of the workforce is thus unionized, although there are substantial variations among occupational groups.

Consequences of the Divisions among Workers' Unions   The division of the workers' unions has been detrimental to workers' interests. Employers and governments have been able to play one union against the other. This also has led unions to make demagogic proposals in order not to be overtaken and convinced many French workers that unionization was not necessary. There are exceptions to these divisions, admittedly. In printing, for instance, all the members belong to the CGT. In many firms and offices, one or at most two unions predominate. The CGT is strong mostly on the docks and in mechanical engineering (particularly around Paris). The CFDT's strength tends to be in light industry and among white-collar workers. *Force Ouvrière* leads among textile workers in the north and among civil servants everywhere, though it is not, as is sometimes claimed, the main trade union among civil servants. Competition between two unions

is common. At the national level, all three major unions take stands and are involved in consultations among themselves, with the government, and with employers.

The combination of this traditional weakness of unions and of legislative efforts to integrate the working-class representatives into the rest of society led to a mixture of compulsory cooperation at the top and of semi-anarchistic and often ineffective outbursts at the bottom. Formally, unions are often involved, as in the social security system, which is largely administered by them; there are also factory committees (*comités d'entreprise*) in charge of large sums devoted to leisure and cultural activities; boards of nationalized industries have union representatives. Many advisory committees of the government in the planning field, for instance, include trade union members. Yet unions are often unable to press seriously their claims at the level of the firm, as they often do not agree on a common stand and cannot promise financial help in case of strikes. Many workers thus often continue to work when a strike is called. This occurs despite the fact that the CFDT has regularly campaigned for a new approach to the relationship between workers and society; instead of emphasizing the need for workers' organizations to prepare for an onslaught on the state, as the CGT traditionally tended to do, the CFDT aimed at developing cooperation. It thus played a large part in developing collective bargaining, which came about in France only in the 1950s, although it was legalized in 1936. It was also the first union to place emphasis on the need to improve job conditions, in particular to reduce boredom and repetitiveness.

Yet these moves have not altered patterns of behavior fundamentally. Unions are weak; workers are generally passive. Occasionally, however, there are somewhat anomic massive protest movements which start from the grass roots and extend to a large proportion of the workforce. This was the case in 1968, the catalyst being provided by the student movement. From time to time, especially among students, revolts seemed about to occur, but strikes have become rarer, in part perhaps because of the reforms of the

Socialist government of the first half of the 1980s. The influence of the CGT has markedly declined, as was shown at elections for the social security boards, since the 1980s in particular. The entrenched class antagonism of the past seems to be giving way to more realism and greater moderation.

However, in December 1995, a large movement took place against a proposed governmental reform of pensions and social security. Strikes, in particular in the railways, urban public transport, and to an extent the post office, were on a scale which resembled the 1968 outburst, although the unrest occurred only in the public sector. The movement thus seemed to indicate that some of the old forms of discontent continued to exist, especially as the (conservative) government had tried to impose changes without consultation.

Other Unions   The three major trade union organizations cover, in theory at least, all types of employees. But many white-collar workers, most lower and middle management (*cadres* is the French expression), the professions, and students have typically been organized in different unions (though a minority belong to the three major organizations). There has even been a substantial spread of "autonomous" trade unions among some categories of skilled workers, such as train drivers. Sectional unions have long existed among professionals—doctors, dentists, and lawyers, for instance, who are typically self-employed. Special unions also exist among some other groups, such as school and university teachers. For a while, in the 1950s and early 1960s, students succeeded in creating one of the best and most active French trade unions, the *Union Nationale des Etudiants de France,* but the Algerian war and the events of 1968 led to a radicalization of the leadership, which proved unacceptable to the mass of the students and led to union splits. Finally, much of the employed middle class—the various levels of management in commerce and industry—are organized in a general union, the *Confédération Générale des Cadres* (CGC), which aims at maintaining the pay differentials which *cadres* have acquired in the

growing French economy. Together with the three major workers unions it participates in general government-union discussions, but clashes with workers' unions are frequent in view of status and ideological differences.

Business Organizations

Business organizations are somewhat divided because of the traditional influence of small business and because of the economic changes that have benefited large firms. Before 1945, industrial pressure—mainly from industrialists—on government was frequent, but it tended to occur in secret and outside the framework of organizations. Change began to take place with the first ever French Socialist government, elected in 1936, which initiated general negotiations between government, unions, and business. This led to an overall agreement, the Matignon Accord, which indirectly strengthened the role of business organizations as well as that of trade unions. After World War II the reconstituted *Conseil National du Patronat Français* (CNPF) first started to operate in an unfriendly environment of strong antibusiness ideology. Employers seemed divided among themselves. Though the CNPF was a federation covering all types of firms, small and medium-sized enterprises were organized into a semi-independent confederation, the *Confédération Générale des Petites et Moyennes Entreprises* (CGPME), which because of the larger number and smaller incomes of its members and the prevailing cult of the "petit" in France was often more militant. Meanwhile, a section of the *patronat,* organized into a *Centre des Jeunes Patrons,* now the *Centre des Jeunes Dirigeants d'Entreprise,* displayed a more progressive attitude and criticized their colleagues for their conservatism.

The division between the CGPME and the CNPF—reorganized and renamed *Mouvement des Entreprises de France* (MEDEF) in 1998—has remained a feature of the contemporary French business scene. On the whole, the CNPF used to cooperate with government, but this has been markedly less the case in its new MEDEF incarnation. The earlier cooperation arose in

CGT unionists in Paris at the march in opposition to proposed changes in the 35-hour working week (February, 2005).

part because governments have usually been of the Right or Center, in part because of many personal ties between leaders of large businesses and civil servants. Business leaders and top civil servants tend to go through the same elite schools or be members of the *grands corps,* as we shall see later. Big business has also been broadly sympathetic with the policy of growth and industrialization promoted by French governments since the 1950s, which still prevailed, albeit in a somewhat bruised manner, in the conditions of economic depression of the late 1970s and early 1980s. Relations had been relatively good even with Socialist governments of the 1980s, despite the large-scale nationalization program. They deteriorated to a substantial extent in the late 1990s, the leaders of the MEDEF taking an appreciably more radical,

"free enterprise" line than the leaders of the CNPF had previously adopted.

Defensive Attitudes of Small Business   From the mid-1950s, small businesses, in particular proprietors of small shops and small repair stores, had come increasingly to view with major suspicion both civil servants anxious to rationalize the economy and big businesses that seemed to benefit from the changing economy, in particular supermarkets and discount stores. This led to the development of a number of strong protest movements, the earliest of which, that of Pierre Poujade, the *Union de Défense des Commerçants et Artisans,* became so famous for its populist ideology that it acquired the status of a political symbol. The expression "poujadism" was used widely, in France and abroad, to refer to bodies based on and aiming to represent "small men" fighting against the "tentacles" of the state and of big business. The protest was not just on the economic plane; it was also political (the poujadists obtained 12 percent of the votes at the 1956 parliamentary election). It was often violent, direct action against tax offices being one of the methods used by the movement. The return of de Gaulle to power in 1958 abruptly ended the success of poujadism, but another movement with similar aims and similar tactics was founded in the late 1960s, though that body never had the political success of the prior organization and it quickly faded out. Meanwhile, the CGPME continued throughout the period to voice, in a more responsible manner, the basic grievances of shopkeepers and small businesspeople. Results were indeed occasionally obtained, for instance in the form of restrictions placed on the development of large discount stores.

Outbursts of the underdogs of French business thus did occur in the Fifth Republic, especially in the 1960s, but more sporadically than before 1958, though, under the Socialist governments, truck drivers in particular have more than once adopted direct action and blocked roads and superhighways. On the whole, however, the party system of the Fifth Republic has been better able to contain the activities of these groups. Yet the contrast between the "civilized" forms of pressure exercised by large businesses and the somewhat anomic and occasionally violent actions of small businesspeople shows that traditionalism has not ceased to play a part in the panorama of French social and political life.

Farmers' Organizations

The evolution of agriculture has been rapid, though outbursts of discontent are not unknown among farmers. The flight from the land and the development of mechanization have altered farming conditions everywhere in the country; those who stayed gained more elbow room and some scope for expansion, though they also confronted acute problems of capital and investment. Small farms are the norm except in the north and the Paris area, where wheat and beetroot growers have long constituted an aristocracy, with larger plots, widespread mechanization, and rather high incomes. Elsewhere, the prevailing culture emphasizes, and is adamant to protect, the tradition of the small farm. This culture prevails, not just among the members of the agricultural community, but widely across many segments of the population and in the political world.

The main pressure group of farmers is the *Fédération Nationale des Syndicats d'Exploitants Agricoles* (FNSEA), created in 1945 and originally led by the northern farmers. This body was challenged as agriculture rapidly changed in structure and its relation to the rest of the community. The first anomic protests resembled those of shopkeepers; roadblocks and the dumping of unsold vegetables were fairly common means of demonstrating anger. Gradually, however, a change began to occur when a number of associations, mainly of Catholic origin, started to stress the long-term benefits of the modernization of agriculture, cooperation among farmers being presented as the best way of solving the problems posed by the need to undertake large investments, especially in machinery. The agricultural policy of the European Community, as the European Union was then known, also suggested that huge opportunities were becoming open to French farmers. The *Jeunesse Agricole Chrétienne* and the *Centre National des Jeunes Agriculteurs* (CNJA) thus succeeded in converting large sections of the farming community to their views, to the extent that these eventually came to be adopted by the FNSEA as CNJA leaders took over that organization.

Yet recurring complaints continue to be voiced by farmers. Many of them feared the effect on their incomes of the expansion of the European Community and of the liberalization of farm products on a worldwide basis. On the whole, farmers' unions have succeeded in forcing French governments to support their cause on the international scene, indeed to an extent that seems out of proportion with the size of the farming population.

Other Groups

Since the mid-1960s, interest groups have played a large part in the panorama of French political life, although their development has remained patchy. Until the late 1950s, promotional groups had not been influential. For instance, while the nuclear disarmament campaign was reaching a climax in Britain, there was almost no equivalent in France, though the subject could have become controversial when de Gaulle embarked on a worldwide nuclear strategy.

The Algerian war was instrumental in the development of protest organizations, as political parties seemed impotent and none of them, not even the Communist Party, was able or willing to take a firm line against the war. The end of the Algerian war in 1962 made these protest organizations obsolete, but gradually new groups emerged. Consumer associations started to inquire into the quality of products, forms of marketing, and relative costs. Environmental societies have campaigned against the pollution of the seaside and the development of private beaches, attacked the takeover of vast areas of land for army camps, and opposed plans for highways and, more recently, for new lines for "very rapid" trains. Some groups are purely local and exclusively concerned with one issue; others are national and foster general aims. From the mid-1970s, antinuclear groups have become vocal and often violent, while women's groups have begun to make themselves felt, but both types have remained relatively low-key.

In the late 1960s and early 1970s, there was an upsurge in the activity of regionalist groups. Long limited to the Bretons and (though less so) the Basques, regionalist ideas extended for a while to large parts of the country, particularly the southern half, where the *Mouvement Occitan* stated that the "colonization" of the country by the north and by Paris had to be ended. The strength of most of these movements declined, however, in part probably because the Socialist government of 1981–1986 introduced regionalist and decentralization measures. Only to an extent in French Overseas Territories (in New Caledonia, in the Caribbean) and above all in Corsica did radicalization occur. Yet even in Corsica, the terrorist activities of autonomist movements has remained rather patchy, in part because of the division among these movements. These terrorist activities are beginning to have an effect on politicians' attitudes, however, the Socialist Party being, on the whole, the only party which is truly prepared to grant substantial autonomy to the island. In continental France, the one set of serious terrorist activities which the country has known since World War II occurred during the Algerian war in the early 1960s. In the late 1980s and mid-1990s, however, there were sporadic outbursts of bombing connected with Muslim, and

A CLOSER LOOK 3.2

THE WEAKNESS OF PROTEST GROUPS IN FRANCE

Groups are unquestionably much weaker in France than in other Western democracies. What was true in the nineteenth century continues to be true, despite some changes, at the beginning of the twenty-first. It is not just that trade unions are less strong and more divided than elsewhere; it is that the groups which flourish in other countries do not emerge, or scarcely emerge, in the French context. The huge antinuclear protests in Britain had no counterparts in France, despite the fact that France has nuclear weapons. The limited reactions within France to the bombs exploded in the Pacific in the mid-1990s are a case in point. Moreover, there have also been on balance relatively few demonstrations against nuclear power stations despite the fact that France has more nuclear power stations than other countries. Even feminist groups have been weak, and not because women have made more advances in France than elsewhere, though they have not made fewer advances than elsewhere either. The low level of associationalism in France was mentioned by Tocqueville in his *Democracy in America* in the 1830s and, remarkably, the same trend still prevails. This characteristic is unquestionably among the most important aspects of French political culture.

in particular Algerian, opposition to French government policies.

Groups and the Political System

The Role of Consultation   The Fifth Republic began in 1958 with an anti–interest-group bias. Yet de Gaulle was soon confronted with large waves of protest on the part of veterans and of opponents of church schools. The government took little notice of the huge demonstrations and won. De Gaulle seemed to have proved his point—that when the state is strong, it can withstand the pressure of groups. However, his policy of benign neglect led to an accumulation of grievances which finally exploded in May and June 1968. Since then, leaders of the Fifth Republic have been more cautious and have developed consultation as a means of addressing grievances.

The origin of consultation can be traced to the *ancien régime* and the Napoleonic system. Although it was initially limited to narrow sectors of the population, representation gradually increased. After World War I, it was institutionalized through an economic council that was given constitutional status in 1946. The Economic and Social Council is composed of representatives of all sectors of the population, including consumers and intellectuals. In addition to advising on bills and the more important government regulations, it debates economic and social plans. Together with the many representative bodies on which trade unionists are present (boards of nationalized industries, social security boards, and others) and with the associations of farmers (*Chambres d'Agriculture*) or of business leaders (*Chambres de Commerce*), the council provides a broad formal basis to the consultative process.

Yet what had been lacking until recently was not so much a formal machinery, but a will to discuss or a climate of consultation. Previously partnership existed only in one privileged sector, big business, where personal ties between leaders of industry and higher civil servants made informal discussions possible and indeed frequent. For small business, agriculture, employ-

ees, and consumers, no similar relations existed. Admittedly, the uncooperative and unrealistic attitudes of many trade unions and of many other groups can be blamed, but these uncooperative attitudes were also in part the product of an earlier lack of partnership.

Some change began to occur in the 1970s with Presidents Pompidou and Giscard d'Estaing. Pompidou's first prime minister, Chaban-Delmas, undertook to bring about a partnership between the various "live forces" *(forces vives)* of the nation. Then, in the 1980s, having accused the Gaullists and their associates of not giving enough scope for consultation, the Socialists who

General Charles de Gaulle (1890–1970) was the leader of the Free French movement in London during World War II, the head of government in 1944–1946, the last prime minister of the Fourth Republic in 1958, and president of France 1959–1969.

came to power in 1981 attempted to increase consultation; however, the program of reforms which they undertook was so large in the fields of local and regional government, public enterprise, and workers' participation that the government was primarily anxious to act quickly. The return of the Right to power, first in the late 1980s and subsequently in 1993, did not lead to much change, if any, in the direction of greater consultation. Under the Socialist government of the late 1990s, consultation suffered a setback when the leaders of the new business organization, the MEDEF, declared that they would no longer participate in the management of the social security bodies if major changes in structure were not introduced; no way out of the impasse had been found by the time the Socialists left power in 2002.

The role of interest groups has increased: the civil service can no longer implement its big projects without engaging in discussions with vocal groups. Yet much has still to be done to reconcile the French with the basic need for and the real value of association. As few workers belong to unions, these are weak and their leaders often feel impotent. Much has still also to be done, despite recent changes, to bring government and civil service nearer to the nation. A centralizing spirit and centralized structures are major handicaps to a real partnership between groups and the state. Therein lies perhaps the major problem of French society, a problem which the 1981–1986 Socialist government began to tackle, but to which high priority has not been given since then, although lip service is periodically paid to the need to find a solution.

THE PARTY SYSTEM

Streamlining the Parties: Gaullists and Socialists

Before 1958, French parties were weak, poorly organized, and undisciplined. This was largely due to the traditions that we examined earlier and in particular to the high degree of localism. With the advent of the Fifth Republic, the situa-

tion changed somewhat, but neither regularly nor indeed continuously. In a first period, roughly during the 1960s, the Gaullist party established itself as the dominant party. It won an unprecedented victory in 1968, when it gained a large majority of seats (though only 45 percent of the votes), but this was followed by a decline in the 1970s. The Gaullist party has scarcely polled above 20 percent since the 1980s, most of the votes lost going to groups of the Center, which are only loosely held together.

The election of 1981 changed the party configuration, in more ways than one. The French Socialist Party, for the first time in the history of the country, won an absolute majority of seats; it gained only 38 percent of the votes, admittedly, but never had it obtained before the support of more than a quarter of the electorate. For the first time since 1958, there was a change in the party in power. The victory of the Socialists in 1981 was also remarkable in that it signalled the end of the Communist Party as a major force in French politics. That party declined first to 16 percent and subsequently to under 10 percent.

The 1986 parliamentary election brought about the return of the Right with a small majority, but when reelected in 1988, the Socialist president, Mitterrand, immediately dissolved parliament. The Socialist Party did win, though this time short of an absolute majority. It was to suffer a crushing defeat at the parliamentary election of 1993, in part as a result of a number of financial scandals. The Right confirmed its victory at the 1995 presidential election, which was won by the Gaullist Chirac with a relatively small majority. However, in view of the squabbles within the right-wing coalition in power, Chirac dissolved parliament a year early, in 1997; this led, somewhat unexpectedly, to a victory of the Socialist Party at the head of a coalition including Communists and Greens. Lionel Jospin's tenure as prime minister was to last five years, up to the 2002 election, the longest that any Socialist prime minister in France ever enjoyed. The 1997 election also led to the longest period during which a president of one party (the Gaullists) was to "cohabit" with a government of the other main party (the Socialists).

In the first ballot vote for the May 2002 presidential election, Socialist candidate Jospin came in third, behind extreme-Right candidate Le Pen. Chirac won an easy victory over Le Pen in the run-off, and in June 2002 the Socialists were roundly defeated. As a result, the Right held both the presidency and the government.

In the Fifth Republic, the French party system is somewhat more streamlined than under the two previous Republics. It still has a multiparty character, but these parties come under the umbrella of two main blocs, Center-right, in which Gaullists and Center parties now share power equally, and Center-left, in which the Socialist Party dominates. Thus even when, as in the 1970s and typically in the 1990s, complex coalitions have controlled the government, these have remained more disciplined and cohesive than at almost any time since the beginning of the twentieth century.

The Effect of the Electoral System

The streamlining of the party system was helped by the electoral system that (with the exception of the 1986 parliamentary election) has been in force since 1958. The system is known as the *scrutin d'arrondissement à deux tours,* a two-ballot system within single-member districts taking place on two successive Sundays. This type of electoral system had been in use during most of the Third Republic, but it was replaced in 1945 by proportional representation, traditionally advocated by the Left as being fairer. Proportional representation was reintroduced by the Socialist majority in 1985, but the conservative coalition that won in 1986 returned to the majority system. At the first ballot, only candidates receiving 50 percent or more of the votes cast in a district are elected. At the second round, the candidate who gets the most votes is elected, but only candidates who obtained more than 12.5 percent of the votes at the first round may run. Between the first and second round, deals take place and candidates withdraw voluntarily, sometimes in favor of other candidates better placed in the race.

The effect of this two-ballot system on the French party system has varied somewhat over time and is not entirely straightforward. In some cases, it has the same apparent consequences as the British first-past-the-post system. It has made it possible for one party to be temporarily dominant, as in the case of the Gaullists between 1962 and 1973 and of the Socialists during most of the last two decades of the twentieth century. At other times, the effect has been to create two blocs—on the Right and on the Left—within which agreements are made between component parties. This type of agreement has become truly imperative to governments of the Right. After the decline of the Gaullist party in the mid-1970s, the scene was also occupied by the *Union pour la Démocratie Française* (UDF), a coalition of loosely organized medium-sized and small parties closely connected at the time with President Giscard d'Estaing. This coalition consistently obtained between a fifth and a quarter of the votes at parliamentary elections. On the Left, the Socialist Party has dominated but has tended to associate with some Center-left groupings, some Communists, and increasingly some members of the Green Party.

The French system thus remains multiparty, with only some tendencies toward having dominant parties (see Table 3.3). The effect of the electoral system consists perhaps more in bringing parties within two broad blocs than in forcing the merger let alone the disappearance of parties.

The Right and Center

Unlike Britain, France never had a Conservative party. Yet on at least two occasions, it seemed that the Gaullist party would be able to unite the large majority of the electors of the Right. The first time was in the late 1940s, when de Gaulle created the *Rassemblement du Peuple Français* (RPF), which was pointedly called a "rally" because its founder wanted to indicate that his organization was different from all other political movements. The RPF was for a time very successful. At the municipal elections of 1947, it swept most large towns, obtained nearly 40 percent of the votes cast, and seemed a major challenge to the government of the Fourth Republic. Traditional parties of the Center, however, proved to be resilient and gradually eroded

TABLE 3.3

ELECTIONS TO THE FRENCH NATIONAL ASSEMBLY (SELECTED DATES)

		Party Votes (%)						
	Total (millions)	Communist and Other Left Parties	Socialists	Center-left and Greens	Center	Gaullists	National Front	Other
1962	18.3	22.0	15.0	8.0	29.0	32.0		
1981	25.0	16.2	37.6	1.3	19.1	20.9		4.9
1988	24.0	11.1	37.7	0.3	40.3*		9.9	0.6
1993	25.2	11.0	17.6	10.1	19.2	20.4	12.5	9.1
1997	25.3	12.1	25.5	6.7	14.7	16.8	15.1	9.1
2002	26.3	7.6	25.2	4.4/3.1	4.2	34.2	11.1	4.6

	Total	Seats per Party						
1962	480	41	67	45	89	234	—	4
1981	491	45	289	—	73	84	—	—
1988	577	27	277		—	130	128	112
1993	577	25	67	—	206	242	1	36
1997	577	37	245	37	109	140	1	8
2002	577	21	154	3	22	369	—	8

*Combination of Center and Gaullists for 1988 election only. Before and after 1988 they were separate.

Gaullist strength. At the 1951 general election, the Gaullists obtained little more than one-fifth of the votes; a year later they split, and by 1956 Gaullism as a movement had all but disappeared.

The resurgence of Gaullism was the direct consequence of de Gaulle's return to power in 1958 as a result of the inability of the Fourth Republic's political leaders to deal with the Algerian problem. But this time the return of Gaullism seemed likely to be more than a passing phenomenon. The *Union pour la Nouvelle République* (UNR), as the Gaullist party then came to be named, obtained a quarter of the votes in 1958 and 40 percent in 1962. These successes were repeated at the elections of 1967 and 1968, and by then, the Gaullist party seemed fully established. It was the closest to a mass party on the Right that France ever had, although it did not have a very large membership (unlike the old RPF of the late 1940s)—50,000 members in the early 1960s and about three times this figure in the

early 1970s. Membership drives occurred from time to time, but they were neither pushed hard nor really successful.

The policies of the first Gaullist party—that of the 1940s—were on the whole those of the authoritarian right. De Gaulle ostensibly favored ideas of collaboration between capital and labor and announced a profit-sharing scheme, but its details were not worked out in practice. What was more apparent was a nationalistic tone and a strong anticommunist stance; the policies on colonial issues were somewhat ambiguous. The first Gaullist party also allowed its militants to behave with some brutality against opponents. Fighting often broke out, and local Communist Party headquarters were occasionally burnt. The second Gaullist party, which emerged after 1958, acted more responsibly and its policies were more moderate.

In its heyday in the late 1960s, the Gaullist party seemed able to attract the support of a large proportion of the electorate without having to build a massive organization. It provided de Gaulle and his government with a solid majority, although it ceased to be as monolithic as it was once accused of being. No longer authoritarian as the first Gaullist party had been, the UNR seemed to be based on a discipline that was naturally accepted; whips were not imposed in a ruthless fashion. In parliamentary debates, criticism may not have been voiced on major matters, but it was often expressed on less important questions. This was in part because there was a "community of feeling," or common approach, between de Gaulle and his supporters in parliament and elsewhere. Some may have disagreed on tactics, but most Gaullists agreed on basic aims.

The Decline of the Gaullist Party and Its Recovery in 2002 In part because of the large parliamentary majority which de Gaulle bequeathed to his successor, Pompidou, the dominance of the Gaullist party in French politics survived for a time after the departure and death of the founder of the Fifth Republic. But the beginnings of the decline can be traced to one of the first decisions of Pompidou, which was to appoint to the government a number of members of small fringe parties who had hitherto remained on the sidelines. Unlike Adenauer in West Germany in the 1950s, Pompidou did not attempt to force non-Gaullist parliamentarians of the Right and Center to choose between joining the Gaullist party or abandoning effective political life. He undermined his own party by relying increasingly on non-Gaullist politicians—and in particular on Giscard d'Estaing—to counterbalance the strength of the Gaullists.

The real blow to Gaullist supremacy was administered in 1974 by one of the younger leaders of the Gaullist party at the time, Chirac, who led a substantial group of Gaullist members of parliament to support the candidacy of Giscard d'Estaing for the presidency against the official Gaullist candidate, Chaban-Delmas. Giscard d'Estaing won, and he rewarded Chirac for a while by appointing him prime minister, but the Gaullist party lost its dominant position. It lost the prime ministership in 1976, and the subse-

quent efforts of Chirac, who became Gaullist party leader, to strengthen the organization and to oppose, at times bitterly, the president whom he had so significantly helped to elect proved unsuccessful. The Gaullist party, which had by then been renamed *Rassemblement pour la République* (RPR), had ceased to embody the Fifth Republic. By 1978, the Gaullist party obtained only a quarter of the votes cast, a proportion that did not change markedly during the 1980s and 1990s, despite the efforts of its leader, Chirac. In 2002, in the wake of his presidential victory, he created a new movement, the *Union pour la Majorité Présidentielle* (UMP), which went a long way, but not all the way, toward incorporating all the (non-extreme) Right. This was converted into the Union for a Popular Movement (also UMP).

The Resilience of the Center

France has been characterized traditionally by an undisciplined and loosely organized Center and Right—which curiously seem nevertheless to succeed in staying in power for very long periods. The constant inability of the Right to be organized was accompanied by periodic efforts to streamline the many organizations that belonged to it, the efforts of the Gaullists being in a line of earlier endeavors. Thus, in the late 1930s, a new party, the *Parti Social Français,* seemed for a while poised to make considerable gains, but because of the Second World War, the 1940 election which would have provided the test never took place.

In 1945, when prewar conservative groups had been badly shaken by the fact that many of their members had collaborated with the Vichy regime of 1940–1944, a Christian party, the *Mouvement Républicain Populaire* (MRP), obtained a quarter of the votes. Its policies were not moderate enough to satisfy the conservative electorate, however, and its alliance with the Communists made it somewhat suspect. The emergence of de Gaulle's RPF caused the vote for the MRP to drop to about 10 percent. Yet the strength of the RPF in turn quickly eroded. By 1956, the shopkeepers' party of Poujade seemed on the verge of constituting a new catalyst, but its policies were too crude to attract the bulk of the Right; it gained only 12 percent of the votes and was soon swept away by the second Gaullist tide.

Neither organization nor ideology can provide the real explanation for the resilience or recurrence of groupings on the Center and Right; the explanation can be found only by considering the social base. Before World War II, and to a large extent in the 1950s as well, conservative and center groups were composed of prominent local politicians who had first established their influence at the municipal and county levels and had enough following to be elected to parliament. These developments flourished in a context in which political behavior was highly sectional; they accounted for the fact that parties remained both organizationally weak and undisciplined in parliament. The village and small-town basis of politics thus mirrored the rather static character of the society.

The socioeconomic changes that followed World War II seemed likely to end the dominance of these traditional politicians, especially as the war record of many of them had been poor or downright inadmissible. The old Radical party, which had long ceased to be radical except in name, was thus discredited for having led France during the years that preceded the collapse of 1940. Yet in the late 1940s and early 1950s, the same Radical party as well as other traditional groupings on the Center and Right made a surprisingly rapid comeback. Their leaders showed considerable skill and strength in opposing the first Gaullist party of the late 1940s; they became partners in government with Christian Democrats and Socialists, since those two parties alone could not command a parliamentary majority. The Radical leaders eventually provided most of the prime ministers of the last years of the Fourth Republic, only to show once more, in 1958, their inability to lead the country decisively in times of crisis.

The gradual return of small Center and Right parties to the fore in the 1970s after over a decade of Gaullist dominance is in the French political tradition in spite of major economic and social changes. In order to compete with the

Gaullists, these parties have had to be better organized than in the past. From the 1978 general election, they federated under the label *Union pour la Démocratie Française* (UDF). But the various segments of the UDF have kept their identity, the two strongest elements being the Republican party founded by Giscard d'Estaing but renamed subsequently *Démocratie libérale* under a new leader, and the *Centre démocratique et social* (CDS), which is the heir to the Christian party of the 1940s and 1950s. Overall, the UDF remains an uneasy coalition of somewhat autonomous chieftains joining forces to repulse a common enemy. It is not a true federation, let alone a single party.

From the 1978 general election and throughout the 1980s and 1990s, the Right and Center have been divided into two major forces of about equal strength—the Gaullists and the non-Gaullists. Moreover, since the early 1980s, a challenge to the Gaullists and non-Gaullists has come from the extreme right, with the National Front led by Le Pen, who had been a poujadist deputy of 1956.

The Extreme Right

The National Front has somewhat fascist undertones; its main plank—and source of success—has been an attack against immigrants, mainly those from North Africa. It gained substantial successes in particular in a number of suburban areas. The 10 percent of the votes it obtained at the 1986 election grew to 14 percent at the 1988 presidential election. Support for the Front remained static at the parliamentary elections of 1988, 1993, and 1997 as well as at the presidential election of 1995. The party then split, one of the key lieutenants of Le Pen having decided that Le Pen had become too old and perhaps too soft on some issues. The result was a temporary decline of each of the two parties (and of the votes of both parties jointly) at the 1999 European parliament election and at the 2001 local elections.

But Le Pen recovered, somewhat unexpectedly, at the 2002 presidential election. He recovered so well that he succeeded in beating Jospin, the Socialist candidate, for second place at the first ballot, thus qualifying for the run-off; Le Pen was only three points behind Chirac, scoring 17 percent against Chirac's 20 percent. This result did not mean, however, that the extreme-Right had significantly gained ground in the electorate, although the fact that Le Pen was Chirac's challenger had a great symbolic significance. One result was that it mobilized practically all the rest of the electors (82 percent) behind Chirac at the run-off. Indeed, the National Front suffered a substantial defeat at the June parliamentary election, where it obtained only 11 percent of the votes.

The Left

While the Right and Center were traditionally based on loose, personalized groupings, the Left has long been organized around structured political parties, but always around more than one. Before World War I, the Socialists competed with the Radicals. After World War I, the Communist Party quickly gained votes, reaching 12 percent in 1932 and 15 percent in 1936, and peaking at 28 percent in 1946. Though the Communist Party lost votes when de Gaulle returned to power in 1958, it hovered around 20 percent for about two decades and was a force to be reckoned with, especially because the decline of the Socialist Party was even more pronounced in the 1950s and 1960s. Only in 1981 did the Communist Party's strength substantially diminish again, first to 16 percent, and later to under 10 percent. The party has been marginalized as a result and the Socialist Party has become the dominant party of the Left, although it suffered a major defeat in 1993 when it obtained under 20 percent of the votes. It recovered in 1997 but lost substantial support at the 2002 presidential election, where Jospin obtained only 16 percent of the votes. At the subsequent parliamentary election, it obtained a more normal 25 percent.

The Socialist Party   The victories won by the Socialist Party since 1981 seem almost miraculous, given what the party had been in the 1960s. Born in 1905, and for over half a century called the French Section of the (Sec-

ond) Working-Class International (SFIO), the Socialist Party originated from two groups created in the 1890s, one humanitarian and liberal, the other Marxist. Until 1914, the party practiced "noncollaboration" with bourgeois governments and seemed to be moving gradually toward a commanding position. At the 1914 general election, the party had about 100 deputies, or one-sixth of the chamber. Jaurès, the great humanitarian leader of the party, tried with all his strength to rally the antiwar forces, but he was assassinated just before hostilities started, and French Socialists were made to accept the *Union Sacrée*. Some of their members joined the cabinet.

Early Setbacks of the Socialist Party   As in other European countries, a wing of the Socialist Party split in 1920 to form the Communist Party. This had little immediate effect on the Socialist organization but did hamper its electoral appeal; the party stagnated at the polls during the 1920s and 1930s, gaining votes on its right but losing about the same number on its left. At the 1936 general election, the party emerged apparently as the great winner, having led to victory the Popular Front coalition, which included the Radicals on its right and the Communists on its left, as well as various socialist splinter groups. For the first time a Socialist, Blum, was called to head the government, and for a few tense spring days the dream of the Socialist Party seemed to have become reality. But the victory was in fact small (the Socialist Party obtained only one-quarter of the votes) and hollow.

The expectations of manual workers had been raised so high by the 1936 election result that sit-down strikes soon became the norm in large factories. The Communists pushed for takeovers while the liberals were already backing out. Blum, a follower of Jaurès, a *grand bourgeois* who strongly believed in equality and liberty, made a number of important reforms (the 40-hour week, paid holidays, and collective bargaining), but he did not succeed in retaining the confidence of the workers nor, of course, in acquiring that of the employers. Financial difficulties grew and the government, in difficulty with the upper house of parliament, the Senate, resigned after a year in office.

The Socialist Party then entered a long period of decline. It was divided over the Vichy regime in 1940, and while it took an important part in the Resistance, it was far behind the Communists. It was central to many coalitions of the Fourth Republic after World War II, but perhaps as a result, its support dwindled, falling from 25 percent of the votes in 1945 to 15 percent in 1958. It entered the era of the Fifth Republic as a losing and demoralized party.

Reorganization of the Socialist Party   From the mid-1960s, efforts were made to broaden the base of the Socialist Party and change its image. Hopes were entertained around the creation of a federal organization that was expected to be substantially larger than the Communist Party. The Radicals and the Christian Democrats, as well as representatives of some political clubs, were to belong to the new grouping, sometimes viewed as a potentially large umbrella for the Left, but minor Socialist groups opposed the move, and the Christian Democrats, unsure of their conservative voters, rejected the proposal, while the old anti-Catholic reflex grew in the Socialist Party itself. A smaller and looser grouping comprising Socialists, Radicals, and some tiny organizations was to be a more modest but influential alternative. Its presidential candidate, Mitterrand, polled 45 percent of the votes at the presidential election of 1965, and it returned 121 members of parliament at the 1967 general election, but the old Socialist Party did not survive a crushing electoral defeat in 1968 in the wake of the Gaullist wave following the end of the 1968 "revolt."

Mitterrand was to prove stubborn in his aim to unite and lead the Left, however. Helped by the disarray caused by a further defeat of the Left at the polls at the presidential election of 1969, which followed de Gaulle's resignation, Mitterrand campaigned for the reconstruction of the Socialist Party—now known simply as the *Parti Socialiste*. Having become leader of the new party, he entered a series of negotiations with the Communist Party designed to expand the collaboration between the two organizations. A "Common Program of the Left" was adopted in 1972. It was markedly Socialist but more moderate than the Communists wanted. The result was the first upsurge in Socialist votes in 30 years at the 1973 general election.

The Socialist Party continued to increase its strength. At the 1974 presidential election, Mitterrand was once more defeated, but by a small margin. Hopes were increasingly entertained that economic difficulties and the natural unpopularity of a majority coalition in power for 20 years would result in a victory for the opposition. Divisions between Socialists and Communists appeared to have been buried, with the Socialist Party being the clear leader of the opposition. The "Common Program of the Left" was generally viewed as the natural alternative. The result of an agreement between Socialists and Communists at a time when the Communists were still the stronger partner, it had a radical flavor and included in particular large-scale nationalization proposals. At the municipal elections of 1977 the two opposition parties did particularly well—the Socialist candidates being especially successful.

In late 1977, however, the Communist Party decided to make strong demands for a redrafting of the "Common Program"; it made suggestions for major changes to sharpen the radical character of the program. Negotiations broke down. The Communist Party then endeavored to undermine the Socialist Party at the grass roots but failed. It did, however, undermine the credibility of the Left in general and therefore bore responsibility for its defeat at the 1978 general election. The 1978 result was nevertheless the best result achieved by the Socialist Party since 1945, and for the first time since World War II it was the largest party in the country.

The Socialist Victory of 1981   The breakdown of the "Common Program" led to a short period of stagnation, and divisions within the Socialist Party seemed to point to the reelection of Giscard d'Estaing as president in 1981. Yet, during the winter of 1980–1981, the tables were turned rapidly. Mitterrand declared himself a candidate and rallied the whole Socialist Party behind him. The Communist Party fielded their secretary general, Marchais, whose popularity was low and personal record unappealing. The scandals and arrogance associated with Giscard d'Estaing, coupled with the ever deepening economic recession, meant an upsurge in the fortunes of the Socialist Party, whose slogan (*Une force tranquille*) and whose symbol (the rose) turned out to be clear winners.

At the first round of the presidential election of April–May 1981, Mitterrand was still 2 percent behind Giscard d'Estaing, but the Communists had lost 5 percent of the votes. On the second ballot, two weeks later, when only the top two candidates could stand, Mitterrand edged out as the winner with 52 percent of the votes. A large bandwagon effect then occurred. The National Assembly was dissolved and, in June, for the first time in French history, the Socialist Party won an absolute majority of seats in parliament. The Communist representation had been halved; the Communist Party could be given four seats in the government between 1981 and 1984 without any danger.

Five years of stable government of the Left then followed—for the first time in French history. At first reforms took place rapidly and on a large scale; nationalizations, industrial reforms, and administrative decentralization were among the main changes. By 1983, however, economic difficulties led to a major rethinking, as France could not push for growth in a world in which retrenchment and "monetarism" were dominant. The Socialist government became moderate; this led the Communists to leave the government in 1984.

Ups and Downs of the Socialist Party The Socialist Party lost votes at the 1986 general election but remained the largest party, with 32 percent of the votes. It had gained a reputation for moderation and statesmanship; it had shown greater unity than the conservatives who, while pledged to rule together as they did between 1986 and 1988, displayed a high level of dissension. This may explain in part the second victory of Mitterrand at the 1988 presidential election and of the Socialist Party at the subsequent general election, although the party

this time remained a few seats short of an absolute majority.

The prime minister appointed by the president in 1988, Rocard, practiced a policy of "openness" (*ouverture*) to the elements of the center parties and stressed sound management rather than ideological pronouncements. The head of the government was popular in the country, but not among the party activists throughout his three years in office. He was perhaps for this reason suddenly replaced by Mme Cresson, the first woman French prime minister. Although this was regarded as a rather skillful move by Mitterrand, largely because the new incumbent was a woman, the result proved to be a failure. Cresson was replaced a year later by a faithful supporter of Mitterrand, hitherto minister of finance, Beregovoy. By then, however, the party had become embroiled in a number of financial scandals that seemed to concern both the organization and a number of prominent personalities at national and local levels (but similar scandals also affected the parties of the Right and Center). Defeat at the 1993 parliamentary election was crushing. The Socialist Party received fewer votes than at any time since 1962; yet the result was even worse at the European parliamentary elections one year later.

The party quickly bounced back, benefiting largely from the internal dissensions within the Right and Center coalition in power between 1993 and 1997. At the 1995 presidential election, the candidate of the Socialist Party, Jospin, an ex-minister of education who had become secretary general of the party, obtained 47 percent of the votes. Under Jospin's leadership, the party was then to win decisively the 1997 parliamentary election, admittedly in combination with the Radicals, Communists, and Greens. The policies of Jospin's government were to be moderate, though not to the same extent as those of Blair and Schröder, an example being provided by the introduction of the 35-hour week. Although the prime minister was continuously popular during his five-year term of office, this was not enough to ensure a Socialist victory in 2002. At the presidential election, Jospin was in the third place and decided immediately to quit politics. At the parliamentary election, under the provisional leadership of its secretary, François Hollande, the party suffered a substantial loss of seats (because of the greater unity of the Right and the decline of the other components of the Left) despite the fact that its percentage of votes was about the same as in 1997.

The Greens and the Communist Party

By the turn of the twenty-first century, the French Left included, alongside and indeed under the Socialist Party, a number of groupings, the two most important of which have been the Greens and the Communists. The Greens grew in strength in the 1990s, but in an uneven manner as a result of their weak organization and the serious personality conflicts that characterize them. The Communist Party, however, has a long history and was for three decades the leading party of the Left before its catastrophic decline in the 1980s and 1990s.

The hold of the French Communist Party (PCF) on French politics has much puzzled observers, as France has been one of the few European countries (with Italy, Finland, and Portugal) in which Communist strength has been large for over a generation after World War II. Simple economic explanations are obviously not sufficient: the standard of living is as high in France as in other Western European countries, indeed higher than in some. Moreover, development in France was just as fast, at least until the mid-1970s. Those who in the late 1940s had hoped that an improvement of living conditions would be accompanied by a substantial decrease in Communist Party membership have been disappointed. The Communist vote was to be reduced, but not at that time and not for economic reasons.

The resilience of the Communist Party is found in its history—a history marked in large part by the discredit of the Socialist Party and by that party's subsequent decline. The Communist Party was born of the discontent felt by many Socialists after World War I, as their party had firmly supported the war. The Resistance provided a second boost during World War II. Up to 1941, when the war was labeled bourgeois and

imperialist by the Soviet Union, French Communists refused to participate in the defense of their country (their members of the parliament were dismissed in 1940) and even supported the German occupying forces in the early period. But after the Nazi invasion of the Soviet Union, the Communist Party took a leading part in the Resistance. It gained considerable prestige as a result (nicknaming itself the *parti des fusillés,* the party of the shot), successfully infiltrated the underground trade union organizations, and made inroads in parts of the countryside (particularly in those regions which the Resistance had freed from the German occupying troops long before liberation). The party went into the government in 1944, probably hoping to remain in it for long periods, but in May 1947 the Communist ministers were dismissed. With the intensification of the Cold War, the Communist Party used trade union strength to harass the government (the strikes of November 1947 were among the most difficult episodes of postwar French politics). But the government won, and the Communist challenge became less effective. By the end of the Fourth Republic in 1958, the Communist Party was a nuisance, not a menace; it could help any party to overthrow governments, but it could do little to achieve its own aims.

The Communist Party thus occupied, from the 1950s at least, the comfortable position of being the only real defender of the workers against capitalism; yet it was at the same time (its supporters would say that this was precisely for that reason) a rigid, indeed monolithic organization. Its detractors criticized it for its complacency and total lack of intellectual life as much as for its internal dictatorial methods. Purges had taken place from time to time, enabling the secretary general to remain at the helm of a large machine (potential successors were shown to be wrong or traitors to the party), but vitality was absent, in contrast with what was occurring in the Italian Communist Party.

In the 1960s, some signs of liberalization did emerge. In August 1968, for the first time in its history, the party dared to voice a criticism of the Soviet Union and (though in a somewhat lukewarm manner) attacked the occupation of

Czechoslovakia. After the 1978 defeat at the polls, however, the French Communist Party retreated once more into its characteristic position of faithful and loyal supporter of the "Socialist Motherland."

For a few more years, the tightly knit character of the party organization accounted for its maintained strength, the Communist Party being the only French party that ever created a "society," and a very disciplined and hierarchical one at that. Membership figures have been unreliable, but the party seems to have had about 300,000 to 400,000 paid-up members (about 8 to 10 percent of its voters) in the 1960s and 1970s—more than other parties had. For long periods, these members were tied closely to the party. Thus party decisions, in theory based on "democratic centralism," could be in practice imposed by the secretariat and the executive committee. Resolutions were virtually always adopted unanimously at congresses, and opponents were quickly singled out and in most cases dismissed from the party.

Dissent began to emerge with the decline of the party. This culminated with the fielding of an unofficial Communist candidate alongside the official one at the presidential election of 1988. This type of division did not occur again at the 1995 and 2002 elections and, by and large, the top leadership has been able to remain in control. While the secretary general elected in the 1990s is ostensibly more prepared to accept discussion, real behavior within the party has little changed. Yet this tight organization did not stop the electoral decline. The party's presidential candidate (and general secretary) obtained only 3 percent of the votes in May 2002, in part because of the presence of several extreme-Left candidates. With under 5 percent of the votes at the June parliamentary election of that year, the maintenance of the Communist Party as a significant political force has come into question.

Meanwhile the Greens have not succeeded in making a real breakthrough. Perhaps because of their internal divisions, especially over the leadership, they did not overtake the Communist Party, as they had hoped (they obtained just over 4 percent in June 2002). They never were as influential as their German counterparts, although they had played a significant part in the Jospin 1997–2002 government. The defeat of the Left in 2002 clearly reduced their influence, but they seem likely to see that influence rise again if and when the resurgence of the Left occurs later in the decade.

THE SPIRIT OF THE CONSTITUTION OF 1958

De Gaulle and the Constitution of 1958

The Constitution of 1958 was introduced primarily to strengthen the executive. From 1870 to 1958, French governments had been weak and unstable, except for about a decade at the beginning of the twentieth century, when the campaign against the Catholic Church gave cohesion to the majority and some real strength to the leader of the government. De Gaulle was convinced that chronic instability was one of the major causes of the decline of France; he believed that only by a change in the institutions could the man at the top be able to take a long-term view of the interests of the country. He thus based his cure on constitutional remedies, but the medicine was somewhat unorthodox.

A Hybrid System of Executive Power

De Gaulle did not adhere to any of the constitutional models devised in the eighteenth and nineteenth centuries and broadly adopted in the major democracies. He wanted to ensure governmental stability and executive authority; he was not anxious—to say the least—to give representatives of the people effective means of supervising the executive, nor did he wish to devise an equilibrium between executive and legislature. Thus he proposed neither a revamped cabinet system nor a presidential system, but plumped for a hybrid system giving marked preponderance to the executive. Yet, as the cabinet system and the presidential system are the only two forms of constitutional arrangements (together with a streamlined party system) that seemed effective elsewhere in sustaining liberal democracy, the new French institutions were attacked from the start as being both authoritarian and impractical. Few expected that they would last beyond de Gaulle; indeed, though they were kept alive under the subsequent presidents, there are still doubts about the long-term future of the constitution, in that the hybrid character of the system appears to make it rather vulnerable.

This hybrid system divides executive authority into two sharply distinct segments. The president has the somewhat lofty and almost undefinable task of looking after the long-term interests of the nation; the government, headed by the prime minister, is in charge of the country's affairs. This raises two main problems. First, there is a large gray area of divided responsibility. Because the constitution does not define sectors for the president and the prime minister, clashes between the two are likely. Second, while the president appoints the prime minister, the prime minister needs the support of the legislature. There is, therefore, potential for conflict when the parliament and the presidency are controlled by different parties. This did not occur between 1958 and 1986, but it did between 1986 and 1988 and between 1993 and 1995

A CLOSER LOOK
3.3

DE GAULLE AND MITTERRAND

By far the two most important presidents of the Fifth Republic have been Charles de Gaulle, who founded the regime in 1958, and François Mitterrand, who reorganized the Left and gave it a new strength. Charles de Gaulle, born in 1890, had a military career during which he unsuccessfully attempted to give the French army a more modern outlook. Shocked by the defeat of June 1940, he rallied in London and created the Free French Movement, which was to become the embryo of the government of liberated France in 1944. Having led this government until January 1946, he resigned in disgust at what he considered to be party domination of the regime. He founded a movement called the Rally of the French People in 1947 but remained in the wilderness of the opposition until 1958, when the events of Algeria gave him an opportunity to implement his ideas of a president-led as well as a more nationalistic form of government. Ten years later, in 1968, confronted by massive popular demonstrations, he sought to retake the initiative by proposing to the people in 1969 a reform of the constitution. He was defeated in a referendum, immediately resigned, and retired to his home in eastern France, where he died one year later, in 1970.

François Mitterrand can be regarded as having done for the Left what de Gaulle did for the nation. Born in 1916, he started as a young parliamentarian and minister in the 1940s. At the time, he belonged to a small party of the Center. He opposed de Gaulle from 1958 and moved gradually to the Left, being a strong challenger to the founder of the Fifth Republic at the election of 1965, when he obtained 45 percent of the votes. He was instrumental in giving the Socialist Party a new life in 1971 and boldly agreed to an alliance with the Communist Party in 1972, being determined to overtake that party. The policy succeeded triumphantly at the presidential and parliamentary elections of 1981, when, for the first time, the French Socialist Party gained an absolute majority of seats in the National Assembly. He agreed to appoint a conservative government in 1986, after the Socialist Party had lost its majority, but was reelected president in 1988 for a further seven years. By the early 1990s, however, as de Gaulle's earlier, his popularity began to wane; his political flair, in both internal and foreign policies, seemed to desert him. In 1993, the Socialist Party suffered a crushing defeat: Mitterrand had to appoint, once more, a conservative government with which he "cohabited" during the last two years of his term, which ended in 1995. He died in January 1996 after a long struggle with cancer, which he bore with great courage. His death was viewed as the passing of an era.

under Mitterrand and between 1997 and 2002 but only up to 2002, under his successor, Chirac. Cohabitation was relatively painless in each case, but the role of the president was clearly diminished in the process.

PRESIDENT AND GOVERNMENT

The Formal Powers of the President

Formally at least, the powers of the president are relatively limited. In 1958, de Gaulle had to agree to compromises with the politicians of the time who feared full-scale presidentialism. Whether de Gaulle wanted a presidency on American lines was never clarified; he had in any case to settle for much less in the constitution.

The president of the Republic was elected for seven years, but a constitutional amendment passed in 2000 reduced the term to five years. Presidents can be reelected only once. The president of the Fifth Republic has eight powers which French presidents have traditionally held:

1. Appointment of the prime minister and of the ministers on the proposal of the prime minister (without any formal power of dismissal of the prime minister).

2. Promulgation of laws voted by parliament. The president may ask parliament to reconsider a law within two weeks of its having been voted, but he has no power of veto.

3. Signature of regulations (decrees), but these must have been approved by the council of ministers.

4. Chairmanship of the council of ministers.

5. Chairmanship of the high councils of the armed forces.

6. The right to send messages to the National Assembly.

7. Ratification of treaties, after parliamentary approval.

8. The power of pardon.

As in other Western European countries, the fact that the head of state signs regulations and ratifies treaties merely means that the seal of authority of the state is given to these decisions; however, these decisions must be countersigned by the prime minister and, when appropriate, by some of the ministers. The rule of the countersignature is basic to the operation of the parliamentary system, as the government, not the head of state, is held to be politically responsible. No particular significance must therefore be attributed to the fact that the president of the Fifth Republic signs decrees or ratifies treaties.

Alongside the eight traditional powers, four others are new in the Fifth Republic and constitute the extent of the formal innovation in the regime. These powers affect the dissolution of the parliament, constitutional amendments, referendums, and emergencies. These new powers are the prerogative of the president alone. No countersignature is required, but they can be exercised at rare intervals or in emergencies only. Of these four powers, only one, the right of dissolution, has been really effective and has markedly helped to modify the conditions of political life.

The Presidential Power of Dissolution

Before 1958, the dissolution of the parliament had been used rarely (in fact not at all between 1877 and 1955, when parliament dominated the scene). Because of the ill-organized nature of the party system, the dissolution of 1955 had no effect on political life. On the other hand, since 1958, dissolutions have been used to great effect in 1962, 1968, 1981, 1988, and 1997, in the context of a more streamlined party system. Moreover, the threat of dissolution plays a major part in helping to render governments more stable.

Constitutional Amendments and Referendums

The other three new powers of the president have been used relatively rarely. One gives the president the power to decide that a constitutional amendment proposed by the government need not be approved by referendum after it has been adopted by parliament. In this case, the proposal has to be approved by a joint meeting of the two chambers separately. This provision was used by de Gaulle in 1960 to loosen the links between France and its African ex-colonies, by Giscard d'Estaing in 1976 with respect to the duration of parliamentary sessions, and by Chirac in 1995 to extend the duration of parliamentary sessions and the scope of legislative referendums.

Article 11 of the constitution gives the president the right to refer certain government bills to the electorate. Up to 1995, this concerned exclusively bills dealing with the organization of public authorities, those carrying approval of a (French)

Dominique Galouzeau de Villepin, Prime Minister.

Villepin was born in 1953, obtained degrees in arts and law, and graduated from the Ecole Nationale d'Administration in 1980. His career has been in the diplomatic service. 1980–84, Foreign Ministry, specializing in African and Malagasy affairs; 1984–89, French Embassy in Washington; 1989–92, French Embassy in Delhi; 1992–1993, Foreign Ministry, Deputy Assistant Secretary for African Affairs; 1993–95, Chief of Staff of Minister of Foreign Affairs; 1995–2002, Secretary-General of the Presidency of the Republic; 2002–04, Foreign Minister; 2004–05, Interior Minister; May 2005, Prime Minister. Villepin is also a poet and the author of a number of books on French culture and history.

community agreement, or proposals to ratify treaties that, without being contrary to the constitution, would affect the functioning of the institutions. A 1995 constitutional amendment extended this right to bills dealing with social and economic matters, a right which has not so far been used.

De Gaulle liked referendums, as these enabled him to go directly to the people without having to bother about parties. He used the technique in a highly dubious manner from a constitutional point of view. First, he introduced the practice of bypassing parliament altogether, as if the referendum was an alternative and not merely a complement to the parliamentary approval of bills. The constitution was silent on this point, but the president's interpretation was, to say the least, highly innovative.

Yet de Gaulle went further. According to the constitution, constitutional amendments must be passed in identical terms by both chambers of parliament; a referendum then takes place, though the president has the power to avoid this referendum, as we just noted, by sending the amendment to a joint meeting of the two chambers, in which case the amendment must be approved by a majority of at least three-fifths of the votes cast. It is therefore clearly unconstitutional for an amendment to be approved without a positive vote of parliament. In 1962, however, de Gaulle proposed directly to the people an amendment stipulating that the election of the president would be by direct universal suffrage. This successful but unconstitutional move created considerable stir (including the fall of the government and the dissolution of the National Assembly). It was the last time that the referendum led to an important reform. In 1969, de Gaulle used it again on regionalism, but he lost and left power. His successor, Pompidou, used it only once; Giscard d'Estaing did not use it at all. Mitterrand proposed to use it in 1984, but the constitutional change he sought was blocked by the upper chamber. It was used in 1988 to change the status of the Pacific island of New Caledonia (when only 33 percent voted) and in 1993 to ratify the Maastricht Treaty of the European Union (when the majority in favor turned out to be wafer thin). It was used by Chirac in 2000 to approve the reduction of the duration of the presidential term to five years: there was a large majority in favor (73 percent), but only 30 percent of the electors voted, a record level of abstention.

Emergency Powers

The fourth new power of the president is given by Article 16 of the constitution and concerns emergencies. It was used only once, in 1961, following an attempted coup by four generals in Algiers. A heated conflict had arisen at the time of the drafting of the constitution, because the clause allowed the president to assume full powers in some situations. De Gaulle wanted the power to enable the head of state to take appropriate measures in cases of national catastrophes such as the defeat of 1940. Opponents, however, saw it as a means of installing a legal dictatorship. The experience was mixed, to say the least. Such a clause does not by itself give authority to a president who does not already have it; moreover, parliament is required to meet, a somewhat ludicrous provision in the case of a national catastrophe.

The procedure proved cumbersome when it was put in use, in part because the scope of parliamentary action in the context of Article 16 was not defined. It was in fact a great relief for the government (more than for parliament) when, at the end of the of the summer of 1961, Article 16 ceased to be operative, as those who had benefited most from the emergency powers were the farmers, whose lobby was able to make itself felt in the chamber.

Popular Election of the President

The four new powers point to de Gaulle's main preoccupation, namely that the president should be able to steer the ship of state. For this, authority was necessary. This is why de Gaulle forced a change with respect to the election of the president. He had had to accept in 1958 the setting up of a limited electoral college composed of about 80,000 delegates, mainly representatives of local authorities in which rural areas were overrepresented. By 1962, he had acquired the political strength to launch a referendum introducing the direct popular election of the president (with a two-ballot or run-off system, the second ballot taking place two weeks after the first between the top two candidates only). Opposition to the proposal was fierce, largely due to the fear of Bonapartism. The only popularly elected presi-

A CLOSER LOOK

3.4   THE POPULAR ELECTION OF THE PRESIDENT MAY WEAKEN POLITICAL PARTIES

The election of the French president by universal suffrage contributed to an extent to the streamlining of French politics but may also have led to new divisions between and even within parties. One of the main reasons the Right of the political spectrum is not united is that both the Gaullists and the Centrists (the UDF) have their presidential hopefuls. The Socialist Party avoided major problems in the 1970s and 1980s because of the towering position of President Mitterrand. Difficulties began to arise in the party in the 1990s, however, as there were a number of presidential hopefuls. As a matter of fact, mechanisms of selection of candidates are still unclear. The idea of primaries was to an extent applied in the Socialist Party. In both 1995 and 2002, the mechanism led to the nomination of Jospin, not surprisingly in 2002, since Jospin had been prime minister for five years and was unquestionably the foremost politician of the party. Primaries took place to an extent in other parties, among the Greens in particular. The idea had been rejected by the Gaullist party in 1995, with the result that there were then two candidates of the party at the first ballot, Balladur and Chirac. The problem did not arise in 2002 as the candidate of the Gaullist party could not be other than Chirac, the outgoing president. Overall, the French Fifth Republic has still to devise a nominating mechanism that will make it possible to select presidential candidates smoothly and truly authoritatively.

dent, Louis-Napoleon, made himself emperor after a coup d'etat in 1851.

The fear proved misplaced and outdated. The popular election of the president, however unconstitutional, was approved by the people in 1962 by a majority of over 3 to 2 (62 percent voted yes). Three years later, in December 1965, the first popular election of the president led to a very active campaign. The direct election of the president has remained popular ever since, and the measure clearly enhanced the position of the president in relation to parliament and government, as de Gaulle had hoped.

Presidential elections have become the central event of French politics. It was indeed the presidential election that rendered alternance possible in 1981 when Mitterrand, the Socialist candidate, won. Thus contests have been heated; margins of victory have tended to be small; turnout has been higher than at other contests. Clearly, the Fifth Republic has succeeded in one respect; it has introduced a procedure that is very popular. The Left, which originally opposed it, abandoned its attacks and was a marked beneficiary in 1981 and 1988. The president (of whatever party) has acquired an authority he did not have in the past. The result of the second ballot of the 2002 election proved it once more, as Chirac, who had only obtained 20 percent of the votes at the first ballot, garnered 82 percent against Le Pen two weeks later, on a larger turnout. The point was clearly made by the voters that they rejected the policies and general stand of the extreme-Right. Thus the president is in a position to be a key actor, if not always the main actor, in French political life.

THE GOVERNMENT

The Role of the Prime Minister

The influence of the president on the government stems from his authority alone, as the constitution clearly states that the government, headed by the prime minister, is in charge of the policy; this was rediscovered after the 1986 and 1993 elections, when President Mitterrand had to appoint a government composed of Gaullists and of members of the Center parties, and after the 1997 election, when President Chirac had to appoint a government primarily composed of Socialists.

According to Article 20, "[t]he Government shall determine and direct the policy of the nation. It shall have at its disposal the administration and the armed forces." Article 21 continues: "The Premier shall direct the operation of the Government. He shall be responsible for national defense. He shall ensure the execution of the laws." There is no ambiguity; though the president of the Republic, according to customs dating back to the Third Republic, chairs the council of ministers, the government as a whole, headed by the prime minister, is responsible for national policy.

As in many other countries, the position of the prime minister grew gradually during the course of the twentieth century. The Constitution of 1875 did not formally recognize the premier, but in practice all governments had a head, then known as "president of the council of ministers" (rather illogically, since the president of the Republic chaired the meetings of ministers). However, since French governments were often uneasy coalitions, premiers tended to be compromisers rather than leaders. The Constitution of 1946 sought to increase the authority of the premier by giving him specific powers. He alone was designated by the chamber; he alone appointed the rest of the cabinet. These provisions had no effect; there was little difference between a premier of the 1930s and of the 1950s. In the Constitution of 1958, the premier—now named prime minister for the first time—retained some of these powers. He or she leads the government, has the power to implement the laws (*pouvoir réglementaire*), is responsible for national defense, and makes a number of important appointments. The constitution stresses the leadership role of the premier as much as is compatible with the position of the president of the Republic and with the collective character of the government.

The government remains legally a collective organ. Important measures of the government are taken in the council of ministers (as we noted, decrees are signed by the president after they have been approved by the council). The government as a whole is empowered to "determine and direct the policy of the nation." Collective decision making is also associated with collective responsibility through the mechanism of the vote of censure, which automatically results, if adopted, in the resignation of all the ministers. The conflict between prime ministerial leadership and collective decision making is as difficult to solve in France as elsewhere, but the matter is further complicated by the role of the president.

The Structure and Composition of the Government

Formal arrangements have not markedly modified the internal structure of French governments. Names of ministries change from time to time, but the structure has followed a gradual evolution since the Third Republic. Typically, a government has about 20 ministers (slightly fewer than in the last years of the Fourth Republic); it includes about as many "secretaries of

state" of lower status. A number of changes have markedly affected the decision-making processes and even the nature of the cabinet, however. Three of these changes in particular must be mentioned.

First, prime ministerial instability has sharply decreased. From 1958 to 2002, France has had 16 prime ministers: Debré, Pompidou, and Couve de Murville under de Gaulle; Chaban-Delmas and Messmer under Pompidou; Chirac and Barre under Giscard d'Estaing; Mauroy, Fabius, and Chirac under Mitterrand I; Rocard, Cresson, Bergegovoy, and Balladur under Mitterrand II; Juppé and Jospin under Chirac (see Table 3.4). Only two prime ministers of the Fourth Republic lasted over a year, and no prime minister since 1875 lasted continuously in office as long as Pompidou, Barre, or Jospin. Ministers, on the other hand, change fairly frequently—though rather less than under the Fourth Republic.

TABLE 3.4

PRESIDENTS AND PRIME MINISTERS IN THE FIFTH REPUBLIC

Presidents		Prime Ministers	
C. de Gaulle	1958–1969	M. Debré	1959–1962
(reelected 1965 for 7 years;		G. Pompidou	1962–1968
resigned 1969)		M. Couve de Murville	1968–1969
G. Pompidou	1969–1974	J. Chaban-Delmas	1969–1972
(died in office)		P. Messmer	1972–1974
V. Giscard d'Estaing	1974–1981	J. Chirac	1974–1976
		R. Barre	1976–1981
F. Mitterrand	1981–1995	P. Mauroy	1981–1984
(reelected 1988 for 7 years)		L. Fabius	1984–1986
		J. Chirac	1986–1988
		M. Rocard	1988–1991
		E. Cresson	1991–1992
		P. Beregovoy	1992–1993
		E. Balladur	1993–1995
J. Chirac	1995–2002	A. Juppé	1995–1997
(reelected 2002 for 5 years)	2002–	L. Jospin	1997–2002
		J.-P. Raffarin	2002–2005
		D. de Villepin	2005–

Second, there has been a marked influx of technicians in the government. De Gaulle first brought civil servants into the cabinet in 1958, in part on the grounds that the government should in some sense (like himself?) be above the daily turmoil of political life; the government should run the state, and de Gaulle conceived of politics as an activity divorced from state policy making, a view that probably stems from the part played by the civil service in the running of modern France. Thus, Couve de Murville, successively foreign minister and prime minister, was from the career foreign service; Pompidou, a teacher and a banker, had never been in politics before 1962, except as a personal adviser to de Gaulle; Chirac was a personal adviser to Pompidou before entering politics. Since the early 1960s, civil servants have composed between one-quarter and one-third of the cabinet; many of these subsequently became members of parliament, as Pompidou or Chirac, while successive presidents continued to draw their prime ministers (Barre by Giscard d'Estaing) and ministers (Cheysson or Dumas by Mitterrand) from outside politics.

Third, in order to give the executive more independence, Article 23 of the constitution, introduced at de Gaulle's specific request, stipulates that there shall be *incompatibility* between the function of minister and that of member of parliament. This incompatibility rule also exists in some parliamentary democracies (the Netherlands, Norway, and, since the 1990s, Belgium), but it contravenes the general principle that the executive stems from the majority of the National Assembly and aims at leading it. What de Gaulle wanted was to detach ministers from the legislature, as ministerial crises often occurred in the past to help the personal careers of ambitious men. Though they can come and speak (but not vote) in parliament, ministers no longer belong to the legislature and thus can be expected to take a loftier view of daily politics. Yet the provision has been partly by-passed, as ex-ministers often seek to be reelected. This results in a cascade of by-elections at many ministerial reshuffles, as when Chirac became president in 1995. Yet the rule reduces somewhat the desire of parliamentarians to become ministers.

PRESIDENT, PRIME MINISTER, AND GOVERNMENT IN THE FIFTH REPUBLIC

Institutional changes have brought about a new framework and introduced hurdles that have helped the Fifth Republic give France a stable political system. These institutional changes alone do not explain the whole story, however. In theory, the government is collective; in practice, it is in part hierarchical. From the very start, de Gaulle intervened in governmental life, and Pompidou, Giscard d'Estaing, Mitterrand, and Chirac followed his lead, at least outside periods of cohabitation, although even then, the president's position was never seriously challenged. Let us examine developments somewhat more closely.

The Extent of Presidential Intervention

Until 1986, presidential intervention had gradually increased. In the early period, de Gaulle's involvement was seemingly due to the special problem of the Algerian war and was held to be confined to some fields only. The presidential sector seemed to include foreign affairs, defense, Algeria, overseas France, and key institutional problems. The prime ministerial and governmental sector seemed to comprise the rest, particularly economic and social matters. But these sectors never were recognized by de Gaulle as marking the limits of his area of intervention. De Gaulle intervened in other aspects of internal policy making, possibly because these might have had an impact on the political system. He had said in 1964: "Clearly, it is the president alone who holds and delegates the authority of the State. But the very nature, extent, and duration of his task imply that he be not absorbed without remission or limit by political, parliamentary, economic, and administrative contingencies." This meant a hierarchical distinction rather than a division between sectors. The prime minister was left to deal with those contingencies which are "his lot, as complex and meritorious as it is essential."

Subsequent presidents came to view their role as one of steering important matters affecting the well-being of the nation, directly or by implication. Hence the many instances of direct action by the president in financial matters. De Gaulle decided in 1968 not to devalue the franc; less than a year later Pompidou reversed the decision. Many aspects of regional or cultural policy, economic development, or social security reform can be ascribed to the president's steering.

The Semipresidential Character of the Fifth Republic

The French political system under the Fifth Republic is only half-presidential in that, on many issues, the president remains an arbiter rather than an actor. On various important economic and social problems, especially under de Gaulle and Pompidou, prime ministers and individual ministers initiated policies with the president of the Republic being seemingly neutral. Giscard d'Estaing was also somewhat aloof, although his commitment to the policies of his second prime minister, Barre, was clearer than that of the two previous presidents had been to the policies of their prime ministers. In this respect, the role of the third president was greater, partly also because Giscard d'Estaing had more knowledge of and interest in economics, and economic difficulties made solutions more pressing.

Mitterrand embarked on the same path, keeping some distance from the daily turmoil and letting the prime minister deal with the major economic and social problems resulting from the government's efforts to counter economic depression. But Mitterrand was also closely associated with government policy, and he decided on a major change of economic policy in 1983 from expansion to orthodoxy. His involvement in governmental policy was less apparent but nonetheless deep between 1988 and 1993.

Intervention on such a scale implied the development of a presidential staff. Indeed, in the early period, de Gaulle seemed to want to dismantle the Council of Ministers and replace it with a number of committees chaired by the president. This was not to occur, but the president maintained a large personal staff of *chargés*

de mission and *conseillers techniques* who constitute a parallel organization to that of the prime minister. They cover most important fields of government action and are the sign of the president's interest in a given problem, though they are far less numerous than the members of the American presidential staff.

Cohabitation

The 1986 general election brought about for the first time a parliamentary majority different from that of the president's party. Since the mid-1970s at least, the possibility of such an occurrence had been canvassed; what presidents would then do had remained the object of major speculation. Giscard d'Estaing had promised in 1978 that he would abide by the decision of the people if the Left were to win in parliament. This did not happen and, in 1981, the newly elected president, Mitterrand, could dissolve the chamber and obtain a socialist majority. But in 1986, with Gaullists and Centrists together having a small overall majority, Mitterrand was faced with the decision to abide—or not—by the results of the polls. He had to do so again in 1993, with the difference that the parliamentary victory of the Right and Center was then overwhelming. The same situation obtained in 1997 when Chirac dissolved the chamber and a majority of the Left was returned. As a result, between 1986 and 2002, cohabitation (president and government being from opposite political blocs) occurred during 9 years out of 16—in the years 1986–1988, 1993–1995, and 1997–2002.

Mitterrand's reaction was quick in 1986 and 1993. He appointed the prime minister from among the new parliamentary majority, choosing Chirac, the leader of the Gaullist party, in 1986, and, on the advice of Chirac, Balladur in 1993. In such circumstances, the president's role became limited: a *modus vivendi*—the "cohabitation" idea—was adopted by prime minister and president. The president would accept what the new majority would propose, provided it was within the limits of what could be regarded as fair and honest government. Thus denationalization proposals or changes in the electoral system (in fact the return to the two-ballot system) would be accepted by the president on condition that parliamentary debates not be curtailed and the rights of citizens maintained.

The cohabitation arrangement functioned well, two elements playing a major part. First, the president retained the right of dissolution in case there were conflicts with the prime minister—a threat that was real, as the popularity of the new conservative government tended quickly to decline. Second, as Chirac wished to be a presidential candidate in both 1988 and 1995 (he was to be defeated by Mitterrand in the first case and to win against Jospin in the second), neither the prime minister nor conservative politicians in general wanted to reduce the role and status of the presidency.

Cohabitation became more embedded as a result of the 1997 election, as it was to last for the whole of the five years of the life of a parliament. The system did function well, whatever has been said in the press, especially toward the end of the legislature. There was a division of labor, in that Jospin had a more limited interest in foreign affairs—even in European affairs—while being a very able, if not charismatic, leader who continuously sensed where the nation wished to go (e.g., the 35-hour working week, the need to have only some privatizations, and the desire to obtain more effective security measures). In such a context, Chirac had to concentrate on foreign affairs, including European affairs, though this was probably also his main interest. Moreover, Chirac's room for action was somewhat reduced as a result of a number of alleged scandals linked to his previous position as mayor of Paris. Yet Jospin unquestionably achieved more of what he wanted than Chirac, in part because one should not exaggerate the differences between the two leaders on foreign affairs. They both agreed broadly on the main tenets of foreign policy, whether in relation to world developments, in particular in the context of the world economy, or in relation to European integration. Both were adamant to defend French interests even in matters on which France found almost no allies. Moreover, the French people not only liked cohabitation; they also liked the two leaders who ran the country between 1997 and 2002, as opinion polls continuously showed.

The long-term consequence of the five years of the Chirac–Jospin tandem is probably a reduction of the role of the presidency. The decline of this role led, at the end of the period, to increasing attacks, especially from the Right, against the idea of cohabitation and its end, temporarily perhaps, as a result of the 2002 election after which Jean-Pierre Raffarin, was appointed prime minister.

THE LEGISLATURE

The Traditional Role of the French Parliament

Before the installation of the Fifth Republic in 1958, much of French political life swirled around the lobbies of the Palais Bourbon, the seat of the lower house of parliament, known as the Chamber of Deputies during the Third Republic and renamed the National Assembly in 1946. The Chamber of Deputies came to symbolize the Republic and all its works; it finally became the focus of all criticism aimed at the shortcomings of French politics.

Perhaps because it was the arena where the rights of man were first enunciated and defended, the National Assembly became the repository of republican legitimacy. Inevitably, however, confusion over rights and privileges developed; members became more and more parochial and tended to regard their function as the defense of advantages that had accrued to their district by circumstance, natural good fortune, or government action. From being protectors of civil liberties, the members of the National Assembly slowly became champions of vested and purely local interests, a not uncommon development in legislatures, particularly in the U.S. Congress, whose mores resemble in many ways those of the French parliament before 1958.

In these circumstances, the mark of a promising premier was his ability to deflect or postpone the demands for the extension of special privileges which poured in on the government. Yet to survive, a premier had to nurse along the majority coalition, pleading with his own ministers not to lead an attack against him, while compromising the integrity of his legislative program to maintain the cohesion of his cabinet. To compound difficulties, the premier had to submit the plans of his legislative action to the often hostile committees of the house, whose chairmen were usually more anxious to further their own careers (perhaps by replacing the relevant minister) with brilliant critiques of the legislation under discussion than to contribute to the progress of public business. Here, too, parallels can be drawn with the committees of the U.S. Congress, though the French parliament never resorted to public grilling through hearings. This behavior was based on a supporting philosophy according to which, since the Revolution, there were crucial enemies of republicanism, namely the Church, the bureaucracy, and the armed forces. A kind of rampant anarchism (*le citoyen contre les pouvoirs,* the citizen against the powers) justified the harassment of the government, this harassment being regarded as a republican virtue.

Yet the system, despite its faults, gave France a long period of liberal government, interrupted only by the collapse of the French army in 1940 and by major colonial wars in the 1950s. Admittedly, the Napoleonic bureaucracy did help and, if the regime showed resilience, it never reformed itself. The personal stakes were too high; the life of parliamentarians was too often punctuated by the ritual of government crisis. Reform had to come from outside, as occurred in 1958, and only because of de Gaulle did a substantial curtailment of the rights of parliament take place.

Parliamentary Organization in the Fifth Republic

The framers of the Constitution of 1958 introduced a number of devices designed to enhance the position of the government and to give parliament the power to supervise, but not block, executive action. These devices come under five headings. First, some provisions aim at reducing harassment and diminishing opportunities for conflict. Second, the scope of legislation is reduced and governmental pre-

rogatives correspondingly increased. Third, opportunities for guerrilla warfare in parliament are limited. Fourth, the operation of censure motions is severely restricted. Fifth, parliamentary activity is controlled by the Constitutional Council. To these devices must be added the power of dissolution given to the president of the Republic.

Parliament is composed of two chambers, the National Assembly and the Senate, the upper house having regained the title but not all the powers it had under the Third Republic, while the lower house kept the name given to it by the Constitution of 1946. The National Assembly is elected for five years (if not dissolved before) by direct universal suffrage. The Senate, sometimes nicknamed the "Grand Council of French Communes," is elected for six years (one-third of its members retiring every three years) by a complex electoral college, composed of representatives of local authorities, which favors rural areas and the Center-Right parties. Senators are elected within *département* (county) districts, in part by a two-ballot majority system, in part on a proportional representation basis.

Since the constitutional reform of 1995, parliament meets during nine months of the year (instead of during two sessions of three months each, in the autumn and the spring). The government can also call for special sessions, a procedure that was originally interpreted very restrictively but came to be used more often and led to the 1995 reform extending sittings to nine months.

The speaker of the National Assembly is elected for the duration of the legislature (instead of once a year, as was the case before 1958); thus avoiding the repeated conflicts of the past. The speaker of the Senate is elected after each partial reelection of the Senate every three years. Both speakers are assisted by a *bureau* composed of vice presidents and secretaries drawn from the various parties. The speakers of the houses, who are sometimes but not always drawn from among top politicians, are consulted by the president of the Republic, according to the constitution, in various circumstances (such as dissolution or the use of Article 16). They conceive of their role more as do speakers of the U.S. House of Representatives than as do speakers of the British House of Commons; they attempt to influence the conduct of business by informally talking to members. Indeed, before 1958, these offices were stepping stones toward the presidency of the Republic as in Italy and were strongly contested.

Since 1958, the government plays a major part in the organization of parliamentary business. Previously the order of business was decided by a "Conference of Presidents," a body that is similar to the Rules Committee of the U.S. House of Representatives and which includes chairs of committees and of the parliamentary groups (the parties in the chamber). Before 1958 the government was only represented and had no vote. In the Fifth Republic, the government's power is based on Article 43 of the constitution, which states that "Government and Private Members' Bills shall, at the request of the Government or of the Assembly concerned, be sent for study to committees especially designated for this purpose." Article 48 then stipulates that "the discussion of the bills filed or agreed to by the Government shall have priority on the agenda of the Assemblies in the order set by the Government." Government bills are thus sent automatically to a committee and are then extracted from the committee and presented on the floor of the Assembly by the government.

Scope of Legislation

Traditionally, as in other parliamentary systems, the French parliament could legislate on any matter. Constitutions merely regulated the principles of organization of the public powers; there was no Supreme Court. Statutes (*lois*) were defined merely as texts adopted by parliament, by contrast with decrees (regulations adopted by the whole government) and *arrêtés* (adopted by a minister or a local authority). These documents derived their legal power from each other; the government could not make decrees, and ministers or local authorities could not make *arrêtés* unless a *loi* had given them the authority to do so. Parliament could invade any field and correspondingly decrease the influence of the government, although parliament often had little time to devote to major issues; it therefore often dele-

gated its statutory power to the government by means of *décrets-loi*.

Article 34 of the Constitution of 1958 attempted to provide a solution to the problem. Having stated that "all *lois* (statutes) shall be passed by Parliament," the article defines what the *lois* are by saying that "laws determine the rules" (*règles*) with respect to a list of matters as well as the "fundamental principles" with respect to others. The article then adds that its provisions "may be elaborated and completed by an organic law." Yet there are difficulties over the arrangements. While the list includes all the important matters with which one would expect a parliament to be concerned, the concept of *règle* is not precise in French law; nor is it clear what a "principle" is. Conflicts have arisen, the arbiter being the Constitutional Council. Finally, what "elaboration and completion by an organic law" means is also rather vague.

The drafters of the constitution tried to buttress the system by introducing two new distinctions among the statutes, those of "organic laws" and "ordinances." Organic laws are passed by parliament by a somewhat more stringent procedure and must be deemed to be constitutional by the Constitutional Council before being promulgated. On the other hand, when parliament delegates its legislative powers to the government, the government's texts are known as ordinances, which have to be ratified by parliament at the end of the delegation period. The procedure proved to be of value for governments anxious to pass controversial legislation rapidly, especially in 1986–1988, when the conservative majority was small. Mitterrand then used his presidential authority to ensure that the government did not overstep its rights.

This complex machinery has functioned surprisingly smoothly, although there have been occasional complaints by the opposition, both of the Left, before 1981, and of the Right, since 1981, and for the same reasons.

The Legislative Struggle

In a parliamentary system, the two main activities of a parliament consist in voting laws and in controlling the government, but the two are intertwined. Before 1958 it was through the legislative struggle that the patience, wits, and skills of ministers were tested, as governments needed laws to implement their program. Thus, in 1958, the power of the executive over the legislative process had to be enhanced if the government was to be stronger.

A bill debated in the French parliament goes through the following sequence (not very different from that which bills go through in the U.S. Congress). After having been laid on the table of either chamber by a member of that chamber or by the government (with the exception of finance bills, which must be presented first to the National Assembly), the bill is sent to a committee which then reports to the house (a *rapporteur* from the committee is in charge of presenting this report). The house discusses the bill first in general, then clause by clause, and votes on each clause. A final vote is then taken, at which point the bill goes to the other house, which follows the same procedure. If both houses agree on the same text, the bill is sent to the president for promulgation (he can ask for a second deliberation, but has no veto). If the houses disagree, the bill goes again to each house. If there is still disagreement, a joint committee comprising an equal number of members of each house is set up with a view to drafting a common text. Only if the government intervenes, as we shall see, is there a possibility of breaking the deadlock between the two chambers.

Parliamentary Committees

Before 1958, parliamentary committees were very powerful. Organized, as in the United States, on the basis of specialized subjects (finance, foreign affairs, etc.), the 20 or so committees of the pre-1958 parliaments had great opportunities to make trouble for the government. Their members (elected on the basis of proportional representation of the parliamentary groups) were specialists or more often had electoral reasons to be interested. Their chairs, elected every year (the seniority system never took root in France, though some office holders did remain in office for long periods), were highly influential; they were natural leaders of any opposition in their field and were the real shadow ministers.

Committees made life difficult for governments because the procedure of the chambers gave them full responsibility in relation to bills. These, whether from the government or from private members, became in effect the committee's bills; their substance could be so altered that they became unrecognizable. The government had therefore to ensure that proposed changes were overturned after the bills came on the floor of the house, a process whose outcome was always uncertain.

These practices have become impossible since 1958. The number of permanent committees in each house has been reduced to six; it was hoped these would become so large that they would include more than experts, but despite various rulings from the Constitutional Council, the government could not avoid the setting up of informal subcommittees. More importantly, committees can no longer substitute their bills for those of the government; Article 42 of the constitution states that the discussion on the floor has to take place on the government's text.

The Power of the Government to Curb Debate

Harassment on the floor of the Assembly used to be continuous. For instance, amendments could be withheld to embarrass the government and its supporters at the last moment; this is now forbidden. There used to be no closure and no guillotine; now Article 44 allows the government to request the chamber to vote by a single vote (*vote bloqué*) on the text under discussion. The procedure is harsh, but it is designed to stop the practice of presenting hundreds of amendments that could not be reasonably dealt with but were aimed at halting the progress of bills. As a result, government bills now clearly take precedence over others (see Table 3.5).

The government has two further sets of powers with respect to legislation. First, finance bills used to be much delayed before 1958; parliament has now 70 days to discuss and decide on the budget. If the finance bill is not voted on by then, the government can promulgate it by ordinance, a stringent weapon that has not had to be used.

Second, the government, and the government alone, can end a deadlock between the two

TABLE 3.5

SENATE 2005

In 2004, an election was held for one-third of the members. The number of senators will be increased from 321 to 346 in 2010. Senators will be elected for 6 years by representatives of local administrative councils and deputies. In 2005, the number is 331.

	Number of Members
Union for the People's Movement (UMP)	156
Socialist Party (PS)	97
Union for French Democracy (UDF)	33
Communist Party (PC)	23
Democracy and Social European Rally (RDSE)	15
Others	7
Total	331

chambers by asking for yet another reading by each chamber of the text adopted by the National Assembly. If there is still disagreement between the two chambers, the National Assembly then votes once more, and this decision is final. Thus the Senate is not in a position to block *governmental* legislation. This provision was used frequently between 1981 and 1986, as much of the legislative program of the Socialist government—in particular, but not only, its nationalization program—was strongly opposed by the Senate.

The balance has clearly been tilted. According to some, it has been tilted too much in favor of the government, a view which is arguable in light of the past behavior of parliament. The executive had to be strengthened. Since a variety of clever tricks were used by parliament against the government, tough rules had to be introduced to prevent the recurrence of previous tactics.

The Vote of Censure

Only comparatively recently has the procedure of the vote of censure, in France and elsewhere, appeared to constitute a major problem. Traditionally, as is still the case in Britain, parliaments could censure governments at will. However, in France and some other countries where party discipline was weak and parties numerous, the result

was governmental instability. Yet the problem is complex because censure and legislation are often linked. If the right to censure the government is curtailed but parliament can nonetheless easily reject bills proposed by the government, and in particular reject or delay financial bills, governments will simply resign without having been censured. This was the case in the Third and Fourth Republics. Vote of censure and votes on legislation have therefore to be linked.

The 1958 Constitution does so in a curious provision which stipulates that an absolute majority is needed to defeat the government, but that only those voting for the censure motion (that is, against the government) will record their votes, while government supporters simply do not vote at all. Abstainers are thus counted on the government side. Furthermore, if the government wants to see a bill through but encounters difficulties, it can "pledge its responsibility on the vote of [the] text." In this case, the bill passes without a vote unless a motion of censure is tabled. If the censure is not adopted (the procedure is the one just described), the government is safe and the bill is adopted as well.

Thus the government has the upper hand; governments cannot be suddenly overthrown. Deputies have only two means of curbing the executive. They have the question, which was introduced in the Constitution of 1958, allegedly on the British model, but which has taken the form of short debates, not of a grilling, although its scope has been extended; there is no vote at the end of these debates. The other curb is the motion of censure. These are the Assembly's only means of supervision and control of the government; the rest of its activities are legislative and budgetary. The constitution may have gone too far. The governmental instability of the past suggested that a stringent medicine was needed, but the restrictions may be too strong. Indeed, gradually, some loosening has taken place, from the Giscard d'Estaing presidency of the second half of the 1970s onwards. With more compact majorities, the government can be more ready to make concessions, while parliament recognizes the need for self-discipline.

THE CONSTITUTIONAL COUNCIL

An important new development of the Fifth Republic is the part played by the Constitutional Council in controlling legislation. The Constitutional Council includes nine members appointed in equal numbers by the president of the Republic and the speakers of the two chambers. It also includes the ex-presidents of the Republic. The council was set up in 1958 principally as a means of ensuring that parliament did not overstep its powers; it thus has to approve the standing orders of both houses (a matter which led to conflicts in the late 1950s). It has jurisdiction over referendums and national elections, both presidential and parliamentary, which it must officially declare and settle in cases of dispute.

Yet the main power of the council turned out to be different. Because it was entitled to assess whether laws were in conformity with the constitution, it became gradually a supreme court. Admittedly, it differs from the U.S. Supreme Court in that it can consider the validity of legislation only if the government or one of the houses asks for a ruling and does so in the period immediately following the approval of the bill by parliament, but the impact has been strong.

At first, the Constitutional Council tended to side with the Gaullist government. Gradually, it

became more independent and started to rule that bills or parts of bills were not "in conformity with the constitution." In 1982, for instance, it declared that, subject to a few minor amendments (which were subsequently introduced), the nationalization program of the government was in conformity with the constitution. In 1986, it also adjudicated over the privatization legislation of the conservative coalition. In 1991, it stated that a law could not refer to a "Corsican people" as this would undermine the unity of the nation, but it added that special rules could be introduced for different areas, a major innovation in the context of centralized France. The same line was taken again in January 2002 when it quashed the first clause of the law on Corsica adopted by the parliament a few weeks earlier on the grounds that it was not in conformity with the constitution for a law to allow any body other than parliament (in this case the Corsican regional assembly) to adapt national legislation, even if only on an experimental basis. In 1993, it quashed parts of a law of the conservative government that attempted to make the French language obligatory in many fields, on the grounds that this went against the freedom of expression. It intervened in what was perhaps a more substantial manner in the laws passed under Jospin's Socialist government, in particular in relation to segments of social, economic, and budgetary policies of that government, though not the whole of these policies.

THE NEW EQUILIBRIUM OF POWERS

The Constitution of 1958 profoundly changed the character of French political life. Parliament's power has been reduced (too much, according to some); governmental instability is a thing of the past. For the best part of three decades, the system has been dominated by the president, whose authority was enhanced by the legacy of de Gaulle and by the mechanism of the popular election. This domination has been seriously put in question by cohabitation situations, but the authority of the president has remained high throughout, even if the effective power of the head of state has

A CLOSER LOOK

3.5

THE JUDICIARY AND POLITICIANS

In France as in a number of Western European countries, particularly Italy, the judiciary—and not merely the Constitutional Council—appear prepared to play a large part in relation to politics and politicians. Intervention of this kind has originated primarily, indeed almost exclusively, from examining magistrates (*juges d'instruction*) who, in France (as indeed in Italy), belong technically to the judiciary. A kind of war has resulted, with many examining magistrates apparently convinced of the guilt of many politicians in various scandals, involving in particular the financing of political campaigns. As a matter of fact, these magistrates have often not been followed by the judges themselves, a development that has led some of these magistrates to resign in anger. Perhaps the main example of a case which led to nothing, but after two years of investigation, was that of the first minister of finance of the Jospin government, Strauss-Kahn, who was in effect forced to resign his post as a result of (seemingly very small) accusations made against him but was subsequently acquitted of all charges. This problem has been complicated by the introduction of a law designed to clarify the complex relationship between state prosecutors (*procureurs*) and the minister of justice, a problem which appears as difficult to solve as that of squaring the circle.

diminished. Because of the popular election, the president continues to have authority; even in cohabitation he can both ensure continuity in foreign policy and exercise some supervision over the working of the executive.

Parliament also changed in character. Its social composition has been somewhat altered, although women remain markedly underrepresented and manual and white-collar workers are very few, while lawyers, members of the liberal professions, and teachers are numerous. But there are civil servants, managers, and even farmers in substantial numbers, agriculture and business being particularly represented in Center and right-wing parties. This ensures that at least parts of the active strata of the nation are in the legislature (see Table 3.6). In terms of powers, the pendulum swung originally too far against the assembly, though not quite as far as critics and parliamentarians claimed. Gradually, the right of the legislature to discuss, supervise, and suggest has been recognized, but in exchange, the government's right to lead has been fully accepted by parliamentarians.

Indeed, the constitutional reform of 1995, which increased somewhat the role of parliament by extending its sessions, is evidence that parliament is regarded as having abandoned some of the irresponsible forms of behavior in

which it engaged under previous regimes. Thus, by and through its institutions and the effects these institutions have had on the party system and on the behavior of the actors, and despite the fact that the role of the president is likely to be more limited than it was originally, the Fifth Republic has brought about a real and lasting transformation of French political life.

TABLE 3.6

OCCUPATIONAL BACKGROUND OF FRENCH DEPUTIES, 1997 PARLIAMENT (PERCENTAGES)

Business proprietors	9
Professionals	18
Teachers	26
Civil servants	16
Managers (private sector)	15
Journalists	3
White-collar workers	2
Manual workers	1
Other	10
Women	10
Total (numbers)	577

Source: Rapports Assemblee Nationale. Statistiques, 1999.

Thinking Critically

1. Would you describe the present French system as a presidential one?
2. How would you define "Gaullism"?
3. What have been the effects of centralized bureaucracy?
4. Has the use of referendums in France been successful?
5. How would you explain the vote of between 10 and 15 percent for Jean-Marie Le Pen and his party?

KEY TERMS

Algerian war *(143)*
arrêtés (165)
Chambres d'Agriculture/Chambres de Commerce *(144)*
Jacques Chirac *(148)*
Communist Party *(153)*
Confédération Française Démocratique du Travail (CFDT) *(139)*
Confédération Française des Travailleurs Chrétiens (CFTC) *(139)*
Confédération Générale des Cadres (CGC) *(140)*
Confédération Générale des Petites et Moyennes Entreprises (CGPME) *(140)*
Confédération Générale du Travail (CGT) *(138)*
Conseil National du Patronat Français (CNPF) *(140)*
Constitution of 1958 *(154)*
Constitutional Council *(168)*
Council of Ministers *(159)*
decrees *(165)*
Valéry Giscard d'Estaing *(162)*
European Union (EU), formerly European Economic Community (EEC) *(157)*
Fédération Nationale des Syndicats d'Exploitants Agricoles (FNSEA) *(142)*
Gaullist party (RPF, then UNR, then RPR) *(146)*
interest groups *(138)*
Lionel Jospin *(152)*
François Mitterrand *(151)*
National Assembly/Senate *(164)*
parliament *(164)*
Georges Pompidou *(148)*

Socialist Party *(150)*
Union pour la Démocratie Française (UDF) *(149)*
vote of censure *(167)*

FURTHER READINGS

Groups

Ehrman, H. *Organized Business in France* (Princeton University Press, 1957).

Kesselman, M., ed. *The French Workers' Movement* (London: Allen and Unwin, 1984).

Parties

Anderson, M. *Conservative Politics in France* (London: Allen and Unwin, 1973).

Bell, D. S., and B. Criddle. *The French Socialist Party*, 2nd ed. (Oxford: Oxford University Press, 1988).

Charlot, J. *The Gaullist Phenomenon* (London: Allen and Unwin, 1971).

Converse, P., and R. Pierce. *Political Representation in France* (Cambridge, MA: Harvard University Press, 1986).

de Tarr, F. *The French Radical Party from Herriot to Mendès-France* (New York: Oxford University Press, 1961).

Evans, Jocelyn A. J. *The French Party System* (Manchester: Manchester University Press, 2003).

Irving, R. E. M. *Christian Democracy in France* (London: Allen and Unwin, 1973).

Knapp, Andrew. *Parties and the Party System in France: A Disconnected Democracy?* (New York: Palgrave Macmillan, 2004).

Kriegel, A. *The French Communists* (Chicago: University of Chicago Press, 1972).

Institutions

Hayward, J., ed. *De Gaulle to Mitterrand: Presidential Power in France* (London: Hurst, 1993).

Leites, N. *On the Game of Politics in France* (Stanford University Press, 1959).

Lewis-Beck, Michael S. *The French Voter: Before and After the 2002 Election* (New York: Pelgrave Macmillan, 2004).

Williams, P. M. *The French Parliament* (London: Allen and Unwin, 1967).

C. PUBLIC POLICY

THE ORGANIZATION OF THE STATE

The Civil Service

It is commonplace to contrast the traditional weakness of the French political institutions with the strength of the French bureaucracy. It is also commonplace to stress the virtues of this bureaucracy. There is indeed much evidence to support this praise. The French civil service helped the monarchs build the unity of the nation, actively implemented laws, and intervened in the life of the provinces. It ensured the continuity of the state—indeed embodied the state—throughout the various regimes.

There is, however, another side to the picture. The strength of the bureaucracy has the effect of stifling initiative, breeding irresponsibility, and slowing down moves toward participation and democracy. The bureaucracy's aim is to unify and develop, often against the wishes of the population. This enlightened despotism may have brought about change, but it led to paternalism. Local political and social elites were not encouraged to be entrepreneurial. This is being redressed in part, but many psychological barriers remain, two of which are particularly important: the belief in the need for uniformity, and the overwhelming importance of rules and regulations. As a result, while citizens feel impotent and aggrieved, they also accept bureaucratic canons. The role of the bureaucracy thus is far from being wholly positive.

The Idea of the State

The pervasive nature of the bureaucracy stems from the nature and role of the French state. As in many continental European countries, the state in France is much more than a set of bodies designed to initiate and implement public policies; it is the legal embodiment of the nation. *It thus encompasses all the public organizations and corporations,* both central and local. In the United States and in Britain many public bodies began, and some still are viewed, as groupings of like-minded persons wanting to run a service. Such an associational conception of public bodies has never prevailed in France, where public services are run in the context of a general organization of the state, which can coerce or compel, but also protect citizens, as local authorities and other public corporations are deemed to be better controlled in this way. In the French legal jargon, these are merely "decentralized" entities of the state. For the French, state and law go together because the organization of the state is the embodiment of the principles of the law, and no public authority, large or small, can operate outside this framework.

Moreover, the French state is not only a legal entity; it is a legal entity with a purpose: the well-being of the citizens. From the seventeenth century, and even more so from the early nineteenth century, the tradition of the French state has been one of social engineering. Born from the strong mark that the kings and later Napoleon wanted to make on the nation, an approach that can be described as *dirigisme* (strong management), French social engineering was given its intellectual stamp of acceptability by various writers, philosophers, and sociologists, and in particular by Saint-Simon and Auguste Comte, in the early years of the nineteenth century. Society has to be molded; it is a machine, which can be perfected by appropriate means. In this the *Ecole Polytechnique* is a key element, and characteristically, Saint-Simon and Comte were associated with teaching at that school. Although Saint-Simonism faded out as a doctrine, its influence on attitudes was profound, indeed determining, during most of the nineteenth century (Napoleon III was a Saint-Simonian), particularly in those periods when economic development took place at a rapid rate.

Among the consequences of this tradition, perhaps the most important is state centralization, which includes as its corollary the spreading of public agencies across the whole nation. Another consequence, perhaps not sufficiently stressed, is the greater concern for economic than for social well-being, as the happiness of men is viewed as dependent on the better organization of society for the production of goods and services. Ideas are changing as the potential dangers of economic growth to the health of citizens and the protection of the environment become more widespread, but old ideas die hard.

THE CIVIL SERVICE AND ITS CHARACTERISTICS

The French civil service has high prestige and considerable competence and is widely dispersed throughout the nation, although some of the differences between France and other Western countries have decreased in this respect. The strength of the civil service comes in part from its size: over 2 million men and women are employed by the central government (see Table 3.7). It comes also from the organization and the traditions of the service. The bureaucracy extends widely in the provinces in a pyramidal manner. Ministries are divided into a number of *Directions générales* and *Directions,* which have a large staff in Paris, but most of these ministries also have offices (external services) in regions, *départements* (counties), and sometimes even small towns. These offices are supervised by a prefect on behalf of the government as well as by their hierarchical superiors in Paris.

The *Grands Corps*

Another element in the civil service tradition results from the existence of the *grands corps.*

TABLE 3.7	
CIVIL SERVICE OFFICIALS, 2002 (PERCENTAGES)	
Education	64.7
Economy and finance	10.2
Interior	9.8
Equipment	6.0
Justice	3.6
All other	5.7
(Defense is 18% of total of civil and defense officials.)	

Source: Annuaire statistique de la France, 2004 (p.103).

Indeed, until 1945, the service was not united: the *fonctionnaires* (public servants) had some common rights (pensions for instance), but real unity was achieved only in 1946 by the general code for the civil service (*Statut de la fonction publique*). Before 1945, civil servants were appointed by the various ministries to fill specific jobs, and for the more technical or specialized jobs (not necessarily senior, but at least skilled) they were recruited into groups called "corps." These corps have been the basic cells of the service, with a spirit of their own (*esprit de corps*) marking them differently from other branches and divisions and with a desire to excel.

As these differences were prejudicial to the unity of the service and fostered inequality, post-1945 reforms tried to abolish the corps and replace them by general grades, but the most prestigious of the corps, the *grand corps,* were not abolished. In the economic field (Inspectorate of Finance), the administrative judiciary (Council of State), the home and local government sector (Prefectoral Corps), and various technical branches (Corps of Mines, Corps of Roads and Bridges), these bodies have for generations attracted bright, aspiring civil servants. There was an attempt to link members of these corps to the rest of the service, but it failed. Thus the French civil service continues to be run, in most of the ministries, by members of the *grands corps.* Although they may each have barely a few hundred members, they dominate the civil service and give it its tone.

The *Grandes Ecoles*

The domination of the *grands corps* occurs through the special training given in a few elite schools, the *grandes écoles,* whose members are recruited on the basis of tough competitive examinations and in which high-quality training is given. Some are old (School of Mines, for instance), while others are recent (School of Taxes). Two are particularly important: the *Ecole Polytechnique* and the *Ecole Nationale d'Administration* (ENA). The *Ecole Polytechnique* was set up in 1795 to provide officers for the artillery and engineering branches of the army; it now gives the nation its best technical administrators. The ENA was set up in 1945 as part of the effort to unify the civil service and prepare candidates for higher management jobs in all government departments (including the foreign service). Meanwhile, a school of similar status, the *Ecole Normale Supérieure,* trains the most brilliant of the future secondary school and university teachers. Competition for entry into these schools is fierce.

The ENA is a postgraduate school. Students have first a year of field training (usually in the provinces); this is followed by a year of study in the school itself, and a further training period (usually in a large firm) before the new civil servant chooses where to go. In fact, only top candidates can truly choose; the others are left with less prestigious positions. The final examination, which leads to the posting, decides in particular whether students are to become members of a *grand corps.* Typically, about the first 20 of each class can do so, while the other 100 become *administrateurs civils* and are unlikely to reach the very top posts of the civil service.

The Role of the *Grands Corps* in the Nation

Except for the diplomatic corps, which remains somewhat separate and whose members typically stay in the foreign service all their lives (the service still retains some of its older aristocratic flavor), members of the *grands corps* do not work in the same department for more than a few years. They tend to be "detached" (the official expression) to be posted over a wide range of public bodies (including nationalized corporations). Thus inspectors of finance do not merely serve in the Inspectorate but are in charge of practically the whole of the Treasury and of numerous other divisions and branches in which financial or economic expertise is required. Thus graduates of the *Ecole Polytechnique* who have achieved particular excellence enter one of the two technical *grands corps,* the Corps of Mines and the Corps of Roads and Bridges, and are later detached to run not merely the relevant divisions of ministries, but other government departments and various nationalized industries. This may mean technical excellence, but there is a cost. The rigid distinction created between the very successful elements of the higher civil service and the others can lead to disillusionment and constitutes a waste of early training efforts.

The role of top civil servants does not stop at the civil service itself. The best students of the prestigious schools also provide large numbers of managers to the private sector. The situation is the converse of that which occurs in the United States, where private sector managers often join the federal service for a period. In France, the prestige of the training schools is such that their graduates transfer to business (an operation known as *pantouflage*). This gives the civil service, indirectly, a

A CLOSER LOOK

3.6

EDUCATION: STILL STRONGLY ELITIST

The one element of social policy that is given high priority in France is education, in part because it is traditionally regarded as a ladder for upward mobility and in part because of the massive student protests that take place periodically. The best-known are those of 1968, but these have been followed by further waves of protests, for instance in the second half of the 1980s. The French education system, and in particular the French higher education system, has traditionally been elitist. The *grandes écoles* are regarded as providing their alumni with great careers, hence the tough competitive examinations set up to enter them. The rest of the higher education system tends to be a Cinderella. Despite some changes, universities remain badly provided for, and there is little contact between staff and students (of whom there are about 2 million). Centralization makes matters worse and in particular induces professors to want to reside in Paris (even if they have a post in the provinces). No real reform has as yet taken place to render universities more autonomous and more responsible.

substantial influence on the whole of the economic life of the nation.

Civil Service Control

The quality of the *grands corps* accounts for much of the excellence of the service, but it also leads to conflicts among the various branches, each of which is primarily concerned with its own sector. Supervision and coordination can therefore be difficult, and not surprisingly, control plays a crucial and often frustrating part in the French public sector.

Control takes many forms. Some of these are internal to the civil service and date back to Napoleon. First, there are inspectorates, which are often weak, to an extent because the inspectors general stayed in the service while most of their colleagues of the same age group found a more active and more lucrative life in private business. The main role of inspectors general is now not so much to inspect but to inquire. They are often asked to examine long-term problems, and thus act in a way similar to royal commissions in Britain or presidential commissions in the United States. A second type of control is provided by the administrative courts, headed by the Council of State. These courts started as internal organs of supervision on the model of inspectorates and, as inspectors do, still conduct some inquiries and have advisory functions (on bills and decrees, the Council of State advises the government about legality, opportunity, and effectiveness), but they have become real courts and are at some distance from the active administrators.

*Ministerial Staffs (*Cabinets*)*   Because the civil service's internal controls seemed insufficient, there developed around each minister a staff known as the "ministerial *cabinet.*" Members of the *cabinet* (to be sharply distinguished from the "cabinet" or government) are appointed by the minister. They help him or her remain in touch with constituents and with parliament. They prepare drafts of bills and other reforms; they follow the implementation of policies; they inform their minister about what goes on in the department. They are thus both a protection against undue civil service independence and a brain trust for innovations.

The character of ministerial *cabinets* has changed somewhat in recent decades. These *cabinets* have come to include specialists drawn from the civil service itself, as ministers increasingly need technical advice. The staff of a minister of transport will thus include among others an engineer of roads and bridges, an inspector of finance (to examine costs), and a member of the Council of State (to help draft legal documents). These are civil servants, usually young and loyal to their minister (their future career depends in part on the help they give), but they are civil servants and part of their loyalty is to the civil service, and especially to the corps to which they belong. As other civil servants, they are anxious to foster development, rather than control other civil servants on behalf of constituents or politicians. *Cabinets* thus now provide only a limited check on the bureaucracy.

LOCAL GOVERNMENT

While the civil service and central government agencies were strong, local government was traditionally weak. It was shaped by Napoleon, who, rejecting the early decentralizing schemes of the Revolution, imposed an authoritarian plan. Local authorities were not only supervised but indeed run by agents of the central government. Liberalization slowly took place in the nineteenth century, in the 1830s and 1880s in particular, but there never was a decisive break with the origins. A large amount of central government control was maintained in part for political reasons. Even liberals felt that full devolution of power to local authorities was dangerous, since much of the opposition to the government was opposition to the regime as well. Local government has thus been caught in a vicious circle, as yet not entirely broken, despite some changes in structure and a modification in attitudes, especially since the 1950s when an entrepreneurial spirit began to prevail.

Département and *Commune*

The current structure of French local government dates from the Revolution of 1789, as modified by Napoleon. The French territory is divided into *départements,* of which there are now 96. This entirely artificial creation was designed to break the hold of the old provinces (such as Brittany or Provence); new counties were set up with names drawn from mountains or rivers (Jura, Var, and the like). The *départements* are in turn divided into communes—usually corresponding to the old parishes—of which there are about 37,000. This structure helped centralization and prevented real local autonomy from developing, despite the democratization of the appointment processes, as the average commune is too small to be effective and has to rely on the services of central government agents. No significant reduction in the number of communes has ever taken place, in part because of local resistance, but in part because the strength of the civil service is better maintained by the present structure. Since the 1960s there have been only a few joint authorities (urban districts), linking towns to the suburban communes, and a Paris district, which has a similar purpose for the Paris area.

Communes maintain strong sentiments of local patriotism. Their representatives play a large part in French local life. Elected every six years by universal suffrage, municipal councilors in turn elect a mayor and a number of assistants (*adjoints*). Mayors have some of the authority of the state, while running the local authority. As the basic law of municipal government of 1884 states: "The mayor is in charge of the affairs of the commune." Mayors pass by-laws relating to police or health matters, register citizens, and supervise the maintenance of roads, street lighting, street cleaning, and the like. Aspects of education and housing come directly or indirectly under their jurisdiction. Particularly in large cities, the mayor is a focal point, especially because mayors tend to stay in office for long periods—two or three terms of six years are common. The stability of communal government has always contrasted with the instability of national politics. Communal government is executive centered; the municipal government is typically dominated by the mayor.

Decentralization Efforts   Traditionally, mayors and municipal councils were tightly supervised by central government agents, especially those at the level of the county (*département*). This is in part because counties had, up to the 1980s, a peculiar organization, based on an osmosis between central government agents and locally elected councilors. Until 1982, the executive of the *département* was indeed the prefect, who served both Paris and the elected county council. This helped to perpetuate the dependence of local authorities on the central government and has in particular prevented *départements* from being true local authorities. A major step was therefore taken by the Socialist government of the 1980s: while prefects were retained as agents of the central government, *départements* came to be run by an elected representative, the president of the "general council," the official title of the *département* council. Meanwhile, communes were given greater autonomy; they no longer need prior approval to undertake most activities.

Regionalism

One reform to the system of local government and the problems of centralization took place through regionalism. First, regional councils composed of representatives of *départements,* communes, and economic and social groups were set up. This occurred for the Paris area in 1959, where a government-appointed post of "delegate general" was created. Regional economic development councils were introduced elsewhere in France in 1964. Participation having been one of the main themes of the 1968 revolutionary outburst, a scheme for regionalization was presented to the French people in 1969. It was limited in scope. Being coupled with a reform of the Senate, it was rejected in the referendum, and de Gaulle resigned as a result. In 1972, a regional reform was presented to parliament for approval and passed. Members of the regional councils continued to be drawn from local authorities, while regional prefects were appointed alongside the

A CLOSER LOOK 3.7

THE FRENCH MEDIA

France has not been well-served by its media. For a long period after World War II, state radio and television were closely controlled by the government. A number of private radio stations located at the periphery of the country provided much needed fresh air to information. Improvements took place since the de Gaulle period, the three main channels having become independent networks. Under President Mitterrand's Socialist governments, private television began to flourish. There is now more choice and genuine independence from the government, though the quality of the programs leaves much to be desired.

Most of the press is regional and of indifferent quality. Not surprisingly, the best newspapers are Parisian, *Le Monde* being the outstanding example, though some of the competitors that were set up in the 1970s and 1980s have also endeavored to develop a modern form of journalism. Weeklies have moved in the direction of investigative stories and have uncovered problems and scandals. By and large, the media suffer from the classic French characteristics of nationalistic elitism. Culture is given great emphasis—with such ministers of culture as Malraux under de Gaulle and Lang under Mitterrand—but culture is regarded as being true if it is essentially French. As a result, the Americanization of the media is (officially at least, if not necessarily in reality) markedly frowned upon: it was a strong bone of contention in the discussions leading to the 1995 GATT agreement as well as to problems arising between France and its partners in the successor body of GATT, the World Trade Organization (WTO).

regional presidents and councils; these administered a small portion of the matters hitherto handled centrally by the civil service. Finally, the Socialist government of the 1980s instituted regional elections; the councils in turn elect their executive. Independent political bodies thus exist in each region, though their powers and influence are still limited. Although these moves have been relatively slow and half-hearted, France is at last engaged in a process that may gradually dispose of many of the old habits of centralization.

ECONOMIC INTERVENTION AND PUBLIC ENTERPRISE

The weakness of French local government stems in large part from the widespread belief that France needs a strong civil service if it is to be a modern industrial and commercial nation and the inertia of the provinces is to be shaken. A parallel view has traditionally been adopted with respect to business (see Table 3.8). Hence the large development of public and semipublic

undertakings, often taking the form of mixed companies (*sociétés d'économie mixte*), while large-scale nationalizations took place in 1945–1946 after World War II and in 1982 after the Socialist victory. An attempt was also made to supervise business generally by means of economic plans. The tide then turned. A privatization program was launched by the 1986–1988 conservative government and an effort was undertaken to reduce the traditional role of the civil service in the economy. The Socialist government of 1997–2002 followed suit, though somewhat reluctantly.

The Plan

French economic development from the 1940s to the 1980s has often been associated with the activities of the *Commissariat général au Plan,* although its role is now almost nominal. It started under the leadership of Jean Monnet, a strong-willed ex–civil servant and ex-businessman who was to be crucial to the psychological success of the idea and was later, much in the

TABLE 3.8

BUDGET EXPENDITURE 2000 AND 2001
Euro million (2005 €1 = $1.23)

Expenditure*	2000	2001
General non-salary disbursements (net)	53,916	51,050
Agriculture and fisheries	4,427	5,107
Culture and communications	2,452	2,549
Defence	37,019	37,309
Economy, finance, and industry	13,834	14,143
Employment and solidarity	32,673	31,947
Equipment, transport, and housing	20,945	21,363
Foreign affairs	3,196	3,368
Interior	13,175	16,980
Justice	4,162	4,435
National education	55,030	59,166
Overseas territories, etc.	972	1,040
Research and technology	6,077	6,157
War veterans	3,672	3,627
Total (incl. others)	253,806	260,900

*Expenditure by ministry, according to initial budgetary law.
Source: Ministry of the Economy, Finance and Industry, Paris.

same vein, to foster European unity. The Plan was to be flexible; it was to be run by a team, not by a hierarchical and bureaucratic organization. Its strength came from the intellectual authority of the experts belonging to it.

The character of the Plan changed over the years. It was first concerned with reconstruction and the development of basic industries. It then extended its purview to the whole economy, to regional development (it helped decentralization to an extent), and even to social policies. Originally the Plan was prepared exclusively by officials with little discussion, even in parliament, but large segments of the community later became involved through numerous committees. Employers, leaders of nationalized industries, and trade unionists were associated with the preparation of the Plan. There were also increasingly discussions in the Economic and Social Council, in the regional economic committees, and among the public at large. However, the idea could only suffer in a climate of greater liberalization and free enterprise. With the advent of the Socialist government of 1981, its importance was revived somewhat, but because of the imperative of economic retrenchment, it never had again the importance it once had. By the 1990s, it had effectively disappeared in all but name.

The Size of the Public Sector

The downgrading of the Plan coincided with the first real attempt made by post–World War II French governments to reduce the size of the public sector, which up to 1986 was among the largest in Western Europe and had already been so before the large-scale nationalization measures of the 1981 government. From a base that included, before World War II, the post office, the railways, some shipping lines, and undertakings such as potash mines in Alsace, electricity production in the Rhone Valley, and luxury china in Sèvres, the public sector expanded in 1945–1946 to include the coal mines, the major banks, insurance companies, gas, electricity, and much of aircraft manufacturing. Renault, the largest car manufacturer, was nationalized, as the owner had collaborated with Nazi Germany during the Second World War. Much of air and shipping transport also came under direct governmental control. There was a de facto monopoly of radio and television within France, and the state acquired majority capital in several of the private radio stations that operated at the periphery of the country. A public news agency, *Agence France-Presse,* replaced the private prewar *Agence Havas.* As demand for oil increased (France has very little within its territory), the state created companies, typically as a major shareholder, which engaged in research, production, and distribution of oil and natural gas on a worldwide basis.

This was the situation before 1981. The Socialist government, following to the letter the party's pledge at the election, then carried through parliament the nationalization of practically all the banks (including old, established private ones such as Rothschild) and of five major industrial groups in the chemical and electronic fields, while the major steel companies, already heavily subsidized by the state, were taken over.

These developments took a variety of legal forms that had been perfected since World War I.

Originally state control was direct, as in the case of the post office. Later came the model of the *établissements publics,* whose funds are public and where control is tight, but where a board makes decisions and contracts with third parties on behalf of the agency. The formula has often been adopted by local authorities as well. To increase flexibility, companies and corporations were set up with the same structure, the same rights, and the same obligations as private firms. In the case of the large undertakings nationalized in 1945–1946 and in 1982, special legislative arrangements gave the corporations a somewhat different organization, with boards including representatives of the state, the users, and the employees, for instance. But in many other cases there was simply no difference between private and public firms, thus making it possible for state corporations to combine with private bodies to set up subsidiaries.

The Move toward Privatization

The development of the public sector reached a peak in the mid-1980s. In 1986, for the first time, a government came to power committed both to privatization and to the abandonment of the traditional practice of linking private and public bodies. For the first time, too, the Left no longer wished to modify the new equilibrium by increasing again the public sector when it returned to power in 1988; no new nationalization was even suggested. The French governments of the 1990s thus came to follow the same direction as other European governments. In line with European Union policy, they made moves toward more classical forms of private enterprise at the expense of both wholly public and mixed economy companies, although the latter had been regarded as the way of the future for at least a generation.

Privatization spread in the 1990s and came to include, both before and under the Jospin government of 1997–2002, Air France, Renault, most banks, and television stations. However, a marked reluctance of the Socialists to move too quickly was noticeable. Some utilities, such as gas and electricity, did remain, perhaps for a

while only, in the public sector. This was not merely because of the Socialists' visceral reluctance to go too far along the privatization road, however, but also because of the French tradition according to which the public sector, under the civil service, is expected to play a key part in the life of the nation.

FOREIGN POLICY

De Gaulle's Worldwide Policy

Foreign policy was the main interest of de Gaulle. Even the reform of the institutions was in some sense provoked by the bias of the founder of the Fifth Republic for foreign affairs, as he felt that the instability and impotence of previous regimes had been the cause both of defeat in 1940 and of the generally limited influence of the country in the world ever since. Yet although there were indeed external effects of French internal political uncertainties, de Gaulle markedly underestimated the extent to which the country could any longer be a prime mover in the contemporary world. Thus his efforts at pushing for a strong and independent foreign policy ended in failure. Indeed, he himself may have realized that he could not go much beyond symbolic gestures, such as the effort to build closer links with the Soviet Union or to defend the rights of some countries or groups against Anglo-Saxon imperialism (as he tried to do in Quebec or Latin America). In practice, he kept France within NATO (despite some changes) and within the European Community, despite a continuous emphasis on the fact that Europe should be a "Europe of nations" and despite the fact that he unquestionably retarded the development of European unity.

Pompidou's Greater Realism

De Gaulle's departure from the scene meant a slow, indeed very slow, return to the recognition of France's international position, that of a medium-sized power, with some influence stemming from her cultural and economic ties with parts of Africa and, to a more limited extent, with Latin America. But France cannot have a direct effect on the course of events outside Western Europe. Within the European sphere, the nation has a significant part to play, albeit as a partner and not as a leader. Thus Pompidou, de Gaulle's successor and heir, began to make some moves away from grand world involvement and toward the acceptance of the country's limited European role. His acceptance of British entry into the European Community was partly motivated by the hope that Britain, as France, would reduce the spread of "supranationalism." In this he was proved right. Chirac disagreed strongly with the U.S. over the war in Iraq in 2003.

France's Role in World Affairs

The third President of the Fifth Republic, Giscard d'Estaing, established a close working relationship with the German chancellor of the time, Helmut Schmidt, that continued the rapprochement of de Gaulle with Adenauer a decade or more earlier, but with a different purpose. De Gaulle used Adenauer to assert his leadership over Europe. Giscard d'Estaing was more modest; he recognized the economic superiority of Germany and was primarily concerned with economic association. A step was thus taken toward real collaboration and the abandonment of the (wholly unrealistic) idea that France could do more than partly influence the course of events in Western Europe, let alone in the rest of the world.

With Mitterrand's accession to the presidency in 1981, France's foreign policy ceased to be truly worldwide, although some interest for what had been French Africa and for the "francophonie" lingered on. Not being associated, directly or indirectly, with de Gaulle and Gaullism, Mitterrand was able to assert that France's position was in Europe and, in effect, in Europe only. His successor, Jacques Chirac, seemed torn between traditional Gaullism in words and realism in deeds. He clearly took a Gaullist line over nuclear weapons, at least in a first phase. He insisted that France should have a truly independent nuclear deterrent. He doggedly proceeded with a series of tests in the South Pacific that

antagonized almost every country, not just in the Pacific but in Europe as well. Yet Chirac then stated that the tests conducted up to January 1996 would be the last and that he would from then on act strongly in order to reduce the nuclear threat—not a line that de Gaulle would have readily adopted. As Mitterrand, he came to adopt a more realistic line in favor of Europe. However, there still is more than a lingering desire to play a large part—an unrealistically large part—in worldwide developments, whether in the Middle East, Africa, or Latin America.

France and the European Union

Mitterrand was markedly more realistic than his predecessors about the need for France to concentrate on European affairs. This realism stemmed in part from the economic difficulties (and the consequential social problems of unemployment) of the country. These made it impossible for the president to expect to move at a different pace from his European partners. But his European conviction was also part of a general recognition that if France's commitment to Europe was wholehearted, she could play a key part in the European Community. Perhaps as a result, Mitterrand was able to appoint his ex-minister of finance, Jacques Delors, to the presidency of the European Commission in 1985, a post he was to occupy for ten years in the most able and forward-looking manner. Delors, for instance, was the architect of the single market policy and, indirectly, of the Economic and Monetary Union, which led to the adoption of the single European currency. Mitterrand could thus exercise indirect influence on Union affairs. He was not fully a federalist, but he clearly was a realist. So was Chirac, who, unlike many other members of his party, had previously supported the Maastricht Treaty of the European Union. Once in office, he began to pursue, out of sheer necessity, a European orientation.

French commitment to Europe remains somewhat ambiguous. While Joschka Fischer, the Green German foreign minister under Schröder, stressed the need to move toward a federal system, Jospin, the Socialist French prime minister, repeated that the Union had to be a Union of nations. He was indeed attacked in some quarters for being too lukewarm toward Europe and for being primarily concerned with home affairs—a point that was in some ways correct, as he did leave to Chirac many opportunities to take the lead in European matters. Yet it was under Jospin that the euro became a reality, and the support that his government showed for the move was in no way less active than that of other European governments of the "Eurozone."

Nonetheless, French governments have often been concerned, not just under de Gaulle but consistently afterwards, to use the European Union to defend their economic interests to the hilt, as over the GATT negotiations of 1993–1994, while being rather slow at applying in practice the principles that they claim to support in theory. Such a mode of behavior is perhaps inevitable in a period of transition. However, France, as the other Western European powers, has to recognize that its role in the world must diminish, and that only through a common European policy can the voice of the whole area be of real moment. The dilemma between going it alone and further integration has affected almost daily the actions of French governments over the last decades. It is likely to continue to affect them for a substantial period.

CONCLUSION

In the 1950s and 1960s, the French economy was profoundly transformed; the colonial problems that destroyed one French regime and brought another at times near the precipice were solved and forgotten; the international status of the country was high. Yet social tensions, which seemed to diminish for a while in the 1960s, reemerged dramatically in 1968. This reinforced the feeling of many among the French that the Fifth Republic remained provisional. Yet the departure of de Gaulle one year later, in 1969, did not shake the institutions, and the transition from de Gaulle to Pompidou was smooth. Nor was the regime shaken by the transition from Giscard d'Estaing to Mitterrand in 1981, despite the many predictions made earlier that "alternance" from

Right to Left would be difficult, if not impossible. Nor was the regime at all shaken by cohabitation—twice between a president of the Left and a government of the Right and Center and once between a president of the Right and a government of the Left—despite gloomy predictions made earlier that conflicts would be intense.

In 1981, a Socialist government embarked on a major reform program. This was possible only because of institutions that had been tailor-made for de Gaulle. In 1986, a conservative government undid many of these reforms, but the regime, then too, was flexible enough to make these movements possible and to remain stable through repeated swings of the pendulum, toward the Left in 1988 and 1997, toward the Right in 1993 and 2002. The institutional ambiguity of the 1958 Constitution turned out to be a major asset of the Fifth Republic.

Cynics had claimed that de Gaulle wanted to have it both ways—to be able to run the executive and yet have considerable control over the legislature, to have the elbow room of a U.S. president but the hold over the chamber of a British premier, and, in practical terms, to be immovable for what was then seven years but be able to dissolve parliament and appeal to the people. Others had claimed that de Gaulle was unable to appreciate the importance of constitutional structures, a view which has some truth, though the attitudes of the first president of the Fifth Republic on this matter were complex. He seemed to consider that constitutional arrangements were matters for lawyers who can always find solutions if they are firmly led, and yet he had a simple, naive, almost religious belief in the virtues of constitutional reform to redress the imperfections of a political system. His approach to political analysis was more institutional than behavioral, to adopt the widely used expression of modern political scientists. Yet he made a change that, however ambiguous (or perhaps because it was ambiguous), allowed for a transition to occur and turned out to be adapted to French patterns of political behavior.

De Gaulle was often criticized because he preferred to introduce constitutional change instead of establishing a streamlined and responsible party system as Adenauer had succeeded in

Jacques Chirac was elected president in 1995, the third time he ran for the position. Chirac was mayor of Paris from 1977 to 1995, was leader of the Gaullist Rally for the Republic (RPR), and was twice prime minister.

achieving in West Germany. De Gaulle was indeed old-fashioned in this respect. He did not like parties, which he often referred to as "factions"; he saw them as divisive and as the cause of the ineffectiveness of French political life in the past. Yet, in practice, while concentrating on institutional change and endeavoring to reduce the role of parties, he streamlined the party system. He built a party on the Right, which his successors, Pompidou and Giscard d'Estaing, undermined. Indirectly, too, he enabled Mitterrand to build his popular support and to restart the Socialist Party.

The election of 1981 constituted an historic event in more than one way. In the broadest political sense, more than Pompidou and Giscard d'Estaing, Mitterrand was the heir and the continuer of de Gaulle's approach. Mitterrand, as de Gaulle, defeated the Communist Party on coming to power; he, as de Gaulle, established a strong majority party, since the election of 1981 had the same political effect of streamlining and strength-

ening the party system as the election of 1962; Mitterrand, as de Gaulle, came to power with a mission, albeit a different one. De Gaulle's mission was to solve the Algerian crisis and, beyond this crisis, to bring France back to political and psychological sanity. Mitterrand's mission was to reconcile the French among themselves, to make them no longer fear to take on their own destiny at the grass roots, whether in the regions and the communes or in the firms.

Here the comparison stops. To achieve this tall order, Mitterrand needed to exorcize the twin specters of unemployment and inflation. He reduced the latter, but unemployment probably contributed to the first setback of his party in 1986 and unquestionably led to the major Socialist defeat of 1993. As a matter of fact, Mitterrand could not hope to succeed in his mission without the collaboration of other Western European countries, the United States, and Japan. These nations practiced economic orthodoxy. Mitterrand had to accept the need for retrenchment and, with it, the clipping of many of his ideals. Yet, while the French turned away from the Left in 1993 in view of its relative failures, Mitterrand and the Socialist Party in general gained a central position in French political life of respect and of acceptability which the party had not had before, as the good performance of Jospin at the 1995 presidential election showed. That performance foreshadowed the parliamentary victory of the Socialist Party two years later in 1997. As a result, France has become a country in which pluralism and alternance are firmly established, as the 2002 election result was once more to show.

Observers around the world have tended to admire the British form of government but have been fascinated by the French political system. For a while, under the Fifth Republic, it was fashionable to say that a new French political system, streamlined and dull, had emerged. This was scarcely true at the time of the Algerian war, when virulence added unpleasantness to the political fights of the French; this has not become true with the end of the colonial wars. Since the 1970s, there has been a difficult search for a better equilibrium between the various forces in society, between Paris and the provinces, between employers and workers, as well as between the majority of the French and the many minority groups—immigrants, the young, and others. No doubt the Socialist experiment of 1981 disappointed some and repelled others, but France also changed in the process. The central bureaucracy and the elite groups are no longer able to maintain a hold on society to the extent that they once did.

By 1981 the Gaullist (and Giscardian) phase of the Fifth Republic seemed to have outlived its usefulness. By 1995, the Socialist Party, too, seemed to have proved unable to give France the brave new world that many wanted, while some among its political elite appeared to have succumbed to the lust for money as well as for power. To the lasting credit of de Gaulle, he made it possible for French citizens to bring about responsible changes in policies and changes in personnel, developments which had not been possible for many generations. It is to the credit of the French that they seized this opportunity, though many motivations, from unemployment to scandals, have played a substantial part. Thus France may gradually overcome its social problems while also overcoming the institutional difficulties from which it suffered for almost two centuries. Yet the path is narrow and tortuous. Ingenuity and imagination will no more suffice than a competent bureaucracy. Patience and determination—not the qualities for which the French are best known—will have to be shown if the motto "Liberty, Equality, Fraternity" is to be brought, in full, closer to reality.

Thinking Critically

1. What impact does the educational elite have on the life of France?
2. Has the role of the state been greater in France than in the United States?
3. Is it true to say that France cannot be France without "grandeur"?
4. How would you characterize France's attitude to the European Union?
5. How would you assess the impact of socialist governments on the French economy?

KEY TERMS

adjoints (175)
bureaucracy (171)
ministerial cabinets (174)
civil service (172)
commune (175)
départements (175)
Directions générales/Directions (172)
dirigisme (171)
Ecole Nationale d'Administration (ENA) (172)
Ecole Normale Supérieure (173)
Ecole Polytechnique (172)
Grands Corps (172)
Grandes Ecoles (172)
mayors (175)
prefects (175)
regions (175)
social engineering (171)

FURTHER READINGS

Bauchet, P. *Economic Planning: The French Experience* (London: Heinemann, 1963).

Cerny, P., and M. Schain, eds. *French Politics and Public Policy* (New York: Methuen, 1980).

Chapman, B. *Introduction to French Local Government* (London: Allen and Unwin, 1953).

Chapman, Herrick, and Laura L. Frader, eds. *Race in France: Interdisciplinary Perspectives on the Politics of Difference* (New York: Berghahn Books, 2004).

Crozier, M. *The Stalled Society* (New York: Viking, 1973).

Gregoire, R. *The French Civil Service* (Brussels: Institute of Administrative Science, 1964).

Guyomarch, A., H. Machin, and E. Ritchie. *France in the European Union* (Basingstoke: Macmillan, 1998).

Machin, H., and V. Wright, eds. *Economic Policy and Policy-Making under the Mitterrand Presidency, 1981–1984* (London: F. Pinter, 1985).

Ridley, F., and J. Blondel. *Public Administration in France,* 2nd ed. (London: Routledge and Kegan Paul, 1968).

Suleiman, E. *Politics, Power, and Bureaucracy in France* (Princeton, NJ: Princeton University Press, 1974).

Suleiman, E. *Elites in French Society* (Princeton, NJ: Princeton University Press, 1978).

WEB SITES

www.elysee.fr
Information on the French president
www.premier-minstre.gouv.fr
Information on the prime minister
www.archives.premier-ministre.gouv.fr
Information on the prime minister

www.assemblee-nationale.fr
Information on the National Assembly
www.senat.fr
Information on the Senate
www.fonction-publique.gouv.fr
Information on the ministry for the civil service
www.ena.fr
Information on the National School for Administration
www.conseil-etat.fr
Information on the Council of State
www.archivesnationales.culture.gouv.fr
National Archives
www.conseil-constitutionnel.fr
Constitutional Council
www.parlement.fr
French parliament
www.interieur.gouv.fr
Ministry of the Interior
www.francetresor.gouv.fr
Ministry for Economic Affairs
www.diplomatie.gouv.fr
Ministry for Foreign Affairs
www.lemonde.fr
France's most respected newspaper, *Le Monde*
www.monde-diplomatique.fr
Le Monde Diplomatique
www.lefigaro.fr
Le Figaro
www.permanent.nouvelobs.com
Le Nouvel Observateur
www.rpr.org
RPR
www.parti-socialiste.fr
Socialist Party

CHAPTER

4

THE GOVERNMENT OF
Germany

Donald Kommers and A. James McAdams

INTRODUCTION

Background: As Western Europe's richest and most populous nation, Germany remains a key member of the continent's economic, political, and defense organizations. European power struggles immersed the country in two devastating World Wars in the first half of the twentieth century and left the country occupied by the victorious Allied powers of the United States, United Kingdom, France, and the Soviet Union in 1945. With the advent of the Cold War, two German states were formed in 1949: the western Federal Republic of Germany (FRG) and the eastern German Democratic Republic (GDR). The democratic FRG embedded itself in key Western economic and security organizations, the European Community and NATO, while the communist GDR was on the front line of the Soviet-led Warsaw Pact. The decline of the USSR and the end of the Cold War allowed for German unification in 1990. Since then Germany has expended considerable funds to bring eastern productivity and wages up to western standards.

GEOGRAPHY

Location: Central Europe, bordering the Baltic Sea and the North Sea, between the Netherlands and Poland, south of Denmark

Area: 357,021 sq km

Area—comparative: slightly smaller than Montana

Land boundaries: 3,618 km

> *border countries:* Austria 784 km, Belgium 167 km, Czech Republic 646 km, Denmark 68 km, France 451 km, Luxembourg 135 km, Netherlands 577 km, Poland 456 km, Switzerland 334 km

Climate: temperate and marine; cool, cloudy, wet winters and summers; occasional warm foehn wind

Terrain: lowlands in north, uplands in center, Bavarian Alps in south

Elevation extremes: *lowest point:* Freepsum lake –2 m

  highest point: Zugspitze 2,963 m

Geography note: strategic location on North European Plain and along the entrance to the Baltic Sea

PEOPLE

Population: 82,424,000

Age structure: *0–14 years:* 14.7% (male 6,197,000; female 5,879,000)

  15–64 years: 67.00% (male 28,619,237; female 27,132,000)

  65 years and over: 18.39% (male 6,096,000; female 8,999,000)

Population growth rate: 0.02%

Birthrate: 8.45 births/1,000 population

Sex ratio: 0.96 male/female

Life expectancy at birth: 78.54 years

  male: 75.56 years

  female: 81.68 years

Nationality: *noun:* German, Germans

  adjective: German

Ethnic groups: German 91.5%, Turkish 2.4%, other 6.1% (made up largely of Serbo-Croatian, Italian, Russian, Greek, Polish, Spanish)

Religions: Protestant 34%, Roman Catholic 34%, Muslim 3.7%, unaffiliated or other 28.3%

Languages: German

Literacy: *definition:* age 15 and over can read and write

  total population: 99%

GOVERNMENT

Country name: *conventional long form:* Federal Republic of Germany

  conventional short form: Germany

Government type: federal republic

Capital: Berlin

Administrative divisions: 16 states (Länder, singular—Land); Baden-Württemberg, Bayern, Berlin, Brandenburg, Bremen, Hamburg, Hessen, Mecklenburg-Vorpommern, Niedersachsen, Nordrhein-Westfalen, Rheinland-Pfalz, Saarland, Sachsen, Sachsen-Anhalt, Schleswig-Holstein, Thüringen

Independence: 18 January 1871 (German Empire unification); divided into four zones of occupation (UK, US, USSR, and later, France) in 1945 following World War II; Federal Republic of Germany (FRG or West Germany) proclaimed 23 May 1949 and included the former UK, US, and French zones; German Democratic Republic (GDR or East Germany) proclaimed 7 October 1949 and included the former USSR zone; unification of West Germany and East Germany took place 3 October 1990; all four powers formally relinquished rights 15 March 1991

Constitution: 23 May 1949, known as Basic Law; became constitution of the united German people 3 October 1990

Legal system: civil law system with indigenous concepts; judicial review of legislative acts in the Federal Constitutional Court; has not accepted compulsory ICJ jurisdiction

Suffrage: 18 years of age; universal

Executive branch: *chief of state:* President Horst Koehler (since 1 July 2004)

  head of government: Chancellor Gerhard Schröder (since 27 October 1998)

  cabinet: Cabinet or Bundesminister (Federal Ministers) appointed by the president on the recommendation of the chancellor

  elections: president elected for a five-year term by a Federal Convention including all members of the Federal Assembly and an equal number of delegates elected by the state parliaments; chancellor elected by an absolute majority of the Federal Assembly for a four-year term

Legislative branch: bicameral Parliament or Parlament consists of the Federal Assembly or Bundestag (603 seats; elected by popular vote under a system combining direct and proportional representation; a party must win 5% of the national vote or three direct mandates to gain representation; members serve four-year terms) and the Federal Council or Bundesrat (69 votes; state governments are directly represented by votes; each has 3 to 6 votes depending on population and are required to vote as a block)

Judicial branch: Federal Constitutional Court or Bundesverfassungsgericht (half the judges are elected by the Bundestag and half by the Bundesrat)

ECONOMY

Overview: Germany possesses the world's third most technologically powerful economy after the United States and Japan, but structural market rigidities—including the substantial nonwage costs of hiring new workers—have made unemployment a long-term, not just a cyclical, problem. Germany's aging population, combined with high unemployment, has pushed social security outlays to a level exceeding contributions from workers. The modernization and integration of the eastern German economy remains a costly long-term problem, with annual transfers from western Germany amounting to roughly $70 billion. Corporate restructuring and growing capital markets are transforming the German economy to meet the challenges of European economic integration and globalization in general.

GDP: purchasing power parity—$2,271 trillion

GDP—real growth rate: 0.1%

GDP—per capita: purchasing power parity—$27,600

GDP—composition by sector: *agriculture:* 1.2%
industry: 30.4%
services: 68.4%

Inflation rate (consumer prices): 1.1%

Labor force: 42.63 million

Labor force—by occupation: industry 33.4%, agriculture 2.8%, services 63.8%

Unemployment rate: 10.5%

Currency: deutsche mark (DEM); euro (EUR)
note: in 2002, the euro replaced the local currency for all transactions.

A. POLITICAL DEVELOPMENT

On October 3, 1990, after 45 years of painful division, Germany was once again a united nation. After midnight on that day, East Germany ceased to exist. The territory formerly governed by the German Democratic Republic (GDR) and its hard-line Communist leaders was now an integral part of the Federal Republic of Germany (FRG). For those involved, the magical term was *accession.* According to Article 23 of West Germany's constitution, "other parts of Germany" outside the territory governed by the FRG could join or "accede to" the Federal Republic. Accession meant that these "other parts" of Germany joining the FRG would henceforth be subject to its constitution, better known as the Basic Law or *Grundgesetz.* In this instance, accession took place under the terms of the German Unity Treaty signed by the FRG and the GDR. In signing the treaty the GDR agreed to dissolve itself, to embrace the Basic Law, and to bring its entire social, political, and economic system into conformity with the legal order of the FRG.

Unification did not restore to Germany all the territory lost as a result of World War II. In 1945 the Soviet Union had annexed northern East Prussia, including Königsberg, while all German territory east of the Oder and Neisse Rivers (East Prussia, Silesia, and parts of Pomerania and Brandenburg) was placed under Polish administration. The Allies divided the rest of Germany and Berlin into four zones of occupation: a Soviet zone in the east and three zones in the west occupied by France, Britain, and the United States, respectively. The western zones, united in 1949 to form the Federal Republic of Germany, constituted only 60 percent of the territory of the German nation that existed between 1871 and 1937. The Saarland, annexed by France after World War II, was returned to the FRG in 1957 after its residents voted in favor of reunion. With the GDR's accession in 1990, Germany recovered three-fourths of the territory contained within its 1937 borders.

The division of Germany after World War II recalls the tragic course of German history through the centuries. This history has been marred not only by territorial dismemberment but also by political discontinuity, which has manifested itself in recurrent patterns of revolution and reaction. It has left the German nation with a diverse and fragmented political legacy, punctuated by authoritarian, and even totalitarian rule. But importantly, since the Second World War, the German people have shown that, given the right conditions, democracy can win out.

HISTORICAL BACKGROUND: MOLDING THE GERMAN NATION

The First Reich (800–1806)

Centuries after Britain and France had been unified under strong national monarchs, Germany was still a dizzying patchwork of sovereign powers. In the territory where the German nation-state would eventually arise, there were over 300 feudal states and some 1,300 smaller estates, each with its own political institutions, laws, and customs. No imperial institution was prestigious enough to unify these entities, and no emperor was strong enough to merge them into a single national state. The shape of the Holy Roman Empire of the German Nation (the predominantly German parts of the Empire founded by Charlemagne and restored by Otto I—and quite rightly described as "neither holy, nor Roman, nor an empire") changed repeatedly over its thousand-year history. It stretched in and out like an accordion, depending on the fortunes of war or the outcome of princely rivalries.

Religious and political division matched the severity of Germany's territorial fragmentation. The Reformation (1517–1555) polarized Germans religiously, creating a legacy of intolerance and hatred that lasted well into the nineteenth century. The Thirty Years' War (1618–1648) was equally devastating in long-range political impact. Reputed to be the most destructive war in the first millennium of German history, it decimated the population, wrecked agriculture and industry, and destroyed an emergent middle class that might have formed the nucleus of a nationalizing and moderating force in German politics. Instead, it restored power to the princes, reinvigorated feudalism, and set the stage for the nineteenth-century struggle between feudal and modernizing forces. Moreover, Protestant religious teaching and princely absolutism combined to emphasize the duty of obedience to the State, thus inhibiting popular participation in politics.[1]

Napoleon to Bismarck (1806–1871)

Ironically, the path to German unity was laid not by internal design but by a foreign invader. As part of his plan for European conquest, Napoleon Bonaparte occupied Germany in 1806 and forced hundreds of principalities into a confederation of some 30 states governed by a unified code of civil law. Like so much else in German history, this experience led to contradictory results that certainly Napoleon could never have foreseen, nor desired. On the one hand, French rule stimulated the development of a liberal movement focused mainly in southwestern Germany and rooted in the eighteenth-century revival of classical humanism. On the other hand, it triggered an outburst of German nationalism built almost exclusively on antipathy toward the liberal reforms of the French Revolution—a reaction paralleled in the cultural domain by a literary backlash that glorified tradition over reason, heroism over compassion, and a romantic conception of one's local community over cosmopolitanism.

France's defeat in 1815 led to the Congress of Vienna and the establishment of a new confederacy of 41 states that largely retained Napoleon's extensive remodeling of Germany. In its effort to

strengthen Germany vis-à-vis France, the Congress ceded large possessions in the Rhineland and Westphalia to Prussia, a German state that by then had grown into a formidable power in central Europe. The Prussian-led conservative Hohenzollern monarchy and militaristic Junker caste were destined to finish, through "blood and iron," the work of national unification started by Napoleon. Economically, the Prussian-sponsored customs union (*Zollverein*), which removed most trade barriers among the German states, was an important tool of national integration.

A watershed year in this period was 1848, when revolutions against monarchical regimes broke out all over Europe. German liberals had gathered enough strength to persuade several princes to go along with the election of a national assembly, which convened in Frankfurt am Main. Known as the Frankfurt Parliament, it called for the creation of a united Germany to be ruled under a new federal constitution containing an impressive bill of rights, an independent judiciary, and parliamentary institutions. By the following spring, however, this attempted revolution had been put down and Germany reverted to its traditional pattern of authoritarian governance, increasingly under Prussian domination. In 1866, under the leadership of Otto von Bismarck, Prussia defeated Austria, its closest rival for hegemony in Germany. Austria's defeat led to the creation of the North German Confederation in 1867, also under Prussian domination. Four years later, after conquering France, Prussia successfully established a truly national state in the form of a constitutional monarchy.

The Second Reich (1871–1918)

The constitutional order installed by Bismarck in 1871 was a semi-authoritarian system designed to contain and control all of the contradictory forces unleashed over the previous century. Among its diverse features, it (1) limited the franchise to the wealthier classes; (2) subordinated the popularly elected house of parliament (*Reichstag*) to the executive; (3) established a Prussian-dominated upper parliamentary chamber (*Bundesrat*) composed largely of landed proprietors and members

---

[1]This and the following historical subsections rely heavily on Geoffrey Barraclough, *The Origins of Modern Germany* (New York: Capricorn Books, 1963); Koppel S. Pinson, *Modern Germany*, 2nd ed. (New York: Macmillan, 1966); and H. W. Koch, *A Constitutional History of Germany in the Nineteenth and Twentieth Centuries* (London and New York: Longmann, 1984).

of reigning families; (4) divided executive authority between a chancellor and the emperor (*Kaiser*), with effective political power lodged in the latter; and (5) empowered the emperor (preeminently the king of Prussia) to appoint and dismiss the chancellor, dissolve the Reichstag, declare martial law, and serve as supreme commander of the armed forces.

In the socioeconomic sphere, the imperial era was marked by a similarly precarious balance of forces: (1) an economic revolution that transformed a backward and predominantly agrarian society into a powerful urban, industrialized nation; (2) the establishment of a tenuous alliance between agrarian and industrial interests in foreign policy; (3) the colonization of overseas territories and the launching of an arms race with Britain and France, reflecting many Germans' dreams of a larger and even more powerful global order under German hegemony; and (4) importantly for the later development of the nation's distinctive social and economic values, the adoption of a comprehensive program of state-supported social legislation designed to purchase the loyalty and passivity of the working masses.

The social theorist Ralf Dahrendorf has characterized imperial Germany as an "industrial feudal society,"[2] meaning that, unlike in Britain and France, industrialism in Germany failed to produce a fully modern society. Whereas modernization had brought about liberal traditions of civic equality and political participation in Britain and France, Germany retained many of the features of a preindustrial class society based on rank and status. The state bureaucracy, professional army, landed aristocracy, and patriarchal family remained the central pillars of the social structure. Human rights or other fundamental guarantees of human dignity were conspicuously absent in the imperial constitution. Conflicting social groups were either brutally repressed, or they were simply bought off through state paternalism. These devices reinforced the political compliance of the German people. It induced many to seek the satisfactions of life by turning inward toward themselves and by cultivating private values, such as those to be gained through friends and families, rather than by turning outward toward the cultivation of public and egalitarian virtues.

The Weimar Republic (1919–1933)

Germany's defeat in World War I gave liberals some grounds for hope. The abdication of the monarch led to the establishment at Weimar of the nation's first constitutional democracy since the short-lived National Assembly of 1848. The Constitution of 1919 confirmed the tradition of German federalism, guaranteed numerous social and political rights, and adopted a parliamentary system capped by the popular election of the president. However, it also contained structural features that contributed to the instability of the new polity. The president could dismiss the chancellor, dissolve the Reichstag (the new and increasingly vocal lower chamber), control the armed forces, suspend constitutional rights, and exercise broad emergency powers. The system of proportional representation splintered the electorate, leading to a succession of weak governments. Also, basic liberties were judicially unenforceable, and the ease with which the constitution could be amended or suspended tended to trivialize it.

It is doubtful whether any constitution, however artfully drawn, could have contained the social and political chaos of this postwar period. The disgrace of military defeat and the harsh terms of the Versailles Treaty—for example, the enforced reparations at a time of economic distress and the Allied occupation of the Rhineland—gave birth to yet another round of frenzied nationalism. Against the backdrop of an unchanged social structure, a large segment of Germany's elite failed to be persuaded about the legitimacy of Weimar's republican institutions. At length, these institutions were easily manipulated for antidemocratic purposes as social turmoil grew and the economy collapsed. Violence erupted in the streets as right-wing extremists, often fighting left-wing extremists, gathered strength and influence. This unrest led to Adolf

---

[2]Ralf Dahrendorf, *Society and Democracy in Germany* (Garden City, NY: Doubleday, 1967), p. 62.

Hitler's installation as chancellor on January 30, 1933. Nazi success in the elections of March 5, 1933, following the February burning of the Reichstag, anchored his hold on power. The passage of the Enabling Act shortly thereafter, which granted the government dictatorial powers, ended the life of the Weimar Republic.

The Third Reich (1933–1945)

With Hitler's rise to power, constitutional government succumbed to National Socialist totalitarianism. The popular assemblies of the various states were abolished, political parties banned, autonomous groups and associations suppressed, dissent crushed, anti-Nazi political figures imprisoned, tortured, or murdered, and ordinary citizens deprived of liberty and property without due process of law. Having consolidated his power and in violation of the Versailles Treaty, Hitler took steps to remilitarize the Rhineland and build a war machine that by 1941 would sweep across Europe, threatening the security of the entire world.

Among the many atrocities committed between 1933 and 1945, Hitler engineered what Lucy S. Dawidowicz has called "the war against the Jews."[3] The dictatorship's assault began with campaigns of anti-Semitic propaganda; it continued with decrees to boycott Jewish businesses, remove Jews from the civil service and the professions, divest them of their citizenship, seize their property, and forbid them from marrying non-Jews; it culminated in the "night of the broken glass" (*Kristallnacht*), when gangs of storm troopers all over Germany assaulted Jews on the streets, invaded their homes, destroyed their shops, and set fire to their synagogues. The Holocaust followed as millions of Jews in Germany and in conquered territories throughout Europe, including women and children, were rounded up, herded into cattle cars, and sent to concentration camps designed for their extermination. Six million Jews died in these camps, almost completing Hitler's goal of ridding Europe of its Jewish population.

Although the German dictatorship met with the courageous resistance of a handful of religious and political groups during this time—including even attempts on Hitler's life—it took Germany's total destruction from the outside to topple the Nazis from power. Once again, military defeat resulted in the nation's enforced dismemberment and its occupation by foreign powers. Yet provocatively, for those Germans who yearned for democracy, the situation at war's end was not completely bad. In their 12-year orgy of repression and violence, the Nazis inadvertently succeeded in destroying the old order, including many traditional institutions and values. Thus Hitler's "social revolution," combined with Germany's physical destruction, cleared the way, at least potentially, for the building of a new political order, one that would hopefully be both united and democratic.

TOWARD A NEW FRAMEWORK OF GOVERNMENT

The Occupation (1945–1949)

In 1945 Germany lay smoldering in ruins. Its once powerful military machine was shattered, its industrial establishment heavily damaged, its urban centers demolished, its transportation and communication networks disrupted, its government at all levels in a state of collapse, and its people demoralized and starving. Politically, Germany's future seemed bleak. At the Yalta and Potsdam conferences, the victorious powers had agreed to a number of measures to eliminate the German war threat in Europe, including the nation's total disarmament, the punishment of leaders responsible for war crimes, and the payment of reparations to nations hurt by German aggression.

In each of their zones of occupation, the Allies embarked upon programs of *denazification* and *democratization* as the first steps toward the reconstruction of a new political

---

[3]See Lucy S. Dawidowicz, *The War Against the Jews* (New York: Holt, Rinehart and Winston, 1975). See also David S. Wyman, *The Abandonment of the Jews* (New York: Pantheon Books, 1984).

order. By 1947–1948, however, cooperation among the Allies had ceased. For France, Britain, and the United States, democratization meant parliamentary institutions, competitive elections, civil liberties, and a free enterprise economy. But for the Soviet Union, it meant Communist Party dictatorship and state ownership of the means of production. Furthermore, the Soviet Union had embarked upon a policy of conquest and one-party rule in Eastern Europe, creating satellite states organized in accordance with Marxist-Leninist principles out of the countries it had liberated from the Nazis.

The Cold War was a gathering force with a vengeance, and Germany was its flash point. Unable to reach an agreement with the Soviet Union over the future of Germany, the three Western powers decided to combine their zones of occupation into a single economic unit. The Soviet Union responded by attempting to blockade the city of Berlin, but the famous airlift of 1948–1949 foiled the Soviet attempt to drive the Western powers out of Berlin.

Economic union in the western half of Germany was soon followed by political union. With the establishment of state and local governments and the licensing of political parties committed to democratic constitutionalism, the Allied military governors laid the groundwork for a new West German political system. A constituent assembly dominated by Christian and Social Democrats, elected in turn by the state legislatures, convened with Allied approval to write a new constitution. They called it the Basic Law (*Grundgesetz*), rather than the Constitution (*Verfassung*), to underscore the provisional character of the new polity pending national unification. That would take place, they argued, on the day the German people could make the choice to live together again "in free self-determination." This Basic Law, which created the Federal Republic of Germany, entered into force on May 23, 1949, after its ratification by the legislatures of more than two-thirds of the participating states (*Länder*).

The Soviet Union responded by founding the German Democratic Republic, whose constitution entered into force on October 7, 1949. From that date until 1990, Germany remained a divided nation, and for most of these 40-plus years the FRG and GDR viewed each other with mistrust and hostility. The Berlin Wall, which cut an ugly path through the center of Berlin, stood out as the chief symbol of their mutual antagonism. Although some relaxation in relations between the two German states gradually took place by the late 1960s and throughout the 1970s, as a consequence of the West German government's efforts to ease relations with all of Eastern Europe (*Ostpolitik*),[4] tensions remained. They seemed bound to persist so long as Europe itself remained divided militarily and politically between East and West.

Reunification

Forty-five years after the postwar division of Germany, the "impossible dream" happened. Owing to the rise of the Soviet Union's reformist General Secretary Mikhail Gorbachev, seismic changes in the geopolitics of Eastern Europe, and the subsequent end to the Cold War, the former Allied powers set the stage for Germany's reunification (see Section C for a description of these developments). Today, Germany's political and intellectual leaders often speak as though they clearly saw this event coming. But the truth is that most Germans were fully unprepared for the restoration of national unity in 1990. In earlier years, some like then-chancellor Helmut Kohl and his predecessor had repeatedly remarked that the event, however desirable, would not happen in their lifetimes. This was because they could never imagine the Soviets giving up their prized conquest in East Germany. In contrast, others, like the prominent German novelist Günter Grass, openly expressed reservations about reunification. They feared the creation of a "super-Federal Republic." Nevertheless, on Octo-

---

[4]*Ostpolitik,* which means "Eastern policy," is the term used to describe the efforts of West Germany, especially its Chancellor Willy Brandt, to normalize relations with the Communist countries of Eastern Europe. For the FRG, the high point of these efforts, which took place between 1970 and 1973, was the Basic Treaty between the Federal Republic of Germany and the German Democratic Republic.

A CLOSER LOOK
4.1

INCOMPATIBLE SOCIAL REALITIES?

"There can be no unification of the GDR and the Federal Republic on West German terms; there can be no unification of the GDR and the Federal Republic on East German terms. What blocks such a unification—such a concentration of power—is not only the objections of our neighbors in Eastern and Western Europe, but also the fact that these two social systems are mutually exclusive.... [We] have to recognize not only the territorial and political division, but also the incompatibility of two existing German social realities."

Source: Günter Grass, *Two States—One Nation?* Trans. Krishna Winston and A. S. Wensinger (New York: Harcourt Brace, 1990), pp. 54–55.

ber 3, 1990, the entity came into being—a unified *and* democratic Germany—that had been such a constant subject of debate since the middle of the nineteenth century.

Helmut Kohl, the former chancellor of German unity and a champion of European unification.

SOCIETY AND ECONOMY

An understanding of contemporary German politics requires some attention to the profound social and economic changes that occurred, first in the FRG after 1945 and then in the "new states" (*Länder*) that acceded to the FRG upon the dissolution of the GDR. These five reconstituted *Länder* came with a vastly different political and socioeconomic formation from that of the western *Länder.* Yet it is intriguing to note the determination with which both societies committed themselves to raising the standards of living and of production in the eastern area to parity with those enjoyed in the western area. From the beginning, Germany's more affluent leaders in the West indicated their desire to erase all vestiges of the former GDR's command economy and to replace it with the mixed economy of the advanced social welfare state. In fact, the ideal of a social welfare state has been pursued by nearly all of Germany's governments, with varying degrees of intensity, since the days when Bismarck sought to buy off his working-class and revolutionary critics with state-sponsored welfare programs.

Economic Background

The material foundations to support the policies of a welfare state were surprisingly quick to return to Germany in the postwar period. Within a single decade, West Germany emerged from the wreckage and devastation of World War II to become one of the top industrial giants of the world. Marshall Plan aid in the amount of $4.5 billion; a preexisting industrial base available for the production of capital goods; a burgeoning export trade generated by the Korean crisis; a plentiful supply of foreign workers; and the discipline, skills, and sacrifices of the German people—all contributed to the West German economic revival.

The most important factors setting the FRG on its way to economic recovery were the currency reform of 1948 and the founding of a central bank that in time would become the main pillar of budgetary discipline and monetary stability. These were the initial building blocks of the FRG's celebrated "social market economy" (SME). Other features of the SME are competition and individual entrepreneurship, intervention by the state to ensure the realization of both, and social responsibility. Unlike in the United States, governmental regulation in Germany is not seen as a barrier to the flourishing of the market economy. Rather, the state is seen as both a guarantor of fair competition and a necessary agent in fostering social solidarity among diverse interests.

The FRG's economy percolated at an astoundingly rapid rate without any significant leveling off until the late 1960s. Motor vehicles, precision engineering, brewing, chemicals, pharmaceuticals, and heavy metal products were among Germany's strongest industries. Growth rates in the national economy in each of the four decades since 1950 were 7.96, 4.45, 2.74, and 2.21 percent, respectively,[5] placing the FRG fourth among the world's top industrial nations while transforming the country into a prosperous and mass-consumption society.

During these years, East Germany seemed to experience an economic miracle of its own, if only when compared with the struggling economies of other socialist states in the Soviet bloc. By 1970, concentrating on heavy industry, chemicals, and mechanical engineering, the GDR ranked second, after the Soviet Union, in industrial production within the bloc, outstripping all

other Socialist countries in per capita national income. In the 1970s, its leaders turned their attention to improving the everyday lives of ordinary citizens, offering a greater variety of consumer goods and improved housing. However, the good times were not to last. By the 1980s, as its totally state-owned economy proved unable to innovate and adapt to changing conditions, the GDR's increasingly outmoded industries could no longer compete in the new, postindustrial, global market. The state was on the verge of bankruptcy, workers were becoming restless, and consumer goods were scarce and markedly inferior to West German products.

Accordingly, when reunification came in the early 1990s, the FRG faced an economic challenge more formidable than the effort to revive West Germany after the war. East Germany's instantaneous integration into the FRG exposed serious weaknesses in the GDR's centrally planned economy. Its factories were unproductive and overstaffed, its technological base inferior, and its infrastructure in need of rebuilding from the ground up. The cost of reconstructing the eastern economy would require enormous financial transfers, which in turn resulted in higher taxes for West Germans and increased deficit spending. Only five years into unification, these transfers were amounting to around 640 billion in deutsche marks (DM), and billions more would be required to close the still-large gap in productivity and living standards.

Naturally, all of these changes brought heavy social costs in their wake. The rapidity of the old GDR's transformation resulted in scores of factory shutdowns. Predictably, many areas of the economy collapsed under the pressure of enormous competition from western Germany and as a result of the loss of traditional markets in the former eastern bloc. The result was massive unemployment as the region's industrial output fell by some 40 percent between 1990 and 1993. Although by 1995 over 14,000 East German industries and businesses had been privatized, productivity remained much lower than in the west. Still, for those who were willing to look down the road a bit, the future was far from bleak. Corporate-sector investment in plant and

---

[5]Eric Owen Smith, *The German Economy* (London: Routledge, 1994), p. 9.

A CLOSER LOOK

4.2

THE SOCIAL MARKET ECONOMY

An outgrowth of German neoliberal and Catholic social thought, the social market economy is predicated on the belief that a free market is compatible with a socially conscious state. It seeks to combine the principles of personal freedom and social responsibility in a unified political economy. The production of goods and services is to be left to free choice in an open market, but the marketplace is to function within a social framework created by law. This framework includes general public policies designed to enhance competition, ensure honest trade practices, and protect consumers. It is also government's duty in neoliberal economic theory to stabilize the economy as a whole and to care for the needs of persons not served by the market.

equipment over this period was far stronger in the eastern *Länder* than in the west. Also, as would be expected in the underdeveloped east, the construction industry played a dominant role in the growth of an East German economy whose gross domestic product (GDP) expanded from 5.8 percent in 1993 to 8.5 percent in 1994. By contrast, the growth rates in West Germany for these years were –1.7 and 2.4 percent, respectively. Although East Germany's economy slowed to a growth rate of 5.6 percent in 1995, it was way ahead of the 1.6 percent increase in the west.

During these years, the growth rate in the FRG as a whole bordered on 2 percent. Yet Germany remained an economic powerhouse. By 1994, the country's GDP had reached a record $1,911 billion, ranking it third in the world, just behind the United States and Japan. By 1999, as Table 4.1 shows, Germany had retained this ranking (despite having to weather an economic slowdown) as it stood on the verge of a new century.

Territory and Population

In territorial size, reunited Germany is the fifth largest nation in Europe. Bordered by nine countries ranging from Denmark in the north to Austria in the south and flanked by Poland and the Czech Republic in the east and France and the Benelux countries in the west—a 2,350 mile border—Germany takes up 137,787 square miles in the center of Europe. Geographically, Germany is the third largest nation in the European Union,

behind France and Spain. But even if the Germany of today had the desire or the ability to return to its 1937 borders, it would nonetheless remain a medium-sized state on the global scale, even though as an industrial power, the FRG ranks third in the world.

The more revealing figures for contemporary Germany, both for its place in Europe and in the world, are those concerning its population. Before reunification, the FRG was the most populous state in Western Europe and second on the continent only to the USSR. The acquisition of

TABLE 4.1

GERMANY'S GDP RANKING AMONG SELECTED NATIONS, 2005

Nation	GDP (trillions)	GDP per Capita ($)
United States	$10.99	$37,800
Japan	3.58	28,200
Germany	2.27	27,600
France	1.66	27,600
United Kingdom	1.66	27,700
Italy	1.55	26,700
Canada	0.95	29,800
Spain	0.88	22,000

Source: CIA World Factbook, 2005. www.intellect.org/resources/cia_worldfactbook_00.

some 16 million East Germans did not dramatically change this ranking, although everyone could see that it would eventually make an important contribution to Germany's economic future. Along with expanding its borders and its population, the FRG has gained a new neighbor, Poland, and a new set of demographics. The overall population of over 82 million is now somewhat more East European in origin, and proportionately more Protestant.

The population figures in Table 4.2 represent a fascinating tale of human migration and dislocation. Between 1950 and 1989 the old FRG's population increased by 13 million, while the ex-GDR lost over 2 million of its inhabitants, nearly all of whom migrated or fled to West Germany. The indigenous birthrate had little to do with these statistics. The rapid increase in population recorded over these years resulted mainly from two factors: the influx of 13 million German refugees and migrants from Poland, the Soviet Union, East Germany, and other eastern countries and the arrival of 2.5 million foreign workers who entered under the FRG's labor recruitment program in the 1950s and 1960s. The *German* "immigrants"—not technically foreigners—consisted of Polish and Sudeten Germans expelled from their homes and property (*Vertriebene*), ethnic Germans from Eastern Europe resettling in the FRG (*Aussiedler*), and East Germans who abandoned their homes and careers in the GDR to resettle in the FRG (*Übersiedler*).

Since 1970, an additional 1.9 million *Aussiedler* entered Germany from Poland, Romania, and the former Soviet Union. (Some 1.8 million East Germans moved to the western *Länder* after the collapse of the Berlin Wall.) Finally, some 900,000 asylum seekers arrived in Germany from 1988 through 1991; the figure leaped to 430,191 in 1992 alone.[6]

By 2005, there were 7.2 million foreign residents in reunited Germany, nearly 50 percent of whom had lived there for ten years or more. The FRG's foreign nationalities, which today make up more than 10 percent of the population, include 3.5 million Turks and 1.3 million persons from the former Yugoslavia. Italians, Greeks, Poles, Austrians, Romanians, Spaniards, Iranians, and Portuguese residents account for another 2 million residents, not to mention several hundred thousand British, American, and EU nationals and roughly equal numbers of persons of non-European origin. What is striking about these figures is that they represent a rate of entry relative to the national population that is not only twice the rate of mass immigration to America in the 1920s but, apart from Israel, several times more than that of any other EU country today.

As we shall see, the response of some Germans to these foreign entrants, particularly those from the southern and eastern parts of Europe, was sometimes far from welcoming. Sporadic incidences of violence against foreigners were registered throughout the 1990s. Further, it would prove difficult if not impossible for most of these non-Germans, even those who had lived in the FRG all their lives, to acquire actual German citizenship.

Yet despite the difficulties many foreigners encountered in living and working in the Federal Republic, one interesting fact about the native German population demonstrates just how much the FRG's economy depends on the continued presence of immigrants. Beginning in 1998, the FRG's native German population has shown marked signs of decline. According to current

TABLE 4.2

POPULATION OF GERMANY (MILLIONS)

Year	Old FRG	Ex-GDR	Germany
1950	49.9	18.4	68.3
1960	55.4	17.2	72.6
1970	60.1	17.1	77.2
1980	61.5	16.7	78.2
1993	65.5	15.6	81.1
1999	65.0	17.2	82.2
2005			82.4

Source: Statistisches Jahrbuch für die Bundesrepublik Deutschland 1995, p. 46; Statistisches Jahrbuch, 2001.

[6]"Political Asylum Seekers," *Week in Germany,* January 15, 1993, p. 2.

projections, it is conceivable that these numbers will fall from the current level of 82 million Germans to around 70 million in the year 2050, and perhaps even lower. Generally, the FRG's increasing affluence and typical postindustrial values have combined to foster this problem. Germans (and particularly western Germans) are having far fewer children than they did in the past. Additionally, they (again, particularly western Germans) are getting married at a slower rate than before. At the same time, the major factor holding the total population relatively constant is that, thanks to improved health care and living conditions, the mean age of the country's population has risen correspondingly. Now that average Germans are living longer, there are actually more persons above the age of 65 in the FRG than there are below the age of 15. This fact means that the German social welfare system is increasingly challenged to meet the costly needs of an older and presumably more demanding citizenry which is in the position to exercise considerable political clout.

One effect of this demographic shift has been to increase the demand for skilled labor. Accordingly, the German government has begun to follow the example of Canada and the United States in offering special work permits and other incentives (akin to the American "Green Card") to foreign professionals who are willing to share their talents with the FRG's high-tech industries for extended periods. Not surprisingly, critics of this initiative have been quick to point out that the German government has been much less generous when it comes to opening the country's doors to less skilled immigrants from poorer states outside Europe. As antipathy to these foreigners has risen, the Berlin government has taken strong steps to curtail the number of would-be entrants.

Still, as the native German population as a whole continues to drop in the coming years, one wonders whether the current restrictions on immigration and citizenship can be maintained. It will be interesting to see whether one of two possible outcomes is dominant. One possibility is that the necessity of recruiting labor of all kinds to keep the German economy running at full steam will have the effect of forcing the FRG's leaders to open their borders even wider. The other, more disturbing eventuality is that a greater influx of foreigners will lead to greater resentment and hostility on the part of native Germans.

From Bonn to Berlin and In Between

Berlin is the new capital of united Germany. At last, Germany has a hub like London, Paris, or Rome and one around which the economic, cultural, and political life of the country is likely to swirl. With a population of 3.5 million, it is Germany's largest city. A sprawling urban landscape scarred by 40 years of division—half the city lay in the West and half in the old Soviet zone—Berlin experienced an unprecedented building boom in the 1990s as it prepared for the presence of the national government, parliament, and numerous federal ministries. All of these institutions were moved from Bonn to the city in 1999, marking a striking contrast between those times of national division when Germany's capital had been located in a sleepy village-like setting along the Rhine River. With its major universities, research institutes, cultural institutions, technical industries, and ongoing improvements in transportation, including its incorporation into Germany's high-speed intercity railroad network, Berlin is poised to become the gateway between East and West if not "the de facto metropolis of the new free Central Europe."[7]

Apart from Berlin, the economic and political life of the country is centered in a number of conurbations: in the Rhine-Ruhr (Essen, Dortmund, Cologne, and Düsseldorf), Rhine-Main (Frankfurt) and Rhine-Neckar (Mannheim) regions; in the business-industrial concentrations around the cities of Stuttgart, Hamburg, Hanover, and Munich; and now in the east around Dresden, Leipzig, and Chemnitz. Fourteen cities boast a population of more than 500,000. Although they are catching up, the new eastern German *Länder* remain somewhat less urbanized than those in the west. Of 19 cities

---

[7]John Ardagh, *Germany and the Germans* (London: Penguin Books, 1991), p. 63.

with more than 300,000 inhabitants, not counting Berlin, three (Leipzig, Dresden, and Halle) are in the ex-GDR. Thirty-five percent of the former FRG's population lives in cities with more than 100,000 inhabitants, but only slightly more than 10 percent of former GDR residents live in such areas. In Germany as a whole, 10 percent of the population lives in predominately rural areas—with fewer than 150 inhabitants per square kilometer—although these areas constitute over 60 percent of the national territory. Twenty-eight and 62 percent of the population live in intermediate and concentrated areas, respectively.

Economic and Social Stratification

Germany's occupational structure shows a nation gradually transforming itself from an industrial into a postindustrial society. As is characteristic of postindustrial societies, both the service and trade sectors of the economy have grown the fastest in both western and eastern Germany, clearly overtaking traditional industries and productive enterprises. Most jobs created in West Germany over the past couple of decades have been connected with banking, insurance, education, the health professions, and the civil service. This social transformation has given way to a rising middle class composed of salaried employees associated with the worlds of finance, commerce, and increasingly the high-tech sectors of the economy. These salaried employees, along with 2.5 million public servants and 3.2 million self-employed persons constitute nearly two-thirds of the German workforce. No longer is the holding of property the decisive factor in class distinction, but rather the nature of a person's job and the prestige and income that go with it are what determine status.

The traditional crafts are another declining sector of an increasingly technological society. As in other western European states, tailors, shoemakers, painters, typesetters, and carpenters have seen their numbers dwindle in the face of a far greater demand for the services of building cleaners, automobile mechanics, TV technicians, plumbers, electricians, and hairdressers—underscoring the widespread availability of discre-

tionary income among most occupational groups, including even common laborers. The craft trades still remain an important part of the German economy. In 1994, there were 668,000 craft firms headed by a master craftsman. The crafts employed 15 percent of the workforce, trained 37 percent of apprentices, and accounted for 9 percent of the FRG's economic output.

Of course, one cannot expect that the sort of modernization of the professions witnessed by western Germany would be equally matched in the east. The residue of socialist mismanagement will long remain in the region. The dominance of manufacturing industries in the eastern *Länder*, combined with the pathologies of central planning and the lack of competition, continues to inhibit the emergence of a modern diversified economy as well as the development of new technologies. In 1988, 94.7 percent of all persons employed in the GDR worked for state-owned enterprises. The figure was 99.9 percent in industry, 92.3 percent in construction, and 98.5 percent in agriculture and forestry. Only the traditional crafts (excluding construction) remained under some form of private ownership.

Since unification, however, progress has been made. All crafts, trades, and professions were privatized. More important, they would see their numbers increase dramatically. For example, craft firms in the ex-GDR had doubled by the end of the 1990s. In the professions, only a half-decade after the fall of the Wall, there were four times as many doctors and dentists than before unity. The number of private lawyers has more than doubled, perhaps representing an iron law of modernization, and tax advisors have shot up from only 350 into the thousands. Other professions experienced similar increases. Their number, together with the proliferation of the service trades, promises to accelerate the arrival of the postindustrial age in the eastern *Länder*.

Another major sign of postindustrialism is the increasing replacement of industrial employment by automation and the substitution of moving machines with electronic and communications technology. After years of delay, perhaps betraying an extant cultural conservatism, Germans have finally embraced the Internet revolution and the World Wide Web. These developments have coincided with the emergence of a large techno-cratic and managerial elite. Jobs in highly skilled professional and technical areas are increasing at a much faster rate than unskilled or semiskilled jobs. In the 1970s the number of engineers, com-puter technicians, economists, teachers, accoun-tants, lawyers, and social workers in the FRG almost doubled, while university admissions in the natural and social sciences nearly tripled. By 1995 the professional-technical-managerial class contained 6.2 million persons, representing 23.4 percent of the total workforce.

The socioeconomic changes described here have affected the nature of political cleavages in Germany, largely by making them less and less important and class boundaries more permeable. While the society may reveal residues of a tradi-tional class structure, German politics in recent decades has not been determined by the heated class conflicts of the first half of the twentieth century. The ascendancy of a new professional, technical, and managerial class supported by a vast army of white-collar employees performing highly specified roles in the social economy has blunted the class feeling of earlier generations. Additionally, as a result of Communist rule, the old class structure in the eastern *Länder* has entirely disappeared, and thus the political pres-sure from this part of Germany is likely to be in the direction of greater egalitarianism.

Security and Equality

The portrait of German society sketched up to now is one of general affluence and economic opportunity, particularly in western Germany. If industrial wages, home ownership, and posses-sion of consumer goods are considered, then income and property are widely distributed in the western *Länder*. However, as much as the *social* market economy tries to provide minimum levels of decency for all, the social *market* econ-omy tolerates large disparities in income and economic power. As a result, as Figure 4.1 indi-cates, western and eastern Germany presented two rather different images of social justice and equality in the early years of unification. In the

western areas that had formed the preunification FRG, a significant gap separated the lowest and highest paid persons in the mid-1990s. In con-trast, the bell-shaped curve of the ex-GDR in Fig-ure 4.1 shows much less disparity among income levels than in the west. The figure also under-scores the different levels of prosperity in the east and west. Noticeable, too, is the much larger income gap between the sexes in the west. The higher the income category, the greater the inequality, whereas in the east the inequality is far less at all income levels.

What Figure 4.1 fails to show are unemploy-ment levels. Unemployment in the FRG reached a postwar preunification high of 10.2 percent of the workforce in 1983, tarnishing the image of the FRG's well-run social market economy. Even in 1990, with the economy running at full capac-ity, unemployment persisted at around 6 percent of the workforce, indicating serious structural problems in Germany's export-intensive indus-tries. The unification-induced slump in employ-ment drove this figure up to 9.2 percent in the early 1990s, representing 8.7 percent of unem-ployment in the old *Länder* and as much as 25 percent in the new. By 1996, unemployment in Germany as a whole was on the verge of reach-ing a postwar high of 4 million, or 10 percent of the total workforce. This figure was still lower than the rate of unemployment in France (11.5 percent) and Italy (10.5 percent), but it was significantly higher than in the United States (5.7 percent) and Japan (3.1 percent)[8]. It was over 10 percent in 2005.

Although the unemployment picture would begin to show significant signs of improvement in the 1998–2000 period, this was largely confined to western Germany. In the east, however, the pic-ture remained especially painful, in part because of different attitudes in the region. Emphasizing equality over liberty, the GDR's former leaders had constructed a socialist state where the right to work was guaranteed and where there was little disparity in income among persons employed in various sectors of the economy. Finally, the state's attention to social welfare was universal in the old

[8]*The OECD Observer* (August–September, 1995), p. 49.

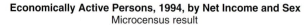

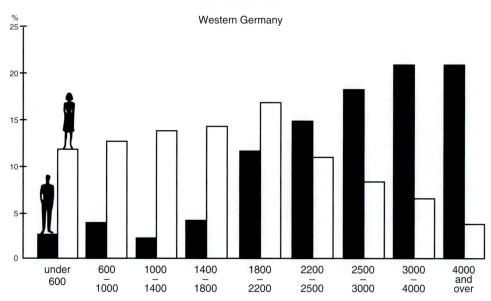

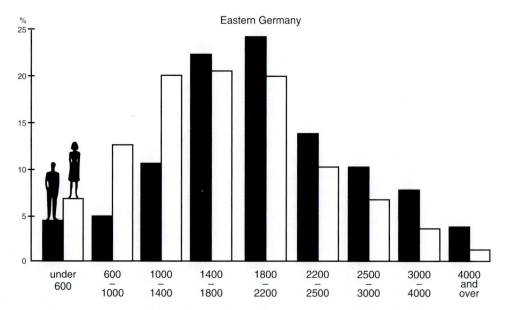

Figure 4.1 WESTERN AND EASTERN INCOME DISTRIBUTIONS IN REUNIFIED GERMANY

GDR, although the system lacked the efficiency and quality of social welfare planning in the FRG. In 1988, the year before the GDR's collapse, pensions and medical care accounted for more than 90 percent of the system's social expenditures. The average old-age pension in the GDR covered about 45 percent of net wages as opposed to about 50 percent in the FRG,[9] but again the latter was of far greater value. The child-care system and leave policy for child-bearing women, however, were more generous in the east (in large part because the Communist government wanted to stimulate population growth).

Despite its weakness, unified Germany's social security system remains one of the most comprehensive in the world. The national pension system alone covers nearly all private sector employees; for example in 1991, just after unification, it accounted for 30 percent of the social budget. Still, based as it is on an income strategy tied to lifetime earnings, its redistributive effect is limited. Elderly persons, especially widows on pensions, are the hardest hit, in part because of a discriminatory policy which allows such persons only 60 percent of the pension to which a living husband would have been entitled. Pensioners are the least well off. In the mid–1970s, approximately 35 percent of pensioners over 65 lived on or below the poverty line and in grossly inadequate housing.[10] Although Germany may not have as large an underclass of destitute persons as some other Western nations, and especially the United States, the pockets of poverty that do exist are a continuing challenge to the nation's social conscience (see Section C for additional details on German social policy).

---

[9]Günter Thumann, "The System of Public Finance in the German Democratic Republic," in Leslie Lipschitz and Donough McDonald, *German Unification: Economic Issues* (Washington, DC: International Monetary Fund, December 1990), p. 159.

[10]For a discussion of the West German social welfare system, see Wolfgang Zapf, "Development, Structure, and Prospects of the German Social State," in Richard Rose and Rei Shiratori, *The Welfare State* (New York: Oxford University Press, 1986), pp. 126–155.

Women, Law, and Society

The West German constitution guarantees equal rights to men and women. In reality, women have not shared equally in the opportunities offered by the social economy. Even more than in many European states, Germany's legacy of male supremacy has been extremely difficult to overcome (even in the reputedly more egalitarian eastern *Länder*). This is especially true in the domain of family affairs, where tradition and law have for generations confined women to hearth, children, and the guardianship of their husbands. Although the tradition persists, the legal structure of gender discrimination has been gradually torn down, thanks in part to the Federal Constitutional Court. Laws favoring the patriarchal family have been invalidated, the last remnant of which fell in 1992 when the court struck down a provision requiring married persons to adopt a single family surname and, in the event of spousal disagreement, the surname of the husband. Already in 1977 a new family code had provided for no-fault divorce, spousal support arrangements keyed to economic status rather than gender, and an equal division of property.

Opportunities for women outside the home can be measured by comparing their participation rates in the workforce, their earnings, and the kinds of jobs they perform to those of men. In 1989 women in the FRG constituted a little more than one-third of the full-time workforce, whereas in the GDR it was about one-half. (Ninety percent of East German adult women were employed in some fashion in 1989.) Yet this was hardly a result of enlightened attitudes. In the GDR's system of state-mandated liberation, women were expected to lead a dual life of both homemaker and working person. The country's labor-intensive economy and low productivity helped to drive women into the working world. But as in the west, women were responsible for most of the household work as well.

Social policy in the GDR was designed to make a dual career possible for women. For example, child-care facilities were everywhere and free of charge, maternity leave with pay (at 75 to 90 percent of wages) was available for up to 26 weeks, and working parents could count on at least 40 days per year of paid time to care for their sick children. Yet significantly, these generous benefits were quickly abandoned in the east after reunification, at precisely the time many eastern Germans were losing their other forms of employment. As businesses remodeled and factories modernized, huge numbers of women were forced to withdraw from the labor market. By 1993, they would constitute nearly 65 percent of the unemployed in eastern Germany. Deprived of child-care facilities and other social benefits for working parents, single women with children were among the hardest hit, while women over 50 who lost their jobs had little hope of reemployment.[11] Many became depressed and bitter, feeling cheated out of their previous lives and deceived by promises of coming well-being in united Germany.

Interestingly, in terms of earning power, women lagged substantially behind men even in the affluent western *Länder,* owing both to wage-rate discrimination and to the lack of promotional opportunities associated with less stable and skilled jobs. Moreover, the disparity showed little improvement between 1983 and 1993, and in some categories of employment the gap actually widened. For example, the average gross monthly salary of female versus male white-collar employees in these years was DM 2541 and DM 3670 respectively, as opposed to more favorable male salaries of DM 4153 and DM 5987. Available household income revealed a similar gap. In 1993, the average income of a female-headed household was 63 percent of that available to a male-headed household.[12] These differences in earnings and disposable income can be attributed in part to the limited number of hours women were able to work because of their child-care and household duties.

Finally, even though the situation would gradually improve over the 1990s as women could be found in every occupation in Germany, gender-based job segregation would continue. The overall representation of women is extremely high in low to mid-level occupational categories. Textiles, retail sales, social services, and health care are almost wholly feminized. Still, the old GDR had a better record of female participation in several distinctive professional categories than West Germany. In fact, by 1985 more women than men were being admitted as students of medicine, mathematics, and economics. With unification, however, the overall figures, except for public school teachers, continue to show significant disparities. Segregation in the job market is often ascribed to employee recruitment mechanisms that, although not always overtly discriminatory, tend to channel women into traditional female roles.

As early as 1980, the West German Parliament sought to remedy these inequalities by imposing certain duties on private employers. The European Community Adaptation Act incorporated EC nondiscriminatory directives into domestic law. The act requires equal pay for equal work; bars gender discrimination in hiring, promotion, and dismissal; eliminates job descriptions based on sex; shifts the burden of proving nondiscrimination to the employer; and requires the latter to display prominently copies of equal rights legislation in the workplace. (These provi-

---

[11]On the other hand, precisely because the right and duty to work in the GDR was state-decreed, "many [East German women] appear[ed] to link self-realization to a life in which homemaking is a preferred option, and employment limited or not necessary at all." See Sabine Hübner, "Women at the Turning Point: The Socio-Economic Situation and Prospects of Women in the Former German Democratic Republic," *Politics and Society in Germany, Austria, and Switzerland,* vol. 3 (1991), p. 26. For other sources on East German women after reunification, see Marilyn Rueschemeyer, et al. (eds.), *Women in the Politics of Postcommunist Eastern Europe* (Armonk, NY: M. E. Sharpe, 1994), pp. 87–116; and Friederike Maier, "The Labor Market for Women and Employment Perspectives in the Aftermath of German Unification," *Cambridge Journal of Economics* 17 (1993), pp. 267–280.

---

[12]"Zur Einkommenslage der westdeutschen Arbeitnehmerinnen," *Wochenbericht* 61 (Berlin: Deutscher Institut für Wirtschaftsordnung, 21 September 1994), pp. 655 and 659.

sions were extended to public employers in 1994.) Nonetheless, the Adaptation Act has not been vigorously enforced, owing in part to the lack of enforcement agencies. Thus, the success rate of individual victims who have initiated actions against their employers under these provisions has been low.[13]

Perhaps the most important victory for women on the employment front was the *Nocturnal Employment* case of 1992. In this landmark decision, the Federal Constitutional Court invalidated as unconstitutional a federal statute that barred women from working at night. Invoking Article 3 (2) of the Basic Law, which declares that "men and women shall have equal rights," the court flatly rejected the gender stereotyping that produced the night-shift ban. *Nocturnal Employment* was decided against the backdrop of a national debate over affirmative action. By now, women were organizing in defense of their interests and the political parties were beginning to pay attention. Efforts were being made to demand more than antidiscriminatory legislation and the dismantling of legal classifications based on sex. In 1994, after years of lobbying for such an amendment, the needed two-thirds parliamentary majority added this sentence to Article 3 (2) of the Basic Law: "The state shall seek to ensure equal treatment of men and women by removing existing disadvantages [between them]."

Whatever progress has been made on behalf of women must be attributed in part to the rise of the Greens in the 1980s and the party's efforts to give greater publicity to the cause of affirmative action. By highlighting feminist issues and by requiring that 50 percent of all their party posts and parliamentary seats be held by women, the Greens effectively became a "woman's party." The Greens drew their electoral support disproportionately from women under 40 years of age. Other parties soon got the message. They grew more

sensitive to women's issues, made an effort to expand their female membership, and placed increasing numbers of women on their ballots. In 1994, 176 women were elected to the Bundestag, representing 26 percent of its membership, the most ever. Four years later, in 1998, the Bundestag elections resulted in even more telling figures, as 207 women entered parliament, an increase of nearly 5 percent in the forum's total membership. In the two major parties, the SPD and the CDU/CSU, women accounted for 35.2 percent and 18.4 percent of their respective representatives (a slight decrease from the preceding election). In contrast, the Greens and the PDS were responsible for the most impressive figures, as women made up 57.4 and 58.3 percent, respectively, of their total Bundestag representation (see Table 4.3). In 2005, 32.8 percent (197) of the Bundestag and 18.8 percent (13) of the Bundesrat were women.

Significantly, in 2000, the moderate-conservative Christian Democratic Union, generally no partisan of progressive causes, elected Angela Merkel as its first female party chairperson. Merkel's ascendancy was notable both because she was a woman and because she was one of only a handful of prominent politicians to emerge from eastern Germany. Moreover, she

---

[13]For a discussion of the effects of the European Community Adaptation Act, see Josephine Shaw, "Recent Developments in the Field of Labor Market Equality: Sex Discrimination Law in the Federal Republic of Germany," *Comparative Labor Law Journal* 13 (1991), pp. 27–41.

TABLE 4.3

WOMEN IN THE GERMAN PARLIAMENT, 1998 ELECTION

Party	Women	Total (Women + Men)	Women (%)
SPD	105	298	35.2
CDU/CSU	45	245	18.4
Alliance 90/ Greens	27	47	57.4
FDP	9	43	20.9
PDS	21	36	58.3
Total	207	669	30.9

Source: Gabriela Metzler, "Women in Politics in Canada and Germany," in *Zeitschrift für Kanada-Studien—online,* v. 19, n. 2, 1999, p. 124, *http://www.kanada studien.org/ZKS/2141-992.html.*

enjoyed the distinction of replacing Helmut Kohl, the so-called Chancellor of German unity, who had heretofore seemed a permanent fixture in the CDU because of his remarkable political longevity.

Finally, whereas women remained under-represented in the judiciary as a whole, they would occupy no fewer than 5 of 16 seats on the Federal Constitutional Court by the mid-1990s, also a new high. In fact, with her election in 1994, Jutta Limbach became the first woman president or "chief justice" of the Federal Constitutional Court, Germany's highest tribunal. Evelyn Haas was chosen as an associate justice in the same year. Her appointment was significant because she was the first woman nominated to the high court by Christian Democrats. Still another woman was among the candidates for election to the high court in 1996. Only the future will tell whether these advances in the nation's highest judicial and legislative arenas will carry over into other areas of law and society.

Ethnic Minorities

While grievances based on sex have been the object of the law's special solicitude, those based on ethnicity have arguably been allowed to fester. Large-scale immigration in the postwar era has transformed the FRG's racially homogeneous society into a nation of ethnic minorities. Most of the older immigrants—notably, the postwar expellees who were mainly ethnic Germans—have been almost wholly integrated into the dominant culture. Yet the story has been much different for those persons who have been unable to claim German ancestry. The new immigrants consist mainly of foreign workers recruited by industry on a massive scale during the 1950s and 1960s, who should properly be credited with playing a large role in sustaining Germany's "economic miracle." By the 1990s, there were over 5,000,000 of these workers and their families—mainly Turks, Yugoslavs, Greeks, and Italians—making up 6.4 percent of reunited Germany's total population, or nearly 8 percent of the population of the western *Länder*. Despite governmental incentives that encouraged nearly a million of these "guestworkers" (*Gastarbeiter*) to

return to their homelands during the mid-1970s recession, higher wages and the promise of a better life prompted most of them to remain in the FRG.

Many of these guestworkers and their families consider the FRG their home, but it has been anything but a "melting pot." Their experience is not unlike that of black or Hispanic Americans in the United States, or the experience of ethnic minorities in other European states like England and France. Occupying low-status jobs that Germans do not want, they live in culturally isolated urban ghettos marked by substandard housing.[14] Even though millions of guestworkers speak German fluently, send their German-born children to German schools, pay taxes, and have no plans to leave Germany, they are denied the right to vote. For them, regardless of their contribution to the FRG's well-being, citizenship is extremely difficult to secure in a nation that still defines itself largely in ethnocultural terms.

Recent waves of *Aussiedler* have also experienced difficulties in adjusting to German life and society. Although their ethnic German roots were often celebrated by the FRG during the Cold War, many have encountered a cooler reception in the period after the Soviet Union's demise. As in the past, these ethnic Germans are economically disadvantaged, come from culturally diverse backgrounds, and often have little or no knowledge of the German language. The pressures of economic reconstruction have left native Germans somewhat less accommodating.

Additionally, as noted in the section on population, hundreds of thousands of persons seeking asylum in West Germany have been added to this multicultural mix. Their presence has triggered not only acts of violence and terrorism against these "foreign elements" but also an explosive national debate over what to do about the increasing numbers of persons seeking freedom and opportunity in Germany. One recent solution has been intergovernmental agreements providing for the deportation of asylum seekers

---

[14]See Ray C. Rist, "Migration and Marginality: Guestworkers in Germany and France," *Daedalus* 108 (spring 1979), pp. 95–108.

A CLOSER LOOK
4.3
NOT QUITE A MELTING POT

"Sustained and lasting progress in integration is only possible if the number of foreigners living in Germany does not increase in a way which threatens to exhaust the resources of the Federal Republic of Germany. For this reason, the immigration of foreigners from non-EU states is restricted.... [In view of the] poor employment chances of less qualified workers, which look set to remain this way, this policy is very much in the occupational interests of the foreign workers and especially to the young foreigners starting their working lives."

Source: German Ministry of the Interior, 2001, at *www.eng.bmi.bund.de/frameset/index.jsp.*

to their country of origin or other deals encouraging their return. By 1992, after extreme right-wing parties entered two state parliaments on their antiforeigner platforms, pressure was building to limit the right of asylum and to adopt an American-style system of quotas on immigration to Germany. (For a discussion of immigration and citizenship policy, see Section C.)

CULTURE: SOCIAL AND CIVIC

Education and the Media

Reunited Germany boasts high levels of literacy, cultural and educational diversity, and opportunities for personal development and leisure. As in Berlin, parks, sport clubs, museums, public libraries, theaters, choral societies, art galleries, opera houses, and multimillion-member book clubs abound in the country at large. There is also a high consumption rate of media output; book and magazine readership is one of the highest worldwide. In the 1990s, in terms of titles alone, Germany was second only to the United States in book publishing. By 2000, Germany had begun to catch up with the United States in terms of the percentage of Internet users among its population. German news broadcasts were also readily available on the World Wide Web.

In contrast to the United States, however, popular culture has been much more heavily funded since, in line with German state-centered traditions, most theatrical groups, orchestras, and opera houses are government-subsidized. In united Germany, for example, there are more than 100 subsidized opera houses. Hence, one could easily predict in this nation of opera lovers a swift end to any government or to the political career of any politician who would have the temerity to advocate an end to these government subsidies.

The wealth of cultural opportunities in the western *Länder* builds on their efficient and diverse educational system. A common four-year primary system splits at the secondary level into three tracks, almost seeming to mimic the country's historical class structure. These tracks are the five-year continuation of primary school (*Hauptschule*), the six-year intermediate school (*Realschule*), and the nine-year senior grammar school (*Gymnasium*); the former two emphasize preparation for vocational and technical jobs, respectively, while the latter offers the prized opportunity to the relative few, university preparation. Originally based in the classics, the *Gymnasium* offers a tough modern curriculum of arts, languages, mathematics, and science, leading to the famous school-leaving certificate, the *Abitur.* This tripartite system of secondary education has been sharply criticized for its tendency to perpetuate social and class differences. Yet its advocates note that the system has produced the most highly trained and credentialed population in Europe. Almost all nonfarm youth outside the universities are in vocational or technical schools of one kind or another. Fifty-nine percent of all German youth are in school until the age of 18, as opposed to 24 percent in England and 41 percent in France, while 44 percent are licensed to practice a trade or craft as opposed to 20 percent in England, 10 percent in Italy, and 6 percent in Spain.[15]

With the accession of the eastern *Länder* into the Federal Republic, Communist ideological control has predictably ended in the schools and universities of the former GDR, as have the jobs of Communist ideologues in law, the humanities, and social sciences. Following their western counterparts, the *Länder* themselves have taken charge. Religious instruction has been reintroduced, western language education expanded, and the humanities and social sciences reconstituted. Independent schools have reopened and the *Abitur* restored to its pride of place. True, national unification, if steered in a somewhat different direction, could have provided the opportunity to reorganize the entire system of German education on a more egalitarian basis. This strategy might have served to break down remaining class distinctions. However, to the dismay of most eastern German educators and many western critics, this opportunity was lost in the rush to reconstruct the old GDR system on the basis of the West German model alone.

Religion and the Churches

National unity has affected Germany's religious make-up. With the accession of the five new *Länder,* the relatively equal numbers of Catholics and Protestants of the earlier FRG have been tilted in favor of the Evangelical Lutheran Church. Thus, on the eve of reunification, the FRG counted official religious affiliation among its permanent residents (German and foreign) as roughly 26 million Roman Catholics, 25.75 million Protestants (both Evangelical Lutheran and "Free Church"), 50,000 Jews, 1.5 million Muslims, 1 million members of other religions, and 4 million with no religious affiliation. Figures from the ex-GDR are more difficult to present. For years, the Communist regime was reluctant to admit any significant religious aspiration in a would-be atheist state, and citizens were reluc-

tant to declare a religious identity that would have reduced them to second-class status at work and in school and barred them from the upper reaches of all professions. Nonetheless, it is clear that what religious activity there was between 1945 and 1989 remained overwhelmingly Protestant. Catholic figures, which remained free of direct government intervention, showed the six bishoprics within the five eastern *Länder* as ministering to only 5 percent of the local population, approximately 800,000 out of 16,000,000 people.

Still, the denominational strife that once buffeted Bismarck's Germany has virtually disappeared, in no small part because new forms of political and social cooperation evolved out of the common struggle of the major churches against the Nazi regime. Even in the purely religious sphere, the major denominations have made great effort to reconcile their differences. An ecumenical high point was the November 1980 meeting of Pope John Paul II with German Protestant leaders in Osnabrück, the site of the signing of the Treaty of Westphalia in 1648, which confirmed the sectarian division of the German lands.

It is difficult to assess the role of religion in contemporary Germany. Figures in the preunification FRG showed a long-term decline in official affiliation. Thus, between 1950 and 1989, the proportion of Catholics decreased slightly from 44.3 to 42.9 percent, while that of Protestants dropped from 51.5 to 42.2 percent. An Allensbach Opinion Research Institute poll conducted in West Germany on the eve of the breaching of the Berlin Wall suggested that this secularization affected not only practice but basic belief. Yet even though formal religious observance in Germany is down, the biennial Catholic and Protestant national "church day" conferences remain well attended and the influence of each denomination within its own worldwide communion remains strong.

The rates of basic religious identification remain high, both in paying the church tax and in choosing a marital partner. The 1989 figures for marrying within one's faith in the preunification FRG showed 68.7 percent for Catholics, 63.0 percent for Protestants, and 32.5 percent for

---

[15]*European Marketing Data and Statistics 1995* (London: Euromonitor International, 1995), p. 411.

Jews. The social impact of the churches likewise remains high. They operate and maintain hospitals, facilities for the handicapped, nursing homes, schools, and large charitable organizations such as the Protestant Diaconal Works and the Catholic Caritas Association.

One distinct fact helps to explain their continued success at such activities. Organized as corporate bodies under public law—a constitutional status carried over from the Weimar period—Germany's organized churches are entitled to state financial support. All wage earners on the official rolls of the main denominations are subject to a church tax equal to about 8 percent of their net tax. A wage earner can escape the tax by formally resigning his or her church membership; by the mid-1990s, around one-half million Protestants and Catholics were doing so every year. Yet many Germans have remained faithful to their obligations. Collected by state revenue officers, these taxes amount to several billion dollars a year and are distributed to the major denominations in amounts proportionate to their total membership. The funds help to pay for ecclesiastical salaries, construction and maintenance, the churches' far-flung social welfare functions, and their immense overseas charitable programs.

This *modus vivendi* between church and state does have critics, both secular and religious. The most radical secular critics fear excessive church influence on politics and would divorce religion altogether from the nation's public life. By contrast, the most radical religious critics see the contemporary church as the captive of the liberal state, having compromised its spiritual mission by adopting middle-class values and copying the latter's bureaucratic forms of organization. They would have the church call society to account for its injustices and hypocrisies, and in the name of faith ally itself with the poor of Germany and the world. Most Germans who have thought about these matters situate themselves between these extremes.

Political Attitudes and Participation

West Germans were often characterized in the first 20 years of the Federal Republic as voting in high numbers but having little feeling for their new polity. Opinion polls showed that older age groups retained some sympathy for monarchy or dictatorship and that most voters were prouder of their economic system than of its political corollary. Yet by the 1980s these attitudes had changed dramatically. The FRG was a proven success and an increasing percentage of the electorate had grown up in it and come to identify with its procedures and institutions. Nonetheless, there was still something missing. Because of the two world wars and the experience with Nazism, national pride remained well below the average for European Community member states. Reunification in 1990 thus posed two issues: Would the East Germans follow the pattern of quick adaptation to democratic practices and slow internalization of democratic feelings? In the meantime, if unforeseen economic difficulties arose, would West German civic culture now prove to be well enough rooted to weather the storm?

One measure of political democracy is the level of participation in elections. The turn-out rate for federal elections in the FRG began at 78.5 percent in 1949, exceeded a spectacular 90 percent by the 1970s, and then fell to a record low of 77.8 percent in the first all-German election of December 2, 1990. It rose again to 79.0 percent in 1994, and in 1998 it reached an impressive 82.2 percent of eligible voters but fell in 2002 to 79.1 percent.

This is a respectable rate of participation for any industrial democracy—and consistently higher than that for U.S. presidential elections. As Section B shows, the results of these elections have given the FRG a highly competitive and relatively stable party system. However, the measure of the health of a civic culture extends beyond formal electoral and institutional arrangements. Since the late 1960s, the FRG has witnessed massive demonstrations against a number of issues—the war in Vietnam, the development of nuclear power, restrictions on university admissions, NATO missiles stationed on German soil, assaults on foreign residents, and airport construction plans that threaten deforestation. These protests and *Bürgerinitiativen* (citizens' initiatives)—rivaled perhaps only by the French—have also championed other forms of democracy, such as referendums and greater popular participation. At times, commentators have asked whether this species of "politics of protest" bespeaks a widening gap between formal democratic institutions and actual grassroots democratic sentiments. For the most part, although very few Germans would support the more violent manifestations of these protests, the consensus seems to be that German democracy is holding together fairly well. Some observers have noted that these demonstrations represent a vital outlet for minority sentiments in their country, an outlet that is perfectly compatible with the functioning of any democracy. Others have contended that they represent an internalization and therefore a triumph of democratic values, while still others have acknowledged that both the Christian Democratic Union (CDU) and the Social Democratic Party (SPD) have successfully remodeled their local party electoral activities along the lines of these same *Bürgerinitiativen.*

In part, the increasingly participatory character of the FRG's civic culture seems related to changes that have taken place in family, school, and society under the impact of advanced industrialization and its accompanying patterns of social stratification—changes likely to be enhanced by the incorporation of the ex-GDR's socialist egalitarian values into the FRG. The entrance of housewives into the labor market, the separation of family and workplace, increased social mobility and income, and the enormous expansion of communications have loosened up old authoritarian structures such as the male-dominated family and the traditional school curriculum. Additionally, important instruments of socialization, such as the family and the schools, appear increasingly to promote values that are more consistent than in the past with the regime's formal values of human dignity, mutual respect and cooperation, and the pragmatic adjustment of social conflict. Generational change has also been an important source of political socialization. By the 1980 federal election, western Germany's postwar generation constituted 48.8 percent of the population and 25.5 percent of adult voters. For them, the liberal-

Supporters of the former Communist Party, the Party of Democratic Socialism (PDS) at the German election in October 1994. The PDS received 4.4 percent of the vote, thus falling below the 5 percent threshold. But it obtained 30 seats in the Bundestag because it won four directly elected seats in East Berlin. In 2002 it obtained only two seats.

democratic FRG was the only political and social order they had ever known. As a consequence of all these factors, while German citizens might be expected, from time to time, to challenge the political practices of one or another government, it is now reasonable to claim that the FRG's democratic system should be in the position to survive any serious threats to its authority.

Politics and Literature: A Footnote

When unified in 1871, Germany had a humanist tradition characterized by the genius of Goethe and Schiller, renaissance men of letters and civic leadership. Yet the predominant cultural expression of the Wilhelmine and Weimar years was one of flight from political affairs as many representatives of the rising bourgeois classes retreated into an "inner freedom" or strictly private and apathetic culture. Without a strong middle class to provide an alternative political vision, persons already in authority were left to conduct public affairs as they saw fit, to define the aims and limits of state power, and to suggest, albeit broadly, the proper form and content of culture.

The works of Hermann Hesse (1877–1962), such as the novel *Siddhartha* (1922), still a favorite at many American colleges, continued the age-old inquiry into the Germanic conflict between Nature and Spirit. But they also did so in the relatively new form of stressing the need for personal, rather than communal or authoritarian, responsibility in selecting values. With Thomas Mann (1875–1955), this need was cast against the backdrop of the violent currents sweeping Germanic society: the degeneration of the great nineteenth-century mercantile order in *Buddenbrooks* (1901), the quest for regeneration and personal understanding through flight from society and its conventions in *The Magic Mountain* (1924), and the descent of artistic creativity into the demonic in *Doctor Faustus* (1947). More than anyone else, Mann gave expression to the struggle between the power and the subtle pessimism of *Germanism.*

During the life of the Federal Republic, the works of Günter Grass, such as *The Tin Drum* (1963), were especially noteworthy for their inquiry into how German culture had fallen into

National Socialism and also what should be retrieved and replanted from the ashes it left in 1945. As we saw earlier, Grass opposed German reunification until the very end, claiming that Germany lacked a sense of responsibility before history and might have served as a beacon for spiritual renewal and the deflation of purely national aspirations.[16] The work of Heinrich Böll (1917–1985) was also popular. His novel *The Clown* (1963) portrayed a sense of the intrinsic worth and redemptive possibilities of life. More recently, a postunification literature has begun to appear as authors such as Martin Walser (*Die Verteidigung der Kindheit,* 1991) and Helga Königsdorf (*Im Schatten des Regenbogen,* 1993) seek to describe and to reflect on the painful changes and disorientation many East Germans have experienced since the collapse of the Berlin Wall. On the western side of the old German divide, Bernhard Schlink, a noted legal scholar, showed that his generation continues to be preoccupied with the memory of the Holocaust by publishing an allegorical novel about the subject. In *The Reader* (*Der Leser,* 1996), which received widespread attention not only in Germany but also in the United States, a young boy is swept into a love affair with an older woman (possibly Germany?) with a secret past. When it is revealed in the book that the woman was once a guard at a concentration camp, the boy is thrown into all the personal turmoil and anguish of anyone who must balance his love for an individual with his recognition of that person's guilt. Yet provocatively in view of its message for Germany, the book leaves open the possibility of reconciliation between the two persons.

In this way, where humanism temporarily failed Germany in the nineteen-century, history—and perhaps now the healing powers of national unification—may have begun to show the German people a path to normalcy. In the wake of two world wars and two major dictatorships, Germans have at least abandoned the turn to "inner freedom" and its concomitant neglect of public

---

[16]Günter Grass, *Two States—One Nation?* Trans. Krishna Winston and A. S. Wensinger (New York: Harcourt Brace, 1990), pp. 12–14.

cultural and civic responsibilities that led to such disastrous consequences. They have acknowledged Hesse's point that responsibility is personal and that, with time, it may have a redemptive effect on the whole human community. Arguably more self-consciously than any other Europeans, the Germans continue to question their values. Some observers will say this is because only the Germans have such a tortuous past to overcome. But this inclination may also have a positive side. By preventing them from taking anything for granted, it can help to extend the breadth and depth of their pluralist democracy.

CONCLUSION

This section has traced Germany's development from a class-based feudal society into a modernized postindustrial order now completed by the accession of the nation's eastern *Länder* into the FRG. The FRG's economy, even before the incorporation of the ex-GDR, was among the richest in the world. Notwithstanding pockets of poverty, measurable discrimination against ethnic minorities, and most daunting, the massive reconstruction and clean-up of the east, the country's social system is marked by extremely high levels of economic security and welfare benefits. Finally, the political system created under the 1949 Basic Law, together with its liberal values, has been a congenial framework for the development of a social market economy. Both the system's durability in the west and its growing acceptance in the east augur well for the future.

Likewise, religious divisions are no longer readily apparent in either part of the reunited country. Also, traditional class and economic divisions have given way to the rise in the west of a new middle class of white-collar employees and professionals generated by ever-expanding service industries and technological enterprises. Western business managers, industrial trainers, and university professors hope to replicate their success in the east. Although some young people and intellectuals continue to reproach their leaders for allowing their society to sink into materialism, most Germans are no different from other Europeans, especially those recently liberated

from Communism. They are by no means willing to forego the manifest advantages of their social and economic system. On the contrary, the more likely challenge for the coming decade will be to redistribute wealth and well-being so as to convince their compatriots in the east that both parts of the nation will share equally in the benefits of unification. Germany has put its political and religious divisions behind it. As it enters the twenty-first century, it must resolve to complete the same process socially and economically.

Thinking Critically

1. What political, social, and economic factors made Germany's adoption of democratic institutions and values in the twentieth century so difficult?
2. How did Hitler's "social revolution" and Germany's physical destruction after World War II ironically contribute to the country's remarkable transformation over the second half of the twentieth century?
3. How will German society change in coming years as a result of its shifting immigration and demographic patterns?
4. What are the characteristics of postindustrialism in Germany? What impact will this socioeconomic trend have on future politics in the FRG?
5. How successful was German reunification in the 1990s? Will the challenge of integrating eastern and western Germany into one united whole continue to be a problem?
6. How successful has Germany been in providing equal social and economic opportunities for all people who live within its geographic boundaries?

KEY TERMS

Abitur (205)
accession *(188)*
Basic Law *(188, 192)*
Bürgerinitiativen (207, 208)
church tax *(207)*
deutsche mark *(194)*

*F*URTHER READINGS

History and People

Barraclough, Geoffrey. *The Origins of Modern Germany* (New York: Capricorn Books, 1963).

Craig, Gordon. *The Germans* (New York: Putnam, 1982).

Fulbrook, Mary. *A Consise History of Germany* (Cambridge: Cambridge University Press, 2004).

Green, Simon. *The Politics of Exclusion: Institutions and Immigration Policy in Contemporary Germany* (Manchester: Manchester University Press, 2004).

Koch, H. W. *A Constitutional History of Germany in the Nineteenth and Twentieth Centuries* (London: Longman, 1984).

Niven, William, and James Jordan, eds. *Politics and Culture in Twentieth-Century Germany* (Rochester: Camden House, 2003).

Peukert, Detlev K. *The Weimar Republic.* (New York: Hill and Wang, 1987).

Schulze, Hagen. *Germany: A New History* (Cambridge, MA: Harvard University Press, 1998).

Stern, Fritz. *The Politics of Cultural Despair* (Berkeley: University of California Press, 1961).

Tripton, Frank B. *A History of Modern Germany since 1815* (Berkeley: University of California Press, 2003).

Third Reich

Bracher, Karl Dietrich. *The German Dictatorship* (New York: Praeger, 1970).

Dawidowicz, Lucy S. *The War against the Jews* (New York: Holt, Rinehart and Winston, 1975).

Gallagher, Hugh G. *By Trust Betrayed* (New York: Henry Holt, 1990).

Müller, Ingo. *Hitler's Justice* (Cambridge, MA: Harvard University Press, 1991).

Snyder, Louis L., ed. *Hitler's Third Reich: A Documentary History* (Chicago: Nelson-Hall, 1981).

Federal Republic

Bork, Dennis L., and David R. Gress. *A History of West Germany,* Vols. 1 and 2 (Oxford: Basil Blackwell, 1989).

Conradt, David P. *The German Polity,* 8th ed. (New York: Longman, 2005).

Jones, Larry E. *German Liberalism and the Dissolution of the Weimar Party System, 1918–1933* (Chapel Hill: University of North Carolina Press, 1988).

Junker, Detlev, et al., eds. *Cornerstone of Democracy: The West German Grundgesetz, 1949–1989* (Washington, DC: German Historical Institute, Occasional Paper No. 13, 1995).

Merritt, Richard L. *Democracy Imposed: U.S. Occupation Policy and the German Public, 1945–1949* (New Haven, CT: Yale University Press, 1995).

Smith, Eric Owen. *The German Economy* (London: Routledge, 1994).

Spotts, Frederic. *The Churches and Politics in Germany* (Middletown, CT: Wesleyan University Press, 1973).

German Reunification

Garton Ash, Timothy. *In Europe's Name* (New York: Vintage Books, 1993).

Grass, Günter. *Two States—One Nation?* trans. Krishna Winston and A. S. Wensinger (New York: Harcourt Brace, 1990).

James, Harold, and Marla Stone, eds. *When the Wall Came Down* (New York: Routledge, 1992).

Maier, Charles S. *Dissolution* (Princeton, NJ: Princeton University Press, 1997).

McAdams, A. James. *Germany Divided: From the Wall to Reunification* (Princeton, NJ: Princeton University Press, 1994).

Quint, Peter. *The Constitutional Law of German Unification* (Princeton, NJ: Princeton University Press, 1996).

Wallach, Peter H. G., and Ronald A. Francisco. *United Germany* (Westport, CT: Praeger, 1992).

B. POLITICAL PROCESSES AND INSTITUTIONS

POLITICAL PARTIES

The Federal Republic of Germany has long been described as a two and one-half party system. For at least the first 30 years of West Germany's existence, social and political circumstances combined to facilitate a remarkable degree of continuity in the parties representing the German population. In the first national election, held in 1949, the three most popular parties— the Christian Democratic Union (CDU) and its Bavarian affiliate, the Christian Social Union (CSU); the Social Democratic Party (SPD); and the Free Democratic Party (FDP)—captured 72.1 percent of the total votes. By the 1970s, these same parties commanded the support of virtually the entire West German electorate.

In 1987, only two years before unification, the three parties still managed to win 90.4 percent of the vote (a drop from their total of 98.0 percent in 1980). But there were already signs that the party landscape was being shaken up. In 1983, a fourth party, the radical-environmentalist Greens, entered parliament for the first time since 1949. Even more surprising, the postunification elections of 1990 and 1994 resulted in the entry of a fifth party—the ex-GDR's old Socialist Unity Party (SED) now recast as the Party of Democratic Socialism (PDS)—into the national parliament. In this sense, national unification had altered German politics, at least for the time being. The established parties would have to devise strategies to recapture the allegiance of voters attracted by the upstarts. Then too, the presence of new parties in the national legislature would complicate the creation and maintenance of stable governing coalitions. But as we shall see, German democracy would prove capable of surviving these tests.

By the federal elections of 1994, observers wondered whether the Greens would replace the FDP as the balance wheel and "kingmaker" in the Bundestag. Yet the three traditional parties still managed to receive 84.8 percent of all votes cast, one sign of the remarkable continuity of German politics. They got 88.8 percent in 2002. This continuity—and stability—has often been traced to the Federal Election Act's 5 percent clause. Enacted early on to avoid fragmenting the electorate, the act grants parliamentary representation only to those parties securing 5 percent or more of the votes cast in a national election or at least three single-member district seats. The 5 percent rule has kept numerous splinter parties out of parliament over the years, thus avoiding the coalition instability that might otherwise have arisen. This bit of institutional engineering shows that given the right set of circumstances, election rules can effectively channel political activity in predetermined directions.

Christian Democrats

The first party to rise to prominence in postwar German politics was the CDU. The CDU (*Christlich Demokratische Union*) was founded in 1945 as a result of the collaboration of old Center Party Catholics with liberal and conservative Protestants who had been members of other pre-1933 political parties. These groups were broadly inspired by Christian principles and the desire to present a strong united front against Leftism. But most indicative of the party's innovative style was that its founders deliberately steered away from the sectarian and dogmatic policies that had led to the ruin of the Weimar Republic. Under the canny direction of the FRG's first chancellor, Konrad Adenauer (ex-mayor of Cologne and Germany's wiliest politician since Bismarck), the CDU was cast as a modern catch-all party, espousing pragmatic values and seeking to gain the support of a majority of the German electorate. So successful was this appeal during the FRG's first two decades that the CDU would represent nearly every major occupational and class grouping in the country and completely dominate West German politics (see Table 4.4).

The party's leadership after Adenauer, however, was not nearly as capable, contributing to declining membership and its first loss of national power in 1969. As part of its recovery program, the CDU launched a major membership drive in the 1970s, leading once again to a larger—and

TABLE 4.4

BUNDESTAG SEATS OCCUPIED BY THE CDU/CSU AND SPD, FEDERAL ELECTIONS, 1949–2002

Year	CDU/CSU (%)	Seats	SPD (%)	Seats	Total Seats
1949	31.0	139	29.2	131	402
1953	45.2	243	28.8	151	487
1957	50.2	270	31.8	169	497
1961	45.3	242	36.2	190	499
1965	47.6	245	39.8	202	496
1969	46.1	242	42.7	224	496
1972	44.9	225	45.8	230	496
1976	48.6	243	42.6	214	496
1980	44.5	226	42.9	218	497
1983	48.8	244	38.2	193	498
1987	44.3	223	37.0	186	497
1990	43.8	313	33.5	239	662
1994	41.5	294	36.4	252	672
1998	35.2	245	40.9	298	669
2002	38.5	248	38.5	251	603

Sources: Peter Schindler, *Datenbuch zur Geschichte der Deutschen Bundestages 1949 bis 1982*, 4th ed. (Baden-Baden: Nomos Verlag, 1984), pp. 34–48; *Statistisches Jahrbuch 1991 für das Vereinte Deutschland*, p. 101; and *Statistisches Jahrbuch für die Bundesrepublik Deutschland 1995*; Federal Election Results, 1998, American Institute for Contemporary German Studies.

much more diverse—membership. Not coincidentally, the 1980s saw the party's return to power under the leadership of Helmut Kohl, a man whom few people were likely to credit with great charisma yet who somehow rallied his party to stunning victories from 1983 onward. His leadership talents were never more evident than in his skillful role in spearheading the drive for German unification—a feat that led to his reelection in 1990 as the first freely chosen chancellor of *all* the German people since 1932.

The CDU's adaptability since the FRG's founding has partly been due to its different constituent groups. Christian social pressures within the party, particularly in its early years, long supported progressive policies such as government-sponsored savings programs and subsidized housing. Yet over time, the party's increasingly prominent business, industrial, and middle-class constituencies have led it to support policies favoring free-market economics. The party has favored tax and spending cuts as

well as government deregulation as a means of boosting an economy overburdened by the cost of unification. The party has emphasized traditional moral values with a heavy accent on law and order. Internally, the CDU has often defended the FRG's federal structure against the centralizing influences of the national government. In foreign policy, it has been an ardent supporter of both the Atlantic Alliance and diverse efforts at European unification. In particular, the German-French axis has long been regarded as a key to European political and economic integration. The leader of the CDU in 2005 is Angela Merkel, a Protestant from East Germany.

Social Democrats

The SPD (*Sozialdemokratische Partei Deutschlands*), one of the largest mass-membership parties in Europe, can trace its roots back to the General Workingman's Association founded in

1863 by the brilliant young radical Ferdinand Lassalle. The first party to organize the working masses on a large scale, the SPD of Imperial Germany won the votes of the emerging industrial proletariat and moved on from that popular base to share power in 7 of the Weimar Republic's 21 governing coalitions.

Unlike the CDU, the Social Democrats were slower to recognize the virtues of identifying themselves with the nonideological orientation of a modern catch-all party. When the party reorganized after World War II, it failed to expand its influence much beyond the industrial working class. For almost a decade, it remained a staunchly left-wing party, openly embracing socialism and calling into question much of the Adenauer government's unabashedly pro-Atlantic and pro-European policies. This stance may have satisfied the dogmatic purists within the SPD, but to the evident satisfaction of its Christian Democratic opponents, it did not win the party any more votes. As a result, when more pragmatic elements gained the upper hand in the party leadership, like Herbert Wehner and the young Willy Brandt, its policies changed accordingly. At an historic meeting in 1959, with the passage of the famed *Godesberg Platform,* the Social Democrats finally embraced the social market economy and the basic outlines of Adenauer's foreign policy. Overnight, the SPD shed the more rigid aspects of its Marxist heritage and transformed itself from a narrow ideological party into a broadly based and pragmatic popular party.

The strategy worked. The party was able to diversify its membership by attracting more white-collar, middle-class members, and by 1966 had wide enough support to become part of a governing coalition with the CDU/CSU. After this achievement, beginning in 1969, the SPD went on, with the help of the Free Democratic Party, to elect the chancellor in four consecutive national elections. For a short period, during the 1980s, the SPD lurched abruptly back to the Left, largely as a result of internal disputes over foreign affairs and growing dissatisfaction with Western (especially American) defense policy. Perceived by voters as faction-ridden, impractical, and unfit to govern, it languished at the polls. In 1989 and 1990, in particular, the SPD blundered by seeming to oppose the immediate reunification of Germany. This costly mistake allowed Chancellor Kohl to seize the initiative and ride to yet another victory in 1990 on the CDU's speeding "unity now" train.

During the early 1990s, as the party struggled to find its way back to power, the SPD went through another series of leadership changes. The Left-leaning, minister-president of Saarland, Oscar Lafontaine, was induced to step down from his post as party chairman after the SPD's election defeat in 1990. The party then turned to Björn Engholm, the pipe-smoking and laid-back centrist minister-president of Schleswig-Holstein, who took on the challenge of ushering the Social Democrats back to the political mainstream until his sudden demise in 1993, following his admission of having given false testimony in a *Land* election scandal. Rudolf Scharping, minister-president of Rhineland-Palatinate, succeeded Engholm as party chairman. Young, intelligent, and tastefully bearded, he projected a professorial image and, given the state of public opinion polls, looked like a sure bet to emerge as chancellor in 1994. However, once again, public opinion experts underestimated Helmut Kohl's skills as a political manager. His reputation as an effective leader appeared to play a significant role in CDU/CSU–FDP victory, albeit by a single vote in the German parliament. Finally, in need of more dynamic and aggressive leadership in the face of rising unemployment and other economic problems arising out of reunification, the SPD desperately turned again, in 1995, to Lafontaine, expecting him to unify the party and produce the magic that would lead to victory in 1998. Yet surprisingly, as we shall elaborate momentarily, it was not Lafontaine but a younger and ostensibly new type of Social Democrat, Gerhard Schröder. He became Chancellor in 1998 and was re-elected in 2002.

Free Democrats

The FDP (*Freie Demokratische Partei*), founded in 1945, is the modern counterpart of the older German liberal parties. Although considerably smaller than the CDU or SPD, the FDP is the third party to have played a consistently influential role in postwar German politics. It is the only minor party to have survived the 5 percent clause in all federal elections (although just barely in 1998), and it has determined the governing coalition in 10 out of 14 such elections. The FDP's success has in large part been a reflection of its leaders' tactical flexibility. Until 1966, it was allied with the CDU, then from 1969 to 1982 with the SPD, and from 1983 through 1994 with the CDU again. Drawing its support primarily from business people, professionals, and the secular middle classes, the FDP has profited by profiling itself as a traditional liberal party, one that stands for free enterprise and individual self-determination in all areas of social life. Thus, it has quarreled with the CDU over foreign policy and with the SPD over spending and social programs, and it has taken strong, independent stands on issues such as education reform, abortion, and church taxes. Because it has so often controlled the fate of governing coalitions, the FDP's impact on German politics has consistently far outweighed its smaller numbers, and it has used its leverage to gain important government positions—on two occasions even capturing the federal presidency.

Splinter Parties

In addition to the three long-established parties, Germany has for years witnessed the rise and fall of numerous splinter parties. In the FRG's first few decades, the most successful of these parties seemed to predominate on the far right of the political spectrum, such as the chauvinistic National Democratic Party and, later, the *Republikaner.* Both of these parties were identified most conspicuously with their campaigns to rid Germany of its large foreign population. By exploiting the fears of the most vulnerable sectors of the electorate, especially in times of economic downturn, these parties have occasionally managed to surmount the minimum electoral hurdle (5 percent) required to gain entry into various *Land* parliaments. On the whole, however, these successes have been short-lived. Right-wing splinter parties have turned out to be localized movements with programmatically untenable platforms, and they have rarely won more than 1 percent of the national vote. The story is rather different for splinter parties on the left.

Greens

It should not be surprising that experts were initially inclined to regard Germany's Left-leaning Greens, which began their ascent to prominence in the late 1970s, as having no better prospects than a typical splinter party. Representing a loose alliance of ecological, antinuclear, and peace groups and disgruntled Social Democrats, the Greens gradually emerged on the German scene in the wake of the student protests of the 1960s and the failed terror campaigns of the 1970s. They were something entirely new for German politics, a Left libertarian party committed to nonviolent methods of protest, which rejected politics as usual and envisioned nothing less than the total transformation of society. Popular with young voters, feminists, and middle-class environmentalists, the Greens accomplished a feat that had long eluded the traditional splinter parties of the Right. In 1983, they shocked the political establishment by attaining 5.6 percent of the national vote and hence earning 34 seats in the Bundestag. Blustery and often disdainful of formal rules of procedure, the Greens prided themselves on being the "antiparty" party. They declared war on the "bourgeois-democratic state," and sought to revitalize grassroots democracy by insisting that their representatives rotate in office and abide by the orders of their local constituencies. They also prided themselves on creating symbolically charged public spectacles, bringing live trees into debates in the Bundestag and, to the consternation of conservative parliamentarians, refusing to wear suits and ties!

After the 1987 election, when they bettered their previous success by winning 8.3 percent of the vote, the Greens began to run into the problems facing any typical protest party. Some of the party's members, the so-called *Fundis* (fundamentalists) insisted that they should brook no compromises in adhering to their original values, even if this rigidity should cost them votes at election time. In contrast, another wing of the party, the *Realos* (realists) questioned this dogmatism, wondering how the party was to survive, let alone bring its policies to fruition, if it failed to find enough loyal voters to return it to office. Slowly, the party's *Realo* wing gained the upper hand in these debates (although never decisively), and the Greens transformed themselves into a more pragmatic party willing to cooperate with other parties in achieving their aims. Having failed to clear the 5 percent hurdle in 1990, in part as a consequence of their internal squabbles, the Greens merged with Alliance 90 (*Bundnis 90*), an East German party consisting largely of citizens-rights groups that helped to topple the old GDR's Communist government. Winning 7.3 percent of the votes in 1994, Alliance 90/Greens, as the party now called itself, entered parliament with 49 seats, but interestingly, nearly all of its popular votes came from the western *Länder.* The party's postindustrial emphasis on environmental and lifestyle issues had little appeal for eastern Germans worried about unemployment and other material concerns. But this time around, undoubtedly because of the party's willingness to portray itself as a modern party of the middle, western voters proved more supportive of its programs. The prize for this conciliatory attitude, as we shall see shortly, was the Greens' inclusion in the governing coalition in 1998 and again in 2002. It won 55 seats in the Bundestag in 2002.

Party of Democratic Socialism (PDS)

According to most experts in 1990, it was inconceivable that the Party of Democratic Socialism (PDS), the successor to East Germany's old Socialist Unity Party (SED), would long survive the fall of Communism. With the implosion of the GDR, the party's membership dropped from 800,000 to 320,000 in 1990 alone, and to 130,000 in 1994. Yet to the astonishment of most observers, this renamed party was able to define a distinctive role for itself in reunified Germany by campaigning for a reformed version of socialism with a human face. In 1994, although the party failed to win the necessary 5 percent of the national vote, it was still awarded 30 seats in the Bundestag by virtue of winning four single-member districts in East Berlin. Then, in 1998, it just exceeded the 5 percent hurdle and received 36 (later, 37) parliamentary seats, but in 2002 it got only 4 percent of the vote.

In retrospect, it is clear why the PDS was able to carve out a semblance of political credibility with certain segments of the electorate. Although many of its early leaders and members were old SED comrades, the party was quickly able to attract voters from a much wider and younger segment of the electorate. While the ex-GDR's old managerial and professional elite were unification's losers and therefore had nowhere else to turn, the PDS's leaders proved skilled in gaining the support of thousands of ordinary easterners who, for one reason or another, were displeased with the course of unification. Many were angered by the seemingly arrogant behavior of their western "colonizers" and by the rapidity with which they were supposedly destroying values, such as solidarity and egalitarianism, romantically associated with the tradition of democratic socialism. Others were simply alienated as a result of the debilitating consequences

---

A CLOSER LOOK

4.4

THE PDS TAKES ROOT

"In their hearts [many older persons] clung to [socialist] values that in their heads they thought to be superannuated. It is precisely this gap between heart and head upon which the PDS has been able to build its nest. That is, the party appeals neither purely to easterners' nostalgia for the past nor to their rational self-interest in the redistribution conflicts of unification. Instead, it reflects their ambivalence about the past and present…. The PDS has succeeded in positioning itself as the defender of this eastern desire to maintain biographical continuity without threatening to disrupt seriously the ongoing integration process."

Source: Lawrence H. McFalls, "Political Culture: Partisan Strategies, and the PDS: Prospects for an East German Party," *German Politics and Society* 13 (1995), p. 55.

of economic reconstruction in the East, mass unemployment, and general insecurity.

The PDS was able to take advantage of all of these currents of displeasure and uncertainty to elude the fate of most small parties in the past. In 1998, it achieved its first major success above the municipal level when it was invited by the SPD to form a coalition government in the eastern *Land* of Mecklenburg–West Pomerania. Of even greater proportions, however, was the successful conclusion of coalition negotiations between the PDS and the SPD in December 2001 about governing the *Land* of Berlin, after the SPD's attempts to create a "traffic light" coalition with the FDP and the Greens had broken down. Thanks to the PDS's strong appeal to voters in Berlin's eastern half, it seemed that even the reform Communists had found a measure of legitimacy in the German political system.

Party Organization

One reason for the historical continuity and stability in Germany's parties, as well as for subtle differences among them, is their success in capturing and channeling popular opinion. The major parties are formally organized at the federal, *Land,* and precinct levels. The CDU bears the imprint of the FRG's federalized structure, with organizational power residing in the party's 13 *Land* associations. Like the American Republican and Democratic Parties, the CDU is a loosely structured party held together by a coalition of interests with a common goal of winning elections. The SPD, on the other hand, is a mass-organized party under a centralized leadership that is served by a large and disciplined core of full-time professionals who are in charge of various district parties (*Bezirksparteien*). The relative power and autonomy of the district associations have permitted the development of strong regional leaders whose views the national leadership cannot ignore with impunity.

The highest formal authority in each party is the national party convention held every two years—although the FDP meets annually—consisting of delegates elected mainly by *Land,* district, and county associations. The convention sets the general outlines of policy, votes on organizational

matters, and elects a national executive committee consisting of the party chairperson, several deputy chairpersons, secretary general, treasurer, and other elected members. At the national level, the SPD's organizational chart also includes a large party council, consisting of *Land* and local party leaders, and a nine-member presidium to supervise the work of the party executive committee.

Parties are such an important part of policy making in the FRG that the Basic Law (Article 21) actually recognizes a privileged role for them in the inculcation and articulation of democratic values. This role has been reaffirmed by the Political Parties Act of 1967. Apart from provisions on the disclosure of finances, the act largely codifies existing party practices and procedures, many of them prescribed in decisions of the Federal Constitutional Court. This act provides for a host of measures to safeguard internal party democracy: (1) the right of all members to vote for party convention delegates; (2) the right of such delegates to vote on party guidelines and programs; (3) a secret ballot for the election of party officers, who must be elected every two years; (4) a reasonable balance of *ex officio* and elected members on the party executive committee; and (5) a written arbitration procedure for the resolution of intraparty disputes.

Party Finance

Unlike the United States, where parties have traditionally been weak organizations, Germany's parties have, at least since Bismarck's time, consistently been able to count upon strong support from their members and the state itself. One key source of support has been in funding. The parties receive their funds from a wide variety of sources, including public subsidies, private donations, receipts from party events and publications, and contributions from individual members and members of parliament. As Table 4.5 shows, some funding comes from their respective constituencies. As a mass-organized party, the SPD relies mainly on membership dues, whereas the CSU and the FDP have relied heavily on donations from corporations and other private groups. These emphases have shifted over time. Private contributions filled the CDU's coffers during the

TABLE 4.5

PARTY FINANCES, 1999 (DM MILLIONS)

Party	Public Subsidies	Donations	Membership	Total Income
SPD	93.9	33.7	157.5	285.1
CDU	76.6	65.3	105.3	247.2
CSU	18.9	15.3	19.8	54.0
FDP	13.4	19.3	10.8	43.5
Greens	17.0	10.1	20.9	48.0
PDS	14.5	7.5	17.5	39.5

Source: Figures based upon *Deutscher Bundestag: Parteifinanzierung,* at *www.bundestag.de/datbk/finanz/pf_einnahmen.htm.*

Adenauer years, but as a result of the party's membership drive in the 1970s, when it first experienced financial difficulties, it began to catch up with the SPD in dues-paying members.

An even greater source of funding over time has been the German state. The state began to reimburse the parties for their election campaign costs in 1959. By 1990, their election campaign costs exceeded DM 400 million, representing approximately 5 DM ($3.13) for each second-ballot vote cast, an amount divided among the parties proportionate to each party's total vote. In a series of decisions, the Federal Constitutional Court has handed down rulings to ensure that the funding provisions treat all parties fairly. In 1968, the court ruled that any party receiving as little as 0.5 percent of the vote is constitutionally entitled to state support at the rate, per voter, established by federal law. The original purpose behind state funding was to help the parties compete on a more equal basis and to liberate them from the excessive influence of interest groups. Yet in the late 1970s, as the cost of campaigning skyrocketed, numerous illegal campaign finance practices dominated the news. In 1983, the Bundestag enacted a legislative reform package to put a stop to practices that deliberately circumvent the law (*Umwegfinanzierung*).[17]

Unable any longer to distinguish adequately between legitimate campaign costs and other party expenditures, a Constitutional Court judgment of April 9, 1992, declared major parts of the existing party finance law unconstitutional and ordered the German parliament to enact a new law. Initiated by the Greens, the case was decided against the backdrop of declining party membership and the increasing public perception that the parties were more interested in shoring up their power than in caring for the public interest. To encourage the parties to revitalize their ossified structures, increase their membership, and raise more funds on a voluntary basis, the court ruled that state subsidies and reimbursements may not exceed the amount of funds the parties raise by themselves. Then, on January 1, 1994, a new law was put into effect by the Bundestag. This statute regularized the distribution of public funds according to a revised standard, the extent to which a given party was institutionalized within society. By measuring institutionalization in terms of two factors—party performance in a variety of recent elections and the combination of membership dues and donations—parliamentarians hoped they had a fair and just means for allocating scarce public resources. Yet even with new legislation, some party leaders could not resist the temptation to cut corners. In 1999, Helmut Kohl was caught up in a well-publicized party finance scandal when he and other prominent CDU representatives were accused of maintaining secret

---

[17]This section on party financing relies heavily on Arthur B. Gunlicks, "Campaigns and Party Finance in the West German 'Party State,'" *Review of Politics* 50 (Winter 1988), pp. 30–48.

bank accounts in Switzerland in order to fund party activities; they were also implicated in kickback schemes involving military sales and the restructuring of East German industry.

INTEREST GROUPS

German constitutional theory regards political parties as the chief agencies of political representation, providing the vital link between state and society that facilitates effective majority rule. In reality, public policy results from the complex interplay of political parties and private interests who seek special favors from the government. This factor too is an important source of political stability in the FRG. Hundreds of national associations, ranging from recreational and fraternal to economic and professional groups, maintain offices and highly skilled professional staffs in the capital on a year-round basis. For decades, Bonn was the site of most lobbying activity because of the central importance of federal executive agencies in making public policy, and now this function has been assumed by Germany's new capital, Berlin.

Contact between interest-group representatives and public officials in the FRG is much more direct and formal than in many other other advanced democracies. This is largely a vestige of the German corporatist tradition that goes back to Bismarck's efforts to preserve political calm during Germany's initial unification in the 1870s. Under corporatist arrangements, the support of major social and economic interests, like trade unions and business associations, is guaranteed by giving them a direct stake in all decisions of consequence to the country's political welfare and its economy. These groups are represented on forums as diverse as ministerial advisory councils, agency consultative committees, regional planning councils, public broadcasting stations, and the parliamentary study groups of the political parties. Additionally, federal ministerial officials meet on a regular basis behind closed doors with the top representatives of industry, banking, agriculture, and labor for the purpose of coordinating national economic policy. Also, the quasi-official compulsory-membership trade and professional associations are still other examples of direct interest-group influence on public policy.

The link between organized interests and Germany's political parties is equally firm. Far more than in the United States, these interests are actually represented by their functionaries in the national and parliamentary parties (*Fraktionen*). Representatives of business, religious, agricultural, and refugee organizations have been conspicuous among CDU/CSU members of parliament, while not surprisingly, trade union officials are to be found in SPD leadership positions at all levels of party organization. Members of parliament associated with trade unions, business associations, and other organized interests actually dominate the membership of parliamentary committees such as labor, social policy, food, agriculture, and forestry.

This complex web of public and private interlocking directorates has prompted political scientist Peter Katzenstein to characterize the FRG as a "semisovereign state."[18] In Katzenstein's view, the FRG is semisovereign because, unlike a country like the United States which has more clearly set lines of demarcation between public and private authority, the central state in Germany shares its sovereignty with private centers of power and influence. In this conception, popular elections do not empower the victors to change policy in strict accordance with an electoral mandate. Rather, politics by consensus is the norm in Germany, a norm promoted by the regular practice of formalized cooperation between a decentralized government and highly centralized private interest associations. Thus "incrementalism rather than large-scale policy change typifies West German politics,"[19] a reality that helps to explain the stability of the FRG's political system as well as the frustration felt by those citizens who believe the system is insulated and biased against change.

---

[18]See Peter J. Katzenstein, *Policy and Politics in West Germany* (Philadelphia: Temple University Press, 1987), p. 10.
[19]Ibid., p. 362.

Citizen Initiatives (*Bürgerinitiativen*)

The sudden appearance on the political scene of urban and rural protest groups in the 1970s and 1980s was one sign that some Germans were not happy with the inherently conservative tendencies of the political structure. Tens of thousands of German citizens staged protest rallies involving quality of life issues such as nuclear power plant construction, urban renewal, air and water pollution, new highway construction, and the cost of inner-city transportation. Their grassroots activism—protest marches, letter-writing campaigns, petition gathering, sit-ins, and other forms of spontaneous action—expressed the disenchantment felt by many citizens with the lack of responsiveness of mainstream political parties, private corporations, and official bureaucracies. These efforts were most effective at the local level, resulting in the rollback of some public transportation prices, delays in the building of nuclear power plants, and the postponement of official decisions to cut new highways through certain residential and open areas.

This culture of autonomous protest precipitated the formation and eventual electoral successes of an alternative party like the Greens. However, as a sign of the robustness of the German political system, the more mainstream parties soon recognized that they could not afford to ignore these extra-systemic protests for long. Notably, the CDU and the SPD took action on citizens' disenchantment by making the *Bürgerinitiativen* models for their local party interelection activities. Both parties were also quick to see the electoral advantage of adopting many of the alternative groups' policies (e.g., on environmental protection and gender equality) as their own.

Major Interest Aggregations

Business   The three largest business associations in the FRG are the German Federation of Industry (BDI), the Federation of German Employers (BDA), and the German Chamber of Trade and Commerce (DIHT). Approximately 90 percent of employers belong to such associations,

a far higher percentage than that of employees in trade unions. For example, the German Federation of Industry, which is dominated by a few large firms, embraces 35 major industrial associations. Its financial resources, expertise, high-powered staff, and close links to the federal ministries make it one of the most effective lobbies. The Federation of German Employers, whose economic experts engage in collective-bargaining negotiations on behalf of nearly 90 percent of all private firms in the FRG, consists of 54 trade associations and 14 *Länder* organizations representing more than 1,000 regional associations. The DIHT, speaking for 82 chambers of commerce, is concerned with the legal and promotional interests of organized business. Collectively, these groups have been heavy contributors to the CDU/CSU, though the BDI's leaders have also donated funds to the FDP, a strategy calculated to secure access to the ruling circles within SPD-FDP coalition governments.

Labor   West German workers are organized into four major unions: the German Salaried Employees Union (DAG), the German Federation of Civil Servants (DBB), the Christian Trade Union Federation of Germany (CGB), and the German Trade Union Federation (DGB). These four unions represent a little more than one-third of the FRG's organized labor force. They are not strictly blue-collar organizations. The DGB, the largest of the unions, consists of 8 affiliated unions with a total membership of 7.7 million persons, only about two-thirds of whom are blue-collar workers. Higher civil servants, middle-level white-collar employees, and many Catholic workers are represented in the DBB, DAG, and CGB, respectively.

The unions serve their members with an extensive infrastructure of educational, social, and political activity, and keep them and the general public informed through a communication network that includes scores of periodicals, newsletters, and a significant presence on the World Wide Web. The unions are also heavily represented in parliament. In the ninth Bundestag (1980), for example, 69.4 percent of SPD and 30.6 percent of CDU/CSU delegates had formal interest-group ties to trade unions or other employee organizations.[20] In the Bundestag in 2005 over a third were members of DGB. Still, membership levels have always fluctuated. For instance, between 1982 and 1990 the CGB grew from 297,000 members to 309,000 members, while between 1980 and 1990 the DBB dropped from 821,000 to 799,000. More important, the fortunes of the trade unions have recently been similar to those of other postindustrial democracies, including the United States. In the first half of the 1990s alone, as a result of the decline of traditional industries, they lost nearly 2 million dues-paying members.

Unlike their European neighbors, German unions have also had to contend with the complicated problem of unification. The entry of East Germany's workforce into the western unions has not been smooth. As eastern workers demanded wage settlements on a par with western levels, western employers became more disinclined to invest in the less productive and all too often antiquated eastern plants. As a result, the largely western leadership of the trade unions often found themselves in the awkward position of having to support lesser wage increases in the hopes of keeping eastern industry alive. Likewise, while western unions have traditionally exercised "a sense of proportion in the national interest" by taking modest raises (e.g., the 6 percent settlement accepted by civil service union leaders in the spring of 1991), their grassroots membership has complained that it is being made to pay for the problems in the east. Calls for western union members to make direct contributions to their eastern fellow members have been particularly poorly received. Hence, the goal of achieving equality in eastern and western living standards not only has proven unsusceptible to quick or easy attainment, but has also come at the cost of union credibility.

Churches   The Basic Law forbids the establishment of a state church. In the consensual spirit that governs other social relations, how-

ever, it reminds the German people of "their responsibility before God." In addition, the Basic Law defines religious communities as "corporate bodies under public law," in which capacity they are entitled to levy taxes and enter into agreements with the state. While the state is constitutionally bound to remain neutral in religious matters, the neutrality that governs church-state relations in Germany is one that leans toward accommodation rather than strict separation. The prevailing view of this relationship acknowledges the important role of religion in the nation's public life. The relationship is governed by *Länder* concordats and church covenants, and they cover matters such as religious instruction in the public schools, observance of religious holidays, establishment of confessional schools, and appointment of chairs in theology at state universities.

The Evangelical Church in Germany (EKD) is an alliance of 24 largely independent Lutheran, Reformed, and United Churches. Their 29 million members include some 5 million eastern Germans. Its top legislative organ, the Synod, takes positions on various social, cultural, and educational issues, in which respect it often cooperates with the Roman Catholic Church. The Catholic Church consists of 27 dioceses, seven of which are archdioceses. Its 26 million members include 800,000 eastern Germans. The Conference of Catholic Bishops is the church's top policy-making organ. It functions independently of the Central Committee of German Catholics, an influential lay organization consisting of more than 100 Catholic associations. Other religious organizations include the Protestant Methodist Church, the Old Catholic Church, the Central Council of Jews, and even Islam. These congregations are relatively small. The Jewish community, for example, consists of around 100,000 members, a far cry from the 530,000 Jews who lived and worked in Germany prior to the Holocaust. However, some cities, like Berlin, have recently experienced an increase in the size of their Jewish communities. At the same time, immigration from Turkey and the Middle East has led to a growing Muslim population in the FRG, in 2005 about 3½ million, which has further tested German understandings of religious tolerance.

[20]Russell J. Dalton, *Politics: West Germany* (Boston: Scott Foresman, 1989), p. 236.

The two major confessions—Evangelical and Catholic—continue to be influential in selected areas of public policy. Both religious establishments are represented on the governing boards of many public agencies, including those of the major public broadcasting stations. The churches are also critical players on the field of social welfare. They spend billions of dollars operating hundreds of kindergartens, hospitals, old-age homes, and homes for the handicapped, all activities that enjoy broad public support. In addition, the churches have a history of involvement in hotly contested political issues such as nuclear missile deployment, compulsory military service, and abortion. The Evangelical Church can even be credited with spearheading the West German peace movement as well as East Germany's peaceful revolution. What the churches seem unable to do today—certainly far less than in the earlier years of the Federal Republic—is to deliver votes in national election campaigns. Unlike in the late nineteenth and early twentieth centuries, German citizens have become modernized and no longer regard their religious and their political identities as inextricably intertwined.

ELECTORAL POLITICS

The Electoral System

In an ingenious but sometimes complicated way, the German electoral system combines single-member districts with proportional representation. This fact, which can be understood in terms of Germany's response to the chaotic conditions of the Weimar Republic, allows the electoral system to include interests across the spectrum without at the same time giving rise to political instability. Each voter receives two ballots. The first is cast for a specific candidate running in a district, the second for a party list. The second ballot includes the names of those candidates nominated by their respective parties, and they are chosen in the order in which they appear on the list. The number of parliamentary seats allocated to a party is determined by second-ballot

votes, that is, by its total share of the nationwide vote. Under this system, which the *Länder* also use, party list candidates would be added to the single-member district winners until the total number of seats equals the percentage of its nationwide, second-ballot vote.

The functioning of the system can be illustrated by the election results of 1983. In winning 48.8 percent of second-ballot votes, the CDU/CSU also captured 180 districts; the figures for the SPD were 38.2 percent and 68 districts; for the FDP and the Greens they were 7.0 and 5.6 percent, respectively, and no districts. These results meant that Christian Democrats were entitled to 244 Bundestag seats. Thus, under the formula, the CDU/CSU was awarded 64 list seats which, when added to its district seats, totaled 244 or 48.8 percent of all second-ballot votes. The SPD, having won 68 district seats, was awarded an additional 125 list seats, totaling 193, whereas the FDP received 34 and the Greens 27 list seats, representing their respective shares of the national (second-ballot) vote. It is possible, however, for a party to win more district seats than it would normally be entitled to by its second-ballot vote. When this happens, such "overhang" seats are retained, thus increasing the total number of parliamentary seats by that much.

The voting system can be skewed by the 5 percent clause, which often results in "wasted" votes but also fosters stability by holding down the number of small parties in parliament. In 1990, for example, the western Greens won 4.6 percent of the votes in the old FRG, just missing the 5 percent requirement. Under "pure" proportional representation, the Greens would have been entitled to 23 seats in the Bundestag but, having failed to win 5 percent of the vote, they received none. The CDU/CSU's ten-seat majority after the 1994 election was due entirely to its overhang seats. The SPD had four such seats.

The 5 percent clause was not regarded as equitable, however, for the first all-German election of December 1990. The Federal Constitutional Court ruled that political parties in the eastern *Länder* would be severely handicapped if the rule were to apply nationwide. For this particular election, therefore, as Table 4.6 indicates, the 5 percent rule was manipulated to apply separately to Germany's eastern and western regions. If seats in the Bundestag had been allocated on a nationwide basis, as is usually the case, neither the Greens (eastern or western) nor the Party of Democratic Socialism (the old SED) would have achieved parliamentary representation. The two-constituency tabulation presented in Table 4.6 was a one-time exception to the 5 percent nationwide rule.

Finally, if a political party fails to get 5 percent of the national vote, it may still obtain proportional representation in the national parliament by winning at least three single-member districts. This happened in 1994. The PDS won 4.4 percent of the national vote, although only 0.9 percent of these votes came from the western *Länder.* However, because it won 4 constituency seats in East Berlin, the party was entitled to 30 seats in the thirteenth Bundestag (see Table 4.7).

TABLE 4.6

FEDERAL ELECTION RESULTS, 1990

Party	Nationwide (%)	Old FRG (%)	Ex-GDR (%)	Seats
CDU	36.7	35.0	43.4	262
SPD	33.5	35.9	23.6	239
FDP	11.0	10.6	13.4	79
CSU	7.1	9.1	—	51
Greens (West)	3.9	4.7	—	—
PDS	2.4	0.3	9.9	17
DSU	0.2	—	1.0	—
Greens (East)	1.2	—	5.9	8
Republicans	2.1	2.3	1.3	—

Sources: Statistisches Jahrbuch 1991 für das Vereinte Deutschland, p. 101; and *The Week in Germany* (New York: German Information Center, December 7, 1990).

Note: The percentages do not include the election results in Berlin. The DSU (German Social Union) ran as the "sister" party of Bavaria's CSU. The Greens (East) were allied with Alliance 90.

TABLE 4.7

FEDERAL ELECTION RESULTS, 1994

Party	West (%)	East (%)	Total (%)	Seats
CDU/CSU	42.2	38.5	41.5	294
SPD	37.6	31.9	36.4	252
FDP	7.7	4.0	6.9	47
Alliance 90/Greens	7.8	5.7	7.3	49
PDS	0.9	17.7	4.4	30
Republicans	2.0	1.4	1.9	—
Other parties	1.9	1.3	1.7	—
Total	100	100	100	672

Split-Ticket Voting

The German system gives voters the unusual opportunity to split their tickets, a method by which coalition partners can help each other. In 1972, for example, the SPD openly encouraged its voters to cast their second ballot in favor of the FDP, while 60 percent of second-ballot FDP voters supported CDU and SPD candidates with their first ballot. Split-ticket voting was also prevalent in the 1987 election when many SPD voters, troubled by their party's military and ecological policies, cast their second ballot for the Greens, whereas many CDU voters cast their second ballot for the FDP. The FDP, in turn, appeared to convince voters that the best way to keep the CDU/CSU on the right course was to ensure its presence in the new government.

As Table 4.8 indicates, large numbers of German voters appear to be leery of one-party government. No fewer than 40.1 percent of CDU/CSU voters and 41.7 percent of SPD voters thought it would "not be good" for their respective parties to win an absolute majority of seats in the Bundestag. The corresponding percentages for the 1983 election were 27.1 and 29.5. These figures point to an increasing tendency on the part of German voters to split their ballots. This preference for governing coalitions over single-party rule contrasts sharply with the attitudes of British voters, who tend to associate responsible parliamentary government with unified party leadership backed by electoral majorities. This split-ticket voting is one indicator of the Americanization of FRG electoral behavior; another is the phenomenon of the "floating voter" who does not owe a deep and consistent attachment to any one party.

Candidate Selection

German parties are strong in part because they monopolize the candidate selection process. Candidates seeking district seats are nominated either directly by party members or by conventions of party delegates. (There is no system of primary elections as in the United States.) In the CDU and SPD parties, executive committees select candidates for the Bundestag. Naturally the party will seek to nominate the candidate with the broadest popular appeal. But invariably he or she is a well-known party loyalist with years of faithful service to the organization. "Independent" candidates who circumvent the party organization are rarely if ever nominated. Party control over *Land* list candidates is even tighter. In principle, these lists are determined by secret ballot in party conferences, but in truth delegates vote mainly to ratify lists already put together by district and *Land* party executive committees in cooperation with national party officials. These lists are usually headed by leading party officials to ensure their election to the Bundestag.

Campaign Styles and Techniques

West German elections have evolved into major media events and highly professionalized undertakings similar to American presidential campaigns. The CDU and the SPD continue to speak in terms of the traditional FRG mass party, the *Volkspartei* (People's Party), but both have been highly Americanized and centralized in their campaigns, especially in the use of new communication technologies and new marketing approaches. (The German courts, however, put an end to U.S.-style direct phone canvassing as an illegal infringe-

TABLE 4.8

VOTERS PREFERRING ABSOLUTE MAJORITY FOR SPD OR CDU/CSU, 1987 ELECTION (PERCENT)					
Absolute Majority	CDU/CSU	SDP	FDP	Greens	Total
Good for SPD	0.0	57.7	1.0	14.3	22.2
Good for CSU/CSU	59.8	0.0	8.5	0.0	26.5
Not good	40.1	41.7	90.5	85.7	50.3

Source: *Bundestagswahl 1987: Eine Analyse der Wahl zum 11. Deutschen Bundestag am 25 January 1987* (Mannheim: Forschungsgruppe Wahlen E. V., 1987), p. 48.

ment of individual privacy.) Campaign advertisements fill newspapers and popular magazines, while election posters and richly colored lifestyle photographs of leading candidates dot the landscape. Lapel buttons, paper flags, T-shirts, and bumper stickers by the tens of thousands convey their partisan messages.

In the 1980s, the art of selling candidates reached new heights of sophistication as public relations firms assumed a central role in mapping campaign strategy. As part of this strategy, each party seeks to establish a "brand image" with matching colors and catchy slogans. For example, the CDU/CSU, in emphasizing the "take charge" quality of its leader, Helmut Kohl, sought to personalize the 1994 campaign by turning the election into a referendum on his chancellorship. One influential campaign poster showed a huge and smiling Kohl under the caption "Politics Without a Beard," referring to the bearded SPD leader at that time, Rudolf Scharping, who was thought by some to be too much of an intellectual to lead the Federal Republic. The SPD countered with its issue-oriented emphasis on "Jobs, Jobs, Jobs" in the face of rising unemployment. The FDP has cultivated itself as a "creative minority" by emphasizing its independence and portraying its leaders as persons of reason and common sense who are concerned about the lot of small businesspeople and the "besieged" middle class. The Greens have drawn upon their name as a powerful symbol of their commitment to environmental preservation.[21]

GERMAN POLITICS IN TRANSITION

The Postwar Years to Reunification

The year 1969 marked the turning point of West German politics in the postwar era. Prior to that year, the CDU/CSU had won five successive

national elections, most of them by wide margins over the SPD. Yet the clearest observable trend, seen in Table 4.9, is the clockwork regularity of SPD gains between 1953 and 1972. The SPD's chance to enter a governing coalition occurred in 1966 when Ludwig Erhard, the CDU chancellor, resigned against a backdrop of discord within his own party and a widening rift between the CDU/CSU and its regular coalition partner, the FDP. There followed the three-year period (1966–1969) of the so-called Grand Coalition under the CDU's Kurt-Georg Kiesinger (chancellor) and the SPD's Willy Brandt (vice-chancellor). In 1969, when the Social Democrats reached a new high of 42.7 percent of the popular vote, the FDP, with 5.8 percent of the vote, decided to join hands with Brandt in producing Bonn's first SPD-led government.

The new coalition ruled with a slim voting edge of 12 votes, which by 1972 had virtually disappeared in the wake of defections from Brandt's controversial Eastern policy (*Ostpolitik*), which had sought to "regularize" the FRG's relations with the communist states of East Europe. Christian Democrats, smelling an opportunity to get back into office, moved for a vote of no confidence, the first time the parliamentary opposition had tried to topple a ruling government between federal elections. On April 27, 1972, the coalition survived the CDU/CSU challenge by a razor-thin margin of two votes. On the very next day the Bundestag rejected Brandt's budget, plunging the government into another crisis. The failure of the budget to win parliamentary approval came at a time of economic downturn and bitter wrangling in the cabinet over fiscal policy. Yet Brandt's personal popularity was at an all-time high, prompting him in late 1972, when the economic news was much brighter, to call for new elections in the hope of increasing his margin of parliamentary support. Accordingly, the chancellor invoked Article 68 and lost his vote of confidence, as planned, whereupon the federal president dissolved the Bundestag and scheduled new elections for November 19.

The 1972 federal election campaign—a bitterly fought contest—resulted in a solid victory for Brandt, marking the first time Social Democrats had exceeded the CDU/CSU in popular votes. Shortly thereafter, however, the party's for-

---

[21]For a study of changing campaign styles in Germany, see Susan Edith Scarrow, *Organizing for Victory: Political Party Members and Party Organizing Strategies in Great Britain and West Germany, 1945–1989* (Ph.D. dissertation, Yale University, 1991), chs. 5 and 10.

TABLE 4.9

FEDERAL ELECTION RESULTS, 1949–2002 (PERCENTAGE OF VOTES CAST)

Year	Turnout	CDU/CSU	SPD	FDP	Greens	PDS	Others
1949	78.5	31.0	29.2	11.9	—	—	27.3
1953	86.0	45.2	28.8	9.5	—	—	16.5
1957	87.8	50.2	31.8	7.7	—	—	11.3
1961	87.7	45.3	36.2	12.8	—	—	6.6
1965	86.8	47.6	39.3	9.5	—	—	5.6
1969	86.7	46.1	42.7	5.8	—	—	4.9
1972	91.1	44.9	45.8	8.4	—	—	0.9
1976	90.7	48.6	42.6	7.9	—	—	0.9
1980	88.7	44.5	42.9	10.6	—	—	1.9
1983	89.1	48.8	38.2	7.0	5.6	—	6.0
1987	84.4	44.3	37.0	9.1	8.3	—	8.9
1990	77.8	43.8	33.5	11.0	5.1	2.4	4.0
1994	79.1	41.5	36.4	6.9	7.3	4.4	3.5
1998	82.2	35.2	40.9	6.2	6.7	5.1	6.0
2002	79.1	38.5	38.5	7.4	8.6	4.0	3.0

tunes declined again as the SPD suffered severe losses in several state and local elections, only to be followed by Brandt's resignation in May 1974. This set the stage, after Helmut Schmidt's takeover, for the 1976 election.[22]

In 1976 the CDU/CSU not only recovered its 1972 losses, but narrowly missed securing the majority that would have toppled the SPD-FDP coalition—a popular victory without power, as many editorial writers characterized the election. The CDU's revival was widely attributed to the expansion of its grassroots membership campaign in the early 1970s under its able general secretary, Kurt Biedenkopf, and to a highly effective national advertising campaign. Yet many spectators saw the election as an issueless campaign, decided mainly by the styles and personalities of the leading candidates.[23]

The 1980 and 1983 elections were largely a replay of 1976. However, the fortunes of Helmut Schmidt's SPD-led government declined rapidly. The popular chancellor's days were numbered in the face of increasing opposition from the FDP over his economic policy and from his own party over his strong pro-American nuclear missile policy. On October 1, 1982, after the FDP pulled out of its coalition with the SPD and switched its support to the CDU/CSU, parliament chose the CDU's leader, Helmut Kohl, as chancellor. The new chancellor pledged forthwith to call new elections in March. It turned out to be a banner year for Christian Democrats. Far ahead of the SPD in the polls, they obtained their highest percentage of the national vote since 1957 but fell just short of a majority. Again in 1987 the CDU/CSU–FDP coalition emerged victorious, this time against the challenge of Johannes Rau, the moderate SPD candidate for chancellor. Although the Greens had been gaining strength on the Left, often at the expense of the SPD, Rau promised the electorate that he would not consider a coalition with the Greens. But as the SPD organization moved steadily leftward in an attempt to draw votes from the Greens, many other voters, par-

[22]For a detailed discussion of the 1972 campaign, see Arnold J. Heidenheimer and Donald P. Kommers, *The Governments of Germany*, 4th ed. (New York: Thomas Y. Crowell, 1975), ch. 5.
[23]A treatment of the 1976 election is Karl H. Cerny, ed., *Germany at the Polls* (Washington, DC: American Enterprise Institute, 1978).

ticularly the swing vote in German politics, supported the Kohl coalition.

With the FRG's economy booming in the summer of 1989, the SPD under Oskar Lafontaine planned a 1990 campaign focusing on "a policy of ecological and social renewal of industrialized society." This postindustrial strategy, they hoped, would provide the Social Democrats with the clear sense of identity they needed to regain voter confidence. Even if this gambit would have worked, however, the Lafontaine wing of the party could not have planned on intervening events in the GDR. Massive antigovernment demonstrations in the east led to the collapse of the Communist regime and the breaching of the Berlin Wall. As East Germans prepared for their first free election in nearly 60 years and as calls for reunification became its defining feature, Chancellor Kohl seized the opportunity at his doorstep. With the active support of his FDP foreign minister, Hans-Dietrich Genscher, who had been born in the east, he obtained Allied support for negotiations with East Berlin and Moscow. By October 3, 1990, these contacts were to reunite the two German states and thereby make Kohl the first chancellor of all Germany since World War II.

Kohl's extraordinary determination and enthusiasm overcame all obstacles and all cautionary notes, including those of the president of the Bundesbank, as to the eventual costs of reunification. Wherever he went in the east, of course, Kohl was welcomed by tumultuous crowds, not least because of his willingness to predict that the integration of the GDR's economy into the FRG would produce "blooming landscapes" throughout the region. Meanwhile, Lafontaine's SPD was thrown onto the defensive by his initiatives and reduced to warning voters, in a Cassandra-like manner, that the chancellor's promises could have unpleasant side effects. Accordingly, the party's cautious support for national unity was popularly perceived in the east as far too little, and much too late. Kohl, ever the shrewd political campaigner, had both the diplomatic power and the deutsche mark to offer; Lafontaine offered voters little more than skepticism.

As a consequence, the elections to the Bundestag of 1990, the first to take place in united Germany, led to a resounding victory for Kohl's government coalition. True, the total national vote for the CDU/CSU dipped somewhat (to 43.8 percent) and was counterbalanced by a gain for Genscher's FDP (which rose to 11.0 percent). Nonetheless, the drubbing the SPD received at the polls, which fell to 33.5 percent of the national vote (its lowest level since 1957), was roundly perceived as a vindication of the chancellor's aggressive pro-unification policy.

A Change of Government

Students of democratic politics agree that one of the most important indicators of a vibrant democracy is a "circulation of elites," an ongoing process by which even the most popular leaders are eventually subject to replacement by their opponents. By the Bundestag elections of 1994, the FRG provided a perfect test case of this proposition because Chancellor Kohl had already governed his country for 12 years. In the eyes of many citizens, it was time for a change.

Additionally, in the two decades prior to the 1994 election, the FRG's electorate had changed in significant ways. In the 1950s, voting patterns could be explained largely in terms of class and religion. By the 1970s these variables, although still important factors, were no longer sure predictors of how Germans would vote. The SPD had begun to advance beyond its labor union support into urban Catholic, white-collar Protestant constituencies, just as the CDU was beginning to broaden its appeal in urban white-collar districts previously weak in CDU affiliation. On the whole, Catholicism and ruralism correlated positively with high CDU/CSU voting, whereas the SPD's success over the long term seemed to lie less with its working-class membership than with the broadening of its base in the middle class.[24]

---

[24]For treatments of the 1969, 1972, and 1976 federal elections, see "The West German Elections of 1969," *Comparative Politics* 1 (July 1970); David P. Conradt and Dwight Lambert, "Party System, Social Structure, and Competitive Polities in West Germany: An Ecological Analysis of the 1972 Federal Election," *Comparative Politics* 7 (October 1974); and Cerny, *Germany at the Polls.*

The most dramatic shift in postwar voting patterns was due to the changing character of the German middle class. The numbers of traditional middle-class voters—property owners and farmers—had dwindled and been replaced by a new middle class of civil servants and white-collar employees connected with the FRG's mushrooming service trades. Highly urbanized, younger, and less attached to traditional values, these voters were more responsive to newer issues centering on environmental matters, educational reform, and alternative lifestyles than to older economic issues. In the 1980s, many of these voters—especially those in districts with high concentrations of students, salaried workers, and civil servants—cast their votes in favor of the Greens, seriously cutting into traditional FDP strongholds. First-time voters and younger voters (18–44) cast their ballots disproportionately for the Greens.

These factors, combined with unprecedented high levels of unemployment, both in eastern and in western Germany, and a rising national debt due to the economic costs of reunification, seemed to prime the SPD for a triumphant return to power during the so-called *Superwahljahr* (super election year) of 1994. Ten key elections would take place between March 13 and October 16, 1994: the European parliament election, eight state (*Länder*) elections, and the Bundestag election. But thanks to some clever campaigning by the CDU/CSU, which emphasized the safe virtues of continuity and stability, as well as some miscues by the SPD, which made the monumental mistake of running on a platform of large-scale income redistribution, the inevitable was postponed. In the end, Kohl inched back into the chancellorship by a single vote. Thanks to the assistance of overhang seats, the CDU/CSU–FDP coalition found a renewed lease on life with a majority of ten seats in the thirteenth Bundestag.

The Kohl government had no reason to be self-satisfied. By this point, it was clear that the German public had developed an appetite for more dynamic leadership and would not long be satisfied with Kohl's weary tributes to a now fading past. Even business leaders were unhappy with the ruling coalition's economic policies. The answer was found in a charismatic new leader of the SPD, Gerhard Schröder, who in a stunning display of political acuity brought his party, in coalition with the Greens, back to power in the Bundestag elections of 1998. This was the first time in the FRG's history a sitting chancellor had lost his job as a result of a general election.

Looking back, there is no great mystery to Schröder's success. The new chancellor seemed to be everything for everybody, especially those in the mood for change. For Germans who had grown tired of Kohl's aging presence, Schröder seemed the epitome of youth: handsome, debonair, and excitingly fresh. More important, by cleverly modeling himself after the personal styles of other prominent left-centrist politicians on the world stage—Bill Clinton in the United States and Tony Blair in Britain—Schröder (referred to by some wits as "Clintonblair") was able to appeal to voters across the political spectrum. For unemployed workers and for easterners suffering under the burdens of unification, Schröder offered the Alliance for Jobs, a plan to create new jobs by fostering increased cooperation, in corporatist fashion, between trade unions and management. For the business community, he portrayed himself as a resurrected Ludwig Erhard (the father of Germany's "economic miracle"), someone who would be committed to the virtues of the social market economy but avoid the socialist temptations of the SPD's left wing. For the FRG's vibrant middle class, his promises of a *neue Mitte* (new middle) were expressly designed to combine postmodern values of environmental protection and equal rights with the assurance of social stability.[25]

Although the arithmetic that led to the governing coalition between the SPD and Greens was actually quite close, the major story of the 1998 election was what it signified for the electoral balance between the SPD and the CDU/CSU (see Table 4.10). The Social Democrats were the

[25]See Russell J. Dalton, "A Celebration of Democracy: The 1998 Bundestag Election," *German Politics and Society* 16(4) (Winter 1998), pp. 1–6; and Gerard Braunthal, "The 1998 German Election," *German Politics and Society* 17(1) (Spring 1999), pp. 32–54.

TABLE 4.10

FEDERAL ELECTION RESULTS, 1994, 1998 (PERCENTAGES) AND 2002 (SEATS)

	1994				1998				2002
Party	West	East	Total	Seats	West	East	Total	Seats	Seats
Christian Democrats	42.1	38.5	41.5	294	37.1	27.3	35.2	245	248
Free Democrats	7.7	3.5	6.9	47	7.0	3.3	6.2	43	47
Social Democrats	37.5	31.5	36.4	252	42.3	35.1	40.9	298	251
Greens	7.6	4.3	7.3	59	7.3	4.1	6.7	47	55
Party of Democratic Socialism	1.0	19.8	4.4	30	1.2	21.6	5.1	36	2
Other Parties	4.1	2.4	3.6	—	5.1	8.6	6.0	—	—
Total	100%	100%	100%	672	100%	100%	100%	669	603
Percent Voting	80.5	72.6	79.0		82.8	80.3	82.2		79.0

Source: Forschungsgruppe Wahlen; Russell J. Dalton, *A Celebration of Democracy: The 1998 Bundestag Election,* p. 4.

Note: Seats include 16 overhang-mandates in 1994 and 13 overhang-mandates in 1998. West Berlin is included within the West, and East Berlin is included in the East.

big winners, able to secure 40.9 percent of the popular vote (up from 36.4 percent in 1994 and their best outcome since 1980), thanks in part to a huge shift of 1.4 million voters away from the CDU. Significantly, nearly a third of these came from the ex-GDR. In turn, the CDU/CSU fell to 35.2 percent of the vote (a loss of 6.3 percent since 1994), and for only the second time in the history of the FRG was relegated to the status of the second-largest party in parliament.

POLICY-MAKING INSTITUTIONS

In this subsection we turn our attention to Germany's major policy-making institutions, its federal system, and its distinctive scheme of separated and divided powers. Upon their accession to the FRG in 1990, the eastern *Länder* brought their governmental systems into complete conformity with the Basic Law. Thus, unless otherwise indicated, the institutions, structures, and policy-making processes discussed here are applicable to all of Germany.

Germany's main legislative institutions are the popularly elected Bundestag (house of representatives) and the Bundesrat, the nonelected upper house of parliament, whose appointed delegates represent the *Länder* governments. The leading executive institutions are the chancellor and cabinet, collectively known as the federal government. The president, once a powerful head of state directly elected by the people, has been reduced to a figurehead akin to the British monarch. One of the most distinctive features of Germany's federal system is that the states are entrusted under the constitution with the administration of national law. This system, often dubbed *administrative federalism,* is a carryover from Germany's nineteenth-century origins. Finally, empowered to enforce the provisions of the Basic Law, the judiciary, at the top of which is the Federal Constitutional Court, serves as a check on the activities of the other branches of government.

The Federal President

The federal president is the FRG's highest-ranking public official, but he functions mainly as a ceremonial head of state, a vestigial reminder of the once thriving presidency under the emperor. Symbolically, he remains important as a spokesman for the nation, an attribute of the office that has been acted upon to differing degrees by holders of the position. Although the presidency is perceived as a nonpartisan office, its occupant is elected for a five-year term—under Article 54 of the Basic Law he may be reelected only once—by a federal convention composed of party representatives from national and state parliaments. The president is chosen as a result of bargaining between the coalition parties forming the majority in the convention. Yet despite the complexity of the process, the office has generally been filled by respected public officials who have won recognition for their fair-mindedness and ability to communicate across party lines. The office has served as a capstone to a successful career in politics.

In May 1999, Johannes Rau, the moderate Social Democratic and former candidate for chancellor, became the FRG's eighth president. He was preceded by Theodore Heuss (FDP, 1949–1959), Heinrich Lübke (CDU, 1959–1969), Gustav Heinemann (SPD, 1969–1974), Walter Scheel (FDP, 1974–1979), Karl Carstens (CDU, 1979–1984), Richard von Weizsäcker (CDU, 1984–1994), and Roman Herzog (CDU, 1994–1999). Until 1979, an incumbent president who was competent and prudent in the exercise of his authority could expect, if he wished, to be reelected to a second term. Some recent elections, however, have been largely an exercise in partisan politics. In 1979, the CDU forced the resignation of Walter Scheel as presidential candidate and elected its own candidate (Karl Carstens) by a slim majority of 26 votes. In 1994, there were three serious presidential candidates. Herzog won on the third ballot when the FDP switched its vote to the CDU candidate. In 1999, Rau was elected when Herzog decided not to stand for another term. In 2004, Horst Köhler, former head of the International Monetary Fund and CDU candidate, was elected, 604 to 589.

The president's powers include the appointment and dismissal of various public officials, including cabinet officials and military officers, and the pardoning of criminal offenders. His exercise of the pardoning power has occasionally caused a public uproar. This happened in 1989 when President Weizsäcker pardoned two imprisoned terrorists—female members of the terrorist Red Army Faction—after they had served 12 years of their prison terms and shown that they could reenter society as responsible citizens. The president's most common official duty, apart from receiving and visiting foreign heads of state, is to promulgate, with his signature, all federal laws.

In one respect, the president may be more than just a figurehead. Although it is disputed whether he can reject a statute on substantive constitutional grounds, presidents have done so on at least five occasions. A president's refusal to sign a properly enacted bill could conceivably bring about a constitutional crisis resulting in demands for his resignation or his impeachment. If the president resigns, dies, or is impeached—or is otherwise unable to perform his duties—the president of the Bundesrat, as the second highest official of the Federal Republic, assumes his powers. In their absence from the country, presidents have often requested the Bundesrat's president to serve as acting president.

Horst Köhler, President of Germany.

Born in 1943, Köhler studied economics and political science, and held various positions in the Ministries of Economics and Finance, including Deputy Minister of Finance. He served as President of the European Bank for Reconstruction and Development, and as Managing Director and Chairman of the International Monetary Fund. In May 2004 he was narrowly elected President of Germany.

The Federal Government

The Chancellor The Basic Law puts the chancellor in firm control of the federal government. He alone is responsible to parliament, whereas his ministers—that is, the members of his cabinet—whom he may hire and fire, are responsible only to him. Constitutionally charged under Article 65 to lay down the guidelines for national policy, he is chosen by a majority of the Bundestag and is usually the leader of the largest party in the governing coalition. Parliament is not empowered to dismiss the chancellor at will, however, as it was able to do in the Weimar Republic. Under the so-called constructive vote of no confidence, prescribed by Article 67 of the Basic Law, the Bundestag may dismiss a chancellor only when a majority of its members simultaneously elects his successor. The stabilizing effect of this provision has led many persons to label the FRG a "chancellor democracy."

The constructive vote of no confidence has succeeded only once, in 1982, when the Bundestag voted Helmut Schmidt out of office after the FDP's withdrawal from the coalition government. A new alliance between the FDP and the CDU/CSU elected Helmut Kohl as chancellor by a vote of 256 to 235, the first time in the FRG's history that a government had been replaced without an election.

Article 68 allows the chancellor to initiate a vote of confidence and to authorize him, if he loses the vote, to request the president to dissolve parliament and call for new elections. Brandt used this procedure in 1972, and Kohl used it again in 1983. Both chancellors planned to lose in the expectation that new elections would

---

REVIEW

4.1

THE BASIC LAW: SELECTED BASIC RIGHTS

ARTICLE 1

1. The dignity of man shall be inviolable. To respect and protect it shall be the duty of all state authority.

2. The German people therefore acknowledge inviolable and inalienable human rights as the basis of every community, of peace, and of justice in the world.

ARTICLE 2

1. Everyone shall have the right to the free development of his personality insofar as he does not violate the rights of others or offend against the constitutional order or the moral code.

2. Everyone shall have the right to life and to the inviolability of his person. The liberty of the individual shall be inviolable. These rights may be encroached upon pursuant to a law.

ARTICLE 3

1. All persons shall be equal before the law.

2. Men and women shall have equal rights. The state shall seek to ensure equal treatment of men and women and to remove existing disadvantages.

3. No one may be prejudiced or favored because of his sex, parentage, race, language, homeland and origin, faith, or religious or political opinions. Persons may not be discriminated against because of their disability.

ARTICLE 5

1. Everyone shall have the right freely to express and disseminate his opinion by speech, writing, and pictures and freely to inform himself from generally accessible sources…. There shall be no censorship.

increase their parliamentary majority and thus their hold on governmental power. In both instances the strategy worked, although some constitutional lawyers argued that these were cynical political moves that circumvented the intent and spirit of the Basic Law. They held that the constitution permits the dissolution of parliament in advance of its regular expiration date only when the chancellor actually loses its confidence or is unable to govern with his current majority. To deliberately contrive a vote of no confidence for the purpose of holding new elections trivializes the Basic Law in their view by undermining the principle of regular elections.

The Chancellor's Office   The most powerful instrument of executive leadership in the FGR is the chancellor's office. Originally a small secretariat serving the chancellor's personal needs, it has evolved into an agency of major political importance, even overshadowing the cabinet. It contains departments corresponding to the various federal ministries as well as a planning bureau, created in 1969, to engage in long-range social and economic planning. Its staff of about 500 persons keeps the chancellor informed of domestic and foreign affairs, assists him or her in setting policy guidelines, coordinates policy making among the federal ministries, and monitors the implementation of cabinet decisions.

The chancellor's office is headed by a chief of staff, usually an experienced public official and close personal advisor. The chief of staff is a person of immense power—his influence often exceeds that of federal ministers. Other chancellery advisors have obtained national prominence in their policy-making role. Two such persons were Egon Bahr, the principal architect of Brandt's *Ostpolitik,* and Wolfgang Schäuble, a principle figure in Kohl's reunification strategy and later his political rival.

The Cabinet   While prescribing a chancellor-led government, the Basic Law (Article 65) also envisions a high level of cabinet responsibility. In practice, however, the cabinet has not functioned as a true collegial body. First of all, the chancellor decides how much authority is to be accorded to each minister. Adenauer and Brandt, for example, virtually served as their own foreign ministers, as

The Social Democratic leader Gerhard Schröder became chancellor in 1998 with the promise of economic and political "renewal." He was reelected in 2002.

did Schmidt in certain areas of foreign policy. On the other hand, certain ministers achieve enormous prominence in their own right and occasionally overshadow the chancellor. Hans-Dietrich Genscher became the dominant figure in foreign affairs under Chancellor Kohl, sometimes to the point of orchestrating his own policy.

Furthermore, cabinet members are not all equal in rank (see Table 4.11). For example, the minister of finance—probably the cabinet's most powerful official in the field of domestic policy—has a qualified veto over proposals affecting public finances. His objection to such proposals can be overridden only by the vote of the chancellor, with whom he is ordinarily closely affiliated, and a majority of the cabinet. The ministers of justice and interior also have special powers of review over cabinet proposals impinging upon their jurisdiction.

In creating the cabinet, a chancellor is constrained by the demands of coalition politics and the interests of groups allied to and rivalries within his party. Often he is required to negotiate at length over the nature and number of ministries to be awarded the minor party in his coalition government. The FDP, the perennial minor party in German coalition governments until recently, has often threatened to withhold its votes for the chancellor (i.e., the head of the major party in the coalition) until it secures agreement on certain policy issues and is assured adequate representation in the cabinet. After the 1994 election, Chancellor Kohl not only had to ensure that the FDP was satisfied with its apportionment of cabinet posts; he was also required to achieve a measure of religious and geographic balance among the CDU's cabinet members, while including members from the eastern *Länder* and granting proportionate representation to Bavaria's CSU.

Parliamentary State Secretaries The office of parliamentary state secretary—to be distinguished from the permanent state secretaries of the various ministerial bureaucracies—was introduced in 1967. Parliamentary state secretaries are

TABLE 4.11

FEDERAL GOVERNMENT MINISTRIES, 2005

Cabinet Minister	Minister's Party
Minister of the Chancellery	SPD
Foreign Minister	Greens
Minister of the Interior	SPD
Minister of Justice	SPD
Minister of Finance	SPD
Minister of Economics and Technology	SPD
Minister of Consumer Protection, Nutrition, Agriculture, and Forestry	Greens
Minister of Labor and Social Affairs	SPD
Minister of Defense	SPD
Minister of Family, the Elderly, Women, and Youth	SPD
Minister of Health	SPD
Minister of Transport, Building, and Housing	SPD
Minister of the Environment, Protection of Nature, and Nuclear Safety	Greens
Minister of Education and Research	SPD
Minister of Economic Cooperation and Development	SPD
Minister of Culture and Media	Non-party

Seven ministers are women.

selected from among the more junior members of the Bundestag to help the ministries run their departments, defend their records in parliament, and maintain contact with the public. A new element in the Schmidt cabinet was the high number of former parliamentary state secretaries who were elevated to cabinet posts. The office is now widely recognized as a training ground for cabinet service by all the major parties.

The Bundestag: Legislative Branch

The Bundestag is the successor to the old imperial (1871–1918) and republican (1919–1933) Reichstag. In those regimes the legislative branch was politically, and in some respects constitutionally, subordinate to the executive establishment, just as elected representatives played second fiddle to professional civil servants. In contrast, as part of Germany's efforts to profit from the experiences of the past, the authors of the Basic Law elevated parliament to first rank among the FRG's governing institutions. Though commentators agree that parliament has fallen short of the founders' vision of a vigorously self-confident body in control of the executive, they agree that the Bundestag has evolved from the rather submissive body of the Adenauer era into an increasingly assertive agency of national policy making. Even in the event of a national emergency, which only it can declare, the Bundestag's authority remains largely intact, thereby ensuring that ultimate power will always reside in the hands of civilian leaders and the elected representatives of the people.

Power and Functions   While playing a role similar to that of the U.S. Congress, the Bundestag is structurally a very different institution. First of all, it is "the parliament of a parliamentary system of government" in that "it [also] determine[s] the political composition and tenure in office of the government."[26] Second, and by

the same token, the highest officials in the executive branch—that is, the chancellor and his ministers—are, at the same time, among the most important and influential members of the Bundestag. This symbiotic relationship between executive and legislative power is not at all like the U.S. notion of separation of powers. In the FRG, the idea of separation of powers is embodied largely in the role of the opposition *within* parliament. As in other parliamentary systems, such as Great Britain, the opposition's task is to call the government—and thus the executive—to account for its policies in the crucible of parliamentary inquiry and debate.

Parliament checks the executive by its power to review the national budget, to pass upon all bills introduced by the government, to hold hearings and investigations, and to confront the chancellor and his ministers in the legislative question hour, a device borrowed from British parliamentary practice. The screening of proposed legislation absorbs most of the Bundestag's time. By far, the largest number of bills are initiated by the government. For example, of the 800 bills received by the twelfth Bundestag (1990–1994), 407 were government bills, 297 originated in the Bundestag itself, and 96 were sent over by the Bundesrat. The government managed to pass 77 percent of the bills it introduced, as compared with a 16 and 7 percent success rate, respectively, for the Bundestag and Bundesrat. As these statistics show, the federal government dominates the law-making process.

Fraktionen *and Committees*   The most important groups in the Bundestag are the parliamentary parties, or *Fraktionen*. In practice, they control the Bundestag's organization and decision-making machinery. Although constitutionally regarded as "representatives of the whole people, not bound to instructions [from any group]," deputies who plan on advancing their legislative careers will not lightly oppose the policy decisions of the party hierarchy, for party unity and discipline are strongly embedded in the parliamentary party system. Party discipline, however, is exercised in only a small number of cases. Most bills—over 85 percent—are the product of group negotiation in which repre-

---

[26]Winfried Steffani, "Parties (Parliamentary Groups) and Committees in the *Bundestag*," in Uwe Thaysen, et al., *The U.S. Congress and the German Bundestag* (Boulder, CO: Westview Press, 1990), p. 273.

The Bundestag meets in Berlin.

sentatives of the federal government, the Bundestag, and the Bundesrat participate, and they are passed unanimously.

Each *Fraktion* divides itself topically into working groups or councils, which parallel the Bundestag's committee structure and serve as instruments for crystallizing party policy and developing the expertise of deputies. Indeed, the deputy who does his homework in the party group to which he is assigned—showing leadership, skill, forensic ability, and mastery of subject matter—often winds up as an influential member of a corresponding legislative committee and eventually a parliamentary state secretary. The Bundestag also has a differentiated committee system, including standing, investigating, and special committees. Of these, the 23 standing committees are the most important. Comparable to the committees of the U.S. Congress, they and their numerous subcommittees are parliament's workhorses. In the Bundestag, however, committee chairs are shared by all the *Fraktionen* in proportion to their strength in the chamber as a whole and are allocated on the basis of expertise instead of seniority.

Members of Parliament   Typically, having studied law, political science, or economics, members of parliament begin their careers in the youth branch of a political party, frequently assisting established politicians. After fulfilling an apprenticeship in the party apparatus or, as is often the case, in a trade, farm, or labor organization closely linked to their party, they are then, in their late 30s, elected to parliament. They remain there for about 16 years, only to resign in their mid-50s to draw a comfortable pension and to enter the employment of an organized interest group. The careerism and security inherent in this system of political recruitment are not calculated to staff parliament with "movers and shakers," and often to the consternation of reformers insulate deputies against new and evolving trends in society.

Given these circumstances, it is perhaps predictable that not all groups are equally represented in parliament. Yet the Bundestag has made some progress over the past couple of decades in addressing this problem. By the 1980s, women represented about 15 percent of the membership, more than double the number elected in the 1970s. In the Bundestag of 1998, this figure jumped to 30.9 percent, the highest ever. (The PDS and the Greens had more women than men in their delegations.) Of the 207 women elected to the fourteenth Bundestag, 35.2 and 18.4 percent belonged, respectively, to the SPD and CDU/CSU. In 2005, 197 women were members.

The Law-Making Process

Bills may be introduced by any member of the Bundestag or by the Bundesrat. As indicated earlier, however, the overwhelming majority of legislative bills originates with the federal government. A bill sponsored by the latter is first submitted to the Bundesrat, which is required to act on the bill within six weeks. If there are any changes, the Bundesrat must return the bill to the cabinet for its approval or disapproval. (Bills originating in the Bundesrat are submitted to the Bundestag by the cabinet after the latter has expressed its opinion on the bill.) The bill is then submitted to the Bundestag, where it is given a first reading. From there it is assigned to the proper committee. If it survives this stage, together with a second and third reading, it is transmitted to the Bundesrat. If the Bundesrat amends the bill, it may be sent to a joint conference committee for mediation. Any changes by the committee again require the Bundestag's approval of the entire bill. The Bundesrat, however, has a suspensive veto over ordinary legislation and an absolute veto over legislation involving the *Länder*—but any such veto can be overridden by the Bundestag. After final approval, a bill is countersigned by the chancellor or appropriate federal minister and then signed by the federal president, whereupon it is promulgated as law in the *Federal Law Gazette.*

The chancellor, federal and *Land* ministries, and representatives of organized interest groups are the major actors in the law-making process.

They work closely with the *Fraktionen* in hammering out legislative policy, though committees play a critical role in filtering legislation for final passage. So successful are the committees in the performance of this role that few bills, once reported out of committee, are the subject of amendment or even debate from the floor. The intense plenary debates in 1979 on energy policy and in 1996 on cutting social benefits—debates stretching over several days—are exceptions to the customary practice of securing broad interparty agreement on most bills that become law.

Federalism and Bureaucracy

Like the United States, Germany divides power constitutionally between national and state governments. This structure represents a major check on central power. Federalism is in fact one of the unamendable principles of the Basic Law. The 16 *Länder* consist of 13 territorial states and the three city-states of Berlin, Bremen, and Hamburg. Each *Land,* like the national government, has its own constitution based on principles of republican and democratic government. Each has a parliamentary system. A minister president—lord mayor in the city-states—responsible to a one-house popularly elected legislature is the head of government in the territorial states. Historically, however, German federalism differs from the U.S. brand. The crucial distinction is that in the United States both federal and state governments exercise a full range of separate legislative and administrative functions, whereas German federalism confers the bulk of legislative powers upon the national government, with the *Länder* being mainly responsible for the administration of both federal and state laws.

Although federalism has cultural roots in the German past, the boundaries of the *Länder* were drawn without much reference to their ancestral ties. Only Bavaria, Saxony, and Thuringia survived the war with their pre-1945 boundaries relatively intact. In 1952, however, in an attempt to cement its authority, the GDR abolished the *Länder* and replaced them with 14 administrative districts under the control of the central government. These *Länder* were reestablished in July 1990 as one of the conditions of reunification. The *Länder* now range in population from 680,000 in Bremen to 17.3 million in North-Rhine Westphalia, more than eastern Germany's entire population. They also differ vastly in territorial size: excluding the small city-states, they range from Saarland with 2,570 sq km to Bavaria with 70,554 sq km. The largest and richest states, measured in terms of population and geography, are in the west. The eastern *Länder,* by contrast, are relatively smaller and much poorer.

This imbalance between the eastern and western *Länder* has revived proposals to redraw state lines for the purpose of creating larger and more integrated political and economic units. The Basic Law permits the restructuring of the *Länder* so long as the system as a whole remains federal in design. Under the terms of the Basic Law (Article 29), any federal law proposing a state boundary change must be approved by the Bundesrat, and subsequently ratified by referendum in the affected *Länder.* This procedure was first used in 1952 when the states of Baden, Württemberg, and Württemberg-Hohenzollern were consolidated into the single state of Baden-Württemberg. The next change, considered nearly four decades later, was Berlin's incorporation into Brandenburg, but this was rejected by voters.

One possible solution to the enormous disparity among the states in territory and population would be a merger based on the reorganized council of Germany's central bank (Bundesbank). Instead of giving each *Land* a vote on the Bundesbank Council, the system was changed in 1992 to accord representation to nine economically integrated regions that were defined by existing state boundaries but relatively balanced in population and territory. The nine regions consist of Schleswig-Holstein and Mecklenburg-Pomerania; Berlin and Brandenburg; Bremen, Lower Saxony, and Saxony-Anhalt; North Rhine-Westfalia; Hesse; Thuringia and Saxony; Rhineland-Palatinate and Saarland; Bavaria; and Baden-Württemberg. Any such fundamental change in *Land* boundaries, however, would almost surely lack the required popular support

and face resistance by political and economic interests favored by the current system.

The Bundesrat

The Bundesrat, the mainstay of German federalism, was designed to safeguard the vital interests of the *Länder* (see Table 4.12). But it is not a second chamber like the U.S. Senate. First, its powers are not equal to those of the Bundestag; second, its 69 votes are cast by officials who serve at the pleasure of the *Länder.* Thus each *Land* delegation votes as a unit and in accordance with the instructions of its government. How a delegation—or the person appointed to represent the state—votes often depends on the party composition of the *Land* cabinet. Nearly all seats in the Bundesrat are occupied by *Land* minister presidents or their delegates.

To accommodate the interests of the eastern *Länder,* the Unity Treaty amended Article 51 of the Basic Law, changing the allocation of seats in the Bundesrat. As before, each state is entitled to at least three votes, but now states with a population of more than 2 million are entitled to four votes, those with more than 6 million receive five votes, and those with more than 7 million receive six votes. (In the past, the largest states had five votes.) This system favors the smaller states. The five largest states, with two-thirds of the population, have 29 votes in the Bundesrat; the remaining states, with one-third of the population, have 40 votes.

The Bundesrat's consent is required for all federal legislation affecting the administrative, financial, and territorial interests of the *Länder.* With respect to other legislation, it has a suspensive veto, as noted earlier. If the Bundesrat objects to a bill by a majority vote, the Bundestag may override by a majority vote; if the former is by two-thirds, the vote to override must also be two-thirds. Additionally, the Bundesrat is authorized to approve all federal action enforcing national law in the *Länder,* to participate in major legislative decisions taken during a national emergency, and to elect half of the members of the Federal Constitutional Court. This last prerogative is important, for the Bundesrat has a

TABLE 4.12

THE BUNDESRAT, SEPTEMBER 30, 2000

Land	Votes	Ruling Coalition	Population (millions)
Baden-Württemberg	6	CDU-FDP	10.51
Bavaria	6	CSU	12.21
Berlin	4	SPD–Alliance 90/Greens	3.38
Brandenburg	4	SPD-CDU	2.60
Bremen	3	SPD-CDU	0.66
Hamburg	3	SPD-PRO-FDP	1.71
Hesse	5	CDU-FDP	6.06
Mecklenburg-W. Pomerania	3	SPD-PDS	1.78
Lower Saxony	6	SPD	7.92
N. Rhine Westphalia	6	SPD–Alliance 90/Greens	18.01
Rhineland-Palatinate	4	SPD-FDP	4.03
Saarland	3	CDU	1.07
Saxony	4	CDU	4.43
Saxony-Anhalt	4	SPD	2.62
Schleswig-Holstein	4	SPD–Alliance 90/Greens	2.79
Thuringia	4	CDU	2.44

record of electing judges with strong federalist leanings, thus giving to the upper house an indirect influence in constitutional cases involving the interpretation of federal laws and ordinances.[27]

An Emerging Instrument of Opposition

In spite of its considerable powers, the Bundesrat largely functioned during its first 20 years in the shadow of the Bundestag, ratifying the latter's policies and those of the government's ruling party or coalition. Its leaders tended to view the Bundesrat as a nonpartisan chamber concerned exclusively with the merits of proposed legislation, an image reinforced by the dominant role of bureaucratic officials in its proceedings.

[27]See Donald P. Kommers, *Judicial Politics in West Germany* (Beverly Hills, CA: Sage, 1976), pp. 128–144.

Since 1969, however, the Bundesrat has risen in political importance and popular awareness. Until then the parties dominating the lower house also controlled the upper chamber. Owing to the distribution of power among the parties within the states, however, the Christian Democrats—the party out of power in the government—enjoyed a 21–20 voting edge in the Bundesrat between 1969 and 1975—an advantage that swelled to 11 votes by 1979—leading to sharp confrontations with the governing parties in the Bundestag.

In the 1990s, however, the tables were turned. The ruling CDU/CSU–FDP coalition in the Bundestag confronted a Bundesrat overwhelmingly controlled by SPD-led coalitions in the *Länder*. Given that all financial legislation and nearly all legislation affecting the administration of federal law require the Bundesrat's consent, this house—contrary to the expectations of the Basic Law's founders—has evolved into a body virtually coequal with the Bundestag. In recent legislation periods, between 50 and 60 percent of all bills passed by the Bundestag required the Bundesrat's consent. The clash between the CDU/CSU-led government coalition was most evident in the twelfth Bundestag. No fewer than 85 government bills had to be taken up by the Mediation Committee, as opposed to 13 in the eleventh and 6 in the tenth Bundestag. Under these circumstances, important policy initiatives cannot be passed into law without considerable give-and-take by the two parliamentary bodies and by the major parties.

The Legal System and the Judiciary

Germany's Legal Tradition and the **Rechtsstaat**   The *Rechtsstaat* or "law state" is a key concept in the German legal order.[28] All just states are based on law, of course, but in its original form the German *Rechtsstaat* placed extraordinary emphasis upon legality. Germans viewed the state as a neutral entity entrusted with the resolution of public issues in accordance with objective standards of law, unsullied by the play of selfish interests or the machinations of political parties. The sovereign state—the axis of the law state—was the guarantor of freedom and equality, just as rights and obligations arose from membership in the state. Liberty did not precede law; rather, law defined it, and the judiciary, staffed by a professional class of impartial and apolitical civil servants loyal to the state, existed to enforce the law as written.

Under the Basic Law the *Rechtsstaat* remains a vital principle of German constitutionalism, but not in its earlier nineteenth-century sense. The *law state* would henceforth be limited by constitutionally guaranteed individual rights enforced by the judiciary, just as it would be moderated by the humanity implicit in the constitutional notion of *Sozialstaat* (freely translated, a *socially conscious state*). In legal theory the sovereign is no longer

---

[28]This subsection on law and the courts draws heavily from Donald P. Kommers, *The Constitutional Jurisprudence of the Federal Republic of Germany,* 2nd ed. (Durham, NC: Duke University Press, 1996).

supreme. Article 20 reads: "All state authority emanates from the people," and further, "Legislation shall be subject to the constitutional order; the executive and the judiciary shall be bound by law *and justice*" (italics added). Finally, Article 20 contains this remarkable provision: "All Germans shall have the right to resist any person or persons seeking to abolish [the] constitutional order should no other remedy be possible."

The Court System   Germany has a uniform and integrated judicial system. All lower and intermediate courts of appeal are state courts, whereas all courts of final appeal are federal tribunal courts. Federal law specifies the structure of state courts, but their administration and staffing, including the training of judges, is under the control of the *Länder.* The trademarks of the German judiciary are collegiality and specialization. Except for courts of minor jurisdiction, all tribunals are multijudge courts. Most operate in panels of three. In addition to the regular courts, which handle ordinary civil and criminal cases, there are separate judicial hierarchies consisting of labor, administrative, social, finance, and constitutional courts. The federal courts, as shown in Table 4.13, cap these hierarchies.

Justice in the FRG is carried out by more than 20,000 judges, nearly 80 percent of whom serve on the regular courts of ordinary civil and criminal jurisdiction. About one-quarter of these sit on the courts of specialized jurisdiction, while the high federal courts consist of under 500 judges. In addition to these legal professionals, the German courts have more than 4,000 public prosecutors. As might be expected of a *Rechtsstaat,* even the more than 50,000 attorneys practicing law in the FRG are regarded as officers of the courts.

The Judges   The training and professional standing of German judges varies from that of their peers in the United States and Britain. In the United States, for example, judgeships are usually awarded to lawyers in their middle years following successful private practice or experience in public office. In Germany, by contrast, lateral mobility of this kind is rare among legal professionals. After six years of study, which

TABLE 4.13

COURTS OF THE FEDERATION AND THE *LÄNDER*

Jurisdiction	Courts of the Federation	Courts of the Länder
Constitutional	Federal Constitutional Court	13 constitutional courts
Ordinary	Federal Court of Justice	25 higher regional courts; 116 regional courts; 717 local courts
Labor	Federal Labor Court	19 higher labor courts; 124 labor courts
Administrative	Federal Administrative Court	16 higher administrative courts; 52 administrative courts
Social	Federal Social Court	16 higher social courts; 69 social courts
Finance	Federal Finance Court	19 finance courts

Source: Wolfgang Heyde, *Justice and the Law in the Federal Republic of Germany* (Heidelberg: C. F. Müller Juristischer Verlag, 1994), p. 9.

includes practical training in various administrative and judicial capacities, law graduates must make their choice of a legal career. Those deciding to become judges go through still another three-year probationary period. Upon the successful completion of this training, they receive a judgeship with lifetime tenure and security. Judges can expect to ascend slowly in the hierarchy of the judicial establishment if they meet with the approval of the *Land* justice ministry; if they are lucky and know the right persons in Berlin, they may end their careers in one of the high federal courts.

The civil service orientation of the judiciary tends to be reinforced by the narrow social base from which judges, particularly those appointed by the *Länder,* are recruited. Almost half are the sons and daughters of parents who have spent their lives in the civil service. Federal judges tend to be more diversified in social background and occupational experience, largely because of the method by which they are selected. They are chosen by a committee of electors composed of 11 members of the Bundestag together with those *Land* and federal ministries whose authority is similar to the federal court to which a judge is to be named. This mechanism allows interest groups, political parties, state and federal agencies, and the public to participate in the selection process, producing a federal bench somewhat less characterized by professional inbreeding and political conservatism than the state judiciary.

The Federal Constitutional Court The Federal Constitutional Court with its sweeping powers of judicial review is only as old as the Basic Law. To the surprise of many observers, this tribunal has developed into an institution of major policy-making importance. Judicial review was a relatively new departure in German constitutional history. Postwar German leaders were of the opinion that, in the light of Germany's authoritarian and totalitarian past, traditional parliamentary and judicial institutions were insufficient to safeguard the new liberal democratic order. They created a national constitutional tribunal, as well as equivalents at the *Land* level, to supervise the judiciary's interpretation of constitutional norms, to enforce a consistent reading of the constitution on the other branches of government, to resolve conflicts between branches and levels of government, and to protect the basic liberties of German citizens. Thus the old positivist belief separating the realm of law from the realm of politics was abandoned, together with the idea that justice could automatically be achieved through the mechanical application of general laws duly enacted by the legislature.

Structurally, the Federal Constitutional Court is divided into two chambers, called senates, each of which is composed of eight justices chosen for single 12-year terms. Half of the justices are chosen by the Bundestag's 12-member judicial selection committee and the other half by the Bundesrat. A two-thirds vote is required in both electoral organs. This method of selection, together with the requirement that the Bundestag and Bundesrat alternate in the selection of the court's president and vice president, usually means that judicial appointments are the subject of intensive bargaining among the parliamentary parties. No one party has been strong enough to make appointments over the objections of the other parties. Thus the court's membership has reflected fairly well the balance of forces in parliament as a whole.

Judicial Review in Operation   The Constitutional Court's jurisdiction includes 14 categories of disputes, nearly all of which the Basic Law prescribes. The Basic Law authorizes both judges and legislators, as well as state governments, to petition the court directly. Judges may initiate a "concrete" judicial review proceeding by asking the court to rule on a constitutional question arising out of a pending case if in their view the law under which a case has arisen is of doubtful validity under the Basic Law. On the other hand, a state government or one-third of the members of the Bundestag may initiate an "abstract" proceeding by petitioning the court to review the constitutionality of a statute. Cases on abstract review tend to draw the judges directly into the arena of political conflict, prompting its harshest critics to deplore what they perceive as the "judicialization" of politics.

Constitutional complaints account for about 95 percent—an average of 5,000 per year—of all cases coming to the court. These cases relate to fundamental rights and freedoms guaranteed by the Basic Law. To encourage Germans to view the constitution as the source of their rights and freedoms, the Basic Law (Article 93 [13]) authorizes ordinary citizens to file complaints with the Federal Constitutional Court in the event that their basic rights have been violated by the state. Such an action involves neither court costs nor even the participation of legal counsel, an ideal situation in which "Hans Everyman" can bring his woes to the attention of the country's highest tribunal.

The Constitutional Court's Impact   Public opinion polls continue to show the high regard German citizens have for the Constitutional Court. In this respect, it outranks all other institutions in the nation's public life, including the civil service and the churches. When the court speaks, Germany's "attentive public" listens; what people hear is often an outspoken tribunal reminding them of their constitutional values, their political morality, and their ethical goals as a nation. This attentiveness is by no means surprising, since the court's landmark cases have involved some of the issues most pressing to the ongoing health of Germany democracy. These have included decisions outlawing extremist parties, overturning certain campaign-finance legislation, prohibiting the display of crucifixes in public school classrooms, and declaring unconstitutional a liberal abortion law.

Thinking Critically

1. How have postwar Germany's laws and institutions contributed to its distinctive record of political continuity and social stability?
2. On balance, have splinter parties served or hindered the cause of building democracy in Germany? Why might these parties and citizen initiatives be important to the good health of any democratic system?
3. Compared to other democracies, how do established political parties play a special role in German politics?
4. What institutional factors reinforce norms of consensus and incrementalism in the FRG? Why do these factors sometimes lead to frustration among German citizens?
5. How does the German electoral system represent an ingenious way of representing interests across the political spectrum?
6. What factors have helped to ensure the routine circulation of elites in the FRG?

KEY TERMS

abstract judicial review *(241)*
Alliance for Jobs *(228)*
Bundesrat *(237)*
chancellor democracy *(231)*
citizen initiatives *(220)*
constructive vote of no confidence *(231)*
Fraktion (234)

Grand Coalition *(225)*
Greens *(215)*
Neue Mitte (228)
new middle class *(228)*
overhang votes *(222)*
PDS *(215)*
Realos (215)
Rechtsstaat (239)
second ballot *(222)*
semisovereign state *(219)*

*F*URTHER READINGS

Baker, Kendall, Russell J. Dalton, and Kai Hildebrand. *Germany Transformed: Political Culture and the New Politics* (Cambridge, MA: Harvard University Press, 1981).

Blair, Philip M. *Federalism and Judicial Review in West Germany* (Oxford: Clarendon Press, 1981).

Braunthal, Gerard. *The German Social Democrats since 1969,* 2nd ed. (Boulder, CO: Westview Press, 1994).

Burkett, Tony. *Parties and Elections in West Germany* (New York: St. Martin's, 1975).

Cerny, Karl H. *Germany at the Polls: The Bundestag Elections of the 1980s* (Durham, NC: Duke University Press, 1990).

Clemens, Clay. *Reluctant Realists: The Christian Democrats and West German Ostpolitik* (Durham, NC: Duke University Press, 1989).

Dalton, Russell J. *Germans Divided: The 1994 Bundestagswahl and the Evolution of the German Party System* (Oxford: Berg Publishers, 1996).

Doering, Herbert, and Gordon Smith. *Party Government and Political Culture in Western Germany* (New York: St. Martin's, 1982).

Dyson, Kenneth H. F. *Party, State and Bureaucracy in Western Germany* (Beverly Hills, CA: Sage Publications, 1977).

Gunlicks, Arthur B. *The Länder and German Federalism* (Manchester: Manchester University Press, 2003).

Heyde, Wolfgang. *Justice and Law in the Federal Republic of Germany* (Heidelberg: C. F. Müller Juristischer Verlag, 1994).

Jesse, Eckhard. *Elections: The Federal Republic of Germany* (Oxford: Berg Publishers, 1990).

Kommers, Donald P. *The Constitutional Jurisprudence of the Federal Republic of Germany* (Durham: Duke University Press, 1997).

Kommers, Donald P. *The Federal Constitutional Court* (Washington, DC: American Institute for Contemporary German Studies, 1994).

Langguth, Gerd. *The Green Factor in West German Politics* (Boulder, CO: Westview Press, 1986).

Loewenberg, Gerhard. *Parliament in the German Political System* (Ithaca, NY: Cornell University Press, 1966).

Muller, Jan-Werner, ed. *German Ideologies since 1945: Studies in the Political Thought and Culture of the Bonn Republic* (London: Palgrave Macmillan, 2003).

Padgett, Stephen, and Tony Burkett. *Political Parties and Elections in West Germany* (New York: St. Martin's, 1986).

Padgett, Stephen, and Thomas Saalfeld, eds. *Bundestagswahl 1998: End of an Era?* (Portland: Frank Cass, 2000).

Spath, Franz. *The Federal Presidency* (Washington, DC: American Institute for Contemporary German Studies, 1996).

Umbach, Maiken, ed. *Germany Federalism: Past, Present, Future* (New York: Palgrave, 2002).

C. PUBLIC POLICY

CIVIL LIBERTIES: AN ORDERING OF CONSTITUTIONAL VALUES

To understand the distinctive culture of public policy making in the FRG, there is no better place to start than with its constitution. The first part of the Basic Law (Articles 1 to 19) is a charter of fundamental rights and an affirmation of human personhood. It is rooted in the natural law thesis that certain liberties of the individual are antecedent to organized society and beyond the reach of governmental power. As interpreted by the Federal Constitutional Court, the Basic Law has established a value-oriented order based on human dignity. Article 1 is no idle declaration. As the Basic Law's "highest legal value," the idea of human dignity—a concept that was clearly lacking in German politics during the period of Nazi dictatorship—has been employed by the Constitutional Court as the defining standard by which to measure the legitimacy of state actions as well as the uses of individual liberty.

Apart from the freedoms guaranteed by Articles 1, 2, 3, and 5, the Basic Law's fundamental rights include the freedoms of religion (Article 4), assembly (Article 8), association (Article 9), privacy (Articles 10 and 13), and movement (Article 11), together with the right to property (Article 14), the right to choose a trade or occupation (Article 12), and the right to refuse military service for reasons of conscience (Article 12a). Additionally, criminal defendants are accorded most of the rights and privileges normally associated with the Anglo-American notion of due process of law.

These rights, however, have been proclaimed with an important German twist—that is, they are to be exercised responsibly and used to foster the growth of human dignity within the framework of the political and moral order ordained by the Basic Law. In this sense, Article 2 is a paradigm of Germany's special approach to basic rights. While individual liberty and personal autonomy are jealously guarded values of the legal order, they are also constrained by the equally important values of political order and social morality. Thus, the right to develop one's personality is limited by the moral code, just as the right to freedom of speech is limited by the inviolability of personal honor. As the Constitutional Court noted in a famous case on communications privacy: "The concept of man in the Basic Law is not that of an isolated, sovereign individual: rather, the Basic Law has decided in favor of a relationship between individual and community in the sense of a person's dependence on and commitment to the community, without infringing upon a person's individual value."[29]

With regard to the polity as a whole, the Basic Law creates what the Constitutional Court refers to repeatedly as a "militant democracy." This means that certain forms of speech and behavior

---

[29]Walter F. Murphy and Joseph Tanenhaus, *Comparative Constitutional Law* (New York: St. Martin's, 1977), p. 660.

A CLOSER LOOK 4.5

ARTICLE 65 OF THE BASIC LAW—THE CHANCELLOR

The Federal Chancellor shall determine, and be responsible for, the general policy guidelines. Within the limits set by these guidelines, each Federal Minister shall conduct the affairs of his department autonomously and on his own responsibility. The Federal Government shall decide on differences of opinion between Federal Ministers. The Federal Chancellor shall conduct the affairs of the Federal Government in accordance with rules of procedure adopted by it and approved by the Federal President.

described as anticonstitutional—activities that would probably be protected under prevailing U.S. constitutional doctrine—may be legally punished. The Basic Law predicates political freedom on the acceptance of certain principles of political obligation. Freedom of association, for instance, is guaranteed, but associations "the purposes or activities of which … are directed against the constitutional order" are prohibited (Article 9). Similarly, political parties "whose aims … seek to impair or abolish the free democratic basic order" may be declared unconstitutional (Article 21). These provisions are not accidental. They spring from the conviction of the FRG's founders, who drafted the Basic Law in the aftermath of Weimar's collapse and Hitler's totalitarianism, that a democracy cannot be an unarmed society but has the right—so long as the rule of law is preserved—to dissolve organizations and prohibit activities aimed at the destruction of republican government.

ASYLUM AND CITIZENSHIP

A portrait of the FRG's civil liberties record, like that of other advanced constitutional democracies, would reveal much light but also some shadows. At various points during the 1990s, the shadows included attacks on asylum seekers and foreign residents by youthful gangs and other acts of aggressive nationalism. Western observers have applauded the government for cracking down on the most xenophobic of these groups, but they also find mixed signals about the FRG's commitment to absorbing the immigrant population into the mainstream of society. As examples of this lack of commitment, they point to German policies on asylum and citizenship.

Until 1993, Article 16 (2) of the Basic Law granted the right of asylum to all persons persecuted on political grounds, a powerful expression of the FRG's constitutional morality in the light of Germany's Nazi past. The policy behind Article 16 (2) was extremely generous. Any person arriving on German soil who claimed asylum on the ground of a well-founded fear of political persecution could have that claim adjudicated, during which time the claimant would be entitled to free housing and other benefits under German law.

In the early 1990s, however, following the influx of over a million asylum seekers, parliament introduced a constitutional amendment to limit the right of asylum. The ensuing debate took place as extreme right-wing parties won seats in a number of *Land* parliaments by pandering to popular antiforeign sentiments. However, mainstream politicians as well were concerned about the strain asylum seekers were placing on the nation's welfare system and the presumed threat to the security of job-seeking Germans in the face of rising unemployment. In the end, parliament reincorporated the right to asylum into the first paragraph of a new Article 16a, but added qualifying paragraphs that some critics thought would seriously vitiate that right.

According to the new article, which parliament ratified in June 1993, aliens may not claim a right to asylum if parliament has designated their country of origin as safe from political persecution (Article 16a [3]). In addition, aliens may not claim a right to asylum if they come to Germany overland from a member state of the European Union or from a third country statutorily defined as politically safe (Article 16a [2]). If such persons fail to seek asylum in the safe country through which they pass en route to Germany—by land or by air—they forfeit their right to apply for asylum in Germany and thus can be summarily turned back at the border or at an international airport. Finally, aliens claiming asylum from a country of origin that has been declared safe will not have their asylum claims heard unless they can overcome the presumption that they will not suffer political persecution or inhumane treatment upon their return.

Article 16a and its implementing statutes had their intended effect, reducing asylum applications to a fraction of their previous number. However, unsuccessful asylum seekers from Ghana, Iran, Iraq, and Togo challenged the constitutionality of the new policy's most controversial features—i.e., parliament's definition of safe countries of origin, the "third state rule," and the possibility of instant deportation at German airports. In a 234-page opinion handed down on May 14, 1996, the Constitutional Court sustained the validity of each of these practices, claiming that they did not violate the Basic Law's guarantee of political asylum in that the petitioners were afforded the opportunity for asylum in secure third countries.

The asylum controversy of the 1990s was part of a larger debate over immigration and citizenship policy. The influx of refugees and the presence of millions of permanent foreign residents and their families, many of whom had lived and worked in Germany for decades, triggered demands to make it easier for resident aliens to acquire citizenship. Under the Nationality Act of 1913, which remains the law today, citizenship is based on the principle of *jus sanguinis* (i.e., by right of blood or descent rather than by *jus soli* or place of birth). Because of this policy, it has been easier for non-German-speaking ethnic Germans from Eastern Europe to acquire German citizen-

ship than for a third-generation resident alien who is fluent in the language and thoroughly privy to German ways but whose ancestors came from Turkey.

In reality, the FRG is a country of immigrants. Foreign residents make up 12 percent of the population, more than in any other European nation (see Figure 4.2). In some large cities, foreign residents exceed one-fourth of the total population. Yet these residents are not permitted to vote or run for public office, they experience discrimination in housing and education, and they are subject to deportation on specified legal grounds. Despite the de facto presence of a large immigrant population and the long-term need for such residents in light of the low native

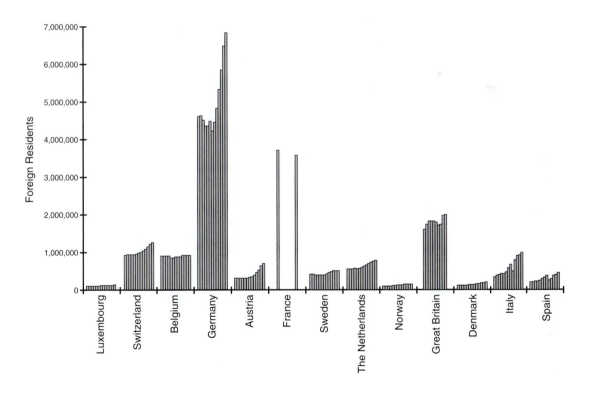

Figure 4.2 FOREIGN RESIDENTS IN SELECT EUROPEAN STATES, 1981–1996

Source: Adapted from "Statistiken zur Migration und Integration von Migranten," *http://www. uni-bamberg.de/~ba6ef3/ds118a_d.htm.*

birthrate,[30] the FRG continues to understand itself in ethnocultural terms, one reason for Germany's low rate of naturalization.

In 1999, the Schröder government successfully passed legislation to ease the terms under which some foreign residents—especially German-born citizens—can obtain citizenship, and the waiting time for many applicants has been shortened. However, in the wake of recent upheavals in the Balkans and elsewhere in Eastern Europe, even the most liberally minded Social Democrats have had to admit that the FRG cannot afford to meet the needs of all immigrants who wish to cross its borders. Some, like the outspoken minister of the interior and former Green, Otto Schily, have gone so far as to advocate draconian measures for keeping additional foreigners out.

PUBLIC ADMINISTRATION: DECENTRALIZED FEDERALISM

There are five levels of public administration in Germany, organized mainly on a spatial or territorial basis.[31] The first is the national level. But here (except for those few functions administered directly by the national government), the various ministries are engaged mainly in formulating general policy. Under Article 65 of the Basic Law, each federal minister is in complete control of his or her department, though it must be run within the limits of the chancellor's policy guidelines. The command hierarchy includes the federal minister, the parliamentary state secretary (the ministry's chief spokesperson in the Bundestag), and the permanent state secretary—a career civil servant who, along with aides, plays a significant rule in the policy-making process. Finally, undersecretaries head the major departments of each

ministry, which in turn are divided into sections, offices, or bureaus.

The ministries work out their programs in accordance with the guidelines and political predispositions of their top executives. Yet the ministries do not shape policy by issuing central directives from on high any more than they shape it from the bottom up on the basis of purely professional considerations. The planning units of the various ministries weave their program recommendations out of clientele demands, the expertise of bureaucrats, and the politics of top executives. In general, policy planning is more of an interactive process, following what some scholars have described as a "dialogue model" of policy making,[32] involving a good deal of discussion and bargaining within and among bureaucracies.

Land governments are the next level of administration. In addition to administering federal law, they enact laws in certain areas within the framework of national policy guidelines and in areas of their exclusive jurisdiction. Public policies at the *Land* level are carried out by *Land* ministries, various functional *Land* agencies, and several self-governing corporations. The last three levels of administration are the administrative district, counties and county-free independent cities, and municipalities. The administrative district, found in the six larger *Länder,* "is a general purpose regional *Land* institution of administration."[33] The county, at the lowest level of *Land* administration, carries out functions delegated to it by state governments. Finally, municipalities or associations of local governments, whose independence is guaranteed by the Basic Law, are responsible, within the framework of *Land* law, for the provision of local public services.

SOCIAL AND ECONOMIC POLICY

Fiscal Policy

The fiscal articles of the Basic Law (Articles 104a through Article 115l) mandate a system of rev-

---

[30]See Rainer Münz and Ralf E. Urich, "Depopulation after Unification? Population Prospects for East Germany, 1990–2010," *German Politics and Society* 13 (1995), p. 1–48.
[31]Arthur B. Gunlicks, "Administrative Centralization in the Making and Remaking of Modern Germany," *Review of Politics* 46 (1984), pp. 336–340.

[32]Ibid., p. 100.
[33]Gunlicks, p. 336.

enue sharing among the federation, *Länder,* and local governments, the administration of which requires close cooperation among levels of government. Total tax revenue in 1993 amounted to DM 748.8 billion, of which federal and state shares were each 42.5 percent and that of municipalities 15 percent. The federal government derives its tax revenues mainly from corporate and personal income taxes, the value-added tax, the turnover tax on imports, and selected excise taxes. The main source of *Land* revenue is from taxes on property, automobiles, beer, and inheritance, whereas local governments depend primarily on real estate and business taxes. In addition, *Land* and local governments draw a portion of their tax revenue from income, turnover, and value-added taxes.

The goal of German fiscal policy is to bring about a "unity of living standards" in the various *Länder* and throughout the FRG. This is the reason for the detailed revenue-sharing provisions of the Basic Law. Income, corporate, and turnover taxes are among the tax receipts shared between levels of government. Federal and state governments have an equal claim to these funds after local governments have received their share. In addition, federal and state governments are constitutionally bound to help each other financially. Under so-called vertical equalization procedures, the federal government redistributes a given proportion of its revenues to the poorer states, just as equivalent horizontal procedures require the wealthier states to share a portion of their revenues with poorer *Länder.*

The new eastern *Länder* did not participate in the revenue-sharing scheme until 1995. The Unity Treaty exempted the new *Länder* from the fiscal provisions of the Basic Law for five years, during which time it was hoped that their deficient economies and substandard social structures could be repaired. In the interim, federation and *Länder* agreed to establish an off-budget plan known as the "German Unity Fund." Under this plan, billions of DM were transferred annually to the eastern *Länder,* 80 percent of which was raised in capital markets and the rest supplied from the federal budget. In one form or another, such special subventions of the east have been maintained.

General Economic Policy

The FRG is noted for its *Sozialmarktwirtschaft* or "social market economy" (SME), a system of free enterprise guided and supported by the strong hand of government and undergirded by a comprehensive scheme of social welfare. In this way, Germany has managed to avoid the extremes of a pure laissez-faire economy and centralized state control.

German federalism has made its own distinctive contribution to the growth of the SME. As Christopher Allen notes, *Land* governments encouraged banks to adjust "their investment and loan policies to improve the competitive position of key industries in various regions" and to "invest heavily in vocational education to provide the skills so necessary for high quality manufactured goods" capable of competing in world markets.[34] *Land* governments also worked closely with business and organized labor, not only to encourage the development of a modern, competitive economy but also to shape the framework of cooperation among trade unions, corporations, banks, and educational institutions, a process of coordination matched at the national level by such major policy initiatives as the Economic Stabilization Act of 1967 and the Codetermination Act of 1975.

The Codetermination Act The issue of codetermination offers an excellent example of the unusual pattern of politics and policy in postwar Germany, one that encourages bargaining and mutual partisan adjustment among state agencies, private groups, and political parties. Codetermination has roots far back in German history. Already in the 1840s workers were demanding a voice in shaping the conditions of their labor. Their influence was gradually solidified and augmented through a series of acts in the late 1800s and the first few decades of the 1900s, so that by 1922 employees were legally

---

[34]"Corporation and Regional Economic Policies in the Federal Republic of Germany: The 'Meso' Politics of Industrial Adjustment," *Publius* 19 (1989), pp. 156–157.

entitled to at least one representative on factory management boards. The progress of workers' rights received a brief setback under the Nazi regime. But following the war all the German *Länder* reestablished work councils—employee groups designed to offer proposals to management—and gave them varying degrees of influence in determining company policies relating to production and operating methods.

Current codetermination policy is based on the Works Constitution Act of 1952 and its successor, the Works Constitution Act of 1972. The 1952 act established one-third employee representation on the management boards of all private industries employing between 500 and 2,000 workers (a principle that was later extended to the public sector), and its 1972 replacement authorized every factory or business with more than five employees to elect a work council to bargain with plant managers over issues not dealt with in collective bargaining agreements.

Finally, in 1976, after four more years of struggle and compromise among various parliamentary groups, an overwhelming majority of the Bundestag passed the Codetermination Act, underscoring the consensus achieved over years of negotiation. This act extended the principle of numerical parity, requiring equal representation of workers on company supervisory boards, to include all enterprises with more than 2,000 employees, affecting about 7 million workers in more than 500 firms. It did this by providing for 12- to 20-member supervisory boards, depending on the size of the plant, with an equal number of shareholders and representatives from the workforce, the latter to include delegations elected separately by blue-collar, white-collar, and managerial staff.

Although the unions were not entirely pleased with the allocation of seats on the boards or with the provision that allows the chairperson—usually a shareholder—to break a tie vote, the act nevertheless gave them a significant foothold in industrial decision making. Not long after the act's passage, it was challenged in the Federal Constitutional Court on grounds that it violated the Basic Law's rights to property, association, and entrepreneurial freedom. But the court cautiously upheld the act, suggesting that codetermination is a legitimate application of the constitutional ideal of a "social federal state" (Article 20).

This example of codetermination illustrates the institutionalized process of bargaining among various interests that create policy in the FRG, a process requiring extensive cooperation, consultation, and compromise. This filtering process means that a large degree of consensus is necessary before any real movement in public policy can be achieved. This is why policy change in the FRG has been aptly described as *incremental* rather than *large-scale,* even in the face of major shifts in electoral politics.

Economic Stabilization Act   Until the mid-1960s, German economic policy contained a strong antiplanning bias. With the adoption of the Economic Stabilization Act, however, long-term fiscal planning became a vital element of the FRG's economy. Influenced in part by Keynesian economic theory, the act authorized the federal government to (1) coordinate the budgetary policies of state and national governments, (2) change, temporarily, rates of taxation on personal and corporate incomes without prior parliamentary approval, (3) stimulate the economy during periods of recession by public expenditures up to specified amounts, and (4) harmonize general fiscal policy with monetary policy.

Here, too, as with codetermination, an enormous amount of cooperation was required within and among governmental and nongovernmental bodies to make the Stabilization Act work. A Fiscal Planning Commission (FPC) consisting of federal and state representatives, as well as representatives from the Federal Bank (Bundesbank), business, and the political parties, was formed to coordinate budgetary policy between the national government and the *Länder.* Over the years, the FPC has contributed to the development of fiscal policy in a number of ways: drawing up draft budgets for national and state governments, setting guidelines for economic growth, coordinating tax policy with cuts in expenditures, and ensuring that federal and state policies complement rather than contradict each other.[35]

[35]See Eric Owen Smith, *The German Economy* (London: Routledge, 1994), pp. 61–62.

A CLOSER LOOK
4.6

GERMANY'S SOCIAL CODE

1. Purposes of the Social Code

(1) The provisions of the Social Code are intended to provide for social benefits, including social and educational assistance, with the object of making social justice and social security a reality. Its aim is to contribute to ensuring an existence worthy of human beings; providing equal opportunities for the free development of the personality, especially for young persons; protecting and encouraging the family; enabling persons to derive a livelihood through freely chosen activity; and averting or compensating for special burdens in life, *inter alia*, by helping persons to help themselves.

Source: Social Code (*Sozialgesetzbuch*), Federal Minister of Labor and Social Affairs, Bonn, 1981; BGBl., I, 1975, 3015.

Social Welfare Policy

Germany has typically spent more than a third of its GNP on social services—among the highest in Western Europe. Social policy expenditures on all governmental levels amount to nearly one-half of total governmental expenditures. As seen in earlier sections, this social welfare system draws upon a long tradition of state-supported social policies. The current system includes generous programs of health insurance, unemployment compensation, industrial accident insurance, pensions, housing benefits, and youth welfare programs. Old-age pensions, the largest of these programs—they typically account for one-third of the social budget—are financed by contributions from the insured and their employers. Adjusted to inflation and other economic indicators, social security payments have increased nearly every year since 1957, and they are extraordinarily generous. The system also includes a number of other benefits: relief payments for the needy, child benefit allowances, rent subsidies, nursing care for the aged, and special reparations for former prisoners of war and persons who suffered losses under Nazism because of their race, religion, or political beliefs.

After unification, the FRG's social policy, like other economic programs, was extended to the new eastern *Länder*. Social benefits, however, particularly unemployment pay and retirement pensions, were adjusted to eastern economic standards and would not reach western levels until the east achieved economic parity with the west. Even so, these benefits resulted in significant increases in pensions for East Germans who were, as in the west, given the option of retiring at 57 years of age at 75 percent of their former gross pay. West Germany would bear most of the social costs for health and welfare, although some advantages associated with the GDR's old system, such as 20 weeks of paid leave for women after giving birth, were phased out. The costs of these programs were met in part by large transfers of public funds from the federal and state governments.

Yet as might be expected in times of economic austerity, the German government has found it steadily more difficult to supply its citizens with such high levels of well-being. This problem has become particularly acute with the FRG's demographic shift, as Berlin struggles with the challenge of financing the health costs and other retirement needs of an aging population. This factor, combined with the continuing task of modernizing the eastern German economy, has caused the Schröder government to consider a variety of cost-cutting measures and the elimination of some marginal programs.

Summary

As noted earlier, social welfare policy in postwar Germany has been the product of consensus politics, as well as a long historical tradition. The CDU, SPD, business organizations, and labor unions can all take some credit for Germany's extensive system of social insurance and welfare benefits. The system represents not only a longstanding accord between these groups but also a social compact between the generations. At times, there have been conflicts among these groups, as some threaten to cross the invisible boundary lines of this consensus. This was the case in 1966, when the CDU/CSU–FDP coalition proposed substantial cuts in corporate taxes and social spending in order to spur economic growth, facilitate the creation of jobs, and reduce a public debt aggravated by reunification. In response, union leaders organized a massive protest demonstration in Bonn and attacked the "savings package" as an assault on the social market economy and a threat to the time-honored consensus between labor, management, and government.

Whatever adjustments are made in the delicate balance of interests governing the FRG's social economy, the German model will continue to be less centralized than the French or the British, while still much more sensitive to social concerns than the American. Government ownership of industry and intervention in the market supply of goods and services are still other features of the social market economy, although by the 1990s, the government had begun to divest itself of ownership in areas such as transportation, the postal services, and communications. In addition, although the German government is unusual in owning stock in hundreds of private companies, here too it has begun to denationalize some of them. At the same time, showing that generalizations about Germany's social economic policy are always risky, several state governments continue to subsidize certain industries, either for the purpose of reviving them or to keep them from moving their plants to other states or countries.

FOREIGN POLICY, NATIONAL UNITY, AND THE ROAD TO NORMALCY

Resolving the "German Problem"

Germany's foreign policy since 1945 may be summarized as having three foundations. The first is the state's rootedness in the security and common values of the Atlantic Alliance, especially its close ties to the United States. The second is its membership in the European community of states, which was founded on the need to end long-standing tensions with France and has now reached its highest point in the FRG's major economic and political contributions to the European Union (EU). Yet the third leg of the FRG's postwar policy—the need to resolve the "German problem"—for decades prevented the country from fully assuming the functions of a "normal" state.

This problem was the fulcrum of the East-West conflict in post–World War II Europe. First of all, the FRG's hostile relationship with the GDR carried over into all of its relations with Eastern Europe. Additionally, West German rearmament within the North Atlantic Treaty Organization (NATO), coupled with the refusal under a succession of Christian Democratic governments to recognize the Oder-Neisse line as a permanent boundary between Poland and Germany, was viewed by the Soviet Union as a dangerous threat to peace in Central Europe. The city of Berlin represented still another component of the German problem. Cleft by concrete and barbed wire and later by the infamous Wall, the city became the most poignant symbol of German separation and Cold War confrontation.

There clearly could be no resolution of the German problem without a relaxation of tension in Central Europe. Moscow was the key to any such resolution. It is significant that both Adenauer and Brandt journeyed to the Soviet Union—the former in 1955, the latter in 1970—in search of "normalized" relations between Bonn and Moscow. For Adenauer, however, normalization meant not only the reestablishment of diplomatic relations with the Soviet Union, which he accomplished, but the reunification of Germany, which he failed to achieve. In his Moscow talks, he spoke of the "abnormality" of Germany's division, leaving his Soviet hosts with the message that "there can be no real security in Europe without the restoration of German unity." A decade and a half later, with Germany still divided, Willy Brandt sought to define the *initial* steps to normalization. He announced that it was time "to reconstitute our relationship to the East upon the basis of the unrestricted, reciprocal renunciation of force, proceeding from the existing political situation in Europe."

Brandt's eastern policy (*Ostpolitik*) was designed to achieve this result. The cornerstone of the new policy was the Soviet–West German treaty on the renunciation of the use of force, signed in Moscow in August 1970. The Warsaw Treaty, signed in November of the same year, rounded out this foundation. Essentially, both treaties recognized existing boundaries in Europe. Another stone in Brandt's rising edifice of detente was the 1971 Quadripartite Agreement on Berlin. In fact, Brandt conditioned Bonn's ratification of the Moscow and Warsaw treaties upon progress toward settlement of the Berlin question. Pledging to resolve their disputes by peaceful means, the four powers reaffirmed their individual and joint responsibility for Berlin.

The capstone of detente was the Basic Treaty between East and West Germany, signed in December 1972. The FRG and GDR both agreed to develop regular ties with each other on the basis of equal rights. The concept of "two German states in one nation," which the FRG urged on the GDR, was conspicuously left out of the treaty. Instead, the right of both German states to "territorial integrity" and "self-determination" was affirmed. In addition, the two states agreed that "neither … can represent the other in the international spheres or act on its behalf." In supplementary protocols both states also agreed to settle their frontier problems, to improve trade relations, and to cooperate in scientific, technological, medical, cultural, athletic, and environmental fields.

Gorbachev and *Glasnost*

The advent of the reform Communist Mikhail Gorbachev in the Soviet Union and the associated policies of *glasnost* (openness) and *perestroika* (restructuring) placed East-West relations in a new light and encouraged many Germans to dream about the prospects of German reunification within a unified Europe. GDR leaders, however, remained adamant in viewing the Basic Treaty as a step toward a fully sovereign and independent GDR—an interpretation the FRG had never accepted. Unlike Poland and Hungary and the Soviet Union itself, the GDR refused to move toward democracy or free markets. The hard-liners in charge of the regime—most of them old men—brooked no opposition to the socialist system of their creation. Yet we have seen that by 1989 this stand was no longer realistic. As thousands of young East Germans fled to the FRG by way of Hungary in search of freedom and employment, GDR leaders seemed increasingly isolated in their own backyard. They accused Hungary of violating various legal treaties and denounced the FRG for encouraging the exodus, but these charges were seen for what they were: feeble attempts to hide the fragility of a regime deeply in trouble in the face of a "new order" emerging in Eastern Europe.

The GDR was caught on the horns of an excruciating dilemma. It could either loosen up the regime and allow its people to move freely in and out of their country or continue its present course. The first option would lead to greater contact between East and West Germans and could undermine its authority. The second option—keeping a tight grip on its people—would lead to another crisis of legitimacy and the continued flight of its most productive citizens. With the collapse of the hard-line Communist regime in October 1989, a hastily reassembled government under younger and more pragmatic leadership chose the first option. In the following weeks, events unfolded with dizzying speed, surprising even close observers of German affairs. By the end of the year the Communist Party had disavowed its leading role, promised to hold free elections, and exposed the corruption of its longtime leaders as an angry and outspoken citizenry demanded their prosecution. In the meantime, the Brandenburg Gate was opened, GDR citizens waved FRG flags in the streets, and East and West German leaders began to talk about a new relationship.

The Progress and Politics of German Unity

The story of German unity is a fascinating tale. On the one hand, the story seems to show that the forces of history, once unleashed, cannot be stopped. On the other hand, unity would not have come about without the cooperation of the Allied powers, especially the United States and the Soviet Union, and the intense negotiations between the GDR and FRG. Although the FRG held most of the trump cards in these negotiations, the GDR managed to extract significant promises from the FRG, including some changes in the Basic Law. The negotiations between the GDR and the FRG, and those between Britain, France, the Soviet Union, and the United States, did not proceed on separate tracks. They were conducted—in coordinated fashion—over many months; hence, they were known as the *two-plus-four* talks. This mix of international and domestic politics, with its interplay of constitutional law and public policy, made the new Germany possible.

Several months earlier, Chancellor Kohl had proposed a ten-point plan for Germany's eventual union. He had envisioned the development of a *contractual community* in which the two Germanys would establish "confederative structures" leading first to social, monetary, and economic union and eventually, perhaps in a few years, to political union. Events, however, overtook him, as well as those East German reform groups who merely wanted to humanize socialism in the GDR. The "bloodless coup" occurred on March 18, 1990, when East Germans voted in their first free election since Hitler was named chancellor in 1933. Unity *now* was their unmistakable message. Fired up, and with Kohl at the controls, the unity train roared toward its destination. One possible route to unity was the formation of an all-German government under the terms of a new constitution ratified by all Germans. Instead, East Germany agreed to become part of the existing FRG under the simple procedure of accession laid down in Article 23 of the Basic Law.

Four landmarks paved the way to reunification. These are the State Treaty on Monetary, Economic, and Social Union (May 18, 1990), the All-German Election Treaty (August 3, 1990), the Unity Treaty (August 31, 1990), and the Treaty on the Final Settlement with Respect to Germany (September 12, 1990). The GDR and the FRG negotiated the first three treaties, though in consultation with the Allies; the last was the product mainly of the two-plus-four negotiations.

A CLOSER LOOK

4.7

AN INDIVISIBLE NATION

On the night of October 2–3, 1990, East and West Germans came together on the *Platz der Republik,* the great lawn before the Reichstag, to celebrate their reunification. Many of them flew the black-red-gold flag of the FRG, which had been the tricolor of the two previous German democracies as well (1848 and 1918). Germany was felt to be reclaiming the best elements of its common past. At the same time, a good number of European Community flags were also in evidence, with the circle of 12 gold stars on a field of blue, seeming to reflect the often-stated aim of the two societies to work together henceforth—not for a "German Europe" but for a "European Germany."

The State Treaty   The State Treaty united the social, economic, and monetary systems of East and West Germany.[36] It effectively extended the FRG's social market economy eastward, installing in all of Germany an economy based on private ownership, competition, and the free movement of goods and services. As of July 2, 1990, the West German deutsche mark became the official currency of the GDR. Under the terms of the treaty, all "[w]ages, salaries, grants, pensions, rents and leases" were to be converted at a rate of one East German mark to one West German mark. All other claims and assets were to be converted at a rate of two to one. One effect of the currency union was to increase the importance of Germany's central bank, already renowned for its control over monetary policy in the FRG.[37] The bank would now take responsibility for all of Germany and sorely test its capacity to fight inflation in the face of price rises that were surely to occur from the transfer of billions of deutsche marks into the east.

The State Treaty covered other areas such as intra-German and foreign trade, agriculture environmental protection, social and health insurance, budgetary planning, and tax policy. For each of these areas, the treaty required the GDR to adopt laws consistent with policies prevailing in the FRG. In some instances, however, transitional arrangements were worked out to ease the pain of the legal and structural changes the GDR would have to make. One of these temporary arrangements was the establishment of an arbitration tribunal to resolve disputes arising under the treaty.

The All-German Election Treaty   The GDR election of March 18, 1990, set the stage for the all-German election of December 2, 1990. The

March election resulted in an impressive victory for the CDU-led Alliance for Germany and thus for German unity. The new parliament went on to create a grand coalition consisting of the Alliance for Germany, the SPD, and the Federation of Free Democrats under the leadership of Lothar de Maizière (CDU). This coalition negotiated the unity treaties with West Germany's CDU-FDP coalition government, one of which was the All-German Election Treaty. The GDR, which had a system of pure proportional representation, objected to the FRG's 5 percent clause, arguing that it would keep smaller parties out of the all-German parliament. Negotiations led to an agreement that would retain the 5 percent clause for all of Germany but permit smaller parties and groups in the GDR to field candidates in alliance with other, larger parties in the west. This plan, however, favored some small parties at the expense of others. In response to petitions by the PDS, Greens, and the far-right Republicans, the Federal Constitutional Court held that the election agreement discriminated against these parties, and it went on to recommend that for this first all-German election, the 5 percent clause should be adopted separately in both east and west. An amended election law followed this recommendation.

The Unity Treaty   The historic Unity Treaty—a massive document consisting of 433 printed pages—provided for the GDR's accession to the FRG and the application of the Basic Law to all of Germany. Its 45 articles, annexes, and special provisions touched almost every aspect of German public policy. The treaty's "Special Provisions on the Conversion to Federal Law" appeared in 19 chapters that dealt with the laws, procedures, and institutions subject to the jurisdiction of the various federal ministries. While extending FRG law immediately to numerous policy areas in the eastern *Länder,* these special provisions also contained transitional and interim measures to accommodate special conditions in the ex-GDR.

Constitutional Amendments   The Unity Treaty amended several provisions of the Basic Law. First, the preamble was amended to delete all

---

[36]Treaty between the Federal Republic of Germany and the German Democratic Republic Establishing a Monetary, Economic and Social Union (New York: German Information Center, 1990 [official translation]).

[37]For a study of the role of the Bundesbank in the FRG's political system, see Ellen Kennedy, *The Bundesbank* (New York: Council on Foreign Relations Press, 1991).

THE PATH TO GERMAN UNITY

1989

July–September	GDR citizens flee to the FRG by way of Hungary.
October 9	100,000 people demonstrate in Leipzig to the chant, "We are the people."
October 18	Erich Honecker is removed as head of the GDR.
November 7	GDR government resigns after 1 million people demonstrate in Berlin.
November 9	Berlin Wall is breached.
November 28	Chancellor Kohl announces his Ten-Point program for unity.
December 1	GDR constitution amended to end the SED's monopoly of power.

1990

March 18	First free election in GDR. Overwhelming victory for parties allied with Kohl's CDU.
April 12	GDR legislature elects first democratic government. CDU's Lothar de Maizière elected prime minister.
May 18	State Treaty on Monetary, Economic, and Social Union.
July 22	GDR legislature reestablishes its five constituent *Länder.*
August 3	All-German Election Treaty signed.
August 31	Unity Treaty signed.
September 12	Treaty on the Final Settlement with Respect to Germany signed.
October 3	Day of German unity. GDR ceases to exist.
October 4	First all-German legislature meets in the Berlin Reichstag building.
October 24	Five eastern *Länder* elect new parliaments.
December 2	First all-German Bundestag elections.

references to the goal of reunification, for "Germans in [the sixteen *Länder*] have [now] achieved the unity and freedom of Germany in free self-determination." Importantly for the FRG's neighbors, this new language effectively froze Germany's present borders, making it legally impossible for Germany to claim other territories lost as a result of World War II. Second, the treaty repealed Article 23—the very provision under which the GDR acceded to the FRG. In short, no "other parts of Germany" were left to be incorporated into the FRG by accession. Third, the treaty added the following italicized words to Article 146: "This Basic Law, *which is valid for the entire German people following the achievement of the unity and freedom of Germany,* shall cease to be in force on the day on which a constitution adopted by a free decision of the German people comes into force." Fourth, Article 135a was amended to relieve the FRG of certain liabilities incurred by the GDR or its legal entities. Finally, the treaty changed the number of votes allocated to the states in the Bundesrat under the terms of Article 51.

In addition to these amendments, the Unity Treaty inserted a new article—Article 143—into the Basic Law. The new article allowed the all-German government to deal flexibly with issues that might otherwise have slowed down or even stopped the unity train. Abortion, property rights, and intergovernmental relations were among these issues. The eastern *Länder,* for example, were unable to abide by the revenue-sharing provisions of the Basic Law or other obligations growing out of its scheme of federal-state relations. There appeared to be no constitutional objection to this particular deviation clause.

Abortion   The deviation clause of Article 143 (1) was another matter. Its incorporation into the Unity Treaty represented a compromise between east and west over abortion. In 1975, the Federal Constitutional Court had struck down West Germany's liberalized abortion law, holding that it violated the right to life within the meaning of Article 2 (1) of the Basic Law as well as the state's duty to protect human dignity under Article 1 (1). In so ruling, the court obligated the state to make abortion a crime at all stages of pregnancy, subject to exceptions specified by law. The GDR, on the other hand, permitted abortion on demand within the first three months of pregnancy. The effect of Article 143 was to allow East and West Germany to follow their respective policies on abortion. The FRG conceded this much to the GDR. But the treaty also required the Bundestag to enact an all-German policy on abortion by the end of 1992 "to ensure better protection of unborn life and provide a better solution in conformity with the Constitution of conflict situations faced by pregnant women" (Article 31 [4]). This was the GDR's concession to the west.

These concessions, however, raised a difficult constitutional issue, for Article 143 bans deviations from the Basic Law in violation of Articles 19 (2) and 79 (3). The first flatly prohibits any encroachment on a basic right; the second bars amendments that contravene principles laid down in Articles 1 (human dignity) and 20 (enshrining the rule of law). The constitutional issue was whether the deviation clause encroached upon the principle of human dignity with respect to abortion. In addition, some wondered whether a treaty could suspend the application of a court ruling. These questions remained unanswered in 1991 as the Bundestag heatedly debated a number of abortion reform proposals. In the end, a compromise law was passed that decriminalized abortions performed during the first trimester of pregnancy, although in a subsequent ruling the Constitutional Court required women contemplating abortions to submit to pro-life counseling before making their final decision.

Property   The deviation clause of Article 143 (1) was also designed to deal with the problem of property rights. On June 15, 1990, the GDR and FRG governments signed a Joint Declaration on the Settlement of Open Property Issues. This agreement provided that property illegally taken by the GDR's Communist government between 1949 and 1989, including expropriated businesses and property placed under state administration, was to be returned to its rightful owner. Compensation would be paid in the event that property could not be returned. The treaty contained some exceptions to this policy of restitution. Expropriated property would not be returned to their former owners if needed for investment purposes—a rule applied mainly to factories and large businesses—if innocently acquired by third parties, or if incapable of being returned in its original form.

The most controversial part of the property settlement was its exclusion from restitution of property expropriated by the Soviet Union in eastern Germany between 1945 and 1949. The Soviet Union had seized all landholdings over 250 acres and distributed most of them to small farmers. Prime Minister de Maizière refused to undo these acts on the grounds that the return of these millions of acres to their former owners would cause enormous social unrest in the east. Yet the right to property, the rule of law, and equality under law are core values of the Basic Law. Accordingly, former owners of land in the east challenged the 1945–1949 exclusion in the Constitutional Court. In this instance, however, the achievement of unity—one of the Basic Law's highest values—outweighed the right to property in the form of its restoration. Further, the court declared that the 1945–1949 takings occurred before the Basic Law entered into force.

Other Treaty Provisions   The Unity Treaty provided for the creation of a special trust agency (*Treuhandanstalt*) charged with privatizing East German businesses and industries, and revised the constitutional formula for intergovernmental revenue sharing. Several additional provisions dealt with the status or continuing validity of GDR treaties, court decisions, and administrative rulings, most of which were to remain in effect

unless incompatible with the Basic Law or federal statutes. GDR school certificates, university
degrees, and titles were to retain their validity,
although only in the eastern *Länder,* whereas
judges and civil servants were required to submit to recredentialing procedures. The treaty
also required the former GDR to adopt regulations in conformity with EU standards, to maintain the church tax, and to decentralize cultural,
educational, and athletic institutions. The German government took responsibility for "[reha-
bilitating the] victims of the iniquitous SED
regime," obliging it to pay compensation for their
suffering. In this connection, and at the insistence of the GDR the 6 million files of the disbanded state security police (*Stasi*) were to
remain in the ex-GDR until an all-German parliament could enact a law regarding their storage
and access. GDR officials were interested in
keeping control of the files and allowing public
access to them, in part to expose the crimes of
human rights violators.

Treaty on the Final Settlement with Respect to Germany
After seven months of
negotiation, the four wartime Allies and the two
Germanys signed the treaty that finally closed the
books on World War II.[38] As part of the treaty—
known as the Two-Plus-Four Treaty—the Allied
powers relinquished all their occupation rights
and restored full sovereignty to a united Germany. Under the treaty, the new Germany (1)
accepted its present boundaries and guaranteed
the border with Poland, (2) renounced aggressive
warfare as well as the production and use of biological, chemical, and nuclear weapons, and (3)
agreed to reduce its armed forces to 370,000 and
to finance the return of Soviet troops to their
homeland by 1995. Germany also agreed to ban
any NATO presence in the east while Soviet
troops remained there, but Moscow's greatest
concession was to allow the FRG to choose its
military alliance.

Finally, in a supplementary letter to the
Allied foreign ministers, Foreign Minister Hans-
Dietrich Genscher and Prime Minister de Maizière noted that Germany would abide by the
agreement excluding property expropriated
between 1945 and 1949 from the general terms
of the Unity Treaty. They pledged on behalf of
Germany to preserve monuments to war victims
erected on German soil and to maintain war
graves. The two German politicians also declared
that in united Germany "the free democratic
basic order will be protected by the Constitution."
It provides the basis, they underscored, "for
ensuring that parties which ... seek to impair or
abolish the free democratic basic order as well as
associations which are directed against the constitutional order or the concept of international
understanding can be prohibited." This language
was taken directly from Article 21 of the Basic
Law, which authorizes the prohibition of antidemocratic parties. In this fashion, reunited Germany would remain a "fighting democracy."

Post-Unification Foreign Policy
When novelist Günter Grass opposed reunification, he did so by arguing that "we Germans
would become, once again, something to be
feared" because a "reunited Germany would be
a colossus loaded with complexes, standing in its
own way and in the way of European integration."[39] Yet the reality has been quite different.
The FRG's political leaders immediately reas-
sured their eastern neighbors that Germany
would honor all treaties respecting its present
boundaries and obligations to the European
Union. This reassurance was underscored in
March 1991 by a treaty between the FRG and the
USSR, reaffirming the two countries' "respect
[for] each other's sovereign equality, territorial
integrity and political independence." Most
important, both powers declared their unquali-
fied adherence to the territorial integrity of all

---

[38]The Treaty on the Final Settlement with Respect to
Germany (New York: German Information Center,
1990).

[39]*Two States—One Nation?* trans. by Krishna Winston
and A. S. Wensinger (New York: Harcourt Brace, 1990),
p. 13.

European states and pledged to have no territorial claims whatsoever.

The FRG has adhered to these principles in the face of the Warsaw Pact's dissolution, the breakup of the Soviet Union, and the collapse of Communism in Eastern Europe. In some ways, as its own situation has become normalized with the restoration of national unity, the FRG has even begun to play a more active role in both Atlantic and European affairs. This was nowhere more apparent than in the decision of the SPD-Greens government in 1999 to fly combat missions in support of NATO's air war in the Kosovo campaign. This was a starting reversal of German military policy, because previous governments, including that of Helmut Kohl, had argued that the Basic Law barred the use of German troops outside of NATO, even for peace-keeping purposes. Yet thanks to a July 12, 1994, decision by the Federal Constitutional Court which freed the way for such deployments, a new generation of German leaders, including the former peace activist and new foreign minister Joschka Fischer (Greens), was able to rationalize a new role for the FRG. The use of the military for restoring peace and preventing massive human rights abuses, they argued, was not only consistent with the lessons of the past; it was a moral obligation for Germans to combat dictators and overcome oppression. Fischer and his colleagues appealed to the same rationale to support the deployment of German troops to Afghanistan in December 2001, though it did not send troops to Iraq in 2002.

This is not to say that Germany thereby became a more aggressive power or, in Grass's words, a "colossus." If anything, as demonstrated in the country's active role in the EU, the FRG of the early twenty-first century is defining its priorities less in terms of a narrow national self-interest than within the context of a broader and more inclusive "European house." There was a time when many Germans—and the Bundesbank in particular—were among the greatest skeptics of the benefits of European monetary integration, largely for fear of losing a pillar of the FRG's postwar economic miracle: the deutsche mark. Moreover, of all of Germany's parties, the SPD had for years been the most outspoken proponent of Euroskepticism. Yet as the German people accepted the introduction of a new currency to their economy in 2002, their attitudes had clearly changed. They were now supporters of the euro, while many of the Bundesbank's previously formidable powers were passed on to a common European Central Bank. Furthermore, in 2001, Germany's Social Democratic chancellor Gerhard Schröder was once again demonstrating his capacity to be a man for all seasons. He endorsed even more ambitious plans than his neighbors for regional integration, such as a stronger European parliament that would eventually lay the foundations for a continental "federation."

These developments did not mean that the FRG would have no occasion in future years for serious differences with either its Atlantic or its

A CLOSER LOOK
4.8

FOREIGN POLICY: A SPECIAL RESPONSIBILITY TO HISTORY

"At the beginning of the new century, the 'never again,' the lesson to be learned from our history, remains the basic principle in German politics and policies: within our country, in Europe, towards Israel and the Jewish communities, in our commitment to peace and respect for human rights around the world. That is the moral obligation, as well as the firm political will, of the generation of those who must shoulder responsibility for the heavy burden of German history."

Source: Joschka Fischer, German Foreign Minister, New York, September 11, 2000.

European allies. Nor did they imply that Germany's leaders were oblivious to their own domestic interests as they underscored the importance of political and economic cooperation in an era of globalism. They did suggest, however, that the Germany that had once been a cause of so many of the world's problems in the first half of the twentieth century had been fundamentally transformed.

CONCLUSION

The portrait of German policy making presented in this chapter is of a polity that has functioned effectively and, in the process, brought about a high measure of stability and prosperity. The Federal Republic of Germany also appears to have come of age politically. Its people are committed to democratic values, its party system is open and competitive, and its policy-making institutions are responsive to public opinion. For all intents and purposes, the transition to democracy has been completed in the eastern *Länder,* although the region must still catch up with the west economically.

Institutionally, the FRG remains a decentralized state marked by a system of administrative federalism, a fragmented bureaucracy, autonomous federal ministries, and a powerful Bundesrat capable of blocking parliamentary action. These institutions, like the political parties and parliament itself, are closely linked to social and economic groups in the private sector, producing a notable politics of compromise and consensus. The Federal Constitutional Court, another independent center of power, watches over this system, keeping the major organs of government within their proper spheres of competence while safeguarding individual rights and liberties. Finally, having regained full sovereignty under the Two-Plus-Four Treaty of 1990, and increasingly confident of its ability to influence world events, Germany can be expected to be a major international actor in the years to come, both within the framework of the Atlantic Alliance and in an expanding European Union.

Thinking Critically

1. What does it mean to say that the FRG is a "militant democracy"? What are the advantages of this type of democratic politics?
2. Overall, how would you assess the FRG's citizenship policy? Is this policy fair to immigrants, asylum seekers, and other non-Germans living in the FRG?
3. What crucial role does "decentralized federalism" play in the German system? What are its advantages in comparison with more centralized democracies?
4. How is "codetermination" an essential feature in the making of German social and economic policy?
5. Did reunification solve the age-old "German problem"? Should the legacies of injustice committed by the National Socialist and communist regimes in the twentieth century continue to concern Germany's leaders in the twenty-first century?

KEY TERMS

abortion compromise *(255)*
Article 16a *(244)*
Article 143 *(254–255)*
codetermination *(248)*
decentralized federalism *(246)*
Economic Stabilization Act *(248)*
"German problem" *(250)*
German Unity Fund *(247)*
Lothar de Maizière *(253)*
militant democracy *(243)*
monetary union *(253)*
Ostpolitik (251)
Two-Plus-Four Treaty *(257)*
vertical equalization procedures *(247)*

FURTHER READINGS

Braunthal, Gerard. *Political Loyalty and Public Service in Germany* (Amherst: Massachusetts University Press, 1990).

Bulmer, Simon, et. al. *Germany's European Diplomacy: Shaping the Regional Milieu* (Manchester: Manchester University Press, 2000).

Childs, David. *The Fall of the GDR: Germany's Road to Unity* (Harlow: Longman, 2001).

Garton Ash, Timothy. *In Europe's Name: Germany and the Divided Continent* (New York: Random House, 1993).

Hanrieder, Wolfram P. *Germany, America, Europe: Forty Years of German Foreign Policy* (New Haven: Yale University Press, 1989).

Katzenstein, Peter J., ed. *Industry and Politics in West Germany* (Ithaca, NY: Cornell University Press, 1989).

Kommers, Donald P. *The Constitutional Jurisprudence of the Federal Republic of Germany,* 2nd ed. (Durham, NC: Duke University Press, 1996).

Markovits, Inga. *Imperfect Justice* (Oxford: Clarendon Press, 1995).

McAdams, A. James. *Judging the Past in Unified Germany* (New York: Cambridge University Press, 2001).

Schweitzer, C. C., et al., eds. *Politics and Government in Germany, 1944–1994* (Oxford: Berghahn Books, 1995).

Smith, Eric Owen. *The German Economy* (London: Routlege, 1994).

Swenson, Peter. *Fair Shares, Unions, Pay, and Politics in Sweden and West Germany* (Ithaca, NY: Cornell University Press, 1989).

Thelen, Kathleen. *Union in Parts: Labor Politics in Postwar Germany* (Ithaca, NY: Cornell University Press, 1991).

WEB SITES

Political Development
www.democ.uci.edu/democ/germany.html
Superb source of information and sites on all aspects of German politics and society.
www.mathematik.uni-ulm.de/de-news/
Compilation of the latest news from Germany.
www.germany-info.org/fgic/index.html
The German embassy in Washington, DC.

www.germany-info.org/relaunch/business/business.html
Background information on the role of business in German society.
www.usembassy.de/
American perspective on German affairs, provided by the U.S. Embassy to the Federal Republic.

Political Processes and Institutions
www.constitution.org/cons/germany.txt
Germany's constitution, or Basic Law (*Grundgesetz*).
eng.bundesregierung.de/frameset/index.jsp
The official Web site of the German government.
www.bundestag.de/htdocs_e/index.html
Up-to-date information about Germany's parliament, the Bundestag.
www.destatis.de/e_home.htm
Useful source of official statistics on the German economy and people.

Public Policy
www.eng.bmi.bund.de/
Germany's Ministry of the Interior, addressing such controversial topics as immigration policy and citizenship.
www.bma.de/
Federal Ministry of Labor and Social Affairs, dealing primarily with labor relations and social security issues.
www.aicgs.org/index.shtml
Analyses of German public policy and decision making, provided by the premier center on Germany in the United States, the American Institute for Contemporary German Studies.
www.foothill.fhda.edu/divisions/unification/
Stimulating teaching guide on the triumphs and perils of German unification.
www.rferl.org/nca/special/10years/germany2.html
Information on the first ten years of German unification.
europa.eu.int/
Official site of the European Union.
www.democ.uci.edu/democ/gread.htm
Further readings on German history, society, economics, and politics.

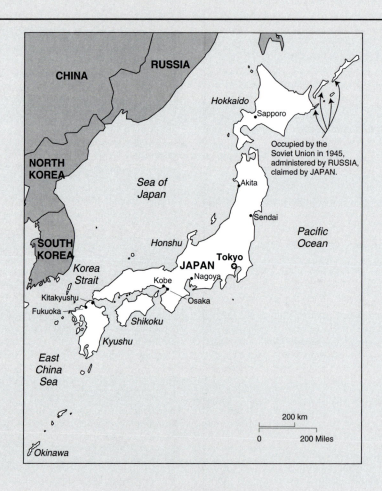

CHINA

RUSSIA

Hokkaido

• Sapporo

Occupied by the
Soviet Union in 1945,
administered by RUSSIA,
claimed by JAPAN.

NORTH
KOREA

Sea of
Japan

Akita

• Sendai

SOUTH
KOREA

Honshu

Pacific
Ocean

Korea
Strait

JAPAN

Tokyo

Kobe

Nagoya

Kitakyushu

Osaka

Fukuoka

Shikoku

Kyushu

East
China
Sea

200 km

0   200 Miles

Okinawa

CHAPTER
5

THE GOVERNMENT OF
Japan

Theodore McNelly

INTRODUCTION

Background: While retaining its time-honored culture, Japan rapidly absorbed Western technology during the late nineteenth and early twentieth centuries. After its devastating defeat in World War II, Japan recovered to become the second most powerful economy in the world and a staunch ally of the United States. While the emperor retains his throne as a symbol of national unity, actual power rests in networks of powerful politicians, bureaucrats, and business executives. The economy experienced a major slowdown in the 1990s following three decades of unprecedented growth.

GEOGRAPHY

Location: Eastern Asia, island chain between the North Pacific Ocean and the Sea of Japan, east of the Korean Peninsula

Area: 377,835 sq km

   Note: includes Bonin Islands (Ogasawara-gunto), Daito-shoto, Minami-jima, Okino-tori-shima, Ryukyu Islands (Nansei-shoto), and Volcano Islands (Kazan-retto)

Area—comparative: slightly smaller than California

Climate: varies from tropical in south to cool temperate in north

Terrain: mostly rugged and mountainous

Elevation extremes: *lowest point:* Hachiro-gata –4 m

   highest point: Fujiyama 3,776 m

Geography note: strategic location in northeast Asia

PEOPLE

Population: 127,330,000

Age structure: *0–14 years:* 14.3% (male 9.3 million; female 8.8 million)

15–64 years: 66.7% (male 42.6 million; female 42.1 million)

65 years and over: 19% (male 10.16 million; female 14.05 million)

Population growth rate: 0.08%

Birthrate: 9.56 births/1,000 population

Sex ratio: 0.96 male/female

Life expectancy at birth: 81.0 years

male: 77.7 years

female: 84.5 years

Nationality: *noun:* Japanese

adjective: Japanese

Ethnic groups: Japanese 99.4%, Korean 0.6%

Religions: observe both Shinto and Buddhist 84%, other 16% (including Christian 0.7%)

Languages: Japanese

Literacy: *definition:* age 15 and over can read and write

Total population: 99%

GOVERNMENT

Country name: *conventional long form:* none

conventional short form: Japan

Government type: constitutional monarchy with a parliamentary government

Capital: Tokyo

Administrative divisions: 47 prefectures

Independence: 660 B.C.E. (traditional founding by Emperor Jimmu)

National holiday: Birthday of Emperor Akihito, 23 December (1933)

Constitution: 3 May 1947

Legal system: modeled after European civil law system with English-American influence; judicial review of legislative acts in the Supreme Court; accepts compulsory ICJ jurisdiction, with reservations

Suffrage: 20 years of age; universal

Executive branch: *chief of state:* Emperor Akihito (since 7 January 1989)

head of government: Prime Minister Junichiro Koizumi (since 24 April 2001)

cabinet: appointed by the prime minister

elections: the monarch is hereditary; the Diet designates the prime minister; the constitution requires that the prime minister must command a parliamentary majority; therefore, following legislative elections, the leader of the majority party or leader of a majority coalition in the House of Representatives usually becomes prime minister

Legislative branch: bicameral Diet or Kokkai consists of the House of Councillors or Sangi-in (242 seats; one-half of the members elected every three years—72 seats of which are elected from the 49 multiseat prefectural districts and 50 of which are elected from a single nationwide list; members elected by popular vote to serve six-year terms) and the House of Representatives or Shugi-in (480 seats—180 of which are elected from 11 regional blocks on a proportional representation basis and 300 of which are elected from 300 single-seat districts; members elected by popular vote to serve four-year terms)

Judicial branch: Supreme Court (chief justice is appointed by the monarch after designation by the cabinet; all other justices are appointed by the cabinet)

ECONOMY

Overview: Government-industry cooperation, a strong work ethic, mastery of high technology, and a comparatively small defense allocation (1% of GDP) have helped Japan advance with extraordinary rapidity to the rank of second most technologically powerful economy in the world after the United States and third largest economy in the world after the United States and China. One notable characteristic of the economy is the working together of manufacturers, suppliers, and distributors in closely knit groups called *keiretsu*. A second basic feature has been the guarantee of lifetime employment for a substantial portion of the urban labor force. Both features are now eroding. Industry, the most important sector of the economy, is heavily dependent on imported raw materials and fuels. The much smaller agricultural sector is highly subsidized and protected, with crop yields among the highest in the world. Usually self-sufficient in rice, Japan must import about 50% of its requirements of other grain and fodder crops. Japan maintains one of the world's largest fishing fleets and accounts for nearly 15% of the global catch. For three decades overall real economic growth had been spectacular: a 10% average in the 1960s, a 5% average in the 1970s, and a 4% average in the 1980s. Growth slowed markedly in the 1990s largely because of the aftereffects of overinvestment during the late 1980s and contractionary domestic policies intended to wring speculative excesses from the stock and real estate markets. Government efforts to revive economic growth have met little success and were further hampered in 2000–2003 by the slowing of the U.S. and Asian economies. The crowding of habitable land area and the aging of the population are two major long-run problems. Robotics constitutes a key long-term economic strength, with Japan possessing 410,000 of the world's 720,000 working robots.

GDP: purchasing power parity—$3.58 trillion

GDP—real growth rate: 2.7%

GDP—per capita: purchasing power parity— $28,200

GDP—composition by sector: *agriculture:* 1.3%
  industry: 25.4%
  services: 73.3%

Household income or consumption by percentage share: *lowest 10%:* 4.8%
  highest 10%: 21.7%

Inflation rate (consumer prices): 0.3%

Labor force: 66.66 million

Labor force—by occupation: services 70%, industry 25%, agriculture 5%

Unemployment rate: 5.3%

Currency: yen (JPY)

A. POLITICAL DEVELOPMENT

DISTINCTIVE CHARACTERISTICS OF POLITICS IN JAPAN

The United States and Japan are both democracies and have the two largest economies of the world. As advanced industrial states they have many social and economic problems in common, problems that may require action by the government. Yet the politics of the two countries are very different.

1. Japan has a parliamentary system of democracy rather than a presidential system. In Japan, the relationship between the chief executive and the legislature is very different from that relationship in the United States. In Japan, the chief executive (prime minister) is elected by the legislature, not by the people. The Japanese chief executive has the power to dissolve the House of Representatives and bring about an election for new members, a power that the American president does not have. Thus, in Japan, the term of office of the chief executive depends very much on the will of the legislators, and vice versa. In America, the president and legislators are elected by the people and serve for fixed terms. Thus it may be said that Japanese politics resembles politics in Western Europe more than in the United States.

2. In Japan, two of the principal political issues are constitutional revision and electoral reform. Although the text of the Japanese constitution has not even once been altered during the 58 years of its existence, proposals for its amendment and controversies over its interpretation have been constantly to the fore. At the same time there have been perennial changes or proposals for change in the electoral systems of the two houses of the parliament (the Diet).

3. Japan occupies a very different place in world politics than does the United States. Japan is not a superpower, or even a great power. The country does not have a permanent seat in the Security Council of the UN. It does not have nuclear weapons, and its military and naval power is modest, certainly not commensurate

with its economic position. The constitutional limits on the nature and scope of Japan's role in world politics are a persistent topic of bitter controversy. At the same time, Japan's relations with its neighbors are even today complicated by bitter memories of Japan's behavior leading to and during World War II.

4. Japan has a unitary rather than a federal system of government. The powers of the governments of Japan's major political subdivisions are largely dependent on the legislation passed by the national Diet. Although the prefectures in practice enjoy some autonomy, there are no inviolable "states rights" that may not be infringed upon by the national legislature (the Diet).

5. The structures of Japanese political parties and the one-party dominant system in Japan are very different from parties and the party system in America.

6. Japan's history, religion, language, and literature originated in Asia and represent the distinctive cultural environment within which the Japanese political system functions.

In Japan, the emperor serves as head of state, and the prime minister serves as head of the government. In the U.S., the president simultaneously serves as head (or chief) of state and as head of the government. Because so much in Japanese politics and culture is rather different from what those unfamiliar with Japan are apt to expect, Japanese phenomena often seem exotic or even unique. Given the social and cultural environment within the country, however, Japanese politics is probably more pragmatic than illogical or exotic.

THE LAND AND THE PEOPLE

In terms of area, Japan is a middle-sized country like Great Britain, France, and Germany, but its population (over 127 million in 2005) is roughly twice that of any of those nations. Today Japan's gross national product (GNP) is the world's third largest, and the GNP per capita is one of the world's highest. The quality of life, however, suffers from overcrowding and long commutes, since one-fourth of the population is jammed into Tokyo and its immediate surroundings alone.

The Japanese are keenly aware that their country lacks the natural resources necessary for modern industry, the most obvious being iron ore, coal, and oil; these must all be imported and paid for by exports. If the present global trading system were to break down and Japan were excluded from it, its now prosperous economy would be threatened with imminent collapse.

Japan is an island nation. Although its total land area is slightly less than that of California, its outlying smaller islands are dispersed over a huge area of the western Pacific Ocean. As the crow flies, the distance from the northern tip of Hokkaido to the southernmost of the Ryukyu Islands (just east of Taiwan) is about 1,800 miles. Japanese territory extends as far south as Okinotori Shima, between the Philippines and the Commonwealth of the Northern Mariana Islands (a U.S. possession), and as far east as Minamitori Shima (Marcus Island), midway between Wake Island (U.S.) and Japan's Izu Islands. The strategic importance of Japan's outlying possessions is substantial, because responsibility for their defense has been assumed by Japan's Maritime Self-Defense Force.

Japan's four principal islands are, from north to south, Hokkaido, Honshu, Shikoku, and Kyushu. They are located in the north temperate zone. Hokkaido and northern Honshu are notable for their cold winters and heavy snows, and much of Japan suffers from rainy springs and smoldering summers. Earthquakes are common and have sometimes resulted in major disasters, as in the case of the Tokyo-Yokohama quake in 1923 and Kobe earthquake in 1995. The Kobe disaster, in which over 6,400 people were killed, has impelled the government to insist on more rigorous standards for the construction of buildings and elevated highways.

Kyushu is separated from Korea, on the Asian mainland, by 100 miles of high seas. Throughout history this location has helped Japan protect itself against foreign invasion. Although at times foreign influence has been intense, the Japanese have developed their culture and institutions largely in isolation. Thus many Japanese cultural characteristics, such as language, architecture, and traditional food and clothing, are very different even from those of the closest neighbors.

Yet modern Japan has much in common with other developed countries: science and industry, nearly universal literacy, a high material standard of living, a large investment in education at all levels, and a fondness for television and automobiles. A western tourist in Tokyo would find that city—with its noise, tall buildings, and traffic jams—disappointingly similar to big cities anywhere in the world. The principal exotic feature would be the Chinese characters on the fronts of stores. The spoken Japanese language is fundamentally different from Chinese, but the Japanese use Chinese characters to write their language. Although English is a required subject in Japanese schools, the percentage of Japanese who can speak it fluently is very small.

PREHISTORY

Ancient Chinese descriptions of Japan written in the third and fifth centuries C.E. suggest that it was originally inhabited by warlike, nature-worshiping people. Archeological and anthropological evidence indicates that the land was originally inhabited by Ainu, a caucasoid race of which only a few thousand still exist in Hokkaido. Later in prehistoric times, mongoloid peoples evidently migrated from northern Asia, and some migrants apparently came from the South Seas.

By the sixth century, one clan and its allies had consolidated their rule over other tribes and established their chief, Jimmu, as the emperor. The imperial clan (perhaps descendants of horse-riding invaders from Asia, possibly Korea) propagated the myth that Jimmu was the grandchild of the sun goddess, Amaterasu, who had commanded her descendants to rule the land. The sacred sword, jewel, and mirror, all of legendary origin, constitute the imperial regalia and are treasured by the imperial court as evidence of the antiquity and legitimacy of the dynasty.

CHINESE INFLUENCE

The coming of Buddhism and Confucianism from Korea and China in the sixth century exacerbated existing clan rivalries as different groups sought either to sponsor the new ideas or to rally around traditional religious beliefs and ideologies. In order to distinguish the traditional nature worship from Buddhism, the old beliefs came to be referred as *Shinto,* or "way of the gods." Gradually, as often seems to be the case in Japan, the foreign ideas gained widespread acceptance, but they were adapted to the needs of the Japanese. For example, the Buddhist pantheon came to be superimposed on the gods of the traditional Shinto faith. One emperor is said to have dreamed that the Hindu deity Vairocana appeared in the form of a bright sun and declared itself to be none other than Amaterasu, the emperor's ancestress.

Late in the sixth century, Crown Prince Shotoku distinguished himself as a scholar of Confucianism. Acting as regent, in 604 he proclaimed his famous "Seventeen-Article Constitution," which was actually a collection of Confucian precepts calling for harmony, obedience, diligence, and honesty in the conduct of administration. Confucian ideology provided a convenient rationale for the establishment of a centralized bureaucratic monarchy in place of quasi-feudal rule by clan chieftains. Emperor Kotoku's Edict of Reform of 646, largely inspired by the ideology of the Seventeen-Article Constitution, formally abolished hereditary guilds, set up a system of imperially appointed governors to rule the provinces, reformed the distribution of land among the people, and set up a system of taxation, usually in the form of rice, that would be paid to the central government. The centralizers cited the Chinese doctrine: "Under the heavens there is no land which is not the king's land. Among the holders of land there is none who is not the king's vassal."

The Taiho Code of 702, compiled by scholars of Chinese law, established a central administrative structure in imitation of the government of Tang China. The old custom of the Japanese court had been to maintain no fixed residence but to move from one place to another. In 710, following the Chinese example, a permanent Japanese capital city with straight streets and Chinese-style buildings was established in Nara. A university was set up where the sons of the nobility could learn the teachings of Confucius. A few years later, apparently to escape the overweening influence of the Buddhist clergy, the capital was moved to Kyoto, which remained the emperor's capital until 1868.

FEUDALISM

Although the imperial court in Kyoto was evidently committed to the ideal of a centralized, bureaucratic monarchy, the Confucian notion of government by merit tended to be overridden in favor of the hereditary principle. The Chinese theory that a wicked imperial dynasty could be overthrown was not adopted by the Japanese, who did not accept the idea that their divinely descended monarch could be anything other than virtuous. The Fujiwara family of hereditary court nobles, who—like the emperor—traced their descent from mythological deities, dominated the court and usually provided imperial consorts, regents, and civil dictators (*kanpaku*). The latter carried on the actual administration of state affairs.

The imperial court and capital soon became the center of intrigues and plots within and among the imperial family, the Fujiwara nobility, and rival Buddhist monasteries. From time to time successive emperors, yielding to political or physical pressures, made large grants of tax-exempt land to presumably deserving members of the imperial family, Fujiwara bureaucrats, Buddhist monasteries, and Shinto shrines. As less and less land provided revenue for the central government, the imperial court gradually became impoverished. Great tax-exempt manors grew into hereditary feudal baronies with their own armies. Unable to finance its own military forces and to maintain order in the provinces and even in the capital, the imperial government became dependent on the barons in order to enforce its rule.

In 1192, the emperor appointed the most powerful feudal baron, Minamoto Yoritomo, as "barbarian-subduing generalissimo," or *shogun,* a title which became hereditary in the Minamoto family. Minamoto Yoritomo, Japan's military ruler, established his own capital at Kamakura in eastern Japan, hundreds of miles from Kyoto. From 1192 until 1868, Japan was ruled not by the emperor or his court but by the military government (*bakufu*) of the successive shoguns. While the emperor, powerless and isolated in Kyoto, sometimes lived in poverty, the military government presided over a full-fledged feudal system. Within the hierarchy of lords and vassals, the chivalrous code of the *samurai* (the ruling caste of hereditary warriors) emphasized loyalty to one's overlord and military discipline. Aided by this discipline, the Kamakura *bakufu* defeated the Mongols, who twice tried to invade Japan by sea in the thirteenth century. The defenders of the nation were reputedly aided by the prayers of Buddhist and Shinto priests and great storms, the "winds of the Gods" (*kamikaze*), giving rise to the tradition that Japan enjoyed supernatural protection and was invincible.

The Tokugawa Regime

Warfare among local feudal lords raged across the land in the sixteenth century, when the country was nominally under the control of the Ashikaga dynasty of shoguns. Finally in 1603, after decades of civil war, Tokugawa Ieyasu, using political guile as well as military strategy, brought the country under his rule. Tokugawa Ieyasu, the first of the Tokugawa dynasty of shoguns, had remarkable political skills. After subduing or making alliances with the other feudal lords (*daimyo*), he established a regime that endured over two and a half centuries. He set up his capital in a swampy town called Edo, in eastern Japan. He required his defeated rivals to support the construction of a huge system of moats around his palace, redistributed their fiefs in such a way that his former enemies were kept separated from one another, and required them to live alternately in Edo and in their fiefs. When the feudal lords left Edo, they had to leave their families behind as hostages. When they returned to Edo, they were forbidden to bring weapons with them.

In order to prevent a possible conquest of the country by the European powers, Christianity was forbidden. In 1636 all Japanese ships without exception were forbidden to leave Japan. Only the Dutch (who were confined to an island in Nagasaki harbor and who agreed not to propagate the teachings of Christ) and the Chinese were permitted to trade with the Japanese. The isolationist policy helped to prevent the conquest of Japan by European imperial powers. The long period of peace enforced by the shoguns combined with the growing use of money in place of rice as a means of exchange encouraged the rise of a large merchant class. By 1772, Edo's population reached 1 million, making it the world's largest city at that time.

THE IMPERIAL RESTORATION

The changes in the economy during the Tokugawa period wrought hardship on many of the samurai and peasants, whose income was in the form of rice and who became indebted to rice brokers and merchants. At the same time, samurai scholars fostered the study of "national literature," which was based on Shinto legends that emphasized the divine origin of the state and the imperial dynasty. Some nationalist scholars contended that the shoguns had usurped the emperor's authority and that the emperor should be restored to his rightful position.

In 1853, during this period of internal division, Commodore Matthew Calbraith Perry came to Japan with a message from the American president demanding that the country open its door to foreign trade. The American fleet steadfastly refused to leave Japanese waters despite military threats, placing Shogun Tokugawa Iesada in a grave predicament. The nationalists and the shogun's feudal rivals demanded that the shogun "expel the barbarian and revere the emperor."

The shogun simply did not have the military and naval resources or the political support needed to resist American demands and had no choice but to make a treaty with the Americans. This provoked the shogun's enemies to intensify their demands that he abdicate. Efforts to work out a compromise of joint rule between the emperor and the shogun failed. Finally Shogun Tokugawa Keiki agreed to a restoration of the emperor, with the understanding that the shogun would be a principal councillor to the throne. When it became clear that the western daimyo, who leagued against him, were determined to exclude him from the new regime, some of the shogun's followers rebelled. A full-scale civil war was averted when the shogun agreed to abdicate, and the imperial regime was restored.

In 1868, the youthful Emperor Meiji established his capital at Edo, took over the shogun's palace and moats, and renamed the city Tokyo, or Eastern Capital. At first, there was much confusion about what the new group of ruling clans wanted. Some of the architects of the restoration would have been happy to leave things as they had been under the Tokugawa shoguns but with themselves as the effective rulers. Others felt that the times called for sweeping economic, political, and military changes. After considerable debate and outbreaks of violence (especially by samurai who were unhappy about the inadequacy of the pensions promised them by the new regime), the advocates of change won out. The feudal system was formally abolished with the return of the land and population from the daimyo to the emperor. The daimyo and the samurai were pensioned off, and their privileged status was abolished. The outcast *eta* (a caste of "untouchables" engaged in hereditary occupations related to the slaughtering of animals, such as the making of leather and leather goods) were declared emancipated, and everyone became equally a subject of the emperor.

During the Meiji period (1868–1911), the Western powers forced the Japanese to sign treaties that prevented Japan from trying foreigners in Japanese courts and from freely setting tariffs on foreign imports. To facilitate negotiations to end these unequal treaties and reassert Japan's independence, the Japanese modernized their legal system using European models.

The Imperial Constitution

During the struggle for power, some samurai leaders had demanded that a representative assembly be established. In 1889, after several false starts, a new constitution was promulgated. The principal author of the Imperial Constitution (usually referred to as the Meiji Constitution) was Count Ito Hirobumi, a leader of the Choshu clan, who hailed the new Japanese constitution as the "Emperor's gift to the Japanese people." Ito had studied constitutions in Europe and had been greatly impressed by the basic law of Prussia, which provided for a powerful executive branch. The autocratic ideology of the Imperial Constitution was explicitly declared in Article 1: "The Empire of Japan shall be reigned over and governed by a line of Emperors unbroken for ages eternal." The theory and interpretation of the document were further clarified in Ito's *Commentary on the Constitution of Japan.* Although the text of the constitution was never altered until the entire document was replaced in 1947, the actual operation of the government, as we shall see, underwent significant changes during the 58 years that the Meiji Constitution was in force.

Japan's new leaders (samurai who had brought about the imperial restoration) were determined to make Japan a rich and powerful country and wanted to ensure that their influence in Tokyo would not be hobbled by the newly established Imperial Diet. The Diet consisted of an aristocratic House of Peers and a House of Representatives composed of members chosen by a small electorate of high-paying taxpayers, but its powers were limited by the constitution. The Diet was powerless to control the executive branch using the power of the purse: If the two houses failed to approve the budget proposed by the government, the government could simply enforce the budget of the preceding year. Prime ministers were appointed by the emperor on the recommendation of the *Genro,* or Elder Statesmen, a powerful group of former samurai not mentioned in the constitution. Until 1918, all prime ministers were appointed from either the samurai class or, in one instance, from the hereditary court nobility. The emperor had "supreme command of the army and navy." This provision largely removed the military from the control of the prime minister and the Diet. The prestige and power of the executive and the military were vastly enhanced during the victorious wars with China (1894–1895) and Russia (1904–1905). These wars resulted in Japan's acquiring Taiwan, Southern Sakhalin, and a foothold in Manchuria. Korea was forcefully annexed in 1910.

TAISHO DEMOCRACY

Political parties emerged in the 1880s, organized by disgruntled samurai who felt that they were being excluded from the Meiji power structure. Their influence in the Diet had to be recognized by the oligarchy. In 1918, a year of widespread rice riots, the emperor and the Genro for the first time chose a commoner, Hara Takeshi, the leader of the *Seiyukai* (Constitutional) Party, to serve as prime minister. With the establishment of party government in 1918 and the agitation for democratic rights after the First World War, party leaders began to talk of the coming of "normal parliamentary government," in which the leader of the majority party (or majority coalition) in the House of Representatives would serve as prime minister. The movement favoring universal manhood suffrage became irresistible.

In 1925, the Diet passed the universal manhood suffrage law, which made the lower house a more democratic body. Some intellectuals and party leaders had hoped that Japan would become a parliamentary democracy like England, but the Diet enacted a peace preservation law that made illegal any attack on the principle of the emperor's sovereignty. The trend toward parliamentary government came to be known as Taisho democracy, referring to the reign of the Taisho emperor (1912–1925). Had it not been for the world depression in the 1930s, which had devastating consequences in Japan, democracy might have become more firmly established in that country.

THE RISE OF MILITARISM

In the 1930s, junior officers in the army, largely drawn from the impoverished peasantry, tended to blame capitalists and the politicians, believed to be controlled by the capitalists, for the plight of the people, who were suffering from the depression. Advocating a "Showa Restoration," or restoration of direct imperial rule, they aspired to a more equitable social order. Several military coups d'état were attempted and leading cabinet ministers were assassinated. Prime ministers lived in fear for their lives. To strengthen control over rebellious junior officers and to appease the militarists, with increasing frequency, the Genro chose military men to serve as prime ministers, and the representation of the political parties in the cabinets was reduced. The ministers of war and navy (who had to be generals or admirals according to an imperial ordinance) would threaten to refuse service in a cabinet or proposed cabinet whose chief or whose policies did not please them. Thus the military exercised an effective veto over the policies and personnel of the government.

The civilian government in Tokyo was unable to restrain the Kwantung Army (the Japanese forces stationed in Japan's basehold on the southern tip of Manchuria, China) from carrying out its own policy. In 1931, Japanese troops seized all of Manchuria and later established a puppet state (Manchukuo) headed by the former emperor of China ("Henry" Pu Yi), who collaborated with the Japanese in order to gain wealth and prestige. Under international condemnation, Japan resigned from the League of Nations, and in 1937 a full-scale war broke out between China and Japan. Japanese forces captured Nanking, the Chinese capital, and brutalized and murdered tens of thousands of civilians. In 1940, Japan allied itself with Germany and Italy to deter American and Soviet opposition, and the three Axis powers announced their intention to establish "New Orders" in Europe and Asia.

War broke out in Europe in 1939, and on December 7, 1941 ("a date that will live in infamy," President Roosevelt called it), Japanese carrier-based aircraft made a surprise attack on Pearl

Harbor in an attempt to prevent American interference with Japan's invasions of the Dutch East Indies, Malaya, and the Philippines. The Japanese attack devastated the American navy and aroused the wrath of the American people, who regarded the attack as unprovoked. Within a few months, Japan conquered the Philippine Islands and the British and Dutch possessions in Southeast Asia.

The Japanese drive was halted in the sea battle with the Americans at Midway Island in June 1942, and the Japanese were thrown on the defensive. By the spring of 1945, the Americans had captured island bases close enough to mainland Japan to launch frightful air attacks on Japanese cities. In August, after two Japanese cities had been destroyed by American atomic bombs and the Soviet Union (with which Japan had a neutrality treaty) had declared war on Japan, the Japanese government accepted the terms set forth by the Allies in the Potsdam Declaration of July 26, 1945.

THE ALLIED OCCUPATION

The main purpose of the Allied occupations of previous Axis countries was to ensure that those nations never again threaten the security of peace-loving countries. Because of the common belief that people, as distinguished from leaders, are peace loving, it was thought that democratic regimes were less inclined to be warlike than autocratic governments. Thus, in addition to completely disarming Germany and Japan, the Allies set about establishing democratic institutions in the defeated countries. Moreover, it was widely thought that fundamental economic and social reforms were essential to provide a lasting basis for democratic political institutions. There was continuing controversy about the need, extent, and precise character of the social reforms that would have to be carried out. The unconditional surrender of the defeated states meant that there was virtually no limit to the authority of the occupying powers to intervene in the internal affairs of Germany and Japan.

The occupations of Germany and Japan differed in two essential respects. First, unlike Germany, which was administered in four zones, one for each Allied power, all of Japan (except Okinawa and Japan's former possessions, Korea and Taiwan) was placed under the unified control of the Supreme Commander for the Allied Powers (SCAP), General Douglas MacArthur, who had been appointed by President Truman with the concurrence of Joseph Stalin. The policies of the United States were in effect controlling, and the other Allies represented in the Far Eastern Commission could do little more than give their advice or complain about measures already taken by MacArthur's staff. Second, in Germany, where no effective national German government existed following the surrender, the Allied authorities directly enacted legislation. In Japan, the emperor and imperial government remained in place, and SCAP issued directives to the Japanese government, which was required to enact laws or issue ordinances to carry out the Allies' (essentially American) policies. Thus the policies of Allied military government in Japan were uniform for the whole country and were administered indirectly.

DEMOCRATIZATION

From the beginning, critics in the United States and the Allied countries complained that the emperor should have been arrested and either tried as a war criminal or made to abdicate, or both, and that the Japanese government, composed of reactionaries, could not be trusted to carry out the sweeping reforms required by the Allies. However, the system worked with a minimum of friction between the Allied (overwhelmingly American) forces and the Japanese, and as we shall see, substantial democratic reform was accomplished in Japan. By contrast, the occupation of Germany was the focus of continual bitter controversy within and among the Allied countries, and at the time of the Berlin blockade (1948–1949), there were fears that war might break out between the Soviet Union and the Western powers. While Germany became the center of the Cold War confrontation, Japan seemed to represent the epitome of tranquillity,

General Douglas MacArthur, Supreme Commander for the Allied Powers, with Emperor Hirohito of Japan at the American embassy in Tokyo in September 1945.

and MacArthur enjoyed wide praise for the smoothness of his operation.

The policies of the Allied occupation of Japan were largely based on the Potsdam Declaration of July 26, 1945. It stated that Japanese military and naval forces were to be disarmed and repatriated, Taiwan was to revert to Chinese rule, and Korea had to be liberated from Japanese control. In addition to trials set up among the East Asian countries for the punishment of Japanese violations of the laws of war, an International Military Tribunal for the Far East (the Tokyo War Crimes Trial) was established for the trial of class A war criminals, those accused of crimes against peace (planning and carrying out aggressive war) and

crimes against humanity, following the precedents of the Nuremberg trial. Officeholders or office seekers who had been military or naval officers or holders of positions in the Imperial Rule Assistance Association (a totalitarian organization) or in other militaristic or ultranationalistic organizations were declared ineligible for public office. This "purge," the administration of which was entrusted to the Japanese government, was intended to clear the way for new leadership in Japan.

Under SCAP guidance, a sweeping land reform was carried out which made virtually every peasant a landowner. Partly as a result, Japanese farmers became politically very conservative because they suspected that Communists might try to deprive them of their land. The government broke up the great family-controlled business and financial combines (*zaibatsu*) and sold their stock publicly, encouraged the unionization of labor, and for the first time, gave women the right to vote. Freedom of speech and of the press was granted.

THE DEMOCRATIC CONSTITUTION

In MacArthur's view, the Allied occupation's most notable accomplishment in Japan was the establishment of a thoroughly democratic constitution. The general first raised the issue of constitutional revision in 1945, but Prime Minister Shidehara publicly stated that it was unnecessary to amend the Meiji Constitution, which he said had failed because it had been abused by the militarists. In his view, all that was needed to democratize the country was the enactment of appropriate legislation. But as it became increasingly clear that the Allied Powers would require drastic reforms, private groups and individuals, as well as the government, began to propose a variety of democratic constitutional amendments.

By February 1946, the Shidehara cabinet was still unable to produce a sufficiently democratic constitution. General MacArthur's Government Section secretly drew up a model constitution which they presented to the cabinet

---

A CLOSER LOOK 5.1

WOMEN IN JAPANESE POLITICS

Doi Takako

Women in Japan were given the right to vote by General MacArthur in 1946, a right confirmed by the democratic constitution adopted later that year. In the 1946 general election, 39 women were elected to the House of Representatives, which then had a total of 464 members. Never since have women candidates for the lower house done so well. The Japan Socialist Party won the 1989 upper house election by a landslide under the leadership of a woman, Doi Takako. In that election, 22 women won seats.

Doi was elected speaker of the lower house, a position that she resigned in 1996 to resume leadership of the ailing JSP. A former college professor, she strongly advocates the preservation of Article 9 of the constitution, which bans war and military forces. The women candidates who emerged in the 1989 campaign were popularly dubbed "madonnas." They were very sensitive to issues of education, consumers' rights, world peace, and the environment, and they had been especially aroused by the imposition of the 3 percent consumption tax on sales.

As of 2005, 67 women were members of the two houses of the Japanese Diet, accounting for 9.5 percent of the total membership. In 2001, the popular and outspoken Tanaka Makiko, a former actress and the daughter of a former prime minister, became foreign minister in the Koizumi cabinet. A member of the Liberal Democratic Party, she was serving her third term in the lower house, representing the Nagano fifth district. Tactless and insubordinate, in 2002 she was fired from her cabinet post by Koizumi.

for its guidance. The Shidehara cabinet, faced with the possibilities that the Far Eastern Commission might insist on abolishing the monarchy, that the Allies might try the emperor as a war criminal, or that MacArthur might submit the draft constitution directly to the Japanese people for their decision, accepted the American proposal as the basis for a new constitution.

The cabinet's constitutional revision bill was submitted to the Diet as an "imperial project" in accordance with Article 73 of the Imperial Constitution concerning constitutional amendment. The imperial project was thoroughly debated, substantially amended, and passed by overwhelming majorities in both houses of the Diet, approved by the Privy Council, and on November 3, 1946, promulgated by the emperor. The new "Constitution of Japan" became effective on May 3, 1947.

Japan's new constitution proclaimed the sovereignty of the people, guaranteed basic human rights, and renounced war and the maintenance of military forces. The emperor was declared "the symbol of the State and of the unity of the people," and would have no "powers related to government." The House of Peers, the Privy Council, and all titles of nobility (save those of the imperial family) were abolished. A parliamentary-cabinet system of democratic government (in which the cabinet was responsible to the lower house of the Diet) was set up. The new upper house, whose members would have six-year terms, would be popularly elected but would be less powerful than the lower house. The constitutionality of legislation and governmental acts would be subject to judicial review. Sexual and racial discrimination were forbidden.

Popular Acceptance
of the Democratic Constitution

The new constitution represented such a radical departure from the previously published conservative (some said "reactionary") views of the Japanese cabinet that the document was obviously the product of urging from occupation officers. Nonetheless, after several decades during which public schools taught the provisions of the new constitution, it gained widespread popular acceptance. The antiwar provision enjoyed popularity from the very beginning, and women, students, intellectuals, journalists, laborers, indeed just about everyone, became attached to their new constitutional rights.

Many Japanese conservatives, however, have been unhappy with the document. They hold that the no-arms clause, if strictly interpreted, makes it difficult or impossible to defend the country. The emperor, they say, should be made head of state and be more respected. The family should enjoy more constitutional protection. The constitution, they assert, overemphasizes people's rights and neglects to set forth their duties. When the occupation ended in 1952, there appeared a spate of articles and books exposing real and purported facts about the occupation that had hitherto been suppressed by SCAP censors. The conservatives began to insist that the constitution had been forcibly imposed on Japan and that an independent Japan should have an "autonomous constitution."

In 1954, the conservative-dominated Diet created a Commission on the Constitution that would examine the origins and operation of the document and make possible recommendations for its amendment. By the mid-1960s when the commission made its report, however, the conservatives were still unable to win the two-thirds majorities needed in both houses of the Diet to amend the constitution. In 2001, both houses of the Diet established Research Commissions of the Constitution. Premiers Nakasone and Koizumi have strongly advocated a controversial amendment to provide that the prime minister be directly elected by the people rather than chosen by the Diet from its membership.

Although several prime ministers publicly declared their support of constitutional amendment as a matter of principle, they have been chary of assigning the highest priority to this issue, given its extremely controversial nature. In the meantime, the government, citing a controversial interpretation to be described later in this chapter, has been able to strengthen the Self-Defense Forces without amending the constitution, thus reducing the urgency of the issue. It must be said that there has been widespread unhappiness in Japan and abroad with the manner in which the government had gradually rearmed the country in apparent violation of the disarmament clause of the constitution and with the reluctance of the Supreme Court of Japan to deal forthrightly with this issue.

The democratic constitution is now 58 years old. Despite the conservatives' drive to amend it, not a word of its text has been altered. Much controversy has surrounded its interpretation and a number of famous constitutional cases have been tried by Japan's Supreme Court. On the whole, however, the document is popular and its principles have been adopted as accepted components of the political culture.

THE RETURN
OF INDEPENDENCE

After the new constitution went into effect in 1947, MacArthur believed that the occupation's only remaining task was to revive the Japanese economy. The time was drawing near for the Allies to sign a formal peace treaty with Japan. As the Cold War worsened, however, American policy makers became reluctant to withdraw their military forces from Japan, given the growing Communist threat in China and North Korea. American policy makers devised a plan whereby the Allied occupation would formally end, Japan's sovereignty would be restored, and the Japanese government would invite the United States to station forces in Japan. The Soviet Union, however, would not consent to this arrangement. Such a treaty would favor the

United States over the Soviet Union and compromise the neutrality of Japan. War broke out in Korea in 1950, and the American negotiators pushed ahead with their proposals in Japan, finally prompting the Japanese government to agree. Japanese socialists and pacifists strongly opposed the "one-sided" peace, asserting that it would alienate Japan's powerful neighbors, the Soviet Union and Communist China, and could drag Japan into a U.S.-Soviet war. The Japanese government asserted that a treaty acceptable to both superpowers was not a possibility. If Japan wished to end the occupation and regain its independence promptly, the best thing to do was to sign the treaty with the non-Communist powers.

The Japanese Peace Treaty was formally signed in San Francisco on September 8, 1951, to become effective on April 26, 1952. The Soviet Union sent a delegation to the conference but it refused to sign the treaty, the details of which had been finalized before the conference was convened. Neither the Nationalist nor the Communist government of China was represented. On the same day that the peace treaty was signed, Japan and the United States signed a mutual security treaty, which provided for the stationing of American forces in Japan. Urged by the United States, the Japanese government negotiated a peace treaty with the Nationalist government of China, based in Taiwan. In April 1952, Japan's independence as a sovereign state was restored and SCAP headquarters in downtown Tokyo was closed, but American forces remained in Japan under the terms of the security treaty.

The peace settlement alienated Japan from both the Soviet Union and Communist China and in effect made Japan an ally of the United States. The Japanese sought to negotiate a peace treaty with the Soviet Union but were unable to do so because of disagreements over the Japanese claims to northern islands under Soviet military occupation. In 1956, the two countries issued a "joint peace declaration" formally ending the state of war between them. The territorial dispute continued unabated, and 60 years after the end of the fighting there was still no formal peace treaty between Japan and Russia.

THE EMPEROR SYSTEM TODAY

According to the 1889 Imperial Constitution, Japan was to "be reigned over and governed by a line of Emperors unbroken for ages eternal." The emperor was "sacred and inviolable." He was "the head of the Empire, combining in Himself the rights of sovereignty."

In the 1930s, militarists exploited the emperor's authority and prestige to mobilize public support for their empire-building efforts in Asia. After World War II, hoping to prevent the revival of Japanese militarism and imperialism, many people in the Allied countries strongly urged that both the system of emperor worship and the imperial throne be abolished once and for all. The incumbent emperor, they believed, should be tried as a war criminal. MacArthur feared that the indictment of Emperor Hirohito would provoke a popular uprising in Japan and that the people's resentment of the occupiers would make it virtually impossible to educate them in the ways of democracy and peace. So the emperor was not tried, and the imperial throne was preserved.

On New Year's Day, 1946, the emperor issued a rescript in which he renounced the notion that he was divine. This statement pleased General MacArthur and was apparently an important factor in the rehabilitation of the imperial institution. Under the postwar democratic constitution, the emperor would be deprived of all powers related to government, and war and the maintenance of armed forces would be banned. The postwar emperor would be a powerless and harmless symbol.

Hirohito

In January 1989, Emperor Hirohito died at the age of 87. He had served as prince regent for five years during the mental illness of his father and in 1926 ascended to the imperial throne. He served as emperor for 20 years under the Imperial Constitution and for over 40 years under the democratic constitution. He survived several assassination attempts and lived through two world wars and seven years of occupation by for-

Emperor Akihito and Empress Michiko on January 9, 1989, when he pledged to uphold the democratic constitution of Japan. His father, Hirohito, had died two days earlier.

eign military forces. Few of the world's statesmen had so closely witnessed or participated in so many great events. With the accession of Emperor Akihito to the throne in 1989, the Showa era ended and the Heisei (Peace Attained) era began. The new emperor pledged to uphold the constitution and to strive for world peace.

The Imperial Family

The name of the imperial reign, rather than the Western calendar, is often used in Japan to designate the year. For example, 2002 is frequently referred to as "Heisei 14," the fourteenth year of the reign of the present emperor. When an emperor dies, his reign name is used to designate him, so that Emperor Hirohito is now called the Showa Emperor. Progressive critics complain that the use of reign names for dates unduly exalts the emperor.

The imperial family, whose popularity was enhanced by the marriage of the present emperor (then the crown prince) to a beautiful and intelligent commoner in 1959, is constantly in the news. Prince Naruhito, the older of the present emperor's two sons, is the crown prince. The crown prince, like his uncle Prince Mikasa, is a serious historian and has given lectures on Japanese history. In 1993 he married Owada Masako, a graduate of Harvard University, who had studied law at Tokyo University and passed the examination to join the diplomatic service. (Her father was a career diplomat.) In December 2001 she gave birth to a baby girl. Under the terms of the Imperial House Law passed by the Diet in 1947, only males can succeed to the throne.

A Modern Monarchy

In Japan, under the democratic constitution, the emperor "appoints" as prime minister the individual chosen by the Diet and "appoints" as chief judge of the Supreme Court the person chosen by the cabinet. The emperor presides over the openings of Diet sessions and his seal is necessary for important state documents.

In 1966, the Diet enacted a law that revived the annual celebration on February 11 of the founding of the state by the mythical first emperor (presumably in 660 B.C.E.). Called "National Foundation Day" (*Kenkoku Kinen no Hi*), this is one of 13 national holidays. This move and other conservative attempts to enhance the status of the imperial throne have been fervently resisted by progressives and pacifists in Japan and viewed with concern by foreign observers.

In 1988, the mayor of Nagasaki publicly blamed Emperor Hirohito for having needlessly prolonged World War II. This statement was made during the emperor's prolonged fatal illness and provoked a nationwide controversy. A year later, a rightist shot and gravely wounded the mayor in front of the city hall. The would-be assassin was tried and sentenced to 12 years of penal servitude. When the mayor ran for re-election in 1991, he was denied the support of the Liberal Democratic Party but was reelected by a narrow margin. In 1995, he was defeated in a bid for reelection.

Many progressive Japanese were especially disturbed by the reactionary implications of the Shinto ceremonies connected with the funeral of the Showa emperor and the formal accession to the throne by Akihito. At the same time, imperial court circles tend to be cautious about doing anything that would make the throne a focus of controversy.

THE BURDEN OF HISTORY

In 1987 Prime Minister Nakasone talked of "closing the books on the postwar [period]." This statement seemed to imply a repudiation of the postwar reforms. Nakasone formally visited the Yasukuni Shrine, where Japan's war dead are deified. For some years, the Ministry of Education has been using its authority to review textbooks so that Japan's aggressions against China and Korea are glossed over. Official visits to Yasukuni and the textbook issue have provoked protests from China, Korea, and others of Japan's erstwhile victims as well as from religious groups, intellectuals, and others in Japan. Since 1985 several Japanese cabinet ministers have been forced to resign because of tactless statements justifying Japan's militaristic record.

In the United States, too, controversy has surrounded the issue of Japanese guilt in World War II. In 1995, the fiftieth anniversary of the end of the war, the Smithsonian Institution set up an exhibit of the *Enola Gay,* the B-29 airplane that had dropped the atomic bomb on Hiroshima. The original plan called for the display of heart-rending photographs and relics of the destruction of Hiroshima and its inhabitants, but protests that the museum was portraying Japan as a war victim rather than as an aggressor forced the museum to forego a display of the materials. Wartime atrocities by the Japanese—the Bataan Death March, the Nanking Massacre, maltreatment of prisoners of war, and the exploi-

tation of "comfort women" and forced laborers—were recalled in the American media. Heated controversies arose in both Japan and the United States concerning Japanese aggression, the morality of the use of the atomic bombs, the purported obligation of one side or the other to apologize, and freedom of historical inquiry. Sixty years after the Japanese surrender, the memory of Japan's war record still complicates relations with its neighbors and trading partners. Japanese intellectuals and politicians continue to debate the meaning of the prewar and wartime policies of their nation and the constitutionality of the Self-Defense Forces or their dispatch as United Nations peacekeepers.

MINORITIES

In Hokkaido, Japan's northernmost main island, there remain several thousand Ainu, a caucasoid people whose ancestors evidently lived in Japan before the arrival of the mongoloids. Some make their livelihood by making and selling souvenirs depicting their picturesque culture to tourists.

In the subtropical Ryukyu Islands reside well over 1 million Okinawans, who until two generations ago were as likely to speak Okinawan as they were to speak Japanese. After coming under Japanese rule in 1879, many intermarried with the Japanese. During the closing stages of World War II, in the bloody battle of Okinawa, thousands of Okinawans lost their lives. While Okinawa was under the American military government from 1945 to 1972, they sought the return of their land to Japanese rule. At the same time, some Okinawans seek to preserve their distinctive language, art, and music from being submerged completely by Japanese culture. The vast majority of American military bases in Japan are concentrated in Okinawa, and the local people bear a disproportionate share of the burden of crimes committed by American servicemen and the noise and danger of American military aircraft.

In addition to Okinawans and Ainu, there are two other substantial minorities. There are over 650,000 Koreans whose families have lived in Japan for several generations. Many are descendants of Koreans brought to Japan during World War II for forced labor. They are not Japanese nationals and insist on the right to Korean-language schools and complain of discrimination, such as, in the recent past, having to be fingerprinted (as are other aliens) by Japanese authorities. Under Japanese law, mere birth in Japanese territory does not automatically confer citizenship. Japanese nationality can only be claimed by blood-descent from a Japanese or naturalization, which is often a difficult procedure.

There are also about 2 million *burakumin* (literally, "village people"), who are the descendants of *eta*. Communities of *burakumin* may be found concentrated in certain areas of large cities, and their occupations and diet as well as other cultural characteristics may distinguish them from majority Japanese. Racially, *burakumin* are indistinguishable from majority Japanese, but employers and the families of potential marriage partners try hard to avoid people with *buraku* ancestries. Discrimination against this minority is illegal, and the Burakumin Liberation League regularly makes political or judicial issues of apparent cases of flagrant discrimination.

All told, fewer than 2 percent of Japan's population may be considered "minority." Except for the importation of 2 or 3 million Korean laborers into Japan during World War II, there has been no substantial immigration to the Japanese islands in recorded history. As a result, the Japanese have a strong consciousness and pride in their racial distinctiveness and homogeneity. Japan, as contrasted with India, the United States, and a number of other countries, is blessed with the relative absence of ethnic strife. Japanese society is not pluralistic nor does it seriously aspire to be. The Japanese government does not encourage immigration in spite of labor shortages. In the past few years, the lure of good jobs in Japan has attracted legal and illegal immigrants from other parts of Asia as well as Brazilians and Peruvians of Japanese ancestry. Given the fact that the Japanese islands are already overcrowded, the relative closing of Japan to immigrants is understandable.

RELIGION

Over the centuries, various religious sects have been introduced to the point that Japan has sometimes been referred to as a "museum of religions." Opinions differ as to how religious the Japanese people really are, and some experts cite the ready tendency of the population to accept new religions or sects as evidence of the shallowness of religious convictions. It is, however, true that for many Japanese, religion is an important force in their lives.

The various religious organizations in Japan report a combined membership of over 220 million. Because this is almost twice the total population, it is evident that many people are adherents of two or more religious persuasions: 108 million Japanese are said to be Shintoist, 89 million are reportedly Buddhist, 1.5 million are Christians, and 11 million belong to other organizations. Most people are married in Shinto ceremonies and are buried according to Buddhist rites. Before the enactment of the postwar democratic constitution, the national government subsidized the indigenous Shinto religion, which asserted the divine origin of the Japanese nation and the divinity of the imperial dynasty. Christianity became widespread, especially in Kyushu during the early seventeenth century, but because of suspicions arising from its foreign origin it was forbidden by the Tokugawa shoguns and its followers were mercilessly persecuted. Although Christians are a small minority in Japan, there are many well-attended Christian colleges in the country, and Christians probably exercise greater influence in the society than their small numbers might suggest. Christians are especially prominent in the peace movement and in the advocacy of other progressive causes. The late Prime Ministers Katayama Tetsu and Ohira Masayoshi were Christians.

Because the new constitution forbade the state from subsidizing religious organizations, Shinto organizations that had received state subsidies (called "state Shinto"), including the Yasukuni shrine, had to become self-supporting. At the same time there emerged numerous "new religions," which were often sects of

Buddhism, that paid special attention to psychological and economic insecurities. The most conspicuous perhaps was the *Soka Gakkai*, a layman's educational and social organization that had been founded in the 1930s in affiliation with the old *Nichiren Shoshu* sect of Buddhism. In the 1960s this organization sponsored the organization of the *Komeito*, a political party that soon became the third largest political representation in the Japanese Diet, as we shall note later in this chapter.

The relation of the state to religious organizations became a very delicate issue in 1995, when members of the *Aum Shinrikyo* sect, led by a domineering guru, were accused of involvement in the placement of sarin gas, a chemical weapon, in several subways in central Tokyo. Twelve passengers were killed and hundreds were hospitalized. Police made mass investigations of *Aum* establishments in scattered parts of Japan and discovered that the sect's members were manufacturing and using hallucinogenic drugs as well as sarin. They had begun experimenting with and making other chemical weapons and firearms. They were implicated in the kidnapping and murders and attempted murders of defectors from the sect and their relatives, and of individuals engaged in exposing *Aum* activities. The *Aum* sect came to be feared as a terrorist organization, and the public began to demand that the government cancel the sect's official designation as a religious organization.

Thinking Critically

1. Is it true, as believed by the reformers in the Allied countries, that democratic states are more peace-loving than nondemocratic states?
2. Should the Allied reformers have insisted that the system of the hereditary monarch be abolished in Japan?
3. Was the present Japanese constitution imposed on the Japanese people by the Allied occupation?

4. Compare the constitutional status of religion in Japan with the constitutional status of religion in another country of your choice.
5. On a practical level, how and to what extent does the Japanese constitution protect the rights of an ethnic or religious group of your choice in Japan?

KEY TERMS

Aum Shinrikyo (278)
Edo *(267)*
burakumin (277)
Fujiwara *(266)*
Hirohito *(274)*
Japanese Peace Treaty *(274)*
kamikaze (267)
Meiji *(268)*
Okinawa *(276)*
purge *(271)*
responsible government *(272)*
SCAP *(270)*
Shinto *(266)*
shogun *(267)*
Taisho democracy *(269)*
Tokugawa *(267)*
zaibatsu (271)

FURTHER READINGS

Allinson, Gary D. *Japan's Postwar History,* 2nd ed. (Ithaca: Cornell University Press, 2004).

Bix, Herbert P. *Hirohito and the Making of Modern Japan* (New York: HarperCollins, 2000).

Conroy, Hilary, and Harry Wray. *Pearl Harbor Examined: Prologue to the Pacific War* (Honolulu: University of Hawaii Press, 1990).

Dower, John. *Embracing Defeat: Japan in the Wake of World War II* (New York: Norton, 1999).

Field, Norma. *In the Realm of the Dying Emperor* (New York: Pantheon, 1991).

Framing the Japanese Constitution: Primary Sources in English, 1944–1949 (Bethesda, MD: University Publications of America, 1989). This is a massive collection of documents on microfilm.

Fujimura-Fanselow, Kumiko, and Atsuko Kameda, eds. *Japanese Women: New Feminist Perspectives on the Past, Present, and Future* (New York: Feminist Press at CUNY, 1995).

Gluck, Carol, and Stephen R. Graubard, eds. *Showa: The Japan of Hirohito* (New York: Norton, 1992).

Gordon, Andrew, ed. *Postwar Japan as History* (Berkeley: University of California Press, 1993).

Hardacre, Helen. *Shinto and the State, 1868–1989* (Princeton, NJ: Princeton University Press, 1989).

Hayes, Louis D. *Introduction to Japanese Politics,* 4th ed. (Armonk: Sharpe, 2005).

Hellegers, Dale M. *We the Japanese People: World War II and the Origins of the Japanese Constitution* (Stanford: Stanford University Press, 2001).

Hong, Wontack. *Paekche of Korea and the Origin of Yamato Japan* (Seoul, South Korea: Kudara International, 1994).

Hook, Glenn D., and Gavan McCormack. *Japan's Contested Constitution: Documents and Analysis* (London: Routledge, 2001).

Ienaga, Saburo. *Pacific War, 1931–1945: A Critical Perspective on Japan's Role in World War II* (New York: Pantheon, 1979).

Inoue, Kyoko. *MacArthur's Democratic Constitution: A Linguistic and Cultural Study of Its Making* (Chicago: University of Chicago Press, 1991).

Ito, Hirobumi. *Commentaries on the Constitution of the Empire of Japan,* trans. Ito Miyoji (Tokyo: Insetsu Kyoku, 1889).

Jansen, Marius. *The Making of Modern Japan* (Cambridge, MA: Harvard University Press, 2000).

Japan: An Illustrated Encyclopedia, 2 vols. (Tokyo: Kodansha, 1993).

Kades, Charles A. "The American Role in Revising Japan's Imperial Constitution," *Political Science Quarterly* (Summer 1989), pp. 215–248.

Kingston, Jeff. *Japan in Transition, 1952–2000* (Harlow: Longman, 2001).

Kodansha. *Constitution of Japan* (Tokyo: Kodansha Bilingual Books, Kodansha International, 1997).

Koseki, Shoichi. *The Birth of Japan's Postwar Constitution,* trans. Ray A. Moore (Boulder, CO: Westview Press, 1997).

Large, Stephen S., *Emperor Hirohito and Showa Japan: A Political Biography* (London: Routledge, 1992).

McNelly, Theodore. *The Origins of Japan's Democratic Constitution* (Lanham, MD: University Press of America, 2000).

Moore, Ray A., and Donald L. Robinson. *The Constitution of Japan: A Documentary History of Its Framing and Adoption, 1945–1947* [CD-ROM] (Princeton, NJ: Princeton University Press).

Moore, Ray A. and Donald L. Robinson. *Partners for Democracy: Crafting the New Japanese State under MacArthur,* (New York: Oxford University Press, 2002).

Nakamura, Masanori. *The Japanese Monarchy: Ambassador Joseph Grew and the Making of the "Symbol Emperor System," 1931–1991,* trans. Herbert P. Bix, Jonathan Baker-Yates, and Derek Bowen (Armonk, NY: M. E. Sharpe, 1992).

Nishi, Toshio. *Unconditional Democracy: Education and Politics in Occupied Japan, 1945–1952* (Stanford, CA: Stanford University Press, 1982).

Pharr, Susan J. *Political Women in Japan* (Berkeley: University of California Press, 1990).

Ruoff, Kenneth P. *The People's Emperor: Democracy and the Japanese Monarchy, 1945–1995* (Cambridge, MA: Harvard University Press, 2001).

Sugihara, Seishiro. *Japanese Perspectives on Pearl Harbor,* trans. Theodore McNelly (Hong Kong: Asian Research Service, 1995).

Supreme Commander for the Allied Powers, Government Section. *The Political Reorientation of Japan,* 2 vols. (Washington, DC: U.S. Government Printing Office, n.d.).

Ward, Robert E., and Yoshikazu Sakamoto, eds. *Democratizing Japan: The Allied Occupation* (Honolulu: University of Hawaii Press, 1987).

Ward, Robert E., and Frank Joseph Shulman, eds. *The Allied Occupation of Japan, 1945–1952: An Annotated Bibliography of Western Language Materials* (Chicago: American Library Association, 1974).

B. POLITICAL PROCESSES AND INSTITUTIONS

Political parties arose in Japan among samurai who felt excluded from the Meiji regime in the 1880s. By organizing and agitating, they sought to pressure the government into establishing an assembly, and the government did so when it promulgated the Imperial Constitution in 1889. That constitution, however, left the executive dominant over the legislative branch, the Diet.

In 1898, the samurai leaders of the two principal political parties joined forces to form the Constitutional Party (Seiyukai). The new party's strength in the House of Representatives was sufficient to pressure the Genro to appoint one of its leaders, Okuma, as prime minister. In 1900 Prime Minister Ito, in order to organize a working coalition in the House of Representatives, accepted the leadership of the Seiyukai Party. Thus political parties proved their usefulness in organizing lower house elections and in mobilizing support in the lower house for the passage of the government's legislation. In 1918, with the appointment of Hara, a commoner and leader of the Seiyukai, as prime minister, it appeared that the power of the samurai oligarchy was greatly weakened and that political parties might come into their own as a dominant factor in politics.

The rise of militarism in the 1930s checked the ascendance of political parties, and beginning in 1932, most of the prime ministers were either generals or admirals. In 1940, the major parties voted to dissolve themselves, and a quasi-totalitarian state, led by the Imperial Rule Assistance Association (IRAA), came into being. At the end of World War II, the IRAA was abolished and the prewar political parties were revived with the strong encouragement of MacArthur's headquarters. Indeed, the Americans hoped that the promise of "normal constitutional government," advocated by the political parties in the 1920s, would be realized.

POLITICAL PARTIES
IN MODERN JAPAN

Political parties seem to be a necessity in modern states, whether they be democratic or totalitarian. Parties initiate and advocate government programs, sponsor candidates who will work for the adoption of these programs, raise money and campaign for their candidates, and provide blocs of votes in the legislature for enactment of their programs or defeat of their rivals' programs. In a parliamentary-cabinet system of democracy such as exists in Japan, the leader of the party or coalition of parties that controls a majority in the parliament normally serves as the prime minister.

From 1945 to 1955, Japan had a multiparty system. In 1955 the two wings of the Socialist Party reunited, and the two conservative parties combined to form the Liberal Democratic Party (LDP), thus inaugurating an essentially two-party arrangement that became known as "the 1955 system." However, the Socialist Party was never able to capture a majority in the lower house, so there was no rotation in office of prime minister between the two major parties. Thus from 1955 until 1993, the "one-party-dominant system" prevailed in Japan. For 38 years, without exception the prime ministers and nearly all their cabinet ministers were members of the Liberal Democratic Party. The other political parties were unable to muster enough votes among the electorate to elect majorities in the lower house of the Diet. Because an acquaintance with Japan's unusual electoral systems is essential to an understanding of party politics in that country, we shall now look at how elections there are conducted.

THE ELECTORAL SYSTEM
FOR THE LOWER HOUSE

Japan's House of Representatives (the lower house) is more powerful than the House of Councillors (the upper house). The term of the members of the House of Representatives is four years, but normally the house is dissolved before the four years have elapsed, so that general elections are normally held once every two or three years. (The term "general elections" refers to elections for the House of Representatives.)

The constitution provides that the qualifications of both the voters and the members of the Diet shall be determined by law, but there can be no discrimination because of race, creed, sex, social status, family origin, education, property, or income. The law provides that to vote one must be a mentally competent, currently unincarcerated Japanese national 20 years of age or older.

Before the reform of 1994, the electoral system for the House of Representatives was different from that of any other major national legislative assembly. At the time of the 1986 and 1990 elections, there were 130 electoral districts as determined by law. The 130 districts altogether sent 512 members to the House of Representatives. Each district, depending on the size of its population, elected from two to five members to the lower house.

Each voter was permitted to vote for only one candidate. The candidates receiving the most votes were declared elected. Thus, in a five-member district, each voter selected only one candidate and the five candidates receiving the most votes were declared the winners and would represent the district. This arrangement made it possible for a minority party to win a seat in the district, and it reduced the possibility that a plurality party would win all the seats in a district. In a single-member district (SMD) system, with which the British and Americans are familiar, the plurality party wins the single seat for the district and the other parties are left with nothing to show for their pains. The Japanese called their setup the "medium-sized district system" and it is known to political scientists as the single nontransferable vote (SNTV) system with multimember districts (MMD). Table 5.1 shows the results of lower house elections since 2000.

The SNTV system worked best for the LDP and the Japan Socialist Party (JSP); they generally

TABLE 5.1

HOUSE OF REPRESENTATIVES ELECTIONS, 2000–2003

Party	June 25, 2000			November 9, 2003		
	Single-Member Districts	Proportional Representation	Total	Single-Member Districts	Proportional Representation	Total
Liberal Democratic Party	177	56	233	168	69	237
Komeito	7	24	31	9	25	34
Social Democratic Party	4	15	19	1	5	6
Japan Communist Party	0	20	20	–	9	9
Democratic Party	80	47	127	105	72	177
Liberal Party	4	18	22	–	–	–
New Frontier Party	–	–	–	–	–	–
Conservative Party	7	0	7	4	–	4
Minor parties and independent	21	0	21	13	–	13
Total	300	180	480	300	180	480

The Liberal Party merged with the Democratic Party in 2003, and the Conservative Party merged with the LDP in 2004.

received more seats than their respective proportions of the vote would justify under proportional representation (PR). The system worked badly for the small parties, which won fewer seats than their proportion of the votes would justify under PR. Another problem was the failure of the government to redistribute seats when some districts lost population and others gained population. The LDP majority in the Diet was reluctant to reduce the representation of rural areas which had been loyally electing conservative candidates. In the 1980s the Japanese Supreme Court declared unconstitutional the apportionment plan then in force, and a new distribution of seats was used for the 1986 election. As things turned out, the reapportionment did no appreciable damage to the LDP, which won a landslide victory in that election.

The ballot did not carry either the names of the candidates or the parties, forcing the voter to write his or her favorite candidate's name on the ballot. This had the effect of emphasizing individual candidates over their parties, because in order to vote the voters had to memorize, and be able to write, the names of their favorite candidates.

Problems with the Single Nontransferable Vote System

In the SNTV system, if a party endorsed too many candidates in a district, the votes of the party's supporters would be spread too thin among too many candidates, and few or none would be elected. Because the LDP usually endorsed several candidates in each district, conservative voters had to choose among the LDP candidates. The pressure in the party to sponsor too many candidates was great, and the LDP leaders sought to restrict the number of its endorsements to assure the optimal result.

Rarely did the JSP have enough supporters to elect more than one Socialist candidate in a district, so it usually endorsed only one candidate. The Communists also endorsed only one candidate per district. In most districts, the Communists usually failed to win a single seat, so many Communist votes were "wasted." (If the Communists had refrained from sponsoring Communist candidates in the hopeless districts, at least their supporters could have voted for candidates of other

progressive parties, but the Communist strategy in recent years has been to oppose the other progressive parties as much as they opposed the conservatives.) The Democratic Socialist Party (DSP) and Komeito each normally endorsed one candidate only in those districts where a fair chance of success existed. The DSP, Komeito, and JSP occasionally made electoral alliances, by which they agreed to support one another's candidates in some electoral districts, thus making the most effective use of progressive votes.

The nature of the electoral system often made it possible to determine the outcome of the election in advance—in broad outline. For example, in the 1990 general election only the LDP endorsed more than 257 candidates, the number necessary to have the possibility of winning a majority (257) of the 512 seats in the lower house. Even if every one of the 148 Socialist candidates had won seats, they still would not have captured a majority of the seats in the chamber. The same could be said of the other parties. Thus, even before the election was held, everyone knew that none of the opposition parties could possibly win a majority of seats. Because only the LDP had a mathematical potential to win a majority of seats, the LDP was the only party that would be able to establish a one-party cabinet, whereas a cabinet made up of the other parties probably would be an unpredictable and unstable combination. Voters desiring political stability would have been inclined to vote conservative in order to produce a single-party cabinet with the stable majority in the House of Representatives necessary to govern effectively. At the same time, many LDP members believed that the single-member district system, in which the winner of a plurality would win the seat, would probably be more favorable to the LDP candidates than the medium-sized district system. Thus from time to time, the LDP sought to change the system to SMD.

Electoral Reform for the Lower House

The Japanese SNTV electoral system was criticized on a number of grounds: (1) It favored large parties over small parties. (2) The size of the electoral districts was too large, which increased the cost of campaigning. (3) LDP candidates found themselves competing against one another for conservative votes, which increased the total cost of conservative campaigns. (It was rare that any other party sponsored more than one candidate in a district.) The high cost of campaigning required politicians to raise large amounts of money, which was a source of corruption. (4) The districts were not promptly reapportioned to take into account changes in the distribution of the population. Thus districts with small populations might have more seats in the lower house than was merited while districts with large populations were underrepresented.

Because of these complaints, every few years serious proposals were advanced to correct these problems. However, reform proposals provoked opposition, as any given proposal was apt to favor certain parties, factions, or individuals over other parties, factions, or individuals.

In 1993, when the reformer Hosokawa became prime minister of a coalition cabinet that excluded the LDP, the Diet enacted a new electoral law and a reapportionment law for the lower house. The radical new law established the total number of seats at 500, with 300 seats to be filled by voting in 300 single-member districts (SMDs), and 200 seats to be filled by proportional representation (PR) in 11 regions, in which the system of party lists would be used.

The 300 SMDs were created by dividing up each of the 47 prefectures (Japan's major political subdivisions) into electoral districts. This was comparable to the system used for the U.S. House of Representatives, according to which each of the states is divided into SMDs.

In order to fill the 200 seats to be elected by proportional representation, the 47 prefectures of Japan were divided into 11 regions, called "blocks." The islands of Hokkaido, Kyushu, and Shikoku were each designated as a block for PR. Honshu was divided into eight blocks (see Table 5.2).

Each voter would cast two votes. One vote would indicate the candidate that the voter preferred to represent the voter's single-member district. The other vote would indicate the party list the voter preferred. (Each party would propose a list of its candidates for seats represent-

TABLE 5.2

PROPORTIONAL REPRESENTATION BLOCKS IN JUNE 25, 2000, HOUSE OF REPRESENTATIVES ELECTION

Region	Number of Seats
Hokkaido	8
Tohoku (northern Honshu)	14
Kita Kanto (northern Tokyo plain)	20
Minami Kanto (southern Tokyo plain)	21
Tokyo	17
Hokuriku-Shinetsu (central Japan seacoast)	11
Tokai (Pacific coast southwest of Tokyo)	21
Kinki (Kyoto-Osaka-Kobe area)	30
Chugoku (western Honshu)	11
Shikoku	6
Kyushu (including Okinawa)	21
Total	180

ing the relevant block.) After an election, the candidates winning pluralities in the 300 SMDs would be declared elected. The 200 PR seats would be assigned to the political parties in proportion to the votes received by their party lists. For example, after the votes for a block party list are counted and a certain party is awarded four seats, the top four individuals named on that party's list are declared elected. The new system bears some resemblance to the electoral system for the German Bundestag.

Campaign financing was also reformed. A law was enacted that, among other things, limited corporate donations to individual politicians, provided public funds to parties for campaigning, and strengthened enforcement of the rules.

The new electoral system was used for the House of Representatives Election in 1996. However, for the 2000 election, the number of PR seats was reduced from 200 to 180. Some candidates ran both in their SMD and in a PR list. If a candidate was unsuccessful in his SMD, he might be elected in the PR race if his name was high enough on that list. Depending on his SMD results, his position in the PR list could be improved.

Unfamiliarity with the operation of the new system and the tricky strategies of the candidates in its operation have not endeared the system to the voters. Moveover there is a great disparity in the number of voters from one SMD to another, seeming to require redistricting. Thus proposals for revamping the system are being widely advocated. The electoral system remains a controversial issue in Japanese politics.

UPPER HOUSE ELECTIONS

Between 1947 and 1970, the House of Councillors consisted of 250 members. Of this number, 150 were chosen by SNTV in electoral districts. (The then 46 prefectures served as electoral districts, often referred to as prefectural constituencies.) The remaining 100 councillors were chosen by SNTV with the entire nation serving as an electoral district (i.e., each voter would vote for one candidate, and the candidates with the most votes were elected). The six-year terms of the members were staggered so that elections were held once every three years to fill one-half of the seats. In 1970 two seats for Okinawa were added to the 150 seats representing the prefectural constituencies. In 1983, the list system of proportional representation (PR) replaced the former SNTV used to elect the 100 members rep-

resenting the nation at large; each political party proposed a list of candidates and the relevant seats would be assigned to each political party in proportion to the number of votes it received in the PR constituency. (If a party list won, say, 12 seats, the seats would be assigned to the 12 individuals highest on the party list.)

In 2000, following an extremely bitter debate and a three-week boycott of the deliberations by opposition members in the Diet, a new electoral law was enacted that reduced the number of seats to be filled by PR from 100 to 96 and the seats to be filled for prefectural constituencies from 150 to 144. At the same time, the system for filling the PR seats was substantially altered. As before, each party would propose a list of candidates for the PR seats. But now the voter was given the option of *either* voting for a party list *or* voting for a single candidate on any of the lists. A vote for any single candidate would count as a vote for the entire relevant party list, to be used in distributing seats to the parties in proportion to their votes. Each party would allocate the seats it had won to the candidates on its list who had won the highest number of votes. As a result of this system, it would become possible for a single candidate's votes to benefit all the candidates on a list. The new system was used in the 2001 upper house election (see Table 5.3).

TABLE 5.3

HOUSE OF COUNCILLORS ELECTION RESULTS, JULY 29, 2001 AND JULY 11, 2004

Party	Seats Not Up for Re-election		Constituency		Proportional Representation		Total	
	2001	2004	2001	2004	2001	2004	2001	2004
Liberal Democratic Party	46	49	44	34	20	15	110	115
New Komeito	10	11	5	3	8	8	23	24
New Conservative Party	4	–	0	–	1	–	5	–
Democratic Party of Japan	33	50	18	31	8	19	59	82
Japan Communist Party	15	4	1	–	4	4	20	9
Liberal Party	5	–	0	–	3	–	8	–
Social Democratic Party of Japan	2	2	2	–	4	2	8	5
Other	11	5	3	5	–	–	14	7
Total	121	121	73	73	48	48	247	242

Also at each election, 76 seats are filled by using the 47 prefectures as electoral districts. Each district is entitled to send to Tokyo from one to four councillors depending on the size of the district. The SNTV is used. Each voter chooses one candidate, and the candidates winning the most votes in each district are declared elected. (For an example of an election, see Table 5.3.)

The 1995 upper house election was notable in two respects. First, the percentage of qualified voters who voted, 44.52 percent, was the lowest ever in any national election in Japan since World War II. The low turnout was usually attributed by most to voter apathy. (The enthusiasm for political reform that had led to the defeat of the LDP and the formation of the Hosokawa cabinet had given way to disillusionment after Hosokawa resigned as the result of a scandal, Hata was unable to establish a stable coalition cabinet of the reform parties, and the SDPJ and LDP compromised their long-held political ideals

when they formed the Murayama government.) Second, the New Frontier Party replaced the SDPJ as the second largest political party in the House of Councillors, inspiring some analysts to conclude that if a lower house election were held at that time, the NFP would win a majority in that house. Actually, the New Frontier Party came far short of winning a majority in the 1996 lower house election, and late the following year the New Frontier Party dissolved. Table 5.4 shows upper house election results since 1992.

The electoral systems for the two houses of the Diet seem complicated when they have to be described to non-Japanese. But the rules of the game have everything to do with who wins and who loses, so that politicians are much preoccupied with purported improvements in the system. The majority party is understandably reluctant to "improve" the system in a way that would enhance the chances of the opposition parties. In Japan, as elsewhere, abstract theories

TABLE 5.4

HOUSE OF COUNCILLORS ELECTIONS, 1992–2004, NUMBER OF SEATS WON

Party	1992	1995	1998	2001	2004
Liberal Democratic Party	68	46	45	64	49
Komeito	14		9	13	11
New Conservative Party				1	–
Democratic Party of Japan			27	26	50
Japan Communist Party	6	8	15	5	4
Liberal Party			6	3	–
Social Democratic Party of Japan	22	16	5	6	2
Democratic Socialist Party	4				
Japan New Party	4				
Ni-in Club	1	1			
Sports Peace Party	2	0			
New Frontier Party		40			
New Party Sakigake		3			
Peace Party		1			
People's Reform League		2			
Minor Parties and Independents	7	9	19	3	5
Total	128	126	126	121	121

Note: Terms of office are six years; every three years, one half of the seats are up for election.

of justice do not always prevail over the realities of political power.

THE LIBERAL DEMOCRATIC PARTY

The Liberal Democratic Party (LDP) was formed in 1955, largely in response to the reunification of the Socialist Party earlier that same year. The big businesses that had been financing the two rival conservative parties, the Liberal and the Democratic, were concerned that these two parties would waste their funds fighting with each other and fail to protect business from the establishment of a socialist government committed to the nationalization of privately owned companies.

The Liberal Democrats stand for private enterprise, protection of the interests of farmers, close economic and strategic ties with the United States, and the maintenance and strengthening of Self-Defense Forces. The top leaders of the party usually are either former bureaucrats or professional politicians. Only a tiny percentage are lawyers by profession. The revision of the constitution to strengthen the status of the military forces and to enhance the position of the emperor has long been a feature of the agenda of this party, but its failure to get the required two-thirds of the seats in both houses and the unpopularity of the proposed amendments have made it unable to achieve this goal notwithstanding its near permanent monopoly of political power.

Factions in the LDP

The LDP is essentially a coalition of the party's factions in the two houses of the Diet. Some LDP factions have more seats in the Diet than do some of the political parties. These factions are groups of politicians working together to raise money and gain political power, and only occasionally do they stand for a particular policy distinct from the policies of the party as a whole. Each faction ordinarily has as its leader one of the faction's most effective fund raisers, usually a senior member in terms of number of times elected to the House of Representatives. No faction is headed by a woman, possibly because few

if any women have been able to acquire the necessary seniority.

Virtually every LDP Diet member belongs to a faction. A politician will affiliate with a faction (1) to use the faction's influence in obtaining sponsorship of the party in an election (sponsorship by the party means that one gets money and publicity from the party headquarters in a campaign), (2) to receive campaign funds from the faction leader, and (3) to get the faction leader's support for nomination to a position as cabinet minister or parliamentary vice minister. The faction leader may hope that his faction and the leaders of several other factions will support him one day for the coveted post of president of the LDP. From 1955 to 1993, the Diet would elect as prime minister whoever happened to be the LDP president.

After a faction leader retires or dies, the faction usually continues in existence under the leadership of another senior faction member. Even while being tried and even after his conviction for corruption in the Lockheed scandal, former Prime Minister Tanaka Kakuei continued as his faction leader and, with no formal title, was the most powerful politician in Japan. His influence in supporting the ambitions of Nakasone to become prime minister was so great that the latter's administration was popularly dubbed the "Tanakasone Cabinet."

For years the factions have borne the brunt of much criticism. On the face of it they seem undemocratic and feudalistic. Political idealism seems to be completely absent in the factions, which are only out for power and money for their members. Every few years, some party leader proclaims that the factions have been abolished, or that a leader's own faction has been abolished, but within a few weeks, newspapers report meetings of the faction members. Factional rivalries have occasionally threatened to tear the LDP apart, but at election time the LDP leaders have usually but certainly not always been able to bring the party together to make a solid stand against the opposition parties.

Until the Socialist landslide in the 1989 upper house election, the LDP never failed to win a majority, or at least a plurality, of seats in every election to the upper or lower house of the Diet. In this sense, Japanese politics was boring, because one always knew in advance that the conservatives would win. Two unpredictable factors were the size of the LDP victory and the size of the victories or losses of each of the LDP factions. The relative strengths of the factions are of vital importance in the intraparty fights for the party presidency, seats in the cabinet, and other benefits for the party members. Thus, after each election, the newspapers report the new factional strengths.

Every two years, the LDP members of the Diet elect their party's president. Because from 1955 to 1993 the LDP president was normally destined to become the next prime minister, the rivalry for the party presidency was very intense. In the past, various procedures have been used to choose the president. Since no single faction leader has enough followers of his or her own to become elected, a leader must make alliances and deals with the leaders of other factions. In the course of the intrigues and maneuvers among the faction leaders, substantial sums of money may secretly change hands and promises may be made that are not always kept. The system is open to corruption and chicanery, and since the stakes are money and power for individual politicians rather than the public good, the LDP's internecine conflicts, frequently discussed in the newspapers, often provoke public disgust. Some critics, paraphrasing Voltaire's description of the Holy Roman Empire, say that the faction-ridden Liberal Democratic Party is misnamed—that it is neither liberal nor democratic nor a party.

A politician's faction may sometimes claim more of his loyalty than does his party, so that once in a great while members of a faction may vote no confidence in a prime minister not of their own faction. A politician's *koenkai* (supporters association) may be sufficiently loyal to the politician that in rare situations he may not feel uncomfortable about leaving the LDP and joining a new political party, as in the early 1990s.

In April 2001, just before the election of the LDP president, the factional strengths in the LDP were as follows (the name of the faction is followed by the number of members of both houses of the Diet who belong to the faction): Hashimoto, 101; Mori, 59; Eto-Kamei, 55; Horiuchi, 43; Yamasaki, 23; Kato, 15.

Scandals

Partly because of the lower house electoral system before 1996, in which candidates from the LDP competed with one another for votes in the general election, enormous amounts of money had to be raised by politicians in order to finance successful campaigns. In 1976 many prominent Japanese politicians, bureaucrats, and businessmen were caught up in a massive scandal in which the Lockheed Company of the United States paid generous bribes and kickbacks in Japan and other countries to bring about the purchase of civilian and military aircraft manufactured by the company. Most conspicuous in Japan was former prime minister Tanaka, whose trial was conducted in court every Wednesday from 1977 to 1983. Tanaka had accepted a 500 million yen (around $1,800,000) "commission" from Lockheed and was sentenced to hard labor in 1983. Although he formally resigned from the LDP, his loyal constituents in the Niigata prefecture third district (the beneficiaries of government largess, including highways, tunnels, and Shinkansen stations) continually reelected him to the Diet with landslide majorities. He continued his political activities while he appealed his case to higher courts, and until his stroke in 1985 was the most powerful man in Japanese politics. (He retired from politics in 1990 and died three years later.)

In 1988, it was revealed that many politicians, regardless of party, and bureaucrats had received from the Recruit Company, a large information-industry firm, generous benefits including low prices for shares of stock in a subsidiary of the company before the stock was placed for public sale. Later, the recipients sold their shares for large profits. Prime Minister Takeshita (leader of the former Tanaka faction) and three members of his cabinet resigned because of their involvement. As most of the principal leaders of the LDP were implicated, it was almost impossible to find a suitable successor to Takeshita. Finally, Foreign Minister Uno Sosuke was offered the LDP presidency, although he was not a faction leader. (He was a member of the Nakasone faction.) On June 2, 1989, he became prime minister.

Almost immediately, a talkative former geisha revealed to the press the shabby details of her ungallant treatment by Uno. The sex scandal, added to the unpopular new sales tax, helped bring about a Socialist landslide in the 1989 upper house election. Uno resigned the party presidency and was succeeded by Kaifu Toshiki (Komoto faction), who had been untainted by the Recruit affair. Kaifu became prime minister on August 9, 1989.

As part of a political reform package, Kaifu proposed a new electoral system that was bitterly opposed not only by the opposition parties but by some LDP politicians as well. The leaders of the major factions who had been compromised in the Recruit affair now decided that the time was ripe to reenter the race for the party presidency, and they contrived to defeat Kaifu's proposals. Although Kaifu was much better liked by the public than were his powerful rivals, he felt that he had no choice but to renounce any effort to win a second term as party president and with it the prime ministership.

Kaifu's successor, Miyazawa Kiichi, had held cabinet positions of foreign minister, finance minister, and deputy prime minister. He had acquired a reputation both as a diplomat and economist, and as a fluent speaker of English he was expected to conduct Japan's relations with the United States effectively.

Former Prime Minister Takeshita had succeeded Tanaka as leader of the former Tanaka faction, but was compromised in connection with the Recruit scandal. Kanemaru Shin, who succeeded as the faction's leader and as a king-maker like Tanaka, became Japan's most powerful politician. While deputy prime minister in the Miyazawa cabinet, he was arrested and found guilty of tax evasion and illegally receiving large sums of money from the Sagawa Kyubin parcel delivery company. Among his records and cash seized by the public prosecutor were 100 kilograms of gold bars. He was incarcerated in March 1993. In June the non-Communist opposition parties proposed a no confidence resolution in the Miyazawa government. A substantial number of LDP members joined the vote against Miyazawa, and Miyazawa dissolved the lower house. In the ensuing election, the LDP lost its absolute majority in that body.

The Splintering of the LDP

In mid-1992, Hosokawa Morihiro, a grandson of Prince Konoe Fumimaro, a prewar prime minister, founded the Japan New Party, which was intended to represent an alternative to the unedifying politics of the recent past in Japan. Although Hosokawa had once been elected as an LDP member of the lower house, later as governor of Kumamoto prefecture he had come to resent the excessive domination of the national government by the bureaucrats in Tokyo and their LDP allies who had stifled private initiative and local autonomy by excessive regulation. The members of the Japan New Party were largely idealists who were new to politics and eager to break with the practices and policies that had characterized the LDP-dominated regime in Tokyo.

Younger members of the LDP had long been unhappy with the monopolization of the leadership of the party by senior members. In June 1993, much of the Tanaka-Takeshita faction under the leadership of Ozawa Ichiro and Hata Tsutomu seceded from the Liberal Democratic Party to form the Japan Renewal Party. It was Ozawa's purported wish to bring into being a two-party system in Japan. In the same month, Takemura Masayoshi recruited a number of LDP members into his new party, the *Shinto Sakigake* (literally "New Party Harbinger," usually referred to as Sakigake, and not to be confused with Soka Gakkai, the Buddhist organization that had sponsored the Komeito Party). In the July 1993 general election, for the first time in 33 years, the LDP lost its majority in the House of Representatives. The LDP leadership scrambled to put together a coalition cabinet that would include its erstwhile and dissident members, but without success.

To the astonishment of nearly everyone, under Ozawa Ichiro's leadership a multiparty coalition cabinet was formed that would be under the leadership of Hosokawa Morihiro, the founder of the Japan New Party. The eight parties in the coalition did not include the LDP. The "1955 system" of conservative one-party dominance had ended.

The parties making up the Hosokawa cabinet's coalition were the following (the number of seats held by each party in the House of Representatives is shown in parenthesis): Japan Socialist Party (70), Japan Renewal Party (55), Komeito (51), Japan New Party (35), Democratic Socialist Party (15), Sakigake (13), Social Democratic League (4), and *Minkairen* (0 seats in the House of Representatives, but 2 seats in the House of Councillors). The LDP, with 223 seats, for the first time in its history found itself in the opposition. The JCP, with 15 seats, also was in the opposition, as was its wont. The composition and policies of the Hosokawa Cabinet were dominated by Ozawa.

Hosokawa and most of his fellow party members had never before served in the Diet. Hosokawa's candid, unpolitician-like manner made him popular among the public, which had tired of the self-seeking and corruption endemic among traditional politicians. Hosokawa promised political reforms and it seemed that a new day had arrived in Japanese politics. Hosokawa presided over the passage of a sweeping electoral reform bill, but he announced controversial proposals for tax reforms without first adequately discussing them with other politicians, and the Socialists seceded from his coalition. Reports that Hosokawa had been compromised in the Recruit affair led to his resignation.

In April 1994, Hata Tsutomu of the Japan Renewal Party with Ozawa's backing succeeded as prime minister and organized a coalition cabinet. It excluded the LDP. The SDPJ, claiming that other coalition parties were intriguing against it, withdrew its support almost from the beginning. Thus the Hata administration could count on the support of only a minority of the members of the lower house. After only two months in office, Hata, threatened by an imminent vote of no confidence, resigned.

The LDP had now been joined in the opposition by their perennial enemy, the Socialists. LDP strategists believed that to remain in the opposition and without power would deprive the LDP Diet members of the ability to provide the necessary benefits (or pork, some might say) to their constituencies and would result in the ruin of their party. They now did what had been unthinkable during the prevalence of the 1955

system. In June 1994, they formed a coalition cabinet under a left-wing Socialist, Murayama Tomiichi, while the majority of the ministers in the cabinet were LDP members.

The New LDP Hegemony

We have noted that the "1955 system" ended in 1993, when for the first time in its history the LDP was completely removed from the cabinet. But in 1996 Hashimoto Ryutaro of the LDP became prime minister, and all subsequent cabinets have been led by LDP members. His coalition cabinet, in addition to the LDP, included the SDPJ and the Sakigake. The LDP was heartened by its victory over the New Frontier Party in the October 1996 lower house election in which the LDP increased its seats to 239. The New Frontier Party, contrary to expectations, won only 156 seats, two seats fewer than it had previously held. In November, Hashimoto formed a new cabinet consisting entirely of members of his own LDP, which held only a plurality of the seats in the lower house, though the government continued

Hashimoto Ryutaro.

to be based on a loose alliance with the Social Democratic Party and the Sakigake. In September 1997, the LDP gained an outright majority in the House of Representatives by bringing a number of legislators who had been independents or members of other parties into the LDP.

The deepening of the recession and the failure of several very important financial institutions resulted in a stunning defeat of the LDP in the July 1998 upper house election. The LDP had become a minority party in the House of Councillors. Hashimoto took the blame and resigned as head of the ruling party.

A presidential election was held in the LDP in which Obuchi Keizo emerged victorious, and on July 30, 1998, he became prime minister. In light of the deepening economic and financial crisis facing the country, Obuchi broke all precedent by appointing to his cabinet a former prime minister, namely Miyazawa Kiichi. Miyazawa, who would serve as finance minister, was known for his expertise in economics and facility with the English language. The Obuchi cabinet, however, was still short of a majority in the House of Councillors. After winning reelection as LDP president, in October 1999, Obuchi formed a new cabinet including the LDP, the Liberal Party, and the Komeito. Since then, coalition cabinets headed by the LDP president have been the order of the day. Thus it may be said that although the LDP has regained its hegemony, it has not regained its majorities in the Diet and its monopoly of cabinet posts, and must therefore depend on coalitions and alliances with other parties in order to rule.

Obuchi was relatively popular and his administration seemed for a while to be making some progress with the economy. But Ozawa Ichiro, the leader of the Liberal Party, became unhappy with the economic policies of the cabinet and withdrew his party from the coalition. In April 2000, apparently overwhelmed by the economic situation and the defection of the Liberal Party, Prime Minister Obuchi suddenly collapsed. He was incapacitated by a stroke and died in May. (A year after he died, the tactless Tanaka Makiko said that Obuchi's death "serves him right" because he had increased the nation's debt 100 trillion yen in a year. "That's why he kicked the bucket," she told a crowd.) Obuchi was suc-

ceeded as prime minister by the LDP secretary general, Mori Yoshiro.

When he formed his last cabinet in December 2000, Mori included Hashimoto Ryutaro as state minister for administrative reform and affairs relating to Okinawa and the Northern Territories. Thus, with Miyazawa retained and Hashimoto newly added to the cabinet, Mori's administration included two former prime ministers.

The apparent inability of the Mori administration to solve the country's economic problems, and Mori's controversial comments about Japan's being a "divine nation with the Emperor at its center," won for his government an unusually low approval rating. In April 2001, a discouraged Mori announced his decision to resign as president of the LDP.

A new party president would be chosen by the votes of individual LDP Diet members together with three votes representing each of the prefectural branches of the LDP. The candidates included former prime minister Hashimoto, whose faction was the largest in the LDP; Kamei Shizuka, head of the second largest faction; Koizumi Junichiro, former health minister and recently of the Mori faction (the third largest faction); and Aso Taro, state minister in charge of economic and fiscal policy.

There were predictions that none of the candidates would win on the first balloting, thus requiring a run-off election. However, at the last moment Kamei pulled out of the contest to support Koizumi, citing his agreements with Koizumi on policy issues and Koizumi's popularity among local party members. Koizumi, who had stood for the party presidency previously, had acquired a following among the general public that would be helpful to the party in the forthcoming upper house election. The rank and file of the LDP membership overwhelmingly preferred Koizumi, and he won the election for the LDP presidency. (The results of the April 24, 2001, LDP presidential election are shown in Table 5.5.)

Koizumi's victory represented the first time that the LDP chose a president who did not have the backing of the largest faction. The number one faction, led by former premier Hashimoto, had controlled party politics since

TABLE 5.5

ELECTION FOR LDP PRESIDENCY, APRIL 24, 2001

Candidate	Diet Members' Votes	Local Votes (Primaries)	Total
Koizumi Junichiro	175	123	298
Hashimoto Ryutaro	140	15	155
Kamei Shizuka	—	3	(3)*
Aso Taro	31	0	31
Total	346	141	487

Source: Japan Times Online, April 25, 2001.

*Votes cast for Kamei were invalidated when he withdrew.

the time when Tanaka Kakuei headed that faction in the early 1970s.

Throughout the history of the conservative party, when it appears that the public is fed up with the LDP's image as self-serving and corrupt politicians, the LDP chooses as its leader an advocate of reform, a maverick young Turk or a "Mr. Clean" who is not a faction leader and has been on the periphery of conventional LDP politics. Premiers Miki Takeo and Kaifu Toshiki were chosen by the effective holders of power in the LDP to present a more positive image of the party to the voters. In this tradition, Koizumi, the reform advocate, was elected LDP leader largely because of his popularity among the grass roots of the party even though the LDP Diet members would have preferred someone of a more traditional stripe.

As the three-party coalition held a majority of the seats in the lower house, it was expected that the Diet would promptly elect Koizumi as prime minister. Koizumi said that he would not make any policy agreements with the LDP's coalition partners—the New Komeito and the New Conservative Party—until after he was elected prime minister, so that he could call for support from the opposition. But the leadership of the two coalition parties, albeit pleased with Koizumi's victory in the presidential election, protested, warning that they could not back Koizumi in the Diet vote on the premiership unless an agreement was made on the coalition's platform. (Because the LDP did not alone have a majority in the lower house, it was necessary to

placate the coalition partners to ensure Koizumi's election.) Members of the Mori faction successfully persuaded Koizumi to harmonize policy positions with the two coalition partners, and he was then elected prime minister by the Diet.

The July 2001 House of Councillors election, which occurred three months after Koizumi established his power, was taken as an indicator of the popularity of the coalition government (see Table 5.3). In this election, the coalition was able to preserve its majority in the upper house. Moreover, the LDP did vastly better than it had three years before. Credited with his party's victory, Koizumi was reelected without opposition to the LDP presidency.

Koizumi

Prime Minister Koizumi's status as a maverick in the LDP is symbolized by his long wavy hair, sometimes compared to a lion's mane, which makes him conspicuous in photographs as very different in personality from rival LDP politicians, whose sparse locks are closely plastered to their craniums. He is known for his fondness for skiing, kabuki, opera, and rock music, and he helped establish a museum in Yokosuka to commemorate the life of a popular guitarist. His hair style, likened to Beethoven's, is regularly permed. He is the divorced father of two children. He has been a leading proponent of reform, especially the privatization of the postal system. Unlike other senior LDP politicians, Koizumi is said to eschew *"ryotei* politics," in which behind-the-scenes negotiations are conducted in *ryotei* (expensive restaurants).

Koizumi comes from a family of politicians. His grandfather served as posts minister and vice speaker of the lower house, and his father headed the Defense Agency. He graduated from the department of economics at the prestigious Keio University and began studying economics at London University but quit the university to run for the House of Representatives. Failing to win office, he worked as a secretary to the late Prime Minister Fukuda Takao (father of Fukuda Yasuo, chief cabinet secretary in Koizumi's cabinet.) He was first elected to the lower house in 1972 and has served ten straight terms.

Koizumi became nominal head of Prime Minister Mori's faction (formerly Fukuda Takeo's faction) when Mori assumed the premiership in 2000. However, early in April 2001, Koizumi ended his 30-year connection with the Mori faction to dramatize his proposals for party reform that he advocated in his platform for the LDP presidential race.

Prime Minister Koizumi's administration got a rocky start when, against the strong protests of Foreign Minister Tanaka Makiko and his Komeito coalition partners, he made a visit to the Yasukuni Shrine, where the spirits of Japan's dead (including convicted war criminals for World War II) are venerated. Also against Tanaka's publicly expressed wishes, Koizumi ordered her to dismiss the ambassadors to the United States and England in connection with the mishandling of government funds. Tanaka failed to carry out the dismissals until rumors spread that she might have to be fired for insubordination. Tanaka, the popular daughter of the late prime minister Tanaka Kakuei, had been one of Koizumi's strongest political allies.

Koizumi's cabinet was pleased by the results of the election in 2001 for half of the seats in the upper house, in which the three coalition parties won 78 of the 121 seats contested, a comfortable majority. In October 2001, two LDP candidates won by-elections for seats in the lower house vacated because of deaths. As a result, the LDP alone now held an absolute majority of 241 in the 480-seat House of Representatives. The LDP-led three-party coalition now had 279 seats in the lower house. The Komeito party leaders stressed their importance in the coalition, because the LDP alone did not have a majority in the House of Councillors.

Critics, however, have pointed out that Koizumi's effectiveness as a reformer is doubtful. Notwithstanding his progressive rhetoric, the LDP is overwhelmingly dominated by conservatives who are, to say the least, unenthusiastic about reform proposals that would alienate their traditional constituencies.

Even while confronted with the persistent ills of the Japanese economy, Koizumi was suddenly confronted with the shock of the terrorist attack on the World Trade Center, in which Japanese numbered among the victims. In the week following the attack, Koizumi discussed the issue with U.S. President Bush in Washington, and later Bush telephoned Koizumi shortly before commencement of the American military response. Koizumi promised Washington full support, and the matter of the nature of the Japanese contribution to the antiterrorist campaign became the major issue of Japanese politics.

THE SOCIAL DEMOCRATIC PARTY OF JAPAN

The Japan Socialist Party (JSP) won a plurality of the seats in the lower house in the 1947 election. As a result, the JSP and the conservatively inclined Democratic Party formed a coalition government under the leadership of Katayama Tetsu, the JSP leader. The coalition cabinet, however, could not survive the defection of left-wing Socialists who differed with Katayama over the budget. The successor coalition cabinet included Socialists but was led by the Democrat Ashida Hitoshi. In 1948 the Ashida cabinet was forced to resign because of a major scandal, and Mr. Yoshida formed a conservative cabinet and remained prime minister until 1954. From 1948 to 1994 no Socialists served in the cabinet. The lack of governmental experience was a substantial handicap to the image of the Socialists among the voters, who place a premium on competence.

In 1950, the JSP split into rival left and right wings because of a dispute over the peace treaty.

When the left and right factions of the JSP reunited in 1955, it appeared that the party had a new lease on life. Most of the party's support came from labor unions and Marxist intellectuals. However, Japan's economic recovery, touched off by the Korean War boom in the early 1950s, deprived the Socialist ideology of its earlier appeal. The Socialists, however, were able to capitalize on the public suspicions of conservative efforts to amend the constitution and the unpopularity of the new security treaty negotiated by Prime Minister Kishi with the United States in 1959. Massive street demonstrations and factional rivalries in the LDP forced Kishi's resignation, and he was succeeded in office by a fellow LDP member (Ikeda Hayato).

Although the LDP won the subsequent general election, the Socialists hoped that they would soon become the governing party. Instead, the economic boom of the 1960s made the LDP virtually invincible. With the secession of Nishio's right-wing Socialists, the emergence of the Komeito, and the revival of the Communists, the JSP was faced with rivals for the leadership of the opposition camp.

The JSP, from its very beginning, was torn by internal strife. An uncompromising doctrinaire left wing refused to accommodate itself to pragmatic realities, and when moderates seceded from the party, the left became even less inclined to compromise. Unlike the Socialist parties of Western Europe, which strongly supported NATO, the JSP long opposed the alignment with the United States, and instead seemed to show a preference for the USSR, Communist China, and North Korea. When the Sino-Soviet dispute broke out in the 1960s, some of the JSP members praised the Chinese and blamed the Soviet Union. The external influences on the party tended to discredit it. When the JSP leadership perennially proposed a coalition of leftist parties, it was faced with the adamant refusal of the Communists to collaborate with the Democratic Socialists and with the latter's refusal to work with the Communists.

In the 1970s as the security treaty with the United States and the existence of the Self-Defense Forces became more widely accepted, the Socialists were no longer able to capitalize so successfully on these issues. Their advocacy of "unarmed neutrality" seemed increasingly irrelevant and had to be deemphasized to make electoral alliances with other opposition parties.

After its 1986 electoral debacle, the JSP, in an uncharacteristically imaginative stroke, elected Doi Takako, a female pacifist law professor, as its leader. Making the unpopular new consumption tax (a sales tax) its principal issue, the JSP won a landslide victory in the 1989 upper house election. Doi announced plans to moderate JSP stands on the security treaty and defense in order to pave the way for a JSP-led coalition cabinet. However, in the 1990 lower house election, the poor showing of the JSP's potential coalition partners (DSP and Komeito) and their alienation from the JSP made a JSP-led coalition cabinet an impossibility. The party formally moderated its opposition to the Self-Defense Forces and changed its English (but not its Japanese) name to Social Democratic Party of Japan (SDPJ). Doi resigned as chair of the party, while tensions continued among the pacifist, leftist, and moderate factions.

The 1993 lower house election was catastrophic for the SDPJ; it won only 70 seats, its fewest seats in any election since 1949. In 2003 it gained only 6 seats.

Murayama's Coalition Cabinet

In 1994, after withdrawing their support from the Hata cabinet, the Socialists found themselves in the opposition together with the LDP. This prompted an event that had been hitherto considered a fantastic impossibility in Japanese politics. The Socialists and the LDP, which had staunchly advocated opposing ideologies and contrasting foreign policies, joined forces in June 1994 to form a coalition government. Murayama Tomiichi, a leftist SDPJ leader, became prime minister of a cabinet that included 13 members of the LDP, 6 Socialists, and 2 members of the Sakigake. (The New Party Sakigake, or Sakigake for short, was made up largely of LDP members who had defected from the LDP before the 1993 general election.) Thus the LDP held a majority of the cabinet posts, and Kono Yohei, then the president of the LDP, served concurrently as deputy prime minister and foreign minister.

When he assumed the premiership of a coalition government in 1994, the Socialist leader Murayama publicly proclaimed that the Self-Defense Forces were constitutional and the security treaty with the United States should be maintained, thus repudiating the most salient policy positions held by the Socialists for decades. The overwhelming majority of the ministers in the cabinet were LDP members, and the Socialist Party had lost much of its distinctive identity.

Decline of the SDPJ

The Socialists' disastrous showing in the 1995 upper house election resulted in their decline to the number three position in that house, with only 38 seats. The SDPJ had lost its position as one of the two major parties to the New Frontier Party. Socialist leaders had already been openly discussing the replacement of the SDPJ by a new political organization. At a meeting with labor leaders in August 1995, Murayama said that the proposed new party should be based on high ideals such as had characterized the SDPJ. He said that the Socialists should be proud of their record and be credited with having prevented the runaway rearmament of Japan and Japan's involvement in the Vietnam War. Murayama resigned as prime minister in January 1996 and was replaced by Hashimoto Ryutaro, the president of the LDP.

In September 1996, Doi resigned the speakership of the lower house to resume the chairmanship of the SDPJ. In the 2000 general election the SDPJ won only 19 seats to become the number six party in the House of Representatives. After the 2001 upper house election, it had only 8 seats left in that body, fewer than half of the seats of the Communists and tying the Liberal Party for fifth place. In 2005 it has 5 seats.

Probably the basic reason for the precipitous decline of the SDPJ is that the dissolution of the Soviet Union and the end of the Cold War largely deprived it of the issues of neutrality and disarmament that had earned it support among much of the middle class in Japan. At the same time, the decline of the influence of labor unions deprived the Socialists of much of their financial and electoral support. The Democratic Party of Japan has succeeded the Socialist Party and the short-lived New Frontier Party as the leading group in the opposition.

THE DEMOCRATIC SOCIALISTS

In 1960, some of the Socialists of the right wing under the leadership of Nishio Suehiro quit the JSP in protest against its ties with the Japan Communist Party (JCP), its use of street demonstrations that sometimes became violent in opposition to the U.S.-Japan Security Treaty, and its apparently pro-Soviet, anti-American posture. The seceding group formed the Democratic Socialist Party (DSP).

In 1989, the dissolution of the Domei labor union federation and the absorption of its members into the newly established Rengo labor union federation deprived the DSP of critical support. The loss of nearly half of its seats (from 26 to 14) in the 1990 general election raised serious questions about the party's viability. In 1994 the DSP merged with other parties to form the New Frontier Party, which by 1998 had dissolved.

THE COMMUNISTS

The Japan Communist Party (JCP) had a very troubled and usually illegal existence before World War II. At the end of the war, occupation officials obtained the release from jail of the Communist leaders, including Tokuda Kyuichi, the prewar party leader. Nosaka Sanzo, who had taught Communist doctrine to Japanese prisoners of war in Yenan, returned from China. The Communists, who had been the prime targets of the discredited Japanese militarists and ultranationalists, were regarded by the left as martyrs and heroes after the war, but they soon made themselves unpopular by demanding an end to the emperor system. Later, under Nosaka's leadership, the Communists moderated their attacks on the emperor.

At the beginning of the Allied occupation, the Communists proclaimed many of the same goals championed by the occupation officers, such as the breakup of the monopolies and land reform. For a while they advocated the formation of a democratic front and aspired to join a coalition cabinet made up of the progressive and moderate parties. Communists won leading positions of leadership in labor unions and in 1947 called for a general strike. A general strike when Japan had not yet restored its war-ravished economy and was dependent on the United States for food imports would have had catastrophic consequences. When MacArthur ordered that the strike be called off, the strike was canceled, and the Communist leaders lost much of their prestige and influence in the labor movement.

In 1950, the Cominform (the Soviet-run organization that directed the policies of Communist parties worldwide) published a devastating criticism of the opportunism of the JCP, and the party became involved in instigating serious riots and sabotage. This provoked MacArthur's headquarters to ban the leaders of the JCP from political activity. The party lost most of its popularity and all of its seats in the Diet. In the 1960s, even as it was embroiled in internal controversies over the Sino-Soviet dispute, the JCP attempted with some success to modify its image.

The JCP has softened its revolutionary rhetoric and adopted issues that immediately concern the voters, such as the environment, railroad fares, and education. Following the 2003 and 2004 elections, there were 9 Communist councillors and 9 Communist members in the House of Representatives. Because the electoral system has operated to the disadvantage of the JCP, the Communists have made a big issue of it.

Increasingly the JCP assumed an image of bourgeois respectability and has asserted its independence from outside control by criticizing the Soviet occupation of Japan's Northern Territories and the bloody suppression of the student democracy movement at Tiananmen in Beijing in 1989. Largely because of revenue from their publications, the JCP is Japan's second richest party, and during electoral campaigns its loudspeaker trucks are a very common sight and sound.

The JCP has had a long record of noncooperation with other parties, including the parties of the left. One possible reason for its strong showing in the 2001 upper house election is that given the near demise of the Socialists, the JCP came to be regarded by some as the only party credibly in opposition to the conservatives.

THE KOMEITO

At the close of World War II, many Japanese were without food or shelter, unemployment was widespread, and people sought refuge in religion. Among the new religions that emerged at this time was the *Soka Gakkai,* or Value-Creating Society. The Soka Gakkai is a lay educational organization founded before the war as an auxiliary to the old Nichiren Shoshu sect of Buddhism. The Soka Gakkai, in addition to emphasizing traditional forms of chanting and scripture study, practices faith healing and stresses a wide variety of social and cultural activities. Evangelism is the duty of all the members, and high-pressure methods are used to recruit converts. The Soka Gakkai has become a global organization and has branches in many countries, including centers in major U.S. cities. (In the United States it is known as Nichiren Shoshu.)

The Soka Gakkai has claimed that faith in its doctrines has brought material prosperity to many believers. The worldly concerns of the Soka Gakkai have involved it in politics. In the 1960s it formed the *Komeito,* or Clean Government Party. This party would be unlike either the LDP or the JSP. It would promote world peace. It would not represent capitalistic interests, nor would it propagate socialism. The formal ties between the Komeito and the Soka Gakkai were officially severed in the 1970s, but in the public mind they remain closely associated. Because of the rapid growth of the Komeito in the 1960s, some observers feared that it might become a mass-based authoritarian party that would try to impose its religious beliefs on the rest of society. In recent years, the party has focused its attention on peace, the environment, and other conventional issues, and it occasionally has made electoral alliances with the Socialists. In the 1990s it became an essential partner in LDP-led coalition cabinets.

The Komeito has normally sponsored candidates only in districts where there is a high probability of victory. As a result, its ratio between number of seats won to number of votes has been the highest among the parties. Where it did not sponsor a candidate, the candidates of other parties were tactful in their treatment of the Soka Gakkai and Komeito. For a number of years the Komeito has been the third largest party in terms of seats held in both the upper and lower houses of the Diet, and it played a leading role in the opposition. In 1995, the Komeito candidates ran for seats in the House of Councillors as members of the New Frontier Party. Resentment of the strong influence of the former Komeito members was a factor in the break-up of the New Frontier Party. The Komeito reemerged as the "New Komeito."

THE DEMOCRATIC PARTY OF JAPAN

The Democratic Party of Japan (DPJ) was founded in September 1996. Initially it elected two coequal chairmen, Hatoyama Yukio and Kan Naoto, both of whom had formerly been members of the Sakigake, which ultimately became extinct in 1998. Following the October 1996 general election, of the DPJ's 52 lower house members, 26 were former Socialists, 15 were former Sakigake members. Hatoyama Kunio had come from the New Frontier Party. The Hatoyama brothers, Yukio and Kunio, were grandsons of former prime minister Hatoyama Ichiro. Kan Naoto had been minister of health early in 1996 in the Hashimoto cabinet, and had become popular when he dramatically apologized for the government's responsibility to the families of hemophiliacs who had suffered or died because of HIV-contaminated blood.

After the October 1996 election, the Democratic Party, with 42 seats, became the second largest party in the opposition, after the New Frontier Party, which had won 156 seats. However, when the New Frontier Party broke up in early 1998 and many of its members joined the Democratic Party, the Democrats became the largest party in the opposition. As of October 29, 2001, the Democratic Party held 125 of the 480 seats in the House of Representatives. At that time, the LDP had an absolute majority—241 seats—in the lower house, and the three government coalition parties (LDP, New Komeito, and New Conservatives) together held 279 seats. The Democratic Party favored Prime Minister Koizumi's pro-American policy in the war against terrorism, but insisted that the Diet have a say in the deployment of Japanese Self-Defense Forces provided for in the new legislation sponsored by the government. The Democrats favored the kinds of reforms advocated by Premier Koizumi but taunted him with the probability that the LDP members of the Diet would not support the reform program.

THE LIBERAL PARTY

We have described how Ozawa Ichiro together with Hata Tsutomu led a secession from the LDP in 1993 to form the Japan Renewal Party and how they engineered the establishment of the Hata cabinet. Ozawa had a vision of a more flexible and modern political system in which a nonsocialist party could challenge the domination of the LDP and in which rotation in office between two parties would be possible. He outlined his views on reform in 1993 in his book *Blueprint for a New Japan*.

In 1994 Ozawa took the leadership in forming the New Frontier Party. In December 1995, a party president was elected. Anyone paying 1,000 yen ($10) could vote, and Ozawa won the election handily over former prime minister Hata. Because of the New Frontier Party's excellent performance in the 1995 upper house election, there were expectations that it might win by a landslide in the subsequent general election.

But in the 1996 general election, the New Frontier Party lost two of its seats, although it remained the leading opposition party in the House of Representatives. Early in 1998 when the New Frontier Party split up, the Democratic Party gained many new members, and Ozawa formed a new group, the Liberal Party.

Ozawa's small Liberal Party joined in a coalition cabinet led by Prime Minister Obuchi, of the LDP. When Ozawa led his party out of the coalition, Liberals who wanted to remain in the government seceded from the Liberal Party to form the New Conservative Party, led by Ogi Chikage. In the 2000 general election, the Liberal Party won 22 seats, to become the fourth largest party in the House of Representatives, and after the 2001 upper house election, the Liberal Party was left with 8 seats in that body, tying with the SDPJ for fifth place.

In October 2001, the LDP, which had been ousted from power largely by Ozawa's machinations in 1993, held by one seat an absolute majority of seats in the House of Representatives, and the premiership was held by the popular LDP president, Koizumi, who led a coalition that excluded the Liberal Party. The Democratic Party was the leading party in the opposition. The Liberal Party merged with the Democratic Party in 2003.

THE DIET

The Japanese call their parliament *kokkai,* which literally means "national assembly," but the English word *Diet* is usually used to render *kokkai.* The Japanese Diet, created in 1889, is the oldest parliament in Asia. Today's House of Representatives represents a continuation of the prewar lower house. But today's House of Councillors (the upper house) is a democratic institution, very different from the prewar House of Peers, an aristocratic body.

While the postwar democratic constitution was being drafted, MacArthur's staff pointed out that Japan did not have a federal system and therefore did not need an upper house (such as the United States Senate) to represent the constituent states. The Japanese believed that a second chamber was needed to act as a check on the popularly elected chamber. They wanted an upper house based on functional (or vocational) representation. The Americans held that functional representation would violate the constitution, which provided that qualifications of both Diet members and electors could not involve discrimination because of "race, creed, sex, social status, family origin, education, property, or income." As enacted, the democratic constitution provided for a House of Councillors but failed to indicate the nature of its composition. Later, a law was passed prescribing the electoral system described earlier in this chapter. The six-year staggered terms of the members of the House of Councillors and the relevant electoral laws were expected to make that body more conservative than the lower house.

From the beginning, the function of the House of Councillors, the product of a compromise, was an enigma. If the House of Representatives was a truly democratic body that accurately represented the people's will, there was no need—from a strictly democratic point of view—for a second chamber, which at best would only confirm the will of the democratic lower chamber and at worst would obstruct the democratic will.

The Legislative Process

To become law, a bill must be debated in both chambers of the Diet. If the House of Councillors does not pass a bill within 60 days after its approval by the House of Representatives, the bill is considered to have been rejected by the councillors. The councillors' veto may be overridden in the lower house by a two-thirds vote. If the councillors refuse to pass the budget or to approve a treaty, and their difference with the House of Representatives is not resolved in a joint committee, the will of the House of Representatives prevails. The amendment of the constitution requires approval of two-thirds of the entire membership of each house and ratification by a majority of the voters. No party, not even the LDP, has ever captured the two-thirds majorities in both houses of the Diet necessary to amend the constitution, and it is very conceivable that the House of Councillors could veto a proposed amendment.

Most bills originate in a ministry of the government, which is sensitive to the demands of big business, agriculture, and the (usually) conservative voters that put it in office. After the ministry has approved a bill, it must be approved by the cabinet. The bill, which may be discussed with the relevant study group in the LDP's Policy Research Council, is circulated among various concerned ministries and is considered by the full Policy Research Council. Especially since 1993, the leaders of opposition parties have been consulted. After the cabinet's approval of a bill, arrangements must then be made to put the bill on the Diet's agenda.

In each house, bills are referred to the appropriate standing (permanent) committees. Each committee specializes in a particular subject matter as in the United States. Thus there are lower and upper house standing committees on foreign affairs, education, agriculture and fisheries, justice, etc. In addition there are special committees working on particular issues. Many important bills are debated in the lower house budget committee, whose proceedings are sometimes televised. In past decades, because the LDP usually commanded a majority in every committee, and often held the chair of every committee, committee approval was assured.

If the bill is sufficiently repugnant to the sensibilities of the opposition, the opposition may use obstructive tactics in either the committee or the plenary session, or both, to prevent a vote from being taken. The use of obstructive measures is not purely the function of emotional outrage; by using boycotts and filibusters, the opposition may sometimes extract concessions from the government. Delaying tactics may prevent a bill from coming to a vote before a Diet session is closed. Faced with enough opposition, which may include massive street demonstrations, the gov-

The Diet building, which houses Japan's two parlimentary chambers in the heart of Tokyo. Photo courtesy Myra McNelly.

Prime Minister Koizumi Junichiro.

ernment might even give up trying to enact its bill. (This happened in 1959, when the government tried to enact its police duties bill.)

Unlike the lower house, the upper house is not subject to dissolution, so the members may serve out their full terms. With longer terms of office and with the system of staggering terms, the composition of the upper house is much more stable than that of the lower house. This stability is enhanced by the fact that incumbents in both houses stand a very strong chance of being re-elected. The incumbency principle is aggravated by the tendency of sons or sons-in-law of retiring or deceased Diet members to stand for election with a very strong prospect for success. A retiring member's *koenkai* is often inherited by a family member.

THE CABINET

Responsible Government

Under the Meiji Constitution, executive powers were dispersed among the *Genro,* the Privy Council, the emperor's ministers, and the military Supreme Command. When needed, the

A CLOSER LOOK
5.2

AUTOMATIC APPROVAL OF TREATIES

Where treaties are concerned, if the decision of the upper house of the Japanese Diet differs from that of the lower and no agreement can be reached in a joint committee of the two houses, the decision of the lower house becomes that of the Diet. Or if the upper house fails to take action in 30 days after receiving the treaty from the lower house, the decision of the lower house becomes that of the Diet. The joint committee option has been neglected in recent decades, so the government may simply wait for the 30-day period to elapse. The procedure is known as "automatic approval" of a treaty. Numerous treaties have been approved automatically, without action by the upper house. Thus, unlike the U.S. Senate, the Japanese upper house cannot veto treaties.

Perhaps the most dramatic case of the automatic approval of a treaty occurred in 1960. The new U.S.-Japan security treaty had been approved at a riotous session of the House of Representatives that the Socialists refused to attend. The House of Councillors failed to deliberate on the treaty because of the boycott of that chamber by the Socialists. On June 18, 1960, the date of the expected automatic approval of the treaty, thousands of demonstrators surrounded the Diet building, protesting against the treaty and the manner of its passage in the lower house. But the parades, speeches, shouts, and placards of the multitude were of no avail against the inexorable ticking of the clock, and the treaty was officially deemed approved by the Diet at the stroke of midnight.

residual power of the sovereign emperor to issue ordinances could be employed. Although executive authority overwhelmed the power of the weak Imperial Diet, the authority of the cabinet, which was not even mentioned as such in the Imperial Constitution, was subject to constant challenge from the Genro, the Privy Council, and the military. Under the postwar constitution, these rivals of the cabinet no longer exist, and "Executive power shall be vested in the Cabinet."

"Responsible government," insisted upon by the Allied Powers, required that the executive be answerable directly to the people or answerable to an assembly elected by the people. Either a congressional-presidential system after the American model or a parliamentary-cabinet system after the British model would have been acceptable to the Allied Powers, but given the existence of a monarch and the precedent of Taisho democracy, the British model was much more compatible with Japanese tradition. At the time of the drafting of the postwar constitution, Japan had a multiparty system. It was apparently anticipated that the cabinet, unsupported by a stable majority, would be subservient to the Diet, which was declared to be the "highest organ of state power."

The Prime Minister

The first business of the Diet after a general election for the lower house is to designate the prime minister from among the Diet members. (In practice, since World War II all prime ministers have been members of the House of Representatives.) An election is held in each house, and if the two

---

REVIEW

5.1 PARLIAMENTARY DEMOCRACY ACCORDING TO THE JAPANESE CONSTITUTION

Article 1. The Emperor shall be the symbol of the State and of the unity of the people, deriving his position from the will of the people with whom resides sovereign power.

Article 3. The advice and approval of the Cabinet shall be required for all acts of the Emperor in matters of state, and the Cabinet shall be responsible therefor.

Article 6. The Emperor shall appoint the Prime Minister as designated by the Diet. The Emperor shall appoint the Chief Judge of the Supreme Court as designated by the Cabinet.

Article 41. The Diet shall be the highest organ of state power, and shall be the sole law-making organ of the State.

Article 65. Executive power shall be vested in the Cabinet.

Article 67. The Prime Minister shall be designated from among the members of the Diet by a resolution of the Diet. This designation shall precede all other business. If the House of Representatives and the House of Councillors disagree and if no agreement can be reached even through a joint committee of both Houses, provided for by law, or the House of Councillors fails to make designation within ten (10) days, exclusive of the period of recess, after the House of Representatives has made designation, the decision of the House of Representatives shall be the decision of the Diet.

Article 69. If the House of Representatives passes a non-confidence resolution, or rejects a confidence resolution, the Cabinet shall resign en masse, unless the House of Representatives is dissolved within ten (10) days.

Article 70. When there is a vacancy in the post of Prime Minister, or upon the first convocation of the Diet after a general election of members of the House of Representatives, the Cabinet shall resign en masse.

Article 71. In the cases mentioned in the two preceding Articles, the Cabinet shall continue its functions until the time when a new Prime Minister is appointed.

Article 81. The Supreme Court is the court of last resort with power to determine the constitutionality of any law, order, regulation, or official act.

houses are unable to agree on a single individual even after deliberation by a joint committee of the two houses, the decision of the House of Representatives prevails. The constitution requires the emperor to "appoint the Prime Minister as designated by the Diet."

The prime minister occupies a position in Japanese politics that is fundamentally different from that of the president of the United States. The American president is elected by the people (via the electoral college) and therefore may claim a popular mandate for his program. His link with the voters is virtually direct. The prime minister, on the other hand, is not directly chosen by the people but rather by the Diet, which serves as an electoral college for this purpose. From 1955 to 1993 because of the LDP's control of the House of Representatives, the president of

that party was invariably chosen for the prime ministership by the Diet. Personal popularity or oration skills were not necessary in order to become prime minister. (Of course if the prime minister is thoroughly unacceptable to the public, the public may choose to punish his party at the next election.)

From 1945 to 2005, Japan had 27 different prime ministers; during the same period, the United States had only eleven presidents and England had only eleven different prime ministers. The Japanese prime minister's average tenure of office was slightly over two years. Koizumi is the eleventh premier to serve in the past 18 years. The prime ministers' short tenures weaken their influence and make it difficult to enforce long-term policies and conduct efficient diplomacy.

REVIEW
5.2

JAPAN'S PRIME MINISTERS, 1945–2005

April 7, 1945	Admiral Suzuki		July 7, 1972	Tanaka
			December 9, 1974	Miki
(August 15, 1945, Japan time, World War II ended.)			December 24, 1976	Fukuda
			December 7, 1978	Ohira
August 17, 1945	Prince Higashikuni		July 17, 1980	Suzuki
October 9, 1945	Shidehara (Progressive)		November 27, 1982	Nakasone
May 22, 1946	Yoshida (Liberal)		November 6, 1987	Takeshita
			June 2, 1989	Uno
(May 3, 1947, new constitution became effective.)			August 9, 1989	Kaifu
			November 5, 1991	Miyazawa
May 24, 1947	Katayama (Socialist)			
March 10, 1948	Ashida (Democrat)		(In 1993, the 1955 system ended.)	
October 19, 1948	Yoshida (Democratic Liberal)			
December 10, 1954	Hatoyama (Democrat)		August 9, 1993	Hosokawa (Japan New Party)
(The political system from 1955 to 1993 was characterized by LDP predominance in both houses of the Diet and an LDP monopoly of the premiership—"the 1955 system.")			April 28, 1994	Hata (Japan Renewal Party)
			June 30, 1994	Murayama (SDPJ)
			January 11, 1996	Hashimoto (LDP)
December 23, 1956	Ishibashi		July 30, 1998	Obuchi (LDP)
February 25, 1957	Kishi		April 5, 2000	Mori (LDP)
July 19, 1960	Ikeda		April 26, 2001	Koizumi (LDP)
November 9, 1964	Sato			

302 PART I Industrial Democracies

Between 1955 and 1993, two formal events were crucial in determining the prime minister's official longevity: elections for the presidency of the LDP (which normally occurred every two years) and lower house elections (which must occur at least once every four years if not more often), after which the Diet designates the prime minister to be appointed by the emperor. Thus the tenure of a prime minister may include successive formal appointments to the office by the emperor. The relatively short tenures of the Japanese heads of government may be explained by bitter interfactional rivalry in the LDP, the short term of office of LDP presidents, and ill health. Since 1945, prime ministers who have served the longest periods in office have been Sato, Yoshida, and Nakasone, in that order. These leaders managed to maintain their influence over their own and rival factions in order to prolong their hold on the office, and thus may be regarded as effective, if not always popular, leaders.

Cabinet Ministers

The constitution requires that all cabinet ministers be civilians and that the prime minister choose a majority of his cabinet ministers from among the members of the Diet. The prime minister is free to appoint and may dismiss whomever he wishes without the formal consent of the Diet. Currently the law limits the size of the cabinet to 18 members including the prime minister. In practice, cabinet members are selected primarily on the basis of political expediency. Most cabinet members are from the lower house, but a few may be members of the upper house, or not be members of the Diet at all. Occasionally, a woman is appointed as a cabinet minister. The prime minister and his advisors try (but do not always succeed) to allocate cabinet posts to members of the different parties or factions of parties in such a way as to assure maximum stability. Diet members strive to become cabinet ministers because the title confers prestige on them for the rest of their lives. It is one of the duties of a faction leader to get as many cabinet posts for his followers as possible. The most prestigious posts are the ministries of finance and foreign affairs. These may serve as stepping stones to the prime ministership.

The cabinet lasts only as long as it is acceptable to the lower house of the Diet. If the House of Representatives votes no confidence in the cabinet, the cabinet must within ten days either (1) resign, in which case a new prime minister must be designated by the Diet, or (2) ask the emperor to dissolve the house, in which case elections are held for the lower house. In practice, it was usually unlikely that the members of the majority party, the LDP, would allow a no-confidence resolution to pass and possibly force an election which might imperil their seats. But this did happen in 1980 and again in 1993 when some LDP members deserted their prime minister after a no-confidence resolution was proposed. A prime minister and his cabinet may resign without waiting for a no-confidence vote if it appears that they are no longer supported by a majority in the lower house. Since Yoshida's time (1948–1954), no individual who has left the premiership has later resumed that office.

Japanese prime ministers, whose terms in office are relatively short, are not necessarily the most influential political leaders of their country. While on trial in connection with the Lockheed scandal and during the appeal of his conviction, a total of eight years, former prime minister Tanaka Kakuei was the leader of the most powerful faction of the LDP and the kingmaker, whose support was critical to aspirants to the premiership. Tanaka's strength was based on the enormous amount of money at his disposal to dispense to his followers. (Much of the money came from contractors, the builders of highways, railways, bridges, and public buildings financed by the government.) Tanaka's successors as "shadow shoguns" were Kanemaru Shin and Takeshita Noboru, who successively took over his faction after his retirement from politics.

The Koizumi Cabinet

Following Koizumi Junichiro's election as president of the Liberal Democratic Party and then his selection by the Diet to the post of prime minister, on April 26, 2001, he was formally appointed prime minister by the emperor. As his party, the LDP, did not have majorities in either the lower or upper houses of the Diet, in order to command the majorities required for the passage of his proposals, like recent prime ministers, he formed a coalition cabinet. The parties belonging to the ruling coalition were the LDP (13 cabinet posts), the New Komeito (1 cabinet post), and the New Conservative Party (1 cabinet post).

Koizumi dubbed his cabinet a "national salvation" government. The seriousness of the economic condition of the country seemed to require an unusual focus on the particular expertise of the cabinet members. Thus three posts were reserved for nonpartisans: the Ministry of Environment; the Ministry of Education, Culture, Sports, Science, and Technology; and the State Ministry for Economic and Fiscal Policy and IT Policy. Five of the ministries were assumed by women. Never before had so many nonpoliticians and so many women been appointed to a cabinet in Japan.

Of the five women, Minister of Justice Moriyama Mayumi was an LDP member of the former Komoto faction, Foreign Minister Tanaka Makiko was a strong Koizumi supporter and LDP member without factional affiliation, and Minister of Infrastructure and Transport Ogi Chikage was a leader of the New Conservative Party. The minister of environment, Kawaguchi Yoriko, and the minister of education, etc., Toyama Atsuko, were not politicians.

Also unusual was the fact that only two ministries were assigned to members of the largest faction in the LDP, the Hashimoto faction. The Mori faction received three posts, and one post each was assigned to the former Komoto, Eto-Kamei, Horiuchi, Yamasaki, and Kato factions. Two of the LDP members belonged to no faction. The prime minister had been a member of the Mori faction, from which he resigned shortly before the LDP presidential election.

The Koizumi cabinet provides numerous Japanese examples of the importance of family dynasties in politics, a phenomenon not unknown in other democracies. Koizumi's father had been an LDP politician who had held ministries in LDP cabinets. Moriyama's late husband had served as a transport minister. Hiranuma Takeo, the minister of economy, trade, and industry, was the adopted son of Hiranuma Kiichiro, prime minister and privy council president before World War II. Ishihara Nobuteru, the state minister in charge of administrative and regulatory reforms, is an LDP reformer without a factional affiliation and is the eldest son of Ishihara Shintaro, the governor of Tokyo. The popular sharp-tongued foreign minister, Tanaka Makiko, is the daughter of former prime minister Tanaka Kakuei and the wife of Tanaka Naoki, a member of the House of Councillors. The director of the Defense Agency, Nakatani Gen, is the grandson of a member of the lower house. Chief Cabinet Secretary Fukuda Yasuo, a lower house member of the Mori faction, is the son of the late prime minister Fukuda Takeo. (Fukuda Yasuo frequently appears on TV as the spokesman for the cabinet.) Early in 2002, Koizumi fired the contentious Foreign Minister Tanaka and replaced her with another woman, Kawaguchi Yoriko, who had been serving as minister of environment. Oki Hiroshi, lower house member of the LDP Hashimoto faction, became the new environment minister.

Dissolutions

The constitutional term of office for members of the House of Representatives is four years, but the cabinet normally does not like to wait that long and prefers to hold general elections when it is politically advantageous for the ruling party. Only once, in 1976, have the lower house members been able to serve out their full four years.

The Constitution does not provide for the dissolution of the House of Councillors. At the same time, the House of Councillors does not have the authority to vote no confidence in the cabinet.

In 1980 and 1986, the government scheduled the lower house elections to coincide with the triennial elections of the upper house. Thus the ruling party was able to make the most politically profitable use of the issues that worked in its favor, citing these issues in the upper house campaign as well as in the lower house campaign. In both of these "double elections" the LDP won resounding landslide victories.

THE BUREAUCRACY

The Confucian tradition exalts the role of bureaucrats, and bureaucrats regulate much of Japan's economy by "administrative guidance." In pre–World War II Japan, bureaucrats selected through competitive examinations were regarded as servants of the revered emperor and enjoyed more power and prestige than did the elected politicians. Although the democratic constitution has enhanced the authority of elected officials, the power of the bureaucracy in Japan remains overwhelming. The short terms of office of the cabinet ministers make them unusually dependent on the bureaucrats for advice in matters of policy. After retiring at a fairly young age, many high-level bureaucrats go into politics (especially in the LDP) or "descend from heaven" to good positions in private business or public corporations that are subject to government regulation. Most of Japan's postwar prime ministers have been former career bureaucrats. Thus the bureaucratic approach permeates much of society.

In recent years, the prestige of the bureaucracy has been severely compromised by the exposure of serious instances of corruption in the ministries of finance and foreign affairs. Also the rise of *zoku* (tribes), groups of politicians representing particular interest groups, have managed to increase the clout of their clients in political and administrative affairs.

THE COURTS

There are several levels of courts: the Supreme Court, 8 high courts, 50 district courts, 50 family courts, and 438 summary courts. All of the courts pertain to the national government. Supreme Court judges are appointed by the cabinet and are subject to the approval of the people at the time of the next general election and every ten years thereafter. No judge has ever been turned down as a result of the popular vote. The chief judge of the Supreme Court is "designated" by the cabinet and "appointed" by the emperor. The imperial appointment presumably places the chief judge on a plane of equality with the prime minister.

Japan's prewar legal system under the Meiji Constitution was heavily influenced by the French and German models, which represented the European civil law tradition. Under Japan's postwar constitution, it is fair to say that while the legal principles introduced by the occupation are clearly evident, old attitudes still exist among the senior members of the judiciary, who are predominantly conservative.

Under the 1948 Code of Criminal Procedure, the former inquisitorial procedure was replaced by the adversary procedure, believed to be more favorable to the interest of defendants. The right of trial by jury, such as prescribed in the Bill of Rights of the U.S. Constitution, does not exist in Japan. In Japan there is no jury system; judges make decisions without the assistance of juries of ordinary citizens. Judges are appointed, not elected. The Japanese Supreme Court has held that capital punishment is not unconstitutional, and convicted criminals may be and have been hanged in Japan.

Judicial Review

A notable power of the courts in Japan is their authority to review the constitutionality of governmental acts and of legislation (see Figure 5.1). In Japan, as in America, it has become customary for the political opposition to challenge the constitutionality of legislation they especially dislike, so the courts may serve political purposes. Although the constitution explicitly grants the power of judicial review, the courts have been rather reluctant to strike down legislation, partly out of deference to tradition and to the Diet, which according to the constitution is "the highest organ of state power," and partly because of concern about the political consequences of a highly controversial decision.

Article 9

The most controversial clause of the constitution, Article 9, which renounces war and the maintenance of military forces, has been the focus of much judicial attention. In 1959 in the Sunakawa case, a district court declared that the security

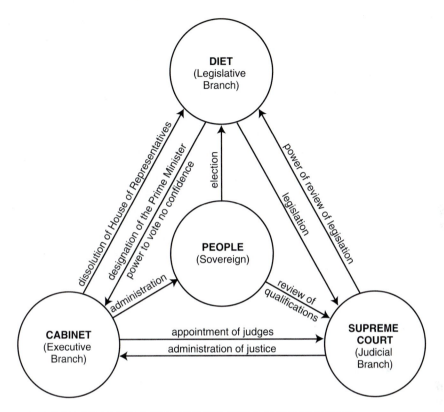

**Figure 5.1 SEPARATION OF POWERS AND CHECKS AND BALANCES IN THE
JAPANESE CONSTITUTION**

Adapted from Kawamata Noboru, *Shakai no Kenkyū* (The Study of Society) (Tokyo: Obunsha, 1960), p. 70.

treaty with the United States was unconstitutional, because it provided for the maintenance
of military forces. If this decision had been
allowed to stand, American forces in Japan
would have had to go home. The Supreme Court,
however, promptly overruled the district court,
ruling that the treaty was not *clearly* unconstitutional and that a political question was involved.

In the Naganuma Nike missile case, a district
court declared that the laws creating the Self-
Defense Force and the Defense Agency violated
Article 9. A high court and finally the Supreme
Court ruled in 1982 that the original plaintiffs
lacked standing to sue. The Supreme Court left
undecided the question of the constitutionality of

the Self-Defense Force, and to this day there is
no definitive ruling on this issue.

For some years it was feared that the failure
of the Supreme Court to come directly to grips
with the interpretation of Article 9 would result
in the ultimate disappearance of the review
authority. But since 1970 the Supreme Court has
found a number of statutes unconstitutional.

LOCAL GOVERNMENT

The political relationship of the national government and the provincial and local governments
has historically been a contended issue in

Japanese politics. The establishment of feudalism in the twelfth century represented a victory over the Chinese theory of an absolute centralized monarch. In 1868, the imperial restoration revived the power of the imperial capital.

Before World War II, the imperial government in Tokyo seemed all powerful. Prefectural governors were appointees of the Home Ministry, which controlled the national police. The Education Ministry controlled the country's system of public schools and universities. As in France and England, Japan's governmental system was unitary rather than federal.

Japan's relatively modest area (about the size of Montana) and the religious, linguistic, and cultural homogeneity of its population seem to argue against the need to establish a federal system. The postwar constitution did not create federalism or a panoply of "state's rights" in Japan, but it did provide that prefectural governors and other local officials, including mayors and assemblymen, be elected. Prefectural governments do not have constitutions of their own (as American states do), but exercise powers delegated to them by the national government, and the laws they enact may not contradict laws passed by the national Diet.

Japan is divided into 47 prefectures, including one metropolitan prefecture (Tokyo), two urban prefectures (Kyoto and Osaka), and Hokkaido prefecture, which includes Hokkaido Island. Most Japanese live in or near the great urban complexes such as the Tokyo-Yokohama area, the Osaka-Kyoto-Kobe area, and the Kitakyushu and Fukuoka area. The urban buildup has largely wiped out the agricultural areas that separated many of the cities and towns from one another. In the 1950s and 1960s, many cities, towns, and villages were legally merged, thus greatly reducing the number of local government entities.

The main concerns of prefectural and local governments are education, roads, sewage, garbage collection, police, and protection of the ecology. The public continuously complains about the inadequate management of these concerns, yet local governments often do not have adequate financial resources to run them effec-

tively. The dependence of the local governments on the aid of the national government for up to 70 percent of their finances severely limits the scope of local authority.

In 1995, apparently out of disgust with the political parties, the voters of both Tokyo and Osaka prefectures elected as their governors nonpartisan TV personalities who had served terms in the House of Councillors. More recently, Ishihara Shintaro, a popular novelist who had once been elected to the Diet as a member of the LDP, was elected to the Tokyo governorship. He had left the LDP in 1995 when it was plagued with scandal. A strong nationalist frequently interviewed on television, he was coauthor in 1989 of *The Japan That Can Say No,* which called into question Japan's close ties to America. A citizen's federation formed to make Ishihara the prime minister, but he would first have to be elected to the parliament, which might not be difficult for him.

Thinking Critically

1. What are the advantages and disadvantages of proportional representation?
2. Why has the Liberal Democratic Party with rare exceptions dominated politics in Japan since 1955?
3. How do the factions in Japan's Liberal Democratic Party resemble and differ from the factions in the parties of a country of your choosing?
4. What characteristics are necessary in order to become Japan's prime minister?
5. Is the Japanese system of government federal or unitary? Explain your answer.

KEY TERMS

Democratic Party of Japan *(296)*
Doi Takako *(293)*
factions *(286)*
Hashimoto Ryutaro *(289)*
"highest organ of state power" *(304)*
judicial review *(304)*

FURTHER READINGS

Bayley, David H. *Forces of Order: Policing Modern Japan* (Berkeley: University of California Press, 1991).

Baerwald, Hans H. *Party Politics in Japan* (Boston: Allen and Unwin, 1986).

Christensen, Ray. *Ending the LDP Hegemony: Party Cooperation in Japan* (Honolulu: University of Hawaii Press, 2000).

Curtis, Gerald, ed. *Policymaking in Japan: Defining the Role of Politicians* (Tokyo: Japan Center for International Exchange, 2002).

Curtis, Gerald. *The Logic of Japanese Politics: Leaders, Institutions, and the Limits of Change* (New York: Columbia University Press, 1999.

Flanagan, Scott C., Shinsaku Kohei, Ichiro Miyake, Bradley M. Richardson, and Joji Watanuki. *The Japanese Voter* (New Haven: Yale University Press, 1991).

Hayao, Kenji, *The Japanese Prime Minister and Public Policy* (Pittsburgh: University of Pittsburgh Press, 1993).

Hrebenar, Ronald J. *Japan's New Party System* (Boulder, CO: Westview Press, 2000).

Ishida, Takeshi, and Ellis S. Krauss, eds. *Democracy in Japan* (Pittsburgh: University of Pittsburgh Press, 1989).

Ishihara Shintaro. *The Japan That Can Say No* (New York: Simon and Schuster, 1991).

Itoh, Hiroshi, and Lawrence Ward Beer, eds. *The Constitutional Case Law in Japan: Selected Supreme Court Decisions, 1961–1970* (Seattle: University of Washington Press, 1978).

Johnson, Chalmers. *Japan: Who Governs? The Rise of the Developmental State* (New York: Norton, 1995).

Kishima, Takako. *Political Life in Japan: Democracy in a Reversible World* (Princeton, NJ: Princeton University Press, 1991).

Koh, B. C. *Japan's Administrative Elite* (Berkeley: University of California Press, 1991).

McCormack, Gowan, and Yoshio Sugimoto, eds. *Democracy in Contemporary Japan* (Armonk, NY: M. E. Sharpe, 1986).

Maki, John M., ed. *Court and Constitution in Japan: Selected Supreme Court Decisions, 1948–1960* (Seattle: University of Washington Press, 1964).

Mitchell, Richard H. *Political Bribery in Japan* (Honolulu: University of Hawaii Press, 1996).

Pharr, Susan. *Losing Face: Status Politics in Japan* (Berkeley: University of California Press, 1990).

Reed, Steven R. *Japanese Electoral Politics: Creating a New Party System* (London: Routledge Curzon, 2003).

Scalapino, Robert A. *The Japanese Communist Movement, 1920–1966* (Berkeley: University of California Press, 1967).

Schlesinger, Jacob M. *Shadow Shoguns: The Rise and Fall of Japan's Political Machine* (New York: Simon and Schuster, 1997).

Shinoda, Tomohiko. *Leading Japan: The Role of the Prime Minister* (Westport, CT: Praeger, 2000).

Tanaka, Hideo, ed. *The Japanese Legal System: Introductory Case Studies and Materials* (Tokyo: Tokyo University Press, 1976).

Thayer, Nathaniel. *How the Conservatives Rule Japan* (Princeton, NJ: Princeton University Press, 1969).

Weinstein, Martin E. *The Human Face of Japan's Leadership: Twelve Portraits* (New York: Praeger, 1989).

C. PUBLIC POLICY

THE JAPANESE ECONOMY

In the Meiji era (1868–1912), the imperial government fostered the establishment of modern industries in Japan, often using funds borrowed from abroad and employing Europeans as advisors. Once the industries were brought to a profitable basis, they were sold to private companies. Thus, it was the government, not private entrepreneurs, who launched the industrial revolution in Japan. While England was preoccupied with World War I, the Japanese took over a large share of the British market in Asia and became a leading manufacturer and exporter of light industrial goods. But in the last year of World War II, American bombers destroyed the factories in Japanese cities.

The Economic Miracle

After defeating Japan, the Allied powers did not regard the reconstruction of the Japanese economy as their responsibility. They believed that the Japanese were to blame for the war that had brought disaster to their country and should be made to learn from the experience. Moreover, they held, industries that would facilitate Japanese rearmament such as the manufacture of aircraft should be banned.

This tough policy, however, proved impractical. In 1946 when there were severe food shortages in the cities and Communist agitators were capitalizing on the food crisis, General MacArthur imported food from America. If only to relieve the American taxpayer of the burden of feeding Japan, the Japanese economy would have to be rehabilitated. The United States opposed the policy of extracting reparations from Japan, as it was believed that the Americans would be indirectly footing the bill. Labor unions fostered by Allied policies increasingly fell under the domination of Communists, and they scheduled a general strike for February 1, 1947. The strike would have had disastrous consequences for the war-ravished economy and MacArthur ordered that it be canceled, causing leftist leaders to lose prestige and influence. The American occupiers belatedly began to foster the economic revival of Japan. The labor relations law was modified to forbid strikes by government employees. Poor in natural resources and overpopulated, Japan would have to "trade or die." The honeymoon between the political left and MacArthur's headquarters began to come to an end. In 1948, the program of breaking up Japan's family monopolies, the *zaibatsu,* was halted in midstream.

The Korean War Boom

By 1950 neither the policies of the Japanese government nor of the occupation had been able to rescue Japan from unemployment, inflation, and every kind of shortage. When war broke out in Korea in June of that year, the American military hired Japanese firms to repair damaged equipment and manufacture uniforms, blankets, trucks, and other war materiel. "The Korean War boom" nudged the Japanese economy off dead center, and soon prewar levels of production were achieved. From 1950 to 1973, the average annual growth rate of Japan's GNP was over 10 percent, possibly the highest sustained rate of increase that the world had ever seen.

The Japanese no longer had to maintain a costly military establishment, and—unlike the British, French, and Dutch—they were not encumbered with rebellious colonies; it thus became easier to raise funds for economic reconstruction. Most of the money needed for rebuilding Japanese enterprises was obtained as loans from banks, rather than from the sale of shares. After World War II, the nationally regulated banking system directed funds to companies for the construction of new factories, replacing those destroyed by the war. Thus Japan's postwar industrial plants were more up-to-date and efficient than those of other countries.

Government Involvement

Although Japan is often said to be a capitalist country with a free-market economy, there seems to be no ideological commitment to the notion that government should not involve itself in the economy. Quite the contrary, the government is expected to and is ready to intervene not only to correct economic imbalances but also to take the lead in directing national economic change. The conservative rulers of Japan, notably LDP politicians, not only take pride in their effective oversight of the capitalist system, but also, with their pork-barrel spending, bring economic benefits to their local constituents.

The Ministry of International Trade and Industry (MITI) played a conspicuous role in fostering the development of Japanese industry and foreign trade since the 1960s. Government bureaucrats, who enjoy substantial prestige, are often longtime school friends of business and political leaders. It is not necessary for the Diet to continually pass new laws to facilitate government's involvement in the economy. *Administrative guidance* is the term usually used to denote the great influence of the bureaucracy on business activity. Businesses are aware that the bureaucracy has at its disposal effective, albeit informal, rewards and punishments to ensure conformity to government policies. The common practice of retiring government officials to assume administrative positions in private businesses or public corporations that they had previously regulated is known as *amakudari,* or "descending from heaven." Obviously this custom strengthens the ties between the bureaucracy and business, and opens the door to possible conflict of interest or even corruption.

In recent decades, members of the Diet have become increasingly involved in policy making. Groups of legislators belonging to Diet committees who are experts in the policies of particular government agencies are noticeably influencing policy. Known as *zoku* (literally, tribes), they act as lobbies at the highest level of government. The growing influence of the *zoku* suggests that the democratically elected Diet and the political parties are increasing their influence in relation to the bureaucracy.

Globalization

In the 1950s, Japanese and American entrepreneurs set up joint ventures in Japan, which facilitated the introduction of advanced American technology. Later the Japanese, rather than attempt to duplicate in their laboratories what had already been discovered elsewhere, purchased the most recent American technology. In the 1970s, Japan became the world's leader in the application of modern technology to industrial production. The Japanese pioneered the development of fully automated assembly lines and led the world in the use and manufacture of robots.

Over the decades, Japanese businesses gradually changed the mix of their manufactures. From textiles they moved to transistor radios and cameras. They then went to steel, ships, and automobiles. Japan has led the world in the manufacture and export of automobiles, musical instruments, photocopiers, cameras, and VCRs. With vast amounts of currency from exports and savings, Japanese banks became the leaders in global finance. Japan became the world's leading donor of development assistance to third world countries.

Japan is afflicted with many of the same economic and social problems that plague the other postindustrial countries in Europe and North America. Constant modernization of production processes requires that new jobs or retraining be provided to those who become unemployed because of technological advances. South Korea, Taiwan, Hong Kong, and Singapore have become "Little Japans" by manufacturing and exporting many goods, including automobiles, TV sets, and computers, that compete with Japanese exports. Japan is faced with serious competition from industries in China, India, and Brazil, which have large populations and substantial natural resources. Because of the high cost of labor and land in Japan, Japanese entrepreneurs, like their American counterparts, have established overseas sites for the plants. The appreciation of the yen in relation to the dollar accelerated Japanese acquisition or construction of manufacturing plants in the United States.

Japanese firms are becoming increasingly multinational as the structure of the Japanese economy is undergoing rapid change. These changes are imposing great stress not only on the Japanese people but also on the people of the world who do business with them. For example, Japan's trade imbalances and the appreciation of the yen may require that the Japanese—who are money rich but whose actual standard of living is modest—save and produce less but consume more. In the 1980s the average Japanese household saved over 15 percent of its disposable income, whereas American families saved only 3 or 4 percent. The expansion of the Japanese market that would accompany an increase in Japanese consumption might reduce Japan's reliance on exports and increase imports.

The Structure of the Japanese Economy

The holding companies of the prewar *zaibatsu* were partly broken up during the Allied occupation of Japan. However, many of the businesses formerly controlled by the family-owned holding companies are still affiliated in various ways and now are often referred to as *keiretsu* (economic groups). The names of some of the prewar *zaibatsu* (Mitsubishi, Mitsui, Yasuda, Sumitomo) may still be found attached to leading Japanese companies. There are, for example, the Mitsubishi Bank, Mitsubishi Chemical Industries, Mitsubishi Electric Corporation, Mitsubishi Heavy Industries, Mitsubishi Mining and Cement Company, Mitsubishi Motor Corporation, Mitsubishi Paper Mills, Mitsubishi Steel Manufacturing Company, and Mitsubishi Trust and Banking Corporation (not to be confused with the Mitsubishi Bank), to mention only some of the Mitsubishi affiliated companies.

Most major Japanese corporations are connected with one or another *keiretsu*. The name of a company may not necessarily indicate what its affiliations are. The directorships of the affiliated companies often interlock, and companies often own stock in affiliated companies. The varied enterprises (including banks) making up a *keiretsu* often prefer to do business with one another rather than with outsiders, without regard to cheaper prices or rates tendered by the outsiders. Sensitive to the hazards of cutthroat competition and economic instability and the need to compete in global markets, the Japanese government has not always been zealous to engage in trustbusting. Foreigners often find the system very difficult to penetrate.

Business associations such as the *Keidanren* (Federation of Business Organizations), *Keizai Doyukai* (Committee for Economic Development), and *Nikkeiren* (Japanese Federation of Employers Associations) effectively lobby both the Liberal Democratic Party and the bureaucracy on behalf of their interests. Japan's financial leaders, usually referred to as *zaikai,* are the nation's economic elite. The LDP and its factions get most of their funds from Japanese business. It is often said that Japan is run by a triumvirate of big business, the LDP, and the bureaucracy. But small business and agriculture are often able to use their electoral clout with the LDP to extract benefits from the state.

Banks (many with *keiretsu* affiliations) play a leading role in the growth of Japanese business. Interest rates in Japan have long been lower than elsewhere and the Japanese are great savers, so that companies are able to obtain money cheaply for the improvement and expansion of their facilities, or sometimes for stock or land speculation. In the late 1980s, the price of stock and of land had been driven to unprecedented heights, and these were used as collateral to obtain loans for more speculation.

The Collapse of the Bubble Economy

In the 1980s the growth rate of the economy amounted to a healthy 4 percent a year. In December 1989, the Nikkei stock market average reached its all-time high, ¥38,916. It then began to drop precipitously, hitting several false bottoms until it reached a low in June 1995 of ¥14,485. Thus within five years, Japanese stocks lost 63 percent of their value. From time to time the economy seemed to recover, but during the 1990s the economic growth rate dropped to about 1 percent a year. In November 2001, the stock market fell to ¥10,431, losing almost three-fourths of its 1989 value. There was a similar collapse in land prices.

This phenomenon was referred to as the collapse of "the bubble economy." Obviously, individual investors and land owners were hard hit by these events, but the effects went far beyond individual distress. Much of the stock and land had been bought with money borrowed from banks and housing loan companies, stock and land being used as collateral. When the value of these largely disappeared and the borrowers were unable to repay their loans, the financial institutions found that the collateral was no longer adequate. The banks themselves owned shares of stock and land which had lost much of its value. Loans that the banks had made were in too many cases "non-performing" (interest was not being paid on them). As a result, banks did not have sufficient money available to loan even to prospering enterprises. In August 1995, depositors began runs on several leading financial institutions, demanding the return of their deposits. The Ministry of Finance and the Bank of Japan became involved in the takeover of weak banks by stronger ones. In 1998, the Diet pumped $500 billion of public money to rescue troubled banks.

As a result of corporate restructuring, unemployment (which had hovered between 1.1 and 1.4 percent between 1961 to 1974) reached 5.4 percent in October 2001. In 2000, the economy showed signs of deflation, which further depressed the economy. As a result, some economists have advocated the inflation of the money supply to reduce the relative value of the yen and increase the competitiveness of Japanese exports.

Financial scandals were exposed when individuals and institutions that had borrowed money in violation of legal requirements failed to repay their loans. The borrowers may have planned to repay the money when their investments increased in value—as they usually had in the past—but the collapse of the bubble economy

sent them to prison or bankrupted them and was disastrous to the lenders.

In 2001, Japanese government bonds were assigned lower ratings on the international market. Some observers held that the government finances were on the verge of bankruptcy.

Reform and Privatization

Given the many notorious scandals in Japanese politics, unhappiness with the electoral system, the many inefficiencies in the economy and the government, and the persistent economic depression following the collapse of the bubble economy, it is not surprising that Japanese politicians of every ideological persuasion have been touting the mantra of "reform." However, determining precisely what needs reform and then how to reform it is no simple matter. Any reform program is bound to hurt the vested interests of somebody, and resistance to any change is built into the system.

Japan has long had a very extensive system of railroads, both publicly and privately owned. Most of their revenue comes from passenger traffic, as commuters in Japan's sprawling metropolitan centers depend on them to get to work. Until the 1980s most, but by no means all, of the railroads were owned and operated by the national government. The *shinkansen* trains (known as "bullet trains") were introduced by the Japan National Railways in the 1960s. They became world famous for their speed and convenience, linking most of the major cities and running at 15- and 20-minute intervals. In their frequency of operation they resemble a city subway system but operate much faster and on a national scale. Their bureaucratic structure and politicized national railroad workers union, however, acted as dampers on efficiency, and the system ran up enormous deficits. In 1987, the Japan National Railways was divided into privately owned and operated regional segments. The Nippon Telegraph and Telephone Public Corporation had been privatized in 1985.

In 2005 there were 77 public (government-affiliated) corporations. They were often criticized for inefficiency, for offering cushy jobs to retired bureaucrats, and for their lack of financial transparency.

During his campaign for the LDP leadership in 2001, Koizumi Junichiro strongly advocated the privatization of the national postal system. In November 2001, the Koizumi administration decided to kill or privatize seven public corporations, expecting to save 1 trillion yen. The Housing Loan Corporation would cut back its operations over a five-year period and go out of existence. The Housing and Urban Development Corporation would halt new housing projects and be dismantled in 2005. The Japan Oil Corporation would be abolished. Private companies would take over the functions of these corporations. Four public highway construction corporations would be abolished or their functions taken over by one corporation.

The reforms that the Koizumi government intends to carry out would result in the short run in more unemployment and alienate many of the traditional constituents of LDP Diet members. It is feared that many of the reforms, in order to garner the necessary support, will be merely cosmetic or will have to be greatly watered down. Because of Koizumi's pledge to limit the issuance of government bonds to ¥30 trillion a year, his administration would find it very difficult if not impossible to continue the generous stimulus spending indulged in by its predecessors.

THE WELFARE STATE

After World War II, although Japan had lagged behind the other leading industrial states in the development of welfare programs, such programs were vastly expanded in the 1970s, and Japan became a welfare state. The LDP stresses the importance of a prosperous capitalist system in order to finance welfare programs and social security. With one of the world's most modern medical and hospital systems and with nationalized health insurance, the Japanese now have the longest average life span among the nations of the world.

In the traditional farm villages common in prewar times, grandparents lived with their children and grandchildren, but in the modern urban environment, the expensive apartments are barely large enough to accommodate two generations, and separate living quarters must be provided for the elderly with or without some measure of government subsidy. As people live longer and as the percentage of the working-age population declines, a great strain is imposed on pension systems, and the medical and hospital costs for the elderly rise.

Because of Japan's unusually low birthrate and the longevity of its people, the number of people 65 and older will nearly double by 2020 to 32 million people. Senior citizens will then make up 25 percent of Japan's population, the highest proportion in the industrial world.

To lower costs, the government has raised the age for receiving national pensions from 60 to 62, and eventually it will be 65. The consumption tax of 3 percent (a kind of national sales tax) was introduced in 1989 to supplement revenues from individual and corporate income taxes largely in order to meet the increased cost of caring for the aged. It was later increased to 5 percent. A principal issue in contemporary Japanese politics as in the other industrialized countries has been the question of how the needs of the growing numbers of elderly will be met.

EDUCATION

Japan's leaders have long been keenly conscious of the importance of education in the development of their country's economic strength. During the Meiji period, the imperial government established a system of public education to indoctrinate the population in patriotism and to train a literate workforce. By 1940, Japan had one of the world's highest literacy rates.

The Allied occupation sought to democratize the content of education and reduce the role of the national government in its administration. Elected school boards and parent-teacher associations were established. Later, when members of the leftist National Teachers Union were being elected to the school boards, these institutions were made appointive.

Although schools are locally administered, national standards must be maintained. About half of the cost of public education is borne by the national government, and expenditures per pupil are essentially equal nationwide.

The Japanese regard their schools as the key to individual and national economic success. Although some foreign observers view the Japanese educational system as a model to be emulated, the Japanese are keenly aware of its shortcomings. Because entrance to a prestigious university is necessary for entrance into the best careers, parents are determined that from kindergarten on, their children will pass the competitive examinations allowing them to move upward from one reputable school to the next. The first nine years of education are compulsory, and no tuition is charged for admission to public schools. After the ninth grade, nearly every child attends high school, although it is not legally required.

School meets on alternate Saturday mornings as well as all day Monday through Friday, and summer vacation lasts only one month. Homework assignments begin in first grade, and helping the child with his or her schoolwork is a principal duty of every parent. To prepare for examinations to enter a good high school or a university, about half of the children attend *juku*, privately operated schools, after regular school hours. The examination system tends to stress rote memory of information rather than creative thinking. It generates great stress on both children and parents, and the "examination hell" is generally believed to interfere with the wholesome physical and moral development of children. Just as there have been efforts to reduce the working week for adults, there have been recent attempts to eliminate Saturday morning classes for children, an idea resisted by some parents. There is general agreement that the examination system must be radically reformed or replaced with something else, but there is no consensus as to which specific changes should be made.

Higher Education

In Japan, about half of all college-aged young people attend colleges or universities. (Men outnumber women by a ratio of about 1.6 to 1.) The most prestigious is the University of Tokyo—Todai—followed by the other former "imperial universities," most notably Kyoto. There is at least one national university in each prefecture, and some prefectures and municipalities support their own public universities. The most famous private universities are Keio and Waseda, in Tokyo, together with a number of reputable private institutions established before World War II. Many private universities were established during the 1960s when the national government encouraged their proliferation with substantial subsidies.

The academic demands on undergraduates in Japan are modest, and there is a tendency for the students to spend much of their time trying to enjoy life and to recover from the rigors of the examination system that got them into university. In the 1960s, Japanese universities, like those of other leading industrial nations, were seriously disrupted by mass student demonstrations. Students nowadays are apt to be politically conservative. One-third to one-half of all top positions in the government bureaucracy and in big business are occupied by products of Todai, and graduation from a leading university is regarded as a sine qua non for success in life.

FOREIGN POLICY

Alignment with the United States

When Japan made a peace treaty with the United States and other non-Communist countries in 1951, it also entered into a mutual security treaty with the United States, which permitted American forces to remain at bases in Japan. Since then until the 1990s, Japan's debate over foreign policy revolved largely around the two poles of unarmed neutrality on the one hand and rearmament and the American alignment on the other.

Japan's position as America's "junior partner" in a world divided by the Cold War largely determined Japan's orientation toward the rest of the world. In 1960, the U.S.-Japan Security Treaty was replaced by a revised security treaty more favorable to Japan. But there was widespread opposition to it in Japan. Demonstrations opposed to the new treaty and to President Eisenhower's scheduled visit to Japan resulted in the death of a coed (regarded as a martyr by activists), the "postponement" (in effect the cancellation) of Eisenhower's visit, and the resignation of Prime Minister Kishi. Japan remained loyal to its commitments to the United States and did not recognize Communist China until after Nixon made his famous trip to China in 1972.

Continuously since the end of the occupation in 1952, American military, naval, and air forces have been stationed in Japan. They have served as a deterrent against invasion or attack and in that sense have advanced the cause of Japan's security. American air bases in Japan were used during the Korean War to launch raids against North Korea, provoking fears that the Communist powers might make retaliatory air attacks on the Japanese bases, which are uncomfortably close to Japanese cities.

It would be virtually impossible to defend Japan's great cities from air attack, especially from nearby Russian, Chinese, or North Korean aircraft or missiles, and a war against a major country to defend Japan would likely be suicidal. Japan is sheltered by the American "nuclear umbrella," which implies that any nuclear attack on Japan would be met by retaliation by the United States. Thus the presence of Japanese and American forces in Japan is primarily designed to *deter* a possible attack against Japan. After the American withdrawal from Vietnam, there were nagging doubts—reinforced by President Carter's talk of withdrawing American forces from Korea—that the United States would have the will or the perseverance to defend Japan if the need arose.

The end of the Cold War in 1990 has seemed to reduce the importance of Japan's strategic affiliation with America. During the 1991 war in the Persian Gulf, American requests for Japanese assistance at first evoked little more than a passive response from Prime Minister Kaifu. After prolonged and largely public negotiations between the United States and Japan, Japan contributed $13 billion as its share in the costs of the war against Iraq. However, both foreigners and Japanese ridiculed Japan's "checkbook diplomacy" and advocated a larger role for Japan's military forces in the world.

About 40,000 American troops are stationed in bases in Japan, and much of the cost of maintaining them is paid by Japan. Most of the Americans are stationed in Okinawa, where American bases cover one-fifth of that prefecture's territory. The rape of a school girl by three American enlisted men in Okinawa in 1995 precipitated a reconsideration of the status of U.S. forces in Japan. The governor of Okinawa called for the removal of American bases from his prefecture, and the national government began negotiations concerning the scaling down or transfer of American bases from Okinawa to other places in Japan.

Some of Japan's neighbors as well as many Japanese approve of the American troop presence in Japan because that presence is a disincentive to Japanese rearmament. So long as the Americans remain in Japan in force, there would seem to be less likelihood that Japan would again become a military power and a threat to her neighbors.

Japan's relationship with the United States is economic as well as military. In 2005, 24 percent of Japan's exports went to the United States, and the United States provided 15 percent of Japan's imports. Michael Mansfield, American ambassador to Japan from 1977 to 1988, is noted for saying that the U.S.-Japanese relationship is "the most important bilateral relationship in the world bar none."

Relations with Russia

After the conclusion of the Hitler-Stalin nonaggression treaty of 1939, it was widely believed that the Soviet Union might join the Axis powers (Germany, Italy, and Japan). In April 1941, Japan entered into a Neutrality Treaty with the Soviets.

Two months later, Japan's ally, Germany, invaded Russia, but at that time Japan and the Soviet Union did not go to war, nor did the outbreak of war between Japan and the United States result in hostilities between Japan and the Soviet Union. However, in the spring of 1945, the Soviets alarmed the Japanese by informing them that they would not renew the Neutrality Treaty, which would expire in 1946.

After the war in Europe had ended, the Japanese tried to enhance their relations with the Soviets and induce Stalin to mediate a peace between Japan and the Allied powers. Stalin replied to this request on August 8 (two days after the atomic bombing of Hiroshima) with the announcement that on the next day the Soviet Union would be at war with Japan. The treacherous attitude of the Soviet Union toward its commitment in the Soviet-Japanese Neutrality Treaty was regarded by Japanese diplomats as outrageous. After the war, hundreds of thousands of Japanese prisoners of war were detained for several years in the Soviet Union, many as laborers, and indoctrinated with Leninism-Stalinism. In 1956 the Soviet Union and Japan issued a joint peace declaration, but because of the dispute over the "Northern Territories," to be discussed later, the two countries have thus far failed to conclude a peace treaty for the conclusion of World War II.

The arguments for unarmed neutrality after the dreadful war were very compelling to the Japanese. But the Soviet record of almost unrelieved hostility toward Japan provoked anti-Soviet suspicions and a popular reluctance to scuttle the tie with America. In any event, once the alignment with America had been in place for several years, a Japanese withdrawal from it would seem to appear pro-Soviet and anti-American rather than neutral. But more than appearances were involved. The U.S.-Japan Security Treaty has long been a key factor in the balance of power in the Far East.

After the United States had returned Okinawa to Japanese administration in 1972, the pressure in Japan for the return of certain northern islands occupied by the Soviet Union intensified. In the Japanese Peace Treaty with the non-Communist countries, Japan gave up its claims to Karafuto (Southern Sakhalin) and to the Kurile Islands, but the Japanese insist that the islands of Habomai, Shikotan, Kunashiri, and Etorofu (from which the attack on Pearl Harbor had been launched) do not pertain to the Kuriles and are rightfully Japanese. These islands had served as important fishing bases and as homes for several generations of Japanese. These "Northern Territories" are part of a chain of islands extending from Hokkaido to the Kamchatka Peninsula and limit the access from Siberia to the Pacific Ocean. They are now highly fortified by the Soviets.

The buildup of the Soviet fleet and air force in the Western Pacific in the 1980s and spy scandals involving Soviet agents and Japan Self-Defense Forces personnel deepened Japanese distrust of the Soviet Union. Relations were not improved when in 1983 the Soviet air force shot down a Korean airliner that had wandered over Soviet territory (near the disputed islands), with the loss of 269 passengers including 28 Japanese.

From time to time, the Soviet government hinted that a negotiable solution might be found for the Northern Territories dispute. A complication was the presence of thousands of Soviet citizens in the disputed territory, who may have reservations about coming under Japanese rule or emigrating. The dissolution of the Soviet Union in 1991 and the apparent end of the Cold War inspired some hope that Russia would be more responsive to Japan's desires in the near future. Visits by Japanese to the Northern Territories have been permitted, and trade relations have developed between these territories and Hokkaido. However, apparently fearful that the return of the disputed areas to Japan would encourage secessionist tendencies in other Russian possessions, the Russian government has taken a hard line on this issue.

Relations with the Two Chinas

The People's Republic of China   In the 1960s and 1970s, the security tie with the United States involved Japan in the American political and economic boycott of Communist China. However, Japan, with a policy of "separation of politics and economics," engaged in limited trade with Communist China through unofficial channels and informal cultural contacts. Beijing encouraged these unofficial contacts with its policy of "people's diplomacy," which eschewed normal diplomatic channels. The official Japanese boycott of the Beijing government ended in 1972 with Prime Minister Tanaka's visit to Communist China and the establishment of formal diplomatic relations between his country and the People's Republic of China (PRC).

After prolonged and difficult negotiations, a Sino-Japanese peace treaty was finally signed in 1978. It contained an "antihegemony" clause, insisted upon by the Chinese, which was regarded as provocative by the Soviet Union. China had been complaining of the Soviet military buildup on China's border, the invasion of pro-Chinese Kampuchea by Vietnam (a Soviet ally), and the Soviet invasion of Afghanistan. When the Carter administration recognized Communist China the following year, there was speculation that a U.S.-China-Japan alliance aimed against the Soviet Union was in the making.

Before Japan's rapprochement with Communist China, Japanese progressive intellectuals harbored romantic notions about the high ideals of the Communist revolution in China while many businessmen fondly expected a boom in exports to the PRC when trade restrictions were lifted. These attitudes were encouraged by a sense of guilt for Japan's past aggressions against China, the concept of cultural indebtedness to China, the idea that China's radicalism was an understandable response to America's hostility, the notion that, as Asians, the Japanese could understand the Chinese better than the Americans could, and the view that American Cold War diplomacy was to blame for the alienation between Japan and China.

After 1972, when the PRC was officially opened for visits by the Japanese people, the excesses of Mao's cultural revolution and the trial of the "gang of four" in China disillusioned Japanese intellectuals. At the same time, China's poverty and backwardness seriously obstructed

the growth of trade with that country. In 1989 the ruthless suppression of the prodemocracy demonstrators in Beijing's Tiananmen Square shocked the Japanese and reminded them of the blessings of their own democratic system. There has been, however, a substantial infusion of Japanese capital and tourists into China.

In 1995, China resumed nuclear testing in spite of Japanese protests. In 1996, the Beijing regime carried out missile tests and military exercises in the vicinity of Taiwan. When President Clinton and Prime Minister Hashimoto announced plans for closer military cooperation between America and Japan, Chinese commentators accused them of conspiring to enforce a containment policy against the People's Republic.

At the same time, China's economy was expanding at a phenomenal rate. China, with an area more than 25 times that of Japan, has enormous quantities of natural resources and her population is 9.5 times that of Japan. In 2004, China contributed 18 percent of Japan's imports, more than the United States. In the early 2000s, Japan was faced with a growing flood of cheap Chinese goods in the Japanese and world markets. More worrying, perhaps, was the increasingly high level of Chinese technology. Chinese entrance into the World Trade Organization was expected to enhance China's competitive position in world trade. A miniature trade war erupted in 2001 when the Japanese government sought to check the import of Chinese agricultural goods and the Chinese sought to hamper imports of Japanese vehicles. Thus the Japanese are becoming increasingly conscious of possible strategic and economic threats from China.

Taiwan   Taiwan had been a part of the Japanese Empire from 1895 until Japan's defeat in 1945, when it reverted to Chinese rule. After its defeat by the Communists in 1949, the National Government of China moved its capital to Taipei, in Taiwan. When Japan officially recognized the Beijing regime in 1972, it simultaneously withdrew its formal recognition of the Republic of China (ROC) in Taiwan. Quasi-official relations, however, continue between Japan and the ROC, and the economic and cultural ties between the two countries are very important to them. Taiwan is one of Japan's largest customers. In Japan, as in the United States, political conservatives and some commercial interests have been unhappy with the treatment that has been meted out to the ROC by their government. The continuing close relationship between Japan and Taiwan has been a source of irritation and complaint by the Beijing government.

Relations with the Two Koreas

Japan's relations with Korea are still poisoned by the memory of Japanese colonialism. The events leading to the annexation of the Korean kingdom in 1910 and the cruelty with which Japanese authorities suppressed the national independence movement are still fresh in the minds of Korean patriots. Although the country gained its independence in 1945 with Japan's defeat, it was immediately divided between U.S. and Soviet occupation zones, in South and North Korea, respectively. When American and Soviet troops withdrew from Korea, they left behind anti-Communist and pro-Communist governments in their respective former zones, and the Korean War broke out in 1950.

The Japanese were fearful that their own country might be engulfed in the war, but when it ended in 1953, the Japanese economy had been invigorated by the Korean War boom. American policy discouraged the Japanese government from establishing relations with Communist North Korea. The fact that both South Korea and Japan have security treaties with the United States did not seem to mitigate the distrust between the Japanese and the Koreans. In 1965, 20 years after the attainment of Korean independence, South Korea (the Republic of Korea, ROK) and Japan negotiated an agreement that normalized relations between the two countries. Although there was agreement that Japan should grant economic assistance to Korea (and it did), the Koreans made their claim on the basis of their right to reparations, a moral assertion that the Japanese were reluctant to concur with. The treaty was bitterly attacked by neutralists and leftists in Japan on the ground that it was

aimed against the Communist states in Asia, especially North Korea and Communist China, and would further alienate Japan from her Asian neighbors and involve Japan in American anti-Communist adventures.

Bad feelings between Japan and South Korea are perpetuated by reports of discrimination against the Korean minority in Japan, the apparent revival of Japanese nationalism, and the tendency of Japanese governments to maintain informal relations with North Korea. The South Koreans believe they bear a disproportionate share of the burden for the defense of the Free World in the Far East and that the Japanese should recognize this. Trade friction has risen between the two countries, as the South Koreans accuse the Japanese of refusing to buy from South Korea although South Korea imports large amounts of Japanese goods. At the same time, South Korean automobiles, steel, ships, TVs, VCRs, and computers compete with Japanese products on the world market.

With the end of the Cold War, Japan became involved in efforts to assist with Korean reunification and the reduction of tensions in northeast Asia. Japan, like the United States, has been deeply concerned about the development of North Korea's nuclear capability, which could directly or indirectly threaten Japan's security. The United States maintains some 36,000 personnel in South Korea. Should war break out in Korea as it did in 1950, the American forces there would immediately become involved, with the possibility of entangling Japan, where the United States maintains major air and naval bases.

In August 1998, North Korea test fired its Taepodong ballistic missile over Japan, and in March 1999, North Korean spy boats invaded Japanese waters. For Japan, North Korea has been a difficult neighbor.

THE UNITED NATIONS

The Japanese had mixed feelings about the United Nations involvement in the Korean War in which Japan-based American forces were participating. After that war was over and Japan had regained its independence, Japan was admitted as a member of the UN in 1956. Japanese participation in the UN has enjoyed almost unanimous support in Japan. The UN provided a vehicle for Japanese participation in world affairs outside of the confining framework of the U.S.-Japan Security Treaty. Membership in the global organization appealed to the neutralist and pacifist tendencies of the political left in Japan as well as to the internationalist tendencies of the right.

Largely because of constitutional restraints, only since the passage of the International Peace Cooperation Law in 1992 has Japan contributed to UN noncombatant peacekeeping operations, notably in Cambodia. On the other hand, Japan's economic contributions have been very substantial. In 1986, Japan's contribution to the UN budget exceeded that of the Soviet Union, so that Japan became the second largest contributor, after the United States. The United Nations University (primarily a research institution) has its headquarters in Tokyo. In a speech at the UN in 1994, Foreign Minister Kono Yohei not only affirmed Japanese interest in disarmament, nuclear nonproliferation, and human rights but also called for a permanent seat in the Security Council for Japan. If Japan obtained such a seat, it would be the only permanent member without nuclear weapons. Of course, the debate over a permanent seat for Japan would provoke protests from Japan's World War II victims and perhaps more importantly raise the issue of permanent seats for other important countries, most notably India.

NATIONAL DEFENSE

Article 9

"Realists" tend to evaluate Japan's defense policies in terms of the global distribution of power and Japan's diplomatic and strategic position. Many Japanese, however, tend to begin their discussion of Japan's defense in terms of Article 9, the "pacifist clause," of their postwar constitution, which they dub the "Peace Constitution."

Article 9 of the Japanese constitution reads:

> Aspiring sincerely to an international peace based on justice and order, the Japanese people forever renounce war as a sovereign right of the nation and the threat or use of force as a means of settling international disputes.
>
> In order to accomplish the aim of the preceding paragraph, land, sea, and air forces, as well as other war potential, will never be maintained. The right of the belligerency of the state will not be recognized.

The actual text of the Constitution is cited here because it is often misquoted.

When the constitution was adopted in 1946, it was generally believed that Article 9 prohibited *defensive* as well as offensive wars and banned *defensive* as well as offensive arms. Most constitutional scholars insist on this strict interpretation, but the Japanese public has over time come to accept the existence of the Self-Defense Forces (SDF) as legitimate. However they interpret its technicalities, the majority of the Japanese people approve of and support the no-war no-arms clause of their constitution. They do not want to repeat the horrors of the 1930s and 1940s and view Article 9 as a formidable obstacle to militarism and war.

THE SELF-DEFENSE FORCES

In 1950, shortly after the outbreak of war in Korea, General MacArthur directed Japan's prime minister to create a 75,000-member "National Police Reserve," evidently to help maintain internal security in Japan while the American occupation forces were fighting in Korea. The Police Reserve was shortly renamed the Security Force. In 1954, the Land, Maritime, and Air Self-Defense Forces (incorporating the former Security Force) and the Defense Agency were brought into being by acts of the Diet.

In 2000 the International Institute for Strategic Studies reported in *The Military Balance, 2000,* that there were 242,600 regular and 48,600 reserve personnel (including women) in Japan's Self-Defense Forces. They were equipped with 1,070 tanks, 13 frigates, 42 destroyers, and 16 submarines. Japan has 12 air squadrons, but no aircraft carriers. Japan has no nuclear military capability.

In number of personnel, Japan's Self-Defense Forces rank 25th among the world's nations, but Japan has the world's third largest defense budget, a figure that reflects the high cost of salaries where civilian salaries have made it impossible to completely fill the ranks of the military. It is notable that Japan's defense budget consumes less than 1 percent of the nation's gross national product (an unusually small percentage), but the Japanese GNP is the world's second largest. About 40,000 American military personnel are stationed in Japanese territory, and Japan is protected by America's nuclear umbrella. Japan's own military forces are very modest compared with those of its close neighbors, Russia, North Korea, South Korea, and China.

The Japanese government has said that the Self-Defense Forces did not constitute "war potential" prohibited by the constitution because they were not capable of fighting a modern war. In more recent years, the government has been saying that the defense of Japan is not forbidden by the constitution, and that although offensive weapons and the dispatch of the SDF combat forces overseas are banned, the minimum force needed for Japan's defense is permissible. During the national debate over Japan's participation in the UN military actions against Iraq in 1991, the public looked more favorably than before on sending SDF personnel overseas provided their purpose was to enforce UN-sponsored peace-keeping operations and they were not involved in combat. Japan's Supreme Court has avoided ruling directly on the constitutionality of the Self-Defense Forces and has thus avoided saying that they are unconstitutional.

The prime minister has supreme control over the SDF and is advised by the National Defense Council, which includes the director of the Defense Agency (a cabinet minister), the foreign and finance ministers, and the director of the Economic Planning Agency. Because the prime minister is a civilian and is responsible to the Diet, this system, the government contends, assures civilian control.

There has been much debate over whether Japan should become a "normal nation." Ozawa Ichiro popularized this expression. By this he meant a nation that is willing to assume the responsibilities regarded as natural in the international community. The implication is that Japan should arm to defend itself and participate in United Nations military activities.

The Mission of the Self-Defense Forces

The Japanese government's position has been that the SDF may fight only in the defense of Japan. They may possess only defensive weapons and their personnel may not be sent overseas into combat. These and related questions were thoroughly aired during the debate over the dispatch of SDF personnel to the Gulf War in 1991. The SDF is often mobilized to deal with earthquakes (such as the Kobe earthquake in 1995) and other natural disasters, and in the minds of many Japanese such humanitarian projects represent their most appropriate use.

The officially announced mission of the SDF in the event of an invasion of Japan would be to fight for up to two weeks while the United States came to Japan's rescue. Japan would provide America with intelligence and protect shipping lanes. Because a modern war in Japan would be calamitous, it is hoped that the American commitment to defend Japan together with Japan's defensive capability would constitute a credible deterrent against a potential aggressor.

With the breakup of the Soviet Union and the end of the Cold War, the possibility of a Soviet attack on Japan seems remote. The issue in 1991 was the nature and extent of Japan's participation in the UN-sponsored liberation of Kuwait after its invasion by Iraq. After bitter and confusing debate, in addition to sending humanitarian aid and making a very substantial financial contribution to the anti-Iraq coalition ($13 billion), the Japanese sent a minesweeping mission to the Persian Gulf—after the fighting had ended.

Only rarely—and after much debate—has the cost of Japan's military establishment exceeded 1 percent of Japan's gross national product. However in 1995, notwithstanding the costs of the peacekeeping operations, the Defense Agency recommended a 5 percent reduction in the Defense Forces budget as well as substantial reductions in their personnel.

Meeting President Clinton in Tokyo in 1996, Prime Minister Hashimoto agreed on closer logistical and intelligence cooperation between American and Japanese forces and a larger role for Japan in maintaining peace and security in Asia. Later, apparently responding to criticism that Japan's new policy might allow the United States to drag Japan into a war, Hashimoto announced that his government continues to hold that the constitution forbids Japan from entering collective self-defense arrangements.

The Japanese government's policy is that although Article 9 permits *individual* self-defense, it forbids *collective* self-defense. The principle of collective self-defense, legitimate under Article 51 of the UN Charter, holds that if a nation is not itself directly attacked, it may go to war to defend one of its allies from an aggressor. Japan's security agreement with the United States obligates the United States to defend Japan but does not obligate Japan to defend the United States. A law in 2001 expanded the role of the SDF, allowing troops to provide noncombat support in Afghanistan: another in 2004 allowed similar deployment in Iraq.

Two questions remain unanswered. (1) In the defense of Japan's interests and international responsibilities, can economic prowess serve as a substitute for military might? (2) Will Japan, an economic superpower, become a military superpower?

NUCLEAR NONPROLIFERATION

In 1970, Japan signed and in 1976 ratified the Nuclear Nonproliferation Treaty, committing the country not to make or acquire nuclear weapons. Japan maintains the three principles that the nation will (1) not produce nuclear weapons, (2) not acquire them, and (3) not allow their introduction into Japanese territory. There have been reports over several decades that American vessels visiting Japanese ports carry nuclear weapons in contravention of the three principles. The United States government refuses as a general principle to confirm or deny the presence anywhere of its nuclear weapons. The Japanese government has not tried to publicly embarrass the United States by insisting on an unequivocal denial of the presence of American nuclear weapons on Japanese territory. Japan is shielded by the American nuclear umbrella.

MILITARY TECHNOLOGY

Japan manufactures fighter planes under American licenses. In the 1980s the point was reached where the American military began to ask for Japanese technology. In 1991 a prominent Japanese politician asserted that America's sensational victory over Iraq would not have been possible without Japanese technology.

As Japan develops its own fighter planes and other weapons systems, it may feel the need to export them to help defray development costs. The export of military technology and weapons has become an extremely controversial issue in Japan, involving as it does very delicate diplomatic and economic questions as well as the spirit of the "Peace Constitution." Japan's rules for the export of military technology have been: (1) not to Communist countries, (2) not to countries where the UN prohibits exports, and (3) not to countries involved in international conflicts (except the United States). In 1991, the Japanese proposed that the United Nations oversee a program for making public all international weapons sales.

Even though the Japanese may now possess or may obtain the necessary technology for independently producing a massive modern military establishment, it does not presently possess the manufacturing capacity needed to do so. Economic, demographic, and diplomatic considerations as well as constitutional limitations inhibit, but may not absolutely prevent, Japan from becoming a military superpower.

THE WAR AGAINST TERRORISM

The terrorist attacks on the World Trade Center in New York and on the Pentagon in Washington, D.C., on September 11, 2001, and the American response forced the Japanese government to revise their defense policy in light of the new global situation. How would the Japanese respond to American calls for cooperation in the war against terrorism?

The Japanese had had experience with domestic terrorism, most notably the sarin gas attack launched by the Aum Shinrikyo against the Tokyo subway system in 1995, in which hundreds of people were hospitalized and 12 died. In the September 11 terrorist attack on the World Trade Center, 24 Japanese died or were missing, including 19 who were employed by Japanese companies. The Japanese were keenly conscious of the widespread criticism of their lukewarm response to the Gulf War in 1991, when they had made nothing more than a monetary contribution.

In the days immediately following the Trade Center attack, Prime Minister Koizumi telephoned President Bush and visited Bush in Washington. From the beginning there was a consensus in Japan that Japan would have to make a very substantial contribution to the antiterrorist effort, including military support in some form or other. There was serious debate and some partisan wrangling over the precise nature of the Japanese contribution, constitutional limitations on the use of Japan's Self-Defense Forces, and the role of the Diet in the making of military policy.

On October 29, 2001, after 60 hours of deliberations, the Diet enacted an antiterrorism bill which would allow the Self-Defense Forces to lend an unprecedented level of noncombatant support to U.S.-led forces overseas. The Democratic Party opposed the bill because it does not require the government to seek Diet approval before the SDF is dispatched. However, as revised in the House of Representatives, the bill does require the government to ask for Diet approval within 20 days of an SDF dispatch. The revision also allows the SDF to transport weapons and ammunition by sea.

On November 25, three Maritime SDF vessels departed on a mission to provide rear-area support and carry relief supplies for refugees. They would be joined by three other vessels that had left earlier for information gathering under the provisions of the Defense Agency Establishment Law. On December 3, the Defense Agency announced that an MSDF supply vessel had started supplying fuel to U.S. ships involved in military operations in Afghanistan. It was expected that some 1,400 SDF personnel would participate in the logistical operations by sea and air, to destinations in Guam, Australia, the Indian Ocean, and the Persian Gulf. The positive response of the new prime minister and the public to the need for meaningful action in Afghanistan and in 2004 in Iraq stood in striking contrast to the response of Prime Minister Kaifu Toshiki to the Gulf Crisis in 1990.

The paradigm of global politics assumed a new configuration as the dramatic improvement of United States relations with the Soviet Union and China and the intimacy of British-American military collaboration seemed to threaten the relative importance of Japan's alignment with America. Some politicians suggested that the Japanese, whose relations with Arab countries had always been friendly, might assume a significant role in the mediation of a peaceful settlement.

Thinking Critically

1. Should Japan be awarded a permanent seat in the Security Council of the United Nations?
2. Explain the collapse of the "bubble economy."
3. What needs to be done to restore the Japanese economy to health?
4. Should Japan abandon its strategic ties with the United States to pursue a policy of neutrality?

5. Explain the positions of the relevant governments concerning any one of Japan's territorial disputes.

KEY TERMS

administrative guidance *(309)*
antihegemony clause *(316)*
Article 9 *(318)*
juku (313)
keiretsu (310)
MITI *(309)*
Northern Territories *(315)*
Okinawa *(314)*
Self-Defense Forces (SDF) *(318)*
Todai *(313)*
U.S.-Japan Security Treaty *(313)*
Zoku (309)

FURTHER READING

Allinson, Gary D., and Yasunori Sone. *Political Dynamics in Contemporary Japan* (Ithaca, NY: Cornell
University Press, 1993).

Bouissou, Jean-Marie. *Japan, the Burden of Success*
(Boulder: Rienner, 2002).

Calder, Kent E. *Crisis and Compensation: Public Policy
and Political Stability in Japan, 1949–1986*
(Princeton, NJ: Princeton University Press, 1988).

Chan-Tiberghien, Jennifer. *Gender and Human Rights
Politics in Japan* (Stanford: Stanford University
Press, 2004).

Cowhey, Peter F., and Mathew D. McCubbins, eds.
*Structure and Policy in Japan and the United
States* (New York: Cambridge University Press,
1995).

Dobson, Hugo, and Glenn D. Hook, eds. *Japan and
Britain in the Contemporary World: Responses to
Common Issues* (London: Routledge Curzon, 2003).

Farrell, William R. *Blood and Rage: The Story of the
Japanese Red Army* (Lexington, MA: D. C. Heath,
1990).

Ishida, Takeshi, and Ellis S. Krauss, eds. *Democracy in
Japan* (Pittsburgh: University of Pittsburgh Press,
1989).

Johnson, Chalmers, ed. *Okinawa: Cold War Island*
(Cardiff, CA: Japan Policy Research Institute,
1999).

Krauss, Ellis S., and T. J. Pempel, eds. *Beyond Bilater-
alism: US–Japan Relations in the New Asia–Pacific*
(Stanford: Stanford University Press, 2004).

LeBlank, Robin. *Bicycle Citizens: The Political World
of the Japanese Housewife* (Berkeley: University
of California Press, 1999).

Lincoln, Edward J. *Arthritic Japan: The Slow Pace of
Economic Reform* (Washington, DC: Brookings
Institution, 2001).

McKean, Margaret A. *Environmental Protest and Citizen Politics in Japan* (Berkeley: University of California Press, 1981).

Milly, Deborah. *Poverty, Equality, and Growth: The Politics of Economic Need in Postwar Japan* (Cambridge, MA: Harvard University Press, 1999).

Morley, James W., ed. *Driven by Growth: Political
Change in the Asia-Pacific Region,* 2nd ed.
(Armonk, NY: Sharpe, 1998).

Okimoto, Daniel I., and Thomas P. Rohlen, eds. *Inside
the Japanese System: Readings on Contemporary
Society and Political Economy* (Stanford, CA:
Stanford University Press, 1988).

Packard, George R., III. *Protest in Tokyo: The Security
Treaty Crisis of 1960* (Princeton, NJ: Princeton
University Press, 1966).

Pempel, T. J. *Policy and Politics in Japan: Creative
Conservatism* (Philadelphia: Temple University
Press, 1982).

Prestowitz, Clyde V., Jr. *Trading Places: How We
Allowed Japan to Take the Lead* (New York: Basic
Books, 1988).

Schoppa, Leonard James. *Education Reform in Japan:
A Case of Immobilist Politics* (New York: Routledge, 1991).

Tabb, William K. *The Postwar Japanese System: Cultural Economy and Economic Transition* (New
York: Oxford University Press, 1995).

Van Wolferen, Karel. *The Enigma of Japanese Power:
People and Politics in a Stateless Nation* (New
York: Knopf, 1989).

WEB SITES

www.lib.duke.edu/ias/eac/wwwjapan.html/
Links to a vast number of sites, each concerned with a particular aspect of Japan, including English versions of Japanese newspapers, governmental agencies, political parties, economics, history, and culture.

www.jinjapan.org/
Many links to political parties and governmental agencies, etc.

www.people.virginia.edu/~ljs2k/webtext.html
Links especially helpful to students on Japanese politics, including Japanese newspapers.

jguide.stanford.edu
Stanford University guide to Japan information sources. Includes lists of Web sites relating to many aspects of Japan. Especially strong on science, technology, business, and government.

www.japantimes.co.jp/
Japan Times, an English-language daily newspaper in Tokyo, helps to make Japanese politics understandable for foreign readers.

history.hanover.edu/texts/1889con.html
Constitution of the Empire of Japan, 1889.

www.uni-wuerzburg.de/law
Japanese constitution compared with other national constitutions.

www.nobuteru.or.jp/english/
Web site of Ishihara Nobuteru, a cabinet minister and member of the lower house.

www.feer.com
Far East Economic Review.

www.japaneseimperialfamily.net/imphous.html
Describes the imperial family in detail.

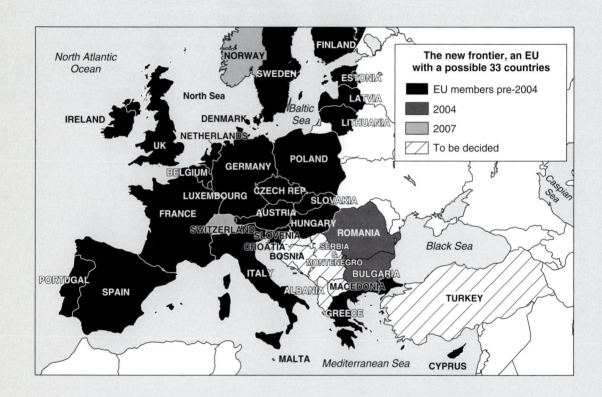

The new frontier, an EU with a possible 33 countries

EU members pre-2004
2004
2007
To be decided

THE
European Union

Michael Curtis

INTRODUCTION

The European Union (EU) is the new name of the organizations engaged in the process of European integration that began in 1952 when the European Coal and Steel Community was established by six member states. Since then it has undergone four enlargements and now consists of 25 member states; another 3 are candidates for accession to the EU. The combined member states give the European Union the third largest population in the world.

GEOGRAPHY
Member states: Austria, Belgium, Cyprus, Czech Republic, Denmark, Estonia, Finland, France, Germany, Greece, Hungary, Ireland, Italy, Latvia, Lithuania, Luxembourg, Malta, Netherlands, Poland, Portugal, Slovakia, Slovenia, Spain, Sweden, United Kingdom
Area: 3.9 million sq km

PEOPLE
Population: 456 million
Age structure: *0–14 years:* 16.3%
   15–64 years: 67.2%
   65 years and over: 16.6%
Sex ratio: 0.95 male/female
Life expectancy at birth: *total population:* 78 years
  male: 75 years
  female: 81 years

ECONOMY

GNP: $11,323 billion

GNP—per capita: $25,700

Share of world GNP: 28.3%

Share of world trade: 36.2% imports; 36.7% exports

Trade as % of GDP: 12.2% imports; 10.9% exports

Major imports: *oil:* 7.9%
electrical machinery: 7.8%
office machines: 7.6%

Major exports: *road vehicles:* 9.2%
electrical machinery: 7.5%
industrial machinery: 6.0%

Labor force by occupation: *agriculture:* 4.3% highest, Greece 20.8%; lowest, Britain 2.1%
industry: 29% highest, Germany 37%; lowest, Netherlands 23.3%
services: 66.8% highest, Netherlands 72.7%; lowest, Greece 55.6%
high-tech manufacturing: 7.8%

HISTORICAL BACKGROUND

The diverse proposals since World War II for some kind of union of Western European countries reflect the complexity and richness of European history and politics. Europe is not a given entity with a single past or tradition. Eastern and Western Europe are both heirs to Roman and Christian traditions, but the Byzantine Empire, Orthodox religion, and Islamic Arabs have made Europe more than a predominantly Romanic and Germanic group of peoples.

After the fourteenth century, the word "Europe," until then rarely used, tended to be identified with "Christendom." But there was never a single political organization for the whole of Christendom or a medieval international order, and Latin and Greek were not really universal languages. In the sixteenth century, the influence of the humanists and the new cartography, which emphasized political authority in territorial areas rather than ecclesiastical rule, began to challenge Europe's identification with Christendom.

European culture cannot be simply defined or described by a single formula. Rationalism, individualism, the devotion to economic activity, industrialism, and the preoccupation with ideals of democracy, communism, fascism, and socialism have all contributed to the pattern of European behavior. Political concepts such as the rule of law and constitutional government, social concerns such as care for the handicapped and the distressed, personal qualities of tolerance and a reliance on persuasion rather than coercion, and shared cultural values exemplify those characteristics still confined largely to European nations or their direct descendants.

The movement for European integration has a long lineage, going back to the Greeks and continuing in various ways throughout history and up to the present. Although the motives have always been complex, the essential reasons have remained largely the same: the preservation of peace, the need for a common defense, the ambition to act as a stronger power bloc, the conservation of a common European culture, the wish to create greater material well-being, and the easing of restrictions on trade.

The development of the European Union has been influenced not only by these same motives, but also by significant external factors. The role of the United States as common friend, supplier of material aid in the immediate postwar years, defensive protector of the West, and now economic competitor, has given an Atlantic dimension to the European story. The fear of Soviet expansion and the threat of Communism to western democracies after 1945 led Western Europe, in association with the United States, to common defense and security arrangements.

The new Europe has been impelled by both positive and negative factors. Europe needed to recover from the devastation and depletion of material resources caused by World War II, and economic growth and social improvements would be advanced by European cooperation. The small, separate European markets compared poorly with the size and economic strength of the United States, as individual countries were politically weaker than before the war, less significant internationally, and obliged to end their colonial empires.

Political factors also spurred the moves toward a more united Europe. Many thought that, after two world wars in one generation, it was imperative to prevent the possibility of further intra-European conflict, especially between Germany and France. (The German problem seemed incapable of solution except within the framework of a larger community.) The economic and military dependence of Western Europe on the United States created a desire for protection against a possible American recession, and inspired awe of American strength. Europe recognized that it was no longer the political center of the world, that apart from Britain and France it did not possess nuclear weapons, and that it would be difficult for it to play an independent political role or act as a third force in world politics. In addition, there was a strong fear of expanding Soviet imperialism, which had reached to Berlin and Prague and had substantial ideological support in the West, where one-third of the Italian electorate and one-quarter of the French had voted Communist.

The interrelation of political, economic, and military factors explains the large spectrum of alternative proposals concerning the new Europe and the various institutions that have been constructed. Politically, the proposals ranged from regular meetings of heads of governments, to regional and functional conferences on specific problems, to a confederal and finally a federal political system. Economic alternatives ran from a tariff and customs community to a full economic union. Possibilities for integration also existed in military alliances among individual sovereign states, collective alliances with common leadership, and integrated defense forces.

A United States of Europe?

European proposals for integration took account of differing attitudes toward the United States. Some favored an Atlantic alliance, partnership, or community with the United States, whereas others called for an independent Western European political entity, economically sound and militarily strong, capable of acting as a third force without ties to the United States or anyone else.

At the core of the different views toward European integration have been attitudes toward the continued existence of sovereign nation-states. The European nation-state has been a constructive force in the creation of political unity, cultural homogeneity, patriotic feeling, and personal identity. But the destructive twentieth-century wars, partly resulting from militant nationalism, led Europeans to question whether the sovereign nation-state could provide the basis for a peaceful Europe. Some still argue that only the nation-state can be responsible for its own protection and welfare, and that nations should be associated only in some framework of intergovernmental cooperation, with unanimity as the procedure for decision making. This view that sovereign power should largely remain with nation-states was reflected in the policies of Charles de Gaulle and Margaret Thatcher. Others hold that limited cooperation of this kind, while useful, is inadequate for solving problems of peace, order, and economic well-being in modern life. They argue that the solutions will come not from the nation-states but from some form of European integration or unity, or a United States of Europe.

The movement toward European integration was created by intellectuals and political elites rather than by mass demand. The postwar attempt to influence the citizen body and make European integration a popular movement, in fact, hardly lasted after 1949 and the institution of the Council of Europe. All other European organizations have been formulated and organized by elite political groups or key political actors whose dedication to Europe is strong and whose idealism has been tempered by political reality. But even if the integration idea does not enflame millions as communism and nationalism have done, it nonetheless attracts increasing support by the success of these European organizations.

The impetus to European integration began simultaneously in the political, economic, and military fields. In September 1946, Winston Churchill, then leader of the opposition in Britain, talked of "recreating the European family, or as much of it as we can" by building "a kind of United States of Europe." Representatives of a number of organizations aiming at such a result met in The Hague in May 1948 and agreed on the establishment of an assembly of representatives of European parliaments, a European charter of human rights, a European court, an economic union, and the inclusion of Germany into a European community.

During this time the United States, for a number of political and economic reasons, took a historic initiative. In June 1947, Secretary of State George Marshall, in a commencement speech at Harvard, proposed American aid for a Europe still suffering from physical destruction, economic dislocation, and lack of productivity, and suggested "a joint recovery program based on self-help and mutual cooperation." Moscow forced Poland and Czechoslovakia to withdraw their requests to be included among the Marshall Plan recipients, and none of the Eastern European countries, then under Soviet control, accepted the Anglo-French invitation in July of 1947 to join an organization of European economic recovery. The Iron Curtain had effectively divided Europe. In April 1948, after 16 Western European governments agreed that cooperation would continue even after Marshall Plan aid had ended, the Organization for European Economic

Cooperation (OEEC) was established, and a series of bilateral agreements was concluded between the United States and OEEC countries.

Western Europe, meanwhile, was concerning itself with its military defense. In March 1947, the Treaty of Dunkirk was signed by France and Great Britain for mutual protection against any renewed aggression by Germany. As a result of changing international relationships, this pact was extended to include the Benelux countries—Belgium, the Netherlands, and Luxembourg—in the Brussels Treaty Organization (BTO) set up in March 1948. The BTO was set up under Article 51 of the United Nations Charter as a regional organization able to undertake individual or collective self-defense if an armed attack occurred. The Organization was a 50-year alliance based primarily on the principle of collective defense; members agreed to take steps in the event of renewed German aggression and pledged automatic mutual military assistance. The BTO was intended not as a supranational organization, but as an intergovernmental one in which the chief policy organ was the Consultative Council of the five foreign ministers.

The Communist capture of power in Prague raised the possibility of the whole of Western Europe being at the mercy of the Russian forces. With the advent of the Berlin blockade in April 1948, it rapidly became apparent that the BTO was not strong enough to resist the Communist threat. Already in March 1946 Winston Churchill, in a speech at Fulton, Missouri, talked of an "iron curtain" in Europe and called for a military alliance between the United States and the Commonwealth. In April 1948 the Canadian Foreign Minister, Louis St. Laurent, suggested an Atlantic defense system. After the Vandenberg Resolution in the U.S. Senate, which ended the historic American policy of no entangling alliances, the Truman Administration went ahead with negotiations throughout the summer of 1948. On April 4, 1949, the North Atlantic Treaty Organization (NATO), with twelve members—Belgium, Britain, Canada, Denmark, France, Iceland, Italy, Luxembourg, the Netherlands, Norway, Portugal, and the United States—was established.

From the beginning of the discussion on the new Europe, differences existed between the "fed-eralist" and the "functionalist" points of view about the nature of a European political institution. The federalists believed that the best way to encourage collaboration among European nations and deal with the problem of sovereignty was to set up a constitutional convention and a European constitution. The functionalists argued that vested interests, multilingual nations, and diverse customs and traditions prevented such a radical step, and that any new organization must be based on the power of the states. At the same time, however, they recognized the need to subordinate the separate national interests to the common welfare.

The issue was decided with the establishment of the Council of Europe in August 1949. In the debate on the nature of the council the federalists, who argued for an elected bicameral legislature and an executive federal council responsible to the legislature, were defeated. The council has remained an intergovernmental organization.

European Coal and Steel Community

The first step to a European community came in May 1950 with a proposal for a common market for coal and steel. The proposal was made by French Foreign Minister Robert Schuman, on the suggestion of Jean Monnet, the French public servant often regarded as the inspiration of the European movement. From an economic standpoint, the plan could lead to joint Franco-German control over the Ruhr and assure the French a coke supply, and could end the struggle between the two countries over the Saar's coal and steel. It would also increase the internal market needed for economic expansion. But above all, the motivations were political. National antagonisms could be transcended, and the reconciliation of the two old enemies could lead to a closer European political association. The plan could thus be the first concrete step toward the goal of European unity. For Germany, the plan meant the removal of Allied controls over the German economy; for German Chancellor Konrad Adenauer, it meant the realization of an idea of friendship he had proposed 30 years earlier.

The plan was greeted enthusiastically in some European countries, but Britain refused to participate. After a year of negotiations, the

REVIEW 6.1

KEY TERMS IN EUROPEAN INTEGRATION

ACP Countries—78 African, Caribbean, and Pacific region countries associated with the European Union through the Lomé Agreements

CFSP—Common Foreign and Security Policy; a pillar of the EU

Coreper—committee of permanent representatives of the states to the EU

Council of Europe—founded 1949, located in Strasbourg, now has 43 democratic European states including Russia

EC—European Community, incorporates the EEC, ECSC, and Euratom

ECB—European Central Bank, in Frankfurt, responsible for monetary policy in the EU countries

ECJ—European Court of Justice

ECOSOC—Economic and Social Committee composed of employers, employees, and various groups to give advice

ECSC—European Coal and Steel Community, founded 1952

EEA—European Economic Area, started 1994, includes the 15 EU states and EFTA except Switzerland and provides for free movement of goods, capital, services, and labor across national borders

EEC—European Economic Community, set up in 1958 to create a common market

EFTA—European Free Trade Association, in Geneva, has agreements with EU to create single market

EMU—Economic and Monetary Union

EP—European Parliament, directly elected

EU—European Union, created 1993 by the Maastricht Treaty

Euratom—founded 1965 for common European research on nuclear energy

Euro—single currency in effect 2002 in several EU member nations

Eurocorps—military unit organized by France and Germany for joint military security, which will be open to other countries

European Research and Coordinating Agency—founded 1985 for greater cooperation in research and technology; participants are the EU and EFTA countries and Turkey

European Social Fund—the EU unit to finance common social policy, including help and training for unemployed youth, adults, and migrant workers

Europol—European police authority, in The Hague, supervises activities against organized crime and narcotics trade

Maastricht—treaty on European Union signed 1992

Nice—treaty concluded in December 2000 to extend qualified majority voting and prepare for the extension of the EU

PHARE—European assistance to countries in Central and Eastern Europe

Schengen—border agreements started in 1985 and now part of the EC

SEA—Single European Act, in force 1987 to complete the single market

Subsidiary Principle—the principle that issues should be dealt with by higher levels of government only if they cannot be handled at a lower level

WEU—Western European Union, founded 1954, a European defense organization linked to NATO

governments of six countries—France, Germany, Italy, Belgium, the Netherlands, and Luxembourg—signed the Treaty of Paris in April 1951, and in July 1952 the European Coal and Steel Community (ECSC) came into existence, the first European body in which any institution had supranational powers. The six nations set up the ECSC High Authority, a unique institution to which member governments transferred part of their sovereign powers in the area of coal and steel. ECSC had a Council of Ministers, an Assembly (to be renamed a Parliament), and a Court of Justice, and it could act directly on the citizens and businesses of the member states. ECSC achieved quick success with the increase of coal and steel trade among the six countries by 129 percent in the first five years.

Monnet regarded the ECSC as the first of several concrete achievements which would be the building blocks of the new Europe in military, political, and economic matters. Even before ECSC came into operation, another proposal was put forward for a European army, and in May 1952 a treaty for a European Defense Community (EDC) was signed by the six ECSC nations. The EDC would be supranational with common institutions, common armed forces, and a common budget. The six countries also began discussing proposals for an even more ambitious European Political Community (EPC) which would include a European Executive Council, a council of ministers, a court, a bilateral assembly, and an economic and social council. But when the French Parliament refused to ratify the EDC treaty in August 1954, both plans failed.

At this point Anthony Eden, Foreign Minister of Britain—which had refused to participate in EDC or to put its forces under supranational control—proposed that the BTO be enlarged to include Germany and Italy in a new organization, the Western European Union. Britain pledged to keep some forces on the European mainland, and Germany would be admitted to NATO and

supply troops to it. But with the defeat of EDC and EPC, the European integration process had been temporarily checked. Defense policy for the moment would remain a national responsibility. The advocates of European unification then decided that the best policy was to pursue economic integration.

The European Economic Community

The unsuccessful EPC proposal had included provisions for a common market with free movement of goods, capital, and persons. Two organizations already existed to facilitate trade. On the international level, the General Agreement on Trade and Tariffs (GATT), concerned with reduction of tariffs and quantitative restrictions on goods and setting up a common set of trade rules, was signed by 23 nations in October 1947. A narrower agreement in 1944 by Belgium, the Netherlands, and Luxembourg created a customs union (Benelux), which actually came into operation in 1948. Benelux abolished tariff barriers among the three countries and imposed a common tariff on imports from nonmember countries.

In May 1955 the Benelux countries, aided by Monnet and others, proposed a wider common market and other steps toward European integration. These proposals for organizations to deal with a common market and customs union, and with atomic energy, were discussed by the six ECSC countries, with Britain again refusing to participate. In March 1957 the Treaties of Rome were signed, and on January 1, 1958, the European Economic Community (EEC) and the

A CLOSER LOOK

6.1

THE COUNCIL OF EUROPE

The Council of Europe was set up in 1949 with headquarters in Strasbourg to foster European cooperation, to protect human rights and fundamental freedoms and the rule of law, and to promote awareness of European cultural identity and diversity. Starting with ten members, in 2002 it has 43 member states. This intergovernmental organization is primarily a forum for discussion by a Council of Ministers, the foreign ministers of the states, and a Parliamentary Assembly. Its main achievements have been the 1950 European Convention on Human Rights, the European Court of Human Rights set up in 1959, and cultural activities.

REVIEW 6.2

THE SINGLE EUROPEAN ACT (SEA)

- Signed in 1986; operative in 1987.
- Amends the Treaties of Rome.
- Qualified majority voting in Council of Ministers on certain subjects.
- Establishes cooperation procedure to give Parliament more input into legislative process.
- Timetables set up to implement a common market by 1992.
- Formal recognition of European Political Cooperation (EPC).

European Atomic Energy Community (Euratom) came into existence. The EEC would merge separate national markets into a single large market that would ensure the free movement of goods, people, capital, and services, and would draw up a wide range of common economic and social policies. Euratom was designed to further the use of nuclear energy for peaceful purposes. In 1965, the three executive bodies of ECSC, EEC, and Euratom were merged into the European Community (EC).

Britain, wanting an organization with no common external tariff or objective for economic or political unification, led the move toward the establishment in 1960 of the European Free Trade Association (EFTA). This body, consisting of Austria, Great Britain, Denmark, Norway, Portugal, Sweden, and Switzerland, was to be concerned with liberalization of trade, not with political objectives. Within two years, however,

Britain changed its mind because of the obvious success of the EEC and applied for membership in July 1961. After being rebuffed twice, Britain became a member of the European Community on January 1, 1973, together with Denmark and Ireland. The government of Norway had also agreed to join, but the parliament refused ratification after the Norwegian electorate voted against accession. Greece joined the EC in 1981, Spain and Portugal in 1986. The Single European Act (SEA), signed in 1986 and operative in 1987, amended the EC treaties and proposed that a single market be established by 1992.

The Maastricht Treaty

In 1991, the heads of the governments of the 12 EC member states agreed to the Treaty on European Union at Maastricht in the Netherlands. This agreement, known as the Maastricht Treaty, was signed in February 1992 but ratification

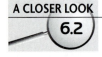

A CLOSER LOOK 6.2

THE EUROPEAN ECONOMIC AREA (EEA)

The agreement establishing the European Economic Area (EEA) was signed in 1992 by the EU and three of the four EFTA countries (Norway, Iceland, and Liechenstein, but not Switzerland) and enforced in 1994. This intergovernmental organization was established to administer the single market—now of 380 million people, accounting for 17 percent of world imports and 20 percent of world exports—and ensure freedom of movement of goods, persons, capital, and services.

MAJOR FEATURES OF MAASTRICHT

- The EC will now be known as the EU.
- Single currency by 1999, but optional for Britain and Denmark, and transition to an Economic and Monetary Union with a central bank.
- Eventual European defense, but in collaboration with NATO.
- Common foreign policy and security making, and implementation by majority vote.
- Some more legisiative power given to the European Parliament with a veto on some items.
- Common citizenship of European Union: citizens can vote and be candidates in all the countries.
- More majority voting in the Council of Ministers.
- European Social Community accepted by all states except Britain.
- Fund set up to help poorer EC countries in transport and environment.
- Cooperation on justice and home affairs, immigration, drugs, and terrorism.

was delayed because of a lack of enthusiasm in some of the member states, especially Denmark, France, and Britain. Concessions were made to Britain, which did not accept the Social Charter of the Treaty that will deal with employment, working conditions, social security, and minimum wages.

The Maastrich Treaty came into force on November 1, 1993, creating the European Union (EU). The EU is not founded on a constitution but on international treaties. It can enact rules that directly bind all citizens of the countries in the EU that have relinquished part of their national sovereignty to the EU institutions. The treaty provides the basis for a European citizenship; citizens of a member state can vote and be a candidate for office in any EU country in which they reside.

THE BASIC STRUCTURE OF THE EUROPEAN UNION

With the signing of the Maastricht Treaty in 1992, the 12 member states of the EC became the European Union. Austria, Finland, and Sweden joined in 1995, bringing the membership to 15 nations. Ten more were admitted in 2004. The EU now stretches from the Mediterranean to the Arctic Circle. The criteria for EU membership are democracy, a market economy, ability to compete in the single market, and ability to apply the laws and treaties of the EU (see Table 6.1). Enlargement of the EU means that it will become more diverse economically, geographically, and culturally (see Figure 6.1).

The EU countries vary widely in population, from Germany with 82 million to Luxembourg with 400,000, and in GDP (see Table 6.1). Some states, Britain and the Netherlands in particular, are more enthusiastic about free trade than others, such as France and Spain.

The EU is not a federal political system, but it is considerably more than an intergovernmental agreement or commercial arrangement. Its objective is integration, not merely cooperation among states, which makes it different from other regional organizations (see Table 6.2). Its institutional structure and procedural rules do not fit easily into any of the categories of political systems discussed in the introduction of this book. It was developed to provide an economic and monetary union, a common foreign and security policy, and action on common problems of justice and internal affairs.

TABLE 6.1

COUNTRIES ADMITTED IN 2004

Members Admitted 2004	Area (thousand km)	Population (millions)	GDP (billion)
	Country	Country	Country
Cyprus	9	728	11
Czech Republic	79	10,211	78
Estonia	45	1,351	7
Hungary	93	10,115	69
Latvia	65	2,319	9
Lithuania	65	3,447	15
Malta	4	400	0.3
Poland	313	38,194	202
Slovakia	49	5,318	26
Slovenia	20	1,997	23
Total	738	77,143	444

Candidates for admission: Albania, Bosnia–Herzegovina, Bulgaria, Croatia, Macedonia, Romania, Serbia and Montenegro, and possibly Turkey.

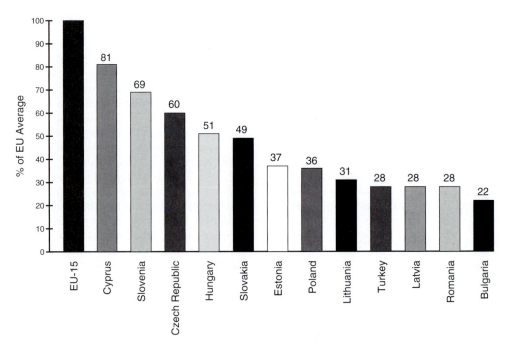

Figure 6.1 INCOME DIFFERENCES BETWEEN THE EU AND NEW MEMBER COUNTRIES
Source: Eurostat.

REVIEW
6.4

KEY EVENTS IN EUROPEAN INTEGRATION

1947   Treaty of Dunkirk linked Britain and France
        Marshall Plan proposed as joint recovery program for Europe
        General Agreement on Trade and Tariffs (GATT) ratified
1948   Benelux began to operate
        Organization for European Economic Cooperation (OEEC) formed
        Brussels Treaty Organization set up
1949   North Atlantic Treaty Organization (NATO) formed
        Council of Europe established
1950   Robert Schuman proposed that coal and steel be put under a common European authority
1952   European Coal and Steel Community (ECSC) formed
1954   European Defense Community (EDC) defeated
        Western European Union (WEU) formed
1958   European Economic Community (EEC) and European Atomic Energy Community (Euratom) established
1960   European Free Trade Association (EFTA) formed
        Organization for Economic Cooperation and Development (OECD) replaced OEEC
1962   Common Agricultural Policy (CAP) adopted
1963   Yaoundé Convention between EEC and 18 African states
1967   Merger of Commissions of ECSC, EEC, and Euratom in European Community (EC)
1968   EEC customs union completed
1973   Great Britain, Denmark, and Ireland joined EC
1974   European Council met for first time
1975   Lomé Convention between EC and 46 African, Caribbean, and Pacific states which gained preferential
        trading arrangements
1979   Direct election of European Parliament
        European Monetary System (EMS) became operative to achieve exchange rate stability
1981   Greece joined EC
1986   Portugal and Spain joined EC
        Single European Act signed, became operative in 1987, amended the EC treaties and proposed a
        European single market by 1992
1989   EC countries endorsed a plan for European Monetary Union
        EC coordinated Western assistance to Poland and Hungary
1990   Two intergovernmental conferences on economic and monetary union and on political union opened
        Schengen Convention formalized 1985 agreement of five countries introducing freedom of movement
        for their nationals
1991   Europe Agreements with Poland, Hungary, and Czechoslovakia to include political dialogue and free
        trade area
1992   European Economic Area (EC and EFTA) proposed
        Maastricht Treaty on European Union signed
1993   Single market enters into effect
1994   EEA comes into force
1995   Austria, Finland, and Sweden join EU
1997   Amsterdam Treaty signed, amending Maastricht

(continues)

REVIEW

6.4

KEY EVENTS IN EUROPEAN INTEGRATION (continued)

1998	Single currency (euro) agreed to by 11 of the 15 EU members; European Central Bank established
	Accession process to EU starts for 10 applicant states and Cyprus
1999	Schengen agreements incorporated into EU
	European Commission resigned after reports of fraud and mismanagement
2000	Treaty of Nice extended majority voting and preparation for EU expansion
	Fifth Lomé Convention signed; Lomé now renamed Cotonou Convention for preferential trading arrangements
2002	The euro became sole currency in the 12 countries participating
2004	Ten more countries join EU
	Constitution for EU signed, but not yet ratified

The EU does not operate on the basis of a clear separation of powers. It is founded on international treaties (of Paris, Rome, and Maastricht) among sovereign nations, not on a constitution. Yet it is more than an international organization because it has power in certain fields to enact laws and regulations that are directly binding and applicable to citizens of the member states, and to adjudicate cases in certain topics in its court. The voting arrangements by ministers, allowing some decisions to be made by simple or weighted majority rather than by unanimity, means qualification of national sovereignty, as does the obligation of members to take specific common actions and decide on common policies. The legislative power of states is limited by their commitment to achieve coordination of economic and monetary policy and harmonization of social legislation. The EU method is to seek communally devised solutions rather than individual or bilateral state action.

In recent years, the EU has said that it operates on the basis of "subsidiarity." This term, drawn from Catholic socioeconomic doctrine, means that the EU is granted jurisdiction and is responsible only for those policies that cannot be handled adequately at the state, national, regional, or local level.

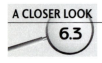

A CLOSER LOOK

6.3

THE EUROPEAN COMMUNITIES AND THE EU

There are three European communities governed by separate treaties: the European Coal and Steel Community (ECSC), by the Treaty of Paris, 1951; and the European Economic Community (EEC) and the European Atomic Energy Community (Euratom), by the Treaties of Rome, 1957. The term "European Communities" was used in legal documents to refer to the three bodies, but the generally accepted term was "European Community" (EC). According to the Maastricht Treaty the term "European Union" (EU) is now used.

The European Economic Community (EEC) provided a framework, to which legislation and policies have been added, calling for a customs union, ending cartels and monopolies, guaranteeing free movement of people, services, and capital, and a common policy for agriculture and transport. The treaties have been amended by the Single European Act, signed in 1986, and amplified by case law resulting from determinations made on the basis of the treaties, and by regulations, directives, decisions, recommendations, and opinions.

TABLE 6.2

OVERLAPPING MEMBERSHIPS OF THE EU AND OTHER EUROPEAN AND REGIONAL ORGANIZATIONS, 2005

Country	EU	Council of Europe[1]	NATO	OECD[2]	EFTA	WEU	EEA
Austria	X	X		X			X
Belgium	X	X	X	X		X	X
Bulgaria			X				
Denmark	X	X	X	X			X
Estonia	X		X				
Finland	X	X		X			X
France	X	X	X	X		X	X
Germany	X	X	X	X		X	X
Greece	X	X	X	X		X	X
Ireland	X	X		X			X
Italy	X	X	X	X		X	X
Luxembourg	X	X	X	X		X	X
Netherlands	X	X	X	X		X	X
Portugal	X	X	X	X		X	X
Spain	X	X	X	X		X	X
Sweden	X	X		X			X
United Kingdom	X	X	X	X		X	X
Canada			X	X			
Cyprus	X	X					
Czech Republic	X			X			
Hungary			X	X			
Iceland		X	X	X	X		X
Latvia	X		X				
Liechtenstein		X			X		X
Lithuania	X		X				
Malta	X	X					
Mexico				X			
Norway		X	X	X	X		X
Poland	X			X			
Slovakia	X		X				
Slovenia	X		X				
Switzerland		X		X	X		
Turkey		X	X	X			
United States			X	X			

[1]Council has 46 members and 5 observers.
[2]OECD has 30 members.

Revenue (%)		Expenditure (%)	
VAT	38.3	Agriculture and fisheries	45.0
Customs duties	14.8	Structural funds	34.5
Member states	43.0	External action	8.4
Agricultural duties and sugar levies	1.8	Administrative costs	5.2
		Reserve, energy	4.1
		Consumer protection	1.2
		Training, employment	1.0
Total revenue 95 billion (euro).			

Figure 6.2 GENERAL EU BUDGET IN 2002

EU FINANCIAL STRUCTURE

The European communities have been financed in different ways. The ECSC is financed by a levy on the value of coal and steel production paid directly to the EU. The EEC and Euratom were originally financed by differing amounts from the member states, but in 1970 the EC decided to raise its own resources for additional revenue. Its income now comes from a number of sources, levies on imports of agricultural produce, customs duties on other imports from non-EC countries, a small part of the Value-Added Tax (VAT) collected in member states, and contributions based on a proportion of the GNP of the states (see Figure 6.2 and Table 6.3).

The European Commission—the administrative core of the EU—prepares the preliminary budget and presents it to the European Council, which amends and adopts this draft budget. This is then forwarded to the European Parliament (EP), which can propose changes in some areas and can amend it in other areas. The Council then examines it again before the EP adopts the final budget. If the EP and the Council cannot agree, the EP can reject the budget as a whole.

THE INSTITUTIONS OF THE EU

As in the original ECSC, there are four major institutions in the EU: the European Commission, the Council of Ministers, the European Parliament, and the Court of Justice. Other bodies, such as the European Council, the Committee of Permanent Representatives (Coreper), the Economic and Social Committee, and the Court of Auditors, also play roles of different kinds.

The European Commission

The central institution of the EU is the European Commission, which is both an executive and a civil service as well as the body that prepares and formulates the budget, policy proposals, and legislation for approval. It is the driving force in the legislative process. It is responsible for administering EU policies and for ensuring that

TABLE 6.3

EU TRADE, 2004

EU 15 exported 20.5% of world exports; imported 18.6% of world imports.

EU and US are each other's main trading partner; together: 37% of world merchandise trade and 45% of world trade in services.

EU exports to US 25.8% of its total exports; imports from US 16.8% of its total imports.

EU investments in US is 52% of its total direct investments.

US investments in EU is 61% of its total direct investment.

EU–China trade has been increasing: two-way trade of $180 billion in 2003, and $210 billion in 2004.

José Barroso.

decisions are carried out. It has authority to bring legal action against persons, companies, or states that have violated EU rules. The Commission is the guardian of EU treaties, seeing that the treaties and rules are correctly applied and properly implemented. In addition, its task is to defend the interests of the EU and represent it in international negotiations (see Table 6.4).

There are now 25 commissioners—two each from Britain, France, Germany, Italy, and Spain, and one each from the other ten countries—who are nominated by their governments and approved by agreement of the 25 states for a renewable five-year term. Five of the 25 are women. The European Parliament approves the Commission as a whole but has not yet been given the power to approve individual nominations. The president is chosen from among the commission-

ers by the governments of the member states subject to approval of the European Parliament.

All commissioners are expected to act in the interest of the EU rather than in defense of national interests, although they have not always followed this rule. The Commission acts in collegiate fashion with decisions made by majority, not unanimity. Each commissioner is assigned a specific policy area or areas of main responsibility, and each has a "cabinet" or small staff of aides. The Commission as a whole has a staff, based mainly in Brussels, of about 13,000 people, a third of whom are employed in translation and interpretation services.

The Commission's chief role as initiator is to propose new policies and regulations to the Council of Ministers; EU decisions can only be taken on the basis of these proposals, which are agreed on by the Commission as a whole at its weekly meetings. The Council of Ministers can accept or reject these proposals, or it can modify them by a unanimous vote. The Commission has often amended its own proposals to meet criticism by the Council, but the Single European Act and the Maastricht Treaty have strengthened the position of the Commission in many areas. The Council will be able to make more decisions by majority vote rather than by unanimity, and the Commission always tries to find a consensus.

The Commission also is charged by the Council to negotiate on behalf of the EU in some areas: competition policy, farming, trade policy, and customs duties. It does not have power over fiscal or monetary policies or over central banking, though it has been trying to extend its general authority. Since 1993 it shares in initiatives in foreign policy.

A CLOSER LOOK

6.4

JOSÉ MANUEL BARROSO—PRESIDENT OF THE EUROPEAN COMMISSION

José Manuel Barroso was born in Lisbon, Portugal, in 1956. He was a lawyer and a political scientist, a member of parliament, a foreign minister, and prime minister of Portugal. In 2004, he became president of the European Commission.

TABLE 6.4

THE EUROPEAN COMMISSION, 2005

25 persons, one from each member country,
appointed by accord of the governments of
the member states for a term of 5 years. The
president is José Manuel Barroso.

	Responsibilities		
Proposing	**Monitoring**	**Administering**	**Representing**
Legislation for development of EU policy: must consult two advisory bodies, the Economic and Social Committee (representatives of employers and trade unions), and the Committee of the Regions (representatives of local and regional authorities)	Guardian of the treaties: observance and proper application of EU law	Administers and implements EU legislation and budget: assisted by the Court of Auditors	Negotiates international agreements and represents the EU in international organizations

The Council of Ministers

The main forum for policy making is the Council of Ministers. The Council consists of representatives of the 15 states and must approve proposals of the Commission before they can be implemented. The Council, unlike the Commission, is not a fixed group of people. Its membership changes according to the subject being discussed, such as finance, agriculture, transportation, or the environment; the ministers responsible for these activities in the member states will make up the Council. But most often the Council consists of ministers responsible for foreign policy who meet once a month (see Table 6.5).

The Council differs from international organizations that require unanimity to make decisions. The logic of European integration was that the Council would increasingly decide by majority vote. This was stalled by the Luxembourg Compromise of 1966 (a concession to the nationalism of President de Gaulle), which said that the other governments would not overrule a member state that opposed proposals it held to be contrary to its national interest. This veto power by a state has rarely been used since 1966, because the Council has generally acted by consensus. Since the Single European Act in 1987, greater

use has been made of either simple or qualified majority voting in the Council, though unanimity is still needed for certain matters. Most of the important EU policies are now decided by a qualified majority—approval by a majority of states and at least 72.3 percent of the total vote.

An essential part of the decision-making process has the Committee of Permanent Representatives (Coreper)—the representatives of the member states who hold ambassadorial rank—which meets weekly to prepare meetings of the Council of Ministers. Coreper has played a significant role in coordinating the attitudes of the states with the proposals of the Commission. Most of those proposals go to Coreper before going to the Council, and decisions on some issues have been reached by the states at the Coreper level.

Other Executive Bodies

Two other significant bodies have been acknowledged by the Single European Act. One is the European Council (not to be confused with the Council of Ministers), which consists of the 25 heads of state or government assisted by their foreign ministers and the president of the Commission, and since 2001 by a political and

TABLE 6.5

THE COUNCIL OF MINISTERS, 2005

	Representatives of the Governments of the Member States 25		
	Permanent Representatives Committee (Coreper)		
	LEGISLATION		

Weighting of Votes		**Weighting of Votes**	
Germany, France, Italy, and the United Kingdom	29	Denmark, Ireland, Lithuania, Slovakia, and Finland	7
Spain and Poland	27	Cyprus, Estonia, Latvia, Luxembourg, and Slovenia	4
Netherlands	13	Malta	3
Belgium, Czech Republic, Greece, Hungary, and Portugal	12	Total	321
Austria and Sweden	10		

The Council passes European laws; together with the parliament, coordinates the broad economic policies of the 25 states, concludes international agreements, approves the budget (with the parliament), develops the Common Foreign and Security Policy.

security committee, a military committee, and staff. The European Council meets at least once every six months, primarily to discuss foreign policy, defense, and important economic subjects. Since 1993 the European Council is an official body of the EU.

The second body is the European Political Cooperation (EPC), which began in 1970, was acknowledged in the Single European Act, and is now part of the EU institutional arrangements. The EPC is a forum in which the 15 foreign ministers meet regularly to discuss coordination of foreign policy and the political and economic aspects of security. Assisted since 1981 by a small secretariat in Brussels, the EPC has coordinated the policy of the 15 countries at several meetings of the United Nations and on a number of international issues, beginning with the 1980 Venice Declaration on the Middle East.

The EPC, like the Council of Ministers and the European Council, is chaired by one of the states every six months. The overlap between the different executive groups, which are all trying to coordinate the opinions of the national foreign ministries, has sometimes made it difficult to differentiate the working of EPC from that of the European Council. The Single European Act recognized the EPC and suggested it would play an even more important role in the future, a development which may help to resolve the question of who makes foreign policy in the EU. It could also decide whether nonmember states such as the United States should deal with officials from the Commission, the European Council, or the individual 15 countries, a problem that is complicated by the fact that a different country assumes the presidency of the European Council and the EPC every six months. However, the EPC is superseded by the common foreign and security policy.

Members of the Commission and others at the European Union meeting in Brussels.

THE EUROPEAN PARLIAMENT

The European Parliament, renamed from the Assembly established under ECSC, is composed of 732 members (directly elected in the 25 states for a five-year term) in approximate proportion to the size of the different populations (see Fig-ure 6.3). The Parliament meets one week in each month in plenary sessions in Strasbourg, France, but its committees meet in Brussels and its sec-retariat of 3,600 meets in Luxembourg. Its mem-bers come from over 60 political parties and almost always come together in political groups—eight in 2005—not in national blocs.

A CLOSER LOOK

6.5

WHO MAKES EU POLICY?

Policy making is shared by the different EU institutions. Ministers of the individual states set long-term policy and request the Commission to deal with certain issues. The Commission has sole initiative in proposing legis-lation, regulations, and budgetary expenditure.

There are three general kinds of procedure:

1. *Consultation:* now less important than in earlier years. The Commission presents a proposal and consults other EU institutions. Decision is taken by the Council.

2. *Cooperation:* Commission proposal is sent to both the Council and EP, and sometimes to other bodies. Council adopts a common position, which is sent to EP, which either accepts, rejects, or amends. Commis-sion and Council decide after getting EP opinion.

3. *Co-decision:* now the most important procedure. On certain issues (internal market, transport, environ-ment, research) Commission proposal must be approved by both the EP and the Council acting by quali-fied majority.

They can use any of the 20 official languages of the EU.

The Parliament has been useful as an arena for the discussion of EU matters and as a representative of over 450 million people. But its powers go beyond giving its opinion on draft directives, proposals, and regulations coming from the Commission. The latter may decide to amend its proposals as a result of that opinion. The Parliament has power to dismiss the Commission on a vote of censure by a two-thirds majority, but this has never been done. It also must approve or reject the budget that is prepared with its help by the Commission for decision by the Council of Ministers; it has amended or rejected the draft budget on three occasions. Since 1975 the Parliament has helped the Commission draw up the budget, and can make amendments in limited areas. The Parliament has no formal powers of control over the Council of Ministers. But it is now consulted before governments nominate the president of the

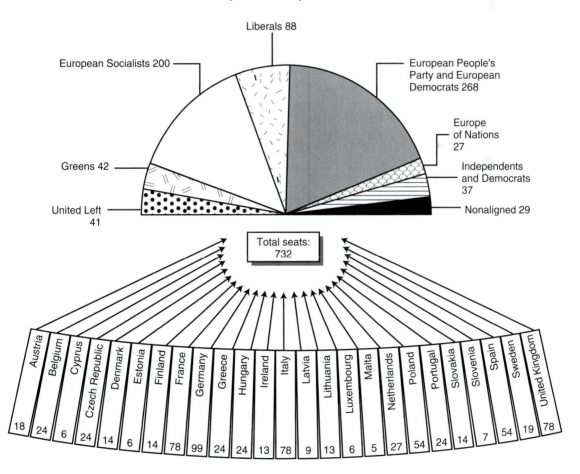

Political Groups in the European Parliament, 2005

Liberals 88
European Socialists 200
European People's Party and European Democrats 268
Europe of Nations 27
Independents and Democrats 37
Greens 42
Nonaligned 29
United Left 41

Total seats: 732

Austria	Belgium	Cyprus	Czech Republic	Denmark	Estonia	Finland	France	Germany	Greece	Hungary	Ireland	Italy	Latvia	Lithuania	Luxembourg	Malta	Netherlands	Poland	Portugal	Slovakia	Slovenia	Spain	Sweden	United Kingdom
18	24	6	24	14	6	14	78	99	24	24	13	78	9	13	6	5	27	54	24	14	7	54	19	78

Figure 6.3 GROUPS AND NUMBER OF MEMBERS IN THE EUROPEAN PARLIAMENT

Commission, and approve the Commission as a body.

The Single European Act has increased the Parliament's legislative role, allowing it to accept, reject, or amend some legislative proposals. The act has also given it power to ratify new international agreements and even veto some agreements concluded by the Council of Ministers and the admission of new members to the EU. In the complicated process of decision making, the Commission can accept or reject any amendment asked for by the Parliament, and the Council of Ministers can overturn the result only by unanimity. The Parliament is now allowed to question or dismiss members of the Commission and to question the Council.

The Amsterdam Treaty, implemented in 1999, gave more power to the EP in the legislative process and in scrutinizing members of the Commission. This increase in authority was immediately illustrated in January 1999 when a censure motion against the Commission was introduced and only narrowly defeated and when in March 1999 the Commission resigned as a bloc after an independent committee found evidence of fraud and wrongdoing, the same allegations made in the EP.

THE COURT OF JUSTICE

The European Court of Justice (ECJ), located in Luxembourg, consists of 25 judges—one from each state and the president of the Court—appointed for six years. By the Single European Act, a junior Court of First Instance was set up in 1989 to assist the Court. The Court of Justice differs from two other bodies: the International Court of Justice in The Hague (the World Court), and the European Court of Human Rights, which was established by the Council of Europe in Strasbourg. Member states of the EU must accept the final decisions and judgments of the ECJ but have no legal obligation to accept those of the other two courts, which are not part of the EU.

The essential functions of the ECJ are to ensure that EU law is properly applied and to resolve disputes between governments, EU institutions, and citizens over that law (see Table 6.6). It works by unanimity and thus, unlike the U.S. Supreme Court, no public dissent is registered. All member states are obliged to accept its rulings and its powers which are stated in the Treaties of Paris and Rome. The states have accepted that EU law is now also national law in their countries, that EU law prevails over national law if there is a conflict between them, and that the ECJ's decisions overrule those of national courts. The ECJ has by now laid down a body of law that applies to the EU institutions, states, and citizens. Its decisions are not subject to appeal. It has an increasingly large case load.

OTHER AGENCIES

The Economic and Social Committee consists of 344 persons representing employers, workers, and various interests such as consumer groups and professional associations. It meets once a month in Brussels to give its opinion on policies and legislative proposals in certain fields. It has the right to be consulted, but has no right of amendment.

The Court of Auditors, based in Luxembourg, consists of 15 members appointed by the Council of Ministers. It supervises expenditure, checking all EU revenue and spending, and has investigated cases of mismanagement and fraud.

The Committee of the Regions, established in 1993, comprises 222 members, representing local and regional authorities, and is consulted before decisions affecting regional interests are adopted.

The European Investment Bank provides loans in many economic sectors to help less-developed regions of the EU, to modernize enterprises, and to create employment.

Two new agencies, the Institute for Security Studies and a satellite center, became operational in 2002 within the framework of the Common Foreign and Security Policy.

TABLE 6.6

THE COURT OF JUSTICE, 2005

Governments of the member states appoint the 25 judges and 8 advocates general by common accord for a term of six years

Court of Justice created 1952

Full court of 25 judges

Also sits as a chamber of 11

Judgments by majority

Types of Proceedings

Actions for failure to fulfill obligations under the treaties (Commission vs. member state)	Actions on grounds of failure to act (against Council or Commission)	References from national courts for preliminary rulings to clarify the meaning and scope of Community law
Actions by one member state against another		Claims for damages against the Community
Actions to annul a EU law if it is considered illegal	**Court of First Instance created 1989**	
	15 judges	
	Staff cases	
	Actions in the field of competition law	
	Actions under antidumping law	
	Actions under the ECSC Treaty	

THE SINGLE OR COMMON MARKET

The original objectives of the EC stated in the Treaties of Rome were the development of economic activities, a balanced expansion, greater stability, a higher standard of living, and closer relations between the member states. The members were therefore supposed to establish a common market and to try for similar economic policies.

The first step was a customs union among the original six countries, which meant removing tariffs on internal trade and imposing a common external tariff against nonmember countries. The tariff is paid once on goods entering the EU; the goods then circulate within the EU without fur-

ther tariff. By 1968 the union had been completed but other barriers to trade continued, preventing the establishment of a real common market. In the late 1980s the EC proposed new measures to eliminate barriers to free trade and movement. These included ending customs checks and border controls within the EC, harmonization of technical standards, mutual acceptance of professional qualifications and diplomas, a Community market for financial services such as banking and insurance, and approximate taxation rates. The Single European Act, with its important amendments to the EC treaties, has facilitated the implementation of most of these measures to complete the internal market.

The essential objective of the SEA was the creation of a common market in which goods, services, people, and capital can move without obstacles such as frontier delays, fiscal barriers (including Value-Added Tax [VAT] rates and excise taxes), or technical obstructions such as national health and safety regulations. Tariffs and direct trade barriers have been ended since the mid-1960s.

In 2005 the EU is responsible for about 80 percent of all rules on the production, distribution, and exchange of goods, services, capital, and labor in the European market. It has removed barriers to the free movement of goods, put restrictions on state aids to enterprises, and fostered competition. Most of the provisions of the single market have, by the EEA, been extended to Norway, Iceland, and Liechtenstein. The EU has also acted to harmonize existing national standards and set common minimum standards in areas such as health, safety, environment, and consumer protection.

The proposed constitution for Europe, agreed in Brussels, June 18, 2004 has as its main features:

- Power of EU extended to new areas, such as justice policy, asylum, immigration
- Principle of voting by qualified majority (QM) generally accepted, but a veto by states possible in foreign policy, defense, taxation
- President elected by QM of states for term of 2½ years, renewable once; Parliament must approve
- Foreign minister appointed by QM to conduct EU's Common Foreign and Security Policy (CFSP)
- EU can define and implement CFSP
- European Commission transitional membership of 25, to be reduced to 18
- European Parliament has powers of "codecision" with Council of Ministers where policies require QM
- Charter of fundamental rights and freedoms to be incorporated into EU law
- The Constitution and EU laws will have primacy over the law of the member states: The EU has a "legal personality"

Figure 6.4 indicates the EU's sizable share of world trade.

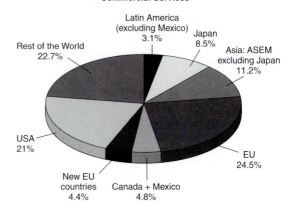

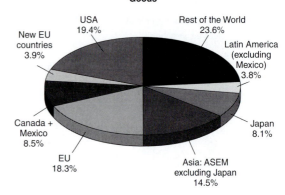

Figure 6.4 SHARE OF WORLD TRADE, 1999
Source: Department of Commerce; World Bank.

EU POLICY ISSUES

A Common Currency

Since 1979 the European Monetary System (EMS), now the EMU, attempted to coordinate economic policies and to stabilize the currencies of the EC countries. The exchange rate mechanism of the EMS obliged member states to limit fluctuations in the value of their currency to small amounts. Central banks of the states ensured that these limits were kept by raising or lowering interest rates, buying and selling currencies, and adjusting fiscal policies. The EMS helped to keep inflation and interest rates low and rates of investment high.

Not until the Maastricht Treaty was a basic plan for a single currency agreed on. A ten year process then began with a European exchange rate control mechanism. In 1999 a virtual currency, the euro, was used in electronic transfers by banks and international businesses, and brokers. The currencies of 12 participating EU countries were pegged to the euro. On January 1, 2002, the euro became the official single currency of those 12 countries, with banknotes and coins replacing the existing individual currencies. Changes of exchange rates are abolished, and money can now move freely across the frontiers between member states. The European Central Bank (ECB) in Frankfurt aims to maintain price stability and to support the EU's general economic policies, and sets interest rates. The European Monetary Union (EMU) urges that states pursue policies that impose fiscal discipline in order to get balanced budgets.

Security and Defense

Under the Maastricht Treaty, a common European foreign and security policy is to be decided by the member states by unanimity and intergovernmental cooperation. In certain areas, such as control of arms exports, decisions can be made by qualified majority. The treaty recognized the European Political Cooperation and the Western European Union (WEU).

The EPC is now superseded by the ESDP (CFSP in English), a common foreign and security policy. The ESDP is operational and has a planned strong rapid reaction force of 60,000. The ESDP is supposed to complement rather than duplicate NATO. It may also foster multinational coproduction of military equipment. The EU also plans to have a 5,000 strong police force as well as crisis management capabilities. The military strength and defense expenditures of the EU member nations are shown in Table 6.7.

TABLE 6.7

EU COUNTRIES AND DEFENSE, 2004

Country	Number in Military (thousands)	Defense Expenditure as % of GDP
Austria	40.5	0.85
Belgium	41.8	1.3
Denmark	24.3	1.6
Finland	31.7	2.0
France	317.3	2.6
Germany	332.8	1.5
Greece	165.6	4.3
Ireland	11.5	0.9
Italy	265.5	1.9
Luxembourg	0.8	0.9
Netherlands	56.4	1.6
Portugal	49.7	2.3
Spain	186.5	1.2
Sweden	53.1	2.1
United Kingdom	212.4	2.4
New Members, 2004		
Cyprus	10	
Czech Republic	49.4	2.82
Estonia	5.5	0.57
Hungary	33.4	1.43
Latvia	5.5	1.08
Lithuania	13.5	2.6
Malta	2.1	0.7
Poland	163.0	2.43
Slovakia	26.2	2.59
Slovenia	9.0	2.04

Source: EXXUIV 2004.

Justice and Home Affairs

Policies in the areas of justice and home affairs, according to the terms of the Maastricht Treaty, are to be decided on an intergovernmental level. They include immigration, asylum, drug trafficking, and other international crimes. The

Maastricht Treaty provides for a central police office (Europol).

The Maastricht Treaty was amplified by the Amsterdam Treaty, signed in 1997, in effect in 1999. This pledged the EU members to combat discrimination on the basis of gender, race, religion, age, or sexual orientation. It also called for coordination in policies on unemployment and social matters. The treaty further argued for more shared decision making between the Council of Ministers and the European Parliament; and extended both the scope of qualified majority voting in the Council and the powers of the EP.

Common Agricultural Policy

In 1950 Robert Schuman said that "Europe will not be made all at once or according to a single general plan. It will be built through concrete achievements, which first create a de facto solidarity." Among the most significant achievements has been the Common Agricultural Policy (CAP).

The objectives of the CAP are to maintain food supplies at stable and reasonable prices, to improve agricultural productivity, and to ensure a fair standard of living for farmers. The CAP initially accounted for about 90 percent and

---

REVIEW
6.5

A TALE OF EIGHT CITIES

City	Signed (and in force)	Number of Countries	Major Decisions
Paris	1951 (1952)	6	Set up ECSC; pooling of some powers; Supranational High Authority
Rome	1957 (1958)	6	Set up EEC and Euratom (nuclear energy)
Luxembourg	1986 (1987)	12	Single European Act: abolished internal barriers to trade; cooperation procedure for some legislation; extended qualified majority voting
Maastricht	1992 (1993)	12	Set up the EU; agreement on monetary union and euro; cooperation in justice and home affairs, and future common foreign and security policies (CFSP); more qualified voting; powers of EP enhanced
Amsterdam	1997 (1999)	15	Common strategies in some areas and countries; extended scope of co-decision
Helsinki	1999	15	Summit agreement on rapid reaction force to be established by 2003 with ability to deploy 60,000 troops
Nice	2000 (2001)	15	Agreement to prepare EU institutions for future expansion; more scope for qualified majority voting and enhanced cooperation
Rome and Brussels	2004	25	Constitution for EU agreed

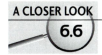

A CLOSER LOOK 6.6

NO MORE FRANC, NO MORE LIRA—NOW THE EURO

The EU countries using the euro are Austria, Belgium, Finland, France, Germany, Greece, Ireland, Italy, Luxembourg, the Netherlands, Portugal, and Spain.

Euro banknotes are available in denominations of €5, €10, €20, €50, €100, €200, and €500. The official symbol of the euro is €; the official abbreviation is EUR.

Each euro denomination has its own color and size. The higher the value, the larger the banknote.

Pictures of windows and gateways on the front of the banknotes symbolise openness. Pictures of bridges on the back symbolize cooperation.

EURO banknotes. The new money in the EU.

accounted for about 40–45 percent of total EU expenditure and covers about 90 percent of farm output in the 25 countries. A number of goals underlie the CAP: price guarantees for farmers, common prices for agricultural commodities, variable import levies to raise import prices to the EU level, and subsidies to EU farmers to enable them to export and sell at world prices, which are generally below the internal EU market.

The CAP has been successful and important for the farming community, now a much smaller part of the employed than 30 years ago, but it has also been severely criticized on several grounds. It is expensive, and some argue that it takes too large a part of the EU budget. Prices of agricultural commodities are higher than world market prices. The high prices stimulated production, resulting in surpluses that were very costly to store. These "wine-lakes" and "butter mountains" distorted competition and depressed world prices. Many outside countries, especially the United States, have accused the CAP of being protectionist by preventing or reducing imports. They have called in particular for the elimination of EU subsidies that encourage excessive and inefficient production.

In the mid-1980s, the EC reduced financial support for agricultural products in surplus, and

price cuts were made in 1988. Further reforms of the high-cost CAP came in 1992 with sharp price cuts to restrict overproduction and the break of the links between price support and production. In 2005, less emphasis is being put on subsidizing production of basic foodstuffs, and more on direct payments to farmers as the best way to guarantee farm incomes, food safety and quality, sufficient production, and on enviromental rules. The CAP in 2005 accounted for 45 percent of the EU budget.

FOREIGN AFFAIRS

Trade

The EU is the world's largest trading unit accounting for about 20 percent of world trade. (see Figure 6.5). It therefore played a significant role in GATT and now has an important role in the World Trade Organization. The European Commission, on behalf of the EU, negotiates all external trade arrangements, which are then formally accepted by the Council of Ministers by majority vote.

The United States is the European Union's major trading partner, and the two cooperate on numerous issues, not only on bilateral matters but also an international forums including the UN, WTO, NATO, and the G-8, the major developed countries. The EU and the United States account for over a third of the global economy. Each is the other's largest single trading partner and source of, and destination for, foreign investment.

Diplomatic Relations and Development Programs

The EU has diplomatic relations with over 140 countries, varied trade agreements with countries throughout the world, and association agreements with others. Two of these external links are particularly interesting. One is the relationship between the EU and the European Free Trade Association (EFTA), which now includes four countries with a combined population of 12 million. Both the EU and EFTA have abolished customs duties and restrictions on trade in manufactured goods in a free trade area, and in 1991 the two bodies agreed on the creation of a European Economic Area (EEA). This involves a single market with free movement of goods, services, people, and capital, but without EFTA having any vote on EU laws.

A second important link is with the countries of the third world. Since the Yaoundé Convention of 1963, the EU has extended special preferential trading arrangements to the ex-colonies of EU countries. The EU is now linked to 78 African, Caribbean, and Pacific (ACP) countries through a series of Lomé Conventions (now renamed Cotonou) the latest of which was renewed in 2000. The ACP countries are freed from customs duties

---

REVIEW

6.6

MAJOR FEATURES OF THE EUROPEAN UNION

EUROPEAN COMMUNITY AND SINGLE MARKET

- Democratization of institutions; common European citizenship; qualified majority voting in some issues.
- Enhanced powers of European Parliament.
- Economic and monetary union: single currency; European Central Bank; single monetary policy; economic policy coordination.
- Principle of subsidarity, decisions taken at lowest possible level.

FOREIGN AFFAIRS AND DEFENSE

- Common foreign policy: systematic cooperation; joint positions and actions.
- Common defense policy based on the Western European Union (WEU).

JUSTICE AND HOME AFFAIRS

- Enhanced cooperation: customs asylum policy; rules governing the crossing of external borders of the member states; immigration policy.
- Combating drug addiction; combating international fraud.
- Judicial cooperation on crime and terrorism; European Police Office (Europol).

on almost all their exports to the EU and also receive financial aid from the EU.

Most of the EU's external aid at first was concentrated on former colonies; now much more goes to Central and Eastern Europe. The EU also has multilateral relations with international organizations and with other regional groupings. The EU has been the largest donor of nonmilitary aid to the Palestinians.

Not only is the EU the largest single donor of official development assistance in the world; it now also focuses on the reduction of poverty in third world or developing countries, and on institution building in those countries. The EU is the leading importer of goods from the third world and provides full market access in EU countries for products originating from those countries.

The EU has concluded cooperation arrangements with many other countries, including 12 Eastern and Southern Mediterranean nations, which have been given duty-free access for their industrial exports and agricultural trade and have received financial grants and loans. The EU has also entered into a Euro-Arab dialogue, discussing agricultural, trade, and technical matters with Arab countries.

Since the decline of Communism and the end of Soviet control in Eastern Europe, the EU has become involved in the affairs of Eastern Europe in a number of ways. It coordinated the 1989 PHARE program in which 24 countries sent aid to Poland, Hungary, and other Central and Eastern European countries. It entered into bilateral trade agreements with each of the Eastern European countries and assisted in addressing their environmental problems. This has meant allowing these states a degree of free trade with the EU, granting them aid and loans, and providing for a number of joint projects, including funds for reconstruction programs and humanitarian aid.

THE EU'S FUTURE

The European Union has as official objectives the creation of "an organized and vital Europe," laying "the foundations of an ever closer union among the peoples of Europe," and combining together to "contribute to the prosperity of the peoples." The EU has already become an important part of European politics and well-being. Many decisions have been made that affect the states and their citizens in important ways (see Table 6.8).

At this point the nature of the EU has not been clearly defined. It is still a confederation of independent states that have pooled some powers and some aspects of sovereignty in economic matters, but that retain their authority to deal internally with law and order, foreign policy, and defense. The EU, however, can act in some areas, including trade, agriculture, competition, transport, research and technology, environment, and education.

Strong differences exist between those calling for more supranational government and more EU impact on citizens and those who think that active cooperation between sovereign states is the best way to build a successful European community, and would be content with little more than an intergovernmental body. Some favor a single market without a political union; others prefer a political union with a wide range of centralized policies. Some want a community focused mainly on deregulation, competition, and capital mobility; others call for a more positive role in world affairs in security as well as economic matters.

Differences on two matters are of great concern to the United States. The first is the dispute about the EU's subsidies on agricultural exports and the degree of European protectionism. The United States claims that these subsidies are unfair and that they distort markets in the rest of the world. The EU in the past, in a dispute now largely resolved, restricted imports of bananas from American companies, and also genetically modified foods produced by American farmers. Yet the EU in 2004 took some 18 percent of U.S. exports and accounts for half of all direct foreign investment.

The second issue is that of defense. Some in the European Union believe that there should be a strong European pillar in NATO on which

TABLE 6.8

COMMON FOREIGN AND SECURITY POLICY (CFSP)

1954 European Defense Community failed

1970 European Political Cooperation: European countries try to coordinate their positions on foreign policy issues by making joint statements, but no common action

1992 Maastricht Treaty: principle of CFSP formalized

1999 Position of High Representative for Foreign and Security Policy created to assess crisis situations; assisted by a political and security committee and a military committee

2003 European Security and Defense Policy (ESDP) to create a common defense structure: agreement on priority areas for action, humanitarian missions, and crisis management

Rapid reaction force created

Police officers to participate in civilian aspects of crisis management

2004 New proposed constitution suggests a foreign minister

Source: Eurostat.

Europe could rely for its defense. Others argue that Europe should be responsible for its own security and defense, and suggest that a European force would be the best organization for this purpose. France and Germany proposed in 1991 a joint military brigade that would be the basis for a European corps.

There are also important disagreements within the EU over questions such as the relative merits of free trade and protectionism; a complete market economy or one with the state intervening to a considerable degree; the cost of the CAP, the cost of regional aid, the extent of welfare systems and of social rights; the enlargement of the EU to embrace new members, in particular Central and Eastern European states, the weight of voting allotted in the Council to the new states, the number of working languages, and the problem of democratic control over the work of EU institutions. Resolution of these questions will not come easily to a group of states that have had such a long and complex history, and that now must reformu-

late their attitudes toward the former Soviet Union and Central and Eastern Europe and toward policies on many issues, such as arms control, nuclear proliferation, the Middle East, the United Nations, and the United States. The political dimension of the EU is still to be decided.

That dimension will be affected in a variety of ways. France in 2005 is no longer dominant in the EU with 25 present and more future members and with Germany as a united country. Dramatic international affairs have led to calls for collective European military action, combining joint operations, rationalizing defense and other expenditures, and a European peacekeeping force. New members of the EU have to be incorporated while decision making may be changed, and obtaining a consensus may be more difficult with those countries at different economic levels and different degrees of familiarity with democratic practice. The EU faces an open, interesting, and challenging future for its hybrid structure, which includes some federal features and many intergovernmental ones, and many forms of cooperation in different policy areas, and with sharing power between the institutions of the EU and between those institutions and the member states.

What lies ahead? The EU has been a unique success economically, as shown by its growth in GDP and trade, and by its low tariffs, its low nontariff barriers to trade, and its open services sector. In return, the EU wants all its trading partners to eliminate or reduce their import duties and barriers such as technical regulations, dumping of goods, subsidies by governments and other public authorities which reduce production costs or costs of exports to the EU, and barriers to a global market in services.

The question now is whether the EU can be an equally potent political and military presence. It has ambitions to play an important role in world affairs. Javier Solana, currently high representative for the CFSP and secretary general of the Council, as virtual foreign minister is anxious to coordinate the foreign policies of the EU members. Already, the EU has intervened in some global issues; among them are environmental policies, ratification of the Kyoto Protocol, conservation of biodiversity, and emergency assistance and relief to victims of natural disasters or armed conflict outside the EU. It has acted in various international crises, imposing sanctions on the Ivory Coast for rigging the election in 2001, and sanctions on Robert Mugabe in Zimbabwe in 2002 for his expulsion of the EU election observer mission. The EU helped enforce peace in Sierra Leone and Macedonia. It aims at promoting and protecting human rights, developing and consolidating democracy and the rule of law, and combatting discrimination and racism.

To advance progress, a constitutional convention was launched in February 2002 to propose changes to make decision making in the EU more efficient. Chaired by former French president Valéry Giscard d'Estaing, this convention presented its draft constitution which was agreed on by the EU in Brussels in 2004.

The constitution is in the process of being reviewed and ratified by the 25 members of the EU.

Is the EU at a crossroads or en route to an "ever closer union?" It will not be easy to resolve the competing views of federalists, wanting stronger powers for the European Commission and Parliament, and those members who are reluctant to increase those powers.

Thinking Critically

1. Do you think that a Euro-identity is emerging? How might it be affected by immigration into the EU countries?
2. To what extent has the EU diluted the traditional strength of national sovereignty? What does the pooling of sovereignty in the EU mean?
3. Can the EU become a body that can use military force and play a role in foreign policy? Is it time to reinvent NATO?
4. What are the main reasons for EU criticism of the United States?
5. How does the role of the European Commission compare with that of the Council of Ministers in decision making in the EU?
6. Is the EU likely to develop into a federal system? How will the entrance of the present candidate nations into the EU affect this?

KEY TERMS

Benelux *(329)*
Committee of Permanent Representatives (Coreper) *(340)*
Common Agricultural Policy (CAP) *(348)*
Common Foreign and Security Policy (CFSP) *(347)*
Common Market *(345)*
Council of Europe *(329)*
Economic and Monetary Union (EMU) *(346)*
European Atomic Energy Community (Euratom) *(332)*
European Central Bank (ECB) *(347)*

European Coal and Steel Community
(ECSC) *(330)*
European Community (EC) *(332)*
European Economic Area (EEA) *(332)*
European Free Trade Association (EFTA) *(332)*
European Parliament *(344)*
General Agreement on Trade and Tariffs
(GATT) *(331)*
Maastricht Treaty *(333)*
North Atlantic Treaty Organization
(NATO) *(329)*
Organization for Economic Cooperation and
Development (OECD) *(335)*
Schengen Agreements *(335)*
Single European Act *(332)*
Treaty of Nice *(348)*
Treaty of Paris *(330)*

*F*URTHER READINGS

Cowles, Maria Green, and Desmond Dinan, eds. *Developments in the European Union 2* (New York: Palgrave Macmillan, 2004).

Cram, Laura, et al., eds. *Developments in the European Union* (New York: St. Martin's, 1999).

Dehousse, Renaud. *The European Court of Justice* (New York: St. Martin's, 1998).

Dinan, Desmond. *Europe Recast: A History of European Union.* (New York: Palgrave Macmillan, 2004).

Duchêne, François. *Jean Monnet: The First Statesman of Interdependence* (New York: Norton, 1994).

Edwards, Geoffrey, and David Spence, eds. *The European Commission,* 2nd ed. (London: Cartermill, 1997).

George, Stephen, and Ian Bache. *Politics in the European Union* (New York: Oxford University Press, 2001).

Guttman, Robert J., ed. *Europe in the New Century* (Boulder, CO: Rienner, 2001).

Herrmann, Richard K., et al., eds. *Transnational Identities: Becoming European in the EU* (Lanham; Rowman and Littlefield, 2004).

Kaiser, Wolfram, and Jurgen Elvert, eds. *European Union Enlargement: A Comparative History* (London: Routledge, 2004).

Lasok, Dominik. *Law and Institutions of the European Communities,* 7th ed. (London: Lexis, 1998).

Laurent, Pierre-Henri, and Marc Maresceau, eds. *The State of the European Union* (Boulder, CO: Rienner, 1998).

McCormick, John. *Understanding the European Union* (New York: St. Martin's, 1999).

Nugent, Neill. *The European Commission* (New York: Palgrave, 2001).

Nugent, Neill. *The Government and Politics of the European Union,* 4th ed. (Basingstoke: Macmillan, 1999).

Peterson, John, and Elizabeth Bomberg. *Decision-Making in the European Union* (New York: St. Martin's, 1999).

Pinder, John. *The Building of the European Union,* 3rd ed. (New York: Oxford University Press, 1998).

Pond, Elizabeth. *The Rebirth of Europe* (Washington, DC: Brookings, 1999).

Rhodes, Carolyn, ed. *The European Union in the World Community* (Boulder, CO: Rienner, 1998).

Richardson, Jeremy, ed. *European Union: Power and Policy-Making* (New York: Routledge, 1996).

Smith, Karen E. *European Union: Foreign Policy in a Changing World,* 2nd ed. (Cambridge: Polity, 2003).

Van Gerven, Walter. *The European Union: A Polity of States and Peoples* (Stanford: Stanford University Press, 2005).

Wallace, Helen, ed. *Interlocking Dimensions of European Integration* (New York: Palgrave, 2001).

Wallace, Helen, and William Wallace, eds. *Policy-Making in the European Union,* 4th ed. (London: Oxford University Press, 2000).

Wind, Marlene. *Sovereignty and European Integration: Towards a Post-Hobbesian Order* (New York: Palgrave, 2001).

WEB SITES

www.europa.eu.int
Information on the European Commission.

www.ue.eu.int
Information on the European Council of Ministers.

www.curia.eu.int
Information on the European Court of Justice.

www.europarl.eu.int/groups/
Information on political groups in the European Parliament.

www.europarl.eu.int
Information on the European Parliament.

www.coe.int
Information on the Council of Europe.

www.nato.int
Information on NATO.

www.weu.int
Information on the Western European Union.

www.eurunion.org/infores/euindex.htm
Index of European Web sites.

States of the
Former Soviet Union

1. Russia
2. Belarus
3. Moldova
4. Ukraine
5. Armenia
6. Azerbaijan
7. Turkmenistan
8. Uzbekistan
9. Kazakstan
10. Tajikhstan
11. Kyrgyzstan
12. Estonia
13. Latvia
14. Lithuania
15. Georgia

ALASKA
(U.S.)

ARCTIC
OCEAN

0   500   1000 Miles
0   500   1000 Kilometers

NORWAY
SWEDEN
FINLAND
POLAND
ROM.
TURKEY
IRAQ
IRAN
AFGHANISTAN
PAKISTAN
CHINA
MONGOLIA
JAPAN

Riga
St. Petersburg
Novgorod
Minsk
Moscow
Kiev
Odessa
Kharkova
Kazan
Nizhny Novgorod
Syktyvkar
Yekaterinburg
Volgograd
Astrakhan
Baku
Ashgabat
Tashkent
Alma-Ata

Murmansk
Arkhangelsk

RUSSIA
(Russian Federation)

Magadan
Petropavlovsk-
Kamchatskiy
Sea of Okhotsk

Yakutsk
Kirensk
Lake
Baikal
Irkutsk
Omsk
Novosibirsk

Khabarovsk
Vladivostok
Sea of
Japan

Black
Sea
Caspian Sea
Aral
Sea
Lake
Balkhash

Volga
Ob
Yenisei
Lena

14 13 12
2
3 4
15
5 6
7 8
9
11
10
1

CHAPTER

7

THE GOVERNMENT OF THE
Russian Federation

Roger E. Kanet and John S. Reshetar Jr.

INTRODUCTION

Background: The defeat of the Russian Empire in World War I led to the seizure of power by the Communists and the formation of the USSR. The brutal rule of Josef Stalin (1924–1953) strengthened Russian dominance of the Soviet Union at a cost of tens of millions of lives. The Soviet economy and society stagnated in the following decades until General Secretary Mikhail Gorbachev (1985–1991) introduced *glasnost* (openness) and *perestroika* (restructuring) in an attempt to modernize Communism, but his initiatives released forces that by December 1991 splintered the USSR into 15 independent republics. Since then, Russia has struggled in its efforts to build a democratic political system and market economy to replace the strict social, political, and economic controls of the Communist period.

GEOGRAPHY

Location: Northern Eurasia (or Europe and Asia), bordering the Arctic Ocean, between Scandinavia and the North Pacific Ocean

Area: 17,075,200 sq km

Area—comparative: slightly less than 1.8 times the size of the United States

Land boundaries: 20,017 km

> *border countries:* Azerbaijan 284 km, Belarus 959 km, China (southeast) 3,605 km, China (south) 40 km, Estonia 294 km, Finland 1,313 km, Georgia 723 km, Kazakhstan 6,846 km, North Korea 19 km, Latvia 217 km, Lithuania (Kaliningrad Oblast) 227 km, Mongolia 3,485 km, Norway 167 km, Poland (Kaliningrad Oblast) 206 km, Ukraine 1,576 km

Climate: ranges from dry steppe in the south through humid continental in much of European Russia; subarctic in Siberia to tundra climate in the polar north; winters vary from cool along Black Sea coast to frigid in Siberia; summers vary from warm in the steppes to cool along Arctic coast

357

Terrain: broad plain with low hills west of Urals; vast coniferous forest and tundra in Siberia; uplands and mountains along southern border regions

Elevation extremes: *lowest point:* Caspian Sea −28 m

   highest point: Gora El'brus 5,633 m

Geography note: largest country in the world in terms of area but unfavorably located in relation to major sea lanes of the world; despite its size, much of the country lacks proper soils and climates (either too cold or too dry) for agriculture

PEOPLE

Population: 147,022,000

Age structure: *0–14 years:* 15% (male 11,064,000; female 10,518,000)

   15–64 years: 71.3% (male 49,534,000; female 52,958,000)

   65 years and over: 13.7% (male 6,177,000; female 13,529,000)

Population growth rate: −0.45%

Birthrate: 9.63 births/1,000 population

Sex ratio: 0.87 male/female

Life expectancy at birth: 66.39 years

   male: 59.91 years

   female: 73.27 years

Nationality: *noun:* Russian, Russians

   adjective: Russian

Ethnic groups: Russian 81.5%, Tatar 3.8%, Ukrainian 3%, Chuvash 1.2%, Bashkir 0.9%, Byelorussian 0.8%, Moldavian 0.7%, other 8.1%

Religions: Russian Orthodox, Muslim, other

Languages: Russian, other

Literacy: *definition:* age 15 and over can read and write

   total population: 98%

GOVERNMENT

Country name: *conventional long form:* Russian Federation

   conventional short form: Russia

Government type: federation

Capital: Moscow

Administrative divisions: 49 oblasts, 21 republics, 10 autonomous okrugs, 6 krays, 2 federal cities, and 1 autonomous oblast

Independence: 24 August 1991 (from Soviet Union)

Constitution: adopted 12 December 1993

Legal system: based on civil law system; judicial review of legislative acts

Suffrage: 18 years of age; universal

Executive branch: *chief of state:* President Vladimir Vladimirovich Putin (acting president since 31 December 1999, president since 7 May 2000, re-elected March 2004)

   head of government: Premier Mikhail Fradkov (since March 2004)

   cabinet: Ministries of the Government composed of the premier and his deputies, ministers, and other agency heads; all are appointed by the president

   note: there is also a Presidential Administration (PA) that provides staff and policy support to the president, drafts presidential decrees, and coordinates policy among government agencies; a Security Council also reports directly to the president

   elections: president elected by popular vote for a four-year term; no vice president; if the president dies in office, cannot exercise his powers because of ill health, is impeached, or resigns, the premier succeeds him; the premier serves as acting president until a new presidential election is held, which must be within three months; premier appointed by the president with the approval of the Duma

Legislative branch: bicameral Federal Assembly consists of the Federation Council (178 seats; members appointed by the top executive and legislative officials in each of the 89 federal administrative units—oblasts, krays, republics, autonomous okrugs and oblasts, and the federal cities of Moscow and Saint Petersburg;

members serve four-year terms) and the State Duma (450 seats; half elected by proportional representation from party lists winning at least 5% of the vote, and half from single-member constituencies; members are elected by direct popular vote to serve four-year terms)

Judicial branch: Constitutional Court; Supreme Court; Superior Court of Arbitration; judges for all courts are appointed for life by the Federation Council on the recommendation of the president

ECONOMY

Overview: Russia is still struggling to establish a modern market economy and achieve strong economic growth. Stubborn budget deficits and the country's poor business climate made it vulnerable when the global financial crisis swept through in 1998. The crisis culminated in the August depreciation of the ruble, a debt default by the government, and a sharp deterioration in living standards for most of the population. The economy rebounded in 1999 and 2000, buoyed by the competitive boost from the weak ruble and a surging trade surplus fueled by rising world oil prices. This recovery, along with a renewed government effort to advance lagging structural reforms, raised business and investor confidence. Yet serious problems persist. Russia remains heavily dependent on exports of commodities, particularly oil, natural gas, metals, and timber, which account for over 80% of exports, leaving the country vulnerable to swings in world prices. Russia's agricultural sector remains beset by uncertainty over land ownership rights, which has discouraged needed investment and restructuring. Another threat is negative demographic trends, fueled by low birthrates and a deteriorating health situation—including an alarming rise in AIDS cases—that have contributed to a nearly 2% drop in the population since 1992. Russia's industrial base is increasingly dilapidated and must be replaced or modernized if the country is to achieve sustainable economic growth. Other problems include widespread corruption, capital flight, and brain drain.

GDP: purchasing power parity—$1.28 trillion

GDP—real growth rate: 7.3%

GDP—per capita: purchasing power parity—$8,900

GDP—composition by sector: *agriculture:* 5.2% *industry:* 35.1% *services:* 59.8%

Population below poverty line: 25%

Labor force: 71.68 million

Labor force—by occupation: agriculture 12.3%, industry 22.7%, services 65%

Unemployment rate: 8.5%, plus considerable underemployment

Currency: Russian ruble (RUR)

A. POLITICAL DEVELOPMENT

On 31 December 1999, President Boris Yeltsin surprised the world with the announcement that he was resigning the presidency of the Russian Federation immediately and turning over the reins as acting president to Vladimir Putin, the virtually unknown figure whom Yeltsin had plucked out of political obscurity a few months earlier to serve as prime minister. Actually the unexpected turn in Russian politics had begun already in August 1999. The increasingly embattled and enfeebled President Yeltsin installed as prime minister Vladimir Putin, the fourth replacement in that office in the year and a half since he had fired Viktor Chernomyrdin, who had served in the position since 1992.[1]Yeltsin reputedly selected Putin because he was convinced that none of his other choices as prime minister was a viable candidate to replace him as president. In the final four months of 1999, the new prime minister—and his mentor Yeltsin—moved rapidly and effectively to consolidate his power position in Moscow. The backing of President Yeltsin and the Moscow economic "oligarchs," Putin's successful prosecution of a popular war in Chechnya, the absence of an effective opposition, and Putin's image as a young and forceful new leader all strengthened his position in the months leading up to the presidential election.

As occurred in earlier electoral campaigns in Russia during the 1990s, the media served as a valuable election tool. During the campaign leading up to the Duma elections of December 1999, ORT Television, part of Yeltsin crony Boris Berezovsky's media empire, carried out a vitriolic campaign against those candidates associated with likely presidential candidates Yuri

Luzhkov, mayor of Moscow, and former prime minister Evgeny Primakov. The result was both the election of a Duma far more malleable for the Yeltsin-Putin leadership and the erosion of the political effectiveness of potential opponents in the upcoming presidential elections. The results of the presidential election of April were from the very outset a foregone conclusion; Putin won with 53 percent of the vote in a field of 11 candidates.

Putin inherited an almost unbelievable array of problems, beginning with a political system that did not work effectively and an economy that had virtually ceased to produce. More specifically, the state had become so weak that a combination of province-level politicians and the oligarchs who came to dominate what remained of the economy were able to function independently of the state. Economic collapse, organized crime, widespread corruption, the disintegration of the public health and educational systems, war in Chechnya, and general societal decay, along with the cultural legacies of the past, had characterized the weak and chaotic presidency of Boris Yeltsin. The billions of dollars lent and granted to Russia by the West had not contributed to rejuvenating economic production; rather it was consumed or stolen by so-called reformers turned thieves, both inside and outside the government. State institutions atrophied, crime and corruption exploded. Even before officially taking office as president in May 2000, Putin began to move to deal with some of these issues. The two most serious obstacles to success in revitalizing Russia were the dominant position of provincial governors and the overriding political power of the oligarchs who control most of the economy and, thereby, exercised major influence on government policy. Moscow's weakening grasp on the entire Russian Federation meant a decreasing ability of the central government to set national policy. From tax collection to arms sales, growing Russian regionalism contributed to Russia's domestic and foreign policy problems.

In one of the first major acts of his presidency, Putin announced measures to curb the

---

[1]After the dismissal of Chernomyrdin, Sergei Kiriyenko served from April until August 1998. In August the Duma refused to approve Yeltsin's attempt to reinstate Chernomyrdin. Yevgeny Primakov served as prime minister from September 1998 until the next May, followed by Sergei Stepashin for the next five months until August. Finally, on August 9, 1999, Yeltsin appointed Vladimir Putin.

A CLOSER LOOK
7.1

VLADIMIR PUTIN

Vladimir Putin, a former KGB operative in East Germany, had a meteoric rise to political influence since Russian independence. After returning from East Germany to Leningrad/St. Petersburg to pursue graduate study, he joined the staff of the reform mayor of St. Petersburg. In 1996 he was invited to Moscow to work in the presidential property office; a year later he became head of the Federal Security Service, reportedly in return for suppressing criminal investigations that implicated President Yeltsin's family. In March 1999, Yeltsin appointed him secretary of the Security Council, in August prime minister, and before the end of the year he was acting president. So rapid and unexpected was Putin's political rise that he was not even mentioned in a special September–October 1999 issue of *Problems of Post-Communism* devoted exclusively to the likely major presidential candidates for the presidential elections then scheduled for June 2000. Putin became president in 2000 and was re-elected in 2004, winning 71 percent of the vote.

power of the provincial governors and ensure the coordination of federal policy with that of the provinces and other regions. He called for the establishment of a "strong state" and the powers to sack regional governors and exclude them from membership in the upper house of parliament, the Federation Chamber. Putin's record as president is mixed, but he has succeeded in strengthening the authority of the central government and in dealing with at least some of the political problems that he inherited. Putin has not been able to make nearly so forceful a move against the oligarchs whose domination of the economy has permitted them to dominate politics as well. However, he has curbed, and virtually eliminated, the independent media, generally under the guise of rooting out economic corruption. By January 2002, for example, the last independent national television network was closed by court order.

Russian and Western analysts have questioned Putin's commitment to democracy and human rights. Russian analyst Liliya Shevtsova, for example, "cannot find anything that would be comforting" in the current political situation in Russia.[2] Others view with special concern the "heavy-handed commando raid" on the Media-MOST company, a competitor to Berezovsky's ORT, and the more recent move against Berezovsky and other independent media. The threat to independent media was reinforced by Press Minister Mikhail Lesin's assertion that "The defence of the state from the free mass media is a pressing problem at present."[3]

What is evident in the period since Putin's inauguration as president is his energy and ability to move to accomplish his objectives. He has installed a governing team dominated by those with whom he had worked in St. Petersburg prior to his coming to Moscow, while slowly but systematically removing Yeltsin's appointees. It remains to be seen whether this new team can implement a strategy for reform of the political system that will establish a strong state without simply ignoring the Russian constitution and basic human and democratic rights of the Russian people.

THE POLITICAL SETTING

During the fall 1991, the political structures that for seven decades had made the Soviet Union a highly centralized and authoritarian state and a

[2]Liliya Shevtsova, "Political Conformism Bordering on Lackeydom" (interview by Armen Gasparyan), *Literaturnaya gazeta,* May 24, 2000; cited in *Johnson's Russia List,* no. 4325, May 25, 2000.

[3]"Editorial: Raid Part of Disturbing New Pattern," *Moscow Times,* May 17, 2000.

global superpower crumbled in the face of the failed attempt to reform the system and the growing nationalist sentiment in Russia and elsewhere throughout the huge expanse of Soviet territory. The Soviet political system that had represented revolutionary change and utopian promise in the second decade of the twentieth century was in a profound crisis as it entered the last decade of the century. The failure of centralized economic planning and state ownership to meet the challenges of rapidly expanding external competition and rising international demands and expectations resulted in negative economic growth, empty store shelves, growing inflation, strikes, rising unemployment, and a declining standard of living. After more than four years of increased political and economic turmoil resulting from Mikhail Gorbachev's efforts at reform, the Russian Federation, the largest and most important of the 15 states to emerge from the territory of the former Soviet Union, was still searching for its future.

The Communist Party dictatorship had been replaced by multiparty political competition, but the foundations for a democratic society remained fragile, and many of the key political figures were publicly committed to reestablishing authoritarian political structures. Much of the economy that in the past was state-owned and centrally planned had been privatized, but criminal elements referred to as "mafia," usually in cooperation with government officials whose roots are in the old *nomenklatura* system of party and state officials, controlled much of the economy. Moreover, growing pressures existed to expand the role of the government in the economy, in particular in subsidizing economic enterprises that were not competitive in the new market environment.

Thus, despite the dramatic changes that occurred in the former Soviet Union, Russia and most of the other successor states had yet to establish stable and effective political and economic structures by the end of 2001, although under President Putin clear evidence of an economic turnaround emerged. Moreover, the legacies of the Communist past remained very influential in setting the agenda and determining the ways in which politics emerged at the end of

the twentieth century. Thus, we will begin our examination of Russian government and politics with a review of the Russian and Soviet past, emphasizing those aspects likely to influence political developments in the new Russia.

The Soviet Legacy

In February 1986, General Secretary of the Communist Party of the Soviet Union (CPSU) Mikhail S. Gorbachev used the Twenty-seventh Party Congress to characterize the rule of his immediate predecessors as a period of stagnation and corruption. He warned that "it is impossible to retreat and there is nowhere to retreat" and that "history has not given us much time."[4] Subsequently, in July 1991, Gorbachev noted that in the 1980s the country had been in a "state of depression" and "the previous theoretical and practical model of socialism [had] ... proven to be insolvent." He lamented that "old and new ailments of society were not exposed, let alone treated, but were suppressed, which further aggravated the situation and in the end led to severe crisis."[5] This proved to be a crisis of political leadership and economic policy, social and ethnic conflict, and spiritual and moral degeneration. After six years of ineffective efforts at reform, Gorbachev's Soviet government found itself in disarray, overwhelmed by events and demands as the non-Russian republics and the Russian Republic itself asserted their lack of confidence in the political center and the growing desire for sovereignty.

During 1991 the very name of the Soviet Union (or Union of Soviet Socialist Republics) became a matter of dispute, as its disunity became increasingly evident. Although often mistakenly referred to as a "nation," the Soviet Union was actually a collection of nations and peoples, a multinational empire comprising more than a hundred officially recognized ethnic and linguistic communities. The Soviet crisis thus represented an extraordinary combination of the

---

[4]*Pravda,* January 28, 1987.
[5]*Isvestiya,* July 26, 1991.

collapse of a political system and the disintegration of an empire. In fact, the disappearance of the Soviet Union initiated in the 15 major constituent units a process of "triple transition" characterized by the need (1) to establish new states, in almost all cases where none had ever existed before, with accepted borders and supportive populations among multiethnic societies; (2) to create democratic and representative political institutions and values in place of the authoritarian structures and values of the Soviet and pre-Soviet past; and (3) to lay the foundations for competitive market economies where a centralized command economy had dominated. In varying degrees the challenges of this simultaneous triple transition faced all the former Communist states that emerged in Central and Eastern Europe and Eurasia. Everywhere the task has been daunting, notably in former Yugoslavia, where it has been overwhelming.

The Soviet political order had evolved from its beginnings in military defeat, revolutionary war, and utopianism into a cruel totalitarian dictatorship under Stalin, and subsequently into an oligarchy of aged and ineffective leaders. It had its origins in the Russian Revolution of 1917—one of the most significant events of the twentieth century—and emerged on the ruins of the Russian Empire, which failed to survive the dislocations and crises created by World War I. The Russian Revolution began in February 1917 with the abdication of Tsar Nicholas II and the collapse of the monarchy. Administrative breakdown, war weariness, and an inability to supply the army and feed the population of the capital precipitated the empire's collapse. A weak and indecisive Provisional Government of liberals and moderate Socialists headed by Alexander Kerensky attempted to continue Russia's participation in the war on the side of the Allies (Great Britain, France, Italy, and the United States), meanwhile putting off needed internal reforms until a new constitution could be written and a legitimate government elected. As the war grew more unpopular and the army disintegrated, the Provisional Government was unable to defend itself from the growing discontent and the threat of a seizure of power.

The threat of a takeover of the Russian capital of Petrograd (formerly St. Petersburg, later Leningrad, and now again St. Petersburg) came from the most extreme Russian Marxists, known as the Bolsheviks, under the leadership of Vladimir Ilyich Ulianov, better known as V. I. Lenin. The Bolsheviks succeeded in gaining control of the soviets (or councils) of workers, peasants, and soldiers' deputies in Petrograd and Moscow. The soviets, which were revolutionary organs that arose spontaneously at the very beginning of the Russian Revolution, were only haphazardly representative and not popularly elected. Initially such non-Bolshevik parties as the agrarian Socialist Revolutionaries and the more moderate Marxists known as the Mensheviks controlled them. Although the Russian word *sovet* means "council," the takeover of the soviets in the principal cities by Lenin's Bolsheviks gave the word a distinct political meaning associated with Communist rule and a new type of system based on the dictatorship of a single party.

Lenin succeeded in seizing power from the Provisional Government because it was never fully in command. From the very beginning of the Revolution, it had to share power with the Petrograd soviet, which by the summer of 1917 came under the domination of Lenin's associate Leon Trotsky. The Provisional Government also lacked the intelligence-gathering ability and the security police of the previous imperial regime. It could not rely on the army, because the troops stationed in the capital were not loyal and had come under the influence of Bolshevik agitators. In addition, Lenin's supporters were tightly disciplined and organized. Lenin had the support of the "workers' red guard"—a paramilitary force that could be armed and sent into the streets to intimidate those who opposed the Bolsheviks. Thus, Lenin's takeover of the Russian capital on November 7, 1917 (October 23 by the Julian calendar still in use in Russia at the time), was a relatively easy undertaking, but years of bloody civil conflict followed. In a very literal sense the Soviet system was spawned by war (World War I) and also succeeded in establishing itself by means of war (civil war).

Initially Lenin gained control of only the central portion of European Russia. He established a Russian Socialist Federated Soviet Republic in July 1918 but was confronted with several centers of resistance. Russians who opposed the establishment of a Communist regime, including part of the tsarist military, waged a civil war that Lenin eventually won in 1920–1921 because of the fatigue brought on by Russia's demoralization and the absence of any unified military command or political center among the forces opposed to the Bolsheviks. Lenin had the advantage of having a divided opposition that could not develop an attractive and sufficiently powerful alternative to Bolshevik rule. Political moderates had little chance to succeed in a time of turmoil and simple propaganda slogans, while Lenin's principal Russian opponents were political conservatives or reactionaries who sought to restore the old order.

The more numerous non-Russian peoples who had been subjected to Russian rule within the empire seized the opportunity presented by Russia's collapse and proclaimed their independence in 1917–1918. The Finns, Ukrainians, Georgians, Armenians, Poles, Estonians, Latvians, Lithuanians, and others established independent states. Lenin was ultimately able to establish Soviet (and Russian) rule over most of the non-Russian peoples, and the form and name of the Russian state was changed. In December 1922 the Union of Soviet Socialist Republics was formed as a federation, at least in theory, consisting of separate Soviet republics for the major nationality groups.

The Imperial Legacy

Lenin's Bolshevik Party and the Soviet political system that it created became the successors to the tsarist Russian Empire, although ironically Lenin had dedicated his political life to the overthrow of that empire and its monarchy. The monarchy was not overthrown but collapsed in March 1917 (February in the old Russian calendar) with the abdication of the tsar, a lack of leadership, and a breakdown of the military and administrative systems, which touched off bread riots and disorder in the capital. Eight months

later the overthrow of the Provisional Government gave Lenin the opportunity to extend Soviet rule from the center of the former empire.

Lenin faced the same problem that the Russian autocrats had faced: how to rule a huge ethnically diverse empire from a single distant center. Although the Bolsheviks rejected many traditional Russian values and introduced significant changes in the Russian way of life, in the end they came to represent Russian domination of the USSR. Thus, many Russians who might have had doubts about the nature of Soviet rule came to accept it as the heir to the Russian Empire and as the only available means of preserving Russia's claim to greatness and satisfying its yearning to rule over neighboring peoples—issues seemingly of as great importance in the new Russia of the 1990s as they were after the Bolshevik Revolution, given their importance in the current political debates in Russia.

The Price of Empire

Empire meant neglect of domestic problems. Its very size in territorial terms created large bureaucratic establishments that declined in competence and effectiveness. In addition to costly military forces, it required large police establishments to keep subject peoples intimidated and to impose internal order and an apparent unity. The attempt to govern diverse peoples from a single center (which was also the center of the dominant nationality) bred resentment and resistance. The imperial system was costly and wasteful because of its swollen bureaucracy and apparatus of coercion, and because of its efforts to retain conquests and great-power status. Bigness led to the sacrifice of quality for quantity and to numerous forms of corruption and venality.

The unity of the imperial system, for all of its apparent power, had a synthetic quality and was unstable because it attempted to embrace too many and too much. Because of its size and heterogeneous nature, it was difficult to identify with the imperial system. Yet vast sums were squandered on grandiose public monuments and displays of military might in an attempt to sustain the myth of omnipotence and invincibility.

A CLOSER LOOK

7.2

SOLZHENITSYN ON THE BURDENS OF EMPIRE

The Russians paid a high price for empire if, as Aleksandr Solzhenitsyn contends, the Russian "national way of life" and "national character" were disappearing and if Russian nationhood was being destroyed "without pity" by Soviet leaders who claimed to be of Russian nationality. Winner of the 1970 Nobel Prize in literature, Solzhenitsyn argued that despite greater use of the Russian language, in its Soviet version it became "a sullied and bastardized form." If so, this was a part of the price of empire as the Russian language ceased to be the possession of Russia and was corrupted by non-Russians and Russians alike.

An additional price of empire was the inundation of the metropole and imperial capital by subject peoples and alien elements. In the process the dominant Russians increasingly alienated the subject peoples. Fear of fragmentation of the empire promoted suspiciousness of "subversion" and obsession with security. It also engendered arrogance and blindness, as Russians failed to understand the national ideals and aspirations of subject peoples. Solzhenitsyn, in his essay "Repentance and Self-Limitation in the Life of Nations," counseled his people to withdraw and engage in self-examination and divest themselves of the burdens of empire. He also warned the Soviet leaders that "the aims of a great empire and the moral health of the people are incompatible" and that empire inflicts spiritual harm.

Sources: Aleksandr Solzhenitsyn, *The Mortal Danger: How Misconceptions About Russia Imperil America,* 2nd ed. (New York: Harper and Row, 1981), pp. 28 and 109; *From Under the Rubble* (Boston: Little, Brown, 1975); *Letter to the Soviet Leaders* (New York: Harper and Row, 1974), p. 41.

The Russians, as the dominant and core nationality, paid a high price for empire. In denying non-Russian subject peoples the right of self-determination, Russians greatly limited their own freedom by having to sustain an authoritarian system designed to preserve the imperial patrimony and hold restive subject peoples within its grip. By creating and sustaining the synthetic entity known as the USSR, Russians experienced (and imposed upon themselves) a diminution or loss of original identity. Because of the multinational nature of the USSR, the adjective "Russian" was usually supplanted by "Soviet" and even by the strange adjective "fatherland" (for example, with reference to machine building, medicine, and music). Russians were thus unable to acquire and develop genuine nationhood as part of the USSR. In professing a contrived "internationalism," Russia submerged itself in the union-empire. It is ironic that the Russian Republic in effect surrendered its membership in the United Nations to the union-empire, while Ukraine and Belarus, as charter members of the United Nations, actually acquired greater international and legal recognition than Russia.

THE GEOGRAPHIC SETTING

Tsarist Russia and the former Soviet Union could claim to be, in terms of area, the largest country under a single political regime. It covered one-sixth of the earth's landmass and extended a distance of more than 6,000 miles over 150 degrees of longitude and 11 time zones. Even after the dissolution of the Soviet Union, the Russian Federation, with an area of 6.6 million square miles, continues to rank as the largest country in the world physically, with almost twice the territory of either the United States or China.

Most of this vast landmass has an intemperate continental climate because it is remote from the oceans that would have a moderating effect, warming the land in winter and cooling it off in the summer, and is exposed to the frigid climate of the Arctic. Temperature extremes vary greatly—parts of Siberia have a range of 150°F. Much of the land has limited rainfall, receiving less than 20 inches of precipitation annually.

The land is reasonably well endowed with natural resources, including petroleum, natural gas, and all important minerals, and can be largely self-sufficient. However, transportation costs are often high when oil, coal, natural gas, and raw materials are distant from users. There is heavy reliance on railways that are slow and poorly maintained, and no modern highway system exists, even in the more densely populated regions of European Russia. Moreover, permafrost, which covers two-thirds of Siberia, makes the construction and maintenance of buildings, railroads, and pipelines extremely expensive and difficult.

The area of the former Soviet Union has not been entirely self-sufficient in agriculture and has had to import grain. This has been partially the result of natural conditions such as the limited rainfall and the short growing season, especially in the northern latitudes. Despite the vast size of the country, the amount of land suitable for agriculture is limited. This has resulted in the costly cultivation of marginal lands and reliance on extensive agriculture, bringing more land under cultivation rather than developing intensive agriculture, which would increase crop yields. It has also meant high reliance on irrigation and chemicals, which are both costly and damaging to the environment. Low crop yields have also resulted from the absence of an effective, modern agricultural infrastructure and from the administrative inefficiencies inherent in the collectivized and state-farm systems of the former Soviet Union. The failure to reform the agricultural sector since the collapse of the Soviet system in 1991 resulted in even further declines in agricultural production. The 1995 harvest was the worst since 1963. Grain output, for example, dropped to 63 million metric tons, down from 81 million tons in 1994 and 117 million in 1990. New investments in agriculture at the end of the decade have resulted in growing grain harvests that reached 83 million tons in 2001.

Thus, in geographical terms the Soviet Union possessed both advantages and disadvantages. Its sheer size provided it with a measure of invulnerability, although the region has historically remained open to invaders over the steppe route from the east (the Mongols and Tatars) and the west (Poland, Sweden, France, and Germany). The Russian Federation, which shares most of the former USSR's advantages and disadvantages, claims the world's longest coastline, and yet much of the region faces icebound Arctic waters and the North Pacific. Ice-free ports on the Baltic and Black Seas, many of which are no longer a part of Russian territory, have historically been vulnerable to closure by the countries that control access to them. Such apparent disadvantages have been compensated for in other ways. An excellent year-round ice-free port at Murmansk on the Barents Sea in far northern European Russia provides naval forces and commercial shipping with ready access to the Atlantic Ocean and world sea-lanes, and ports on the northern Pacific Ocean can be kept open during the winter with icebreakers.

Although not landlocked, both the Russian Empire and the USSR historically sought to penetrate such neighboring lands as Poland, the Balkan countries, Turkey, Iran, Afghanistan, Mongolia, China (including Manchuria), and Korea in a bid to gain strategic advantage—including enhanced access to open seas. Some see in recent efforts of the Russian Federation to reassert influence in its new neighbors of the "near abroad"—the Central Asian countries, the Baltics, the Transcaucasian states, Belarus, Moldova, and Ukraine—a continuation of this effort to control neighboring states and gain strategic benefits. However, Russia's limited resource base has caused its leaders to pursue a more cautious approach to exerting influence in recent years.

THE PEOPLE

Nationalities

The Soviet Union possessed the world's third largest population, exceeded in size only by those of China and India, while the Russian Federation ranks sixth in world population (following also the United States, Indonesia, and Brazil). The population of Russia is 144 million (considerably less than the 285 million of the former Soviet Union). This population is not homogeneous and must be viewed in terms of its ethnic and social composition. The principal nationalities (see Table 7.1) in both the former USSR and the present Russian Federation represent highly diverse peoples with distinctive ethnic, linguistic, religious, and cultural qualities. Although the Russians constituted

TABLE 7.1

POPULATION AND PRINCIPAL NATIONALITIES OF THE RUSSIAN FEDERATION/CIS

Nation	Population	Percentage	Nation	Population	Percentage
Russian Federation			Gypsy	153,000	0.1
Population	147,022,000*		Karachai	150,000	0.1
By nationality			Komi-Permiak	147,000	0.1
Russian	119,866,000	81.5	Karelian	125,000	0.1
Tatar	5,522,000	3.8	Adygei	123,000	0.1
Ukrainian	4,363,000	3.0	Korean	107,000	0.1
Chuvash	1,774,000	1.2	Lak	106,000	0.1
Bashkort	1,345,000	0.9	Polish	95,000	0.1
Belarusian	1,206,000	0.8	Other	1,614,000	1.1
Mordvinian	1,073,000	0.7			
Chechen	899,000	0.6	**Armenia**		
German	842,000	0.6	Population	3,305,000	
Udmurt	715,000	0.5	*By nationality*		
Mari	644,000	0.4	Armenian	3,084,000	93.3
Kazakh	636,000	0.4	Russian	52,000	1.6
Avar	544,000	0.4	Other	169,000	5.1
Jewish	537,000	0.4			
Armenian	532,000	0.4	**Azerbaijan**		
Buryat	417,000	0.3	Population	7,021,000	
Ossetian	402,000	0.3	*By nationality*		
Kabard	386,000	0.3	Azerbaijani	5,805,000	82.7
Yakut	380,000	0.3	Russian	392,000	5.6
Dargin	353,000	0.2	Armenian	391,000**	5.6
Komi	336,000	0.2	Other	433,000	6.2
Azerbaijani	336,000	0.2	**Belarus**		
Kumyk	277,000	0.2	Population	10,152,000	
Lezghin	257,000	0.2	*By nationality*		
Ingush	215,000	0.1	Belarusian	7,905,000	77.9
Tuvan	206,000	0.1	Russian	1,342,000	13.2
Moldovan	173,000	0.1	Other	905,000	8.9
Kalmyk	166,000	0.1			

continues

TABLE 7.1 (continued)

POPULATION AND PRINCIPAL NATIONALITIES OF THE RUSSIAN FEDERATION/CIS

Nation	Population	Percentage	Nation	Population	Percentage
Georgia			**Tajikistan**		
Population	5,401,000		Population	5,093,000	
By nationality			*By nationality*		
Georgian	3,787,000	70.1	Tajik	3,172,000	62.3
Armenian	437,000	8.1	Uzbek	1,198,000	23.5
Russian	341,000	6.3	Russian	388,000***	7.6***
Other	836,000	15.5	Other	335,000***	6.6***
Kazakhstan			**Turkmenistan**		
Population	16,464,000		Population	3,523,000	
By nationality			*By nationality*		
Kazak	6,535,000	39.7	Turkmen	2,537,000	72.0
Russian	6,228,000	37.8	Russian	334,000	9.5
Other	3,701,000	22.5	Uzbek	317,000	9.0
Kyrgyzstan			Other	355,000	10.1
Population	4,258,000		**Ukraine**		
By nationality			Population	51,471,000	
Kyrgyz	2,230,000	52.4	*By nationality*		
Russian	917,000	21.5	Ukrainian	37,419,000	72.7
Other	1,111,000	26.1	Russian	11,356,000	22.1
Moldova			Other	2,696,000	5.2
Population	4,335,000		**Uzbekistan**		
By nationality			Population	19,810,000	
Moldovan	2,795,000	64.5	*By nationality*		
Ukrainian	600,000	13.8	Uzbek	14,142,000	71.4
Russian	562,000	13.0	Russian	1,653,000	8.3
Other	378,000	17.4	Other	4,015,000	20.3

Sources: Stephen K. Batalden and Sandra L. Batalden, *The Newly Independent States of Eurasia: Handbook of Former Soviet Republics* (Phoenix, AZ: Oryx Press, 1993). The Bataldens draw on the official Soviet census of 1989 and a variety of more recent statistical estimates.

*More recent estimates put the entire population of the Russian Federation at 143.8 million people. Irina Vorobyeva and Ilya Kharlashkin, "Russia in the Mirror of Statistics," *Profil* 19, June 2002.

**These figures do not reflect the exodus of most Armenians, except about 150,000 in Nagorno-Karabakh, from Azerbaijan since the outbreak of hostilities in Nagorno-Karabakh.

***These figures do not reflect the exodus of much of the European population during the civil war that began in 1992.

approximately one-half of the population of the USSR, their relative weight declined from 58.4 percent in 1939 to 50.8 percent in 1989. They now compose about 82 percent of the population of the Russian Federation.

The eastern Slavic population consists of Russians, Ukrainians, and Belarusians, who together form about 75 percent of the total population of the former Soviet Union. The Ukrainians, the second most numerous Slavic people in the Soviet Union, trace their origins to the Kievan Rus' of the ninth to thirteenth centuries. Subsequently they were part of the medieval Lithuanian states, which united with Poland in 1569. The eastern Ukrainians, who rebelled against Polish rule in 1648, established an independent state that soon came under the influence and then control of Moscow—after making a fatal decision to turn to the Muscovite tsar for military aid in 1654. The Belarusians, who differ from Russians, did not come under Russian rule until the end of the eighteenth century. Only small numbers of Ukrainians and Belarusians remain within the borders of the Russian Federation— less than 4 percent of the total population.

The various Turkic peoples constituted approximately 17 percent of the Soviet population and make up somewhat less than 10 percent of the population of the Russian Federation. They are related to the Osmanli Turks of Turkey and extend from Sakha (Yakutia) in northeastern Siberia across Central Asia to Azerbaijan. Their subjugation by the Russians began in the sixteenth century (in the cases of the Kazan and Volga Tatars) and was not completed until the 1890s in Turkmenistan. The largest groups of Turkic peoples—the Uzbeks, Kazaks, Turkmens, Kyrgyz, and Azerbaijani—now enjoy nominally independent states, although significant numbers of Kazaks and Azerbaijani also live in Russia. The Turkic peoples also include numerous smaller groups, which are part of the population of the Russian Federation itself. The Volga Tatars live along the middle section and east of the river of that name, and the Siberian Tatars in the Tobolsk area of western Siberia. The Crimean Tatars came to the Crimea in the thirteenth century but were forcibly resettled during World War II; their return to their homeland, now officially a part of Ukraine, was long delayed. Other Turkic peoples include the Bashkirs, Chuvash, Kara-Kalpaks, Tuvans, Karachai, and Balkar located variously in southern Siberia and the northern Caucasus region. Inhabiting a rugged mountainous country along the Afghan frontier, the Tajiks are linguistically an Iranian people and are also Muslims.

As a result of several centuries of Russian rule over Armenia, Georgia, and the Baltic states, substantial numbers of individuals from these ethnic communities, especially the Transcaucasians, can also be found scattered across the Russian Federation. The Armenians represent an old culture that flourished long before the Russians emerged as a people. Armenia was also the first Christian state and has a unique national church. The Georgians, neighbors of the Armenians, have a very distinctive language and accepted Christianity in the fourth century. These two peoples came under Russian rule early in the nineteenth century as a result of pressure from their Muslim neighbors and Russian penetration of the area south of the Caucasus Mountains.

The Baltic peoples belong neither to the Slavic nor the Germanic worlds but constitute separate ethnic entities that came under Russian rule in the eighteenth century. They include the Estonians and Latvians, who are Lutherans, and

One of the many people who form Russia's diverse population.

the Lithuanians, who are Roman Catholics. Although the Baltic states obtained their independence after World War I during the Russian Revolution, they were forcibly annexed by the Soviet Union in 1940 and again in 1944. They played a key role in the disintegration of the Soviet state and seceded from the USSR and regained their independence in September 1991, immediately following the abortive coup attempt against the government of Mikhail Gorbachev. Other non-Slavic peoples of the former Soviet Union included the Moldovans, who are actually Romanians of the region of Bessarabia conquered by Russia in 1812 and returned to Romania from 1918 to World War II, after which the Soviet Union reannexed the region.

Among the nationalities that had no union-level Soviet republic were the Jews, Germans, and Poles. The Jewish population came under Russian rule in the late eighteenth-century annexations of Polish-ruled territories. Although one-half of the world's Jewish population lived in the Russian Empire prior to World War I, subsequent events, such as the Holocaust—the mass execution of Jews and others in Nazi-occupied Europe, including Ukraine, Russia, and Belorussia (now Belarus)—repressive practices on the part of Soviet authorities, and emigration caused their number to diminish to the level of 1.3 million according to the 1989 census. Germans in the former Soviet Union are largely descendants of colonists invited by the Russian government to settle there in the eighteenth century; their Volga German Autonomous Republic was liquidated and its population deported to Central Asia in 1941. Since 1985 substantial numbers of ethnic Germans have left for Germany. Among the other peoples who have been under extensive demographic pressure from the Russians are the Finno-Ugric peoples of northern European Russia, including the Mordvinians, the Udmurt, the Mari, the Karelians, and the Komi.

Among the most serious problems facing the Russian government of President Boris Yeltsin was the explosion of ethnically based nationalism among a number of the minority peoples of Russia. The most serious and visible example occurred in the Republic of Chechnya, where, after two years of brutal warfare and the use by Russian troops of their full military arsenal against the Chechen rebels, the Russian government was forced in 1996 to accept a truce that left the area de facto autonomous. Since fall 1999, when then Prime Minister Vladimir Putin began a new campaign in Chechnya, the Russians have been committed to eradicating all military resistance to continued Russian rule over this small Muslim people in the Caucasus. As of 2005, however, pockets of resistance remained, including sucide bombings.

Elsewhere across Russia some ethnically based constituent republics of the Federation—for example, Tatarstan along the Volga River and Buryatia north of Mongolia—have declared their autonomy or independence from Moscow and resisted the imposition of full central authority. Throughout most of the other ethnically based republics within the Russian Federation, nationalist movements have emerged that make various claims for greater autonomy. Overall, however, the Russian government has succeeded in assuaging the most radical demands of the non-Russian peoples of the federation by a combination of granting to them substantial autonomy while simultaneously demonstrating in Chechnya the costs of refusing to cooperate with Moscow. Moreover, President Putin has successfully exerted greater central control over both Russian and non-Russian regions of the country, and the threats of disintegration of the federation widely discussed a few years ago seem to have passed.

Social Classes

Although the Soviet Union claimed to be building a "classless Communist society"—according to the 1977 Constitution—social strata recognized officially included the "working class, the collectivized peasantry, and the people's intelligentsia." Social classes can be distinguished in terms of income levels, status, and prestige, and by the degree of their influence in society. Yet Soviet rulers, for ideological reasons, sought to minimize social differences. Thus, "workers"

Russian troops maintain a strong presence in Chechnya, while civilians try to survive.

were said to constitute 58.8 percent of the population in 1989, collective farmers 11.8 percent, and "salaried" persons 29.3 percent. The self-employed and others were a mere 0.2 percent of the population. Such broad categories blur real social distinction, since each contains numerous subgroups.

Official Soviet social categories also omitted the political class—an elite usually referred to as the *nomenklatura* that consisted of the leading *cadres* (officials) of the ruling Communist Party, as well as government ministers and high-level bureaucrats, economic managers, leading diplomats, military figures, and KGB personnel. This ruling class enjoyed superior housing, country homes, chauffeur-driven automobiles, servants, vacations and foreign travel, and access to special "closed stores" that sold scarce and imported items at discount prices or for "certificate rubles" worth much more than ordinary rubles. There were also fringe benefits such as

medical care in exclusive clinics and hospitals that were far superior to those serving ordinary Soviet citizens.[6] Leonid Brezhnev as general secretary of the Communist Party could acquire a large private collection of expensive foreign automobiles. The elite could accumulate considerable wealth, often by corrupt means, and give their children academic diplomas and arrange prestigious and well-paid positions for them. One of the unfortunate characteristics of post-Communist Russia is that a new elite is emerging, often from among the very membership of the old Soviet *nomenklatura,* that controls an

---

[6]See Mervyn Matthews, *Privilege in the Soviet Union: A Study of Elite Life-Style Under Communism* (London: Allen and Unwin, 1978). See also Michael Voslensky, *Nomenklatura: The Soviet Ruling Class* (Garden City, NY: Doubleday, 1984).

ever-growing percentage of economic resources which it uses to buy political influence and flaunt its economic success.

In the 1980s the term *mafia* gained currency in the Soviet Union and was used in several senses. It applied to CPSU officials and to members who held key positions in nonparty organizations and participated in networks based on mutual advantage and self-enrichment. *Mafia* also referred to those engaged in large-scale black market activity. With the emergence of individual and private (nominally cooperative) enterprise resulting from changes in economic policy in the Gorbachev period, another type of mafia appeared—racketeers engaged in extortion and theft at the expense of successful legitimate businesses. As quoted by *Izvestiya* (July 2, 1988), Boris Yeltsin observed at the Nineteenth CSPU Conference that "the decay is evidently deeper than some have assumed, and I know, on the basis of Moscow, that a mafia definitely exists." He also noted that there were "millionaire bribetakers" among CPSU officials at the republic and oblast levels who were not being punished by the Committee of Party Control. The expansion of organized crime and its influence on society continued unabated during the first decade of the new Russian Federation. In 1995, for example, reported murders rose to 32,000, up from 15,500 five years earlier. Moreover, organized crime exercises substantial influence within government and control over the economy—some estimates place it at more than 50 percent in some regions. Links with organized crime abroad have opened up new avenues of activity, such as drug smuggling and money laundering, for the Russian mafia.

Soviet society came to be characterized by significant inequalities of income, education, and educational opportunity, despite official claims to the contrary. The intelligentsia—which included professional, scientific, scholarly, educational, artistic, and literary persons—represented great differences in rewards. Thus, physicians, two-thirds of whom were women, were poorly paid. Many Soviet citizens, including unskilled workers and pensioners, fell below the poverty level by the early 1990s. At the same time there emerged a new class of "ruble millionaires" as a result of increased corruption, severe goods shortages, and a developing market. By the turn of the twenty-first century, upwards of two-thirds of the population found itself below the official poverty level, as inflation eroded the buying power of all those on government incomes, such as teachers, government employees, and retirees, and governments social services contracted for a lack of funding.

The Soviet population was long characterized by a disparity in the sex ratio. Women significantly outnumbered men as a result of famine, the bloody Stalinist purges, and World War II, apart from longevity differences. There were 17.6 million more women than men in 1979 and 15.7 million more in 1990—at a time when the effects of events in the 1930s and 1940s were beginning to lose their impact. The USSR experienced a steadily declining birthrate that was especially evident in Russia and Ukraine. The natural increase declined from 17.8 (per thousand population) in 1960 to 7.6 in 1989, with current estimates indicating that deaths have outnumbered live births ever since the early 1990s. However, the rate of population increases in the Muslim areas of the former Soviet Union were four to eight times greater than among the European population groups.

One of the great ironies of the post-Communist period across Central and Eastern Europe and the former USSR concerns the position of women. While governmental coercion has been greatly reduced and political systems have become much more open, the economic and political situation of women has deteriorated. First of all, the impact of economic depression has hit women harder than men. They have been the first to be laid off from work, and two-thirds of all officially registered employed workers are women; even more than in the Communist period they continue to find it difficult to achieve senior positions of leadership within the economy. Although they form 47 percent of the workforce, 48 percent in the state sector, they make up only a quarter of the workforce in the dynamic new private sector. An indication of the official place of women's issues in the new Russia is the response of Russian Labor Minister Melikian to questions about tackling the problem of unemployment among women: "Why should we employ women when men are out of work? It is better that men work and women take care of children and do housework. I don't think women should work when men are doing nothing."[7]

In the political sphere, the position of women has also declined dramatically. In the Soviet Union prior to the initiation of political reforms, women usually made up 30–35 percent of those in leadership positions in the Communist Party and in governmental bodies at the regional, republic, and federal levels, excluding the very top CPSU organs and the Council of Ministers. Women were also visible in upper-level positions in governmental ministries, even though the equality of women in the Soviet system was often more apparent than it was real. In the Supreme Soviet, elected with substantially more openness in 1989, however, only 5.4 percent of the deputies were women (57 of 1,063). In the first two elections to the newly created Duma in 1993 and 1995, the number of women who emerged victorious was well below 10 percent. Although women continue to dominate in numbers of employees in such governmental ministries as Finance and Public Health, very few are in leading positions.

In an attempt to ensure that issues of special importance to women—such as escalating violence against women (15,000 were murdered by their husbands or lovers in 1994), drastic declines in the quality of health care and in the availability of affordable childcare, skyrocketing unemployment, and related issues—a political party called Women of Russia was created to focus especially on these issues. The party generated only 4.6 percent of the popular vote in the parliamentary elections of December 1995 and elected only three candidates. Public opinion polls in Russia indicated that even a high percentage of women do not support the idea of women in positions of political leadership.

Summarizing the political situation of women in Russia, sociologist Galena G. Sillaste

emphasizes that political reforms and democratization in the former Soviet Union and Russia have provided broad political rights and freedoms for women and a real (not verbal and formal) abolition of sexual discrimination in all spheres of social life, but they have also resulted in the deliberate expulsion of women from power and political decision making.[8] Economic and social developments in Russia in the past few years have done little to change this situation.

RUSSIAN POLITICAL VALUES AND SOVIET POLITICAL CULTURE

In the midst of society-wide transitions that appear chaotic and unpredictable, the Russian population has been required to change its expectations of government and of the broader political environment. Just as political forces in Russia are required to contend with the difficulties of the triple transition from old methods of political, economic, and social orientation and organization, the population at large finds itself facing changes of monumental proportions that challenge the belief system, or political culture, that dominated the Soviet past. A political culture reflects the ideals, beliefs, and values that a people hold in common. It defines a people's attitudes toward authority, relations between the government and the governed, and the degree of trust accorded leaders and what they are permitted or not permitted to do. The degree of loyalty that a political system elicits will depend on the extent to which it is in accord with the dominant political culture.

However, certain reservations must be kept in mind. Various subcultures (regional, social, ethnic, religious) may be in conflict with the dominant political culture. St. Petersburg traditionally has represented somewhat different values from those accepted in Moscow. The numerous non-Russian nationalities have not necessarily shared the values and preferences of the Russians. Also

[7]Cited in Anatasiya Posadskaya, "Demokratiya minus zhenshchina—ne demokratiya," *Ogonëk,* no. 398 (1993), pp. 8–9.

[8]G. G. Sillaste, "Sotsiogendernye otnosheniya v period sotsial'noi transformatsii Rossii," *Sotsiologicheskie issledovaniya,* no. 3 (1994), pp. 15–22.

culture represents learned behavior; it is acquired, being transmitted from generation to generation, and is not biological or based on racial attributes. As learned behavior, cultural patterns and values can be changed over time; the degree and speed of such change will depend on circumstances and on a willingness to reappraise and modify existing values.

No people or political system can escape its past. Each people possesses a political tradition and fund of experience that influence its institutions, practices, values, and norms of political conduct. The Russian political experience reflects certain unique traits, issues, and problems that can be characterized as syndromes. The question under debate among analysts of contemporary Russian politics is the degree to which Russians are attracted to and supportive of authoritarian political institutions and leaders. Many believe that Russians lack most of the values that are essential for the effective functioning of political democracy—a sense of political efficacy, a willingness to compromise with those with different views, and so on. They note that the Communist successes in the elections of December 1995 and the tone of the political rhetoric and directives emerging from the political leadership—especially authoritarian in tone since the political rise of Vladimir Putin—belie the democratic institutions that have been created in Russia. They raise serious questions concerning the interaction of new and old methods of political behavior. However, other analysts argue that Russia has long possessed an alternative political culture that derived from community-based activism, and that Soviet totalitarianism did not represent continuity in Russian political traditions. Prospects for the growth and acceptance by the Russian population of the underlying attitudes and values associated with democracy are favorable, they maintain.

Although the answers to the argument concerning existing political culture in Russia are not self-evident, what is clear is that, for a stable democratic system to emerge in Russia, the peoples of Russia must accept and internalize the assumptions about politics and government that are necessary for a functioning democracy—

assumptions that diverge significantly from the Russian autocratic tradition that was, in the words of noted historian Robert V. Daniels, "reincarnated in Stalinism and perpetuated in Brezhnevism."[9] In his study of the concentration of power in the hands of the Russian presidency under Boris Yeltsin, Eugene Huskey also emphasizes the importance of the authoritarian legacy in the emergency of Russian political structures.

KEY RUSSIAN SYNDROMES

Closely associated with Russian political culture and central to an understanding of the patterns of political organization and behavior that have characterized Russia in the past are several persistent traits or key syndromes: (1) centralized power and absolutist rule; (2) truth seeking; (3) resistance, sectarianism, and anarchic tendencies; (4) alienation of the intelligentsia; (5) Russia's identity and its appropriation of foreign ways; and (6) pretense and mendacity. Let's look at each one in more detail.

Centralized Power and Absolutist Rule

Centralized power and absolutist rule form one of Russia's most persistent traits.[10] The Russian political tradition emerged from the Muscovite state, which developed an autocratic order originally headed by princes, one of whom, Ivan IV ("the Terrible"), adopted the title of tsar, a Russian version of *caesar*. The Muscovite state and its rulers gained an advantage over neighboring principalities by collaborating with the Mongol-

[9]Robert V. Daniels, *Is Russia Reformable? Change and Resistance from Stalin to Gorbachev* (Boulder, CO: Westview Press, 1988), p. 48.
[10]A perceptive effort to compare traditional patterns of Russian political behavior with those of the Soviet Union can be found in Edward L. Keenan, "Moscovite Political Folkways," *Russian Review* 15(2) (1986), pp. 115–181.

Tatar conquerors who had subjugated much of Eastern Europe in 1240. By serving as collectors of tribute and by being outwardly servile, the Muscovite princes succeeded in establishing a power base that enabled them to subjugate their neighbors, including Finnish peoples living to the east and north of Moscow. Muscovite princes learned much from the Mongols and Tatars regarding taxation, intelligence gathering, military organization, census taking, and the importance of the postal system and communications. Mongol rule gradually weakened, but it lasted nearly two and a half centuries until 1480.

The rulers of Muscovy were also influenced by the autocratic political system of the Eastern Roman (Byzantine) Empire, in which Orthodox Christianity was the state religion and the emperors posed as defenders of religious doctrine. Muscovy received Christianity from the early Rus', but Byzantium taught the Russians that the West (Rome) was heretical and not to be trusted. Orthodox Christianity also meant that Muscovy would develop in cultural isolation from the West. After Constantinople fell to the Turks in 1453, Muscovite rulers could depict themselves in the sixteenth century as the "Third Rome." As the successor of the first two Romes, both of which had fallen, and the only Orthodox Christian state free from Ottoman Turkish and Muslim domination, Muscovy allegedly was specially chosen. This sense of exclusiveness and self-satisfaction helped to motivate Muscovite expansionism and the urge to acquire an empire.

Russian political development was fated to adopt an autocratic pattern when Muscovy annexed the principality of Novgorod in 1478. Novgorod had been the most prominent Russian polity for three centuries prior to the emergence of Muscovy. It was an important commercial center, but it also had a unique political order. Novgorod developed as a republic with nonhereditary princes and with other elected officials. A popular assembly met in the marketplace, but actual power was exercised by a limited number of local magnates. If Novgorod had prevailed instead of Muscovy, Russian political culture might not have developed in the autocratic pattern of absolutist

rulers but would probably have assumed a republican form.

Absolutist rule in Muscovy was also made possible or even necessary by the steady territorial expansion of the Muscovite state. Muscovy is first referred to in the chronicles in 1147. By the fifteenth century it covered 15,000 square miles, but in the course of the subsequent four centuries it expanded approximately 570 times to an area of 8.5 million square miles by the end of the nineteenth century. The Muscovite state was renamed the Russian Empire in 1721 by Peter I ("the Great"). Empire building meant the subjugation of other peoples. The Volga Tatars were conquered in 1552, and within a century Siberia, with its alien peoples, was acquired. Eastern Ukraine came under Muscovite influence in 1654 as a result of a treaty of alliance against Poland between the Ukrainian Cossack state and the Muscovite tsar—the terms of which were then systematically violated by the Russians. The Baltic peoples (Estonians, Latvians, and Lithuanians) were annexed during the eighteenth century, as were the Belarusians, more than half the Poles, and the Crimean Tatars, along with the central and western Ukrainians. During the nineteenth century the Russian Empire annexed the Caucasus, Georgia, Armenia, Azerbaijan, Finland, and Turkestan (Central Asia). The end of the nineteenth century saw the empire seeking gains at the expense of a weakened China, in Manchuria especially, and in Korea—an effort that was thwarted as a result of Russia's military defeat at the hands of Japan in 1905.

Russian territorial expansionism, pursued on an unparalleled scale, could hardly have been accomplished without an autocratic political order. The fact that the Russian emperors ruled large numbers of alien subjects—the Russians were a minority of 43 percent in their own empire at the turn of the twentieth century—guaranteed the perpetuation of autocratic rule. The last emperor, Nicholas II, remained an autocrat even after the 1905 Revolution, when he was compelled to agree to the establishment of a weak legislative body, the Imperial Duma.

The idea of service to the ruler who personified the state was well established in the Russian political experience. Strong monarchs such as Ivan IV were able to keep the nobles (boyars) subordinate by making land ownership of estates dependent upon service to the state and unconditional obedience to the tsar. When the monarchs were weak personalities, the autocracy functioned through the bureaucracy, whose officials were just as arbitrary and demanding as the absolute monarch.

It is not surprising that the heavy weight of Russian autocratic rule doomed the brief experiment with democracy under the Provisional Government in 1917. Russians had failed to develop any effective restraints on autocratic power, and it was relatively easy for Lenin and his Bolsheviks to adapt the Russian tradition of centralism and absolutist rule to their own purposes. The Communist ruling class claimed the right to rule on the basis of its professed monopoly of philosophical truth, wisdom, justice, and moral good. The Communist Party assumed the role of a collective counterpart or successor to the Russian tsars and emperors, who in their claim to total power ruled on the basis of divine right. The Russian autocrats were said to be responsible to God and to their own conscience, whereas the Communist rulers claimed to be responsible only to "history" as understood in the Communist philosophy.

In the decade that has passed since the collapse of the Communist system in 1991, it has been evident that the roots of authoritarian political culture run deep in the Russian population. In the face of growing social and economic problems in post-Soviet Russia, a majority of the population has voiced its preference for strong and stable political leadership. President Putin has drawn effectively upon these views to gain widespread support for his rather authoritarian approach to restructuring Russia and dealing with its problems.

Truth Seeking

Truth seeking and the claim to possess truth have characterized the Russian understanding of political values. In Russia, political power has traditionally been wedded to ideology based on total solutions, sweeping assertions, absolute values, and the notion of official truth. The claim to possess truth and to be pursuing maximal goals in its name promoted a brand of unyielding politics that tended to reject moderation and compromise.[11] It also favored the adoption of "devil" theories of politics emphasizing enemies and "dark" and "impure" forces seeking to destroy Russia—behavior that has reemerged in Russia to explain the purported role of Western intelligence organizations and corporations in the collapse of the Soviet Union and the emergence of the problems facing Russia. In imperial Russia, the truth was embodied in the official Russian Orthodox Church, and it served as a major source of support for the autocratic political order, with the emperor serving as guardian of the faith. In the past decade the Orthodox Church has made serious efforts to reestablish its role in Russia and has been among the more xenophobic influences in Russian politics.

The official "truth" of the Soviet political system—Marxism-Leninism—represented different values from those of the tsarist regime; however, the notion of official truth remained a basic attribute of both regimes. The Russian philosopher Nikolai Berdyaev contended that the Russians are an "apocalyptic people" concerned with ultimate ends and total solutions and with the prophetic element in life. If this is the case, it is easier to understand why Marxism-Leninism could be accepted as the ideological basis of the Soviet system. Marxism-Leninism offered predictions in the guise of social science and depicted the ultimate triumph of good, as represented by the Communist Party, over evil. Social justice would supposedly triumph, and the Russians would serve as interpreters and guardians of the doctrine and could claim to be carrying out the will of history. Marxism-Leninism and its

---

[11]This point can be illustrated with the complaint of Gorbachev that "we do not yet have enough ethic of debate" and that some writers "tend to settle old scores with others or tag offensive labels on them." Mikhail Gorbachev, *Perestroika and New Thinking for Our Country and the Whole World* (New York: Harper and Row, 1987), p. 74.

vision of the future could claim to have universal application and to be internationalist in outlook. It had wider appeal abroad than the official truth of the Russian Empire and served to rationalize Russian imperial ambitions and expansionism in the Soviet period. Many of the tenets of the doctrine continue to attract widespread support, as the showing of the Communist Party in parliamentary and presidential elections has shown.

One of the problems that have faced reformers as they attempt to generate support for democratic and free-market ideals relates to the immensity of the economic and social problems facing Russia and the lack of familiarity of most Russians with the values associated with democracy. Moreover, the patent opportunism and corruption that have characterized Russian politics since 1991 have contributed to the weak societal enthusiasm for democratic reform and the market economy.

Resistance, Sectarianism, and Anarchy

Resistance, sectarianism, and anarchic tendencies have represented a reaction by the Russians to the harsh absolute rule of political centralism. There is much evidence to indicate that Russians have not submitted totally or unquestioningly to their rulers. Historically there has been a wide and deep gulf separating the rulers and the ruled. Authority has been distrusted and resisted when circumstances have permitted. The *veche* (popular assembly) in the pluralistic eastern Slavic society of Rus' in the pre-Mongol period opposed princes, especially in Kiev and Novgorod. Russia witnessed the great peasant revolts of Ivan Bolotnikov and Stenka Razin in the seventeenth century and Emelian Pugachev in the eighteenth century. However, Bolotnikov claimed to act in the name of the tsar and both Razin and Pugachev claimed to be true tsars come to reclaim their thrones from usurpers; none presented himself as a challenger to the existing order. In the nineteenth century the fierceness of Russian revolt prompted the greatest of Russia's poets, Aleksandr Pushkin, to characterize it as "senseless and ruthless." The twentieth century

saw the burning of the manor houses and the murder of estate owners and the bursting forth of peasant wrath during the revolutionary upheavals of 1917 that preceded the Bolshevik seizure of power.

Russian resistance is also evident in a rich tradition of religious sectarianism that flourished despite the existence of an official Russian Orthodox state church. The seventeenth century saw a great schism between the official church and the Old Ritualists (Old Believers), who refused to accept a revision of religious practices. Subsequently a variety of exotic sects emerged, including the *Dukhobory* (Spirit Fighters), who refused to accept political authority, perform military service, or pay taxes. In the Soviet period, various Protestant sects made their appearance in opposition to the regime's official atheism and the subordination of the Russian Orthodox Patriarchate to the Soviet rulers.

Russian interest in anarchism prompted Berdyaev to observe that anarchism was largely a Russian creation and that the Russians do not really like the state, but either meekly submit to it or rebel against it as circumstances dictate or permit. It is significant that such prominent Russians as Mikhail Bakunin, the novelist Leo Tolstoy, and Prince Peter Kropotkin contributed to the theory of anarchism. Bakunin's anarchism was violent and atheistic, based on "creative" destruction; Tolstoy's was nonviolent and religious; and Kropotkin's anarchic communism was based on mutual aid in place of the wage system. If Russians have had an inclination toward anarchism and resisting the state, as Berdyaev contends, the existence of harsh and repressive authoritarian systems in Russia becomes more understandable. The fear of anarchy may explain why Soviet rulers insisted on "moral political unity," and some current Russian leaders call for a return to strong central authority.

Alienation of the Intelligentsia

Alienation of the intelligentsia was a problem for both the tsarist imperial and Soviet Russian regimes. The term *intelligentsia* is one of the few Russian words to be adopted into foreign languages. It originally referred to the nineteenth-century "men of ideas" who criticized contemporary conditions on the basis of abstract ideas. In rejecting prevailing values, the intelligentsia became alienated from the Russian state, church, nation, and way of life and instead often embraced foreign ideas, including Marxism. The Soviet rulers created a large intelligentsia of specialists, but alienation persisted among political dissidents and persons who sought to emigrate. It is ironic that Svetlana Alliluyeva, the only daughter of the late Soviet dictator Joseph Stalin, defected in 1967, rejecting the Soviet system and its values and renouncing her membership in the Communist Party, as well as her Soviet citizenship.[12] The effort of Mikhail Gorbachev to co-opt the intelligentsia by allowing it greater freedom of expression was designed to obtain its support for his reforms and deal with its alienation.

Russia's Identity

Russia's identity and its appropriation of foreign ways have also contributed to its reliance on a severe and demanding political order. Russians have persistently debated the question of Russia's relationship to Europe and Asia, what Russia is, and whether or not it has some special historic mission to fulfill. The problem of Russia's identity was complicated by its efforts to subjugate and assimilate neighboring peoples and by the scale of its borrowing and appropriation of foreign technology beginning with the reign of Peter I. The Russian elite has contained many non-Russians or assimilated elements. Peter I recruited Baltic Germans to carry out his reforms and hired foreigners to develop a Russian navy. Many Russian explorers in the eighteenth and nineteenth centuries were actually Germans. The Russian ruling dynasty, known as the House of Romanov, became ethnically German after 1762 during the reign of Catherine II, a German princess, and her ill-fated husband, Peter III. Italians constructed much of the Kremlin, and Italians and other foreigners erected most of the imposing structures of the new capital of St. Petersburg. The Muscovite state, in its expansion and transformation into the multinational Russian Empire, developed an imperial consciousness prior to the emergence of a Russian national consciousness and thus created a persistent identity problem that is still evident today in the debates about the very nature of Russia and its orientation toward both Europe and Asia. As the noted philosopher Aleksandr Tsipko has argued, "without Kiev there can be no Russia in the old, *real,* sense of the word."[13]

Russia's heavy reliance on borrowing is reflected in the presence of large numbers of English, French, and German loan words in the Russian language as common nouns for household objects. All languages contain foreign loan words, but the degree of their presence in the Russian language is vivid testimony to the Russian ability to borrow and appropriate. Yet this practice and the Russian effort to dominate and assimilate non-Russian peoples have resulted in the need for an imposed identity—such as the notion of a "Soviet people" or the recent revival of the distinction between *Russkie* (ethnic Russians) as opposed to *Rossiiskie* (inhabitants of Russia)—and have posed the related threats of "contamination" and fragmentation. Russia's unity has been complex and synthetic, and its rulers have traditionally resorted to extreme measures in attempting to preserve it—as illustrated currently by the policies of President Putin in Chechnya.

Pretense and Mendacity

Pretense and mendacity have been employed to justify and maintain the political order and society. Fedor Dostoevsky, in an essay entitled "Something on Lying" (1873) published in his *Diary of a Writer,* posed the unusual question: "Why does everyone among us [in Russia] lie and

---

[12]See Svetlana Alliluyeva, *Only One Year* (New York: Harper and Row, 1969).

[13]Aleksandr Tsipko in *Komsomotskaya pravda,* January 14, 1992. For an extended discussion of the question of Russians' sense of identity see Alesander Yanov, *The Russian Challenge and the Year 2000* (Oxford: Basil Blackwell, 1987).

without exception?" The writer contended that lying was engaged in "out of hospitality" and for effect, noting that the truth is "for us too boring and prosaic, insufficiently poetic, too commonplace."[14] The reliance on pretense, deception, and self-deception was evident in the claims of Soviet political leaders, who for decades maintained that Soviet society was "superior" and that its political system under a party dictatorship was "democratic." The Soviet Union, based on coercion and territorial aggrandizement, was said to be "voluntary." Concealment was evident in such matters as the denial of the famines of 1932–1933 and 1947, official statistics on Soviet fatalities in World War II, the size of the Soviet military budget, the declining life expectancy of males, fatalities resulting from the Chernobyl nuclear catastrophe, the claim that there were budget surpluses when there were actually large deficits, and the inflated official exchange rate for the ruble in the absence of convertibility.

The revelations made by Nikita Khrushchev in his campaign against Stalin's dictatorship and by Gorbachev regarding his predecessors served to confirm the role of mendacity and pretense in Soviet politics. The Communist Party's reliance on resolutions and proclamations reflected a preference for verbal "solutions" and claims, with assertions being equated with achievement but actually reflecting problem avoidance. Aleksandr Yakovlev, who as an adviser to Gorbachev investigated the party's crimes and rehabilitated large numbers of victims, told the Twenty-eighth Party Congress, "Over the course of seventy years we have too frequently permitted ourselves to ignore everything that was not to our liking. Even today … we sometimes continue to deceive ourselves and play the hypocrite."[15] Ample evidence exists in post-Soviet Russia to indicate that

this attribute of Russian political culture still flourishes; official treatment of the effort to regain control over Chechnya militarily is a clear example of the effort to avoid full disclosure and even to deceive.

PSYCHOCULTURAL THEORIES

Theories of the Russian character, which have been used to explain Russian and Soviet political behavior, have been based on various hypotheses and on a limited amount of clinical psychological evidence. Some observers have noted contradictions in the Russian character evidenced in "mood swings" and in sudden shifts in attitude and behavior—as from activity to passivity, from euphoria to melancholy, or from friendship to hostility. The philosopher Berdyaev saw the Russian character as a "combination of opposites" including such contradictory traits as individualism and collectivism, nationalism and universalism, God-seeking and militant atheism, humility and impudence, and slavery and rebellion.[16] Similarly, Russians have been both attracted to and repelled by the West.

Other observers have noted the presence of guilt, hostility, and fear in Russians. Preoccupation with enemies (internal and external) and "dark forces" has played an important role in Russian life. The Soviet media readily denounced such "enemies" as capitalists, fascists, Trotskyites, Maoists, imperialists, neocolonialists, bourgeois nationalists, monopolists, revisionists, and dogmatists. In much the same way, current nationalists, including key figures in the Russian Orthodox Church, have emphasized the corrupting role of Western influence in Russia, the direct role of Western intelligence agencies in the downfall of Soviet power, and the current problems of Russia. Such allegations are indicative of the Russian tendency to blame their ills and failings on foreigners. Moreover, guilt feelings persisted in the Soviet practice of "criticism and self-criticism" and in the

[14]"Nechto o vran'ye," in Fedor M. Dostoevsky, *Polnoe sobranie sochinenii* (St. Petersburg: izd. A. F. Marska, 1895), vol. 9, pp. 320–322 and 330. Dostoevsky noted that lying was largely a male phenomenon in Russia and that women were "more serious" and less likely to engage in it. See also Ronald Hingley, *The Russian Mind* (New York: Scribner's, 1977), pp. 90–104.
[15]*Pravda,* July 4, 1990, p. 3.

[16]Nicolas Berdyaev, *The Russian Idea* (London: Geoffrey Bles, 1947), p. 3.

inability of Soviet citizens to fulfill all the demands made upon them by the authorities (including the numerous obligations incorporated into the 1977 Soviet Constitution).[17]

LENINISM—THE RUSSIAN VERSION OF MARXISM

An official state doctrine meant to explain social reality and provide a blueprint for the future, Marxism-Leninism lost its preeminent position with the collapse of the Soviet Union in 1991. For more than 70 years, however, it had inspired much Soviet organization and behavior and served as the political language of communication. For many it continues to serve these functions. The core of Soviet ideology was the Marxian critique of capitalism and the call for violent revolution by workers to replace capitalism with a stateless and classless society. Based on the writings of the German philosopher, historian, and social scientist Karl Marx, Marxism provided a doctrine that claimed to explain all of history and human behavior and to be "scientific" as well. Russian intellectuals under Lenin's leadership appropriated Marxism and modified it to suit Russian needs. Thus, the Soviet Union acquired an official ideology that can be said to have replaced the Russian Empire's state religion of Orthodox Christianity.

Marxism-Leninism as an ideology is a system of thought, a "world outlook" that attempts to explain or rationalize all of reality. It is a method of political analysis that offers a plan of action and a vision of the future. It acquired some of the characteristics of a sectarian or quasi-religious movement despite its claim to be scientific and its advocacy of militant atheism. It promised humanity a form of secular salvation and claimed to be the sole source of truth and ultimate knowledge. It required converts to master the Marxist-Leninist "scriptural" writings, as understood in their current interpretation, and to accept Communist Party discipline. In insisting upon ideological orthodoxy, party leaders employed the practice of condemning deviationist movements, which were the Communist counterpart of religious heresies. Leninists even made Lenin's embalmed body in the Red Square mausoleum an object of veneration comparable to a religious relic.

Tenets of Leninism

Although Lenin reinterpreted and developed the thought of Karl Marx (1828–1895), Leninism reflected the basic tenets of Marxism and its view of capitalism. Marxism provided a Communist analysis of capitalism rather than a clear blueprint for a Communist society. In the Communist version of capitalism and of precapitalist societies (feudalism and slaveholding societies), the class struggle is seen as the principal motive force. History evolves as the result of a dialectical conflict, which emphasizes the interdependence of all phenomena and objects, the centrality and irreconcilability of conflict in human existence, and the ultimate victory of Communist society social structures in human society.

Marxism has assumed different forms in various countries. Marx and Engels provided a general appraisal of the capitalism of their time, but they did not offer any specific advice concerning the political form that the Communist revolution would assume. Leninism provided not merely a Russian version of Marxism, but also a means by which Marxists could establish a Communist political order. The vehicle for this purpose was the party of professional revolutionaries established by Lenin. As early as 1902, in his booklet *What Is to Be Done?* Lenin advocated the formation of a unique type of elite political party composed of a limited number of

---

[17]These behavioral traits have been attributed originally to the traditional Russian patriarchal family, which is said to have bred tension between fathers and sons and to have produced a male personality type that was both domineering and servile in accordance with circumstance. For a discussion of various theories of the Russian character, see John S. Reshetar Jr., *The Soviet Polity: Government and Politics in the USSR*, 3rd ed. (New York: Harper and Row, 1989), pp. 33–44. On the neofascist and anti-Western tendencies within the Russian Orthodox Church, see Stephen D. Shenfield, *Russian Fascism: Traditions, Tendencies, Movements* (Armonk, NY: M. E. Sharpe, 2001), pp. 60–72.

dedicated, disciplined, tested, and trained professional Communists. The party was to be the vanguard of the working class and of the industrial proletariat. In practice, Lenin substituted his Communist (Bolshevik) Party for the working class because he distrusted the "spontaneity" of the masses. He established a new type of highly centralized party that was trained in conspiratorial methods and capable of acting unquestioningly under the leadership's direction.

Priority of the political struggle was a basic tenet of Leninism, largely because its founder warned against the "dangers" of having the workers settle for mere economic benefits and reform through trade unions and strikes. Leninism was also to give meaning to the term "dictatorship of the proletariat." The notion of the dictatorship of any ruling class is basic to Marxism-Leninism, whether it is the slaveholding class, the feudal lords, or bourgeois interests. In Marxism-Leninism, the economic order determines the political order, and each ruling class is said to use the instrument of the state and its laws to oppress and exploit. Although Marx had used the term "revolutionary dictatorship of the proletariat" in his writings (in his *Critique of the Gotha Program*), it was left to Lenin to establish the first one-party dictatorship in the name of the industrial working class. The dictatorship of the proletariat was really to be the dictatorship of Lenin's Bolsheviks for the purpose of completing the revolution by crushing the bourgeoisie and establishing socialism. Lenin could promise the "withering away" of the state in 1917 (in *State and Revolution*), but his successor, Stalin, would boast in June 1930 that the Soviet dictatorship of the proletariat was "the strongest and most powerful of all state authorities." He justified the Soviet dictatorship in dialectical terms "for the purpose of preparing the conditions *for* the withering away of state authority."[18]

Leninism was also characterized by tactical flexibility, which accepted the notion of temporary retreat for the purpose of future gains—as in the conclusion of a peace treaty with the Central

Powers in 1918 at any price and the granting of concessions to small-scale capitalism associated with the New Economic Program of 1921 as a means of reviving the war-damaged economy.

Lenin's theory of imperialism was developed hastily in 1916 from the writings of others in an effort to explain why World War I had occurred and why most Socialists were supporting their countries' war efforts. In *Imperialism, the Highest Stage of Capitalism,* Lenin argued that a new type of "finance capital" (as opposed to industrial capital) had arisen as a result of the merger and concentration of banking and industry. It exported capital abroad because of domestic stagnation, in order to benefit from abundant raw materials and cheap labor. Capital was reportedly exported because of the domestic stagnation that resulted from the growth of monopolies, declining profits, and shrinking markets at home. The export of capital led to colonialism, and the competition for colonies and redivision of the spoils were said to lead to military alliances and wars.

Lenin's theory of imperialism was based on very limited historical evidence and did not fully explain the phenomenon of war. However, Lenin used it to attempt to explain why proletarian revolutions were not occurring in the most industrially developed countries, as they were supposed to occur according to the teachings of Marx and Engels. According to Lenin, the increased profits from colonialism made it possible for the capitalist ruling class to "buy off" important parts of the working class with high wages and other concessions, thereby creating "privileged sections" that became bourgeois in outlook (a "labor aristocracy"), and postponing or even preventing proletarian revolution led by Communists. He concluded that Communist-led revolutions were more likely to occur in economically underdeveloped countries with no industrial proletariat.

Leninism was subsequently modified by Lenin's successors—but always in the name of Leninism. For more than seven decades, Marxism-Leninism was the official ideology of the Soviet Union, and dialectical materialism was the officially recognized philosophy. Marx and Engels were acknowledged in the Soviet Union, but the Soviet rulers suppressed their many statements critical of imperial Russia.

---

[18]I. V. Stalin, *Sochineniya,* vol. 12, pp. 369–370 (Moscow: Gosudarstvennoe izdatelstvo, 1949).

Relevance of Marxism-Leninism

From the very beginning there were those who raised many questions concerning the validity of Marxism-Leninism. Because it reduced all of human history to several stages and based them on a materialistic theory of history, Marxism-Leninism is seen as oversimplifying and neglecting the importance of nonmaterial factors such as sex, nationalism, and religion in human behavior. Critics also pointed out that, while claiming to be a science, Marxism-Leninism has also served to make moral judgments and to declare one social class evil and another the source of virtue. Moreover, as many critics have noted, virtually all of the predictions of Marxism-Leninism have been inaccurate; for example, neither the industrial proletariat nor the middle class has become impoverished, and nationalism did not disappear.

Yet for Soviet rulers, Marxism-Leninism was more than a philosophy or theory, since it served to justify and legitimize their system of rule. For seven decades Soviet leaders sang the praises of their ideology, as Gorbachev did at the Twenty-seventh Party Congress in 1986:

> Marxism-Leninism is the greatest revolutionary worldview. It has substantiated the most humane objective that humankind has ever set for itself—the creation of a just social system on earth. It points the way to the scientific study of the development of society as a single, law-governed process in all of its vast many-sidedness and contradictoriness, and it teaches [us] to understand correctly the nature and interaction of economic and political forces, to select the correct directions, forms and methods of struggle, and to feel self-confident at the decisive turning points in history.[19]

So long as the Soviet system appeared to function successfully, the adherents of Marxism-Leninism could claim that their ideology was correct. They could also find confirmation of it in the competition for markets between capitalist countries, in the growth of corporate mergers and "monopolies," strike activity, bankruptcies, business failures, inflation, and unemployment in capitalist countries.

The ideology was the source of much Soviet political practice. The Communist Party used it to justify its claim to a monopoly of political power and its role as the chosen instrument of "history" and the source of official truth. It also justified by means of the concept of "socialist internationalism" Soviet domination over other Communist states and parties. Ideological requirements dictated many Soviet government policies: the nationalization of all land, state ownership of the economy, collectivization of agriculture, forced industrialization, the refusal to permit even small private business enterprises based on hired labor (as distinct from cooperatives), and the global confrontation with the United States and other capitalist countries. The teaching of "scientific atheism" as an obligatory subject in Soviet schools was based on Marxism-Leninism. Ideology prompted the Communist Party to dictate standards in literature and in the arts and to influence the writing of historians and social scientists. In the past, ideological tenets even dictated acceptable findings in the natural sciences. Censorship was justified by the Marxist-Leninist view that ideas are important and have consequences.

Leninism in Retreat

Although Mikhail Gorbachev, as party leader, continued to profess belief in Marxism-Leninism, he ceased quoting from Lenin's writings because they provided no prescriptions for the Soviet malaise and were incompatible with the market economy that Gorbachev claimed to be establishing. Marxism-Leninism, which for decades had suffered from increasing irrelevance to sociopolitical and economic reality in the USSR, came under attack in the intense discussion prompted by Gorbachev's reformist policies. The acknowledgment by Gorbachev of widespread failure on the part of his predecessors contributed further to discrediting the ideology.

Statues of Lenin, regarded as the symbol of the totalitarian dictatorship, were removed by democratically elected non-Communist officials, initially in the Baltic states, Georgia, and western

---

[19]*Pravda,* February 23, 1986. Gorbachev's views on the importance of Marxism-Leninism permeate the argument presented in his book *Perestroika.*

Ukraine, but subsequently elsewhere. In some jurisdictions the police and military guarded statues of Lenin in a futile effort to defend an old and exhausted ideology that was incapable of providing solutions to the problems that it had created. Indeed, in an effort to solicit popular support, Communist leaders abandoned the blatant propagation of militant atheism as state policy and sought to co-opt religious leaders and appear with them in public. Marxism-Leninism had been able to claim credibility only so long as the Soviet leadership was able to demonstrate some degree of competence in problem solving and claim that the ideology had a certain relationship to reality. As the Soviet economy deteriorated and the society became more fragmented, the claims made for the ideology proved to be vacuous and irrelevant. The abandonment of Marxism-Leninism by the East European countries in 1989 and also by Angola, Ethiopia, Nicaragua, South Yemen, and other states also served to discredit it.

Russians who desired to perpetuate the empire and the rule over other peoples had found Marxism-Leninism a convenient artifice for justifying their dominance and claiming to be adherents of internationalism. However, the inadequacies of the ideology made it necessary for Gorbachev in 1991 to undertake another revision of the 1986 revised Communist Party program "to include in our arsenal of ideas all of the wealth of the fatherland and world Socialist and democratic thought."[20] But the swift pace of events nullified this effort. Russians, in their claim to an empire, have lacked a suitable replacement for Marxism-Leninism, although Russian security concerns and the welfare of the ethnic Russians living outside the Russian Federation have been used as a justification for reestablishing the linkages broken in 1991. (Of the 25 millions ethnic Russians who found themselves outside the borders of the Russian Federation in December 1991, only an estimated 10 percent had returned to Russia by the end of 1996.)

Gennadi Zyuganov and other Communists have succeeded in selecting and modifying portions of the old dogma that seem to apply to the current problems of Russia and implied calls for reinstituting some of the old imperial order. Most importantly, they have married elements of the old ideology to Russian nationalism. While neither the democrats nor the radical nationalists have developed a message that gives hope to the demoralized population of Russia, Zyuganov and the new Communist Party emphasize both a new Russian patriotism and a call for social equity. They are not clear on whether the state should renationalize those parts of the economy that have been privatized. Rather, they argue for guarantees of income and living standard and a more equitable distribution of income in Russia. Yet in advocating social guarantees, they also cynically advocate subsidies from an empty state treasury.

Marxism-Leninism did not die in 1991, as so many in Russia and the West declared. Rather, it continues to have a strong hold on a substantial portion of the population and even tends to shape the way that its opponents conceptualize reality. But the segment of the population that so strongly supported the Communists in the 1995 elections is aging, and the appeal of Zyuganov's party in the parliamentary elections of 1999 dropped to 24 percent of the votes. Since Putin's rise to power, the attractiveness of the Communists has weakened further. In the 2000 presidential contest, Zyuganov was a distant second behind Putin.

Thinking Critically

1. Compare the major features of the tsarist political system with those of the communist period. To what extent do they prepare, or hinder, Russia's current attempt to create a democratic political system?
2. What relevance has geography had for the history of the Russian people and their political systems?
3. What are the major elements of Russian political culture as it evolved in both the tsarist and the communist periods?
4. What is the relevance of "imperialism" in Russians' sense of their own identity?
5. What is the relevance of Marxism-Leninism for an understanding of the current Russian political system?

---

[20]*Izvestiya,* July 26, 1991, p. 2.

KEY TERMS

Bolsheviks *(363)*
cadres *(371)*
Communist Party of the Soviet Union
     (CPSU) *(362, 372)*
intelligentsia *(372)*
mafia *(362, 372)*
Marxism-Leninism *(376, 380, 383)*
Muscovite state *(374, 375)*
nomenklatura *(362, 371)*
Novgorod *(375)*
Russian Empire *(361, 366)*
soviet *(sovet) (363)*
triple transition *(363)*

FURTHER READINGS

Anderson, Thornton. *Russian Political Thought: An Introduction* (Ithaca, NY: Cornell University Press, 1967).

Avrich, Paul. *Russian Rebels, 1600–1800* (New York: Schocken, 1972).

Berdyaev, Nicolas. *The Russian Idea* (London: Geoffrey Bles, 1947).

Bremmer, Ian, and Ray Taras, eds. *Nations and Politics in the Soviet Successor States* (Cambridge: Cambridge University Press, 1991).

Brown, Archie, and Jack Gray, eds. *Political Culture and Political Change in Communist States* (New York: Holmes and Meier, 1979).

Carrère d'Encausse, Hélène. *The End of the Soviet Empire: The Triumph of the Nations* (New York: Basic Books, 1993).

Conquest, Robert. *The Great Terror: A Reassessment* (New York: Oxford University Press, 1990).

Cracraft, James, and Daniel Rowlands, eds. *Architectures of Russian Identity: 1500 to the present* (Ithaca: Cornell University Press, 2003).

Daniels, Robert V. *The End of the Communist Revolution* (London: Routledge, 1993).

Dmytryshyn, Basil. *USSR: A Concise History,* 4th ed. (New York: Scribner's, 1984).

Evtuhov, Catherine, et al. *A History of Russia: Peoples, Legends, Events, Forces* (Boston: Houghton Mifflin, 2004).

German, Tracey C. *Russia's Chechen War* (London: Routledge, 2003).

Hunczak, Taras, ed. *Russian Imperialism: From Ivan the Great to the Revolution* (New Brunswick, NJ: Rutgers University Press, 1974).

Huskey, Eugene. *Presidential Power in Russia* (Armonk, NY: M. E. Sharpe, 1999).

Kaiser, Robert J. *The Geography of Nationalism in Russia and the USSR* (Princeton, NJ: Princeton University Press, 1994).

Kirkow, Peter. *Russia's Provinces: Authoritarian Transformation versus Local Autonomy?* (Houndmills, UK: Macmillan, 1998).

Lewin, Moshe. *Russia, USSR, Russia: The Drive and Drift of a Superstate* (New York: New Press, 1995).

Lieven, Dominic. *Empire: The Russian Empire and Its Rivals* (New Haven, CT: Yale University Press, 2000).

Lynch, Dov. *Russian Peacekeeping Strategies in the CIS: The Cases of Moldova, Georgia, and Tajikistan* (Houndmills, UK: Macmillan; New York: St. Martin's, 2000).

Meyer, Alfred G. *Leninism* (Cambridge, MA: Harvard University Press, 1957; reprint, Boulder, CO: Westview Press, 1986).

Nove, Alec. *The Soviet Economic System,* 3rd ed. (Winchester, MA: Allen and Unwin, 1986).

Petro, Nicolai N. *The Rebirth of Russian Democracy: An Interpretation of Political Culture* (Cambridge, MA: Harvard University Press, 1995).

Pipes, Richard. *The Formation of the Soviet Union: Communism and Nationalism, 1917–1923,* rev. ed. (Cambridge, MA: Harvard University Press, 1964).

Pipes, Richard. *Russia under the Old Regime* (2nd ed. New York: Penguin, 1995).

Reddaway, Peter, and Dmitri Glinski. The *Tragedy of Russia's Reforms: Market Bolshevism against Democracy* (Washington, DC: United States Institute of Peace Press, 2001).

Riasanovsky, Nicholas V. *A History of Russia,* 7th ed. (New York: Oxford University Press, 2005).

Rumer, Boris. *Soviet Central Asia: "A Tragic Experiment"* (Winchester, MA: Unwin Hyman, 1989).

Rywkin, Michael. *Moscow's Muslim Challenge,* 2nd ed. (Armonk, NY: M. E. Sharpe, 1990).

Shatz, Marshall S. *Soviet Dissent in Historical Perspective* (New York: Cambridge University Press, 1980).

Treadgold, Donald, ed. *Twentieth-Century Russia,* 7th ed. (Boulder, CO: Westview Press, 1989).

Tucker, Robert C., ed. *Political Culture and Leadership in Soviet Russia* (New York: Norton, 1987).

White, Stephen, et al., eds. *Developments in Central and East European Politics 3* (New York: Palgrave Macmillan, 2003).

B. POLITICAL PROCESSES AND INSTITUTIONS

The Communist Party of the Soviet Union (CPSU) enjoyed a legal monopoly of political power from the establishment of the Soviet political system in 1917–1918 until it formally relinquished that monopoly in 1990. In the aftermath of the unsuccessful coup of August 19–21, 1991, by several top political leaders and part of the military and the security police, the CPSU experienced a precipitous collapse with the resignation of Mikhail Gorbachev as its general secretary, his dissolution of the Central Committee on August 24, the suspension of all party activity, and the confiscation by the governments of most of the republics of its real property and other resources. For over seven decades the CPSU had shaped the institutions and political practices of the Soviet system. It also brought it to its deplorable condition in the 1980s and to its final collapse.

The transformation from an absolutist dictatorial party to a beleaguered political dinosaur, stubbornly seeking to retain its leading role while steadily losing credibility, can be understood in terms of the CPSU's development and its methods of operation. It had emerged from the small Bolshevik wing of the All-Russian Social Democratic Labor Party (RSDLP), founded by Vladimir Ilyich Lenin. While in exile in 1898 for his involvement in establishing the party, Lenin developed a plan for organizing it more effectively, and after completing his sentence in 1900 he joined several emigrés in Western Europe in establishing a revolutionary newspaper, *Iskra* (The Spark).

Lenin planned to have the newspaper published abroad and smuggled into Russia for the purpose of developing a leadership that could be used to recruit members for his conspiratorial underground party of tested, dedicated, and disciplined professional revolutionaries. At the second RSDLP Congress, held in Brussels and London in 1903, a momentous division developed between Lenin's Bolsheviks and the more moderate Mensheviks. The division centered on such issues as the size of the party, membership requirements, and centralism in its organization. Lenin favored a smaller party and a more rigid definition of membership qualifications and demanded complete centralism and denial of local autonomy. Contrary to the Jewish Marxists in the party, he opposed the notion of a party organized along ethnic lines and consisting of separate nationality groups.

Other issues that later divided the Bolsheviks and Mensheviks included disagreement about retaining an illegal underground organization after the 1905 Revolution. While Lenin favored the use of both legal and illegal means to achieve revolutionary goals, the Mensheviks advocated greater reliance on legal and open forms of activity. In general, the Mensheviks were willing to let the bourgeois revolution and the development of capitalism in the Russian Empire run its course, whereas Lenin was very impatient and wished to accelerate the revolutionary process. To a large extent the disagreement between the two factions was over methods and tactics rather than goals. All efforts to heal the widening gulf between the Bolsheviks and Mensheviks failed. Lenin maintained his separate Bolshevik organization and factional treasury and heaped scorn on the Mensheviks, his fellow Marxists, denouncing them as "Liquidators" (for wanting to liquidate the underground party organization) and opportunists. The break became complete in January 1912 when Lenin held a conference of his followers (with only 14 voting delegates) in Prague. He formed a new central committee, declared his conference to be the "supreme party body," and designated himself leader of the "RSDLP (of Bolsheviks)."

However, Bolshevism was not a fully united faction, since Lenin had disagreements with his closest followers. These disagreements persisted even after the establishment of the Soviet regime and throughout the first ten years after the Revolution. Lenin was opposed by leftist Bolsheviks on the issue of concluding a peace treaty with the Central Powers in March 1918; the leftists wanted to conduct a revolutionary war, even though Russia lacked an effective army and was likely to be overpowered by German troops. Others opposed Lenin's decision to hire bourgeois specialists, especially tsarist military officers, and to create a standing army. The Democratic Centralist Opposition criticized the development of a party bureaucracy and the appointment (rather than election) of party officials. The Workers' Opposition was dissatisfied about the influx of nonproletarian elements into the party—which in their view had ceased to be a workers' organization. In May 1921 at the Tenth Party Congress, Lenin took measures to outlaw all such oppositionist groups by adopting a formal ban on factions. This action, which failed to eliminate factions, was followed by a purging of the party membership that resulted in the expulsion of 170,000 members, most of whom were seen as careerists.

PARTY LEADERSHIP

The Communist Party of the Soviet Union had remarkably few leaders when compared with European democratic countries or the United States. During more than 70 years only seven men held the top leadership position. Lenin was unique as the party's founder; he never held the position of first (or general) secretary that would become the top political position in the USSR, but each of his successors headed the Secretariat. Originally the Secretariat was regarded as a service organization charged with keeping the party's records, but Stalin converted it into a powerful vehicle for his personal dictatorship, and it eventually became the principal means for achieving ultimate power in the Soviet political system. Joseph Stalin became general secretary in 1922 and, after Lenin's death two years later, ruled until his own death in 1953. He used the Secretariat and the Central Committee administrative apparatus to reward followers and punish opponents. Lenin, during his final illness, called for Stalin's removal from the post in January 1923, but his "Testament" was suppressed in the Soviet Union for more than 30 years.

Lenin established the Soviet security police, originally known as the *Cheka* and eventually as the KGB, in late 1917 to deal with opponents to his regime both inside and outside the country. Stalin would expand and use this instrument as one of the pillars of his cruel and bloody dictatorship. Lenin also provided Stalin with the organizational means of disposing of political opponents by outlawing factions and conducting purges of the party's membership. Nonetheless, Stalin had to wage a fierce power struggle from 1923 until 1927, first against Leon Trotsky, then against the Left Opposition headed by Grigorii Zinoviev and Lev Kamenev, and finally against the Right Opposition led by Nikolai Bukharin. Stalin first allied with the Right of Nikolai Bukharin and others who favored greater economic concessions to the peasantry, a slower rate of industrialization, and a continuation of the moderate New Economic Program (NEP), introduced by Lenin in 1921. After ousting Trotsky and the Left, Stalin adopted their program of centralization of the economy and rapid forced industrialization and defeated his erstwhile allies of the Right. He thus proved to be a master at dissimulation and at creating a party apparatus that became his personal political machine.

Stalin's name is correctly associated with full-blown totalitarian rule in the Soviet Union and the attempt to have the Soviet state equate itself with the totality of society and with control over all aspects of life. He employed terror and blood purges on a massive scale, established a huge network of forced-labor camps in which millions perished, and embarked on a program of forced industrialization and collectivization of agriculture which, in turn, resulted in famine and additional millions of deaths. The justification for this totalitarianism was social discipline so that the process of socialist development could be speeded up. Rapid economic growth was based on deprivation and forced savings and on the lives of tens of millions of Soviet citizens.

Besides living in great fear and personal insecurity, Stalin's subjects were required to praise his wisdom and genius. He proclaimed the establishment of socialism in the Soviet Union in 1936 and made himself the supreme authority in ideological matters. Under Stalin the central party institutions ultimately declined in importance and were replaced by his personal secretariat and the secret police. In addition to being repressive, Stalin's rule was socially conservative in making divorce extraordinarily difficult and in banning abortions while coming to terms with the Russian Orthodox Church during World War II, and favoring Russian nationalism at the expense of the non-Russian nationalities.

During the 30 years that he ruled the Soviet Union, Stalin presided over a profound socioeconomic transformation of the country. He eliminated whatever capitalism remained when he took power; he pushed industrialization and urbanization, led the country through the devastations of World War II against Nazi Germany (when more than an estimated 20 million Soviet citizens perished), and created a massive military machine after World War II with which to challenge the United States for global dominance.

Stalin's death in March 1953 ended his ruthless and arbitrary dictatorship. Following the arrest and execution of Lavrenti Beria, who had headed Stalin's repressive secret police, and a period of collective leadership of several senior party officials, a power struggle ensued in which Nikita S. Khrushchev, who had replaced Stalin as first secretary, became the head of government. In February 1956, at the Twentieth Party Congress, Khrushchev, himself a longtime lieutenant of Stalin, launched an attack on Stalin's system of rule in a "secret speech" delivered at a dramatic late-night session, in which the dead dictator was depicted as an evil psychopath. The criticism of Stalinism (which Khrushchev called the "cult of personality") was accompanied by a fresh political style, with Khrushchev traveling about the country, offering impromptu statements and advice, and permitting some relaxation of the rigid censorship. Khrushchev also revived the various central bodies of the party, including the Congress and the Central Committee. Instead of physically eliminating political rivals, Khrushchev had them forcibly retired with a pension paid for by their silence.

Khrushchev attempted a variety of reforms affecting economic policy and administrative reorganization. He virtually eliminated the reliance on indiscriminate mass terror and initiated an increase in popular involvement in government, although the basic dictatorial and coercive nature of the system remained, as his reinvigorated attacks on religion indicated. He also oversaw the emergence of the Soviet Union

as a world power, by emphasizing the development of a blue-water navy, strengthening the Soviet nuclear missile arsenal, and expanding Soviet political, military, and economic commitments to many of the newly independent states of the third world. Unlike Stalin, he traveled abroad extensively. Khrushchev's domestic and foreign politics, his efforts to replace party officials, and his political style resulted in considerable instability and opposition and led to his abrupt ouster on October 14, 1964, by his associates, most of whom he had elevated to high office.

The plotters who removed Khrushchev in a palace coup formed a collective leadership with Leonid I. Brezhnev, Khrushchev's former protégé, as first secretary of the party. The new oligarchy repealed Khrushchev's major administrative and economic reforms and criticized him and his policies. As part of the effort to emphasize discipline and ideological orthodoxy both inside and outside the party, it substantially toned down his anti-Stalin campaign, partially rehabilitated Stalin's reign, and raised a monument over the dictator's grave (Khrushchev had removed Stalin's embalmed body from Lenin's Red Square mausoleum in October 1961). His former associates and lieutenants treated Khrushchev as an "unperson." His numerous published speeches were withdrawn from circulation, and he was denied a state funeral and burial near the Kremlin Wall when he died in September 1971.

Brezhnev assumed Stalin's title of general, rather than first, secretary of the party in 1976, although he could not acquire Stalin's powers. Brezhnev reaffirmed political centralism by restoring a large number of central government ministries, but he did not become head of government, as Khrushchev had. The general secretary became chief of state, largely a ceremonial position, in June 1977 and also had a new constitution adopted in that year. As party leader, Brezhnev sought a consensus in the Soviet oligarchy and tried to obtain prior approval for his actions, thus avoiding Khrushchev's method of publicly advocating highly controversial policies prior to any high-level discussion. As a result of the search for consensus, decision making under Brezhnev became slower and more cumbersome, and needed reforms were neglected.

In the international sphere, Brezhnev continued the expansion of the Soviet role and, by the mid-1970s, the USSR reached the maximum extent of both its military power vis-à-vis the West and its involvement in the developing world. The later years of Brezhnev's rule, called "the period of stagnation" by Gorbachev, witnessed a considerable downturn of economic growth and a deterioration of living conditions for most Soviet citizens. The refusal to move away from the Stalinist approach to economic management meant continued inefficiency in the use of the natural and human resources of the country.

Brezhnev died in November 1982. However, the oligarchy of aged party officials who still dominated the Soviet political system was unwilling to face the realities of the problems facing the country or to turn to the next generation of potential leaders. Rather, two aging and ill leaders followed in succession before the selection in March 1985 of Mikhail Gorbachev as first secretary of the party. Yuri Andropov, a party official who for 15 years had headed the security police (KGB), replaced Brezhnev. In addition to his experience in the security police, Andropov had served as Soviet ambassador to Hungary (where he oversaw the suppression of the Hungarian rebellion in 1956) and as a CPSU secretariat official responsible for relations with East European Communist parties from 1957 to 1967. As KGB chief, he had intensified both overt and covert Soviet foreign intelligence operations and employed repressive measures against political dissidents at home. As would befit a security police chief, Andropov attempted to deal with flagging economic production and growing social problems by emphasizing discipline and order and by launching an anticorruption campaign within the party and governmental apparatus. Andropov's brief tenure of only 15 months as general secretary ended with his death in February 1984, after he had disappeared from public view for nearly six months because of illness.

Konstantin Chernenko, at the age of 72, succeeded Andropov. His election probably resulted in part from the inability of two rivals, Mikhail Gorbachev and Grigori Romanov, to obtain sufficient support. His election was the last collective act of the gerontocratic "old guard," and it pro-

vided a respite for officials threatened by Andropov's anticorruption campaign. Chernenko's poor health limited his tenure to 13 months—a period used to advantage by his successor, Mikhail Sergeyevich Gorbachev.

The election of Mikhail Gorbachev as general secretary on March 11, 1985, represented an important leadership change. Relatively young at age 54, Gorbachev would initiate needed reforms. He had become a party member while a student at the age of 21. From 1955 (when he graduated from the Moscow State University's faculty of law) until 1978, his career was confined entirely to his native Stavropol Territory (*krai*), north of the Caucasus Mountains. He first served in the local Communist youth organization and in 1963 assumed the first of several posts in the territory's Communist Party organization. In 1970 at the age of 39 he became the first secretary of the Stavropol Party Committee, a post that entitled him to Central Committee membership. Unlike his predecessors, Gorbachev had no experience in any of the non-Russian republics—a distinct disadvantage in dealing with troubling nationality issues that would later test his leadership abilities. He also had limited experience in Moscow, having served there for less than seven years before becoming general secretary. As a Secretariat member, he acquired full membership in the Politburo in 1980.

Gorbachev proved to be an articulate, shrewd, and reasonably sophisticated leader. In his career he also benefited from some fortunate circumstances, including friendship with Andropov, also a native of Stavropol. Although he had significant abilities, Gorbachev obtained the post of general secretary almost by default. His two principal rivals were Central Committee Secretary Grigori Romanov and Moscow Secretary Viktor Grishin. Romanov was a weak contender because of various indiscretions, lack of polish, and inexperience and ineffectiveness in foreign policy. Grishin, who had arranged Chernenko's election as general secretary, was vulnerable because of his age and corruption in the large Moscow party organization that he headed.

Gorbachev also had the advantage of organizing and presiding over the Twenty-seventh Party Congress in February 1986, asserting his leadership there and in summit meetings with President Ronald Reagan in Geneva, Reykjavik, Washington, and Moscow. His vigorous but controversial reform efforts prompted him to publish a book *Perestroika: New Thinking for Our Country and the World* (Harper and Row, 1987). Designed to appeal to foreign readers, the book was also available to the Soviet public. Although less candid than some of the speeches on which the book drew, the work reflected his determination to make the Soviet system more effective. Yet Gorbachev's leadership style, policies, and reorganizational efforts also elicited uncertainty, skepticism, and resistance among critics who were alarmed by rapid change. The need for change and "new thinking" meant that the Soviet system confronted very serious difficulties. Gorbachev issued a revised version of the 1961 Party Program (a response to the many extravagant claims and unfulfilled promises made by Khrushchev), and enhanced his powers in October 1988 by assuming the chairmanship of the Supreme Soviet and then by establishing for himself the presidency of the USSR.

THE FAILED MODEL

The Soviet political and governmental system was based on the Leninist-Stalinist model that, according to the conventional wisdom of many observers, would be able to perpetuate itself. Its principal components were the mass membership CPSU and its auxiliary, the Leninist League of Communist Youth (*Komsomol*), which was to serve the party as a ready recruiting and training ground for young members. The CPSU apparatus (staffed by generalists, usually with specialized technical training and a narrow educational experience) operated through republic, province (*oblast*), district (*raion*), and city party committees. The more than 3,000 district party committees were directed by 122 province party committees and, in turn, supervised the more than 440,000 primary party organizations (p.p.o.) that were charged with carrying out party directives in factories, collective and state farms, educational institutions, government ministries, military units, embassies abroad, and housing developments.

The p.p.o. was charged with attempting to promote productivity, reduce waste, and meet output quotas. It also organized campaigns and mass meetings to mobilize public opinion in accordance with party directives and provided information for superior party bodies, serving as their eyes and ears. It enlisted new members, supervised their training, and expelled members (with the approval of the district or city party committee to which it was subordinate).

Advancement was based on a partisan patronage system known as the *nomenklatura,* representing the lists of positions in all institutions and enterprises that could be filled only with the approval of the responsible CPSU (territorial) committee—each at its own level—from lists of approved prospective candidates. Promotion under this system generally depended more on compliance and acceptability to party officials than on the competence of candidates. Acquaintance, connections, and verbal support for party positions tended to determine advancement. Party dominance was also based on the administrative-command economy that established and enforced economic priorities and utilized scarcities to reward the faithful and bind them to the system.

The Partocracy

The Soviet political system was aptly termed a "partocracy"—a system of rule by and in the interests of a single political party that Lenin had immodestly deemed to be "the intelligence, honor, and conscience of our epoch."[21] The partocracy functioned either through an individual dictator, like Lenin or Stalin, or by means of an oligarchy (a collective dictatorship) consisting of a small group of men who comprised the Politburo and Secretariat of the CPSU Central Committee.

The Party Congress held every five years elected the Central Committee, as the parent body. The Central Committee was authorized "to direct all party activities and local party bodies" in the lengthy intervals between party congresses but

---

[21]V. I. Lenin. *Polnoe sobranie sochinenii,* 5th ed. (Moscow Gospolitizdat, 1962), vol. 34, p. 93.

would usually meet only twice a year because of its large size. In its place the Politiburo (political bureau or "executive committee") served as the Soviet Union's supreme policy-making body; it held weekly meetings and usually consisted of 11 or 12 voting members and half as many (nonvoting) candidate members. The chief oligarch in this body was the CPSU general secretary, who was elected by the Central Committee. He headed its Secretariat, a collective body that varied in size and was responsible for the functioning of the various administrative departments of the CPSU apparatus. These departments were concerned with the various sectors of the Soviet economy and with personnel matters, as well as the supervision of science, education and culture, the media, the security police, the courts, prosecuting agencies and the legal profession, foreign policy, and relations with foreign Communist parties. In effect, the departments of the Secretariat oversaw and regularly meddled in the activities of the parallel and larger governmental bureaucracy. The Secretariat also administered the party's central fund, controlled its press organs and journals, and was responsible for placing personnel in both party and governmental positions.

The CPSU had its own central bureaucracy with headquarters in the center of Moscow. The entire CPSU administrative apparatus had approximately 250,000 full-time officials and employees of 4,625 territorial party committees at various levels. Prior to 1991 it also had the full-time services, at no cost, of secretaries and officials of 52,000 larger p.p.o.'s. These officials remained on the payrolls of enterprises but did no productive work, instead distributing Communist propaganda among the workers, holding endless meetings, and often interfering with management or colluding with it in various forms of corruption.

The Reckoning

According to conventional wisdom, the partocracy would attract the "best people" and its longevity would be assured by the self-perpetuating oligarchy. Marxism-Leninism would provide answers and solutions to its problems. The massive Soviet governmental and economic bureaucracy, backed by the security police and the

military, would muddle through by means of sheer weight and omnipresence. However, the agonizing and seemingly endless "moment of truth" that Gorbachev was compelled to initiate in 1985–1986 was a consequence of profound systemic failure.

In trying to explain what went wrong, we can note that Marxism-Leninism promoted closed minds and a form of rote learning that, combined with Russian self-satisfaction and complacency, produced a very debilitating condition. Under the aging Brezhnev oligarchy, many Soviet citizens could be deceived into believing that the Soviet Union was an advanced society representing "developed socialism" with a viable and advanced economic system. Information that did not fit this image—such as rising infant mortality rates and rampant environmental pollution—was simply purged from the public record. Under Gorbachev, the elaborate, costly, and self-deluding notion that the Soviet leadership had been capable of solving problems could not be sustained. Indeed the CPSU was, for the most part, not attracting the best people but was actually attracting and rewarding some of the worst types: self-seekers, careerists, opportunists, and sycophants who could be counted on to sustain the exercise in mass pretense. This was a long-standing problem noted earlier by Nikita Khrushchev, who said that the CPSU had "many people without principle, lickspittle functionaries and petty careerists [who] seek to get much more out of our society than they put into it."[22] Thus, the CPSU rewarded mediocre hangers-on and apparently had no place for honest persons of intellect with questioning and inquiring minds. As a result, it paid a high price in the end.

GORBACHEV: REFORMER IN SPITE OF HIMSELF

A fundamental contradiction in the reform process was that *perestroika* was undertaken in defense of Marxist-Leninist socialism in its Russ-

---

[22]Nikita Khrushchev, *Khrushchev Remembers* (Boston: Little, Brown, 1970), pp. 17, 57, 182.

ian version that had brought the Soviet empire to economic, political, and moral bankruptcy. Gorbachev was convinced that the system was still viable and hoped to save its essentials, especially the dominant role of the party and the planned economy, by opening up the system to controlled democratization and limited marketization. In almost any other country, a political party that had brought about such deplorable conditions would have resigned in disgrace, but the CPSU arrogantly entrusted itself with the task of remedying all of the folly that had resulted from its own ideology, leadership, and policies.

This unenviable and even impossible task fell to Mikhail Gorbachev, who as CPSU general secretary developed a tripartite approach to reform based on *perestroika* (economic restructuring), *glasnost* (openness), and democratization. *Perestroika* was depicted as an effort to loosen the dead hand of the state's economic bureaucracy by giving plant managers greater authority regarding wages and hiring, placing greater reliance on sales and profits, and requiring self-financing (elimination of subsidies and interest-free investment capital) and economic accountability. Gorbachev sought to reduce (but not eliminate) centralism, especially as it impinged upon details of management and resulted in what was condemned as "petty tutelage." He permitted various producer cooperatives, as well as self-employment in the small-scale manufacturing and services sectors. Private housing was encouraged, while social leveling in the form of consumption and wage egalitarianism was condemned. Joint economic ventures with foreign investors were authorized. Thus, the aim of *perestroika* was to make Soviet socialism less inefficient and somewhat competitive.

The *glasnost* component of Gorbachev's reform effort was intended to promote discussion of economic problems and to develop support for *perestroika*—a sort of alliance between reformers at the top of the political system and the masses of Soviet citizens against the opposition to change of the ingrained bureaucrats. Yet, in admitting the corruption, mendacity, and failures of the Brezhnev era, Gorbachev could not confine the discussion to economic issues. Decades of repression, intolerance, and historical censor-

ship had created a tidal wave of frustration, resentment, and anger that led to demands that all the ugly carbuncles and cancers on the Soviet body politic be confronted and revealed.

Gorbachev's democratization approach was initially more tactical in nature, since it definitely did not involve abandonment of the CPSU's political monopoly. The plan was to have party secretaries and even plant managers elected in an effort to introduce some accountability into the bureaucracy, get rid of the most odious Communist officials, and restore some modicum of public confidence. Gorbachev also sought to involve more non-Communists and women in the work of the local soviets (government councils). As with *glasnost*, there could not be just a little democratization. Demands were made for religious freedom, for legalization of opposition parties, and for sovereignty and independence for the union republics.

In fact, Gorbachev's reform program contained yet another important element: namely, a dramatic restructuring of the foreign and security policy of the Soviet Union. Gorbachev noted the tremendous costs and the counterproductiveness of the arms race, as well as of the competition with the West for political, economic, and military influence in developing countries. He pointed to the commitment of ever-increasing amounts of resources to the arms race and to supporting unpopular Communist regimes in Eastern Europe and self-proclaimed Marxist allies throughout the developing world that had contributed to weakening the Soviet economy. Breaking with the traditional Soviet view of class conflict as the sole basis of Soviet foreign policy, he argued for "new thinking" in foreign and security policy based on the assumption that all peoples share certain overriding interests that take precedence over class. The result was a major reorientation of Soviet foreign policy between 1986 and 1989, including major initiatives in relations with the West and pathbreaking agreements on arms reductions, the withdrawal of Soviet troops from Eastern Europe, and the acceptance in 1989 of the anti-Communist revolutions throughout the region. The Soviet Union even supported the military operations of the United States and its Western allies in 1991 that drove the troops of its erst-while ally Iraq from occupied Kuwait. These initiatives contributed substantially to the liberation of the Communist states of Eastern Europe from Soviet dominance and to ending the global confrontation between the Soviet Union and the United States. They also resulted in the opening up of political and economic contacts between the Soviet Union and the West.

Contradictions in the Reform Process

Gorbachev's reform program developed in four major phases.[23] During 1985 and 1986, as Gorbachev outlined the breadth of the problems facing the Soviet Union, he tried to rely on traditional Soviet methods of stimulating the economy—greater investments in key sectors of the economy and, picking up on the earlier efforts of Yuri Andropov, an emphasis on labor and social discipline. The second phase of reform, from the January 1987 plenary meeting of the Central Committee to the Nineteenth Party Conference in late June 1988, was characterized by a movement away from mere reform from the top to greater democratic involvement and the focus on *glasnost* and democratization. Rather than strengthening the system or helping to resolve the serious problems, the revelations about the past actually undercut even more the legitimacy of the system as a whole.

After the party conference, a third stage of reform set in that included the development and actual implementation of programs of reform. Plans were developed to create a one-party democracy based on single-party parliamentarianism, and the establishment of a state governed by law. In the political sphere the elections of March 1989 for a restructured parliament were marked by a relative openness that resulted in the defeat of many Communist Party officials and the election of some democrats. Plans were discussed for radical restructuring of the economy. However, it became increasingly evident that

Gorbachev and the CPSU were losing control of the reform process. On February 4, 1990, influenced by the collapse of the Communist systems in Eastern Europe during the final months of the prior year, an estimated half million people marched in Moscow in support of a multiparty political system. A few days later a Central Committee plenum agreed to eliminate the constitutional monopoly that was guaranteed to the Communist Party. One-party rule was over.

The fourth and final stage of *perestroika* stretched from March 1990 until the abortive coup of August 1991. The period was characterized by growing conflict over economic policy and escalating political and nationalist demands across the entire policy spectrum. Gorbachev, whose commitment to reform had shown signs of flagging since the very beginning and whose "new thinking" was often negated by "old thinking," began to move away from reform as he faced growing opposition during the course of 1990 and 1991. During this period, reformers, most conspicuously Boris Yeltsin, emerged in the Russian Republic to demand sovereignty and to challenge the decaying Soviet system. On December 20, 1990, Foreign Minister Eduard Shevardnadze, Gorbachev's closest political ally who along with Gorbachev had been instrumental in revamping Soviet foreign policy, announced his resignation on the floor of Parliament. He accused Gorbachev of having abandoned his own reform program and of allying himself with the very individuals committed to seizing power and reinstating the policies of the past.

Probably the most sinister side of Gorbachev, and one that contributed to his undoing, was his strange relationship to and reliance on the KGB. His role as the protégé of KGB chief Yuri Andropov was consummated with KGB sponsorship of him as CPSU general secretary. For Gorbachev, the KGB was above criticism; he simply ignored the numerous crimes perpetrated by its agents and maintained its privileged status, and promoted its chiefs Viktor Chebrikov and Vladimir Kryuchkov to full membership in the Politburo. He made it clear that the KGB was the mainstay of his regime, along with OMON—the interior ministry's special deployment forces under the command of Boris Pugo, a KGB general whom

[23]This periodization of *perestroika* draws upon the discussion of Richard Sakwa, *Russian Politics and Society* (London: Routledge, 1993), pp. 1–10.

Gorbachev appointed to head the ministry. The OMON (*otdely militsii osobogo naznacheniiy*) militia units for special assignment were also known as the "black berets" and played a key role in the repressive operations of 1990–1991.

Gorbachev countenanced the use of armed force against peaceful civilian demonstrations in Tbilisi (Georgia) in April 1989, in Baku (Azerbaijan) in January 1990, and in Vilnius (Lithuania) and Riga (Latvia) in January 1991, with considerable loss of life. *Glasnost* and democratization did not eliminate KGB disinformation and calumny against opposition leaders and groups such as Boris Yeltsin, the democratic Ukrainian *Rukh* organization, and Lithuania's nationalist movement, *Sajudis*. Police brutality was employed against peaceful demonstrators, and police provocation and violence were used against democratically elected deputies.

Gorbachev's Errors and Failures

The six and a half years of Gorbachev's leadership left a profound impression on all the republics of the USSR and offered great opportunities for change. Yet his popularity plummeted from 80 percent approval for his program of reforms in 1988 to 10 percent in 1990 and about 3 percent in December 1991 at the time that the Soviet Union was dissolved. In part this was related to the series of errors that prevented him from fully utilizing these opportunities. These errors and failures had their source in Gorbachev's initial mistake: his gross underestimation of the seriousness of the malaise plaguing the Soviet system and what would be required to deal with it. The very concept of "restructuring" implied that a mere reordering or rearrangement of Soviet management and administration and some concessions to small-scale entrepreneurship in the service sector would suffice to unbind the flywheel of the Soviet economy. However, if the Soviet structure was fundamentally unsound and its structural integrity was in question, no amount of restructuring would suffice. In effect, Gorbachev wasted the first two years of his tenure as party leader before he initiated real reforms, and even then, he failed to develop a coherent program of economic reform or to curb the political forces

committed to maintaining the old system—as indicated by the attempted overthrow of Gorbachev in August 1991 by a conspiracy of reactionary forces representing the military, the security police, and the central government bureaucracy whom he himself had put into office.

A second error was Gorbachev's failure to establish clear priorities. Although he called for the need to "accelerate" the economy, in 1988 Gorbachev shifted positions and undertook political, rather than economic, reform measures that rapidly undermined the political structures of the Soviet state, destroyed whatever authority the system retained among the people, and opened up a Pandora's box of demands. Had he been able, as were his political counterparts in China, to concentrate on improving production of agricultural goods and of certain everyday household commodities—sectors of the economy in which improvements would have been readily evident—he would have been able to claim some credit as an economic reformer, at least in the short term.[24] After establishing as part of his political reforms an ineffective presidential system, Gorbachev shifted to a new priority: the preservation of the deteriorating union-empire. In the face of opposition from the republics that was possible because of the opening up of the political system, he made an ill-advised attempt to force the signing of a "new union treaty." This move precipitated the August 1991 coup, as the forces of reaction concluded that he had made too many concessions to the republics and weakened the power of the political center. Each of Gorbachev's priorities, then, was dissipated and led to diametrically opposite results from those that he had intended.

Gorbachev's third error was in his lack of appreciation of the utter failure of the CPSU's nationalities policies and for the seriousness of the non-Russian peoples' grievances against

---

[24]For a comparison of the experiences of the Soviet Union/Russia and China in the reform area that emphasizes the overall benefits of the Chinese approach, see Peter Nolan, *China's Rise, Russia's Fall: Politics, Economics and Planning in the Transition from Stalinism* (New York: St. Martin's, 1995).

Moscow's centralist rule. Speaking in 1987, for example, he declared, "We have settled the nationalities question" and proclaimed the USSR's nationality policy "one of the greatest triumphs of the October Revolution."[25] As a Russian Communist official whose entire career was limited to Russia, Gorbachev was ill prepared to deal with these crucial issues. His stubborn refusal to understand the republics' demands for sovereignty and independence cast him in the reactionary role of guardian of an anachronistic empire, even as it was disintegrating. Indeed, his efforts to impose a new union treaty in 1991 directly contributed to his downfall and to the final dissolution of the Soviet imperial system.

Gorbachev's fourth failure resulted from his indecisiveness and his attempt to placate hard-line Communists, neo-Stalinists, and other reactionary forces. Gorbachev's reform-minded economic advisers came and went as through a revolving door, while he first embraced and then rejected new economic reform proposals put forth every few months. He attempted in vain to reconcile irreconcilable reform plans in the name of "market socialism." He could not adopt the "shock therapy" of rapidly introduced market conditions in April 1990 that he had publicly advocated. This accelerated his loss of credibility, ironically at a time when he was acquiring greater presidential powers. Gorbachev's temporizing and his unwillingness to remove from party political leadership positions those, such as Yegor Ligachev, who strongly opposed the economic and political reforms to which he was supposedly committed, contributed to his declining

authority. As it was, the record of economic performance under Gorbachev was dismal, as GNP declined 10 percent in 1990 and 14 percent the next year. Budget deficits soared from 25 billion rubles in 1985 to 200 billion rubles five years later. Shortages, black market expansion, inflation, increased criminality, growing poverty—these were the fruits of Gorbachev's attempts at economic reform.

A fifth failure was Gorbachev's inability to abandon Marxism-Leninism and his ideological illusions regarding the CPSU. While conceding that "deformities" had occurred in the party and its policies, he remained committed to "more socialism" and to an "improved socialism."[26] Despite a pragmatic bent and a certain appreciation of realities, Gorbachev expressed this continued commitment as late as 1991: "I adhere to the Communist idea, and with this I will leave for the other world."[27] Even on his return from house arrest after the August 1991 coup attempt, Gorbachev's immediate response was to assign to the Communist Party the task of regenerating the reform. Not until the extent of party officials' complicity in the coup and the loss of credibility of the party were clear to him did Gorbachev abandon his hope that the party would be the engine of reform in the USSR. Gorbachev's commitment to the party and to Marxism-Leninism created a mental block that diluted every serious reform effort. Gorbachev remained bound by the CPSU and served as its head for too long, thus failing to develop the strength of his presidency, which had the potential of providing him with a power base independent of the Communist Party and the political forces that were resistant to change.

Gorbachev's excessive reliance on verbal pronouncements, legal decrees, and Communist Party resolutions was his sixth error. His prolix and rambling style were often evident at press conferences and in speeches, and he tended to

[25]Cited in Hélène Carrère d'Encausse, *The End of the Soviet Empire* (New York: Harper and Row, 1993), which provides an excellent overview of the ineptitude of Soviet nationalities policy. Gorbachev's and the Party's Russian "blind spots" on nationalities were evident in the Central Committee's platform adopted in September 1989. It called for the "international solidarity of the Soviet peoples," a "strong Union and strong republics," the "development of internationalist processes of mutual interaction of cultures," and "legal consolidation of the Russian language as the common state language." *Izvestiya,* September 24, 1989.

[26]M. S. Gorbachev, *Perestroika i novoe nyshlenie, dlia nashei strany i diia vesgo miru* (Moscow: Politizdat, 1987), pp. 32–33.
[27]Cited by Serge Schmemann, *New York Times,* February 28, 1991.

treat verbal pronouncements as a substitute for decision and to equate the written word with action. The result was a lengthy period in which effective action was not taken, despite the evidence of dramatic deterioration, as in the economy.

A seventh failure was both political and moral in nature and resulted from Gorbachev's association with the KGB and its longtime chief, Andropov, and its sponsorship of the rise to power of both men. Gorbachev failed to condemn explicitly the horrendous crimes perpetrated by the security police and did not bring responsible officers to justice. *Glasnost* did not extend to the heinous activities of the KGB or its predecessor organizations—except for the publicity given some of them by part of the media and by branches of *Pamyat* (Memory), a public, non-Communist nationalist organization. Gorbachev's poor judgment in casting his lot with the organs of repression in the fall of 1990 and betraying his reform-minded supporters became evident in the abortive military and police putsch of August 19–21, 1991, when he experienced the humiliation of house arrest.

A related error was Gorbachev's refusal to obtain a mandate based on popular election. His election as a member of the Soviet Parliament in 1989 was as a representative of the CPSU Central Committee, and proved to be a handicap. A mandate that Gorbachev could have obtained in 1988 or 1989 as a popularly elected president could have provided decisive support for a coherent program of radical reform—if he had developed such a program.

Success in Failure

Gorbachev's critics pointed out that he presided over a deteriorating economy in which ordinary citizens were driven to engage in "speculation" (reselling of goods at a higher price); standing in line in front of stores became a form of "employment" as purchasers of goods in short supply could sell them at a profit. Boris Yeltsin and others accused him of pursuing contradictory policies and half-measures. However, Gorbachev did have success in terms of the long-range impact of his actions, whether they were intended or

not. He was a qualitatively different Soviet leader from his predecessors and the first to acknowledge the symptoms of decay and degeneration. He could be criticized for treating symptoms rather than causes, but his admissions and policies had a profound effect on both Soviet ideology and policy. In fact, Gorbachev may have been more successful as a debunker of the Soviet system than as its reformer. He failed to preserve the system and made possible (often unintentionally) the many profound changes that led to its demise.

The reduced fear, especially among the youth, created a different political climate. It even resulted in the ouster of the prime minister of Ukraine, Vitali Masol, in October 1990 by hunger-striking students who demanded fulfillment of the July 16, 1990, Ukrainian declaration of sovereignty. Gorbachev introduced a substantial degree of freedom of speech and press, which resulted in an outpouring of frustrations, grievances, and suppressed information and historical evidence. Yet many complained that free speech had little effect on the KGB and police provocations or on local Communist Party bosses who were reluctant to change their old ways. Although independent newspapers emerged, they often had difficulty obtaining newsprint and access to printing facilities. Despite the difficulties, however, the ferment of opinion and the questioning of old ways had a long-term salutary effect.

Soviet citizens were permitted to travel abroad, although usually with hard-currency restrictions, as part of Gorbachev's effort to make the Soviet Union a more normal or "civilized" country. Various taboos were abandoned; this included a truce in the Soviet war against political émigrés and especially against the politically active Ukrainian diaspora. The costly and only partially effective jamming of foreign radio broadcasts was suspended, including that against Radio Liberty, in November 1988. In addition, foreign tourists were permitted greater freedom of movement.

The holding of republic elections in March 1990 gave citizens a degree of choice between Communists and democrats despite certain electoral irregularities and intimidation, especially in rural areas. This resulted in the election of anti-Communist governments in the Baltic states and in western Ukraine and Georgia. Democratic oppositions emerged in various legislative councils (soviets) and parliaments. Former political prisoners who had been arrested for being unappreciated forerunners of *glasnost* and democratization were elected as parliamentary deputies in Ukraine.

The political dissidents were vindicated when Gorbachev acknowledged the need for "pluralism" and the right to establish unofficial "informal" organizations not controlled by the Communist Party or the KGB. The recognition of a multiparty system in July 1990 (which had been stubbornly opposed by Gorbachev in 1989) placed the CPSU increasingly on the defensive. Yet the partocracy sought to delay change by requiring (and obstructing) the official registration of political parties and organizations by the Ministry of Justice.

The acknowledgment of pluralism made it necessary to recognize freedom of religion and to reduce the dependence of the Russian Orthodox Church (Moscow Patriarchate) on the Soviet government and its use by the KGB. In 1989 the Ukrainian Greek Catholic (Uniate) Church emerged from more than four decades of underground existence, and conducted mass demonstrations demanding that it be legalized and regain control of its church properties. Gorbachev's visit to the Vatican in 1989 resulted in a promise of religious freedom and the recognition of all religious bodies. The Ukrainian Autocephalous Orthodox Church, which had also been banned by Stalin, reemerged in the same year demanding legal recognition, as its clergy and parishes rejected the Moscow Patriarchate; in 1990 it established its own Patriarchate of Kiev and All Ukraine. Since 1989, significant friction has emerged among the three Ukrainian churches—that portion which has remained loyal to the Moscow Patriarchate and the revitalized Greek Catholic and the Ukrainian Autocephalous churches—as they have jousted for control of parishes and church property.

These developments and reforms constituted the most substantial and pervasive legacy of Gorbachev's efforts. Yet while Gorbachev basked in

his image abroad as a reformer—influenced, no doubt, by the central role that he played in bring to an end the global arms race and superpower confrontation with the United States—his ability to control the course of domestic events diminished. His declining popularity at home was a consequence of his failure to consummate radical economic and political reforms as well as reform of the legal system.

The New Office of President

Gorbachev, as Communist Party chief, avoided any direct role in the Soviet government until he became chairman of the USSR Supreme Soviet in October 1988. He then introduced an unusual presidential system that culminated in the new office of President of the USSR established in March 1990. The new presidency was created by a simple amendment to the Soviet Constitution of 1977, the fourth Soviet constitution.

As a would-be political reformer, Gorbachev established an unusual and unwieldy legislative structure. In place of the bicameral Supreme Soviet that had been created by Stalin in 1937 but had exercised extraordinarily little political authority, Gorbachev established a large Congress of People's Deputies of 2,250 members elected for five-year terms. The Congress, in turn, was to elect the two chambers of the Supreme Soviet, the Soviet of the Union and the Soviet of Nationalities, each with 271 members. In contrast to the Supreme Soviet of 1937–1989, which met for only about one week of the entire year to approve policies already decided upon within the Communist Party hierarchy, the new legislative bodies were to hold both spring and autumn sessions of several months' duration. The new Supreme Soviet elected the USSR Supreme Court and appointed the Procurator General, the highest legal officer of the government. It also formed the Defense Council and could order mobilization and declare war. However, the Supreme Soviet was subordinate and accountable to the Congress of Deputies.

Gorbachev's legislative creation proved to be cumbersome, and much of its membership was of such a character as to cause the new parliament to lose legitimacy. Fewer than half (1,101) of the deputies were popularly elected in contested elections; 399 were elected without opposition in accordance with the Stalinist-Brezhnevist practice of single-candidate elections. The electoral results could hardly be democratic when 87 percent of the deputies were CPSU members (party membership never exceeded 6.8 percent of the population and was declining dramatically in response to political revelations and the growing irrelevance of the party) and 5.9 percent of the deputies were *Komsomol* members. Such disproportion reflected Gorbachev's massive blind spot regarding the CPSU and its role as the "political vanguard." Thus the overwhelming mass of the population that was not Communist was, in effect, accorded 7.1 percent of the seats in the Congress. The 353 women deputies (15.6 percent) represented Gorbachev's pledge to give women an enhanced role in public life. The Congress also included 82 active-duty military officers. Despite the heavy concentration of members of the *nomenklatura* in the Congress, clear divisions appeared: a pro-reform Interregional Group, clearly defined nationality and republic groups, economic interests, and the backward-looking, anti-reform *Soyuz* (Union) group of hard-line Communists and military officers.

In March 1990 the Congress elected Gorbachev to a five-year presidential term, with 41 percent of the deputies opposed to his election. On the surface this was a strong presidency with extensive decree-issuing and emergency powers. Gorbachev wanted his presidency to serve as a counterweight to the CPSU Politburo, but instead found that his broad—even quasi-dictatorial—powers were not sufficient either to solve the economic problems or to curb the rebellious republics and prevent the disintegration of the union-empire. In fact, over the course of the next 17 months until the August 1991 coup, *Soyuz* and other conservative groups mounted a relentless attack on Gorbachev. They regularly berated him and Foreign Minister Shevardnadze for their failures in foreign policy and came close to charging them with treason—in particular, for having abandoned traditional Communist foreign policy dogma, for having "lost" Eastern Europe, for initiating "unilateral disarmament" of the country in arms control agreements signed

with the United States, for abandoning long-term Soviet allies, as in the Gulf war against Iraq, and for permitting the erosion of the Soviet state. By 1991, as Gorbachev moved to resolve the growing conflicts between the federal government and the republics, the reactionaries moved to more drastic measures, culminating in the abortive coup, to reverse developments.

As the principal Soviet executive and head of state, Gorbachev was unable to gain adequate control over the central government. Although he often presided over parliamentary sessions and wagged his finger at critics, he failed to dismantle the centralized bureaucracy that obstructed his reform efforts in the economic ministries and in the military-industrial complex. He also lost any ability to control the activities of republic parliaments and oblast and city governing councils. He was ineffective in attempting to abrogate laws and acts of republic authorities, and he found himself in the unusual position of issuing "legal" pronouncements regarding the alleged unconstitutionality of various acts of democratically elected republic and oblast authorities, while at the same time being unable to prevent or rescind them.

By late 1990, Gorbachev found himself the target of attacks from both the conservatives and the democratic reformers. In response to the former, Gorbachev had since 1989 increasingly stepped back from his support for radical reform. Rather than supporting the pro-reform elements in his government, he removed many of them and appointed to top positions—as prime minister, vice president, and minister of internal affairs, for example—the very reactionaries who in summer 1991 would attempt to topple him from power. Thus, the reformers gave up on Gorbachev and turned to Boris Yeltsin, who by 1990 had replaced Gorbachev as the champion and symbol of reform in the Soviet Union.

THE RISE OF BORIS YELTSIN

The contradictory nature of Soviet reform was reflected in the tense relationship between Gorbachev and his nemesis and rescuer in 1991, Boris Nikolaevich Yeltsin. These two Communist officials clashed because of profound differences in personality and temperament, in their perceptions of events, and in the policies that they advocated. The early careers of these two leaders were very different, despite a common peasant background. While Gorbachev entered Communist Party work as a bureaucrat at age 24, Yeltsin pursued a successful career as a construction engineer after completing his studies in civil engineering at the Urals Polytechnic Institute in 1955, becoming the head of a large housing construction firm in Sverdlovsk (now renamed Yekaterinburg). He did not join the CPSU until 1961 (at age 30) and did not enter party work as an official until 1968. He became a Central Committee member in 1981, ten years after Gorbachev. As a native of western Siberia, Yeltsin was far closer to the Russian heartland than Gorbachev, who came from the Russian periphery.

In 1986, after heading the party organization in the province of Sverdlovsk and establishing a reputation as a pragmatic, innovative, and honest manager, Yeltsin was named head of the Communist Party organization in Moscow, and was thus chosen to deal with the rampant corruption and economic woes of the municipal administration. When Yeltsin attacked these problems directly and forcefully, he encountered much opposition from entrenched venal interests. He purged almost the entire Communist Party and city bureaucracy in Moscow and arrested the most corrupt retail managers. Yeltsin faulted Gorbachev for the slow pace of his reform efforts and criticized conservative Politburo member Yegor Ligachev for obstructing reform. He did not endear himself at the Twenty-seventh Party Congress in 1986 when he attacked the "social injustice" of the benefits and material advantages that separated the party privileged from the Soviet public.[28]

In order to appease the corrupt but ideologically orthodox in Moscow and rid himself of an

outspoken critic, Gorbachev supported the conservative Ligachev and removed Yeltsin from his Moscow city post and as candidate member of the Politburo in November 1987. Yeltsin accepted a junior ministerial post and appeared to be just another minor loser in the game of Soviet hardball politics. When he requested that the Nineteenth CPSU Conference "rehabilitate" him in July 1988 (while he was alive, rather than posthumously, as was usually the case in party practice), he was once again humiliated, as Gorbachev rejected his request. But Yeltsin achieved a dramatic comeback in August 1991 when, in a remarkable turn of events, Gorbachev was forced into the role of a hapless supplicant, depending on Yeltsin to rescue him from house arrest and from the conspirators who sought to depose him. Yeltsin had been able to acquire support as an outspoken populist while Gorbachev and the KGB sought to discredit him.

Yeltsin's growing political strength during 1989–1991 derived from his advocacy of radical reform at the very time when Gorbachev maneuvered and meandered in his search for an unattainable "consensus." Yeltsin also acquired popularity as a defender of the interests of ethnic Russia and of the Russian Republic against the union-center represented by Gorbachev, who stubbornly continued to advocate and personify a thoroughly compromised and ineffective centralism. Yeltsin's reputation for forthrightness won him favor among those who perceived Gorbachev as guileful and evasive.

Despite opposition from Gorbachev, Yeltsin was elected from Moscow to the USSR Congress of People's Deputies and played a key role in the developing parliamentary opposition. In March 1990, Yeltsin was elected with 90 percent of the vote in a contest with Gorbachev's candidate to represent the city of Moscow in the new Russian Parliament; two months later he was elected its chairman. In June 1990, he demonstrably withdrew from the CPSU at the Twenty-eighth Party Congress before a national television audience.

Yeltsin called for Gorbachev's resignation in February 1991 after the attacks by Soviet troops on civilians in the Baltic republics, but he subsequently sought an accommodation with the

[28]*Pravda,* February 27, 1986, p. 3. For a discussion of Yeltsin's role as head of the Communist Party organization in Moscow see Timothy J. Colton, *Moscow: Governing the Socialist Metropolis* (Cambridge, MA: Belknap Press, 1995), pp. 572–583.

USSR president on an ill-fated plan to reform and rescue the divided union. When Gorbachev sought to ban a pro-Yeltsin demonstration in March 1991 (to counter Communist efforts to unseat Yeltsin in the Russian Parliament), he was successfully defied, and the mass demonstration took place despite the presence of troops in the capital.

When the Russian Republic opted for a popularly elected president, Gorbachev again sought covertly to prevent Yeltsin's election. However, Yeltsin easily won 57 percent of the vote against five opponents in June 1991 and became the first popularly elected president in the history of Russia. As president, Yeltsin began to express the long-repressed grievances of Russians against the union-center. Already on November 19, 1990, in Kiev he had signed a treaty with the government of Ukraine that acknowledged the sovereignty of both Ukraine and Russia and recognized their existing borders.

Yeltsin insisted that the Russian Republic have its own KGB free of union control and its own defense ministry and military forces; he claimed the republic's right to control all its natural resources, which the union-center had used for its own purposes while flagrantly neglecting the republic's domestic needs. Yeltsin called for an end to Soviet aid to Cuba, and exacted a ban on Communist Party organizations in the workplace and their control of patronage, promotions, and various benefits. Earlier, in January 1991, when the Kremlin sought to employ violence against the seceding Baltic states, Yeltsin had directed an appeal to Soviet troops in Lithuania (delivered while he was in Estonia) warning them not to be used by the forces of reaction and not serve as "a pawn in a dirty game, a grain of sand in the Kremlin's building of an imperial sand-castle." He appealed to the troops not to believe the political officers and not to betray their own generation, warning that "dictatorship is arriving, and it is you who is bringing it, sitting with a submachine gun in a tank!"[29]

---

[29]"Don't Shoot," *Moscow News,* no. 4, January 27–February 3, 1991, p. 5.

THE AUGUST 1991 COUP

A cabal representing the KGB (Vladimir Kryuchkov), the military (Marshal Yazov), the interior ministry or MVD (Boris Pugo), and the military-industrial complex organized the August 1991 Coup against USSR President Gorbachev. It included the premier, Valentin Pavlov, and had as its spokesman Vice President Gennadi Yanayev, whom Gorbachev had insisted be elected to that post after he was initially rejected by the Congress of Deputies. The gang of eight constituted a self-proclaimed State Committee for the State of Emergency in the USSR. It claimed mendaciously that Gorbachev was unable to exercise the duties of the presidency for unspecified reasons of health and announced that Yanayev would serve as acting president. It soon became clear that Gorbachev was being held under house arrest in his Crimean vacation retreat at Foros, near Yalta, and was cut off from all means of domestic communication and had to obtain news of events from foreign radio broadcasts.

The putsch extended far beyond the self-proclaimed junta; it included numerous higher military officers and was supported by many CPSU apparatus officials at the republic and oblast levels. The coup, a futile attempt to prevent the breakup of the empire, was precipitated by Gorbachev's plan to return to Moscow for the signing on August 20 of the "new union treaty" with nine of the constituent republics of the Soviet Union. The putsch leaders claimed that Gorbachev's reform policies had reached a dead end, but promised to pursue a "consistent policy of reform." In a vague and confusing statement, the plotters condemned the turmoil and the "extremist forces" that allegedly sought to destroy the Soviet Union. They objected to the "war of laws" between the republics and the president and the "destruction of the unified machinery of the national economy which has taken decades to evolve." The plotters contended that "the country has become ungovernable" and condemned the alleged use of power as "a means of unprincipled self-assertion" with the aim of establishing "an unbridled personal dictatorship" (although they did not specify whether this was the sin of

Yeltsin or Gorbachev).[30] Although it promised to act against "the octopus of crime and scandalous immorality" as well as the "propagation of sex and violence" and the "tyranny of those who plunder the people's property," the junta had no specific program for rescuing either the economy or the empire. Its offer to conduct a public debate on Gorbachev's new union treaty reflected its misplaced suspicion of that instrument.

The coup of August 19–21, 1991, proved to be poorly planned and the plotters ill-prepared. They apparently assumed that the removal of Gorbachev would be as easy as the 1964 ouster of Khrushchev, which was accomplished by hauling him before a Central Committee that was insistent on his removal. The junta contented themselves with a televised press conference that revealed to viewers a motley assortment of undistinguished and unattractive bureaucratic types. Interior Minister Pugo sat beside the principal spokesman, acting president Yanayev, whose hands shook visibly as he attempted to cope with the barbed and ironic questions of correspondents.

The junta sent tanks and armored personnel carriers into the streets of Moscow and issued orders to all military forces and CPSU organizations in a vain effort to intimidate the opposition. But they miscalculated in relying on the divided and dispirited military establishment and in not obtaining the support of the elite Alpha force of the KGB. They also failed to obtain the acquiescence of Gorbachev or to arrest or assassinate Boris Yeltsin, who quickly moved to lead the widespread opposition to the coup. Although they were able to control the major media, they could not control foreign radio broadcasts, the independent press, and recently developed nongovernmental information networks. In the end, the plotters experienced a failure of nerve.

Yeltsin defied the plotters and took refuge in the government house of the Russian Republic—

the White House—with aides and armed guards, as tens of thousands of supporters surrounded the building day and night and erected barricades for its defense. Military, KGB, and interior ministry forces loyal to Yeltsin refused to move against the government house and instead took up its defense. The plotters failed to cut off Yeltsin's communications and utilities, and he was able to communicate with world leaders and to project an image of the defender of constitutional government.

The plotters failed largely because of their inability to rely on the military, their ineptitude and questionable reputations, and their failure to inspire public confidence in the unanticipated confrontation with the popularly elected Russian president, Boris Yeltsin. The plot unraveled within 72 hours (despite the failure of Yeltsin's call for a general strike), and a shaken but not entirely chastened Gorbachev was able to return to Moscow to denounce the coup. Interior Minister Pugo committed suicide, and the other plotters were arrested. Gorbachev's military adviser, the old-line Marshal Akhromeyev, also committed suicide.

An intriguing question prompted by the coup was that of Gorbachev's unwitting complicity in it. Had he been less self-assured and more perceptive, he would have heeded the various warnings and ominous events that should have alerted him to the danger of a coup. Foreign Minister Eduard Shevardnadze had warned of the threat of dictatorship when he resigned in December 1990. In June 1991, in an attempted "constitutional coup," Premier Pavlov had sought unsuccessfully to have the Supreme Soviet grant him some of Gorbachev's presidential powers, and KGB chief Kryuchkov, Defense Minister Yazov, and Interior Minister Pugo had expressed profound dissatisfaction with political and economic developments in a closed session of the Supreme Soviet.

Gorbachev cannot be viewed as an innocent victim of the coup. He appointed and promoted all of the plotters and had to know their political positions. It can be argued that Gorbachev implicitly encouraged the plotters by his shift toward their position in the autumn of 1990, relying on coercive methods, police provocations, and intimidation. Gorbachev permitted Kryuchkov, Pugo, and the military a free hand in the Baltic states and reimposed media control and news blackouts. Thus Gorbachev, in casting his lot earlier with the KGB, the military, and the interior ministry, apparently led the plotters to believe that he relied upon them, condoned their methods, and would be prepared to join them when presented with a *fait accompli.*

In a sense, Gorbachev was an unwitting or silent accessory to the plotters. He demonstrated poor judgment in selecting, promoting, and relying on the plotters. He handpicked men of middling abilities and questionable character, possibly because he felt more compatible with them than with the various aides and advisers of superior intellect whom he had alienated. Several of his closest staff cooperated with the plotters. Gorbachev became a victim of his own guile and equivocation as well as his ego, his excessive self-confidence, and his carelessness. Some have speculated that Gorbachev cynically sought to utilize the very real threat from the anti-reform hard-line Communists as a means of extracting economic and financial aid from the West and Japan. In possibly seeking to use this threat as an undesirable alternative to his own leadership, Gorbachev became its victim.

THE END OF THE SOVIET UNION

The outcome of the failed August 1991 coup was the very opposite of the plotters' intentions. It greatly accelerated the dissolution of the Soviet Union and once again demonstrated the endemic incompetence, mismanagement, and potentially dangerous nature of the center and of the CPSU. Yet the coup proved to be a remarkable turning point for Russia and the republics, paid for with the lives of three young men who died on the barricades in Moscow. It was very literally a coup d'état in which part of the Communist state—indeed, some of the very highest officials who presumably enjoyed the unquestioned confidence of the USSR president—struck a fatal blow at the entire fabric of the Soviet polity. It also created a vacuum in the center, which gave Russia and the other republics a freedom of action they had not enjoyed since 1917–1918.

The coup and the resistance to it were essentially Russian phenomena; the plotters were all ethnic Russians (except for Boris Pugo, a Russified Latvian) and the immediate decisive resistance to the coup was largely Russian. The coup represented a conflict between Moscow and the Kremlin, between Russia and the Union. Boris Yeltsin emerged from the coup as the de facto political leader of the country and the leading force committed to destroying the old political order, while Gorbachev returned to Moscow in a greatly weakened and isolated position. Initially, Gorbachev did not comprehend the profound changes caused by the failure of the coup. Indeed, the coup demonstrated the irrelevance of the CPSU as a constructive factor in the political system.

Yeltsin, as the leader of Russia, issued various decrees appointing new military commanders for Moscow and Leningrad (St. Petersburg) and placing troops of the army, KGB, and interior ministry in the Russian Republic under the jurisdiction of his office. The Russian Republic assumed ownership of all economic enterprises and properties on its territory, and Yeltsin restored the imperial Russian tricolor as the republic's flag, abandoning the red banner and the hammer and sickle (although he later reinstated the red flag with star but minus the hammer and sickle as a co-equal national flag), and he suspended all activities of the Russian Communist Party. Yeltsin insisted that Gorbachev approve all decisions taken by the Parliament and president of the Russian Republic during the coup, and Gorbachev had no choice but to give his assent.

The lack of support for Gorbachev within the central party apparatus during the coup prompted him to dissolve the Central Committee and the central party organization on August 24. Similar bans were imposed throughout the former USSR. However, several republic Communist parties sought to change their names and continue in existence, many party leaders at the oblast level, who were locked out of their party offices, continued to hold local or regional governmental posts and issue orders in an attempt to retain their powers and privileges. The USSR Supreme Soviet, by a vote of 283 to 29 with 52 abstentions, suspended all CPSU activities on August 29, 1991.

Gorbachev's new union treaty could not be signed as a result of the coup, and the USSR president was compelled to witness the adoption of declarations of national independence by nearly all of the former union republics. The process that had begun with Lithuania's abrogation of the Communist monopoly of power on December 7, 1989, and its declaration of independence and secession from the USSR on March 11, 1990, was largely consummated when Ukraine proclaimed its independence on August 24, 1991. But Russia, though insisting on its sovereignty, proclaimed on June 12, 1990, was reluctant to secede from the defunct Union.

The Baltic republics, where the drive for secession and independence had begun, made clear throughout 1991 that they were not interested in a revamped union treaty or a restructured Soviet Union and had not participated in the discussions concerning a new union treaty. Estonia and Latvia declared their full independence during the August coup; after the coup, all three Baltic states, with support from the West and from Yeltsin's Russia, demanded their full separation from the USSR. On September 6, 1991, the Kremlin granted full independence to the three states. Almost immediately separatists in the other republics speeded up their efforts at independence. By mid-October, Ukraine announced that popular demands for greater sovereignty precluded its signing the union treaty that had been negotiated in the spring.

With the collapse of the coup and the union treaty proposal, Gorbachev was compelled to employ other tactics in his tattered strategy of imperial revival. His dissolution of the USSR cabinet of ministers because of its support for the coup meant that there was no longer a central union government. The Congress of People's Deputies was convened early in September 1991 in an effort to preserve some semblance of a political center. Yeltsin told the Congress that "the collapse of the empire is final, but the republics

have got to take its place."[31] The Congress balked at legislating itself out of existence but agreed to a new transitional center. The compromise, enacted at the insistence of Gorbachev and ten republic leaders, created a new interim executive body, the State Council, consisting of republic representatives and Gorbachev as chairman.

The transitional arrangement was actually a terminal arrangement. Republics that had proclaimed their independence were suspicious of possible collusion between Gorbachev and Yeltsin and were apprehensive that the Russian Republic would usurp or seek to restore the role of the collapsed center. When the restructured Supreme Soviet met, four republics (Ukraine, Azerbaijan, Georgia, and Moldova) refused to participate. In a referendum held on December 1, 1991, more than 90 percent of voters in Ukraine, including most of the ethnic Russians, approved secession from the Soviet Union and the establishment of an independent country. By this time Boris Yeltsin had come to the conclusion that further efforts to hold the Soviet Union together were fruitless. Moreover, he had also decided that Russia could be more successful alone in implementing effective economic reform.

On December 8, 1991, the presidents of the three Slavic republics of the Soviet Union—Russia, Belarus, and Ukraine—which together contained 73 percent of the Soviet population and 80 percent of its territory, met in Minsk, the capital of Belarus, to announce their secession from the Soviet Union and the creation of Commonwealth of Independent States (CIS). Ignoring Gorbachev's criticisms of their actions, the three presidents submitted their agreement to their respective parliaments for ratification; on December 10, 1991, the Commonwealth officially came into existence. Ten days later, the five Central Asian republics joined the CIS after gaining assurances that they would be treated as fully equal members, and on December 22, three more republics (Armenia, Azerbaijan, and Moldova) joined, leaving only Georgia, which was

---

[31]See excepts of his speech in *New York Times,* September 4, 1991.

THE DECLINE OF EMPIRE

The decline of several great continental empires has been a twentieth-century phenomenon. The collapse of the Austro-Hungarian, Ottoman, and Russian empires after World War I was as remarkable and consequential as the collapse of the USSR. Attempts to reform and preserve empires have failed because of their essentially anomalous nature, and many were not acknowledged to be aberrational until the process of implosion was evident. Major characteristics of imperial decline include the following:

1. Widespread corruption, including theft and embezzlement; officials at all levels expect bribes for performing their duties.

2. The imperial bureaucracy not only proves incapable of initiating reforms, but actually obstructs and sabotages such efforts and seeks to preserve its privileges, opting for stagnation rather than innovation.

3. The military may suffer outright defeat or retreat and have serious morale problems, especially if it must rely on unwilling and unreliable conscripts from subject nationalities. In addition it often faces the dilemma of whether to serve as an instrument of repression against its own people.

4. Imperial rule proves to be excessively costly and ultimately exhausts revenue sources. Military power and economic bankruptcy provide an incongruous combination when the empire becomes dependent on foreign capital and technology.

5. Imperial decline is accompanied, and to a degree concealed, by hubris—the arrogance, overweening pride, insolence, and self-deception on the part of the ethnic hegemon that the early Greeks recognized as preceding decline and fall. Hubris reflects the corrupting and perverse nature of imperial rule as the ethnic hegemon demonstrates loss of a sense of reality.

6. The quality of the empire's political leadership is crucial as its efforts at modernization, reform, and empire preservation fail.

7. The final stage in the collapse of empire is a failure of nerve and a crisis of confidence, as it finally becomes evident that the attempted solutions for crises and defeats are ineffective.

---

preoccupied with a bloody civil war, outside the new Commonwealth.

On December 20, the Russian Federation took formal jurisdiction over virtually all of the governmental bodies and resources of the Soviet state. On December 25, Gorbachev informed a national television audience of his resignation as president and the formal demise of the Soviet Union. The next day the Supreme Soviet passed a resolution acknowledging the dissolution of the Soviet state. A little more than 74 years after Lenin and the Bolsheviks seized power in Petrograd and began laying the foundations for a new social, political, and economic order, that order crashed to an ignominious end.

The August 1991 coup proved to be the denouement of Gorbachev's singular achievement: the introduction of significant democratic conditions and the partial dismantling and weakening of the centralized bureaucratic structures of the empire's metropol-center. Prior to this, the entire Soviet political system had been based on a triadic structure consisting of the following principal components: the CPSU oligarchy and its administrative apparatus that determined basic policy and conducted propaganda on its behalf, the governmental bureaucracy that managed the state-owned economy, and the organs of repression—military, police, and internal security organs (the MVD and the KGB). Gorbachev's reform efforts challenged and weakened an exhausted power structure but did not develop a viable substitute and the new personnel needed to give such an alternative life and substance. The ultimate source of this enormous failure must be sought in the policies pursued by the CPSU leadership for decades and the methods that it chose to employ.

BUILDING THE RUSSIAN FEDERATION

Over the first decade of the Russian Federation, the U.S. media have presented an expansive picture of drug dealers and mafia hit men, corrupt businessmen, destitute pensioners, an embittered and impoverished intelligentsia—all providing a plausible explanation of the initial growth of support for extremists of the right (such as Vladimir Zhirinovsky) and the return of the Communist Party as the leading force in Russian politics. The euphoria of the early 1990s, when Russian and foreign observers alike assumed that the collapse of the authoritarian and centralized structures of the Soviet state would usher in a period of stable participatory government and expanding economic welfare, has given way to the realities of creating new social, political, and economic structures in Russia and in the other successor states of the USSR. Russia and the other post-Soviet states are engaged in a complex process that analysts have called a "triple transition." They are attempting simultaneously to create new states and national

identities, establish new political institutions based on the rule of law, and build the foundations for effective and productive market economies. In many respects the demands associated with one of these three areas—for instance, expanding political participation—may conflict with the prerequisites for success in another—such as the unemployment that may result from introducing market mechanisms into the economy.

Russia is not alone in attempting to deal with the multiple demands of sociopolitical and economic modernization. At least in the political sphere, it is part of what Samuel P. Huntington has referred to as the "third wave" of democratization.[32] Between 1972 and the year 2000, the number of countries in which authoritarian political systems have been overthrown and efforts initiated to establish democratic political systems almost tripled, from 44 to 120. Countries in Southern Europe, Latin America, East Asia, Africa, and most recently the former Communist states of East-Central Europe and Eurasia have joined the list of mature and fledgling democratic states. However, most of them have found the process of transition from authoritarian to stable democratic rule a long and difficult one. Most of the countries currently making the transition to democracy are doing so in the context of established geographic borders, a relatively homoge-

---

[32]Samuel P. Huntington, *The Third Wave: Democratization in the Late Twentieth Century* (Norman: University of Oklahoma Press, 1992).

A CLOSER LOOK

7.3

RENAMING THE USSR

Post-Soviet states or *Soviet successor states* refers to all 15 of the states that emerged from the former Soviet Union, including the Baltic states of Estonia, Latvia, and Lithuania.

CIS, or *Commonwealth of Independent States,* refers to the Russian Federation and the other 11 Soviet successor states that have attempted to create political, security, and economic linkages among themselves: Belarus, Ukraine, Moldova, Armenia, Georgia, Azerbaijan, Kazakhstan, Kyrgyzstan, Turkmenistan, Uzbekistan, and Tajikistan.

neous population, and an economy that even during the period of authoritarian rule operated on the basis of market principles. For most of the post-Communist states, however, the situation is much more complex.[33] The negative legacies of the past are especially strong and deeply rooted throughout much of the post-Communist world. The political values essential for a functioning democracy are weak among both the population and the political elites; hostilities across ethnic communities create special problems for political transition and state building; moreover, many of the infrastructural prerequisites for market economics are absent. Thus, the process of transition in the post-Communist states, including the Russian Federation, has proven to be especially difficult and problematic.

Nation Building in the Russian Federation and the CIS

For the most part, neither Russia nor the other CIS states have existed historically within their current boundaries. In fact, tsarist Russia emerged over the course of several centuries as a result of imperial conquest and expansion into territories populated by a diverse mixture of peoples. At the end of the tsarist period, ethnic Russians were a minority of 43 percent in their own empire. Territorial and population losses after World War I brought the figure to 58 percent in 1939; additional territorial changes after World War II and demographic developments over the next 50 years reduced the percentage of ethnic Russians in the Soviet Union to only slightly more than 50 percent in 1989. Moreover, the boundaries of the post-Soviet states were based on purely administrative determinations of the Stalinist period and have little to do with the historical borders of earlier states or with the ethnic composition of the new states. For example, the Crimea, populated largely by ethnic Russians and originally a part of the Russian Republic, was

given to Ukraine by Khrushchev in 1954 during the celebrations of the tercentenary of the Pereyaslavl Treaty that brought much of Ukraine under Russian rule. The portion of eastern Moldova whose Russian and Ukrainian plurality have de facto seceded from Moldova since 1992 was transferred from Ukraine to the new Soviet Republic of Moldavia by Stalin after World War II.

Besides the fact that existing territories and populations of the post-Soviet states have for the most part not existed historically as independent political units, there are several other, primarily psychological, factors that influence the process of nation and state building in Russia. A significant portion of Russians, including members of the political elite, find it difficult to accept the existence of Russia without its former non-Russian territories and are committed to reestablishing the old empire in some form. As former Vice President Aleksandr Rutskoi put it, "the historical consciousness of the Russians will not allow anybody to equate mechanically the borders of Russia with those of the Russian Federation and to take away what constituted the glorious pages of Russian history."[34]

Two serious issues emerge that relate directly to the view of what constitutes Russia and Russians. First, there is the issue of the millions of ethnic Russians who remain in the countries of the "near abroad" (the other post-Soviet states) and the impact that this has had on Russian relations with those states. For the most part their presence results from the policies of Stalin and his successors to bring Russians into areas depopulated by the famine and purges of the 1930s (e.g., in Ukraine), the "Virgin Lands" program of the 1950s in Kazakhstan, and the overall commitment to ensuring Moscow's control over non-Russian populations. Russian leaders, including former Foreign Minister Andrei Kozyrev and more recently President Putin, have made clear that they view the well-being of these populations as a central concern of the Russian state. They point to real and alleged discrimination against Russians in the neighboring countries as a justification for greater Russian

[33]For a discussion of the special problems of democratization in post-Communist states, see Valerie Bunce, "Comparing East and South," *Journal of Democracy* 6(3) (1995), pp. 87–100.

[34]*Pravda,* February 30, 1993.

influence in these countries—and even for reintegrating the independent post-Soviet states into a new Russian-led political entity. One must distinguish between ethnic Russians who are indeed natives of the new states and those who were in effect recent colonists. The Soviet policy of demographic inundation of indigenous populations, as in Estonia and Latvia, was accompanied by discriminatory language policies of various kinds that favored Russian speakers. Hence, it is not surprising that tensions exist in the post-Soviet environment. What is surprising

is that greater tension does not exist. Moreover, there is ample evidence that various political figures in Russia seek to provoke ethno-linguistic hostilities in the "near abroad" as a pretext for intimidation and destabilization, if not subversion and intervention.

The second issue regards the place of non-Russian minorities in the Russian Federation and the possible impact of ethnic hostility and separatist tendencies on the political processes and institutions being developed (see Table 7.2). The most serious of Russia's problems in this

TABLE 7.2

ETHNO-TERRITORIAL UNITS OF THE RUSSIAN FEDERATION, INCLUDING THE SHARE OF TITULAR NATIONALITY AND RUSSIANS IN THE POPULATION

Unit	Total Population	Titular Nationality (%)	Russians (%)
Republics			
Adygei	450,000	22.1	68.0
Altai	2,672,000	—	89.5
Bashkortostan	4,111,000	21.9	39.3
Buryatia	1,046,000	24.0	69.9
Checheno-Ingushetia	797,000*		24.8
Chechens		66.6	
Ingush		2.3	
Chuvashia	1,359,000	67.8	26.7
Dagestam	2,095,000	15.6	9.2
Kabardino-Balkaria	792,000		31.9
Kabardians		48.2	
Balkars		9.4	
Kalmkia	317,000	45.4	37.7
Karachai-Cherkessia	436,000		42.4
Karachais		31.2	
Cherkess		9.7	
Karelia	776,000	10.1	73.6
Kharkassiay	566,861	11.1	79.5
Komi	1,161,000	23.3	57.7
Mari-El	763,000	43.3	47.5
Mordvinia	944,000	32.5	60.8
North Ossetia	663,000	53.0	29.9

continues

TABLE 7.2 (continued)

ETHNO-TERRITORIAL UNITS OF THE RUSSIAN FEDERATION, INCLUDING THE SHARE OF TITULAR NATIONALITY AND RUSSIANS IN THE POPULATION

Unit	Total Population	Titular Nationality (%)	Russians (%)
Sakha (Yakhutia)	1,003,000	33.4	50.3
Tatarstan	3,774,000	48.5	43.3
Tuva	310,000	64.3	32.0
Udmurtia	1,636,000	30.9	58.9
Autonomous Oblast			
Jewish AO			
Autonomous Okrugs**			
Aga Buryat (Chita oblast)	1,277,000		91
Koriak (Kamchatka oblast)	31,000	16.5	62
Chukchi (Magadan oblast)	246,000		72.4
Nenets (Arkhangelsk oblast)	47,000	11.4	65.6
Evenki (Krasnoyarsk oblast)	20,000	14.1	67.5
Taimyr (Krasnoyarsk oblast)	862,100		67.1
Khanty-Mansi (Tyumen oblast)	1,358,000		66
Khanty		.9	
Mansi		.6	
Ust' Orda Buryat (Irkutsk oblast)	144,000	35.7	56.7
Komi-Permiak (Perm oblast)	154,000	61.2	34.9
Yamalo-Nenets (Tyumen oblast)	497,000	4	79.2

Source: Robert W. Orttung, *The Republics and Regions of the Russian Federation,* (New York: EastWest Institute, 2000). Population estimates as of 1 January 1998.
*Separate data for the two republics of Chechnya and Ingushetia, which separated officially in 1992, are not available.
**Autonomous okrugs are under the administrative jurisciction of provinces (*oblasti*) that are not territorially defined; the names of these provinces are given in parentheses.

regard are to be found in the Caucasus, where numerous ethnic groups have long coexisted, although divided by language, religion, and a history of feuding with one another and opposing domination by the Russians. During the Soviet period these antagonisms were kept under control primarily by coercive measures. With the collapse of Soviet power, however, conflicts broke out between the Christian Ossetians and the Muslim Ingush, who had refused to secede from Russia along with the Chechens, a fellow-Muslim people, with whom they had shared the Chechen-Ingushetia autonomous

republic until 1992. In late 1992 President Yeltsin sent Russian troops into the region to separate the warring sides. The situation was complicated by the issue of Chechnya, and after a year of confrontation and fruitless negotiations, Yeltsin decided to put down the Chechen secession by military force. In December 1994, he sent in thousands of Russian troops, backed by tanks, heavy artillery, and aircraft. Only after months of brutal battle, during which the Russians killed thousands of civilians and destroyed the cities and villages of Chechnya, did the Russians declare victory—prematurely, as it turned out. A cease-fire negotiated in June 1996 broke down several months later, and the conflict festered for the next three years.

Soon after his appointment as prime minister in late summer 1999, Vladimir Putin responded to Chechen insurgent incursions into neighboring areas of Russia and to bombings in Russian cities that he claimed were the work of Chechen terrorists with a massive military intervention. Although Chechen cities and the countryside have been devastated, sporadic fighting continues in 2005.

The challenges to Russian control over Chechnya, and the Caucasus more generally, were but one part of a much broader problem faced by President Yeltsin as he attempted to create the constitutional foundations for the new Russia. Other ethnically based republics scattered across Russia, including especially Tatarstan, also declared their sovereignty soon after the collapse of the Soviet Union. The Tatars, a Turkic Muslim people living about 500 miles east of Moscow on the Volga River, voted overwhelmingly in March 1992 in favor of complete independence from Moscow. Like the Chechens, they refused to hold nationally scheduled elections on their territory, claimed control over their national resources, and refused to send tax payments to the federal government in Moscow. Similar developments have occurred elsewhere across Russia, as in Buryatia, north of Mongolia, and in the Republic of Sakha (Yakutia) comprising most of the gold- and mineral-rich northeastern portions of Siberia. Yet in none of these three republics is the titular nationality a majority (49 percent Tatars; 24 percent Buryats; 33 percent Yakuts). In these and other cases, ethnic Russians have supported the call for sovereignty, which they view largely in terms of greater economic and political independence from the heavy administrative hand of Moscow.

With the major exception of Chechnya, however, the Yeltsin government resolved the most significant issues dividing the central government in Moscow and the 21 ethnic republics of the Federation, for the time being. This major achievement in state building was accomplished by a combination of the forceful example of Yeltsin's coercive policy in Chechnya and the simultaneous granting of substantial amounts of autonomy to the republics. The constitution approved in a national referendum in December 1993 and agreements negotiated between Moscow and various republics have helped create a degree of stability in relations between the federal government and the constituent units of the federation. For example, although Russian tax laws apply in the 59 nonautonomous Russian provinces and territories and approximately 60 percent of local tax revenues from these provinces flow to Moscow, the governments of the autonomous republics negotiate with Moscow the amount of taxes to be paid to the center—usually at rates 80 percent lower than for the provinces.

As a result of this permissive approach, however, legislation of the republics—and the other provinces—increasingly conflicts with the federal constitution. For example, the Republic of Tuva, along the northwestern border of Mongolia, outlaws private land ownership, although the Russian constitution permits it. Legislation in 75 of Russia's constituent provinces (including the 21 republics and one autonomous oblast) is reportedly at odds with the federal constitution.[35] Thus, the constitutional issues have not been worked out fully, and the relationships between the central government and the republics are evidence of the larger and more general problem of weak governmental institutions and a continued lack of established rules for conducting the business of government.

Although the demands for independence of the republics have been muted, in part because of the flexibility of the policies of President Yeltsin, the chaotic set of relationships between the central government in Moscow and the regional political systems inherited by Putin represent a serious problem. To date, Putin appears to have had some success, but his efforts to reimpose strong central control have the potential of encouraging renewed separatist tendencies that will challenge the nation- and state-building requirements of the Russian Federation.

---

[35]According to then Head of the Presidential Administration Sergei Filatov. Interfax, December 27, 1995.

In many respects the problems of state and nation building are even greater in most of the other Soviet successor states. For example, Ukraine, Moldova, and Kazakhstan all have substantial Russian minorities, most of whom are geographically concentrated, who represent a real or potential threat to national unity. In Moldova, the central government lost control of Transdniester to Russian secessionists soon after independence. In Ukraine, the Russian majority of Crimea has called for reunion with Russia, which may only be an attempt to obtain better terms from Kiev (Kyiv). In fact, accepting Moscow's rule would interfere with the plans of certain groups within the very diverse Russian population, which consists of an assortment of carpetbaggers, retired *nomenklatura* types (including KGB, MVD, and military retirees), and people associated with various forms of corruption. It is also important to recognize that a quarter million Crimean Tatars (roughly half the number brutally exiled by Stalin during World War II as a security threat) have returned to Crimea. Generally they fear Russia and wish to remain in Ukraine. The unresolved conflict between Armenia and Azerbaijan over control of Nagorno-Karabakh and the devastating civil wars in Georgia are further evidence of the seriousness of the problem of creating political loyalties to the new states of the CIS among their diverse populations.

Democratization and Political Institution Building

Besides the problems associated with nation and state building in Russia and the CIS, there are also those related to the creation of a stable representative or democratic political system. The Russian Federation has established a complex political system that, although it includes a strong presidency, also establishes, in principle at least, the separation of powers. Therefore, presidential-parliamentary (executive-legislative) relations have been at the very center of Russian politics. The first two years of Russian independence witnessed a move toward parliamentary democracy in Russia with a parliament that increasingly attempted to exert its authority in

the legislative process relative to the power of the executive. The result was a growing confrontation between President Yeltsin (and his government) and a parliament elected in March 1990, prior to the collapse of the Communist system, that represented the old bureaucratic interests and opposed the dismantling of state enterprises. The conservative forces aligned against Yeltsin also charged him with being too supportive of the West and with undermining the strategic security interests of Russia. They opposed the rapid and widespread introduction of economic policies of the sort that the majority of Western analysts now argue were a major contributing factor to the collapse of the Russian economy. These included privatization of state industries in a manner that many have argued verged on robbery by well-positioned individuals. Many of the critics were also strong nationalists for whom the collapse of the Soviet empire and the emergence of independent states on the territory of the former USSR were unacceptable.

By 1993, various factions or groupings had emerged within the Russian Supreme Soviet and Congress based on political and ideological differences concerning the breadth and timing of economic reforms. Increasingly the factions attempted to exercise some control over their members, much as occurs in Western parliamentary systems. These factions, in turn, were joining in much broader coalitions. Three broad coalitions emerged: the democratic left, representing about 225 members (with Democratic Russia the most important party) who usually fully supported Yeltsin's economic reforms and his foreign policy oriented toward emphasizing ties with the democratic West; an ideological center of about 200 members (headed by the Civic Union) who opposed some of the specifics of the reforms and called for greater attention to relations with the other post-Soviet states; and a bloc of right and left extremists of about 375 members (including both Communists and extreme nationalists) who opposed almost all aspects of Yeltsin's domestic and foreign policy agenda.

President Yeltsin himself contributed to the opposition that he faced in Parliament by ignoring the legislature's views concerning many of his initiatives and by ruling by presidential degree when he could not get parliamentary support. His authoritarian approach to rule meant that he often acted contrary to the existing Russian constitution, which gave limited authority to the president. An indication of the style of Yeltsin's leadership can be seen in the fact that, although Russia has a much smaller population and controls less territory than the former Soviet Union, the Russian government is in fact larger than its Soviet predecessor was in 1991. For example, a presidential apparatus modeled after the Central Committee apparatus of the old CPSU evolved in order to permit Yeltsin to get around the state bureaucracy that was still dominated by former Soviet bureaucrats. This apparatus continues to flourish under President Putin. One especially important element of the new presidential bureaucracy has been the National Security Council, which has played a key role in both domestic and foreign security policy. Immediately after the first round of the presidential elections in June 1996, President Yeltsin appointed General (ret.) Aleksandr Lebed—who ran a strong third to Yeltsin and Zyuganov—to head the council, in return for the latter's support against Zyuganov in the July runoff. Soon after his reelection, Yeltsin fired Lebed.

The large multistory White House, the home of the Russian Parliament until its partial destruction by Yeltsin's troops in October 1993, is now filled with members of the presidential staff. In the words of one American analyst, "The problem of the presidency is that it is now beginning to take on many of the characteristics of the entrenched bureaucracy that it was designed to supersede."[36]

By the end of 1992, Yeltsin faced increasing defection from among his past supporters and allies and growing confrontation with Parliament. The central issue that divided the Russian political elite concerned the type of government that would be established by the new Russian constitution. While Yeltsin insisted that it must be based on a strong presidency along the lines of that of the Fifth Republic in France, a majority in Parliament favored a parliamentary system

of government in which the legislature would play the major role.

By early 1993 a stalemate ensued, with the president and Parliament pushing for the approval of very different drafts of a new constitution. Moreover, Yeltsin insisted that, until such time as a new constitution was enacted, he had the right and obligation based on his popular election to rule by decree in order to ensure the country's well-being. In April 1993, Yeltsin called a referendum in which Russian voters were given the choice to indicate who should rule the country: Yeltsin or Parliament. After a bitter three-week electoral campaign, 59 percent of those voting (with only 39 percent of registered voters casting ballots) indicated that they had confidence in Yeltsin's leadership.

Despite the referendum, the constitutional crisis continued throughout the summer, since the Constitutional Court whose members had been appointed by Yeltsin had ruled prior to the referendum that it would require a majority of all registered voters to force Parliament to disband and call new elections. Although 64 percent of those voting called for early parliamentary elections, they were only 43 percent of registered voters; thus, their preferences were not deemed legally binding. The confrontation continued throughout the summer, with the pro-Yeltsin members of the Congress and the Supreme Soviet boycotting all sessions. Finally, on September 21, 1993, President Boris Yeltsin ordered the dissolution of both the Supreme Soviet and the Congress of Peoples' Deputies—an act that the Constitutional Court declared illegal. Simultaneously he suspended the existing constitution and scheduled elections for a new parliamentary body, the State Duma, and a referendum on his version of a new constitution.

Led by Vice President Rutskoi and parliamentary Speaker Khasbulatov, 400 Congress deputies (289 less than a quorum) met in Parliament and voted to impeach President Yeltsin and replace him with Rutskoi; they then barricaded the White House, or parliament building, against a feared attack by Yeltsin. The attack, by Russian paratroopers and elite militia units loyal to Yeltsin, complete with tanks shelling the White House, came on October 4, 1993, and was wit-

---

[36]Eugene Huskey, "Weak Russian State Expanding Exponentially," *Meeting Report,* Kennan Institute for Advanced Russian Studies, 12(18) (1995).

TABLE 7.3

FINAL RESULTS OF DUMA ELECTION, 2003

			Seats		
	% List Vote	List Seats	SMD Seats	% Total Seats	Total Seats
United Russia[1]	37.57	120	102	49.3	222
Communist Party	12.61	40	12	11.6	52
Liberal Democrats	11.45	36	0	8.0	36
Motherland[2]	9.02	29	8	8.2	37
People's Party	1.18	0	17	3.8	17
Yabloko	4.30	0	4	0.9	4
Union or Right Forces	3.97	0	3	0.7	3
Agrarian Party	3.64	0	2	0.4	2
Other parties[3]	11.56	0	6	1.3	6
Independents	—	—	68	15.1	68
Against all	4.07	—	3[4]	0.7	3

Turnout: 55.6% (1999 turnout: 61.7%)   450

Notes: [1]United Russia was formed by the merger of Unity and Fatherland-All Russia in 2001. Unity's list vote in 1999 was 23.3%; Fatherland-All Russia's list vote in 1999 was 13.3%. [2]Motherland-People's Patriotic Union is an electoral bloc formed in autumn 2003 and led by Sergei Glaz'ev and Dmitry Rogozin. [3]Six seats were won by smaller parties, including Rebirth of Russia with 3 seats, and one each for New Course-Automobile Russia, Development of Enterprise, and Great Russia-Eurasian Union.
[4]Repeat ballots will be held in three districts where the number of votes against all exceeded votes for any one candidate.

nessed worldwide on television. During that ten-day interval the rump Parliament called on the armed forces to oppose Yeltsin and support Parliament. In effect, the leaders in the White House set up a competing government and called for an overthrow of President Yeltsin's government.

On October 3, "President" Rutskoi harangued supporters in the streets outside Parliament. That evening the crowd responded to his call to seize the office of the Mayor of Moscow and the state television and radio. The next morning troops loyal to Yeltsin launched a counteroffensive against the parliament building. By late afternoon Rutskoi, Khasbulatov, and their supporters surrendered. The "Battle of Moscow" resulted in 150 deaths, 1,000 wounded, 2,000 jailed, the defeat of those opposing Yeltsin, and Yeltsin's success in convincing the West that he alone was committed to economic and political reform and that all who opposed his bid for power also opposed political and economic reform.

Little more than two years earlier Boris Yeltsin—along with political allies who included Rutskoi and Khasbulatov—had achieved political prominence in Russia by opposing, at this very same location, the forces committed to reversing the changes underway in the Soviet Union. In the intervening two years, Yeltsin had managed to alienate these men, and others, in part because of his authoritarian approach to political leadership. However, political and ideological differences, as well as aspirations for political leadership among many politicians, contributed to the split. For the next two months after the storming of the White House, Yeltsin ruled with a heavy hand, banning radical opposition groups and parties and removing the members of the Constitutional Court and provincial political leaders who had opposed his dissolution of Parliament.

Yeltsin attempted to stay above the politics of the election campaign for a new parliament scheduled for December 12. He did not associate himself with any of the political parties maneuvering for position prior to the elections in the attempt to present himself as the president of all of Russia who was above party politics. As the elections drew near, scores of parties and factions competed for positions on the ballot. Eventually more than 2,000 candidates registered to run for the new Federal Assembly. Of these more than 1,500 competed for the 225 single-mandate seats that would compose half the membership of the lower house, or State Duma (the remaining 225 Duma seats would be distributed proportionately to those parties or election blocs that received at least 5 percent of the national vote). The remaining 500 candidates were competing for the 178 seats in the Federation Council, the upper chamber of the Federal Assembly.

Thirteen parties and blocs ended up winning the 5 percent of the national vote required to be represented on the party lists. Four of these represented the reformist wing of the political spectrum and were associated with major political figures. The key issues dividing these three parties were the personalities of their leaders, more than major differences of political perspective, as well as the long-standing tendency among Russians, even those whose views are similar, to emphasize the importance of ideological differences over areas of agreement. This appears to be an ingrained aspect of Russian political culture that historically has made agreement or compromise on political matters very difficult, even among individuals or groups whose positions are close together.

The political center for parliamentary elections was represented by six parties and blocs, the most important of which was Civic Union, the party of former Vice President Rutskoi, who had been imprisoned after Yeltsin's attack on the White House in early October. The extremes of the political spectrum were held on the left by the relegalized Russian Communist Party and the Agrarian Party, and on the right by Vladimir Zhirinovsky's radical nationalist Liberal Democratic Party. In the 1991 elections for the presidency of Russia, Zhirinovsky had received 6 million votes and placed third.

The results of the parliamentary election of December 1993 represented a serious political defeat for the reformers and, in effect, for President Yeltsin, even though he had not voiced his support for any of the parties that competed in the elections. Although Russia's Choice emerged with the largest number of seats in the Duma (96

combined single-member and party-list seats of the total 450 seats), the other reform parties together won only 68 additional seats. The real winners in the December 1993 election were Zhirinovsky's extreme nationalist Liberal Democrats, who received almost 23 percent of the popular vote and 59 seats on the party lists, and the anti-reform Russian Communist and Agrarian Parties, which together won an additional 53 seats on the party lists. Since the three parties that opposed most of the reforms that had been introduced by the Yeltsin government also won 70 single-member seats, they controlled 182 of the 450 seats in the Duma and represented the largest single group of delegates.

The elections of December 1993, therefore, did nothing to resolve the problems of executive-legislative relations in Russia that had resulted in confrontation between President Yeltsin and Parliament. In fact, very early in its existence and over the strong protests of President Yeltsin, the new parliament provided a general amnesty to those arrested and imprisoned on criminal charges for their roles in the violence of October 1993, including both Aleksandr Rutskoi and Ruslan Khasbulatov. The Parliament also released from prison and dropped all charges against the plotters involved in the August 1991 attempt to overthrow Soviet President Gorbachev.

The most unexpected result of the 1993 parliamentary elections was the emergence of radical nationalist Vladimir Zhirinovsky as a major political force in Russian politics. Zhirinovsky had campaigned on a platform that opposed the economic reforms, emphasized law and order, and advocated an assertive and nationalistic foreign policy. The support for Zhirinovsky, as well as that for the Communist and Agrarian Parties of the left, indicated the widespread alienation of large portions of the Russian population that resulted from the collapse of the Soviet Union and the resulting deterioration of economic conditions throughout the country. Two years later, again confounding the political pundits, Zhirinovsky's nationalists would hold onto a larger percentage of the vote than had been expected (with the third largest number of total seats of any party). At the same time, the Communists

RUSSIAN GOVERNMENTAL INSTITUTIONS

The Russian Federation, as its name implies, has a federal system of government, with authority divided between a national government in Moscow and regional governments in 89 subnational units of various types. Moreover, it has a strong presidential system of government, complemented by a two-chamber legislature. The constitution that provides the legal framework for the Russian Federation was approved in a national referendum in December 1993.

The Russian federal system differs significantly from that of the United States because the rules that regulate relations between the central government and each of the constituent units differ from case to case, depending on individual agreements negotiated during the 1990s. Yet the resulting flexibility has probably contributed to the growing stability in center-periphery relations in Russia.

The Russian presidency has strong powers. In fact, the president has the authority to rule by decree without parliamentary approval, as did President Yeltsin during much of his administration. Yet the president does not have dictatorial powers and is subject to parliamentary oversight and to public scrutiny in periodic competitive elections.

The Russian Federal Assembly is a bicameral legislature. The lower house, called the State Duma, has 450 members, 225 of whom are elected by party list and 225 elected from single member districts. The upper house, called the Federation Council, has 178 members—the executive and the legislative heads of each of the 89 constituent units of the federation. Parliament has the authority to pass laws and to override the president's veto. The State Duma must approve presidential administrative appointments and has the authority to impeach the president and dissolve the government. The Federation Council must approve presidential appointments for major judicial posts.

---

would emerge as the dominant political force in the second State Duma. However, in the parliamentary elections of 1999, with the rise to power of Vladimir Putin, both of these parties lost support—with Zhironovsky's party receiving only six percent of the vote and 18 seats (down from 51 seats in 1995) and the Communists losing 34 seats in the Duma, down to 123 and to 52 in 2003.

Already in 1991 in his first campaign for the Russian presidency, Zhirinovsky voiced support for extreme measures in foreign policy. Over the next five years he regularly made the most outlandish nationalist claims for Russia and ethnic and racist attacks on others, including advocating the use of force to reconquer for Russia the territory of the former Soviet Union and threatening the devastation of those countries that opposed Russian "interests."

Although the election of December 1993 did not resolve the problem of confrontation between the legislature and President Yeltsin, compromises often were worked out. In fact, throughout the next two years political forces within the legislature were fairly equally divided between those who in general supported the policies of the president and those who opposed them. Moreover, given the evidence of public support for parties that opposed the central elements of the early domestic and foreign policy orientation of Yeltsin's government, his policies in several areas shifted, especially in foreign policy. While still claiming to be committed to a policy of cooperation with the West and treatment of the countries of the "near abroad" as sovereign equals, Russia became visibly more assertive on issues as wide-ranging as behavior toward the former republics, policy toward former Yugoslavia, arms sales to countries viewed as international pariahs by the West, and the entry into full NATO membership of the countries of Central Europe.

Since the general confrontation between President Yeltsin and the Parliament continued to dominate Russian politics, the run-up to the parliamentary elections of December 1995 were filled with charges and countercharges among the major political figures, as well as widespread speculation about the growing strength of antireform political forces in Russia. However, the election process was much more open, fair, and clean, according to virtually all Russian and foreign observers, than the election two years earlier. This time the Duma was elected for a full four-year term. No political parties were prevented from running candidates, and a total of 42 parties and movements participated in the political race. The new Duma included 157 members who had served in the former Duma. The number of women declined from 58 members to 46, thus continuing the very visible trend since the Gorbachev reforms of the reduced presence and role of women in positions of political importance in Russia.

The results of the election represented a major defeat for democratic and reform forces and for President Yeltsin (see Table 7.4). Antireform parties of the left, with 188 seats in the 450-seat Duma, and of the right, with 56 seats, controlled a majority in the Duma. Democratic parties fared especially poorly, with a total of 54 seats, while centrist parties gained 58 seats. Overall the results of the election indicated even more clearly than those of 1993 that the Russian

TABLE 7.4

TRENDS IN RUSSIAN STATE DUMA ELECTIONS, 1993–1999

	% Vote on Party List District Seats			Party List Seats		Single Member		Total Seats	
	1993	1995	1999	1995	1999	1995	1999	1995	1999
Communist Party of the Russian Federation	12.4	22.7	24.3	99	67	58	56	157	123
Unity			23.3		64		8		72
Fatherland–All Russia			13.3		37		30		67
Union of Right Forces			8.5		24		5		29
Zhirinovsky Bloc	22.9	11.4	6.0	50	17	1	1	51	18
Yabloko*	7.9	7.0	5.9	31	16	14	4	45	20
Communists–Workers' Russia		4.6	2.2	0	0	1	0	1	0
Women of Russia	8.1	4.7	2.0	0	0	3	0	3	0
Our Home Is Russia		10.3	1.2	45	0	10	9	55	9
Russia's Democratic Choice**	15.5	3.9		0		9		9	
Agrarian Party	8.0	3.8		0		20		20	
Others	20.9	28.8	10.0	0	0	31	10	31	10
Independents								78	101
Against All	4.3	2.8	3.3						
Total	100.0	100.0	100.0	225	225	225	224	450	449
Turnout	54.8	62.5	61.9						

Source: Matthew Wyman, "Elections and Voters," in Stephen White, Alex Pravda, and Zvi Gitelman, eds., *Developments in Russian Politics* (Durham, NC: Duke University Press, 2001), p. 68.

* 1993 and 1995, Liberal Democratic Party of Russia.

** 1993, known as Russia's Choice; in 1999 a constituent party of the Union of Right Forces.

population, especially in areas outside the major metropolitan areas of Moscow and St. Petersburg that the positive results of market reforms had not yet reached, did not trust the government's program of reforms, which they associated with the dramatic collapse of the Russian economy and of their standard of living. They were tired of escalating crime and corruption that had taken over much of Russian society.

The impact of the election results on the Russian government and its policies was evident early in 1996 as President Yeltsin removed from his government the last officials and advisors committed to significant economic reform. New government subsidies were allocated for government-owned industries, major wage concessions were made to striking coal miners, and additional financial commitments were announced for the beleaguered Russian defense industries. These shifts in policy—which followed a pattern of movement away from the reform policy in place since 1993—when considered in the context of the more assertive foreign policy rhetoric of new Foreign Minister Yevgeny Primakov, indicated a shift in policies of Yeltsin's government. During the electoral campaign, President Yeltsin continued to make budgetary commitments that were viewed as potentially inflationary and to make various promises about reasserting Russia's role in world affairs.

Indicative of the new distribution of political power in the Duma, Gennadi Seleznev, former editor of *Pravda,* deputy speaker in the prior Duma, and a key figure in the Communist Party of Russia, was elected speaker of the Duma, with 231 votes (5 more than the required 226). His support came from his own Communist Party, the Agrarian Party, Power to the People–Communists, and some Liberal Democrats (Yabloko). The comeback of the Communists, who were banned in 1991 after the failed coup attempt and declared dead by many analysts, can be explained in part by the success of Gennadi Zyuganov and others in the party to take up the call of Russian nationalism, while also supporting the interests of the ordinary Russian whose entire existence has been disrupted by events of the past decade. The image of the new Communist Party is one

that mixed elements of traditional Marxism with Great Russian nationalism. In the mid-1990s, Zyuganov and his party responded more effectively than either the democrats or the radical nationalists to provide the Russian people, disillusioned and demoralized by the collapse of their imperial state and of much of the social net that had undergirded their personal existence, with hope for the future. The results of the 1995 parliamentary elections indicate that millions of Russians have found this message attractive. Four years later the stagnation of the institutional base of its support, the aging of its core supporters, and most important, the rise of an alternative in Vladimir Putin combined to reduce appreciably the relative electoral success of the Communist Party.

In early 1996, Zyuganov announced his candidacy for the presidential elections of June 1996. Most of the other parties of the left announced their willingness to support his candidacy. On February 14, despite the opposition of Yegor Gaidar and other Yeltsin supporters and public opinion polls that indicated that his support among Russian voters remained below 10 percent, President Yeltsin announced from his home city of Yekaterinburg that he would run for reelection. With the takeover of the Duma by political forces opposed to a continuation of the reform policies of the prior four years, led by the Communists, the election of Zyuganov would likely have resulted in a reversal of many of the political and economic developments of the past decade. Duma speaker Seleznev, for example, noted the Communist Party's commitment to eliminating the presidency and the Duma and reestablishing a Soviet-style governmental system with a Council of Ministers accountable to a reinstated Supreme Soviet.

The presidential election campaign of spring 1996 presented two quite different perspectives on the direction that Russia should take. For example, in mid-May Gennadi Zyuganov outlined the main points of an economic program committed to a centrally managed economy. Although some forms of private ownership would be permitted, the state would own a controlling share in various sectors of the economy,

REVIEW 7.2

KEY POLITICAL FIGURES IN RUSSIA 2005

President of the Russian Federation	Vladimir V. Putin
Prime Minister	Mikhail Fradkov
Minister of Foreign Affairs	Sergey Lavrov
Minister of Defense	Sergei Ivanov
Secretary of the Security Council	Vladimir B. Rushailo
Chairman of the State Duma	Boris Gryzlov
Chairman of the Federal Council	Sergei M. Mironov

CHAIRMEN OF MAJOR POLITICAL PARTIES

Communist Party of the Russian Federation	Gennadi A. Ziuganov
Unity and Fatherland Party	Sergei Shoigu, Yuri Luzhkov, and Mintimer Shaimiyev, co-chairs
Union of Right Forces	Boris Nemtsov
Liberal Democratic Party of Russia	Vladimir Zhironovsky
Yabloko	Grigory A. Yavlinsky

including energy, transport, military industry, education, and science. Zyuganov's program envisaged strong state intervention to stimulate investment, control prices, and protect domestic producers. Zyuganov also called for forms of censorship to protect Russian culture and morals. Yeltsin, on the other hand, committed himself to a continuation of the policies of the prior four and a half years, although he seldom spoke of privatization, and he made a vast array of expensive commitments that threatened to undermine economic stabilization and contradicted commitments made to the International Monetary Fund. Only in the foreign policy area, where Russian policy had already become much more assertive than it was in the first year of independence, were the differences in policy minimal.

In some respects Russia had by 1996 made substantial progress in establishing the bases for a functioning democratic system. The constitution approved in December 1993 provides the framework for a political system and for the legal transfer of political power. Despite serious political differences among political parties and between the executive and the legislature, legislation was passed and political compromises reached. Less positive, however, was the lack of

evidence that democratic values had taken root among the majority of the Russian population, including the political elites. Moreover, the development of stable institutions—such as political parties, an effective legal system, and other institutions that are essential components of democratic systems elsewhere—remains retarded.

Russian politics during the last four years of the Yeltsin era were characterized largely by a continuation of the politics of stalemate and inaction that had characterized the earlier years of his administration. Yeltsin's periodic absences from public view because of illness did not help the establishment of a stable political environment. Throughout this period the most serious political issues facing the government related to continuing economic problems, rampant corruption and crime, and the dramatic loss in public confidence in President Yeltsin and in the political system itself. As we shall discuss below, the financial disaster of August 1998 that resulted in Russia's defaulting on its massive international debt represented the nadir of its economic problems.

In early 1998, Yeltsin fired his entire cabinet, including Prime Minister Viktor Chernomyrdin, who had held the post for more than five years. Although Yeltsin justified the move as an effort to push through more effective economic reforms, some analysts explained it as a result of Chernomyrdin's growing political strength in relationship to the president, as well as the strong opposition to Yeltsin's policies by members of the Duma. In fact, despite his more conservative political credentials, Chernomyrdin completed much of the radical privatization campaign initiated by Yegor Gaidar.

Many saw the privatization policy as a giveaway of state assets and an essential part of the explosion of corruption by government officials, including Chernomyrdin himself. Two noted analysts of Russian politics, Peter Reddaway and Dmitri Glinski, argue that early in Yeltsin's rule the real democrats—those who were committed to the creation of a political system basic of democratic principles—were effectively maneuvered to the sidelines so that important remnants of the old *nomenklatura* who surrounded Yeltsin could consolidate their economic and political control over Russia. They summarize their assessment of the economic "reforms" as follows: "Thus, instead of pursuing an equitable denationalization of property and a level playing field for law-abiding new entrepreneurs, the regime accelerated Soviet-era elites' and the criminal underworld's rush to conduct what Soviet history textbooks called 'the primitive accumulation of capital,' something that was supposedly an inevitable stage in the building of a capitalist society." Rather than building the foundations of a democratic society, they conclude, Yeltsin and his associates imposed on Russia "a regime of Byzantine authoritarianism."[37]

Chernomyrdin's replacement was the unknown 35-year-old Sergei Kirienko, who proved not to be up to the task of running the country and the economy. Yeltsin tried to bring back Chernomyrdin in August 1998 after the financial crisis that forced Russia to default on its debts and devalue its currency. Strong opposition in the Duma resulted in his appointing Yevgeny Primakov, a moderate with extensive

political experience who had the support of many parliamentarians.

However, by spring 1999, despite some evidence of the stabilization of the economy, Yeltsin dismissed Primakov. The Duma immediately brought impeachment proceedings against the president. Although majorities supported all five sets of charges against him, they did not reach the two-thirds level required to remove him from office. Yeltsin's next choice as prime minister, Sergei Stepashin, a long-term Yeltsin supporter, lasted a mere three months in the office.

Finally in August 1999, Yeltsin appointed the virtually unknown Vladimir Putin as prime minister with the explanation that he saw in him his own successor as a candidate in the presidential elections scheduled for summer 2000. As we have already seen, Putin moved rapidly and successfully to consolidate his position during fall 1999. His forceful action against Chechen terrorists elicited widespread popular support, although questions remain whether Chechen rebels were actually responsible for several bombings. In addition, the media associated with Yeltsin's supporters carried out devastating attacks on those likely to be important political challengers in the presidential elections.

The parliamentary elections of December showed Putin's growing strength. A hastily organized political movement to support Putin, called Unity, came in second in the elections, after the Communist Party, with almost 24 percent of the vote and 16 percent of the parliamentary seats. The elections showed that the Russian political party system is still in flux, although on the positive side, a lower percentage of the total vote went to marginal parties unable to pass the 5-percent threshold required to gain representation.

After Yeltsin's resignation on 31 December and the appointment of Putin as acting president, the date of the presidential election was pushed up to April 2000. Although eleven candidates vied for the office, the race was really a two-man affair between Putin and Zyuganov, head of the Communist Party. With 53 percent of the votes, Putin won on the first ballot, while Zyuganov polled 29 percent.

Even before his formal inauguration in May, Putin began to move against regional political

---

[37]Peter Reddaway and Dmitri Glinski, *The Tragedy of Russia's Reforms: Market Bolshevism Against Democracy* (Washington, DC: United States Institute of Peace Press, 2002), p. 638.

forces and the oligarchs who controlled much of the economy to reconsolidate the authority of the political center. Two years later it can be said that he has had significant success in both areas. However, serious questions continue to exist concerning his commitment to political democracy and the rule of law. He has been heavy-handed in dealing with political opponents and has seemingly focused his attack on corruption against those who controlled independent national media, especially television networks. By early 2002, for example, all independent TV networks had been shut down because of "financial irregularities." Moreover, Russian policy in Chechnya has been especially brutal in dealing with real and suspected opponents of Russia's continuing role in the region.

On the other hand, Putin continues to command the support and respect of the vast majority of Russian citizens. In addition, he has successfully attacked some of the most serious of Russia's problems. Finally, under his presidency the economy has flourished—for the first time since the collapse of the Soviet state. It is far too soon to assess the overall contributions of Putin's leadership to the rebuilding of the Russian state and economy. However, at the beginning of 2002, many analysts, both in and outside Russia, gave him a cautiously positive grade.

Political developments elsewhere throughout the Commonwealth of Independent States generally have been less positive than those in Russia from the perspective of establishing functioning democratic systems and effective market economies. Many of the countries have very weak national governments that have found it virtually impossible to govern. Civil war, sectionalism, and virtual anarchy have characterized large portions of Georgia, Moldova, and Tajikistan, for example. Across Central Asia, presidential dictatorships of the right and the left have emerged as the predominant form of government. In a referendum in Kyrgyzstan in February 1996, with voting statistics akin to those of the Soviet past, more than 90 percent of the population voted, with over 95 percent of the voters favoring expanded powers for President Askar Akaev. In Tajikistan the old Communist *nomenklatura* rules the country and is carrying

out, with Russian assistance, a relentless struggle against its political and religious enemies. Uzbekistan under President Islam Karimov and, increasingly, Kazakhstan under Nursultan Nazarbayev are ruled by presidential decree. In the Transcaucasus, continuing warfare and ethnic strife make any semblance of political stabilization and democratization a virtual impossibility. Politics in Belarus under the authoritarian leadership of President Lukashenka resembles Brezhnev's USSR, with the widespread use of police brutality to cow political opponents.

Prospects for long-term stability and for the resolution of serious underlying problems remain questionable. Throughout the region, the two central political questions of importance concern the relationship with Russia, including the degree to which effective independence can be maintained, and the creation of productive economies from the residue of the old Soviet system.

Toward a Market Economy

The third major task facing Russia and the other post-Communist states—after state and nation building and the establishment of democratic institutions—has been the creation of the institutions needed for a productive market economy. It is important to recall that prior to the Gorbachev reforms—and, in fact, in most respects at the time of the implosion of the Soviet Union—Russia lacked most of the prerequisites for a market economy. Central planning, price controls, the absence of a real banking system, and the lack of a sense of entrepreneurship were but a few of the characteristics of the old economic system that impeded the emergence of a market economy. Moreover, the efforts at reform, both under Mikhail Gorbachev and Boris Yeltsin, resulted in precipitous declines in production in both the industrial and the agricultural sectors. By 1995, estimated gross national product for the Russian Federation had fallen to less than 53 percent of the figure for 1989 and industrial output was only 47 percent as high—although production data for 1995–1997 gave some evidence that the depression had bottomed out. Indeed, production in certain areas, such as the iron and steel and chemical and petrochemical industries, actually rose for the first time since the collapse of the Soviet Union. This was but a prelude, however, to the financial and economic crash of August 1998. Since then the economy has begun to expand, as world energy prices rose and less expensive Russian goods became attractive in world markets (see Table 7.5). By the time Vladimir Putin took over as acting president, growth rates in both Russian industrial and agricultural production were quite high. But already by the end of 2001, data indicated a substantial falloff in the rate of Russian economic growth.

Despite the disastrous collapse in Russian production, there are those who view President Yeltsin's economic reform program as "Russia's Success Story," to cite the title of an article by Anders Åslund, a noted Swedish economist and former economic advisor to the Russian government. The gist of his argument is the following:

The Western caricature of Russia as a destitute country on the verge of either collapse or falling into the hands of fascists could not be more wrong. Naturally, things are far from perfect, but no one thought communism would go away without costs. In a new openness all problems

are discussed in the Russian media, and often exaggerated. But few in the West write about Russia's successes, like the end of shortages and the risk of famine. Moreover, the true disaster of other former Soviet republics is often confused with Russia's. Of course major problems such as crime and inflation remain in Russia, but even monthly inflation fell to five percent in June [1994].[38]

Even after the disastrous financial collapse of August 1998, Åslund and others support their argument by noting that much of the supposed depression of the Russian economy was not real. Under Communism, overreporting of production was notorious; under the current capitalist system, underreporting to avoid taxes is even more prevalent. Åslund maintains that the consumption

[38]Anders Åslund, "Russia's Success Story," *Foreign Affairs* 73(5) (1994), p. 58. Åslund develops his arguments more fully in *How Russia Became a Market Economy* (Washington, DC: Brookings Institution, 1995). For a similar positive assessment, see Brigitte Granville, *The Success of Russian Economic Reforms* (London: Royal Institute of International Affairs; distributed by Brookings Institution, Washington, 1995).

TABLE 7.5

KEY ECONOMIC TRENDS IN RUSSIA, 1990–2001

Main Macroeconomic Indicators of Russia

as % of thee previous year

	1995	1996	1997	1998	1999	2000	2001	2001	2003	2004
Gross domestic product	95.9	96.4	101.4	94.7	106.4	110.0	105.1	104.7	107.3	107.1
Industrial production	97	96	102	95	111	112	105	104	107	106.1
Agricultural production	92	95	102	87	104	108	108	102	102	101.6
Capital investments	90	82	95	88	105	117	110	103	112.5	111

Sources: Interstate Statistical Committee of the CIS.

of electricity is probably a better indicator of actual industrial production than the output statistics. Here one finds decreases one-third to one-half those of production statistics. The central problems of the emerging capitalist economy in Russia, according to Åslund, result from the rise of organized crime and its growing role in controlling an ever-increasing portion of the economy and the unfettered domination of the workers by management in the workplace. He concludes that Yeltsin and Prime Minister Chernomyrdin, to whom he gave much of the credit for the success, created the foundations for a functioning free-market economy. The issue is not the impending collapse of Russia, but rather the direction that it will take in the future. Slow and limited reforms, not shock therapy, were the main cause of Russia's economic woes, he has maintained.

Other analysts—mainly those who emphasize the negative impact of the changes on the lives of individual Russians and the degree to which public assets were virtually stolen—paint a very different picture of the results of the economic restructuring that has occurred in Russia since independence. They note that the costs of the shock therapy approach to economic reform introduced by Yeltsin were extraordinarily disruptive and contributed to severe dislocations in the economy. Shock therapy refers to a set of short-run policies that were designed to create a free and open economic market and to achieve macroeconomic stability. As the first part of this program, Yeltsin deregulated prices on most consumer goods on January 2, 1992. Producers could set whatever price they pleased on their goods, with distributors adding an additional 25 percent. As a result, prices soon quadrupled on foodstuffs. However, the reformers expected that the increased prices would encourage all producers to bring their products to market, thereby eliminating shortages and thus reducing prices once again. The expectation was that after an initial period of inflation, supply would catch up with demand. However, this did not occur, for in many areas of the economy—including large segments of the consumer sector—monopolies that did not respond effectively to factors of supply and demand dominated production or distribution.

A second important aspect of the shock therapy was the attempt to stabilize the Russian ruble and make it fully convertible on international financial markets—the latter in response to the demand of the International Monetary Fund as a precondition for financial assistance. By the standards of free-market economies, the Communist monetary system was exceptionally stable. Prices and currency exchange rates were fixed by decree and often did not change officially for decades. Inflation was allegedly eliminated, which facilitated long-term planning. In fact, this was but an illusion. The Russian ruble was a mysterious entity that had no monetary value outside the Soviet Union and had multiple rates of exchange for convertible world currencies. Initially the Russian Central Bank, under the direction of Viktor Gerashchenko, continued to provide enormous credit to enterprises that otherwise would have gone bankrupt, thereby contributing significantly to the hyperinflation that Russia suffered in 1992 and 1993. Only after July 1993 did President Yeltsin and Prime Minister Chernomyrdin bring the Central Bank under government control. The tight money policy of the next two years contributed to bringing inflation down and stabilizing the value of the Russian ruble. The attempt to deal with this issue required major government budget cuts, especially in the military sector where earlier cuts had reduced military spending from about 25 percent of GNP in the USSR to less than 5 percent. Despite these efforts, the Russian government until 1995 consistently ran budget deficits in the neighborhood of 9–10 percent per year of GNP, thereby contributing to the explosive inflation that characterized the economy through 1994.

A third major aspect of the radical economic reforms introduced in Russia in early 1992 was privatization of Russia's state-owned industries. Privatization of the consumer service sector of the economy proceeded relatively smoothly. It has been quite a different matter with the large industrial enterprises, most of which went to well-placed individuals at bargain prices in 1995–1996. The privatization of these large industrial complexes brought with it a whole series of potentially explosive social and political problems. First, the fact that most industrial enterprises in the former

USSR were not really competitive and did not incorporate contemporary technology into their production meant that they would not be competitive in a market economy. The privatization of large industrial enterprises, therefore, would likely bring with it widespread unemployment for workers considered redundant. A related matter concerned housing and social services, much of which in the former Soviet Union was provided by employers. As enterprises were privatized, or as state enterprises lost portions of their government subsidy, responsibility for housing and for other social services devolved on local governments ill-prepared to deal with them.

One group in Russia that has benefited greatly from privatization is the former Soviet *nomenklatura.* The liberalization of state control over the prices of commodities and consumer goods, as well as the legalization of domestic and foreign trade, opened up substantial opportunities for the "new Russians"—Russia's new entrepreneurial class, which includes a disproportionately large percentage of former state and party officials. These officials commanded the expertise and were positioned to take advantage of the new opportunities. As Jerry Hough has pointed out, the transfer of state assets was done in a manner that guaranteed major economic benefits to inside traders. This led to economic behavior that downplayed production and contributed to a form of corruption that did not contribute to economic growth. Russia's first generation of capitalists behaved much as their predecessors had in other early capitalist systems. Moreover, the remaining wealth of the nation ended up, to a very substantial degree, in the hands of a very small number of individuals.[39]

---

[39]See Jerry F. Hough, *The Logic of Economic Reform in Russia* (Washington, DC: Brookings Institution, 2001). Studies done by sociologist Olga Kryshtanovska indicate that 61 percent of the new business elite in Russia come from the old Soviet *nomenklatura,* while 75 percent of the political elite come from the old bureaucracy. *Izvestiya,* January 10, 1996. For information on favoritism in the privatization of Russian industry, see Alessandra Stanley, "Russian Scandal Threatens Future of Privatization," *New York Times,* January 26, 1996.

Until the end of the 1990s, policy changes in the agricultural sector of the Russian economy lagged far behind those in the service and industrial sectors. In fact, it is in agriculture that the strongest resistance to change can be found in Russia, and it is in rural Russia that the Communist and Agrarian Parties of the left find major support. The Russian government has lacked a coherent plan for agriculture, and what efforts were made to privatize land holdings and develop effective market mechanisms have proven counterproductive. In part, this results in the continued dominance of the old Soviet *nomenklatura* at the district level in Russia. The government's tight money policy and the high cost of credit and production resulted in a drop of agricultural production and of food processing.

A fourth element of the reform program put into place by the Russian government, one closely related to monetary reform, was the creation of a modern banking system. Although banks existed in the former Soviet Union, their primary function was to distribute governmental subsidies to enterprises. They did not play the role, as they do in market economies, of taking risks by supporting entrepreneurial projects. They played no role in decision making about the directions that the economy would take. After Russian independence, a whole new system of banking emerged in Russia—not without serious problems of corruption and an unhealthy role of organized crime—that is essential to the emergence of a functioning market economy.

Possibly the most serious problem that has resulted as a side effect from the economic reforms has been the emergence of organized crime, or so-called mafia groups, across Russia. The objective is control of the lucrative private economic activity that, in many areas of Russia, is flourishing. Among their major targets have been the private banks that have mushroomed in Russia in an environment with very few and very inadequate regulatory controls. These have provided great opportunities for sophisticated swindling and scams. Smuggling, protection rackets, and extortion are other widespread forms of economic crime, as well as prostitution, drug smuggling, and gun running. Much of the new criminal class finds its roots in unemployed or underpaid members of the former Soviet security forces. They also have close ties to supposedly legitimate businessmen and politicians. Moreover, they are not loath to execute or assassinate bankers, politicians, and journalists who resist their activities or report on them. Governmental bodies at the federal, provincial, and local level have devoted major resources to combating organized crime; however, according to one Russian analyst, "the wave of organized crime continues to sweep across Russia.... There is ample evidence to support the MVD's [Ministry of Internal Affairs] declaration that 70 percent of the country is ruled by the mafia."[40] Despite President Putin's initial efforts to create a stable foundation for the Russian economy, as of early 2002 there is little evidence of success in undercutting the role of organized crime.

Although many serious problems have been associated with the efforts of the Russian political elite to create a market economy, they have made progress in laying the foundations for such an economy, although that progress has been exceedingly slow and sporadic. During 1999 and 2000, inflation dropped significantly—from 84 percent in 1998 to 20 percent in 2000. But the decline virtually stopped in 2001 (18.6 percent). The economy grew significantly during the past three years at annual rates of between 8.5 and 4.5 percent. But even after ten years it is still too soon to predict with any degree of reliability whether or the Russian economy has entered a period of long and stable growth.

In general the economic situation in the other post-Soviet states—except in the Baltics, where developments have been unexpectedly positive—is bleaker than that in Russia. Most of the other countries have suffered severely because of the break-up of the single economic space that characterized the USSR, created to tie regional economies together and ensure Moscow's control. Their access to needed raw mate-

rials and energy, as well as their access to markets, has been disrupted. Moreover, the focus of government policy throughout most of the CIS has been on issues of internal security or ways to assure independence from Russia rather than on economic reform. Not until 1995, for example, did the government of Ukraine begin to look seriously at the question of economic reform, although economic trends in 1995 were generally quite positive. The depression suffered by all the post-Soviet states has been even more severe throughout the other CIS states than in the Russian Federation. Only in several of the countries of Central Asia, where oil and gas reserves are significant and Western companies and countries are helping to fund development, do medium-term economic prospects look favorable.

Toward the Future

Since independence, Russia has made progress in the triple requirements of state building, democratization, and marketization—although most other post-Soviet states outside the Baltics have seen little success in one or more of the areas. However, much more remains to be done if the successes of the first decade are not to founder and be lost. With the major exception of Chechnya, the most serious challenges to Russian authority in the ethnically based republics have been resolved. Moreover, the issue of federal relations with both the republics and the provinces is less a concern than it was only a few years ago.

Significant progress has also been made in Russia in creating some of the institutions associated with democracy. However, it is in this area that Russia has the most yet to accomplish. First, there is the appeal among many in the Russian political elite—including President Putin himself—for authoritarian approaches to solving problems. Moreover, the costs of change have fallen disproportionately on various groups in Russian society. Although significant strides have been made in rehabilitating the Russian economy, the benefits are not falling equally to all groups. Those displaced by the changes or for whom the presumed security of the Communist past remains an overriding concern—including

---

[40]Aleksandr Zhilin, "Russian Organized Crime—A Growth Industry," *Prism: A Bi-Weekly on the Post-Soviet States* 1(26) (December 22, 1995).

especially the elderly, industrial workers, and the rural population—blame the central government and its so-called reforms. They, as well as those dismayed by the decline in Russia's world status and the loss of the old empire and by the pervasive influence of organized crime, are attracted to the supposedly easy solutions offered by the Communists of Gennadi Zyuganov. It is ironic that the very democratic institutions that have been put in place in Russia are being used by those committed to reestablishing a more authoritarian system that would return to many of the policies of the past.

Another indication of the weakness of democracy in Russia—and a problem that was highlighted during all presidential election campaigns—relates to government ownership of much of the mass media and printing plants and the continued existence of partial censorship. With the suppression by President Putin of most remaining private media, the problem has grown.

Finally, despite many serious problems that remain in the Russian economy, progress was made in a very short period of time in dismantling the old command economy and creating a functioning market economy. What remains to be done is to deal with the problems of income distribution and the collapse of the social network, corruption and the role of criminal elements in the economy, and the depressed status of rural areas and many provincial cities. The key questions are whether the government of President Putin is committed to dealing with these problems and whether the Russian people have the patience to wait for the solution within the context of a democratic political system.

Thinking Critically

1. What were the major reasons for Mikhail Gorbachev's failure to reform the political and economic systems of the USSR?
2. What are some of the special problems faced by post-Communist states, compared with other former authoritiarian states, in making the transition to democratic politics and market economies?

3. What is meant by "nation building" in the context of the Russian Federation?
4. What is the relevance in Russia of institution building for the process of democratization?
5. How successful has Russia been in establishing a functioning market economy? What are the major problems still facing the economy?

KEY TERMS

"Battle of Moscow" *(411)*
Bolsheviks *(385)*
Central Committee *(389)*
Cheka (386)
Commonwealth of Independent States (CIS) *(404, 405)*
CPSU (Communist Party of the Soviet Union) *(383)*
cult of personality *(387)*
democratization *(404)*
General Secretary *(385)*
glasnost (391)
hubris *(403)*
KGB (Committee for State Security) *(388)*
Komsomol (389)
Mensheviks *(385)*
nation building *(405)*
nomenklatura (397, 418, 421)
oblast *(389)*
oligarchy *(387)*
partocracy *(389, 396)*
perestroika (389, 390, 391)
Politbureau *(390)*
p.p.o. (primary party organization) *(389)*
Secretariat *(390)*
shock therapy *(394)*
State Duma *(412, 413)*
totalitarian rule *(386)*
triple transition *(404)*
Workers' Opposition *(381)*

FURTHER READINGS

Adelman, Jonathan R. *Torrents of Spring: Soviet and Post-Soviet Politics* (New York: McGraw-Hill, 1995).

Andrew, Christopher, and Oleg Gordievsky. *The KGB: The Inside Story of Its Foreign Operations from Lenin to Gorbachev* (New York: HarperCollins, 1990), ch. 14.

Åslund, Anders. *Russia's Economic Transformation in the 1990s* (London: Pinter, 1997).

Armstrong, John A. *The Politics of Totalitarianism* (New York: Random House, 1961).

Blasi, Joseph R., Maya Kroumova, and Douglas Kruse. *Kremlin Capitalism: Privatizing the Russian Economy* (Ithaca, NY: Cornell University Press, 1997).

Boettke, Peter J. *Why Perestroika Failed: The Politics and Economics of Socialist Transformation* (London: Routledge, 1993).

Breslauer, George W. *Khrushchev and Brezhnev as Leaders: Building Authority in Soviet Politics.* (London: Allen and Unwin, 1982).

Brown, Archie, ed. *Contemporary Russian Politics: A Reader* (Oxford: Oxford University Press, 2001).

Conquest, Robert. *The Great Terror: A Reassessment* (New York: Oxford University Press, 1990).

Conquest, Robert. *Power and Policy in the USSR* (New York: St. Martin's, 1961).

Carrére d'Encausse, Hélène. *The End of the Soviet Empire: The Triumph of the Nations* (New York: Basic Books, 1992).

Daniels, Robert V. *The End of the Communist Revolution* (London: Routledge, 1993).

Dawisha, Karen, and Bruce Parrott, series and individual volume eds. *Democratization in Postcommunist Societies* (Cambridge: Cambridge University Press, 1997). Two of the four volumes in this series, are directly relevant to Russia and the CIS: *Democratic Changes and Authoritarian Reactions in Russia, Ukraine, Belarus, and Moldova,* vol. 3, and *Conflict, Cleavage, and Change in Central Asia and the Caucasus,* vol. 4.

Dawisha, Karen, and Bruce Parrott, series eds. *The International Politics of Eurasia,* 10 vols. (Armonk, NY: M. E. Sharpe, 1994–1997). A ten volume series with the following titles: *The Legacy of History in Russia and the New States of Eurasia,* ed. S. Frederick Starr, vol. 1 (1994).

National Identity and Ethnicity in Russia and the New States of Eurasia, ed. Roman Szporluk, vol. 2 (1994).

The Politics of Religion in Russia and the New States of Eurasia, ed. Michael Bourdeaux, vol. 3 (1994).

The Making of Foreign Policy in Russia and the New States of Eurasia, eds. Adeed Dawisha and Karen Dawisha, vol. 4 (1995).

State Building and Military Power in Russia and the New States of Eurasia, ed. Bruce Parrott, vol. 5 (1995).

The Nuclear Challenge in Russia and the New States of Eurasia, ed. George Quester, vol. 6 (1995).

Political Culture and Civil Society in Russia and the New States of Eurasia, ed. Vladimir Tismaneanu, vol. 7 (1995).

Economic Transition in Russia and the New States of Eurasia, ed. Bartlomiej Kaminski, vol. 8 (1995).

The End of Empire? The Transformation of the USSR in Comparative Perspective, ed. Karen Dawisha and Bruce Parrott, vol. 9 (1997).

The International Dimension of Post-Communist Transitions in Russia and the New States of Eurasia, ed. Karen Dawisha, vol. 10 (1997).

Fainsod, Merle. *How Russia Is Ruled,* rev. ed. (Cambridge, MA: Harvard University Press, 1967).

Gerson, Lennard D. *The Secret Police in Lenin's Russia* (Philadelphia: Temple University Press, 1976).

Gill, Graeme, and Roger D. Markwick. *Russia's Stillborn Democracy? From Gorbachev to Yeltsin* (Oxford: Oxford University Press, 2000).

Granville, Brigitte, and Peter Oppenheimer, eds. *Russia's Post-Communist Economy* (Oxford: Oxford University Press, 2001).

Hough, Jerry F. *Democratization and Revolution in the USSR, 1985–1991* (Washington, DC: Brookings Institution, 1997).

Hough, Jerry F. *The Logic of Economic Reform in Russia* (Washington, DC: Brookings Institution, 2001).

Hough, Jerry F., and Merle Fainsod. *How the Soviet Union Is Governed* (Cambridge, MA: Harvard University Press, 1979).

Huskey, Eugene. *Presidential Power in Russia* (Armonk, NY: M. E. Sharpe, 1999).

Jack, Andrew. *Inside Putin's Russia* (New York: Oxford University Press, 2004).

Kempton, Daniel R., and Terry D. Clark, eds. *Unity or Separation: Center-Periphery Relations in the Former Soviet Union* (Westport, CT: Praeger, 2002).

Khrushchev, Sergei N. *Nikita Khrushchev and the Creation of a Superpower* (University Park: Pennsylvania State University Press, 2000).

Knight, Amy W. *Spies Without Cloaks: The KGB's Successors* (Princeton, NJ: Princeton University Press, 1996).

Leggett, George. *The Cheka: Lenin's Political Police* (Oxford: Clarendon Press, 1981).

McCauley, Martin, ed. *Khrushchev and Khrushchevism* (Bloomington: Indiana University Press, 1988).

McFaul, Michael, et al. *Between Dictatorship and Democracy: Russian Post-Communist Political Reform* (Washington, DC: Carnegie Endowment for International Peace, 2004).

McNeal, Robert H. *Stalin: Man and Ruler* (New York: New York University Press, 1988).

Nagy, Piroska Mohácsi Nagy. *The Meltdown of the Russian State: The Deformation and Collapse of the State in Russia* (Cheltenham, UK: Edward Elgar, 2000).

Reddaway, Peter, ed. *The Dynamics of Russian Politics* (Lanham: Rowman and Littlefield, 2004).

Sadwa, Richard. *Putin: Russia's Choice* (London: Routledge, 2004).

Schapiro, Leonard. *The Communist Part of the Soviet Union,* rev. ed. (New York: Random House, 1971).

Steele, Jonathan. *Eternal Russia: Yeltsin, Gorbachev, and the Mirage of Democracy* (Cambridge, MA: Harvard University Press, 1996).

Ulam, Adam B. *The Bolsheviks: The Intellectual and Political History of the Triumph of Communism in Russia* (New York: Macmillan, 1965).

Ulam, Adam B. *Stalin: The Man and His Era* (New York: Viking, 1973).

PUBLIC POLICY IN THE SOVIET UNION

The Soviet Union acquired the status of a super-power not only by being on the victorious side in World War II, but also as a consequence of deliberate policies pursued by its leadership after 1945. These policies, as well as the Soviet (Marxist-Leninist) view of international relations, served to maximize Soviet power and caused many countries to be suspicious or fearful of Soviet intentions, just as other countries in the past had feared tsarist Russian intentions. The Soviet Union's human and material resources were mobilized and its military capabilities rapidly developed so that it could acquire nuclear parity or even superiority. The Soviet rulers were unashamedly power-oriented, and the 1977 Soviet Constitution (Article 62) obligated all citizens to strengthen the "might and authority" of the Soviet State.

The policies and actions of other countries also contributed to the Soviet Union's emergence as a great power. The Soviet Union was sought as an ally by the French and Czechs in 1934; negotiations with the British in 1939 eventually broke down at the time when the Soviet Union was faced with the possibility of a two-front war—in Asia where they were already fighting Japanese troops based in the Japanese province of Manchukuo (occupied Manchuria) and also in Europe against Nazi Germany. Eventually Stalin concluded a nonaggression pact with Nazi Germany in August 1939. Two weeks after Germany invaded Poland and precipitated World War II, the Soviets joined in the military campaign that led to the destruction of the Polish state. The Nazi-Soviet Pact enabled the USSR to annex western Ukraine and western Belorussia (Belarus), as well as Estonia, Latvia, Lithuania, and the region of Bessarabia (which had been part of Romania between 1918 and 1940)—territories with a non-Russian population of more than 22 million. Hitler's invasion of the Soviet Union in June 1941 involved Stalin's regime in World War II, despite efforts to remain neutral.

The war was very costly to the Soviet Union (resulting in more than 20 million deaths) and initially involved a year and a half of military retreat. It was won, but not solely because of Soviet patriotism, Russian nationalism, or belief in Marxism-Leninism. The Soviet victory was also the result of other factors, including brutal German occupation policies that provided no attractive alternative to Stalin's rule, and in part to $12 billion of U.S. Lend-Lease aid made available unconditionally to Stalin's dictatorship by the Roosevelt administration. In addition, the USSR was spared having to fight a war on two fronts in Europe and in the Far East in 1941–1945 thanks to the decision of the Japanese militarists to attack the United States at Pearl Harbor and to seize Southeast Asia, Indonesia, and the Philippines in 1941–1942, instead of attacking Siberia at the time that Soviet forces were retreating in the West.

The total defeat of Germany and Japan in 1945 and the weakened condition of France and Italy added to the Soviet Union's advantage and resulted in a U.S.-Soviet bipolarity in place of the prewar multipolar international situation. The failure of Britain and the United States to prevent the establishment of Communist regimes in eight East European countries and in North Korea (largely as a result of Soviet military occupation) led to the emergence of a Soviet bloc under Moscow's leadership. The wartime United Nations military alliance that defeated Nazi Germany and Japan deteriorated quickly, as Stalin moved to consolidate power in the territories "liberated" by the Red Army and launched an intensive campaign to end the U.S. atomic weapons monopoly. The Soviets succeeded in detonating an atomic bomb in 1949 and acquired the hydrogen bomb in 1953. In the 1960s and 1970s Soviet military power was deployed in Cuba, Angola, Ethiopia, Vietnam, South Yemen, and Afghanistan.

The Soviet Union's lead in the acquisition of the heaviest intercontinental ballistic missiles, the largest nuclear warheads, a limited antimissile defense capability, a hunter-killer satellite, the largest submarine fleet in naval history, and the first mobile intercontinental ballistic missiles did not prove the success or even the viability of the Soviet system. In fact, as Gorbachev was later to admit, the arms race resulted in a profligate waste of scarce resources in the Soviet Union and contributed significantly to the economic crisis that he inherited in 1985.

The Soviet View of International Relations

Soviet leaders understood international politics largely in terms of Marxism-Leninism, although traditional Russian expansionism and a sense of a special Russian role in history (Russian messianism) also affected the Soviet view of foreign countries. Marxism-Leninism emphasized conflict and the class struggle as the motive force in historical development. Class warfare was extended into the realm of international relations, and a certain level of tension and conflict was regarded as a normal condition in relations between states; however, tension was to be kept within limits in order to avoid high-risk military confrontations or "adventurist" undertakings. By the 1970s, after the U.S. military defeat in Vietnam and the emergence of a growing number of countries in the developing world that proclaimed the establishment of Marxist-Leninist regimes, the Brezhnev leadership was especially confident about the future. As late as 1986 the CPSU Program declared, "The dialectics of development are such that the very same means that capitalism puts to use with the aim of strengthening its positions inevitably lead to an aggravation of all its deep-seated contradictions. Imperialism is parasitical, decaying and moribund capitalism; it marks the eve of the socialist revolution."[41]

In the Soviet view of international politics, at least until the late 1980s, quantitative changes were seen as leading to qualitative change that favored the Soviet Union. International developments were depicted and analyzed in terms of the

concept "correlation of forces," which reflected the relations between the great powers—actually, the strategic balance. Foremost among the Soviet Union's objectives was the enhancement of its strategic power and its ability to influence the actions of other states and play a prominent, if not dominant, role in the world.

Soviet foreign policy makers sought to prevent the formation of coalitions that could be directed against the Soviet Union and result in its isolation. Moscow attempted to divide its capitalist opponents by driving wedges between them and disrupting alliances, such as NATO, which had been established to deter the possible threat of Soviet aggression. The Soviet Union always attempted to isolate the state that it regarded as its principal enemy: Great Britain was cast in this role in the 1920s, Nazi Germany in the 1930s, and the United States after World War II.

The Soviet Union also sought to retain primacy in the Communist world. This claim was first asserted in 1919 when Lenin founded the Communist International (Comintern). Although this organization was dissolved in 1943, the CPSU continued its practice of interfering in the affairs of foreign Communist parties and governments. The USSR intervened militarily in Hungary (in 1956), in Czechoslovakia (in 1968), in Afghanistan (in 1979–1989), and threatened to intervene in Poland (in 1981) in order to overthrow Communist leaders and install or keep in power others deemed more loyal to Moscow. The CPSU rejected the Yugoslav Communist attitude that approved of polycentrism (the existence of several centers of Communism), but had to acquiesce in the fragmentation of the international Communist movement while claiming a special role as the world's first socialist state.

The accumulation of serious, even debilitating, domestic problems and a costly arms race were important factors that prompted Gorbachev at the Twenty-seventh Party Congress in 1986 to present a far more sobering picture of world affairs than that proclaimed by his predecessors:

> The present-day world is complex, diverse, dynamic, permeated with contending tendencies, [and] full of contradictions. It is a world of very complex alternatives, anxieties and

---

[41]*The Programme of the Communist Party of the Soviet Union. A New Edition* (Moscow: Novosti, 1986), p. 18.

hopes. Never before has our earthly home
been subjected to such political and physical
overloads. Never has man exacted so much
tribute from nature, and never has he proved
to be so vulnerable to the might that he himself has created.[42]

This was a harbinger of Gorbachev's "new thinking" which led to a general reappraisal of Soviet
foreign policy and had profound consequences
for both that policy and for the world at large.

Strategic Retreat: From Superpower to Supplicant

When Gorbachev assumed the Soviet leadership
in 1985, he appointed as foreign minister an out-
sider, Eduard Shevardnadze, former head of the
Communist Party of Georgia, for the purpose of
undertaking a thorough reorganization of the foreign ministry and a reorientation of foreign policy. As Gorbachev probed into the morass of the
Soviet Union's internal and foreign affairs, he
apparently concluded that the empire's foreign
commitments greatly exceeded its capabilities.
He sought to end the "isolation of Socialist countries from the common stream of world civilization."[43] He undoubtedly understood that the
assertive and aggressive policies of his predecessors had set the Soviet Union apart as an abnor-
mal entity that lacked respect in the international
community and fell further behind the technologically advanced world—and in some areas
behind the industrializing states of East Asia.

Central to the reassessment in Soviet foreign
policy (termed "new thinking" by Gorbachev)
was the recognition that the domestic economic
and political reforms necessary to rejuvenate the
Soviet state simply did not permit continued
profligacy in Soviet foreign policy. Rather, a cut-
back in commitments abroad and the redirection
of resources to domestic needs, as well as
improved relations with the West and a less
threatening international environment, were

essential for the success of Gorbachev's domestic reform program.

The Reagan administration's decision to
pursue an antiballistic missile defense (Strategic
Defense Initiative) posed the fundamental question of whether the Soviet Union could afford to
compete in this new stage in the arms race. In
the 1970s the USSR had unwisely deployed
intermediate-range SS–20 missiles in Europe
and had mistakenly thought that this would not
elicit an effective response from NATO. When it
did, the Kremlin was forced to rethink its entire
missile deployment strategy and much more.
This led to the December 1987 and July 1991
agreements between Washington and Moscow
that for the very first time significantly reduced
intermediate and strategic missiles.

Gorbachev's foreign policy also included
abandonment of the Brezhnev Doctrine, under
which the Soviet Union engaged in armed intervention in foreign countries to prevent the overthrow of Communist rule. The doctrine failed its
most crucial test in Afghanistan, from which the
Kremlin had to withdraw its forces in 1989
when the cost of occupation became prohibitive.
In 1986–1987 Gorbachev had attempted to
crush the Afghan resistance by means of a punitive aerial offensive directed against the civilian
population. This offensive failed because of the
antiaircraft missiles provided to the resistance
by Western and Muslim countries, but it did not
prevent Gorbachev from being awarded the
Nobel Peace Prize in 1990.

The Soviet failure in Afghanistan demonstrated its vulnerability and fueled resistance to
Communist rule in Eastern Europe. In 1989,
when semicompetitive elections in Poland forced
by domestic opposition resulted in the emergence of a government dominated by the Solidarity trade union movement, the Soviets
accepted the results. When thousands of East
Germans sought refuge in the West via Hungary
and Czechoslovakia, where officials proved to be
tolerant of the exodus, and more still demonstrated for democracy in East German cities,
Gorbachev advised the East German authorities
that Soviet troops would not come to their support. If Gorbachev had invoked the Brezhnev

---

[42]*Pravda,* February 26, 1986.
[43]*Izvestiya,* February 6, 1990.

Doctrine, he would have faced a disruption in relations with the West which could have led to an economic embargo and general condemnation, and he would have destroyed the foundations of his attempt at reform in the USSR. Rather, Gorbachev had to acquiesce in the collapse of communist regimes throughout all of Central Europe and the Balkans in 1989–1990, including the demolition of the Berlin Wall, the dissolution of the German Democratic Republic, and the unification of Germany within an expanded NATO. He agreed to the withdrawal, in stages, of Soviet troops from Germany. Moreover, the pullout of Soviet troops from Czechoslovakia and Hungary in 1990–1991 presaged the dissolution on March 31, 1991, of the Warsaw Pact, the Soviet Union's Eastern European military alliance. All of this was done while the Soviet Union accepted the continued existence of NATO as a defensive alliance and the extension of NATO into eastern Germany after German unification.

The Council for Mutual Economic Assistance (CMEA or Comecon), Moscow's organization for controlling the Eastern European economies for almost four decades, also unraveled, as the Soviets were forced to cut those countries loose because of increasing difficulties in their own economy. CMEA had been based on unrealistic planned pricing that made it impossible to determine real costs. It also lacked viable terms of trade because of the inconvertibility (and uncertain value) of the ruble, resulting in a reliance on barter arrangements.[44] Another aspect of the dramatic reorientation of Soviet foreign policy was the establishment of diplomatic relations between Moscow and the Vatican in March 1990.

The decision to retreat from the external Soviet empire in Eastern and Central Europe—despite objections from some in the military—was not accompanied by a comparable willingness to give up the internal empire that consisted of the 14 non-Russian republics and the many ethnically based regions of the Russian Federation. This

intransigence on the part of Gorbachev and his cohorts could only prolong the agony that would confront the Soviet Union as it sought to cope with its insoluble domestic problems.

Coordination of Foreign and Domestic Policies

Soviet foreign and domestic policies were always closely related. Ambitious and costly foreign policies influenced domestic policies, and domestic conditions necessitated changes in foreign policy. Initially, in order to save the Soviet regime and his dictatorship in 1918, Lenin had to accept a very unequal peace treaty with the Central Powers. Following years of war that greatly damaged the economy, he had to improve relations with some of the capitalist countries, especially Germany, to promote economic recovery. The Soviet Union joined the League of Nations in 1934, at a time when Stalin was engaged in costly industrialization and increasingly concerned about German expansion. Several years later, when the Soviet Union needed to avoid or postpone a war for which it was not prepared (as a result of the purging of the military and domestic dislocations), Stalin signed a pact with Nazi Germany.

Although the Soviet Union was a victor in World War II, the wartime alliance was replaced by the Cold War; Stalin closed the country to foreigners and lowered the "iron curtain" to conceal the country's weakness and extensive wartime losses and to ensure control over the population. When domestic conditions improved, the iron curtain was partly lifted in the mid-1950s. The detente of the 1970s was prompted, in part, by the need to import foreign technology and obtain financial credits. In the 1980s, Gorbachev advocated a "dialog" and reaffirmed the "peaceful coexistence of states with different social systems" because of the deplorable state of the Soviet economy. The Soviet need for more butter rather than more guns required a degree of international stability and a reduction of tensions.

The crisis that confronted the Soviet leadership in the late 1980s was, to a considerable extent, a consequence of its costly foreign policy

---

[44]See Jan Winiecki, *The Distorted World of Soviet-Type Economies* (Pittsburgh: University of Pittsburgh Press, 1988).

and excessive preoccupation with military power. Such priorities resulted in the development of a "command economy" with all basic economic policy decisions made by political authorities and central economic planners. Wages and prices, capital investment, and consumption levels were centrally determined rather than left to market conditions. Nevertheless, consumer resistance developed as buyers refused to purchase goods of inferior quality. The "second economy" (termed by Gorbachev the "shadow economy") produced more expensive goods of better quality but with materials obtained in questionable ways through illegal diversions, embezzlement, and barter.

The command economy reflected a fear and distrust of market forces associated with capitalism, whether they represented consumer choices, the money market competing for available investment capital, or the supply market that provided the raw materials and components needed by industry. Such an economy could produce (and waste) large quantities of steel, coal, petroleum, and cement. It enabled the Soviet Union to engage in space exploration and to undertake costly large-scale projects, such as the heavily subsidized Baikal-Amur Mainline (BAM), a new rail line 3,200 kilometers long, linking central and eastern Siberia along a route north of the Trans-Siberian Railroad farther removed from the Chinese frontier. It enabled the Soviet Union to acquire a large modern merchant fleet and to develop several cities within the Arctic Circle.

However, the imbalances, the system of administratively fixed prices that did not reflect real costs, and the heavy subsidization of rents, food, public transportation, and other items led to a grossly distorted economy. In the absence of a money market (with capital investments often based on grants), capital was frequently wasted and not put to work quickly. Gorbachev criticized "laughable interest rates" that made efficient use of investment capital impossible and that resulted in the absence of a financial credit system.[45] Construction projects chronically lagged.

A prominent factory director told the Nineteenth CPSU Conference: "With us it is regarded as normal to take 15 to 20 years to build a factory—and no one shoots himself, no one goes insane."[46] Wages rose ahead of productivity, and workers were paid to produce goods of inferior quality that consumers refused to buy. Savings bank deposits grew at a rapid rate from 18.7 billion rubles in 1965 to 337.8 billion rubles in 1989. This economic factor reflected an oversupply of money in relation to goods and services available. It also testified to a large pent-up demand, inflationary pressures, and the ability of Soviet citizens to obtain additional income. In the 1971–1985 period, the ratio between the growth in the money supply and the increase in consumer goods was 3.1 to 2.0.

Soviet leaders had claimed for years that the governmental budget had annual surpluses. This claim proved false, and Gorbachev informed the Central Committee that revenues were only able to cover expenditures by several extraordinary means. These included the sale on the world market of petroleum and other energy and material resources and the appropriation or transfer of funds belonging to enterprises and organizations (probably including tapping the reserves of the state insurance monopoly of the Ministry of Finance). The budget deficit was also dealt with by increasing the highly profitable production and sale of vodka and other spirits. Tax revenues from the sale of alcohol during the Eleventh Five-Year Plan were 169 billion rubles.[47] Gorbachev summarized the unsatisfactory financial condition of the Soviet Union when he told the Nineteenth CPSU Conference: "Over a period of many years expenditures of the state budget grew more rapidly than revenues. The budget deficit exerts pressure on the market, undermines the stability of the ruble and monetary circulation, [and] gives rise to inflationary processes."[48]

---

[45]*Izvestiya,* February 6, 1990, p. 2.

[46]*Izvestiya,* July 1, 1987.

[47]See Vladimir G. Treml, *Alcohol in the USSR: A Statistical Study* (Durham, NC: Duke University Press, 1982).

[48]*Izvestiya,* June 29, 1988.

The priorities of the Soviet oligarchy resulted in serious dislocations in such areas as housing, public health and medical care, and ecology. In 1961, the CPSU Program promised that by 1980 every Soviet family would have its own apartment or dwelling. In 1986 the revised CPSU Program promised that by the year 2000 every Soviet family would have its own apartment or house. More than 35 million new apartments and dwellings were needed to fulfill the goal.

For years leading Soviet officials had acknowledged the "bitter truth" of inadequate expenditures for health care but had stated that there were higher priorities. Minister of Public Health Yevgenii Chazov revealed in 1988 that as a result, in terms of the portion of gross domestic product devoted to public health, the USSR ranked in the middle of the seventh decile among 126 countries. In infant mortality it ranked fiftieth in the world—after Mauritius and Barbados—and in average life expectancy it ranked thirty-second. Dr. Chazov noted that a hospital for handicapped war veterans in Moscow had been under construction for 11 years. He complained of the shortage of pharmaceuticals. He pointed out that "as a result of poor water supply and a low sanitary-hygienic level in many dairies and meatpacking enterprises ... annually in the country 1.7 million persons suffer from severe gastro-intestinal ailments."[49] Dr. Chazov resigned from the ministry because Gorbachev would not provide the resources needed to improve the health care system.

Under perestroika, serious ecological problems were finally acknowledged, including soil depletion and loss of humus content, cutting of forests without reforestation, and air pollution in 102 cities—often exceeding safe levels by ten times. Major rivers were badly polluted and the damming of the Volga and Dnieper (Dnipro) Rivers to form large reservoirs had deleterious ecological consequences. It was reported that the principal polluters of air, soil, and water were the enterprises of seven central economic ministries. Such costly ecological disasters

resulted from unsound planning and false priorities, as well as from the Soviet leadership's neglect of domestic problems.

Seven decades of Communist rule exacted a horrendous toll in material, ecological, and human terms, and contributed to the degradation of Soviet society. The problems were exacerbated by the older population's willingness to accept an economy based on rationing, low wages, dependency, and artificial egalitarianism; any wealth was suspect unless it was acquired under Communist Party auspices. These conditions promoted cynicism, the stifling of initiative, and the decline of the work ethic and self-reliance.

If the Soviet system quite literally self-destructed, it was for a variety of reasons. State ownership of the economy had spawned a wasteful and inefficient central government bureaucracy staffed by surly, self-aggrandizing, and only marginally competent officials. The system provided tragic examples of what happens when the center imposes its power-driven priorities at the expense of republics and cities. The metropole's priorities ignored the development of the infrastructure and resulted in inadequate and crumbling utilities systems in the largest cities. In St. Petersburg—a city with a population of more than 4 million—the water system became a disgraceful source of infectious disease and toxicity.

The peoples of the Soviet Union bore the enormous costs of an assertive foreign policy. Maintaining the empire involved spending more than 25 percent of the Soviet gross domestic product for military purposes. It meant reliance on conscription and the rejection of conscientious objection. Non-Russian conscripts were frequently abused while in military service, and homicide and suicide rates among them were excessively high. Service in the Soviet army was reduced from three to two years in 1967, and service in the navy was reduced from four to three years. At that time, compulsory military training with weapons practice for both sexes was introduced into the secondary schools.

Vast sums were expended on excessive military programs, and space technology was given priority (largely for military purposes) at the expense of civilian needs. The security

[49]*Izvestiya,* June 30, 1988.

police organs expanded beyond real needs, and their employees were overpaid in comparison with other occupations. The extension of financial credits to a variety of third world and Communist countries left the Soviet Union an unsatisfied creditor, as recipients such as Cuba, North Korea, and Vietnam expressed ingratitude. Ironically, Lenin's denunciation of the capitalist "bureaucratic-military institutions which subordinate everything to themselves and suppress everything" was actually applicable to the Soviet bureaucracy and the military and security establishments.[50]

BUILDING A NEW PUBLIC POLICY

The Soviet empire collapsed as a result of political and economic breakdown, as well as moral failure. The August 1991 coup was followed by the collapse of the ruble in late 1991 as a result of enormous government deficits. Proposals to save the nearly worthless ruble with foreign aid and an international hard-currency stabilization fund simply demonstrated the pathetic plight of the Soviet economy. The collapse of the ruble was preceded by a secret depletion of the Soviet gold reserve and hard-currency stocks. Many CPSU officials had converted their vast ruble holdings into gold and hard currencies and had made deposits in European banks. Others had taken advantage of the developing market in the USSR to buy up enterprises at deflated ruble prices, sell their resources for hard currency at world market prices, and deposit the immense gains—usually abroad.

In Moscow rubles were being printed around the clock to finance the deficits of Gorbachev's shadowy "Union government." The grievances of the non-Russian peoples had been systematically ignored by Moscow as a matter of course. Uzbekistan had been converted into a gigantic cotton

plantation for the Russian textile industry, with Moscow setting the price of cotton. The irrigation required for cotton cultivation effectively dried up the Aral Sea to less than half its former size, with attendant loss of soil, and the careless use of pesticides created catastrophic health problems. In Ukraine the metropole-center constructed 22 nuclear power plants without the consent of the people; it also constructed gas and oil pipelines across Ukrainian territory without obtaining permission or paying any fees. In both cases electricity and fuel were exported to neighboring countries and the revenues were appropriated by Moscow. The horrendous aftermath of the Chernobyl nuclear catastrophe serves as a constant reminder of the costs of tolerating arbitrary rule from an external center.

Ukraine adopted an incremental approach in extricating itself from the Soviet Union. The process was spearheaded by the Ukrainian Parliament, the Supreme Rada, elected in March 1990. The Communist majority became divided, and on many issues some of its members sided with the democratic bloc, which held nearly one-third of the seats. Following the proclamation of Ukraine's sovereignty on July 16, 1990, a number of measures were adopted. Ukrainian laws were declared to have primacy over Soviet laws, and Ukraine declared its neutrality and its commitment to being a nuclear-free country. The Rada's Presidium and the Ukrainian ambassador to the United Nations condemned Moscow's use of force against Lithuania in January 1991. Ukraine reduced its financial payments to the union by 80 percent in 1991, established its own National Bank of Ukraine, and concluded bilateral agreements with other republics. Following the August 1991 coup, Ukraine established its own defense ministry and commenced formation of its own armed forces and national guard. It reorganized the KGB in Ukraine, renaming it the National Security Service (SNB). It also took steps to introduce its own currency.

The death knell of the Soviet Union was sounded by the Ukrainian referendum of December 1, 1991, which approved the August 24, 1991, declaration of Ukraine's independence by a 90 percent majority, including a high percent-

---

[50]In chapter 3, section 1, of *State and Revolution*. See also Robert C. Tucker, ed., *The Lenin Anthology* (New York: Norton, 1975), p. 337.

age of the Russian-speaking population. Leonid M. Kravchuk was also elected president of Ukraine by a 61 percent majority against five other candidates. President Kravchuk, armed with a clear mandate, asserted that Ukraine would not join any new union. In Moscow, Yeltsin stated that if Ukraine rejected Gorbachev's union, Russia would also refuse to join.

However, Yeltsin was apparently reluctant to have Russia formally declare its independence from the USSR as the other republics had done. Kravchuk seized the initiative by proposing the formal dissolution of the union and the formation, instead, of a Commonwealth of Independent States (CIS) that would not replace the defunct union but would serve as a consultative and coordinating forum for the former Soviet republics. The Soviet Union was dissolved by a declaratory act of the three remaining signatories of the December 1922 treaty that formally established the USSR. The heads of state of Belarus, Russia, and Ukraine met at a government estate in the Belovezha Forest Reserve near Brest, Belarus, and in Minsk on December 7–8, 1991, and declared that "the U.S.S.R. as a subject of international law and as a geopolitical reality ceases its existence."[51] The act and the formation of the CIS were approved by the parliaments of the three countries. The commonwealth decision was a means of removing Gorbachev and eliminating his presidency in the disappearing government of a disintegrated empire. It also negated Moscow's claim to be the imperial metropole. Gorbachev's presidency came to a belated end on December 25, 1991, with his resignation. The red flag with its hammer and sickle was lowered from the Kremlin and replaced with the Russian tricolor.

The CIS was established to facilitate cooperation among its members in the fields of foreign policy, economic relations, the environment, and immigration policy, and in combating organized crime. Coordinating bodies of the CIS were to be located in the Belarus capital of Minsk. Yeltsin and Kravchuk asserted that the CIS was not a state

and its bodies would not constitute a government. The commonwealth was joined almost immediately by all the other former Soviet republics except Georgia, which was involved in a bloody civil war, and the Baltic states, which had achieved full independence in September 1991.

The CIS began in difficulties and distrust. Yeltsin's decision to administer shock therapy to Russia's economy by freeing prices on January 2, 1992, meant that the other member states had no choice but to comply, as their lower prices would have resulted in massive outflows of food and goods to Russian purchasers. Yeltsin's higher prices provided little impetus for the development of a market economy in Russia in the absence of widespread privatization and competition, as the state enterprises remained the principal suppliers and maintained a sellers' market. However, the price increases did reduce the Russian government's budget deficits.

Russian Foreign Policy

During the first decade of its existence, the foreign policy of the Russian Federation, toward both the countries of the CIS (or "near abroad" as Russians initially called the region) and the world beyond, has shifted appreciably. Almost immediately after President Yeltsin and Foreign Minister Kozyrev proclaimed a policy that emphasized Russia's full integration into the Western-dominated international community, voices arose in Russia that condemned them for abandoning the interests of the Russian state and pursuing policies determined in Washington.

For millions of Soviet people who proudly regarded the USSR as their own state and homeland, its disappearance was seen as a disaster. But for imperial-minded Russians, it was also a national catastrophe that caused a deep psychological trauma. Russian grievances over the collapse of the USSR were further intensified by the highly publicized stories (both true and false) of violations of human rights of those ethnic Russians who found themselves outside the boundaries of the Russian Federation after the Soviet disintegration. Various constraints on acquiring citizenship imposed by local authorities, alleged

---

[51]*Izvestiya,* December 9, 1991, p. 1.

language discrimination, the loss of former privileges, and other explosive issues concerning the rights of the Russians in the "near abroad" substantially radicalized the political process within Russia itself, thus providing a fertile soil for the growth of nationalist sentiments. According to the Federal Migration Service, in spring 1996 there were some 9 million forced migrants on the territory of the former Soviet Union (see Table 7.6). Forced migration totaled more than one-third of the 3 million people who have moved to Russia since 1993. More than 70 percent of the migrants have come from Central Asia, especially Uzbekistan and Kazakhstan, and two-thirds of the arrivals have been ethnic Russians.[52]

Officially Russian leaders have denied any desire to reestablish dominance over the newly emerging states. Yet it has been difficult for them to adjust to the new reality in which they are expected to negotiate as equals with independent political elites in Kiev and Almaty, rather than merely issue instructions, as in the past. This is part of a much larger psychological problem of redefining Russia's statehood and establishing a new concept of Russian identity.

Despite Russia's decidedly pro-Western policy during 1992 and into 1993, Moscow began to pursue aspects of a more independent policy orientation. It proposed expanding the role of the

all-European CSCE peacekeeping organization as an alternative to enhancing NATO's activities; it negotiated a collective security pact with some members of the CIS to deal with potential and existing challenges to stability; it continued the normalization of relations with China based, in part, on arms exports. It began to reestablish relations with former partners in the developing world, some of which were viewed as rogue governments by Washington. Moreover, after initially accepting the idea of Poland's entering NATO, President Yeltsin soon began to criticize any effort to expand NATO into East-Central Europe.

Although the rhetorical emphasis on the importance of Russia's ties with the West remained largely constant, the reality of that policy had already begun to shift by 1993 as Moscow played a much more assertive role within the CIS—significantly before Yeltsin replaced Kozyrev with Yevgenii Primakov as foreign minister in January 1996. The shift in policy was inevitable, since Russia's initial policy orientation was based on unrealistic assumptions of a coincidence of interests between Russia and the West and a level of Western support for the economic and political rehabilitation of Russia. Until Kozyrev was replaced as foreign minister in early 1996, Russian foreign policy emphasized the central importance of relations with the West, while simultaneously engaging in more assertive policies within the CIS and rebuilding some of the relationships with devel-

---

[52]Reported in *Omri Daily Digest,* May 27, 1996.

TABLE 7.6

NET MIGRATION TO RUSSIA FROM POST-SOVIET STATES, 1990–1996 (IN THOUSANDS)

	1989	1990	1991	1992	1993	1994	1995	1996	Total 1990–1996
Total Net Immigration	162.6	287.2	104.9	355.7	553.8	914.6	612.2	439.8	3,430.8
Of which from CIS	158.4	275.0	90.5	299.0	500.3	872.5	588.0	425.6	3,209.3
Of which from Baltics	4.2	12.2	14.4	56.7	53.5	42.1	24.2	14.2	221.5
Net Immigration of Ethnic Russians	—	199.9	117.7	360.1	419.4	612.4	388.4	263.8	2,361.7

Source: Zhanna Zayonchkovskaya, "Recent Migration Trends in Russia," in George J. Demko, Grigory Ioffe, and Zhanna Zayonchkov-skaya, eds., *Population under Duress: The Geodemography of Post-Soviet Russia* (Boulder, CO: Westview Press, 1999), pp. 115, 120.

oping countries that had been abandoned in recent years. During this period, most groups within the Russian political elite reached agreement on the general guidelines of Russian foreign policy. Top priority went to the geographic region of the former Soviet Union, "the near abroad." Besides agreeing on the importance of Russia's continued role as the regional hegemon, they also were committed to the retention of Russia's status as a nuclear power and to the reestablishment of Russia as a world power.[53] These objectives remain at the center of Russian policy today under President Vladimir Putin.

The nationalist shift in Russian foreign policy was seen in the expansion of Russia's influence in the "near abroad," often in the guise of peacemaker, as Dov Lynch has argued.[54] Agreements with both Georgia and Armenia—extracted by Russia only after covert Russian military intervention in local conflicts helped to undermine the stability of these governments—resulted in the continued presence of Russian troops in the Caucasus. Relations with Ukraine involved periodic confrontations over issues such as the disposal of Ukraine's nuclear arsenal, the disposition of the Soviet Black Sea Fleet, and Russian claims to Crimea, administratively a part of Ukraine for four decades but with a majority Russian population. Nationalists in both Moscow and Kiev (Kyiv) have made resolution of these problems difficult, although the influence of nationalists in Moscow has been much greater than that of Ukrainian nationalists. Moreover,

acceptance of Russian demands for dual citizenship and declaring Sevastopol (in Crimea) would serve to negate Ukrainian sovereignty.

In Central Asia the Russians were active in coordinating security-related activities with the countries of the region. Russia continues to view the borders of CIS members in the south as Russia's borders and has committed the military personnel to defend them. In Azerbaijan the Russians were reportedly involved in the overthrow of the elected president in early 1993, in his replacement with an old Kremlin hand, Heydar Aliev, and in late 1994 in efforts to undermine the latter when he refused to abrogate a deal with Western oil companies for the exploitation of Caspian Sea oil. More recently, Russian policy toward its neighbors became much less assertive, in large part as the leadership in Moscow recognized that it no longer commanded the resources to pursue assertive policies throughout the territory of the former Soviet Union.

Russian foreign policy shifted in the mid-1990s on a number of other issues. On the matter of the civil war in former Yugoslavia, for example, Russia consistently supported Serbia and the Bosnian Serbs against Western pressures and strongly opposed Western intervention against Serbia in 1999–2000 at the time of the chaos in Kosovo. Although Russia had initially voted for economic sanctions, it soon began calling for their reduction or elimination. Moreover, as part of an effort to have Iraq and Libya pay large outstanding debts to Russia, the Russians have improved relations with the two countries and have worked to have U.S.-sponsored international sanctions modified or lifted. Throughout the late 1990s, Russia was often at odds with the United States on policy toward these countries.

Despite opposition to the impending expansion of NATO eastward, Russia joined the U.S.-initiated Partnership for Peace Program in 1994 and engaged in joint exercises with the United States on several occasions. At the same time Russia completed the withdrawal of its military forces from East-Central Europe and the Baltics, reached a cooperation agreement with the European Union, became a member in 1996 in the

[53]This policy orientation was outlined in the foreign policy statement signed into law by President Yeltsin in April 1993. Although "The Fundamental Positions of the Concept of the Foreign Policy of the Russian Federation" was never published, Leon Aron cites an unpublished version in his possession: Leon Aron, "Foreign Policy Doctrine of Postcommunist Russia," in *The New Russian Foreign Policy,* ed. Michael Mandelbaum (New York: Council on Foreign Relations Press, 1998), p. 25.
[54]Dov Lynch, *Russian Peacekeeping Strategies in the CIS: The Cases of Moldova, Georgia, and Tajikistan* (Houndmills, UK: Macmillan, 2000).

Council of Europe, continued to receive Western economic support, joined in 1998 the G–7 club of leading industrial states, and despite growing opposition at home, supported U.S.-led initiatives to impose a settlement on the conflict in Bosnia-Herzegovina. All these activities were part of the continuing Russian effort to integrate itself into Western political, economic, and security institutions.

However, Russia's increasingly vocal claims about its status as a global nuclear power and some of its policy initiatives, especially toward its near neighbors, began to generate concern and criticism in the West. These included Russia's evident meddling, including military support for secessionist groups, in the domestic affairs of other CIS countries, and the decision to use military force to crush the rebellion in Chechnya. Although Western states did not challenge Russia's legitimate concerns about territorial integrity, the massiveness of the response raised serious reservations in the West, as well as throughout East-Central Europe.

In addition to Russian concerns about Western policy in Yugoslavia and Iraq, an even more serious problem was the Western commitment to moving ahead with the eastward expansion of NATO. Driving the expansion was NATO members' perceived need to find a new rationale for an organization whose original mission had disappeared. Russian leaders expressed concerns that NATO expansion would create a new division in Europe and sow distrust that could lead to a new confrontation. In response to the Poles and others whose motives for entering NATO included a concern about the longer-term security threat that a revitalized Russia might present, the Russians denied that such a concern was warranted and noted that the inclusion of Central European states in NATO broke promises made by the West at the time of German reunification. Apparently recognizing the futility of its opposition and hoping to have some influence on NATO policy, Moscow finally implemented its agreement to participate in the Partnership for Peace in summer 1995.

Although Foreign Minister Kozyrev shifted the focus of Russian policy increasingly in support of Russian interests during his final two years in office, his policies failed to meet the demands of the nationalists and the Communists. After their successes in the December 1995 Duma elections, President Yeltsin replaced Kozyrev with Primakov, whose past activities in the intelligence community and as a Middle East specialist generated the support of a broad spectrum of the Russian political elite, including within the left.

When President Yeltsin plucked Aleksandr Putin from political obscurity in August 1999 and began to groom him as his successor, the state of Russia's relations with the United States and the West in general had reached a plateau. While Russia pursued policies that were in direct conflict with Western foreign policy objectives, the central component of bilateral Russian relations with the United States remained stable. Moreover, given its generally weak position because of its economic dependence on the West, Moscow often was forced to back down when faced with opposition.

The government of President Yeltsin continued to command the support of the United States—although strong criticism arose of the corruption, political and economic chaos, and failure of real reform that characterized his administration. This support, however, was based almost solely on the view that the present government was the only real alternative to a return of the Communists. On the other hand, Russia continued to pursue other aspects of its foreign policy—within the CIS, in Yugoslavia, in Asia, and on issues such as arms exports—that challenged U.S. and Western policies.

Closely related to developments in Russia's foreign policy have been military issues, some of which have served as a source of tension with other Soviet successor states. Ukraine had made it clear from the beginning that it would organize its own armed forces, and it was joined by Azerbaijan and Moldova. Belarus and Uzbekistan expressed reservations concerning a common CIS military force. Yeltsin and the Russian-dominated military command in Moscow wanted to have the divided services of the former union recognized as the armed forces of the CIS, but under the old ethnic Russian command. Ukraine and other states saw this as a scheme to maintain what they regarded as occupation forces in their territories. In March 1992, Yeltsin announced that Russia would establish its own defense ministry—as Ukraine had done on October 22, 1991.

The nuclear weapons on the territories of Russia, Ukraine, Belarus, and Kazakhstan added to the disagreement, since there was skepticism regarding Russia's ability and willingness to destroy nuclear weapons transferred to it by the other countries. President Kravchuk of Ukraine insisted that Russia not be given exclusive control of nuclear weapons but that they be under joint control of the four states. The issues concerning nuclear weapons were eventually worked out with the assistance of the United States, and the nuclear weapons of Belarus and Kazakhstan have been transported to Russia for destruction, as have most of those on Ukrainian territory.

Military relations among the CIS member states are quite mixed. Although agreement does not exist among all CIS members for joint border protection, the Russians have signed bilateral agreements with several other CIS states (for example, Armenia, Georgia, Kyrgyzstan, Tajikistan) that provide for the stationing of Russian troops in those states. What emerges from the information available on CIS military relations is a Russian commitment to reestablish its military superiority across the geographic space of most of the former Soviet Union.

Another area of special significance of the military in the new Russia concerns military reform and emerging civil-military relations in the Russian Federation. In 1992 a new military force of the Russian Federation was established to replace the Unified Armed Forces of the Commonwealth of Independent States, which had replaced the Soviet military. Almost immediately, Defense Minister General Pavel Grachev outlined plans for a comprehensive reform of the military, including a reduced military force and expanded capabilities. In the first years of the twenty-first century, President Putin is still struggling to begin to implement these objectives.

Overall, the process of reintegration of the states of the CIS has moved forward piecemeal and sporadically—pushed by Russia's use of various forms of military and economic coercion to force its partners into expanded cooperation, but countered by the general refusal of many of the member countries to implement agreements that had been reached. Russia has used a range of weapons from covert support for secessionist movements to overt economic blackmail to reassert a dominant position within the CIS under the guise of multilateral cooperation. The decision of the Russian State Duma in March 1996 to denounce the December 1991 dissolution of the Soviet Union gave clear evidence of the long-term objective of important political forces in Moscow. The Russian Council on Foreign and Defense Policy, headed by Sergei Karaganov, Deputy Director of the Europe Institute of the Russian Academy of Sciences, released in June 1996 a draft document entitled "Will the [Soviet] Union Revive by 2005?" The council, whose past publications have provided the basis for official Russian foreign policy, emphasizes the centrality of Ukraine in the revival of the Union. Increasing Ukraine's economic dependence on Russia is the key to Russia's policy.[55] Ukraine, on the other hand, continues to insist on policies within the CIS that emphasize the full sovereignty of the member countries and rely on bilateral rather than multilateral agreements.

The decision to deploy troops in Chechnya to put down the de facto secession by former President Dudayev and the Chechen government demonstrated the degree to which Russian military preparedness had declined. Not only was the Russian Army unable to enforce peace after more than a year and a half of fighting, but many of its troops proved inadequately trained, and it was forced to rely on mercenaries (*kontraktniki*, "contract soldiers"), many of whom became notorious for looting.

In the months leading up to Putin's appointment by President Yeltsin in August 1999 as

---

[55]Volodymyr Zviglyanich, "Russia Discusses Plans to Restore the Soviet Union by 2005," *Prism* 2(4) (June 14, 1996).

prime minister, several developments occurred that were especially relevant for Russian policy. First and probably most important was the renewed challenge from Chechen separatists that provided the new prime minister with the opportunity to present himself as the forceful political leader needed to stabilize the political and economic situation in Russia. The massive government campaign in fall 1999 that brought Moscow de facto control of most of the secessionist republic generated support among the majority of the Russian population and played a role in Putin's resounding electoral victory in spring 2000—even though the brutality of the policy raised serious criticism in the West, including censure by the Council of Europe.

Relations with the West had also been seriously strained over the U.S. and British bombing of Iraq and, even more, because of NATO's campaign against Yugoslav President Slobodan Milosevic and his attempt to expel the majority of the ethnic Albanians from Kosovo. The United States and its NATO allies simply ignored strongly stated Russian opposition. When Putin took over as interim president on January 1, 2000, he inherited an entire series of additional issues in Russia's relations with the West that included the restructuring of the Russian debt, NATO and EU expansion, the U.S. commitment to move forward with a missile defense system, and the future of Yugoslavia and the Balkans.

Yet the general parameters of Russian policy were clearly set early in Putin's presidency and derived from earlier policy. Putin is committed to reestablishing the place of Russia as the preeminent regional power and an important international actor. He has argued that, as an essential precondition for the fulfillment of these objectives, Russia must ensure against separatism, national and religious extremism, and terrorism.[56] Putin has moved forcefully and in many

cases effectively in reasserting central governmental control in Russia, and the economy has shown significant signs of turning around with growth rates of 4.5, 10, and 5.0 percent in the years 1999–2001. These gains, however, have been made with little regard for civil liberties and democratic processes.

In the foreign policy arena, Putin continued to seek allies who shared Russia's commitment to preventing the global dominance of the United States that Russia views as a threat to international security and to Russia's goal of serving as a major center of influence in a multipolar world. Of the issues on which Russia and the United States disagreed already in the mid-1990s—the erosion of democratic guarantees in Russia itself, Russian policy in Chechnya and toward its near neighbors, the various conflicts in Yugoslavia and other Balkan states, Russian sales of sophisticated arms to particular developing countries, and NATO expansion—only policy toward Yugoslavia and general Russian policy toward the CIS were no longer issues of immediate concern. To the others were added, after the election of George W. Bush as U.S. president, Russia's strong opposition to the U.S. development of a missile defense system and disagreements about Russia's involvement in the exploitation of the oil and gas reserves of the new states of the Caspian Basin.

Thus, by summer 2001, little more than half a year into the presidency of George W. Bush and one and a half years into Vladimir Putin's presidency, U.S.-Russian relations were apparently on a collision course. The leaderships of the two countries had established political objectives that they viewed as important to their national interests that were in direct conflict with one another. Russians were increasingly frustrated by Washington's clear disregard for their importance in world affairs and by apparent U.S. disregard for

[56]*The Foreign Policy Concept of the Russian Federation,* Approved by the President of the Russian Federation V. Putin, June 28, 2000. *http://www.mid.ru/mid/eng/econcept.htm*; also available in *Johnson's Russia List,* no. 4403, July 14, 2000. *http://www.cdi.* *org/russia/johnson.* The same basic points are included in Russia's new security concept; "Kontseptsii natsional'noi bezopasnosti Rosiiskoi Federatsii," *Nezavisimoe voennoe obozrenie,* no. 1, January 14–20, 2000.

The terrorist attacks of September 11, 2001 changed the Russian–U.S. relationship from one of possible collision to cooperation.

Russian interests and its unilateralist approach to foreign and security policy. Large-scale diplomatic expulsions of early spring 2001 initiated by Washington were but the most visible indication of the serious tensions in bilateral relations.

Yet virtually overnight, the terrorist attacks of September 2001 changed all of this—at least for the short and medium term. Immediately after the attacks, President Putin was the first foreign government leader to offer his and his people's condolences to the American people and to pledge full support for whatever responses the United States might take. Less than two weeks later he announced a five-point plan to support the United States in its war on terrorism: the Russian government would (1) share intelligence information with the United States, (2) open Russian airspace for U.S. flights, (3) cooperate with Russia's Central Asian neighbors to provide similar overflight rights, (4) join in international search and rescue efforts, and (5) increase direct humanitarian and military assistance to the Northern Alliance in Afghanistan. Over the course of the next nine months, and often despite strong opposition at home, Putin responded in other ways that would have been virtually unthinkable in summer 2001. This included expanded Russian cooperation with NATO that culminated in spring 2002 in the creation of the new relationship between Russia and NATO; the agreement in principle announced at the November 2001 summit meetings in the United States between Putin and Bush of the dramatic reduction in nuclear arsenals which was then formalized in Moscow six months later; the basic Russian acceptance of the U.S. decision to withdraw from the ABM treaty of 1972 and to move forward with the development of a national missile defense system; Russia's resistance to OPEC's decision to cut global oil production and the adverse effects that this would have on the West; and basic acceptance of NATO's impending decision to admit a number of new Central and East European states to full membership.

The questions that arise concern the reasons for the shift in Russian policy and the likelihood that the change is likely to lead to a long-term stable Russian-U.S. relationship. Various explanations have been given for Putin's response, ranging from the view that this is but a short-term tactical move to the position that Russian policy since September 2001 is but the logical outcome of the major changes in Russian domestic politics that have occurred during the past decade, as argued most forcefully by Leon Aron. Putin has recognized that Russia's future lies with Europe and the West. The attempt to rebuild Russia as an independent power center juxtaposed against the United States and Western Europe is not a feasible short- or long-term strategy. Moreover, in coming decades the interests of Russia are likely to diverge significantly from those of China, thus making a long-term alliance with that country questionable. "If Russia's foreign policy has changed," Aron maintains, "it is because in the past decade Russia itself has become a changed country. Russia's voters in the 1990s decisively chose the pro-reform and pro-Western Yeltsin, despite his many flaws, over his nationalist communist alternative. Currently a stable pro-reform majority continues to support the creation of the underpinnings of a functioning free market economy and a political democracy—flawed though they both may be."[57] In other words, Putin has recognized, as have many others in Russia, that Russia's future lies in and with the West. Immediately after the terrorist attacks of September 2001, he seized on the opportunity to revamp Russia's relations with the United States and the West and to accelerate the normalization of Russia's relations with the West and of integrating Russia into Western institutions. Putin has seemingly accepted the realities of the post–Cold War world, in which the United States is the dominant state and in which Russia will have to play by the rules established by the West during the past century, and more.

Most of the improvements in Russian-U.S. relations since September 2001 are attributable to shifts in Russian policy, not changes in Washington. Virtually across the board, Moscow has stepped back from positions that it had taken in the past—as recently as the first year of Putin's presidency. A second round of NATO expansion that will likely include one or more of the Baltic states, a development of a U.S. missile defense system and the renunciation of the 1972 ABM Treaty, a nuclear arms reduction agreement that lacks detail and specificity of the sort initially expected by Vladimir Putin and the Russians, and a U.S. military presence throughout former Soviet Central Asia all represent issues on which the Russians have withdrawn, or at least muted, their opposition in order to facilitate the objective of reestablishing Russia's economic and political stability and its long-term role in the international community. In return Russia has experienced the virtual disappearance of Russian policy in Chechnya from the U.S. political radar screen. Questions in official Washington of Russian human rights violations in Chechnya, and elsewhere, have virtually disappeared. Moreover, in April 2002 the United States suspended remaining Cold War restrictions on trade with Russia and accorded the designation of Russia as a market economy—with the economic benefits that come with that designation.

Putin understands that Russia needs the West and needs to be integrated into Western institutions if it is ever to regain a measure of its former greatness. He recognizes as well that the U.S.-led war on international terrorism is of immediate interest to Russian security, given its geopolitical location along the northern edge of the Muslim world and its substantial number of Muslim citizens. So long as the Russian leadership is willing to act as a junior partner to the United States—much as the countries of Western Europe have done during the past half-century, at least in the security arena—the emerging relationship is likely to remain stable.

---

[57]Leon Aron, "Putin's Progress: Russia Joins the West," *Weekly Standard* 7(25), March 11, 2002. *http://www. weeklystandard.com/content/public/articles/000/000/ 000/971yvonj.asp.*

Russian Domestic Policy

At the base of many major policy issues in Russia is the question of the economy and of government policies introduced to stimulate economic growth. We have already examined the general outlines of the reform policies of the 1990s and their impacts—positive and negative—on the Russian economy. We have noted, as well, the intense unpopularity of many of the economic policies introduced by President Yeltsin that was used most effectively by the Communists and other groups to build a strong political base in Russian politics, to gain control over the parliament in the December 1995 elections, and to position themselves in the unsuccessful presidential election campaign in summer 1996. During 1995 and early 1996, Yeltsin backed off from some of the earlier reforms, and his cabinet no longer included individuals committed to economic reform. As the presidential election campaign heated up in spring 1996, Yeltsin made numerous commitments that could only undercut the process of economic reform—including extending subsidies to state enterprises, granting inflationary wage increases to government employees, and promising expanded expenditures of state funds in numerous areas of the economy.

Despite serious concerns voiced both within and outside Russia about the level of Vladimir Putin's commitment to economic reform when he came to office, he has in fact moved rather effectively to carry out many of the reforms that Yeltsin had never managed to implement. His policies have resulted in renewed economic growth (which began before he replaced Yeltsin as president), a balanced government budget, reduced inflation, and a major balance of trade surplus. The most important contributions to economic growth made by the Putin government are in the political sphere, where greater stability and central authority have been established. Moreover, Putin has taken on some of the tycoon-politicians (such as Vladimir Gusinsky and Boris Berezovsky) who played an important and often negative role during the Yeltsin years.

Putin is also aware of the continuing need to establish the legal foundations essential for a modern market economy. Putin periodically speaks of the need for an improved and fair system of justice in Russia, but there is little evidence that the justice system will anytime soon gain the political independence needed to achieve such a goal.

Given the immensity of the problems facing Russia and its leaders, it is doubtful that they will be able in the near future to deal effectively with more than a few of those problems. For example, it would require growth rates of at least 8 percent a year for 15 years for Russia to reach the level of economic development and standard of living of even the poorest of the European Union's current members.

Directly relevant to the economic concerns that have faced Russia during the past deacde are a whole series of environmental and health problems. One of the worst legacies of the Communist past throughout Central Europe and Eurasia is the ecological and environmental devastation left behind by politico-economic systems that for decades were committed to expanded industrial and agricultural production at virtually any cost. The result has been a level of environmental degradation unmatched anyplace else on earth. In Poland, for example, rivers from which the drinking water of major cities is drawn were so polluted that they did not meet the minimum standards for industrial water use in Western Europe. Much of northern Ukraine and more than 20 percent of all Belarusian territory has been made uninhabitable for the foreseeable future by the Chernobyl nuclear disaster. A substantial portion of the territory of Uzbekistan east of the Aral Sea has been turned into a toxic wasteland as a result of extensive irrigation that prevents 90 percent of water from reaching the Aral and has resulted in the exposure of more than 11,000 square miles of seabed covered with salts and other chemicals largely from the runoff of agricultural chemicals. In regions immediately adjacent to the Aral, infant mortality rates reached twice the Soviet average, maternal mortality rates tripled between 1984 and 1989, and

80 percent of all pregnant women were found to suffer from anemia.[58]

These represent but a handful of stories concerning the devastation inherited by the Russian Federation and the other Soviet successor states. As Murray Feshbach and many other specialists have demonstrated, Russia is a giant country awash with nuclear materials, whose northern seas are threatened by radiation pollution, whose Siberian forests lose millions of acres a year to fire, pollution, and overcutting, and whose people face serious dangers from polluted water and contaminated food. Because of the economic disaster, however, Russia is financially unprepared to begin tackling the problems of control and cleanup. Russian factories continue to pollute, nuclear power plants as dangerous as those at Chernobyl continue to operate throughout the territory of the former Soviet Union, and the billions of dollars required to clean up the waters and air of Russia are unavailable. Just as important, given the immediacy of problems of economic decline, ethnic conflict, and related matters, environmental concerns have not been high on the agenda of government priorities.

The horrendous state of the health of the population and the precipitous decline in health care are closely related to the ecological devastation of much of the territory of the Russian Federation and the other post-Soviet states. The USSR devoted an inadequate and declining percentage of its GNP to health. The government, which controlled the entire health care system, had refused to make the investments that would have permitted it to keep up with technological developments in health care. Moreover, basic medical supplies—from medicines to thermometers and needles—were in disastrously short supply.

Male life expectancy dropped almost annually until in 1990 it had reached 63.8 years. Four years later it was at 57.5 years (even lower in the countryside), but rose to 66.3 in 2004. Poor diet, alcoholism, cigarettes, and air and water pollution were among the major causes of this decline. But since the collapse of the Soviet Union, an increase in unnatural deaths (murder and suicide, for example) was the primary source of the decline in life expectancy. Infant mortality rates in Russia are also the highest in the industrial world, up from 17.4 per thousand live births in 1990 to 19.9 per thousand in 1993, though it fell to 16.9 per thousand in 2004. The maternal mortality rate was 63.5 per 10,000 live births in 1994—and a full 75 percent of Russian women experience complications during pregnancy. Only 45 percent of Russian births qualify as normal by Western medical standards.[59]

Throughout Russia, deaths have been outpacing births by nearly two to one—9.6 births and 15.1 deaths per thousand in 2004. Major diseases long thought to be under control have reemerged at epidemic levels throughout the country. The factors underlying these developments are many and complex. However, environmental, economic, and social disintegration are at the root of the problem. The drop in the birthrate is directly related to the economic collapse and the bleak prospects for the future for most Russian citizens. The rising death rate results from growing alcoholism in a country in which this was already a serious problem, increased stress that has resulted in a suicide rate three times that of the United States, a col-

[58]Feshbach and Friendly, *Ecocide in the USSR,* pp. 74–75. Murray Feshbach has long been among the most knowledgeable of specialists on the Soviet environment. His book represents a terrible indictment of a system that destroyed much of the environment of a substantial portion of the globe.

[59]Toni Nelson, "Russia's Population Sinks," *World Watch* (January/February 1996), pp. 22–23. See also Anatoly Vishnevsky and Vladimir Shkolnikov, "Russian Mortality: Past Negative Trends and Recent Improvements," in George J. Demko, Grigory Ioffe, and Zhanna Zayonchkovskaya, eds., *Population under Duress: The Geodemography of Post-Soviet Russia* (Boulder, CO: Westview Press, 1999), pp. 59–72.

lapse of the already inadequate health care system, and widespread environmental contamination. Presumably economic improvements will help to stabilize the demographic situation in Russia. However, the public health crisis, including the impact of the high levels of deadly pollution, are problems that the Russian government will find it difficult to overcome.

An area of public policy of special importance as an indicator of the degree of commitment of the Russian government to democratization concerns human rights. Although the Bolsheviks who came to power in Russia in 1917 expressed high ideals in this area and the Soviet constitution included the protection of citizens' rights, and although the Soviet government was always a strong advocate of international human rights agreements, actual practice fell far short of minimum world standards in protecting civil and human rights. Millions of Soviet citizens died in the terror campaigns initiated by Stalin. Even after the reforms introduced under Khrushchev in the 1950s, Soviet citizens were still subject to widespread abuses of their human rights. Political dissidents were harshly treated. Many were imprisoned on trumped up charges; others were declared mentally unstable and sent to psychiatric hospitals.

This approach to human rights must be understood within the context of the view of Soviet authorities that the collectivity was more important than the individuals who comprised it. In the Marxist-Leninist view, individuals were not endowed from birth with "inalienable rights." Rather, the individual gained meaning and, therefore, rights, only through membership in the larger community. The state took precedence over the individual, and individuals gained their rights through the state. As we have seen, this situation changed significantly during the Gorbachev reform period, when a whole series of guarantees were put into place that provided greater protections against the state for citizens of the Soviet Union.

After a decade of an independent Russia, some remain concerned about the commitment of the government to strengthening human

rights. In early 1996, after issuing a very critical report on the state of human rights in the Russian Federation which noted "a visible retreat from democratic achievements," a majority of the members of the Presidential Commission for Human Rights resigned their positions. Subsequently President Yeltsin abolished the commission. The last report of the commission, as well as reports by Freedom House, raises concerns about the declining commitment to human and civil rights. The Kovalev Commission referred to the increasing militarization of society (with special reference to Chechnya), the growing tendency to resolve internal conflicts by force, and the rise in racial discrimination and intolerance.[60] A Freedom House report for the year 2001 shows Russia's performance declining from the mid-1990s on almost all the criteria used to assess a country's commitment to political freedom and civil liberties. For example, among all post-Communist states, Russia falls in the middle category of "transitional" governments (along with Georgia, several Central Asian states, and rump Yugoslavia.[61] In 2004, Freedom House downgraded Russia to "not free."

Evidence has mounted that democratic activists have been prosecuted for political reasons and that government agencies have moved to try to silence some of the criticism by the media. Although it appears that most of the cases refer to the actions of individual officials, there is growing concern about a government that looks the other way. In his campaign to root out corruption, President Putin has seemingly targeted the owners of the independent

---

[60]Reported in *Monitor,* February 7, 1996. On June 12, 1996, Amnesty International sent an open letter to all the candidates in the presidential election deploring the continuation of human rights abuses in the country. See *Omri Daily Report,* June 13, 1996.

[61]Adrian Karatnycky, Alexander Motyl, and Armanda Schnetzer, eds., *Nations in Transit 2001: Civil Society, Democracy and Markets in East Central Europe and the Newly Independent States* (New Brunswick, NJ: Transaction Publishers, for Freedom House, 2001), p. 27.

media. By early 2002 all independent nation-wide television networks had been closed and journalists were under pressure to reduce criticism of the government. These developments and the continuing brutal policy in Chechnya were among the most important indications of Russia's continuing weak record on civil liberties and human rights.

TOWARD THE FUTURE

The two decades beginning with the selection of Mikhail Gorbachev as leader of the CPSU in 1985 brought with it revolutionary changes in the Soviet Union and its successor states. With the failure of Gorbachev's efforts to reform the Soviet system and the implosion of the Soviet state, the new Russian leadership faced the daunting task of creating a new state, new political institutions based on democratic principles, and a market economy. Over the next eight years, President Yeltsin and his supporters succeeded in establishing the foundations for a new society. A constitution was in place that provided the ground rules for a presidential republic, but one in which for the first time in Russian history the power of the executive was balanced by representatives of popular interests. Moreover, after serious initial challenges to Moscow and despite the ongoing catastrophe in Chechnya, the relationship between the political center and the regions that compose the Russian Federation has been stabilized—in particular in the short period of Vladimir Putin's presidency. The political battles being fought in Russia are contested in elections and through the ballot box. In the economic realm, the basic foundations for a functioning market economy have been put into place and, after a long period of drastic economic decline and personal disaster for much of the population, indicators for the future are positive—for the first time since before the collapse of the former USSR.

However, besides these basically positive indications of Russian success in the triple transition of state building, democratization, and marketization, there exist many important negative indicators. The constitutional arrangements that define relations between the federal government and its constituent parts remain fragile. Moreover, the horrors of the war in Chechnya indicate the continuing willingness of the political center to use virtually any means to accomplish its objectives, although the majority of Russian citizens support government policy.

President Putin has brought to Russia a sense of commitment and order, along with the expectation that things will improve after a decade of political chaos, economic decline, and widespread crime and corruption. Many Russians long for the stability of the past and fear the widespread uncertainties of a democratic and market-oriented future. Thus, they are more concerned with the stability and improving economy that they associate with Putin than they are with his failure to pursue all of his objectives within the context of Western conceptions of democratic procedure.

In the economic area, although positive indicators exist about future growth in the Russian economy, the disasters associated with the market reforms of the initial years of the Russian Federation and with the financial collapse of August 1998 undermined public support for economic reform policies. However, President Putin has pushed forward with a whole range of reforms that have begun to pay off in terms of improved economic performance. The economic future of Russia is not rosy, but it is much more attractive than it was only a few years ago.

Russia appears to have selected its path for the future—a path that will combine a commitment to a basically market economy with a political system that incorporates competitive elections, elements of public participation, and accountability. The political system, however, is not likely in the foreseeable future to meet the standards of Western democratic procedure and practice. It will be characterized far more by top-down authority and decision making than by bottom-up political influences. But compared with past Russian political systems, it will continue to be more open and more representative of the interests of a broad spectrum of the population.

Life in Russia for the vast majority of the population is bleak and will remain bleak in the coming years. But, assuming no new economic disasters, gradual economic improvements should occur over the next decade. The state should begin to collect the revenues that will permit it to begin rebuilding the infrastructure and social services—electricity, heating, water supply, education, medical care—essential for an improved standard of living. But even the most optimistic picture of the future is not very positive. In the concluding words of a recent analysis:

> In the short and medium term, the likeliest outcome is that the economy will grow just enough to keep the country from collapsing, postponing any crunch. If so, Russia will stagger on much as it is now: a large, poor, mostly backward place with a maddening habit of wasting its potential. If the decline worsens, though, all the old fears about Russia that haunted the 1990s—disintegration, unrest, loose nukes, disease, and pollution—will re-emerge, with even fewer hopes of recovery.[62]

Thinking Critically

1. How did the Soviet view of international relations differ from the current views that underlie Russian foreign policy?
2. How have domestic and foreign policy been interrelated in the Soviet Union and in the Russian Federation?
3. What were the benefits and the costs of empire for the Soviet Union?
4. What were the implications of the September 11, 2001, terrorist attacks on the United States for Russian foreign and domestic politics?

---

[62]"Putin's Choice: A Survey of Russia," *The Economist,* July 21, 2001, p. 16.

5. How would you evaluate the overall success of the post-1991 Russian leadership in dealing with economic reform?

KEY TERMS

Brezhnev Doctrine *(428–429)*
Comintern *(427)*
command economy *(430)*
Commonwealth of Independent States (CIS) *(433)*
Council for Mutual Economic Assistance (CMEA) *(429)*
correlation of forces *(427)*
global dominance *(438)*
Lend-Lease *(426)*
new thinking *(428)*
Partnership for Peace *(435)*
Russian Federation *(433)*
Warsaw Pact *(429)*

FURTHER READINGS

Allworth, Edward, ed. *Ethnic Russia in the USSR: The Dilemma of Dominance* (New York: Pergamon Press, 1980).

Black, J. L. *Russia Faces NATO Expansion: Bearing Gifts or Bearing Arms?* (Lanham, MD: Rowman and Littlefield, 2000).

Blasi, Joseph R., et al. *Kremlin Capitalism: Privatizing the Russian Economy* (Ithaca, NY: Cornell University Press, 1997).

Bremmer, Ian, and Ray Taras, eds. *Nations and Politics in the Soviet Successor States* (Cambridge: Cambridge University Press, 1993).

Bridges, Olga, and Jim Bridges. *Losing Hope: The Environment and Health in Russia* (Aldershot, UK: Averbury, 1996).

Brudny, Yitzhak, et al., eds. *Reconstructing Post-Communist Russia* (Cambridge: Cambridge University Press, 2004).

Brzezinski, Zbigniew. *The Grand Failure, The Birth and Death of Communism in the Twentieth Century* (New York: Scribner, 1989).

Conquest, Robert, ed. *The Last Empire: Nationality and the Soviet Future* (Stanford, CA: Hoover Institution Press, 1986).

Demko, George J., Grigory Ioffe, and Zhanna Zayonchkovskaya. *Population under Duress: The Geodemography of Post-Soviet Russia* (Boulder, CO: Westview Press, 1999).

Donaldson, Robert H., and Joseph L. Nogee. *The Foreign Policy of Russia: Changing Systems, Enduring Interests* (Armonk, NY: M. E. Sharpe, 2002).

Dunlop, John B. *The Rise of Russia and the Fall of the Soviet Empire* (Princeton, NJ: Princeton University Press, 1993).

Ebel, Robert, and Rajan Menon, eds. *Energy and Conflict in Central Asia and the Caucasus* (Lanham, MD: Rowman and Littlefield, 2000).

Feshbach, Murray, and Alfred Friendly Jr. *Ecocide in the USSR: Health and Nature under Siege* (New York: Basic Books, 1992).

Garthoff, Raymond L. *Detente and Confrontation: American-Soviet Relations from Nixon to Reagan,* rev. ed. (Washington, DC: Brookings Institution, 1994).

Hoffman, David E. *The Oligarchs: Wealth and Power in the New Russia* (New York: Public Affairs, 2002).

Kanet, Roger E., and Alexander V. Kozhemiakin, eds. *The Foreign Policy of the Russian Federation* (Houndmills, UK: Macmillan, 1997).

Kolodziej, Edward A., and Roger E. Kanet, eds. *The Limits of Soviet Power in the Developing World: Thermidor in the Revolutionary Struggle* (Houndmills, UK: Macmillan; 1989).

Kolsto, Pal, and Helge Blakkisrud, eds. *Nation-building and Common Values in Russia* (Lanham: Rowman and Littlefield, 2004).

Laitin, David D. *Identity in Formation: The Russian-Speaking Populations in the Near Abroad* (Ithaca, NY: Cornell University Press, 1998).

Matlock, Jack F. *Autopsy on an Empire: The American Ambassador's Account of the Collapse of the Soviet Union* (New York: Random House, 1995).

Motyl, Alexander J., et al., eds. *Russia's Engagement with the West* (Armonk: Sharpe, 2005).

Petro, Nicolai N., and Alvin Z. Rubinstein. *Russian Foreign Policy: From Empire to Nation-State* (New York: Longman, 1997).

Pilkington, Hilary. *Migration, Displacement and Identity in Post-Soviet Russia* (London: Routledge, 1998).

Rowen, Henry S., Charles Wolf Jr., and Jeanne Zlotnick, eds. *Defense Conversion, Economic Reform, and the Outlook for the Russian and Ukrainian Economies* (New York: St. Martin's, A RAND Study, 1994).

Rule, Wilma, and Norma C. Noonan. *Russian Women in Politics and Society* (Westport, CT: Greenwood Press, 1996).

Sanders, Deborah. *Security Co-Operation between Russia and Ukraine in the Post-Soviet Era* (Houndmills, UK: Palgrave, 2001).

Shearman, Peter, ed. *Russian Foreign Policy Since 1990* (Boulder, CO: Westview Press, 1995).

Truscott, Peter. *Russia First: Breaking with the West* (London: I. B. Tauris, 1997).

Ulam, Adam B. *Expansion and Coexistence: The History of Soviet Foreign Policy, 1917–1973,* 2nd ed. (New York: Praeger, 1974).

Trenin, Dmitri. *The End of Eurasia: Russia on the Border between Geopolitics and Globalization* (Washington, DC: Carnegie Endowment for International Peace, 2002).

Waller, J. Michael. *Secret Empire: The KGB in Russia Today* (Boulder, CO: Westview Press, 1994).

Zevelev, Igor. *Russia and Its New Diasporas* (Washington, DC: United States Institute of Peace Press, 2001).

WEB SITES

www.carnegie.ru
Carnegie Moscow Center. This site has minimal graphics and current news, but much in-depth research analysis.

www.csis.org
Center for Strategic and International Studies. An archive of publications, working papers, and policy memos.

www.ku.edu/~herron
Guide to Eurasia and the Baltics on the Web. Comprehensive guide to materials on the Internet that deal with Russia and the other Soviet successor states.

www.itar-tass.ru
ITAR-TASS, Telegraph Agency of Russia. Rich source of news and information on Russia.

www.cdi.org/russia/johnson
Johnson's Russia List. Daily compendium of news items and informed commentary on Russia.

www.indiana.edu/~reeiweb/webresources/libraries.html
Library Collections and Bibliographical Resources of the Russian and East European Institute. Excellent guide to Internet sources dealing with Russia and Eastern Europe.

www.moscowtimes.ru
Moscow Times. Newspaper for English-speaking expatriates and business types living or working in Moscow.

www.rferl.org/newsline/search/
RFE/RL Newsline. Daily news items and analysis on Russia and Eastern Europe.

www.ucis.pitt.edu/reesweb/
Russian and East European Studies Virtual Library, University of Pittsburgh.

www.strana.ru
Russian Federation, National Information Service. Official Russian government website.

www.worldpolicies.com/english/world___newspapers.html
World Policies, 150 world newspapers online.

Territories claimed, but not controlled
by the People's Republic of China
(applies to Hong Kong untill 1997)

Ethnic Tibetan Area

RUSSIA

KAZAKSTAN

KYRGYZSTAN

TAJIKISTAN

PAKISTAN

MONGOLIA

INNER MONGOLIA

HEILONGJIANG
Harbin
Changchun
JILIN

Sea
of
Japan

Ürümqi

XINJIANG

Hohhot

LIAONING

NORTH
KOREA

BEIJING
TIANJIN
HEBEI

SOUTH
KOREA

TIBET
AUTONOMOUS
REGION
(OUTER TIBET)

QINGHAI

INNER TIBET

NINGXIA

Xining

GANSU

Taiyuan

Jinan

Xi'an

SHANXI

SHANDONG

JIANGSU

SHAANXI

HENAN

ANHUI

Nanjing

SHANGHAI

CHINA

HUBEI
Wuhan

ZHEJIANG

East
China
Sea

NEPAL

Lhasa

Chengdu

SICHUAN

Changsha

Nanchang

JIANGXI
Fuzhou

FUJIAN

Taipei

BHUTAN

INDIA

HUNAN

GUIZHOU

INDIA

BANGLADESH

YUNNAN

Kunming

GUANGXI
ZHUANG

GUANGDONG
Canton

TAIWAN

Nanning

Hong
Kong

South China
Sea

0   200   400 Miles

0   200   400 Kilometers

Bay of
Bengal

BURMA
(MYANMAR)

VIETNAM

LAOS

THAILAND

HAINAN

CHAPTER

8

THE GOVERNMENT OF
China

Joseph Fewsmith

INTRODUCTION

Background: For centuries China has stood as a leading civilization, outpacing the rest of the world in the arts and sciences. But in the first half of the 20th century, China was beset by major famines, civil unrest, military defeats, and foreign occupation. After World War II, the Communists under Mao Zedong established a dictatorship that, while ensuring China's sovereignty, imposed strict controls over everyday life and cost the lives of tens of millions of people. After 1978, his successor Deng Xiaoping gradually introduced market-oriented reforms and decentralized economic decision making. Output quadrupled in the next 20 years and China now has the world's second largest GDP. Political controls remain tight even while economic controls continue to weaken.

GEOGRAPHY

Location: Eastern Asia, bordering the East China Sea, Korea Bay, Yellow Sea, and South China Sea, between North Korea and Vietnam

Area: 9,596,960 sq km

Area—comparative: slightly smaller than the United States

Land boundaries: 22,147.24 km

   border countries: Afghanistan 76 km, Bhutan 470 km, India 3,380 km, Kazakhstan 1,533 km, North Korea 1,416 km, Kyrgyzstan 858 km, Laos 423 km, Macau 0.34 km, Mongolia 4,676.9 km, Myanmar 2,185 km, Nepal 1,236 km, Pakistan 523 km, Russia (northeast) 3,605 km, Russia (northwest) 40 km, Tajikistan 414 km, Vietnam 1,281 km

Climate: extremely diverse; tropical in south to subarctic in north

Terrain: mostly mountains, high plateaus, deserts in west; plains, deltas, and hills in east

Elevation extremes: *lowest point:* Turpan Pendi −154 m

highest point: Mount Everest 8,850 m

Geography note: world's fourth-largest country (after Russia, Canada, and United States)

PEOPLE

Population: 1,298,000,000

Age structure: *0–14 years:* 22.3% (male 153 million, female 135 million)

15–64 years: 67.66% (male 469 million; female 443 million)

65 years and over: 7.5% (male 46.3 million; female 50.7 million)

Population growth rate: 0.57%

Birthrate: 12.98 births/1,000 population

Sex ratio: 1.06 male/female

Life expectancy at birth: 71.96 years

male: 70.4 years

female: 73.72 years

Nationality: *noun:* Chinese (singular and plural)

adjective: Chinese

Ethnic groups: Han Chinese 91.9%, Zhuang, Uygur, Hui, Yi, Tibetan, Miao, Manchu, Mongol, Buyi, Korean, and other nationalities 8.1%

Religions: Daoist (Taoist), Buddhist, Muslim 2%–3%, Christian 1%

Languages: Standard Chinese or Mandarin (Putonghua, based on the Beijing dialect), Yue (Cantonese), Wu (Shanghaiese), Minbei (Fuzhou), Minnan (Hokkien-Taiwanese), Xiang, Gan, Hakka dialects, minority languages

Literacy: *definition:* age 15 and over can read and write

total population: 81.5%

GOVERNMENT

Country name: *conventional long form:* People's Republic of China

conventional short form: China

abbreviation: PRC

Government type: Communist state

Capital: Beijing

Administrative divisions: 23 provinces (sheng, singular and plural), 5 autonomous regions (zizhiqu, singular and plural), and 4 municipalities (shi, singular and plural); China considers Taiwan its 23rd province

Independence: 221 B.C.E. (unification under the Qin or Ch'in Dynasty 221 B.C.E.; Qing or Ch'ing Dynasty replaced by the Republic on 12 February 1912; People's Republic established 1 October 1949)

Constitution: most recent promulgation 4 December 1982

Legal system: a complex amalgam of custom and statute, largely criminal law; rudimentary civil code in effect since 1 January 1987; new legal codes in effect since 1 January 1980; continuing efforts are being made to improve civil, administrative, criminal, and commercial law

Suffrage: 18 years of age; universal

Executive branch: *chief of state:* President Hu Jintao and vice president Zeng Qinghong (since March 2003).

head of government: Premier Wen Jiabao (since March 2003)

cabinet: State Council appointed by the National People's Congress (NPC)

elections: president and vice president elected by the National People's Congress for five-year terms; elections last held March 2003 (next to be held March 2008); premier nominated by the president, confirmed by the National People's Congress

Legislative branch: unicameral National People's Congress or Quanguo Renmin Daibiao Dahui (2,985 seats; members elected by municipal, regional, and provincial people's congresses to serve five-year terms)

Judicial branch: Supreme People's Court (judges appointed by the National People's Congress); Local People's Courts (comprise higher, intermediate, and local courts); Special People's Courts (primarily military, maritime, and railway transport courts)

ECONOMY

Overview: In late 1978 the Chinese leadership began moving the economy from a sluggish Soviet-style centrally planned economy to a more market-oriented system. Whereas the system operates within a political framework of strict Communist control, the economic influence of non-state managers and enterprises has been steadily increasing. The authorities have switched to a system of household responsibility in agriculture in place of the old collectivization, increased the authority of local officials and plant managers in industry, permitted a wide variety of small-scale enterprise in services and light manufacturing, and opened the economy to increased foreign trade and investment. The result has been a quadrupling of GDP since 1978. In 2005, with its 1.29 billion people but a GDP of just $5,000 per capita, China stood as the second largest economy in the world after the United States (measured on a purchasing power parity basis). Agricultural output doubled in the 1980s, and industry also posted major gains, especially in coastal areas near Hong Kong and opposite Taiwan, where foreign investment helped spur output of both domestic and export goods. However, the leadership has often experienced in its hybrid system the worst results of socialism (bureaucracy and lassitude) and of capitalism (windfall gains and stepped-up inflation). Beijing thus has periodically backtracked, retightening central controls at intervals.

GDP: purchasing power parity—$6.44 trillion

GDP—real growth rate: 9.1%

GDP—per capita: purchasing power parity—$5,000

GDP—composition by sector: *agriculture:* 14.8%

industry: 52.9%

services: 32.3%

Population below poverty line: 10%

Labor force: 778 million

Labor force—by occupation: agriculture 50%, industry 22%, services 28%

Unemployment rate: urban unemployment roughly 10%; substantial unemployment and underemployment in rural areas

Currency: yuan (CNY)

A. POLITICAL DEVELOPMENT

China, the world's most populous nation, is also the oldest continuous civilization in the world. Moreover, it is historically the most self-conscious society in the world, and the legacy of its history and civilization plays an important role, consciously and unconsciously, in the way that China is governed. When Mao Zedong, the leader of the Communist revolution, sought guidance on governing his nation, he turned not to the works of Marx and Lenin, whose philosophy he espoused, but to China's dynastic histories to better understand the way in which China's emperors had ruled the nation.[1] He did so even as he excoriated China's imperial past as feudal (see Table 8.1).

The legacies of imperial China are many. Here we can outline some basic features that have resonated clearly in the contemporary period. First, China for two millenia has had a tradition of unified rule under a strong ruler, even if that tradition has often been honored only in the breech as domestic turmoil or foreign conquest engulfed China. This tradition stretches back at least to the first emperor of the Qin Dynasty (Qinshi Huangdi), who unified China in 221 B.C.E. A ruthless ruler, the emperor ended feudalism in China, starting China on a path remarkably different from that of Europe or Japan. The legacy of this crushing of local autonomy has been a powerful belief that China can be unified only under strong, central rule; the idea of federalism, although now advocated by some intellectuals, is alien to China's political tradition.

Second, this system of centralized rule was complemented and implemented by the most developed bureaucratic structure in the premodern world. China may have invented bureaucracy, but imperial China could hardly be considered a bureaucratic society. On the contrary, it was a rather lightly administered society (which does not mean that the government could not suppress rebellion by military force if neces-

TABLE 8.1	
MAJOR PERIODS IN CHINESE HISTORY	
Zhou Dynasty	B.C.E. 1122–255
Qin Dynasty	B.C.E. 255–206
Han Dynasty	B.C.E. 206–221 A.D.
Period of disunion	221–589
Tang Dynasty	618–907
Song Dynasty	951–1280
Yuan (Mongol) Dynasty	1280–1368
Ming Dynasty	1368–1644
Qing (Manchu) Dynasty	1644–1911
Republic of China	1912–1949
People's Republic of China	1949–

sary). Throughout the late imperial period, China's bureaucracy remained nearly constant in size, at around 20,000 officials. This meant a ratio of 1 official for every 11,000 people in 1650 and only 1 for every 20,000 people in 1850.[2]

Third, the bureaucracy was staffed by officials trained in the Confucian tradition. The ideas of Confucius (551–479 B.C.E.) identified moral conduct as the core concern of governance. Thus, although the Chinese created perhaps the most rational bureaucratic structure of the premodern world, it did not generate a notion of rule of law. The stress in Confucianism was on the cultivation of "gentlemen" (*junzi*) who would know intuitively what correct behavior demanded in any given situation; laws were seen as inimical to the development of such moral knowledge. This tradition left a legacy of "rule by men" (rather than law), but it also created a sense of duty among intellectuals that they must serve as the conscience of society, as well as its natural rulers.

Officials were recruited into the bureaucracy through an examination system that tested the

---

[1]Li Zhisui, with Anne Thurston, *The Private Life of Chairman Mao* (New York: Random House, 1994).

[2]John R. Watt, *The Chinese Magistrate in Late Imperial China* (New York: Columbia University Press, 1972).

candidate's knowledge of the Confucian classics. The Confucian classics included the instructions of Confucius, some of his followers, and other texts that Confucians took as illustrating important moral principles. The examination system consisted of three major levels, and candidates reaching the highest level were appointed to the most prestigious positions in the land. Thus the notion of a bureaucracy staffed by people well indoctrinated in a particular worldview stretches back millenia. The examination system also created a legacy of rule by educated elites; even today, many people think of "democracy" as choosing the "right" person (an educated, capable person) for the job rather than in procedural terms.

Finally, bureaucratic officials were drawn from the scholar-gentry class. The term "scholar-gentry" is a somewhat awkward importation of the British concept of "gentry" to the Chinese scene. But whereas British gentry were beneficiaries of landed titles, China's scholar-gentry attained their social status through a combination of wealth and scholarship. A successful farmer could send his sons to school in the hopes that one might succeed in the examination system, thus conferring status and opportunities to acquire greater wealth on the family. There were always many more aspirants to official positions than the bureaucracy could employ, so the majority of China's scholar-gentry stayed in their local areas, sometimes serving as secretaries for officials who came to rule that area and more often becoming the pillars of local society. Such people had a vested interest in maintaining the institutions of Confucian learning that underpinned their own standing in the community and legitimated their aspirations for themselves and their offspring.

Thus Confucianism was deeply embedded in both China's social structure and political institutions. This combination explains why Chinese society could remain stable while governed by such a small bureaucracy. It also explains why dynasties could come and go without fundamentally disrupting the social order.

China's imperial legacy leaves a clear, if sometimes indirect, imprint on contemporary China. More immediate as shapers of contemporary China's political institutions and behavior have been the decline of imperial China and the history of the national and social revolutions of the nineteenth and twentieth centuries. It is to that history that we now turn our attention.

THE DECLINE OF IMPERIAL CHINA

By the mid-nineteenth century, China was suffering from population pressures and the resulting decline in social order and from a weakening of imperial vigor caused in part by efforts to suppress domestic rebellion. A long period of peace following the establishment of the Qing (Manchu) dynasty in 1644, and the spread of new foods such as yams allowed China to experience a population explosion unique in the premodern world. The population nearly doubled from 125 million in 1650 to 225 million in 1750, then nearly doubled again, increasing over the next century to 410 million in 1850.[3] This growth in China's population meant that ever larger numbers of people were cultivating increasingly marginal land, with the result that more people than ever before were vulnerable to the vagaries of nature, and the prospect of starvation.

A series of rebellions starting in the late eighteenth century gradually drained the central treasury and the vigor of the dynasty. By the middle of the nineteenth century, when the largest rebellion in human history—the Taiping Rebellion—broke out, the central government no longer had the fiscal strength and military organization to effectively meet the challenge. As the armies of the Taiping rebels swept northward from their origin in southwest China, the Qing allowed a number of provincial officials to organize armies in their home localities. Although this effort to raise local armies eventually succeeded in suppressing the Taiping Rebellion, it also brought about a localization and militarization of Chinese society that would eventually undermine the foundations of China's last

---

[3]Ho Ping-ti, *Studies on the Population of China* (Cambridge, MA: Harvard University Press, 1959).

dynasty and lead to warlordism in the 1910s and 1920s.[4]

The Taiping Rebellion not only reflected domestic pressures but also the coming of the West. Many peasants were driven to join the rebellion by the deflation of copper currency that was caused, at least in part, by the export of silver to the West in exchange for opium. At the time, China had a bimetallic currency system, copper for small transactions and silver for large. Peasants generally earned copper when they sold their crops, but they had to pay the tax collector in silver. As silver rose in value, the effective tax burden on peasants increased, driving many to the point of rebellion. Western influence was also present in the ideology of the Taipings. The leader of the rebellion, Hong Xiuquan, had come into contact with Christian tracts and had become convinced (following a nervous breakdown) that he was the younger brother of Jesus Christ. The ideology of the Taiping Rebellion was a combination of erzatz Christianity and native Chinese traditions. Despite its strange origins, it presaged many trends that would later be present in the Communist movement. In particular, the Taipings called for communal ownership of land and an equalization of wealth. In this sense, the Taiping Rebellion really marks the beginning of an enormous social revolution that swept over China from the mid-nineteenth century to at least the mid-twentieth century.

The coming of the West was apparent in one other way. As the Taipings looked like they might genuinely threaten the existence of the dynasty, a Western led and financed "Ever Victorious Army" was organized to help defeat the Taipings. The Qing may have eventually succeeded in defeating the Taipings, but the Ever Victorious Army nevertheless played a significant role.

Thus, by the time the Taiping Rebellion was ultimately suppressed in 1864, China's final dynasty and the Confucian society on which it was based were slowly disintegrating. Chal-lenged from below, the dynasty responded by devolving authority to an increasingly active and organized society. Confronted by the intrusion of the West, the dynasty responded by adopting half-hearted Westernization. Unlike in Japan, no new elite emerged to reform the state, so West-ernization efforts could only be sporadic, supported by a handful of reform-minded officials and declining when those officials moved or were removed. Neither emulated nor effectively challenged, the Western presence slowly chipped away at the efficacy of Confucian institutions and beliefs that had been the core of the Chinese system for 2,000 years.

The Self-Strengthening Movement

The decline of the Qing turned out to be a lengthy process. Beginning in about 1860 a remarkable group of men in Beijing and in the provinces made an effort to breathe new life into the dynasty. They tried to restore the vigor of Confucianism while borrowing selectively from the West. This period, known as the self-strengthening movement, lasted nearly a quarter of a century until the Sino-Japanese War of 1894–1895 ended the hope of gradual transition.[5]

The self-strengthening period is important not only because it began a process of introducing Western technology and ideas, first in the military field and then gradually in industry and other areas, but also because it reflected a desire to integrate Chinese culture and Western learning selectively. The approach was expressed by the well-known scholar-official Zhang Zhidong as "Chinese learning as the essence, Western learning for practical use." This sense that Chinese culture could remain fundamental to the system while Western technology could be grafted selectively onto it has been a theme that has repeated itself throughout modern Chinese history, including in the reform period introduced by Deng Xiaoping in 1978. It has never worked well; the

---

[4]Philip Kuhn, *Rebellion and Its Enemies in Late Imperial China* (Cambridge, MA: Harvard University Press, 1970).

[5]Mary C. Wright, *The Last Stand of Chinese Conservatism: The T'ung-chih Restoration, 1862–1874,* rev. ed. (Stanford, CA: Stanford University Press, 1966).

technology that was being introduced carried with it cultural values that could not be isolated from Chinese culture.

Nevertheless, the self-strengthening impulse remains strong in part because it has proven more successful in modernizing China than two other forces: cosmopolitanism and nativism. Cosmopolitan impulses, which grew strong in the early twentieth century, have sought to integrate China into the world by a wholesale adoption of foreign ideas. But cosmopolitanism has always run aground on nationalism, the most powerful force in modern Chinese politics. In contrast, the nativist tradition has tried to reject Westernization. Nativism has frequently merged with nationalism to produce radical movements. It was this combination that the Communist movement tapped so effectively in its rise to power, and it remains a potent force in China today.

Toward Social and National Revolution

The decline and fall of the Qing dynasty opened up a range of political questions and historical trends that reverberate to the present day. As noted above, China had traditionally been ruled by a combination of monarchy and Confucian-based bureaucracy. Even the institution of the monarch (emperor) was tied to the Confucian value system through the notion of the "mandate of heaven." According to the ideology, the monarch did not rule simply because of blood, but also because he embodied virtue and earned the right to rule by winning heaven's favor. When the monarchy fell in China, it took with it the values and institutions that had upheld imperial rule. The fall of the monarchy meant the corresponding fall of Confucian-based knowledge and associated institutions. Therefore, any new system that would come into being would not have to simply transform old ideologies into modern ideologies but to legitimize political rule on the basis of a new ideology.

The fall of the Qing also ushered in a social revolution that would ultimately span the next half century. Efforts to overthrow the Qing were led by people who had been marginal in the old

social order. Typical of these was Sun Yat-sen, China's first professional revolutionary and the leader of the Revolution of 1911 that ended the Qing dynasty. Sun was born into a middle-peasant family in the southeastern province of Guangdong. When he was still a boy, he followed his elder brother to Hawaii, where he acquired a command of English and a familiarity with a range of Western ideas, including Christianity. As someone who had not followed the traditional path of immersing himself in the Confucian classics in the hopes of passing the examination system but instead went abroad for a foreign education, Sun was of a different social class and background than his contemporaries in officialdom. The success of the Revolution of 1911 thus heralded the rise of a new type of political leader.

This combination of the decline of the old order and revolution by a new class of people reflected the fact that in China, the national revolution (political change) and social revolution would proceed hand in hand. State building in China would not be a top-down process as it was in Japan.

NATIONALIST REVOLUTION

Mass Nationalism

If events of the late nineteenth and early twentieth centuries determined that China's efforts to modernize were going to be far more wrenching than those of its neighbor to the east, the eventual success of the Communist revolution was brought about by two other factors. First was the rise of mass nationalism. The impact of nationalism on Chinese politics might be dated from 1895 when Japan defeated China in a short but decisive war that destroyed China's nascent navy and brought its self-strengthening efforts to a close. A radical scholar by the name of Kang Youwei, then in Beijing to take the highest level of the imperial examination, led 800 of his fellow examinees in signing a petition demanding that the Qing government reject the peace treaty (which the Qing signed) and undertake fundamental reform. This initial nationalist movement, modest as it was, suggested the link between nationalist passion and the demand for radical political action on the one hand and foreshadowed the rise of far more powerful mass nationalism on the other.

The rise of mass nationalism in China can be dated from the May Fourth Movement of 1919. The cause of this movement was the decision of the Versailles Conference to turn over German concessions in the eastern Chinese province of Shandong to Japan (which claimed them because of a secret agreement it had signed with the warlord government in Beijing during World War I). When news of this agreement reached Beijing, students took to the streets demanding that the Chinese delegation refuse to sign the peace treaty. When government troops arrested some of the students involved, the movement spread throughout China. Moreover, in a sign of China's rapidly changing society, the movement quickly drew support from merchants and workers as well as intellectuals. Political participation would never be confined to a small elite again.

The May Fourth Movement boosted an intellectual revolution in China that was radically critiquing China's Confucian past, thus ushering in a period of new thought. At the same time, the movement ushered in a demand for political action. The May Fourth Movement led not only to the reinvigoration of the Chinese Nationalist Party (Guomindang, GMD), but also to the founding of the Chinese Communist Party (CCP) in 1921.

The Nationalist and Communist Revolutions

Under the auspices of the Communist International (Comintern), the GMD and the CCP joined together in a united front. The GMD was the larger, older, and better-known party, while the CCP brought in a core of highly dedicated young activists—as well as foreign aid from the Soviet Union. In 1926, the GMD led a Northern Expedition from its base in the southeastern city of Guangzhou (Canton) to defeat the warlords and reunify the country under its rule. The Northern Expedition progressed remarkably rapidly toward

the middle of China, but then paused when it reached the east coast metropolis of Shanghai.

For nearly two years after the 1925 death of Sun Yat-sen, who had led the GMD and forged the alliance with the CCP, tensions had built up between the GMD and the CCP and within the GMD itself. In 1927 the military commander of the Northern Expedition, Chiang Kai-shek, decided the time was right for him to take overall leadership of the movement. He did so by launching a bloody purge of the Communists, an action that ultimately claimed thousands of lives. Chiang was successful in establishing his own leadership over the GMD (although he was repeatedly challenged in the ensuing years) and in reunifying China, at least nominally, under the control of the GMD. Communist leaders who survived the purge of 1927 had little choice but to adopt a radically different strategy.

Rural Revolution

After several ill-fated efforts to launch urban insurrections and military uprisings, Mao Zedong and a handful of other party leaders headed for the mountainous areas of the south central province of Jiangxi. In the mountains of Jiangxi, Mao and his followers slowly worked out a different model of revolution. Instead of basing themselves on the urban working class, Mao and his followers exploited rural discontent to develop a powerful and remarkably well-disciplined guerrilla movement. The development of this path of rural revolution, however, did not come easily. In 1934, surrounded by a well-organized assault on their base area by the Nationalist army, the CCP was forced to retreat from the area. Breaking out of their encirclement in October 1934, the CCP headed southwest on what turned into an epic military retreat that ultimately would carry them 6,000 miles to the isolated and impoverished areas of northwestern China. Militarily this Long March was a disaster. Overall, the party lost some 90 percent of its strength.

Nevertheless, the Long March did two things for the CCP. First, it took on mythological proportions as the tale of the march was told and retold, thus creating an image of CCP members as being of heroic stature and their movement as invincible. Second, the battle-toughened veterans who survived the Long March became the core of the CCP in the years ahead. All the major leaders of the CCP, including Mao Zedong, Liu Shaoqi, Zhou Enlai, and Deng Xiaoping participated in the Long March. The hand of this Long March generation was still felt in party councils up until the death of Deng Xiaoping in 1997.

Mao Zedong Thought

In the course of their revolutionary history, which spanned 22 years from the retreat into Jiangxi in 1927 to ultimate victory in 1949, the Chinese Communist Party evolved a number of military and political tactics that became deeply imprinted in the party's behavior in the years after it came to power. This collection of experience is often summed up by the term "Mao Zedong Thought."

Mao Zedong was a complex and contradictory man who ultimately towered over his age and left a legacy that will take the Chinese political system and people generations to digest and come to grips with. He insisted on investigation and research but repeatedly ignored reality to impose his own utopian visions. A man of great intelligence, he despised intellectuals as a class, and he led a peasant revolution only to oversee the deaths of millions of peasants in his ill-fated effort to bring crash industrialization to China.

In the revolutionary period when Mao and the movement he led were still confined to their rural base areas, Mao continuously stressed the need to combine theory and practice. Mao was not, initially at least, a sophisticated Marxist theoretician. On the contrary, he came to Marxism already committed to revolution; in Marxism he found confirmation and reaffirmation of his own natural inclinations. For instance, his famous 1926 "Report on the Peasant Movement in Hunan" is most noted for its absence of Marxist vocabulary. What gave the essay its power was Mao's conviction that he had found in those peasant uprisings a powerful current that could carry the revolution to victory. Indeed, it was not until Mao reached Yanan (in northwestern Shaanxi province) in 1935 that he had any time to study Marxism-Leninism on a systematic basis. Even then his close associates could not get him to read more sophisticated Marxist writings. Mao preferred the Communist Manifesto, the meaning of which he summed up as "Class struggle! Class struggle! Class struggle!"[6]

Mao was vulnerable to criticism from the more sophisticated Marxists in the CCP, many of whom had studied in Moscow. They criticized Mao as an unsophisticated leader who would never be capable of doing more than leading a peasant uprising. In response, Mao heaped scorn on his critics, accusing them of not understanding the realities of China. Mao asserted that all understanding arose from practice, and accused his opponents of being "lazybones."[7]

For Mao, the critical thing was to be able to combine the "universal truth" of Marxism-Leninism with the concrete reality of China. Mao asserted that Marxism-Leninism did not exist as an abstract entity but could only exist in concrete manifestations. That is to say, there was only Russian Marxism or Chinese Marxism, not abstract Marxism. This idea of rooting the abstract formulations of Marxism-Leninism in the specific reality of China was part of a process known as the Sinification of Marxism, in which the language of Marxism was translated into the idiom of Chinese reality.

The ideas of practice and the Sinification of Marxism were closely connected with the idea of the mass line. Because knowledge derived from practice and because Marxism had to be made comprehensible in terms of Chinese reality, peasants could only be mobilized if cadres took the message of the revolution to the grass roots and

---

[6]Stuart Schram, ed., *Mao's Road to Power: Revolutionary Writings, 1912–1949, Vol. 1: The Pre-Marxist Period, 1912–1920* (Armonk, NY: M. E. Sharpe, 1992) p. xvii.

[7]Mao Zedong, "On Practice," in *The Selected Works of Mao Tse-dong* (Peking: Foreign Language Press, 1966), vol. 1.

Mao Zedong (1893–1976) reviewing a rally of over a million Red Guards composed of students and schoolchildren, during the Cultural Revolution. Mao, chairman of the Chinese Communist Party from 1935 until his death, established the People's Republic of China in 1949.

made it comprehensible to the peasants. This was not an easy process, and the ideal was often violated in practice. Nevertheless, the mass mobilizational tactics of the CCP during the revolutionary war required an integration of party policy with reality. This meant a process of getting cadres to understand local realities and trying to integrate the concerns of peasants with party policy. The mass line, in Mao's words, was a matter of "from the masses, to the masses." That is, the party would take the scattered concerns of the peasants and try to integrate them with party policy so that when policy was implemented at the local level it could be accepted by the peasants.

Another idea that proved vital to the CCP's success was that of the united front. The idea of the united front was to try to bring together the majority of people in a common cause and thereby isolate those who were in opposition. In order to win the support of people who were not Marxists, it was necessary for the party to play down its most radical ideas and stress ideals that it had in common with the majority of Chinese—

such as nationalism during the Sino-Japanese war of 1937–1945.

These four ideas—practice, the Sinification of Marxism, the mass line, and the united front—acted as a restraining mechanism on the party's more radical tendencies. In the face of hostile forces—the GMD on the one hand and the Japanese on the other—the CCP had no choice but to act in a prudent manner and thereby attract as much support as it could. In such a wartime atmosphere, there was an immediate and obvious test of policy: whether the party gained support and won battles or whether it lost support and suffered defeat. Such an environment forced the party to pay great attention to the realities of China.

One can view the radicalization of the CCP in the years between its victory in 1949 and the end of the Cultural Revolution in 1976 as the result in part of the removal of a hostile environment and hence of the factors that had led the party to adhere to a prudential course during the revolutionary years. In other words, the victory of the CCP in 1949 was overwhelming, indeed too much so. As the party consolidated power in the early 1950s, it destroyed and silenced all opposition. As a result, there was no countervailing force to check the radical tendencies of the party.

Among the most damaging of Chairman Mao's thoughts was his lifelong belief in the intrinsic value of struggle. Mao's faith in struggle served him and the party well in wartime, but very poorly in peacetime. Yet Mao was convinced that "contradictions" lay everywhere and that resolving them through struggle would have a purifying effect on the party. In fact, it had a debilitating effect. Accompanying Mao's belief in struggle was his faith in mass mobilization. Again, organizing and mobilizing people was very effective during the revolutionary struggle, but it proved a very poor way of building a modern economy. To these notions of struggle and mass mobilization, one can add that of will. Mao repeatedly demonstrated a will that carried him to the top of the CCP and the CCP to victory against great odds. Mao seemed convinced that with sufficient will China could achieve any goal. Combined with revolutionary romantic notions about building a classless society, Mao's faith in will, struggle, and mass mobilization would prove disastrous to China's modernization.

Consolidation and Radicalization

The end of China's civil war concluded a period of over 30 years in which the country had been more or less continuously divided and at war. The sense of stability and unity gave the CCP something that its Soviet counterparts never experienced, namely widespread support and popularity. There was a hope and a belief that the CCP would be China's salvation. This period of domestic stability also brought a resuscitation of China's agriculture and industry. Despite the widespread damage to China's infrastructure, by 1953 China had restored both agricultural and industrial production to prewar highs. This rapid revival of the economy also rebounded to the party's favor, giving hope that it could indeed lead the country to prosperity.

Part of the new government's success in providing stability and restoring production was due to its ability to penetrate society and establish its

power within every corner of society. This process was accomplished first through land reform and then through the socialization of the urban and rural economies. In the course of land reform, the CCP systematically destroyed the old social structure in the countryside. Landlords, social elites, those who had supported the GMD or, during the war, the Japanese, were systematically identified, criticized, and frequently eliminated physically. A new elite of activists was created, one whose basis of power was due entirely to their support of the CCP.

Through its penetration of local society, the CCP was able to establish unprecedented political authority and to mobilize resources on behalf of the state. The new government established an economic system that systematically distorted prices in a way that would funnel resources to the state. This was remarkably effective. In the pre-Communist period, economists estimate that the GMD was able to extract only about 4 percent of national income. By the mid-1950s, the Chinese Communist government was able to extract some 30 percent of national income. That is approximately the same rate that the Soviet Union was able to extract in the mid-1930s, but China in 1950 had a per capita income of only one-fourth that of the Soviet Union in 1928.[8] Such figures testify to the degree of political power possessed by the new state and its ability to use that power on behalf of the state.

In the 1950s, the CCP used that power to support the First Five-Year Plan. This plan, which was heavily supported with aid from the Soviet Union, was extremely successful in terms of creating industrial production. Industrial production grew at an average annual rate of 18 percent.[9] Nevertheless, by the end of the First Five-Year

[8]Nicholas Lardy, "Economic Recovery and the First Five-Year Plan," Roderick MacFarquhar and John K. Fairbank, eds., *The Cambridge History of China, Vol. 14: The People's Republic,* Part I: The Emergence of Revolutionary China, 1949–1965, pp. 144–184.
[9]Carl Riskin, *China's Political Economy: The Quest for Development Since 1949* (Oxford: Oxford University Press, 1987), p. 57.

Plan, problems were mounting in the Chinese economy. Although industry had expanded rapidly, agriculture had lagged behind. Food grain is estimated to have grown 3.7 percent per annum during the First Five-Year Plan period, but that rate fell short of the demands created by rapid industrialization and urbanization. Moreover, there is evidence that the government had simply extracted too many resources from the Chinese economy, leaving the countryside bereft of inputs. It was also obvious that the centralization of economic authority in the First Five-Year Plan had created many inefficiencies as a newly created bureaucratic system grappled with problems that were beyond its capabilities.

In short, as China summed up the results of its First Five-Year Plan, it was apparent that China could not continue to follow the Soviet model. Something would have to give. Either the rate of economic growth would have to slow in order to allow agriculture to develop, or new ways of managing the economy would have to be found.

Political Factors

Rethinking China's course of development was also heavily influenced by political factors. In 1956, Khrushchev shocked the Communist world by harshly denouncing Stalin as a person who had created a personality cult and condemned millions to their deaths. This speech, which caught the Chinese leadership completely off guard, had profound ramifications for China. "Mao Zedong Thought" had been written into the Chinese constitution as the fundamental guideline of the party, and a cult of personality had grown up around Mao (though not on the same scale as around Stalin or as would later develop around Mao). At the CCP's Eighth Party Congress in 1956, the party deleted the reference to Mao Zedong Thought from the party constitution, and Mao stepped back from day-to-day management of the system, allowing more managerial powers to flow to Liu Shaoqi and Deng Xiaoping. This opened up questions about Mao's role in the system, and wittingly or unwittingly opened a gap between the person of Mao and the bureaucratic organization of the party.

At the same time, the rigidities of political control in the 1950s had given rise to many complaints of abuses of power and corruption. Contrary to the desires of his party colleagues, Mao decided to address these problems by opening up the door to public criticism of the party. Accordingly, in February 1957, Mao delivered a speech called, "On the Correct Handling of Contradictions among the People," which argued that "nonantagonistic contradictions" could be handled through a public airing of complaints. This speech and subsequent urgings by the party leadership ushered in a period known as the "Hundred Flowers" movement (after the slogan "Let a hundred schools of thought contend, let a hundred flowers bloom").

The Hundred Flowers campaign soon brought forth a torrent of criticism that shocked the party leadership, and apparently embarrassed Mao since he had urged such a campaign against the advice of his colleagues. Mao had apparently felt confident that he and the party enjoyed overwhelming public support; after all, their accomplishments seemed evident. But people in general, and intellectuals in particular, chafed at the political controls that had been imposed and suggested opening up the political system, even allowing other political parties to compete with the CCP. Embarrassed and angered by this outpouring of criticism (and the organization of some demonstrations), Mao moved quickly to reverse himself. In June 1957, the party launched an "anti-rightist" campaign against those who had spoken out. In the ensuing campaign, organizations were told to ferret out 5 percent of their members as "rightists," so even units that felt they could find no rightists still turned over 5 percent of their members as rightists. Altogether, at least 500,000 people were named as rightists; many of them would not have their labels reversed until the end of the Maoist era two decades later.

In sum, by the late 1950s, both economic trends and political events were combining in ways to launch China on a path that was distinctively different from the Soviet model and far more radical. The result was the Great Leap Forward, one of the greatest economic and human policy failures in the history of the world.

The Great Leap Forward

Although the Great Leap Forward (GLF) was an unprecedented disaster, at least some aspects of it made sense. The GLF called for a decentralization of the economy and an expansion of local authority at the expense of China's central bureaucracies. This kernel of economic rationality (which has ripened in the post-Mao reforms) was distorted by other policies, which led the GLF to disaster. First, economic decentralization was accompanied by a belief in local autarky. Under the assumption that central planning had failed to effectively coordinate the economic activities of the nation, radicals urged that each locality develop local self-sufficiency. This led to a great deal of duplicative construction and a loss of economic efficiency through a diminution of interregional trade. Second, accompanying this decentralization was an undercutting of the central bureaucracies. No doubt critics were right that the central bureaucracies were stifling growth and local initiative through overcentralization and bureaucratic rigidity, but their efforts led China to the other extreme, in which the central bureaucracies lost most of their coordinative functions. In other words, instead of paring the central bureaucracies to a size and function that they could reasonably expect to fulfill, the GLF destroyed their oversight function and left no constraints on the economic irrationalities that would follow.

It was, however, the radicalization of the political atmosphere that gave the GLF its character. In the wake of the anti-rightist movement, no one dared speak out against the policies. On the contrary, the atmosphere was such that the political demands of the center were inflated as they went down the hierarchy, with cadres at each level trying to prove their devotion to Mao and socialism by overfulfilling their quotas.

In short, the GLF was the apotheosis of the mobilizing techniques developed by the CCP during the revolutionary period and the early years of the People's Republic of China (PRC). Unchecked by either opposition forces or the normal bureaucratic restraints that would have occurred had there not been an anti-rightist campaign and a radicalization of the political atmosphere, the GLF threw tremendous human resources into enormously wasteful projects.

The campaign to develop backyard furnaces came to symbolize the wastefulness of the GLF. Determined to surpass England and catch up with the United States in steel production, Chinese leaders called for the creation of thousands of small-scale iron smelters. By late 1958, there were several hundred thousand small blast furnaces scattered throughout the country. Into these furnaces went every bit of scrap steel that peasants could locate—sometimes including their own cooking implements.

The result was wasteful in the extreme. The quality of the iron produced was so poor that most of it had to be discarded. In many instances, perfectly good iron and steel products had been dumped into the blast furnaces only to produce useless lumps of iron. Moreover, forests were destroyed in this ill-fated effort to industrialize, causing an ecological disaster from which China has yet to recover.

If the economic effects of the GLF were bad, the human results were disastrous. The backyard furnaces, for instance, were erected at the time of the fall harvest, and some 20 percent of the rural labor force was diverted to build and maintain them. Moreover, in their zeal to bring about the "transition to communism," most localities built common dining halls. There people ate as much as they wanted, and pretty soon food supplies were depleted.[10] Because localities had sold excessive amounts of grain to the state to cover up the lies they told about their production "successes," there were no grain reserves. Particularly after 1959, when the political atmosphere was further radicalized by a challenge to Mao's policies, people began to starve in large numbers. By the time the GLF finally ended in late 1961, at least 20 million people had died.

---

[10]Dali Yang, *Catastrophe and Reform in China: State, Rural Society, and Institutional Change since the Great Leap Famine* (Stanford, CA: Stanford University Press, 1996).

The Cultural Revolution

The Great Leap Forward marked a critical turning point that has affected all subsequent development of the Chinese Communist Party. Given the disaster of Mao's policies, he had no choice but to turn to others, indeed to those whose counsel he had rejected when he had launched the GLF, to restore the economy. Mao, however, would not, and perhaps could not, admit that he had been wrong in launching the GLF. The result was a period of policy oscillation in which party moderates implemented policies designed to rationalize the economy, while Mao continued to emphasize the socialist and egalitarian values that he had championed during the GLF.

Finally, Mao became convinced that others were creating a bureaucratic society inimical to his vision of a revolutionary society. Accordingly, Mao launched the country on one last nightmare, the Cultural Revolution. In 1966, Mao mobilized the youth of the country, who were formed quickly into Red Guard units. Under the banner of opposing the "four olds" (old customs, old habits, old culture, and old thinking), Red Guards ransacked people's homes, confiscating or destroying anything deemed "feudal" in nature (including old books, paintings, and ceramics), persecuting individuals deemed "bourgeois" or "rightist," and denouncing party leaders who were accused of opposing Chairman Mao. This phase of the Cultural Revolution, which cost thousands their lives, lasted about two years before Mao intervened to restore order. Millions of former Red Guards were sent to the countryside, where they were told to learn from the peasants. Disbanding the Red Guards, however, did not end the Cultural Revolution, for instead of admitting defeat and restoring the party, Mao called on the military to restore order throughout the country.

In the end, the Cultural Revolution dragged on for ten years until Mao died in September 1976. The human suffering caused by the Cultural Revolution was staggering, the waste appalling. Finally, a month after Mao died, veteran party and military leaders moved to arrest Mao's wife, Jiang Qing, and her cohorts, who collectively became known as the "Gang of Four." As Deng Xiaoping later put it, China had wasted 20 years.

CHINA UNDER REFORM

The death of Mao and the arrest of the Gang of Four did not immediately bring a change to China's economic and political policies. Hua Guofeng, a 56-year-old vice premier, succeeded Mao as chairman of the party. He had been chosen by Mao as a compromise candidate who might maintain the balance between radical leftist and moderate forces that Mao had established in his last years. Hua, however, did not have the seniority within the party or the leadership abilities to maintain the top job for long. Soon, veteran party members purged during the Cultural Revolution demanded to be restored to their jobs, and many old revolutionaries still in power (known as "survivors") supported their efforts. The leader of this veteran cadre group was Deng Xiaoping.

In 1977, Deng Xiaoping was restored to his position as a vice premier, but he was not content with a second-tier position. Deng deeply felt the loss of time and believed that China must act quickly to develop its economy or it would never achieve its century-old dream of attaining "wealth and power." He also believed that China could not modernize its economy if it continued to adhere to the ideological dogmas espoused during the Cultural Revolution. In 1978, Deng supported a nationwide discussion on the theme of "practice is the sole criterion of truth." The campaign harkened back to the theme of "practice" that had served the party so well during the revolution, arguing that policies could not be determined a priori to be socialist but rather had to be tested in practice.

The campaign on practice as the sole criterion of truth radically changed China's political atmosphere. Intellectuals, excoriated as the "stinking ninth category" during the Cultural Revolution, were restored to their positions and considered part of the working class. Deng Xiaoping spoke to the 1978 National Congress of Science and Technology and declared science and technology to be the "primary forces of production." More movingly, he declared himself willing to serve as the "logistics" officer for their research.

In December 1978, the party convened the Third Plenary Session of the Eleventh Central Committee. In the resulting communiqué, the party declared that large-scale class struggle was over and that the focus of the party's work would shift to economic modernization. The "four modernizations" of industry, agriculture, science and technology, and national defense were to be given top priority. A number of veteran party leaders were restored to high-level positions. Hua Guofeng was allowed to stay on as chairman until 1981, but the era of reform had clearly begun.

Some of the specific policies adopted under reform will be discussed in the next section. Here, it is important to point out that reform covered the whole range of state-society relations as well as foreign policy. Not only was the content of the CCP's ideology changed from Mao's romantic revolutionary notions of building a socialist state to Deng's far more pragmatic ideas of "building socialism with Chinese characteristics," but the role of ideology within the polity changed dramatically. Mao sought to modernize China through the mobilizing lever of ideology; Deng sought economic growth by reducing ideology to a set of prescriptions intended to uphold the authority of the party. This much more limited notion of ideology both reflected and promoted a depoliticization of society. In the Maoist period, especially during the height of the Cultural Revolution, the most private of thoughts and acts were considered politically relevant. With the inauguration of the Dengist period, the state largely withdrew from society, allowing a "zone of privacy" to develop around individuals. Although there have been periodic attempts to prevent the growth of this zone of privacy, it has nevertheless continued to be enlarged throughout the Dengist period and beyond. The public expression of political ideas remains restricted, but the definition of what constitutes a political idea has constantly shrunk. Into the space vacated by the state has blossomed a vibrant popular culture that does not generally challenge the authority of the state but does restrict the

impact of state ideology.[11] Exceptions to this rule occurred during the student movements of the late 1980s and the *Falun Gong* movement in the late 1990s. These are discussed below.

Opening up to the outside world has reinforced this retreat of the state and diminution of the role of ideology. With the inauguration of reform, serious ideas and frivolous notions alike flooded into China, and were sometimes taken with the same degree of seriousness. Although Western notions including such weighty concepts as democracy and human rights and less serious thoughts as expressed in Hollywood movies have poured into China, popular culture has been more influenced by Taiwan and Hong Kong, Chinese cultural areas that have developed strong and vibrant film and entertainment industries. The impact of outside ideas has often been decried, but it is clearly unstoppable.

There is no question that the reform and development of the economy as well as the opening up of Chinese society have generated forces that challenge the political status quo. The usual cliché that China has engaged in economic reform but not political reform contains both truth and exaggeration. In fact, the breakdown of the commune system in the countryside, the development of an economy beyond Beijing's direct control, the development of law and the role of China's legislative organ, the National People's Congress (see Section B), and the greater role of experts in policy formation all suggest that China's political system has evolved a great deal. It is nevertheless true that all power continues to reside in the CCP and that direct expression of contrary political opinions is not tolerated.

The tensions between an emerging society and a still-closed political system burst into international view in the spring of 1989 as thousands, then over a million Beijing residents took to the streets to demand a more open political system. After six weeks of confrontation, and occasional

[11]A wonderful account of popular culture is given by Jianying Zha in *China Pop* (New York: New Press, 1995).

Deng Xiaoping, 93 years old when he died in 1997, did more than any other Chinese leader to secure China's dream of wealth and power.

again. As described in more detail in the next section, Deng Xiaoping in January 1992 traveled to the controversial Shenzhen Special Economic Zone (SEZ) to once again praise reform and opening up. Deng's trip jump-started a new wave of reform and a new period of high economic growth. In October 1992, the party reaffirmed its commitment to economic reform by adopting the most liberal document in its history. Brushing off conservative objections, the document called for developing a "socialist market economy"—the first unambiguous statement that the goal of reform was a market economy.

With power passing to a new generation of leaders, there remain many uncertainties about China's political evolution. For all the difficulties of the reform period, including the tragedy of Tiananmen, China has been more successful in engineering an economic takeoff than any other socialist country. Indeed, China appears to be attaining its century-old goal of "wealth and power" (though many economic problems remain), and it is that success which legitimizes the government's claim to power, not Marxism-Leninism. That change only underscores the evolution the CCP has undergone from its founding to the present time.

movements toward conciliation, the protests were crushed by the military at the cost of some 700 lives. The images of tanks and armored personnel carriers moving into the center of Beijing, guns blazing, remains firmly planted in the minds of millions. It also obscures a complex reality. Indeed, controversy over the tactics of student leaders and the associated debate over how political change in China is best achieved came to wider public attention with the release of the films *The Gate of Heavenly Peace* and *Moving the Mountain* and the publication of the *Tiananmen Papers*.

The suppression of the 1989 protests appeared for a while to mark the end of reform, as the reform-minded General Secretary Zhao Ziyang and other officials were purged from office and as intellectuals and others were subjected to investigation. As the immediate crisis passed, however, pressures for reform grew once

Thinking Critically

1. What legacies did China's long imperial rule leave for twentieth-century China?
2. What is meant by the terms "national revolution" and "social revolution"?
3. What are the chief characteristics of "Mao Zedong Thought"?
4. What were the implications of the CCP's overwhelming victory in 1949?
5. Why did Chinese politics become increasingly radical until Mao's death in 1976?

KEY TERMS

cadre *(457–458)*
Chiang Kai-shek *(456)*
Chinese Communist Party (CCP) *(456)*
Confucius *(452)*

FURTHER READINGS

Ash, Robert, et al., *Hong Kong in Transition: One Country, Two Systems* (London: Routledge Curzan, 2003).

Barnett, A. Doak. *Cadres, Bureaucracy, and Political Power in Communist China* (New York: Columbia University Press, 1967).

Belden, Jack. *China Shakes the World* (New York: Monthly Review Press, 1949).

Bianco, Lucien. *Origins of the Chinese Revolution: 1915–1949* (Stanford, CA: Stanford University Press, 1971).

Chang, Jung. *Wild Swans: Three Daughters of China* (New York: Simon and Schuster, 1991).

Chow, Ts'e-tung. *The May Fourth Movement: Intellectual Revolution in Modern China* (Cambridge, MA: Harvard University Press, 1969).

Eastman, Lloyd. *The Abortive Revolution: China under Nationalist Rule, 1927–1937* (Cambridge, MA: Harvard University Press, 1974).

Fewsmith, Joseph. *Party, State, and Local Elites in Republican China* (Honoloulu: University of Hawaii Press, 1985).

Hsiao, Kung-Chuan. *Rural China: Imperial Control in the Nineteenth Century* (Seattle: University of Washington Press, 1960).

Johnson, Chalmers. *Peasant Nationalism and Communist Power: The Emergence of Revolutionary China, 1937–1945* (Stanford, CA: Stanford University Press, 1961).

Kuhn, Philip A. *Rebellion and Its Enemies in Late Imperial China* (Cambridge, MA: Harvard University Press, 1970).

Law, Kam-yee, ed. *The Chinese Cultural Revolution Reconsidered: Beyond Purge and Holocaust* (Houndmills: Palgrave Macmillan, 2003).

Li, Zhisui, with Anne Thurston. *The Private Life of Chairman Mao* (New York: Random House, 1994).

Lieberthal, Kenneth. *Governing China: From Revolution through Reform* (New York: Norton, 1995).

McLaren, Anne E. ed. *Chinese Women: Living and Working* (London: Routledge, 2004).

Schram, Stuart R. *The Political Thought of Mao Tse-tung* (Middlesex, CT: Penguin, 1963).

Spence, Jonathan D. *The Search for Modern China* (New York: Norton, 1990).

Spence, Jonathan D . *The Gate of Heavenly Peace* (New York: Penguin, 1981).

Schwartz, Benjamin. *Chinese Communism and the Rise of Mao* (Cambridge, MA: Harvard University Press, 1951).

Shiffrin, Harold. *Sun Yat-sen and the Origins of the Chinese Revolution* (Berkeley: University of California Press, 1968).

Stuart-Fox, Martin. A Short History of China and Southeast Asia (Australia: Allen and Urwin, 2003).

Thomson, James C. *While China Faced West: American Reformers in Nationalist China, 1928–1937* (Cambridge, MA: Harvard University Press, 1969).

Watt, John R. *The Chinese Magistrate in Late Imperial China* (New York: Columbia University Press, 1972).

Wright, Mary C. *The Last Stand of Chinese Conservatism: The T'ung-chih Restoration, 1862–1874*, rev. ed. (Stanford, CA: Stanford University Press, 1966).

B. POLITICAL PROCESSES AND INSTITUTIONS

From the overview of China's political development presented in the previous section, we turn here to the basic institutions and processes through which China is governed. Because China is ruled by the CCP, we start with the party. We consider first how its historical legacy affects its behavior and then look at the formal structure of the party. Then we turn to the organization of the state and to China's legislative body, the National People's Congress. In order to understand how these institutions function, we look at the implementation of reform, which began in the late 1970s. Finally, we look at the social tensions generated by reform.

THE PARTY

Historical Legacy

The Chinese Communist Party (CCP) lies at the core of the Chinese political system. As suggested in Section A, the CCP arose in reaction to a number of interlocking crises facing China in the early and mid-twentieth century: the breakdown of political authority, the humiliations suffered at the hands of foreigners, the failure of Confucianism to provide an effective ideological framework, and the growing belief that social revolution was a necessary component of any effective response to these problems. Moreover, in its revolutionary period, the CCP suffered repeated setbacks, some of which almost destroyed the party. This background left important legacies in the organization and functioning of the CCP.

First and foremost, the CCP inherited the mantle of nationalism. Born of the May Fourth Movement, the CCP was one (and ultimately the most successful) expression of the nationalist aspirations that were deeply held by the population. In this sense, Marxism-Leninism provided Chinese nationalists with a template for action, a belief that in adopting certain intellectual and organizational orientations they could realize their broader nationalist objectives. This sense of

nationalism has pervaded the CCP throughout its existence, permitted it to survive such incredible policy failures as the Great Leap Forward and the Cultural Revolution, and been the anchor on which the party based its continued existence following the failure of Communism in the former Soviet Union and Eastern Europe.

Second, the party developed organizational techniques that continue to affect the life of every Chinese even today, though some of these techniques are beginning to loose their hold. Chief among these was the division of society into *danwei* ("units"). Under the *danwei* system, all Chinese are attached to specific bureaucratic, industrial, or agricultural organizations. Such organizations encompass every aspect of an individual's life. In the cities, until recently, housing was owned and assigned by specific units, and medical care and other social benefits have been allocated by units. Employment was for life, and it was very difficult to move from one unit to another. In recent years, this system has begun to break down as the economy diversifies, as housing reform has privatized living units, and as labor mobility has increased, but it nevertheless remains an important part of Chinese life. In the countryside, prior to the inauguration of the reforms, peasants were bound tightly to the land through the commune system and migration was not permitted. In recent years, peasants have been allowed to travel and migrate (though generally not to change their legal residence), which has brought about new problems (discussed below).

The *danwei* system was enforced by the household registration (*hukou*) and dossier systems. Every Chinese was assigned a household registration that assigned him or her to a specific physical location, and until recently it was very difficult to move from one area to another. More important, a dossier was maintained on each Chinese citizen. Such things as the person's family background (thus making class background an inherited characteristic), his or her educational and employment history, as well as a complete record of one's political thought and activities were included in the dossier.

The combination of the *danwei, hukou,* and dossier systems allowed the state to impose very tight control over the population. In recent years, these controls have begun to break down as the opening up of the economy has necessitated greater internal population movement and migration and as the decline of political criteria have made the dossiers less threatening. Nevertheless, these features continue to exist, particularly in the cities, and provide the means by which the state can tighten control over individuals when it seeks to do so. At higher levels of the state and party bureaucracies, the dossier system allows the Organization Department of the CCP to exercise tight control over the advancement of individuals.

Third, the party developed in strong reaction to the social and political disintegration of the earlier period. Its mission was to unify China. Internally, although a legacy of personal relations was inherited from the past, a strong norm against factionalism, in the sense of a group of people working together in an organized fashion to achieve a common aim, developed within the party. The corollary of this norm against faction, ironically, has been the belief that it is possible and necessary for one viewpoint ("line") to win complete victory against all others.[12]

Organizationally, this legacy has found expression in one person dominating, and in some sense transcending, the party. This feature of the party dates from at least 1943 when the party appointed three people, including Mao Zedong, to the Secretariat but authorized Mao to make decisions on his own if he disagreed with the others.[13] In a well-known speech, Deng Xiaoping referred to the leader of the party as the "core," evoking an image of a leader whose position is based on a combination of formal and informal authority. This feature appears attenu-

ated under Jiang Zemin, though his campaign for the "Three Representatives" (see below) suggests its continued importance. Nevertheless, with each succeeding leader it will become more difficult to assert personal dominance over the party.

This outline of some of the features of the CCP suggests that to understand its functioning and role in Chinese society, it is necessary to have an understanding of it in historical, ideological, formal, and informal terms. Having dealt with the party's historical development, we turn here to its formal organization.

Organization

The CCP, as befits a party that developed as a clandestine organization struggling to overturn the social and political order, is hierarchical in structure (see Figure 8.1). At the top of the system is the supreme leader (in Deng's phrase, the "core"). In the later revolutionary period and the first 28 years of the People's Republic of China, this was Mao Zedong, who held the title chairman. The 1982 party constitution, adopted after Mao's death, abolished the position of chairman in order to prevent another person from so completely dominating the political system. In the reform period, the top party position has been that of general secretary, but real power was been retained in the hands of Deng Xiaoping and other party elders. Hu Yaobang was general secretary from 1980 to 1987, when he was ousted and replaced by Zhao Ziyang. After the Tiananmen incident in 1989, Zhao was ousted and Jiang Zemin took over as general secretary. He was succeeded in 2002 by Hu Jintao.

The supreme leader generally serves on the Politburo Standing Committee (PSC). The PSC is usually composed of around seven people, generally men, who make up the inner circle of political power. The actual power of the PSC as a policy-making body varies over time. In the early reform period (until 1987), Deng Xiaoping served on the PSC but generally did not rule through it (Deng insisted on being the third ranked member). In fact, to circumvent the PSC and the broader Politburo, which was dominated by a number of superannuated and conservative party elders, much authority was shifted to the

---

[12]Tang Tsou, "Chinese Politics at the Top: Factionalism or Informal Politics? Balance-of-Power Politics or a Game to Win All?" *China Journal* 34 (July 1995): pp. 95–156.

[13]Stuart Schram, *Mao's Road to Power, Revolutionary Writing, 1912–1949, Vol. 1: The Pre-Marxist Period, 1912–1920* (Armonk, NY: M. E. Sharpe, 1992), p. xix.

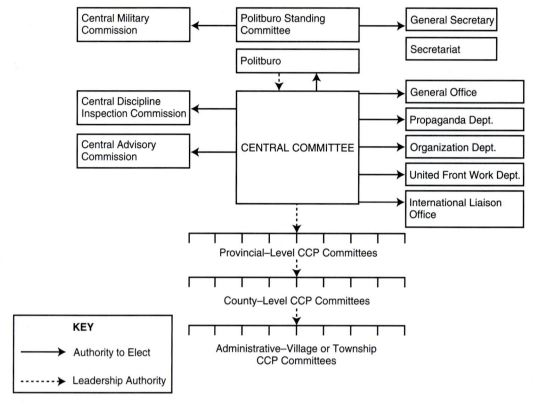

Figure 8.1 ORGANIZATION OF THE CHINESE COMMUNIST PARTY

Source: Adapted from *Policy Conflicts in Post-Mao China,* ed. John P. Burns and Stanley Rosen (Armonk, NY: M. E. Sharpe, 1986), pp. 360–361.

CCP Secretariat. Since 1987, power has generally shifted back to the PSC, though as the Tiananmen crackdown vividly demonstrated, the power of elder cadres could eclipse the formal policy-making process. In recent years, power has passed to a younger generation, and the PSC has been restored as the center of decision making.

Each member of the Politburo Standing Committee is in charge of a particular functional responsibility. For instance, the highest-ranking member of the PSC is in charge of overall party affairs (including ideology) and the military, giving him the most powerful and far-reaching brief of all the leaders. The second or third ranking member of the PSC usually serves con-

currently as premier of the State Council (to be discussed later) and generally has overall responsibility for management of the economy (although this portfolio can be subdivided in a variety of ways). Another leader will be in charge of legal affairs, a broad area of responsibility that includes internal security. Yet other leaders will take charge of such areas as propaganda and organization.

This division of labor among the highest-ranking officials in the country reflects the organization of the Chinese polity into various *xitong,* or systems. Six distinct systems have been identified: Party Affairs, Organization and Personnel, Propaganda and Education, Political and Legal Affairs, Finance and Economics, and the Military.

Each of these systems combines several bureaucratic organizations that run from the top of the system to the bottom. In other words, almost everyone in China belongs to one *danwei* or another, and almost every *danwei* is encompassed in one of these various *xitong*.[14]

The PSC is elected by the membership of the whole Politburo. The Politburo, generally composed of around 20 people, ratifies decisions made by the PSC. On less critical issues, individual members of the Politburo will have responsibility for a particular issue area and will report on that issue to the whole membership, which then makes a decision.

The Politburo is selected by the Central Committee, a body composed of approximately 200 people, which is elected by a party congress. Party congresses are supposed to meet every five years, but in the pre-reform era they were held only irregularly. For instance, the Seventh Party Congress was held in 1945 as the party prepared for its final push on power, but the Eighth Party Congress was not held until eleven years later in 1956. The Ninth Party Congress then was not held until 1969—three years after the start of the Cultural Revolution and after Mao's main adversaries in the party had been purged and denounced publicly. After Mao's death, however, party congresses have been held on a regular basis, starting in 1977, a sign of the increasing institutionalization of the party.

Delegates to a party congress are supposed to represent lower levels of the party organization and number around 4,000–5,000. After the party congress is over and a new Central Committee is selected, the delegates to the party congress no longer play any political role (they may or may not be selected to attend the next party congress). In between party congresses, the Central Committee will meet periodically in plenary session (hence the term *plenum*). In the reform period, such plenums have generally been held once a year, though sometimes there have been two or more plenums a year. The first plenary session of a

Hu Jintao, born in 1942, was named general secretary of the Chinese Communist Party in fall 2002, and president in 2003.

newly selected Central Committee is normally held immediately following the end of a party congress and is for the sole purpose of selecting the party leadership, particularly the members of the Politburo, the PSC, the Secretariat, and the Central Military Commission (CMC). Central Committees are numbered according to which party congress selected them (there have now been 16 party congresses since the party began in 1921), and plenary sessions of the Central Committee are numbered during the tenure of that Central Committee. Thus, for example, the plenum that inaugurated the reform period in December 1978 was the Third Plenary Session of the Eleventh Central Committee.

In formal terms, the party is organized from the bottom up, with lower-level party organizations selecting delegates to higher-level meetings to select the party's leadership, but the selection of delegates from lower levels is heavily influenced by

[14]Kenneth Lieberthal, *Governing China: From Revolution through Reform* (New York, Norton, 1995), pp. 194–208.

the opinions of higher-level bodies. Moreover, for most of the party's history, delegates to party congresses have had no choice in candidates for Central Committee, just as the members of the Central Committee have had no choice in whom they select for the Politburo. Such sensitive personnel decisions have always been heavily influenced, if not absolutely controlled, by the highest-level leaders. Beginning in 1987, there has been some loosening up of this system. There are now a few more candidates for the Central Committee than there are seats on the Central Committee, so some people fail to be elected. In at least two instances, candidates widely reported to have been slated to take a position on the Politburo have failed to be elected to the Central Committee, thus ending their chances of taking a position on the party's top policy-making body. Although very limited, this "inner-party democracy" has begun to have an impact on the way the party works, and there are indications that inner-party democracy may be expanded in the coming years.

The influence of higher levels of the party over lower levels of the party derives largely from the practice of democratic centralism. In theory, democratic centralism means that all party decisions can be discussed fully by lower-level party members before a decision is made, but that once a decision is made all party members must carry it out without dissent. Thus there is supposed to be a combination of "democratic" decision making and centralized implementation. In practice, the system has never worked in this fashion. Higher-level party members, particularly the party secretary at any given level, monopolize decision making, so that the decision-making process is centralized and top-down.

There are also several important organizations that nominally are under the Central Committee but, in fact, are run by the central party leadership. The most important is the Secretariat. The primary purpose of the Secretariat is to oversee the implementation of Politburo decisions. It plays an important role in drafting documents and overseeing the propaganda that promotes central policies. As noted above, in the 1980s it took on an even more important role by becoming deeply involved in policy making itself.

In addition, there is the Propaganda Department, which directly oversees publication of articles supporting the party and makes sure that publications not under direct control of the central party organization nevertheless do not deviate from the party line. There is also an Organization Department that vets all appointments to senior positions. The United Front Work Department has the difficult task of trying to persuade nonparty intellectuals of the correctness of the party's policy. It attempts to do this through the Chinese People's Political Consultative Conference (CPPCC), an organ that includes many prominent nonparty intellectuals and meets annually in conjunction with the National People's Congress (NPC) to listen to reports by government officials. The International Liaison Office is not as important as it used to be, for its function is to develop relations with foreign political parties, particularly socialist and communist parties. Finally, there is the General Office that overseas and coordinates the work of the central party, particularly that of the general secretary. It is also in charge of the security of China's top leadership.

In order to enforce control within the party, there is a Central Discipline Inspection Commission (CDIC), the main function of which is to root out violators of party discipline, primarily those involved in corruption, but it has also been used at times to rein in reformers. Between 1982 and 1992 there was a Central Advisory Commission (CAC), which served as a vehicle for easing veteran party cadres into retirement. Members of the CAC had to retire from their other party and state positions but were allowed to retain important privileges, including access to important party documents and, in the case of Standing Committee members, the right to attend Politburo meetings. Although formally retired, members of the CAC played an important role from time to time, including in the dismissal of General Secretary Hu Yaobang in January 1987 and in the decision to use military force to suppress the Tiananmen demonstrations in 1989.

Central Military Commission

Standing in a category of its own is the Chinese military, the People's Liberation Army (PLA).

From its origins in the mountains of the Jiangxi base area, the PLA has always been the party's army. All military commanders and many of the troops are party members, and a system of political commissars, serving alongside professional military commanders, ensure the loyalty of the army. Control over the military has always been one of the keys to CCP rule, and personal leadership of the military has always been essential to attain the position of supreme leader. Mao Zedong was a co-founder of the PLA and one of its chief strategists during the revolutionary period; Deng Xiaoping was a political commissar in one of the five field armies during the civil war.

This control is maintained through the Central Military Commission (CMC), an organ that reports directly to the Politburo. Mao was head of the CMC until his death. After a brief interregnum during which Hua Guofeng served as head of the CMC, Deng Xiaoping took over. Deng continued to retain this position two years after he retired formally from the Politburo in 1987 (a change that necessitated a rewriting of the constitution). After Deng retired as head of the CMC in 1989, Jiang Zemin was named to this position. Jiang was the first wholly civilian head of state since the overthrow of the Manchu (Qing) dynasty. This transfer to civilian control of the military has, so far, gone smoothly (despite reports of occasional friction between the military and civilian leaderships over such issues as Taiwan), and is one of the least heralded political developments of recent years.

Local Party Organizations

The organization of the party described above is generally replicated at lower levels of the system, albeit somewhat less elaborately. Each of China's 30 provinces is headed by a party committee, which has a standing committee and party secretary. Members of the standing committee have a division of labor much like their counterparts at the central level. There are also provincial-level propaganda, organization, and other departments as well as a provincial-level discipline inspection commission.

Below the province, there are party organizations in each county (there are over 2,000 counties in China) or, in cities, in each district. Below the county there is the administrative village or township, where the party structure is replicated. In the Maoist period, this was the commune level. Below the administrative village or township, there is a party organization at the village level.

THE STATE

The state apparatus in China can be thought of as consisting of two main parts, the administrative side and the legislative side. According to the Chinese constitution, the highest organ of state power is the National People's Congress (NPC), although the NPC historically never played a role anywhere comparable to its constitutionally stated authority. In recent years, however, the NPC has begun to play a more prominent role in the Chinese political system, and its role is discussed below. It is appropriate to discuss first the administrative side of the state—the State Council and its subordinate ministries—because they have been and continue to be the most important organs overseeing the management of the country.

State Council, Ministries, and Commissions

The State Council is presided over by the premier, who is formally elected by the NPC upon the recommendation of the CCP Central Committee, a recommendation that has never been rejected (though in recent years there have been votes cast in opposition). In the Maoist period, the premier was Zhou Enlai; in March 2003 Wen Jiabao was appointed to the position. Normally, the premier is the second or third ranked person on the PSC. Under the premier are several vice premiers (currently numbering four), who have a specific division of work (normally industry, agriculture, finance and banking, and foreign policy).

Traditionally the primary role of the State Council is to oversee the work of the various ministries and commissions that have administered the country. Most of these ministries and commissions (which numbered 45 in the 1990s)

REVIEW
8.1

KEY ABBREVIATIONS IN CHINESE POLITICS

CAC	Central Advisory Committee		IMF	International Monetary Fund
CCP	Chinese Communist Party		NPC	National People's Congress
CDIC	Central Discipline Inspection Commission		PLA	People's Liberation Army
			PPP	Purchasing Price Parity
CMC	Central Military Commission		PSC	Politburo standing committee
CPPCC	Chinese People's Political Consultative Commission		SOEs	state-owned enterprises
			TVEs	township and village-owned enterprises
GLF	Great Leap Forward			
GMD	Guomingtang (Kuomintang)		WTO	World Trade Organization
GNP	Gross National Product			

oversaw the economy, but other important areas of concern include foreign affairs, education, and science and technology. Each of these bureaucracies is headed by a person who holds at least ministerial rank. In the case of the most powerful commissions, the head might be a person who concurrently serves as a vice premier as well as on the Politburo or even its Standing Committee.

Historically, this organization of the state mirrored the organizational structure developed in the Soviet Union, and its primary purpose was to administer the planned economy. The planned economy in China, as in the Soviet Union, was based on the idea that the state could and should mobilize resources from throughout the society for investment in areas deemed to be in the long-term interest of the country. This mobilization of resources was largely accomplished through a highly distorted price system that drew resources to a relatively small number of large state-owned enterprises, which then delivered profits and taxes to the state. This distorted price system largely substituted for a tax system, and collecting taxes is perennially one of the most difficult tasks in developing countries.

In 1998, this structure was substantially reformed. The number of ministries was reduced to 29, though increased in 2003 to 36; economic functions were concentrated in the State Economic and Trade Commission; and half of the

cadres staffing the State Council were let go. The thrust of this administrative reform has been to remove the state from the direct management of most of the economy (though it continues to oversee the functioning of the largest enterprises) and to strengthen its ability to use macroeconomic tools (such as fiscal and monetary policy) to manage the economy. The old State Planning Commission, which used to run the planned economy, has been renamed the State Development and Planning Commission, and its functions have been curtailed greatly. This administrative reform underscores the distance China has traveled from a traditional planned economy to a modern market economy.

Party Control of the State

As in the Soviet model, the party and state hierarchies are parallel to each other in China. The party maintains control over the state through two mechanisms. First there is a *nomenklatura* system in which the party appoints people to the most important bureaucratic (and industrial) jobs in the country.[15] Second, there are party

---

[15]John P. Burns, *The Chinese Communist Nomenklatura System: A Documentary Study of Party Control of Leadership Selection* (Armonk, NY: M. E. Sharpe, 1989).

groups (*dangzu*) at different levels in the state bureaucracy. For instance, in the typical ministry, the minister is usually the party secretary of the ministry's party group. Regardless of the formal rankings of different officials, it is this party group that sets policy for the ministry. It is also the party group's responsibility to carry out broader party policy, though frequently bureaucratic interests make the formulation and implementation of coherent policy difficult.

The National People's Congress

Although formally part of the state apparatus, the NPC is a distinct part of the system and therefore deserves separate discussion. Like national party congresses, the NPC is supposed to be elected every five years, a schedule that has been adhered to in the reform period, though not before. Delegates to the NPC are elected from geographical and functional organizations (such as industry and the military). Though most delegates are members of the CCP, they do not have to be. Indeed, one of the functions of the NPC is to bring party and nonparty people together in a so-called united front in order to promote party policy among nonparty people.

Although the state constitution of the PRC calls the NPC the highest organ of state power, it has never played such a powerful role. The selection of delegates is highly influenced by party preferences, and the NPC has never wielded a truly independent role. The NPC meets in full session once a year, usually in March. Its primary function is to listen to and ratify various government reports. These normally include the Government Work Report, which is presented by the premier, the budget report presented by the minister of finance, and a social and economic development plan presented by the head of the State Development and Planning Commission.

In between annual meetings of the NPC, a Standing Committee meets at regular intervals. In recent years, Standing Committee meetings have been held approximately every two months. The task of the Standing Committee, like that of the full NPC, is to consider legislation and "supervise" the government. The NPC Standing Committee is generally headed by a member of the Politburo;

prior to the Cultural Revolution and since 1993 it has been headed by a member of the PSC (the head is Wu Bangguo, the outgoing vice-president and second ranked member of the PSC).

Although frequently referred to in the Western press as a "rubber stamp" legislature, the NPC in recent years has taken on an increasing role as a sounding board as well as a body of opinion that has to be taken into account. In the reform period, as the regime has increasingly emphasized the development of the economy, the pace of legislation has been stepped up and the role of the legislature has accordingly become more important. Like other legislatures around the world, the NPC has developed a committee structure (especially for law and economics), which has given it a level of expertise that it did not previously have. These committees play an important role in drafting legislation, and their growing role has reflected both the greater role that expertise plays in policy making and the broader input that currently goes into the formulation of law.

The NPC has also played a safety-valve role of registering dissatisfaction with government policies. Policies and leaders are routinely subjected to skeptical questioning by delegates, although much of these interventions are done in separate discussion meetings that are not open to public scrutiny. Throughout the reform period, the NPC has routinely amended the Government Work Report. Although many of these amendments are minor in nature, some of them are clearly substantive. This does not mean that China is on the verge of becoming a parliamentary democracy, but it does suggest that the NPC can increasingly play a role in reflecting public opinion.

THE EMERGENCE OF ECONOMIC REFORM

The Cultural Revolution left China politically, economically, socially, and spiritually exhausted. If there was any one impulse that dominated society at the time, it was a desire to return to normal, to stop the ceaseless political campaigns that destroyed families and lives. Reform responded to this societal desire. It also responded to another, but parallel, desire, namely the widely felt belief that China had wasted two decades. In the 20 years since Mao had launched the Great Leap Forward, Japan had emerged as a major world economic power. Following very much in the path of Japan were the "four small dragons" of South Korea, Taiwan, Singapore, and Hong Kong. All were achieving the prosperity that China had long hoped for. It was apparent that despite the frenetic efforts of the Chinese people, the gap between China and the outside world was widening—and widening quickly.

In launching its reforms, China had many advantages not enjoyed by the Soviet Union or Eastern Europe. First and foremost, China had not destroyed its party elite as Stalin had. Many party leaders, including state president Liu Shaoqi, had died during the Cultural Revolution, but most had survived. Moreover, the Cultural Revolution had had a sobering effect on them. It allowed them to see just how far out of control an overemphasis on ideology could go. It also gave them a taste of the party dictatorship that they themselves had inflicted on others. For some, the Cultural Revolution provided contact with ordinary Chinese citizens for the first time in years. For instance, Deng Xiaoping worked in a tractor factory in Nanchang, the capital of Jiangxi province, and the experience appears to have given him at least some sense of the feelings of ordinary Chinese. In short, there was a heartfelt desire on the part of the party veterans who returned to power following the Cultural Revolution to return to the goals that had motivated them in their youth: the desire for China to become "wealthy and powerful."

Moreover, as party veterans returned to power, they had something of a party program on which to build—the Eighth Party Congress program of 1956. That congress had laid out the basic theme of turning away from class struggle to concentrate on economic development that was subsequently adopted to much greater effect at the Third Plenary Session of the Eleventh Central Committee in December 1978. This background provided returning veterans with something of a consensus on policy and direction.

Although the decisions of the Eighth Party Congress had not lasted long before Mao launched the country onto the disastrous course of the Great Leap Forward, there were many policy legacies from the 1950s and 1960s (when China was recovering from the GLF) that could be built on in the reform era. One was in agriculture. At various times in the 1950s and early 1960s, when the party had retreated temporarily from its efforts to implement collective agriculture, the peasants in many areas had turned to various forms of contracting land from the local collective. In other words, instead of restoring private ownership, which was forbidden, they had adopted a type of tenant farming with the local collective acting as the landlord. This type of household responsibility system, as it would become known in the reform era, was particularly widespread in 1960–1961 in the wake of the Great Leap famine.

Another policy legacy of the 1950s and 1960s was the effort to promote various forms of accountability in industry. Intellectuals and industrial bureaucrats had long struggled with ideas about reforming industrial relations within the framework of socialism. For instance, the famous economist Sun Yefang had advocated increasing enterprise decision-making authority and giving the "law of value" a greater role in the management of the economy. These were ideas for which Sun was condemned to seven years in jail during the Cultural Revolution, but he emerged from jail in 1977 with his ideas intact—and many new converts.

In short, there was a history of ideas and policy experimentation that predated reform by many years. Without this repository of ideas and experience, it is unlikely that reform could have been undertaken so quickly or succeeded so well.

Another advantage that China had in the late 1970s, though few central bureaucrats would have considered it as such at the time, was the decentralization of the economy. During the Cultural Revolution, much authority over economic activity had been decentralized to local governments. That meant that when veteran cadres, purged during the Cultural Revolution, returned to office and began to focus on restoring production, they had to try to recentralize economic authority in Beijing. But they could only do so to a certain extent. Local governments which had acquired authority over economic activities, and invested local economic resources in them, were not willing to yield easily.

One area in which this test of strength between local and central authorities became apparent was in the reform of the tax system. Desiring to step up investment in industry, the central government needed greater tax revenues. However, a simple demand to remit greater revenues to the center would have encountered local resistance. Central authorities tackled this problem by means of a compromise. In 1980, a tax reform was instituted that provided localities with a financial incentive for increasing revenues by allowing them to retain for local purposes a portion of the new taxes raised. This revenue system, which was subsequently extended to some sectors of industry as well, gave localities an incentive to develop new sources of revenues, particularly in those areas where they would be permitted to retain the receipts.

This was one of the main reasons industries in China's rural areas, known as township and village enterprises (TVEs), took off. Although there was some basis for such industries in the pre-reform period, it was the new financial arrangements (along with the new emphasis on developing the economy) that stimulated local interest in developing industry. The TVE sector has been one of the great success stories of China's reform period, and one that distinguishes China's path of reform from that of other socialist countries. In 1978, there were approximately 28 million people employed in TVEs, which produced only 9 percent of China's total industrial output. Moreover, such industries were extremely backward in terms of technology and concentrated in such heavy industries as iron and steel, cement, farm implements, and so forth. By the mid-1990s, the situation had completely changed. In 1992, for the first time, TVEs produced more than 50 percent of China's industrial output. They employed approximately 120 million workers and accounted for some 20 percent of China's exports. Although many TVEs remained technologically unsophisticated, others were producing advanced electronic products and precision instruments.

Rural Reform

China's reform began with the rural sector. This was more a matter of happenstance than design. The area in which rural reform advanced earliest and most quickly was the province of Anhui in central-east China. Anhui was a pioneer in rural reform in part because it had suffered more perhaps than any other province during the Great Leap Forward and had implemented the household responsibility system (although under a different name) more widely than any other province following the GLF. In 1977, Wan Li, a close associate of Deng Xiaoping, was appointed the leading party official in the province, and he quickly came to support agricultural reform there.

Bottom-up initiative was as important as top-down support in the inauguration and spread of rural reform. A severe drought in 1978 provided an incentive, and a rationale, for adopting new forms of organization. Peasants in several areas demanded to contract their own land. In one famous instance, 18 families signed a secret pledge to engage in household production (which was still illegal) and to support the families of anyone (particularly local cadres) who was arrested as a result of their actions.

The household responsibility system soon proved a great success in Anhui and elsewhere. The reform of agriculture went against everything that Mao Zedong had tried to accomplish in over two decades of rural collectivization and, therefore, encountered stiff resistance from many quarters. Nevertheless, the demonstrable success of the system, as well as the support of officials committed to reform, eventually overcame all opposition. In 1983, the household responsibility system was universalized throughout China, and the commune system was officially abolished. The Maoist era had clearly come to an end.

The household responsibility system was successful in promoting the development of agriculture. Grain production increased by a third, from 305 million metric tons in 1978 to 407 million metric tons in 1984. In addition to resolving a food crisis that had beset China for three decades, rural reform had a number of other effects that not only changed rural life but also the visage of China as a whole. First, the increased rural incomes that came from increased grain output as well as the cultivation of other crops and the restoration of sideline production permitted peasants to purchase more goods, thus stimulating the growth of industry (this was particularly true of building materials as peasants began to build new homes throughout the country). Second, agricultural efficiency increased greatly, thus freeing millions of people from agricultural labor and allowing them to enter the growing TVE sector (which further supported the growth of rural incomes).

Third, the breakdown of communes and the emancipation of rural labor quickly fed the growth of new circulation channels as peasants began traveling both locally and nationally to buy and sell goods. This activity brought new concepts of commerce even as it undermined the old, inefficient state channels of commerce. Finally, the success of the early rural reforms and the breakup of the communes changed the way state related to society in the countryside and provided an important success for reform, thus fueling the demand for reform in other parts of the economy.

Industrial Reform

Industrial reform began almost as early as rural reform, but it progressed more slowly. It developed slowly for a number of reasons. First, given the decentralization policies followed during the Cultural Revolution, there was at least as much of an impulse to recentralize and strengthen the State Planning Commission's control over the economy as there was to reform. Second, industrial reform is intrinsically more difficult because of the interrelatedness of the urban economy. Unlike the rural reforms in which different areas could undertake reforms without adversely affecting other areas, a reform in one industry could have an effect on the supply of materials or the purchasing of products from another industry as well as on revenues delivered to the state.

Thus, there was a tendency to retreat from any reform that proved disrupting—and most did. Third, unlike the rural economy, the industrial economy was managed by a huge bureaucratic apparatus composed of the ministries and commissions outlined previously. This meant that a great deal of bureaucratic coordination, and bureaucratic obstruction, was involved in any effort to reform.

However, there were also great incentives to reform industry. There was widespread recognition among economists, who were then being restored to positions of influence, that China's industries were highly inefficient and in need of reform. In particular, most economists accepted the notion (which had been sharply criticized during the Cultural Revolution) that enterprises needed to have incentives in order to increase efficiency. Apart from pressures from economists and policy makers to reform industry, there were also pressures from enterprises themselves, as well as from some of the bureaucracies in charge of industries. Such bureaucracies recognized the difficulties the enterprises under their control were facing and hoped to alleviate some of their problems so that production would increase.

Thus, at the beginning of the reform period, there were pressures both in favor of reform and against reform, and these pressures led industrial reform to progress in fits and starts. In general, the period from 1979, when industrial reform got under way, to 1984 was a period in which initial reform efforts were followed by retreat. There were, however, two features of this period that merit particular attention. The first was that initial reform efforts created a foundation for reform on which later efforts could be based. Second, ironically, during the retreat from reform (1980–1982), cutbacks in government expenditures forced many industries to try to stimulate demand for their products by developing and marketing new products. Thus, marketization advanced precisely in a period when central planners were trying to tighten control over the economic system.

In 1984, spurred on by the success of the rural reform and better than expected conditions in industry, the CCP adopted a major reform document entitled, "Decision on the Reform of the

Economic Structure." This document, along with efforts to create new institutions to support reform, inaugurated a new era of reform in which market forces advanced significantly.

The key reform, though few thought of it as such at the time, was the adoption of a dual-track price system. Everyone realized that price reform was essential to the whole reform effort, but policy makers could not agree on how to go about it. The compromise was to allow above-quota production to be marketed by enterprises at prices higher than the state-set price. This immediately created an incentive to increase production so that a greater percentage of output could be marketed at the higher price. Economists have argued that this arrangement provided an incentive for enterprises to orient their behavior increasingly toward the market because their marginal increase in revenues would be derived from the market. In other words, products produced under the plan acted as a large tax, while enterprises were able to earn increasing amounts of income from sales on the market.

The other factor that came into play at this time was the TVE sector discussed previously. It was precisely at the time of the "Decision on Economic Structural Reform," 1984, that township and village enterprises really took off. Since TVEs had never been included in the plan in the first place, their behavior from the beginning was determined by the market. They purchased their raw materials on the market and sold their produce on the market. When market demand changed, their product mix changed.

Moreover, by the mid- and late 1980s, the rise of the TVE sector was great enough to erode the profits of large state-owned enterprises. Under the planned economy, large state-owned enterprises had enjoyed monopoly profits. As new enterprises entered the market and as other enterprises reformed and began to compete with state-owned enterprises, the profit margins of the latter began to decline. This decline then put fiscal pressure on the state, which derived most of its revenues from large state-owned enterprises. One result of such pressures was that state-owned enterprises began to undertake reforms and become more efficient and market-oriented—though not

enough to stave off deficits and the need for drastic restructuring in the 1990s.

The result of the rise of the TVE sector and the relative decline of the state-owned sector has meant that the plan has become much less important in China. By the mid-1990s, the market determined the prices of almost all consumer goods and most industrial goods. In short, China's economy "grew out of the plan."[16]

The Politics of Economic Reform

The process of economic reform in a socialist state is intrinsically difficult. This difficulty is in part because of the economic changes required. Prices must be reformed, markets must develop, ownership relations must be changed, and macroeconomic structures must be reformed. Even under the best of circumstances, this is a daunting list of changes. Frequently a change in one area causes difficulty in another area. Smooth reform of the economic system is probably impossible; the best one can hope for is to contain difficulties within certain parameters.

In addition to the intrinsic economic problems involved in reform, there are inevitable political difficulties. In part, these difficulties derive from different visions of the goal of reform. In the case of China, there were sharp disagreements about whether the goal of reform was to restore, with appropriate improvements, the old planned economy that had prevailed in the 1950s and 1960s or whether that model of the economy was inherently flawed and should be fundamentally changed. Some thought that the basic problem in the Chinese system was the radicalism associated with Mao, particularly the Great Leap Forward and Cultural Revolution. If such radicalism was abolished, these people argued, the old system could be made to function. Others saw the problem as far deeper, believing that the basic patterns of a socialist economy had to be changed. Accordingly, they were willing to countenance far-reaching changes.

---

[16]Barry Naughton, *Growing Out of the Plan: Chinese Economic Reform, 1978–1993* (Cambridge: Cambridge University Press, 1995).

TABLE 8.2

THE CHANGING COMPOSITION OF THE CHINESE WORKFORCE (IN MILLIONS)

	Total Employed	Sub-total	TVE	Rural Private	Individual	Sub-total	SOE	Urban Collective	Joint-stock*	Private	Foreign-invested	Individual
1978	401	306	28			95	74	20				0.15
1980	424	318	30			105	80	24				0.81
1985	498	370	70			128	90	33	0.38		0.06	4.50
1990	639	473	93	1.13	15.0	166	103	35	0.96	0.57	0.31	6.60
1995	678	488	129	4.71	30.5	190	113	31	3.70	4.85	5.13	15.60
2000	711	499	128	11.40	29.0	213	81	15	13.40	12.70	6.42	21.40

Source: Zhongguo tongji nianjian (China Statistical Yearbook), 2001 (Beijing: China Statistical Publishing House, 2001).
*Note: "Joint Stock" combines cooperatives, Joint Ownership, Limited Liability Companies, and Share-Holding Corporations, each of which has different ownership characteristics but all of which divide profits on the basis of shares owned.

Disagreements about how much reform was appropriate were not limited to the economic realm but had implications for party organization, propaganda, ideology, and even political structures. In short, reform was not just about changing economic arrangements but about changing the whole range of state-society relations. Such changes went to the core of what Marxism-Leninism was about and thus raised highly emotional questions about the type of society that should be created. Such questions are highly political.

In general, "conservatives" wanted to restore and preserve the basic parameters of the socialist system as they understood it. Led by economic policy specialist and party elder Chen Yun, these conservatives were indeed part of the reform coalition that came to power in 1978, but they had a much more limited notion of reform than their more radical counterparts. Chen Yun's slogan was "planned economy as primary, market economy as supplementary." He had believed this in 1956 when he had first raised the issue of expanding the role of markets, and he believed it in 1980 when he sought to limit the role of markets. But while Chen Yun had remained constant, the center of gravity of the political spectrum had shifted greatly. In the 1950s and 1960s, he was considered a "rightist" for his willingness to countenance market measures; by the 1980s he was considered a conservative or a

"leftist" for his unwillingness to countenance a greater role for markets.

Deng Xiaoping, the paramount leader from 1978 until his physical decline in the mid-1990s (he died in 1997), was willing to contemplate much more far-reaching measures to reform the economy and even the political system than was Chen. Although there is evidence to suggest that Chen Yun as well as Deng Xiaoping supported the early rural reforms, Deng was far more willing than Chen to countenance far-reaching change in the countryside. For instance, in late 1981, Chen expressed concern that the rural reforms were undermining state planning, but Deng continued to support the deepening of rural reforms. This support included such things as the hiring of labor by private and quasi-private enterprises that grew up in the countryside, permitting peasants to engage in long-distance transport (which challenged the state monopoly over circulation), and in 1983 the dissolution of communes. Deng was also far more supportive of the emerging TVE sector than was Chen, who feared that it would erode the position of state-owned enterprises.

Opening to the Outside World

Perhaps the most important area of disagreement between Chen Yun and Deng Xiaoping revolved around the issue of opening China to the outside world, both politically and diplomatically. On the political level, it was Deng who saw ties with the United States as an essential support for China's reforms. Chen, on the other hand, never met with Western leaders throughout the reform period, though he did meet with the Russian economic planner Ivan Arkipov in late 1984, thereby expressing indirect criticism of Deng's close ties with the West. Similarly, it was Deng who insisted on opening the Special Economic Zones (SEZ) that were created in Shenzhen (opposite Hong Kong) and three other locations. Deng also wanted to open an SEZ in Shanghai but yielded to Chen's objections to doing so. Years later, Deng expressed regret, calling the failure to open an SEZ in Shanghai one of his greatest mistakes.

The decision to open up China and forge economic and political links with the outside world was perhaps the single most important element of Deng's reforms. As important as the other reforms were, they could not have spurred either the degree of marketization or the rapid rate of economic growth in the absence of the international market and the access to technology, capital, and managerial know-how of foreign areas. In 1978, China's foreign trade amounted to only $20.6 billion; a decade later it had reached $80.5 billion, and in 2004 it totaled $833 billion (see Table 8.3). China had become a major trader in the world economy, one of the top ten trading nations in the world.

Much of China's success in opening up to the outside was due to Hong Kong and Taiwan. By the time China was ready to open up, Hong Kong had developed to the point where its labor costs were rising and it had to find new paths to continue its economic growth. The opening of China provided the perfect complement to Hong Kong's managerial talent, financial resources, and marketing expertise. Before long, Hong Kong manufacturers began setting up joint ventures in neighboring Guangdong province and in the Shenzhen SEZ to tap the rich labor resources of the mainland. The products could then be sold on the international market, frequently in the United States. Already by the late 1980s, Hong Kong enterprises employed more workers in manufacturing jobs in Guangdong than in Hong Kong.[17]

As tensions began to ease across the Taiwan Straits during the 1980s and as labor costs in Taiwan began to increase, Taiwanese entrepreneurs began to emulate their Hong Kong counterparts. Just as Hong Kong entrepreneurs relied on their knowledge of the Cantonese dialect to develop business ties in Guangdong, so Taiwan merchants gravitated toward Fujian province, the province from which many Taiwanese migrated to Taiwan and where the dialect spoken

[17]Ezra Vogel, *One Step Ahead in China: Guangdong under Reform* (Cambridge, MA: Harvard University Press, 1991).

TABLE 8.3

CHINA'S ECONOMIC DEVELOPMENT UNDER REFORM

	GNP (in billion yuan)	Per Capita Income (in yuan)		Foreign Trade (in billion U.S. dollars)
		Rural	Urban	
1978	362.4	138	615	20.6
1980	451.8	178	762	38.1
1985	899.5	347	1148	69.6
1990	1859.8	571	2140	115.4
1995	5749.5	1578	4283	280.9
2000	8818.9	2253	6280	475.0

Source: Zhongguo tongji nianjian (China statistical yearbook), 2001 (Beijing: China Statistical Publishing House, 2001).

A CLOSER LOOK

8.1

HOW WEALTHY IS CHINA IN 2004?

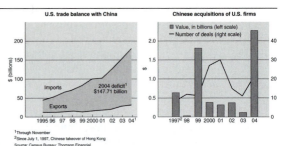

U.S. trade balance with China

Chinese acquisitions of U.S. firms

□ Value, in billions (left scale)
— Number of deals (right scale)

[1]Through November
[2]Since July 1, 1997, Chinese takeover of Hong Kong
Source: Census Bureau; Thomson Financial

In 1993 the International Monetary Fund (IMF) issued a report that substantially increased the estimated size of China's economy, setting off both increased business interest in this new economic giant and fears of the role an economically and perhaps militarily powerful China would play in Asia and the world. The IMF undertook to estimate the size of the Chinese economy on the basis of purchasing power parity (PPP), a way of trying to compare economies by calculating the cost of a comparable basket of goods. This method is used when distortions in the exchange rate make the usual method of comparing economies by simply converting their gross national product (GNP) into U.S. dollars ineffective. The conclusion of the IMF study was that China's economy was nearly four times larger than previously believed.

The IMF study has provoked other agencies and scholars to calibrate the size of China's economy. Nicholas Lardy, in *China in the World Economy,* calculates that China's per capita income in 1990 was probably around $1,000, almost three times the official figure of $370 (figured according to the exchange rate), but still more modest than the IMF figures. A per capita income of $1,000 would mean that China's GNP in 1990 was about $1.25 trillion. In 2004, GDP was assessed at $6.4 trillion.

Purchasing price parity is a useful methodology for comparing living standards in very different economies and for controlling for the effect of fluctuations in exchange rates. However, only currency that can be exchanged can be used to purchase goods abroad, so for measuring China's economic size one also needs to calculate the GNP in terms of the exchange rate. By this measure, China's GNP of 8,818 billion yuan in 2000 has only just crossed the $1 billion threshold—about the size of Italy's economy. In 2004, it grew by over 9%.

When thinking about China's economic size, it is important to remember the vast differences in income between the relatively prosperous east coast and the poor areas in the interior. There are an estimated 80 million people still living in dire poverty in China.

---

is the same as that of the majority of Taiwanese. Over the years, investment in China from Hong Kong and Taiwan has developed steadily, now totaling over $40 billion from the former and another $70 billion or more from the latter.

POLITICAL AND SOCIAL TENSIONS

Despite several oscillations between high growth and retrenchment and several periods of relatively high inflation (reaching 30 percent in 1988), China's transition from a planned economy to a market-oriented economy has been smoother and more successful than that of most rapidly modernizing nations. Nevertheless, such rapid

changes have generated considerable economic, social, and political tensions in China. These tensions have derived from the very different expectations of reform held by different leaders within the party, from conflicts of interests as reform produced economic "winners" and "losers," and from the rapid change in state-society relations and from the maturation of a new generation of youth who had little memory of the Maoist period.

One way to understand why the reform process has generated such tension within Chinese society is to look at the impact of the rapid growth of the TVE sector. As noted before, the growth of TVEs is one of the great success stories of Chinese economic reform, contributing both to China's economic development and to the marketization of the economy. Their growth nevertheless proved controversial. The growth of the TVE sector reduced the profitability of state-owned enterprises, which in turn created fiscal difficulties for the central government. Central revenues as a percentage of GNP fell from 31.2 percent in 1978 to 22 percent in 1987 to only 14.7 percent in 1992. At the same time, central government revenues as a percentage of all government revenues fell from about 60 percent at the beginning of the reform era to 33 percent in 1993. These figures reflect both the diminished role of the central government in the overall economy and the gradual shift of economic power from the capital to the provinces. The relative decline in central government revenues was reflected in continuous deficits (which in turn contributed to inflation) as well as in the declining ability of the central government to exercise macroeconomic control.

In the minds of conservatives, these trends were ominous and directly attributable to reform. Reform in their minds was undermining the role of state-owned enterprises in the economy and thus eroding the ability of the government to exercise both economic and political control. The increasing financial strength of the localities, and their increasing willingness to evade or reject controls on their behavior, led many to believe that it was necessary to recentralize authority in Beijing.

At the core of these concerns was not simply the technical matter of revenue and macroeconomic control but the political and ideological question of what type of system was being built. As noted above, the gulf between conservatives and reformers widened after 1984. Reformers tried to solve one problem after another by continuing to deepen reform, while conservatives believed that each such effort led the country further away from socialism.

This dispute over economic matters was exacerbated by ideological conflict. From the beginning of the Dengist period, conservatives tried to maintain a rein on the reform process by stressing orthodox socialist values. Reformers, intent on creating a political and social atmosphere that would allow ever greater experimentation, were just as intent on breaking through one ideological barrier after another. As noted in Section A, the reform era was launched with a major effort to open up the ideological atmosphere and thus break free of the ideological shackles of the Maoist era. The discussion on "practice is the sole criterion of truth" broke through Maoist dogma by subjecting every program to the fundamental question: Does it work? This was a major break with the Maoist practice of asking: Is it socialist? It thus provided intellectuals with a much broader area of inquiry and protected reforms such as those in agriculture from ideological counterattack.

Such divisions within the party were greatly exacerbated by the changing relationship between state and society and by the emergence of a generation that had little memory of the Maoist period and great hopes for more personal freedom. Despite periodic efforts to clamp down on the expression of opinion, the dominant trend in the 1980s was toward an ever expanding expression of ideas. As the state became less involved in people's day-to-day lives and as economic reform took hold, the relevance of the old ideas of Marxism-Leninism faded rapidly and were soon in disrepute in many sectors of society. Efforts to reimpose more orthodox patterns of thought, such as during the campaign against spiritual pollution, evoked an ever greater sense of repulsion among the people, particularly intellectuals and college students.

At the same time that official ideology became less relevant to the lives of most people, many of the bureaucratic rigidities of the old system remained. Bureaucrats came to be resented for their constant but largely inefficient and ineffective interference in people's lives. They were also increasingly resented for their corruption. Economic reform, particularly the dual-track price system, had opened up enormous opportunities for corruption, and many state bureaucrats could not resist the opportunity of using their power to line their own pockets.

Popular resentments became visible in China's public life in the fall of 1985 when many students took to the streets to protest Japan's supposed "economic invasion" of China in the 1980s. Triggered by official commemorations of nationalistic demonstrations half a century earlier, such student activism suggested a newfound willingness to take to the streets in protest.

The following year, beginning in December 1986, students in Hefei, Anhui, took to the streets to protest the disqualification of candidates who had been nominated for the local people's congress by the students. The demonstrations soon spread to Shanghai, where over 50,000 students protested the heavy hand of government.

These demonstrations had major repercussions within the party. On January 13, 1987, Hu Yaobang was officially removed as general secretary, and a far-reaching campaign against bourgeois liberalization made an example of three intellectuals who were purged from the party and criticized repeatedly in the press. The virulence of the 1987 campaign against bourgeois liberalization reflected deepening divisions within the party, suggesting that Deng's long-standing efforts to hold conservatives and reformers together in an uneasy coalition were coming undone.

As soon as Hu Yaobang was ousted, Deng named Zhao Ziyang, who had served as premier since 1980 and had been largely responsible for the implementation of economic reform, to replace Hu as general secretary. Zhao had developed a reputation as a reformer who, like Deng, preferred to concentrate on economic reform rather than ideological liberalization. With the support of Deng, Zhao moved rapidly to bring the campaign against bourgeois liberalization under control and thereby create an atmosphere for further economic reform. However, Zhao also believed that economic reform could only proceed with a certain degree of political reform, and his reform program angered conservatives.

Tiananmen

The tensions and political conflict evident in 1986–1987 soon reprised themselves in a far more dramatic and serious fashion in 1988–1989. Zhao Ziyang seems to have underestimated the seriousness of the political crisis of 1987 and overestimated his ability to control events. With Hu gone, Zhao inevitably became the sole target of conservatives' criticism. As conservatives would soon demonstrate, they were not opposed to bourgeois liberalization alone but

to economic reform itself. As they sometimes stated openly, they believed that economic reform bred bourgeois liberalization. What they wanted was a major effort to recentralize the economy and strengthen planning. Now only Zhao (and his patron Deng) stood in their way.

Conservatives did not have to wait long to strike. In the spring of 1988, with inflationary pressures heating up, Deng Xiaoping made an enormous error. Apparently frustrated with the slow pace of reform and the criticism of conservatives, Deng called for an effort to carry out comprehensive price reform. This was interpreted by many people as a signal that prices would soon be going up, so they immediately set out to protect the value of their money by purchasing consumer durables (such as washing machines and television sets). This spending spree added enormously to inflationary pres-

Protest demonstration in Beijing in spring 1989.

sures, and the rate of inflation shot up to around 50 percent in August 1988. With the economy spiraling out of control, conservatives were able to scapegoat Zhao. A variety of administrative measures were put into place to control inflation, and Zhao's authority over economic affairs was ended. Conservatives called for Zhao's ouster, and Zhao clung to power only by the good graces of Deng Xiaoping. The party was thus deeply divided and the distribution of power among top leaders highly uncertain as China entered 1989.

The decade of reform had also brought about major tensions between state and society, which soon became visible to the whole world. Many intellectuals worried that the pace of reform was slowing; they contrasted the relative failure of China to bring about political reform with the policy of *glasnost* (opening) being pursued by Gorbachev in the Soviet Union. Students reflected a similar frustration with the pace of reform and had little appreciation of how far and how fast China had gone. Memories of the Cultural Revolution were dim for people who had been perhaps seven or eight years old when the reforms got underway; what they saw was not the progress but the obstacles in the way of faster reform. Students, influenced by the pop culture of Taiwan, Hong Kong, and the West, yearned for more freedom and self-expression. They resented the dull commentaries that appeared in the official press and the petty interference in their lives by low-level bureaucrats. Perhaps most of all, they resented the corruption that they saw around them. Finally, workers and those on fixed incomes had seen their standards of living eroded by the rate of inflation. Everywhere citizens had complaints about corruption. The atmosphere was highly combustible.

The match that set off the firestorm was the death of Hu Yaobang. Hu, who had been permitted to stay on the Politburo in an inactive role following his dismissal as general secretary, was apparently attempting to make a political comeback. In the midst of a heated argument during a Politburo meeting, Hu was struck by a heart attack. Efforts to save him failed and he died on April 15, 1989.

The timing could not have been worse. Students had already been organizing for a commemoration of the seventieth anniversary of the May Fourth Movement, so they had the rudiments of an organization already set up. On the morning of April 16, students headed to Tiananmen Square in the center of Beijing to pay tribute to the fallen reformer. Much as people had headed to Tiananmen Square 13 years previously to pay their respects to Zhou Enlai, so students began to leave wreaths and poems in honor of Hu Yaobang.

The situation took a turn for the worse when on April 26 the party's newspaper, the *People's Daily,* ran an editorial that labeled the student movement as causing "turmoil" and as "antisocialist." A major crackdown appeared to be in the offing. The following day, however, large numbers of students marched toward police and finally broke through police lines. Moderates within the party had prevailed in heated internal debates the night before over the use of violence. As students proceeded toward Tiananmen Square, they were joined by thousands of Beijing residents. Students decided to occupy the square and continue their protest.

General Secretary Zhao Ziyang made a major effort to diffuse the situation on May 4. In a speech delivered to the Asian Development Bank, which was meeting in Beijing that day, Zhao described the motives of the students as patriotic. That was as far as Zhao could go, and he had bent party rules to go that far. Students, however, wanted an explicit retraction of the April 26 editorial. Their desire was perhaps natural. If they left the square without an explicit change in party policy, then they would have been highly vulnerable to arrest after public order was restored. More serious was that the student movement had developed a logic of its own in which more moderate leaders were denounced and ousted by more radical leaders.

The situation deteriorated further on May 13 when student leaders, fearing that the movement was losing momentum, started a hunger strike. The strike evoked sympathy from all over Beijing. Workers began to show up on the square in ever greater numbers, and small vendors and others began contributing sums of money to the students. The sounds of ambulance sirens were heard throughout the city as students collapsed from hunger.

Soviet leader Gorbachev arrived in Beijing on May 15 to signify the normalization of Sino-Soviet relations after nearly three decades of hostility. China's leadership was deeply embarrassed and angered that they could not hold as planned a welcoming ceremony for Gorbachev in Tiananmen Square. The day after Gorbachev left China, the State Council declared martial law. Zhao Ziyang, unwilling to go along with the decision, was removed from power. He died in 2005.

As the situation headed toward a violent resolution, moderates tried desperately to mediate. The situation, however, had gone on too long with both sides too deeply entrenched to permit compromise. The outspoken journalist Dai Qing tried to persuade student leaders to leave the square, but she was contemptuously dismissed. Her efforts were not appreciated by hardliners within the party either. After the Tiananmen crackdown, Dai was sentenced to a year in jail for trying to prevent a tragedy. It was symbolic of how the middle had dropped out of Chinese polities.

The crackdown finally came on the night of June 3–4. Under orders to take and clear the square by dawn, the PLA shot its way into the center of Beijing. Most of the violence was not in the square itself—students there were allowed to leave peacefully after prolonged negotiations—but in the approaches to the square. The toll may never be known, but it was clearly heavy. Perhaps 700 people died that night.

THE POST-TIANANMEN ERA

It was frequently assumed that Tiananmen would bring about either the downfall of the CCP or the end of reform. In fact, neither happened, although Tiananmen touched off one of the deepest crises in the party's history. The continued presence of the aging patriarch, however, eventually ameliorated the crisis and set off a new round of even more far-reaching reform.

Deng's presence was critical to the post-Tiananmen political situation because even though his prestige within the party declined sig-

nificantly following Tiananmen, no one else was able to challenge his position as the core of the party, and thus he was eventually able to dominate the political agenda once again. Even at his weakest, in the weeks and months following Tiananmen, Deng's views were decisive on critical issues. In particular, Deng was able to deny the fruits of victory to the conservatives who had led such a determined campaign to oust Zhao Ziyang. Indeed, four days before the crackdown, Deng called in Premier Li Peng and Politburo Standing Committee member Yao Yilin, both conservative leaders who might reasonably expect to succeed Zhao as general secretary of the party, and told them almost contemptuously, "The people see reality. If we put up a front so that people feel that it is an ossified leadership, a conservative leadership, or if the people believe that it is a mediocre leadership that cannot reflect the future of China, then there will be constant trouble and there will never be a peaceful day."[18] Accordingly, Deng informed them that Jiang Zemin, then the party secretary of Shanghai, would be named general secretary. Thus, even as his long-standing efforts to carry out reform seemed to be destroyed by Tiananmen and the purge of Zhao, Deng set about building a new coalition, carefully balancing divergent forces within the party.

It would take Deng a full three years to restore reform to its former prominence. In January 1992, Deng went on a well-publicized tour of the Shenzhen SEZ, where he harshly criticized conservatives within the party, called for deepening reform, and urged Guangdong province to catch up with the "four small dragons" within 20 years. The following fall, the Fourteenth Party Congress ratified a document that called for the creation of a "socialist market economy," thus firmly identifying the party with a market economy.

Deng's trip to the south and the subsequent decision of the Fourteenth Party Congress inaugurated another period of high-speed growth in

---

[18]Deng Xiaoping, "Zucheng yige shixing gaige de you xiwang de lingdao jiti" (Organize a reformist, hopeful leadership collective), in *Deng Xiaoping wenxuan, disanjuan* (Selected works of Deng Xiaoping, vol. 3) (Beijing: Renmin chubanshe, 1993), p. 296.

China, one that caught the attention of economists and businesspeople the world over. In 1992 China's economy grew by 11 percent, and then grew 12.9 percent in 1993, 12 percent in 1994, and 10.2 percent in 1995. For a large economy the size of China's to sustain such growth rates was unprecedented. At the same time, China was drawing in vast sums of foreign capital—$30–40 billion dollars a year, more than any other country in the world except the United States.

The resumption of reform in the wake of Deng's trip to the south did not mean a simple replication of trends of the 1980s. On the contrary, the 1990s took on a very different look than the preceding decade. This was in part because economic growth and the continued difficulties of state-owned enterprises (SOEs) basically ended the debate between planners and reformers—there was no way to restore the old planned economy. But building a new market-oriented economy was no easy task. Restructuring SOEs, either by laying off workers, selling shares, or privatizing them, inevitably would demand government funds to create a social security system. But central government coffers were largely drained by the decentralization of the 1980s. In 1994, the government finally carried out a major tax reform that began increasing Beijing's tax revenues. This was not simply recentralization, as conservatives had called for in the 1980s, but a combination of strengthening the central state in certain respects and an increased reliance on the market in others.

Moreover, the government went about reestablishing legitimacy by emphasizing nationalism—or, as the government would say, patriotism. A new emphasis was placed on cultivating pride in the nation. This new emphasis was not limited to the "heroic" deeds of the CCP, as past propaganda had often had it, but was extended to the glories of China's past. This marked a genuine departure in cultural politics. It will be recalled that the May Fourth Movement, which gave rise to the CCP, was an iconoclastic movement that called for "striking down Confucius' shop." By the 1990s, however, Confucius and much else about China's cultural tradition was revived and lauded; indeed, people talked about a "national studies fever" (*guoxuere*), which focused attention on China's tradition. Sometimes there was cultural chauvinism present in these discussions, as Chinese lauded their own culture and denigrated that of the West.

Full-scale commercialism also emerged in the 1990s. As citizens became wealthy, at least in the cities, they turned their attention to consumer goods and away from politics. Upscale shopping malls proliferated in cities like Beijing, Shanghai, and Guangzhou, and people became far more interested in the latest music trends than in the CCP's latest ideological pronouncement. Consumerism is a complex phenomenon. In some ways it deflected citizens' attention away from the tragedy of Tiananmen, while in other ways it was seen as leading to a decay of public morality. Not only had the idealism of the Maoist era disappeared, but it seemed that all ideals had—and that was troubling to many people.

At the same time, there was a rapid increase in income inequality between regions and between different population groups within the same region. Income inequalities had started to emerge in the latter part in the 1980s, but they accelerated and became more politically salient in the 1990s. The east coast has moved rapidly ahead of the interior regions, especially after China joined the World Trade Organization in 2001. Meanwhile, the *nouveau riche* who have emerged in the cities co-exist with workers who have lost their jobs. These inequalities are frequently blamed on government officials who are too intent on feathering their own nests to pay attention to those left behind.

Moreover, corruption has become a major public issue in the 1990s. Corruption grew in the 1980s—indeed, that was one of the issues that drew students and citizens out onto the streets of Beijing in spring 1989—but it became much more pervasive and the amounts involved much greater in the 1990s. There are few issues that outrage hard-working citizens (and especially those who are laid off) more than corruption. Public opinion surveys rate corruption as the number one concern of the populace, and it is frequently the cause of riots and other disturbances.

These and other issues have contributed to the rise of nationalism in contemporary China. To some extent, as suggested above, nationalism is promoted by the government to enhance its legitimacy, but there is a populist, antigovernment edge to much nationalism. Nationalists see the government as too corrupt, too incompetent, too undemocratic—and too yielding to the demands of the West, particularly the United States. As we will see in the next section, resentment of corruption, growing income inequalities, and China's place in the world economic system have fed into a critique of globalization and China's participation in the World Trade Organization.

These and other problems continue to press the government to undertake more and farther reaching reforms, including in the political area. In 2000, Jiang Zemin began to campaign for a new ideological vision, the "Three Representatives" (the idea that the CCP represents the fundamental interests of the vast majority of the people, the advanced productive forces, and advanced culture). The Three Representatives play down traditional Marxist notions such as class struggle in favor of co-opting emerging social forces—as was made evident by the party's call in summer 2001 to admit capitalists into the party. Under the rubric of the Three Representatives, the CCP discussed a wide range of possible political reforms, and many small-scale experiments have taken place. Before his resignation in 2002, Jiang stated that the protection of private property and wealth generated by private entrepreneurs was important for Chinese economic policy.

Thinking Critically

1. What is meant by the term "democratic centralism"? Why does the CCP not operate democratically?
2. What are the *danwei* (work unit) and *hukou* (household registration system) and how have these systems come under challenge in recent years?

3. What is a planned economy, and how has economic reform reduced the importance of planning in the Chinese economy?
4. What is the National People's Congress (NPC), and why has it become more important in recent years?
5. What was the impact of the Tiananmen crackdown on economic and political reform in China?

KEY TERMS

bourgeois liberalization *(477)*
Chinese People's Political Consultative Conference (CPPCC) *(470)*
Central Advisory Commission (CAC) *(470)*
Central Discipline Inspection Commission (CDIC) *(470)*
Central Military Commission (CMC) *(469, 471)*
Chen Yun *(478)*
consumerism *(485)*
danwei (units) *(466–467)*
dangzu (party groups) *(473)*
democratic centralism *(470)*
dual-track price system *(477)*
hukou (household registration) *(466)*
Hu Yaobang *(470)*
Jiang Zemin *(471)*
Li Peng *(468)*
National People's Congress (NPC) *(473)*
nationalism *(485–486)*
People's Liberation Army (PLA) *(470–471)*
Politburo *(469)*
Politburo Standing Committee (PSC) *(467–469)*
Secretariat *(468–470)*
state-owned enterprises (SOEs) *(472, 485)*
State Planning Commission *(472, 476)*
Tiananmen *(483–484)*
township and village enterprises (TVEs) *(475–477)*
Three Representatives *(486)*
xitong (systems) *(468)*
Zhao Ziyang *(482)*
Zhou Enlai *(471)*
Zhu Rongji *(471)*

FURTHER READINGS

Bachman, David M. *Chen Yun and the Chinese Political System* (Berkeley: University of California Press, 1985).

Baum, Richard. *Burying Mao: Chinese Politics in the Age of Deng Xiaoping* (Princeton, NJ: Princeton University Press, 1994).

Burns, John P. *The Chinese Communist Party Nomenklatura System: A Documentary Study of Party Control of Leadership Selection* (Armonk, NY: M. E. Sharpe, 1989).

Chan, Anita, Richard Madsen, and Jonathan Unger. *Chen Village: The Recent History of a Peasant Community in Mao's China* (Berkeley: University of California Press, 1984).

Fewsmith, Joseph. *Dilemmas of Reform in China: Political Conflict and Economic Debate* (Armonk, NY: M. E. Sharpe, 1994).

Fewsmith, Joseph . *China since Tiananmen: The Politics of Transition* (Cambridge: Cambridge University Press, 2001).

Friedman, Edward, Paul G. Pickowicz, and Mark Selden. *Chinese Village, Socialist State* (New Haven, CT: Yale University Press, 1991).

Goldman, Merle. *China's Intellectuals: Advise and Dissent* (Cambridge, MA: Harvard University Press, 1981).

Goldman, Merle . *Sowing the Seeds of Democracy in China* (Cambridge, MA: Harvard University Press, 1994).

Goldman, Merle, and Roderick MacFarquhar, eds. *The Paradox of China's Post-Mao Reforms* (Cambridge, MA: Harvard University Press, 1999).

Hamrin, Carol Lee. *China and the Challenge of the Future* (Boulder, CO: Westview Press 1990).

Harding, Harry. *Organizing China: The Problem of Bureaucracy, 1949–1976* (Stanford, CA: Stanford University Press, 1981).

Harding, Harry. *China's Second Revolution: Reform after Mao* (Washington, DC: Brookings Institution, 1987).

Lardy, Nicholas. *China in the World Economy* (Washington, DC: Institute for International Development, 1994).

Lee, Hong Yung. *From Revolutionary Cadres to Technocrats in Socialist China* (Berkeley: University of California Press, 1991).

Lieberthal, Kenneth, and Michel Oksenberg. *Policy Making in China: Leaders, Structures, and Process* (Princeton, NJ: Princeton University Press, 1988).

Link, Perry. *Evening Chats in Beijing: Probing China's Predicament* (New York: Norton, 1992).

Manion, Melanie. *Retirement of Revolutionaries in China: Public Policies. Social Norms, Private Interests* (Princeton, NJ: Princeton University Press, 1993).

Nathan, Andrew J. *Chinese Democracy* (New York: Knopf, 1985).

Naughton, Barry. *Growing Out of the Plan: Chinese Economic Reform, 1978–1993* (Cambridge: Cambridge University Press, 1995).

Oi, Jean. *Rural China Takes Off: Institutional Foundations of Economic Growth* (Berkely: University of California Press, 1999).

Preston, P. W., and Jurgen Hancke, eds., *Contemporary China: The Dynamics of Change at the Start of the New Millennium* (London: Routledge Curzon, 2003).

Rosenbaum, Arthur Lewis, ed. *State and Society in China* (Boulder, CO: Westview Press, 1992).

Smith, Tony. *Governance and Politics of China* (Houndmills: Palgrave Macmillan, 2004).

Thurston, Anne F. *Enemies of the People* (Cambridge, MA: Harvard University Press, 1988).

Tsou, Tang. *The Cultural Revolution and Post-Mao Reforms: A Historical Perspective* (Chicago: University of Chicago Press, 1988).

Unger, Jonathan, ed. *The Nature of Chinese Politics: From Mao to Jiang* (Armonk: Sharpe, 2002).

Vogel, Ezra. *One Step Ahead in China: Guangdong under Reform* (Cambridge, MA: Harvard University Press, 1989).

Wassertrom, Jeffrey, and Elizabeth Perry, eds. *Popular Protest and Political Culture in Modern China* (Boulder, CO: Westview Press, 1992).

Womack, Brantly, ed. *Contemporary Chinese Politics in Historical Perspective* (Cambridge: Cambridge University Press, 1990).

C. PUBLIC POLICY

The Chinese government faces a long list of public policy issues. Economic inequalities need to be addressed and an adequate social security system constructed even while the economy continues to undergo readjustment. The financial system remains shaky (the banks carry a high percentage of nonperforming loans), which makes economic readjustment more difficult. Corruption fuels public discontent even as it makes addressing the bureaucratic and legal inadequacies that give rise to corruption more difficult. State capacity—including the state's fiscal resources, its bureaucratic efficiency, its level of expertise, its decision-making process, and its legitimacy—needs to be enhanced, but issues of political participation, especially as new social groups come into being and as new sources of discontent build up, need to be addressed. These and other issues, including human rights, the environment, ethnic tensions, and gender equality, all need to be faced at a time when globalization is increasing pressures from the outside world. Thus, the political system and its adaptability lie at the center of China's public policy difficulties. Some argue that the Chinese political system has not changed at all, while others maintain that China is likely to democratize within the foreseeable future. We start our discussion with the pressures on the political system to change—some stemming from generational change and others from the evolving political economy—and then move on to consider China's response to globalization. Finally, we look at human rights conditions and ethnic conflicts, which are both major public policy issues and important aspects of the evolving political situation.

A CLOSER LOOK

8.2

TENSION IN THE TAIWAN STRAITS

In the summer and fall of 1995 and the spring of 1996, the PRC mounted a series of military exercises in the Taiwan Straits that were designed to convince the people and authorities of Taiwan (as well as those of other nations) that efforts to secure international recognition for Taiwan would bring full-scale military assault. These tensions have resulted from several factors. When the United States decided to extend diplomatic recognition to the PRC in 1979, Taiwan began to exist as a largely unrecognized but nevertheless independent political unit. This anomalous status prevailed for many years, but as the government on Taiwan moved toward democratization in the late 1980s, cries for independence or some sort of international recognition as a "political entity" began to grow louder.

The then-president of Taiwan, Lee Teng-hui, launched a vigorous effort to secure greater status for Taiwan, including a return to the United Nations, though in what capacity was left unstated. In June 1995, the Clinton administration, in a change of long-standing policy, granted a visa to Lee Teng-hui for a "private" visit to the United States so that he could return to his alma mater, Cornell University. Because the United States is widely viewed by both the PRC and Taiwan as the key to any change in Taiwan's international status, this change in policy provoked an angry response from the PRC, which saw it as the latest and most significant in a series of moves that could lead to the permanent separation of Taiwan from the mainland.

The election of Chen Shui-bian in 2000 further raised tensions because his political party, the Democratic Progressive Party, has a plank in its charter calling for holding a referendum on Taiwan's independence. Although Chen in his inaugural remarks promised not to hold such a referendum, suspicions between Taiwan and the PRC remain high. In order to deter Taiwan from declaring independence, China has placed short-range ballistic missiles in Fujian province across the straits from Taiwan. In response, the United States, especially under the Bush Administration, has stepped up military cooperation with Taiwan.

PRESSURES FOR POLITICAL CHANGE

Generational Change

China's political process has been dominated by a small number of elite actors relatively unconstrained by formal institutions. This was particularly true in the Mao era, but Deng Xiaoping also stood above the rest of the political system even as he inaugurated economic and, to a lesser extent, political changes. Jiang Zemin was a less dominating political leader, often compromising with his PSC colleagues.

China appears to be evolving a more corporate style of management in which the general secretary acts more like a corporate head than a towering charismatic figure like Mao Zedong. The general secretary continues to hold the most important levers of power, including the ideology portfolio, but the trend toward greater equality and institutionalization in the decision-making process is noteworthy, given not only China's imperial history but also the domination by individual leaders throughout the twentieth century. How does one explain this apparent transformation?

At least two processes appear to be at work. When Deng came to power in the late 1970s, he inaugurated a process of bureaucratic rejuvenation. Born in 1904, Deng was 74 years of age when he took the helm of Chinese politics, and most of his senior colleagues were of the same generational cohort. Moreover, those who were younger in the political system had risen largely through their role in the Cultural Revolution—hardly the sort of people Deng wanted to promote. So Deng called for making the leadership younger and better educated. This changed the criteria for recruitment and promotion, and throughout the 1980s and 1990s China's political elite, both within the CCP and the state bureaucracy, became better trained and more professional. Regulations were established governing retirement, and gradually these became increasingly effective and moved up the hierarchy so that even the general secretary of the CCP does not have life-long tenure. Jiang Zemin remained as chair of the party and chair of the

central military commission after his retirement in 2002.

Second, at the same time that bureaucratic regulations were being institutionalized, generational succession was taking place. Generational succession inevitably creates problems of legitimacy even as it brings to the fore younger leaders with different experiences. Deng Xiaoping liked to call himself the core of the "second generation" of leaders, but in fact he was the second leader of the first generation. A mere decade younger than Mao, Deng had made the Long March and fought for victory in the war against Japan and the civil war. His legitimacy derived from his revolutionary accomplishments. Jiang Zemin was of a very different generation. His only revolutionary experience prior to the establishment of the PRC was as a student leader in Shanghai. After the establishment of the PRC, he furthered his education as an engineer by studying in Moscow and then rose through a series of bureaucratic posts. He had no military experience and had not engaged in such party activities as propaganda or personnel promotion. He, like other leaders of his generation, was a technocrat.

In 2003, Hu Jintao succeeded Jiang as general secretary and this transformation to a technocratic political elite was complete. Hu, born in 1942, graduated from China's top technological school, Qinghua University, just as the Cultural Revolution was breaking out. He rose to power by serving in a number of posts, including head of the Communist Youth League and party secretary of Tibet and Guizhou provinces. His education almost entirely postdates the founding of the PRC, and he has deep awareness of the consequences of the Cultural Revolution. Hopefully, these experiences, along with his technical training, will make him a very pragmatic leader. In any event, this brief sketch of his life illustrates the vast difference between his upbringing and those of the revolutionary generation of leaders.

Technocrats cannot derive legitimacy from their revolutionary accomplishments; they must emphasize their ability to solve problems. A problem-solving approach to administration changes the tenor of administration and politics.

Administration is more consultative—which does not obviate political conflict, particularly on major issues or in times of crisis. Politics is based more on "procedural rationality" (whether the correct procedures have been followed)—which does not mean that leaders never violate procedures to promote their own interests. This process can perhaps be seen in terms of Max Weber's famous notion of the "routinization of charisma." According to Weber, when a charismatic leader passes from the scene, the organization he or she leaves behind inevitably becomes bureaucratized and routinized, features alien to charismatic leadership. Thus, a charismatic leader like Mao gives way to a leader like Deng, who begins to rationalize the bureaucracy and then yields to a leader like Jiang, who is more of an administrator than an inspirational leader.

This process seems likely to continue, and it opens up interesting questions. Revolutionary leaders are relatively easy to compare (who led the revolution? who led the biggest military?), but technocratic leaders are not (the question of who led the biggest bureaucracy hardly seems relevant). The inability to judge who should succeed to power inevitably leads to demands for some sort of rule for selecting the leader. It is possible for a leader to choose his or her own successor, but this is not very Leninist (even if Kim Il Song was able to promote his son Kim Chong Il in North Korea) and has been widely criticized in China. Deng Xiaoping labeled the practice "feudal." The ruling party in Mexico, the PRI, adopted a form of this type of succession for 70 years (before it fell from power), but the trade-off was that each leader received a single, six-year term.

Another possibility is for the CCP to more openly recognize and legitimate factions within the party, rotating the leadership among factions as the strength of factions waxes and wanes. A third possibility is to open up a limited degree of "inner-party democracy," allowing a limited number of party leaders (for instance, the Central Committee) to vote on the party leadership (which is what the Central Committee should be doing according to party statutes). China may adopt some combination of these or other mech-

anisms. But it seems clear that generational succession creates pressures for institutionalization even as its creates difficulties for leadership legitimacy. This conundrum seems difficult to work out within an authoritarian context and is one of the pressures propelling political evolution.

State-Society Relations

A second force propelling continued evolution of the political system is state-society relations, including the rapid development of the private economy, tensions between local party cadres and citizens, and corruption. One of the great changes in recent years in China has been the growth of a private economy. The need to provide employment for China's large and growing population was one force that propelled the emergence of a private economy in the 1980s. People who could not find employment in the country's state or collectively owned economies were allowed to set up their own enterprises. Such people became known as "individual entrepreneurs" (*getihu*), and their enterprises initially were very simple trades: peddling, giving haircuts, opening family restaurants, and the like. A social stigma initially clung to such individual entrepreneurs because they often came from marginal elements in society who could not get more stable jobs, but that has dropped away as increasingly sophisticated people such as lawyers, computer specialists, and economic consultants have joined the ranks of individual entrepreneurs. In numerical terms, individual entrepreneurs (those whose enterprises consist of no more than eight people) make up the bulk of the private economy; there were over 60 million such people by the end of the twentieth century.

There has also been a very large upsurge in the number of "private enterprises" (*siying jingji*—consisting of more than eight people). At the beginning of the 1990s, there were only about 1.5 million people employed in such enterprises. By the beginning of the twenty-first century, that figure had grown to around 20 million. In addition, a growing number of people were employed in foreign-owned enterprises of one sort or another (either joint venture or wholly owned by overseas investors). Altogether, there were approximately 90 million people employed in private enterprises by the end of the twentieth century—and that figure does not include the millions who work in TVEs that have been privatized in recent years.

The political impact of these socioeconomic changes is likely to be far ranging, but still uncertain. Although some expect that such privatization will lead to democratization, there is no indication of such a trend at this time. The evidence available at this time suggests those involved in China's private economy would rather work with the state than against it. While this tendency may reflect the continued strength of China's political culture (which has never pitted private interests against the state), it also suggests both the strength and the arbitrariness of the political system vis-à-vis the economy as well as the weakness of the legal system. Thus, most entrepreneurs seem to try to secure a stable and predictable environment for their business operations by cultivating local officials, a process that involves wining and dining as well as outright bribery, instead of challenging the political system.

Nevertheless, most of China's private economy is outside the scope of the *danwei* (work unit) system, through which the CCP has traditionally controlled society. This has caused much concern in the CCP and led to Jiang Zemin's call, in the summer of 2001, to allow private entrepreneurs to join the CCP. In fact, many private entrepreneurs had already joined the party (and many CCP members had opened private businesses), but the policy reversal suggests that the party will try to maintain its political control by co-opting the leaders of China's most dynamic sector. This will no doubt have an effect on the CCP (making it more business friendly), but it will not necessarily lead to democratization, at least not in the short term.

Another force fostering political change has been the growth of tensions between peasants and cadres in the countryside. These tensions derive primarily from three factors: (1) the breakdown of the commune system, which has made peasants less dependent on local cadres,

(2) the unequal distribution of economic development, and (3) the political pressure on cadres to develop their localities. In the previous section we described the growth of the TVE sector and its importance to the Chinese economy but also noted that it was unequally distributed geographically. The TVE sector has flourished in those areas with long entrepreneurial histories, with good local infrastructure, and with access to international markets—and such areas lie disproportionately along the east coast of China. The middle section of China—ranging from Hebei in the north to Hunan and Jiangxi in the south—is predominantly agricultural. Although rural industries exist there, they tend to be smaller scale, less technologically advanced, and less well run.

Therefore, tax revenues for local government must be extracted from largely agricultural areas that do not have the thriving economies of the east coast. But local cadres are under pressures—both those from higher levels and those that are self-imposed by local cadres who want to demonstrate their "achievements" so that they can be promoted—to demonstrate that they can generate economic development. Such cadres squeeze the local population so that they can build roads or new enterprises that they can show off to higher ups. Often they pocket a portion of the proceeds. Or local cadres will monopolize opportunities to build enterprises for themselves, requisitioning land from peasants who have no choice but to sell at low rates. It appears that it is this arbitrary use of political power to enrich oneself at the expense of the local population that generates the greatest amount of resentment. In economic terms, such local cadres are "rent seekers"—people who are able to extract above market rates of return through their use of political power.[19]

In the 1990s, resentment at such behavior reached dangerous levels. In 1993, Wan Li, then head of the NPC, spoke emotionally about peasants, saying they wanted another Cheng Sheng

[19]Tom Bernstein and Xiaobo Lu, *Taxation without Representation* (Cambridge: Cambridge University Press, 2003).

and Wu Guang, the legendary leaders of the peasant rebellion that led to the fall of the Qin; half a million people participated in a wave of rural riots in May and June 1997.[20] There has been a major increase in the number of petitions, both individual and collective, since 1997. A recent book edited by the CCP Organization Department confirms that collective actions have become larger and better organized over time; such actions sometimes involve thousands of people, and they actively seek the support of the media.[21]

One reason that peasants and workers are willing and able to organize larger and better-coordinated protests is that they are no longer as dependent on the state as they used to be. With the breakup of the commune system and the dissolution of many SOEs in urban areas, and with the rise of incomes and education, peasants and workers know more about areas outside their own, have new sources of income, and resent efforts by cadres to monopolize economic opportunities for themselves. The level of social discontent is significant enough that the CCP needs to worry about restructuring local government to tackle problems of corruption, accountability, and public goods. This is a formidable public policy challenge for the central state, and it is one of the forces behind the expansion of village elections in recent years.

Corruption is another force that generates discontent and forces political change but which nevertheless makes political change difficult. In recent years, major smuggling scandals have erupted in port cities such as Zhanjiang in Guangdong province and Xiamen in Fujian province that revealed the enormous stakes involved and the extensive human networks that

[20]Thomas P. Bernstein and Xiaobo Lu, "Taxation without Representation: Peasant, the Central and Local States in Reform China," *China Quarterly*, no. 163 (September 2000): 753–754.

[21]*2000–2001 Zhongguo diaocha baogao: Xin xingshi xia renmin neibu maodun yanjiu* (2000–2001 China Investigation Report: A study of contradictions among the people under new historical conditions). Beijing: Zhongyang bianyiju chubanshe, 2001.

have protected these smuggling operations. Approximately one-third of the 42 million barrels of oil believed to be smuggled into China annually in the mid-1990s went through the port of Xiamen. Some $10 billion worth of goods were allegedly involved. Those caught up in the subsequent investigation included not only local customs and military figures, but also leaders of Fujian province and apparently the wife of a Politburo member. This case was of sufficient scale that it provoked the central authorities to take a series of measures to reorganize the customs service and remove the military from business operations.

While such measures give hope that the central state is finally serious about cracking down on corruption, corruption has become so embedded in many of the institutions of China—including the judiciary—that it will take many years of concerted efforts to bring the problem under control. Corruption is so difficult to control partly because, as in the Xiamen case, large webs of people tend to be involved, so cracking a case threatens to expose leaders at fairly senior levels of government, and hence is resisted.

VILLAGE DEMOCRACY

With the breakup of the commune system in the early 1980s, the development of the TVE sector, and greater migration to find jobs, villagers became less dependent on rural cadres. Income from farm production now goes first to the villager and then, through taxes and fees, to village cadres (under the commune system, cadres kept account books and distributed income to villagers at the end of the year). Villagers thus became more aware of the cost of village government and the amounts that cadres were extracting. It was a volatile combination. Peasants began to resist the extraction of taxes, to oppose local corruption or wasteful spending, and to resist the implementation of policies that they believed unfair. By the late 1980s, tensions between local villagers and cadres reached a critical point; the central government began to think of ways to ameliorate this social discontent.

Within the CCP there has always been a tradition, embodied in the mass line and other policies, of local self-rule. In the late 1980s, several high-ranking political leaders, most notably Peng Zhen, the head of the Standing Committee of the NPC, began pushing for local elections as a way to bolster local autonomy. He saw elections as a way to get both greater compliance from villagers (because they would have selected their own leaders) and to reduce social tensions. Peng's support led to the adoption of the Organic Law of Villagers Committees in 1987, which lay the foundation for village elections.

Such elections were for the village head, not the local party secretary, so they were limited in their implications for party control. Nevertheless, they encountered opposition both from central party officials, who feared that elections would mean the loss of control over local areas, and from county and township-level officials, who worried that freely elected officials would be less willing to carry out the tasks assigned by those levels of government. In the aftermath of the Tiananmen crackdown, there was an effort to abolish village elections, but Peng and other senior officials continued to support the law. In 1998, the Organic Law of Villagers Committees was revised to emphasize the competitive nature of elections and secret ballots. By the first years of the twenty-first century, some areas of China already had five rounds of voting.

Despite steady progress in the implementation of elections, there has also been widespread resistance. In many areas, local party cadres use a variety of tactics to manipulate the elections. Estimates on the percentage of villages that have reasonably competitive elections on a regular basis varies widely; some put it as low as 10 percent, others considerably higher.

Whatever the extent of implementation, it is clear that village elections have begun to change life at the local level, at least in some locations. For instance, although the village head is supposed to be subordinate to the local party secretary, many village heads assert their authority on the basis that they are the only ones actually elected by all the villagers. Such disputes not only cause conflict in villages but also undermine the authority of the local party organization, and they have forced the party to find ways to compete. One method has been to adopt what is called a "two-ballot system." Under this system, people being considered as party secretaries are voted on by local villagers in what is technically an opinion poll. Then, the second ballot, in the party organization, follows the results of the opinion poll. In this way, party secretaries are indirectly elected by villagers. Another method is to combine the posts of the party secretary and the village head. Then the party secretary has to run for election as village head. If he (or sometimes she) fails to be elected, he is then forced to step down as party secretary and is replaced by the winner of the election. In general, villagers are more willing to follow state policies—everything from birth control to tax payments—if they are administered by people they have elected and trust than if they are simply ordered to carry them out by an unpopular party secretary.

Elected village leaders often develop conflicts with township officials (the next highest level of government). Township officials are subject to many demands from higher levels of government (county and province), so they depend on village leaders to carry out assigned tasks. Elected officials frequently object to certain tasks, especially when, as is often the case, those tasks violate central regulations (such as the amount of revenue that can be lawfully collected). This conflict between village and township authorities has led many to argue that elections should now be raised to the township level, and several township elections have been carried out on an experimental basis. But developing elections at the township level is much more complicated than at the village level. First and foremost, townships are big enough that most voters would not know the candidates personally (as is usually the case in villages), so some sort of campaign organization is likely necessary. This sounds very close to competitive party politics to many people, and they have, so far, successfully resisted the expansion of elections to this level. Nevertheless, as elections become more institutionalized at the village level, it seems likely that pressures will mount for similar elections to be held at the township level.

GLOBALIZATION

Globalization has become one of the most hotly debated issues in the world today, as the anti-WTO (World Trade Organization) demonstrations in Seattle, Ottawa, and Genoa and discussions of the "clash of civilizations" suggest.[22] This mingling of national identity and economic questions has not been foreign to China, either early in the twentieth century or in the contemporary period. The Chinese revolutions of 1911, 1927, and 1949 all involved questions of cultural identity and national independence. It was anti-Manchu sentiment that finally united Han Chinese revolutionaries behind Sun Yat-sen's movement at the beginning of the century, and it was nationalism and cultural iconoclasm (the radical critique of China's Confucian heritage) that fueled the May Fourth Movement of 1919. Opposition to foreign domination (whether the Japanese invasion during World War II or the continued force of imperialism before and after the war) united many Chinese behind the Communists' drive for self-determination and their own route to national development. In all these periods, there have been divisive arguments (political and intellectual) over what it means to be Chinese and how and to what degree to distinguish that "Chineseness" from the "West" (often left undifferentiated).

These issues have been rejoined in post-Mao China. In the 1980s, many reform-minded intellectuals drew on the country's "enlightenment" tradition (that tradition stemming from the May Forth Movement that stressed science, democracy, and Western-style rationalism) to argue that China needed to emulate the West, including its free-market economics and its political democracy, in order to pursue its century-old dream of wealth and power. In the 1990s, however, having watched the breakup and economic decline of the former Soviet Union, the increasing social inequality in China as market-oriented policies are implemented, and the sometimes antagonistic attitude of the United States (as in the 1993 opposition to China's bid to host the 2000 Olympics and the effort to link human rights to trade privileges), many have embraced a new nationalism and a new stress on Chinese cultural identity (which, however, remains quite undefined). Perhaps ironically these attitudes among some intellectuals and a portion of the urban population have opened up a gap between the populace and the government, which has embraced globalization in economic if not political terms.

The issue on which this gap of understanding has become most apparent and could lead to political conflict is that of China's entry into the WTO. In November 1999, the United States and China, after 13 years of on-again, off-again negotiations, finally reached an agreement on terms for China's accession to the world trade body. Reaching agreement with other nations (most notably the EU) and translating all the separate accession agreements into one binding document took another two years, but finally in November 2001 all the member states of the WTO agreed to China's joining. Debates about the impact of the WTO on China have been as cantankerous as they are inconclusive. Those in favor of China's accession see many benefits deriving from WTO membership. For the first time in history, these people say, China will have a seat at the table when the nations of the world sit down to negotiate trade agreements, and that will protect China from unfavorable agreements being adopted. Moreover, economic reformers see the pressures of international competition as essential to bring about further reform of the economy. They also see WTO membership as reassuring foreign investors of China's intention to "play by the rules" and therefore encouraging foreign investment to continue to pour into the country. With investment will come increased managerial know-how and technology. In addition, belonging to the WTO will assure Chinese exporters of access to foreign markets that might otherwise come under protectionist pressures.

Critics argue that these gains, even if they do materialize, are long-term and diffuse. In the short term, China will face the costs of economic

---

[22]Samuel Huntington, *The Clash of Civilizations and the Remaking of World Order* (New York: Simon and Schuster, 1996).

readjustment, some of which might be quite high. In recent years, China has cut some 39 million workers from the payrolls of its state and collective enterprises. With WTO entry that figure could go higher, especially in vulnerable sectors like automobiles and manufacturing. Most controversial are the effects on agriculture. Although many agricultural experts disagree, critics in China argue that millions of agricultural jobs will be lost to cheap imports from the United States, Australia, and Canada. It might seem unlikely at first glance that agricultural producers in the advanced economies can undercut the prices of Chinese farmers, but the fact is that the average farmer in China has very little land. Like family farms elsewhere in the world, their scale is not sufficient to be economically viable. As a result, the price of Chinese agricultural products hovers around that of world agricultural prices, and in some cases is even higher. Considering that China already has an estimated 150 million redundant agricultural workers, there could be even more pressure to move workers off the land and into the cities. But will there be jobs to absorb them? The TVE sector was vital for job creation in the 1980s and early 1990s, but in recent years, as it has become technologically more sophisticated, it has been cutting back on employment, not creating new jobs.

It is likely that the impact of WTO membership on China will be both complex and debated. Most economists agree that the macroeconomic effects will be good, but there will no doubt be enough pain from economic readjustment to fuel continued debate on the benefits of WTO entry.

It should also be kept in mind that the WTO is not merely an economic issue. For many people it is a cultural and political issue as well. At this level, the issue of the WTO joins with the century-old debate about China's relationship with the rest of the world. Certainly China's accession to the WTO represents an acceptance of Western economic thinking about international economic relations. Many argue that it (as well as other recent reforms) represents a wholescale acceptance of neoliberal economic thought (that is, *laissez-faire* economics). Since neoliberal economic thought is so much a part of the

fabric of Western culture—including individualism, notions of law, freedom, and perhaps democracy as well—some critics see the WTO as part of Western cultural imperialism. Such people argue for the preservation of Chinese culture against this onslaught, though given the turbulent history of the twentieth century, even they have a difficult time defining the cultural values that are uniquely Chinese.

Critics go beyond this cultural critique of the WTO (and globalization more generally), arguing that the WTO is merely an extension of the old imperialist order in new garb—that it represents neocolonialism. As one critic put it:

> The U.S. controls the regulations that have been formulated by the international economic organizations; all are designed to accord with the interests and needs of the institutional model of the strong capitalist states. As soon as China joins the WTO, the U.S. can at any time find an excuse to interfere in, sanction, and intimidate our country into accepting so-called "international norms" that do not accord with our national characteristics. And to help the multinational companies to control China's industrial and financial lifelines, it [the U.S.] will usurp our economic sovereignty and force us to carry out suicidal reforms just as it has in Latin America, Russia, Southeast Asia and elsewhere.[23]

In short, in accepting globalization, these critics argue, China is committing itself to a subordinate position in the world economic order, an order controlled by the advanced capitalist nations. This is an argument that draws on world systems theory, which argues that the world is divided into core and peripheral areas, and that it is very difficult, if not impossible, to move out of the periphery. The experience of East Asian nations since World War II, and of China over the past two decades, argues strongly

---

[23]Shao Ren, "Zhongguo: Ruguan bu rutao" (China: Join the WTO, but don't fall into a trap), *Tianya* (Frontier), no. 3 (May 1999), p. 6.

against any such economic determinism, but it remains a popular argument.

If the economic impact of globalization and the WTO is difficult to assess, the political impact is even more so. Many believe that WTO membership will pave the way for political democratization in China. It may do so eventually, but it is unlikely to happen soon. WTO membership is likely to increase pressures for expanding the private economy (if only because inefficient SOEs and collective enterprises will have to close) and to reinforce the legal system. But it should be remembered that China has a long way to go in these regards. Those who live in free-market economies take for granted many of the institutions that make such economies work: a judicial system that can enforce its decisions, a stock market that generally has little insider trading, a host of financial institutions and credit agencies that keep an eye out for the financial well-being of firms. China, like many developing countries, does not have such institutions, and it takes time for such institutions to develop. They do not appear automatically with the declaration of a free market, as Russia and the countries of Eastern Europe found out.

Moreover, the immediate impact of the WTO is likely to reinforce the strength of the central state in China. The WTO demands adherence to rules, and it is only the central government that is likely to have the expertise and willpower to supervise the implementation of WTO policies. In addition, there will be a strong demand that the central government smooth some of the dislocations, particularly regional inequalities, that are likely to increase under the impact of the WTO. So it may be quite a while before either the government feels confident enough or the society feels strong enough to bring about a turn to democracy.

ETHNIC CONFLICT AND HUMAN RIGHTS

Closely related to these issues of political evolution are the issues of ethnic relations and human rights. These are often emotional issues on which different observers differ a great deal. Although human rights received some attention in the 1980s, it was the Tiananmen crackdown that drew widespread attention to the issue. Definitions of human rights differ greatly, as do assessments of both general trends in China; some stress political rights such as free speech, free association, free elections, while others include social and economic rights such as living standards, personal safety, education, health care, and life expectancy. If one emphasizes improvements in living standards and even in the realm of personal freedom (such as the ability to candidly express opinions within the privacy of one's own home), there is no question that Chinese today live better and with greater freedom from direct interference in their lives than at any time in modern history.

If one takes a narrower approach, however, there is certainly a great deal of room for improvement. The Chinese government continues to forbid the direct expression of political dissent, much less the organization of opposition groups. Often the boundary between what is acceptable speech and what is not is unclear or changing. In times of relative political relaxation, writers publish works that challenge established orthodoxies, whether in the realm of historical understanding, contemporary public policy, or lifestyle issues. When the political system tightens up, however, many authors find it difficult to publish their works. Nevertheless, the scope of public expression of ideas is much greater in the early twenty-first century than it was in the late 1980s (a period of relative openness). However, other forms of public expression, from forming labor unions to public demonstrations, remain forbidden.

An area that is highly controversial is that of religious freedom. There is no question that there is much greater tolerance of religious belief today than at any time under the PRC, but there are periodic crackdowns on certain forms of religious expression. For instance, many Protestants and Catholics gather for worship in "house churches" rather than the officially recognized churches. Usually this is permitted, but if a group becomes too large or if a local leader does not like it, then the practitioners are subject to arrest. The government is also not tolerant of Catholic priests who publicly profess allegiance to the pope in Rome rather than to the official church (which has no ties to the Vatican).

In recent years, *qigong,* a traditional form of exercise and medicinal practice with spiritual underpinnings, gained great popularity. It was accepted by the government as an expression of traditional Chinese values, and many government and party cadres took up the practice as well. In the 1990s, however, one such group, the *Falun Gong,* came into conflict with the government. In 1999, some 10,000 members of *Falun Gong* surrounded *Zhongnanhai,* the government compound in Beijing, demanding that *Falun Gong* be recognized by the government. Such a direct challenge to government authority was not tolerated, and beginning in the summer of 1999 the government cracked down harshly on *Falun Gong,* calling it a "cult." There are some cultlike features of *Falun Gong,* but most of its practitioners were involved for medicinal reasons or the uplifting spiritual message of the group. When the government cracked down, many practitioners openly defied the government, but eventually the government prevailed. At the same time that the government shut down the *Falun Gong,* it also prohibited the practice of *qigong* altogether, fearing that it could be used by other groups to challenge the government.

In some ways, the appearance of *Falun Gong* reflected the complex development of contemporary Chinese society. With the end of the political campaigns of the Maoist era and the growth of the economy, citizens have much greater time and resources to spend on leisure activities, whether going to the movies or practicing martial arts. At the same time, there is a widespread sense of the absence of spiritual values, and that has led many to pursue religion, whether of the Western or Eastern sort. In many ways, *Falun Gong* builds on China's tradition of folk religion and provides an alternative to official, and tainted, avenues of belief.

Ethnic issues are also contentious in China, and they frequently overlap with religious issues. Altogether, 55 different ethnic minorities make up about 8 percent of the total population. Although the size of this minority population is relatively small by the standards of most nations, China's minorities are concentrated in strategically sensitive parts of the country that often do not have large concentrations of Han Chinese, the dominant ethnic group. These areas are primarily in the southwestern and western parts of the country, including the provinces of Yunnan, Guizhou, Xizang (Tibet), Sichuan, Qinghai, Xinjiang, and Ningxia.

In recent years, the Tibetan situation has attracted a lot of international attention, and the spiritual leader of Tibet, the Dalai Lama who has been in exile since 1959, received the Nobel Prize for peace in 1989. Although Tibetans resent the rule of the Han Chinese, no nation has ever challenged the Chinese claim to rule Tibet, a recognition that dates back at least to the Anglo-Chinese Convention of 1906 and the Anglo-Russian Treaty of 1907. The vital security role played by the Tibetan highlands suggests that no Chinese government is likely to surrender control over the area. Mutual suspicion between the Chinese government and the representatives of the Dalai Lama make resolution of this issue extremely difficult.

Although the Tibetan issue has received the most attention in recent years, with the attack on the World Trade Center and Pentagon in September 2001, attention shifted to the Muslim populations of the northwest, particularly the Uyghurs, Uzbeks, and Tajiks of Xinjiang province. These populations are of Turkish origin and have retained their Muslim beliefs. With the opening of China, and particularly since the breakup of the Soviet Union, there has been a revival of Islam in this area, as there has been throughout Central Asia. Along with moderate Islam there has also been Islamic militance, which has built on and reinforced separatist feelings in the area. In the 1990s, there were several acts of violence, including bombings, attributed to Islamic extremists. Some Muslims from Xinjiang apparently trained in the al Qaeda training camps of Afghanistan, with which China shares a border.

Thus, with the war on terrorism, China quickly aligned itself with the United States and other countries to oppose Osama bin Laden's al Qaeda network. Since that effort has begun, there have been allegations that China has taken advantage of the war to carry out large-scale repression in the area. If so, it seems likely to bury the seeds of ethnic hatred even more deeply in the minds of ethnic minorities who otherwise would not have been inclined toward violence. It thus seems likely that there will be continued violence in that part of China for years to come.

Ethnic tensions and especially violence make any turn toward democracy more difficult. If the Chinese government believes that new rights and freedoms are likely to be used to support the cause of territorial separation, it will no doubt move very cautiously, which in turn may well fuel the conflicts that Beijing worries about. Dealing with ethnic and religious issues is thus a major challenge to Beijing, one that will affect social stability, political evolution, and China's relations with other countries.

Thinking Critically

1. What are the pressures for and against political change in the contemporary period?
2. Why did village elections emerge, and how are they changing life at the local level in China?
3. How will China's membership in the World Trade Organization (WTO) affect China's economic and political systems?
4. What are the sources of ethnic conflict in contemporary China?
5. What are some different dimensions of human rights, and how do you evaluate China's record along these various dimensions?

KEY TERMS

clash of civilizations *(494)*
globalization *(494–496)*
Hu Jintao *(489)*
individual entrepreneurs *(490)*
inner-party democracy *(490)*

institutionalization *(489)*
neoliberal economic thought *(495)*
Organic Law of Villagers Committees *(493)*
procedural rationality *(490)*
rent seeking *(491)*
routinization of charisma *(490)*
state capacity *(488)*
world systems theory *(495)*
World Trade Organization (WTO) *(494)*

FURTHER READINGS

Fewsmith, Joseph. *Elite Politics in Contemporary China* (Armonk, NY: M. E. Sharpe, 2001).

Finkelstein, David M., and Maryanne Kivlehan, eds. *China's Leadership in the 21st Generation: The Rise of the Fourth Generation* (Armonk: Sharpe, 2003).

Goldman, Merle, and Roderick MacFarquhar, eds. *The Paradox of China's Post-Mao Reforms* (Cambridge, MA: Harvard University Press, 1999).

Harding, Harry. *The Fragile Relationship: The United States and China since 1972* (Washington, DC: Brookings Institution, 1993).

Harris, Lillian Craig. "Xinjiang, Central Asia, and the Implications for China's Policy in the Islamic World," *China Quarterly* 133 (March 1993): 111–29.

Lampton, David M. "Chinese Politics: The Bargaining Treadmill," *Issues and Studies* 23(3) (March 1987): 11–41.

Lampton, David M., ed. *The Politics of Policy Implementation* (Berkeley: University of California Press, 1987).

Lardy, Nicholas R. *China and the World Economy* (Washington, DC: Institute for International Economics, 1994).

Li, Cheng. *China's Leaders: The Next Generation* (Lanham, MD: Roman and Littlefield, 2001).

Lieberthal, Kenneth, and David M. Lampton, eds. *Bureaucracy, Politics, and Decision-Making in Post-Mao China* (Berkeley: University of California Press, 1992).

Smil, Vaclav. *China's Environmental Crisis* (Armonk, NY: M. E. Sharpe, 1993).

So, Alvin Y., ed. *China's Developmental Miracle: Origins, Transformations, and Challenges* (Armonk: Sharpe, 2003).

Walder, Andrew. *Communist Neo-Traditionalism: Work and Authority in Chinese Industry* (Berkeley: University of California Press, 1986).

Zagoria, Donald S. *Breaking the China-Taiwan Impasse* (Westport: Praeger, 2003).

WEB SITES

www.scmp.com/
South China Morning Post (Hong Kong's leading English language paper).

http://news.bbc.co.uk/1/hi/world/asia-pacific/default.stm
British Broadcasting Corporation's Far East news coverage.

english.peopledaily.com.cn/
People's Daily is the official organ of the Chinese Communist Party.

http://www.xinhua.org/english/index.htm
Xinhua (or New China) News Agency gives China's official views on events, both domestic and foreign.

www.taipeitimes.com/news
For Taiwan's views, the *Taipei Times* is a useful source.

usinfo.state.gov/regional/ea/uschina/
American government views, including policy statements, can be found on the U.S. Department of State's Web site.

www.pacom.mil/
Site of the U.S. Pacific Command, based in Hawaii; often contains information relevant to China and broader regional issues.

www.savetibet.org
The International Campaign for Tibet.

www.chinaonline.com/
Business news regarding China.

www.chinabusinessreview.com/
U.S.-China Business Council monthly magazine, *China Business Review,* and links for WTO-related material.

www.cartercenter.org
The Carter Center.

www.iri.org
The International Republican Institute.

chinanews.bfn.org/
A good starting point for doing research on China; links to dozens of sites on a variety of issues.

www.nbr.org/
National Bureau of Asian Research.

www.chinaleadershipmonitor.org
China Leadership Monitor site offering special research reports on China.

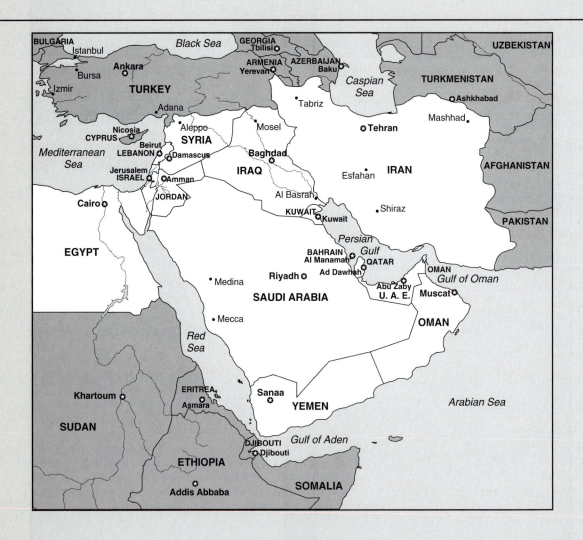

CHAPTER

9

GOVERNMENTS OF THE
Middle East

Michael Curtis

INTRODUCTION

Background: Collective portrait of 15 states in the Middle East: Bahrain, Egypt, Iran, Iraq, Israel, Jordan, Kuwait, Lebanon, Libya, Oman, Qatar, Saudi Arabia, Syria, United Arab Emirates, Yemen. Most of the states are relatively recent creations of European colonial powers during the twentieth century. They are, apart from Israel and Iran, members of the Arab League and the Islamic Conference. The peoples and governments are troubled by problems of development, legitimacy, identity, and ethnic, religious, and national issues.

GEOGRAPHY

Area: 7.6 million sq km: the world's most arid region; about half is desert, which has spread over time

Land: Agriculture is limited; the area is the largest proportional importer of food of any region in the world. Highest percentage of arable land: Syria (28%); lowest: Iran, Kuwait, and UAE

Water: Resources are limited, leading to conflicts over the use of the Tigris, Euphrates, Jordan, and Nile rivers

The Middle East is located on major trade routes between Europe and Asia. It is an area of major waterways: the Suez Canal which links the Mediterranean and the Red Sea; the Turkish Straits; the Strait of Hormuz at the mouth of the Persian or Arabian Gulf; Bab al-Mandab at the entrance to the Red Sea from the Indian Ocean and dominated by the port of Aden; the Gulf of Aqaba, which terminates at the Israeli port of Eilat and the Jordanian port of Aqaba.

PEOPLE

Population: 208 million
  largest: Egypt 76 million
  smallest: Bahrain 0.6 million
  most dense: Bahrain 977 per km
  least dense: Libya 3 per km
Urban: *highest:* Kuwait 97%
  lowest: Yemen 24%
Life expectancy at birth: *highest:* Israel 78
  lowest: Iraq 62
Literacy: *highest:* Israel 95%
  lowest: Yemen 43%
Female literary: *highest:* Israel 93%
  lowest: Egypt 40%

ECONOMY

Overview: The Middle East, one of the world's leading oil-producing regions, accounts for about one-third of the world's crude oil production and 10 percent of refined product. Saudi Arabia has about one-quarter of the world's reserves known at present. The area is also rich in natural gas reserves, phosphates, copper, and iron ore.

GDP ($ million): *highest:* 478,000 in Iran
  lowest: 15,000 in Yemen

GDP—per capita ($): *highest:* 25,000 in Kuwait
  lowest: 800 in Yemen

Petroleum reserves (billion barrels): *highest:* 260 in Saudi Arabia
  lowest: 3.7 in Qatar

Imports ($ billion): *highest:* 31.5 in Israel
  lowest: 4 in Jordan

Exports ($ billion): *highest:* 35.1 in Israel
  lowest: 0.7 in Lebanon

HISTORICAL BACKGROUND

The area known as the Middle East, a term that began to be used by the British in the early twentieth century, has no specific geographical delineation but is generally recognized as the territory stretching from Libya in the west, Turkey in the north, Yemen in the south, to Iran in the east, though sometimes other countries such as Sudan and Afghanistan are included. Other terms have been used in the past, and some still are used, to designate the area or parts of it. One favorite term was the Near East, used to differentiate the area from the Far East. Another was the Levant, which now signifies the eastern end of the Mediterranean, the countries of Syria, Lebanon, and Israel. Outside these borders is the Maghreb, the western region of the Arab Islamic countries; the states of Algeria, Morocco, Tunisia, and sometimes Libya are included. The Gulf (Arabian or Persian) states are Iran, Iraq, Kuwait, Saudi Arabia, Qatar, United Arab Emirates, Oman, and Bahrain.

The Middle Eastern states, with the exception of Turkey, Iran, and Israel, are part of the 22-member League of Arab States, formed in 1945 with headquarters in Cairo. These same states plus Iran are part of the 57-member Organization of the Islamic Conference, formed in 1969 to promote the well-being of Muslims. A crucial feature of the Middle East and Turkey is thus the interrelation between politics and religion.

The present map of much of the area dates from the breakup of the Ottoman Empire after World War I, when new states were constituted under the League of Nation mandates administered by France and Britain, who introduced parliamentary institutions and constitutional arrangements. These Western powers revived names long obsolete, including *Palestine,* a term that had been used by the Romans when they abolished the names of Judea and Samaria, but that had disappeared by the time the Crusaders arrived in the eleventh century.

The Middle East has been the location of ancient civilizations of the world—Sumerian, Babylonian, Assyrian, Egyptian, Iranian, Jewish, and Arabic—and of the three great monotheistic religions, Judaism, Christianity, and Islam. Its geographic setting between the land masses of Europe, Africa, and Asia made the Middle East the crossroads of the world, thereby engendering

---

A CLOSER LOOK

9.1

LEAGUE OF NATIONS MANDATES

At the end of World War I, the Allied Powers did not incorporate conquered territories into their own empires. On the basis of the Covenant of the League of Nations (Article 22), they set up mandates for the non-Turkish parts of the defeated Ottoman Empire and for the imperial possessions of defeated Germany. The mandatory power was given the task of preparing the mandate area for independence and self-rule. The system for the Middle East was agreed to in the Treaty of San Remo in 1920 and formally came into force in 1922. Britain and France divided the area into new states with new frontiers and new names, establishing regimes modeled on their own. The central, northern area, the Levant, was assigned to France, which then set up two republics, Syria and Lebanon. Britain established a monarchy in Iraq, an emirate of Transjordan, and directly administered the western area known as Palestine.

REVIEW

9.1

ORGANIZATION OF THE ISLAMIC CONFERENCE

The Organization Islamic Conference was established in 1969 and currently has 57 member and 3 observer states.

The OIC Charter states that its aims are to:

- Strengthen:
  Islamic solidarity among member states.
  Cooperation in the political, economic, social, cultural, and scientific fields.
  The struggle of all Muslim people to safeguard their dignity, independence, and national rights.

- Coordinate action to:
  Safeguard the Holy Places.
  Support the struggle of the Palestinian people and assist them in recovering their rights and liberating their occupied territories.

- Work to:
  Eliminate racial discrimination and all forms of colonialism.
  Create a favorable atmosphere for the promotion of cooperation and understanding between member states and other countries.

The charter also enumerates the principles governing OIC activities:

- Full equality among member states.
- Observation of the right to self-determination and non-interference in the internal affairs of member states.
- Observation of the sovereignty, independence, and territorial integrity of each state;
- The settlement of any dispute that might arise among member states by peaceful means such as negotiations, mediation, conciliation, and arbitration.
- A pledge to refrain, in relations among member states, from resorting to force or threatening to resort to the use of force against the unity and territorial integrity or the political independence of any one of them.

(continues)

trade and a mixture of people and cultures, but also leading to frequent conflict and waves of invasion. The Middle East in whole or in part has been subjected to the control of a variety of rulers throughout history. Conquest by military victories led to the spread of Islam from its Arabian homeland into what were then Christian countries, and the attempt at a Christian reconquest by Crusaders from Western Europe in the eleventh and twelfth centuries was unsuccessful. The strategic importance of the area has long been recognized. Napoleon Bonaparte invaded the Middle East to block British control of India. In its turn Britain supported the Ottoman Empire, which lasted until 1918, to prevent Russian expansion southward. Germany, before World War I, competed with other powers to obtain a foothold in the area. In the post–World War II era, the vital importance of the Middle East has been enhanced by Western dependence on the area for oil—two-thirds of the world's known resources lie in the area—and by the rivalry between the United States and the former Soviet Union for influence.

ORGANIZATION OF THE ISLAMIC CONFERENCE, (continued)

MEMBER STATES (YEAR OF ACCESSION)

Afghanistan (1969)	Guyana (1998)	Pakistan (1969)
Albania (1992)	Indonesia (1969)	Palestine (1969)
Algeria (1969)	Iran (1969)	Qatar (1970)
Azerbaijan (1991)	Iraq (1976)	Saudi Arabia (1969)
Bahrain (1970)	Jordan (1969)	Senegal (1969)
Bangladesh (1974)	Kazakhstan (1995)	Sierra Leone (1972)
Benin (1982)	Kuwait (1969)	Somalia (1969)
Brunei Dar-us Salaam (1984)	Kyrgyzstan (1992)	Sudan (1969)
Burkina Faso (1975)	Lebanon (1969)	Surinam (1996)
Cameroon (1975)	Libya (1969)	Syrian Arab Republic (1970)
Chad (1969)	Malaysia (1969)	Tajikistan (1992)
Comoros (1976)	Maldives (1976)	Togo (1997)
Côte d'Ivoire (2001)	Mali (1969)	Tunisia (1969)
Djibouti (1978)	Mauritania (1969)	Turkey (1969)
Egypt (1969)	Morocco (1969)	Turkmenistan (1992)
Gabon (1974)	Mozambique (1994)	Uganda (1974)
Gambia (1974)	Niger (1969)	United Arab Emirates (1970)
Guinea (1969)	Nigeria (1986)	Uzbekistan (1995)
Guinea-Bissau (1974)	Oman (1970)	Yemen (1969)

The OIC observer states: Bosnia and Herzegovina, Central African Republic, and Thailand.

The geography of the Middle East—desert, river valleys, mountains, and fertile plain—has given rise to a diversity of cultural and behavioral patterns. Much of the area is desert, resulting primarily from lack of rainfall but also to some degree from past misuse, and little land can be cultivated. Under present conditions, the area cannot feed itself, a situation that is being aggravated by the increase in population. The desert has been a barrier to unity. The consequence of this and other geographical factors has been the clustering of families around places where water is available, thus creating isolated self-sufficient settlements adhering to particular ways of life. Historic rivalry has existed between herdsmen living in the desert and those living from agriculture. At an early stage, rulers had to provide for the policing of desert borders and the security of desert routes.

The mountain ranges have been barriers to unified control, protecting religious and ethnic minorities and linguistic differences. For this reason, religious groups—including the Druze, Maronites, Yezidis, and Alawites—tribes such as the Bakhtiari in Iran, and a people such as the Kurds in Iran, Turkey, and Iraq have been able to survive in the midst of an overwhelming Arab control and Islamic majority (see Table 9.1). Farsi (Persian) has remained as a separate language in Iran. The historic rivals, Egypt and Iraq, result from river valleys and the area surrounding them. Both are ancient civilizations, skilled at agricultural production and in the use of artificial irrigation, and experienced in the art of centralized government. The geographic boundaries of modern Turkey and Iran coincide approximately with the great plateaus. By contrast, the modern states of Israel, Jordan, Syria,

TABLE 9.1

ELEVEN STATES IN THE MIDDLE EAST, 2005

Country	Area (sq km)	Population (millions)	Muslim Religion (%)	GDP per Capita ($ thousand)	Occupation Sector (%)		
					Agr.	Ind.	Services
Bahrain	620	0.65	100 Shi'a (70) Sunni (30)	14	1	46	53
Egypt	1 million	76	94 Mostly Sunni	3.9	29	22	49
Iran	1.6 million	68	99 Shi'a (89) Sunni (10)	7	30	25	45
Iraq	437,000	24	97 Shi'a (63) Sunni (34)	2.4	6	13	81
Israel	20,700	6.1	15 Mostly Sunni	19	3	37	60
Jordan	92,000	5.4	92 Mostly Sunni	4.3	5	12.5	82.5
Kuwait	17,800	2.3	85 Shi'a (40) Sunni (45)	15	0	55	45
Lebanon	10,400	3.6	70 Mixed groups	5	12	27	61
Libya	1.7 million	5.2	97 Sunni	8.9	7	47	46
Saudi Arabia	1.9 million	24.2	100	10.5	12	25	63
Syria	185,000	17.5	74 Sunni Alawite, Druze, and other Muslim sects (16)	3.5	29	22	49

and Lebanon are political entities whose geographic features do not correspond with the natural geography of the region.

The largest linguistic group in the Middle East is the Semitic language group. Most in this group speak Arabic, though a relatively small number—about 5.5 million—speak Hebrew. For centuries, Islam and Arabs have dominated the area. As is often the case in political analysis, terms of this kind do not lend themselves to easy definition. One can talk of an Arab people as composed of individuals who are bound together by the Arabic language and civilization, with a distinctive culture and literature, though it may include individuals of different races and religions. Arabs do not constitute a single physical type or race, and although nine-tenths of Arabs are Muslim, some are Christians and Jews. As a corollary, Arabs constitute only about one-fifth of the world's 1.2 billion Muslims. Language was therefore the most important single factor binding together the approximately 120 million in the Middle East geographical triangle who are regarded as Arab. Nevertheless, if Turkey is included in the definition of Middle East, about half of the population in that extended area speaks Turkish or Farsi (the language of Persia, now Iran).

For some 400 years, from the seventh to the eleventh century, the Arabs were the center of political power, commerce, and learning in the area. Yet for a long time a single Arab state that includes all Arab people has not existed in political terms. The Arabs have been nationals of a number of countries, including, since 1948, Israel. The Arab-dominated Middle East has always been the setting for fierce competition and rivalry among the individual states.

Two proposals for the creation of an Arab nation have been made. One is to weld existing states together to form a larger Arab union. Though a number of attempts have been made, such as the United Arab Republic of Egypt and Syria between 1958 and 1961, all have quickly failed. The other argument is to create a pan-Arabic state, based on the idea that all Arabic speakers form one nation with Common rights, aspirations, and national attributes. In this view, each territorial nation is only a partial representative of the Arab people, often based on the ambition of the political ruler. As a political movement, pan-Arabism dates from the late-nineteenth century, largely originating from Christian Arab thinkers. At first pan-Arabism was directed against the Ottoman Empire. After World War I, the new targets were the European countries, Britain and France, which had entered the area, and the increasing immigration of Jews into Palestine.

As a language, Arabic only became important with the rise of Islam. For many centuries, Arab and Islamic consciousnesses were difficult to distinguish. Not until the late-nineteenth century were the arguments made by Christian Arabs that Arab identity was not synonymous with religious identification, and that national loyalty should be given higher priority than adherence to Islam. The dialogue continues in the contemporary world between those advocating the primacy of Islam and those arguing that nationality should be the bond among Arabs.

In all Arab states except Lebanon, Islam is the established religion of the state, religious instruction is given in the schools, and religious institutions are financially supported by the state. Islam, the dominant faith for 14 centuries in the Middle East, has provided a sense of common identity, resting on the fundamental principles that "God is one and Mohammed is his prophet," and that the Koran, the messages revealed to Mohammed in the early seventh century, and the traditions of the prophet should form the basis not only of theology but also of law, though commentators differ on interpretation of that law or *sharia*. For Islam, the sole source of political legitimacy is God, and the state and military power are to be employed in the service of God. In this view, the world is seen as divided into the House of Islam, those lands in which the *sharia* is dominant, and the House of War, those lands that did not accept or resisted Islam. In theory, Islam is pledged to a *jihad,* sometimes translated as holy war, against those territories not under Muslim rule. Islamic theory also suggests that the ruler, whose main obligation is to implement religious law, is absolute; the notion of popular participation, as in representative democratic systems, is unfamiliar.

In spite of any clear distinction in Islam between the religious and the secular, two factors are pertinent to contemporary affairs. The first is the division within Islam between the majority group, the Sunnis, and the minority Shiites who honor Ali, the fourth caliph after Mohammed. The Shiites regard Ali, the martyred leader, as the first true imam (religious leader) who passed on the valid interpretation of the Koran to his descendants, who see themselves as having the legitimate right to the mantle of the prophet. Constituting 80 million in all, outside as well as within the Middle East, the Shiites constitute about 8 percent of the total Muslim population. In the Middle East, they form the dominant majority in Iran, a majority in Iraq, the largest single community in Lebanon, and important groups in the Gulf States, Yemen, and other places.

The second factor relating to contemporary affairs is the existence of other religious affiliations. The Druze, an Islamic sect, exist in Lebanon, Syria, and Israel. The Alawites, holding certain deviant religious views but nonetheless regarded as being close to the Shiites, currently form the ruling group in Syria, though they constitute only 14 percent of the total population. Christianity, the majority religion in medieval times, has now dwindled to a small and largely powerless minority except in Lebanon, where numerous sects—Maronites, Greek Orthodox, and Greek Catholics—remain. The largest Christian group, the Copts, form about 8 percent of the Egyptian population. In Iran, small groups of Zoroastrians and Bahais remain.

Judaism is the oldest surviving faith in the region. Jews live primarily in Israel now that ancient Jewish communities in Arab countries have almost come to an end. Though dispersed at different times by the Babylonians, Assyrians, and Romans, and at times persecuted by both Christian and Muslim rulers, Jews have always been present in varying numbers in the area of the Holy Land. Jewish immigration from the Mediterranean countries in the sixteenth century led to an increase of intellectual as well as religious activity in towns such as Jerusalem and Safed. At the beginning of the nineteenth century, Zionists from Central and Eastern Europe began immigrating as pioneers and settled on the land. By 1914 this immigration by Zionists of different kinds led to about 85,000 Jews residing in Palestine, a number that had grown to half a million when the state of Israel was established in 1948. With the new state came the recognition of Hebrew, together with Arabic, as the official language and the accepted form of communication.

Despite the religious divisions, a pan-Islamic movement, whose political goal was the unity of all Muslims, emerged in the latter part of the nineteenth century among the Young Ottomans, who saw the Ottoman Empire as the natural center of such a union to ward off European influence. A more militant form of pan-Islamism in other countries after World War I, when there was a more active concern with religion, argued

that Islam should be united as a world power, reasserting Islamic principles and values against Western power and culture. But it was not successful in leading to an effective political organization based on religious solidarity. After World War II, the reassertion of Islamic principles, appealing to the lower classes, resulted in the creation of religious leagues, the most important of which has been the Muslim Brotherhood, originally founded in 1928 by Hasan al-Banna. The Brotherhood is part of the larger Islamic fundamentalist movement, which at first sought to transform the Muslim world by religious revival and return to the ethics of Islam. It soon became politicized and engaged in actions that included terrorism. Since 1948 a major factor in the Islamic movement has been hostility to Israel. Strong in Egypt in the 1930s and 1940s, the Brotherhood provided a focus for opposition to economic and political control by foreign powers as well as for attack on the Egyptian monarchy. Suppressed by President Nasser in 1954, the Brotherhood reemerged under President Sadat, who saw it as helpful in the internal fight against Communists. Saudi Arabia also viewed the Brotherhood as such and has provided it with financial assistance.

Countries and political regimes can be classified in a number of ways. For the Middle East, the three most important distinctions are religion, historical development, and political development.

THE ROLE OF RELIGION

The Middle East is the birthplace of three major religions: Judaism, Christianity, and Islam. The vast majority of inhabitants are Muslims. Jews have dwelt in the area for several thousand years in the land of Israel. For a time after the end of the kingdom of David and Solomon in the tenth century B.C.E., they lived in two states: Judah with Jerusalem as its capital in the south and Israel (later Samaria) in the north.

The kingdom of Judah came to an end and the Jewish Temple was destroyed with the capture of Jerusalem by Babylon in 586 B.C.E. and the exiling of Jews. Cyrus, the Persian ruler, defeated Babylon and allowed the return of Jews to the

A CLOSER LOOK

9.2

THE KURDS

The Kurds, mostly Sunni Muslims, are a non-Arab ethnic group with their own culture and language, akin to Farsi. Numbering about 20 million, they are the largest ethnic group in the Middle East without a state of their own but live in an area generally called Kurdistan, which embraces parts of Iraq, Iran, Armenia, Syria, and above all Turkey, where about 8 million live. The Kurds are an ancient people whose history goes back several thousand years. The most famous Kurd is Saladin, who fought against the Christians in the Crusades. In the absence of a unified Kurdish government, their organization is still largely tribal in Kurdistan. The Kurds were conquered by the Arabs in the seventh century and were then subject to different empires, the Seljuk Turks, the Mongols, the Safavid and Ottoman Empires. The Kurds seemed to have been promised a state of their own by the Treaty of Sèvres (1920) following the end of the Ottoman Empire. The Treaty did lead to the creation of the modern states of Iraq and Syria, but Kemal Ataturk, who put down Kurdish revolts in 1925, 1930, and 1937–1938 with brutality, rejected the provision for an autonomous Kurdish state. The Treaty of Lausanne (1923), which replaced Sèvres and set Turkey's borders to include most of Kurdistan, did not mention a separate state.

The Kurds in Iran rebelled in the 1920s. For a short time in the 1940s, a Kurdish republic was established, with the help of the Soviet Union, in part of the territory of Iran, but the shah crushed it. The Islamic Republic, which supplanted him in 1979, launched a campaign against Kurdish inhabitants. In Iraq, agitation for an autonomous Kurdistan led in the 1960s to fighting; the Iraqi offer of limited autonomy was rejected in the 1970s and fighting resumed. During the Iran-Iraq war (1980–1988), some Kurds supported Iran and were attacked by Iraqi forces, who used poison gas against them in 1988 and killed over 200,000 Kurds at various times. After the Gulf War of 1991, the United Nations organized humanitarian relief for the displaced Kurdish population in northern Iraq and set up a no-fly zone for the Iraqi air force north of the 36th parallel to protect the Kurds. Nevertheless, Iraq's president, Saddam Hussein, crushed a Kurdish uprising; about half a million Kurds fled to the frontier with Turkey and over a million to Iran. In 1992 the Kurds set up an autonomous regime in northern Iraq but were split into two groups, the Kurdistan Democratic Party led by Mustafa al-Barzani, and the Patriotic Union of Kurdistan, with internecine violence between them.

In Turkey, those Kurds who are assimilated play a role in social and political life. They account for about a quarter of the population of Istanbul and, through the Social Democratic Populist Party, have representation in parliament and in the government coalitions. Those who are not assimilated continue their struggle for a state of their own. Fighting has occurred in the 1980s and again in the 1990s between Turkish troops and the Kurdistan Workers Party (PKK), a Marxist movement set up in 1978. Fights in 1992 against the PKK camps in northern Iraq by the Turks led to over 200,000 killed, and in 1999 to the death of the PKK leader. Changing alliances, political and ideological differences, and rivalries between the Kurdish clans make the emergence of a Kurdish state unlikely at the present time.

---

land of Israel. The Jewish states came to an end with invasions by the Macedonian ruler of Syria and then by the Romans, who captured Jerusalem in 70 C.E. and destroyed the second Temple, built by the exiles who returned from Babylon. Sixty-five years later, after a revolt by Jews, the Romans exiled them; Jerusalem was renamed Aelia Capitolina, the names of Judea and Samaria were abolished, and the area was renamed Palestine, referring to the ancient Philistines. During the Ottoman Empire, Palestine was never a state but, from 1517, a military and administrative district. The name reappeared with the post–World War I British Mandate to administer the area. Jews began immigrating to the area and later established the state of Israel, in May 1948.

REVIEW

9.2

THE LEAGUE OF ARAB STATES

- The League of Arab States was established in March 1945 by the governments of Egypt, Iraq, Lebanon, Saudi Arabia, Syria, Transjordan, and North Yemen.
- Any independent Arab state can apply for membership, which in 2005 numbered 22.

The member states are:

Algeria	Iraq	Mauritania	Saudi Arabia	United Arab
Bahrain	Jordan	Morocco	Somalia	Emirates
Comoros	Kuwait	Oman	Sudan	Yemen
Djibouti	Lebanon	Palestine	Syria	
Egypt	Libya	Qatar	Tunisia	

Christians have been in the area for two thousand years, not forming a state of their own but spreading the faith. With the conversion of the emperor Constantine, the Roman Empire became Christian, thus establishing the supremacy of Christianity over other religions. Today, Christians constitute a small and diminishing proportion of the population in Middle Eastern countries (see Table 9.2).

Islam emerged in the seventh century in the Arabian Peninsula with its essential creed of obedience to God's law and to the Koran as the word of God, and acceptance of Mohammed (570–632) as God's last prophet and messenger. Some Arab tribes accepted the religion by a process of con-

version and conquest following the death of Mohammed in 632. The ancient empires of Byzantium and Persia were overthrown, and large areas of Asia, Africa, and Europe were taken, though Charles Martel checked the Arab forces in 732 at the gates of Poitiers. The Moors were in Spain, the Tatars in Russia, and the Turks in the Balkans.

At its height, the Arab Islamic world expanded from Arabia and stretched from Spain to central Asia, constituting a great multiracial and international civilization, the scientific center of the world. The Arabic language was synonymous with learning and science. Today, about 1.25 billion people throughout the world adhere to the Muslim faith, the fastest growing religion.

One of the more controversial concepts of Islam is *jihad,* which has been variously translated as "struggle" or "striving in the path of God" or "holy war," putting God's will into practice. The question is whether *jihad* is understood in a spiritual or moral sense, or is seen as necessitating armed struggle against infidels and apostates. In the latter sense, it would be perceived as a religious obligation that would continue until the world adopted the Muslim faith or submitted to Muslim rule. Mohammed led the first *jihad* against pagans in Arabia. All people who submit to Islam are part of the *umma* (the community), but Islam has been differently interpreted since its emergence, and generalization is not simple, though the *sharia* or law is important for all.

TABLE 9.2

CHRISTIANS IN THE MIDDLE EAST, 2005

Country	Christians (millions)	Population (%)
Egypt	5.5	8
Syria	1.7	10
Lebanon	0.9	30
Iraq	0.7	3
Jordan	0.1	2
Israel	0.1	1
Palestine	0.04	2

Muslims are divided into the majority group Sunnis, who identify with the *sunna,* a body of legal and moral principles stemming from Arabian custom law, and the minority Shiites, followers of Mohammed's son-in-law Ali and his daughter Fatima. After the death of the prophet, Mohammed, two dynasties of caliphs ruled over a united *umma,* the members of which acknowledged the divine mission of the prophet. But this unity broke down because of local rivalries and personal ambitions, and above all by internal divisions over Ali as the caliph chosen on the murder of his predecessor in 656. In his turn, Ali was murdered, and his supporters, the Shiat Ali or Shi'a, became the first schism in Islam. The Islamic community, at first one state with one ruler, was split into a number of states, ruled by dynasties and with no clear boundaries.

The most extreme form of Islam, often referred to as radical, militant, or fundamentalist, is Wahhabism, launched by Mohammed ibn Abd al-Wahhab (1703–1792) in Arabia in 1744. Wahhabism advocates a puritanical religion, returning the Muslim world to the authentic Islam of the prophet, severe punishment for transgressors, and murder of opponents. Wahhabism emanated from the area known as Nejd, where the capital of Saudi Arabia, Riyadh, is today, and it was embraced by the tribe of al-Saud in a part of Arabia. The descendents of the tribe and the first king of Saudi Arabia, Saud, made Wahhabism the official creed of the regime. The al-Saud family and tribe ran the political regime, and the holy men (sheikhs) provided religious legitimacy. The Wahhabi doctrine and the al-Saud family joined again in the early part of the twentieth century with Saud's conquest of the Hejaz, including Mecca and Medina. The most modern manifestation of the Wahhabi view was Osama bin Laden and his al Qaeda network, which attacked the United States on September 11, 2001, calling for holy war against the infidels and for the removal of U.S. forces from the soil of Saudi Arabia and Iraq.

Islamic militant radicalism rejects modernization and the ways of the West in its search for a purely Islamic way of life. In recent years it has called for a reassertion of and return to "authentic Islam" as the basis of society. Politics and religion are thus inextricably intertwined if the religious law, *sharia,* is acknowledged as the fundamental legal system, stemming from the rulings (*fatwas*) of clerics rather than from decisions of elected legislatures and executives. In a number of Middle Eastern countries—Saudi Arabia, Kuwait, Syria, and Iran—Islam is declared the state religion and the *sharia* or the Koran the major source of law. Mullahs, imams, and religious dignitaries often control Islamic activity and education. According to the Koran, leaders should consult (*shura*) before important decisions are taken, but no precise procedure is prescribed. The general method is to have an appointed council, which is advisory to the ruler, though some states have taken some steps toward a more parliamentary form of deliberation. Experiments with democratic institutions, Western-style parliaments, and political parties have not proved successful, with the exception of Turkey. A new departure was the multi-party election in Iraq in 2005.

HISTORICAL DIVISIONS

The Middle East included two creative empires, those of Egypt and Persia (a non-Arab land). However, with the conquest of Baghdad by the Mongols in 1258, the Turks from central Asia dominated the leadership of the Islamic world; their hereditary sultans also became the caliphs. The adaptable Ottoman Empire, which captured Constantinople and defeated Byzantium in 1453, lasted over four centuries and ended in World War I.

After the eleventh century, Muslims encountered strong opposition in various parts of the territory they controlled. In 1492, Ferdinand and Isabella of Spain defeated the Moors and ended the last Islamic kingdom of Granada. The strong Ottoman Empire was defeated at the gates of Vienna in 1683, and again by Napoleon, who landed in Egypt in 1798. The Arab Muslim world began declining politically and militarily and was dominated by the rule or influence of four empires, those of Britain, France, Russia, and the Netherlands.

For most of the last two centuries, European states dominated the area, economically and militarily, and often ruled through colonies and protectorates. Since World War II, the United States has replaced European countries as the influential outside power in the region. For 30 years, until its end, the Soviet Union was a competitive power.

Most states in the Middle East are of recent origin, with their present boundaries dating from the end of World War I and the end of the Ottoman Empire, and some after World War II. Two states, Turkey, which succeeded the Ottoman Empire that was defeated in World War I, and Iran, are old independent states that never fell under imperial control. Three areas—Egypt, Lebanon, and the Arabian Peninsula—had considerable autonomy under the nominal control of their imperial rulers. Egypt was for centuries part of the Ottoman Empire and then under British control; however, it had its own political identity, with a local ruler, government, and administration. Lebanon, also a part of the Ottoman Empire, had some autonomy and separate identity as mostly Christian (Maronite) with Druze and Shiite minorities and it was ruled by local chiefs. After World War I, France enlarged Lebanon by adding a number of neighboring areas, mostly Muslim, to the original territory. The Arabian Peninsula was largely autonomous under the Ottomans and ruled by local tribal dynasties, one of which became the ruling dynasty of what is now Saudi Arabia.

Other states emerged from the mandates of the League of Nations in 1922 and from the areas governed by local leaders, often with undefined borders. Essentially, Britain was given the mandate to administer the areas of Palestine, Transjordan, at first a part of Palestine, and Iraq; France was given control over Syria and Lebanon. The two colonial powers revived the names Syria and Palestine from the past. Italy merged the ancient province of Tripolitania and Cyrenaica and called it Libya, a colony from 1911 to 1943. The most recent state is Yemen, which in 1990 merged the People's Democratic Republic of Yemen (South) with the Arab or North Republic to form the Islamic Republic of Yemen.

Israel was established in the area of Palestine in 1948 but has only been accepted by Egypt (1979) and Jordan (1994) in peace treaties. The Zionist movement founded under the leadership of Theodor Herzl in Basel in 1897 had declared: "The aim of Zionism is to create for the Jewish people a home in Palestine secured by public law." The British government's Balfour Declaration of November 2, 1917, announced its support for "the establishment in Palestine of a national home for the Jewish people." Recognizing the political difficulties of this, the declaration continued: "it being clearly understood that nothing shall be done which may prejudice the civil and religious rights of existing non-Jewish communities in Palestine."

Jewish settlements in Palestine, inspired by the various Zionist theories and the persecution of Jews by Nazi Germany after 1933, led to an increase in the area's Jewish population to 413,000 in 1938, and to 620,000 in 1948. Britain, which controlled Palestine under the League of Nations mandate, could not resolve the conflict between Jews and Arabs and passed the issue to the newly created United Nations. The United Nations by a resolution of the General Assembly on November 29, 1947, approved the partition of Palestine into independent Arab and Jewish states. The Arab League Council on December 17, 1947, refused to accept the UN proposal, and troops from five Arab countries began moving toward Palestine. The Jewish community in Palestine accepted the UN plan, and the People's Council representing that community (Yishuv) declared the independence of the state of Israel at a meeting in Tel Aviv on May 14, 1948. The next day Arab armies invaded the state. The question of Israel and of Palestine has not yet been resolved.

The Middle East has been the arena of turbulent conflicts. Over 20 border wars have taken place since 1945 as well as five clashes between Arabs and Israel. Differences are still acute not only over territory but also because of the aridity of the land, the growth of population, and the scarce water supply. The dominant economic factor remains oil. The Middle East accounts for one-third of the world's crude oil production, 10 percent of refined production, and much of the world's reserves. Partly because of oil wealth, the authoritarian regimes in the area have spent heavily on arms, importing more weapons than any other region in the world.

POLITICAL DIVISIONS

The most useful way to discuss the states of the Middle East is to divide them by the nature of their political regimes. They can be analyzed as democratic, partly democratic, authoritarian but not dictatorial, authoritarian or dictatorial, monarchies (hereditary or otherwise), and theocratic. The history, religious, and political conflicts of the region, however, are other factors that must be considered when forming an understanding of Middle Eastern political systems.

Democratic States

In the Freedom in the World 2005 survey issued by Freedom House, countries are listed as "free," "partly free," or "not free." These categories are related to the presence or absence of characteristics such as free expression, electoral democracies, free and fair voting, pluralistic societies, multiparty political structures and the ability to vote governments out of office peacefully. No Middle East Islamic or Arab country is in the "free" category. Among the least free are Egypt, Lebanon, Iran, Qatar, Oman, UAE, Iraq, Libya, Saudi Arabia, Syria, and Sudan. Among the "partly free" are Jordan, Kuwait, Turkey, and Yemen.

Only two countries in the Middle East, Israel and Turkey, with some qualification, can be characterized as democratic with direct, free elections for the executive and legislature and multiparty competition. Lebanon has an unstable political life in which the constitutional provisions for democracy have been only partly implemented. The other countries are highly centralized authoritarian systems of various kinds: monarchy, military dictatorship with the army as the ultimate source of power, one-party state, or theocracy run by clerics. Rulers include kings, emirs, sheikhs, sultans, and religious dignitaries. Democracy in the Western sense is still absent, though some countries such as Qatar and Bahrain have taken or promised to take steps to introduce some kind of parliamentary forum, and Iraq had an election in 2005.

Oil wells in Saudi Arabia.

Israel Israel is a republic established on May 14–15, 1948, with a parliamentary-cabinet system. It has a unicameral parliament (Knesset) of 120 members elected every four years by proportional representation and no individual constituencies. Until 1996, the prime minister and the cabinet, as in the British political system, came from the political party or coalition of parties that could control a majority of the Knesset. This was changed in 1996 with a law that the people would directly elect the prime minister in a separate election from that of the parliament. However, in 2001, the Knesset voted to restore the old system under which the legislature approves the prime minister. The president, an essentially ceremonial figure, is chosen by parliament for a five-year, renewable term.

Like Britain, Israel does not have a written constitution in a single document. It has a number of basic laws, starting with the Law of Return (1950), and dealing with important, specific issues. The official languages are Hebrew and Arabic. The present population is about 6 million: 80 percent are Jews, and 20 percent Arabs and Druze. Of the non-Jews, 15 percent are Muslim and 2 percent are Christian. The Jews come from over a hundred countries in the world, mostly from Europe and other Middle Eastern countries; the former Central and Eastern Europeans are Ashkenazim (the Hebrew word for German), while the Middle Eastern and North Africans are Sephardim (from the Hebrew word for Spain). Ethiopian Jews are known as Falashas (from the Amharic word for "dispossessed").

Since its creation, Israel has fought four wars (1948–1949, 1956, 1967, 1973) with Arab countries and an ongoing conflict with Palestinian Arabs. This conflict is significant not only in itself but also because it has become a symbolic unifying issue for the Arab and Islamic world. History, religion, and politics are all factors in the conflict in which Arabs, in general since 1949, opposed the state of Israel and called for a Palestinian state in the disputed territories. The Palestine Liberation Organization (PLO) was founded in 1964, merging eight guerrilla groups, of which al Fatah, led by Yasir Arafat, was the main one. The PLO's National Covenant, amended in 1968, speaks of Palestine as the homeland of the Arab people, claims the whole mandate area of Palestine, calls for a struggle to liberate Palestine, and declares the establishment of the state of Israel "null and void." The Arab leaders at a conference in Rabat in 1974 declared that the PLO was the sole legitimate representative of the Palestinian people. The United Nations General Assembly in October 1974 recognized the PLO officially.

Following the Six-Day War between Israel and Arab states in June 1967, the UN Security Council adopted Resolution 242, which called on all the belligerents to end the fighting and to respect the sovereignty, territorial integrity, and political independence of every state in the area and their right "to live in peace within secure and recognized boundaries free from threats or acts of force." It also called on Israel to withdraw from "territories occupied in the recent conflict"—the West Bank, Gaza, the Sinai Peninsula, and the Golan Heights. The resolution was not implemented. As a result of the 1973 Arab-Israeli War, the UN Security Council on October 22, 1973, adopted Resolution 338, which called for cessation of hostilities, for the implementation of 242, and for negotiations to aim at establishing a "just and durable" peace in the Middle East. Resolution 338 led to a cease-fire and a UN police presence in the area.

If a comprehensive peace has not been achieved, some adversarial relationships have ended. In March 1979, Egypt and Israel ended their state of war when the two leaders, Anwar Sadat and Menachem Begin, signed a peace agreement witnessed by President Jimmy Carter in the White House. Israel withdrew completely from the Sinai and dismantled all Jewish settlements in the Peninsula. In October 1994, King Hussein of Jordan signed a peace treaty with Israel.

No peace treaty or final agreement has yet been reached between Israel and the Palestinians, though some agreements were signed in the 1990s. The agreement reached in Oslo in 1993 led Israel to withdraw from parts of the West Bank and Gaza, and to the creation of a Palestinian Authority. At first the Palestinian Authority was composed of members of the PLO but later included members of the Palestinian Legislative

Council (PLC) and the Palestinian National Council (PNC). The inhabitants of territories in the West Bank and Gaza elect the 88 members of the PLC. The PNC, with 422 members, represents those outside these territories. By these arrangements, a formal link exists between Palestinians living in the territories and those living abroad. The president of the Palestinian National Authority, and long-time head of the PLO, Yasir Arafat, died in 2004 and was replaced in 2005 by Mahmoud Abbas, who was elected with 62 percent of the vote.

Turkey Turkey's encounter with political democracy has been troubled. The Republic of Turkey came into existence, replacing the Ottoman Empire, after World War I. An uprising led by Mustafa Kemal, later called Ataturk, led the way to a new government and the creation in October 1923 of Turkey as a republic. The caliphate of Islam was abolished in 1924; religious courts were abolished and replaced by secular jurisdiction.

Ataturk was both president of the new Republic and leader of the new political party, the Republican People's Party (RPP), the two roles being interrelated. Ataturk imposed a mix of nationalism and secularism on the country; the Turks would give up the Ottoman past and look to Europe. The RPP designated itself as republican, nationalist, secular, populist, and as favoring a kind of state socialism. Ataturk assumed dictatorial powers in 1925 after a revolt by the Kurdish minority and problems with Muslim clergy. Modernization and Westernization were introduced: religious orders were closed; the fez was forbidden and Western headgear substituted; women were told not to wear the veil; the Latin alphabet and the Western calendar were adopted; new codes of civil, criminal, and commercial law were formulated; women were given the vote. In 1928, Turkey officially became a secular state when the words "the religion of the Turkish State is Islam" were eliminated from the constitution adopted in 1924. Ataturk, who died in 1938, had transformed Turkish society and politics, attempting to make the country more Western than Middle Eastern.

After World War II, Turkey had its first genuine democratic experiment with elections based on secret ballot and new independent parties (although Communist and Islamic parties were not allowed). The result in 1950 was an overwhelming victory for the opposition Democrat Party, defeating the RPP, which had held power for 27 years. Since then, the democratic process has been interrupted four times (1960, 1971, 1980, and 1997), by military coups or interventions caused by various factors: divisive party activities, political extremism, terrorism, Kurdish revolts, corruption, Islamic activity, and a faltering economy. The military regarded itself as the guardian of the country and the group that would safeguard democracy. At different times the military set up a National Unity Community of senior military officers which at various times conducted government (1960), declared martial law, set up State Security Courts (1970), dissolved Parliament and trade unions (1980), and arrested political leaders and even executed some of them (1961). Yet each intervention by the military was temporary and transitional to foster a democratic system.

The constitution was changed in 1961 and again in 1982, the latter allowing the return of political parties. Competitive free elections have resulted in different parties gaining power. One of them is the Islamic party, set up in 1970 as the National Order Party and renamed in 1989 as Refah (Welfare Party). This party benefited from a certain amount of religious revival, religious education in schools and universities, a network of schools for training imams and preachers, increased attendance at mosques, and Islamic study groups. It won the mayoralties of Istanbul and Ankara in 1994 and got one-fifth of the votes for the National Assembly in 1995, becoming the largest single party. Its leader Necmettin Erbakan became prime minister in 1996. His program of Islamization, however, led to pressure from the military, without the use of violence, for his resignation in 1997. His party was dissolved but reappeared under another name, Wisdom Party. Since 1997, Turkey has experienced coalition governments under a number of different prime ministers.

Turkey has confronted a number of difficult issues: the Kurdish demand for autonomy, religious fundamentalism, and political instability with the constant change and fragmentation of coalitions and parties. Politics in Turkey have been unusual in that the military has intervened, restored order, and then withdrawn after facilitating the democratic process and the changing of governments by free elections. In the effort to overcome traditionalism in political and religious matters, Turkish democracy has been relatively successful, and its experiment in parliamentary democracy, with all its setbacks and problems, is a striking example of the move to modernization. It is still forbidden to wear a headscarf in a government building or a public university, and a crime to use ethnic or religious symbolism for political purposes. In 2001, the state closed the main Islamicist party, but its members soon formed other groups, including the Justice and Development Party, led by a former mayor of Istanbul. This party won the election in 2002 and formed the government.

Partly Democratic States

Lebanon had an autonomous existence in the Ottoman Empire. In 1922, France was given the League of Nations mandate over it and increased the size of the country by adding areas from surrounding territories. To the original mainly Maronite Christian population (Arabic-speaking members of a Uniate Church) was added a substantial Muslim population in the new "Greater Lebanon." It became a republic in 1926, though not fully independent until 1946. Politics in Lebanon has been acutely affected by the conflicts between the different religious communities: the various Christian groups, Maronites, Greek Orthodox; Greek Catholic, Armenian Orthodox; and the Muslim groups, the Shiites in the south and the Sunnis.

In 1943, the concept of "confessionalism" was implemented—the sharing of political representation, in a fixed fashion, on the basis of the size of each religious community according to the 1932 census. Positions in the executive, legislature, administration, judiciary, and armed forces were allotted on this formula. The legislature

was fixed at six Christians for every five non-Christians. The president was to be a Maronite, the prime minister a Sunni Muslim, and the speaker of the parliament a Shiite. The result was a bargaining process involving not only the Christian, Muslim, and Druze religious groups, but also the leaders of the different clans and notable families in the Christian community, each with its own paramilitary force. The mathematical distribution of offices and the consequent minority position of non-Christians remained, even though it seemed clear that by the 1960s the Muslim population was larger than the Christian. This discrepancy, and economic disparities between the wealthier Christian community and the poorer Muslims, led to daily conflicts in the streets and finally to civil war in 1975, when hostilities began between the Christian Phalange and the Palestine Liberation Organization, which had established its headquarters in Beirut after being forced to leave Jordan in 1970. Syrian forces intervened in the conflict and remained to occupy part of the country. The war led to about 60,000 deaths and many thousands injured.

The war also halted the democratic process in Lebanon, which had been an open society in spite of the religious, ethnic, and political differences. The imperfect democracy became a system in which political authority was unclear, Syria was influential, and the PLO was active until the invasion by Israel in 1982 forced its withdrawal from West Beirut. Resulting from the conflict was the assassination of Bashir Gemayel, the Phalangist president-elect on September 14, 1982. In reprisal, on September 17–18, Phalange militia entered the Palestinian refugee camps of Sabra and Shatilla, killing hundreds of inhabitants before Israeli forces were able to stop the killing. The Lebanese civil war continued into the 1990s.

In 1990 the constitution was amended, changing the 1943 power-sharing arrangement. A Christian would still hold the presidency, but the cabinet would be equally divided between Christians and Muslims, as would seats in the legislature. The unicameral national assembly of 128 members is elected by proportional representation reflecting the sectarian groups. Assembly members serve for four years. The assembly elects the president for a six-year term, and the president in consultation with the assembly appoints the prime minister. Israel withdrew from its security zone in southern Lebanon in May 2000; Syria still maintains about 25,000 troops in Lebanon.

Authoritarian but Not Dictatorial States

Egypt   The outstanding example of a regime that is authoritarian but not dictatorial is Egypt, which has a history going back 5,000 years. It became part of the Islamic empire in the seventh century, ruled first by representatives of the caliph and then by independent dynasties. In 1517, Egypt became a province of the Ottoman Empire, which conquered it and retained jurisdiction over it. Mohammed Ali was sent to govern the area and remained to set up a dynasty under the sovereignty of the Ottoman sultan, but it was virtually autonomous. Britain in 1882 invaded the area, setting up a military occupation and a form of protectorate, which was only formally declared in 1914 and which lasted until 1922. At this point, Egypt became an independent, sovereign state with a monarch. Britain kept a military presence there and controlled foreign policy, but, in a treaty with Egypt, agreed in 1936 to withdraw its troops except for those guarding the Suez Canal.

Growing dissatisfaction with the monarchy and a desire for national reform led a group of young officers, the Free Officers Organization, led by Gamal Abdel Nasser, to mount in July 1952 a bloodless coup seizing power and abolishing the monarchy. Egypt became a republic in February 1953. At first a collegial Revolutionary Command Council under General Mohammad Naguib exercised powers; in 1954, Nasser replaced him as the leader. For 15 years, Nasser was the dominant figure in the Arab world and in the pan-Arab national movement. He attempted to change both domestic and foreign policy. Internally, he called for a form of "Arab socialism," agrarian reform, nationalization of banks and major corporations, and a minimum wage. In foreign policy he advocated the struggle against European colonialism and imperialism, a neutralist position in the Cold War though he

accepted weapons from the Soviet Union in 1955, and support for the Palestinians in the conflict with Israel. He also played a leading role in the nonaligned movement. Not all of his endeavors were successful. His intervention in Yemeni civil war failed, as did an attempted merger among Egypt, Syria, and Yemen. The union with Syria, forming in 1958 the United Arab Republic with Nasser as president, ended in 1961. The country kept the UAR name until 1971, when it was renamed the Arab Republic of Egypt. Egypt's participation in the Arab-Israeli conflict in 1956 and 1967 led to the loss of the Sinai Peninsula. Nasser's nationalization of the Suez Canal in July 1956 led to a British-French attack and to invasion by Israel.

Nasser ruled with the support of a network of officers loyal to him. He also set up a one-party system, abolishing all existing parties and establishing at first a Liberation Rally and a National Union and then in 1962 the Arab Socialist Union. The ASU tried to mobilize the population, bringing together different groups in the country and assisting peasants, workers cooperatives, and trade unions. It was an anticapitalist party, but one that excluded Communists or Marxists. In 1965, Nasser became secretary of the ASU, which overlapped with his position in the government.

At first Nasser sought support from Islamic activists. The Muslim Brotherhood, with a creed of strict observance of Islamic doctrine, originated in Egypt in 1928 and was to become the most prominent Islamicist organization in the Arab world. Part of the Brotherhood became an extreme group engaging in terrorism against Western influence and was suspected of trying to assassinate Nasser. This violence led Nasser to change policy and to struggle against fundamentalists. The Brotherhood was suppressed after 1954.

Nasser, who died in 1970, was succeeded by Anwar Sadat, who had engaged in anti-British military conspiracies in the 1940s. Sadat had been a junior officer with Nasser and a government official after the army took power. Sadat modified Nasser's radical policies and launched an "Open Door" policy to tie Egypt's economy to the West and encourage foreign investment. He got rid of political and military rivals in 1971, a number of whom were sentenced to death, though Sadat commuted the sentences to life imprisonment. He allowed rival bodies first as groups within the ASU and then as separate organizations. The ASU in 1979 was transformed into the National Democratic Party, the ruling group that was powerful in government, security, and media organizations. A multiparty system was intended, but Communist, Islamic, and Nasserist groups were banned, and trade unions were controlled.

Sadat also changed foreign policy. In 1971 he signed a treaty of friendship with the Soviet Union but the next year expelled Soviet advisers from the country. He launched war against Israel in October 1973, making some initial gains, though losing in the end. Nevertheless, he emerged a national hero. Sadat goes down in history as the first Arab leader to make formal peace with Israel, first with his visit to Jerusalem in November 1977, then through the Camp David Accords, bringing him together with Menachem Begin of Israel during the presidency of Jimmy Carter in September 1978, and then the treaty with Israel in March 1979. The state of war between the two countries was terminated. Israel withdrew its troops from the Sinai Peninsula and from Sharm al-Shaykh. Sadat was acknowledged internationally and shared the Nobel Peace Prize with Begin.

Internal opposition had not ended, however. His economic policies reducing state subsidies in 1977 led to riots. More crucial was the opposition of Islamic fundamentalists to his attempts at modernization. In 1981, a Muslim extremist assassinated him at a military parade. Hosni Mubarak, his vice president, who emphasized continuation of existing policies and sought social and political stability, succeeded Sadat. This has meant maintaining the peace with Israel and a continuing transition to a market economy.

The authoritarian Egyptian regime is underpinned by the military, from which all the rulers since 1953 have come. The leader, the president, is nominated by the People's Assembly for a six-year term and approved by a national referendum. He appoints all senior political posts and sets general policy.

Egypt's bicameral system is composed of the People's Assembly and the Advisory Council. Most of the 454-members assembly is elected by popular vote; the president appoints ten of the members. The official party, the National Democratic, largely bureaucrats, usually dominates the Assembly. However, at the election in 2000, one generally regarded as fair, some surprises occurred. One was that the NDP, which was divided because of internal differences leading many members to run as independents, only got 175 seats. The other surprise was the presence in the Assembly of fundamentalists. The Muslim Brotherhood is still banned, but some of its members ran as independents and were elected to 17 seats.

Two-thirds of the Advisory Council is elected by popular vote and one-third is appointed by the president. The Council provides advice on legislation before it is presented to the Assembly.

Among the many issues confronting Egypt is that of a rapidly increasing population: 40 million in 1980 and 76 million in 2005. Egypt has about 15 million teenagers. About 33 percent of the population is under 15.

Yemen   A new unified country, Yemen, is undergoing a process of transition but presently can be characterized as an authoritarian state. The Republic of Yemen was established in May 1990 with the merger of the traditional, conservative, and secular Yemen Arab Republic (North Yemen) and the Marxist-dominated People's Democratic Republic of Yemen (South Yemen). North Yemen, with 80 percent of the total population of 13 million, had ties to the West, while South Yemen was regarded as an ally of the Soviet Union and was controlled by a communist party, the Yemeni Socialist Party. Sana, the former capital of the North, became the capital of the new state, while Aden, the former capital of the South, is the commercial capital. The head of the Socialist Party, Ali Abdullah Saleh, was elected by the combined parliaments of the two countries as president of the new state.

Differences over power sharing led to a civil war in 1994, but the conflict was over within months when the North gained control. The president's party, the People's Congress, won a landslide parliamentary victory in the 1997 election, and in 1999 Saleh was elected president with 96.3 percent of the popular vote. By a constitutional amendment of February 2001 a bicameral legislature was established: the Shura Council of 111 is nominated by the president, and the House of Representatives of 301 is elected by popular vote. The country however remains troubled by Islamic militants who have attacked tourists, government officials, oil workers, and in October 2000 the U.S. Navy destroyer *Cole* in the Port of Aden. Progress to privatization in the economy has been slow, though the government is required by the IMF and World Bank to initiate such a program. Export of oil remains the main source of hard currency revenue. In the 2005 ranking by Freedom House, Yemen is classified as partly free with low scores in political rights and civil liberties.

Authoritarian States or Dictatorships

Iraq under Saddam Hussein, Libya under Muammar Qaddafi, and Syria under Hafez al-Assad and his son Bashar al-Assad are all dictatorship or under authoritarian rule. These rulers have been supported not only by the military but also by the single party allowed: the Baath in Iraq and Syria, and the Arab Socialist Union in Libya.

Iraq   The territory of Iraq was for over five centuries ruled by various dynasties, mostly based in Persia and then, from 1534 to 1918, by the Ottoman Empire. Under the post–World War I British mandate, a monarchy was set up under Faisal, a Hashemite prince originally from the Arabian Peninsula and the brother of the emir Abdullah in Transjordan. The Hashemite dynasty was overthrown by a military coup in 1958 and King Faisal II murdered. For a number of years, turmoil and military rule followed. General Abdel Karim Kassem took power but was unable to reconcile internal differences and resorted to repressive measures. Another coup in 1963 brought Colonel Abdul Salam Mohammad Arif to power; he executed Kassem and set up the National Council of the Revolutionary Command in which the Baath party played a prominent role.

The Baath party developed from a movement in Syria that advocated Arab unity, theoretical socialism, and a centralized secular state transcending tribal links and local loyalties. Initially the party cooperated with the military. However, differences between the party and Arif led him to disband the Baath paramilitary organization and create a one-party state through the Arab Socialist Union and the National Revolutionary Council. After Arif's death in a plane crash in 1966, and a short interregnum by his brother, a coup in 1968 by General Ahmad Hassan al-Bakr brought another military ruler and the entrance of the Baath into prominent positions, though still a minority.

Al-Bakr came from the small town of Takrit, about 100 miles north of Baghdad. Many of his associates came from the same area, one of whom was Saddam Hussein, leader of the Iraqi Baath party. In 1979, Saddam replaced the sick al-Bakr, becoming president, head of state, chair of the Revolutionary Command Council, head of the Baath, prime minister, and commander in chief. Protected by a strong security apparatus, Saddam eliminated his rivals in politics, the military, and the party. As a Sunni Muslim ruling over a largely Shiite population, Saddam faced the ire of the new leader in Iran, the Ayatollah Khomeini, who called on the Iraqi Shiites to oppose the anti-Islamic policies of Saddam and the Baath party. The result was a long war (1980–1988) between the two countries, causing heavy casualties.

In 1990, Saddam invaded Kuwait, declared it annexed as Iraq's nineteenth province, and threatened Saudi Arabia. In response the United States sent military forces to the Gulf States, culminating in Operation Desert Storm, the offensive in January 1991 by a coalition led by the United States against Iraq. After a month of air bombing and 100 hours of land warfare, the Iraqis retreated and Kuwait was declared liberated. Saddam Hussein remained in power, supported above all by the Takriti clan. Russia did not support Iraq, as the Soviet Union did in the 1970s with political help, military weapons, technicians, and advisers. The Baath party constituted the only important political organization in the country.

In Iraq, as in Syria, the ruling personnel chosen
by the authoritarian leader came from a small
group: in Iraq from the city of Takrit, and in Syria
from the sect of Alawis, the unorthodox Muslim
group located in the northwest of the country. The
U.S-led military campaign in Iraq in 2003 led to
the downfall of the regime of Saddam Hussein,
who was later arrested, to the establishment of
an interim Iraqi government and to a free election in the country.

Syria   The Arabs, bringing with them the religion of Islam, conquered Syria, a province of the
Byzantine Empire. Damascus became the capital
of the first caliphate at the time of the Omayyads
in 661, and the center of the Islamic Empire.
After World War I, France administered the
League of Nations mandate from 1923 to 1946.
Families of the Sunni Muslim majority and military persons dominated the country. In the
1950s, the Baath (Resurrection) movement
began, first in Syria and then in Iraq, arguing for
the removal of foreign influence, nationalization
of industry, and provision of social services, and
for Arab unity. In Syria the Baath resulted in
1953 from the merger between the Arab Socialists and the Arab Resurrection Party. Ten years
later the underground committee of military officers, of whom Hafez al-Assad was one of the
main leaders, staged a successful coup. After
becoming general secretary of the Baath Party,
Assad played a major role in another shift in
power in 1966, eliminating rivals and ending
conflicts in the party. By a 1964 constitution,
Syria became a Democratic Socialist Republic,
though Islam was declared the state religion, and
the chief political body was the National Revolutionary Council. A 1969 constitution made the
Baath the only legal party. Another constitution
introduced in 1971 was approved in 1973.

In November 1970, Assad became prime
minister, and then president by a referendum in
March 1971, and he was confirmed as general
secretary of the party. Assad had been minister
of defense and commander in chief of the air
force before becoming president. By the new secular constitution, Assad as president was given
power to appoint all ministers. He was soon
chair of the National Progressive Front, which

combined all political parties under the leadership of the Baath. Syria had established a virtual
one-party system. The NPF controlled a majority
of the seats in the People's Assembly, an elected
group, but one that did not initiate legislation.

The Baath controls the choice of candidates
as well as the media and institutions and organizations throughout the country. Assad was an
Alawi, the Shiite group that constitutes about 10
percent of the population and who are generally
regarded as a deprived minority. Effective power
is in the hands of the armed forces and the internal security agencies, all of which are led by officers from the Alawi sect. Many Alawites,
including Assad, a fighter pilot, had joined the
military as a means of advancement, and the
Alawites occupied prominent positions under
Assad. The secular Baath party was useful to justify the Alawite control over the Sunni majority.
It was also useful to bolster Assad's call for a
"greater Syria," which would include Jordan,
Lebanon, Israel, and parts of Turkey.

Relying on his security group, the praetorian
guard, and the military, Assad dealt with the
threat to his regime from Islamic fundamentalists
first by making membership of the Muslim Brotherhood a capital offense in 1981, and then in February 1982 bombing the fundamentalists in the
town of Hama, ruining the city and killing perhaps
as many as 20,000 people. In February 1999,
Assad was re-elected to his fifth term as president
by 99.98 percent of the vote, similar to his support
in earlier elections. He died a year later. Hereditary succession is a familiar method in the Middle
East, dating back to antiquity. In Muslim countries, the usual practice was for the ruler to nominate not necessarily his eldest son, but the person
seen to be most appropriate. The last four
Ottoman sultans (1876–1922) were all brothers.

The son of Hafez al-Assad, Bashar, was the
designated heir after the death of his elder
brother. He had studied ophthalmology in England but returned to Syria on his brother's death
and was appointed colonel and commander in
chief of an armored division. An immediate
problem was that Bashar was 34 when his father
died, and the 1973 constitution had set 40 as the
minimum age for a president. Parliament immediately assembled to amend the constitution by

lowering the minimum age for the presidency to 34; the vote was unanimous and took 15 minutes. Bashar was nominated to and confirmed as president by referendum in July 2000, getting 97 percent of the vote.

Libya The ancient province of Tripolitania was renamed Libya by Italy, which administered it as a colony from 1911 to 1942. The country in December 1951 gained independence as a monarchy under King Idris, who had lived in Egypt for 30 years. Libya, historically a very poor area, was transformed by discovery of oil in its territory in 1959. The king was deposed in September 1969 by a military coup headed by a junior officer in the signal corps, the 27-year-old Muammar Qaddafi, born in a tent to a Beduin family. The monarchy was abolished and replaced by the Socialist Libyan Arab Republic. At its head was Qaddafi, the unpredictable man who remains the head of state. He created a Revolutionary Command Council and, strongly influenced by Nasser, sought Arab unity. He purged the bureaucracy and emphasized Islamic law.

Qaddafi's idiosyncratic political thought and a system he called Jamahiriyah (state of the masses) are outlined in his "Green Book." Critical of Western-style democracy, he advocated bringing the true Islam to Libya and to the whole Islamic world, envisaging himself as creating a new order. That order was to include temporary unions with Egypt and Tunisia, both of which ended quickly. Qaddafi received weapons from the Soviet Union into the early 1980s, encouraged international terrorism, supported the various factions of the PLO, and invaded the neighboring Chad in 1988. Qaddafi's activities led President Reagan to order the shooting down of Libyan aircraft by U.S. Navy fighters over the Gulf of Sidra, and a raid on his headquarters in Tripoli in 1986.

Qaddafi is the authoritarian leader of the country, but the political system has been rather confusing. Political parties are banned on the grounds that they are specific interest groups. Also banned are parliamentary government and majority rule. The Revolutionary Command Council for a time (1969–1977), with Qaddafi's supporters, dominated the decision-making process

throughout the country. In its place are sets of committees to which all citizens belong. These 2,000 Basic Popular Congresses discuss policies and elect delegates to the General People's Congress, which meets twice a year and elects the General Popular Committee, the executive, of which Qaddafi was president until 1979. He also set up the Revolutionary Committee movement that is directly responsible to him and has been a method of repression. Another important power level is that of tribal groups whose members occupy all crucial positions. The indispensable figure, Qaddafi, who has encountered problems with many parts of his society, including intellectuals, disillusioned young officers, and Islamicists, has not had any formal title since 1979.

Monarchies with Limited Consultation

Some Middle East states are monarchies in which the people have no system of democratic representation, but in which the monarch or ruling family may consult with a council or assembly. The major example of this form of regime is Saudi Arabia. Similar monarchies exist in Oman, Qatar, Bahrain, and the United Arab Emirates (UAE).

Saudi Arabia The crucial fact concerning Saudi Arabia is that it currently supplies 10 percent of the world's oil and contains two-thirds of all known oil deposits in the Middle East. The discovery of oil in 1938 transformed the country economically and established significant contact with the United States, which presently imports 50 percent of Saudi Arabia's oil. But traditional Saudi values remain: men and women are separated in many public places and in schools, and a police force ensures "public decency."

Saudi Arabia is a kingdom proclaimed by Abdul Aziz (ibn Saud) in 1932, put together by a confederation of tribes and family groups after he conquered rival tribes in the Arabian Peninsula and consolidated them, partly by marrying into them. Saudi Arabia is the only country named after a family, the al-Saud tribe, which still rules and which now has at least 7,000 members.

The authority of the Saudi family largely rests on its role as the upholder of Islamic values

ORGANIZATION OF PETROLEUM EXPORTING COUNTRIES (OPEC)

OPEC, established in 1960, is an international organization of 11 developing countries that are heavily reliant on oil revenues as their main source of income. Membership is open to any country that is a substantial exporter of oil and shares the ideals of the organization. The current members are Algeria, Indonesia, Iran, Iraq, Kuwait, Libya, Nigeria, Qatar, Saudi Arabia, the United Arab Emirates, and Venezuela. Twice a year, or more frequently if required, the oil and energy ministers of the OPEC members meet to decide on the organization's oil output and consider whether to adjust the level of output in light of recent and anticipated oil market developments. OPEC's members collectively supply about 40 percent of the world's oil output and possess more than three-quarters of the world's crude oil reserves.

and the guardian of the Islamic holy shrines of Mecca and Medina. It also offers financial aid to Islamic causes and foundations, schools, and charities and has funded over 1,600 mosques throughout the world. The al-Saud family became more important in the Arabian Peninsula with its alliance in 1744 with Mohammad Abdul Wahhab, the puritanical theologian who advocated the strict application of Islamic law. Saud, the son-in-law of Mohammad Abdul Wahhab, accepted the doctrine of discipline and piety and began the campaign of spreading the Islamic fundamentalist Wahhabism throughout Arabia, defeating other local tribes in the process and establishing a capital at Riyadh in 1824. The country is governed on the basis of the *sharia,* Islamic law.

The Saudi family rules the regime, and the holy men descended from Mohammad Abdul Wahhab provide religious legitimacy. Representation is limited to the Shura council, a consultative assembly with no legislative powers. Clerics have authority over functions such as school curriculums and building codes. No political parties are allowed, but the consultative council was formalized in 1992 with a mix of clan and religious leaders, government officials, business and professional men, including academics who advised the king in the 1990s. The king rules but needs consensus from leading figures in his family and in society.

Saudi Arabia is important not only because of its vast reserves of oil, but also, for the Islamic and Arab world, because it controls the holy cities and is custodian of the two holy mosques. One of the five pillars or religious duties of Muslims is to make a pilgrimage (*Haj*) to Mecca and Medina at least once in a lifetime. About two million made the pilgrimage in 2005.

The Gulf States Bahrain, Qatar, and the seven smaller Gulf State emirates, Abu Dhabi, Dubai, Sharjah, Ras al-Khaimah, Fujairah, Umm al Qaiwain, and Ajman, were protectorates of Britain, which provided them with political advisers and supervision by a Resident. In all of them, essentially emirates, politics revolve around the ruling family and wealthy merchants with some consultative group. Wealth resulting from oil supplies strengthened the position and authority of the ruler. The states became independent in the 1970s. Each of the emirates has had a turbulent history of factional rivalries within the ruling family, including assassinations and overthrow by coup of the ruler.

Bahrain is ruled by a single family that shares official positions, aided by some Western-educated persons associated with wealthy merchants. A sheikh is at its head. The National Assembly was dissolved in 1975 and was not reinstated in spite of the demand by Shiite activist clergy. However, a consultative assem-

A CLOSER LOOK
9.4

GULF COOPERATION COUNCIL

The members of the Gulf Cooperation Council are Bahrain, Kuwait, United Arab Emirates, Qatar, Saudi Arabia, and Oman. The council was created in 1981 to coordinate economic, political, cultural, and security policy in the face of threats from fundamentalist Iran, from Iraq, and from the Soviet Union, at that time intervening in Afghanistan. In 1991 the council joined with Egypt and Syria to create a regional peacekeeping force.

bly has been promised by 2004. Qatar, with about 100,000 citizens and a population of 650,000, is the wealthiest country per capita in the Middle East. It is headed by a sheikh who deposed his father in 1995, after years of internal dissent among family leaders. It is supposed to have an advisory council but dissenters have been discouraged.

The United Arab Emirates, a federation of seven emirates, was formed in 1971–1972. It has a ruler presiding over the Supreme Federal Council of the seven rulers, which protects the rights of the seven states, electing the president, ratifying federal legislation, and approving the appointment of ministers. Real power lies with the senior members of the ruling families. A consultative Federal National Council debates issues but does not initiate legislation. The most important of the emirates are Abu Dhabi and Dubai, which fund and supply the members of the bureaucracy.

Oman is governed by a sultan, Qabus, who overthrew his father in 1970 and holds most of the political positions: prime minister, foreign minister, minister of defense, minister of finance, and chair of the central bank. He dramatically increased the per capita income of his 2.6 million people to about $8,000. Qabus announced in 1980 the appointment of the Consultative Council to advise him. An elected council replaced this in 1991, but the sultan approves who is nominated to be candidates. A noticeable feature is that some women are on the council as well as holding professional and government jobs. However, no opposition parties exist, and no public criticism is allowed of the sultan.

Monarchies with Representative Elements

Some Middle East states are monarchies that allow for a level of representative government. The chief examples of this type of regime are Jordan and Kuwait.

Jordan   Jordan stems from the eastern part of the League of Nations mandate for Palestine, which was detached from the rest by Britain in 1922 to become the emirate of Transjordan under Abdullah, a member of the Hashemite family. This family claims descent from the prophet Mohammed's tribe and ruled Mecca and the Hejaz section of the Arabian Peninsula from the tenth century to the early twentieth. They were the protectors of the holy cities of Mecca and Medina, but the army of ibn Saud defeated the family of Hashemites in 1925. Ibn Saud incorporated the Hejaz into his own rule and soon became ruler of the new Saudi Arabia.

The Hashemites under Hussein ibn Ali had helped Britain in World War I in the fight against the Ottoman Empire. In return, after the war, Britain installed one of Hussein's sons, Faisal, first as king of Syria and then, after he was forced to leave in 1920, king of Iraq. Another son, Abdullah, was given Transjordan, an area largely populated by Beduins and protected by Britain with financial aid and with the Arab Legion led by a British officer. The country was autonomous but not independent until 1946, when it became the kingdom of Transjordan. During the Arab-Israeli war of 1948–1949, it seized east Jerusalem and the West Bank (the area west of the Jordan River). In 1950 the king annexed the West Bank and renamed the country the kingdom of Jordan. Jordan gave citizenship to Palestinian refugees, the only country to do so. (During the 1967 Arab-Israeli war, Jordan was forced to withdraw from the West Bank, which then came under Israeli occupation.)

Between 1949 and 1967, Jordan ruled over Palestinian Arabs some of whom, concerned about the policies of a Hashemite king, assassinated Abdullah in July 1950. A brief reign by Talal, son of Abdullah, ended in 1952 because of his mental disorder. His son Hussein, who became king in 1953 on his eighteenth birthday, succeeded him. Jordan has been troubled by internal problems occasioning the imposition of martial law for ten years over a 16-year period, by the presence of Palestinian refugees who now constitute over half the population, by the immigration of 600,000 foreign workers, by the struggle with the Palestinian Liberation Organization within its territory, by rivalries with surrounding Arab countries, and by the wars with Israel in 1948–1949, 1967, and 1973. King Hussein accepted the invitation to discuss peace with Israel and in 1994 signed a peace treaty. Hussein had a precarious personal as well as political life. After surviving a number of assassination attempts, he died of natural causes in 1999 after a reign of 46 years. He was succeeded by his son, the present King Abdullah II, who was educated in Britain and the United States.

From the start, the king in Jordan has dominated policy making and has depended on support of loyal Beduin citizens who form the bulk of the Royal Jordanian Army. Though King Hussein was obliged to recognize the PLO as the sole legitimate organ of the Palestinians, he did not accord any significant role to the Palestinians resident in Jordan. He controlled the legislation, the military, and foreign policy. However, Jordan has had to face not only the possible conflict over the question of Palestine, but also economic difficulties and Islamic fundamentalism. To help deal with these, Hussein proposed a more pluralistic society with a multiparty system and repeal of martial law, in effect since 1967, but his attempt at creating a consensus was frustrated by opposition to his peace treaty with Israel and his support for United States policies toward Iraq. Between 1991 and 1999, eight cabinets failed to create the desired consensus. The new King Abdullah faces many difficulties.

Jordan has a bicameral National Assembly. The upper house, the Senate, consists of 55 members appointed by the king from various categories of public life for a four-year term. The lower house, the House of Representatives, is composed of 110 members elected for four years by popular vote on the basis of proportional representation. The House has been convened and dissolved by the monarch on a number of occasions.

Kuwait Kuwait has been dominated by the al Sabah family for 250 years and became an independent state in 1961. The head of state must be a member of the al Sabah family, according to the 1962 constitution, which can be amended or suspended by the emir. The rule has alternated between two branches of the family, the Jaber and Salim branches.

The present emir, Sheikh Jaber, has held the position for almost 30 years, can issue decrees, and generally rules through a Council of Ministers headed by a prime minister who is chosen by the emir. The constitution also provides for a National Assembly, which is partly elected and partly appointed. On a number of occasions, the assembly has been dismissed by the emir because of criticism from political opponents and Shiites which was felt to endanger national security. The army and security services have been used to suppress the Islamicist movement, removing Shiites from official and military positions.

Theocracy

The only Middle Eastern state that can be designated as theocratic—government by clerics claiming to rule with devine authority or claiming that power comes from God, the ultimate source of authority and sole source of legislation—is Iran, which was officially proclaimed an Islamic republic in 1979. Before this, for over 2000 years, a monarch, a shah, had ruled Iran, the territory known in the West as Persia until

1935. The last shah was Mohammad Reza, who adopted the dynastic name of Pahlavi. He was overthrown in 1979 by a revolt bringing the exiled Shiite theologian Ayatollah Khomeini to power. Khomeini instituted a regime based on Islamic fundamentalism, with the *sharia* as the fount of law and God as the sole source of power. The use of power is based on God's will and can be delegated to spiritual leaders. The ruling theologian (*wali faqih*) is the chief religious authority in Iran, both judge and leader of the Shiite community, issuing legal edicts. Khomeini, who held power until his death in 1989, was the absolute authority, making all important decisions and in control of the army, security, and judiciary. Khomeini, the imam (spiritual leader), was selected by a group of senior clerics (the Assembly of Experts) whom he had chosen.

In the republic, a number of political institutions are present: the president (the head of state), the prime minister (the head of government), and an elected assembly (*majlis*). But all are subordinate to the leading theologian (*wali faqih*) or to the council of spiritual leaders, the Revolution Council, composed of the chief ayatollahs. The title of ayatollah (literally "sign of God"), which was created in Iran in the nineteenth century, is bestowed on important religious leaders. The chief political party is the Islamic Republican Party, which is the political arm of the Shiite dignitaries who also control the operation of the secret police (*Savama*), the revolutionary committees (*Komitehs*) that are groups of religious extremists throughout the country, and the Revolutionary Guard (*Pasdaran*), a paramilitary organization. The leadership of the military is also controlled by the clerics (the mullahs). The Guardian Council, a conservative group, supervises elections. It has annulled some election results, blocked parliamentary legislation, and prevented candidates from running.

In recent years, differences between ideological and political factions have arisen. The courts have banned a number of publications that called for reform and more freedom, and they jailed political dissenters. Religious minorities have been subjected to restrictions and persecutions.

The Kurds, Sunni Muslim minorities who live in the western part of the country, have suffered from these restrictions. The differences in Iran are reflected by two current figures: the supreme leader, Ayatollah Ali Khamenei, appointed for life, who is regarded as a conservative hardliner, and President Mohammad Khatami, who is viewed as a reformer. Khatami was re-elected in 2001 with 77 percent of the vote.

THE ARAB-ISRAELI CONFLICT AND THE PEACE PROCESS

By the Lausanne agreement of 1923, Turkey transferred all claims to the area of Palestine, which the Ottoman Empire had ruled, to Britain acting on behalf of the League of Nations as the administrator of the Palestinian Mandate. The area included what is now Jordan, Israel, and the areas occupied by Israel after 1967. Britain in 1922 granted about 80 percent of the total area of Palestine to the newly created Transjordan, the area east of the Jordan River. Continuing hostility and violence between Jews and Arabs in the remaining area led Britain in 1946 to abandon the mandate and pass the problem of Palestine to the United Nations to propose a solution to the conflict. The UN General Assembly on November 29, 1947, proposed the partition of the area west of the Jordan River into two separate states, one Jewish and the other Arab, and the internationalization of Jerusalem. The Arab League Council rejected the plan on December 17, 1947, and Arab irregular forces began moving toward Palestine. The representatives of the Jewish community (Yishuv) in Palestine met in Tel Aviv on May 14, 1948, declared the independence of the state of Israel, and set up a provisional government. The next day, regular armies from five Arab countries under the banner of the Arab League invaded Israel. In May 1949 armistice agreements were signed by Israel with Egypt, Syria, Lebanon, and Jordan; Iraq refused to sign any agreement. From 1948 to 1967 the West Bank, including East Jerusalem, was incorporated into and annexed by Transjordan (which later became the Kingdom of Jordan), and Egypt occupied the Gaza Strip. Israel occupied and annexed West Jerusalem within the state of Israel. The conflict continued with wars in 1956, 1967, 1973, and continuing violence.

In October–November 1956, Israel went through the Sinai and reached the Suez Canal. It withdrew from the area when a United Nations Emergency Force (UNEF) was interposed between Egypt and Israeli forces. Israel insisted on its right to navigate the straits of Tiran and the Gulf of Aqaba. The Six Day War of June 1967 took place after President Nasser of Egypt requested the withdrawal of the UNEF force and ordered the closing of the Straits of Tiran to ships bound for Israel. As a result of the Israeli victory, Israel occupied the West Bank, the Gaza Strip, the Sinai Peninsula, and the Golan Heights, and unified the city of Jerusalem.

The UN General Assembly on November 22, 1967, approved Resolution 242, which called for "a just and lasting peace in which every State in the area can live in security," pointed to need for "secure and recognized boundaries" and called on Israel to withdraw "from territories occupied in the recent conflict." Further hostilities between Egypt and Israel were halted by a cease-fire in September 1970 which lasted three years.

In 1970 Nasser died and was succeeded as Egyptian president by Anwar Sadat. On October 6, 1973 (Yom Kippur), Egypt attacked Israeli forces in the Sinai; Israel was also attacked by Syria in the Golan Heights. The war ended with a cease-fire and the UN Security Council Resolution 338 of October 21–22, 1973, calling on all parties to end military activity, to implement Resolution 242, and to begin negotiations for a "just and durable peace" in the Middle East. In 1974 and 1975, agreement was reached on Israeli withdrawal from Sinai, and disengagement between Israel and Syria.

In November 1977 Anwar Sadat made an historic trip to Israel, during which he spoke to the Israeli parliament (Knesset). This led to the Camp David Accords on Israeli withdrawal from Sinai and future peace between Israel and Egypt. A peace treaty was signed on March 26, 1979; the agreement provided for mutual recognition and full diplomatic relations. It also envisaged

negotiations between Israel and other Arab neighbors. In 1994 a peace treaty was signed between Israel and Jordan, ending all hostilities. To some extent this was the consequence of an agreement between Israel and the PLO in 1993.

In 1964 the Palestinian Liberation Organization (PLO) was established under the sponsorship of the Arab League, bringing together a number of Palestinian groups, the most important of which was Fatah, founded in 1958 and headed by Yasir Arafat. He had been born in Cairo, though some suggest in the Gaza Strip, in August 1929. Arafat was educated as an engineer in Cairo, worked in Kuwait, and then led his group in advocating armed struggle against Israel. In 1969 Arafat became chair of the PLO executive, a position he has retained until the present. After the September 1969 conflict between Palestinians and King Hussein in Jordan, the PLO was expelled and moved to Lebanon, where it remained until its headquarters was destroyed in Beirut as a result of Israeli invasion in June–August 1982. Arafat and the PLO left for Tunisia. In May 1983, Israel signed a peace treaty with Lebanon, but Syria forced the Lebanese president to renege on it. Negotiations between Israel and Palestine took place under various auspices and in different places in the 1990s, starting with the Madrid conference in October 1991, which proposed a framework for a Middle East peace process. Discussions in Oslo in 1993 led to a meeting in Washington in September 1993 between Arafat and Israeli Prime Minister Yitzhak Rabin and to a Declaration of Principles which set out a framework in which the parties could move to a final settlement, starting with strengthening of bilateral cooperation, building mutual trust, and intentions to reach a permanent status agreement within five years. The parties agreed it was time to end the conflict and to set up a Palestinian Interim Self-Government Authority and then an elected Council for the Palestinian people in the West Bank and Gaza. (Arafat was elected President (Ra'ees) of the Palestinian Authority in January 1996.)

In May 1994 the Cairo accord was signed by the two sides, laying down procedures for Israeli withdrawal from the Gaza Strip and the Jericho area and for transfer of authority including public order and internal security to the Palestinians. The Palestian Authority would be responsible for all legislative and executive powers, and for administration of justice in the two areas, except for Israeli settlements. In 1994, Arafat shared the Nobel Peace Prize with Prime Minister Rabin and Shimon Peres. (Rabin was assassinated by a fellow Israeli in Jerusalem on November 4, 1995.) On August 29, 1994, an agreement was signed by Israel and the Palestinians on the transfer of powers and responsibilities in areas of education, culture, social welfare, tourism, and taxation; in August 1995 additional subjects were added.

A subsequent Interim Agreement, Oslo II, of September 28, 1995, outlined the three types of area in the occupied territories and a complex formula for Israeli withdrawal of control over them. The Palestinian National Council convening in Gaza in April 1996 amended the Palestine National Charter by removing articles implicitly calling for the end of Israel.

Further agreements—Wye River Memorandum of October 23, 1998, signed in Washington, and the Sharm el-Sheikh Memorandum of September 4, 1999—followed. Wye called for resumption of negotiations on permanent status which had begun in Taba in May 1996 and which would deal with remaining issues, including Jerusalem, refugees, settlements, security, borders, and relations with neighboring countries.

The July 2000 meeting at Camp David between Arafat and Prime Minister Ehud Barak to discuss permanent status in accordance with Oslo ended with no agreement; another attempt in December 2000 was equally unsuccessful. The result was a wave of violence beginning in September 2000 that was more intense than the 1987 intifada (uprising). This led to a breakdown in negotiations and to Israeli incursions into Palestinian territory.

The reason for the September 2000 intifada is disputed. However, a visit by Ariel Sharon to the Temple Mount in Jerusalem in September 2000 was seen by Palestinians as a provocative act, and they reacted with violence. The United States attempted to act as intermediaries. A fact-finding assessment by George Mitchell in April

2001 urged an end to violence and said that terrorism was unacceptable, that security cooperation should be resumed, that Israel should withdraw to positions held before September 2000, and that confidence-building measures should be started. CIA director George Tenet in the Middle East in June 2001 tried to obtain a comprehensive cease-fire and called for an end to all violent activity. But the violence, including suicide bombings and counterviolence, did not stop and led to an Israeli military operation in the occupied territories.

The first major Arab intervention was by Saudi Crown Prince Abdullah, who presented a peace initiative, subsequently revised and adopted by the Arab League in March 2002, offering Israel "normal relations" in return for withdrawal of Israel to the 1967 borders, the resolution of the Palestinian refugee question, and the creation of a state of Palestine. The search continues for an end to the Israeli-Palestinian conflict. In the summer of 2002, a group known as the Quartet—the United States, the United Nations, the European Union, and Russia—met to discuss the crisis. In 2005, it reaffirmed its commitment to a just, comprehensive, and lasting settlement.

REGIONAL ISSUES

The contemporary Middle East is marked by a number of political characteristics: a low level of political community; authoritarian governments of various kinds in almost all systems; political instability, conflict, and frequent resort to violence; and unpredictability. The low level of political community and the unlikelihood of a common national loyalty is partly the result of the perpetuation of ethnic, tribal, or communal-religious divisions, and partly the heritage of boundaries laid down by colonial powers.

In Lebanon, political positions have, since 1943, been allocated on the basis of religious affiliation; politics is therefore marked by fierce tribal disputes and the primacy of religious sects and clans. The Muslim perception of its position and perquisites as unjustifiably inadequate underlies the internal disarray in Lebanon that began in 1975. Throughout the Middle East, ethnic groups see each other as rivals. Lacking legitimacy through popular election, rulers have frequently appointed relatives, members of their extended family (*hamula*), and tribal allies to senior political and military positions as in Syria, Iraq, and formerly in Yemen. Those appointed may not be representative of the majority of the population.

The boundaries of a number of Middle Eastern states were shaped in the early twentieth century by decisions of Britain and France and were more the result of their strategic interests than of local ethnic or religious factors. The ensuing individual state may not therefore be the recipient of national support. In any case, most of the states are relatively new; only Saudi Arabia and Yemen predate 1936 as full, independent states in their present limits.

Economic and social changes, such as movement in employment away from agriculture, where only half the population now works, have not yet changed adherence to ethnic and religious loyalty into loyalty to the state. Even the growing urbanization—the rapid move to the cities has led to about 45 percent of the population being urban—has not altogether weakened the local bond because rural migrants to the cities have tended to move closer to other migrants from similar backgrounds.

In general, political power tends to be exercised in the Middle East in an autocratic, often highly personalized fashion. The very lack of national loyalty has been one factor explaining the continuation of authoritarian systems in which the dominant political and economic decisions are in the hands of traditional monarchs or of leaders who have emerged from the military hierarchy. Aided by a bureaucracy and security service, their rule is limited only by respect for religious law. Except in the political democracy of Israel, in Turkey intermittently (since democracy there has been interrupted by military coups four times in the last 40 years), and to some extent in Lebanon, representative democracy and the idea of popular participation in the sharing of power have been unsuccessful in the region. At best, informal assemblies (*majlis*) have been the tradi-

tional way for demands to be considered. Where they do exist, parliaments have not been significant bodies, nor has meaningful opposition been tolerated. Lacking legitimacy in the Western sense of a government based on popular election, some rulers have been tempted to strengthen their internal support by foreign adventures, as with Libya's incursions under Qaddafi into neighboring African countries, or Iraq's invasion of Iran in 1980 and Kuwait in 1990.

Because political activity is largely confined to the entourage of the ruler, those outside the elite can only challenge the regime through insurgency, conspiracy, and assassination. Recent rulers in Jordan, Egypt, Saudi Arabia, and Lebanon were assassinated; other rulers have survived assassination attempts. In 1982, Saddam Hussein of Iraq eliminated the town and inhabitants of Ad Dujayl after such an unsuccessful attempt.

The authoritarian regimes take different forms. Dynastic monarchies of the traditional kind still exist in Jordan, Saudi Arabia, and the Gulf countries, and existed in Iran until 1979, with political power shared among the royal family and its advisers. Some regimes came into being as a result of military coups, as in Egypt in 1952, Iraq in 1958, and Libya in 1969. The core of these regimes is the military, a highly politicized unit and often the body that decides on political succession. Rulers in these regimes have often used organizations such as unions, militias, and the media to bolster their rule and prohibit any competing organizations.

These military regimes have sometimes evolved into a third type in which a party or a movement is based, or purports to be based, on some ideological concept. Examples of this third type are the regimes in Egypt, Syria, Iraq, and previously in South Yemen. In 1962 President Nasser of Egypt created the Arab Socialist Union, with a doctrine called Arab socialism, to become the instrument of power and the basis for the mobilization of his people. Syria since 1966 and Iraq since 1968 have had an ideology of Arab Baath socialism which stresses the need for unity, the mission of the Arab nation in the fight against colonialism, and the need for a new Arab consciousness, as well as a claim that public utilities and natural resources should be in the hand of the state. Some who participated in the overthrow of the shah of Iran hoped that the new regime under the Ayatollah Khomeini and the mullahs would embody a kind of Islamic socialism, a combination of socialist ideals and Islamic principles. Except in Israel, communist parties in the Middle East have been outlawed, though some intellectuals have been attracted to Marxism.

Though the Arab-Israeli dispute has received the most regional and international attention, it is only one of the many conflicts and potential conflicts in the area. Historic animosities, conflicting ambitions, personal rivalries, religious differences, and territorial disputes have all played a role in the pattern of continuing violence. They account for the considerable proportion of gross national product spent on defense.

Some of the conflicts stem from differences over the demarcation of borders and territorial issues. A number of boundaries are loosely defined or may not be fully accepted by other countries. Syria and Iraq dispute the distribution of the Euphrates Dam waters and the pipeline for the transport of oil. Syria claims the Hatay province incorporated into Turkey in 1939. Yemen has not given up its claim to the fertile Asir region of Saudi Arabia, which it lost in 1934. Border clashes between North and South Yemen erupted in war in 1972 before the two states merged in 1990. Islands in the Persian Gulf have been the subject of disputes and sometimes hostilities between Bahrain and Qatar, Qatar and Abu Dhabi, and Iran and Iraq. The destiny of the area of Palestine has not been resolved.

Other disputes arise out of rivalry for leadership, both national and personal. In recent years Egypt, Syria, and Iraq have competed for domination of the Fertile Crescent or for controlling influence in the Middle East. These three countries differ from others in their ability to take initiatives and introduce new policies, though dependence on Saudi Arabia for financial aid may place some limit on this. Sadat in going to Jerusalem and then making peace with Israel, Iraq in attacking Iran in 1980, and Syria in supporting Iran against a fellow Arab state all showed independence of action. Other states, however, such as Jordan and Saudi Arabia, are more likely to take account of existing local factors, align with the mainstream Arab position, and rarely move in important matters except in accordance with an Arab consensus, which thus would bestow legitimacy on any action. Since 1948 opposition to Israel has provided such consensus; a deviation such as the initiative by Sadat in reaching peace with Israel subjected Egypt not only to criticism but also to rupture of diplomatic relationships and temporary exclusion from the Arab League.

A third type of dispute arises over religious differences or over the relationship of a secular Arab nation and Muslim identity, or over interpretation of the *sharia,* the religious law. The Iran-Iraq war begun in 1980 was a struggle between the Sunni ruling group in Iraq and the militant Shiite regime in Iran, though it was also a contest between an Arab state (Iraq) and a non-Arab state (Iran), and a war over disputed territory. The civil war and hostilities in Lebanon since 1975 have involved all the religious groups in differing combinations. In the Arab intellectual world, particularly in the universities, clashes between adherents of religious fundamentalism and secular radicals have sometimes caused violence. Tensions cannot easily be resolved between advocates of allegiance to Islam, loyalty to the individual territorial state and concern for its national interest, and arguments for the creation of a greater Arab nation, transcending the present states.

As in other developing regions, conflicts and social tensions have occurred as result of the different levels reached in economic modernization and political development. The Middle East countries are differing mixtures of modernity and tradition, wealth and poverty, with enormous disparity in resources, varying from per capita gross national product of $820 in Yemen to $23,000 in the United Arab Emirates. The region is marked by rapid economic change in some countries largely due to the wealth stemming from the discovery and production of oil, a high rate of population growth, and internal migration from rural to urban areas, and external migration from the poorer to the richer countries. These factors have already brought social dislocation. They may similarly imperil the social order or destabilize existing institutions in other countries, particularly the major oil producing lands in the Gulf. Much of the world depends on that oil: Saudi Arabia is said to have reserves of 260 billion barrels, a quarter of known reserves, and Iraq has 110 billion barrels. The United States imports some one-sixth of its crude oil from Saudi Arabia. Other factors contributing to political difficulties are the high rate of unemployment in Middle East countries, and the high birthrate, which currently means that two-thirds of the population is under 18.

Political relations in the Middle East have often been fluid, and political actions unpredictable. Alliances between the countries have normally been loose and short-lived. Syria intervened in the civil wars in Lebanon from 1975 on, supporting first one side and then the other. Jordan in the 1970s allied with Syria against Iraq, then in the 1980s adopted a more nuanced position. Saudi Arabia supported some North Yemen tribes that opposed the central government in Sana, yet it also financed the deficit of the central government, which often took positions critical of Saudi Arabia.

Some of this unpredictability arises out of contradictions within the societies, some from changing events, and some from external pressures. If there have been a return to the veil by women in certain countries, the installation of a religious elite in power in Iran, and a high rate of illiteracy in most countries except Israel, Turkey, and Lebanon, there have also been an unprecedented increase in wealth, accumulation of modern sophisticated weapons, rapid increases in the general educational level, the establishment of advanced social services, and competing ideologies of territorial nationalism, socialism, and Marxism from the West to compete with Islamic fundamentalism. If radicalism of the left seemed to gain support between the mid-1950s and the mid-1960s, religious militancy has been more significant in recent years.

Governments in the Middle East face the same dilemma as other Islamic countries, an increase in fundamentalism that wants to make religion central to life and the essential determinant of identity and behavior. They are experi-

encing internal and external conflicts. These arise from large, increasing populations; highly populated cities; dependence on Western aid in a number of ways; the impact of Western culture through television, films, radio, and the Internet; and the growing gaps in wealth inside Muslim societies and between richer and poorer Arab states. Most disturbing has been the emergence of Islamic terrorism and violence organized by individuals from Middle Eastern states and constituting a threat to those states as well as to the West.

Relations between the individual Middle Eastern countries and the superpowers, who have sought to influence the area, have also fluctuated over the last 40 years. These changing relations may not reflect or be as dramatic as the kaleidoscopic picture of internal affairs. Nevertheless, the shifts in the relationship between Iran and the United States indicates that these relationships are not completely predictable or to be taken for granted. In studying the Middle East, it is wise not to oversimplify a complex reality.

THE ARAB HUMAN DEVELOPMENT REPORT 2002

The Arab Human Development Report (2002), published by the United Nations Development Program together with the Arab Fund for Economic and Social Development, was written by a group of distinguished Arab intellectuals with advice from policy makers in the Arab world. It examines the progress and the problems of development in 22 countries of the Arab world, from the Maghreb to the Gulf, 11 of which are dealt with in this chapter. Though the countries vary widely in population, area, GDP, income per capita, and human development, they share a common language and cultural heritage.

The main device used is the Human Development Index, which is discussed in the introduction to this book. The HDI is based on a number of variables in countries: life expectancy at birth, adult literacy, education and knowledge level, GDP per capita, empowerment of women, and availability of civil and political liberties (see Figures 9.1 and 9.2). On this index the Arab

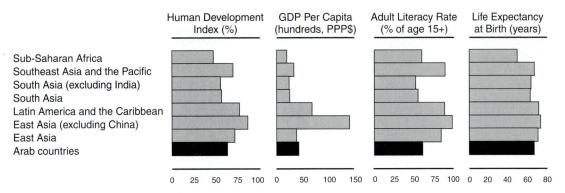

	Human Development Index (%)	GDP Per Capita (hundreds, PPP$)	Adult Literacy Rate (% of age 15+)	Life Expectancy at Birth (years)
Sub-Saharan Africa				
Southeast Asia and the Pacific				
South Asia (excluding India)				
South Asia				
Latin America and the Caribbean				
East Asia (excluding China)				
East Asia				
Arab countries				

Figure 9.1 HUMAN DEVELOPMENT IN ARAB COUNTRIES AND OTHER REGIONS, 1998
Source: Arab Human Development Report, 2002.

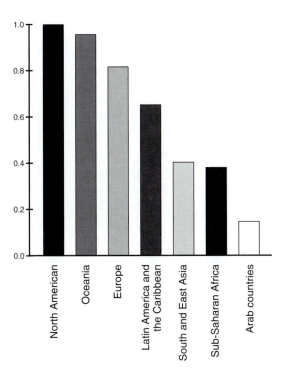

Figure 9.2 FREEDOM SCORES OF ARAB COUNTRIES AND OTHER REGIONS, 1998–1999
Source: Arab Human Development Report, 2002.

states rank low. In the report's Arab HDI, somewhat different from the general HDI, Jordan ranks highest of the Arab countries at number 68, and Iraq worst at 110 (see Table 9.3). The report urges the need to create a cycle "whereby economic growth promotes human development, and human development in turn promotes economic growth."

The report notes the expansion of education of the young, the increase in life expectancy, and the reduction in infant mortality rates. However, growth in per capita income is low, productivity has declined over the last 30 years, and real wages have declined. The main conclusion is that the Arab region is hobbled not only by poverty of income, but also by "poverty of capabilities and of opportunities." Three fundamental factors are lacking: freedom, women's empowerment, and knowledge. These and other factors are traced in the report. Their findings in the areas of population, health, education and knowledge, economics, women's empowerment, and politics are presented below.

Population

At present the Arab region has a population of 280 million—5 percent of the world population, a share that has doubled over the past 50 years. Some 38 percent are under 14 years old, a

TABLE 9.3

RANKING OF SELECTED COUNTRIES ON THE HUMAN DEVELOPMENT INDEX (HDI), 2004, AND THE ARAB HUMAN DEVELOPMENT INDEX (AHDI)

	HDI Ranking 2004	AHDI Ranking	Education Index, 1998	LE,* 2002	Freedom Scores, 1998	GEM,* 1995
Sweden	2	1	0.99	80.0	1.00	0.76
Switzerland	11	2	0.93	79.1	1.00	0.51
Canada	4	3	0.99	79.3	1.00	0.66
Netherlands	5	4	0.99	78.0	1.00	0.63
United States	8	11	0.97	76.8	1.00	0.62
United Kingdom	12	12	0.99	77.3	0.98	0.48
France	16	15	0.97	78.2	0.98	0.43
Italy	21	15	0.93	78.3	0.98	0.59
Japan	9	18	0.94	80.0	0.98	0.44
Mexico	53	45	0.84	72.3	0.65	0.40
Turkey	88	67	0.76	69.3	0.48	0.23
Jordan	90	68	0.82	70.4	0.48	0.23
Kuwait	44	70	0.73	76.1	0.35	0.24
China	94	72	0.79	70.1	0.02	0.47
Lebanon	80	73	0.82	70.1	0.18	0.21
United Arab Emirates	49	74	0.73	75.0	0.18	0.24
India	127	80	0.55	63.7	0.82	0.23
Bangladesh	138	83	0.39	61.1	0.80	0.29
Pakistan	142	90	0.44	60.8	0.48	0.15
Egypt	120	92	0.60	68.6	0.17	0.24
Islamic Republic of Iran	101	101	0.73	69.5	0.17	0.24
Syrian Arab Republic	106	103	0.68	71.7	0.00	0.29
Nigeria	151	107	0.55	51.6	0.20	0.20
Iraq	80 (2002)	110	0.52	63.8	0.00	0.39

Source: Arab Human Development Report, 2002; Human Development Reprint, 2004.
*LE—life expectancy; GEM—gender empowerment measure.

younger population than the global average. Depending on the scenario of future development adopted, the anticipated population in 2020 will be 410–459 million. Fertility rates, though declining, are still high by international standards. The new demographic profile will present both a challenge and an opportunity for Arab countries.

Health

Average life expectancy is 67, an increase by 15 years since 1980. Arab women have a lower life expectancy than world average partly due to maternal mortality ratios. Mortality rates for children under five have fallen by two-thirds. About 4 percent of GDP of the region is spent on health.

Lebanon spends 10 percent of GDP, while Somalia spends 1.5 percent on health matters.

Education and Knowledge

Some progress has been made in literacy. Adult illiteracy dropped from 60 percent in 1980 to 43 percent in the mid-1990s; female literacy tripled since 1970. Yet 65 million adults are illiterate, two-thirds of whom are women. Ten million children are out of school. However, over 90 percent of males and 75 percent of females are enrolled in primary schools, and nearly 60 percent of males and 50 percent of females are in secondary education. Enrollment in higher education is about 13 percent of the age group; the comparable figure in industrialized countries is 60 percent and in North America 85 percent. The report also maintains that the quality of education has deteriorated, implying a decline in analytical and creative skills.

The region has a low level of research funding and a shortage of knowledgeable people who can meet the needs of accelerating or cutting edge technology. Only 0.6 percent of the population at present uses the Internet. Scientific research and development at between 0.4 and 0.5 percent of GDP is weak compared with 1.2 percent for Cuba and 2.9 percent for Japan. Investment in research and development is only one-seventh of the world average. No exact figures are available for the number of new writings, but the number of translations of books is small. The Arab world translates about 300 books a year, about one-fifth of the number in Greece. Spain translates every year as many books as have been translated into Arabic in the last thousand years.

Economics

The GDP of the 22 countries combined was $531 billion, less than that of Spain with $595 billion. The region had slow growth rates. Total productivity declined at an annual average of 0.2 percent between 1960 and 1990 while it accelerated in other parts of the world. The productivity of Arab industrial labor in 1960 was 32 percent of the North American level; by 1990 it had fallen to 19 percent. The rich Arab countries owe their wealth to oil, which accounts for 70 percent of exports, but oil revenues are not always reinvested productively. In both quantitative and qualitative terms, Arab countries have not developed as quickly or as fully as elsewhere. Over the past 20 years the growth in per capita income (annually at 0.5 percent) was the lowest in the world except in sub-Saharan Africa. The real income of the Arab citizen on average is 14 percent of that of citizens in OECD countries. About 20 percent of Arabs live on about $2 a day. Unemployment is calculated at 12 million or 15 percent of the labor force. If present trends continue, the number is expected to rise to 25 million in ten years time.

The region is also troubled by water shortage. Arab countries account for 15 of the 22 countries identified by the World Bank as below the water poverty line, less than 1,000 cubic meters per person per year. The countries suffer from increasing scarcity of usable water. Cultivated land per capita in Arab countries dropped by half in the last 30 years.

Women's Empowerment

"The utilization of Arab women's capabilities through political and economic participation remains the lowest of any region in the world." About 50 percent of Arab women cannot read or write, and female enrollment rates in education are lower than males. Though improvement in female education has occurred, this has not countered gender-based social attitudes and norms that exclusively stress women's reproductive role. Women occupy only 3.5 percent of all seats in assemblies of Arab countries. They suffer from unequal citizenship and legal entitlements, inequity of opportunity, less employment status, and lower wages than males.

Politics

The Arab world has been slow to move to liberalization and democratic systems. The report indicates that the region suffers from low levels of government effectiveness, from corruption and political instability, from the lack of participation and of the rule of law, and from lack of governmental accountability. Political participation is less advanced in the Arab world than in other developing countries. Out of the world's seven regions (sub-Saharan Africa, South and East Asia, Latin America and the Caribbean, Europe, Oceania, North America, and Arab States), the Arab region has the lowest freedom score in the late 1990s, by reference to civil liberties, political rights, independence of the media, and government accountability. The Freedom Survey 2001, issued by Freedom House, reported that no Arab society had genuinely free media, and only three Arab states had partly free media. "The wave of democracy that transformed governance in most of Latin America and East Asia in the 1980s, and Eastern Europe and much of Central Asia in the late 1980s and the early 1990s has barely reached the Arab states." Freedom of expression and association are curtailed. In many cases government is by a powerful executive branch that exerts significant control over all other branches of the state and may be free of institutional checks and balances.

Some changes have taken place in recent years with more political participation or with an increasingly active civil society in some countries such as Bahrain, where freedom of the press and of association has increased. In Kuwait and Qatar, representatives are elected in national assemblies, and in two other Gulf countries, Bahrain and Oman, citizens have been promised this right in the near future.

The report concludes there is a need to reform governmental institutions and to activate the voice of the people. This requires political representation in effective legislatures based on free, honest, and regular elections, reforming public administration, governments to perform in an effective and transparent manner, reform of public sector institutions, implementation of the rule of law, human rights, an independent judiciary, freedom of expression and association, and strengthening local government. Full respect for human rights and freedoms are "the cornerstones of good governance that can unleash cre-

ativity and serve empowerment and participation leading to human development."

Thinking Critically

1. In what ways are governments in the Middle East extensions of the leader of the country?
2. Making use of economic and cultural factors mentioned in the chapter, how would you define identity in the Middle East? How would such a definition differ from that for Western countries?
3. Using economic and cultural factors, how would you explain the status of women in the Middle East?
4. What would you consider an equitable and workable solution to the Arab-Israeli conflict?
5. How were political policies in the Middle East influenced by the Cold War between the United States and the Soviet Union, and have they changed since the end of the Cold War?
6. Which countries of the Middle East do you think are likely to become democratic systems?

KEY TERMS

al-Saud *(521–522)*
Arab Human Development Index *(530–534)*
Arab Socialist Union *(517)*
Kemal Ataturk *(515)*
Baath *(520)*
fundamentalism *(525)*
Gulf Cooperation Council *(523)*
Saddam Hussein *(519–520)*
jihad *(510)*
Ayatollah Ruhollah Khomeini *(525)*
Koran *(511)*
League of Arab States *(510)*
League of Nations *(512)*
mandate *(512)*
Gamal Abdel Nasser *(517)*
Organization of the Islamic Conference *(504–505)*
Organization of Petroleum Exporting Countries (OPEC) *(522)*
Ottoman Empire *(512)*

FURTHER READINGS

Anderson, Roy R., Robert Seibert, and Jon G. Wagner. *Politics and Change in the Middle East: Sources of Conflict and Accommodation,* 6th ed. (Upper Saddle River, NJ: Prentice-Hall, 2001).

Arian, Asher. *Politics in Israel: The Second Republic* (Washington: CQ Press, 2005).

Bergen, Peter L. *Holy War, Inc: Inside the Secret World of Osama bin Laden* (New York: Simon and Schuster, 2001).

Cleveland, William L. *A History of the Modern Middle East,* 3rd ed. (Boulder: Westiers, 2004).

Dalton, Elton L. *The History of Iran* (Westport, CT: Greenwood, 2001).

Davidson, Lawrence. *Islamic Fundamentalism* (Westport, CT: Greenwood, 1998).

Doumato, Eleanor A., and M. P. Posusney, eds. *Women and Globalization in the Arab Middle East* (Boulder: Rienner, 2003).

Fuller, Graham E., and R. R. Francke. *The Arab Shi'a: The Forgotten Muslims* (New York: Palgrave, 2001).

Hopwood, Derek, ed. *Arab Nation, Arab Nationalism* (New York: St. Martin's, 2000).

Houston, Christopher. *Islam. Kurds, and the Turkish Nation State* (Oxford: Berg, 2001).

Jabar, Faleh, and Horsham Dawod, eds. *Tribes and Power: Nationalism and Ethnicity in the Middle East* (New York: Palgrave, 2002).

Kechichian, Joseph A., ed. *Iran, Iraq, and the Arab Gulf States* (New York: Palgrave, 2001).

Kedourie, Elie. *Politics in the Middle East* (New York: Oxford University Press, 1992).

Kramer, Martin S. *Arab Awakening and Islamic Revival: The Politics of Ideas in the Middle East* (New Brunswick, NJ: Transaction, 1996).

Lewis, Bernard. *The Multiple Identities of the Middle East* (New York: Schocken, 1998).

Lewis, Bernard. *What Went Wrong? Western Impact and Middle Eastern Response* (New York: Oxford University Press, 2002).

Martin, Leonore G., ed. *New Frontiers in Middle East Security* (New York: Palgrave, 2001).

O'Brien, Conor Cruise. *The Siege: The Saga of Israel and Zionism* (London: Weidenfeld and Nicolson, 1986).

Ovendale, Ritchie. *The Middle East Since 1914,* 2nd ed. (New York: Longman, 1998).

Peretz, Don, and Gidion Doron. *The Government and Politics of Israel* (Boulder, CO: Westview, 1997).

Reich, Bernard, and David H. Goldberg. *Political Dictionary of Israel* (Lanham, MD: Scarecrow, 2000).

Vatikiotis, P. J., *The Middle East: From the End of Empire to the End of the Cold War* (New York: Routledge, 1997).

White, Paul J., and William S. Logan, eds. *Remaking the Middle East* (Washington, DC: Berg, 1997).

WEB SITES

www.arab.net
Arab net

www.gpo.gov.il
Israeli Government Press Office

www.arabnews.com/arabnews
Arab news

www.Knesset.gov.il
Israeli Parliament

www.amconline.org
American Muslim Council

www.adl.org
Anti-Defamation League

www.ipsjps.org
Institute for Palestine Studies

www.washingtoninstitute.org
Washington Institute for Near East Policy

www.nacusar.org
National Council on U.S.-Arab Relations

www.aipac.org
American Israel Public Affairs Committee

www.pna.org
Palestinian Authority

www.wzo.org.il
World Zionist Organization

www.iap.org
Islamic Association for Palestine

www.opec.org
Organization of Petroleum Exporting Countries

www.beiruttimes.com
Beirut Times

www.jpost.com
Jerusalem Post

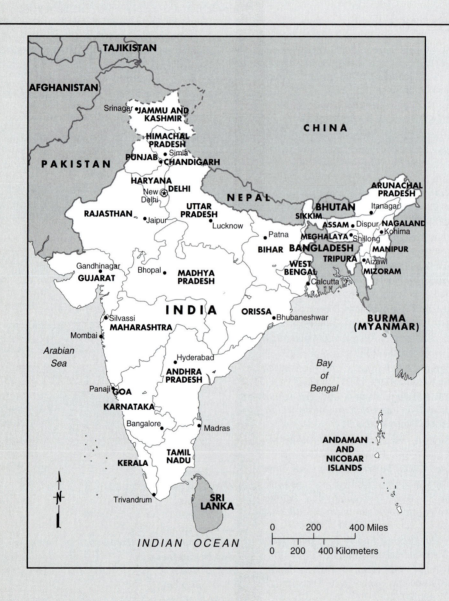

TAJIKISTAN

AFGHANISTAN

Srinagar •JAMMU AND
KASHMIR

CHINA

HIMACHAL
PRADESH

PUNJAB • Simla
CHANDIGARH

PAKISTAN

HARYANA

New ⊛ DELHI
Delhi

NEPAL

ARUNACHAL
PRADESH

BHUTAN
SIKKIM • Itanagar

RAJASTHAN
• Jaipur

UTTAR
PRADESH
• Lucknow

• Patna

ASSAM NAGALAND
• Dispur • Kohima
MEGHALAYA
• Shillong MANIPUR

BIHAR
BANGLADESH
TRIPURA • Aizawl

Gandhinagar
• Bhopal
GUJARAT

MADHYA
PRADESH

WEST
BENGAL
• Calcutta

MIZORAM

• Silvassi

INDIA

ORISSA
• Bhubaneshwar

BURMA
(MYANMAR)

MAHARASHTRA
Mombai •

Arabian
Sea

• Hyderabad

Bay
of
Bengal

ANDHRA
PRADESH

Panaji•GOA

KARNATAKA

ANDAMAN
AND
NICOBAR
ISLANDS

• Bangalore
• Madras

KERALA

TAMIL
NADU

• Trivandrum

SRI
LANKA

INDIAN OCEAN

0   200   400 Miles

0   200   400 Kilometers

CHAPTER

10

THE GOVERNMENT OF
India

Bernard E. Brown

INTRODUCTION

Background: The Indus Valley civilization, one of the oldest in the world, goes back at least 5,000 years. Aryan tribes from the northwest invaded about 1500 B.C.E.; their merger with the earlier inhabitants created classical Indian culture. Arab incursions starting in the eighth century and Turkish in twelfth were followed by European traders beginning in the late fifteenth century. By the nineteenth century, Britain had assumed political control of virtually all Indian lands. Nonviolent resistance to British colonialism under Mohandas Gandhi and Jawaharlal Nehru led to independence in 1947. The subcontinent was divided into the secular state of India and the smaller Muslim state of Pakistan. A third war between the two countries in 1971 resulted in East Pakistan becoming the separate nation of Bangladesh. Fundamental concerns in India include the ongoing dispute with Pakistan over Kashmir, massive overpopulation, environmental degradation, extensive poverty, and ethnic strife, all this despite impressive gains in economic investment and output.

GEOGRAPHY

Location: Southern Asia, bordering the Arabian Sea and the Bay of Bengal, between Myanmar and Pakistan

Area: 3,287,590 sq km

Area—comparative: slightly more than one-third the size of the United States

Land boundaries: 14,103 km

> *border countries:* Bangladesh 4,053 km, Bhutan 605 km, China 3,380 km, Myanmar 1,463 km, Nepal 1,690 km, Pakistan 2,912 km

Climate: varies from tropical monsoon in south to temperate in north

Terrain: upland plain (Deccan Plateau) in south, flat to rolling plain along the Ganges, deserts in west, Himalayas in north

Elevation extremes: *lowest point:* Indian Ocean 0 m

highest point: Kanchenjunga 8,598 m

Geography note: dominates South Asian subcontinent; near important Indian Ocean trade routes

PEOPLE

Population: 1,065,000,000

Age structure: *0–14 years:* 31.7% (male 173,869,000, female 164,003,000)

15–64 years: 63.5% (male 349,785,000; female 326,281,000)

65 years and over: 4.8% (male 25,885,000; female 25,235,000)

Population growth rate: 1.44%

Birthrate: 22.8 births/1,000 population

Sex ratio: 1.07 male/female

Life expectancy at birth: 63.99 years

male: 63.25 years

female: 64.77 years

Nationality: *noun:* Indian, Indians

adjective: Indian

Ethnic groups: Indo-Aryan 72%, Dravidian 25%, Mongoloid and other 3%

Religions: Hindu 81.3%, Muslim 12%, Christian 2.3%, Sikh 1.9%, other groups including Buddhist, Jain, Parsi 2.5%

Languages: English enjoys associate status but is the most important language for national, political, and commercial communication; Hindi is the national language and primary tongue of 30% of the people. Official languages include Bengali, Telugu, Marathi, Tamil, Urdu, Gujarati, Malayalam, Kannada, Oriya, Punjabi, Assamese, Kashmiri, Sindhi, Sanskrit. Hindustani is a popular variant of Hindi/Urdu spoken widely throughout northern India

Literacy: *definition:* age 15 and over can read and write

total population: 59.5%

male: 70.2%

female: 48.3%

GOVERNMENT

Country name: *conventional long form:* Republic of India

conventional short form: India

Government type: federal republic

Capital: New Delhi

Administrative divisions: 28 states and 7 union territories

Independence: 15 August 1947 (from UK)

Constitution: 26 January 1950

Legal system: based on English common law; limited judicial review of legislative acts; accepts compulsory ICJ jurisdiction, with reservations

Suffrage: 18 years of age; universal

Executive branch: *chief of state:* President A. P. J. Abdul Kalam (since July 2002)

head of government: Prime Minister Manmohan Singh (since May 2004)

cabinet: Council of Ministers appointed by the president on the recommendation of the prime minister

elections: president elected by an electoral college consisting of elected members of both houses of Parliament and the legislatures of the states for a five-year term; vice president elected by both houses of Parliament for a five-year term; prime minister elected by parliamentary members of the majority party following legislative elections

Legislative branch: bicameral Parliament or Sansad consists of the Council of States or Rajya Sabha (a body consisting of not more than 250 members, up to 12 of which are appointed by the president, the remainder are chosen by the elected members of the state and territorial assemblies; members serve six-year terms) and the People's Assembly or Lok Sabha (545 seats; 543 elected by popular vote, 2 appointed by the president; members serve five-year terms)

Judicial branch: Supreme Court (judges are appointed by the president and remain in office until they reach the age of 65)

ECONOMY

Overview: India's economy encompasses traditional village farming, modern agriculture, handicrafts, a wide range of modern industries, and a multitude of support services. More than a third of the population is too poor to be able to afford an adequate diet. India's

international payments position remained strong in 2000 with adequate foreign exchange reserves, moderately depreciating nominal exchange rates, and booming exports of software services. The economy grew an average of 6 percent annually since 1990.

GDP: purchasing power parity—$3.03 trillion

GDP—real growth rate: 8.3%

GDP—per capita: purchasing power parity—$2,900

GDP—composition by sector: *agriculture:* 23.6%

   industry: 28.4%

   services: 48%

Population below poverty line: 25%

Labor force—by occupation: agriculture 60%, services 23%, industry 17%

Currency: Indian rupee (INR)

A. POLITICAL DEVELOPMENT

India's population passed the 1 billion mark at the dawn of the twenty-first century, having doubled in a little over 30 years. If current trends in childbirth and mortality rates continue, India will become the world's most populous country by the mid-twenty-first century, surpassing China (which now has 1.3 billion people). In the absence of economic development, a huge population may equate with mass poverty, misery, and helplessness. For many in the West, India still summons up images from Rudyard Kipling—colorful bazaars, fabled palaces and temples, worshipers bathing in the waters of the sacred Ganges, snake charmers, cows wandering through streets, elephants as a means of transport, and red-coated English officers maintaining European customs in a completely alien land. Part of India's continuing fascination for outsiders is that aspects of the world described by Kipling may still be found.

But alongside and more and more displacing the traditional culture is a modern, industrial, Internet-connected society. India now ranks among the six largest economies in the world, producing and exporting a wide range of products, including locomotives, diesel engines, jet aircraft, and computer software. India's gross national product ($3.03 trillion) exceeds that of the United Kingdom ($1.66 trillion). Per capita income in India, measured in purchasing power units, is $2,900, about 8 percent of that in the United Kingdom. The Indian middle class is perhaps the largest in the world in absolute terms, numbering between 150–250 million people. In 1980, India entered the space age by becoming the sixth nation to launch a rocket and communication satellites. It is a major participant in research on telecommunications, space exploration, and nuclear energy. Twelve nuclear power plants are now in operation. Agricultural production has increased dramatically, spurred by a large research structure in universities and government. Life expectancy has gone up since independence from 32 to about 63 years, reflecting improvements in medical science and hospital care.

The contrast between the omnipresent bullock cart and the nuclear power plant makes India a compelling subject of study. The politics of modernization are spread out on a large canvas: the historical culture and society, the forces that penetrate and shatter that traditional synthesis, the dynamic tension between traditional and modern groups, the kinds of policies that facilitate modernization, and the problems thereby created. Students of politics are also drawn naturally to Indian affairs because they are concerned with power; by virtue of its vast population, geographical location, industrial plants, and military strength, India is among the leading actors on the world stage.

The differences between Indian and European society are brought out in Table 1.4 of the introduction to this volume. Compared to European democracies, India is markedly poorer; the GDP per capita of Indians is about 8 percent of that of Western Europeans. Moreover, India remains an overwhelmingly agricultural country, with 60 percent of its population engaged in agriculture. By comparison, in the industrial societies of Western Europe only 2 to 7 percent of the people are still engaged in agriculture, and the agricultural sectors of modern economies are far more productive than in preindustrial economies.

In cultural life and social structure, India is closer to the classic model of traditional societies. It has a much lower literacy rate, a less developed educational system, and a lower life expectancy than modern industrialized nations. Although India has many of the same institutions that exist in Western Europe—parliament, prime minister, cabinet, president, supreme court, political parties, and the like—these institutions serve and are responsible to a society that is still in an earlier stage of economic development.

Most political observers have assumed that there is a correlation between education and high per capita income and democracy. Two reasons are suggested for this correlation: (1) Parliamentary democracy is based on competition among political parties and their leaders, with the electorate deciding among them after considering all arguments. If the governors are to be ultimately responsible to the people, there must be a widespread belief that the people are capable of making informed and rational choices. Such a political process presumably requires a high degree of literacy and of general education. (2) The delicate compromises worked out among interest groups and political parties in democracies reflect a social agreement on how the national income is to be divided. An expanding economy should make it easier to satisfy all claimants.

However, the correlation between democracy and education and prosperity is not undisputable, as proven by the case of Germany. In the late-nineteenth and early twentieth centuries, Germany was in the forefront of the industrial and scientific revolutions—as advanced in literacy, education, and national wealth as Great Britain or France—and yet did not establish a parliamentary democracy until after World War I. Following the collapse of the Weimar Republic, this same "advanced" European nation produced a Fascist regime. Clearly a high level of scientific and economic development is an insufficient condition for the emergence of democracy. The case of India is equally critical. Here is a society that after World War II was far less developed than those of Western Europe. Yet India—almost alone among the nations of the third world—created a parliamentary democracy that has endured. No one interested in the theory of democracy can ignore the case of India.

As was pointed out in the introduction to this volume, the terms *traditional* and *modern* are generally used to help explain economic, social, and political differences. The typology of Max Weber (see Chapter 1) implies that transition between traditional and modern (or bureaucratic) systems is often facilitated by the rise of a charismatic political leader. We shall now survey the Indian experience of modernization, using roughly the Weberian categories. First, India will be considered as a traditional society (before the arrival of the British), then as a transitional society (under British rule), and finally as a modernizing society (since independence).

TRADITIONAL SOCIETY IN INDIA

When the British first arrived in India in the seventeenth century, they found a vast, sprawling congeries of peoples whose historical unity went back five millennia. Recent archaeological discoveries indicate that great cities developed in the Indus Valley from 4000 to 2500 B.C.E. that had a level of civilization equal to or exceeding that of Egypt, Mesopotamia, and China during the same era. Some elements of the Indus culture somehow managed to survive the catastrophe that brought about the destruction of this civilization, and later reappeared in Hunduism. Beginning about 1500 B.C.E. the northern and central plains of India were invaded by waves of nomadic Indo-Aryans. The light-skinned Aryans gradually pushed the native Dravidian people, generally dark-skinned, farther and farther south. A fusion of culture took place, out of which emerged the Hindu way of life. It was during this time that the caste system developed, probably in order to maintain an appropriate distance between Aryan invaders and the native inhabitants. Our knowledge of this period comes largely from the epic literature of the ancient Vedas (religious hymns handed down by word of mouth) and the later Gita (a long poem on war and duty).

The early Hindu society resulting from the Aryan-Dravidian synthesis proved durable and resilient. Successive invaders, including the Greeks under Alexander the Great, were either ignored or absorbed into the national life. A serious challenge was posed, however, by Muslim incursions beginning about 1000 C.E. For 700 years the Muslims, with their militant ideology, were a formidable force. They succeeded in governing most of the country under the Mogul dynasty, founded in 1526 by a Turkish descendant of Genghis Khan. Some of the Mogul emperors, particularly Akbar, were men of considerable skill and talent. But by 1700 C.E. the Mogul empire was in an advanced state of decay. The stage was set for a new period—that of European or, more specifically, British domination.

The economy, social structure, ideology, culture, and politics of India in the seventeenth and eighteenth centuries, at the time of the British invasion and conquest, constituted in every respect a model of the traditional type of society. The masses of India lived in some 700,000 villages, each a virtually self-sufficient, self-governing entity with its own class and caste divisions. A few towns or cities developed as centers of royal authority, trade, or pilgrimage, but the overwhelming majority of the people lived in the villages. Royal authority might be concentrated in the hands of some mighty personage in Delhi or Lahore, but his power was barely felt in the villages except through the intermediary of the inevitable tax collector. In general, a committee of elders, or *Panchayat,* was responsible for order and justice within the village. Minor matters of a personal nature were usually settled by caste councils, whereas more serious crimes, such as cattle stealing and murder, went before the elders. Invaders, revolutions, monarchs, and empires came and went, but the Indian village endured because of its self-sufficiency. In the face of a hostile army, the villagers would arm and defend themselves; if attacked by superior force, they fled, only to return later and take up cultivation again. The astonishing stability of this village system enabled the inhabitants of the Indus Valley to till their land and maintain their culture through 5,000 years of turmoil and troubles.

The dominant activity was agriculture, although some handicraft industries developed, along with the manufacture of cloth, under the Moguls. Finished products of cotton and silk and handcrafted silver objects were exported to Europe, and a small merchant class came into being. Yet these activities probably did not involve more than 2 or 3 percent of the population, nor were the merchant and trader accorded much respect in Indian society, which was led by Brahmins (the priests) and noblemen. Indian farmers produced barely enough for subsistence, husbanding the rainwater that fell during the four months of monsoon. In the event of drought, reduction of fertility, or desolation caused by invaders, famine was practically unavoidable. The lack of a more advanced technology made it difficult to expand the country's resources to feed a rapidly growing population, let alone improve its lot.

As in all traditional societies, Indian economic and social institutions were pervaded by family values. Individuals did not own the land; rather, the village families enjoyed rights of occupation as a consequence of clearing and cultivating their tracts. In the event that a family died out, all rights concerning their land reverted to the village. The male played the dominant role, and the household consisted of all his sons, grandsons, and their womenfolk, except insofar as the women married and entered other households or the sons left the village to strike out on their own. The villagers, in a sense, constituted one large or joint family, with the committee of elders playing a paternal role.

An element of cardinal importance in traditional Indian society was Hindu ideology. Hinduism developed mainly during the period of fusion between Aryan and Dravidian cultures, but some of its elements can be traced as far back as the Indus Valley civilization. Like any traditional ideology, it affects and regulates all aspects of human behavior. It is more than a theology; it is a way of life, a code that determines how people shall live, eat, marry, cultivate land, share produce, and raise children. Much of the morality that informs Hindu ideology may be found in the Vedas and the Gita, and in the religious prose of the Upanishads (the main source of information on the formative period of Hinduism).

The central concept in Hindu ideology has been that of salvation, which is considered a release or deliverance of the soul from the endless cycle of birth and death. Life is miserable and evil. Material things are an illusion. The object of religion is to permit individuals to free themselves of evil and illusion and to merge with the Absolute, or the World Soul. Until release is obtained, the soul is condemned to wander about the earth incarnated in one body after another—the kind of body depending on the soul's record in its previous existence.

There are many varieties of Hindu beliefs, some stressing the importance of ritual and others emphasizing the gods, such as Brahma, Vishnu, and Shiva (representing, respectively, creation, preservation, and destruction). But the theme is constant: Life is a mystery; nature is to be accepted, not mastered; earthly existence is inherently evil; the true destiny of man is to escape from the melancholy cycle of birth and death through ultimate deliverance. Hinduism provided a scheme of thought that made life a little more tolerable in a society where the average individual could expect to live about 20 years, where famine was regular and catastrophic, and where hunger and unadulterated misery were the everyday lot of the great mass of people. But the striking drawback of Hindu thought, as of most traditional ideology, was that it offered little incentive to improve material conditions, to master and transform nature, to make more bearable the fate of humans on earth. Hindu society was able to endure as a consequence of its stability and the widespread acceptance of its values, but it was not able to keep up with the rest of the world in technological development.

A distinctive feature of Hinduism as a way of life is the division of its Indian followers into over 3,000 castes and subcastes, each with its own rules for eating, marriage, and general behavior. The institution probably derives from the efforts of learned Aryans to preserve their racial purity and culture from contamination by the Dravidians. In terms of the theory of birth, rebirth, and incarnation of the soul, caste marks the progression from a lowly to a higher state and, presumably, to total liberation from the cycle. There are four main classes or orders in the caste system, each containing numerous separate castes. In order of nobility or grace these groups are the Brahmins (the learned or priestly class), Kshatriyas (the warriors and rulers), Vaisyas (the traders and merchants), and Sudras (the serfs).

In the past, certain wild tribes and people who performed menial tasks were considered outside this general scheme of things—even below the Sudras—and were called untouchables, or outcastes. (Over half a million people make their living, for example, by emptying latrines and chamber pots.) There were about 60 million of these unfortunate people in 1950, when untouchability was abolished by the new constitution, and their number has more than doubled since. Members of the scheduled castes—as they are officially designated—continue to suffer social discrimination in spite of the special legislation designed to protect them. They now amount to about 16 percent of the population. An additional 8 percent of the population are members of "scheduled

tribes." They live generally in reserved "scheduled areas" (mainly in the northeast and hill country elsewhere), where their rights are protected by the central government. Sudras, known as "backward castes," make up about 25 percent of the population and receive some privileges separate from those given to the scheduled castes. Thus, members of the scheduled castes and tribes, and of the "backward castes" make up about half the population. Together with the non-Hindus (about 18 percent of the population), those outside the high and middle Hindu castes constitute a clear majority.

The caste system doubtless served a useful social purpose in a land subject to ceaseless invasion. Numerous races at different levels of development settled in India, and the caste system permitted each group to preserve its identity and yet somehow coexist with the others. Within a caste, no matter how lowly its general status, members found themselves accepted and helped. During periods of foreign occupation, there was a natural tendency for the Hindus to defend themselves passively by withdrawing more and more deeply into their separate world of ritual and *dharma* (sacred law or duty that often involves minute regulations concerning food and relations among the castes). They were thus able to maintain their Hindu way of life against the foreigner. But the price paid for survival of the culture was high, as popular energies were devoted to theology and *dharma* rather than to the development of science and technology and the improvement of economic and social conditions. The caste system also created deep divisions within society, and greatly reduced the effectiveness of central institutions in achieving national objectives in an increasingly competitive world.

THE IMPACT OF BRITISH RULE

By 1700, the Mogul power in India had virtually disintegrated. No native chiefs or groups at that time were capable of conquering or unifying the nation. The political vacuum was filled at first by European trading companies and then by the European nations themselves. After a period of economic and military rivalry among Britain,

Portugal, France, and Holland, the British emerged as the paramount power in India. Their dominance, registered by the decisive victory of Robert Clive and his Indian allies over an Indian army aided by the French at Plassey in 1757, was recognized by France in the Treaty of Paris of 1763. The British steadily extended their power into the interior, defeating one native ruler after another, sometimes permitting an Indian prince to retain his throne, sometimes assuming direct control themselves. The Mahrattas, Gurkhas, Sikhs, and Burmese were all crushed in battle. By 1840 the whole Indian subcontinent was in British hands, with the exception of a few small enclaves retained by France and Portugal.

Thus, the inhabitants of a small island off the coast of Europe were able to extend their rule over a vast subcontinent in the other hemisphere of the globe, teeming with several hundred million people, and maintain their power there for almost two centuries. British supremacy was achieved by an amazingly small number of men. During the entire nineteenth century, the British ruled India with about 500 administrators and 65,000 troops. The disparity in numbers—at the most, 100,000 Britons ruling 200 or 300 million Indians—reflected the difference between these nations in military potential and economic power. The British had complete control of the sea, an immense superiority in military equipment and tactics, and above all, surplus wealth that could be used to recruit and pay large numbers of Indian troops. They also created a far more efficient administrative system than had existed previously. Divisions between the Muslims and Hindus and among the princely states also enabled the British to play one region or community against another— sometimes deliberately adding fuel to the fire of ethnic and religious rivalries—and to succeed eventually in subduing them all. Their successes were made possible in part by their advanced technology, which produced the necessary wealth, ships, and firearms.

India had managed to absorb all of its previous conquerors with the single notable exception of the Muslims. But even at the height of Muslim rule, the Hindu way of life in the villages was hardly affected by events at the imperial court, except insofar as hostile armies might march through the countryside. British rule, however, profoundly transformed India—economically, socially, and culturally. In the course of the century and a half leading up to independence in 1947, India had changed more than during the preceding five millennia. Large portions of Indian society had been wrenched out of the traditional mold, and an irreversible process of modernization had begun.

Some of the earliest British social reforms dealt with the custom of *suttee* (the burning of widows on the funeral pyres of their husbands), the institution of *thagi* (organized robbery and murder), and slavery. Gradually a system of English law was established that profoundly affected relations among the castes. Perhaps the most important of the early British measures were the creation of a new education system and the introduction of English as a kind of national language. Fifteen major languages and more than 800 dialects are spoken by the people of India. With the introduction of the English language, the Indians were brought into contact with English literature and law and the whole new universe of Western science and technology. In the British scheme, as it was conceived originally, the educated Indians were to form a huge intermediary class between the governing elite and the masses and thus constitute a bulwark of the regime. In fact, this Indian middle class deliberately created by the British eventually led the movement to overthrow British rule. But in any case, English education became an abiding source of Western influence in India, upsetting old ideas, introducing modern knowledge, and helping to form a distinct new social class.

British rule also stimulated economic growth. A network of railroads covered the nation by the end of the nineteenth century, and for the first time in 5,000 years the life of the village masses began to stir and change. The railroads opened regions to one another and India to the world. The mobility of the population was vastly increased; transport of agricultural products made it possible to avert or at least deal with famine; capital flowed into the country; and a few industries, including coal, iron, jute, and cotton, began to develop. The postal system and the telegraph likewise provided part of the framework for a more modern economy. Population drifted into the urban centers of Calcutta, Bombay, and Delhi. By 1940, there were 58 cities with more than 100,000 inhabitants, and there was a total urban population of over 16 million. Thus, although India remained overwhelmingly rural, urbanization had become a significant social phenomenon. In foreign commerce, by 1940 India ranked sixth in the world and had the eighth most important industrial economy, employing over 2 million workers in large-scale industry. Nevertheless, agriculture was still the direct occupation of over 70 percent of the population, and 90 percent of the population continued to live in villages.

These changes—political, administrative, social, and cultural—shook Indian society to its roots. How did the Indians react to the challenge thrown down by the West? Perhaps the first, instinctive reaction was to exalt traditional values and seek refuge in a revival of orthodoxy. Some Indians, however, sought to adapt the values of Indian life to the new conditions. Still others, members of the educated elite, became completely Anglicized and lost touch with their ancient traditions. All these movements eventually merged into a nationwide drive for independence.

One of the early strongholds of religious orthodoxy was, curiously enough, the Indian troops in the pay of the British. These troops were mercenaries and had great pride in their military prowess, but no identification with the British regime. Their discipline took the form of a fanatic devotion to religious ritual. When British administrators began to reform Indian society, however, the reliability of the native troops was subjected to great strain. All the irritations and frustrations of the traditional groups burst into the open in the Sepoy Mutiny of 1857. Its immediate cause was the introduction of the new Enfield rifle, the cartridges of which were smeared with animal fat—said by outraged Hindus and offended Muslims to come from the cow, sacred to the one group, or the unclean pig, abhorred by the other. Native troops refused to accept the new cartridges, killed their officers, and seized control of large areas of the country.

It took a year of bitter fighting to restore order, and the British thereafter were far more cautious in enacting reform measures. Other manifestations of the retreat into orthodoxy were the denunciation of everything European and the glorification of traditional Hindu or Muslim values and society. Among the new middle classes and intellectuals, the view became widespread that the West was materialistic, inhuman, and crass, while the East was spiritual and humane.

But a number of keen Indian observers realized that traditional India could not resist the new invaders and that the only way to preserve the old values was by reform and purification. Most notable of the early Indian reformers was Ram Mohan Roy, who discerned in the Upanishads a central theme of reason with which practices like *suttee,* polygamy, and infanticide were declared incompatible; that is, Roy urged social reforms for Hindu reasons, not Western reasons. He contended that the role of the West was to supplement, not to supplant, the values of the East. Roy gave Indian intellectuals a new measure of self-respect and pride. Religious and theosophical movements mushroomed, all advocating a return to the essential values of Hinduism or Islam purged of irrational customs.

The various groups within Indian society were initially divided over the questions of Hindu orthodoxy, reform, and the extent of imitation of the West. But they were united in their desire for self-government. In shattering traditional Indian society, the British had let loose the forces that inevitably would turn against them. Members of the new Indian middle and professional classes were humiliated by social slights and discrimination, and angered by policies that favored British over Indian economic interests. Resentment evolved into defiance.

At first, the demand for dignity and self-government took the form of requests that more Indians be recruited into the civil service. The Indian National Congress, founded in 1885, was essentially a middle-class reformist organization during its early years. At annual meetings it respectfully petitioned for increased Indian representation in the civil service and legislatures, all the while affirming loyalty to the British Empire. The negative British response to these entreaties strengthened the hand of militants who turned against the empire, calling instead for self-rule *(swaraj)*. In 1906 the Congress officially endorsed the goal of *swaraj,* and many extremists urged a resort to violence in order to achieve that goal.

Nationalism in India remained largely a middle-class movement until the emergence of Mohandas Gandhi as its undisputed leader around 1920. Gandhi's father, a member of the Vaisya caste (traders and merchants) was the head minister of a small princely state in Gujarati. Gandhi was educated in Bombay, then studied law at the Inner Temple in London. After a brief stint in legal practice in India, he went to South Africa to represent Indians in their protest against discriminatory legislation and stayed there for 20 years. Upon his return to India in 1915, he was hailed as "Mahatma," or Great Soul. Gandhi's contribution was to reach out to and arouse the great masses of the people. He understood the Indian mind and with a sure instinct always formulated political demands in a manner the people easily understood. Under his leadership the Congress was reorganized as a mass party extending across the entire nation and reaching down into the villages. Gandhi built up national pride by exalting native Indian languages and religious values, and by defending the spirituality of Indian village life in contrast to the materialism of Western civilization.

The technique Gandhi developed for advancing the cause of independence represented a masterly compromise between the policies of the liberal reformers, who wanted simply to register protests and sign petitions, and those of the extremists, who sought to oust the British by force and violence. Gandhi's supreme achievement was to involve the masses in the struggle against British rule while avoiding a direct challenge to British arms—that is, to keep the protest nonviolent. Although his preference for nonviolence was couched in religious and ethical terms, it probably did not escape Gandhi's attention that British superiority in military technology made a successful uprising an exceedingly doubtful prospect.

His technique of political action was far from passive, however, and indeed the term *nonviolence* is not an accurate translation of *Satyagraha*—a combination of two Sanskrit words meaning truth-force. Elements of his doctrine were derived from Hindu practices; however, they also fit quite nicely the particular needs of the Indian nationalists. The object was to win over the enemy by sympathy, patience, and suffering—by "putting one's whole soul" against the evil-doer.[1] The essence of the technique was noncooperation. Under British rule in the last century, 400 million Indians were governed by about 1,000 British civil servants and 50,000 British troops. It would have been utterly impossible for the British to deliver the mail, run the railroads, police the streets, suppress crime, educate children, or administer the economy without the cooperation of Indian civil servants, troops, teachers, nurses, and so on. Hence, in political terms, Gandhi's insight was correct: Foreign rule could maintain itself against violence but would founder if the Indian people simply refused to cooperate.

Gandhi's first call for nonviolent noncooperation, immediately after World War I, led to large-scale rioting, which was stopped by the Mahatma himself. During World War II the British were increasingly reliant on Indian cooperation and thus vulnerable to the threat of noncooperation. Indian support for the war effort came to depend on a British commitment to independence—which was conveyed as early as 1942 by a special emissary of the British government, Sir Stafford Cripps, though at that time the discord between Muslims and Hindus made it impossible to work out an agreement. To understand the reasons for partition of the subcontinent between India and Pakistan, and the subsequent conflicts between the two nations, it is necessary to review the circumstances under which the British terminated their rule.

---

[1]From Gandhi's article, "The Doctrine of the Sword," written in 1920, cited in *Toward Freedom, The Autobiography of Jawaharlal Nehru* (Boston: Beacon Press, 1958), p. 82.

TOWARD INDEPENDENCE

The proposal by Sir Stafford Cripps, on behalf of the British cabinet, was to create a dominion of India with the power to choose independence at any time. Under his proposal, the British were to be responsible for India's defense for the remainder of the war, but otherwise the Indians were to govern themselves. Plebiscites were to be held in certain princely states and in Muslim areas to determine what role these regions would have in the future dominion. It was specifically provided that any province could choose not to enter the new Indian Union and instead create its own independent government. In his discussions with representatives of the Muslim League and the Congress, as well as associations of untouchables, Sikhs, and Anglo-Indians, Cripps came up against the bitter divisions that were to plague relations among all these groups in the future.

Congress rejected the Cripps proposal, demanding instead immediate creation of an independent national government; it termed the principle of nonaccession for provinces a blow to Indian unity. The Muslim League also rejected the Cripps proposal, but because nonaccession did not go far enough. The League insisted on a partition of India into two zones, stating that it would be unfair to Muslims if they were under any constraint at all to negotiate their status within, or their exit out of, an Indian Union. The leader of the Muslim League, Mohammed Ali Jinnah, declared soon after the outbreak of war that the Muslims were a nation, not a minority within a Hindu nation. Said Jinnah, "We are a nation of a hundred million, and what is more we are a nation with our own distinctive culture and civilization, language and literature, art and architecture, … customs and calendar, history and tradition, aptitudes and ambitions. In short we have our own distinctive outlook on life and of life."[2]

To further complicate matters, the untouchables (or depressed classes) expressed the fear that the Cripps proposal would place them at the mercy of Hindu militants, and the Sikhs of the Punjab vowed that they would never permit themselves to be separated from the Indian motherland by the secession of Muslim provinces. After the failure of the Cripps mission, political debate in India became even more rancorous, ruling out any possibility that the British could extricate themselves gracefully from the subcontinent. Gandhi came to the conclusion that Japan was on the way to winning the war in Asia; the best course for India, he decided, was to invite the Allied forces to leave and then negotiate peace with Japan. As an ultimate weapon, he proposed using nonviolence if the Japanese insisted on invading and occupying India—a tactic that inspired little confidence among those familiar with the ruthless behavior of Japan's victorious army elsewhere. Under Gandhi's prodding, the Congress adopted a "Quit India" resolution; when the British thereupon arrested Gandhi, Jawaharlal Nehru, and other Congress leaders, the Indians responded with widespread civil disobedience.

The Muslim League and Jinnah spurned the Quit India movement, supported the Allied war effort, and insisted at every turn on the need for a separate Muslim state. As Jinnah put it in a speech in 1941: "It is as clear as daylight that we are not a minority. We are a nation. And a nation must have territory…. A nation does not live in the air. It lives on the land, it must govern land, and it must have a territorial state and that is what you want to get."[3]

After the war, the new Labour government in Britain discovered, to its shock, that the Indian problem could not be resolved simply by proclaiming independence. Elections held for the central and provincial legislatures immediately after the war revealed a dangerous polarization of communal groups. The Muslim League won almost all the seats in Muslim areas, and the Congress almost all the seats in Hindu areas. The League and the Congress became increasingly

[2]Cited in T. Walter Wallbank, *A Short History of India and Pakistan* (New York: Mentor, 1958), p. 196.

[3]Ibid., p. 213.

irreconcilable. Jinnah vowed after these elections that the Congress flag would fly in the North "only over the dead bodies of Muslims."[4] The statement was prophetic. Independence for India was to be achieved only at the price of one of the greatest bloodbaths of modern times.

Physically unable to reinstitute imperial rule and politically unwilling to do so in any case, the British Labour government was intent upon granting independence somehow, and as rapidly as possible. In March 1946, Prime Minister Clement Attlee dispatched a cabinet mission to India with the task of finding a constitutional solution. Immediately the cabinet mission was confronted with the incompatible demands of the Muslims, who wanted the British to divide India and then quit, and the Hindus, who wanted the British to quit and leave it up to the Indians (and their Hindu majority) to decide on a division. Unable to secure agreement, the cabinet mission made its own proposals. Pointing out that partition would leave huge minorities in each new nation and was therefore unworkable, the mission recommended that India not be divided, but that predominantly Muslim and Hindu areas should enjoy extensive autonomy within a very complex political structure with weak central power. A constituent assembly was to be elected, with representation from all areas, to assume responsibility for government and draft a constitution. The Muslim League and the Congress Party both agreed, reluctantly and all the while laying down stringent conditions, to participate in the elections to this constituent assembly. In these elections, once again the League swept almost all seats in Muslim provinces and the Congress almost all seats in Hindu provinces. Amid much confusion, the League and the Congress continued to stake out incompatible political claims; Jinnah called for a "Direct Action Day" to protest "Hindu treachery." That day—August 16, 1946—saw one of the most murderous communal uprisings of the twentieth century: almost 5,000 people killed in Calcutta alone, many more

[4]Ibid., p. 217.

thousands hurt, and 150,000 people in flight. At least another 7,000 people were killed in the following months as communal rioting spread from Calcutta to nearby regions.

In despair, Clement Attlee announced in February 1947 that the British government intended to transfer power to Indian hands no later than June 1948, urging Indians to settle their differences before then. He sent Lord Louis Mountbatten to India as the new viceroy, with the mission of finding a way out. After fruitless consultation with League and Congress Party leaders, Mountbatten concluded that there was no alternative to partition; with misgivings, the Congress Party finally accepted the principle of partition. But now began a race against the clock. A thoroughly scrambled government of India had to be dissected, separated, and reconstituted over a territory in which most Muslims and Hindus were concentrated in separate areas but mixed together in some. In July 1947, the British Parliament finally passed the India Independence Bill, providing that power should be transferred to the two new nations on August 15, 1947. That day in New Delhi, Lord Mountbatten became governor general of India and Nehru prime minister; the previous day, in Karachi, Jinnah took office as governor general and Liaquat Ali Khan as prime minister.

Both new states were immediately confronted with enormous problems. At the moment of independence, Pakistan consisted of two geographically separated areas. West Pakistan had some 34 million people living in a dry climate, while East Pakistan had 46 million people living in a wet, tropical climate—in an area only one-fifth as large as the western province. The peoples of West and East Pakistan spoke different languages and reflected wholly different cultural traditions. On top of the exceedingly difficult political and administrative problem of coordinating these two geographically separated areas there was a formidable challenge. Only three-quarters of the population of the new state was Muslim; some 20 million Hindus were now ruled by their traditional Muslim rivals. Conversely, at least 40 million Muslims found themselves in the new state of India, subject to the rule of over 300 million Hindus.

The question immediately posed was, what would be the fate of 20 million Hindus at the hands of 60 million Muslims in Pakistan, and of 40 million Muslims confronted by 300 million Hindus in India? Would toleration and good sense prevail? Unfortunately, communal hatreds exploded immediately after independence. Violence was especially widespread and murderous in the Punjab, where whole villages were decimated and their inhabitants slaughtered or dispersed. Hundreds of thousands and then millions of terrified Muslims and Hindus fled for their lives, toward the sanctuary of either Pakistan for the former or India for the latter. But as those millions moved across hostile territory, they were fair game for thieves and killers. Almost 12 million people (slightly more Muslims than Hindus) fled from one state to the other, almost entirely to and from the Punjab. The situation remained relatively quiet in Bengal and East Pakistan. As many as 1 million people were killed in this humanitarian disaster.

In this climate of mutual hatred and killing, a territorial dispute pushed the new states of Pakistan and India into hostilities. The Muslim ruler of one princely state, Junagadh, disregarded the wishes of the overwhelmingly Hindu population and acceded to Pakistan. After the population rebelled, the ruler took refuge in Pakistan and Indian troops occupied the state. A similar situation existed in Hyderabad, a princely state in the middle of India where a small Muslim elite ruled over a largely Hindu population. India, refusing to accept the Nizam of Hyderabad's demand for independence, took control of foreign affairs and defense as a first step toward complete annexation. In Kashmir, 80 percent of the population was Muslim, ruled over by a small Sikh and Hindu minority. When rioting broke out, New Delhi declared that the area would be taken over by India to restore order and hold a plebiscite on the state's future. An uprising by Muslims, supported by neighboring tribesmen, was countered by the Hindu ruler's own troops; to quell the revolt, New Delhi dispatched Indian troops to join the fighting. At the height of the tension created by communal rioting and armed conflict in Kashmir, the apostle of nonviolence and tolerance, Mahatma Gandhi, was struck down by an ultramilitant Hindu. In announcing the news, Nehru declared, "The light has gone out of our lives and there is darkness everywhere."[5] The first year of independence was a terrible ordeal for all the inhabitants of the subcontinent, Muslims and Hindus alike.

An enormous task confronted Jawaharlal Nehru and the Congress Party as they set about creating order out of chaos. Consider briefly the dimensions of that task in August 1947. First, they had to provide for the safety of Muslims on Indian territory (of whom perhaps half a million were killed in a few months), assist and protect the millions of Muslims fleeing to Pakistan, and receive and care for the millions of Hindus who in turn were escaping to India. Second, they had to create a viable constitutional system out of the crazy quilt of princely states and provinces. In 1947 there were some 600 princely states, containing one-fourth of the population of India. Somehow this incoherent mass of governmental units had to be restructured, and something had to be done about the pretensions of Hyderabad to autonomy if not independence. Eventually Hyderabad was forcibly occupied by the Indian army.

The new political system had to be designed for a society far more heterogeneous than any in Europe. Although Great Britain, France, and Germany contain minorities (linguistic, religious, ethnic, and so on), each country has only one dominant, official language. The dimensions of the language problem in India are staggering (see Table 10.1). About 36 percent of the population speaks Hindi, and another 10 percent either Urdu or Punjabi (which are similar to Hindi). But the other half of India's people speak completely different languages. In all there are some 800 languages or dialects in India, of which over 60 are non-Indian languages. Most of these

---

[5]Michael Brecher, *Nehru: A Political Biography* (New York: Oxford University Press, 1961), p. 149.

TABLE 10.1

MAJOR LANGUAGES OF INDIA

	Users (millions)	% of Population
Indo-Aryan Languages		
Hindi	354.2	36.2
Bengali	69.1	7.6
Marathi	66.5	7.3
Gujarati	44.5	4.9
Oriya	30.7	3.4
Punjabi	24.9	2.7
Assamese	15.0	1.6
Dravidian Languages		
Telegu	72.7	8.0
Tamil	60.0	6.6
Kannada	36.0	4.0
Malayalam	34.8	3.8
Other		
Urdu	47.4	5.2
English (first language)	0.3	0.1
English (lingua franca)	30.0	3.3

Source: World Data, *1995 Britannica Book of the Year,* p. 780. Percentages calculated on basis of a total population of 914 million.

linguistic groups are fairly small, but about 100 of these languages or dialects are spoken by more than 100,000 people each.

The constitution provided that Hindi would become the official language of India after a transition period of 15 years. When that provision took effect in 1965, widespread rioting was triggered in the south. The government then amended the Official Languages Act to permit the continued use of English as an alternative language. In practice, instruction in schools is mainly in regional languages. Drawing the lines of states to take into account linguistic patterns, while maintaining national unity, is a formidable and delicate task.

In other respects, at the time of independence, India presented a social profile typical of any Asian developing country: an extremely low per capita income, an overwhelming mass of the people engaged in subsistence agriculture and mired in poverty, an average life expectancy of about 32 years, and a literacy rate of only 16 percent. However, by 1947 India also had created at least the rudiments of an industrial base, especially in textiles, with an earnest start in chemicals, iron and steel, and engineering. Through the educational system, opportunities were afforded for training an economic, scientific, and political elite.

The independent India that emerged in 1947 was thus vastly different from the nation first ruled by the British almost two centuries earlier. In spite of Gandhi's idealization of village life and Hinduism (perhaps necessary for political purposes), the economy and social structure had undergone profound transformations. Industries and cities had sprung up among India's 700,000 villages, and a new middle class had come into existence. Independence did not mean restoration of the society that had existed in 1757; it was rather the signal for a new departure.

Political energies in India now had to be redirected. Instead of overthrowing authority, the problem was to create it; instead of glorifying the village and denouncing material goods, the goal now was rapid industrialization; instead of opposing power, the need now was to rally popular support behind the government. The construction of a national authority was undertaken by the Constituent Assembly (chosen indirectly by provincial legislators), which first met in December 1946. A constitution was promulgated in November 1949 and took effect formally on January 26, 1950 (the date now celebrated annually as Republic Day). The political institutions outlined by the constitution are inspired directly by the British parliamentary system. The Indian president, House of the People (Lok Sabha), Council of States (Rajya Sabha), Council of Ministers, cabinet, and prime minister were intended to be the counterparts, respectively, of the British monarch, House of Commons, House of Lords, ministry, cabinet, and prime minister. The major departure from the British model is the provision for a federal system dividing power

KEY EVENTS IN THE HISTORY OF INDIA BEFORE INDEPENDENCE

1500 B.C.E.	Invasion of Indus Valley by Vedic Aryans.
327–325 B.C.E.	Incursion into northwest India by Alexander the Great.
300–600 C.E.	Golden age of Hindu culture under Gupta dynasty.
1192	Establishment of first Muslim kingdom, the Delhi Sultanate.
1510	Portuguese conquer Goa.
1526	Babur founds a Mogul empire, later consolidated by Akbar.
1612–1690	British East India Company establishes trading stations at Surat, Bombay, and Calcutta.
1757	Victory of Robert Clive over the Nawab of Bengal at Plassey. Beginning of British Empire in India.
1857	Sepoy Rebellion (or Mutiny), leading to abolition of East India Company and establishment of crown rule through a viceroy.
1877	Queen Victoria crowned empress of India.
1885	Creation of the Indian National Congress.
1919	First nonviolent resistance campaign organized by Mohandas Gandhi.
1942	Sir Stafford Cripps offers a British commitment to independence.
1947	British Parliament passes India Independence Bill. Power is transferred to India and Pakistan. Assassination of Mohandas Gandhi (January 1948) by a Hindu militant.
1949	Promulgation of the constitution of India.
1950	Constitution goes into effect on January 26 (Republic Day).

between the central government and the states. The main powers, however, are held by the center, so that India has many of the characteristics of a unitary system.

Democratic institutions were created by the Constituent Assembly; then the structure had to be given its democratic content through the electoral process, with the full participation of competing political parties. The first national elections were held over a period of four months in the winter of 1951–1952. The largest electorate in the world was mobilized in order to choose its first elected government under the new constitution.

Thinking Critically

1. Is India a developing country or a modern industrial society? What difference does this make for an understanding of the political system today?
2. How did traditional society in India differ from traditional society in any of the European countries treated in this volume? What are the political consequences of such differences today?
3. Max Weber used the term "charismatic" to denote leadership based on personal magnetism and devotion. Such leadership, he suggested, can facilitate the transition from traditional to modern society. (See the Introduction for a treatment of Weber's theory.) Which Indian leaders (past and present) do you consider "charismatic"? Justify your choices.
4. Is Mohandas Gandhi's message of nonviolence universally valid, or relevant only in the Indian context?
5. Was British rule in India positive or negative, good or bad? Justify your criteria.

KEY TERMS

Brahmins *(543)*
caste system *(543)*
Mohandas Gandhi *(546–547, 549–550)*
Hindus *(537–538, 541–544, 548–549)*
Lok Sabha *(539, 550)*
Muslims *(537–538, 541, 547–549)*
Jawaharlal Nehru *(547, 549)*
Rajya Sabha *(538–539)*
Satyagraha (546)
Sikhs *(547)*
untouchables *(543)*

FURTHER READINGS

Bose, Sugata, and A. Jalal. *Modern South Asia: History, Culture, Political Economy* (New York: Routledge, 1998).

Brecher, Michael. *Nehru: A Political Biography* (New York: Oxford University Press, 1961).

Brown, Judith M. *Modern India: The Origins of an Asian Democracy,* rev. ed. (New York: Oxford University Press, 1994).

Brown, Judith M. *Gandhi: Prisoner of Hope* (New Haven, CT: Yale University Press, 1989).

Forbes, Geraldine. *Women in Modern India* (New York: Cambridge University Press, 1996).

Harrison, Selig S., P. Kreisberg, and D. Kux, eds. *India and Pakistan: The First Fifty Years* (Washington, DC: Woodrow Wilson Center Press, 1999).

Judd, Dennis. *The Lion and the Tiger: The Rise and Fall of the British Raj, 1600–1947* (New York: Oxford University Press, 2004).

Nanda, B. R. *Mahatma Gandhi: A Biography* (New York: Oxford University Press, 1981).

Nehru, Jawaharlal. *The Discovery of India* (Garden City, NY: Doubleday, 1959).

Sarkar, Sumit. *Modern India, 1885–1947,* 2nd ed. (New York: Macmillan, 1989).

Sathyamurthy, T. V., ed. *Social Change and Political Discourse in India* (Delhi: Oxford University Press, 1994).

Singh, G. B. *Gandhi: Behind the Mask of Divinity* (Amherst: Prometheus Books, 2004).

Stein, Burton. *A History of India* (Oxford: Blackwell Publishers, 1998).

Tharoor, Shashi. *Nehon: The Invention of India* (New York: Arcade, 2003).

Wallbank, T. Walter. *A Short History of India and Pakistan* (New York: Mentor, 1958).

Wolpert, Stanley. *A New History of India,* 7th ed. (New York: Oxford University Press, 2004).

Wolpert, Stanley. *Nehru: A Tryst with Destiny* (New York: Oxford University Press, 1996).

B. POLITICAL PROCESSES AND INSTITUTIONS

In India, as in the other parliamentary democracies treated in this volume, the people express their interests and convey them to government through a network of professional associations (or interest groups) and through political parties. In organizing themselves for elections, the Indians have adopted an electoral procedure very similar to that of the British. But the context in which groups and parties function in India is radically different from that in Great Britain. A segment of the Indian community, inspired mainly by orthodox Hindu values, views the secular institutions with suspicion if not contempt. Another element in the community identifies itself with the Communist movement, many of whose leaders in the past denounced bourgeois democracy and sought to forward revolutionary goals (all the while being drawn into electoral politics that reduces ideological fervor). Thus, the consensus about political institutions and values on which the British system is based is narrower in India, and in most other developing nations.

Furthermore, the cleavages and contrasts in Indian society are far deeper and more intense than in Great Britain or any other industrial society. A relatively small though rapidly growing elite, Western in education and taste, is set off sharply from a largely illiterate mass attached to a traditional way of life. The gaps tend to be greater all along the line: between the rich and the poor, between urban life and village life, between language groups, and between religious groups (see Table 10.2). There is also a stronger tradition of violence and impulse to resort to violence, in spite of Gandhi and perhaps because of the effort required to overthrow British rule. Above all, India is still largely a traditional society only on its way to modernization, with all the social, economic, cultural, and political characteristics of such a society.

The evolution of the Indian party system was profoundly affected by the struggle for self-rule. Given the prestige of the Congress Party as leader of the national independence movement, a competitive party system could hardly have been expected to emerge immediately. As the Congress brought about unification of Indian society, inevitably economic, social, and communal groups began to affirm their identities and express their concerns. A process of interaction between party and society, characteristic of all democratic nations, was underway. The dominant party mobilized and developed the economy and society, and the diverse groups in turn made demands that led to the transformation of the ruling party and of the party system as a whole. Under democratic conditions, no one party can reconcile all interests. The coming of a multiparty system was a natural development. We shall now review the changing role of interest groups and the movement from a one-party dominant to a multiparty system in which two parties (Congress and the Bharatiya Janata Party) are now dominant.

TABLE 10.2

MAJOR RELIGIONS IN INDIA

	Members (millions)	% of Populations
Hindu	827	80.5
Muslim	138	13.4
Christian	22	2.3
Sikh	19.2	1.9
Buddhist	8	0.8
Jain	5	0.5
Other	29	3.1

Source: World Data, *2004.*

INTEREST GROUPS

There are trade unions, agricultural groups, business associations, and numerous professional societies in India, as in any democracy. But most Indians continue to gain a livelihood in the traditional sectors of the economy. As of 2005, 60 percent of the Indian workforce of 472 million is engaged in agriculture, 17 percent in industry, and 23 percent in services (in France, 71 percent of the workforce is in services, 24 percent in industry, and 2.7 percent in agriculture).

From this rough social profile, it is evident that the highly organized interest groups of business and labor so characteristic of Western democracies cannot draw on similarly massive social forces in India. Nonetheless, workers and businesspeople, as well as peasants, have organized in order to promote their interests. In structure, Indian interest groups resemble more the French than the British or German, inasmuch as working-class and peasant groups are divided along political and ideological lines. The Bharatiya Mazdoor Sanga (BMS), now the largest union, is linked to the Bharatiya Janata Party; the Indian National Trade Union Congress (INTUC), now the second largest union, is a creation of the Congress Party; and both Communist parties have their own trade union affiliates. Similarly, each of these parties has created peasant groups and student associations.

Trade unions together have a membership of some 12 million, which is a small percentage of the total workforce of 472 million. Twelve million unionized workers, nevertheless, could play an important role in the political process if they were disciplined, united, well organized, and well led. But such is not the case. Few union members pay dues regularly, and inadequate financing makes it difficult for unions to recruit, train, and pay competent leaders from within their own ranks. Leadership positions therefore tend to be assumed by intellectuals and politicians who are primarily interested in using the unions for personal or political ends rather than creating efficient structures through which the interests of workers might be defended.

Hence unions are not properly organized for the task of collective bargaining with employers; militancy takes the form of short, sometimes violent strikes. Because most unions are either the creation of or affiliated with a political party, most demands for higher wages and improved working conditions are conveyed directly to the government. When the Congress Party has been in power, it has been in the government's interest to make INTUC a transmission belt of its own economic plan, putting pressure on the workers

to accept discipline in order to contribute to economic growth and higher productivity. Similarly, it is important for the Communist Party to utilize AITUC for its own political purposes—either to embarrass, subvert, or cooperate with the government, depending on the Communist Party's relations with the Congress Party. Indian labor unions vigorously opposed the privatization program introduced by the Rao government in 1992, as well as moves to close down inefficient state-owned enterprises. Unions wish to protect jobs of their members, even though economic expansion in the long run will lead to more employment. Two developments have led to greater militancy and strike actions: the rise of coalition governments has somewhat lessened the ability of political parties to control their trade union affiliates, and the expansion of the private sector has made strikes less of a direct challenge to state authority. Management in both public and private sectors so far has been quite successful in defeating or at least containing strikes and maintaining tight control of the workplace.

Business groups in India are organized for political purposes mainly through a great number of local associations and chambers of commerce, which are linked together loosely in national federations. The most important of these business groups is the Federation of Indian Chambers of Commerce and Industry, whose members include some 2½ million enterprises. Unlike the trade unions, the federation is not affiliated directly with any political party, but the business community as a whole tends to offer financial and other support to the more conservative wings of the Congress, the BJP, and opposition parties. The business community in India labors under several severe handicaps in its attempts to influence public opinion and the government. First, there is historic distrust of and disdain for commercial and business activity, characteristic of any traditional society. Aristocratic Brahmins have always looked down upon businesspeople as particularly unworthy, interested only in profits and accumulation of material objects (as opposed to more noble and uplifting spiritual activity). The lower classes and castes have generally believed that they are exploited by businesspeople and resent their opulent lifestyle. In addition, the founding fathers of modern India adopted socialism as an official policy and were openly contemptuous of the business or capitalist class.

Some business leaders created or supported a Forum for Free Enterprise, later affiliated with the Swatantra Party, in an attempt to shape a more favorable public attitude toward the private sector and market economy. Business groups also regularly protest against expansion of the bureaucracy and of the nationalized sector. But the business associations tend to devote most of their efforts to consulting with administrative agencies and try to stay out of the public limelight. Lobbying is not a well-developed institutional practice. Individual business leaders, however, contribute large sums to political parties, thereby ensuring access to the state. In the mid-1970s, the climate of opinion became somewhat more favorable to business. Under Rajiv Gandhi, V. P. Singh, Narasimha Rao, and A. B. Vajpayee there has been greater recognition of the need for entrepreneurial ability and professional management.

By far the largest single occupational group in India are the peasants, as is natural in any developing nation. But the peasant organizations of India are a far cry from comparable groups in Great Britain, France, and Germany. They have practically no structure and are little more than outreach agencies created by the major political parties to mobilize electoral support. The weakness of peasant groups and the absence of professional leadership among them reflects the lack of education and income of the peasants themselves. Both Communist parties have made a major effort to exploit peasant unrest, especially among landless agricultural workers and poor Muslims. In some areas, Naxalite revolutionaries (almost entirely middle-class intellectuals) have managed to gain peasant support for their program of violent insurrection.

An unusual feature of Indian politics is the proliferation of community associations that defend and further the interests of a caste or of a linguistic or religious group. Among the most important are the associations of Sikhs (the Akali Dal), Dravidians, Nagas, and assorted linguistic groups. These community associations have suc-

ceeded in bringing about a redrawing of state boundaries in order to accommodate linguistic groups and are sometimes powerful forces in regional politics. In principle, the secular political parties have sought to avoid creating any associations that would strengthen the caste system, but they are frequently compelled to acknowledge the popularity and power of the existing community associations. The emergence of the BJP as one of the two leading parties and the eruption of violence in Kashmir have led to renewed emphasis on the religious factor in politics. Hindu militance has been soft-pedaled by the BJP leadership in order to break out of political isolation and negotiate alliances, but Muslims distrust the BJP, throwing their support generally to the Congress.

In short, the Indian interest groups are rarely as well organized, well led, well financed, or effective as their European counterparts. Although the Indian interest groups offer some opportunity for political action, more often than not they serve the purposes of political parties rather than of their members. The functions of the interest groups have thus been largely absorbed by the major actors within the political system—the political parties.

VOTING

Popular interest and participation in elections are unusually high in India. Turnout in the first two general elections was over 45 percent of the eligible voters. Since then turnout has averaged between 56 and 63 percent of eligible voters (55 percent in 2004). The level of participation is all the more remarkable considering that almost half of the Indian electorate, according to official statistics, is illiterate, and it may be assumed that many of those classified technically as literate are not able to read campaign literature with ease. Candidates must therefore reach the overwhelming majority of their supporters directly—through personal canvassing and mass meetings—or by radio; they cannot rely on the press. In order to permit illiterates to choose among candidates, the ballot lists not only the names of the candidates in each constituency but also the symbols of their parties (or, in the case of nonparty candidates, personal symbols). Voters then secretly mark one of the symbols with a rubber stamp, fold the ballot, and drop it in a box. Most observers agree that the system works reasonably well.

The electoral procedure is otherwise quite simple and straightforward, inspired largely by British practice. The size of the Lok Sabha (House of the People) is now fixed at 545 (2 members may be named to represent Anglo-Indians), so that each member represents almost 2 million people. The country is divided into single-member districts; the candidate who wins the largest number of votes wins the seat. Some districts are reserved for members of the scheduled castes (outcastes or untouchables) or tribals. Candidates are required to file nomination papers and also put up a deposit, which is returned if the candidate garners over one-sixth of the vote. Campaign finances are scrutinized by the Election Commission, but many contributions and expenditures go unreported.

The percentage of women voting in elections has increased dramatically, going from perhaps only one-half the rate for men in 1952 to two-thirds in 1962, and three-quarters in 2004. Women are also participating in greater numbers as candidates for office. In recent years the number of women elected has ranged from 27 to 47. A number of women have been ministers in states and at the center, most notably Prime Minister Indira Gandhi. In 1999 and 2004 the Congress Party campaign was led by a woman, Sonia Gandhi.

ELECTION RESULTS AND PARTY SYSTEM

The single-member district system always works to the advantage of large parties. In the first five general elections (1952, 1957, 1962, 1967, and 1971) that advantage was enjoyed by the Congress Party—associated in the popular mind with the national independence struggle through the person of its leader, Jawaharlal Nehru. Its opponents were scattered among a number of smaller parties, representing conservatives, Socialists,

Communists, orthodox Hindus, and ethnic and linguistic groups. In the first five general elections the Congress Party won a clear majority of the seats in Parliament, but it was not at any time a majority in the country as a whole. Its popular vote ranged from a high of 48 percent in 1957 to a low of 41 percent in 1967. The Janata Party, which won 55 percent of the seats in the Lok Sabha in 1977, was also a minority party (with 43 percent of the popular vote). In the election of January 1980, Indira Gandhi's Congress Party won almost 70 percent of the seats with 42 percent of the total vote. Under Rajiv Gandhi, the same party swept a record 79 percent of the seats in 1984 with just under 50 percent of the vote. Congress scored 39.5 percent of the vote in 1989, but the opposition parties were fairly united; Congress won only 197 seats (out of 543) and was blocked from power.

In 1991 the split between the Janata Dal and the Bharatiya Janata Party (BJP) enabled Congress, with only 37.3 percent of the vote, to gain 225 seats, so that it could form a government with external support. In the contests of 1996 and 1998, the electoral system did not produce winners with solid majorities, because regional parties were able to win enough votes to make their support necessary in any governing coalition. In 1998, even with 37.4 percent of the vote, the BJP and its allies won only 252 seats. But in 1999, the fragmentation of some regional parties enabled the BJP and allies to gain full advantage from the working of the electoral system. With only a slight increase in the popular vote (to 41.3 percent) the BJP-led alliance gained 296 seats, making it possible to form a reasonably stable government. In 2004, the alliance lost to the Congress Party.

Despite the apparent confusion of the Indian party system (half-a-dozen officially designated national parties, about 40 state parties, and around 5,000 candidates in most elections) three distinct phases in the evolution of party conflict can be identified: (1) *Domination by the Congress Party* (1952–1977), (2) *The Center Does Not Hold* (1977–1998). The opposition to Congress becomes better organized, but the center does not hold, leading to political instability, a cyclical return to Congress domination, and turmoil. (3) *The Center Holds—For Now* (1999). A center-right alliance headed by the BJP and its leader, Atal Bihari Vajpayee, won a comfortable and reasonably coherent majority of seats (296 out of 537 at stake) in the election of 1999, which may usher in a period of relative or at least greater stability. The BJP and the Congress emerged as the lead parties in two rival alliances that could conceivably alternate as government and opposition. After the 2004 election, the BJP government was replaced by one led by Congress.

Domination by the Congress Party

In the first 30 years of independence, the Congress Party dominated the political arena and furnished the prime ministers of the nation, an era interrupted in the election of 1977 when a coalition of opposition forces, coming together as the Janata Party, succeeded in ousting the Congress Party and Indira Gandhi from power. The victory of the Janata Party followed upon, and was a reaction against, the imposition of emergency rule by Prime Minister Gandhi in June 1975. The 19 months of emergency rule that followed were a watershed in the political evolution of India.

Emergency rule was proclaimed following a decision by the Allahabad High Court in June 1975 that Indira Gandhi had violated several provisions of the electoral law during the preceding campaign. The prime minister headed off opposition demands that she resign by declaring an emergency. When a portion of the Congress Party defected, Mrs. Gandhi succeeded in securing the support of the Communist Party of India, thereby maintaining her majority in Parliament. The government silenced the opposition by imposing press censorship, banning political demonstrations, and jailing critics. When Mrs. Gandhi decided to permit elections to take place in 1977, it was generally expected that the Congress Party would go on to an easy victory because the rate of inflation had been reduced and other economic gains were registered. But the opposition leaders came out of their prison cells, exploited deep popular dissatisfaction with censorship and other authori-

tarian features of the emergency, coordinated efforts through the newly formed Janata Party, and won an astounding victory.

The Center Does Not Hold

The contrast between the pre- and postemergency party systems was striking. In 1971 the Congress Party won 43.7 percent of the popular vote but 67.7 percent of the seats in the Lok Sabha, because it could exploit divisions within the opposition. The 1977 election was contested by only four All-India parties: the Congress Party; the Janata Party, a coalition of the former opposition groups, united in their hostility to Indira Gandhi and emergency rule; the Communist Party of India, which supported the emergency; and the Communist Party of India (Marxist), which opposed the emergency. This time the Janata Party, with about 43 percent of the popular vote, was able to benefit from the winner-take-all electoral system as the Congress Party went down to about 35 percent of the vote.

One of the leaders of the Janata Party, 81-year-old Morarji Desai, became prime minister. However, the contradictions within the Janata soon came to the fore, and the government began to drift. There was a sudden increase in inflation, communal violence, labor and student unrest, and—ominously—strikes by the police. Personality rivalries within the Janata led to unbearable tensions only a year after its landslide electoral triumph. In the summer of 1979 the Janata Party fell apart. Morarji Desai, anticipating a no-confidence vote, resigned as prime minister. The leader of a Janata splinter party, Charan Singh, was appointed prime minister but failed to win a majority, so President Reddy dissolved the Lok Sabha. The election of 1980 was a resounding victory for Congress (I), which supported Indira Gandhi and won 351 out of the 525 seats at stake (elections having been cancelled in 17 districts because of violence). The squabbling Janata and Lok Dal went down to separate and ignominious defeats, reduced respectively to 31 and 41 seats.

Only a few months after Mrs. Gandhi took office, her 33-year-old son and obvious successor, Sanjay, was killed in the crash of a stunt plane he was flying. Shortly thereafter Mrs. Gandhi prevailed upon her elder son, Rajiv, to enter politics and take on responsibility for reorganizing the Congress Party. Her government was being buffeted by charges of corruption and an increasingly unmanageable situation in the Punjab, where militant Sikhs were demanding autonomy. On October 31, 1984, two Sikh members of Indira Gandhi's personal bodyguard assassinated her, triggering a wave of violence in New Delhi.

India was in a state of shock. Rajiv Gandhi, designated immediately as the new prime minister by President Zail Singh, benefited from an outpouring of popular sympathy and support. He called for parliamentary elections in December 1984 (about the time they were due in any case). The result was a great personal victory for Rajiv, and a new lease on life for Congress (I). Out of 508 seats at stake in the Lok Sabha (elections were postponed in Assam and the Punjab because of continuing violence), Congress won 401 seats, more than in any previous election, with almost 50 percent of the vote.

The 1984 election seemed to mark a return of the Indian party system to its historically dominant model: a Congress Party able to govern, despite its lack of a popular majority, because of the fragmentation of the opposition. But the party system continued to evolve. Rajiv Gandhi's government was rocked by charges (and evidence) of corruption, by unrest among Sikhs in the Punjab, and by a surge of Hindu fundamentalism. In the election of November 1989, a reconstituted Janata Dal under the leadership of V. P. Singh won 17.8 percent of the popular votes and 143 seats, whereas Congress (I) won 39.5 percent of the popular vote and 197 seats. Although Congress (I) had the largest bloc of seats, it could not command a working majority. President Venkataraman asked V. P. Singh to form a government after receiving assurance of outside support for Singh from the BJP (the militant Hindu party), which had won 85 seats, and the Left Front (mainly Communist parties) with 51 seats.

V.P. Singh's government lasted barely one year. It foundered on its internal contradictions—liberals versus Socialists, Communists, and Populists; secular forces versus Hindu militants and fundamentalists; and lower castes and outcastes versus higher castes. The BJP withdrew its support in November 1990 because the government ordered the arrest of its leader (who was demonstrating in favor of building a Hindu shrine on the site of a mosque), and the government fell. President Venkataraman asked Chandra Shekhar, leader of an anti-Singh faction within the Janata Dal, to form a government, which was supported by Congress (I) and allied parties. This government, India's least representative, lasted only four months. After a relatively minor dispute between Shekhar and Rajiv over police surveillance of political activities, Congress (I) boycotted Parliament. Both the prime minister and Rajiv recommended new elections in order to resolve the impasse, and the president then dissolved Parliament.

As India prepared for its tenth general election, Congress (I) was still the dominant party and its leader, Rajiv Gandhi, the center of public attention. The opposition was neither united nor fragmented. Instead, it had evolved as two well-organized, mutually hostile parties—the Janata Dal, still led by V.P. Singh, and the Bharatiya Janata Party, whose best-known leader and potential prime minister was Lal Kishan Advani. India's party system entered into a new phase, that of tripolarity, modified by the existence of some locally dominant regional parties (the Communist parties in West Bengal, the Telugu Desam in Andrha Pradesh, and the AIADMK in Tamil Nadu). Of the three leading parties that squared off in 1991, the Congress (I) was present almost everywhere; the BJP was its leading opponent in northern India, and the Janata Dal its main adversary in Uttar Pradesh, Bihar, and Orissa. Thus, in every state there was usually a two-way contest, but nationwide there were three major parties.

The voting was scheduled to take place over three days—May 20, 23, and 26, 1991—in order to permit security forces to move from region to region. The day after the first round of voting, Rajiv Gandhi made a campaign appearance in Sriperumbudur, a town in Tamil Nadu, near Madras. Horror once again struck the heart of India as Rajiv was assassinated by a bomb, which also killed over a dozen other people, including the person carrying the concealed device. This was the culminating act of violence in an election that had already left over 100 killed during the campaign and another 50 on the first day of balloting. Rajiv's assassination was carried out by a Tamil nationalist suicide squad, seeking revenge for the Indian army's attack against Tamil rebels in Sri Lanka.

Voting was postponed to allow for burial of Rajiv and a respite from campaigning, then resumed on June 12 and 15. Violence continued unabated, and an additional 200 people were killed. Elections were postponed in the Punjab (later cancelled), and cancelled in the state of Jammu and Kashmir. Congress (I) did better than expected, winning 37.3 percent of the vote and clearly outpolling its two major rivals. With fewer votes than in 1989, Congress (I) won 28 additional seats because the major opposition force was now split into two separate parties. The big surprise was the increase in popular vote by the BJP, which almost doubled its share, going from 11.4 to 19.9 percent. The Janata Dal went down dramatically to 10.8 percent of the vote, from 17.8 percent in 1989. Out of the 503 members of the Lok Sabha elected in May–June 1991 (the other seats remained vacant because of postponed or cancelled elections), the Congress (I) had swept 225.

Nonetheless, even with the support of a few small parties, Congress fell short of a working majority. The leaders of the major opposition parties—National Front and Left Front—announced that they would make no attempt to topple a Congress government but would rather seek to work out a "consensual" approach on specific issues. A newly elected leader of Congress, Narasim Rao, took over as prime minister and to the surprise of most observers was able to govern for a full five-year term. He introduced liberalizing economic reforms, coped with religious conflict and ethnic unrest, and kept the opposition parties off balance.

In the eleventh general election (1996), Indian voters had to decide whether to continue or modify the economic liberalization reforms of the Rao government and whether to preserve or

change the secular nature of the state. The three major parties entered the campaign under the cloud of an ever widening corruption scandal. In January 1996, the Central Bureau of Investigation (a federal agency) brought bribery charges against three Congress ministers, the leader of the BJP (L. K. Advani), and several important figures in the Janata Dal Party.

The election was a severe setback for the Congress, which lost about one-fourth of its popular support (going from 37 percent of the vote in 1991 to about 28 percent in 1996) and almost half its seats in Parliament (down from 225 to 136). Although the BJP stagnated at about 20 percent of the vote, it was the major beneficiary of the Congress's decline. It won 186 seats (up from 119), the largest bloc in Parliament. BJP strength was concentrated in large northern states, enabling it to take many seats that had previously gone to the Congress. A coalition of center and left parties, including the Janata Dal and the two Communist parties, won some 20 percent of the vote and 111 seats; and regional parties, garnering perhaps 25 percent of the vote, won 101 seats. No single party or alliance came close to the majority needed to form a government.

Negotiations among party chiefs, at the behest of the president, resembled those of the Third and Fourth French Republics, when various combinations had to be tried, put to the test of votes of confidence, and then tried again. Two leaders of the National Front, former prime minister V.P. Singh (now a Janata Dal chief) and Marxist Communist Party chief minister of West Bengal state, Jyoti Basu, both refused to try to form a government, as did outgoing prime minister Rao (Congress). President Sharma then appointed a centrist member of Janata Dal and chief minister of Karnataka, H. Deve Gowda, as prime minister. But Gowda could govern only with the support of the Congress, which was withdrawn abruptly in March 1997 (on the grounds that the government was harassing Congress party leaders by filing unwarranted charges of corruption). Another United Front leader, I. K. Gujral, received the backing of Congress. But Gujral lasted only seven months; he was forced to resign when Congress withdrew its support because the DMK, a party in the governing coalition, was implicated by an official report in the assassination of Rajiv. New elections were then called in 1998.

Again, no clear winner emerged from the contest among the Congress Party, the BJP and its allies, the United Front (including the remnants of Janata Dal and the two Communist parties), and a large number of regional and caste-based parties. Congress continued to decline, wining only 25.8 percent of the vote and 147 seats. The BJP scored impressive gains, with 25.5 percent of the votes (an advance of some 5 percent) and 179 seats (up from 161 in 1996). BJP allies brought 73 additional seats (with 11.9 percent of the vote) to the coalition. Even though the BJP-led alliance did not command a working majority, it was able to form a government with support from a few small parties. The United Front lost ground (down 7 percent of the vote, and going from 174 to 97 seats). Regional and caste parties increased their seats from 28 to 42, making them even more important members of any governing coalition. BJP leader Vajpayee became prime minister, winning confidence by a vote of 274 to 251.

Vajpayee took a number of strong initiatives. In February 1999, he traveled to Lahore by bus to confer with the Pakistan prime minister, Nawaz Shari. Relations with the United States slowly improved as discussions continued concerning India's acceptance of international arms controls, and the budget sailed through Parliament. But the government's narrow majority left little room for maneuver. The leaders of an allied party, the AIADMK, insisted that corruption charges against them be dropped, and another minor party withdrew from the coalition over a local quarrel. The government was then defeated by a single vote. But the Congress and various left parties could not agree on the formation of an alternative government, and the BJP-led coalition was asked instead to form a caretaker government until new elections (the third in only three years) were held. The caretaker period lasted from March through September–October because of the difficulty of holding elections in the rainy season. During this transitional period, a major crisis exploded in Kashmir. Fighting broke out between Muslim insurgents (backed, India claimed, by the Pakistan army) and Indian forces in the mountains of Kargil. After fierce battles, the insurgents withdrew, and war between India and Pakistan was barely averted.

The Center Holds—For Now

The 1999 campaign was seen by many as "presidential," pitting two major candidates for prime minister against one another: the BJP's leader and sitting prime minister, Atal Behari Vajpayee against the Italian-born leader of the Congress, Sonia Gandhi (widow of former prime minister Rajiv, and daughter-in-law of the formidable Indira). Vajpayee ran under the slogan of "tried, tested, and trusted," which seemed to resonate with the voters. The two large parties did not differ sharply over any specific issue. Both favored liberalization of the economy and fiscal restraint. Two factors were important: leadership (Vajpayee was perceived as more effective and experienced than Sonia Gandhi), and the ability to form alliances (BJP proving more adept than the Congress).

The BJP-led National Democratic Alliance (NDA) won 41.3 percent of the popular vote, and 298 seats (up from 253) in the Lok Sabha, offering the prospect of stable government. The margin of victory was provided by the allies, rather than the BJP itself, and reflected developments in the states rather than at the center. The BJP popular vote actually declined slightly (from 25.5 to 23.8 percent), and it won 182 seats. The BJP fared better than the Congress Party in the more established and favored sections of society. It gained the support of 52 percent of the members of upper castes (Congress won 18 percent), 42 percent of the urban population (28 percent for Congress), and 41 percent of males (25 percent for Congress). It also was backed by 41 percent of Hindus (23 percent for Congress), while Congress did better among Muslims (45 percent versus only 10 percent for the BJP).

Thus, three general elections took place in the space of three years: in May–June 1996, February–March 1998, and September–October 1999. For the results of the 1998, 1999, and 2004 elections, see Table 10.3.

ing in 1999), the two Communist parties, and regional parties.

THE MAJOR PARTIES

The Congress Party

Founded in 1885, the Congress Party was the spearhead of the national independence movement, sharing in the glory and triumph of Indian nationalism. It was supported during the preindependence period by a broad coalition of interests, including the rising intellectual elite and business class, and enjoyed genuine popularity. Under Nehru's leadership, the Congress Party after independence pursued a policy of "democratic socialism" in the domestic arena and of nonalignment in foreign affairs. A key element of the party's democratic socialism has been reliance upon a series of national five-year plans, so that economic development and capital investment will proceed in a rational or, at any rate, deliberate manner. Despite the verbal emphasis on socialism, a planned economy, and nationalization of key sectors of the economy (especially the banks), after 30 years of Congress rule a large private sector continued to exist and even flourish. The Congress is also a party of social reform, seeking to eliminate patterns of caste discrimination

BJP leader Atal Bihari Vajpayee before addressing the public from the ramparts of the seventeenth century Red Fort in Delhi, August 15, 2002, to mark the 53rd anniversary of India's independence from Britain.

Let us now take a closer look at India's major political parties: the Congress Party, Bharatiya Janata Party (BJP), Janata (virtually disappear-

TABLE 10.3

MAJOR PARTY ELECTIONS, 1998, 1999, 2004

	1998		1999		2004	
	Popular Vote (%)	Seats	Popular Vote (%)	Seats	Popular Vote (%)	Seats
BJP + Allies (National Democratic Alliance)	40.1	253	41.3	298	34.83	185
Congress (INC) + Allies	31.3	147	34.7	136	34.59	220
Others	28.9	143	23.9	109	30.58	137

2004 *Distribution of seats within blocs.*
NDA (185): BJP 138, Shiv Sena 12, BJD 11, JD 8, SAD 7, TDP 5, AITC 2, NPF 1, MNF 1.
INC alliance (220): INC 145, RJD 24, DMK 16, NCP 9, PMK 6, TRS 5, JMM 5, MDMK 4, LJSP 3, MLKSC 1, RPI(A) 1, JKPDP 1.
Left Front (59): CPI-M 43, CPI 10, AIFB 3, RSP 3.
Others: SP 36, BSP 19, and 13 others.

and increasing opportunities for self-advancement by the disadvantaged. As a mildly left-of-center party, the Congress was able to retain broad support from peasants, workers, and members of the lower castes without alienating the business class as a whole. Given the deep divisions among the opposition parties—Socialist, conservative, Communist, and orthodox Hindu—the Congress appeared during the postindependence period to be the only party capable of governing.

When Nehru died in 1964, a group of state party leaders, who became known as "the Syndicate," secured the election of Lal Bhabur Shastri as prime minister, heading off the powerful Morarji Desai. By 1969, internal divisions and factionalism became a characteristic of the Congress Party as well as of the opposition; it was the beginning of the end of Congress domination. The split within the Congress Party began as a dispute between Prime Minister Indira Gandhi and the established party leaders over a candidate for the presidency. Mrs. Gandhi and the leadership supported different candidates. The leadership (or "the Syndicate") denounced Mrs. Gandhi for breaking party discipline; in turn, Mrs. Gandhi called a special meeting of the All-India Congress Committee, which vindicated her own position. Each group then expelled the other, with the courts finally deciding that neither faction had the right to use the symbol of the former Congress Party. The break was clean and complete; the Syndicate called itself the Congress (O)—for organizational or opposition, while the Gandhi faction called itself Congress (R)—for ruling. Defection of the Congress (O) members of the Lok Sabha left Mrs. Gandhi short of an absolute majority. She was compelled to seek allies, mainly the Communist Party of India. Mrs. Gandhi turned sharply to the left, advocating nationalization of banks and—a popular measure—elimination of allowances to former rulers of the princely states.

In the fifth general election in 1971, Congress (R) scored a clear victory over Congress (O), winning 352 seats in Lok Sabha (with 44 percent of the vote); the Syndicate won only 16 seats. But the popularity of Congress (R) was fleeting, reflecting largely national pride in the performance of the Indian army in "liberating"

Bangladesh and defeating the historic enemy, Pakistan. Mrs. Gandhi's political position became tenuous in the early 1970s, owing to runaway inflation, inability to avert a famine, and increasing cooperation among the opposition parties. The defeat of Congress (R) in 1977 was followed by another split between the faithful supporters of Indira Gandhi and those in the party who now condemned her authoritarian policies during the emergency. Mrs. Gandhi then created a new party, Congress (I)—for Indira—which went on to victory in 1980 while the anti-Gandhi Congress won only 13 seats.

The very name of the new party signaled the predominance of its powerful leader. Decisions were made at the top by Indira Gandhi and her immediate advisers. Mrs. Gandhi relied increasingly on her younger son, Sanjay, who had created a mass Youth Congress and played a key role in selecting candidates and organizing the 1980 election campaign. In recognition of Sanjay's power, and to designate him as the intended successor, he was appointed general secretary of Congress (I).

Mrs. Gandhi suffered a political as well as personal loss when Sanjay was killed in June 1980. Her other son, Rajiv, then started a political career. In a by-election he won the Lok Sabha seat left vacant by his brother's death, and was appointed as one of the secretaries of Congress (I). When supporters of Sanjay found themselves out of favor, political and family intrigues crisscrossed. Sanjay's young widow, Maneka, attended and spoke at a convention of Sanjay's followers in defiance of her mother-in-law's wishes. After being ordered out of the prime minister's house, Maneka continued her political activities, inveighing against the corruption of her mother-in-law's party and government. She helped found a rival political party, the National Sanjay Organization, eventually becoming an ally of the BJP and a minister in the government formed by A. B. Vajpayee in 1999.

Rajiv took control of Congress (I), tried to soothe the nation, dissolved Parliament, and led his party to an unprecedented victory. Considering himself a spokesman for a new generation, Rajiv sought to introduce a more pragmatic style in Indian politics, emphasizing the importance of modern management techniques and results. He declared war on corruption, demanding instead professional devotion to the public interest. Rajiv vowed also to free business of bothersome government regulations, which would eliminate the need or temptation to bribe officials.

The anticorruption campaign was led by the finance minister, Vishwanath Pratap Singh, a poet and painter who was a loyal follower of Rajiv. V. P. Singh took his mandate seriously. To make tax reductions acceptable to the public, he insisted on vigorous enforcement of existing rules. Frequent raids by revenue agents at the homes and offices of India's richest families aroused both wonder and hostility. Among those targeted were powerful business leaders with close connections to Congress (I), including personal friends of Rajiv. In January 1987, at a time of heightened tension with Pakistan, V. P. Singh was moved from finance to defense; this change also had the effect of stopping those controversial investigations. But as defense minister, Singh continued his anticorruption drive with renewed vigor. He discovered evidence that a large bribe (some $25 million) had been paid in 1981 by a German arms manufacturer in order to secure a contract to build two submarines. Singh's by-now numerous enemies accused him of revealing information that might weaken India's defense. V. P. Singh was forced to resign.

Congress (I) was losing momentum as the elections of November 1989 approached. Rajiv's bold new initiatives, announced with much fanfare at the beginning of his term, were not always followed up. He was accused by critics within the party of suppressing dissent and weakening state and local party structures. After his defeat in 1989, Rajiv bided his time, awaiting the collapse of the Janata Dal government under the weight of its own contradictions. In the 1991 campaign he seemed confident of regaining power, if only because the split of the National Front into two rival independent parties—Janata Dal and BJP—condemned both to minority status. Rajiv spoke of the need for vision, promised a more assertive Indian role in South Asia and the world, and defended Nehru's legacy of secularism. But his

economic policy remained hesitant; he called for more deregulation of the economy and reduction of government expenditures, but also pledged to roll back prices on essential goods and build housing for the poor (requiring regulation of the economy and an increase in expenditures).

Immediately after Rajiv's assassination, the 70-year-old Narasimha Rao was elected hastily as the provisional leader. (Rajiv's widow, Sonia, firmly refused to be considered for the post.) After Congress won a near majority of the seats, Rao was asked by President Venkataraman to form a government. For the first time since independence, no member of the Nehru-Gandhi dynasty was at the helm or in the wings of the Congress Party.

Rao, reputedly in poor health and considered a transitional figure at the outset, demonstrated remarkable ability to negotiate with the opposition, asserting himself as leader of both Congress and the government. He acted forcefully in adopting a program of economic reforms that moved India away from its historic commitment to democratic socialism (characterized by bureaucratization, stagnation, and corruption as well as good intentions) and toward a market economy. Although communal conflict erupted again when militant Hindus attacked the mosque at Ayodha in December 1992, Rao persuaded activists on both sides to agree to let the courts handle the issue. Violence in the Punjab was brought under control, but continued to flare up in Kashmir. Rao surmounted one crisis after another, and presided over his government for a full term.

But Rao was not the dynamic leader needed by Congress, weakened by internal strife and corruption scandals, in the 1996 election. A coalition of left and regional parties together with rising support for the party of Hindu nationalism, the BJP, produced a resounding defeat for Congress, which went from 37 percent of the vote down to 28 percent and from 225 seats to 136. Implicated in several corruption cases, Rao stepped down as party leader in September 1996. (Four years later he was convicted and imprisoned on a charge that he had bribed leaders of a small party to vote for him on a confidence motion). His replacement as party leader, the 77-year-old Sitaram Kesri, withdrew his support twice from United Front governments. The result was not the nomination for prime minister for which he hoped, but rather at first a cabinet reshuffle, and then, in November 1997 dissolution of the Lok Sabha and new elections (held in February–March 1998).

In a dramatic move, the Italian-born widow of Rajiv, Sonia Gandhi, agreed to campaign on behalf of the Congress Party. She galvanized party faithful and became the focus of frenzied media attention. The party went down by 2 percent in the 1998 election (to 27 percent of the vote). Sonia then assumed the presidency of the Congress, and led the party in the 1999 elections. Although Congress increased its popular vote slightly, going up to 28.3 percent, it won only 112 seats (28 fewer than in 1998). The glamorous heritage of the Nehru-Gandhi dynasty was not enough to overcome the reluctance of many Indians to have a foreign-born prime minister. However, in 2004 the Congress-led alliance won 220 seats.

The Janata Party

Although the Janata (or People's) Party was only founded in 1977, shortly after the sixth general election, most of its component members long had an independent existence, particularly the Socialist Party (itself a merger of parties dating from 1947 and later), the Jana Sangh (founded in 1951), and the Swatantra (founded in 1959). The Socialists had previously supported the Congress Party when it pursued socialist policies. Jana Sangh was dedicated to preservation of the Hindu way of life, focusing on defense of the Hindi language (in opposition to English), hostility toward Pakistan, and legislation protecting religious practices of the Hindu majority (such as the ban on slaughter of cattle). It had special appeal in those areas of northern India with a large population of Hindu refugees from Pakistan. The Swatantra was a conservative party, sympathetic to free enterprise and favoring closer relations with the West (though some members rejected Western materialism altogether). Diversity was at once the strength and the vulnerable point of the Janata. Most important was the common opposition to emergency

rule and a determination to undo Mrs. Gandhi's authoritarian measures (limitations on the judiciary, suspension of civil rights, press censorship, and forcible sterilization).

The Janata's fragile unity collapsed when the party assumed the responsibilities of office. Some leaders wanted to press forward toward rapid economic development; others considered modernity the ultimate expression of spiritual corruption and sought instead to favor home industries and agriculture. One group wished to assimilate the science and technology of the West; another group rejected Western materialism and resolved instead to revive and fortify Hindu culture. Some defended the outcastes, poor, and oppressed; others spoke out for wealthy business leaders and farmers. Opposition to the emergency rule turned out to be an inadequate program for a governing party.

After its rout in January 1980, the Janata Party split. Each fragment of the former Janata campaigned separately in 1984, and all went down separately to crushing defeat. The party name was continued by the rump that remained after the others had defected. After pondering their loss, opposition leaders rallied and began to cooperate. The opposition got a big boost when Rajiv's former finance and defense minister, V. P. Singh, created a new party, the Jan Morkha (People's Platform). In August 1988, four opposition parties—Jan Morkha, Janata, Lok Dal, and Congress (S)—decided to form the Janata Dal (People's Party). This party in turn took the lead in creating, along with some powerful regional parties (including Telegu Desam and Dravida Munnetra Kazhagam), a National Front. With V. P. Singh as general secretary and Rama Rao (chief minister of Andrha Pradesh and a former movie star) as chairman, the National Front went on to win the 1989 election.

V. P. Singh formed a Janata Dal government, with the support of the BJP and the Communist parties. But the prime minister had to perform an impossible balancing act. Committed to a secular and pragmatic program, V. P. Singh favored liberalization of the economy, opposed concessions to religious militants, and also sought to advance the interests of the lower castes and the outcastes. He thereby aroused the opposition of key elements in the coalition on whose support his government depended. Communists and small farmers were suspicious of liberalization and privatization; militant Hindus resented Singh's defense of secularism and of the rights of Muslims; and members of the higher castes were outraged by his affirmative action policy.

In October 1990, communal violence exploded over the issue of building a Hindu shrine on the site of a Muslim temple in Ayodhya. L. K. Advani, leader of the BJP, decided to place himself at the head of a religious pilgrimage to Ayodhya, which resulted in violence and fierce fighting between Hindus and Muslims. When Singh ordered the arrest of Advani, along with several hundred thousand demonstrators, the BJP withdrew its "outside" support for the government. Singh lost a vote of confidence by an overwhelming (3 to 1) margin.

The Janata Dal declined rapidly, becoming only one small party in a loose coalition of secular parties opposed to both the Congress and the BJP. Taking the cumbersome name of National Front/Left Front, the coalition won fewer seats (110) than either the BJP (161) or the Congress (140) in the election of 1996. When the BJP government had to resign after 13 days because it could not muster a majority, the coalition (now called simply the United Front) was called upon to form a government under H. D. Deve Gowda (Janata Dal chief minister of Karnataka) as prime minister, with the support of the Congress from outside. But Janata Dal had only 43 seats, the Samawadji party 17 seats, the Marxist CPI 33 seats, the CPI 12 seats, and various regional parties about 60 seats; the coalition was inherently unstable. Dogged by charges of corruption, the Janata Dal then split into four separate factions with the rump, allied to the BJP, winning only about 3 percent of the vote in the elections of 1998 and 1999. The two Communist parties and regional parties won 59 seats in 2004.

The Bharatiya Janata Party (BJP)

The BJP has its origins in the Jana Sangh, the militant Hindu movement that was a major opponent of the Congress Party under Nehru. As we have seen, Jana Sangh was one of the founding members of the Janata Party in 1977. When Janata splintered two years later, the former leaders of Jana Sangh created the BJP. They wanted to retain the dynamism of Hindu militants, but extend the appeal of the party to the center. Tensions between Hindu nationalists and more secular leaders have remained a continuing problem for the BJP, with the balance swinging back and forth between the two factions. Exploiting and perhaps contributing to the rise of communal strife, the BJP increased its share of the popular vote from 7.4 percent in 1984 to 11.4 percent in 1989, and then almost doubled its vote in 1991 to about 20 percent, gaining 119 seats.

The meteoric rise of the BJP in 1991 seemed to call into question India's status as a secular society. The militant Hindu sects, especially the Shiv Sena, are more anti-Muslim than fundamentalist, but their hostility toward "special privileges" for Muslims, when pushed to an extreme, is expressed through devotion to Hindu ritual or culture. During the 1991 campaign, the leader of the Shiv Sena, Bal Thackeray, hailed the Hindu terrorist who had assassinated Mohandas Gandhi because "he saved the country from a second partition." A fiery female tribune of the "Hindu Awakening," Uma Bharti, saw the issue before the voters in simple terms: "whether this country belongs to Rama or to Babur!" (Rama is the incarnation of the Hindu deity, Vishnu; Babur is the founder of the Mogul Empire in India.)

The moderate leaders of the BJP—in particular the parliamentarian Lal Kishan Advani, and former foreign minister and amateur poet Atal Bihari Vajpayee—deny that the BJP is a religious party, arguing that Hinduism by its nature is an all-encompassing and nondogmatic religion. But they believe it is important to assert the Hindu identity of India and, as Vajpayee has put it, "to take note of the changing Hindu psyche." A principal support of the BJP, perhaps surprisingly, is the upwardly mobile middle class, including successful small shopkeepers and artisans seeking to improve their social status through emulation of the behavior of higher castes. The BJP moderates are in favor of deregulation of the economy, privatization, and an infusion of foreign capital—all of which appeals to the progressive middle class. Another attractive feature of the BJP is that it seems to present a healthy or clean alternative—rooted in religion—to the perceived corruption of mainstream parties. The BJP's devoted volunteers present a sharp contrast to the hired toughs and rented crowds associated in the public mind with some of its competitors.

The episode that most clearly defined the character of the BJP was the pilgrimage it sponsored to the town of Ayodhya, the presumed birthplace of the Hindu deity Rama, the mythical character who is the central figure of the Ramayana. According to Hindu militants, a mosque (the Babri Masjid) was built on the precise spot where Rama was born. The shrine to Rama they have in mind can be constructed only if the mosque is destroyed or moved, and they have a long list of other mosques destined for a similar fate. L. K. Advani, usually thought of as a moderate, launched a Rath Yatra (march of Rama's chariot), making its way through the solidly Hindu areas of north India to the town of Ayodhya. Mounted on a chariot made up to look like that of Rama, Advani was surrounded by men dressed as the monkeys of Hanuman's army. (Hanuman was the head of an army of monkeys who helped Rama rescue his wife, Sita, from the clutches of the demon, Ravana.) The Rath Yatra, portrayed as a means of reuniting Hindus and making them proud of their culture, led to communal rioting between Hindus and Muslims wherever it went. Advani had organized it in response to V. P. Singh's proposal to reserve almost one-half of government jobs for the lower castes, which the BJP denounced as an attack on the integrity of Hindu society and a recipe for civil war.

One of Rao's first acts as prime minister was to hold talks with BJP leaders in order to avert a showdown, but no agreement was reached. At the prime minister's request, the Supreme Court issued an order prohibiting damage to the mosque or building of a temple. No measures were taken to protect the site, even though Hindu fundamentalist organizations and the BJP called upon militants to begin building a temple at 12:26 P.M. on December 6. At the appointed time, the mosque was attacked and reduced to rubble,

triggering six days of communal violence, particularly against Muslims in BJP-dominated Bombay, with a death toll of over 200. Several thousand people were arrested or placed in preventive detention. The Rao government was shaken but did not fall. It defused the conflict at Ayodha, at least temporarily, by making use of the courts, and the BJP was willing to go along. But the issue had already served the purpose of firing up Hindu militancy, enabling the BJP to win victories in elections for state governments and to solidify its position as a national force.

BJP leaders realized that in order to govern they would have to tone down their Hindu nationalism. The need for an alliance strategy was evident in the aftermath of the 1996 election. The BJP, as the largest party (with 161

The sixteenth-century mosque at Ayodha was destroyed by Hindu extremists in December 1992. They were incited by the BJP and other political groups.

seats), was asked to form a government. But Vajpayee had to resign after only 13 days when he could not marshall a majority. The rival United Front coalition took over, and with Congress support held office for 18 months. The BJP remained the largest party in the 1998 elections, with 176 seats, but was still well short of a majority until the Telugu Desam party abandoned the United Front and joined the BJP-led coalition. Vajpayee sought a consensus on economic reform and an assertive foreign policy (including the development of nuclear weapons). But the defection of a Tamil regional party led to a defeat of the government by one vote, and new elections in 1999. This time Vajpayee improved his coalition-building technique and benefited from a favorable public perception of his leadership in dealing with renewed fighting in Kashmir. A BJP-led coalition went on to score an impressive victory in the 1999 election, but lost in 2004.

Reaffirmation of Hindu identity, according to BJP leaders, will cleanse and strengthen Indian society. But it also leads to increased demands for autonomy and even separation by Muslims and other ethnic minorities, adding to the already formidable strains on the political system.

The Communist Parties of India

The Communist movement of India is split between an orthodox party, the CPI; a rival party originally sympathetic to the Chinese, the CPI (M), for Marxist; and several militant and even terrorist groups inspired by Trotskyism, Maoism, and peasant violence—mainly the CPI (M-L), for Marxist-Leninist, and the Naxalites. The Communist movement has deep roots in Indian society and considerable success in appealing to intellectuals, workers, and poor and landless peasants, especially in West Bengal and Kerala. Since the election of 1952, the combined Communist vote has averaged about 10 percent of the total, falling slightly in 1977 to a little over 7 percent, returning to almost 10 percent in 1980, dipping again to 8.6 percent in 1984, and remaining steady since (6.9 percent in 1999).

The Communist Party of India (CPI), founded in 1928, was closely linked to the Soviet Union.

The CPI cooperated with the Congress Party during the struggle for independence in the 1930s, but relations between the two parties became strained with the outbreak of World War II. After the German invasion of the Soviet Union in 1941, the CPI and the Congress went separate ways: the Communists supported the war effort and the nationalists opted for noncooperation. Immediately after independence, the CPI pursued a militant policy of organizing the workers for revolution, but Communist tactics were moderated as relations between India and the Soviet Union improved. In the 1950s, the CPI endorsed aspects of Nehru's foreign policy and pledged to achieve socialism by peaceful means.

However, the revolutionary elements in the party were restive. Pro-Chinese leftists refused to condemn China when the border conflict with India broke out, and withdrew from the party secretariat in 1962; two years later they broke away completely and formed the Communist Party of India (Marxist). The CPI (M) hailed the Chinese as opposed to the Soviet model of Communism, and sought to use elections as a means of mobilizing workers and peasants for revolutionary action. In 1969 another fission took place. The extreme left created the Communist Party of India (Marxist-Leninist), committed to a Maoist tactic of immediate armed struggle and terrorism. Indian Maoists called themselves "Naxalites" in honor of the tenant peasants of Naxalbari (a hill town in West Bengal), who were then forcibly seizing and occupying their land.

After the secession of the Marxists, the policy of the orthodox CPI remained the pursuit of its objectives through the electoral process, seeking alliances with all progressive forces. It collaborated with Indira Gandhi and her Congress (R) in 1969, providing the government the margin of support needed to stay in power. The Congress subsequently refrained from running candidates in about one-third of the districts where the CPI had a reasonable chance of winning. Cooperation with the Congress paid off for the CPI in 1971, enabling it to win 23 seats; but in 1977 the tactic backfired and the CPI was reduced to under 3 percent of the popular vote, retaining only 7 seats in the Lok Sabha. In 1980 the CPI did not collaborate with Indira Gandhi's Congress (I) but still managed to win 11 seats. It went down to 6 seats with 2.6 percent of the vote in 1984, and up to 13 seats with 2.5 percent in 1991. In 2004, it was down to 1.4 percent of the vote and 10 seats.

Far from supporting Indira Gandhi during the emergency, the CPI (M) cooperated with the Janata, winning 4.3 percent of the vote in the 1977 election and 22 seats in the Lok Sabhal, thus forging ahead of the orthodox party. The Marxists gradually toned down and finally abandoned Maoist policies. In 1980 they upped their vote to 6.1 percent, winning 35 seats. In 1984 they retained 22 seats with 6 percent of the vote, going up to 33 seats in 1989 and 43 seats in 2004, and seemed to be on the road to integration within the parliamentary system. The two Communist parties remained distinct, however. The CPI continued to acclaim the international leadership role of the Soviet Union, denouncing both Maoism and Eurocommunism. The CPI (M) refused to align itself with the Soviet Union, but became increasingly critical of China. Both Communist parties were critical of Gorbachev's reforms, rejoiced when hardliners arrested Gorbachev in August 1991, and lamented the triumph of Yeltsin.

Despite the crisis of Communism elsewhere in the world, both Indian Communist parties have maintained their strength, mainly because of their grip on local governments. The CPI (M) has been the ruling party in West Bengal (which includes Calcutta) since 1977, and has taken turns at governing in two other states (Kerala and Tritura). The Communist parties are functioning more and more like Social Democratic parties—accepting a mixed economy and devoting their energies to defense of their constituents, rather than making a revolution. Both Communist parties announced after the 1991 election that they would not vote to bring down the Congress government formed by Narasimha Rao. After fighting against the liberalization policies instituted by the Rao government, the CPI (M)–led government of West Bengal in September 1994 formally adopted the cause of economic reform, throwing itself with fervor into a campaign to attract foreign capital and promote free

enterprise. CPI (M) Chief Minister Jyoti Basu traveled to the United States in order to urge bankers and corporate executives to invest in West Bengal. India's Communist parties thus seem to be adopting the Chinese tactic of encouraging expansion of the private sector while retaining political control whenever possible.

Regional Parties

In addition to the All-India parties just described, there are several locally important regional parties, especially in the Punjab, West Bengal, and Tamil Nadu. These parties focus on ethnic, religious, or linguistic identity and occasionally enter into alliance with national parties for mutually profitable reasons. Many regional parties disappear once immediate demands are met, but a few have become firmly established.

The Dravida Munnetra Kazhagam (DMK) and its rival secessionist All-India Anna DMK (AIADMK) both agitate in favor of the Tamil language and greater autonomy for Tamil Nadu. The popular film star, M. G. Ramachandran, broke away from the DMK in 1972 and founded the AIADMK to protest policies of the party after the death of its creator, C. N. Annaduri ("Anna"). The AIADMK was allied with the Congress in 1984, while M. Karunanidhi, head of the DMK, joined the National Front in 1988. After the death of M. G. Ramachandran in 1987, the AIADMK was rent by factionalism but remained allied to the Congress.

The Telegu Desam, created by film star T. N. Rama Rao in 1982, urges a stronger role for states. The TDP has consistently supported the opposition to Congress, playing an important role in creation of the Janata, later joining the United Front. However, after the 1998 elections the TDP withdrew from the United Front and supported the BJP in a vote of confidence. It won 25 seats in the 2004 election as a BJP ally.

The Akali Dal—defender of the Sikh faith— has been a major force in the Punjab, usually winning about 25 percent of the vote in that region. After a period of factionalism in the 1980s, the Akali Dal was gradually rebuilt by moderate leaders, in alliance with the BJP.

The Bahujan Samaj Party (BSP) was created in 1984 to defend the interests of Dalits, lower castes, and Muslims. It is a major force in Uttar Pradesh, frequently cooperating with the BJP (though not in 1999). It won 19 seats in 2004.

EVOLUTION OF THE PARTY SYSTEM

Surveying a half-century of party evolution in India, some long-term trends are evident despite the cacaphony of fragmented parties and shifting alliances. (1) India has moved from one-party dominance to a competitive party system in which there are now two leading parties. The BJP and the Congress each wins roughly 25 percent of the popular vote, and each requires support from allies in order to govern. (2) Regional parties are now firmly established in many state governments and are playing an ever larger role on the national scene as well. (3) A defining issue in India, as in Western nations, is where to draw the line between the state and the market. The collapse of Communism in Europe has discredited the command economy, and social democratic parties are more open to the role of the private sector in fostering economic growth and prosperity. (4) Along with the increase in the pace of modernization in India, there is an increase also in political militancy by the disadvantaged and the poor, particularly members of the Scheduled Castes, Scheduled Tribes, and Other Backward Castes (OBCs), who constitute from one-fourth to one-half (depending on definitions) of the population. As the Dalits (the "oppressed") move out of their traditional and even tribal structures, their expectations are aroused, and they become politically active. In 1996, H. D. Deve Gowda became the first member of a low caste to be elected prime minister, and half the members of his short-lived government also were members of low castes. (5) Immediately after independence, the Congress championed secularism and appealed to Muslims as well as Hindus. Nehru was a scathing critic of Hindu militancy, particularly the Jana Sangh. But the explosion of ethnic violence in the Punjab and Kashmir has gone hand in hand with the rise of militant Hindu parties, like the BJP.

Indian politics now bears some resemblance to French politics, to take one of the European systems treated earlier in this volume. In both countries there are now two rival coalitions, each led by one or two large parties (the Gaullist RPR and centrist UDF on the Right and the Socialist party on the Left in France, BJP and Congress in India). Major issues in both revolve around the respective roles of state and markets in the economy, and ethnic identity versus social integration. In both countries, Muslims now constitute a substantial minority (11 percent in India, perhaps 8 percent in France), posing special problems concerning assimilation.

The Indian party system is hardly distinctive because of the number of major parties or because of the importance of the Communist movements. After all, there are four major parties in France, and the Communist Party has been even stronger in France than in India. But there is a distinct style of politics in a country in which half the electorate is illiterate, the per capita income is just $2,900 a year (it is $27,600 in France), and most people are still attached to traditional culture. That is, the Indian parties reflect not only the modern conflict among advocates of capitalism, liberalism, socialism, and Communism, but also the still lively clash between a preindustrial and in many instances primitive society and the rapidly evolving, highly sophisticated industrial and scientific society. The conflict between secular forces and ethnic and religious movements has intensified with the rise of the BJP. Crosscutting currents of the primitive, traditional, and modern merge into a mix that is potentially more explosive than in the parliamentary democracy of any Western society.

THE CONSTITUTION OF INDIA

The political institutions through which Indians govern themselves were created by the 1949 Constitution of India—the product of almost three years' deliberation by the Constituent Assembly (whose members were originally elected by provincial legislatures). One reason for the long delay in promulgating the constitution is that the Assembly also functioned as the Provisional Parliament immediately following independence, and therefore members had to conduct the business of the nation at the same time that they were drafting a basic law. The leaders of the Congress party—especially Nehru, Rajenda Prasad, Sardar Vallabhbhai Patel, and M. A. K. Azad (a Muslim)—dominated debates and presided over the drafting of the document.

The new constitution went into effect on January 26, 1950. It incorporates much of the Government of India Act of 1935, adding considerable detail on civil liberties and the federal system. With its 395 articles and 8 schedules, the Constitution of India holds the distinction of being one of the longest in the world. The Indians essentially adopted the British parliamentary system but modified it to suit their own circumstances. They could hardly replicate an English constitution that had evolved over several centuries and is expressed in unique medieval and early modern statutes and documents such as the Magna Carta (1215), the Bill of Rights (1689), and the Act of Settlement (1701). Instead, they followed the practice of all other democratic governments in the world by enacting a basic law. The preamble of the Indian Constitution reflects the philosophy of the movement for national liberation and is reminiscent as well of the Declaration of Independence and preamble to the Constitution of the United States.

> WE, THE PEOPLE OF INDIA, having solemnly resolved to constitute India into a SOVEREIGN, DEMOCRATIC REPUBLIC and to secure to all its citizens:
>   JUSTICE, social, economic and political;
>   LIBERTY of thought, expression, belief, faith and worship;
>   EQUALITY of status and opportunity; and to promote among them all
>   FRATERNITY assuring the dignity of the individual and the unity of the Nation;
>   IN OUR CONSTITUENT ASSEMBLY … DO HEREBY ADOPT, ENACT AND GIVE TO OURSELVES THIS CONSTITUTION

The basic commitment of the Constituent Assembly was to a parliamentary system (that is, a cabinet responsible to the lower house); a republic (hence, an elected president would play the role of head of state); a federation with a strong center (striking a balance between national authority and provincial assemblies); and a secular system (not a state divided between Hindus and Muslims). Republican institutions and Commonwealth membership were made compatible when India agreed to recognize the British monarch as the symbol of free association and as such the head of the Commonwealth, without otherwise acknowledging any allegiance to the Crown.

One respect in which the Indians departed from British practice and reflected American tradition was in guaranteeing civil liberties (called Fundamental Rights) and making them enforceable through courts. The rights thus protected under the constitution make up an impressive catalog: equality, freedom, freedom of religion, and the right to property, as well as some not specifically set forth in the American Bill of Rights—for example, freedom from exploitation, and cultural and educational rights. Especially important in Indian society are the abolition of untouchability, guarantees of equal opportunity in public employment, and prohibition of discrimination on grounds of religion, race, caste, or sex.

Balancing off the declaration of fundamental rights of citizens against the state are the "directive principles" that set forth the duty of the state toward the citizens. The constitution enjoins the state to promote the welfare of the people by creating social, economic, and political justice. These principles are difficult to carry out because all political parties proclaim the promotion of the public welfare as their goal, but disagree on how to go about doing it. Similarly, abolition of untouchability and guarantees of full employment do not depend exclusively on constitutional provisions. Such measures become effective only under appropriate political, economic, and social conditions.

The Constitution of India goes further than most similar documents in stipulating that freedoms may be suspended or abrogated during an emergency. Part XVIII (Emergency Provisions) of the Constitution specifically gives the president the power to suspend the right to freedom in a national emergency, though the president may act only on the advice of the prime minister. After the Chinese incursion in 1962, a national emergency was declared—and lasted officially for six years. During this emergency, Parliament passed a Defense of India Act (modeled on the Defense of the Realm Acts in Britain), which empowered the government to detain any person it suspected on reasonable grounds to be "of hostile origin" or to be "likely to act" in a manner harmful to Indian defense, state security, maintenance of public order, India's relations with foreign states, or the efficient conduct of military operations.

The balance between individual rights and national unity or law and order swings decidedly toward the latter in an emergency. After the emergency relating to the conflict with China was finally lifted, Parliament passed an Unlawful Activities Prevention Act which continued many of the restrictions of the previous period. The power of the executive to override individual rights was further strengthened by the Maintenance of Internal Security Act of 1971. The most spectacular use of emergency power since the founding of the Indian Republic was the emergency rule invoked by Mrs. Indira Gandhi in 1975–1977.

After the decision of the Allahabad High Court in June 1975 that Mrs. Gandhi had violated the electoral law, the opposition parties began a mass campaign of civil disobedience to force the prime minister to resign. One of India's most colorful political leaders, Jaya Prakash Narayan, pointedly urged the army and police to refuse to obey "unjust orders." The prime minister thereupon advised the president to proclaim, by virtue of the power vested in him by Article 352 of the constitution, that "a grave emergency exists whereby the security of India is threatened by internal disturbance." During the one year and nine months of the emergency, some 110,000 people all told were arrested and imprisoned without trial. Newspapers were forbidden to publish reports affecting India's relations with foreign countries, denigrating the office of the prime

minister, causing disaffection among members of the armed forces or government employees, or bringing the government into hatred or contempt. These regulations were strictly enforced. The government also banned several militant Hindu organizations and the CPI (M).

Through the amending process, the constitution was changed so drastically that it became virtually a different system of government. Amendments can be added to the constitution by a majority vote of both houses with at least two-thirds of the members of each house present and voting; in addition, amendments relating to the political institutions must be ratified by the legislatures of a majority of the states. Three amendments (the 39th, 40th, and 41st) were passed in rapid succession by Parliament and ratified soon after the emergency was declared. These amendments provided that the president's reasons for proclaiming an emergency could not be challenged in any court; also that all matters relating to the election of the president, vice president, speaker of the Lok Sabha, or the prime minister should be referred to a new authority to be created by Parliament and not be judged by the regular courts; that this authority not be questioned by any court; and that all pending proceedings against the president, vice president, speaker, and prime minister were null and void.

In addition, a Maintenance of Internal Security (Amendment) Bill was passed in 1976. It provided that the grounds on which a person had been detained should not be disclosed to the detainee or any other person. President Ahmed ordered the suspension for the period of the emergency of any person's right to apply to the courts for enforcement of Article 19 of the constitution—that is, the rights to freedom of speech and expression and to peaceable assembly. The Supreme Court also held that the government could suspend habeas corpus. One justice declared that the public safety was the highest law in time of crisis.

The most sweeping change of all was instituted by the Constitution (42nd Amendment) Bill, known as A42. This amendment was passed by Parliament on November 11, 1976, by a vote of 366 to 4 in the Lok Sabha and 191 to 0 in the

Rajya Sabha; it was ratified by the legislatures of more than half the states within a month, received the assent of President Ahmed on December 18, 1976, and took effect a few weeks later. A42 amended 37 articles, repealed 4, and introduced 13 new articles. Among the most important provisions were the following:

1. *Preamble:* India was now described as a "sovereign socialist secular democratic republic."

2. *Fundamental rights:* No law giving effect to the "directive principles" might be declared unconstitutional on the ground that it infringed on the fundamental rights guaranteed by the constitution. No law prohibiting antinational activities should be nullified on grounds of violating individual liberties. Antinational activities were broadly defined to embrace advocacy of secession; threatening the sovereignty or integrity of India or "the security of the state or the unity of the nation"; overthrowing the government by force; creating internal disruptions; and fomenting communal and caste hatred.

3. *Fundamental duties:* A new article was inserted into the constitution, stating that every citizen has the duty to abide by the constitution, cherish the ideals of the national struggle for freedom, defend the country, promote social harmony, and strive toward excellence.

4. *The executive:* The article stating that the Council of Ministers would "aid and advise the president in the exercise of his functions" was amended to read that the Council of Ministers would aid and advise the president, "who shall, in the exercise of his functions, act in accordance with such advice."

5. *Amendments:* It was stated that no amendment to the constitution can be called into question "in any court on any ground."

Most of the provisions of A42 were reversed by two constitutional amendments adopted under the Desai government in 1977. Specifically, the provision empowering Parliament to legislate

Congress Party President Sonia Gandhi (widow of former Prime Minister Rajiv Gandhi) at an election rally.

against antinational activity was repealed, and the president was given the right to ask the Council of Ministers to reconsider its decisions. Restrictions were also imposed on the use of emergency powers. A proclamation of emergency can now be issued only when the security of India is threatened by external aggression or armed rebellion. Internal disturbances not amounting to armed rebellion are an insufficient ground. The Council of Ministers must forward its request for an emergency to the president in writing; the proclamation must be approved by Parliament within a month by a two-thirds majority, can remain in force for only six months, and can be extended only after another vote by a two-thirds majority. Even though the main structures of the 1949 Constitution were restored, the emergency is a reminder of the fragility of civil liberties in India.

THE PRESIDENT AND VICE PRESIDENT

The constitution vests the executive power in a president, who is elected for a five-year term by an electoral college consisting of members of Parliament and state legislative assemblies. The voting procedure is complex in order to maintain a rough parity among the states based on population, with electors casting a preferential ballot. The vice president is elected for a five-year term by both houses of Parliament in a joint session. As in the United States, the vice president presides over the upper house of Parliament (the Rajya Sabha). The vice president's main function, of course, is to take the place of the president in case of death or incapacity; in that event a presidential election must be held within six months.

In theory, the president is given vast powers under the constitution. The president may dissolve Parliament, declare an emergency in a state, and rule that state by decree. The president may refuse to assent to a bill, although the veto may be overridden if the bill is repassed by both houses. Also, the president is commander-in-chief of the armed forces and appoints state governors and Supreme Court justices. It was understood by the framers of the constitution that the president would act only on the advice of the prime minister, and this understanding

has been respected in practice. The vast powers of the president have devolved largely upon the prime minister. Nonetheless, the president has considerable influence within the political system. The president is entitled to be informed and consulted by the prime minister, has recently been accorded the power to ask the Council of Ministers to reconsider a decision, and must sign all legislation.

Perhaps the most important function of the president is to appoint the prime minister (who must then win a vote of confidence in the Lok Sabha). During the period of Congress Party dominance (until the election of 1977), the president had little discretion, because the leader of the Congress was the only person who could have the confidence of Parliament. But with the emergence of a more competitive party system, elections frequently produced parliaments where no party or even coalition of parties had a clear majority. Presidents under such situations had considerable leeway in calculating which party leader had the best chance to secure a majority, or whether to dissolve parliament and call new elections. The presidental selection process therefore became more intensely partisan. When the Janata Party disintegrated in 1979, President Reddy asked Charan Singh, of Janata, to form a government. It lasted only three weeks. Rather than ask another Janata leader to succeed him, President Reddy made the controversial decision

---

REVIEW 10.2

PRESIDENTS OF INDIA

President	Election	President	Election
Rajendra Prasad	1950	Neelam Sanjiva Reddy	1977
Rajendra Prasad	1952	Zail Singh	1980
Rajendra Prasad	1957	R. Venkataraman	1987
Dr. S. Radhakrishnan	1962	Shankar Dayal Sharma	1992
Dr. Zakir Hussain	1967 (died 1969)	K. R. Narayanan	1997
V. V. Giri	1969	A. P. J. Abdul Kalam	2002
Fakhruddin Ali Ahmed	1974 (died 1977)		

to dissolve Parliament. When Mrs. Gandhi was assassinated in 1984, President Zail Singh (a loyal follower of Mrs. Gandhi) skipped the usual consultations with party leaders; he simply asked Rajiv Gandhi to form a government. Afterwards, President Singh and Prime Minister Rajiv did not get along, attacking each other in public. Singh's successor, R. Venkataraman, also backed by the Congress, played a larger than usual role in deciding who should be named prime minister, because no political party received a majority in the elections of 1989 and 1991.

In 1997 the first Dalit (or untouchable), K. R. Narayanan, was elected president. A scholar and member of the Congress, Narayanan became a highly active president, returning to the Cabinet for reconsideration a decision to place Uttar Pradesh under president's rule, and urging the appointment of members of the Scheduled Castes and Tribes as judges. In July 2002, the BJP backed the presidential candidacy of a scientist who had supervised creation of India's nuclear missile program, A. P. J. Abdul Kalam. An ethnic Tamil, a Muslim, and author of a best-selling autobiography, Kalam won 90 percent of the votes of the legislators. The new president called for transformation of India into a "developed" and "prosperous" nation.

THE PARLIAMENT

There are two chambers of Parliament: the lower house, Lok Sabha (House of the People), which now has 543 members, and an upper house, Rajya Sabha (Council of States), whose membership is limited to 250. The president appoints 12 members to the Rajya Sabha as representatives of the arts and professions, and all the other members are elected by the state legislatures; hence the upper house serves as a direct link between the state and national governments.

The Lok Sabha members are elected on the basis of single-member constituencies. Its normal term is five years, although it may be dissolved at any time by the president (on advice of the prime minister). According to the constitution, the Lok Sabha must meet at least twice a year, with no more than six months between sessions. Most members speak in either English or Hindi but may use other languages if they wish. As in the British House of Commons, the Speaker is elected from among the members and is supposed to be nonpartisan once in office. Unlike the House of Commons, the Lok Sabha has a system of standing committees that covers the whole range of government operations—including a Rules Committee and others that oversee the budget, exercise of delegated power, and general performance of the ministries. In recent years, up to half of the members of each new Parliament have never before served in that body. Inexperience and lack of office space and staff have contributed to the relative weakness of Parliament in its dealings with the cabinet and the civil service.

Legislative procedure in the Indian Parliament is similar to that in the British Parliament, though the Rajya Sabha has a more important role than the House of Lords. Legislation is drafted and introduced by the government; a severely limited amount of time is reserved each week for bills presented by private members (those who are not members of ministries). As in Britain, there are three readings. The first reading is of the title only and with no debate. The Speaker then assigns the bill to a select (or ad hoc) committee, made up with the advice of party leaders, just to consider that bill. The second reading is based on the report of the select committee; it is at this stage that debate and voting on each clause take place. The third reading is merely on the formal motion that the bill be passed. Money bills can be introduced only in the Lok Sabha; other legislation can originate in either house, although in practice most bills are presented first in the Lok Sabha.

If the two houses do not agree, the bill may be sent back and forth until all differences have been resolved. If there is still no agreement, the president may call a joint session of Parliament, where the matter is settled by a majority vote, thus giving the more numerous Lok Sabha members the upper hand. Joint sessions are rarely necessary, however. If the Rajya Sabha rejects a money bill, it can be enacted into law simply by having the Lok Sabha repass it.

Another feature of Indian legislative procedure based directly on British practice is the question period, which begins each daily session of Parliament. Members are permitted to ask questions of ministers concerning most matters of public policy; replies are generally of interest to the press. Members may ask follow-up questions that test the minister's ability to think under pressure. Occasionally, ministers have been forced to resign because of incompetence or scandal brought out during the question period.

The central notion in parliamentary government is that the cabinet is responsible to Parliament and must resign when it loses the confidence of that body. The Lok Sabha possesses one important weapon in its relations with the cabinet: Any 50 members may introduce a motion of censure; if it carries, the cabinet must resign. The cabinet is not responsible to the Rajya Sabha, which has no power to censure the government. The opposition in the Lok Sabha has been so fragmented in the past that motions of censure were rare because no single opposition party had as many as 50 members. As in Britain, it is expected that the governing party will "manage" the deliberations of Parliament and in so doing will be supported by its members. Parliament plays an important role, not so much as policy maker, but as the forum in which declarations of government policy are made and government and opposition engage in structured debate.

THE PRIME MINISTER AND COUNCIL OF MINISTERS

The effective executive in India—the prime minister, Council of Ministers, and cabinet—is based squarely on the British model. Exactly the same distinctions are made in India as in Britain among all three groups; they have the same relationship to Parliament, but the dominance of the executive over Parliament is perhaps even greater in India. The prime minister is chosen by the president, but in general the president has no choice. He or she must nominate the leader of the majority party in the Lok Sabha, otherwise

the government would not have the confidence of that body.

The prime minister chooses ministers, who are then officially appointed by the president. Ministers must be members of Parliament; nonmembers may be appointed if within six months they become members of Parliament through a by-election. The Council of Ministers is collectively responsible to Parliament for all decisions of the government; as in Britain, however, this collective responsibility does not mean that each minister is fully aware of decisions made by colleagues, for the good reason that the Council of Ministers never meets as a collective entity. The ministry is a large group that includes heads and deputy heads of all the departments. By tradition, the most important ministers (usually from 12 to 18 in number) are invited by the prime minister to join the cabinet, which is not mentioned in the constitution. The cabinet meets regularly once a week and is responsible for formulation and coordination of all government policy. By invitation, other ministers or experts can attend cabinet sessions for discussion of matters in which they have special interest or expertise.

Even the cabinet is too unwieldy for policy making, so all prime ministers have created specialized committees consisting of a few ministers responsible for a specific area or problem. The prime minister, who usually chairs these committees, is in a position to dominate their deliberations. Nehru formed an emergency committee of the cabinet with six members as the equivalent of the "inner cabinet" in Britain; it virtually replaced the larger cabinet as a decision-making body for important policy. Since then each prime minister has continued the practice of consulting regularly with some sort of inner cabinet. As in Britain, a special agency of the civil service is assigned to the prime minister and cabinet to furnish secretarial and administrative assistance in preparing agendas, recording decisions, following up on implementation, and coordinating the various special committees of the cabinet. The central secretariat, headed by a cabinet secretary, thus provides an indispensable element of professionalism and continuity in cabinet deliberations. In view of the secretariat's reputation for irreproachable professionalism, it came as a shock when it was revealed in 1985 that one of its trusted and most important members had long been a spy in the service of a foreign power.

The prime minister is the "buckle that binds" the president, Council of Ministers, cabinet, and Parliament. The dominance of the prime minister within the system was especially evident during the tenure of the first occupant of the office, Jawaharlal Nehru. As leader of the national independence movement and the Congress Party, Nehru was the towering figure of Indian politics in the years following independence. Many feared that his departure would usher in a period of chaos, but no succession struggle took place immediately after Nehru's death in May 1964. The Congress Party unanimously chose one of Nehru's close collaborators, Lal Bahadur Shastri, as prime minister. When Shastri died suddenly in January 1966, the Congress Party turned to Nehru's daughter, Indira Gandhi (no relation to Mohandas Gandhi), a former president of the party. Thereafter she was at the center of the political stage, except for the period between the defeat of the Congress Party in 1977 and its triumphant comeback in 1980. The two prime ministers who served from 1977

to 1979—Morarji Desai and Charan Singh—were not able to fashion a solid majority. Indira Gandhi's elder son, Rajiv, continued the tradition of leadership by a member of the Nehru family after his mother's assassination. The successors to Rajiv—V. P. Singh (1989–1990) and Chandra Shekhar (1990–1991)—were at the mercy of their outside supporters and could not fully wield their power.

Narasimha Rao (Congress) came close to a working majority after the election of 1991 but still depended on outside support from other parties to carry out his program. He proved surprisingly adept at negotiating with opposition leaders in order to arrive at consensual policies. Although he served a full five-year term, Rao lost popular support when consensus seemed to turn into passivity, and when evidence accumulated of widespread corruption. Congress went from 37 to 28 percent of the vote in the election of 1996, losing almost half of its seats. In the period of instability that followed, there were four prime ministers in three years. Atal Behari Vajpayee, the leader of the BJP, was asked to form a government after the indecisive 1996 election, but he resigned after 13 days when he could not secure a majority. The next two prime ministers,

REVIEW 10.3

PRIME MINISTERS OF INDIA

Jawaharlal Nehru	1947–1964	Congress
Lal Bahadur Shastri	1964–1966	Congress
Indira Gandhi	1966–1977	Congress
Morarji Desai	1977–1979	Janata
Charan Singh	1979–1980	Janata
Indira Gandhi	1980–1984	Congress
Rajiv Gandhi	1984–1989	Congress
V. P. Singh	1989–1990	Janata Dal
Chandra Shekhar	1990–1991	Samajwadi Janata
Narasimha Rao	1991–1996	Congress
Atal Bihari Vajpayee	May 15–28 1996	BJP
H. D. Deve Gowda	June 1996–April 1997	Janata Dal
I. K. Gujral	April 1997–1998	Janata Dal
Atal Bihari Vajpayee	March 1998–May 2004	BJP
Manmohan Singh	May 2004	Congress

H. D. Gowda and I. K. Gujral, were Janata Dal leaders dependent on support from Congress to remain in office. Both were hobbled by the need to keep an unstable coalition together. Gowda was replaced by Gujral in April 1997 when Congress withdrew its support, and Gujral suffered the same fate in November 1997, necessitating new elections in 1998.

Again Vajpayee, as leader of the largest party, was asked to form a government. This time he downplayed the BJP's militant Hinduism, received the backing of an important regional party (Telegu Desam), and governed for 18 months before another regional party defected, leading to his defeat on a vote of confidence by

one vote, and new elections in 1999. Vajpayee achieved new popularity for his decision in May 1998 to develop nuclear weapons, his forceful action in resisting an attack by insurgents in Kashmir in the spring of 1999 while head of the caretaker government, and his skill in building an electoral coalition. Following the 1999 election, Vajpayee was able to form a government that had a comfortable majority, offering hope for a return to political stability. The office of the prime minister has remained the major source of policy making and the chief political prize sought by all contenders. After the 2004 election, Manmohan Singh was appointed as India's first Sikh and non-Hindu prime minister.

An Indian dynasty. Prime minister Jawaharlal Nehru, together with his daughter and future prime minister, Indira Gandhi, and her two sons Sanjay and Rajiv (who became prime minister after his mother's assassination in 1984). This photo was taken in 1956 during Nehru's state visit to West Germany. Chancellor Konrad Adenauer is directly behind Nehru. Rajiv was assassinated in 1991.

THE SUPREME COURT

The constitution creates a Supreme Court, consisting of a chief justice and 25 associates, appointed by the president after consultation with sitting members of the court and of state courts. The Indian Supreme Court, unlike its British counterpart, may declare an act of Parliament unconstitutional. It is relatively easy, however, for Parliament to reverse decisions by the Supreme Court through the amending process. Several court decisions invalidating land reform legislation were overridden.

During the 1975–1977 emergency, the Supreme Court pointedly sided with the government, damaging its reputation as a judicial

A CLOSER LOOK

10.1

STRUCTURE OF GOVERNMENT IN INDIA

The chart below shows the channels of political responsibility within the government of India. The voters directly elect the Lok Sabha and the state legislatures; the state legislatures select the members of the upper chamber, the Rajya Sabha (except for 12 members selected by the president, not indicated on the chart). The president is elected by an electoral college, consisting of elected members of both houses of Parliament and of the legislatures in all the states, with the vote weighted on the basis of population. The president selects a prime minister, who is normally the leader of the majority party in the Lok Sabha, or enjoys the support of a majority. The prime minister selects the ministers. The president, after consulting with existing judges of the Supreme Court and of high courts of the states, appoints the judges of the Supreme Court.

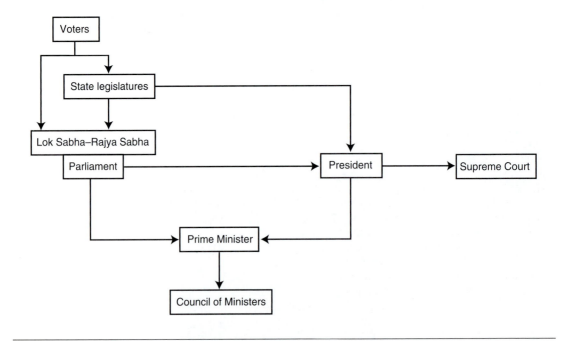

guardian of civil liberties. In 1976 the Forty-second Amendment prohibited the Supreme Court from reviewing changes introduced by constitutional amendment. But in 1980 the Court reaffirmed its power to safeguard the "basic structure" of the constitution, even in amendments. Beginning in the 1980s the Court has encouraged litigation to defend the rights of the poor, and to promote the public interest. It has also assumed an active role in probing and prosecuting government corruption. The understaffed courts are struggling to carry out their program of judicial activism, and many critics charge that the courts are encroaching upon the domain of elected officials.

THE BUREAUCRACY

Indians have long believed that their political system is more effective than those of other developing countries because of the bureaucratic structures inherited from the British; the belief may be at least partly correct. After independence, the old Indian civil service of the British period was refashioned as the Indian Administrative Services (IAS). The membership of the IAS is only about 4,000 people—a minuscule fraction of the 13 million civil servants in India—but they are the steel frame of the whole edifice.

Recruitment into the IAS (approximately 140 annually) and into a few central services of individual ministries, such as the foreign service, is supervised by a Union Public Service Commission. As in Great Britain, an attempt is made through examinations and interviews to select young people of exceptional intelligence and talent, who are then given special training and form a policy-making stratum within the huge civil service establishment. One advantage of this system is to guarantee the competence of the higher civil service. However, the middle and lower levels of the civil service are generally far below the standard set by the top stratum. The explosive growth of the private sector in the past two decades has made it more difficult to recruit and retain bright young university graduates, who are tempted increasingly by the high salaries and greater rewards of management positions in business.

In sum, the Indians have gradually adapted British-style institutions to their own circumstances. These institutions have become familiar to all Indians and are increasingly considered an appropriate mechanism for resolving political conflicts and working out compromises. The greatest crisis of the democratic system probably was the emergency; had it endured, the character of the constitution as originally conceived would have been altered. But the Indian public brought the emergency to an end, and its verdict was accepted by Mrs. Gandhi and her supporters. Some observers have expressed concern that the personalization of power under both Indira and Rajiv Gandhi has led to an erosion of institutions, including the Congress Party as well as Parliament and state governments. Atul Kohli has attributed institutional decay to "the destructive and self-serving acts of leaders who find institutions a constraint on personal power," as well as to mounting social pressures.[6] Without strong institutions as intermediaries between state and society, he contends, policy making has become arbitrary and ineffective.

Certainly we should not underestimate the difficulty of maintaining viable democratic government in any developing country. Yet the constitution held firm in the first 50 years of its existence and acquired genuine legitimacy. Every year that passes increases the chances that the system will be able to meet critical new challenges in the future, despite the heterogeneity of Indian society and the intensity of its political divisions.

---

[6]Atul Kohli, ed. *India's Democracy: An Analysis of Changing State-Society Relations* (Princeton, NJ: Princeton University Press, 1990), p. 309.

Thinking Critically

1. How does the caste system in India differ from the class system in Europe?
2. Are there any significant differences between the interest group structures in India and in Europe?
3. Would you characterize the Indian party system as one-party dominant, two-party, or multiparty? How important are these distinctions?
4. What are the most important differences today between the Bharatiya Janata Party (BJP) and the Congress Party?
5. Is the Indian government basically a federal system, or a unitary system with a large measure of decentralization?

KEY TERMS

L. K. Advani *(565–566)*
Bharatiya Janata Party (BJP) *(553–554, 559–560, 563, 565–567)*
Communist Party of India (Marxist)—
CPI (M) *(557, 559, 567–568)*
Congress Party *(553–554, 557–564)*
Congress (I) *(558–564)*
Council of Ministers *(575–576)*
emergency rule *(570–572)*
Indira Gandhi *(556–557, 562, 571–572, 576, 579)*
Rajiv Gandhi *(555, 558–560, 562–563, 574)*
Indian Administrative Services *(579)*
Janata Party *(557, 564–565)*
A. P. J. Abdul Kalam *(574)*
Lok Sabha *(556, 560, 574–575)*
Naxalites *(567)*
president *(573–574)*
president's rule *(573–574)*
prime minister *(574–577)*
Rajya Sabha *(574–575)*
Narasimha Rao *(555, 563, 566, 576)*
V. P. Singh *(555, 558, 563–564, 566)*
Supreme Court *(578–579)*
Atal Bihari Vajpayee *(555, 557, 560–561, 565, 567, 576–577)*

FURTHER READINGS

Ahmed, Ishtiaq. *State, Nation and Ethnicity in Contemporary South Asia* (London: Pinter, 1996).

Austin, Granville. *Working a Democratic Constitution: The Indian Experience* (Delhi: Oxford University Press, 1999).

Brass, Paul R. *The Politics of India since Independence*, rev. ed. (Cambridge: Cambridge University Press, 1994).

Frank, Katherine. *India: The Life of Indira Nehon Gandhi* (Boston: Houghton Mifflin, 2002).

Gould, Harold A., and S. Ganguly, eds. *India Votes: The Quest for Consensus, 1989 and 1991* (Boulder, CO: Westview Press, 1993).

Hansen, Thomas B., and C. Jaffrelot, eds. *The BJP and the Compulsions of Politics in India* (Delhi: Oxford University Press, 1998).

Hardgrave, Robert L., and S. A. Kochanek. *India: Government and Politics in a Developing Nation*, 6th ed. (New York: Harcourt College Publishers, 2000).

Jaffrelot, Christophe. *The Hindu National Movement and Indian Politics, 1925 to the 1990s* (London: Hurst, 1996).

Kohli, Atul, ed. *India's Democracy: An Analysis of Changing State-Society Relations* (Princeton, NJ: Princeton University Press, 1990).

Kohli, Atul, ed. *The Success of India's Democracy* (New York: Cambridge University Press, 2001).

Manor, James, ed. *Nehru to the Nineties: The Changing Office of Prime Minister in India* (London: Hurst, 1994).

Pylee, M. V. *Constitutional Government in India*, 4th ed. (Bombay: Asia Publishing House, 1984).

Sen Gupta, Bhabani. *Rajiv Gandhi: A Political Study* (New Delhi: Kanarak Publishers, 1989).

Vora, R., ed. *Indian Democracy: Meanings and Practices* (New Delhi: Thousand Oaks, 2004).

Weiner, Myron. *The Indian Paradox: Essays in Modern Indian Politics* (New Delhi: Sage, 1989).

Zavos, John, et al., eds. *The Politics of Cultural Mobilization in India* (New York: Oxford University Press, 2004).

C. PUBLIC POLICY

Political institutions are not ends in themselves; they are designed to formulate policy. The ultimate test of a political system is its effectiveness in permitting a people to attain collective goals. The leaders of the independence movement in India were determined to modernize their nation and conquer poverty through democratic means. An appraisal of the political system they created, then, calls for a review of the effort by Indians to fashion a modern state, society, and economy.

MODERNIZATION: A BALANCE SHEET

In the first decade after independence was won in 1947, Indians succeeded beyond the expectations of most observers in endowing themselves with a rational and workable structure. Their constitution was drafted, promulgated, and implemented. The key position within this structure was occupied by a charismatic leader who had led the struggle of national independence, a struggle which was shared by a political party that stood ready to shoulder the burden and responsibility of power. Buttressing the system was a civil service of considerable competence, inherited from the days of British rule.

Almost immediately those bothersome remnants of feudalism, the princes, were cast aside, and the vast territory of the subcontinent was at last integrated under one authority. Almost 600 territorial units were consolidated into 27 states. Further reorganization took place in 1956 when the government of India created 14 states out of the earlier 27, mainly along linguistic lines. Agitation by linguistic groups in Bombay, the Punjab, and Nagaland subsequently resulted in the creation of more states, and there are now 28 states and 7 union territories in the Indian Union. The new states are organized around dominant languages, and therefore have greater cultural unity than the previous states (which had been created mainly for administrative convenience).

Each state is a replica of the Union government, with a governor (usually from a different state, appointed by the president for a five-year term), a state assembly, and a chief minister who chooses and heads a council of ministers responsible to the assembly. States are created, and may have their borders redrawn, by the central government. The constitution gives the Center exclusive power to act in the domain of foreign affairs, defense, banking, and income taxation; states are accorded power to deal with police and public order, health, education and welfare, industry, agriculture, and property taxes; and the Center and the states share a number of concurrent domains, such as the legal system, and planning. The Center depends on the states to administer most of its programs. Residual power remains with the Center, which prevails in any conflict with states.

Under Nehru the Center clearly dominated the periphery. But after the initial reorganization along linguistic lines in 1956, power began to flow toward the newly cohesive states. Indira Gandhi reasserted central authority, leading to heightened tension within the federal system. After her death, the balance of power within the system began to shift once again to the states. As the grip of the Congress Party weakened, opposition and independent regional parties came to power in many states. Strong regional parties include notably the CPI (M) in West Bengal, the DMK and AIADMK in Tamil Nadu, the Telegu Desam in Andrha, and the Akali Dal in the Punjab. These parties have become forces also in national politics, using their bargaining power within coalitions to demand expanded jurisdiction for the states. Liberalization of the economy since the 1980s has also enabled the states to play a larger role in creating incentives for investment and economic development.

By and large the delicate technical task of reconstructing the polity along linguistic lines was fairly well done, but ethnic tensions continue to plague the nation. In 1948, Nehru expressed the fear that basing regional units on language would let loose the forces of "disruption and dis-integration." In some measure his somber prediction came true. Demands for state autonomy have often been accompanied by violent demonstrations, calling forth counterdemonstrations and police action that further embitter feelings. A particularly difficult problem developed in Assam in the 1970s, when the influx of Bengali refugees from Bangladesh was viewed by Assamese as a threat to the integrity of tribal cultures. A state election in 1983, boycotted by most Assamese voters to protest the participation of Bengali immigrants, led to rioting in which several thousand people were killed. Tribal unrest, punctuated by armed uprisings, has continued in the Northeast. The United Liberation Front of Assam killed almost 100 people in the last months of 1991 alone, including a number of Congress (I) politicians.

An even more serious challenge to national unity came in the 1980s from the Sikh population of the Punjab. The Sikh religion, which emerged in the fifteenth century, was an attempt to reconcile Islam and Hinduism. A series of gurus (teachers)—equivalent in Sikhism to Islam's Muhammad and Judaism's Moses—fashioned a monotheistic creed, holding that all religions are fundamentally alike. The gurus opposed idolatry, priesthood, and the caste system. Persecuted by Mogul emperors, Sikhs became bitter enemies of Muslims, despite their many religious similarities, and created a warrior society to defend themselves. After combating the British in the early nineteenth century, Sikhs served in large numbers in the British army in India, and subsequently in the Indian army. In 1947, Sikhs joined with militant Hindus in fighting Muslims. Since then, however, they have sought to maintain their distinctive identity in opposition to Hindus.

In 1966 the Akali Dal—or Sikh political party—attained its major demand for the creation of a Punjabi language state with a Sikh majority. But conflict persisted regarding the status of the capital city, Chandigarh (on the border between the Punjab and Haryana), and control of river waters. The Akali began to demand autonomy for the Punjab; Sant Jarnail Singh Bhin-dranwale (leader of a religious institution) galvanized many Sikh militants, who later formed an insurgent movement. Sikh militants resorted to acts of terrorism (shooting Hindus at random, for example), and the central government declared an emergency, imposing president's rule. The deadly cycle of terrorism and police repression continued, and hundreds of people were killed in the first months of 1983 alone.

Bhindranwale directed activities from his headquarters in Amritsar's Golden Temple. The Indian army finally moved in, triggering a three-day battle in which almost 1,000 people were killed, including Bhindranwale and over 80 Indian soldiers. Dozens of Sikh religious institutions were raided by the Indian army in their search for extremists. Several thousand Sikh soldiers mutinied, in some cases setting off armed confrontations with the regular army, and there was a surge of support among Sikhs for an independent Khalistan. On October 31, 1984, the horror reached a climax when Indira Gandhi was struck down by two Sikh members of her personal bodyguard. Mobs in the capital went on a rampage, killing almost 3,000 Sikhs.

After calling for an end to the violence, Rajiv Gandhi sought a political solution. Assuming that the Akali Dal had been seeking participation in power rather than autonomy, much less independence, he gambled on state elections permitting the Sikh party to win and govern. In May 1987, the central government imposed president's rule on the Punjab once again, on the ground that the Akali Dal ministry had permitted terrorists and advocates of independence to take over. Sikh militants went on robbing banks, killing Hindus at random, and assassinating politicians. On the final day of balloting in 1991, Sikhs attacked a train in the Punjab, killing 68 Hindu passengers. The elections were rescheduled, finally taking place in February 1992. But the threat of violence by Sikh militants kept voter turnout down to about 22 percent of the electorate; most of those who voted were Hindus, giving Congress (I) 12 of the 13 seats at stake. In 1996 the moderate Akali (Badal) won 8 seats, then forged an alliance with the BJP and gained control of the state assembly. Since then the

Akali (Badal) has been an ally of the BJP and a dominant force in the Punjab. Violence in the Punjab subsided, but the ethnic problem is far from being resolved.

Ethnic conflict also flared in Jammu and Kashmir, the only state with a Muslim majority. India and Pakistan had gone to war over Kashmir at the time of partition, when its Hindu ruler acceded to the Indian Union over the opposition of the Muslim population. Many Muslims in Kashmir remained receptive to cultural and political influences from Pakistan, and a special effort was needed to secure their participation in Indian parties and government. The conflict between Muslims and Hindus in Kashmir is part of a larger struggle between Pakistan and India (to be treated below). The effort required to maintain a proper and workable balance between national unity and state autonomy is taxing the governing ability of the political class.

Remaking the map of India has gone hand in hand with an attempt to reorganize Indian society. The constitution abolished untouchability and asserted the equality of women. This amounted in practice to a declaration of intent, because the status of 60 million untouchables and of women could not be changed overnight. Nonetheless, an act of Parliament unified marriage laws for the entire nation, permitting marriages between members of different castes and providing for divorce. The Untouchability Offences Act of 1955 made it illegal and punishable to discriminate against members of the untouchable class. But here, too, the enforceability of a statute was limited. More important are other developments that have the effect of undermining the traditional caste system. The design of new industrial towns does not take caste differences into account. The growing urbanization and industrialization of the nation are creating new patterns of life that weaken the millennia-old social structures. In addition, the Community Development Program is a positive force in furthering social change.

Despite undeniable progress in the past 50 years, caste remains a central fact of Indian life. Outcastes are still the victims of discrimination, beatings, and even killings if they enter high-caste neighborhoods, use Brahmin temples, or violate any of the numerous rituals consigning them to inferior status. In the 1991 election, V. P. Singh made reform of the caste system a major campaign issue. Indian democracy cannot advance, nor can modernization be achieved, he argued, so long as three-fourths of the population (outcastes and Sudras) are kept down. His specific remedy—reserving almost half of government jobs for the lower castes—provoked a virulent reaction by higher-caste Hindus. The backlash helped the militant Hindu BJP to virtually double its vote and become the second party of India in 1991. The Rao government in October 1991 decided to add 10 percent of central government jobs to those reserved for Muslims, Christians, and the poor.

Seats in the Lok Sabha and state assemblies are reserved by the constitution for members of Scheduled Castes and Tribes in proportion to their population. Hence, 119 of the 543 seats of the Lok Sabha are assigned to them, even if they do not constitute a majority in most reserved constituencies. There has been since the 1990s an upsurge of political activity, for good or for ill, by Dalits and members of the "Other Backward Castes" (OBCs). Dalits and OBCs have won control of some state governments, and are increasingly a presence as ministers in the central government. The sheer increase in the number of lower-caste members in government and politics has been a force in favor of legislation intended to help the disadvantaged. On the other hand, upper-caste Hindus complain that they are now victims of discrimination, and many critics argue that establishment of quotas in government service rewards people for being and remaining backward.

As part of the Community Development Program, the Indian government has revived a tradition of village rule by elders that had existed before the advent of the British—the *Panchayat* (council of five). Mohandas Gandhi praised the *Panchayats* as agencies of local democracy, but his plea to reinstitute them was turned down by the Constituent Assembly. In 1958 the government asked each state to create a system of *Panchayati Raj* as a way of involving village residents in democratic decision making; most areas in India are now covered. Basically, each village elects a council of about a dozen members; the heads of these councils within a large area, together with other members, form a second-level group; and the heads of all the councils within a district, along with elected legislators in that district and others, constitute the highest-level group. The *Panchayati Raj* have brought about impressive popular participation in local political life, but instead of the consensus dreamed of by Gandhi, local elections reflected national party conflict. Nor did the *Panchayats* assume responsibility for economic development and planning, as originally hoped. In 1991 the Rao government required states to transfer to the *Panchayats* jurisdiction over some aspects of economic development and welfare, and assign them financial resources. Given the diversity of local and regional politics, results so far have been mixed.

It is in the economic domain that the heritage from the past has weighed most heavily. Modernization of the social structure is ultimately possible only with simultaneous modernization of the economy, each process being indispensable to the other. The great leader of the national independence movement, however, was unalterably opposed to industrialization. Gandhi once said,

> India's salvation consists in unlearning what she has learned during the last fifty years. The railways, telegraphs, hospitals, lawyers, doctors and such-like have all to go; and the so-called upper classes have to learn consciously, religiously, and deliberately the simple peasant life…. Every time I get into a railway car or use a motor bus I know that I am doing violence to my sense of what is right.[7]

This attitude may have been sound political tactics during the period when British rulers, in the eyes of the nationalists, were exploiting the Indian economy. It also represented a concession to Hindu culture, which seeks salvation in liberation from earthly existence, not in improvement thereof. After independence, however, Gandhi's successors had to face the problem of India's mass poverty. Some continued to exalt the virtues of village life and of a poor but spiritual existence, but the leadership of the Congress Party, particularly the group around Prime Minister Nehru, broke completely with the Gandhian tradition. They set about deliberately to create a modern economy through a series of five-year plans. A noted Indian journalist observed, in this connection: "Posterity will probably rate Gandhi as one of history's magnificent failures."[8]

A five-year plan in India covers a multitude of activities, both governmental and private. A planning commission in Delhi establishes certain targets and goals, measures progress, and calls attention to shortcomings. The process is relatively relaxed, involving little discipline over the economy. The goal is to launch India into a take-off period so that the economy will gain momentum and expand on all fronts. The First Five Year Plan, adopted in haste in 1951, emphasized expansion of agricultural production and public works, laying the groundwork for more systematic and serious efforts in the drafting of the Second and Third Five Year Plans (1956–1966). Considerable progress was made during that decade in creating the infrastructure of a modern economy; by 1959 industrial production had increased by more than 50 percent over 1951. Among the bright spots was striking growth in such industries as iron ore and steel (63 percent increase), chemicals (114 percent), and machine tools (324 percent). Modern forms of business enterprise began to spread in the private sector, displacing the older artisans and speculator-capitalists. But agricultural production faltered during this period, and severe food shortages materialized in some parts of the country. Poor harvests caused hoarding, looting of granaries, and widespread hunger riots. In 1965, the United States shipped one-sixth of its total wheat crop to India as an emergency measure in order to alleviate hardship. Since then, the five-year plans have been primarily attempts to set goals that will stimulate national effort. They have not

---

[7]Cited in Wallbank, *A Short History,* p. 157.

[8]Frank Moraes, *India Today* (New York: Macmillan, 1964), p. 89.

served as realistic guides to economic development. The emphasis has shifted to liberalization of the economy, antipoverty programs, and development of social services.

The five-year plans originally reflected Nehru's belief that the Soviet model of centralized planning offered the best hope for rapid industrialization and social justice. He distrusted capitalism, equating it with speculation, greed, and economic stagnation. Indian business leaders resisted Nehru's brand of socialism, demanding instead encouragement of private enterprise. Their spokesperson within the Congress Party was the powerful S. V. Patel. The conflict between socialism and capitalism, which is fought out in Europe generally by separate political parties, took place in India within the Congress Party. By the mid-1950s, a compromise was reached. A mixed economy would exist in which the state would have direct control of some key sectors (armaments, nuclear energy, railroads), and the exclusive right to start new ventures in such sectors as iron and steel, shipbuilding, aircraft production, and telecommunications; the state would closely regulate most other key industries but would otherwise recognize and protect a large private sector. As a concession to the heritage of Mohandas Gandhi, village industry would also be encouraged.

But within this mixed economy, where would the line be drawn between public and private? Under Nehru, the emphasis was on state control and socialist values. But in the mid-1960s, there was growing dissatisfaction with the Nehru model and a widespread desire to better serve consumer interests. The Swatantra Party, expressing the views of business, attacked the very concept of central planning and demanded the relaxation of government controls. Reflecting changes in public opinion, some measures to liberalize the economy were adopted by Nehru's successor, Lal Bahadur Shastri (1964–1966), and continued by Mrs. Gandhi.

In 1969 a split took place between Indira Gandhi and her more traditional rivals within the Congress. Mrs. Gandhi then swung to the left, sought allies among Socialists and Communists, and revived the socialist policies of her father. Her government nationalized banks and insurance companies, the coal industry, textile mills, railroad car manufacture, and iron and steel production. Government control over the private sector was extended and strengthened. But the results of this sudden swing toward state ownership and control were disappointing: inflation, shortages and black markets, corruption and bribery, and economic stagnation. Mrs. Gandhi changed direction, loosening some controls. During emergency rule from 1975 to 1977, economic liberalization was given a boost by Sanjay Gandhi, who criticized the bureaucracy and lauded private enterprise.

After her return to office in 1980, Mrs. Gandhi resumed a policy of gradual deregulation of the economy. Her successor and son, Rajiv, determined to cut down the size of the public sector. The challenge was formidable. To take one example, the nationalized Steel Authority of India employed 250,000 people in producing 8 million tons of steel a year, at double the international price. In South Korea, the private Pohang steelworks produced 9 million tons of steel with 14,000 workers. Air India employed 17,000 people in 1987 to run 20 aircraft while racking up a loss of $40 million. In contrast, Singapore Airlines ran twice as many aircraft with half as many workers, and at a profit. Rajiv became the apostle of professional management and deregulation—all the while proclaiming his devotion to the goal of social justice.

The trend toward liberalization of the economy continued under V. P. Singh. But his successor, Chandra Shekhar, pledged to stop liberalization, contending that the ills of India were caused by multinationals. When Congress (I) returned to power in June 1991, several factors favored a liberal rather than a socialist approach to economic development. India requested a loan from the International Monetary Fund to meet a shortage of foreign exchange; and the IMF strongly recommended expansion of the private sector. Also, the collapse of Communism in Europe, the decision of the Chinese Communist regime to encourage private enterprise, and the crisis of social democracy in Western industrial societies had brought about a change in political culture. It was now widely believed that complex economies could not be managed from one central point; the emphasis became decentralization, flexibility, and deregulation.

In its first months in office, the Rao government adopted sweeping measures to attract foreign investment and abolish many licensing requirements. Finance Minister Manmohan Singh declared that 90 of India's 244 huge state-owned enterprises were "patently unviable" and should be shut down. These 90 enterprises had about 800,000 employees and cost the taxpayers $750 million annually in subsidies. The Indian government gave virtually automatic approval to foreign companies creating joint ventures, and the massive, intricate system of controls and permits was at least partly dismantled. By 1994, industrial production increased by 8 percent annually, exports by 15 percent annually, and total foreign investments by $6 billion. The Bombay stock exchange boomed, as foreigners invested heavily in the Indian market. India's foreign reserves, down to almost nothing in June 1991, amounted to $24 billion in 1998.

Entry policy (opening the economy to entry of foreign capital) was quite successful, though also stirring nationalist reactions. Less progress was made in exit policy (getting the state out of unprofitable business). The government was able to sell equity in several profitable state-owned companies (in steel, petroleum, and machine tools primarily), raising about $1 billion. But no one will buy into companies producing at a loss, and organized labor, supported by opposition parties, energetically opposes closing or downsizing of these firms. One extreme example is the Hindustan Fertilizer plant, which employs 1,550 workers. After it was opened in 1986, this plant produced nothing at all! One observer commented: "There is a canteen, a personnel department, and an accounts department. There are promotions, job changes, pay rises, audits, and in-house trade unions. Engineers, electricians, plumbers and painters maintain the equipment with a care that is almost surreal."[9]

Finance Minister Singh observed that beyond a certain point, "absolute cuts in expenditures may not be possible in a democracy. We cannot throw people into the pool of unemployed."[10] It also proved politically impossible to cut food and fertilizer subsidies, which add enormously to the budget deficit. As the 1996 election approached, forces opposed to globalization and foreign investment became more assertive, and the Rao government virtually abandoned exit policy.

The era of political instability ushered in by the elections of 1996 and 1998, which did not yield a solid majority for any party or coalition, brought a halt to the reform process. The Gowda government adopted a budget that promoted liberalization of the economy, but little else was accomplished by the United Front coalition. The Vajpayee government adopted economic policies that reflected the contradictions within its 14-party coalition. It proposed a combination of encouragement of village economies (in the spirit of Mohandas Gandhi), massive public spending to jumpstart the economy (in the tradition of Nehru), and at the same time speeding up the processes of liberalization, privatization, and welcome of foreign investment.

Despite a movement in fits and starts, the momentum in favor of reforms is now so great that no major party openly favors a return to the bureaucratized, stagnant economy of the past. As the Indian middle and professional class, already among the world's largest, continues to grow, political pressures in favor of market-oriented economic development are bound to increase. The Indian political class has come a long way from the heady days just after independence, when many Congress Party leaders hoped that socialism would create a highly productive, classless society with equal opportunity and a "good life" (as Nehru put it) for all. It is increasingly accepted that there is no easy way to industrialize an overwhelmingly traditional society, that

---

[9]*The Financial Times,* London, June 6, 1994. Cited by Meghnad Desai, "Economic Reform: Shattered by Politics?" in Philip Oldenburg, ed., *India Briefing: Staying the Course* (Armonk, NY: M. E. Sharpe), p. 91. Desai

added: "Like China, India may live with an inefficient public sector for a long time."
[10]Interview with Finance Minister Manmohan Singh, *India Today,* October 15, 1995, pp. 28–29.

social discipline is an essential ingredient in any policy of modernization, and that economic progress often produces heightened social strains and pressures.

MODERNIZATION AND DEMOCRACY

In any democracy, social and economic groups make claims upon the state; these claims constitute the raw material of the political process. Peasants, landlords, workers, managers, capitalists, merchants, and professionals, as well as ethnic, religious, and linguistic groups, press for satisfaction of their demands and participate in the process of working out compromises embodied in legislation. This continuing "crisis of participation" is a difficult challenge to political leaders even in long-established and prosperous democracies. When political systems are overloaded with claims and counterclaims, they become ineffective and unstable.

The burden on Indian democracy by any standard is enormous. A large part of the electorate is opposed to modernization because it threatens traditional religious beliefs; others are primarily concerned with promotion of their caste, linguistic, or regional interests; still others call for the revolutionary transformation of society. Many Indians have wondered whether democracy is not a luxury for their nation, to be subordinated to other considerations. In a deeply divided society, democracy may permit so much criticism and obstruction that government can no longer function. This classic issue of democratic theory—the point at which the right of minorities to express themselves subverts the right of the majority to rule—was posed with special force by Prime Minister Indira Gandhi during the emergency.

Mrs. Gandhi at first justified her policy of suppressing the opposition as necessary to assure the nation's security. "The actions of a few," she declared in a radio broadcast to the nation, "are undermining the rights of the vast majority." India's enemies were rejoicing, she warned, at the sight of a nation tearing itself apart. In the following months, Mrs. Gandhi pre-

sented a more fully developed explanation of her resort to coercive means in order to attain democratic ends. The real challenge facing India, she said, is not how to maintain the right of an opposition to oppose anything and everything, but how to eliminate poverty, backwardness, and social abuses. She declared in a radio and television broadcast on November 10, 1975: "We want to fight and eliminate the poverty in our country prevailing since time immemorial. We want to remove backwardness. We can do so only if there is stability in the nation. And stability is impossible to achieve if unity gets weakened.... That was the problem before us." What was needed, above all, were "simple measures" to stamp out social abuses and anarchy.

Democracy is desirable, Mrs. Gandhi assured the nation, on one condition—that opposition be constructive. "But no one could claim that in the name of democracy anyone could do what he pleased and that such license was more important than India's progress, more important than the good of the Indian people." What was to be done? "There is only one magic which can remove poverty, and that is hard work sustained by clear vision, iron will, and the strictest discipline."

Many Indians agreed that poverty could never be alleviated in a climate of permissiveness and indiscipline. On the other hand, there was widespread dissatisfaction with authoritarian rule during the emergency—in particular, the arrest of opposition leaders and censorship of the press. Ample opportunities were afforded to members of the ruling party to suppress legitimate criticism, make arbitrary decisions, and even profit personally from their expanded political power. Public prosecutors under the Desai government claimed that the prime minister's son, Sanjay Gandhi, took advantage of his position to forward his career and finances. Democracy without consensus and social discipline may be ineffective (as seemed to be shown when the Janata Party proved incapable of governing after its victory in 1977), but authoritarianism invites the abuse of power evident during the emergency. It is in India, perhaps more than any other nation, that the ability of democracies to cope with the problems of modernization in developing countries is on trial.

FOREIGN AFFAIRS

The terrorist attack against New York and Washington on September 11, 2001, had immediate and far-reaching repercussions in India. Before 9/11 India, as the dominant power in South Asia, sought to insulate the entire region from the influence of foreign nations, particularly the United States and the Soviet Union during the Cold War, and then the United States afterwards. India was especially concerned about American and Chinese support for Pakistan, with which it has fought three wars since independence. Consider the situation after 9/11. An American battle fleet cruised the Arabian Sea, sending fighter-bombers over Pakistani territory, with the approval of the Pakistan government, raining destruction on Taliban forces in Afghanistan, historic gateway to the subcontinent. American heavy bombers based on the island of Diego Garcia in the Indian Ocean also participated in this campaign. American ground forces then moved into Afghanistan, and within three months routed the Taliban regime and largely dismantled terrorist networks and training camps. The United States projected its military power directly into India's backyard. Pakistan had become an indispensable American ally, receiving massive economic and military aid. But there was a bright spot for India in this picture. The United States also needed India's diplomatic and moral support for its campaign.

Then, barely three months after the attack on the United States, a group of five armed men tried to shoot their way into the Indian Parliament in New Delhi. The attackers and nine other people were killed. India charged two Islamic militant groups, backed by Pakistan, with the deed. These groups were carrying the armed struggle for Kashmiri self-determination into the heart of India. Based on the precedent established by the United States, and approved by the United Nations, India asserted the right to use its military power against terrorists, the organizations which supported them, and most pointedly, any country that harbored them. The Pakistani government arrested the leaders and dozens of members of the two Islamic militant groups involved but pledged continuing diplomatic and moral support for Kashmiri Muslim "freedom-fighters." India deployed hundreds of thousands of troops along the border and demanded that Pakistan put a stop to all "cross-border terrorism." There is now a new power alignment in South Asia, with the United States directly involved as a major player. Kashmir is, as always, an explosive issue, fostering the imminent danger of war between India and Pakistan (both nuclear weapons states since 1998). Strategic rivalry between India and China is a long-term prospect. Yet for the first time, the possibility of action by both India and Pakistan against a common enemy, Islamic fundamentalism, offers the glimmer of hope for a dialogue on Kashmir.

Mainsprings of Indian Foreign Policy

From its preindependence period, India inherited Mohandas Gandhi's advocacy of nonviolence, and also the geopolitical concerns of the British Raj. These two principles or policies have proved incompatible. In order to secure its borders, head off potential threats to its security from neighbors and their allies, and assert its claim to be the dominant power of South Asia, India created and used powerful military forces and engaged in traditional diplomacy. The manufacture and underground explosion of an atom bomb in May 1974, making India the sixth nation to become a nuclear power, dramatically illustrated India's resolve to safeguard its interests by military means. In May 1998, India took the next step, conducting full-scale nuclear testing. Prime Minister Vajpayee proudly declared before the Lok Sabha, "India is a nuclear weapons state." Pakistan immediately conducted its own nuclear tests, raising the diplomatic stakes dramatically in South Asia. There is widespread agreement that keeping up with advances in military technology requires a solid industrial and scientific base. The drive to modernize the Indian economy and society is intimately linked to the overall objectives of Indian foreign policy. This is a far cry from the Gandhian vision of village economy, spirituality, and conversion of enemies by persuading them of the evil of their ways.

Independent India's first prime minister, Jawaharlal Nehru, formulated the major principle of Indian foreign policy, to which all of his successors subscribed—nonalignment. For Nehru, nonalignment meant a refusal to become part of the military alliance structures of either superpower, but it did not mean isolation or withdrawal from the international scene. On the contrary, the independence of India would enable it to intervene even more forcefully on specific issues in the cause of world peace. By avoiding alliances with either the United States or the Soviet Union, Indian leaders explained, they retained freedom of maneuver to defend their own national interests. Also, any alliance inevitably would cause divisions within Indian public opinion, create political instability, and divert attention from the pressing problem of dealing with poverty at home. For some Indians, moreover, each superpower represented a perceived evil—either capitalism or oppressive communism—and India represented a 'third way' in which concern for humanity and social justice is combined with freedom. Critics of Indian foreign policy may express skepticism concerning Indian aspirations to (or illusions about) a higher idealism, but the ideals are nonetheless constantly invoked.

Since independence, India has been engaged in three wars with Pakistan, one war with China, military action against the remnants of Portuguese rule in Goa, frequent military activity in restive frontier areas, and military intervention in Sri Lanka. The most pressing foreign policy problem confronting India in the aftermath of independence was its dispute with Pakistan over Kashmir; relations with Pakistan remained thereafter a constant preoccupation. In 1947, partition was accompanied by communal violence and the forced movement of millions of refugees. Kashmir, with a population 80 percent Muslim, was ruled by a Hindu maharajah. In the face of resistance by Muslims, aided by tribesmen from across the border in Pakistan, the Hindu ruler called upon India for protection, and war broke out between Pakistan and India in the winter of 1947.

Both sides accepted a cease-fire arranged by the United Nations in June 1948, with about one-third of the Kashmir area held by Pakistan. Both sides agreed to a plebiscite permitting Kashmiris to decide which nation to join. At the time the Kashmiri leader, Sheik Abdullah, was an ally of Nehru (though he was later jailed by Nehru when he advocated independence). A plebiscite might have gone either way. But neither India nor Pakistan withdrew troops, a precondition for the plebiscite. Nehru subsequently held that local elections confirmed the will of Kashmiris to remain within the Indian Union.

In 1965, conflict flared up between India and Pakistan in the Punjab, though a cease-fire took hold a few months later. In August guerrillas from Pakistan joined Muslim rebels in Kashmir. Indian and Pakistani forces entered the fray, and Indian forces struck out towards Lahore, in Pakistan itself. China came out in support of Pakistan, and both parties accepted a call by the UN Security Council for a cease-fire. The leaders of Pakistan (President Ayub Khan) and India (Prime Minister Lal Shastri) agreed to attend a conference chaired by Soviet Prime Minister Kosygin in Tashkent in January 1966. Partly as a tribute to Shastri, who died during the conference, India agreed to pull its forces back. But Pakistan appeared to be the victim of aggression; it began receiving military aid from China, and to a lesser extent, the Soviet Union.

In 1971 a popular uprising took place in East Pakistan against a virtual military occupation imposed by West Pakistan leaders who refused to accept the legitimacy of an election there. Many Bengals were killed by the Pakistani military, and some 10 million refugees, most of them Hindus, sought sanctuary in India. The Indian government assisted the rebels, Pakistan retaliated, and a full-scale war erupted. In a lightning campaign, Indian forces occupied the East Pakistan capital, Dhaka, forced the surrender of the Pakistan army in the East, and declared a unilateral cease-fire in the West. Three months later the Indian army withdrew, refugees began to return, and Bangladesh became an independent nation. The secession of Bangladesh virtually assured India of dominance over Pakistan, whose hostility remained, however, a thorny problem. In 1984, India accused Pakistan of giving aid and succor to Sikh nationalists in the Punjab, and provocative military exercises were conducted by both countries. Clashes continued along the border in Kashmir, and India renewed its charges that Pakistan was behind the rebellion there.

A turning point was reached when local elections in 1988 were rigged by the Indian government. Outraged Kashmiri nationalists launched a guerrilla movement. The Indian army and police countered with massive repressive measures, which fueled more resentment. The insurgency had broad support among Muslims and was reinforced by well-armed Islamic militants, trained in Pakistan and Afghanistan. Since 1989, about 35,000 people have been killed in this insurgency according to Indian authorities, many more according to others.

The Kashmir dispute is about more than territory. It is at the core of the national identity of both Pakistan and India. The reason for the creation of Pakistan in the first place was to enable Muslims to live in their own country, free from domination by Hindus. But the resolutely secular Nehru, who was born into a Brahmin family in Kashmir, was opposed to borders based on religion. Many Indians today believe that to permit secesssion by Kashmir would call into question India's multiethnic democracy, and its ability to integrate large minorities (including over 100 million Muslims and almost as many other non-Hindus).

After India and Pakistan developed nuclear weapons in the spring of 1998, the leaders of both countries held talks at a regional meeting in July, hoping to defuse mounting hostilities, but could not reach an agreement. In February 1999, in what appeared to be a breakthrough, Prime Minister Vajpayee made a widely hailed trip to Lahore, Pakistan, and hopes were raised that the two sides would continue discussions to reduce tensions. But only a few months later, Islamic militants crossed into Kashmir and occupied key positions in the Kargil mountains. Major battles then raged between Indian forces and the armed militants, who were finally forced to withdraw. Prime Minister Vajpayee, then heading a caretaker government preparing for new elections, won considerable popular support for his firm response to the Kargil intrusion. In the aftermath of the September 11 attack against the United States, and the December 13 attack on the Indian Parliament, the Kashmir dispute became even more dangerous and a pressing concern to the international community.

War with China in 1962, ending in a rout of Indian forces, came as a shock to India. Nehru had been eager to secure the friendship of the Chinese, despite uneasiness over their occupation of Tibet. In 1954, India and China agreed on five principles, notably nonaggression and peaceful coexistence, as defining a mutually beneficial friendship. But growing revolt against Chinese rule in Tibet undermined this friendship. Even more disturbing were claims by China to about 40,000 square miles of Indian territory that it argued had never been within the authority of Great Britain to hand over. The Chinese were intent on securing lines of communication to Tibet, applying pressure also along the Northeast Frontier. India declared a state of emergency, and Chinese forces struck. After pushing back the Indian army, the Chinese announced a cease-fire, withdrew their forces in the Northeast, but retained control of roads to Tibet. In 1987 a threat of renewed hostilities was averted by diplomatic talks and a visit to China by Rajiv Gandhi. But the quarrel over borders was not settled, remaining a sticking point in relations between the world's two most populous nations. Indian Defense Minister George Fernandes just before the Indian nuclear tests in May 1998 called China "potential threat number 1." After the tests, Prime Minister Vajpayee in a letter to President Clinton explaining his action referred to China as a strategic threat; he also deplored the distrust created by the unresolved Sino-Indian border problem.

India's continuing conflict with both Pakistan and China has been a fundamental determinant of its foreign policy. As the Chinese became embroiled with the Russians in a territorial as well as an ideological dispute in the 1960s, India was drawn closer to the Soviet Union. Russians and Indians saw in each other allies of a kind against a common foe—China. Similarly, India became less friendly to the United States as the Americans joined the Chinese in offering military and economic aid to Pakistan (which, in turn, was a valuable military asset in the Sino-American confrontation with the Soviet Union). In 1971, India signed a treaty of peace, friendship, and cooperation with the Soviet Union that reflected also Indira Gandhi's growing collaboration with the Communist Party of India. The friendship treaty, it was argued by Indian leaders, did not represent a departure from nonalignment because no military alliance was involved.

The tilt toward the Soviet Union did not prevent India from seeking and receiving massive aid from the United States to avert famine and help develop its economy. With the virtual elimination of Pakistan as a military threat, India became less sensitive over the U.S. program of aid to Pakistan, and relations between India and the United States improved markedly after the Janata Party's victory in 1977. The Russian invasion of Afghanistan in 1979 confronted Prime Minister Gandhi with an exceedingly delicate problem: how to prevent the United States from reinforcing and rearming Pakistan without at the same time endorsing Russian military intervention in an area of concern to India.

India was drawn into an ethnic conflict in Sri Lanka (formerly Ceylon) supposedly to protect the Tamil minority, but also to ensure that no foreign powers would exploit the situation and establish their influence in the region. Tamils, who make up one-fifth of the population of Sri Lanka, receive sympathetic support as well as material aid and arms from the Tamils of India, just across the strait. When the ethnic conflict worsened in 1987, Rajiv Gandhi took the lead in negotiating a peace agreement that in principle

put an end to the turmoil. Nevertheless, some 50,000 Indian troops, dispatched to Sri Lanka to establish law and order, soon became involved in hostilities with the very Tamil militants whose interests they were originally supposed to safeguard. A suicide squad of Tamil terrorists (the Liberation Tigers) took revenge four years later by assassinating Rajiv Gandhi.

In drawing up a balance sheet of independent India's foreign policy, the record of achievement is impressive. After a long period of stalemate, India emerged victorious from its historical rivalry with Pakistan and is now the dominant power in South Asia. However, India continues to accuse Pakistan of supporting Sikh nationalists in the Punjab and Muslim rebels in Kashmir, and is concerned that Pakistan is a wedge of American and Chinese influence in the region. The northern frontier is vulnerable to Chinese pressure, and memories of India's defeat by the Chinese in 1962 still rankle. Until 1991, India adhered to its policy of nonalignment, avoiding alliances with either the United States or the Soviet Union, receiving economic and military aid from both, and reserving the right to disagree with both. In practice, India tended to be more free in its condemnation of the United States than of the Soviet Union (for example, defending Soviet intervention in Hungary in 1956).

With the growing crisis of Communism in the 1980s, and the collapse of the Soviet Union after the failed coup of August 1991, a pillar of Indian foreign policy crumbled. Nonalignment can no longer have the same meaning in a world with one dominant superpower and an ascendant Western economic model. When Iraq invaded Kuwait in 1990, the Indian government at first leaned toward Iraq, which had given India support on the Kashmir question and also was a major supplier of oil. After the Soviet Union gave its support to the United Nations, India went along with sanctions against Iraq. India seemed caught in a time warp during the attempted overthrow of Gorbachev by old-line Communists. Both Indian Communist parties applauded the coup, and the Indian government did not denounce it. Gorbachev's return and Yeltsin's triumph required a complete recasting of Indian policy toward Russia and the other successor states.

Distrust of the United States, which for much of the intellectual class represents materialism and imperialism, runs deep. But the Rao government mounted a major effort to attract American capital, particularly in the form of joint ventures. Even the Communist-led government of West Bengal joined in the campaign to persuade Wall Street to invest in the Indian economy. Also, the almost 1 million people of Indian origin residing in the United States are beginning to serve as an important interactive channel between the two countries. With Russia no longer a counterbalance, India has a great incentive to improve relations with the industrial West, including the United States. But the heritage of Gandhian principles, Nehru's non-alignment policies, and solidarity with developing countries is weighty. The United States is now directly involved in the geopolitics of South Asia, as a consequence of the attack of September 11 and its close cooperation with Pakistan as well as Tajikistan and Uzbekistan in the war that followed against the Taliban regime in Afghanistan and against Saddam Hussein in Iraq in 2003. The equation of power in South Asia has changed, ushering in a new era for Indian foreign policy.

Thinking Critically

1. A constitutional amendment adopted in December 1976 declared that India is a "socialist secular democratic republic." Are "socialist" and "secular" accurate descriptions of India today?

2. Nehru feared that basing regional units on language would let loose the forces of "disruption and disintegration." Have his fears become a reality?

3. What are the issues between India and Pakistan over Kashmir? Can you see any basis for mediation or settlement of this dispute?

4. What have been the consequences of the terrorist attacks on September 11, 2001, for the

structure of power in South Asia, and for Indian foreign policy?

5. A recent symposium volume is entitled *The Success of Indian Democracy*. Has Indian democracy been a success?

KEY TERMS

Akali Dal *(582–583)*
Sant Jarnail Singh Bhindranwale *(582)*
the Emergency (1975–1977) *(587)*
five-year plans *(584–585)*
nonalignment *(589, 591–592)*
Panchayat (583–584)
Punjab *(582–583, 590)*

FURTHER READINGS

Agnes, Flavia. *Women and Law in India* (New Delhi: Oxford University Press, 2004).

Ahluwalia, Isher J., and I. M. D. Little, eds. *India's Economic Reforms and Development: Essays for Manmohan Singh* (Delhi: Oxford University Press, 1998). Note especially essays by Jagdish Bhagwati and Amartya Sen.

Bayly, Susan. *Caste, Society and Politics in India from the Eighteenth Century to the Modern Age* (New York: Cambridge University Press, 1999).

Bouton, Marshall, and P. Oldenburg, eds. *India Briefing, 1999* (Armonk, NY: M. E. Sharpe, 1999).

Byres, Terence J., ed. *The Indian Economy: Major Debates since Independence* (Delhi: Oxford University Press, 1998).

Cohen, Stephen P. *India: Emerging Power* (Washington, DC: Brookings Institution Press, 2001).

Dréze, Jean, and Amartya Sen. *India: Development and Participation* 2nd ed. (Oxford: Oxford University Press, 2002).

Ganguly, Sumit. *The Crisis in Kashmir: Portents of War, Hopes of Peace* (Washington, DC: Woodrow Wilson Center Press, 1997).

Kohli, Atul. *The State and Poverty in India: The Politics of Reform* (New York: Cambridge University Press, 1987).

Kux, Dennis. *Estranged Democracies: India and the United States* (Washington, DC: National Defense University, 1993).

Nayar, Balder Raj, and T. V. Paul. *India in the World Order: Searching for Major Power Status* (Cambridge: Cambridge University Press, 2003).

Oldenburg, Philip, ed. *India Briefing: Staying the Course* (Armonk, NY: M. E. Sharpe, 1995).

Palmer, Norman D. *The United States and India: The Dimensions of Influence* (New York: Praeger, 1984).

Rudolph, Lloyd I., and S. H. Rudolph. *In Pursuit of Lakshmi: The Political Economy of the Indian State* (Chicago: University of Chicago Press, 1987).

Vijay, Joshi, and I. M. D. Little. *India's Economic Reforms, 1991–2001* (Oxford: Clarendon Press, 1996).

Weiner, Myron. *The Child and the State in India* (Princeton, NJ: Princeton University Press, 1991).

Wirsing, Robert G. *India, Pakistan, and the Kashmir Dispute* (New York: St. Martin's, 1994).

WEB SITES

www.timesofindia.com/
The Times of India (Bombay, New Delhi).
www.hindustantimes.com/
The Hindustan Times (New Delhi).
www.india-today.com/
India Today, a good weekly news magazine (New Delhi).
bas.umdl.umich.edu/b/bas/
Bibliography of Asian Studies, prepared by the Association for Asian Studies. Listings for India are by category, for example: biographies, economics, history, and politics and government.
asnic.utexas.edu/asnic/countries/india/index.html
Asia Studies Network Information Center, University of Texas at Austin.
www.nic.in/
India Informatics Centre: information provided by the Indian government on the political structure.
www.bjp.org/
Bharatiya Janata Party.
indiancongress.org/
Indian National Congress.

UNITED STATES
OF AMERICA

PACIFIC
OCEAN

Gulf of California

Ciudad
Juárez

Hermosillo

Chihuahua

NORTH

CENTER-NORTH

MEXICO

Monterrey

Gulf of
Mexico

San Luis
Potosí

WEST

Lerma

Guadalajara

L. de
Chapala

Pánu

Mexico
City

Puebla

Veracruz

Mérida

SOUTH-
EAST

CENTRAL

Balsas

EAST

BELIZE

SOUTH

Oaxaca

GUATEMALA

EL SALVADOR

Rio Grande

0   125   250 Miles
0   125   250 Kilometers

THE GOVERNMENT OF
Mexico

Martin C. Needler

INTRODUCTION

Background: The site of advanced Amerindian civilizations, Mexico came under Spanish rule for three centuries before achieving independence early in the 19th century. A devaluation of the peso in late 1994 threw Mexico into economic turmoil, triggering the worst recession in over half a century. The nation continues to make an impressive recovery. Ongoing economic and social concerns include low real wages, underemployment for a large segment of the population, inequitable income distribution, and few advancement opportunities for the largely Amerindian population in the impoverished southern states.

GEOGRAPHY

Location: Middle America, bordering the Caribbean Sea and the Gulf of Mexico, between Belize and the United States and bordering the North Pacific Ocean, between Guatemala and the United States

Area: 1,972,550 sq km

Area—comparative: slightly less than three times the size of Texas

Land boundaries: 4,538 km

    border countries: Belize 250 km, Guatemala 962 km, United States 3,326 km

Climate: varies from tropical to desert

Terrain: high, rugged mountains; low coastal plains; high plateaus; desert

Elevation extremes: *lowest point:* Laguna Salada –10 m

    highest point: Volcán Pico de Orizaba 5,700 m

Geography note: strategic location on southern border of United States

PEOPLE

Population: 104,959,000

Age structure: *0–14 years:* 31.6% (male 16,913,000; female 16,228,000)

15–64 years: 62.9% (male 31,975,000; female 34,090,000)

65 years and over: 5.5% (male 2,618,000; female 3,133,000)

Population growth rate: 1.8%

Birthrate: 21.44 births/1,000 population

Sex ratio: 0.97 male/female

Life expectancy at birth: 74.94 years

male: 72.18 years

female: 77.83 years

Nationality: *noun:* Mexican, Mexicans

adjective: Mexican

Ethnic groups: mestizo (Amerindian-Spanish) 60%, Amerindian or predominantly Amerindian 30%, white 9%, other 1%

Religions: nominally Roman Catholic 89%, Protestant 6%, other 5%

Languages: Spanish, various Mayan, Nahuatl, and other regional indigenous languages

Literacy: *definition:* age 15 and over who can read and write

total population: 89.6%

male: 91.8%

female: 87.4%

GOVERNMENT

Country name: *conventional long form:* United Mexican States

conventional short form: Mexico

Government type: federal republic

Capital: Mexico City

Administrative divisions: 31 states *(estados)* and 1 federal district *(distrito federal)*

Independence: 16 September 1810 (from Spain)

Constitution: 5 February 1917

Legal system: mixture of U.S. constitutional theory and civil law system; judicial review of legislative acts; accepts compulsory ICJ jurisdiction, with reservations

Suffrage: 18 years of age; universal and compulsory (but not enforced)

Executive branch: *chief of state and head of government:* President Vicente Fox Quesada (since 1 December 2000)

cabinet: Cabinet appointed by the president; appointment of attorney general requires consent of the Senate

elections: president elected by popular vote for a six-year term; election last held 2 July 2000

Legislative branch: bicameral National Congress or Congreso de la Unión consists of the Senate or Cámara de Senadores (128 seats; 96 are elected by popular vote to serve six-year terms, and 32 are allocated on the basis of each party's popular vote) and the Federal Chamber of Deputies or Cámara Federal de Diputados (500 seats; 300 members are directly elected by popular vote to serve three-year terms; remaining 200 members are allocated on the basis of each party's popular vote, also for three-year terms)

Judicial branch: Supreme Court of Justice or Corte Suprema de Justicia (judges are appointed by the president with consent of the Senate)

ECONOMY

Overview: Mexico has a free market economy with a mixture of modern and outmoded industry and agriculture, increasingly dominated by the private sector. The number of state-owned enterprises in Mexico has fallen from more than 1,000 in 1982 to fewer than 200 in 2005. The administrations privatized and expanded competition in seaports, railroads, telecommunications, electricity, natural gas distribution, and airports. A strong export sector helped to cushion the economy's decline in 1995 and led the recovery in 1996–2000. Private consumption became the leading driver of growth in 2000, accompanied by increased employment and higher real wages. Mexico still needs to overcome many structural problems as it strives to modernize its economy and raise living standards. Income distribution is very unequal, with the top 20% of income earners accounting for 55% of income. Trade with the United States and Canada has tripled since NAFTA was implemented in 1994. Mexico completed free trade agreements with the EU, Israel, El Salvador, Honduras, and Guatemala in 2000, and is pursuing additional trade agreements with countries in Latin America and Asia to lessen its dependence on the United States.

GDP: purchasing power parity—$941.2 billion

GDP—real growth rate: 1.3%

GDP—per capita: purchasing power parity—$9,000

GDP—composition by sector: *agriculture:* 4%
   industry: 26.4%
   services: 69.6%

Population below poverty line: 40%

Labor force: 34.11 million

Labor force—by occupation: agriculture 18%, industry 24%, services 58%

Unemployment rate: urban 3.3% plus considerable underemployment

Currency: Mexican peso (MXN)

A. POLITICAL DEVELOPMENT

Mexico is a distinctive country in many ways. When the astonished Spaniards first laid their eyes on the capital city, Tenochtitlán, at the beginning of the sixteenth century, they were looking at a city probably greater in population than any in Europe at the time. Counting methods vary depending on how much of the metropolitan region is included, but by some modes of reckoning Mexico City is today, with over 24 million people, again the largest city in the world.

The ancient Aztecs had one of the distinctive civilizations of the ancient world, and some of that distinctiveness is apparent today in the way of life of their descendants. To its Spanish conquerors, Mexico offered a deluge of products which have since made their way into the diets of people all over the world; today Mexico may be known abroad for its cuisine, its twentieth-century school of mural painting, or its considerable petroleum production. Politically, as we shall see, Mexico is significant in having pioneered the political system now found throughout Africa and Asia, that of the dominant single party, sometimes known as the hegemonic party or the democratic single-party system.

Mexico City has all the ills of a metropolis in a developing country—impossible traffic jams, overcrowded buses, slums, and pollution. It contains about one-quarter of the national population, currently estimated at 104 million. Although the metropolis is the country's preeminent city in commerce, culture, and communications, as well as in politics, five other Mexican cities have over 1 million inhabitants, and about two-thirds of the national population is considered urban. But that also means that a third of the population continues to live in the country's villages, of which there are more than 50,000 distributed over the 761,000 square miles of the national territory.

The rural population is not spread evenly over the country, however. Much of Mexico is arid; perhaps 10 percent of the land surface receives rainfall adequate for unirrigated agriculture. Nevertheless, vast irrigation schemes have made possible the development of farming in these arid zones (especially in the northern region of the country, which has emerged as a center for the export of fruit and vegetables to the United States), along with cattle raising, light industry, and tourism in the coastal resorts. Moving south, as the breadth of North America narrows toward the Central American isthmus, one encounters the mountainous, semiarid center-north region, whose principal economic activity has always been mining; copper has overtaken silver as the leading product of this industry.

The central region, focused on the national capital and the Federal District, has always had the densest concentration of population. In the rural areas there is dense settlement throughout the mountain valleys and the soils have been continuously worked for centuries, deteriorating in quality and providing no more than a bare subsistence for those who try to eke out a living on their tiny plots of land. A more productive agriculture is found in the western region of the country, centering on the country's second largest city, Guadalajara. Its interconnected river valleys draining toward the Pacific provide rich soils and a long growing season. This rich area is a focus of Spanish colonial tradition and a stronghold of the Catholic Church. The eastern region, on the coast of the Gulf of Mexico, resembles areas of the Caribbean; it has plantations growing tropical products such as rice and sugar cane, and in the past African slaves were brought to the region, which today has a large mulatto population.

What the Mexicans call the south, the mountains lying south and west of the capital city, is a region of small cultivators and only slowly growing population. Its principal state, Oaxaca, is the most Indian state of Mexico; it is only recently that a majority of the population of the state has come to use Spanish and not one of the Indian languages by preference. The Yucatán peninsula, the "southeast," which juts out into the Caribbean, is also firmly Indian in culture, although the Indians there are Maya—akin to the people of Guatemala rather than those of central Mexico—and still hold to a distinctive way of life.

It should be noted that in Mexico, as in the rest of Latin America, "Indian" is a cultural rather than a physical or genetic category. Physically, most Mexicans are Indian or mixed Spanish and Indian, that is, *mestizo*. A person ceases to be an Indian by acculturating to dominant national norms and abandoning specifically Indian characteristics, such as going barefoot, sleeping in a hammock or on the floor, and especially speaking an Indian language rather than Spanish. Clearly, it is difficult to remain culturally Indian in a city, but many Mexicans in rural areas are in transition from one way of life to another, changing their style of dress, using Spanish predominantly, and modifying their diet to include bread and canned goods.

However, although the national culture and way of life are predominantly modern and European, with only an admixture of Indian elements, psychologically most Mexicans identify with their Indian past more than with the Spanish conquerors. There are statues in Mexico of Moctezuma and Cuauhtémoc, the last Aztec emperors, but not one of Hernando Cortés, the Spaniard who conquered them. In fact, the tale of how heroic but doomed Indians were conquered by ignoble but technologically superior Spaniards has provided some interesting paradigms by which Mexicans understand their national history. As Mexican psychologist Jorge Carrión has put it, "The history of Mexico is full of stories which endure in it more because of their psychological value than because of the authenticity of their testimony."

HISTORICAL SUMMARY TO 1910

Traditionally, most Mexicans thought about the country's history as a pattern, repeated over and over. The pattern is that of heroic Mexicans trying to defend themselves against more powerful foreigners and being defeated, partly because of betrayal by some Mexicans who have sided with the foreigners. The conquest was made possible because Cortés had the assistance of some of the indigenous tribes and of his mistress and inter-

preter, Malinche. The original movement for independence, led at the beginning of the nineteenth century by Father Miguel Hidalgo and Father José María Morelos, who were defeated and killed by the Spaniards, was finally successful when the upper classes, afraid that their privileges would be taken away by a liberal Spanish government, joined the cause of independence. Their leadership, however, nullified the original populist impulse of the independence movement, and their military leader, Agustín Iturbide, proclaimed himself emperor.

During the chaotic period of revolts, rigged elections, and foreign interventions that constituted the first half century of Mexican independence, law and order broke down, the economy decayed, and the country's finances were looted. The United States, under President James K. Polk, took advantage of the situation to provoke a war in which U.S. troops occupied Mexico City. The war was concluded in 1848 by the Treaty of Guadalupe-Hidalgo, which led, together with the subsequent Gadsden Purchase, to the annexation by the United States of present-day Texas, New Mexico, Arizona, and California, approximately half of what had been the territorial area of Mexico.[1]

A few years later Napoleon III of France used the Mexicans' suspension of payments on their foreign debt as a pretext to send an army to Mexico whose real purpose was to create a French-dependent Mexican empire with Archduke Maximilian of Austria as Emperor. Maximilian and his bride, Carlotta, apparently believed in all innocence that the opportunistic reactionaries who came to his palace outside Trieste to offer him the crown represented the popular will of the people of Mexico.

In fact, they were simply looking for a way out of the anticlerical and anti-elite program,

---

[1]Texas (as, for a few days, did California) had a period of existence as an independent republic before joining the United States. Mexico had been willing to tolerate the secession of Texas as an independent republic, but its refusal to accept the annexation of Texas to the United States was one of the causes of the war.

Pyramid of the Sun, Teotihuacán.

known as *La Reforma,* being put into effect by a Liberal government under Benito Juárez. Juárez led the military resistance against Maximilian, who was finally executed after his May 1867 surrender. Juárez, regarded by most Mexicans as their greatest president, only survived his triumph by five years, and his successor as president was overthrown in a successful revolt in 1876. The new *caudillo*—the dominant personalist leader—who took power and dominated the politics of Mexico for 35 years was Porfirio Díaz. Díaz was to serve as president for all but one term of the period until he was overthrown in 1910. He began in politics as a Liberal and follower of Juárez, but his regime reinterpreted the idea of progress embodied in Liberalism to mean social and economic development brought about by the encouragement of foreign investment and the suppression of Mexico's Indian character. Díaz imposed a "law and order" that involved intimidating the lower classes, especially Indian peasants. He promoted economic development—

railroad building, mining, communications, and power generation—on the basis of special concessions for foreign investors. Large estates were built up, sometimes in foreign hands, and traditional Liberal anticlericalism was abandoned.

The Díaz regime was a great success, at least in the eyes of foreigners. But Díaz's fatal mistake was maintaining control with the same closed group that had come to power with him and leaving no openings for new middle- and upper-class elements. There were sectors of the population with legitimate grievances against the Díaz regime—Indians who were discriminated against, peasants who had lost their land to cronies of the president, workers in the new industries who were not allowed to organize and seek better conditions, business people whose competitors had better government connections. But just as a hydrogen bomb can only be set off by the explosion of an atom bomb that acts as its trigger, the great social movement that was the Mexican Revolution of 1910 needed a smaller revolution to get it going, the initial uprising against Díaz. This was an upper-class movement led by Francisco Madero, who came from a land-holding family in the northern state of Coahuila.

Madero's original political goal had been limited to getting Díaz to open his regime to some new blood, but it was treated by Díaz as subversion, and Madero's movement became an open revolt. Taken by surprise by the support garnered by the uprising, Díaz resigned. An interim government held elections, which were won by Madero. However, Madero made the mistake of not being revolutionary enough, leaving in office the officials and generals who had served under Díaz; subsequently, some of them conspired with the ambassador of the Taft administration to overthrow Madero's government. Madero was removed and then shot by order of military commander General Victoriano Huerta, known for his brutality, corruption, and drunkenness. A revolution against the Huerta government was not long in coming. It did not have a single leader, however, and the division among the revolutionary forces led to fighting among them after Huerta was defeated and overthrown.

THE MEXICAN REVOLUTION: THE EARLY YEARS

The principal revolutionary forces were led by figures that have become legendary in Mexican history. Emiliano Zapata, from the state of Morelos, continued to fight, as he had since the Díaz administration, on behalf of small land-holders whose land had been taken from them by force or fraud; he had opposed Madero once it became clear that Madero was not serious about land reform. In the northern border state of Chihuahua, an army was raised by Francisco "Pancho" Villa (Doroteo Arango). Villa was a former soldier in the federal army who had escaped from the military prison where he had been placed for disobeying orders. Vaguely populist in ideological terms, Villa attracted followers—including intellectuals who wrote his political material—by his colorful and forceful personality, but he repelled others by his cruelty and opportunism. Villa's historical reputation

has never been secure, and only belatedly, and after much discussion, did the Mexican Congress agree to include him in the pantheon of revolutionary heroes whose names are inscribed in its hall. Zapata, on the other hand, is regarded in Mexican history as a man of noble and unselfish ideals.

Venustiano Carranza was the leader closest, historically and politically, to Madero. When Carranza was a senator and acting governor of Madero's home state of Coahuila under Porfirio Díaz, his support of Madero was important in giving credibility and impetus to the original revolution. Moderate and quite unrevolutionary in his aims, Carranza always regarded himself as the authentic heir to Madero and his logical successor. Carranza's claims were finally vindicated; he was recognized in October 1915 as de facto president by the United States and was formally elected constitutional president in March 1917 under terms of a new constitution.

This result was only achieved after much fighting, however. After the defeat of Huerta's forces, an interim national government representing all of the revolutionary factions was dominated by a coalition between Villa and Zapata. Carranza refused to accept the authority of this government; his armies, commanded by the best military strategist the revolution produced, Alvaro Obregón of the state of Sonora, defeated Villa's forces in a series of battles. Villa finally made peace and was allowed to retire. He was later assassinated, presumably with Obregón's complicity, when he was preparing to resume political activity. Zapata—like all the leaders of the first phase of the Mexican Revolution—was also assassinated.

Carranza's election took place under the terms of the new revolutionary constitution. This document had been drafted by the radical majority of the constituent convention and represented a progressive social democratic perspective. Ownership of mineral resources was vested in the national government, not in the owner of the surface of the land; labor's rights to organize and strike were guaranteed; and religious bodies were forbidden to own property. Carranza ran a moderate administration, however, and the social provisions of the constitution

Emiliano Zapata (1879–1919), the Mexican revolutionary leader who advocated land reform, was killed by government troops in 1919.

were only implemented by the succeeding presidency of Obregón.

Obregón announced his presidential candidacy with criticisms of the moderation of the Carranza government, making it impossible for Carranza to support him. Given traditional Mexican political practices, under which the candidate favored by the incumbent administration always won the election, there was plausibility to Obregón's charge that Carranza was planning to rig the elections to impose his own choice of successor, and Obregón led a revolt. Against Obregón's instructions, Carranza—like the other major revolutionary figures—was assassinated. An interim government under Obregón's fellow-Sonoran, Adolfo de la Huerta, organized elections which were duly won by Obregón.

The administration of Alvaro Obregón (1920–1924) was especially significant. The revolt that made it possible was the last successful revolt in Mexican history, as Obregón himself

foresaw. Of an unsuccessful revolt against his government in 1923, he wrote "a progressive evolution has been slowly taking place; … it is no longer possible to start a revolution in Mexico and immediately thereafter find popular support.… I feel strongly that this will be the last military rebellion in Mexico."[2] This was so in part because Obregón reorganized the guerrilla armies of the revolution—which had consisted of bands haphazardly recruited, trained, and organized, and owing loyalty to specific individuals—into a regular army based on discipline, hierarchy, and loyalty to the constitutional authorities. More important, he pursued policies that won broad popular support so that in a future crisis the great majority of the population would actively support the government, rather than remain passive bystanders or support armed insurrection. The Obregón administration took a clear position in favor of the efforts of labor unions to organize, establish a national trade union confederation, raise wages, and improve working conditions. Moreover, Obregón began to implement land reform legislation passed under Carranza, thus winning over the former supporters of Zapata.

The payoff came in the rebellion of 1923. Obregón chose as his successor General Plutarco Elías Calles, the third of the revolutionary leaders from Sonora. This was resented by the former interim president, de la Huerta, who thought the nomination should rightfully have gone to him, and in the traditional fashion he began a revolt. The army, not yet thoroughly reorganized, split about evenly, but one of the major factors that tipped the balance of power in favor of Obregón was the participation on his side of volunteer battalions and irregular forces of workers and peasants. Something new had occurred in Mexican history: Workers and peasants fought on behalf of an incumbent government instead of against it.

The coalition that Obregón had put together degenerated somewhat under Calles. Although Calles started from a radical revolutionary position, this was soon modified by his

---

[2]Obregón to Frank Bohn, February 12, 1924.

REVIEW
11.1

PRESIDENTS OF MEXICO

1917–1920	Venustiano Carranza	1952–1958	Adolfo Ruiz Cortines
1920	Adolfo de la Huerta	1958–1964	Adolfo López Mateos
1920–1924	Alvaro Obregón	1964–1970	Gustavo Díaz Ordaz
1924–1928	Plutarco Elías Calles	1970–1976	Luis Echeverría
1928–1930	Emilio Portes Gil	1976–1982	José López Portillo
1930–1932	Pascual Ortiz Rubio	1982–1988	Miguel de la Madrid
1932–1934	Abelardo Rodríguez	1988–1994	Carlos Salinas de Gortari
1934–1940	Lázaro Cárdenas	1994–2000	Ernesto Zedillo
1940–1946	Manuel Avila Camacho	2000–	Vicente Fox
1946–1952	Miguel Alemán		

growing conservatism and connivance in financial irregularities. A strong pro-labor position became in fact acquiescence in labor racketeering and allowing companies to buy their way out of labor difficulties. The threatened resumption by the Mexican state, under the terms of the new constitution, of mineral rights ceded to foreign oil companies was somehow negotiated through the good offices of the U.S. ambassador to allow companies active before 1917 to retain their oil concessions. Calles became disillusioned with the land reform program, coming to believe that land was more productive when privately owned than when collectively owned by Indian communities, which was the mode in which most of the expropriated land had been redistributed.

Calles, a former school teacher, nevertheless continued Obregón's program of expansion of the educational system and the building of schools. He also followed up the program of the professionalization of the military; purging of the officers who had supported de la Huerta's rebellion made it possible to reduce the size of the military budget, the officer corps, and the army as a whole. Moreover, Calles went further than Obregón in enforcing the anticlerical provisions of the constitution. Catholic resistance to the harsh measures taken by Calles included the suspension of religious services, and indeed a guer-

rilla war broke out against the government, centered in the devout Bajío region of western Mexico. The government conducted a ruthless counterinsurgency campaign against these "warriors of Christ the King" or *cristeros,* which was not called off until the end of Calles's term.

The country was in fact ready for a return to the more conciliatory and pro-agrarian policies of Obregón, and the former president indicated that he was ready to return for a new term. For this to happen, the constitution had to be amended because it had enshrined the principle of no presidential reelection that had been the banner of Madero's revolution against Porfirio Díaz. Accordingly, Congress passed an amendment making the prohibition of reelection apply only to consecutive reelection.[3] Thus Obregón would be eligible for the term that began in 1928. Moreover, another amendment extended the presidential term from four to six years. Elections were held and the popular Obregón was reelected, although not before a revolt by three frustrated would-be candidates had been put down. The Cristero War, however, was to claim its last victim. A group of religious fanatics, under the mistaken impression that

---

[3]This was subsequently reamended so that anyone who has served as president can never be elected again.

Obregón was responsible for the anticlerical policies of Calles, organized the assassination of the president-elect, and Obregón joined the long line of revolutionary heroes brought to an untimely end.

At this point Calles rose to the occasion with an act of statesmanship. It was generally expected that he would use the pretext of Obregón's assassination to extend his own term; in fact, some disgruntled proagrarian supporters of Obregón went so far as to claim that Calles himself was behind the assassination. Calles, however, made clear that constitutional procedures, which called for the Congress to elect a provisional president until new popular elections could be organized, would be followed. Moreover, he took the assassination as a lesson that the political system of the Revolution should not have to depend on individual personalities, arguing that the time had come to place the regime on a more stable institutional footing by organizing a political party that would embody the aspirations of the revolution in permanent form. Up to that point, different leaders had organized ad hoc parties of their followers, while other parties represented major interest groups. Following the end of his term, accordingly, Calles organized the National Revolutionary Party, *Partido Nacional Revolucionario* (PNR), the precursor of the party that ruled Mexico until the end of the twentieth century.

For the provisional presidency, Congress elected Emilio Portes Gil, a young pro-agrarian former state governor acceptable to both Obregón and Calles supporters. The president elected to serve out Obregón's term was Pascual Ortiz Rubio, who turned out to be conservative, weak, and inconsistent. He referred all major decisions to Calles, who came to be regarded as Mexico's strong man and the real ruler of the country. Finally, the country's leading political figures refused to serve in Ortiz Rubio's cabinet, so he followed Calles's last piece of advice: He resigned. The remaining two years of the first six-year presidential term were filled by a moderate former general and associate of Calles, Abelardo Rodríguez, who had developed extensive business interests, especially in the North.

THE CARDENAS ERA

The first president to serve out the full six-year term (1934–1940) was General Lázaro Cárdenas, regarded by most Mexicans as the greatest president produced by the Revolution. He was also its most leftist president. Land reform proceeded at a pace that was probably the maximum technically feasible and was no longer merely a question of restoring land wrongfully taken from Indian communities. Land could be expropriated from a landholder owning more than a certain amount and then assigned to any group of landless agricultural workers living in the vicinity. As with the Indian communities, however, ownership was vested in the group rather than in the individual, although—under an amendment to the law passed during the Calles administration—the right to farm specific plots of land could be inherited within a family. Under Cárdenas, however, some lands that were producing hemp (for rope and fabric) and cotton were set up as collective farms after expropriation, rather than being subdivided for individual family farming.

The Cárdenas administration was strongly pro-labor, promoting labor organization and consistently favoring workers in industrial disputes. The racketeering head of the principal labor federation, Luis Morones, who had been a major political figure under Calles but was cut off from government favor by Portes Gil, was now overshadowed as the dominant figure in organized labor by a leftist intellectual named Vicente Lombardo Toledano.

Although generally pragmatic on economic questions, Cárdenas inclined to nationalism and socialism and was responsible for setting up some state corporations. The railroads were nationalized, as was the oil industry, after an industrial dispute in which most of the foreign-owned oil companies had made themselves thoroughly unpleasant and unpopular. The oil nationalization in 1938 and the setting up of a state oil corporation, today called *Petróleos Mexicanos,* or PEMEX, is generally regarded as one of the high points in Mexican nationalism. After the expropriation, the foreign companies, which were vertically integrated—that is, they controlled the industry from exploration and development through processing and retailing—organized an international boycott of Mexican oil; the role of the state company was thus limited to supplying Mexico's own domestic needs.

Cárdenas also followed a left-wing line in foreign policy. He was president from 1934 to 1940, a highly emotional era in which the coming battle between democracy and the Fascist powers was taking shape. Cárdenas took a strong pro-Republican position in the Spanish Civil War and refused to recognize the Franco government at the war's conclusion. Mexico became the home of the Republican government-in-exile, and diplomatic relations with the government of Spain were not resumed until after Franco's death many years later.

Cárdenas also reorganized the ruling party to fit his leftist and nationalist principles. The party was renamed the Mexican Revolutionary Party, *Partido Revolucionario Mexicano* (PRM); it was reorganized explicitly as an alliance of classes, with separate sectors representing organized labor, collective peasant landholders, and progressive elements of the middle class. This last sector, called "popular," consisted primarily of unions of teachers and government white-collar workers, along with smaller associations of professionals, small private farmers, and small-business people. Cárdenas also included the armed forces as a full sector of the party, but this was not popular within the military itself, and the military sector was abolished by Cárdenas's successor after two or three years of existence.

THE ERA OF
STABLE DEVELOPMENT

The moderate Manuel Avila Camacho, who served from 1940 to 1946, was the last general to be elected president of Mexico. He continued the work of his predecessors in reducing the political role of the army. A staff officer rather than a heroic leader in battle, Avila Camacho was little known before his nomination for the presidency; in fact, some called him "the unknown soldier." In the presidential elections he was opposed by an extremely popular general, the highest-ranking officer on active duty before he

resigned to enter politics, Juan Andreu Almazán. With support gathered from the interests alienated either by Calles or by Cárdenas—devout Catholics, business interests, disgruntled elements in the military, and even labor factions opposed to Lombardo Toledano—there seemed to be a chance that Almazán might get a majority of the vote. Unwilling to accept a victory for what looked like a coalition of the forces defeated by the revolution, Cárdenas agreed to the announcement of a fraudulent result. Apparently, Almazán won a majority in the Federal District, although not in the country at large, but in any case those were not the results announced.

Avila Camacho showed that the Mexican rule of no presidential reelection allows for the kind of flexibility that has enabled the system to survive; the tree that is able to bend with the wind does not break. Another popular analogy had it that a presidential succession resembled a pendulum: incoming presidents usually swung away from the unpopular or unviable policies of their predecessors, making concessions to the groups most dissatisfied with their predecessors' policies.

What this meant for the president who followed Cárdenas was a position of greater moderation. The pace of land reform was slowed down, and no other industries were nationalized. Avila Camacho did begin a social security system for workers, but its coverage is still limited to employees of government and larger modern firms and does not extend to all Mexican workers. Hostilities against the church were called off, and good relations were fostered with the United States. Mexico participated in its first war on the same side as the United States when an air squadron was sent to fight the Japanese in the Pacific. Arrangements were worked out for the *bracero* program, under which Mexican laborers were contracted to work in the United States for fixed periods. Lombardo Toledano was eased out of his leadership position in the CTM, the Mexican Confederation of Labor, and replaced by the more moderate Fidel Velázquez, who remained secretary general of the CTM until his death over 50 years later.

Avila Camacho capped his policies of national reconciliation and government from the center of the political spectrum by again reorganizing the ruling party, this time renaming it the *Partido Revolucionario Institucional* (PRI), the Institutional Revolutionary Party, symbolizing the final coming to maturity of the revolution. Indeed, since Avila Camacho the country has been run by civilian presidents on the basis of centrist economic policies and a modus vivendi with the Church and with the United States. Stimulated first by the wartime lack of consumer goods to import, and then by the boom that followed World War II, the Mexican economy entered a long and sustained period of stable economic growth that ended only with the economic collapse that followed the fall in oil prices at the beginning of the 1980s.

The following president, Miguel Alemán (1946–1952), carried the pendulum further away from the Cárdenas years. Strongly pro-business, he presided over a threefold increase in Mexico's exports, a doubling of the value of agricultural production, and a 42 percent increase in industrial activity. At the same time, the state sector of the economy expanded and Mexico enjoyed a substantial increase in tourism. The increase in agricultural production resulted from the irrigation of vast expanses of dry land, especially in the north. This newly productive land was sold to private agribusiness interests, not distributed to landless peasants, who in any case lived mostly in the center of the country. But the land reform program dwindled and some categories of large landholding were made exempt from expropriation. These were golden years for private business interests, including the personal interests of the president and his associates. Lombardo Toledano quit the PRI in disgust and founded his own *Partido Popular,* later to become the *Partido Popular Socialista* (PPS) or Popular Socialist Party. It must be said that then, as in future years, Lombardo's tactics responded not only to Mexican realities but also to the international position being taken by Moscow-line Communists and fellow travelers, which at this time was to withdraw from wartime popular front coalitions.

If the three presidents—Carranza, Obregón, and Calles—who presided over the initial period under the new constitution were responsible for the establishment of the country's basic institutional framework, then the three presidents who were the first to serve six-year terms—Cárdenas,

Avila Camacho, and Alemán—established policies that set the parameters for their successors. On the left, Cárdenas's policies favored labor and promoted land reform; in the center, Avila Camacho's policies advanced pacification, political reconciliation, and cooperation with the United States; and on the right Alemán's policies fostered economic growth through favoring export-oriented industry, agribusiness, and tourism. These policies provided the basic mix their successors followed, with differences of emphasis, to be sure.

These differences in emphasis are what gave rise to the concept of a pendular swing between one president and the next. Sometimes, in fact, a candidate was chosen because his reputation made it politically plausible that he would move in the required direction.

This was the case with the president who succeeded Alemán, Adolfo Ruiz Cortines. Alemán was becoming notorious for enriching himself illegally, in those years of economic boom, and former president Cárdenas, who was still the most popular political figure in the country, made it clear that he would find unacceptable any continuation of the situation, either in the form of a constitutional amendment and the reelection of Alemán (which a presidential emissary suggested to him) or in the succession of one of Alemán's close associates. Ruiz Cortines, the candidate who was picked, had a reputation for honesty that went back to his early days in politics handling payrolls for revolutionary armies. His presidency was conservative and unimaginative, however, and he left office the oldest man to have served as Mexican president since Porfirio Díaz.

The succeeding president, Adolfo López Mateos, again provided a contrast with his predecessor. He was relatively young, and indeed was the first president to have been born after Madero first raised the standard of rebellion. He was politically on the left and had been secretary of labor in the cabinet. Tactically, a more left-wing orientation was called for; Fidel Castro's coming to power in Cuba aroused enthusiastic support in Mexico, and Lázaro Cárdenas had come out of retirement to head a movement supporting the Cuban revolution.

In the tradition of Cárdenas, López Mateos stepped up the pace of land distribution. Electricity generation and motion picture production were nationalized; significantly, however, López Mateos showed that his leftism was within the system and served to support it. His actions with respect to the labor movement showed that his service as secretary of labor had prepared him not merely to represent labor, but to manage the labor movement in the interest of the maintenance of the political system. A worker's profit-sharing program was legislated, but López Mateos showed no sympathy for unauthorized or politically motivated strikes and invoked the antisubversion laws to jail the leader of the railroad workers' union. Similarly, López Mateos continued Mexico's policy of being the only member of the Organization of American States to refuse, despite U.S. pressure, to break off diplomatic relations with Cuba, but he cooperated amicably with the United States in the resolution of various border problems. In addition, the electoral system was modified to guarantee the opposition parties a few seats in the Chamber of Deputies.

After López Mateos, the pendulum swung again. The unauthorized railroad strike and growing support for Fidel Castro suggested that law and order issues and the control of "political subversion" might be the key issues of the succeeding presidential term, so López Mateos chose his minister of governance, Gustavo Díaz Ordaz, as his successor. Although the economy continued to grow, helped by Mexico's membership in the new Latin American free trade area, the Díaz Ordaz administration became a spectacular failure precisely with respect to the law and order issue. The late 1960s was the time of worldwide student protest movements sparked by the war in Vietnam. Díaz Ordaz was particularly nervous because Mexico would be hosting the Olympic Games in 1968; the focus of world attention would be on Mexico and political disruption would be a possibility. In this atmosphere, a trivial student dispute escalated until the government was facing huge demonstrations of students and sympathizers demanding political liberalization. In a stunning overreaction, participants in a massive demonstration taking place in a large public square in the Tlatelolco district were attacked by soldiers with tanks and automatic weapons, resulting in hundreds of deaths and universal repudiation of the Díaz Ordaz government.

After this incident the pendulum clearly needed to swing to the left, and the new nominee for the presidency was Luis Echeverría, a career administrator who had been born in the Federal District and had never been a candidate for elected office before. Echeverría attempted to model himself on Cárdenas and run a pro–labor, pro–land reform, leftist government. He particularly tried to reconcile students to the regime by appointing ambassadors and other high officials who were barely out of the university. Despite his good intentions, Echeverría's hyperactive leftism proved counterproductive and self-defeating. The president had to back down on neutralist and pro–third world foreign policy positions when these earned the disfavor of the United States and foreign tourists and investors. Speeches against foreign capitalism simply led to the flight of foreign investment, forcing Mexico to borrow heavily abroad and become more dependent on the world capitalist system. The resulting weakness of the peso forced its first devaluation in almost 25 years. The attempt to liberalize the regime met with opposition from entrenched party bosses and labor leaders, who organized gangs in universities that attacked the left-wing student groups thought to be the biggest agitators in favor of liberalization.

THE SYSTEM ENTERS PERMANENT CRISIS

For the next presidential term, the pendulum swung to José López Portillo, the moderate minister of finance and a well-regarded author of books on administrative law, and even of novels. The increase in world oil prices forced by the Organization of Petroleum Exporting Countries (OPEC) made it worthwhile for Mexico to undertake the considerable costs of exploration in order to become an oil exporter. Exploration proved fabulously successful: Mexico surpassed Venezuela to become the world's fifth largest oil producer. Oil wealth gave Mexico the resources and self-confidence to follow a strong foreign policy independent of the United States; López Portillo backed

Panama's efforts to renegotiate the Panama Canal Treaty and favored popular liberation movements in Central America. In the end, however, oil proved a curse as well as a blessing. Reckless spending of oil income provoked an inflation that hurt the poorer sectors of society; the flood of foreign exchange made it easy to import everything, and Mexico's own industries withered. The temptations of easy money led to vast corruption, including that of the president himself. Meanwhile, consumer nations responded to higher oil prices by cutting back consumption, and prices began to drop. Instead of adjusting to the reduced levels of income, the López Portillo government assumed that the price drop was only temporary and maintained its high level of spending, then borrowed abroad to cover the difference. But the price drop continued, and Mexico's debts became astronomical before the government appreciated the seriousness of the situation. People with money read the signs correctly before López Portillo did, however; they converted their pesos to dollars and sent them out of the country before the government gave up defending the value of the peso. Eventually the peso was devalued, and Mexico witnessed runaway inflation that rapidly dropped the living standards of the poor.

In an attempt to recuperate politically what he had lost economically, López Portillo decreed the nationalization of the banking system. The subsequent burst of leftist and nationalist euphoria soon wore off, however, leaving Mexicans still burdened with unemployment, inflation, and debt. The feeling of despair that settled on the country was made complete in September 1985 when Mexico City was rocked by a devastating earthquake, which was not only disastrous in itself but also revealed that legal construction standards had not been followed. Poor construction was especially evident in government buildings, implying once again corruption and kickbacks. Under López Portillo's successor, various financial services the banks had provided, along with industrial interests they had controlled, were split off and privatized, and eventually the banks were returned to private hands completely.

This successor was Miguel de la Madrid, whose nomination took control of the system by career bureaucrats one step further. Like his two immediate predecessors, de la Madrid had never held elective office before being nominated for the presidency. A technician in administration, programming, and budgeting, de la Madrid had a Harvard M.P.A. and had served as minister of programming and budget in the López Portillo cabinet. Inheriting a collapsed economy, a demoralized population, and a regime that had forfeited much of the prestige of its earlier achievements, de la Madrid had little room for political maneuver. His government's weakness was demonstrated by its failure to follow up on pledges to fight corruption after initially managing to make examples of the notoriously corrupt head of PEMEX and the Mexico City police chief. Mexico's opposition to Ronald Reagan's counter-revolutionary policies in Central America died away, and the government cut back living standards even more in an attempt to reduce inflation and pay off the foreign debt. It seemed bitterly ironic that the bill for the spending spree of the oil-boom years was being paid by those Mexicans who had benefited least from it. Foreign exchange became scarce and Mexican wages became cheap in international terms, leading to steady growth in export industry, especially the *maquiladoras,* in-bond assembly plants located in the northern border area. Inflation eased somewhat and oil consumption crept up once more in the industrialized societies of the world, thus providing some faint rays of hope for improvement in the economic situation.

The president who received credit for the subsequent economic improvement was Carlos Salinas de Gortari, who was elected in 1988. He was an example of the presidential nominee who could now be expected: a career administrator from the Federal District specializing in administrative and financial questions, with a foreign degree but without previous service in electoral office. Like his sponsor, de la Madrid, Salinas had an M.P.A. from Harvard but had carried the process a step further by earning a Ph.D. in political economy. Characteristically, he came from a family committed to the public sector; in fact, at the time of his nomination his father was serving as senator from the state of Nuevo León.

Concluding that there was no realistic alternative to a free-market strategy, in which his economic training in any case led him to believe, Salinas embarked on a radical reorientation of the Mexican economy, joining with the United States and Canada in a North American Free Trade Area, continuing de la Madrid's privatization of state enterprises, balancing the budget, and renegotiating foreign debt. Inflation was brought down to single digits, and the burden of debt service was reduced, while economic growth resumed. Moreover, budgetary savings and the income from the sale of state enterprises was used to finance a poverty-reduction program, known as Solidarity, which followed the most advanced thinking on development by stressing bottom-up grassroots participation in the formulation and administration of projects, avoiding centralization and bureaucratic waste. Salinas apparently hoped that the Solidarity program would provide him with an alternative cadre of political organizers that would enable him to replace the entrenched national and regional political machines that formed the PRI.

But there were severe weaknesses in the Salinas formula. First, his economic policy rested on attracting a continuous flow of foreign investment in government bonds denominated in dollars, thus encouraging an overvaluation of the peso. Second, he tried to extend free-market principles to agriculture, which seemed to landless peasants to betray the agrarian principles of the revolution and caused disaster in coffee-producing areas when the withdrawal of government supports and guaranteed purchases coincided with a collapse in world market prices. Third, Salinas allowed opposition victories in gubernatorial elections, but only when opposition protests threatened a breakdown of public order, which had the effect of encouraging violent protests rather than leading to fair election procedures. Fourth, his government sold privatized state enterprises on very favorable terms to people with good political connections.

But it wasn't only the privatization program that created instant billionaires. The "war on drugs" certainly did not close down direct routes from Colombia to the United States, but it harassed them enough to make it worthwhile to develop connections through Mexico. Enormous drug-trafficking cartels grew, became wealthy, corrupted officials, and used violence with impunity. Drug money purchased and intimidated its way into the halls of power, and the business methods of drug dealers entered Mexican politics. The year 1994 was a terrible one for Mexico: Assassination claimed the lives of the presidential candidate of the PRI, Luis Donaldo Colosio; the party's newly appointed leader in Congress, José Luis Ruiz Massieu; and Cardinal Jaime Posadas. An armed rebellion of Indians in the state of Chiapas, hurt by the crash in the coffee market and angered by the abandonment of land reform, raised the banner of Emiliano Zapata. When, shortly after Salinas left the presidency, his brother Raúl was arrested on suspicion of having ordered the killing of Ruiz

Vicente Fox Quesada, the first opposition candidate elected to the presidency in Mexico's history.

The Zócalo, the principal square in Mexico City and the site of major political demonstrations.

Massieu, questions about Salinas's complicity or at least his cover-up of the murder were raised. Moreover, the investigation suggested that the Salinas family had enriched itself hugely at public expense. Carlos Salinas established residence in Ireland, from where he could not be extradited to Mexico. Most Mexicans were willing to believe that Salinas had also been responsible for ordering the assassination of his own hand-picked nominee for the succession, Luis Donaldo Colosio, after Colosio indicated he wouldn't follow orders; no evidence to that effect was uncovered, but the investigation of the crime was never brought to a full and satisfactory conclusion.

Ironically, the arrest of Raúl Salinas was the good news for the president who took office at the end of 1994, Ernesto Zedillo, because it lent plausibility to his claim that he was determined to implant the rule of law and end impunity, no matter how politically powerful and well-connected the culprit. Zedillo's popularity needed all the

help it could get. He had not been one of the leading candidates for the succession; the heavyweights of the Salinas administration were constitutionally ineligible, the law (to prevent *continuismo*) requiring that an incoming president not have held public office for 12 months prior to his inauguration. Zedillo had fortuitously resigned from the cabinet at the same time as Colosio in order to manage Colosio's campaign, which also identified him with the assassinated popular leader and might well have positioned him to become Colosio's successor. But his sudden elevation to the candidacy seemed to come six years too early.

Already in a weak position, Zedillo inherited a party facing its strongest opposition yet. Cuauhtémoc Cárdenas, son of Lázaro, was a lackluster candidate for the leftist Democratic Revolutionary Party but retained the magic of his family name and was supported by the feeling that the PRD was closer to the values and ideals of the Revolution than the new-model PRI, whose economic policies now seemed closer to those advocated by the right-wing National Action Party (PAN). Moreover, the assassination of Colosio could be interpreted as suggesting that powerful factions within the PRI were unhappy with the direction the party had taken: Colosio had been president of the PRI when it accepted the loss of the governorship of Baja California to the PAN, and it was in Baja California that the assassination took place. Colosio had also indicated that he would discontinue Salinas's tolerance of, if not complicity in, drug trafficking.

Zedillo was weakened even further by an incompetently managed devaluation of the peso shortly after he assumed office. The peso sank like a stone, huge amounts of capital fled the country, and his finance minister was replaced after less than a month in office. The resulting bailout by the U.S. government and international financial institutions meant another heavy burden of debt repayment, crippling financial austerity at home, and the abandonment of any possibility of an independent foreign policy.

In his weakened political position, Zedillo had no alternative but to make a virtue out of necessity and attempt to go down in history as the president who had brought full democracy to Mexico. Under pressure to resolve the question of culpability for the assassinations, he championed the implantation of the rule of law and the cleansing of the republic's corrupt police and judiciary systems, even appointing a member of the opposition PAN as attorney general. Facing strengthened opposition parties able to protest effectively against rigged elections, he espoused a constitutional reform that would implant a system of fair and honest elections. Unable to control local party organizations, he announced support for a more authentic federalism that would devolve power from the center to the state governments. When the inevitable finally happened and the 2000 elections were won by the presidential candidate of the opposition PAN, Vicente Fox, Zedillo moved quickly to recognize Fox's victory and preempt any attempt by PRI hardliners to falsify the count.

Thinking Critically

1. Was the Mexican Revolution a positive development?
2. Is there much difference between what *development* meant in the era of Porfirio Díaz and what it means today?
3. How was it possible for Mexico to go beyond the stereotypical Latin America behavior of revolutions and military dictatorship?
4. To what extent is Mexico today an "Indian" country?
5. How have social changes in Mexico led to political change?

KEY TERMS

caudillo (600)
land reform *(601–602, 604–607)*
mestizo (599)
Partido Revolucionario Institucional (PRI) *(606, 609, 611)*
the pendulum *(606, 607)*
La Reforma (600)
single-party system *(598)*

FURTHER READINGS

Calvert, Peter. *Mexico* (London: Ernest Benn, 1973).

Gentleman, Judith, ed. *Mexican Politics in Transition* (Boulder, CO: Westview Press, 1987).

Hellman, Judith Adler. *Mexico in Crisis,* 2nd ed. (New York: Holmes and Meier, 1988).

Joseph, Gilbert M., and Timothy J. Henderson, eds. *The Mexico Reader: History, Culture, Politics* (Durham: Duke University Press, 2002).

Rodríguez, Jaime, ed. *The Evolution of the Mexican Political System* (Wilmington, DE: SR Books, 1993).

B. POLITICAL PROCESSES AND INSTITUTIONS

It appeared that President Zedillo had been chosen by history to preside over the final long-awaited transformation of the single-party system into one of genuine competition. Skeptics could argue, however, that there was still a lot of life in the hegemonic-party model and the PRI might be able to stage a comeback at some point in the future. After all, the opposition to the PRI was split between a major party to its right and one to its left, each of which had more in common with the PRI than it did with each other, and thus could not be expected to ally permanently against it. Moreover, despite the outcome of the 2000 presidential elections, probably more Mexicans sympathized with the centrist policies of the PRI than with those of either of its more extreme rivals. The PRI moreover retained the inertial force of several generations of identification with the party among voters and an organizational structure that extended to every hamlet of the republic. So the PRI might be expected to win victories even under the newly adopted standards of fair electoral competition.

At the state level, in many jurisdictions, PRI party machines continue in place, and it would be premature to expect the consistent application of such standards, however. Opportunities will continue to exist for many of the techniques in which the PRI's "alchemists" had become expert: the electoral roll on which the names of known voters for opposition parties mysteriously fail to appear, the election-day breakdowns of public transportation in districts dominated by the opposition, the well-financed "illnesses" that suddenly inflict election observers of the opposition parties and prevent them from showing up at the polling places.

Yet it seems likely that at the state and local levels, too, circumstances will change so that it will be increasingly difficult for PRI stalwarts to act in the traditional manner. Most importantly, President Fox has made clear that he will play by the democratic rules and not seek to impose a new single-party hegemony of the PAN. But before we say goodbye to the single-party regime

that ruled Mexico for most of the twentieth century, let us examine its major features. After all, a modified version might yet be revived; in any case it forms the necessary background to understanding the situation today.

THE SINGLE-PARTY SYSTEM

As Mexico developed economically and socially, with a rise in general political sophistication and will to participate, sustained especially by a growth in the business and professional middle classes and the numbers of university students, the PRI's monopoly of power could be expected to erode; governments handled the problem by yielding political space to the opposition, but always managing to maintain not only the substance of power but also the PRI's dominant position at the center of the political spectrum and some appearance of openness and democratic procedure.

During the 1920s and 1930s, the dissenting tendencies both inside and outside the ruling party had been genuine, lively, and intermittently violent. With the great pacification operation of Avila Camacho and the onset of the boom years of stable development, the regime's management of politics became smooth and largely efficient. The opposition party to the right, the National Action Party, *Partido de Acción Nacional* (PAN), had at first seemed not just anti-PRI, but anti-system, vaguely threatening violence on occasion, but the small left and center-left parties had generally been well-behaved satellites of the PRI; their moderate opposition activities were genteel and regularly scripted beforehand, and their façade-strengthening merit was recognized with covert subsidies. During the 1970s, the PAN was taken over by a more modern, more moderate leadership and began to win some local elections.

As opposition grew stronger and more autonomous, the regime's overall strategy became to build up the importance of the opposition to the right, which it then identified in its electoral propaganda with the elements that had ruled Mexico before the revolution, thus enabling the PRI to campaign as the defender of revolutionary principles and obscure how far it had actually departed from those principles. Tame and subsidized microparties of the left and center-left were used to draw support away from uncontrollable opposition groups on the left, and their cooperation with the PRI after the elections served to validate the PRI's claim of being the authentic representative of the revolutionary tradition.

These political strategies were implemented by giving opposition parties seats in the Chamber of Deputies; originally this was done in a rather fraudulent manner, by disqualifying or withdrawing PRI candidates in selected seats to allow candidates of the cooperative minor parties on the left to win by default. López Mateos put this practice on a constitutional basis by introducing a proportional-representation feature into the electoral law, which gave the minor parties some representation in the Chamber in proportion to their total percentage of the national vote. This provision was amplified under successive presidents, so that 200 of the 500 seats in the Chamber are now awarded on a regional-list rather than an individual-district basis, so as to give each party a share of the 500 total chamber seats more proportionate to its popular vote. (Table 11.1 shows the party affiliations of members of the current Congress.)

Opposition candidates regularly competed in presidential elections, and the regime was particularly disappointed when the PAN was unable to agree on a candidate and did not contest the presidential election of 1976. By the time of the presidential candidacy of Carlos Salinas, however, such tolerated and even encouraged opposition activities, which lent credibility to the system's democratic façade, had actually become threatening to continued national control by the PRI. Salinas's own victory in the presidential election had to be carefully managed so that his victory was convincing in two ways: His majority had to be large enough to make his mandate to rule seem clear, yet small enough to make it plausible that all of the opposition's votes had indeed

TABLE 11.1

MEMBERSHIP OF CONGRESS, 2005

Party	Senate	Chamber of Deputies Election July 6, 2003
PRI (Institutional Revolutionary Party)	59	223
PAN (National Action Party)	45	155
PRD (Democratic Revolutionary Party)	17	96
PVEM (Green Ecology Party)	5	17
PT (Labor Party)	1	6
PCD (Party of the Democratic Center)	1	—
Other	0	3
Total	128	500

Source: Federal Election Institute.

been counted. The officially announced margin of his victory—50.36 percent—was not really convincing in either way. Most people assumed Salinas had won less than a majority—perhaps less than a plurality—and the numbers had then been adjusted upward.[4] For Zedillo, the situation was even worse: he received slightly over 50 percent of the "valid" votes—that is, if blank and spoiled ballots were included, his total was under 50 percent. Clearly, the democratic single-party system had entered its twilight years.

Major Features of the Single-Party System

The major features of Mexico's democratic single-party system were:

1. The outgoing president essentially picked the party's nominee as his successor, taking into

[4]According to a poll reported by the *Los Angeles Times* on August 20, 1989, 68 percent of Mexican respondents believed that Salinas had not actually won the election.

account not only the skills of the different possible candidates but also their ability to carry on his own work and to handle emerging problems. However, each incoming president, while representing continuity, was also concerned with distinguishing himself from his predecessor and making his own mark on history, with the result that change was as much a feature of the system as continuity.

2. A politically stable system was achieved. Although revolts or military interventions in polities were talked of from time to time, in fact governments served out their allotted terms with a regularity unmatched not only elsewhere in the third world but also, when the effects of World War II and its aftermath are considered, unmatched in most of Europe. On the whole, military men were subordinated to civilians.

3. The system became institutionalized, as Calles wanted. The president was virtually an all-powerful figure only until his successor was chosen. It was the formal office that conferred authority, not charisma or deeds of daring.

4. Although different presidential administrations varied in their policies, the variation took place within the generally accepted framework of a mixed economy that resembled the economies of Western Europe. There were some nationalized industries and a framework of government regulation, but most economic activity was in private hands. The Salinas administration—in keeping with world trends generally—moved the balance decisively in the capitalist direction with the dismantling of part of the state sector and the revision of trade laws to open Mexico to foreign products and capital.

Economic and Social Changes during the Single-Party Years

Mexico experienced the social changes typical of developing countries. That is, mortality was reduced and life expectancy lengthened; illiteracy declined and the number enrolled in universities increased strikingly; a massive movement to cities shifted the balance so that a majority of the population became urban; rates of population growth at first increased dramatically, but started to level off as a result of urbanization and attitudinal changes (see Table 11.2).

The mix of economic policies followed by Mexican governments before the oil boom of the 1970s was particularly productive, and between 1940 and the early 1980s the country achieved a record of sustained economic growth whose duration was unmatched elsewhere in the world. This record was brought to an end by the collapse of oil prices in 1981, and was succeeded by an alternation between periods of decline and retrenchment, and readjustment and growth.

As the country developed economically and urbanized, its class structure changed. The benefits of economic growth went disproportionately to a new urban bourgeoisie, with a standard of living and pattern of consumption resembling those of the middle class in the United States. Alongside this new bourgeoisie in the modern sector of the urban economy there developed a growing lower middle class of sales clerks and office workers and an industrial working class holding down factory jobs. More significant and much more numerous, however, was the mushrooming urban underclass, the great number of people underemployed and self-employed in what has been called the "informal economy"—people who live in substandard housing, work in small establishments that evade the tax and minimum wage laws, peddle merchandise in the streets, and work as maids, shoeshine boys, or prostitutes. In this respect, Mexico presented a classic third-world profile.

TABLE 11.2

CHANGE IN SOCIAL INDICATORS, 1970–2004

	1970s	1997–2000	2004
Life expectancy (years at birth)	62.4	72.2	74.9
Urban population (% of total)	59.0	74.0	75.2
Daily per capita supply of calories	2,706.0	3,097.0	
Daily per capita supply of protein (grams)	68.0	83.0	

Source: UN, *Human Development Report*, 2000.

POLITICAL AND SOCIAL ISSUES OF WOMEN IN MEXICO

In the political and social position of women, Mexico presents the picture of a traditional society only beginning to modernize. This is not due directly to the strength of the Catholic church, since Mexican governments were officially anticlerical until recently, and the promotion of family planning through birth control, despite Church opposition, has been national policy since President Echeverría. Women could not vote or run for office in national elections until 1953. Thereafter, women's organizations were formed within the PRI, but they were primarily self-promotional gimmicks for their leaders. Women have constituted less than 20 percent of the membership of the national Congress. The tendency toward improvement is clear, however. Under Zedillo, one woman became foreign minister and another president of the PRI.

The contemporary feminist movement was stimulated by developments in the United States and has campaigned for legalized abortions and against rape and domestic violence. But the situation remains dispiriting. Abortions, though illegal, are common (estimated in 1987 at 2 million per year, with perhaps 10,000 fatalities). Even in Mexico City, estimates are that in 1990, when penalties were increased from their previous trivial level, only 1 in 30 rapes was reported to the police, and only 1 in 20 rape complaints resulted in conviction and sentence. The Federal District has started to fund a few rape victims' counseling centers. Despite the extreme frequency of domestic violence, it has not been recognized as a problem for public policy.

Although women's participation in the workforce has increased steadily—about one-third of the paid labor force consists of women—traditional wage discrimination still obtains, as does routine sexual harrassment and the stereotyping of women's work roles. Nevertheless, girls now attend primary and secondary schools in the same numbers as boys, and the infant mortality and life-expectancy figures suggest that women's health has been improving.

How the System Evolved, Struggled to Survive, and Failed

As the single-party system evolved over time, it could be said that Mexico was more or less ruled by a new class, similar to what Milovan Djilas described when writing of the bureaucratic elites that had arisen in Communist Eastern Europe.[5] This was a postrevolutionary ruling group of career administrators recruited on the basis of connections, but also on merit, that is, by academic standing at the university. To some extent a hereditary element developed, as holding public office became a tradition in many leading families. The breeding ground for Mexico's national political leadership was the

national university, the *Universidad Nacional Autónoma de México,* or UNAM. This resulted in an almost complete segmentation of elite career patterns: the public sector elite trained in the national university just as members of the Roman Catholic church hierarchy train only in seminaries and military officers train only in service academies; the leadership of the private business sector is educated in the technological institutes and schools of business, which are also privately owned and managed. Prior to the Salinas administration, it was unheard of in Mexico for a political leader to be a graduate of a private institute of technology or school of business; a military academy background would be extremely rare, and a religious seminary out of the question. Salinas's policy of moving Mexico decisively in a capitalist direction, however, had opened up the possibility of leadership that came from private schools of business even

[5]Milovan Djilas, *The New Class* (New York: Harcourt, Brace, 1957).

before the Fox administration arrived, with MBA's and graduates of Catholic schools.

In the early days after the Revolution, much of the political leadership emerged from the revolutionary army, in those days still an amateur political army and not the professionalized, academy-trained service it has since become. As the political system stabilized during the 1920s and 1930s, and as the fighting of the revolutionary era receded into memory, the military gradually withdrew from the political sphere. The ruling party had established its legitimacy, the political forces favoring the regime had become united, there was no power vacuum, and fighting was no longer a real possibility. The last military man to serve as president left office in 1946; the last military officer to hold a cabinet post not dealing with military affairs left office in 1970. As the generals and colonels retired from the political scene, their place was taken by the professional politicians, many of them lawyers, who had been active in organizing and operating the ruling party. Typically, they had come up through the ranks of state politics, sometimes in staff positions but often in elective posts.

With the final consolidation of the regime in its institutional phase, however, the central tasks of statecraft were no longer to foil uprisings or to weld a set of disparate regional politicians into a coherent national party, but became instead those of managing an expanding economy in the interest of maintaining economic growth. Then the character of the country's leadership underwent another mutation, and the politicians yielded ground to the technocrats. The field was not surrendered without a struggle, and one of the constant themes of political commentary, especially around the time when a new party candidate for the presidency had to be picked, was the conflict between politicians and technocrats, or *políticos* and *técnicos*. This contest was always won by the technocrats, and Mexico was presented with the extraordinary spectacle of a series of presidents, beginning in 1970 with Luis Echeverría, and ending in 2000 with Ernesto Zedillo, who had never held elective office before being nominated for the presidency. In their careers, service in the higher

reaches of the policy-making bureaucracy was relieved by occasional spells of teaching at the national university.

Until the inflations of the late 1980s and early 1990s shrank the value of the peso, service of this kind was generously compensated in salary and additional stipends of various kinds. A tradition of laxity in the handling of public funds and an absence of effective policing of conflicts of interest contributed to illegal and semi-illegal self-enrichment, especially in the lower reaches of the bureaucracy, but often touching the highest levels as well. During the easy-money years of the petroleum boom of the late 1970s and early 1980s, the defalcations of President José López Portillo were notorious. The anticorruption campaigns mounted with great fanfare by each new president typically petered out after a couple of spectacular symbolic arrests that often happened coincidentally to be of the president's political opponents.

The political system had several means of maintaining itself. Toward potential leadership elements in its own natural constituency, such as university students, the regime followed a strategy of co-optation. Toward the population as a whole, the regime attempted to maintain its legitimacy by means of public relations, propaganda, and indoctrination. Toward the country's economic sectors and interest groups, the regime followed a strategy of reconciliation, attempting to spread around specific benefits to the extent that resources were available. To irreconcilable hard-core critics, exemplary punitive strategies were used as a last resort. We will now consider these strategies in more detail.

The leadership elements in the party's natural constituency were the politicians and the technocrats we spoke of earlier. The technocratic leadership came directly from the public universities, especially the national university in the capital city. The politicians emerged from local and state party organizations and from functional organizations affiliated with the PRI: labor unions, the peasants' syndicates (federated into the *Confederación Nacional Campesina*), neighborhood associations, and leagues of professionals. Co-optation occurred primarily through the

CORRUPTION AND ABUSE OF POWER IN MEXICO

The international human rights organization Amnesty International has verified many reported cases of abuse of power by the various police forces in Mexico, including beatings, torture, and even murder. Such reports, which previous governments often denied or swept under the rug, have been taken more seriously by recent governments, which have ostensibly made the establishment of the rule of law a goal for the modernized Mexico of the future. Because the mistreatment of prisoners occurs frequently in the attempt to extract confessions, the government introduced a law, passed by the Congress in August 1990, under which confessions are only valid if they are made in the presence of the suspect's lawyer or a judge. It is not clear that the new law has had any effect in ending police brutality, however.

Campaigns have been mounted by the elected PRD mayors of Mexico City to try to reduce corruption, but the task is enormous. The first city prosecutor from the PRD estimated in 1998 that 40 percent of the city's annual revenue was routinely being stolen—among other methods by private appropriation of city property, including buildings and vehicles, and even by electronic diversion of city funds to private accounts by unauthorized use of passwords. "We are just looking at the tip of the iceberg," he said. One anti-corruption organization, *Transparencia México*, estimated that Mexicans paid $2.5 billion annually in bribes, an average of $100 per family.

concession of benefits that were personal in nature, that is, a job for the leader rather than a change in the legislation that would benefit the group he represented. Jobs were available for the politicians in the party itself and in elective government positions.

When the presidency changed hands every six years there was tremendous turnover as individuals were promoted, retired, or lost favor. University graduates generally went straight into federal bureaucratic jobs in some specialty; some professional graduates set themselves up in private practice, with a sideline as consultant to a ministry or public corporation, or with a part-time teaching position at the university or one of its preparatory schools. A striking demonstration of this kind of co-optation was the appointment of young university graduates to government positions by incoming President Luis Echeverría while they were still in jail cells for having taken part in the 1968 Tlatelolco demonstration.

The politician and technocrat career tracks converged in the cabinet and subcabinet, in positions in public corporations and nationalized industries, and sometimes in state governor-

ships, when the holder of a subcabinet or minor cabinet position might be assigned the governorship nomination by the central party authorities. The co-optation of group representatives and regional political leaders included an averted gaze with respect to money-making activities which might not be altogether legal. This was especially true for labor leaders, who were bought off or pressed not to push their constituents' demands too strongly in order not to accelerate inflation or raise the costs of nationalized industries or the expenses of well-connected industrialists. It was also true of local and regional political bosses, many of whom built up powerful political machines that could be challenged only with a great deal of difficulty.

Of course, the regime claimed legitimacy as a constitutional democracy that functioned in accordance with the norms generally accepted throughout the Western world: elections were held, laws were passed by the legally constituted legislature, an opposition press functioned, and so on. But the regime's claim to legitimacy on these grounds was regarded with increasing skepticism. Although opposition parties won a share of the seats in the

Chamber of Deputies and of municipal offices it was generally believed that the regime lost only those elections it wanted to lose or was forced to concede by popular pressure.

That pressure grew over time, along with the growth of the middle class and the number of university students; with the split in the PRI after Cuauhtémoc Cárdenas was denied the party's presidential nomination; with the Zapatista revolt and the sympathy it aroused in the cities; and especially with the series of economic and financial crises that swept the country during the 1980s and 1990s. The final collapse of the PRI regime was a long time coming, however, because the regime could also claim legitimacy as the heir to the great Mexican Revolution and the sacred values it embodied: nationalism, universal free public education, the restoration of the land to those who work it, and protection of the rights of the poor and humble—what is thought of in Mexico as a vindication of Indian Mexico, the true Mexican nation, against foreign interests and the selfish and opportunistic Mexicans who joined with them in exploiting the country.

After all, the presidential succession had been continuous since Obregón himself. The PRI and its predecessors had distributed the land, built the schools, and nationalized the oil industry. The regime identified itself with the forces regarded generally in Mexico as the truly patriotic ones in the country's history. Of course, the government controlled the content of education, specifying which approved history texts were to be used, so it was no wonder that school children in Mexico were taught to identify patriotism and the country's major achievements with the "party of the Revolution." It was no accident that the party's colors were the same as those of the national flag. Moreover, the dominant television network, TELEVISA, although privately owned and conservative in political orientation, always presented government and PRI in a favorable light—as well it might, in view of its very advantageous tax situation.

But Mexicans became increasingly skeptical of the party's claim to incarnate the values of the Revolution. As a long-entrenched regime, the PRI government spawned a distinctive class, or caste, with unrevolutionary privileges. Whether

for reasons of sound economic policy, or because of pressure from "the north," or because so many PRI leaders became wealthy investors, its policies became increasingly favorable to business interests, including foreign interests, and acceptable to international bankers. Because of evasion of the law and corruption, the land reform was weakened, compromised, and finally watered down to nothing. Well-connected individuals, many of them former government and party officials, held large estates in violation of the land reform laws.

The PRI regime also resorted to intimidation and repression. Agrarian dissidents and suspected urban subversives were sometimes assassinated by army and police units. Several journalists met with foul play. While such acts were committed by low-level government personnel or PRI partisans, presidents cannot always be presumed innocent of direct or indirect complicity.

Normally, however, it was unnecessary to resort to such extreme measures. The discretion that is necessarily involved in the implementation of the laws was usually adequate to co-opt individuals and organizations or to penalize those who proved uncooperative. Uncooperative businesses might experience labor difficulties. But ironically repression fell most heavily on potentially radical elements of lower-status groups that were ostensibly the regime's own constituency—labor, peasants, and students—and it was against them that the most spectacular instances of repression were directed. The removal of the PRI from the presidency has not meant the disappearance of the apparatus of repression, which continues to operate, for example, in trying to prevent those responsible for atrocities from being brought to justice, taking revenge on those thought responsible for the system's downfall, and pursuing vendettas against dissidents. In October 2001, a well-known human rights lawyer, Digna Ochoa, was assassinated; she had been threatened previously and had left messages saying that if she were killed, military officers would be responsible.

The military was one of the basic supports of the regime. The major arena for political struggle during the early years after the Revolution, the army was gradually depoliticized during the 1920s and 1930s. Nevertheless, its primary mission, which is the maintenance of internal order rather than border defense, had political implications, and presidents were always careful to give the military special treatment in pay increases and fringe benefits. Like civilian administrators, military officers were able to increase their incomes in ways not troubled by provisions against conflict of interest. Sometimes, retired military officers were in demand as candidates for lesser elective offices. Yet it is worthy of note that, despite relatively favorable budgetary treatment, the lack of a serious international defense assignment long made it possible to limit the size of the armed forces and to limit military expenditures to levels that, on a per capita basis, were much lower than those common in Europe and elsewhere in Latin America. However, the onset of the Zapatista insurgency in 1994 gave the military arguments for a substantial budgetary increase which the weak Zedillo administration could not withstand, and military expenditures on new "counterinsurgency" functions started to rise. Zapatista insurgents were among those defended by assassinated lawyer Digna Ochoa.

INTEREST GROUPS

In classic Latin American fashion, economic interest groups are organized in an almost corporatist manner. Two organizations, the Confederation of Chambers of Industry, known as CONCAMIN, and the Confederation of Chambers of Commerce, or CONCANACO, group together local chambers of commerce or industry. Membership in one or the other organization is compulsory for manufacturing or commercial businesses, respectively, which have assets in excess of a rather low threshold. There are several other significant business associations, in which membership is voluntary: the Entrepreneurs' Coordinating Council, or CCE; the National Chamber of Manufacturing Industry, or CANACINTRA; and the Mexican Employers' Confederation, or COPARMEX. The CCE tries to speak for the private sector as a whole, which makes its voice very strong when the private sec-

tor is united on an issue. Many questions, however, create splits in the business community, which weakens the position of the CCE and throws into relief the views of the more homogeneous organizations, especially CANACINTRA and COPARMEX. CANACINTRA primarily represents manufacturers producing consumer goods, and thus has an interest in the expansion of the domestic market. It is willing to accept a higher general level of wages and salaries, as this increases its customers' purchasing power. COPARMEX has in recent years taken an active political role in favor of free enterprise and against government control of the economy, which put it in tune with the revival of neoclassical economic thinking in the United States and Western Europe.[6] In 1988 the conservative party, the PAN, nominated a former president of COPARMEX, Manuel Clouthier, as its presidential candidate.

During the era of PRI rule, most of Mexico's labor unions were affiliated with the ruling party through membership in confederations that belong to the party's labor sector, although the government workers' and the teachers' unions were affiliated with the popular sector. Some unions, especially those with leftist political views, were always independent of the party. But as part of the general decline of the PRI that set in as the twentieth century drew to a close, independent-minded leaders arose within several unions affiliated with the PRI, loosening their ties with the party or forming new independent unions. The future evolution of the Mexican labor movement will probably be in the direction of independence from party affiliation.

Labor organization is highly regulated, as is the case with most Latin American countries. In order to enjoy the protections of the country's labor code, unions must be registered with the Ministry of Labor, which can control them in

---

[6] A good discussion of the organization can be found in Luis Felipe Bravo Mena, "COPARMEX and Mexican Politics," in Sylvia Maxfield and Ricardo Anzaldúa Montoya, *Government and Private Sector in Contemporary Mexico* (San Diego: Center for U.S.-Mexican Studies, University of California, 1987).

various ways. For example, the law stipulates that a strike may only be called after certain procedures have been followed, such as a membership vote; only if the strike is declared legal are strikers eligible for benefits during the period of the strike. Moreover, if stipulated conciliation procedures have not reached a mutually satisfactory result, the government may settle the dispute by decree. The government, through the Ministry of Labor, thus has great discretion in handling labor cases. To be sure, at a time of economic distress any interruption in production through a strike is to be avoided, so labor retains influence. However, labor leaders have often used that influence for their own personal advantage rather than that of the membership, so the rank and file have not benefited as much as labor's potential bargaining power should have made possible. Nevertheless, for most of the twentieth century, labor in Mexico probably did better economically by working within the ruling party than labor in the rest of Latin America did by fighting against governments.

POLITICAL PARTIES

Even while the PRI was the dominant party in the political system, the minor parties performed important functions. A former minister of governance, Jesús Reyes Héroles, once said, "Opposition is a form of support." He meant that by competing in elections, the opposition parties signified their acceptance of the system as legitimate. For a long time, the dominant party had the best of both worlds. Unlike the single party in a dictatorship, it did not have to operate in a police regime that stamped out any sign of opposition, ruling by force over a sullen and resentful population. On the other hand, it did not run the risk, as it would in a completely competitive system, of losing office—with the attendant loss of jobs, contracts, and the whole structure of policy that embodied its values and aspirations. Thus, paradoxically, it used to encourage and subsidize opposition parties.

The major party on the right of the political spectrum is PAN, the National Action Party. Founded in 1939 as a party opposing the funda-

mental principles of the Revolution, that is, proclerical and pro-business, its tactical line fluctuated, but from the 1960s on it played the role of loyal opposition. It competed in elections, abided by the rules of the game, and stated that it "accepted" the Revolution. In religious policy, it wanted anticlerical laws changed to remove provisions that the Church could not hold property or operate schools—provisions that have in any case been ignored in practice. It wanted the communal landholding units, or *ejidos* (discussed in Section C), broken up and converted into private landholdings—a change that was actually legislated under Carlos Salinas. In fact, the drastic shift in government economic policy to the right under Salinas aligned the PRI's policies with those advocated by the PAN, so that on economic issues the two parties often voted together in the Congress.

As an opposition party that had success primarily at the municipal level, PAN criticized electoral fraud and supported greater autonomy for local government. The party's vote increased fairly steadily, reaching a little over 17 percent in the 1988 presidential election, then rising to 26 percent in 1994 when its presidential candidate, Diego Fernández de Ceballos, made a strong favorable impression, and peaked in 2000 with the election of its candidate Vicente Fox of Guanajato. Its support at first came from religiously inclined members of the middle class then added "*neopanista*" entrepreneurs especially after López Portillo's nationalization of the banks in 1988, then finally broadened out in the 2000 election to draw voters from all levels as it became regarded as the principal alternative to the discredited PRI. It is strongest in the Federal District and in the northern border states, where it has held some governorships.

The principal party on the left is now the PRD, the *Partido Revolucionario Democrático,* or Democratic Revolutionary Party, formed by Cuauhtémoc Cárdenas after the 1988 elections, using as his base the old Mexican Communist Party. (The PCM had taken a line independent of Moscow as far back as 1968, when it condemned the sending of Soviet troops into Czechoslovakia.) The PRD is strongest in Michoacán, the home state of Cárdenas, in the southern states that are more heavily Indian, such as Oaxaca and Chiapas, and in the Federal District. Although initial enthusiasm for the presidential candidacy of Cárdenas gave the PRI a scare in 1988, his wooden performance as a campaigner in 1994 and 2000, and his inability to formulate a clear position on international trade and other economic policy questions left the PRD clearly in third place. In general, the party favors the traditional revolutionary positions now abandoned by the PRI leadership—agrarian reform, state ownership of industry, and subsidies for mass consumption—but has been unclear or inconsistent on some specific issues. The party has also split over leadership questions, with PRD cofounder Porfirio Múñoz Ledo unsuccessfully seeking to take the party's presidential nomination from Cárdenas. However, prospects seem brighter under the party's new leader, the third successive PRD occupant of the mayoralty of Mexico City, Manuel López Obrador.

The PRI has been strongest among the less sophisticated elements of the population, the rural and urban masses that accept the image the party has tried to project of itself as altruistic, the source of progress and material benefits, the embodiment of revolutionary ideals, and the bearer of legitimacy, democracy, and patriotism. As Mexico developed a more literate, better educated urban society, however, the constituency for opposition parties grew. The PAN draws votes from the middle class in the private and business sectors, and the PRD draws from the intellectual and professional members of the middle class, while both parties draw some support from lower-class elements as well.

In the face of these changes, the PRI modified its tactics. Until 1988 and the breakaway of Cárdenas, its line of policy was to treat the PAN as the principal opposition, identifying it with the forces that were defeated in the Revolution and implying that it had U.S. support. This reinforced the PRI's revolutionary and nationalist credentials and induced some people to vote for the PRI as the strongest bastion against counterrevolution and imperialism. However, after the rise of the PRD and the decline of PRI strength in the Chamber of Deputies to below two-thirds of the membership, it became necessary for the PRI to form an implicit alliance with the PAN in order to pass any of President Salinas's pro-capitalist economic reforms that required amendment of the constitution.

Thus although—or rather because—the PRD espoused the revolutionary rhetoric that had long been the stock in trade of the PRI, it was the PRD rather than the PAN that drew the ruling party's especial animus. The PAN mostly attracted votes from those who were, for religious or historical reasons, not predisposed to vote for the PRI anyway, but the PRD seemed at its origin to have the potential of replacing the PRI altogether by taking away its core constituency. Accordingly, the PRI drew on its traditional repertoire of political tactics, providing monetary and other incentives to co-opt sectoral leaders who might be drawn to the PRD, and encouraging minor left-wing parties that might cut into its vote. In Chiapas especially, hard-line elements within the local PRI representing landowner interests have assassinated PRD activists.

At the local level, the PRI shifts its position toward left or right depending on the nature of the challenge in a specific locality. Thus in the northern states, where business interests are strong, the PRI has nominated local business leaders as its candidates for mayoralties. As a result, in the north, there has developed an effective two-party system, with PRI and PAN competing. In the more Indian southern states, the competition is between PRI and PRD. In the Federal District, all three parties are close contenders, but with the PRD usually the strongest and PRI the weakest. The minor left and center parties are today without electoral significance, except for the PVEM, a "Green" ecology-minded party that has managed to elect a Senator from the Federal District.

VOTING AND ELECTIONS

As opposition support among voters grew, the regime modified the electoral law several times to increase opposition representation in the federal legislature so as to give the opposition parties the illusion that they were gaining actual political power and give them an incentive to play the electoral game instead of rejecting the existing political system. For a long time, this tactic seemed to contain no danger for the PRI regime. But when the pillars of the temple began to crack, with the economic disasters and earthquake of the 1980s, and the assassination and corruption scandals of the 1990s—and more economic disasters—the cumulating minor victories of the opposition parties gave them the credibility to mount an effective challenge and to insist that the elections be fair and the vote count unsullied. IFE—the Federal Elections Institute—did a splendid job of running fair elections in 2000 (see Table 11.3 for the presidential election results).

The formal institutions of Mexican government are clearly based on those of the United States, but they have been modified in several respects. This is a system of separation of powers; the president is popularly elected separately from the two houses of the legislature, the Senate and the Chamber of Deputies. The Senate now has three members elected by each state and by the Federal District (in the U.S. Senate the District of Columbia is not represented).

Voting in Mexico is legally compulsory. This means that for various dealings with government agencies a voting credential, stamped to indicate that one has complied with his civic duty, is among the various papers and forms required legally, though the requirement is enforced only sporadically. Partly because it is compulsory, but also because there is a strong feeling that voting is an important civic duty, electoral turnout is high, generally over 80 percent in presidential elections.

In a speech early in his campaign, Carlos Salinas acknowledged implicitly the existence of

manipulation in previous elections, saying that the credibility of electoral democracy had suffered significant blows: "I want to win and I want also for people to believe in our victory, even if we suffer some defeats." In keeping with those sentiments, in the 1988 elections the PRI accepted the unprecedented loss of four senatorial seats, and in 1991 the president went further and forced the resignation of the governors-elect of Guanajuato and San Luis Potosí after the PAN mounted popular protests against obviously rigged elections.

The lesson learned by this, however, was not that elections could be fair, but that the outcome could be changed by massive and disruptive enough street violence. The PAN continued such protests and was successful on occasion, irrespective of the actual merits of its charge that the election was stolen. However, hard-liners within the PRI learned the same lesson. When President Zedillo, who was less hostile to the PRD than Salinas, was about to recognize the victory of the PRD in the governorship election in Tabasco, street demonstrations and building occupations by the local PRI forced him to back down. President Fox has indicated that he will stay out of any such electoral disputes in the future and leave them to state authorities to settle.

Years before opposition parties posed any kind of threat to the hegemony of the PRI, more progressive elements in the ruling party, believing that the maintenance of the system was better served by flexibility than by rigidity, convinced President Adolfo López Mateos to introduce legislation adding a proportional representation feature to the electoral law for the Chamber of Deputies, which gave opposition parties seats in the Chamber reflecting their percentage of the national vote. Today, electors vote twice in Chamber elections, once on each half of a divided ballot. On one side they vote for candidates in their individual districts, and on the other side they vote for a party to share seats in the proportional distribution.

When they were established, it seemed unlikely that the proportional provisions for opposition representation could ever get out of hand and threaten PRI control. The system was based on the premise of a single dominant party

TABLE 11.3

PRESIDENTIAL ELECTION RESULTS, 2000

Party	Candidate	Percentage
PAN	Vicente Fox	42.52
PRI	Francisco Labastida	36.10
PRD	Cuauhtémoc Cárdenas	16.64
	Other candidates and blank and null votes	4.74

Source: CIA, *The World Factbook,* 2001.

that won a majority of the seats, with a minority of the seats earmarked as a concession to smaller parties, which remained in permanent opposition. What the changes in the electoral law signified at first was the PRI's intention to exercise its hegemony in subtler ways, requiring a more delicate touch. The democratic façade was to be given greater plausibility; the opposition was to be encouraged through its small victories, thus guiding dissidence into safe channels. However, changes have a way of outrunning the intentions of those who introduced them, and that is what happened in Mexico.

Federal elections in Mexico are on three- and six-year cycles. Deputies are elected every three years. Senators, like the president, have six-year terms that coincide with his.

CONSTITUTIONAL STRUCTURE AND NORMS

The Constitution of 1917 addresses itself to three substantive areas. It establishes the structure of national government, including the federal system and separation of powers; it provides for the defense of individual rights; and it establishes various principles and goals for public policy. Individual rights are guaranteed by the first 29 articles, which specify the rights and immunities of citizens with respect to government power of the states and localities as well as of the federal government.

The president is prohibited reelection. Members of Congress may be elected only after skipping terms—that is, consecutive reelection to the same office is not possible. Some members of the legislature have actually alternated for several periods between the Senate and the Chamber of Deputies. The "no reelection" rules were established in their present form through congressional amendment in the aftermath of the assassination of Obregón; the constitution had previously been amended to allow Obregón to run for reelection.

So long as the president was dominant in a single-party system, it did not matter that the turnover in legislative seats was so complete. With the ending of one-party hegemony, however, the Congress has become an active decision-

making body and not just a rubber stamp, and so it makes sense for there to be career legislators who become experts in parliamentary politics as well as in policy subject matter. It seemed likely that one of the changes introduced under the Fox administration would be to end the "no reelection" rule, at least as it applied to Congress, but this was not done.

President Fox might like the change to extend to the presidency too, but the prohibition of presidential reelection is one of the most significant features of the system. It avoids personal dictatorship and forces a policy review and change of direction every six years. It secures the loyalty of those whose immediate careers do not seem promising but who know they will shortly get another chance. The Revolution of 1910 broke out, after all, over the issue of the perennial reelection of Porfirio Díaz. The Bolivian Revolution, similar in many ways to the Mexican, finally came to grief when President Víctor Paz Estenssoro had the constitution amended to permit consecutive reelection. The "no reelection" rule allows for continuing renewal, adjustment, and hope. Of course, it is more necessary in a system of single-party hegemony, since in competitive systems an incumbent may run for reelection but be defeated. Nevertheless, the advantages of incumbency are so great that the "no reelection" rule is healthy for the presidency in any system. After all, in Mexico the presidential term is six years, so a president shouldn't need a second term to implement his program.

Amendments to the constitution must be approved by a two-thirds vote of the Congress meeting in joint session and must then be approved by a majority of the state legislatures. When the Congress is not in session, a commission, composed of 29 members drawn from both houses, may act on behalf of Congress on matters too urgent to be left over for the next session.

Partly because of constitutional disposition and partly because of legislation, the president has considerable legislative power of his own. Constitutionally, as head of the executive branch, he has authority to issue decrees regulating the manner in which legislation passed by Congress is to be enforced. In addition, Congress has voted him the power to issue decrees in other matters—

for example, the authority to transfer funds among different budgetary categories and to incur expenses beyond the amounts appropriated by the original budget.

Under the PRI regime, the judiciary in Mexico normally did not play a significant political role. Most of the time, the judiciary stays away from political questions in any case. Judges are appointed by the president, and if the executive branch is interested in the outcome of a particular case, judges might therefore be responsive to its wishes. However, there were cases on record even under the PRI regime in which a court rendered decisions against the executive branch. This occurred by means of the granting of a writ of *amparo,* a judicial order forbidding acts of administrative officers that violate a specific guaranteed right of an individual, or ordering an official to take an affirmative action called for by the exercise of such a right. *Amparo* has no exact equivalent in Anglo-Saxon common law; it combines features of the injunction with those of specific writs such as *habeas corpus* or *mandamus.* One accustomed to the subtleties of politics in Mexico, however, may be inclined to suspect that on some occasions when a court ruled against the executive branch, its decision might have been requested by the executive, attempting to get itself out of a situation that had become politically untenable, or wishing to take a position for the record that contravened the results it really hoped to achieve. With the growth of party competition in the Congress, the courts developed more independence of the executive and now seem to be progressing toward the fully autonomous role appropriate in a constitutional democracy.

Below the Supreme Court are six circuit courts and 46 district courts in the federal system. The Federal District and the states have their own judiciaries.

STATE AND LOCAL GOVERNMENT

The 31 state governments have their own distinctive constitutions; however, they all have elected governors and single-chamber legislatures, the number of members of which varies from state to state. Each state is on its own elec-toral cycle, and only one governor happens to be elected at the same time as the president. Until 1989, all governors were from the PRI, and before the presidency of Ernesto Zedillo all were nominees of the president. Yet even under the PRI regime, presidents inherited governors nominated by their predecessors, and it was only in their last two years of office, when they were already about to become lame ducks, that presidents had a complete set of governors of their own choice. The governor of the Federal District, effectively the mayor of greater Mexico City, used to be an appointee of the president and a member of his cabinet, but a 1996 all-party agreement provided that the position would be elective in the future. All three occupants of the position since it was made elective have been from the PRD.

Under the PRI regime, commentators used to refer to the Mexican federal system as fraudulent, but this was never altogether the case. Because the federal government was engaged in a continuous balancing act, trying to proceed with its objectives while conciliating a variety of entrenched interests with a minimum of open dissension, a well-managed local political machine could normally run a state pretty much as it liked. On the average of once or twice in a presidential term, however, the behavior of a specific state governor reached such publicly scandalous proportions—because of either monumental embezzlement of public funds, use of state power to promote private business interests, or the assassination of dissidents—that he was removed by the federal government. Impeachment by the state legislature is legally possible, but is a long, drawn-out operation that is likely to be unedifying. Normally such governors simply resigned under pressure from the president. When one governor's position became disputed during the first year of his term, however, Vicente Fox resisted those who wanted him to intervene to impose his own choice as governor, and he indicated that the state would have to resolve its own problems. At the beginning of 2001, only 19 of the 31 state governorships were held by the PRI.

The basic unit of local government is the *municipio,* which resembles a North American township or consolidated city-county government. That is, it consists of a town plus the surrounding rural area. The *municipio* elects a mayor and council, who are not eligible for immediate reelection.

Opposition parties were successful first at the municipal level. Politics at the local level is fairly fluid; an upcoming election will see new alignments and factional shifts, with leading figures crossing party lines, and parties trying to recruit prominent local editors or business leaders as candidates.

The funding of local government is very flexible. Municipalities receive subsidies from state governments but can also raise their own funds by charging fees for municipal services and licenses; for some purposes, federal funds are available. Some economic development expenditures are financed by partnerships between the municipality and the private sector.

Authorities at all three levels of Mexican government have concurrent jurisdiction in several subject areas. Coordination of their activities is effected by a federal delegate; there is normally one such delegate per federal ministry per state capital. State governments are financed partly by federal subsidies and partly by their own taxing powers. Typical state taxes are those on property, sales, inheritance, and income.

The position of state governor (there are no lieutenant governors, just as there is no federal vice president) is an important one, not only administratively but also politically. Conflicts frequently occur between local interests supporting a popular local candidate and a national party wanting to place its own candidate in the position. While the PRI was in power, the national party was normally successful in imposing its choice in such situations. Its candidate was usually a nationally well-connected figure for whom the state governorship was an important stepping stone, perhaps between a subcabinet and a cabinet position. Such imposed candidates were often people who were born in the state but had made their careers entirely in the Federal District. Some aspirants for governor planned to carve out local empires for themselves and become rich and powerful on the local scene, but for most career politicians the major league was the president's cabinet, which was the pool from which future presidents were drawn. With the

ending of the old system of PRI rule, it becomes more likely that future aspirants for the presidency will, like Vicente Fox, have made their political reputations as state governors. So far, legislative leaders have not been major figures, but this should change as the rule against reelection to the Congress is changed, making legislative careers possible.

Outside the cabinet departments are many independent agencies and public corporations, which seem to run their own affairs with a minimum of presidential supervision. In some cases, most notoriously in the case of the petroleum monopoly, PEMEX, the agency officials became involved in racketeering and embezzlement on a large scale.

Corruption has always been present in Mexican public administration. In the early years after the revolution, allowing graft was a deliberate policy of President Obregón to co-opt possible military rebels into the political system. "No one can withstand a cannonade of 200,000 pesos," he is reported to have said. Even after the danger of military insurrection receded, though, corruption continued to play a significant role in the political system. "Moralization" campaigns were waged periodically, especially after graft had become particularly notorious, as during the administrations of Miguel Alemán, José López Portillo, and Carlos Salinas. Sometimes a new governor of the Federal District has launched an anticorruption campaign. Some presidents may have intended such campaigns seriously; for others, they were for show only. In either case, they have not gotten very far.

THE PRESIDENT AND THE PRESIDENCY

The characteristics of Mexican presidents, like the characteristics of the leadership group in general, underwent striking modification over the years, most noticeably in family background, geographic origin, training, and career pattern.

The institutionalization of the Revolution brought about the development of a distinctive ruling group. The castelike features of this group became especially apparent over time, and it has been common to find people in political leadership positions who are the sons and grandsons of government officials and politicians in the dominant party. In fact, all three leading contenders for the PRI presidential nomination in 1988—Carlos Salinas, Manuel Bartlett, and Alfredo del Mazo—were the sons of important regime political figures, as was the leading opposition candidate, Cuauhtémoc Cárdenas.

Another symptom of the shrinking of the pool from which the ruling group was drawn was its dominant Mexico City flavor. In the early postrevolutionary years, Mexico was ruled by generals, who were usually from the provinces and usually from the north; the politicians who followed had made their careers in state and local politics. But the technocrats who ruled during the last years of the PRI regime were overwhelmingly products of the capital.

The shift in academic training was also significant. The generals of the early revolutionary years, and their colleagues in government, frequently lacked higher education; the politicians who succeeded them were typically lawyers. In the technocratic era, there was an increase in cabinet members trained in a technical specialty other than law, first in engineering or architecture, then in administration and fiscal management. This shift in skill and training among cabinet members was reflected, with a slight time lag, at the presidential level. From 1920 to 1946, all popularly elected presidents were generals (although two civilians, Adolfo de la Huerta and Emilio Portes Gil, served as provisional presidents). From 1946 to 1976, with the exception of Adolfo Ruiz Cortines, presidents were all lawyers by training; the four presidents from 1976 to 2000 were specialists in public administration and finance.

In terms of career immediately prior to the presidency, between 1920 and 1940 the incoming president had served as secretary of war or defense, except for the three presidents who shared the term Obregón was unable to serve, from 1928 to 1934. With the exception of Adolfo López Mateos, who had been minister of labor, from 1946 to 1976 the position held by each candidate prior to his election had been minister of governance (*Secretario de Gobernación*). (*Gober-*

nación is usually translated as "Interior," a common designation for the equivalent ministry in continental Europe, but which has different functions from the U.S. Department of the Interior.) The Ministry of Governance, among other things, was in charge of organizing elections and managing relations between federation and states, so it was the key ministry for handling political questions—just as the Ministry of War or Defense was the most important during the preceding era, when the possibility of an armed revolt was always present. But José López Portillo, who served from 1976 to 1982, was selected while serving as minister of finance, and the three succeeding presidents had served as minister of programming and budget, which only became a cabinet department during the López Portillo administration.

This shift in skills and career backgrounds clearly indicates the evolution of the character of the PRI regime as the revolution became institutionalized and foreshadowed the atrophy of the regime as its leadership finally lost touch with the people and their aspirations. We take the presidents in chronological sequence: Obregón, Calles, and Cárdenas were revolutionary generals, heroic leaders in war; Avila Camacho was a desk general, a military administrator. Alemán was a politician rather than a career administrator; Ruiz Cortines, López Mateos, and Díaz Ordaz combined bureaucratic careers with periods of elective office. Echeverría was a career administrator born in the Federal District who never held an elective office before the presidency. López Portillo, de la Madrid, and Salinas combined administrative with academic careers, teaching at the national university concurrently or intermittently while holding their administrative jobs. All four of the final PRI presidents had gone abroad for advanced degrees after completing a first degree at UNAM—López Portillo to the London School of Economics, de la Madrid and Salinas to Harvard; Ernesto Zedillo went to the University of Pennsylvania. The skills required evolved from combat to elective politics, to general administration, to fiscal management; presidents became technocrats more in touch with the thinking of the international financial centers than with the feelings of the

Mexican masses. Carlos Salinas was aware of the problem and prepared his successor, Luis Donaldo Colosio, by putting him in charge of the popular social-welfare Solidarity program, after an earlier period as the key official in the PRI. The popular Colosio might have saved the regime if he had been able to serve as president. With his death, the regime continued its atrophy and decline.

Each time a new president comes to office in Mexico, there is an extensive turnover in government jobs. Even under the PRI, the fact that the ruling party did not change did not make much difference in this, nor did the fact that the incoming president was picked by the outgoing one. Indeed, the fact that new presidents were picked by their predecessors seemed to impose a psychological obligation on them to demonstrate that they were independent and not simply puppets. Moreover, they wanted to demonstrate that they would avoid the errors of their predecessors, and so ostentatious change in personnel and policy orientation was mixed in with the inevitable continuity from incumbent to incumbent.

Even though Vicente Fox represented a different party from the PRI, there was nevertheless a great deal of continuity with the previous regime. Economic policy remained similar, the PRI already having switched to favor a market economy, membership in the North American Free Trade Area, and the closing down of agrarian reform. Fox also continued Zedillo's approach of superficially trying to reach an accommodation with the Zapatista rebels but dragging his feet on implementation of the accords reached.

Appreciating that his party did not have a majority in the Congress, Fox endeavored to work with the opposition parties. On some legislative measures, he drew more support from the PRI than from his own PAN, which contained many ultra-conservatives and others who had not been enthusiastic about Fox's gaining the party's presidential nomination in the first place. Fox also tried to reach out to the PRD on issues of separating government from the PRI apparatus that had dominated it. He wisely emphasized breadth in his cabinet appointments, even including some independent leftist figures, such as the new foreign minister, Jorge Castañeda.

The keystone of the political system is the presidency. As in other presidential systems, the president is the dominant figure, prime mover, inspirer, motivator, and tone setter for all government activity. Of course, the president cannot do everything himself, but everything is done in his name and, on the whole, within the guidelines he has laid down and by the personnel he has selected. A key power is the appointment of cabinet members, and the supervision of their work and that of the ministries they head. Nevertheless, some government departments build up their own point of view and *esprit de corps,* and they may go their own way without reference to the president.

The president also has the significant power to issue decrees with the force of law. These decrees are legally supposed to be limited to the matters within the president's own competence, as specified by the constitution, or to provide for the implementation of legislation passed by Congress. However, on occasion the president has exceeded his legal powers, and the situation has been brought into conformance with the law only retroactively. For example, President López Portillo nationalized the banks by decree, a procedure that seemed to have no legal warrant. Legislation was then hastily prepared and passed by Congress subsequently to regularize the situation from a legal point of view.

The centralization of power in the president was at its highest during the middle third of the twentieth century, from about 1935 to 1968. In the 1920s, the president was the dominant *caudillo,* but there were other strong figures, regional bosses, and leaders of major interest groups. Pro-revolutionary forces were represented in several political parties, and competition among parties for legislative seats and governorships was lively and sometimes violent. This competition, although it then became competition for the nomination of the ruling party, continued after Calles founded the National Revolutionary Party in 1929, and some preexisting organizations continued their separate identities within the PNR. Cárdenas reorganized the affiliated groups, consolidating them into four sectors when he transformed the party into the PRM, or Mexican Revolutionary Party, in 1938.

With Avila Camacho's term, toward the end of which the party's name was changed to the Institutional Revolutionary Party, the system was streamlined and conflict reduced to a minimum. The presidential candidate who ran against Avila Camacho in 1940, General Juan Andreu Almazán, was the last to threaten a revolt. The electoral law, which had previously stipulated that the first citizens to arrive at a polling station to vote would be sworn in as electoral officials, and had thus led to battles between supporters of rival candidates over who was to be first in line when the polls opened, was changed. After 1940, genuine competition within the PRI over nominations was restricted mainly to local offices, with party headquarters in Mexico City deciding on the party's candidates for the federal congress and governorships. Then power started to drift from the presidency following Díaz Ordaz's repression of the Tlatelolco demonstration in 1968. Opposition parties and the constituent organizations within the PRI became stronger, and state party organization gained more autonomy in the choice of candidates. The three major parties traditionally picked their presidential nominees at conventions, but in 2000 Zedillo tried to reinvigorate the PRI by holding a primary election (although he clearly indicated his choice for the nomination).

The election takes place on a Sunday in July, and the new president is inaugurated on December 1.

Thinking Critically

1. What is the significance of the federal system in Mexico?
2. How faithful has the PRI been to the original values and aims of the Revolution?
3. Can the major Mexican political parties be described as representing different economic classes and interests?

4. How might the PRI leadership have acted differently in order to stay in power after 2000?
5. What arguments would you make to support or to oppose the "no reelection" rule?

Key Terms

amparo (624)
Chamber of Deputies *(623)*
Constitution of 1917 *(623)*
co-optation *(616, 617)*
Federal District *(620, 621, 624, 625, 626)*
Ministry of Governance (*Gobernación*) *(626)*
Ministry of Programming and Budget *(626)*
municipio (624–625)
the "new class" *(615)*
Partido de Acción Nacional (PAN) *(620)*
Partido Revolucionario Democrático
(PRD) *(620–621)*

Further Readings

Camp, Roderic A. *Politics in Mexico*, 4th ed. (New York: Oxford University Press, 2003).

Cornelius, Wayne. *Mexican Politics in Transition: The Breakdown of a One-Party Regime* (San Diego: UCSD Center for U.S.-Mexican Studies, 1996).

Needler, Martin C. *Mexican Politics: The Containment of Conflict,* 3rd ed. (New York: Praeger, 1995).

Philip, George. *The Presidency in Mexican Politics.* (New York: St. Martin's, 1992).

Rubio, Luis, and Susan K. Purcell, eds. *Mexico under Fox,* (Boulder: Rienner, 2004).

Tulchin, Joseph S., and Andrew D. Selee, eds. *Mexico's Politics and Society in Transition* (Boulder: Rienner, 2003).

C. PUBLIC POLICY

AGRICULTURE AND LAND REFORM

Land reform policy has traditionally been regarded as the litmus test of the revolutionary character of Mexican governments. A government genuinely committed to alleviating the plight of the poorest Mexicans was one most wholeheartedly committed to land reform; conversely, a government that diminished the pace of reform, provided for limits, exceptions, or exemptions from the program, or placed maximum agricultural production ahead of social justice was a government that had betrayed revolutionary principles. Thus the government of Lázaro Cárdenas has been regarded as the most revolutionary for maximizing the rate of land distribution, and—until the presidency of Carlos Salinas—that of Miguel Alemán as the least revolutionary for promoting agribusiness rather than *ejido* communities. The leader of the early phase of the revolution who remains with most honor in Mexican history books is Emiliano Zapata, the agrarian leader from Morelos who never sold out, who never compromised, who never deviated from his goal of restoring land to those who worked it. So it was entirely logical that the Indians who rose in rebellion in the state of Chiapas on January 1, 1994, rejecting the drastic changes in the agrarian laws introduced by Salinas, should have called themselves Zapatistas.

Nevertheless, the drafters of the constitution and of the statutes of the PNR, the earliest incarnation of the present ruling party, seem to have intended a mixed policy for agriculture. Such a policy would promote land reform for the benefit of Indian communities and poor landless subsistence farmers, but bearing in mind the consumption needs of city populations and the country's requirements for foreign exchange, it would at the same time promote efficient production for the market. Thus a modern commercial sector would exist alongside a subsistence sector. In the early days, when land was relatively plentiful, this kind of mixed policy presented no difficulties.

The laws governing land reform have been modified over the years, but the basic premise had until 1991 remained that if a single landowner held land above a specific size, then the surplus could be expropriated by the state. This land was then given to what may have been an actual village but was more likely to be a fictitious community, the members of which had to be adults whose primary economic activity was farming but who did not own land. The community, real or fictitious, which then became the owner of the land was called the *ejido,* and its members were known as *ejidatarios.* The land was then divided up among the *ejidatarios,* who farmed it as though they owned it outright—since the Calles administration, the right to farm a specific plot can be inherited—except that until the Salinas reforms of 1991–1992, the land could not be sold or mortgaged. In the event that it was abandoned or even improperly farmed by the *ejidatario,* the plot reverted to the *ejido,* whose elected management committee might then assign it to someone else.

The rule that the land could not be sold or mortgaged guaranteed that the *ejidatario* could not lose the land, and avoided reconcentration. In a situation of absolute private ownership, the vagaries of agricultural production often mean that over time land steadily passes into the ownership of banks, moneylenders, or simply more efficient farmers, thus creating a situation in which a small landed elite coexists with a great number of landless laborers. The purpose of land reform, then, is (1) economic, because it ensures at least the means of subsistence to those engaged in agriculture; (2) moral and social, in the sense that landless laborers previously wholly dependent on the goodwill of landowners for whom they worked would now be independent and able to make their own decisions; and (3) political, because the peasants who had received land would become supporters of the government, and agitation would not threaten government stability.

Although a point was reached at which almost 50 percent of the nation's land area planted in crops consisted of *ejidos,* the *ejidos* could not absorb all agricultural workers, and today probably over 4 million people work in agriculture without owning land either as members of *ejidos* or privately.

In the early days, there seemed to be no contradiction between the goals of land reform and those of maximum economic production; Mexico was regarded as an underpopulated country with an unlimited supply of available land, adequate for all purposes. Population, however, grew to the point where the supply of land available for distribution under the land reform program was virtually exhausted—especially in the areas of central Mexico that contained the bulk of the population qualified and eager to receive land. New land was brought into production by large irrigation projects, but primarily in the north of the country, where desert land and usable water supplies were available. This land made fertile by irrigation was sold to larger-scale farmers able to invest in mechanization, who produce crops such as winter vegetables for export to the United States and thus provide the country with one of its major sources of foreign exchange.

In fact, wholesale violations of the land reform laws occurred. Large properties were exempted from expropriation by the simple device of subdividing them on paper, so that legally the situation was that of a series of properties owned by different individuals, perhaps members of the same family, each below the maximum amount allowed and thus safe from expropriation, even if in fact all these properties were still owned by a single individual and continued to be farmed as a unit. Where land was expropriated, the law provided for compensation, but in fact compensation was given only in a few cases in which the former owner had good political connections; otherwise, claims for compensation gathered dust in the files. Until recently the law provided that *ejidal* property could not be rented, but that provision was generally violated and was subsequently repealed.

Controversy has been continuous in Mexico over the merits of the *ejido* system. Those farther

to the right in the political spectrum, who support private property on principle, have argued that the *ejidos* should be broken up so that the plots are held as absolute private property by the members, thereby enabling them to raise money by mortgaging properties, giving them incentives to improve the land, and in general bringing the benefits of capitalism to that sector of agriculture. Some left-wing critics, on the other hand, have argued that the *ejidos* should not only be held collectively, but should also be farmed collectively by large-scale mechanized methods, like a Soviet *kolkhoz.* All across the political scale, criticisms have been made of how the *ejido* system works in practice, and *ejido* management committees have often been guilty of abuse of power, extortion, and diversion of funds.

What merits do the various criticisms have? Arguments in favor of a Soviet-style collective farm management system seem ignorant of the actual drawbacks of Soviet collective farms, which are generally regarded as failures. Arguments that individual ownership would be more productive than *ejidos,* on the other hand, often make comparisons that ignore differences of scale, land quality, and amount of capitalization of private as opposed to *ejidal* farms. It does seem to be true, however, that when these factors are held constant, privately owned land units, even very small ones on land of similar poor quality to that of most *ejidos,* do have somewhat higher productivity.

Attempts by pro-agrarian governments to make capital available to *ejidatarios* were not successful. The difficulty is that *ejidatarios* were not able to mortgage their land as security for payment of the loan, and the special banks set up to serve *ejidos* had the authority to write off a loan that was not repaid. The temptation was then very great for officials of such banks to loan the funds to their friends and relatives and take kickbacks when the loan was written off. There thus seems to be no foolproof way of trying to provide capital to the *ejidos,* even though there is no reason to expect that the bulk of such loans would not be repaid if they could be made.

In 1991 and 1992, as part of his program of modernizing the economy, President Salinas sponsored legislation making it possible for *ejidatarios* to sell their plots of land. He had clearly accepted the argument that outright private ownership would be more productive despite the risk of negative political effects arising from any resulting tendency to reconcentration of land. Salinas's speeches on the topic suggested that he believed the agrarian problem no longer had significant weight in Mexican politics, now that the country's urban population had grown, reaching close to 80 percent by the year 2000. Alleviating the plight of the poor now meant dealing with the problems of urban slums, not maintaining unproductive structures in the countryside. The Zapatista rebellion showed that he had made a political miscalculation, and Zedillo indicated that he would ease up on pressures to privatize *ejido* lands, although their voluntary privatization would be possible where the members of the *ejido* agreed.

Traditionally, the government acted to stabilize the level of food prices through price controls and a commodities purchasing program. After minimal processing, foodstuffs and other articles of prime necessity are retailed by the government through a network of stores and mobile outlets operated as CONASUPO, the National Commission on Popular Subsistence.

Although Salinas originally raised the subsidized price of corn and beans, leading to an increased production that eliminated the politically embarrassing necessity of having to import those basic elements of the Mexican diet, the general tendency of his policy was to eliminate subsidies and fixed prices, for reasons of both free-market ideology and fiscal austerity. The problem of maintaining rural incomes would be met not by high fixed prices, but by direct payments to farmers, in a program called PRO-CAMPO, which opposition parties denounced—with good reason, since such payments seemed to be made unsystematically, in key states just prior to elections.

The drastic drop in coffee prices following the removal of price guarantees, both economically and politically a miscalculation by Salinas, was clearly a catalyst in the Zapatista insurgency in Chiapas. During the 1990s food prices rose sharply, however, imposing very severe hardships on the poor.

GENERAL ECONOMIC POLICY

Like most governments in the modern world, the Mexican government attempts to fix the general parameters of economic activity. It tries to maintain the value of the national currency unit by fiscal and monetary means; it aims for sustained economic growth through planning and investment strategies; it attempts through welfare programs to mitigate the effect of inequality in income distribution; and it tries to maintain the autonomy of national decision-making processes by the regulation of foreign investment and international trade. Until the beginning of the 1970s, these objectives were achieved rather well. Except for a burst of inflation under Alemán, the peso remained fairly stable while, in one of the world's best economic performances, the economy grew fairly steadily at a high and sustained rate. Industry expanded on the basis of import substitution and production for the domestic market, protected by a system of tariffs and controls, while adequate amounts of foreign exchange were earned through agricultural exports and tourism. The rate of foreign investment, primarily from the United States, was high.

Although (with the exception of the crisis period during the 1980s) there were no restrictions on foreign exchange or on the repatriation of profits, there were controls on the types of activity in which foreigners could invest. Some industries were reserved for public enterprise, such as power generation, railroads, telephones and telegraphs, and petroleum. Between 1982 and 1990, banking was added to the list of industries from which foreign capital was excluded.

In addition, the general rule applied that individual firms had to have majority Mexican ownership; that is, foreign participation was limited to 49 percent of ownership in most economic areas, and 34 percent in areas thought to be politically sensitive, such as mining. In practice, there was a great deal of administrative discretion in how the rule was applied, and there were ways of evading its intent, if not its letter. As part of Echeverría's more nationalist and socialist program, legislation was passed regulating the payments that could be made to foreign entities for imported technology and the use of brand names, and limiting patent rights. Although this legislation caused grumbling on the part of foreign businesspeople, who regarded it simply as providing a framework for the extortion of bribes, it by no means prevented them from doing business in Mexico; the legislation was subsequently repealed.

One of the areas of investment that particularly flourished was that of the so-called *maquiladoras,* the assembly plants built in a special customs zone along the border with the United States, in which materials could be imported free of duty if the finished product was then reexported. Essentially, this was a method of exporting Mexican labor without its having to cross national borders, and it attracted European and Asian investment as well as American. The decision of the Salinas administration to form a free trade area with the United States promised, in effect, to extend this system to all of Mexico.

Even during the years of rapid growth, however, the number of jobs in the modern sector never kept up with population growth and migration to the cities. Mexico faced the problems of unemployment and disguised unemployment—that is, the proliferation of self-created forms of economic activity such as guarding parked cars, shining shoes, and selling lottery tickets, which produce very small incomes and add nothing to the nation's production.

Even before the boom and bust in petroleum that began in the middle 1970s, it was becoming clear that there were serious limitations to the country's strategy of development based on import substitution. Apart from the irrationalities, inefficiency, and excessive costs that such a policy entails, employment was not expanding fast enough to cope with the number of new job seekers each year, let alone absorb the backlog

A CLOSER LOOK 11.3

THE NORTH AMERICAN FREE TRADE AREA

Traditionally, Mexico's economic development was based on protection and import substitution. After the economic downturn of the 1980s, drastic remedies seemed to be needed. The international climate favored free-market ideas, and Mexico elected a president who believed in the promotion of free trade and close relations with the United States. As a result, a free trade area embracing Mexico, the United States, and Canada was established, though it has not yet been fully implemented—U.S. truckers have used safety arguments to impede the free entry of Mexican trucking to the United States, and of course labor cannot move freely.

With justice, some Mexicans feared a loss of political autonomy in return for what might prove a limited income gain. A concern on the U.S. side was that a free trade agreement would result in the loss of jobs in the United States. But without the new system they might be equally as likely to move anyway to Thailand or Malaysia or China. Meanwhile, American consumers need lower prices, and Mexico needs all the jobs it can get.

Another objection to NAFTA as it was actually set up is more to the point: the agreement should have included effective guarantees that particularly polluting industries would not be able to relocate to Mexico to avoid U.S. environmental legislation, and that Mexican labor would have decent conditions of work and genuine rights to organize and bargain collectively. During the 1992 election campaign, Bill Clinton conditioned his support for NAFTA on the stipulation of such guarantees, but in the end he settled for weak provisions without serious enforcement mechanisms.

The more important effects of NAFTA are primarily psychological: investors are more likely to keep their money in Mexico if they feel more confident that the rules of the game will not be changed, and American workers will be deterred from asking for higher wages because they are afraid their jobs may go south if they do.

of unemployed.[7] Even when the economy was doing well, only one-third of those entering the labor force each year found regular jobs in the formal sector of the economy.

The López Portillo administration tried to expand Mexico's exports by placing more emphasis on agriculture and the processing of Mexico's own raw materials, as well as promoting manufactured exports. This meant removing tariff protection and subsidies to internationalize Mexican manufacturing, a change of orientation which made it possible under de la Madrid for Mexico to join the General Agreement on Tariffs and Trade, the international association of states promoting greater international trade by eliminating tariff barriers. Mexico had previously resisted U.S. pressure to join GATT, which in 1995 became the World Trade Organization.

With the oil boom, however, many of these policy problems were overtaken by events. The very rapid increase of petroleum production and export multiplied many times over the foreign exchange available, and thus led to an overvaluation of the peso. This made Mexican goods too expensive to export and foreign goods very cheap to import, which in turn led to a decline in Mexican manufacturing because everything the country needed could be imported more cheaply. Wealthy Mexicans took advantage of the relative cheapness of the dollar to buy property in the United States and build up dollar bank accounts. The size of the national government bureaucracy, and official corruption, increased greatly. When petroleum prices dropped later in López Portillo's term, the president gambled that the decline was only temporary and continued the same high levels of government spending with borrowed money. More capital left Mexico as it became clear to everyone except the president that a devaluation of the peso would have to come. Subsequent governments had very little freedom in managing the economy once the decision not to repudiate the foreign debt had been made.

[7]See Ruth Berins Collier, *The Contradictory Alliance: State-Labor Relations and Regime Change in Mexico*, International and Area Studies Research Series, #48 (Berkeley: University of California, 1992).

The body blows to the economy represented by the decline in oil prices, the drop in the value of the peso, the need to pay huge amounts of interest on the new foreign debt, and the Mexico City earthquake of 1985 meant that the de la Madrid administration was one long period of austerity and reduced living standards for the poor. The Salinas administration was able to stage a recovery on the basis of the almost complete adoption of the norms of the international capitalist system and the abandonment of most traditional policies of protection, subsidy, and state ownership.

This new model depended for its success on an inflow of capital, foreign and repatriated Mexican, and the renegotiation of debt. To maintain the appearance of success, Salinas built long-term structures on short-term capital while again allowing the peso to become overvalued. This hollow structure collapsed at the beginning of Zedillo's term, when a badly managed devaluation led to a massive flight from the peso and another even more drastic round of austerity and cruelly reduced living standards.

The Fox administration began during good economic times, although in reality the world economic boom of the Clinton administration had passed its peak. Fox's natural inclinations, the constituency he represented, and the economic situation he inherited all conspired to make him place his economic bets on a policy of openness to world markets and wholehearted cooperation with U.S. interests. He looked for cooperation from the new U.S. administration of George W. Bush, who was ideologically similar and conscious of the growing importance of the Hispanic vote in the United States.

FOREIGN DEBT AND INCOME DISTRIBUTION

Mexican governments have believed that in order to maintain the credit necessary for continued international trade, it is not possible to contemplate repudiating the debt. Given orthodox economic assumptions, this has in recent years meant a policy of deflation, reduction in rates of economic activity, cutbacks in government spending, wage freezes, and the channeling of any surplus to foreign debt payment—a policy, in effect, of redistributing the income of poor and middle-class Mexicans to foreign bankers. One of the planks in the 1988 election platform of Cuauhtémoc Cárdenas was repudiation of the foreign debt, but Cárdenas never presented a consistent and credible economic policy, and he attracted fewer votes in 1994 and 2000 than in 1988.

The capitalist system has a tendency to distribute income increasingly in the form of returns on capital—that is, as rent, profits, dividends, and interest—rather than in the form of wages and salaries. In other words, left to itself, the tendency of the capitalist system is to make the rich richer. To counterbalance this tendency, efforts can be made by labor unions in the form of wage demands, or by government through a variety of tax and welfare measures, that redistribute income to the less affluent members of society. Some programs of this character are permanent features of policy in Mexico, such as the system of distributing basic goods through government retail outlets. Some governments, however, have been especially notable for this left-wing character of their policies—that of Cárdenas, of course, and those of López Mateos and Echeverría. Among other measures, the government of López Mateos introduced legislation providing for companies over a certain size to distribute a percentage of their profits to their employees.

Given the parameters of the world economic system, however, it is extremely difficult to pursue left-wing policies successfully. Capital can go on strike just as much as labor. Within a week of the inaugural speech of López Mateos, in which he identified his government as on the left, $250 million in funds was transferred out of the country. Echeverría achieved the same results in more contradictory form. Attempting to reduce Mexico's foreign debt, he made anticapitalist remarks that resulted in capital flight and forced him, paradoxically, to borrow more money abroad.

In fact, the course of economic development in Mexico had left the country with a very unequal distribution of wealth and income even before the economic crisis that began in the early 1980s. The long period of stable economic growth created a small, comfortably well-off, urban middle class and a small superrich elite; urban workers also benefited, but much less. Workers in agriculture and the marginal unemployed and underemployed people in the cities benefited little. The economic crises of the 1980s and 1990s hit particularly hard at those social elements least able to afford it, wiping out years of moderate economic improvement.

THE MEXICAN OIL INDUSTRY

Petroleum is a particularly sensitive subject in Mexico. The expropriation of foreign oil companies by Lázaro Cárdenas was a great symbolic act of national self-assertion, and the national oil company became a special object of patriotic pride. In fact, the symbolism goes back further than that; one of the policies of Porfirio Díaz that earned his government the charge that it was *entreguista*—that it had sold out to foreigners—was allowing foreign companies to own subsurface minerals, contravening the traditional Hispanic doctrine that ownership of land meant only ownership of the surface, while rights to the products of the subsoil remained with the sovereign. It was thus the traditional Hispanic law on this point, abrogated by Díaz, that was restored by the Constitution of 1917. Under Díaz the oil companies operating in Mexico, like other mineral companies, were predominantly British; with the Revolution, favoritism to British companies ended, and American companies maneuvered themselves into a leading position.

The oil business has some characteristics that make it distinctive. The exploration phase requires large expenditures, which may all be lost if no oil is found. The production phase requires minimal expenditures but produces colossal revenues. Government concession to an oil company of a specific territory to operate in is necessary, but in the absence of competitive bidding for blocks of territory the award to one company or another is arbitrary. Once production has started, the revenues that are rolling in are a tempting target for government; the immobility of the production facilities means that the company is in effect a hostage to government demands.

The combination of these factors meant that oilmen in the early years were strong-willed, adventurer types who became hugely wealthy if successful. Their absolute dependence on essentially arbitrary government favor inevitably meant that they would try to reduce their risks through bribery, in one form or another, which meant that some politician would gain wealth for himself or his cause at the cost of the country's foregoing much larger amounts of wealth. It could hardly have been coincidental that the son of Porfirio Díaz served as a member of the board of directors of the major British oil company in Mexico, or that the U.S. Standard Oil Company contributed funds to the Madero revolution, after which the lawyer who represented Standard's interests in Mexico became Madero's attorney general. With one or two exceptions, the oil barons were too arrogant and cynical to know how to deal with a sincere revolutionary like Cárdenas, and their expropriation in 1938 owes much to their mishandling of relations with him. Their previous difficulties with a revolutionary government, that of Calles, had been satisfactorily resolved, no doubt by the usual methods.

After the expropriation, the companies organized an international boycott of the purchase of Mexican oil, so that the state corporation limited its role to supplying the domestic market from established producing wells. The world's growing need for petroleum was met from production in the Middle East, Venezuela, Romania, and the United States. With no competition, and with established sources of production in a guaranteed and growing domestic market, PEMEX became mismanaged, wasteful, and vastly corrupt. During the 1960s, PEMEX had three or four times as many employees, in terms of the size of its operations, as comparable companies elsewhere. Corporation executives took kickbacks from suppliers, sometimes on quite unnecessary purchases; union leaders took kickbacks from the wages of people hired through their influence; both executives and union officials were part owners of favored supplying firms.

Until the early 1970s, domestic oil prices were deliberately kept low to encourage the development of the economy, even lower than retail prices in other countries, based as they then were on a wholesale price of $3 or $4 a barrel. In the early 1970s OPEC, the Organization of Petroleum Exporting Countries, was able to get its act together to limit oil supply and thus force world prices up—with the implicit prior approval of U.S. Secretary of State Henry Kissinger, in a typical example of that myopic "statesmanship" that inexplicably never deflated Kissinger's overblown reputation. Kissinger apparently believed that this would enable the shah of Iran, a U.S. protégé ironically soon to be overthrown, to buy vast numbers of weapons that would make him a bulwark of anti-Communist stability in the Middle East.

The rise in oil prices, which eventually approached $40 a barrel before dropping back to under $10—since then they have fluctuated between $15 and $30—made it worthwhile for Mexico to incur the considerable expense involved in exploration. These efforts were fabulously successful, as they could hardly fail to be: It transpired that as much as 70 percent of the entire territory of Mexico consists of the sedimentary basins in which hydrocarbon deposits are found. Exploration of less than 10 percent of the national territory showed that Mexico had the potential to become a producer on the scale of Saudi Arabia.

OIL POLICY

Because of the sensitive character of petroleum from the point of view of national pride, various policies were adopted to make sure that Mexico's oil remained in Mexican hands. PEMEX developed the technical capabilities to handle most phases of the industry, except for some specialized tasks involved in offshore drilling. On occasion, PEMEX has even given technical assistance to foreign state oil corporations. Prior to the Salinas administration, the law provided that all oil exploration and development on Mexican national territory were the responsibility of PEMEX; offshore drilling had to be conducted by Mexican companies. (In fact, however, the so-called Mexican companies involved in offshore drilling were actually mere legal and financial shells for what were, in their technical aspects, essentially foreign operations. This arrangement provided lucrative possibilities for some Mexicans who served as fronts and provided legal cover—many of them relatives and associates of PEMEX executives.) In keeping with its general economic policy line, the Salinas administration changed the rules to allow some onshore development activity by foreign oil companies. Given his ideological orientation, Vicente Fox is no doubt in favor of opening up the Mexican oil industry further to foreign enterprises. Because of the sensitive political nature of oil, however, and his lack of a clear congressional majority, any changes in oil policy will have to come slowly and gradually.

Logically, Mexican oil that is exported should find its principal market in the United States, which it can reach by pipeline. However, in defense of national autonomy, Mexican policy makers were at first concerned to limit the dependence of the United States on Mexican oil supplies, fearing that such dependence would give the United States a major reason for interfering in Mexican affairs and even, in the event of an interruption of supply, for occupying the oilfields. Accordingly, policies were adopted under López Portillo to limit any country to no more than 50 percent of Mexico's oil exports, which should constitute no more than 20 percent of that country's oil imports. Given fluctuating conditions of supply and demand in the world market, it has not been possible to keep consistently within these guidelines. Mexico has diversified its export markets fairly successfully, however, with purchasers in Japan, Western and Eastern Europe, and the Caribbean region. In fact, to save shipping costs, some of this oil ends up in the United States anyway, swapped for shipments bought elsewhere for U.S. accounts, with Middle East oil going to Europe and Alaskan oil to Japan.

FOREIGN POLICY

In its foreign policy, Mexico finds itself in a difficult and delicate position. Placed by fate next to the strongest country on earth, its economic well-being is heavily dependent on its relations with the United States. Yet because of its unhappy history, and because of the nationalist principles that its government claims to represent, Mexico even more than other countries must assert its independence from its powerful northern neighbor. Approximately two-thirds of Mexico's exports go to the United States, and almost two-thirds of its imports come from the United States. Moreover, apart from oil, Mexico's largest foreign-exchange earner, by far, is tourism and border transactions, which are extremely sensitive to the quality of relations with the United States. Yet the United States is the country, let us remember, that has repeatedly intervened in Mexican affairs; its representative conspired in the overthrow of Francisco Madero; it waged aggressive war against Mexico and annexed half of Mexico's national territory.

Mexican governments thus find themselves under the dual necessity of maintaining good relations with the United States while making clear the distinctiveness of their values and objectives in foreign policy, and maintaining their independence of action. Which tendency appears strongest depends partly on the relative strength of the two governments. When Mexico felt economically strong during the oil boom, López Portillo staked out a policy clearly opposed to that of the United States with respect to Central America. In the waning days of the Reagan administration, de la Madrid also made his opposition to U.S. policies clear. But between those times, when Reagan was at his peak and the Mexican economy at its weakest, Mexican governments kept a low profile in Central American policy.

Nevertheless, given Mexico's economic dependence on the United States, it is surprising how independent of American wishes Mexican foreign policy has sometimes been. Mexico refused to sign the Declaration of Caracas, pushed through the Organization of American States (OAS) by U.S. pressure, which provided the ideological basis for the U.S.-backed exile invasion that helped to overthrow the leftist government of Guatemala in 1954. Mexico refused to go along with the other members of the OAS in breaking relations with Cuba, and declined to support the sending of an "Inter-American peace force" into the Dominican Republic in 1965. Mexico also resisted pressure from the Reagan administration to join in its crusade against the Sandinista government of Nicaragua, which resembled early postrevolutionary Mexican governments in many respects, and joined with other Latin American countries in trying to bring peace to Nicaragua. It made clear its sympathy with rebel forces in El Salvador, where the United States supported the conservative government side in a long-drawn-out civil war that neither side seemed capable of winning. Foreign Minister Jorge Castañeda was heavily criticized in Mexico—including by cabinet colleagues—when he pledged unconditional support to the United States following the World Trade Center bombing of September 11, 2001.

U.S. administrations have usually shown understanding for the Mexican government's need to demonstrate autonomy from the United States and have not gone to the most extreme lengths to secure Mexican adherence to purely symbolic measures, such as votes in OAS meetings. When U.S. governments have felt very strongly about specific questions, however, they have usually been able to secure Mexican compliance. For example, at one point President Nixon secured Mexican cooperation with U.S. drug policies by ordering a tightening of customs inspections at the border which, in effect, brought border traffic to a standstill.

Traditionally, Mexican governments handled the conflicting requirements of national autonomy and pressure from the United States by resorting to the same calculated policies of deliberate ambiguity that they applied to domestic policy areas. Thus the Mexicans refused to break diplomatic relations with Cuba, but their secret services cooperated with the CIA in keeping track of travelers to and from Cuba through Mexico. Conversely, Mexico has respected U.S. wishes that it not join OPEC, but it has followed OPEC policies with respect to pricing without being a member.

A series of problems in Mexican-U.S. relations grow out of the common border. Indeed, for some time the demarcation of the border was itself in doubt after the Rio Grande changed course; a final solution to that problem was reached during the late 1960s. The two countries have various cooperative mechanisms for attempting to solve other border problems, some of which have proved capable of solution, while others are perennial sources of difficulty. Some principal problems in recent years have been the division of the waters of the Colorado River, which both countries share; problems connected with Mexican migration to the United States; air pollution by industries on one side of the border which drifts across into the other country; the negative impact of U.S. food regulations on imports of vegetables from Mexico; the allocation of airline routes between the airlines of the two countries; fishing problems; and drug trafficking. From time to time, the U.S. government and U.S. public opinion fix on one of these issues and blow it up into a crisis. For several of these issues, such as illegal immigration and drug trafficking, no satisfactory permanent solution has appeared possible, although intelligent joint management of policy may reduce the damage the situations create.

It is true that the long border, which is after all, as President López Portillo once said, the border between the first world and the third world, should give rise to a range of problems. It also gives rise to benefits and opportunities for both countries. The volume of tourism and retail sales to nationals of the other country is considerable on both sides; it constitutes a significant item in Mexico's balance of payments, about 25 percent of Mexico's total foreign income in an average year. At the same time, Mexicans contribute about one-fourth of all the income the United States derives from tourism. Mexican immigrants, legal or not, contribute their labor to the U.S. economy and pay taxes greater than the value of public services they receive. At the same time, the money they bring back to Mexico from jobs in the United States is a significant source of capital for the founding of small businesses.

In fact, the whole "illegal immigration" situation has become something of a racket, as agriculture and the restaurant industry in California and other western states could not function without the labor of illegal immigrants. The U.S. Immigration and Naturalization Service knows this and takes no action against employers of undocumented workers. Because such workers are afraid to complain—and think that if they do, employers are ready to turn them in to the INS and have them deported—they work for low wages and without benefits; even if social security contributions are deducted from those wages, the undocumented know they dare never claim social security benefits.

Under President Carter, an amnesty was declared and immigrants were allowed to legalize their status retroactively. Vicente Fox has made the regularization of the status of undocumented workers a priority of his foreign policy. At least partial amnesty and an increased number of temporary work permits—a system like the bracero system in place at earlier periods—seems likely to be adopted.

In recent years, a significant and growing part of the Mexican economy has been the in-bond assembly plants, or *maquiladoras,* located in the border region.

CONCLUSION

Mexico has had one of the most stable political systems in the world. The constitutional succession has been unbroken since 1934; each president has served the full term for which he was elected and yielded his office to an elected successor. There are no more than a handful of other countries in the world about which a similar statement can be made. Yet the country has been in a state of continual change. Mexico's population has increased enormously; it has gone from a predominantly rural to a predominantly urban society; a vast land reform program has been carried out; illiteracy has decreased almost to the vanishing point; the role of the military in politics has shrunk dramatically; the role of opposition parties has grown.

The country has now embarked on a period of transition toward a fuller democracy. This was always to be expected. Political systems reflect social and economic systems, and it is not possible to rule a literate and urban country the way a land of illiterate peasants is ruled.

But transition does not occur smoothly, and reversals and setbacks can be expected. The tasks to be faced can be listed as follows:

1. The country's constitutional structure is fundamentally sound and democratic, and a reliable system of election monitoring is in place, though it needs fine-tuning at the local level. The only major change needed is to permit reelection of members of Congress.

2. The structure of policy is generally viable. However, progress needs to be made with respect to the movement of people across the U.S. border, improvement of the economic welfare of the poorest, and recognition of the cultural rights of indigenous people.

3. The PRI needs to be disentangled from the civil service, the judiciary, the unions, and the newspapers, all of which need to acquire genuine autonomy of action, a process already started.

4. Perhaps the most difficult issues are those of crime and corruption. The various police forces of the Republic probably commit more crimes than they prevent. Drug trafficking wealth and violence have corrupted prosecution systems and some of the judiciary. It is not clear how realistic it is to hope for substantial improvement in this respect; if improvement does take place, it will probably take two or three generations.

Thinking Critically

1. How free is the president of Mexico to implement his preferred policies and how much is he constrained by circumstances?
2. Does "Poor Mexico! So far from God and so close to the United States" ring true today?

3. Would you agree with the way in which NAFTA was conceived and implemented?
4. Does the *ejido* system of landholding have merit?
5. Was Mexico's economic policy effective in the last quarter of the twentieth century?

KEY TERMS

CONASUPO *(631)*
disguised unemployment *(632)*
ejido (629)
maquiladora (632, 638)
North American Free Trade Area (NAFTA) *(632)*
Organization of American States (OAS) *(636)*
Organization of Petroleum Exporting Countries (OPEC) *(635, 637)*
PEMEX *(604, 635)*

FURTHER READINGS

Foweraker, Joe, et al. *Governing Latin America* (Cambridge: Polity, 2003).

Gwynne, Robert N., and Cristobal Kay, eds. *Latin America Transformed: Globalization and Modernity* (New York: Oxford University Press, 2004).

Needler, Martin C. *Politics and Society in Mexico* (Albuquerque: University of New Mexico Press, 1971).

Paz, Octavio. *The Labyrinth of Solitude,* trans. Lysander Kemp (New York: Grove Press, 1961).

Peschard-Suerdoup, Armand B., ed. *Forecasting Mexico's Democratic Transition: Scenarios for Policymakers* (Washington: Center for Strategic and International Studies, 2003).

Rodríguez, Victoria, ed. *Women's Participation in Mexican Political Life* (Boulder CO: Westview Press, 1998).

WEB SITES

www.laopinion.com
The newspaper *La Opinión,* published daily in Los Angeles for Spanish speakers, carries in its "Latinoamérica" section each day's three or four leading stories from Mexico.

www.gobernacion.mex
Web page of Mexico's *Gobernación* department, in charge of internal administration and political matters.

www.df.gob.mex
Mexico City, the Federal District, Web site.

www.sre.gob.mex
The Secretariat of Foreign Relations ("*Relaciones Exteriores*") gives English-language versions of key foreign policy documents.

www.oas.org
Organization of American States site giving news of major events in Mexican politics (and other countries of Latin America) in four languages, including English.

www.state.gov
Web site of the U.S. State Department.

www.coha.org
Council on Hemispheric Affairs site covers economic and political activity and is frequently critical of U.S. policy.

wola.org
Washington Office on Latin America, a nongovernmental organization with some church connections, monitors Latin American events.

www.usmex.ucsd.edu
Center for U.S.-Mexican Studies, University of California at San Diego.

socrates.berkeley.edu:7001
Center for Latin American Studies, University of California at Berkeley.

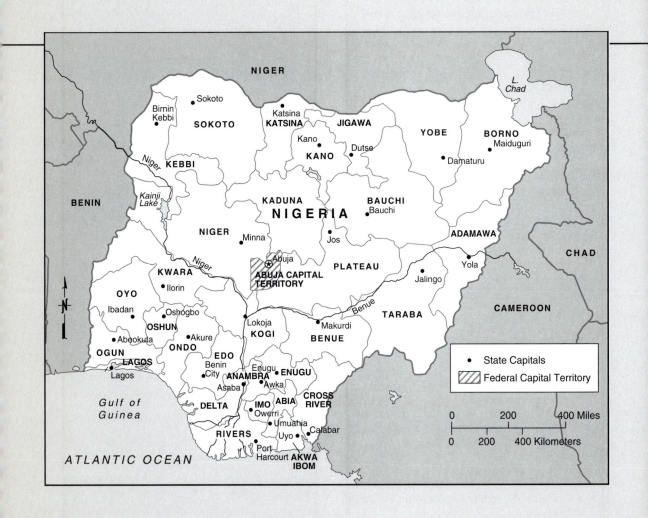

CHAPTER
12

THE GOVERNMENT OF

Nigeria

Stephen Wright

INTRODUCTION

Background: Following nearly 16 years of military rule, a new constitution was adopted in 1999 and a peaceful transition to civilian government completed. The new president faces the daunting task of rebuilding a petroleum-based economy whose revenues have been squandered through corruption and mismanagement, and institutionalizing democracy. In addition, the Obasanjo administration must defuse long-standing ethnic and religious tensions if it is to build a sound foundation for economic growth and political stability. The April 2003 election result marked the first civilian transfer of power.

GEOGRAPHY

Location: Western Africa, bordering the Gulf of Guinea, between Benin and Cameroon

Area: 923,768 sq km

Area—comparative: slightly more than twice the size of California

Land boundaries: 4,047 km

   border countries: Benin 773 km, Cameroon 1,690 km, Chad 87 km, Niger 1,497 km

Climate: varies; equatorial in south, tropical in center, arid in north

Terrain: southern lowlands merge into central hills and plateaus; mountains in southeast, plains in north

Elevation extremes: *lowest point:* Atlantic Ocean 0 m

   highest point: Chappal Waddi 2,419 m

PEOPLE

Population: 137 million

note: estimates for this country explicitly take into account the effects of excess mortality due to AIDS; this can result in lower life expectancy, higher infant mortality and death rates, lower population and growth rates, and changes in the distribution of population by age and sex than would otherwise be expected

Age structure: *0–14 years:* 43.4% (male 29.9 million; female 29.6 million)

15–64 years: 53.7% (male 37 million; female 36.2 million)

65 years and over: 2.9% (male 1.9 million; female 1.9 million)

Population growth rate: 2.45%

Birthrate: 38.24 births/1,000 population

Sex ratio: 1.02 male/female

Life expectancy at birth: 50.49 years

male: 50.35 years

female: 50.63 years

Nationality: *noun:* Nigerian, Nigerians

adjective: Nigerian

Ethnic groups: Nigeria, which is Africa's most populous country, is composed of more than 250 ethnic groups; the following are the most populous and politically influential: Hausa and Fulani 29%, Yoruba 21%, Igbo (Ibo) 18%, Ijaw 10%, Kanuri 4%, Ibibio 3.5%, Tiv 2.5%

Religions: Muslim 50%, Christian 40%, indigenous beliefs 10%

Languages: English (official), Hausa, Yoruba, Igbo (Ibo), Fulani

Literacy: *definition:* age 15 and over can read and write

total population: 68%

male: 75.7%

female: 60.6%

GOVERNMENT

Country name: *conventional long form:* Federal Republic of Nigeria

conventional short form: Nigeria

Government type: republic transitioning from military to civilian rule

Capital: Abuja; on 12 December 1991 the capital was officially transferred from Lagos to Abuja; most federal government offices have now made the move to Abuja

Administrative divisions: 36 states and 1 territory

Independence: 1 October 1960 (from UK)

Constitution: 1999 new constitution adopted

Legal system: based on English common law, Islamic Shariah law in some northern states, and traditional law

Suffrage: 18 years of age; universal

Executive branch: *chief of state and head of government:* President Olusegun Obasanjo (since 29 May 1999)

cabinet: Federal Executive Council

elections: president is elected by popular vote for no more than two four-year terms

Legislative branch: bicameral National Assembly consists of Senate (107 seats, three from each state and one from the Federal Capital Territory; members elected by popular vote to serve four-year terms) and House of Representatives (346 seats, members elected by popular vote to serve four-year terms)

Judicial branch: Supreme Court (judges appointed by the Provisional Ruling Council); Federal Court of Appeal (judges are appointed by the federal government on the advice of the Advisory Judicial Committee)

ECONOMY

Overview: The oil-rich Nigerian economy, long hobbled by political instability, corruption, and poor macroeconomic management, is undergoing substantial economic reform under the new civilian administration. Nigeria's former military rulers failed to diversify the economy away from overdependence on the capital-intensive oil sector, which provides 20% of GDP, 95% of foreign exchange earnings, and about 65% of budgetary revenues. The largely subsistence agricultural sector has failed to keep up with rapid population growth, and Nigeria, once a large net exporter of food, now must import food. Following the signing of an IMF stand-by agreement in August 2000, Nigeria received a debt-restructuring deal from the Paris Club and a $1 billion loan from the IMF, both contingent on economic reforms. It pulled out of its IMF program in 2002 after failing to meet spending and exchange rate targets. In 2003 the government deregulated fuel prices and announced the privatization of the country's four oil refineries.

GDP: purchasing power parity—$114.8 billion

GDP—real growth rate: 7.1%

GDP—per capita: purchasing power parity—$900

GDP—composition by sector: *agriculture:* 30.8%

    industry: 43.8%

    services: 25.4%

Population below poverty line: 60%

Household income or consumption by percentage share: *lowest 10%:* 1.6%

    highest 10%: 40.8%

Labor force: 54 million

Labor force—by occupation: agriculture 70%, industry 10%, services 20%

Unemployment rate: 28%

Currency: naira (NGN)

A. POLITICAL DEVELOPMENT

Nigeria is Africa's most populous country and also one of its most unpredictable. Since its independence from British colonial rule on October 1, 1960, Nigeria has struggled to survive through numerous political crises, including a bitter civil war between 1967 and 1970, and military governments have ruled for 28 years (see Table 12.1). Three heads of state have been assassinated in office, and numerous successful and attempted coups d'état have occurred. With such instability and rapid change, the development of the country's political process and institutions has been seriously affected; hence, the continuity and rhythm of government found in more developed countries is not present.

Nigeria's experience is somewhat typical within an African context. Many countries on the continent continue to face severe challenges to their economic and political development, and some remain ruled by authoritarian regimes despite the burst of democratization in Africa over the last decade. The current civilian government of President Olusegun Obasanjo was elected to office in February 1999 after the country had withstood 16 years of despotic military rule. Despite its best efforts, the Obasanjo government has found it difficult to generate major gains in political and economic stability.

Many resources are allocated by the federal government on the basis of population indicators, and so political manipulation and intrigue have prevented an accurate census from being taken since independence, although the military government concluded a relatively uncontested one in 1993. This census calculated the population to be 88.5 million, down from the previously accepted estimate of 115 million. More recent estimates place the population between 130 and 140 million, and it is expected to double over the next 20 years.

There is a strong undercurrent of diversity and division within contemporary Nigeria, and this provides a significant challenge for peaceful democratization and political development. The country comprises about 250 ethnic and linguis-

TABLE 12.1

NIGERIAN GOVERNMENTS, 1960–2002

Period	Head of State	Ethnicity/Region	Type of Government	How Ended
1960–1966	Tafawa Balewa	Hausa-Fulani	Civilian	Attempted coup/assassination
1966	Aguiyi-Ironsi	Igbo	Military	Coup/assassination
1966–1975	Gowon	Middle Belt	Military	Coup
1975–1976	Muhammed	Hausa-Fulani	Military	Attempted coup/assassination
1976–1979	Obasanjo	Yoruba	Military	Elections
1979–1983	Shagari	Hausa-Fulani	Civilian	Coup
1984–1985	Buhari	Hausa-Fulani	Military	Coup
1985–1993	Babangida	Middle Belt	Military	Palace coup
(1993)	Abiola	Yoruba	Civilian	Election annulled
1993	Shonekan	Yoruba	Interim	Coup
1993–1998	Abacha	Hausa-Fulani	Military	Died in office
1998–1999	Abubakar	Hausa-Fulani	Military	Elections
1999–	Obasanjo	Yoruba	Civilian	

A CLOSER LOOK

12.1

THE CENSUS

The inability to count its population accurately indicates a relative immaturity in the Nigerian polity and provides difficulties in drawing up development plans to address adequately the people's needs. The fact that numbers influence both electoral district and revenue allocations has led to incessant intrigue, making accurate head counts impossible. Since 1863, there have been 12 census attempts, but none has brought results to inspire confidence. Prior to the 1990s, two postindependence censuses had been attempted, with little success. The 1991–1993 census was undertaken in difficult circumstances, namely in the middle of a fierce electoral contest. Organization was a logistical nightmare. In order to minimize corrupt activities, millions of dollars were spent on computers and transport, and the country was divided into 250,000 enumeration areas, with close to 600,000 enumerators employed. Pre-census trials were undertaken in selected areas to smooth out administrative difficulties.

The census results were received in 1993 fairly calmly in contrast to those of the past. That should not necessarily indicate acceptance of the result. The total population was calculated at 88.5 million, considerably below expectation. Census projections had in fact estimated the population at 96.1 million in 1985. For the first time ever, it was acknowledged that the southern population was larger than that of the North, a shift that has significant implications for the country's political economy and is still disputed by many Nigerians. The rural population stood at just under 60 percent of the total. The growth rate of 2.1 percent per year was low by African standards, casting doubt on the figures. Some northern states had incredulously grown by 100 percent since the last census. Few believe that this census provided the true story of Nigeria's population.

In 2005, the population is estimated at 137 million.

---

tic groups, but three large groups have predominated: the Hausa-Fulani in the North, the Yoruba in the West (though geographically this is the southwest of the country), and the Igbo in the East (geographically the southeast). Nigeria's political economy has been influenced by the mutual suspicions, rivalries, and alliances between and within these groups, who account for some 60 to 65 percent of the total population. The smaller groups, including the Nupe and Tiv clustered in the country's "Middle Belt" region, as well as the Edo, Ijaw, Kanuri, and Ogoni, have increasingly striven to exert influence on the political life of this multi-ethnic state.

This complex picture of sociocultural cleavages and diversity is compounded by crucial religious differences within the country. The North is predominantly Muslim (roughly 48 percent of the national population), and the South is predominantly Christian (with 34 percent), although a number of traditional religions have also survived, and the true picture is certainly more complex than this. The historical reasons for this division will be discussed later, but these religious differences, superimposed upon ethnic cleavages, have provided a most difficult issue for the Nigerian state to resolve. In the early 2000s, there were numerous religious clashes between Muslims and Christians, exacerbated by the creation of *sharia* states in the North, in which Islamic law prevails.

It is important to point out that British colonial administrators deliberately sought to divide these various groups and mobilize them against each other. Moreover, the British model of parliamentary government inherited by Nigerians at independence quickly proved to be a poor framework for local political conditions and only served to heighten competition and rivalry. Climatic, linguistic, and cultural differences were also responsible for sowing the seeds of discord that have weakened the country. Nigeria developed not with any real internal logic, but as a conglomerate of ethnic and religious groups.

Such problems greatly influenced the path of political development.

Unlike the British and American political systems, which have evolved gradually, the Nigerian system has made several radical readjustments in attempts to resolve internal tensions and create a suitable style and structure of government. Nigeria has had nine constitutions in less than a century. Four of these came during the colonial period, but five have been since independence (1960, 1963, 1979, 1989, and 1999). Is this a pattern followed by other countries in this volume? Such an abundance of constitutions is an indication of serious political problems within the body politic. To some extent, Nigeria provides a case study to fulfill a political scientist's dream (or nightmare) because several distinct types of political structure have been utilized since independence. The First Republic (1960–1966) operated on a parliamentary system modeled after Britain's, whereas the Second Republic (1979–1983) adopted an American-style presidential system, complete with Senate and House of Representatives. The Third Republic, annulled in 1993 before it became operational, was also to have an American-style system. In 1995, the military government of General Sani Abacha announced that the Fourth Republic scheduled to begin in 1998 would follow a hybrid French/Russian model of mixed presidential and parliamentary structures. However, the Fourth Republic, which began in 1999, followed an almost identical system to that of the Second Republic.

If the Nigerian panorama already appears to be complex, then its political development is further complicated by two fundamental factors. First, although the country is federal in structure, there has been a constant political struggle between federal and state centers. At independence, the three regional governments (North, West, and East) were powerful enough to disrupt the effectiveness of the federal government, contributing to the downfall of the First Republic in 1966. Sociopolitical cleavages and political necessity forced a devolution of regional power to four regions in 1964, then to 12 states in 1967, 19 states in 1976, 21 states in 1987, 30 states in 1991, and 36 states in 1996. Superficially, the creation of states appears to promote the agenda of local democracy, but a political economy perspective highlights the competition between elites to gain access to federal funds, which the creation of a new state facilitates.

Second, the influence of the federal government over the states has been dramatically increased by its centralized control of the country's oil wealth. During the 1970s, Nigerian oil production rapidly increased, making the country then the sixth largest producer in the world and Africa's preeminent member of the Organization of Petroleum Exporting Countries (OPEC). At the end of the decade, Nigeria was the wealthiest country in sub-Saharan Africa, with a strong voice on the world stage, but the subsequent oil glut, economic depression, and failure to diversify in the 1980s and 1990s caused serious political and economic problems for the country. In addition, this oil wealth was seized upon by military and civilian elites, and greed and corruption became predominant features of Nigerian political economy.

HISTORICAL INFLUENCES ON POLITICAL DEVELOPMENT

Nigeria in its contemporary geographical form was created only in the early part of the twentieth century, following the amalgamation of northern and southern colonial provinces for the convenience of British colonial administrators. The name "Nigeria" was, in fact, coined in Britain in 1897 in a letter to *The Times* of London; it was not decided upon by indigenes of the "new" country. In some sense, then, it could be said to be an "artificial" country, at least historically. The earlier historical development in western Africa concerns empires and competing kingdoms or principalities that no longer exist today, but whose former territories now comprise Nigeria as well as neighboring states such as Cameroon, Niger, and Benin. These kingdoms traded and competed with each other for many centuries prior to European colonization; they had reached advanced stages of technical, political, and cultural development—achievements overlooked in the arrogance and plunder of the colonial powers. The Benin empire, to take one case, was a classic example of a society developing from the twelfth century; its internal political system had pattern, legitimacy, and stability, while its bronze statues and sculptures are still widely recognized for their high artistic merit. The Oyo empire, which dates from the thirteenth century, has a similarly strong cultural history.

Cultural differences between these kingdoms were reinforced by geographical factors, as well as early contact with outsiders. In the southern areas, the tropical rain forest influenced the style of farming and living patterns and led to the development of what has been described as a "gun" society, a feature common after 1600 with the expansion of the slave trade in these areas. In the North, in contrast, the drier, open savanna lands led to the development of a "horse" society; the global slave system made less inroads here.

For the last thousand years, Islam has influenced the northern savanna lands as trade by camel across the Sahara desert, to and from the Middle East and North Africa, made these people look inward toward the desert, in contrast to the southern kingdoms which looked outward toward the Atlantic Ocean. Islam has a much longer presence in Nigeria than has Christianity, and its influence in the North was reinforced and expanded in the early nineteenth century by the radical zeal of Usman Dan Fodio, who promoted the concept of jihad and Islamic expansion. Christianity first appeared with the Portuguese influence and missionaries along the coast some 300 or so years ago. Lagos (named after the Portuguese port) became a major port and later capital, and along with Calabar was used heavily in the slave trade, which was the dominant economic activity at that time. The British presence grew steadily through the nineteenth century, with Lagos annexed in 1861. Following the 1884 Berlin conference—which carved up Africa indiscriminately among the European powers—the British consolidated their grip on the disparate regions of what was to be the artificially created nation of Nigeria. At no time were the interests of "Nigerians" themselves considered.

British Colonial Rule

Although Nigerians were exposed to European and Middle Eastern influences for many centuries, the period of direct British colonial control lasted for less than 70 years. Nigerian resistance to British expansion was fierce, and the whole country did not come under British administration until the early 1900s. The British, like other colonizers elsewhere in Africa, had little idea of whom they had conquered or of the social complexity of those societies. For some colonizers there was a sense of mission—the "white man's burden"—to improve the standard of living among Africans, but in reality the colonial period became more concerned with exploitation than development. The impact of colonialism on the economic and political fabric of the country was immense, and the repercussions have had serious implications for contemporary Nigeria.

Although slavery was officially outlawed, the British showed little hesitation in restructuring the Nigerian economy to suit their own requirements. This policy altered the position of Nigeria within the international economy and set Nigerian elites in competition with each other. The three nascent regions became identified with individual cash (export) crops: The North was dominated by groundnut (peanut) production, the West by cocoa, and the East by palm oil. Possessing distinct economic bases, the regions were further separated from each other by the policy referred to as "indirect rule." Although colonial administrators retained the controlling influence, this policy allowed chiefs and emirs to control local affairs within their own areas of jurisdiction. Distinct regional identities began to develop, with each looking inward for support and increasingly competing with the others for favors from the central colonial administration. Cultural differences were also reinforced in education, where southerners became deeply influenced and motivated by Western Christian, missionary, or secular education and values, while northern children (or the minority who received any formal education) were educated in a more traditional and conservative environment of Islam.[1] Prior to independence, this uneven educational pattern left many northerners feeling threatened that they would be unable to compete successfully for jobs with southerners, a valid fear which has still not been fully resolved, although quotas and federal initiatives (similar in some ways to the principle of affirmative action in the United States) have helped to maintain a balance to some extent.

By 1946 three regions had been formally established by the colonial authorities, with commodity boards also at regional levels to purchase produce from within the region. Following World War II, nationalist agitation increased by building on the prewar activity of groups such as Herbert Macauley's Nigerian National Democratic Party and the Nigerian Youth Movement. Such agitation became more successful as Britain's ability and willingness to maintain its colonial possession diminished. Nationalist movements formed nominally at the national level, but their activities were heavily influenced by regional and ethnic factors. Political parties established in the 1940s and 1950s were essentially monoethnic, and elections in the 1950s reinforced regional/ethnic rather than national orientations. Politicians competed for control of the regional commodity boards because these held the key to finances and future political success. As postcolonial theories suggest, colonialism created ethnicity in Nigeria as a basis of political identity and conflict.

A series of constitutional changes during the 1940s and 1950s paved the way for independence. In 1946, the governor of Nigeria, Sir Arthur Richards, consolidated the process of regionalism by establishing three assemblies in the North, West, and East. In 1951, the MacPherson Constitution (named after another governor) allowed these regions to make their own laws and to elect their own representatives and ministers, and the three regions were given equal status in the central legislature. By 1954, problems had emerged that required a further readjustment of the political structure by the Lyttleton

Constitution. Under this, a federal structure was organized dividing power between the federal government and the three regional governments. Direct elections were used to provide equal numbers of representatives for each region in the federal legislature. Regional orientation and identity, however, were strengthened by giving taxation powers to each region, as well as by restricting administrators and bureaucrats to work only in their "region of origin."

This constitutional framework totally ignored the wishes of minority ethnic groups (approximately 40 percent of the population), a problem which was not addressed for more than a decade. The eastern and western regions gained self-government in 1957, but the North delayed this until 1959 in an attempt to buy more time to prepare for the competition and rivalry set to take place after independence was declared on October 1, 1960. At this time the North, which accounted for two-thirds of the territory of Nigeria and 40 to 45 percent of the population, benefited from the alteration of electoral provisions from one that had seats shared equally among the three regions to one that awarded seats on the basis of population. The North managed to emerge at independence as the dominant partner within the federation, as well as have its own representative, Sir Alhaji Abubakar Tafawa Balewa, as prime minister. This desire to maintain Northern preeminence over political life has been an important theme and problem of Nigerian political development down to the present.

THE FIRST REPUBLIC, 1960–1966

Nigeria emerged in October 1960 as a fragile amalgam of distrusting partners. Ethnic divisions accentuated during the colonial period were now magnified as groups vied with each other for patronage from and control over the federal center. Single political parties dominated the regional governments—the Northern People's Congress (NPC) in the North, composed essentially of Hausa-Fulani; the Action Group (AG) in the West, made up of Yoruba supporters; and the National Convention of Nigerian Citizens (NCNC) in the East, composed almost exclusively of Igbo

---

[1]See Robert Heussler, *The British in Northern Nigeria* (London: Oxford University Press, 1968).

people.[2] Minority ethnic groups could not get their voices heard. Within three or four years, the federal government had lost its control over the West, where political chaos became prevalent. Elections were rigged, thuggery and intimidation became widespread, and opposition leaders, notably the Yoruba spokesperson Chief Obafemi Awolowo, were imprisoned. The fragile political machinery of the country failed.

Against this political backdrop, other important developments were taking shape. The armed forces were becoming Africanized—at independence, only 10 percent of the officers were African, but by 1965 only 10 percent remained expatriate. Rapid promotion within the ranks brought many southern, and specifically Igbo, officers to positions of leadership. These officers were predominantly trained in Britain and were supposedly inculcated with the philosophy of nonintervention in politics. However, their skills of organization and discipline, combined with their increasing concern over the political chaos in the country, helped to draw the military nearer to political involvement. The Igbo officer corps was also unhappy with what it considered to be northern domination of Nigeria, and the failure by Igbos to get a fair slice of the Nigerian pie.

These tensions came to a head on January 15, 1966, when the country's first military coup took place, installing a government perceived by many to be Igbo-dominated and assassinating the North's two most powerful leaders, Tafawa Balewa and Sir Alhaji Ahmadu Bello, the Sardauna of Sokoto and premier of the North. In recent years, some scholars have interpreted the coup as having been nationalist in origin, striving to rid the country of ethnic (northern) domination. Evidence for this view is inconclusive, but there was no hesitation within northern Nigeria in perceiving this to be an outright assault on its people. The collapse and overthrow of the First Republic led, within 15 months, to a bitter civil war and an unbroken 13 years of military rule.

---

[2]The National Convention was also known as the National Congress. The NCNC was also known before independence as the National Council of Nigeria and the Cameroons.

MILITARY GOVERNMENT, 1966–1979

The seizure of power by the military on January 15–16, 1966, indicated the failure of Nigerian political development. The military, however, initially fared little better than the civilians, and the social fabric of the country rapidly deteriorated. The junior officers who perpetrated the coup proved to be badly organized, and so leadership reverted to the Army Chief of Staff, Maj. Gen. J. Aguiyi-Ironsi. Although he was already in a precarious position, his decision in May 1966 to abolish the regions and federalism in favor of a unitary system of government inflamed northern opinion and provided the grounds for a counter-coup on July 29, 1966, in which Igbo officers were removed from power. Lt. Col. (later General) Yakubu Gowon, a 32-year-old, was chosen as a compromise candidate for leadership, both because he was from a minority ethnic group and because he was a Christian northerner.

Gowon attempted to defuse the tensions within the country by calling a constitutional conference in August–September 1966 to resolve regional differences. The North initially sought secession from the Republic, but in the end its leaders were persuaded against this, influenced by significant pressure from the United States and Britain. The East, however, came to favor secession, a desire strengthened by the massacre of many thousands of innocent Igbos in northern Nigeria during May and September–October 1966, causing millions to flee the North to the relative safety of the East. The East was also the center of the developing oil industry and thus had considerable economic potential; moreover, Igbos were renowned for their economic resourcefulness and expertise.

On May 26, 1967, Gowon attempted to preempt secession by splitting the regions into 12 states, but four days later the Eastern Region declared its independence as Biafra, and the civil war, or the "war of national unity," was begun. The war claimed the lives of untold millions of Nigerians and proved to be the ultimate test of unity and loyalty for the nascent state. The complex problem of national integration was one faced by many African states, and so the war was watched closely by the rest of the continent. Only four African countries formally recognized Biafra, and many Western states would provide only humanitarian assistance to the secessionists. The rest of the Nigerian federation united against this challenge and, with large military assistance from the Soviet Union and other Eastern European countries, and after 1967 from Britain, finally crushed the rebellion in January 1970.[3]

Gowon, to his credit and Nigeria's benefit, was magnanimous in victory and sought the reconciliation of all the warring factions. Although Biafran soldiers were excluded from further military service, many officers were reintegrated into the Nigerian army, which had grown to over 250,000 troops by 1972—a significant social and political problem in itself. Economic reconstruction was facilitated by the rapid increase in oil production and revenues, which were further boosted by the OPEC "revolution" of October 1973. Such was the confidence of the country by the mid-1970s that Nigeria cultivated its image as a continental leader, and the country appeared to be awash with oil money and large development projects. Across-the-board pay raises fueled inflation, but nobody seemed to worry. Indeed, the military leaders were at the front of the line helping themselves to Nigeria's wealth.

The vast corruption of the military leaders, the inefficiency and apparent lack of direction of development goals, the squandering of the oil wealth, and the failure to provide a program for return to civilian rule all helped to stir up divisions within the military. These contributed to Gowon's overthrow by fellow officers on July 29, 1975, exactly nine years after he had come to power. Gowon's successor, Murtala Muhammed, set out to tackle the worst excesses of corruption and fixed a timetable to return to civilian rule by October 1979. Murtala's radical and crusading zeal led to the dismissal of 10,000 government officials and 150 officers, and naturally upset many Nigerians who had gained illicitly from the

previous regime. Murtala also threatened to trim the armed forces by 50 percent. Consequently, Murtala was assassinated on February 13, 1976, by disgruntled officers, many of whom were found to be from Gowon's home area.

Returning to Civilian Rule

Lt. Gen. Olusegun Obasanjo, the first head of state of Yoruba ethnicity, continued to implement the political transition program. A Constituent Assembly met in 1976 to draw up a new constitution and political framework for the country that would allow for potentially greater stability. Differences emerged between delegates, especially concerning the status of *sharia*, or Islamic, courts within the federation, but the constitution when implemented in 1979 proved to be a balanced document, and it was generally welcomed by Nigerians.

Nigerians accepted that a federal system had to be maintained, and the discredited parliamentary system of the First Republic was replaced by an executive presidential system, balanced by a National Assembly of two federal houses, namely, the Senate and House of Representatives. Like their American counterparts, the Senate gave equal representation to the states of the federation (increased to 19 in 1976 following the report of the Irikefe Commission), and the lower House had its members distributed and elected on the basis of population. Government at the state level was to be under a governor and a single or unicameral assembly. Following elections held in mid-1979, the Second Republic was born on October 1, 1979, and a whole new experiment in political and social engineering was begun.

THE SECOND REPUBLIC, 1979–1983

Only five political parties had been allowed by the military to register under guidelines for the 1979 elections, and of these the National Party of Nigeria (NPN) emerged as the dominant one. The new president, Alhaji Shehu Shagari, was elected on the NPN ticket, and the party was able to secure a majority in both houses of the

---

[3]E. Wayne Nafziger, *The Economics of Political Instability. The Nigerian-Biafran War* (Boulder, CO: Westview Press, 1983).

National Assembly. At the state level the picture was more complex, as the smaller parties were able to gain control of nine state governments. Although the military had forced all five parties to be of national rather than ethnic origin, the election results confirmed fears that ethnicity could not be suppressed so easily. The Unity Party of Nigeria (UPN) was backed predominantly by Yoruba supporters and won the states of the Southwest, whereas the Nigeria People's Party (NPP), closely linked to Igbo support, won the three states in the Southeast.

The NPN did succeed to some extent in cutting across ethnic barriers and striking bargains with southern elements, primarily at the elite level, although it found it difficult to completely shed its image as the party representing northern interests. The electoral process was not as violent or combustible as it had been some 15 years earlier, but tensions grew in the early 1980s between a number of states and the federal government, and within a few states where the governor was not a member of the majority party. Pressure for the creation of more states rose dramatically as political elites around the country attempted to access federal resources. The NPN utilized patrimonial politics to maintain its grip on the country, but opposition to the government grew substantially. Such antagonism was exacerbated by political economy factors, notably the chronic condition of the economy following the collapse in oil prices, as well as by the rampant and blatant corruption associated with the NPN.

Elections held in mid-1983 returned the NPN to office, but allegations of widespread ballot rigging cast serious doubts upon the results. Given the debates within the democratization literature, it is very evident in this case that elections per se do not constitute an acceptance by the elites of the principles of democracy. Riots broke out in areas supported by opposition parties, particularly in the southwestern states, and the federal government lost control and direction. Against this background, and with the fear of further bloodshed in the local government elections slated for January 1984, the military intervened on New Year's Eve 1983 and started its second period in government.

MILITARY GOVERNMENT AND TRANSITION PROGRAMS, 1984–1999

Military government under Muhammadu Buhari (1984–1985) was a bitter experience for most Nigerians. Top civilian leaders, including the former president and vice president, were jailed, and tribunals were organized for those suspected of corrupt practices. A severe clampdown on press freedom was instituted and a "War Against Indiscipline" (WAI) started to attempt to instill better behavior and moral values in the population. Set within the acute economic hardship faced by most Nigerians—accentuated by falling oil revenues and deteriorating terms of trade—the initial euphoria that had greeted the overthrow of the civilians was soon displaced by a distaste for the military leaders. Such unease was felt within the military itself, and in August 1985 Buhari was removed by his colleagues in a "palace coup," and Gen. Ibrahim Babangida took over the reins of office.

Babangida's government initially relaxed some of the harsher policies of its predecessor and introduced economic measures in an attempt to alleviate the severe hardship faced by the majority. Although Babangida did not accept direct assistance from the International Monetary Fund (IMF), the policies implemented followed programs suggested by the IMF and enabled Nigeria to receive large World Bank loans. The most significant structural adjustments included an initial 60 percent devaluation of the national currency, the naira, the abolition of commodity boards, the privatization of many inefficient government-owned corporations (or *parastatals*), the relaxation of import-export regulations, and the gradual reduction of government subsidies. These were difficult and unpopular reforms, and in the long term had marginal success at best. With hindsight, it appears that Babangida had very little genuine interest in altering the status quo that benefited the military and civilian elites.

On political reforms, Babangida (after surviving a coup attempt in December 1985) announced in January 1986 a plan to return the country to civilian rule by 1990 (though it is again indicative of his real intentions that this transfer did not finally take place until 1999, six years after he had left office). Significantly, the presidential system of government was to be retained, but eventually only two government-created parties, the National Republican Convention (NRC) and the Social Democratic Party (SDP), were allowed to compete. All politicians and military personnel who served in federal or state governments or assemblies from 1960 to 1991 were initially barred from contesting for office in 1992 in an attempt to recruit a different political elite, though this ban was lifted in 1992.

Babangida postponed the presidential elections slated for 1992, claiming that northerners had been selected as candidates for both parties. A new transition timetable was drawn up for 1993, and after a tortuous process, new presidential candidates were nominated by their respective parties. The NRC selected Bashir Othman Tofa, a Muslim northerner, as candidate, whereas the SDP nominated Bashoru Moshood Abiola, a Muslim Yoruba southerner and publishing tycoon.

The presidential election took place on June 12, 1993. The National Electoral Commission (NEC) announced that Abiola had received 58 percent of the vote, and won 19 of 30 states. Abiola's victory stunned the northern establishment, and on June 23, 1993, the military government annulled the election result and the Third Republic, claiming various irregularities in polling. A more pressing reason for the annulment was the fear within the Northern/military establishment that their influence over Nigeria's political economy would be severely undermined. Babangida, who had allegedly received financing from Abiola to launch his 1985 coup, was isolated within the military's inner circle and forced to relinquish office on August 27, 1993. An interim government was established under the nominal leadership of Chief Ernest Shonekan, a prominent Yoruba businessman, and fresh presidential elections were promised for March 1994. These never occurred, as General Sani Abacha overthrew this government on November 17, 1993, basically abandoning the transition program and much of the structural adjustment, and returning the country to military rule.

Abiola returned from exile in June 1994 to claim his presidency and was immediately jailed. In February 1995, more than 300 senior military and retired officers were rounded up, including former head of state Obasanjo, after allegations of a coup attempt by them. In October 1995, Abacha announced a program to return to civilian rule by October 1998. A new constitutional framework of "zoning" of top political offices was to facilitate ethnic/regional balance, as was a hybrid presidential and parliamentary framework of government. Abacha was criticized from inside and outside the country for such a long drawn-out program, and few had any confidence that it would be adhered to. The transition program appeared to be used to placate international pressures on the Abacha administration, but there seemed to be little desire to implement it.

The period 1994–1998 was probably the darkest period of Nigerian political development (outside the civil war), as Abacha's draconian style intimidated opposition and drove many into exile. The transition was dragged out, and the political process manipulated to serve the interests of Abacha—classic tactics of an authoritarian leader attempting to cling to power. Five political parties were established to contest the elections of 1998, but the scale of manipulation was such that Abacha was "selected" as the presidential candidate for all five parties. His unexpected death (murder?) from heart failure in June 1998 was a very significant point of departure for Nigerian political development, and after a caretaker year in office by General Abdulsalam Abubakar, including the dissolution of the five political parties, fresh elections brought a Fourth Republic in 1999.

THE FOURTH REPUBLIC

During the transition program started in July 1998, some 25 political associations vied for approval by the military to become legal political parties. Only three were granted legal status, namely the People's Democratic Party (PDP), the All-People's Party (APP), and the Alliance for Democracy (AD). The PDP won significant majorities in the state elections in January 1999, forcing the APP and AD to form an electoral alliance.

This move was insufficient to prevent the PDP from winning majorities in elections to both federal houses, the Senate and the House of Representatives, in February 1999. Olusegun Obasanjo, the former military head of state, ran on a PDP platform and was elected president in February also, winning 62.8 percent of the votes cast. The new civilian government was sworn into office in May 1999, thus ending a bleak period of political development in Nigerian history. The April 2003 election result marked the first civilian transfer of power in Nigeria's history.

The opening of the democratic space within Nigerian politics since 1999 has led to serious challenges to political stability. Ethnic and religious tensions have been exacerbated by the increasing intolerance within society. Economic malaise and the impoverishment of the majority have contributed to serious unrest. Efforts to curb the excessive corruption of civilian and military elites have struggled to bring much success. Are the challenges to Nigerian society too much to overcome at this stage of its political development?

SOCIETAL AGENDAS

It should be evident that Nigeria is a volatile and unpredictable country. The fluidity of Nigeria's political structure, and the experimentation with different styles of government and constitutions, is indicative of numerous social and political problems to which the country is striving to find solutions. How best can these issues be tackled? How have other countries found solutions to these issues? Does Nigeria have a unique set of problems, or are they just more difficult to solve than for most countries?

A National Identity

Probably the most serious and difficult task facing the country since independence has been making people loyal to the concept of Nigeria, rather than allowing diverse ethnic sympathies to predominate over a national orientation. This concept of developing "social capital," where relations between individuals help build societal stability, has been elaborated upon by Francis Fukuyama.[4] Unfortunately, in the Nigerian context, such social capital resides at the ethnic or clan level and can be used to promote actions on behalf of the ethnic group rather than the national group. This task of nation building, or building social capital at the national level, is common to many African countries, where artificial state boundaries often force people of differing cultural backgrounds to live together. Since 1960, Nigeria has provided an arena for the struggle between ethnic identities and national identity as defined by the federal center, where the former has often won to the detriment of the common good.

Efforts by successive governments to control and weaken ethnicity have had some impact. "Federal character" is a term widely used in employment and political circles (and in the constitutions) to denote fair and equitable opportunities for all ethnic groups within the federation, so that discrimination is officially discouraged. Military recruitment also follows this guideline. Political parties can no longer legally be regionally or ethnically biased and must open offices in and recruit candidates from regions all over the federation. As we have seen, this did not prevent ethnic sentiment from surfacing in the Second Republic, and primordial ethnic tendencies resurfaced as a critical factor in the politics of the 1990s transitions. Interestingly, Chief Abiola appeared to break the mold of ethnicity by winning significant support across the whole country, and not just in one region. Such success only served to frighten those elites who gain from the manipulation of ethnic sentiments to serve their own political ends. President Obasanjo, in contrast, is a Christian southerner leading the PDP political party dominated by traditional northern interests. Such an outcome is more the result of very careful ethnic mediation and brokering, rather than the development of a more outwardly national conscience.

The role within Nigeria of traditional rulers, chiefs, and emirs has declined as their powers have gradually diminished, though they still remain important ethnic and religious intermediaries. The

---

[4]Francis Fukuyama, "Social Capital, Civil Society and Development," *Third World Quarterly* 22(1) (2001), pp. 7–20.

rapid changes taking place within the country mean that there is little continuity in government or precedent by which to act. The longest any civilian government has survived to date to develop such traditions is only six years (1960–1966).

The dynamics of growth and change have generated pressures from a variety of sources to increase the number of states in the federation from 3 to 36 (see Table 12.2). The creation of new states has alleviated some sociocultural tensions and allowed smaller ethnic groups greater control over their affairs, though minorities within these states continue to suffer discrimination. Unfortunately, the creation of new states and more apparent local democracy has not automatically led to any more efficient control over resources or their use, and this multiplicity of government has become a major drain on the country's limited finances. These new states have also not provided more honest and capable leadership, and this has seriously hindered the development of a true national consciousness. There is also little evidence to suggest that the increase of states has placed the country in a stronger position to withstand the external pressures emanating from globalization and the changing nature of the international political economy.

Religious Tolerance

Nigeria contains almost equal numbers of Christians and Muslims, who together account for 60–70 percent of the national population. Christianity provides the major religion of the South, with Protestants concentrated in the Southwest and Catholics in the Southeast. Numerous sects and denominations further divide Christians and make the religious scene more complex. Islam is the predominant religious force in the North, though there are many Muslims within the Yoruba community. There have been periods of extreme tension between Muslims and Christians, but general toleration has minimized the impact of differences on Nigerian political development. An example of such tolerance is to be seen in Yoruba families, where siblings often possess different religious affiliation. Religion has been used to reinforce divisions between competing political groups, but it has rarely been the sole or even fundamental issue of division. In this respect, Niger-

ian leaders have displayed both tolerance and maturity—or fear of the consequences to national unity should religious intolerance develop.

With the relative success in minimizing religious differences in the 1970s, it was somewhat surprising that intolerance increased in the 1980s and 1990s, and reached fever pitch in the early 2000s. This was partly influenced by the surge of Islamic fundamentalism. In December 1980, the first violent fundamentalist outbreak claimed at least 4,000 lives in the northern city of Kano, and continued outbreaks of fundamentalist agitation in other cities show the factionalism within Islam and challenges to the established order. The establishment was in disarray when the domestic leader of the Islamic faith, Sultan Abubakar III, died in 1988 after 50 years in office, and bitter rivalries emerged over the choice of his successor, Alhaji Ibrahim Dasuki, who was dismissed by Abacha in April 1996.

In 1987, violent clashes between Christians and Muslims flared up in northern Nigeria, with many lives lost and hundreds of churches burned to the ground. Similar riots occurred throughout the 1990s and resulted in thousands dead, disrupting the transition process. Relations between communities had been sensitive after Nigeria joined the Organization of Islamic Conference (OIC) in 1986, as some Christians feared the creeping Islamicization of national affairs. Religion was deliberately used to inflame passions and destabilize the military government.

Relations deteriorated badly at the end of the 1990s as several states in the North decided to implement *sharia* as the basis of their legal system. Even though Christians were formally exempt from *sharia*, the decision to implement religious laws in an otherwise secular country alarmed Christians and provoked large-scale riots in the early 2000s.[5] President Obasanjo's government was unable to promote a pluralistic environment for religious tolerance, and some elite groups manipulated these tensions for their own narrow political gains. How will Nigeria be able to defuse this escalating religious violence?

---

[5]Simeon O. Ilesanmi, "Constitutional Treatment of Religion and the Politics of Human Rights in Nigeria," *African Affairs* 100(401) (October 2001), pp. 529–554.

TABLE 12.2

NIGERIA'S REGIONS AND STATES, 1963–2006

1963	1967	1976	1987	1991	1996
Northern Region	Northwestern	Sokoto	Sokoto	Sokoto	Sokoto
					Zamfara
				Kebbi	Kebbi
		Niger	Niger	Niger	Niger
	Northeastern	Borno	Borno	Borno	Borno
				Yobe	Yobe
		Bauchi	Bauchi	Bauchi	Bauchi
					Gombe
		Gongola	Gongola	Adamawa	Adamawa
				Taraba	Taraba
	North-Central	Kaduna	Kaduna	Kaduna	Kaduna
			Katsina	Katsina	Katsina
	Benue-Plateau	Benue	Benue	Benue	Benue
		Plateau	Plateau	Plateau	Plateau
					Nassarawa
	West-Central	Kwara	Kwara	Kwara	Kwara
				Kogi	Kogi
	Kano	Kano	Kano	Kano	Kano
				Jigawa	Jigawa
Eastern Region	East-Central	Anambra	Anambra	Anambra	Anambra
				Enugu	Enugu
		Imo	Imo	Imo	Imo
				Abia	Abia
					Ebonyi
	Southeastern	Cross River	Cross River	Cross River	Cross River
			Akwa Ibom	Akwa Ibom	Akwa Ibom
	Rivers	Rivers	Rivers	Rivers	Rivers
					Bayelsa
Western Region	Western	Oyo	Oyo	Oyo	Oyo
				Oshun	Oshun
		Ogun	Ogun	Ogun	Ogun
		Ondo	Ondo	Ondo	Ondo
					Ekiti
Midwestern Region	Midwestern	Bendel	Bendel	Edo	Edo
				Delta	Delta
Federal Capital Territory	Lagos	Lagos	Lagos	Lagos	Lagos
			Abuja	Abuja	Abuja

Note: The Federal Capital Territory was transferred from Lagos to Abuja under the 1979 Constitution. Abuja became the capital in December 1991 and is a federal capital territory rather than a state. (Six new states created in 1996 appear in boldface.) Nigeria now has 36 states and 1 federal capital territory.

Political Economy

Nigerian development plans have unequivocally directed the country toward being a capitalist society. Drawing from colonial experiences, successive Nigerian governments supported capitalist economic strategies and refused to countenance socialist alternatives. Although there are minimum wage policies in force and health and education schemes provide some assistance for the needy, there are few constraints on the market economy. Initially at independence, British influence over the economy was paramount, but gradual indigenization and Africanization policies during the 1970s and 1980s placed more influence in Nigerian hands, although certainly only in the hands of an elite and still with very strong influence by multinational corporations (MNCs). These linkages with MNCs have enriched government representatives and businesspersons with privileged access but have not really developed the administrative, technical, and entrepreneurial skills of the average Nigerian. During the last decade, as part of a neoliberal strategy imposed on Nigeria by the World Bank and IMF to produce economic change, renewed emphasis has been placed on foreign investment and participation in enterprises. Federal and state governments have sold off many *parastatals* to the domestic and foreign business elites. Such a strategy to compete within a world economy influenced by the changes brought about by rapid globalization has brought little change to the overall national economy and has had marginal impact at best on the livelihood of the average Nigerian.

This overtly capitalistic strategy has concentrated wealth in the hands of the few and has been constructed in cooperation with the interests of international capital. Within the country, there has been widespread, though ineffectual, criticism of the development strategy. The universities provide the major source of radical opposition, with academics and students alike pushing for socialistic and egalitarian alternatives, but scant regard is paid to them. The Nigeria Labour Congress (NLC) has also been outspoken in support of workers' rights, but successive governments have ignored it or, worse still, detained its leaders and restructured the labor groups—only to restructure them again at a later date when they become outspoken.

The Babangida government expressly refused to adopt socialism as the national ideology to be followed after 1992, but the government did not recommend any strategy, stating that it would "eventually evolve with time and political maturity."[6] In essence, successive elites have prevented a more egalitarian economic and development strategy from emerging and have controlled through manipulating ethnic, "prebendal" patrimonial tendencies.

The prevailing economic structure of Nigeria provides other strains. Agriculture traditionally provided the backbone of economic wealth, but the oil boom from the late 1960s led to the neglect of the agricultural sector. Investment was poured into expensive prestige projects, often industrial (and often with large kickbacks for business and government elites), and these did not bring much real benefit to the majority. In contrast, the rural areas received little investment and were allowed to decay. In the early 1990s, the government desperately tried to rectify these policies, revitalize rural areas, and prevent the rural-urban population drift that has placed increasing strains on the urban areas. However, these policies recorded minimal success.

Nigeria remains a society of great inequalities—a factor which successive governments have failed to tackle. Class divisions are pronounced, but they have not been the basis of large-scale political action to date. Although there have been political parties that claimed to provide for working-class concerns and espoused class-conscious ideologies, none has been truly class-based, and they have all tended to rely on residual ethnic support for their votes. Indeed, party leaders often have exploited ethnic sentiments in order to reduce the possibility that a true national working-class solidarity would develop.

The urbanized middle class, which was emerging strongly during the oil boom years of the late 1970s, was badly hit by austerity in the 1980s and all but disappeared in the 1990s. The wealthy business and political elites, however, maintained their own privileged positions, and

---

[6]*Government's Views and Comments on the Findings and Recommendations of the Political Bureau* (Abuja: Mamser, undated), Section 53.

A CLOSER LOOK 12.2

A NIGERIAN DEVELOPMENT MODEL?

Nigeria's political and economic development since independence in 1960 provides a confusing picture to those unaccustomed to Africa. In the political arena, experimentation with a British parliamentary model between 1960 and 1966, an American presidential model from 1979 to 1983, and again after 1999 (with a French/Russian hybrid proposed model shelved after 1998), highlights attempts to find a suitable pattern of government. Military governments, which have been in office for more than two-thirds of the postindependence era, have occurred because of failed civilian governments and, especially in the 1990s, a simple desire to retain power.

On the economic side, Nigeria has pursued a capitalist development model, officially scorning socialism. Over the last decade, successive governments have followed fairly closely economic programs laid down by the IMF and the World Bank. These programs, while bringing few short-term benefits, have contributed to extreme societal inequalities and hardship. Earlier efforts at economic indigenization have also been reversed, as Nigeria has been forced to open its companies to foreign ownership. Corruption, at high levels throughout postindependence, appears to have increased in the 1990s, with large amounts of money derived from the international drug trade supplementing more routine revenues from cross-border smuggling and trade. An internal government report, as one example, found $12 billion "lost" from official coffers during the Babangida administration.

Is there a Nigerian development model that has been followed? To a certain extent Nigeria's political and military elites have sketched out a "mixed economy" path of capitalism to follow. Unfortunately, corruption undermines the realization of the country's full economic potential and makes one conclude that the Nigerian model serves to benefit those in power, not the vast majority of citizens.

---

society has become even more divided socially and economically. Class perspectives were vaguely worded into the two parties of the early 1990s but did not provide for class-based politics and elections, and there is little class-based politics in the Fourth Republic.

Will the ideological orientation that has prevailed since independence be altered under the Obasanjo civilian government? As money and patronage tend to control Nigerian politics, a preliminary assessment would conclude in the negative.

SOCIALIZATION AND GENDER

Socialization, the process by which people learn the values and beliefs of their society, is influenced by many factors within the Nigerian context. The novelty of national identity contrasts with the pressures from long-standing traditions, while competing socialization processes take place to promote potentially mutually exclusive

allegiances at ethnic and federal-national levels. The first language of most Nigerians is their own ethnic tongue, with English used as the only national language. Great emphasis in schools is placed on developing a national consciousness with loyalty pledges and instruction of national values, but this can run into conflict with learning experiences within the home or local community, where the belief that the state or federal apparatus has been discriminatory may prevail.

Military governments have attempted to instill greater self-discipline and national awareness among Nigerians, but with varied results. They have also stressed the need for greater honesty in society and have attempted to stamp out the corruption that plagues all levels of Nigerian life. Unfortunately, the armed forces have been guilty of the very things they are attempting to erase in the civilian population, and so the values of society have been slow to change.

The status of women within the domestic power structure is also shaped by the traditions and norms of society. Generally, women suffer discrimination by males in access to positions of authority, as well as in opportunities for economic development. For example, Catherine Acholonu, vice president of the Association of Women in Politics and an aspiring female presidential candidate, was detained in 1993 by the military for several weeks to prevent her registering for the election. But the scale of this discrimination is not uniform across the country. In many southern areas, for example, women have controlled market enterprises for many years and have significant input into the economy; in the North, Islam tends to limit women's active participation in social and economic life because purdah tends to keep them confined to the home. Women were also denied the vote in northern states until 1979. Family planning, seemingly crucial in a country where women on average have six children each, tends to be given low priority by male administrators. In Islamic circles, many males are openly opposed to any form of family planning, charging it is a Christian conspiracy to hold down Islamic population growth.

Against the background of these and other agendas, Nigeria is struggling to develop a collective conscience and political processes and institutions that will be able to withstand the pressures that have plagued all previous governments.

Thinking Critically

1. Why has ethnicity continued to be a politically divisive issue in Nigeria? How strong was the legacy of British colonial rule in strengthening ethnic identity and identification?
2. What advantage has Nigeria gained by having its political institutions modeled on external/Western patterns?
3. Is federalism a positive or negative force in the Nigerian political landscape?
4. Why did civil war break out in 1967? Do you think another civil war in the country is possible?
5. What are the causes of corruption in Nigeria? How has corruption affected political development?

KEY TERMS

Biafra *(649)*
civil war *(649)*
colonialism *(647–648)*
coup d'état *(649)*
ethnicity *(644–645)*
federal character *(643)*
Hausa-Fulani *(645, 648–649)*
Igbo *(645)*
Middle Belt *(645)*
nation building *(648)*
parastatals (651)
regionalism *(648)*
religious tolerance *(654)*
secession *(649)*
socialization *(657)*
Yoruba *(645, 648–649)*

FURTHER READINGS

Ake, Claude, ed. *Political Economy of Nigeria* (London: Longman, 1985).

Balewa, B.A.T. *Governing Nigeria: History, Problems and Prospects* (Lagos: Malthouse Press, 1994).

Chazan, Naomi, Robert Mortimer, John Ravenhill, and Donald Rothchild. *Politics and Society in Contemporary Africa* (Boulder, CO: Lynne Rienner, 1992).

Dudley, B. J. *Instability and Political Order: Politics and Crisis in Nigeria* (Ibadan: Ibadan University Press, 1973).

Falola, Toyin. *The History of Nigeria* (Westport, CT: Greenwood Press, 1999).

Graf, William D. *The Nigerian State: Political Economy, State Class and Political System in the Post-Colonial Era* (London: James Currey; Portsmouth: Heinemann, 1988).

Ihonvbere, Julius O. *Nigeria: The Politics of Adjustment and Democracy* (New Brunswick, NJ: Transaction, 1994).

Kieh, George K., and P. O. Agbese, eds. *The Military and Politics in Africa* (Aldershot: Ashgate, 2004).

Osaghae, Eghosa E. *Crippled Giant: Nigeria since Independence* (Bloomington: Indiana University Press, 1998).

Wright, Stephen. *Nigeria: Struggle for Stability and Status* (Boulder, CO: Westview Press, 1998),

B. POLITICAL PROCESSES AND INSTITUTIONS

Understanding political development and democratization can be challenging, given the array of theoretical models and constructs available to the scholar of comparative politics. Can one anticipate that African states will follow the path to democracy trodden by the United States or countries in Western Europe? Is democracy a universal goal with universally acceptable elements? Will African states actually accomplish a democratic transformation, or will they be relegated to relative obscurity in the apparent rush of globalization and homogenization?

Nigeria has obviously made attempts to develop a democratic framework of governance, though with few clear successes. What factors can we isolate to explain this? The political process in Nigeria is complex, and attempts to study and comprehend it are complicated by several factors. Accurate information concerning actors and decision making is often not present, so it can be difficult to isolate the forces at work. Severe problems such as ethnicity, religion, the civil war, economic inequalities and structural adjustment, and military coups impinge directly on political development. There has been no direct or official continuity of political parties within the country. Parties were banned in 1966 after the collapse of the First Republic, and new parties were formed for the Second Republic in 1979. Likewise in 1983, these parties were proscribed, and two new parties were created for the Third Republic. These parties, in turn, were banned in 1993 and three new parties drawn up for the Fourth Republic in 1999. At the 2003 parliamentary election, 30 parties fielded candidates. Naturally, some of the leading political figures, ideologies, ethnic identities, and policy bases have remained influential throughout.

To a considerable extent, Nigeria differs from more developed political structures in that the political process has been dominated by personalities rather than by parties or policies. Admittedly, vague promises and programs have been enunciated by parties, particularly on education, health, and the economy, but voters have been far more interested in who the leaders of each party are and, more crucially, what their ethnic identifications are. Party alliances and allegiances are forged on ethnic considerations rather than social class identification. In many elections, ballot rigging has occurred on such a grand scale that it has been difficult to gauge real winners and losers.

Has long-term military control had a positive or negative impact on the political process? Should military rule be seen as an integral part of the political process itself? A favorite comment is that the Nigerian system contains only two parties, the civilians and the military, and that both are integral to the political process. Let us consider the validity of that argument.

Since independence in October 1960, Nigeria has struggled to find a stable framework of political institutions through which to govern. The country has experimented with parliamentary (1960–1966), presidential (1979–1983, 1999–), and military (1966–1979 and 1984–1999) structures of government, which have all operated within a federal system encompassing initially three regions and now 36 states. Many commentators, both in Nigeria and abroad, argue that it is not the political institutions that have been at fault—particularly during the Second Republic—but the leaders. How realistic is it to distinguish between political "structures" and political "leaders"?

Before turning in detail to study political parties and institutions, we need to consider the important role in political development of the civilian and military leadership groups.

CIVILIAN ELITE

Politicians around the world do not always have the best of reputations, but Nigerian politicians have been considered especially poor representatives and guardians of the state. The failure of the first two republics (and certain military regimes also) can be at least partially blamed on poor leadership, selfish interests, and gross corruption.

Given this condemnation, who are these politicians and how do they get themselves elected? Most politicians are drawn from the wealthy business communities, professional groups, schools and universities, and government administration, and some hold religious or traditional positions of authority. Increasingly, retired military leaders have also turned to civilian politics. President Obasanjo was a former military head of state; Sani Abacha would have been elected president in 1998 but for his inopportune death; Shehu Musa Yar'Adua, a former military chief of staff under Obasanjo, became a presidential candidate in the 1990s, only to die in jail under mysterious circumstances during the Abacha administration; and Ibrahim Babangida is known to have his sights set on a presidential bid within the Fourth Republic.

Ethnic considerations have been of paramount importance in climbing the political ladder within any given party and have proven to be more important than educational ability or qualifications. Ethnicity has been the major form of political mobilization to distribute benefits of development. The desire to assist people from one's own community provides a very strong impulse for Nigerians. Unlike in the West, values of impartiality and nepotism do not command full respect or are never properly implemented. It has been virtually impossible for politicians to be recruited—and certainly advance—without having the requisite ethnic identification, or at least promising to attract large numbers of his or her own ethnic constituency.

A major weakness of this elite has been the failure to apply a nationalist orientation to policy, with sectionalist or personal interest usually taking priority. In the First Republic, the ruling Northern People's Congress (NPC) was exclusively a mouthpiece of the Northern Region, and the majority of federal spending inevitably went to that region. Its successor, the National Party of Nigeria (NPN), attempted to be more national in outlook but still was biased toward northern states and sectarian interests. This inability of politicians to encompass a truly national orientation is a trait also found in many African states.

Perhaps the critical problem concerning the civilian elite is that its ethical and normative values have proved totally insubstantial. Civilians have unashamedly entered politics to make money. This has been called "extractive" politics, in which politicians merely seek their own personal gain rather than promote societal advancement. Frantz Fanon explicitly condemned such practices in African states, considering it just another form of exploitation under which the African masses have to suffer.[7] It may be unfair to paint all Nigerian politicians with such a broad brush, but they have tended to hold to stereotype. Respected scholars of Nigerian politics appear to be in agreement. Billy Dudley wrote: "For the Nigerian political elite, politics involves not the conciliation of competing demands arising from an examination of the various alternatives entailed by any course of political action, but the extraction of resources which can be used to satisfy elite demands and to buy support."[8] Terisa Turner and Gavin Williams shared a similar view that in Nigeria, "Politics thus comes to be the process of gaining control of public resources for the pursuit of private ends."[9]

Long periods of military rule can exacerbate the corruption of civilian elites when they come to power. The uncertainty of how long they will be in office before the military returns to power can promote what Alex Gboyega has called "fast feeding frenzies." The 1979 Constitution (and its later 1999 version) laid down very clear guidelines against corruption, and politicians at least paid lip service to the need for probity in office. But the record of civilians between 1979 and 1983 was poor, with an estimated $5 to $7 billion embezzled, and arson resorted to in order to prevent official inquiries from finding evidence of such acts. By 1983, a number of important buildings had been burned, including two telecom-

---

[7]Frantz Fanon, *The Wretched of the Earth* (London: MacGibbon and Kee, 1965).
[8]Billy Dudley, *An Introduction to Nigerian Government and Politics* (London: Macmillan, 1982), pp. 62–63.
[9]Gavin Williams and Terisa Turner, "Nigeria," in *West African States: Failure and Promise* (Cambridge: Cambridge University Press, 1978), p. 133.

munications centers in Lagos, as well as the Federal Ministry of Education and the Foreign Affairs Ministry. The Obasanjo government has placed the fight against corruption as one of its highest priorities, but there has been little sign of significant breakthroughs. Corruption scandals continue to envelop federal and state elected officials, and the endemic nature of corruption makes it highly unlikely that a change will occur in the near future. So how can corruption be stopped? Most theorists point to changing aspirations at the grassroots level, and that by developing widespread attitudinal change across society, values can be changed. Little has happened to begin this process in Nigeria.

MILITARY LEADERSHIP

Since independence, the military has controlled the Nigerian government for twice the length of time that civilians have. The most important justification normally put forward by the military for its intrusion into politics (both in Nigeria and in Africa as a whole) is the failure by civilians to maintain political stability and to act in accordance with societal norms.[10] The military itself has had numerous millionaire generals who have flaunted their wealth without hesitation or fear. This wealth was made possible by the rapid increase (and unaccountability) in national revenues accruing from oil. The overthrow of General Yakubu Gowon in 1975 was defended by his successors as necessary to stem this corruption, but they merely made it less conspicuous. Many believe that the outgoing military leadership in 1979 only handed over power to civilians when the latter agreed not to probe into the financial affairs of retiring officers. This seems to have been an issue during the problematic transition in 1992–1993 also, and there is every indication of massive fraud by military officers throughout the 1990s.

The armed forces do help to play a nation-building role, however, in the sense that recruitment and appointments are molded by considerations of federal character, and postings to various parts of Nigeria provide soldiers with greater awareness (and, it is hoped, empathy) of people with different social and cultural backgrounds. National rather than sectional interest is stressed through education and training, and officer recruitment is monitored for equality. Such a balance, however, is a goal rather than a reality, and imbalance has been a focus of bitter controversy in previous years.

At independence in 1960, only 10 percent of the officer corps of the Royal West Africa Frontier Force (RWAFF) was African, as British expatriate officers retained control. This was both for political reasons, because of the pro-Western and pro-British leanings of the federal government, and for practical reasons, in that very few Nigerians had been trained as officers. As was noted earlier, Africanization took place rapidly, so that by 1965 all but 10 percent of officers were Nigerian. This pace of promotion had obvious military significance; young officers rose in the ranks at great speed, leading to what has been termed "professional disorientation." But the political problems were equally severe because the appointments and promotions gave a disproportionate influence to officers from the Eastern Region.[11] The growing frustration with the northern bias of the ruling NPC, combined with the inability of Eastern Region politicians to influence the political process, provided these officers with a justification to use their military muscle to bring an end to the First Republic in 1966.

Few people foresaw such a military intervention, believing that British influence and military training would be sufficient to inspire a nonpolitical stance by military officers and to prevent their interference in the political

---

[10]See William Gutteridge, *Military Regimes in Africa* (London: Methuen, 1975); and Morris Janowitz, *Civil-Military Relations—Regional Perspectives* (Beverly Hills, CA: Sage, 1981).

[11]For a discussion of the military in this period, see N. J. Miners, *The Nigerian Army 1956–66* (London: Methuen, 1971); and Robin Luckham, *The Nigerian Military: A Sociological Analysis of Authority and Revolt 1960–61* (London: Cambridge University Press, 1971).

A CLOSER LOOK

12.3

THE CIVIL WAR

The civil war fought from 1967 to 1970 was one of the worst on the African continent. With more than a million people killed, and with many more homeless and destitute, the war severely tested the unity of the country. The Biafran aim had been to set up their own independent state in southeastern Nigeria, financed by oil revenues, and their claim received significant support within West Africa and from France. The federal side (and northern elites) could not afford to let go of such an economically important area of the country, nor could it allow secession for fear of sparking claims by other dissatisfied ethnic groups.

The internationalization of the war, drawing in the superpowers and some European countries, was also a tragedy, but the end of the war brought an era of reconciliation that few thought possible. The painful memory of the war has probably prevented other secession attempts since, and it provides an incentive to find a viable system of government to bring the whole nation together. However, as the war recedes into history, there are fears that moves to break up the federation will increase.

---

process. But the political awareness of officers had been awakened in 1964, when they were asked by both antagonists to intervene in the constitutional crisis between the president and prime minister, even though this crisis was finally settled by the civilians themselves. The 1966 coup dramatically and irreversibly changed the nature of the political process and set off a chain of events within the military that continues to trouble it. The civil war divided the military into two factions, and although the Biafran secession was defeated, only some officers of eastern origin were allowed to rejoin the federal armed forces. A shift in the profile of the military leadership took place in the 1970s, with Middle Belt officers from the smaller ethnic groups becoming more prominent.

Has military rule had a positive impact on the Nigerian political process? Such a question is value-laden and ambiguous, and it is one that induces significant debate. Military force has been useful in suppressing political violence, but the military did not use excessive force to control society until the 1990s. The military acted in apparent good faith to draw up constitutional programs to return power to civilians in the Second and Fourth Republics, although this was more questionable over the aborted Third Republic. Nevertheless, the military's interven-

tion has not solved the problems inherent in the Nigerian polity, and the military has been unable to solve the deep-seated difficulties in the political system. The military has tended to favor the status quo, shoring up corrupt elites rather than working toward ridding the country of socioeconomic inequalities. In this sense, it could be categorized as conservative rather than reformist. Some have said, perhaps unfairly, that the failure of the Second Republic showed that 13 years of military rule did not affect or improve the political system, attitudes, or institutions, although the civilians must ultimately take the blame for failing to make the system work.[12]

The longer the military stays in office, the more disunity and divisions appear within its ranks. Some factions believe in the importance of military rule, whereas others support civilian control of government. The military's training, discipline, and command structure do not really suit it for political office, and military governments have placed a heavy reliance on co-opted civilians to administer the country. The option to

---

[12]Stephen Wright, "State-Consolidation and Social Integration in Nigeria: The Military's Search for the Elusive," in Henry Dietz and Jerold Elkin, eds., *Ethnicity, Integration and the Military* (Boulder, CO: Westview Press, 1991).

share national leadership with civilians after 1992 was raised and rejected by the military, even though it did occur by default for a few months in 1993 during the Shonekan transition from Babangida to Abacha. Continued training and education are also key factors in trying to keep the military out of civilian politics in the future. Will this prove successful?

THE FIRST REPUBLIC, 1960–1966

Political Parties

The political parties of the First Republic all developed in preindependent Nigeria and thus began their operations within the context of colonial control. Although the first protoparty was formed in the 1920s, it was not until after World War II that parties really began to take the shape and form that made them active players in the political game. As we have already seen, the regionalist philosophy of the colonial administrators served both to create and to reinforce divisions between groups within the country and pushed political parties to seek support largely at an ethnic-regional level.

Northern People's Congress (NPC)   The NPC, established in 1951, controlled the federal assembly in Lagos and had its deputy leader, Sir Alhaji Abubakar Tafawa Balewa, as federal premier. The party's leader, Sir Alhaji Ahmadu Bello, decided to remain as northern premier, indicating his preference as to which was the more powerful institution. The NPC dominated the Northern Region and made it a closed system because of the very tight association of personnel at legislative, executive, and judicial levels. The NPC was blatantly northern rather than national in outlook, and it restricted party membership to people of northern origin. Its policies both at home and abroad reflected the Islamic conservatism of its leadership, promoting steady capitalist growth and no change in Nigeria's external orientation. This philosophy antagonized progressive and non-Islamic factions in the other regions.

The NPC maintained an electoral alliance from 1959 with the major party of the Eastern Region, the National Convention of Nigerian Citizens (NCNC). Rivalry in the South between the NCNC and Action Group over issues and alliances led to bitter electoral contests, the subsequent breakdown of law and order in the Western Region, and eventually to the military intervention of January 1966.

National Convention of Nigerian Citizens (NCNC)   The NCNC, established in 1944, was the oldest party to operate in the First Republic. It was centered on the personality of Dr. Nnamdi Azikiwe, a leading nationalist in the independence struggle who became the first (ceremonial) president of Nigeria in 1963. At independence, the party was almost exclusively based in the Eastern Region, relying largely on Igbo support, and it was more progressive in its economic and social policies than the NPC. The NCNC's pressure and activism in the neighboring Western Region provoked many violent clashes. Frustration over its failure to make a greater impact on the Nigerian political process resulted in the NCNC becoming the primary caucus of the Biafran secessionary movement, although Azikiwe remained loyal to the federal camp.

Action Group (AG)   The Action Group, established in 1948, was founded by and organized around the personality of Chief Obafemi Awolowo, a lawyer. The AG symbolized the cultural and political goals of the Yoruba, and the party's creation helped to formally dissolve a united nationalist movement. Its power center was the Western Region. Awolowo's belief was that the federation could only be kept together by the regions maintaining their own cultural identities and consulting as equal partners at the federal level. The AG strove hard to maintain control over its own region and to expand its influence beyond the West, but in both tasks it was less than successful.

The AG promoted "welfarism," but as the party moved toward adopting democratic socialism, splits appeared within its ranks. These divisions were deepened in 1962 when Awolowo gave up his position as premier of the West to become leader of the federal opposition in Lagos. His successor, Chief S. L. Akintola, was opposed by Awolowo but was able to hold sufficient support in the region to maintain his position. Differences within the Yoruba cultural entity, which have always been strong (and remained strong during the 1990s transition), were exacerbated by these tensions, especially when Awolowo was imprisoned by the federal authorities for treason, a charge he always denied. By 1966, law and order in the West had all but disappeared.

Smaller Parties The NPC, NCNC, and AG represented, to some degree or other, the primary ethnic groups of Hausa-Fulani, Igbo, and Yoruba, respectively. The smaller groups (and their elites) did not perceive their interests to be considered or promoted by these parties or within the regional governments, and so many of them formed their own parties to seek alliances and improve their negotiating position. One such party was the United Middle Belt Congress, which attempted to bring together groups within the country's central areas. Some of these parties held radical perspectives, particularly the Northern Elements Progressive Union (NEPU). NEPU was launched in 1951 under the leadership of Mallam Aminu Kano as a breakaway group and challenger to the NPC. Aminu Kano's radical challenge to the northern establishment continued until his death in 1983, but the effects of NEPU, like those of other smaller parties, were at best localized and at worst ineffectual. At elections in the First Republic, these smaller parties together never polled more than 15 percent of the vote.

Elections

The concern displayed by parties of the First Republic in manipulating the electoral process was partly inspired by negative perceptions of opponents. All parties were perceived as likely to exaggerate their voting support within their own region, and so each reinforced its own intention to do the same. Electoral registers and the census results from 1962 and 1963 were inflated for similar reasons; population was the factor determining seat allocations in the federal lower house (as well as federal revenue paid to the regions). This gave the North a built-in majority and added to the frustration of the

other regions. With each party effectively controlling the electoral process in its own region, sweeping successes were usually recorded (except in the West for specific reasons), as opponents were unable to campaign and ballot boxes were stuffed with false votes. The result of this was that elections served to entrench parties within their own regions, increased sectarianism as a political force, prevented an accurate judgment on party policy, and caused increasing strain and tension in a country already fraught with problems. The elections, then, did not help to defuse tensions or redirect policy as they often do in Western democracies; instead, they helped to fuel a crisis.

The first ever popular, direct elections in Nigeria were held in 1959, a year prior to independence, and based on these results the government was established. The North received a greater allocation of seats than other regions on the basis of population, even though one-half of that population—the female population—was disfranchised by religious custom (and only received the vote in 1979). The NPC was able to win 134 of the 312 seats in the federal lower house, but within a year sufficient numbers had switched allegiances to the NPC so that the party, in an alliance with the NCNC, was able to control a majority.

For the 1964 General Elections, the NPC stood in coalition with Akintola's AG faction, the Nigerian National Democratic Party (NNDP), and together they took 200 seats, with the NPC taking 162 of those. The rump AG had joined in an alliance with the NCNC in the United Progressive Grand Alliance (UPGA), and together they accounted for some 100 seats. The level of violence and intimidation during this campaign led the UPGA to call a boycott of the elections, but this only occurred in the East, which held fresh elections in March 1965. The absence of what could be termed "electoral morality" was evident, and showed that, "for the political elite, power was an end in itself and not a means to the realization of some greater good for the community . . . and that any talk about the rules of the game must be irrelevant."[13]

---

[13]Dudley, *Nigerian Government and Politics,* p. 70.

INSTITUTIONS OF THE FIRST REPUBLIC

The President

To be accurate, Nigeria did not become a Republic until 1963, when Dr. Nnamdi Azikiwe became its first president after having served as leader of the Senate (until 1962) and as governor general (in 1963). For the first three years after independence, Queen Elizabeth II (of England) technically remained the country's head of state, and she was represented in Nigeria by her governor general.

Azikiwe became the country's first ceremonial president after independence, more out of recognition for his leadership of the nationalist movement than from any real political influence he possessed. He was the dominant spokesperson of the East, the Igbo people, and the National Convention of Nigerian Citizens (NCNC), which formed a coalition with the ruling Northern People's Congress (NPC). The NPC would certainly not have allowed Azikiwe to become president if that position had carried any real political clout. The president's role was almost purely ceremonial. Azikiwe was officially able to call on the largest party in the federal House of Representatives to form a government, but he had no effective power to influence that process. In a major constitutional crisis during 1964, Azikiwe refused to accept the federal election results because of blatant malpractices that were detrimental to his own party, and thus would not call on the NPC leader, Sir Alhaji Abubakar Tafawa Balewa, to be premier. Azikiwe called on the army to support him, as did Tafawa Balewa, but in the end it was the president who was forced to back down.

In addition to these weaknesses, Azikiwe was not given authority to conduct foreign policy, even though he was nominally commander in chief of the armed forces. His authority also did not extend to influencing policy in federal or state houses, and he had little ability to prevent any of the conflicts afflicting the Western Region during the latter years of the First Republic.

The Prime Minister

Patterned closely on the British model, the position of prime minister, or premier, was the most important in the federal parliament, and was occupied throughout the First Republic by Tafawa Balewa. The premier, along with ministers selected by him, had ultimate responsibility for initiation and implementation of policy; the premier also used his strength within the federal lower house to ensure that policies were approved. Ultimately, the prime minister held responsibility for both domestic and international policy, including law and order and fiscal policy, but his failure to act decisively in the political problems of the West showed that he was not always willing, or able, to use these powers. It is also worth remembering that Tafawa Balewa was only the deputy leader of the NPC and that the real power broker, Ahmadu Bello, chose to remain as Northern premier.

The House of Representatives

The House of Representatives was the central forum of political debate and was modeled very much on the British House of Commons. The 312 seats were allocated on a population basis, which helped to give the NPC control, and the Action Group (AG) became the official opposition. The parliamentary system requires a toleration of opposition groups, but this was not present. Awolowo was considered a threat to the government, and he and 20 colleagues were imprisoned in 1962 on a spurious charge of treason.

The House held the responsibility for approving all major legislation in the federation. This duty specifically included the budget and other financial matters, as well as aspects of foreign policy. Strict party discipline, at least within the ruling NPC, made votes and victory a certainty for the government. Indeed, during the six years that the House was in existence, the government did not lose a single vote. As in the British system, policy decisions tended to be hammered out in private before being made public on the floor of the House. The presence of ministers and assistant ministers in the House also served to strengthen party unity. The significance of the House is perhaps lessened further when one realizes that it never met for more than 30 days in any one year.

The Senate

The Senate in the First Republic was a non-elected body containing 48 chiefs and elders who were nominated in equal numbers by the federal and regional governments. This upper house had few if any powers of action or initiation but attempted to serve the symbolic purpose of bringing together traditional leaders into the modern political structure. It possessed the ability to delay fiscal bills for 30 days and other bills for six months but was unable to overturn policy.

Regional Houses of Assembly

Each region—North, East, and West (and Midwest after 1964)—possessed its own single assembly with members elected in districts organized according to population. Only the West's assembly was not dominated by a single local party, and it was the scene of violent political controversy and turmoil. The regional government, each with its own premier nominated by the majority party, determined policy within its own jurisdiction, much like state governments do in the United States. These roles extended to areas such as education, the police, and economic planning and fiscal directives for that region. To this extent, they were powerful institutions within their own regions, and in the South this led to clashes with the NPC-dominated federal government over issues of policy implementation.

MILITARY GOVERNMENT, 1966–1979

The intervention of the military clearly had a serious impact on the political process. Political parties were banned, elections became unnecessary, civilian elites were relegated to the sidelines, and the military ruled by decree. The military's claim to be both protector and cleanser of the political system was a dubious one, especially when the country was plunged into civil war in 1967. Following the war, however, the military did help to heal some of the wounds between the warring factions and can reasonably claim some responsibility for maintaining Nige-

ria as one country. In May 1973, General Gowon established the National Youth Service Corps (NYSC) in a further effort to promote integration and to assist with development schemes. Under this program, new university graduates were asked to undertake a year's national service away from their home areas with the hope that this service would provide a greater national awareness and orientation. Unfortunately, the military leadership did not lead by example, and the military-technocratic alliance responsible for running the country accumulated personal wealth at the expense of other concerns.

Gowon had promised in 1970 that the country would revert to civilian rule in 1976. In 1974, however, this program was postponed without explanation or an alternative date offered. Dissatisfaction with Gowon's handling of affairs led to his overthrow in 1975 by a group of officers, who selected Murtala Muhammed as the head of state. Murtala began to act against corruption in society and laid down a timetable to return to civilian rule by 1979. Murtala also established a National Security Organization (NSO) to maintain a network of information and communication within the country, which unfortunately was unable to prevent Murtala's assassination in 1976.

The government of Lt. Gen. Olusegun Obasanjo, Murtala's successor, worked to create a constitution and political process that would tackle the disharmonies of the First Republic. A priority was to ensure that the former political parties were not recreated, and that the new parties would be national in organization, membership, and outlook. The military considered applications by 19 associations, but under its guidelines allowed only five parties to be registered and to contest the 1979 elections. None of these parties was truly socialist, and this reflected the military's own political orientation. It was also assumed that the military would only disengage after passing power to a government that shared similar perceptions and interests. Although these five parties were superficially more nationalistic in composition and policy, many of the dominant personalities of the 1960s returned, and parties quickly became identified with the predecessors of the First Republic.

Institutions of Military Governments

Obviously, military rule is different from civilian rule. There is no attempt made to be democratic, as decisions are issued by decree; there are no elections; there are no political parties; and there is expected to be less debate and criticism, as the military operates by command and obedience.[14] When Maj. Gen. Aguiyi-Ironsi came to power after the coup of January 1966, he established a Supreme Military Council (SMC) of top officers to be the main decision-making forum. In addition, he set up a Federal Executive Council (FEC), which included the top federal permanent secretaries and acted as the bureaucratic arm of the government. Ironsi's decision to scrap federalism and institute a unitary form of government sealed his fate and led to his overthrow in July 1966.

The new head of state, General Yakubu Gowon, continued to use the existing institutions but strengthened the SMC by having it ratify decisions made by the FEC. Gowon resuscitated the federal structure and broke up the four regions into 12 states in May 1967. In the early 1970s, following the civil war, Gowon broadened marginally the base of his government by enlisting civilians to take control of various ministries (though they were still under ultimate control by the military). This infusion of important skills—which the military lacked—did not detract from the negative aspects of Gowon's rule, and he was overthrown in 1975.

Murtala Muhammed (1975–1976) and Olusegun Obasanjo (1976–1979) refined the military institutions of government. Murtala established in 1975 a National Security Organization (NSO) to control opponents of the state, and Obasanjo had a significant impact on government by establishing a third institutional tier, the Council of State. The Council was composed of the military governors of all the states (19 after 1976) who were no longer able to sit on the SMC.

---

[14]A comprehensive survey of the military between 1966 and 1979 is contained in Oyeleye Oyediran, ed., *Nigerian Government and Politics under Military Rule 1966–1979* (London: Macmillan, 1979).

This enabled a distinction to be drawn between state and federal governing bodies and was the pattern adopted by military governments after the demise of civilian rule in December 1983.

THE SECOND REPUBLIC, 1979–1983

Political Parties

To prevent regional identification, each party was required by law to have its headquarters in Lagos and an office in all 19 states of the federation. This regulation ensured some form of national orientation, if not necessarily national support. Membership of the parties was open to all Nigerians and could not be restricted, as had been the case in the First Republic. Similarly, candidates could not be selected on any regionalist, ethnic, or religious grounds, and there had to be regular internal elections for leadership positions. The 1979 Constitution provided all the necessary safeguards and provisions for the maintenance of an equitable system, but political realities strained the system badly and prompted the military's return to government on December 31, 1983.

A fundamental difference in the political process in 1979 was the presence of a total of 19 states in the federation, as the large regional units of the First Republic had been subdivided in 1967 and 1976 to assist democracy and representativeness. The old Northern Region was now broken up into ten states, for example, and the other regions were also divided to give greater expression to minority groups.

National Party of Nigeria (NPN) The NPN drew its strength and support from the states of the North, and bore some resemblance to the old NPC. Its leader, Alhaji Shehu Shagari from Sokoto state, became president of the Second Republic, and the party came to hold a majority in the federal House of Representatives. The party was able to secure victory throughout the North, except in Borno and Kano states, and was able to build alliances in other areas of the country. This was most evident with the selection of the vice president, Dr. Alex Ekwueme, an Igbo from Anambra state in the Southeast, and the chairman of the party, Chief Akinloye, a Yoruba from the Southwest. The party instituted a system of "zoning" by which senior offices would be rotated among the various zones or clusters of states, thus allowing the party to maintain a national image and balance. Some commentators have suggested that this was a ploy to allow a northern elite to rule under a national guise while never losing control over the party or the federation. Non-northerners wanted Shagari to step down after one term in office to rotate the presidency.

The NPN's program was bourgeois in promoting capitalist development, increasing foreign participation in the economy, and preserving the mixed economy developed under the military administration. Unfortunately for the NPN and the country as a whole, the massive oil revenues of the 1970s disappeared rapidly in the early 1980s as the global oil price fell and production and revenue targets were revised downward. Prestige development projects instigated by the NPN became white elephants, and disillusionment set in. Despite the downward economic spiral and the increased hardship faced by the majority, the party's representatives continued their conspicuous consumption of the nation's wealth.

Unity Party of Nigeria (UPN)

The UPN formed under the leadership of Obafemi Awolowo, who had kept the Action Group going as a "social" group during the military era, and was therefore assured of support from the majority of those living in the southwestern states of Ogun, Ondo, Oyo, and Lagos. Awolowo was the party's presidential candidate in 1979 and 1983, running Shagari very close in the 1979 election. The UPN's platform was more radical than that of the NPN, with free schooling, better healthcare facilities, and greater assistance for low-paid labor as its priorities. The party was able to capture the assemblies of the southwestern states, but it was unable in federal elections to make inroads into other parts of the country. Personality and political differences began to eat into UPN support as certain prominent leaders switched loyalty to the NPN, and history appeared to be repeating itself. The 1983 elections showed the NPN allegedly making substantial gains over the UPN, but widespread rioting drew attention to the dubious validity of the result.

Nigeria People's Party (NPP)

The NPP was originally formed by Alhaji Waziri Ibrahim, a wealthy businessman from the northeastern state of Borno. He attempted to pull together a national coalition, but divisions within the party soon made this impossible. Dr. Nnamdi Azikiwe originally stated his desire to remain outside of politics as the "father of the nation," but in December 1978 he agreed to join the NPP and became its presidential candidate, leaving Waziri to form a second party. Most of the NPP's support came from former NCNC members of the old Eastern Region.

The NPP's policies differed little from other parties; they promoted vague ideas of growth and economic development. The party made few inroads into other areas of the country and gained little from its NPN alliance, which was broken in mid-1981.

People's Redemption Party (PRP)

The city of Kano has had a tradition of political radicalism, and the PRP's support was concentrated in that city and in neighboring Kaduna state. Formed under the leadership of Mallam ("teacher") Aminu Kano, the PRP had its roots back in NEPU. The party promoted a progressive platform, particularly on land rights, and thus offered a threat to privilege and established Islamic interests. The NPN eventually managed to draw the PRP into an alliance, and following the death of Aminu Kano in 1983, factionalism weakened its vitality.

Great Nigeria People's Party (GNPP)

The party was formed following the split in the NPP, and the "Great" was added to distinguish between the two. The GNPP was centered on one man, Alhaji Waziri Ibrahim. Waziri was a former NPC minister in the First Republic who had then made his fortune as an arms supplier to the federal government during the civil war. Although the party was registered by the military in 1979, it had little support outside the Northeast.

Nigerian Advance Party (NAP) The NAP had attempted to become a registered party in 1979, but its application was rejected by the military because the party was not nationally organized. The association, under the leadership of Tunji Braithwaite, a Lagos lawyer, set out to establish its organization efficiently and was allowed to contest the 1983 elections as the sixth party. The NAP offered a nonethnic, socialist platform, and its supporters were largely young professionals and students. Although its base was mostly in the Lagos area, it tried to elicit support all over Nigeria, with little success. By refusing to play on ethnic sentiment, the party foundered and was unable to win an election at any level or for any candidate.

The 1979 Elections

Elections took place over five Saturdays in July and August 1979. The first election was for the Senate, and subsequent elections were for the House of Representatives, state assemblies, and state governors. A two-week period was allowed before the election for president. The NPN emerged as the leading party in the elections, taking 38 percent of the votes for the Senate, 37 percent for the House of Representatives, and 36 percent for state assemblies. Shagari polled 5,688,857 votes in the presidential election, over half a million more than his closest rival, Obafemi Awolowo. Despite the appearance of these new parties and competing manifestos, voters still went with old allegiances: "ethnic, regional, religious, and personality-leadership parochialisms"[15] were maximized, and besides the presidential election, "in no election whatsoever did any of the parties present candidates who were not indigenous to the state in which such candidates were contesting."[16]

The results of the presidential election were challenged by Obafemi Awolowo, and the appeal went from an electoral tribunal to the Supreme Court. The constitution called on the presidential victor to win the highest vote as well as score at least 25 percent of the vote in two-thirds of the states. The appeal centered on the question of what was two-thirds of 19. Shagari and the NPN argued successfully that it was twelve and two-thirds states, so he only needed one-sixth of the vote in the thirteenth state. The military government clearly supported Shagari, and "Awo" was again defeated.

The 1983 Elections

The elections in 1983 were the first to be under full civilian control in almost 20 years. The election process cost an estimated $1 billion and involved about 1 million officials. The Federal Electoral Commission (Fedeco) drew up a new electoral register of 65.3 million voters, a staggering increase of 34 percent since 1978. Manipulation of these lists had been so great in some states that increases of 100 percent had been recorded. The NPN acted in its own interests by having the electoral timetable switched to place the presidential election first. The philosophy of this was simple: get Shagari reelected, and then gain from a bandwagon effect in the subsequent elections.

The NPN increased its majorities at all levels and took two-thirds control of the National Assembly. The loosely organized Progressive People's Alliance (UPN, NPP, and GNPP) made little or no advances in NPN territory, but the NPN appeared to make considerable gains across the South. Allegations of electoral abuse brought chaos to the Southwest, where many considered the NPN to have blatantly cheated. This frustration and protest, combined with poor governmental performance and gross corruption, persuaded the military to oust the politicians from power on December 31, 1983, just three months after Shagari had been sworn into office for his second term.

INSTITUTIONS OF THE SECOND REPUBLIC

After four years of consultation and intense debate, Nigerians adopted a new set of institutions for the Second Republic, modeled on the

[15]Ladun Anise, "Political Parties and Election Manifestos," in Oyeleye Oyediran, ed., *The Nigerian 1979 Elections* (London: Macmillan, 1981), p. 89.
[16]Dudley, *Nigerian Government and Politics,* p. 223.

American presidential system. These institutions and respective powers, combined with a redefinition of national values and mores, were enshrined in the 1979 Constitution, which, although suspended after 1983, continued to form the basis of constitutional life in Nigeria until the promulgation of the 1989 Constitution. The 1989 Constitution was never really put into operation, and the 1999 Constitution formed the basis for the Fourth Republic. The 1999 Constitution is very similar to the 1979 Constitution, particularly in terms of the operation of the political institutions. For this reason, the 1979 Constitution is emphasized here, and the structures will not be repeated when we talk about the Fourth Republic.

The 1979 Constitution

The 1979 Constitution appeared to be an excellent document but, unfortunately, its provisions were not fully respected by the politicians. National integration and nation building were stressed as primary political objectives; these goals were to be promoted by encouraging "intermarriage among persons from different places of origin or of different religious, ethnic, or linguistic associations or ties," and by promoting "the formation of associations that cut across ethnic, linguistic, religious or other sectional barriers." Most significantly, the aim was "that loyalty to the nation shall override sectional loyalties."[17] The constitution also guaranteed freedom of speech, information, and association, and provided specific guidelines on the functions and duties of the respective political institutions of the Second Republic.

The President

Unlike in the First Republic, where the president was a ceremonial figure, the 1979 Constitution gave executive powers to the president, similar in range to those of the U.S. president. The pres-

---

[17]The Constitution of the Federal Republic of Nigeria, 1979 (Lagos: Federal Ministry of Information, 1979), Part 1, Section 15.

ident was directly elected by a popular vote throughout the whole country, and would hold office for a maximum of two four-year terms. No electoral college was provided; the president had to win not only the highest number of votes cast, but also one-quarter of the vote in at least two-thirds of the states. Failing that, a second election was to be held within a week with voting restricted to members of the National Assembly and State Houses of Assembly. This was not necessary in 1979 and 1983, because Shagari emerged as winner of the popular ballot.

The president, who had to be a citizen of at least 35 years of age, was officially Head of State, Chief Executive of the Federation, and Commander in Chief of the Armed Forces. The vice president, who was elected on the same party ticket as the president (although some had tried unsuccessfully to have the vice president be the runner-up in the presidential contest), was to succeed the president if the latter became incapacitated or died in office.

The president was able to select his or her own group of ministers, who were not to be members of the National Assembly. The president was responsible for initiating both national and international policies, and held a veto over the legislation passed by the National Assembly, although this veto could be overridden by a two-thirds vote of the Assembly. The process of impeachment against the president could be started by a petition signed by one-third of Senate members, but both a full investigation and final impeachment needed two-thirds support of both houses. This issue never arose in the short life of the Second Republic.

Shehu Shagari was the only president to serve under the 1979 Constitution. Shagari was an experienced politician and wealthy business leader, having initially founded the old Northern People's Congress in his home area in northwestern Nigeria, and then going on to hold three federal ministerial positions between 1960 and 1965. His first cabinet in 1979 contained 42 members reflecting "federal character" (although with only two women), with 23 members from the North (ten states), 4 members from the East (two states), 8 from the West (four states), and 7 from the Middle Belt (three states). Any evenhandedness the NPN government had evaporated as it became dominated by selfish desires and policies and discredited by rampant corruption.

The National Assembly

The National Assembly comprised two houses of equal importance, the Senate and the House of Representatives. The Senate contained 95 members, with 5 representatives from each of the 19 states, irrespective of size or population. The House of Representatives was composed of 449 members whose electoral districts were based on areas of roughly equal population size. Both houses of the National Assembly were responsible for approving legislation before it could be passed on to Shagari for his signature. Each house had equal influence in this task, and each was able to initiate legislation. Senate ratification was necessary for presidential nominations to the Supreme Court, the National Defense Council, and the National Security Council. The Assembly also possessed important influence over the process of creating new states in the federation. Although there were calls for the creation of up to 50 new states, none was able to gain legal recognition in the short tenure of the Second Republic.

Despite the immense effort expended to establish the National Assembly, its operation left much to be desired. The NPN held a majority of seats in both houses through its alliance with the NPP (broken off in 1981), and after the 1983 elections the NPN held this majority by itself. It was never able to control a clear two-thirds majority necessary for constitutional amendments. The failure to implement the Code of Conduct left many Senators and Representatives actively pursuing their business interests from within the Assembly.

State Governments

Each of the 19 states of the federation possessed a governor, deputy governor, and a single House of Assembly. Elections for each assembly were to be held during the same period as federal elections. The constitutional structure operated fairly smoothly in the majority of states, where the branches of government were dominated by a single political party, but serious divisions emerged in Kaduna state, where intense rivalries left an NPN assembly facing a PRP governor. After a series of clashes, the assembly forced through a politically inspired impeachment of the governor, in some ways adapting the presidential system of government to the rules and norms of the former parliamentary system.

MILITARY GOVERNMENTS, 1984–1999

The military's intervention in 1984 was initially well received by Nigerians who had suffered severe economic hardship under the Shagari government. The military could not offer a quick end to that, as chronic debt and deficit problems plagued the country, but it promised a halt to the excessive corruption and abuse of power by the NPN. All political parties were proscribed by the military, the 1979 Constitution was suspended, and political activity in the country was banned.

The government of Muhammadu Buhari (1984–1985) used structures similar to the previous military era but allowed the NSO to run rampant, victimizing many innocent people. When General Ibrahim Babangida came to office in August 1985, he tried to distance himself from Buhari by reshaping the institutions, although some of these changes were cosmetic. He changed the name of the SMC to the Armed Forces Ruling Council (AFRC), but its 29 members (reduced to 19 members in February 1989) remained the central decision makers of the state. Babangida also reorganized the NSO in June 1986 into three bodies: (1) the Defense Intelligence Agency, to oversee defense; (2) the National Intelligence Agency, for intelligence gathering overseas; and (3) the State Security Services, for internal monitoring. In addition, Babangida established two new institutions: the National Defense and Security Council (to provide public security), and the National Defense Council (to ensure territorial integrity).

By integrating a number of civilians into government, though rarely leading politicians, the AFRC gained valuable expertise and presented a softer image of its rule. Nevertheless, the absence of dialogue and the inability to force the AFRC to justify its policies make military governments unacceptable in the long term to most Nigerians.

The military introduced the War Against Indiscipline (WAI) in March 1984 in an attempt to improve national behavior and moral values with a "dose of military discipline." When this program did not have the desired effect, the government revamped WAI in July 1986 to become the National Orientation Movement (NOM). This, in turn, was superseded by the Mass Mobilization for Self-reliance and Economic Recovery (MAMSER) in 1987. All these programs stressed discipline, national consciousness, patriotism, and honesty, but the prevailing social and economic conditions in the country made these goals difficult to achieve, and the military's own example was a poor one.

Babangida's Government

A government white paper, issued on July 1, 1987, followed recommendations made by a National Political Bureau. The 17-person bureau (including one woman), under the chair of Prof. J. S. Cookey, had been established in January 1986 to consider the failures of previous systems and to make recommendations on a successful political framework for the country. Its final report was filed in March 1987, after receiving some 27,000 submissions. Overall, this was an amazing exercise in political development.

Almost every type of political structure was reviewed over the year. Influential commentators favored the breakup of the federation into a confederation, while others recommended the zoning of the country into distinct political units so that each could provide the national leaders in rotation. The idea of joint leadership or "diarchy" of military and civilian elites received noticeable support, even though it had originally been mooted in 1972 by Dr. Nnamdi Azikiwe. This "mixed grill" government, however, did not gain majority support, nor did the idea of "triarchy," somehow bringing traditional leaders—such as chiefs, emirs, and so on—into the institutional framework.

The white paper affirmed that the proposed Third Republic was to inherit many of the institutional features of the Second Republic,[18] including an executive presidential system with a bicameral legislature. In deciding on the retention of this framework, the military rejected the Cookey bureau's majority recommendation that there should be a unicameral legislature. It also rejected the proposal that 10 percent of the seats in the Assembly should be reserved for women and labor unionists. Another major difference with the new framework was that only two political parties were to be registered by the military (and acceptable to it). This novel feature aimed to dissipate ethnic differences by forcing new political alliances.

The ban on political activity was raised on May 3, 1989, along with the promulgation of the new constitution. Within weeks, 49 associations were vying for official registration. Only 13 associations managed to file applications prior to the July 1989 deadline, and after some deliberations the NEC sent a report to the president recommending six associations.

Babangida wanted to screen out radicals and those who threatened to expose the military's corruption. Nevertheless, most observers were surprised in October 1989 when Babangida refused to register any of the parties, claiming that they were residual ethnic parties from previous republics, and announced that the military would organize two new parties and prepare their manifestos. When these were released in December 1989, they followed identical frameworks, except that the Social Democratic Party (SDP) favored somewhat progressive policies, and the National Republican Convention (NRC) supported more conservative, laissez-faire programs. Despite some bitterness about the controlled process, politicians quickly organized to occupy these artificial party shells. The transition program was modified to hold local government elections in December 1990, and gubernatorial

---

[18]*Government's Views and Comments on the Findings and Recommendations of the Political Bureau* (Abuja: Mamser, undated).

elections in December 1991, with national and presidential elections fixed for mid-1992.

The local government elections, held by open ballot in December 1990, were relatively peaceful but had a low turnout. The SDP fared marginally better than the NRC in the country as a whole. Both parties adopted zoning policies, but the bitter divisions within the parties were notable in the 1991 gubernatorial primaries, when fierce intraparty conflicts led the government to postpone the elections twice. Elections for governors and state assemblies were finally held in December 1991, and results showed a fairly even balance between the two parties.

The military's ability to control the transition period undermined the whole process. Increasingly, observers questioned Babangida's intentions. Was it possible for the military to construct democracy within the country, or should that have been left to the civilians themselves? Four attempts in three years to draw up an accurate voter register had brought four different figures. An abortive coup attempt in April 1990 unsettled the military leadership and showed deep divisions within the ranks.[19] The austerity and hardship under the structural adjustment program (SAP) continued to "sap" the economy and promote bitterness and anguish among the populace, especially as stories of high-level corruption multiplied. Workers' strikes increased in intensity during 1991, and religious riots combined with political tensions to provide a volatile atmosphere. The creation of several new states in August 1991, bringing the total to 30, added further impetus to the political race to control the Third Republic and complicated the task of factional balancing.

National Assembly elections held in 1992 gave the SDP control of both federal houses and led to great anticipation for the presidential election slated for December 1992.[20] From a pool of 48 nominees, the parties selected their presidential candidates. The SDP picked Shehu Musa Yar'Adua, a former chief of military staff under Obasanjo, whereas the NRC selected Adamu Ciroma, formerly secretary general of the NPN. The selection of two northerners alarmed many. Even the Sokoto northern establishment was concerned because neither candidate appeared to support its interests. Babangida announced his opposition to the candidates and the postponement of the election in November 1992, raising further doubts about his intentions. A transitional council, headed by Chief Ernest Shonekan, was to help the military run the country until elections could be held and a new president installed in August 1993.

More than 200 candidates for the presidential elections were screened and approved by the military in January 1993. Campaigning began in April 1993, and the parties selected their presidential candidates. The NRC selected Bashir Othman Tofa, a former financial secretary of the NPN, with its vice president being Dr. Sylvester Ugo, from the southeast. The SDP chose Moshood Abiola, a Yoruba Muslim, with its vice president being Babangana Kingibe, a northerner. Tofa had the strong backing of the northern establishment and General Sani Abacha, chief of defense staff.

In the presidential election held on June 12, 1993, Abiola won a clear victory that broke the mold of traditional Nigerian politics. The NEC announced that he had won 8.4 million votes, or 58 percent of the total, and had taken 19 of 30 states, including the key northern states of Kano and Kaduna. Official figures showed that he had gained 97 percent of the military's votes. Despite Abiola's close ties to Babangida, the election results appeared to frighten the northern establishment and senior military officers. Brigadier Hailu Akilu, head of National Intelligence Agencies and a powerful figure in the National Defense and Security Council (NDSC), was quoted as saying, "Abiola will only become president over my dead body."[21] Abacha was also opposed to Abiola.

[19]Julius O. Ihonvbere, "A Critical Evaluation of the Failed 1990 Coup in Nigeria," *Journal of Modern African Studies* 29(4) (1991), pp. 601–626.
[20]William Reno, "Old Brigades, Money Bags, New Breeds, and the Ironies of Reform in Nigeria," *Canadian Journal of African Studies* 27(1) (1993), pp. 66–87.

[21]*New African,* September 1993, p. 13.

TABLE 12.3

PRESIDENTIAL ELECTION, APRIL 2003

Candidate	Party	Votes (million)	% of Vote
Gen. Olusegun Obasanjo	People's Democratic Party (PDP)	24.45	61.94
Gen. Muhammed Buhari	All Nigeria People's Party (ANPP)	12.71	32.19
Gen Emeka Odumegwu-Ojukwu	All Progressive Grand Alliance (APGA)	1.29	3.29
Others		1.03	2.58
Turnout 69.23%			

PARLIAMENTARY ELECTION, APRIL 2003

Senate			House of Representatives		
Party	% of Vote	Seats	Party	% of Vote	Seats
PDP	53.69	76	PDP	54.49	223
ANPP	27.87	27	ANPP	27.44	96
AD (Alliance for Democracy)	9.74	6	AD (Alliance for Democracy)	8.84	34
Others	8.82	—	Others	9.23	4
Turnout 49.23%			Turnout 49.96%		

Babangida announced the annulment of the elections on June 23 and promised that new elections would take place shortly. In early August, these new elections were also canceled, and on August 27 Babangida was forced out of office.

Abacha and Abubakar

Babangida turned over power to a 32-member interim government, headed by Ernest Shonekan, that clearly served only at the military's pleasure. Its mandate was to organize fresh presidential elections and hand over power by March 31, 1994. Chief Shonekan's moderate approach, particularly in economic affairs, was welcomed in the West, but few saw him as holding real power. This was openly revealed on November 17, 1993, when General Sani Abacha appeared to preempt a junior officers coup and took power, overthrowing the interim government and imposing full military rule. This action marked the end of any hope for the rescue of the Third Republic. Abacha had played a critical role in bringing Babangida to power a decade earlier and had remained extremely influential within the military as Babangida's right-hand man.

Abacha moved quickly to gain control. A Hausa, Abacha calmed the fears of the northern establishment by positioning northerners in many top positions, but he aroused the anger of the majority of Nigerians favoring democracy. When Abiola, encouraged by the pro-democracy National Democratic Coalition (Nadeco), returned to the country in June 1994 to claim the presidency, Abacha detained him. Abacha also attempted to appease leading civilians by incorporating them into his government. During the second half of 1994, a two-month strike by oil workers supporting Abiola was beaten down by the military, and a constitutional conference went over the same old ground of considering a framework of government for the country. Issues of federalism and ethnicity were highly debated, but many observers thought the issues ought to be economic development and corruption. The conference called for a transition date of January 1, 1996, but the military forced that date to be withdrawn.

The military received the final report in May 1995 but was preoccupied with other issues. More than 300 officers, including retired generals Obasanjo and Yar'Adua, had been arrested in

February 1995 for allegedly being involved in a coup attempt. There was less evidence of a coup than an attempt by the military to head off dissent by arresting elite officers. Many of those arrested received long-term sentences, including Obasanjo, sparking international criticism.

In October 1995, Abacha announced a new transition program aimed at transferring government to civilians by October 1998.[22] Whereas the constitutional conference had called for the country to be divided into three zones, Abacha announced that six zones would be created: North-East; North-West; Middle Belt; South-West; East-Central; and Southern Minority. Six high-ranking governmental positions would be rotated through the zones. These positions were president, vice president, prime minister, deputy prime minister, senate president, and speaker of the house. No plan was given of how each zone would be demarcated, nor in which order the positions would be rotated.

Furthermore, the presidential system of the Second Republic was to be blended with a parliamentary structure, following along the lines of the French and Russian political structures (observers believed Abacha was attempting to court French financial and diplomatic support). Abacha, with apparent seriousness, announced that this system would operate for a trial period of 30 years. In contrast, few observers were confident that it would even become operational in 1998. Many believed that the military would simply maintain its grip on power, so plunging the country further into chaos. This view remained prominent even after nonpolitical local elections began the transition program in March 1996 and, of course, it turned out to be true.

Abacha manipulated the transition program to allow only five political parties to be registered and then became the presidential candidate of all five parties. His harsh policies left him with many opponents both at home and abroad, but his iron grip on political life positioned him to "civilianize" his military rule in the 1998 elections, just as Jerry Rawlings had done in Ghana, and

Mobutu Seso Seke in Zaire (now Congo). Abacha's death in very suspicious circumstances in June 1998 brought an end to the dark episode in Nigerian political development.

The new military government under General Abdulsalam Abubakar announced yet another transition program. The five political parties were proscribed, and new parties reconstituted. Many political detainees, including Obasanjo, were released, and efforts were made to open dialogue with Western countries which had instituted mild sanctions against the Abacha regime. Unlike other transition programs, this one was scheduled to be completed within a brief twelve months.

THE FOURTH REPUBLIC

As noted earlier, the 1999 Constitution very much followed the 1979 Constitution in terms of the institutional structures to be adopted, and so little will be said here to repeat that information. The reintroduction of the American presidential model of government, complete with Senate and House of Representatives, was perhaps indicative of the widespread support for that system of government, and the inability to alter again the political landscape in such a short period of time. The new constitution was promulgated on May 5, 1999, and Obasanjo sworn in as president on May 29.

Political Parties

The elections had unsurprisingly thrown up new features on the Nigerian political landscape. Three new parties were created to contest the elections.

People's Democratic Party   The PDP, the strongest party, was based on traditional northern political interests (dating back to the NPN of the Second Republic) along with political structures formed by the late Shehu Musa Yar'Adua. This group had urged Abacha not to run in the 1998 elections and developed a powerful financial base, including money from many retired military personnel. Interestingly, the party

[22]*West Africa,* September 25–October 8, 1995, p. 1597; and October 9–15, 1995, pp. 1656–1657.

brought in Obasanjo, a Yoruba, to be their presidential candidate, who beat Alex Ekwueme (the NPN vice president in the Second Republic, and an Igbo) to the nomination. The ticket was balanced with a northerner as vice president, Atiku Abubakar.

All-People's Party   The APP was formed by a number of associations that had been close to the Abacha regime and presumably favored some continuation of the status quo. Much of their support came from the Middle Belt and pockets within the North.

Alliance for Democracy   The AD was formed by associations active in the human rights and democracy movements, who favored a complete restructuring of the political landscape. The AD's power base was primarily in the Yoruba states of the South-West.

The 1999 Elections

At local government elections in December 1998, the PDP took about 60 percent of the councils (the local governments). At the state elections of January 1999, the PDP again performed strongly, and took 21 of 36 governorships. After these elections, the APP and AD agreed on an electoral alliance as their only viable strategy of challenging the PDP. The AD's Olu Falae became the presidential candidate, with the APP's Umaru Shinkafi as his running mate. At elections to the National Assembly held in February 1999, the PDP gained majorities in both federal houses, with 208 seats in the 360-member House of Representatives, and 60 seats in 109-member Senate. The AD took 76 seats in the House and 20 in the Senate, whereas the APP won 69 seats in the House and 24 in the Senate. (Elections in parts of the Delta region were postponed because of security concerns.)

At the presidential elections held on February 27, the two presidential candidates were both Yoruba, an interesting political fact. However, Obasanjo was considered to have sold out to northerners and received little to no support in the South-West, which was carried by Falae.

In Lagos, for example, Obasanjo mustered just 12 percent of the vote. However, such was the national appeal of Obasanjo that he won the election with 62.8 percent of the total vote. He won again in 2003 with 61.9 percent of the vote.

Government Policies

President Obasanjo set out to create a balanced cabinet, which included representatives from most states in the federation, as well as a careful balance of former military and civilian government leaders. Among his first actions was a review of all actions taken by the Abubakar government, many of which were seen as involving corrupt allocation of contracts. Besides his attempts to clamp down on corruption, Obasanjo

Olusegun Obasanjo was elected president in 1999, the first civilian leader of Nigeria since Shehu Shagari was ousted in a coup in 1983. Obasanjo had been a military head of state from 1976–1979. He was re-elected in 2003.

also took aim at the Abacha family, arresting the general's son, Mohammed Abacha, on charges of murdering Kudirat Abiola (Chief Abiola's wife) and Shehu Musa Yar'Adua. He also instigated inquiries into the embezzlement of billions of dollars overseas by the Abacha family.

Political tensions soon engulfed the new civilian government. The adoption of *sharia* law in Zamfara State in October 1999, and similar moves in other northern states (such as Sokoto, Kaduna, Kano, Kebbi, and Katsina) sparked intense religious clashes between Christians and Muslims. New tensions also gripped the Delta region with the increasing militancy of Ijaws, calling for greater distribution of oil revenues back to the region. Calls for Biafran secession resurfaced in 2000, though not with widespread support. The importance of debating the future constitutional framework for the federation took on new urgency, though it was unclear whether such a conference would help or hinder stability.

The future of the Fourth Republic hinges on several difficult issues. Can the government quell the mounting religious differences between Christians and Muslims? Can a long-term settlement be found to the tensions in the oil producing areas of the Niger Delta? Will the country come together for a meaningful debate on the long-term constitutional framework? Can the economy pick up to provide some hope for economic rejuvenation? Democracy is a very difficult form of government to manage, and with such obstacles before it, one must remain uncertain about the future of the Fourth Republic.

JUDICIARY AND LEGAL RIGHTS

Nigeria's legal system has been heavily influenced by norms, traditions, and practices inherited from Britain, but unlike Britain, Nigeria continues to have significant numbers of judicial executions. The country's legal practitioners have retained a relatively high profile and reputation in the country even through long periods of military rule. The judiciary gained credibility during the 1979 and 1983 elections when courts used their constitutional right to amend contested election results. The Nigerian Bar Association (NBA), established as long ago as 1886, attempted to maintain its independence from political pressures by boycotting military tribunals established after the 1983 coup to try politicians suspected of corruption. During the 1980s, the AFRC had at times allowed the legal process to be maintained without excessive pressure. However, the widespread use of military tribunals came under fire in the 1990s for providing poor means of defense for those on trial.

The Civil Liberties Organisation (CLO), founded in 1987, and other groups such as the Committee for the Defense of Human Rights and the National Association for Democratic Lawyers were hounded by the Babangida and Abacha governments. In a damning report published by the CLO in March 1991, the Babangida government was criticized for "executive lawlessness" in its disrespect for court orders, for imposing retroactive legislation, and for taking numerous illegal actions.[23] In mid-1995, the Abacha government preempted possible action in commemorating the second anniversary of Abiola's election victory by arresting about 50 key human rights campaigners. At the end of 1995, the quick military trial and execution of nine Ogoni dissidents led to international condemnation of the judicial process and sanctions against Nigeria by the United States and European Union.

The 1979, 1989, and 1999 Constitutions provided judicial structures at both state and federal levels. At the individual state level, three courts were established: a State High Court, a State Customary Court of Appeal, and a State Sharia Court. A Federal Court of Appeal was inaugurated in 1979 to handle appeals from these three sets of courts. Pressure from Islamic groups to have a Federal Sharia Court was unsuccessful, as only northern states instituted the State Sharia Courts. Also at the federal level was a Federal High Court and a Federal Supreme Court. The Supreme Court was given the power

---

[23]Civil Liberties Organization of Nigeria, *Executive Lawlessness in the Babangida Regime* (Lagos, 1991).

of constitutional review and used it immediately in 1979 to consider the disputed presidential election result and to confirm, in a split ruling, Shehu Shagari as the victor.

LOCAL GOVERNMENT

The structures and role of local governments have varied considerably since independence. During the First Republic, each region had its own system of local government. In the East and West, local governments were loosely organized and relatively weak, whereas in the North they remained strong and influential, particularly when used by emirs as their channel of rule. In the early 1970s, local government structures began to change as the western states instituted a council-manager system of administration and the northern states strove to weaken the powers of traditional rulers. In 1976, the military government introduced the Local Government Edicts, which forced all local governments in Nigeria to adopt similar structural and operating procedures. Decisions of all local governments were to be based on majority voting, and all governments were to be single-tiered, secular authorities. These changes helped to make local governments the natural third level of government in the country after the federal and state levels.

The trends of weakening the role of traditional rulers and increasing the efficiency of these local governments continued in the 1980s and 1990s. The number of local governments increased during the Second Republic, but the military after 1984 cut back the number to 301. The situation was dramatically altered in May 1989, when 148 new local government areas were created, bringing the total to 449. This action was taken to increase the responsiveness of local governments to the needs of the people. More areas were created in August 1991 after the creation of nine new states, bringing the total to 589. Although their powers are often undermined by state governments, local governments remain a primary level of participatory democracy, and it is only at the ward level that party

membership was organized in the transition to the Third Republic. In 1978, 1988, 1990, 1996, and 1998, local government areas provided the initial elections and candidates as the first step to civilian rule.

INTEREST GROUPS

The distinction between interest groups and political parties is blurred in Nigeria, both because of the strong sectional interests, which parties have promoted, and because parties have been banned for more than two-thirds of the postindependence period. Most parties of the Second Republic developed from "social" organizations that were active prior to the raising of the ban on political activity. These groups generally comprised business leaders, high-ranking administrators, professionals, and former politicians. But these are by no means the only type of interest group, and it is useful to consider the most important ones here.

Civil Society Groups

A very significant political development has been the growth of civil society groups, especially during the 1990s. In the face of growing abuse of power by the Babangida and Abacha military regimes, these groups organized to provide societal opposition, both at home and abroad. These groups included civil rights movements, prodemocracy groups, special interest groups, unions and churches, and various umbrella groups. In general, their role in promoting dialogue and pushing toward their goal of greater democracy in the country provided evidence to bolster mainstream theory on the importance of these groups in democratization.

However, two caveats at least must be added. First, many of the more radical groups were perceived to be ethnically based (often Yoruba), and so were resisted by other ethnic groups in the country on those grounds. Second, some groups, especially in the Delta region, had very narrow, sectarian interests at stake in their organizations. So rather than promoting the democracy project, they often served to undermine it by their radical actions.[24] Despite these caveats, the growing importance of civil society groups augurs well for continuing dialogue within the Fourth Republic.

Business Groups

One of the most influential interest groups over the last two decades has been the so-called Kaduna mafia. Kaduna is the former capital of the old Northern Region and remains an important locus of northern Islamic influence in the country. Members of this loosely organized group are prominent businesspeople, retired senior military officers, and others of equivalent stature. Nobody outside of this mafia really knows who belongs to the group, or whether it even exists, but it is a group about whom many have commented in recent years. These influential people are believed to have been inspirational in planning the December 1983 coup by giving backing to the coup leader, Muhammadu Buhari, and by wanting to push aside Shehu Shagari, whose economic mismanagement (despite his northernness) was damaging the infrastructure and business environment of the country. The pro-business mafia received a setback when General Babangida came to office in 1985, but it still casts a shadow over governmental affairs and was considered instrumental in maintaining the Abacha regime in power.

There are, naturally, other groups of businesspeople, including retired senior military officers, throughout the country who have been able to influence state and federal policy. Given the lack of constraints on political leaders seeking economic fortunes while in office, the business community has had a considerable impact on government by ensuring policies to suit their interests. Although not uncommon elsewhere, the open and blatant business group involvement

in the political process has been, and will continue to be, of major significance.

Labor Unions

In contrast to the successful interaction of business and political elites, the Nigeria Labour Congress (NLC) has had little success in influencing the policies of civilian or military governments or in promoting a more socialistic orientation in the country. Divisive internal battles within the labor movement caused the Obasanjo military government to intervene and restructure the labor movement in 1978 into a total of 42 unions, all under the umbrella of the NLC. This has not prevented further internal squabbles. Membership declined considerably in the early 1990s because economic hardship led to unemployment and a growing desperation to cling to a job, whether unionized or not.

The NLC has aligned itself with radical political forces in the past but has been unsuccessful in attempting to make class issues the basis of political conflict, rather than ethnicity. The unions organized their first general strike in 1964, when 800,000 workers gained higher wages and the action by unions was considered a "strike against politicians" to protest the chaotic condition of the country. Strikes were made illegal by the military government after 1966, but numerous strikes nevertheless occurred in the 1970s and beyond. These strikes provided the stimulus for private and public salaries to rise by 30 percent after the Abedo Commission reported in 1971, and then helped provide even larger raises (up to 100 percent for the lowest paid) following the Udoji Commission in 1975.

Generally speaking, however, unions have not been a dominant force within society. As Douglas Rimmer concluded, labor "has been a fitfully active force, lacking sustained political influence and usually inexpert and ineffective in negotiation."[25] The NLC has vehemently protested the

[24]Augustine Ikelegbe, "Civil Society, Oil and Conflict in the Niger Delta Region of Nigeria: Ramifications of Civil Society for a Regional Resource Struggle," *Journal of Modern African Studies* 39(3) 2001, pp. 437–469.

[25]Anthony Kirk-Greene and Douglas Rimmer, *Nigeria since 1970: A Political and Economic Outline* (London: Hodder and Stoughton, 1981), p. 106.

economic reforms implemented since 1986 but with little success. The NLC executive was dismissed by the government in February 1988, and a new structure was organized. The NLC actively supported the creation of a true Socialist Party and the development of a Socialist ideology for the country, but was warned repeatedly by the military to stay out of any political affiliations.

When the presidential election result was canceled in 1993, there were massive strikes across the country, but these failed to change government policy, and workers were forced back to work.

The Media

The media in Nigeria were, until the 1990s, among the most active and independent in sub-Saharan Africa. The media have been outspoken since independence, despite periodic threats and intimidation by various governments. They have not always been impartial, however, as many newspapers or state-controlled radio stations have favored a political party or regional interest, but there has remained a willingness to take firm positions on issues of national importance, particularly corruption.

Recent military governments have attempted to control the media's coverage of events. Babangida introduced Decree 19, under which it became an offense to comment negatively on the government's handling of the transition program, although discussion and positive suggestions were still acceptable. Despite active protests by the National Union of Journalists (which has been in existence since 1955), numerous jail sentences were handed out to journalists in the early 1990s and newspapers closed down for publishing articles embarrassing to the government. One prominent journalist, Dele Giwa, was assassinated in mysterious circumstances in November 1986. Giwa had written several scathing articles on government policy and fell victim to a parcel bomb which appeared to have arrived in a package carrying the government seal. There was intense speculation that the government's security forces were responsible, but no firm evidence was uncovered

at the time (later evidence pointed to the Babangida government). Under the Abacha regime, action against journalists and newspapers increased, but these have since relaxed under the civilian government of Obasanjo.

Book authors have also been major critics of Nigerian development, and their attacks have been much more difficult to contain. There are many excellent Nigerian authors helping to promote political development in this way, most notably Chinua Achebe and Wole Soyinka, the winner of the 1986 Nobel Prize for Literature. Soyinka in particular was outspoken in his condemnation of the Babangida and Abacha regimes.

Religious Groups

It is easier to comment that religious groups have an impact on the political process than to pinpoint the groups involved and the policies influenced. During the First Republic, the Sultan of Sokoto and the Islamic establishment had obvious influence on policy through the sultan's brother, Alhaji Ahmadu Bello, the Sardauna of Sokoto, the Northern Premier, and the leader of the NPC. This influence was less evident in the Second Republic, but Shagari was from Sokoto state and had close connections to the sultan. An indication of the declining influence of the Islamic establishment has been noticed in recent years, particularly during the Babangida administration, when emissaries were dispatched to Lagos to pressure the military to modify policies.

The overall purpose of this lobbying pressure is to maintain the influence and cohesion of Islam, particularly in the North (and especially since the North is no longer a monolithic bloc), to keep the *sharia* system of courts and justice, and to attempt to maintain Nigeria's foreign policy on pro-Islamic-Arab lines. Nigeria's decision to become a member of the Organization of Islamic Conference (OIC) in 1986 was considered to be a concession by Babangida to the powerful northern lobby, both religious and business. At a more popular, domestic level, the Islamic League maintains the loyalty of many Muslims and is outspoken against any policy that threatens the status of Muslims. In recent years, pressure has been exerted over issues such as state creation, education, and family planning. Fundamentalism has been of obvious concern since 1980, with the challenge of its ideology and with the riots that have taken place, but its impact on policy has been minimal.

The Christian Association of Nigeria (CAN) helps to bring together the opinions of a diverse range of Christian churches and groups, and it exerts influence on their behalf. The CAN stands to protect Christian interests against what it considers to be aggressive and expansionist Islam. The organization is also working to maintain the secular disposition of the country and prevent the attachment of Nigeria to Islamic organizations overseas, such as the OIC and the Islamic Bank. During the 1990s, the CAN was at its most active, and Christians sought to oppose the growth of *sharia* law within northern states. The deaths of thousands in religious riots over the past two decades have continued to remind everyone of the political potency of religion.

Universities

Universities provide the base for intellectual challenge to the status quo. By 2004, there had developed 53 federal universities, 6 state universities, and some 250 polytechnics and colleges in the country. The Academic Staff Union of Nigerian Universities (ASUU) has organized numerous actions in the past to attempt to influence a more radical appraisal of Nigerian development. Students have also been highly critical of government policy, notably structural adjustment and the increasing hardship faced by students on university campuses. The military and paramilitary police were involved in many campus clashes with students during the 1990s. For all these challenges, little political headway has really been gained, and the universities have been unable to link up with labor unions to make their views and actions more effective.

Declining financial assistance to higher education has led to deteriorating conditions and a falling standard of education on the campuses. Government harassment of academics during the 1990s combined with low salaries also led to an exodus abroad of many Nigerian faculty. Full professors, on average, earn less than $100 a month.

Universities remain a critical center of action for democracy and consequently will stay very closely involved in efforts to strengthen the prospects for stability under the Fourth Republic. However, the continuing involvement of students in riots, particularly religious-based, will also undermine the Obasanjo government.

Thinking Critically

1. What are the main issues affecting the democratization process within Nigeria?
2. What similarities and differences are there between the civilian and military elites? Which group has done a better job of leading the country, and why?
3. What common threads link political parties through each of the civilian periods of government?
4. Which interest groups are most influential in Nigerian politics? What impact have they had on the political process?
5. Is a presidential system of government best suited for Nigeria?

KEY TERMS

Action Group (AG) *(663)*
Armed Forces Ruling Council (AFRC) *(671)*
ceremonial president *(665)*
civilian elite *(660)*
diarchy *(672)*
electoral systems *(664)*
executive president *(670)*
Federal Electoral Commission (Fedeco) *(669)*
federalism *(659)*
Kaduna mafia *(671, 679)*
military elite *(666–667)*
National Assembly *(671)*
National Convention of Nigerian Citizens (NCNC) *(663)*
National Party of Nigeria (NPN) *(660, 667–668)*
Nigeria Labour Congress (NLC) *(679)*
Nigeria People's Party (NPP) *(668)*

Northern People's Congress (NPC) *(660)*
parliamentary and presidential systems *(675)*
Republics, the First, Second, and Third *(659)*
Supreme Military Council (SMC) *(667)*
triarchy *(671)*
zoning *(668)*

*F*URTHER READINGS

Aborisade, Oladimeji, and Robert J. Mundt. *Politics in Nigeria, 2ⁿᵈ ed.* (New York: Longman, 2002).

Cowen, Michael, and Liisa Laakso, eds. *Multiparty Elections in Africa* (Oxford: Currey, 2002).

Diamond, Larry. *Class, Ethnicity and Democracy in Nigeria. The Failure of the First Republic* (Syracuse, NY: Syracuse University Press, 1988).

Diamond, Larry, Anthony Kirk-Greene, and Oyeleye Oyediran, eds. *Transition without End: Nigerian Politics and Civil Society under Babangida* (Boulder, CO: Lynne Rienner, 1997).

Falola, Toyin, and Julius Ihonvbere. *The Rise and Fall of Nigeria's Second Republic* (London: Zed, 1985).

Ihonvbere, Julius O., and Timothy M. Shaw. *Illusions of Power: Nigeria in Transition* (Trenton, NJ: Africa World Press, 1998).

Joseph, Richard A. *Democracy and Prebendal Politics in Nigeria* (Cambridge: Cambridge University Press, 1987).

Maier, Karl. *This House Has Fallen: Midnight in Nigeria* (New York: Public Affairs, 2000).

Nnoli, Okwudiba. *Ethnicity and Development in Nigeria* (Aldershot, UK: Avebury, 1995).

Odetola, Theophilius O. *Military Politics in Nigeria: Economic Development and Political Stability* (New Brunswick, NJ: Transaction, 1978).

Olorunsola, Victor A. *Soldiers and Power: The Development Performance of the Nigerian Military Regime* (Stanford, CA: Hoover Institution Press, 1977).

Olowu, Dele, Kayode Soremekun, and Adebayo Williams, eds. *Governance and Democratisation in Nigeria* (Ibadan: Spectrum Books, 1995).

Oyebade, Adebayo, ed. *The Transformation of Nigeria* (Trenton: Africa World Press, 2002).

Oyediran, Oyeleye, ed. *Nigerian Government and Politics under Military Rule 1966–1979* (London: Macmillan, 1979).

Oyediran, Oyeleye, ed. *The Nigerian 1979 Elections* (London: Macmillan, 1981).

Panter-Brick, Keith, ed. *Soldiers and Oil: The Political Transformation of Nigeria* (London: Frank Cass, 1978).

Rotberg, Robert I., ed. *Crafting the New Nigeria: Confronting the Challenges* (Boulder: Rienner, 2004).

Soyinka, Wole. *The Open Sore of a Continent: A Personal Narrative of the Nigerian Crisis* (New York: Oxford University Press, 1996).

C. PUBLIC POLICY

Nigeria's economy is dominated by oil. The export of this single commodity has consistently accounted for some 90 percent of the country's total foreign exchange earnings. Since 1970, the country has earned some $320 billion in export revenues from oil. Given oil's critical position in the economy, the commodity has also had a strong influence in shaping the country's foreign policy, especially during the oil boom years of the late 1970s, when Nigeria flexed its nascent muscles on the world stage. The relative demise of the oil market—or more specifically the OPEC oil cartel—in the 1980s and 1990s caused serious economic dislocation, and, when combined with gross mismanagement and corruption, limited Nigeria's ability to strike a bolder profile in world politics. The failure to diversify economic output into high-tech, capital-intensive industry, or any other areas, has stifled aspirations of the current Obasanjo government to move into the ranks of the Newly Industrializing Countries (NICs).

The broad sweep of globalization and neoliberal imperatives laid down by institutions such as the International Monetary Fund and World Bank have had an impact on Nigerian political economy. Pressures to privatize state-owned companies and open up the economy to foreign ownership have increased over the last decade and have intensified for the current Obasanjo administration. Some successes have been achieved, but these have done little to remove Nigeria from the underclass and impoverished within the global economy. Why has an apparently wealthy country, certainly by African standards, been unable to achieve more economic success and distribute more benefits to the majority of its population?

developed, with crops grown not for domestic consumption but for export overseas. During the early part of the twentieth century, Nigeria's agriculture was forged into the classic colonial (or in world-systems theory terminology "peripheral"), export-oriented structure, with groundnuts produced in the North, cocoa in the Southwest, and palm oil in the Southeast. The British built a rail system to freight these commodities (and minerals) to the ports, but not to provide a means of passenger transportation. This rail framework is still used today, although it is in desperate need of repair and modernization.

At independence, these three commodities together contributed the majority of Nigeria's export earnings. The major trading partner was Britain, which retained a controlling hand in many sectors of the Nigerian economy. Minimal horizontal trade was developed with neighboring African states, which had also been geared to cash-crop production and vertical integration with the European colonial powers. During the First Republic, little in the way of structural economic change occurred. Political independence may well have been won, but Nigeria's economic profile remained basically unchanged; British involvement, investment, and areas of control were still being maintained. The impact of European and North American economic forces on the economy altered marginally in the 1970s, but many political economists argue that external factors remain of great significance today in Nigeria. This is especially the case regarding the privatization of state enterprises, the increasing emphasis on foreign investment, the problems of international debt, and the strong role of the IMF and World Bank.[26]

THE ECONOMY

The traditional pattern of agriculture prior to colonial occupation was one of subsistence farming, but British intervention radically altered the nature of production. Cash-crop agriculture was

[26]For a discussion of issues in the Nigerian economy, see Kirk-Greene and Rimmer, *Nigeria since 1970;* Gavin Williams, ed., *Nigeria: Economy and Society* (London: Rex Collings, 1976); and Julius O. Ihonvbere and Timothy M. Shaw, *Towards a Political Economy of Nigeria* (Aldershot, UK: Avebury, 1988).

Farm workers in Nigeria. Over 70 percent of workers are employed in agriculture.

Oil Bonanza

Through geological good fortune, oil has been the single most important factor in Nigeria's economic development over the last 30 years, providing both positive and negative effects. Nigeria's oilfields are concentrated in the South-East, in the Delta region of the Niger river, and a significant proportion of them are off-shore. Oil had been produced in the early 1960s, but the growth of the industry was hampered by the civil war. Once the war was over in 1970, oil production increased rapidly. From a level around the time of independence of 5,000 barrels a day (b/d), production had risen to 1.4 million b/d in 1970, and reached a peak of 2.3 million b/d in 1979. Throughout the 1970s, oil revenues increased by 30 percent a year, and in 1980 rose to $24.94 billion. By early 1989, production had fallen to 1.2 million b/d, and income was only $4.22 billion. The slight boom during the Gulf

crisis of 1990–1991 helped income, but earnings had fallen back again to $5.27 billion in 1998 and remained depressed into the early 2000s.

The government's expenditure levels rose dramatically in the 1970s as a result of the financial bonanza. By 1980, the government was spending more money in one day than its predecessor in 1960 had spent in two months. The tremendous financial gains from oil led, in contrast, to rapid stagnation of other sectors. By the mid-1970s, the contribution to exports of the staple agricultural commodities of groundnuts, cocoa, and palm oil had fallen to zero. Oil ruled.

Nigeria joined the Organization of Petroleum Exporting Countries (OPEC) in 1971 to promote its economic (and political) objectives and established the Nigeria National Oil Corporation (NNOC) to monitor oil production. The NNOC was merged with the Ministry of Petroleum in 1977 to form the Nigeria National Petroleum Corporation (NNPC). The government introduced in 1972 an Indigenization Decree, which prohibited foreigners from certain economic sectors and limited participation to 40 percent in others. The major overseas oil corporations, such as Shell, Gulf, Mobil, and Texaco-Chevron were all limited to a 40 percent stake in the oil sector. Today, this partnership continues, though companies have been allowed slightly higher percentage controls. Superficially, the Indigenization laws appeared to shift economic control into Nigerian hands, but overseas interests remained extremely influential. In addition, leading Nigerian entrepreneurs—both inside and outside government—did not always operate with the national interest at heart, and many simply set out to decimate national wealth. These "lootocrats," as they have been termed, operated within a system of "pirate capitalism" that effectively wasted a golden opportunity to provide real economic development for the country.[27]

Lavish prestige-enhancing projects were undertaken, such as the construction of a new federal capital at Abuja (on the model of Brasilia and Canberra). Abuja was built in the geographical center of the country partly to appease strong northern political interests who were unhappy that the capital was in the southern port of Lagos. Abuja (officially made the capital in December 1991) arguably was more representative of the whole country, being located in its center. A worldwide black arts festival (FESTAC) was hosted in Lagos in 1977 at great expense, and it was held up as a symbol of Nigeria's growing status in the world. By the end of the 1970s, President Shagari was actively threatening to use the "oil weapon" against Western countries to promote foreign policy goals, especially in ostracizing the apartheid government in South Africa.

During this era, there was skewed development or growth without development in the country. Money was often diverted to unnecessary projects and pockets, while deserving schemes, primarily agricultural and infrastructural ones, suffered badly. Urban migration gathered pace while investment in rural areas dwindled. Universities were built at a rapid pace all over the country, but then could not be financially maintained. Overall, efforts to improve the living conditions of the majority of Nigerians fell short. The opportunities offered by oil were squandered by successive governments, and when the oil glut emerged and prices collapsed in the early 1980s, the economy reeled.

Oil Bust: Rethinking Development Priorities

The shrinkage of the economy after the early 1980s was a painful process to watch. In 1990, Nigeria's national earnings were only 20 percent of the 1980 figure. Industries, which had grown in the 1970s, were generally dependent upon imported spare parts, so they ground to a halt as supplies were cut. Nigeria found that its agricultural production had declined to such a level that the country could not feed itself. The rural areas, already depressed, suffered even greater hardship. Formerly in a position of handing out loans to African neighbors, Nigeria now had to look around for loans itself. As with the majority of developing states, Nigeria's debt situation became alarming, and rose to over $30 billion in 2000, with a challenging debt repayment schedule. One of President Obasanjo's earliest tasks in 1999 was to negotiate more favorable terms with foreign lenders.

Though definitions of development vary considerably, there is general acceptance among scholars that development means a reduction in both the absolute level of poverty and the economic inequalities between segments of the population. During the oil boom years, the government appeared to lose sight of these, as growth alone became synonymous with development. Some significant successes were recorded, most notably the provision of education in the country. At the primary school level

---

[27]Sayre P. Schatz, "Pirate Capitalism and the Inert Economy of Nigeria," *Journal of Modern African Studies* 22(1) (1984), pp. 45–57; Nicholas Balabkins, *Indigenization and Economic Development: The Nigerian Experience* (Greenwich, CT: JAI Press, 1982); Thomas J. Biersteker, *Multinationals, the State, and Control of the Nigerian Economy* (Princeton, NJ: Princeton University Press, 1987).

Oil wells in the River Niger Delta. Oil has been the single most important factor in Nigeria's economic development.

(grades 1 through 6), the number of students increased from 2.9 million in 1960 to 11.5 million in 1980. But in the early 2000s, with over 2 million students leaving school and hitting the already saturated job market annually, the underlying economic problems and weaknesses remain just as obvious.

Per capita income figures have worsened in recent years, as have other economic indicators. These problems are accentuated by the rapid growth of the population at about 3.3 percent a year, one of the highest figures in the world. In 2000, according to the United Nations, 45 percent of the population was below 15 years of age, and the average fertility rate stood at a high six children per female (though down from 6.5 two decades earlier). The seriousness of this problem has led to several national drives for population control. Social norms, however, continue to provide resistance. In the Islamic North, for example, men may legally have four wives, and often

are reluctant to limit their family size for economic, status, and religious reasons. In the South, similar social pressures are present, though women's groups increasingly pressure for family planning policies.

One should stress that the country has made developmental gains in a number of sectors. Average life expectancy in 2005 was 50 years, up from 45 years in 1980. Adult illiteracy rates of 25 percent (men) and 40 percent (women) in 2004 were improvements on figures from a decade earlier. The infant mortality rate of 83 per 1,000 live births in 1999 was considerably lower than many African neighboring states, though still painfully high compared with countries such as France (5/1000) or the United States (7/1000). Overall, there were signs of beneficial development. Nevertheless, in 2004 Nigeria is still ranked among the poorest 30 countries in the world on the Human Development Index, based on infant mortality, literacy levels, and real GDP per capita.

Despite the vast oil earnings, the country's GNP per capita of $900 in 2004 is only slightly better than in the 1960s before oil was exported.

A structural adjustment program (SAP) was begun in 1985 to attempt to restructure and diversify the economy, and this has been a stop-go project down to the present. The initial program included the privatization of some state-owned corporations—including the NNPC—as well as the massive devaluation of the naira (the naira immediately fell in value from roughly 1 dollar to 10 cents; today its value is less than 1 cent) and the restructuring of the agricultural sector. Although these have proven marginally beneficial in an economic sense, their social impact on the population has been devastating. Inequality has deepened, as has general poverty and hardship, and environmental problems worsen.

The IMF and World Bank, as well as numerous Western donors, have demanded commitment to SAP from successive governments, resulting in increasing bitterness among the Nigerian populace. The Shonekan administration during 1993 committed Nigeria firmly to IMF policies, but Abacha's first budget in January 1994 reversed structural adjustment, reverting back to fixed exchange rates and tight trade controls. IMF pressure led to a softening of these policies in the 1995 budget (though not necessarily their implementation), but confusion over the government's economic and political policies left it isolated in international financial communities until 1999. Only the death of Abacha and the election of the civilian Obasanjo administration has helped to heal that rift, though Obasanjo's close ties with the West have not brought dramatic domestic developmental benefits.

Revenue Allocation

Revenue allocation has been a divisive issue; it set states clashing against one another over their

Lagos, major port and former capital of Nigeria. Its population in 2005 is 13 million.

A CLOSER LOOK

12.4

THE ENVIRONMENT

Concern for environmental damage has grown dramatically over recent years in the world as a whole, although little concrete action has been taken to date by industrialized powers. In Nigeria, the problems of merely making a living in a severely depressed economy leave little time for concern or money for action on the environment. The government, however, took some action in 1989 by setting up the Federal Environmental Protection Agency (FEPA). The greatest concerns in Nigeria focus on pollution from oil spills, the storage of hazardous and toxic waste, the encroachment of the Sahara desert, and the rapid deforestation linked to rapid urbanization and overpopulation. Ironically for a global oil power, wood still remains the primary source of energy for most, and efforts at reforestation have not kept up with destruction of existing woodland.

Structural adjustment has put even greater strains on the government and has left less money available for a thorough conservation program. Consequently, with the Nigerian population expected to triple over the next 50 years, prospects are grim for the ecological balance of the country.

rights and needs and caused conflict between federal and state governments over respective allocations. The main issue at stake is how the income generated from economic production around the country is collected by the federal government and then how, and on what basis, it is redistributed to the states. Put bluntly, the question is: who owns the oil?[28] At a theoretical level, this raises important questions about the nature of the state. Should the state be constructed to control resources at the national level, or should it be present to facilitate and emphasize the multi-ethnic and subnational elements that exist, focusing on a more pluralist notion of the state?

During the 1950s, there were several changes in revenue allocations given by the colonial administration to the regions. Initially, the North pressed for allocations based on population size, the West on derivation of revenue, and the East on need. These positions reflected the regions strengths and/or needs. As their respective economic profiles changed, and as oil exploration grew in the East, the Western Region

based its claims on uniformity, whereas the East began to favor derivation of income as a major influence on allocation decisions.

After independence the debate on revenue allocation intensified, but successive governments tended to favor derivation of income as a primary factor in assessing federal allocations. In 1970, a Distributable Pool was inaugurated. Using this pool, the federal government shared out payments to states, with half of the amount paid equally to all the states, and the other half paid on the basis of state population size. In 1975, this pool system was modified to receive 80 percent of revenue allocated to states, with the remaining 20 percent paid directly to the state of derivation. Income tax, now under federal control, was also paid back directly to the states. The Shagari government established the Okigbo Commission in 1980—the eighth such commission since 1946 to consider the allocation issue.

The new revenue act, initiated in 1982, decreased the influence of derivation to 5 percent (the NPN-controlled states were essentially nonproducers of oil) and stressed relative need and population size in allocations to states. The act consolidated the strength of the federal government, which kept 60 percent of all revenue generated nationally, with the remaining 30 percent and 10 percent allocated to states and local gov-

---

[28]John Boye Ejobowah, "Who Owns the Oil? The Politics of Ethnicity in the Niger Delta of Nigeria," *Africa Today* 47(1) (2000), pp. 29–47.

ernments, respectively. The Babangida administration changed these figures to 50 percent for the federal government, 35 percent to the states, and 15 percent to local governments, and at the same time allowed local governments more control over their spending. But derivation dropped to 3 percent, sparking off clashes in Ogoniland[29] and other areas of the Delta region during the 1990s. In October 1995, Abacha announced that 13 percent of revenue would be returned to areas of derivation. However, the abject poverty of those living in the Delta region among the oil wells creating Nigeria's wealth continues to provide simmering resentment and agitation.

FOREIGN POLICY

Relations with African states, particularly in western and southern Africa, are considered priority areas of policy. Nigeria does have extensive diplomatic contacts with Western countries, however, and worked through these both to bring improved trade relations for itself and to pressure for change in apartheid South Africa prior to 1990. On the basis of its economic and demographic strength, Nigeria has always considered itself one of the leading countries in Africa, and its foreign policy has been geared to reflect this. Although there are numerous linkages with many African countries, particularly neighboring countries through the Economic Community of West African States (ECOWAS), the level of trade and general economic contacts with them remains relatively low; relations can thus appear to lack a degree of depth and substance.

During the early 1960s, the governing elite was content to play a quiet, conservative role in African and world affairs, and during the civil war (1967–1970) policy was geared toward securing a military victory against the secessionists. With the advent of the oil boom in the 1970s, Nigeria pursued an increasingly forceful and active role in world politics, especially within

international organizations such as the United Nations, but this did not automatically lead to any greater successes. While accepting a degree of generalization, it is possible and constructive to consider foreign policy over the past four decades to illuminate the fluctuations of style, emphasis, and content.

The 1960s

From independence in 1960 until the outbreak of civil war in 1967, Nigeria's foreign policy emphasized caution and a low profile, with a strong reliance placed on close relations with the West, and Britain in particular. This orientation was influenced by the conservative nature of the governing elite, with its strong Islamic roots, but it was also a consciously pursued policy that sought to distance the country from the provocative radicalism of its Anglophone rival in the region, Ghana. The Ghanaian leader, Kwame Nkrumah, advocated a single continental government for Africa, but Nigeria and the majority of African states resisted this and supported closer international cooperation. These moderate states were successful in 1963 in having the new continental association, the Organization of African Unity (OAU), established within a loose, intergovernmental framework. Such conservatism in Nigeria also led to the refusal (on British advice) to allow the Soviet Union to establish an embassy in the country until 1962.

It would be wrong to see Nigerian policy in a completely negative and passive manner, as it contained forceful stands on a number of issues. Its relations with Britain were strained in 1961 after its successful pressure to force South Africa out of the Commonwealth. In the following year, the Anglo-Nigerian Defense Pact, which gave Britain military training rights in Nigeria, was abrogated by the federal government following student protests and active condemnation of this quasi-colonial arrangement by Obafemi Awolowo and the Action Group. This protest contributed to Awolowo's later treason trial (following alleged subversive links with Ghana) and his subsequent imprisonment, but it did little to affect the dominant economic linkages with Britain. British military

---

[29]Eghosa E. Osaghae, "The Ogoni Uprising: Oil Politics, Minority Agitation and the Future of the Nigerian State," *African Affairs* 94 (1995), pp. 325–344.

THE CASE OF OGONILAND

The Ogoni people in southeastern Nigeria account for less than 1 percent of the country's population, but their land hosts some 70 percent of the country's oilfields. Even though much of the country's wealth emanates from Ogoniland, the Ogoni people have seen very little returned, and their standard of living remains poor (and other small Delta ethnic groups face similar dilemmas). Unemployment is estimated at 85 percent, literacy at 10 percent, infant mortality at 40 per 1,000 children born; and chronic pollution has ruined much of the farming land.

During the 1990s, the Ogoni challenged the federal government and oil companies, primarily Shell, to improve their living conditions and local environment, with action spearheaded by the Movement for the Survival of Ogoni People (MOSOP). MOSOP also called for a restructuring of Nigeria into a looser confederation of autonomous (ethnic) states, with each state having considerable control over revenue generated within it. By 1993, Shell, Agip, and Elf were estimated to have lost $200 million as a result of protests, and these companies put pressure on the government to terminate the actions.

The military, directly threatened by these actions, acted ruthlessly in suppressing the Ogoni, and following a military tribunal late in 1995, nine Ogoni leaders, including the internationally renowned writer Ken Saro-Wiwa, were hanged for allegedly inciting others to kill four pro-government Ogoni leaders. Prosecution witnesses admitted being bribed by the military, and those convicted were denied an appeal. Such highly questionable justice provoked outrage around the world; temporary expulsion from the Commonwealth and the freezing of aid and arms transfers by the EU and United States were among the actions taken. The Abacha regime was clearly stunned by the reaction but hardened its siege mentality in 1996. Shell, though battered by hostile public opinion for its actions against the Ogoni, appeared likely to maintain strong investments in the Delta area, particularly in a future $3.6 billion liquefied natural gas project.

Under the current Obasanjo government, problems in the Delta region have continued. An Ijaw activist group has called for the removal of all foreign oil corporations from Nigeria and has intensified violent action in the region. In July 2002, women's groups occupied oil fields in a nonviolent political action that won concessions on hiring and development funding for their villages.

instructors also continued to train Nigerian troops. Nigeria's almost instinctive suspicion of French motivations in Francophone West Africa—all of its neighbors are former French colonies and remain French-speaking today— were intensified in 1961 following France's unscrupulous action in holding atomic tests in the southern desert of its then colonial possession, Algeria. This action outraged Nigerians and led to a break in diplomatic relations with France which lasted for several years.

The civil war, which broke out in mid-1967, forced a reconsideration of both domestic and foreign policy. Western countries, hampered by their own internal pressure groups sympathetic to Biafra's suffering (and oil reserves), were reluctant to sell the large quantities of military supplies requested by the federal government. The French were openly pro-Biafra, hoping to see Nigeria split into weaker territorial units. Consequently, in its time of greatest need, the government perceived it had little option but to turn to the Eastern bloc, at least until Britain added more aid after 1967.

Following the end of the civil war in 1970, policy makers gradually returned to a more sympathetic Western orientation, although this had been undermined to some extent by the experience of the war. The burgeoning economic strength emanating from oil revenues also provided fresh impetus for a more vigorous and foreign policy outlook.

A CLOSER LOOK

12.6

NIGERIA AND ECOWAS

West Africa has traditionally received the highest priority in foreign policy. Surrounded by French-speaking countries, Nigeria has had uneasy relations with them and, partly because of this, sought to bring the region closer together within the Economic Community of West African States (ECOWAS). Founded in 1975 following diplomacy by Nigeria and Togo, ECOWAS developed some cooperative economic linkages but has not brought the region together as hoped. Nigeria dominates West Africa in terms of its economic and military strength, but it has not developed significant trade relations within the region, although smuggling and unofficial trade remain high. Nigeria played a critical role within ECOWAS in peacekeeping efforts in Liberia and Sierra Leone during the 1990s and early 2000s.

Economic hardship facing all the ECOWAS countries has led them to promote national rather than regional agendas, and so cooperation between them seems even more difficult than before. Success of ECOWAS is integral to the ambitious plans for a continent-wide African Economic Community (AEC), which is planned to develop in stages until complete integration is achieved in 2025—a goal that appears to be unattainable at this time.

The 1970s

The 1970s witnessed an increasingly active and committed role in African and world affairs, and this was evident at several levels. Within the African continent, Nigerian diplomats were instrumental in bringing together the majority of countries to negotiate for better terms of trade with the European Union, something needed following Britain's entry into the EU in 1973. Nigeria's economic size, strength, and potential—and the country's willingness to use these in the bargaining process—enabled African countries, as well as others in the Caribbean and Pacific Ocean areas, to be more influential in the negotiations; thus, favorable trade arrangements for these states were agreed upon at the Lomé Convention in 1975, as well as in subsequent agreements in 1980, 1985, and 1990.

Nigeria also took the lead in organizing West African states in a grouping to boost intraregional trade and increase industrial and development opportunities through regional cooperation. These states formed the Economic Community of West African States (ECOWAS) in 1975, a 15-member organization, of which Nigeria is by far the strongest economically. Unfortunately, there have been problems in increasing the level of cooperation among the states, and Nigeria did not

help matters by its expulsion of "aliens"—some 2 million unwanted West Africans in 1983 and another 750,000 in 1985. These events, combined with the smaller states' suspicions of the disproportionately stronger Nigeria, the civil wars in the 1990s in Liberia and Sierra Leone, as well as residual linguistic and cultural divisions within the community, have slowed the pace of progress.

Following the removal of General Gowon from office in 1975, foreign policy took on a sharper focus. The watershed event occurred in 1975 when the Murtala government decisively backed the Popular Movement for the Liberation of Angola (MPLA), a communist movement struggling to gain control of Angola, despite the opposition of many African states and Western powers, particularly the United States. Nigerian support for the liberation movements in Mozambique, Namibia, Zimbabwe, and South Africa also flourished at this time, and the "oil weapon"—the threat to cut supplies to Western countries to persuade them to support liberation movements—was a vocal policy. This was apparently used by Shagari in 1979 when, in an attempt to pressure Britain to allow Zimbabwe its independence, British Petroleum's operations in Nigeria were nationalized (significantly, BP was allowed back into the market in 1991).

South Africa proved to be a much tougher nut to crack, and Nigeria's attempts to pressure that country both directly and indirectly brought little success. Nigeria was a principal agitator behind the boycotts of the Olympic Games in 1976 and the Commonwealth Games in 1978 (and again in 1986), to maintain the international isolation of the South African regime. But it lacked the capability to bring dramatic results in South Africa, and partly out of frustration Nigerian policy makers and the public talked openly of acquiring nuclear weapons—both to provide stiffer support of black African claims in South Africa and to increase Nigeria's own status and bargaining position over this and other issues. Given the fact that South Africa's population is 80 percent black African, it appeared unlikely that Nigeria could credibly plan to use nuclear weapons against the country, as its aim was to protect rather than destroy the African majority.

The 1980s

The rise in economic fortunes and external influence in the 1970s proved transitory and was quickly countered by the country's demise in the 1980s. Economic buoyancy was replaced by a host of problems that diminished external interventions and muted antagonism toward Western powers. The government became increasingly preoccupied with trying to solve its debt problems and seeking international financial assistance and investment. With an increased dependence on Western countries such as Britain and the United States, and faced by a global oil glut, it was impossible to talk of the oil weapon or to pursue provocative policies toward the West, as it had done in the 1970s.

The Soviet Union maintained cordial relations and still sent military advisors to Nigeria and worked toward completing the iron and steel complex at Ajaokuta. Military leaders, however, believed that greater benefits could accrue from seeking aid and investment from the West, although they remained critical of its manipulation of the global economy. The military's policies did not resemble the docile, pro-Western approach of the 1960s. Relations with France improved significantly after the mid-1980s, as

both countries agreed on the importance of preventing the expansion of Libyan interests in Chad (and further afield), and political and military cooperation greatly increased. The French were anxious to maintain their friendly contacts and position in this large Anglophone market, which remained France's most important trading partner in Africa.

The growing strength of French and German interests in Nigeria threatened the position of the traditional dominant trading partner, Britain. Antipathy toward Britain in general, and Prime Minister Margaret Thatcher in particular, over British support for South Africa caused a stormy relationship, but Thatcher's visits to Nigeria in January 1988 and January 1989 seemed sufficient to secure Britain's position as Nigeria's largest supplier of goods.

Nigeria's relations with the United States similarly ebbed and flowed, reaching their greatest heights in the late 1970s, when President Jimmy Carter paid the only visit to the country ever made by a U.S. president. This was as much an indication of the style and preferences of Carter's foreign policy as of the economic strength of Nigeria, which was then the second largest supplier of oil to the United States. The subsequent economic downturn in Nigeria, combined with President Ronald Reagan's downplaying of regional arenas and reemphasis of global politics and neocontainment, relegated the African "giant" to a lesser role.

The 1990s

The 1990s were a period of mixed fortunes. On the positive side, the Gulf War temporarily boosted oil revenues and gave fleeting relief to the beleaguered economy. Nigeria's hosting in 1991 of both the annual Organization of African Unity summit and the ECOWAS summit reinforced Nigerian perceptions of the country as the center of Africa. Babangida's position as chair of the OAU for 1991–1992, combined with Chief Emeka Anyaoku's promotion to the position of secretary general of the Commonwealth in 1991, and Olusegun Obasanjo's strong run at the top job in the United Nations, enhanced this perception. Nigeria's leadership of the ECOWAS military peacekeeping force in Liberia and later Sierra Leone (Ecomog) showed that the country continued to be a dominant force in West Africa, even though the Ecomog operation was not all that successful and became increasingly controversial at home. All these factors did little to translate into real political influence for Nigeria.[30]

On the negative side, a number of problems, both old and new, afflicted foreign policy. Despite the mini oil boom, the economy remained in dire straits, with negligible improvement in diversification. Official nonoil exports in 1994 were a paltry $244 million. The national debt of over $30 billion drained the economy, and the turmoil of the transition program proved to be an equally draining political issue. But other serious fears developed because of events in Europe and Asia. The integration of the EU market in 1993, the more general trend of globalization, and the vast economic opportunities opening up in the markets of Central and Eastern Europe, and Asia, left Nigeria—and most of Africa—very much on the sidelines for potential investment. The post–Cold War new world (dis)order gave little importance to sub-Saharan Africa, except perhaps to postapartheid South Africa, which overtook Nigeria in both economic and political terms as the champion of Africa.

The cancellation of the presidential election results of June 1993 led to increasing isolation in international circles. The United States, partly in response to domestic political pressures from lobbies such as TransAfrica and exiled Nigerian human rights activists, applied limited sanctions to Nigeria in efforts to pressure movement toward democracy. The EU also froze official contacts and arms sales to Nigeria. The imprisonment of Obasanjo, among many others, early in 1995 heightened international anxieties, but the judicial executions of nine Ogoni dissidents in November 1995 led to Nigeria's temporary dismissal from the Commonwealth and further ostracism of the regime. However, sanctions fell

short of blocking Nigeria's oil trade, and Shell remained committed to investing in a future $3.6 billion gas project, also in the Delta region. Most significant, perhaps, in all this was the fact that South Africa's president at the time, Nelson Mandela, was the most outspoken in condemning the Abacha regime and seeking sanctions against Shell, an interesting turn of events in African politics. The death of Abacha in June 1998 and the transfer of power to the elected President Obasanjo in May 1999 brought an end to sanctions and international ostracism.

The 2000s

The birth of the Fourth Republic opened new opportunities for the civilian government to pursue. High on the list was attempting to restructure existing debts and attracting new foreign investment into Nigeria. Obasanjo toured the world to drum up support for Nigeria, though his successes made only a small difference. Continuing external pressures to privatize and cut subsidies were felt within the country, but domestic resistance slowed the pace of economic restructuring. An attempt to cut fuel subsidies in January 2002, for example, brought the country to a grinding halt in a national strike.

The continuation of civil wars in Liberia and Sierra Leone remained a high priority issue for the Obasanjo administration, but little evidence of progress was forthcoming. Foreign policy issues such as illicit drug trafficking, and health issues such as AIDS, came to more prominent positions on the foreign policy agenda. Attempts by civil society groups to influence foreign policy debates and outcomes added a further layer of complexity to government policy making. Efforts by the new government to recover some of the stolen billions stashed in overseas accounts by the Abacha family also became an important foreign and domestic policy issue. Relations with the World Bank and IMF became more cordial and open, but full implementation of policies remained beyond reach. Still, a small semblance of normality (at least in contrast to the excesses of Abacha) allowed Nigeria to again seek a leadership position within the continent, or at least to jostle with South Africa for that role.

---

[30]Julius Emeka Okolo and Stephen Wright, "Nigeria," in Timothy M. Shaw and Julius Emeka Okolo, eds., *The Political Economy of Foreign Policy in ECOWAS* (New York: St Martin's, 1994), pp. 125–146.

CONCLUSION

Nigeria has experienced dramatic changes in its political, social, and economic life since independence in October 1960. It is correct to conclude that instability is a constant theme underpinning Nigerian politics. But it is possible to perceive some of this as a result of the transition, via experimentation, from a country dominated by a colonial power to one searching for a system of government best suited to its needs and those of its people. The long periods of military rule can be seen as part of this trial-and-error experimentation, though in the 1990s the military's deliberate disregard for democracy made its rule less and less justifiable.

Critical questions now are whether the military will actually remain outside of political life, and whether the civilian politicians of the Fourth Republic can be more nationalistic, more honest, and less corrupt than previous political classes. Such improvements would allow the new republic to survive and work to provide the basis for future stability. From the evidence at hand, it is difficult to answer these questions with any certainty.

Against this political backdrop, an agenda of crucial social, religious, and economic issues also has to be resolved. Such actions would help to minimize inequalities and provide the basic human needs of the majority of Nigerians, and restructure the economy to put the country on a more secure footing in the new millennium. Given the current economic insecurity, corruption, and political uncertainty, the next few years raise challenges perhaps as equally daunting as those faced at any time since independence.

Thinking Critically

1. How has oil been both a blessing and a curse to Nigeria?
2. What has been the overall development strategy in Nigeria, and which goals have been achieved?

3. Has Nigeria fulfilled its potential as the leader of West Africa, and perhaps the continent as a whole?
4. What have been the main elements of U.S.-Nigerian relations since 1960?
5. What economic and foreign policy challenges face the post-1999 civilian administration under President Obasanjo?

KEY TERMS

Anglophone *(689)*
cash crops *(683)*
devaluation *(687)*
development *(686)*
Economic Community of West African States (ECOWAS) *(689)*
Francophone *(690)*
Human Development Index *(686)*
Indigenization Decree *(687)*
national debt *(693)*
nuclear power *(692)*
Organization of Petroleum Exporting Countries (OPEC) *(684)*
population growth *(686)*
privatization *(683, 693)*
revenue allocation *(687–688)*
structural adjustment program (SAP) *(687)*

FURTHER READINGS

Aluko, Olajide. *Essays in Nigerian Foreign Policy* (London: Allen and Unwin, 1981).

Babarinde, Olufemi A., and Stephen Wright, "Leadership and Ambition in Nigerian Foreign Policy," in Ryan K. Beasley, Juliet Kaarbo, Jeffrey S. Lantis, and Michael T. Snarr, eds., *Foreign Policy in Comparative Perspective: Domestic and International Influences on State Behavior* (Washington, DC: CQ Press, 2002), pp. 233–255.

Forrest, Tom. *The Advance of African Capital: The Growth of Nigerian Private Enterprise* (Charlottesville: University of Virginia Press, 1994).

Forrest, Tom. *Politics and Economic Development in Nigeria* (Boulder, CO: Westview Press, 1995).

Gambari, I. A. *Theory and Reality in Foreign Policy Making: Nigeria after the Second Republic* (Atlantic Highlands: Humanities Press International, 1989).

Gordon, April A. *Nigeria's Diverse Peoples: A Reference Sourcebook* (Santa Barbara: ABC-CL10, 2003).

Ihonvbere, Julius O., and Timothy M. Shaw. *Towards a Political Economy of Nigeria: Petroleum and Politics at the (Semi-) Periphery* (Aldershot, UK: Avebury, 1988).

Kane, Ousmane. *Muslim Modernity in Postcolonial Nigeria* (Leiden: Brill, 2003).

King, Mae C. *Basic Currents of Nigerian Foreign Policy* (Washington, DC: Howard University Press, 1996).

Lewis, Peter. "From Prebendalism to Predation: The Political Economy of Decline in Nigeria," *Journal of Modern African Studies* 34(1) (1996), pp. 79–103.

Lewis, Peter M., Pearl T. Robinson, and Barnett R. Rubin, *Stabilizing Nigeria: Sanctions, Incentives and Support for Civil Society* (New York: Council on Foreign Relations, 1998).

Magyar, Karl P., and Earl Conteh-Morgan, eds. *Peacekeeping in Africa: ECOMOG in Liberia* (London: Macmillan, 1998).

Musakikagile, Godfrey. *Ethnic Politics in Kenya and Nigeria* (Huntington: Nova Science Publishers, 2001).

Okolo, Julius Emeka, and Stephen Wright, eds. *West African Regional Cooperation and Development* (Boulder, CO: Westview Press, 1990).

Olayiwola, Peter O. *Petroleum and Structural Change in a Developing Country: The Case of Nigeria* (New York: Praeger, 1987).

Saro-Wiwa, Ken. *Genocide in Nigeria: The Ogoni Tragedy* (Port Harcourt: Saros, 1992).

Shaw, Timothy M., and Olajide Aluko, eds. *Nigerian Foreign Policy: Alternative Perceptions and Projections* (London: Macmillan, 1983).

Shepard, Robert B. *Nigeria, Africa and the United States: From Kennedy to Reagan* (Bloomington: Indiana University Press, 1991).

Soremekun, Kayode. *Perspectives on the Nigerian Oil Industry* (Lagos: Amkra Books, 1995).

Zartman, I. William, ed. *The Political Economy of Nigeria* (New York: Praeger, 1983).

WEB SITES

memory.loc.gov/frd/cs/ngtoc.html
Library of Congress site containing very helpful information on all aspects of Nigeria.

www.nigeriainfonet.com
Search engine for information on Nigeria.

www.nigeriacentral.com
An independent news service on Nigeria.

www.nigeria.indymedia.org
An independent news service on Nigeria.

www.Nigeria.com
A news service on Nigeria.

www.netnigeria.com
A regular email news service on Nigeria.

www.ngrguardiannews.com
News from a leading Nigerian newspaper.

www.vanguardngr.com
News from a leading Nigerian newspaper.

allafrica.com
A general news service on Africa.

www.bbc.co.uk
News from the British Broadcasting Corporation.

Conclusion

THE LARGER QUESTIONS ON THE AGENDA OF HUMANITY

The preceding chapters introduced students to a number of major foreign powers in different parts of the world and thus to the history, cultures, and politics of much of humanity. Students will soon realize there is no royal road to knowledge or an easy shortcut to the understanding of other countries. Such understanding requires long and careful study. But students must avoid the peril of being overwhelmed by details and facts, important though they are, of foreign systems and must not lose sight of the larger questions with which this study is concerned. Four major themes that students should keep in mind are the politics and problems of modernization, the different attempts to establish democratic systems in the world, the reconciliation of power and freedom in the different countries, and the relevance of the nation-state in an international system interconnected in a variety of ways.

In all of the countries presented in this book, there has been an inexorable, if uneven, march away from traditionalism and toward modernity. In Europe the traditionalism is the feudal society that existed up to the late eighteenth century, elements of which continued to exist through the nineteenth century and even up to the present. Feudal society was undermined by complex developments. The technology of warfare, especially the invention of gunpowder, deprived the feudal aristocracy of its military dominance; increased trade and commerce brought about a massive expansion of the middle classes, who could not be easily fitted into the two-way relationship between lords and serfs; and the cultural climate throughout Europe was transformed by the coming of a scientific revolution. In an age of experimentation and scientific advance, the essential notions of feudalism—which based the right to rule on heredity—began to crumble. Whether one believes that science, technology, and industry represent progress or degradation is a separate question; the French Revolution and the Industrial Revolution were major facts of life that condemned feudal regimes and led to the creation of new political systems—the substance of our study.

697

In China and India, the traditional societies that preceded the creation of the present political systems were even less developed than the European feudal societies. By "less developed" we do not imply that there was an inferior civilization or culture in Asia (which is demonstrably false), but merely that the scientific, technological, and political movements that characterize twentieth-century societies were delayed in Asia. One measure of the distance between Europe and Asia was the relative ease with which Europeans were able to conquer and colonize the more traditional peoples of the world, and one indicator of the modernization of Asia was the ability of formerly subject peoples to overthrow European rule.

However, the desire to achieve institutions and practices of modernity is not universal. The terrorist attacks of September 11, 2001, on the United States made clear that champions and ideological guides of radical and militant Islamic movements in countries such as contemporary Iran, Sudan, and Afghanistan under the Taliban were opposed to secularization in education, law, and the judicial system and resistant to the general desire to move to modernity, which they regard as less significant than an Islamic order.

Our country studies reveal the development of modern conditions in Britain, France, Germany, Russia, Japan, Mexico, Nigeria, China, India and the Middle East. Modern political study is largely an attempt to understand why and how this march took place, why peoples have chosen different political systems to attain their objectives, and what price is paid for development as well as for stagnation.

In the nineteenth and twentieth centuries, three major types of political systems were created during rapid modernization: liberal or constitutional democracy, Fascism and Nazism, and Communism. Where a self-confident middle class emerged, mainly in Northern Europe and North America, a social base existed for systems whose political leadership was determined by free and fair elections and in which a constitutional order guaranteed protection of human and property rights. But failure of the middle class to assume political power often paved the way to authoritarian rule or to totalitarianism as in Germany and Italy.

With the Russian Revolution in 1917, Communism represented a third possibility. Under the leaders of the new state of the Soviet Union, Communism was the basis for forced industrialization under the control of the one political party that acted in the name of the proletariat. In 1989 the Soviet Union collapsed, one of the defining moments of recent years. Its command economy became too complex to be managed successfully by the centralized one-party regime. The relaxation of political controls after 1989 allowed forces of ethnicity and nationalism to become prominent.

As mentioned in the Preface, this updated edition appears at a time of unusual flux in a number of countries in the world, including Russia and China. This book has suggested generalizations about comparative politics and has also divided the countries into groups for analytical convenience. But rapidly changing political, social, and economic factors suggest caution concerning such analytical categories.

Some developing countries or areas such as Hong Kong or Singapore have a higher income per capita than some major industrialized Western European countries. Moreover, many developing countries are more industrialized than the "industrial" countries in which industry now accounts for less than one-third of total output. About two-thirds of the world's 6 billion population live in Asia and account for about a quarter of gross world product. In the developing countries, the process of economic modernization and technical aspects of modernity have not generally resulted in democratic political systems or in respecting human rights.

Moreover, that process has been uneven and unpredictable. If Pakistan in October 1999 reverted to military rule after a coup by General Pervez Musharraf, other countries such as Mexico (after 71 years), Ghana, Yugoslavia, and Nicaragua during the last few years experienced a peaceful, democratic transfer of political power.

Russia and China present similar problems for comparative analysis. Russia has transformed itself, at least legally, from a Communist, one-party political system to a "democratic, federative, law-governed state with a republican form of government" according to its constitution. It is supposed to guarantee human rights—including freedom of conscience, movement, and the press—and rights to private property and ownership of land. After its long autocratic past, can Russia sustain a democratic system capable of overcoming the combined forces of tradition, ethnicity, and nationalism? This will be a central concern for students of comparative politics into the next millennium.

In China, the one-party dictatorship—the self-selected group of Communist leaders—has presided over some decentralization of the economy, the movement of millions from farms to cities, an increase in consumption goods, private retailing, and a stock market. But if China has free prices, it does not have a free press. It has ended central economic planning, but still has central political dictatorship. Thus, single-party rule with centralized decision making is presently combined with market competition.

Earlier in the book, we discussed societies and political systems characterized as democratic. They embrace certain similar features: freedom of speech, organization, belief, and travel; free and fair elections with universal suffrage and competitive political parties; the rule of law and human rights; peaceful transition of political power; legal political opposition; free associations and groups in civil society, such as the media, universities, and business; controls over and accountability of leaders. The paths to these societies and systems have varied over time and space. One, as in Britain, the Scandinavian countries, and the United States, has been a continuous, generally stable process. A second, as in many European countries such as France, Germany, Italy, Austria, and Spain, has been the successful restoration of democracy after a period of war or totalitarian or authoritarian rule that had ended democratic institutions and values. A third is the attempt, if hesitant and uneven, of countries such as Russia and of previously authoritarian systems in South Korea, Latin America, Asia, and of African countries after independence, to establish democratic regimes. The welcome news is that in the 2004 index of regimes published by Freedom House, 89 of the 192 countries were listed as "free" and another 54 as "partly free."

Do these figures suggest a pattern of history rather than a series of unique events? In his influential book, Francis Fukuyama wrote, as communism was collapsing in 1989, of "the end of history," meaning the move to modernity, liberal democracy, capitalism and the free market, and the rejection of other systems such as socialism, communism, fascism, monarchy, and authoritarian rule. Yet modernization as a process has been difficult, uneven, and interrupted, without an automatic congruence between economic and technical aspects of modernity and democratic politics and values.

At every stage of the modernizing process, all peoples confront the challenge of reconciling power and freedom. Power is necessary in order to orchestrate the activities of millions of individuals, to avoid anarchy, and to enable a people to achieve their collective goals. But the coercive state that is needed for defense, domestic tranquillity, and the general welfare may also deprive people of the fruits of their labor, their freedom, and their very lives. This is the permanent dilemma of all government—whether in primitive, feudal, or industrial societies. Is it possible to reconcile power and freedom, and, if so, under what conditions? It is not enough merely to speculate in the abstract or to dream up ideal solutions. We must review the historical developments of the major societies to be able to convert speculation into theory and theory into testable propositions.

The terrorist attacks of September 2001 lead us to review the ever changing balance between the desire for civil liberties and the need for security in societies with open borders. Defense policies may require alliances and external commitments to address concerns for global security. These policies raise concerns about the extent of the powers of the executive authorities, which because of the nature of war and defense measures tend, as Alexander Hamilton wrote, "to increase at the expense of the legislative authority."

A fourth theme of this book relates to rapid changes in the world. Is the nation-state still viable or have changing technological, economic, and military factors limited its autonomy? The ease of transport and communication within and between countries has meant a vast increase in international trade. It has also resulted in a considerable share of the world's capital being owned by multinational companies operating in different countries, and also money being easily transferred in the international financial market. Those international money flows affect interest rates and investment in the individual nation-states. The world seems a smaller place with the dramatic information revolution through which people everywhere can know a great deal about other countries through television, films, and the Internet.

Yet, in spite of these changes, the world is still divided into nation-states, each with its own interests. The members of the European Union have not yet created a superstate or a federal system. Nor have countries supposedly belonging to a particular cultural area—such as the Confucian Chinese culture, the Slavic Orthodox, the Latin American, the Middle Eastern, or the African, whose members share common religious or philosophic beliefs and historical experience—combined to form a political unit transcending the individual states. After reading this volume it will be up to you, the reader and student, to make your own contribution to the understanding of these major themes and central problems on the agenda of humanity.

Credits

Unless otherwise acknowledged, all photographs are the property of Scott, Foresman and Company.

Photos

Index

Page references followed by t and f refer to tables and figures respectively.